For a summary of general treatment categories, see the Chapter 16 Summary. For a summary of research techniques, see Tables 7-2 and 7-3.

AN INTRODUCTION TO
BRAIN AND BEHAVIOR

ABOUT THE COVER

Dr. Greg Dunn (artist and neuroscientist) and Dr. Brian Edwards (artist and applied physicist) created the artwork *Self Reflected* to elucidate the nature of human consciousness, bridging the connection between the macroscopic brain and the microscopic behavior of neurons. This work of art and science is not a scan of any kind, but was meticulously made from scratch through a complex process of hand drawing, deep neuroscience research, algorithmic simulations, photolithography, gilding, and strategic lighting design. *Self Reflected* offers an unprecedented insight of the brain into itself, revealing through a technique called reflective microetching the enormous scope of beautiful and delicately balanced neural choreographies designed to reflect what is occurring in our own minds as we observe this work of art. *Self Reflected* was created to remind us that the most marvelous machine in the known universe is at the core of our being and is the root of our shared humanity. As of 2018, *Self Reflected* is the most complex artistic depiction of the brain in the world.

You can find more information about the project including video, images, prints, and descriptions of the process, as well as other brain and mind themed artwork, at gregadunn.com.

Self Reflected was funded by the National Science Foundation, #ISE/AISL #1443767.

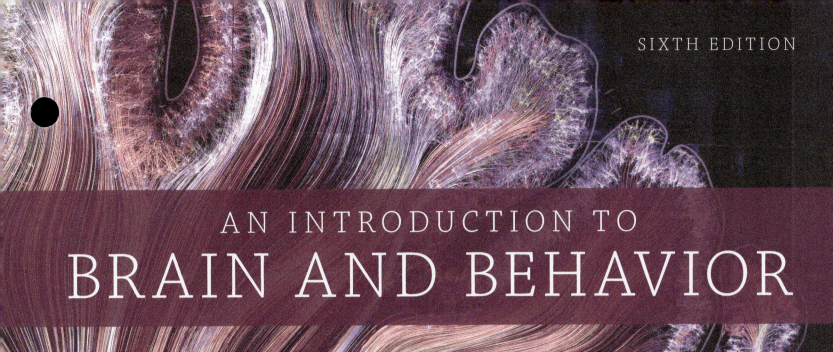

SIXTH EDITION

AN INTRODUCTION TO
BRAIN AND BEHAVIOR

BRYAN KOLB · IAN Q. WHISHAW · G. CAMPBELL TESKEY

University of Lethbridge   University of Lethbridge   University of Calgary

worth publishers
Macmillan Learning
New York

This book is dedicated to our longtime collaborator and friend Timothy Schallert, a Professor of Psychology at The University of Texas at Austin, who passed away on May 30, 2018, with Parkinson disease. Tim loved playing basketball and throwing the football, which he did with his children and with us. He also loved studying behavior. Tim had a gift for behavioral analysis and was the best rat whisperer. He could watch an animal that was not moving and ask, "Why?" Then later, he could tell you why. He traveled the world, collaborating with both neurologists and neuroscientists, showing others how to properly analyze behavior. His research, focused on Parkinson disease, resulted in numerous novel observations and insights about the behavior of a rat model of Parkinsonism. He had a wonderful sense of humor and is widely missed by the neuroscience community.

Senior Vice President, Content Strategy: Charles Linsmeier
Program Director, Social Sciences: Shani Fisher
Executive Program Manager for Psychology: Daniel DeBonis
Development Editor: Andrew Sylvester
Editorial Assistant: Anna Munroe
Marketing Manager: Clay Bolton
Marketing Assistant: Chelsea Simens
Media Editor, Social Sciences: Stefani Wallace
Director, Content Management Enhancement: Tracey Kuehn
Senior Managing Editor: Lisa Kinne
Senior Content Project Manager: Vivien Weiss
Project Managers: Andrea Stefanowicz & Misbah Ansari,
    Lumina Datamatics, Inc.
Media Project Manager: Joe Tomasso
Senior Workflow Project Manager: Paul Rohloff
Senior Photo Editor: Cecilia Varas
Photo Researcher: Richard Fox, Lumina Datamatics, Inc.
Director of Design, Content Management: Diana Blume
Design Services Manager: Natasha Wolfe
Cover Design Manager: John Callahan
Art Manager: Matthew McAdams
New Illustrations: Eli Ensor and Lumina Datamatics, Inc.
Composition: Lumina Datamatics, Inc.

Printing and Binding: King Printing Co., Inc.
Cover Art: *Self Reflected*, 22K gilded microetching under multicolored
    light, 2014-2016. Greg Dunn and Brian Edwards

Library of Congress Control Number: 2018958217

ISBN-13: 978-1-319-10737-6
ISBN-10: 1-319-10737-0

5 6 7 8 9   26 25 24 23 22

Worth Publishers
One New York Plaza
Suite 4500
New York, New York 10004-1562
www.macmillanlearning.com

Deborah Muirhead

Bryan Kolb received his Ph.D. from Pennsylvania State University in 1973. He conducted postdoctoral work at the University of Western Ontario and the Montreal Neurological Institute. He then moved to the University of Lethbridge in 1976, where he is Professor of Neuroscience and holds a Board of Governors Chair in Neuroscience. His current research examines how neurons of the cerebral cortex change in response to various factors—including hormones, experience, psychoactive drugs, neurotrophins, and injury—and how these changes are related to behavior in the normal and diseased brain. Kolb has received the distinguished teaching medal from the University of Lethbridge. He is a Fellow of the Royal Society of Canada and of the Canadian Psychological Association (CPA), the American Psychological Association, and the Association of Psychological Science. A recipient of the Hebb Prize from the CPA and from the Canadian Society for Brain, Behaviour, and Cognitive Science, Kolb has also received four honorary doctorates. He is a Senior Fellow of the Experience-Based Brain and Behavioural Development program of the Canadian Institute for Advanced Research. In 2017, he was appointed as an Officer of the Order of Canada. He and his wife train and show horses in Western riding events.

David Benard

Ian Q. Whishaw received his Ph.D. from Western University and is a Professor of Neuroscience at the University of Lethbridge. He has held visiting appointments at The University of Texas at Austin, the University of Michigan, Cambridge University, and the University of Strasbourg. He is a fellow of Clair Hall, Cambridge, and of the Canadian Psychological Association, the American Psychological Association, and the Royal Society of Canada. Whishaw has received the Canadian Humane Society Bronze Medal for Bravery and the Ingrid Speaker Gold Medal for Research, as well as the Distinguished Teaching Award from the University of Lethbridge and the ASTech Award for Distinguished Science. He has received the Key to the City of Lethbridge and has honorary doctorates from Thompson Rivers University and the University of Lethbridge. His research addresses the neural basis of skilled movement and the neural basis of brain disease, and the Institute for Scientific Information includes him in its list of most cited neuroscientists. His hobby is training horses for Western performance events.

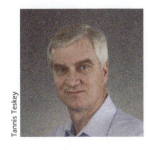

Tannis Teskey

G. Campbell Teskey received his Ph.D. from Western University in 1990 and then conducted postdoctoral work at McMaster University. In 1992 he relocated to the University of Calgary, where he is a professor in the Department of Cell Biology and Anatomy and at the Hotchkiss Brain Institute. His current research programs examine the development, organization, and plasticity of the motor cortex, as well as how seizures alter blood flow, brain function, and behavior. Teskey has won numerous teaching awards, has developed new courses, is a founder of the bachelor of science in neuroscience program, served as Education Director for the Hotchkiss Brain Institute, and chaired the Education Committee of Campus Alberta Neuroscience. His hobbies include hiking, biking, kayaking, and skiing. He refuses to wear cowboy hats.

CONTENTS IN BRIEF

CONTENTS

CHAPTER 1

Callista Images/Cultura/Getty Images

What Are the Origins of Brain and Behavior? 1

CHAPTER 2

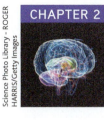

Science Photo Library - ROGER HARRIS/Getty Images

What Is the Nervous System's Functional Anatomy? 31

CHAPTER 3

What Are the Nervous System's Functional Units?.....73

CHAPTER 4

How Do Neurons Use Electrical Signals to Transmit Information?...............107

Bill Diodato/Getty Images

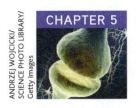

CHAPTER 5

How Do Neurons Communicate and Adapt?

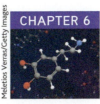

CHAPTER 6

How Do Drugs and Hormones Influence Brain and Behavior?

ANDRZEJ WOJCICKI/ SCIENCE PHOTO LIBRARY/ Getty Images

Meletios Verras/Getty Images

CHAPTER 7
How Do We Study the Brain's Structures and Functions?

CHAPTER 8
How Does the Nervous System Develop and Adapt?

CHAPTER 9
How Do We Sense, Perceive, and See the World? 281

CHAPTER 10
How Do We Hear, Speak, and Make Music? 319

CHAPTER 13

Ashima Narain/Getty Images

Why Do We Sleep and Dream? 437

RUSSELL KIGHTLEY/SCIENCE PHOTO LIBRARY/Getty Images

CHAPTER 14

How Do We Learn and Remember? 475

CHAPTER 15

Movus/Getty Images

How Does the Brain Think?

PREFACE

As with prior editions, this sixth edition of *An Introduction to Brain and Behavior* incorporates the latest research and technological advancements to give students a foundation in behavioral neuroscience as it is understood and practiced today. New material on genetics and epigenetics, genetic mutations, connectomics, brain imaging, genetic engineering and transgenic techniques, and our understanding and categorization of diseases and disorders of the brain are included throughout the text.

In addition to these updates, we have also made some significant changes within some sections to reflect the current understanding of the concepts and better communicate that knowledge to the student. For example, the discussion of the allocortex in Section 2-3 has been revised and expanded. The discussion of neurotransmitters in Section 5-2 has been broadened to include subsections on purines and ion transmitters. The presentation of psychoactive drugs in Section 6-2 has been revamped to emphasize the primary transmitter system that these drugs affect. The discussion of hierarchical organization in Section 11-1 has been revised to include a discussion of parallel organization. Chapter 12 has been reorganized to present a clearer picture of motivated, regulatory, nonregulatory, sexual, reward, and emotional behavior. Chapter 13 has been reorganized to incorporate the new nomenclature and understanding of sleep. Chapter 16 has also seen some significant reorganization to the discussions of psychiatric and neurological disorders and their treatments, including an expanded discussion of the field of clinical neuroscience and the classification systems used by the DSM and RDoC.

The range of updates and new coverage in the sixth edition exposition and Focus features is listed, chapter by chapter, in the margins of these Preface pages. You can easily see the breadth and scope of the revision. Yet these changes have not added to the length of the text. To keep the student focused, judicious cuts have been made throughout to compensate for the new material.

Changes in each new edition are always made with the goal of maintaining the voice and style that have helped make *An Introduction to Brain and Behavior* successful, and this sixth edition preserves the tools and features developed in the prior editions. With encouraging feedback from readers, the book's learning apparatus continues to feature sets of self-test questions at the end of the major sections in each chapter. These Section Reviews help students track their understanding as they progress through the text and the course. Answers appear at the back of the book.

We continue to expand the popular margin notes. Beyond offering useful asides to the text narrative, these marginalia increase the reader's ease in finding information, especially when related concepts are introduced early in the text and then elaborated on in later chapters. Readers can return quickly to an earlier discussion to refresh their knowledge or jump ahead to learn more. The margin notes also help instructors move through the book to preview later discussions.

In this edition, we've also highlighted with margin callouts those places where the 10 principles of nervous systems functioning, introduced in Chapter 2, correspond directly to the material in each chapter. Although this feature is by no means comprehensive, by reiterating these principles in key places where the connection is sharpest, we help to give the student a deeper understanding of these core concepts and the nervous system functioning they reflect.

The illustrated Experiments, another of the book's most popular features, show readers how researchers design experiments—that is, how they approach the study of brain–behavior relationships. The Basics features let students brush up or get up to speed on their science foundation—knowledge that helps them comprehend behavioral neuroscience.

SIXTH EDITION KEY REVISIONS

CHAPTER 1

REVAMPED Section 1-1, which presents PVS and MCS earlier in the chapter and is updated with a discussion of Adrian Owen's work in this area

REVISED discussion of Mendel's experiments and Experiment 1-1

NEW subsection on brain cell connections, including an introduction of the connectome, in Section 1-4

EXPANDED discussion of the hominid genome in Section 1-4

NEW discussion of the role of cell number in relationship to brain size in mediating behavior

CHAPTER 2

EXPANDED discussion of cerebral spinal fluid in Section 2-1

REVISED and EXPANDED discussion of the allocortex in Section 2-3

UPDATED Clinical Focus 2-2, Meningitis and Encephalitis; Clinical Focus 2-3, Stroke; and Clinical Focus 2-4, Bell Palsy

UPDATED discussion of Principle 9: Brain functions are localized and distributed

CHAPTER 3

REVAMPED discussion of the cells of the nervous system in Section 3-1

NEW subsection on acquired genetic mutations in Section 3-3

UPDATED discussion of transgenic techniques and NEW subsection on gene modification and CRISPR in Section 3-3

CHAPTER 4

UPDATED Clinical Focus 4-2, Multiple Sclerosis

NEW discussion of optogenetic techniques in mice in Research Focus 4-3, Optogenetics and Light-Sensitive Ion Channels

REVISED Clinical Focus 4-4, ALS: Amyotrophic Lateral Sclerosis

We have made some big changes, but much of the book remains familiar. In shaping content throughout, we continue to examine the nervous system with a focus on function, on how our behavior and our brain interact, by asking key questions that students and neuroscientists ask:

- Why do we have a brain?
- How is the nervous system organized—functionally as well as anatomically?
- How do drugs and hormones affect our behavior?
- How does the brain learn?
- How does the brain think?
- Why do we sleep and dream?

Every chapter's central question highlights the brain–behavior relationship. When we first describe how neurons communicate in Chapter 5, for example, we also describe how synaptic plasticity serves as the basis of learning. Later, in Section 14-4, we expand on plasticity as we explore learning and memory.

As it was when we wrote the first edition, our goal in this new edition is to bring coherence to a vast subject by helping students understand the big picture. Asking fundamental questions about the brain has another benefit: it piques students' interest and challenges them to join us on the journey of discovery that is brain science.

Scientific understanding of the human brain and human behavior continues to grow at an exponential pace. We want to communicate the excitement of recent breakthroughs in brain science as well as relate some of our own experiences from a combined 125+ years of studying brain and behavior, both to make the field's developing core concepts and latest revelations understandable and to transport uninitiated students to the frontiers of physiological psychology.

Areas of Emphasis

To convey the excitement of neuroscience as researchers understand it, we interweave evolution, genetics, and epigenetics; psychopharmacology; and neural plasticity and connectivity, including CNS and ENS interactions, throughout the book.

EVOLUTION Our perspective—neuroscience in an evolutionary context—recurs in almost every chapter. By focusing on comparative behavior and anatomy, we address nervous system evolution in depth in Chapters 1 and 2, evolution of the synapse in Section 5-1, and evolution of visual pathways in Section 9-2. We discuss how evolution might have influenced behaviors related to aggression and mate selection in Section 12-1, the evolutionary theories of sleeping and dreaming in Section 13-4, and the evolutionary origins of memory in Section 14-3. We describe the evolution of sex differences in spatial cognition and language in Section 15-5 and links between our evolved reactions to stress and anxiety disorders in Section 16-2.

GENETICS AND EPIGENETICS We introduce the foundations of genetic and epigenetic research in Sections 1-3 and 2-1 and begin to elaborate on them in Section 3-3. Chapter 5 discusses metabotropic receptors and DNA, as well as learning and genes. The interplay of genes and drug action is integral to Chapter 6, as are the developmental roles of genes and gene methylation to Chapter 8. Section 9-4 explains the genetics of color vision, and the genetics of sleep disorders anchors Section 13-6. Section 14-4 includes the role of epigenetics in memory. Section 16-3 considers the roles of genetics and of prions in understanding the causes of behavioral disorders.

PSYCHOPHARMACOLOGY Chapter 6 investigates how drugs and hormones affect behavior, topics we revisit often throughout the book. You will find coverage of drugs and information transfer in Section 4-3, drugs and cellular communication in Section 5-3, and synthetic biology in Section 7-1. Section 12-6 covers drugs and emotional behavior; Section 13-6, drugs and sleep disorders; and Section 14-4, neuronal changes with drug use. Section 16-3 discusses the promise of the liposome as a delivery vehicle in pharmacological treatments, while Sections 16-2 and 16-3 explore drugs used as treatments for a range of behavioral disorders.

CONNECTIVITY Neural plasticity is a hallmark of this book. We introduce the concept in Section 1-5, define it in Section 2-1, develop it in Section 2-6, and expand on it throughout. At the conclusion of Section 14-4, we elaborate seven guiding principles of brain plasticity. In Section 1-4, we introduce the emerging field of connectomics, which we explore further throughout Chapter 15. The new field of psychobiotics, which identifies the connection between the gut microbiome and its effects on the enteric nervous system—as well as on the central nervous system—appears in Sections 2-5 and 12-5.

Scientific Background Provided

We describe the journey of discovery that is neuroscience in a way that students just beginning to study the brain and behavior can understand; then they can use our clinical examples to tie its relevance to the real world. Our approach provides the background students need to understand introductory brain science. Multiple illustrated Experiments in 13 chapters help them visualize the scientific method and how scientists think. The Basics features in 6 chapters address the fact that understanding brain function requires understanding information from all the basic sciences.

These encounters can prove both surprising and shocking to students who come to the course without the necessary background. The Basics features in Chapters 1 and 2 address the relevant evolutionary and anatomical background. In Chapter 3, The Basics provides a short introduction to chemistry before the text describes the brain's chemical activities. In Chapter 4, The Basics addresses electricity before exploring the brain's electrical activity.

Readers already comfortable with the material can easily skip it; less experienced readers can learn it and use it as a context for neuroscience. Students with this background can tackle brain science with greater confidence. Similarly, for students with limited knowledge of basic psychology, we review such facts as stages of behavioral development in Chapter 8 and forms of learning and memory in Chapter 14.

Students in social science disciplines often remark on the amount of biology and chemistry in the book, and an equal number of students in biological sciences remark on the amount of psychology. More than half the students enrolled in the bachelor of science in neuroscience program at the University of Lethbridge switched from an initial biochemistry or psychology major after taking this course. We must be doing something right!

Chapter 7 showcases the range of methods that behavioral neuroscientists use to measure and manipulate brain and behavior—traditional methods and cutting-edge techniques such as optogenetics, optical tomography, resting-state fMRI, chemogenetics, DREADD, and CRISPR. Expanded discussions of techniques appear where appropriate, especially in Research Focus features, including Focus 4-3, Optogenetics and Light-Sensitive Ion Channels; Focus 7-2, Brainbow: Rainbow Neurons; and Focus 16-1, Posttraumatic Stress Disorder, which includes treatments based on virtual reality exposure therapies.

Finally, because critical thinking is vital to progress in science, select discussions throughout the book center on relevant aspects. Section 1-2 concludes with The Separate Realms of Science and Belief. Section 15-2 discusses the rise and fall of mirror neurons, demonstrating how the media—and even scientists—can fail to question the validity of research results. Section 12-5 introduces the idea that gender identity comprises a broad spectrum rather than a female–male dichotomy. Section 7-7 considers issues of animal welfare in scientific research and the use of laboratory animal models to mimic human neurologic and psychiatric disorders.

Clinical Focus Maintained

Neuroscience is a human science. Everything in this book is relevant to our lives, and everything in our lives is relevant to neuroscience. Understanding neuroscience helps us understand how we learn, how we develop, and how we can help people with brain

SIXTH EDITION KEY REVISIONS

CHAPTER 10
NEW Clinical Focus 10-2, Tinnitus

REVAMPED Section 10-5, including a NEW subsection on whale songs

CHAPTER 11
REVISED discussion of hierarchical organization, including NEW discussion of parallel organization, in Section 11-1

NEW discussion of position-point theory in Section 11-2

NEW subsection on the secondary somatosensory cortex in Section 11-5

CHAPTER 12
NEW Section 12-1, Identifying the Causes of Behavior, built from previous Sections 12-1 and 12-3

REVAMPED and REORGANIZED discussions of motivated, regulatory and nonregulatory, sexual, and emotional behavior in Sections 12-3, 12-4, and 12-5

NEW Clinical Focus 12-2, Diets and Rhythms

EXPANDED coverage of hormones and cognitive influences in Section 12-5

NEW discussion of mapping pleasure and pleasure electrodes in Section 12-7

CHAPTER 13
UPDATED presentation, including a NEW subsection on chronotypes, in Section 13-2

REVISED presentation of the stages of waking and sleeping, including NEW classification of waking and sleep states, in Section 13-3

UPDATED discussion of sleep and memory storage in Section 13-4, including a NEW subsection on the synaptic homeostasis theory of sleep and memory

REVISED and REORGANIZED presentation of sleep disorders in Section 13-5

CHAPTER 14
UPDATED Clinical Focus 14-1, Remediating Dyslexia

NEW discussion of Binder's noninvasive imaging studies looking for an engram of semantic memories, in Section 14-1

and behavioral disorders. Knowledge of how we learn, how we develop, and the symptoms of brain and behavioral disorders provides insights into neuroscience.

Clinical material also helps make neurobiology particularly relevant to students who seek a career in psychology, social work, or another profession related to mental health, as well as to students of the biological sciences. We integrate clinical information throughout the text with Clinical Focus features, and we expand on it in Chapter 16, the book's capstone, as well.

In *An Introduction to Brain and Behavior*, the placement of some topics is novel relative to traditional treatments. We include brief descriptions of brain diseases close to discussions of basic associated processes, as exemplified in the integrated coverage of Parkinson disease through Chapter 5, How Do Neurons Communicate and Adapt? This strategy helps first-time students repeatedly forge close links between what they are learning and real-life issues.

To provide a consistent disease nomenclature, the sixth edition follows the system advocated by the World Health Organization for diseases named after their putative discoverers. "Down syndrome," for example, has largely replaced "Down's syndrome" in the popular and scientific literature. We extend that convention to Parkinson disease and Alzheimer disease, among other eponymous diseases and disorders.

The nearly 150 disorders we cover are cross-referenced in the Index of Disorders inside the book's front cover. Chapter 16 expands on the nature of neuroscience research and the multidisciplinary treatment methods for neurological and psychiatric disorders described in preceding chapters.

We emphasize questions that relate to the biological bases of behavior. For us, the excitement of neuroscience lies in understanding how the brain explains what we do, whether it is talking, sleeping, seeing, or learning. Readers will therefore find nearly as many illustrations about behavior as illustrations about the brain. This emphasis on explaining the biological foundation of behavior is another reason we include a mix of Clinical, Research, and Comparative Focus features throughout the text.

Abundant Chapter Pedagogy

Building on the innovative teaching devices described so far, numerous in-text pedagogical aids adorn every chapter, beginning with an outline and an opening Focus feature that draws students into the chapter's topic. Focus features dot each chapter to connect brain and behavior to relevant clinical or research experience. Within chapters, definitions of boldface key terms introduced in the text appear in the margins as reinforcement, margin notes link topics together, and end-of-section Review self-tests help students check their grasp of major points.

Each chapter ends with a Summary—several of them including summarizing tables or illustrations to help students visualize or review big-picture concepts—and a list of Key Terms, each referenced to the page number on which the term is defined. Following this Preface, the Media and Supplements section describes the wide array of supplemental materials designed exclusively for students and teachers using the sixth edition.

Superb Visual Reinforcement

Our most important learning aid appears on nearly every page in the book: an expansive and, we believe, exceptional set of illustrations. Overwhelmingly, readers agree that, hand in hand with our words, the diagrams describe and illuminate the nervous system. Important anatomical illustrations are large format to ease perusal. We have selected relevant and engaging photos that enliven and enrich the discussion, ranging from a dance class for Parkinson patients in Section 5-3 to the dress that sparked a social media controversy to illustrate color constancy in Section 9-4 to a seniors' bridge game to illustrate the discussion of cognitively stimulating activities in Section 16-3.

Illustrations are consistent from chapter to chapter in order to reinforce one another. We consistently color-code diagrams that illustrate each aspect of the neuron, depict each structural region in the brain, and demark nervous system divisions. We include many varieties of micrographic images to show what a particular neural structure actually looks like. These illustrations and images are included in our PowerPoint presentations and integrated as labeling exercises in our Study Guide and Testing materials.

Teaching Through Metaphors, Examples, and Principles

If a textbook is not enjoyable, it has little chance of teaching well. We heighten students' interest through abundant use of metaphors and examples. Students read about patients whose brain injuries offer insights into brain function, and we examine car engines, robots, and prehistoric flutes for the same purpose. Frequent illustrated Experiments, comparative biology examples, and representative Comparative Focus features help students understand how much we humans have in common with creatures as distant from us as sea slugs and as close to us as chimpanzees.

We also facilitate learning by re-emphasizing main points and by distilling sets of principles about brain function that offer a framework to guide students' thinking. Thus, Section 2-6 introduces 10 key principles that explain how the parts of the nervous system work together. Section 14-4 summarizes seven guiding principles of neuroplasticity. These sets of principles form the basis of many discussions throughout the book. Frequently, margin notes remind readers when they encounter these principles again—and where to review them in depth.

Big-Picture Emphasis

One challenge in writing an introductory book on any topic is deciding what to include and what to exclude. We organize discussions to focus on the bigger picture—a focus exemplified by the 10 principles of nervous system function introduced in Section 2-6 and echoed throughout the book. Any set of principles may be arbitrary yet nevertheless afford students a useful framework for understanding the brain's activities.

In Chapters 8 through 16, we tackle behavioral topics in a more general way than most contemporary books do. In Chapter 12, for instance, we revisit experiments and ideas from the 1960s to understand why animals behave as they do, then we consider emotional and motivated behaviors as diverse as eating and anxiety attacks in humans. In Chapter 14, the larger picture of learning and memory is presented alongside a discussion of recovery from traumatic brain injury.

This broad focus helps students grasp the big picture that behavioral neuroscience paints. While broadening our focus requires us to leave out some details, our experience with students and teachers through five earlier editions confirms that discussing the larger problems and issues in brain and behavior is of greater interest to students—especially those new to this field—and is more often remembered than are myriad details without context.

As in preceding editions, we are selective in our citation of the truly massive literature on the brain and behavior because we believe that too many citations can disrupt the text's flow, distracting students from the task of mastering concepts. We provide citations to classic works by including the names of the researchers and by mentioning where the research was performed. In areas where controversy or new breakthroughs predominate, we also include detailed citations to papers (especially reviews) from the years 2013 to 2018. An end-of-book References section lists, by chapter, all the literature used in developing the book, reflecting the addition of many new citations in this edition and elimination of other, now superseded, research.

Acknowledgements

We sincerely thank the many people who contributed to the development of this edition. The staff at Worth Publishers is remarkable and makes doing revisions a joy. We thank our program manager, Daniel DeBonis, more than ably assisted by Anna Munroe; our senior content project manager, Vivien Weiss; and senior workflow project manager Paul Rohloff; as well as project managers Andrea Stefanowicz and Misbah Ansari, and the composition team at Lumina. Andrew Sylvester replaced our long-time development editor Barbara Brooks, and he had big shoes to fill. He did so admirably and provided a new set of eyes that brought a fresh perspective to this edition.

We thank cover design manager John Callahan for a striking cover and design manager Natasha Wolfe for a fresh, inviting, accessible new interior design. Thanks also to Cecilia Varas for coordinating photo research and to Richard Fox, who found photographs and other illustrative materials that we would not have found on our own. We are indebted to Macmillan art manager Matt McAdams and medical illustrator Eli Ensor for their excellent work in creating new illustrations.

Our colleagues, too, have helped in the development of every edition. We would like to thank the following colleagues and students for making important contributions: Mike Antle, Jaideep Bains, Nicole Burma, Tim Bussey, Richard Dyck, Jonathan Epp, Paolo Federico, Richard Frayne, Matthew Hill, Lisa Siksida, Simon Spanswick, Peter Stys, Catherine Thomas, Roger Thompson, Tuan Trang, and Alicia Zumbusch.

And for their help in shaping the sixth edition, we are especially indebted to the reviewers who provided extensive comments on selected chapters and illustrations: Karen Atkinson-Leadbeater, *Mount Royal University*; Richard Brown, *LaGuardia Community College, CUNY*; Richard Conti, *Kean University*; Carol DeVolder, *St. Ambrose University*; Benjamin DeVore, *Virginia Tech*; Francine Dolins, *University of Michigan–Dearborn*; Evelyn Field, *Mount Royal University*; Merage Ghane, *Virginia Polytechnic Institute and State University*; Bradley Gruner, *College of Southern Nevada*; Sandra Holloway, *Saint Joseph University*; Adam Hutcheson, *Georgia Gwinnett College*; Eric Jackson, *University of New Mexico*; Daniel Kay, *Brigham Young University*; Lisa Lyons, *Florida State University*; Vincent Markowski, *SUNY Geneseo*; Michael Nadorff, *Mississippi State University*; Michael Neelon, *University of North Carolina–Asheville*; Carlos Rodriguez, *The University of New Mexico*; Neil Sass, *Heidelberg University*; Andra Smith, *University of Ottawa*; and Richard Straub, *University of Michigan–Dearborn*.

Likewise, we continue to be indebted to the colleagues who provided extensive comments during the development of the fifth edition: Nancy Blum, *California State University, Northridge*; Kelly Bordner, *Southern Connecticut State University*; Benjamin Clark, *University of New Mexico*; Roslyn Fitch, *University of Connecticut*; Trevor Gilbert, *University of Calgary*; Nicholas Grahame, *Indiana University–Purdue University Indianapolis*; Kenneth Troy Harker, *University of New Brunswick*; Jason Ivanoff, *St. Mary's University*; Dwight Kravitz, *The George Washington University*; Ralph Lydic, *University of Tennessee, Knoxville*; Paul Meyer, *The State University of New York at Buffalo*; Jaime Olavarria, *University of Washington*; Christopher Robison, *Florida State University*; Claire Scavuzzo, *University of Alberta*; Sarah Schock, *University of Ottawa*; Robert Stackman, *Florida Atlantic University*; Sandra Trafalis, *San Jose State University*; Douglas Wallace, *Northern Illinois University*; Matthew Will, *University of Missouri, Columbia*; and Harris Philip Zeigler, *Hunter College*.

We would also like to thank those reviewers who contributed to the development of the fourth edition: Mark Basham, *Regis University*; Pam Costa, *Tacoma Community College*; Russ Costa, *Westminster College*; Renee Countryman, *Austin College*; Kristen D'Anci, *Salem State University*; Trevor James Hamilton, *Grant MacGewn University*; Christian Hart, *Texas Woman's University*; Matthew Holahan, *Carleton University*; Chris Jones, *College of the Desert*; Joy Kannarkat, *Norfolk State University*; Jennifer Koontz, *Orange Coast College*; Kate Makerec, *William Paterson University of New Jersey*; Daniel Montoya, *Fayetteville State University*; Barbara Oswald, *Miami University of Ohio*; Gabriel Radvansky, *University of Notre Dame*; Jackie Rose, *Western Washington*

University; Steven Schandler, *Chapman University*; Maharaj Singh, *Marquette University*; and Manda Williamson, *University of Nebraska–Lincoln*.

We'd also like to thank the reviewers who contributed their thoughts to the third edition: Chana Akins, *University of Kentucky*; Michael Anch, *Saint Louis University*; Maura Mitrushina, *California State University, Northridge*; Paul Wellman, *Texas A&M University*; and Ilsun White, *Morehead State University*. The methods chapter was new to the third edition and posed the additional challenge of taking what easily could read like a seed catalog and making it engaging to readers. We therefore are indebted to Margaret G. Ruddy, *The College of New Jersey*, and Ann Voorhies, *University of Washington*, for providing extensive advice on the initial version of Chapter 7.

In addition, we thank the reviewers who provided their thoughts on the second edition: Barry Anton, *University of Puget Sound*; R. Bruce Bolster, *University of Winnipeg*; James Canfield, *University of Washington*; Edward Castañeda, *University of New Mexico*; Darragh P. Devine, *University of Florida*; Kenneth Green, *California State University, Long Beach*; Eric Jackson, *University of New Mexico*; Michael Nelson, *University of Missouri, Rolla*; Joshua S. Rodefer, *University of Iowa*; Charlene Wages, *Francis Marion University*; Doug Wallace, *Northern Illinois University*; Patricia Wallace, *Northern Illinois University*; and Edie Woods, *Madonna University*. Sheri Mizumori, *University of Washington*, deserves special thanks for reading the entire manuscript for accuracy and providing fresh ideas that proved invaluable.

Finally, we must thank our tolerant wives for putting up with sudden changes in plans as chapters returned, in manuscript or in proof, with hopes for quick turnarounds. We also thank our colleague Robbin Gibb, who uses the book and has provided much feedback, in addition to our undergraduate and graduate students, technicians, and postdoctoral fellows, who kept our research programs moving forward when we were engaged in revising the book.

Bryan Kolb, Ian Q. Whishaw, G. Campbell Teskey

An Introduction to Brain and Behavior, Sixth Edition, features a wide array of supplemental materials designed exclusively for students and teachers of the text. For more information about any of the items, please visit the Macmillan Learning catalog at www.macmillanlearning.com.

For Students

LaunchPad with LearningCurve Quizzing

A comprehensive Web resource for teaching and learning psychology

LaunchPad combines Macmillan Learning's award-winning media with an innovative platform for easy navigation. For students, it is the ultimate online study guide, with rich interactive tutorials, videos, interactive e-book, and the LearningCurve adaptive quizzing system. For instructors, LaunchPad is a full-course space where class documents can be posted, quizzes are easily assigned and graded, and students' progress can be assessed and recorded. Whether you are looking for the most effective study tools or a robust platform for an online course, LaunchPad is a powerful way to enhance your class.

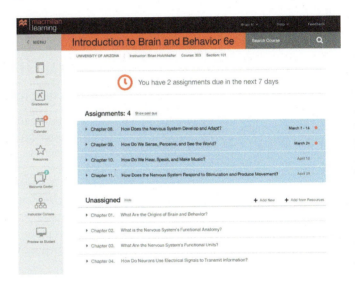

LaunchPad for *An Introduction to Brain and Behavior*, Sixth Edition, includes the following resources:

- **NEW! NEUROSCIENCE ACTIVITIES, VOLUME I,** is a brand-new collection of online activities that enables students to understand neuronal processes in action. Over a dozen new activities show in vivid animations the foundational processes that the reader can only imagine when reading the text. Students come away with a fuller understanding of topics such as the conduction of the action potential, the integration of neural inputs, synaptic transmission, and the action of neurotransmitters. A perfect accompaniment to an online or hybrid course, each activity is fully assessable with multiple-choice questions. This collection is indispensable for bringing fundamental neuroscience concepts to life.

- **THE LEARNINGCURVE** adaptive quizzing system is designed based on the latest findings from learning and memory research. It combines adaptive question selection, immediate and valuable feedback, and a gamelike interface to engage students in a learning experience that is unique to them. Students experience learning that is customized to their level of knowledge, and instructors receive state-of-the-art reporting on the progress of each student, as well as the class as a whole.

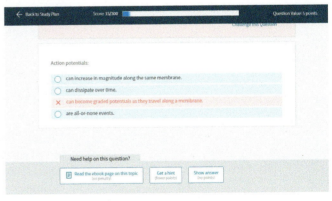

- **PRACTICE QUIZZES** provide another way for students and instructors to rehearse their knowledge. Each quiz is written on the topics discussed throughout each chapter and features a variety of multiple-choice questions presented to students randomly from question pools. Valuable to both student and instructor, these practice quizzes are fully editable and make robust assessment quick and easy to set up.

- **AN INTERACTIVE E-BOOK** allows students to highlight, bookmark, and make notes, just as they would with a printed textbook. The search function and in-text glossary definitions make the text ready for the digital age.

- **STUDENT VIDEO ACTIVITIES** include engaging modules that instructors can easily assign for student assessment. Videos cover a variety of topics and are sure to spark discussion and encourage critical thinking.

- **THE *SCIENTIFIC AMERICAN* NEWSFEED** delivers weekly articles, podcasts, and news briefs on the very latest developments in psychology from the first name in popular science journalism.

- ***PSYCHOLOGY AND THE REAL WORLD: ESSAYS ILLUSTRATING FUNDAMENTAL CONTRI-BUTIONS TO SOCIETY*, SECOND EDITION** is a superb collection of essays by major researchers describing their landmark studies. Published in association with the not-for-profit FABBS Foundation, this engaging reader includes Bruce McEwen's work on the neurobiology of stress and adaptation, Jeremy Wolfe's look at the importance of visual search, Elizabeth Loftus's reflections on her study of false memories, and Daniel Wegner's study of thought suppression. A portion of the proceeds is donated to the FABBS Foundation to support societies of cognitive, psychological, behavioral, and brain sciences.

For Instructors

INSTRUCTOR'S RESOURCES

This invaluable tool, for new and experienced instructors alike, was revised by Catherine Smith of Carleton University. It includes chapter-by-chapter learning objectives and chapter overviews, detailed lecture outlines, thorough chapter summaries, chapter key terms, in-class demonstrations and activities, springboard topics for discussion and debate, ideas for research and term paper projects, homework assignments and exercises, and suggested readings from journals and periodicals. Course-planning suggestions and a guide to videos and Internet resources are also included. The Instructor's Resources can be downloaded from LaunchPad at launchpadworks.com.

Assessment Tools

COMPUTERIZED TEST BANK

The Test Bank includes a battery of more than 1300 multiple-choice and short-answer test questions. Each item is keyed to the page in the textbook on which the answer can be found. All the questions have been thoroughly reviewed and edited for accuracy and clarity. The Test Bank files can be downloaded from LaunchPad at launchpadworks.com.

Presentation

ILLUSTRATION SLIDES AND LECTURE SLIDES

Available for download from LaunchPad at launchpadworks.com, these slides can either be used as they are or customized to fit the needs of your course. There are two sets of slides for each chapter. The Illustration slides feature all the figures, photos, and tables. The Lecture slides feature main points of the chapter with selected figures and illustrations.

What Are the Origins of Brain and Behavior?

CHAPTER 1

Living with Traumatic Brain Injury

Fred Linge, a clinical psychologist with a degree in brain research, wrote this description 12 years after his head injury occurred:

> In the second it took for my car to crash head-on, my life was permanently changed, and I became another statistic in what has been called "the silent epidemic."
>
> During the next months, my family and I began to understand something of the reality of the experience of head injury. I had begun the painful task of recognizing and accepting my physical, mental, and emotional deficits. I couldn't taste or smell. I couldn't read even the simplest sentence without forgetting the beginning before I got to the end. I had a hair-trigger temper that could ignite instantly into rage over the most trivial incident. . . .
>
> Two years after my injury, I wrote a short article: "What Does It Feel Like to Be Brain Damaged?" At this point in my life, I began to involve myself with other brain-damaged people. It brought me an enormous outpouring of letters, phone calls, and personal visits that continue to this day. Many were struggling as I had struggled, with no diagnosis, no planning, no rehabilitation, and most of all, no hope. . . . The catastrophic effect of my injury was such that I was shattered and then remolded by the experience, and I emerged from it a profoundly different person with a different set of convictions, values, and priorities. (Linge, 1990)

Each year, between 2 and 7 million people in the United States suffer from **traumatic brain injury (TBI)**—a wound to the brain that results from a blow to the head or a **concussion** (Kisser et al., 2017). Most of these people have to cope, at least to some degree, with Linge's forecast of "no diagnosis, no planning, no rehabilitation, and most of all, no hope."

TBI and the many other disorders of the brain that we will present in this textbook (see the index of disorders on the inside cover of this book) are major challenges faced by individuals working in the field of *neuroscience*, the multidisciplinary study of the brain. Neuroscience looks not only at the anatomy of the brain but also at its chemistry, physics, computational processes, influences on psychological functioning, influences on sociological and economic factors, and diseases.

Neuroscience can address the challenges outlined by Linge via, for example, improved diagnosis by imaging the anatomy, chemistry, and electrical activity of the brain and rehabilitation through computer-assisted training and prosthetics. Fred Linge's life has been a journey. Before the car crash, he gave little thought to the relationship between his brain and behavior. After the crash, adapting to his injured brain and behavior dominated his life.

The purpose of this book is to take you on a journey toward understanding the link between brain and behavior and how the brain is organized to produce behavior. The knowledge that is emerging from the study of the brain and behavior is changing how we think about ourselves, how we structure our education and social interactions, and how we aid those with brain injury, disease, and disorder.

Illustrated Experiments throughout the book reveal how neuroscientists conduct research, beginning with Experiment 1-1 in Section 1-2.

1-1

The Brain in the Twenty-First Century

The purpose of this chapter is to describe the relationship between brain and behavior: how the brain is organized to produce behavior. We will first present the ideas that led to our current understanding of the role of the brain in behavior. Next, we will describe the evolution of brain and behavior in diverse animal species, including humans. We will end by discussing ideas about why the human brain is special.

Why Study Brain and Behavior?

The *brain* is a physical object, a living tissue, a body organ. *Behavior* is action, momentarily observable but fleeting. Brain and behavior differ greatly but are linked. They have evolved together: one is responsible for the other, which is responsible for the other, and so on. There are three reasons for linking the study of the brain to the study of behavior:

1. *How the brain produces behavior is a major scientific question.* Scientists and students study the brain to understand humanity. A better understanding of brain function will allow improvements in many aspects of our world, including educational systems, economic systems, and social systems.

2. *The brain is the most complex organ on Earth and is found in many groups of animals.* Students of the brain want to understand its place in the biological order of our

planet. This chapter describes the basic function and evolution of the brain, especially the human brain.

3. *A growing list of behavioral disorders can be explained and treated as we increase our understanding of the brain.* More than 2000 disorders may be in some way related to brain abnormalities. As indexed on the inside front cover of this book, we detail relationships between brain disorders and behavioral disorders in every chapter, especially in the Focus features.

None of us can predict how the knowledge we gain about the brain and behavior may prove useful. A former psychology major wrote to tell us that she took our course because she was unable to register in a preferred course. She felt that, although our course was interesting, it was "biology, not psychology." After graduating and getting a job in a social service agency, she has found to her delight that understanding the links between brain and behavior is in fact a source of insight into many of her clients' disorders and the treatment options available for them.

What Is the Brain?

Brain is the Anglo-Saxon word for the tissue found within the skull, and it describes a part of the human nervous system (**Figure 1-1**). The human nervous system is composed of cells, as is the rest of the body. About half of these brain cells (87 billion of them) are called **neurons** and are specialized in that they interconnect with each other and with the muscles and organs of the body with fibers that can extend over long distances. The other half of these brain cells (86 billion) are called **glial cells**, and they support the function of the neurons. Through interconnections, the neurons send electrical and chemical signals to communicate with one another, with sensory receptors in the skin, with muscles, and with internal body organs. Most of the interconnections between the brain and body are made through the spinal cord, a tube of nervous tissue encased in our vertebrae. The spinal cord in turn sends nerve fibers out to our muscles and internal body organs and receives fibers from sensory receptors on many parts of our body.

Together, the brain and spinal cord make up the **central nervous system (CNS)**, the part of our nervous system encased in bone. The CNS is called *central* because it is both the nervous system's physical core and the core structure mediating behavior. All the processes that radiate out beyond the brain and spinal cord constitute the **peripheral nervous system (PNS)**.

As shown in **Figure 1-2**, the human brain comprises two major sets of structures. The **cerebrum (forebrain)**, shown in Figure 1-2A, has two nearly symmetrical halves, called **hemispheres**, one on the left and one on the right. The cerebrum is responsible for most of our conscious behaviors. It enfolds the **brainstem** (Figure 1-2B), a set of structures responsible for most of our unconscious behaviors. The second major brainstem structure, the **cerebellum**, is specialized for learning and coordinating our movements. Its conjoint evolution with the cerebrum shows that it assists the cerebrum in generating many behaviors.

So far, we have been describing the major components of the brain and nervous system, but there is more to the story. For his postgraduate research, our friend Harvey chose to study the electrical activity of the brain. He had decided that he wanted to live on as a brain in a bottle after his body died. He expected that his research would allow his bottled brain to communicate with others who could read its electrical signals. Where does Harvey's proposed experiment lead us in understanding behavior and the brain?

Harvey clearly wanted to preserve not just his brain but his *self*—his consciousness, those processes such as language and

traumatic brain injury (TBI) Wound to the brain that results from a blow to the head.

concussion Damage to the brain caused by a blow to the head.

neuron Specialized nerve cell engaged in information processing.

glial cells Brain cells that support the function of neurons.

central nervous system (CNS) The brain and spinal cord, which together mediate behavior.

peripheral nervous system (PNS) All the neurons in the body outside the brain and spinal cord; provides sensory and motor connections to and from the central nervous system.

cerebrum (forebrain) Major structure of the forebrain that consists of two mirror-image hemispheres (left and right) and is responsible for most conscious behavior.

hemisphere Literally, half a sphere, referring to one side of the cerebrum.

brainstem Central structure of the brain; responsible for most unconscious behavior.

cerebellum Major brainstem structure specialized for learning and coordinating movements; assists the cerebrum in generating many behaviors.

FIGURE 1-1 **Major Divisions of the Human Nervous System** The brain and spinal cord together make up the central nervous system. All of the nerve processes radiating out beyond the brain and spinal cord and all of the neurons outside the CNS connect to sensory receptors, muscles, and internal body organs to form the peripheral nervous system.

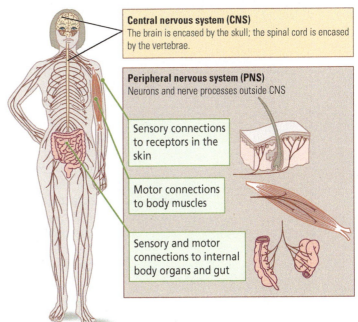

Central nervous system (CNS)
The brain is encased by the skull; the spinal cord is encased by the vertebrae.

Peripheral nervous system (PNS)
Neurons and nerve processes outside CNS

Sensory connections to receptors in the skin

Motor connections to body muscles

Sensory and motor connections to internal body organs and gut

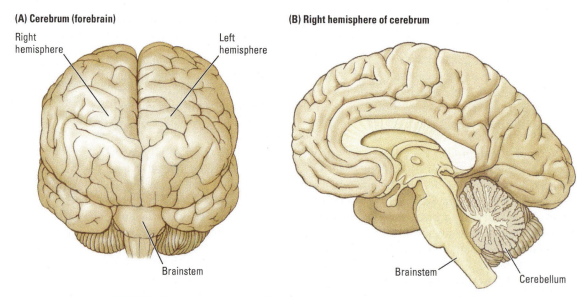

(A) Cerebrum (forebrain)

Right hemisphere

Left hemisphere

Brainstem

(B) Right hemisphere of cerebrum

Brainstem

Cerebellum

FIGURE 1-2 **The Human Brain (A)** Shown head-on, as oriented within the human skull, are the nearly symmetrical left and right hemispheres of the cerebrum. **(B)** A cut through the middle of the brain from back to front reveals the right hemispheres of the cerebrum and cerebellum and the right side of the brainstem. The spinal cord (not shown) emerges from the base of the brainstem. Chapter 2 describes the brain's functional anatomy.

memory that gave him self-awareness and allowed him to interact with others. This meaning of *brain* refers to something other than the organ found inside the skull. It refers to the brain as the body organ that exerts control over behavior. It is what we intend when we talk of someone smart being "a brain" or when we speak of the computer that guides a spacecraft as being the vessel's brain. The term *brain*, then, signifies both the organ itself and the fact that this organ produces behavior.

To return to Harvey's experiment, the effect of placing even the entire CNS in a bottle would be to separate it from the PNS and thus from the sensations and movements the PNS mediates. Could the brain remain awake and conscious without sensory information and without the ability to move? A number of fascinating experiments present us with information relevant to this question.

One line of research and philosophical argument, called **embodied behavior**, proposes that the movements we make and the movements we perceive in others are central to our behavior (Prinz, 2008). That is, we understand one another not only by listening to words but also by observing gestures and other body language. We think not only with silent language but also with overt gestures and body language. According to this view, the brain as an intelligent entity cannot be divorced from the body's activities.

In the 1920s, Edmond Jacobson wondered what would happen if our muscles completely stopped moving, a question relevant to Harvey's experiment. Jacobson believed that, even when we think we are entirely motionless, we still make subliminal movements related to our thoughts. The muscles of the larynx subliminally move when we think in words, for instance, and we make subliminal eye movements when we imagine or visualize some action or a person, place, or thing. In Jacobson's experiment, then, people practiced "total" relaxation and were later asked what the experience was like. They reported a condition of mental emptiness, as if the brain had gone blank (Jacobson, 1932).

Woodburn Heron took Jacobson's investigations a step further when, in 1957, he conducted experiments on sensory deprivation, a form of torture used in the Korean War (1950–1953). How would the brain cope without sensory input? Heron examined the effects of *sensory deprivation*, including feedback from movement, by having student volunteers lie on a bed in a bare, soundproof room and remain completely still. Padded tubes covered their arms so that they had no sense of touch, and translucent

embodied behavior Theory that the movements we make and the movements we perceive in others are central to communication with others.

goggles cut off their vision. The participants reported that the experience was extremely unpleasant, not just because of the social isolation but also because they lost their focus. Some even hallucinated, as if their brain were somehow trying to create the sensory experiences that they suddenly lacked. Most asked to be released from the study before it ended.

Evidence from people who have suffered nervous system injury has added further insights to the relationship between overt behavior and consciousness. When Martin Pistorius was 12 years old, his health began to deteriorate. Eventually, he lapsed into a coma, a condition in which he seemed completely unconscious. His parents placed Martin in a nursing home, where over a number of years he became conscious of his condition, although he remained completely paralyzed and unable to communicate. Martin suffered from **locked-in syndrome**, a condition in which the brain is intact, functioning, and sensitive to the external world but with its nerve fiber pathways that produce movement inactivated.

Martin's condition persisted until, when he was 25, a nurse noticed him making some small facial movements. He seemed to be trying to communicate. With rehabilitation, he made excellent progress toward recovering movement, including using a voice synthesizer. His 2011 book *Ghost Boy* describes his frustration and helplessness during years of enduring locked-in syndrome. Pistorious's story shows that consciousness can persist in the absence of most overt movement; Pistorious was conscious of the world and could make small facial movements.

Another patient's case study offers further insight into the relationship between behavior and the brain: that consciousness is important. The patient, a 38-year-old man, had lingered in a **minimally conscious state (MCS)** for more than 6 years after an assault. He was occasionally able to communicate with single words and occasionally able to follow simple commands. He could make a few movements but could not feed himself despite 2 years of inpatient rehabilitation and 4 years in a nursing home.

Nicholas Schiff and his colleagues (Schiff & Fins, 2007) reasoned that, if they could stimulate their MCS patient's brain by administering a small electrical current, they could improve his behavioral abilities. As part of a **clinical trial** (a consensual experiment directed toward developing a treatment), they implanted thin wire electrodes in his brainstem so they could administer a small electrical current.

Through these electrodes, which are visible in the X-ray image shown in **Figure 1-3**, the investigators applied electrical stimulation for 12 hours each day—a procedure called **deep brain stimulation (DBS)**. The researchers found dramatic improvement in the patient's behavior and ability to follow commands. For the first time since his assault, he was able to feed himself and swallow food. He could even interact with his caregivers and watch television, and he showed further improvement in response to rehabilitation. Clearly, for someone in a minimally conscious condition, when his wakefulness was improved, so was behavior.

Another line of inquiry indicates that consciousness can be present in the absence of all voluntary movement. Patients who have received brain injury so severe that it places them in **persistent vegetative state (PVS)** are alive and show signs of wakefulness, but they are unable to communicate or show signs of any cognitive function. Adrian Owen (2015) and his colleagues asked whether by imaging the brains of some of these patients they could assess the extent to which the patients were conscious. Using a magnetic resonance imaging (MRI) procedure that measures brain function in terms of oxygen use, Owen's group discovered that some comatose patients are conscious and can communicate when given the opportunity.

These investigators devised ways to communicate with their patients by using the signals in their brains' activity patterns. When imaging the brains of control subjects, Owen's group asked them to imagine hitting a tennis ball with a racket. When they did so, it was observed that their brain activity changed in association with the imaginary act. When, next, Owen's PVS patients were asked to imagine hitting a tennis ball,

locked-in syndrome Condition in which a patient is aware and awake but cannot move or communicate verbally because of complete paralysis of nearly all voluntary muscles except the eyes.

minimally conscious state (MCS) Condition in which a person can display some rudimentary behaviors, such as smiling or uttering a few words, but is otherwise not conscious.

clinical trial Consensual experiment directed toward developing a treatment.

deep brain stimulation (DBS) Neurosurgery in which electrodes implanted in the brain stimulate a targeted area with a low-voltage electrical current to facilitate behavior.

persistent vegetative state (PVS) Condition in which a person is alive but unaware, unable to communicate or to function independently at even the most basic level.

Note: We refer to healthy people who take part in research studies as *participants* and to those with brain or behavioral impairments as *subjects* or as *patients*.

FIGURE 1-3 **Deep Brain Stimulation** X-ray image showing electrodes implanted in the thalamus, a structure deep in the brain near the tip of the brainstem, for DBS. DBS can treat disorders such as Parkinson disease and depression (see Section 16-3) and aid recovery from TBI (see Section 14-5).

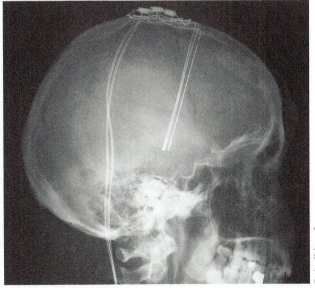

Zephyr/Science Source

More research on and treatments for MCS and TBI are discussed in Sections 7-1, 14-5, and 15-7. Concussion is the topic of Clinical Focus 16-3.

some patients did exhibit activity similar to that of the control participants, showing that they understood the instructions. Owen's study demonstrates that some patients were conscious and so allowed him to proceed with further communication and rehabilitation.

Taken together, these studies reveal that the brain can be conscious to a great extent in the absence of much overt behavior. They also show that in the absence of overt behavior, the brain can communicate through the signals generated by its activity, as Harvey proposed. Whether the brain can maintain consciousness with the absence of *all* sensory experience and movement—one of the challenges of Harvey's brain in a bottle experiment—remains a question for further research.

Some of this future research may come from advances in artificial intelligence (AI). Contemporary AI research shows that computers can do amazing things, including beating master players at the complex games chess and GO. Could a computer that directly experiences the world in the way we do, such as going to school, checking social media, playing sports—in short, sensing and responding in the way we do each day—be conscious in the same way that we are? The answer to the question of whether a computer can be conscious in the absence of embodied behavior is at the heart of our friend Harvey's experiment.

What Is Behavior?

Irenäus Eibl-Eibesfeldt began his classic textbook *Ethology: The Biology of Behavior* (1970) with the following definition: "Behavior consists of patterns in time." These patterns can be made up of movements, vocalizations, or changes in appearance, such as the facial movements associated with smiling. The expression *patterns in time* includes thinking. We cannot directly observe someone's thoughts. As we have described above, however, the changes in the brain's electrical and biochemical activity that are associated with thought show that thinking, too, is a behavior that forms patterns in time.

The behavioral patterns of animals vary enormously, and these variations indicate the diverse functions of the brain. Animals produce behavior that is described as inherited, meaning they can perform a behavior with little or no previous experience. For these behaviors, their brains come equipped with the requisite organization to produce these behaviors. Animals also produce learned behaviors, which are behaviors that require experience and practice. These behaviors depend on the brain's *plasticity*, its ability to change in response to a learning experience. Most behaviors consist of a mix of inherited and learned actions and so involve a preorganized brain that is modifiable through experience.

Figure 1-4 illustrates the contributions of learning in the eating behaviors of two animal species, crossbills and roof rats. A crossbill's beak seems awkwardly crossed at the tip, yet it is exquisitely evolved for eating pine cones. If its shape is changed even slightly, the bird is unable to eat the pine cones it prefers until its beak grows back. For crossbills, eating does not require much modification through learning. Roof rats, in contrast, are rodents with sharp incisor teeth that appear to have evolved to cut into anything. Pine cones are an unusual food for the rats, although they have been found to eat them. But roof rats can eat pine cones efficiently only if an experienced mother teaches them to do so. This eating is not only learned, it is *cultural* in that parents teach it to offspring. We expand on the concept of culture in Section 1-5.

Generally, animals with smaller, simpler nervous systems exhibit a narrow range of behaviors that depend mainly on *heredity*. Animals with complex nervous systems have more behavioral options that are more dependent on *learning*. We humans believe that we are the animal species with the most complex nervous system and the greatest capacity for learning new responses. Most of our most complex behaviors, including reading, writing, mathematics, and using smartphones, were learned long after our brain evolved its present form.

The lesson from the variation exhibited by different animal species with respect to learning is that, in much of its organization, the brain comes prepared to produce behavior but also prepared to change. Like other animals, humans retain many

A crossbill's beak is specifically designed to open pine cones. This behavior is innate.

A baby roof rat must learn from its mother how to eat pine cones. This behavior is learned.

FIGURE 1-4 **Innate and Learned Behaviors** Some animal behaviors are largely innate and fixed (top). Others are largely learned (bottom). Learning is a form of cultural transmission. Top: Information from Weiner (1995). Bottom: Information from Terkel (1995).

inherited ways of responding, such as the sucking response of a newborn infant. But later in life, eating is strongly influenced by learning and by culture.

1-1 Review

Before you continue, check your understanding. Answers to Self-Test appear at the back of the book.

1. _____ and _____ are wounds to the brain that result from a blow to the head.

2. The brain and spinal cord together make up the _____. All the nerve fibers radiating out beyond the brain and spinal cord as well as all the neurons outside the brain and spinal cord form the _____.

3. One major set of brain structures, the _____, or _____, has nearly symmetrical left and right _____ enfolding the _____, which connects to the spinal cord.

4. A simple definition of *behavior* is any kind of movement in a living organism. Every behavior has both a cause and a function, but behaviors vary in complexity and in the degree to which they are _____, or automatic, and the degree to which they depend on _____.

5. Explain the concept of *embodied behavior* in a statement or brief paragraph.

For additional study tools, visit ≋ **LaunchPad** at launchpadworks.com

---

1-2

Perspectives on Brain and Behavior

Let's return to our central topic: how the study of brain and the study behavior are related. Many philosophers have reasoned about the causes of behavior. Their speculations can be classified into three broad approaches: mentalism, dualism, and materialism. After describing each, we explain why contemporary brain investigators subscribe to the materialist view. In reviewing these theories, you will recognize that some familiar ideas about behavior derive from these long-standing perspectives.

Aristotle and Mentalism

The hypothesis that the mind (or soul or psyche) controls behavior can be traced back more than 2000 years to ancient Greco-Roman mythology. Psyche, a mortal, became the wife of the young god Cupid. Venus, Cupid's mother, opposed his marriage, so she harassed Psyche with almost impossible tasks.

Psyche performed the tasks with such dedication, intelligence, and compassion that she was made immortal, thus removing Venus's objection to her. The ancient Greek philosopher Aristotle was alluding to this story when he suggested that all human intellectual functions are produced by a person's **psyche**. The psyche, Aristotle argued, is responsible for life, and its departure from the body results in death.

Aristotle's account of behavior marks the beginning of modern psychology—and the brain played no role in it. Aristotle thought the brain existed to cool the blood. Even if he had thought that the brain ruled behavior, as did some other philosophers and physicians of his time, it would have made little difference in the absence of any idea of how a body organ could produce behavior (Gross, 1995).

To Aristotle, the psyche was a nonmaterial entity independent of the body but responsible for human consciousness, perceptions, and emotions and for such processes as imagination, opinion, desire, pleasure, pain, memory, and reason. In formulating the concept of a soul, Christianity adopted Aristotle's view that a nonmaterial entity governs our behavior and that our essential consciousness survives our death.

The word *psyche* was translated into English as *mind*, the Anglo-Saxon word for *memory*. The philosophical position that a person's mind (psyche) is responsible for behavior is called **mentalism**. Mentalism has influenced modern behavioral science

psyche Synonym for *mind*, an entity once proposed to be the source of human behavior.

mentalism Explanation of behavior as a function of the nonmaterial mind.

François Gérard, *Psyche and Cupid* (1798)

because many psychological terms that originated with Aristotle—*consciousness, sensation, perception, attention, imagination, emotion, motivation, memory,* and *volition* among them—survive today as descriptions of behavior. Indeed, we use these terms in this book, and they frequently appear as chapter titles in contemporary psychology and neuroscience textbooks.

Descartes and Dualism

In the first book on brain and behavior, *Treatise on Man,* French philosopher René Descartes (1664) proposed a new explanation of behavior in which he retained the mind's prominence but gave the brain an important role. Descartes placed the seat of the mind in the brain and linked the mind to the body. He stated in the first sentence of the book that mind and body "must be joined and united to constitute people."

Descartes's innovation was the insight into how body organs produce their actions. He realized that mechanical and physical principles could explain most activities of body and brain—motion, digestion, and breathing, for example. Descartes was influenced by complex machines, including gears, clocks, and waterwheels, being built in Paris at the time. He saw mechanical gadgets on public display. In the water gardens in Paris, one device caused a hidden statue to approach and spray water when an unsuspecting stroller walked past it. The statue's actions were triggered when the person stepped on a pedal hidden in the sidewalk. Influenced by these clever devices, Descartes developed mechanical principles to explain bodily functions.

But Descartes could not imagine how consciousness could be reduced to a mechanistic explanation. He thus retained the idea that a nonmaterial mind governs rational behavior. Descartes did, however, develop a mechanical explanation for how the mind interacts with the body to produce movement, working through a small structure at the brain's center, the pineal body (*pineal gland*). He concluded that the mind instructed the pineal body, which lies beside fluid-filled brain cavities called *ventricles,* to direct fluid from them through nerves and into muscles (**Figure 1-5**). When the fluid expanded the muscles, the body would move.

Descartes's thesis that the mind directed the body was a serious attempt to give the brain an understandable role in controlling behavior. This idea that behavior is controlled by two entities, a mind and a body, is known as **dualism** (from Latin, meaning *"two"*). To Descartes, the mind received information from the body through the brain. The mind also directed the body through the brain. The mind, then, depended on the brain both for information and to control behavior.

Problems plague Descartes's dualistic theory, however. People who have a damaged pineal body or even no pineal body still display typical intelligent behavior. Today, we understand that the pineal gland's role in behavior is relegated to biological rhythms. Experiments in Descartes's time also showed that fluid is not pumped from the brain into muscles when they contract. Placing an arm in a bucket of water and contracting its muscles did not cause the water level in the bucket to rise, as it should if the volume of the muscle increased because fluid had been pumped into it. We now know that there is no way for a nonmaterial entity to influence the body: doing so requires the spontaneous generation of energy, which violates the physical law of conservation of matter and energy.

The inability of Descartes's theory to explain how a nonmaterial mind and a physical brain might interact is called the **mind–body problem**. Nevertheless, Descartes proposed tests for the presence of mind, the ability to use language and memory to reason. He proposed that nonhuman animals and machines would be unable to pass the tests because they lacked a mind.

The contemporary version of Descartes's tests, the Turing test, is named for Alan Turing, an English mathematician. In 1950, Turing proposed that a machine could be judged conscious if a questioner could not distinguish its answers from a human's. Contemporary computers are able to pass the Turing test. Experimental research also

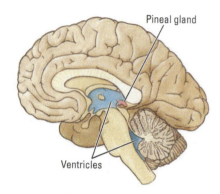

FIGURE 1-5 **Dualist Hypothesis** To explain how the mind controls the body, Descartes suggested that the mind resides in the pineal gland, where it directs the flow of fluid through the ventricles and into the muscles to move the body. The pineal gland actually influences daily and seasonal biorhythms; see Section 13-2.

The 2014 film *The Imitation Game* dramatizes Turing's efforts during World War II to crack the Nazis' Enigma code.

The Speaking Brain

No area of research has generated a literature as diverse and imaginative as the study of human language origins. In their book *Why Only Us*, Robert Berwick and Noam Chomsky (2016) argue that among animals, only humans have evolved language because of their unique ability to "merge" words and concepts to make an infinite number of concepts. In making this argument, they confront evolutionary theory that predicts it is unlikely that language appeared full-blown in modern humans. While accepting the uniqueness of human language, the study of brain and behavior can contribute to our understanding of language origins by asking how the brain plays a role in communication in diverse species of animals. Many animal species with a small cerebrum, including fishes and frogs, are capable of elaborate vocalizations, and vocalization is still more elaborate in species having a large cerebrum, such as birds, whales, and primates.

In language studies with chimpanzees, humans' closest living relatives, scientists have used three approaches: language training, analysis of spontaneous vocalizations and gestures, and study of the anatomy and function of the brain. To show that nonverbal forms of language might have preceded verbal language, Beatrice and Alan Gardner (1969) taught a version of American Sign Language (ASL) to a chimpanzee named Washoe. More recently, Sue Savage-Rumbaugh and her coworkers (1999) taught a bonobo (a chimp species thought to be an even closer relative of humans than others) named Kanzi the symbolic language Yerkish. Kanzi also displayed clear evidence of understanding complex human speech.

Recordings of Kanzi's vocalizations when interacting with people and when eating reveal that he makes many sounds associated with their meanings, or semantic context. For example, Kanzi associates various peeps with specific foods. Chimps are also found to use a raspberry or extended grunt sound in a specific context to attract the attention of others, including people. They have even been shown to use vocalizations and facial and arm gestures, at times in combination, to signal intent. Chimps may also use one distinct call

to attract others to feeding locations and another to initiate a trip. Stewart Watson and colleagues (2015) report that in two chimpanzee colonies, the animals used different referential calls (names) for apples. When the groups were combined, both modified their calls and adopted a common call, an example of gestural drift analogous to people adopting the speech patterns of those around them.

Imaging of brain blood flow associated with the use of the chimpanzeeish language indicates that humans and chimpanzees activate the same brain regions when they communicate. Imaging studies of the pathways in the brain also show that chimpanzees that voluntarily learn to use sounds to attract human investigators show structural changes in these same brain regions compared to chimps that do not use such signals (Bianchi et al., 2016). Taken together, studies on our closest living relatives suggest that we share some key language similarities with them but that perhaps we do not share the critical aspects of language, such as the "merge" ability of humans.

Kanzi

---

casts doubt on Descartes's view that nonhuman animals cannot pass his tests. Studies of communication in apes and other animals partly seek to discover whether other species can describe and reason about things that are not present. Comparative Focus 1-2, The Speaking Brain, summarizes a contemporary approach to studying communication in animals.

Descartes's theory of mind led to some bad results. Based on dualism, some people argued that young children and those who are insane must lack minds because they often fail to reason appropriately. We still use the expression *he's lost his mind* to describe someone who is mentally ill. Some proponents of dualism also reasoned that, if someone lacked a mind, that person was simply a machine, not due respect or kindness. Cruel treatment of animals, children, and the mentally ill could be justified by Descartes's theory. It is unlikely that Descartes himself intended these interpretations. Reportedly he was kind to his own dog, Monsieur Grat.

Darwin and Materialism

By the mid-nineteenth century, another brain–behavior theory emerged. **Materialism** advanced the idea that the workings of the brain and the rest of the nervous system

dualism Philosophical position that both a nonmaterial mind and a material body contribute to behavior.

mind–body problem Difficulty of explaining how a nonmaterial mind and a material body interact.

materialism Philosophical position that behavior can be explained as a function of the nervous system without recourse to the mind.

alone fully explain behavior. It came to prominence when supported by the evolutionary theory of Alfred Russel Wallace and Charles Darwin.

Evolution by Natural Selection

Wallace and Darwin independently arrived at the same conclusion—the idea that all living things are related. Darwin elaborated the position in his book *On the Origin of Species by Means of Natural Selection*, published in 1859, which is why Darwin is regarded as the founder of modern evolutionary theory.

Both Darwin and Wallace were struck by the myriad anatomical and behavioral characteristics common to so many species despite their diversity. The skeleton, muscles, and body parts of humans, monkeys, and other mammals are remarkably similar. So is their behavior: many animal species reach for food with their forelimbs. More important, these same observations led Darwin to explain how the great diversity in the biological world could have evolved from common ancestry. Darwin proposed that animals have traits in common because these traits are passed from parents to their offspring.

Natural selection is the theory explaining how new species evolve and how existing species change over time. A **species** is a group of organisms that can breed among themselves. Individual organisms of any species vary extensively in their **phenotype**, the characteristics we can see or measure. No two individuals of any species are exactly alike. Some are big, some are small, some are fat, some are fast, some are light-colored, and some have large teeth.

Individual organisms whose characteristics best help them to survive in their environment are likely to leave more offspring than are less-fit members. This unequal ability of individual members to survive and reproduce leads to a gradual change in a species' population over time. Natural selection is nature's blueprint for the methods of artificial selection practiced for centuries by plant and animal breeders to produce animals and crops with desirable traits.

Figure 2-1 illustrates this principle of phenotypic plasticity.

Natural Selection and Heritable Factors

Neither Darwin nor Wallace understood the basis of the great variation in plant and animal species they observed. Another scientist, the monk Gregor Mendel, discovered one principle underlying phenotypic variation and how traits pass from parents to their offspring. Through experiments he conducted on pea plants in his monastery garden beginning about 1857, Mendel deduced that heritable factors, which we now call *genes*, govern various physical traits displayed by the species.

Members of a species that have a particular genetic makeup, or **genotype**, are likely to *express* (turn on) similar phenotypic traits, as posited in the Procedure section of **Experiment 1-1**. If the gene or combination of genes for a specific trait—say, flower color—is passed on to offspring, the offspring will express the same trait, as illustrated by the Results section in Experiment 1-1.

The unequal ability of individual organisms to survive and reproduce is related to the different genes they inherit from their parents and pass on to their offspring. By the same token, similar characteristics within or between species are usually due to similar genes. For instance, genes that produce the nervous system in different animal species tend to be very similar.

Interplay of Genes, Environment, and Experience

The principles of inheritance that Mendel demonstrated through his experiments have led to countless discoveries about genetics. We now know that new traits appear because new gene combinations are inherited from parents and that genes change or mutate.

But genes alone cannot explain most traits. Even Mendel realized that the environment participates in the expression of traits; for example, planting tall peas in poor soil reduces their height. Experience likewise plays a part. The experience of children who attend a substandard school, for instance, is different from that of children who attend a model school.

Section 3-3 explains some basic genetic and epigenetic principles, including what constitutes a gene, how genes function, and how genes can change, or mutate.

···> EXPERIMENT 1-1

Question: How do parents transmit heritable factors to offspring?

Procedure

Members of a species that have a particular *genotype* are likely to express similar phenotypic traits. If the gene or combination of genes for a specific trait (say, flower color) is passed on to offspring, the offspring will express the trait. Two white-flowered pea plants produce white-flowered offspring in the first generation, or F1 in the figure below, and purple-flowered parents produce purple-flowered offspring. Observing this result, Mendel reasoned that two alternative heritable elements govern the trait flower color.

Mendel experimented with crossbreeding F1 purple and white pea plant flowers. The second-generation (F2) offspring all expressed the purple phenotype. Had the factor that expresses white flowers disappeared? To find out, Mendel crossbred the F2 purple flowers. The third generation, F3, produced flowers in the ratio of roughly one white to three purple blooms.

Results

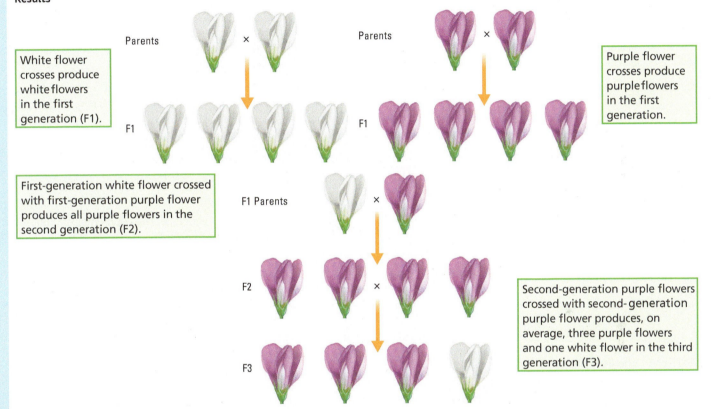

White flower crosses produce white flowers in the first generation (F1).

Purple flower crosses produce purple flowers in the first generation.

First-generation white flower crossed with first-generation purple flower produces all purple flowers in the second generation (F2).

Second-generation purple flowers crossed with second-generation purple flower produces, on average, three purple flowers and one white flower in the third generation (F3).

Conclusion: This result suggested to Mendel that the trait for white flowers had not disappeared but rather was hidden by the trait for purple flowers. He concluded that individuals inherit two factors, or genes, for each trait, but one may dominate and hide (suppress) the other in the individual's phenotype.

We now know that genes and their effects are not static; genes can be active at different times and under different conditions during our life. The field of **epigenetics** (meaning "beyond genes") studies how gene expression is turned on or off at different times and how environment and experience influence our behavior through their effects on our genes.

Epigenetic factors consist of a number of biochemical changes that influence whether a gene is active or inactive. Epigenetic factors can turn on or turn off a gene's function so that the gene influences the function of our body or behavior, or it stops that influence. The epigenetic effects of experience that initiate epigenetic influences on genes can last long after the initial experience and, in some cases, can persist into future generations. Epigenetic factors described throughout this book revolutionize our understanding of behavior–brain relations because they offer an explanation for how our experiences, including studying, influence our brain and the behavior that it subsequently produces.

natural selection Darwin's theory explaining how new species evolve and how existing species change over time. Differential success in the reproduction of different characteristics (phenotypes) results from the interaction of organisms with their environment.

species Group of organisms that can interbreed.

phenotype Set of individual characteristics that can be seen or measured.

genotype Particular genetic makeup of an individual.

epigenetics Differences in gene expression related to environment and experience.

Summarizing Materialism

Darwin's theory of natural selection, Mendel's discovery of genetic inheritance, and the reality of epigenetics have three important implications for studying the brain and behavior:

Section 3-1 describes the varieties of neurons and other brain cells.

1. *Because all animal species are related, their brains must be related.* A large body of research confirms, first, that all animals' brain cells are so similar that these cells must be related and, second, that all animal brains are so similar that they must be related as well. Brain researchers can study the nervous systems of animals as different as slugs, fruit flies, rats, and monkeys, knowing that they can extend their findings to the human nervous system.

2. *Because all animal species are related, their behavior must be related.* In his book *The Expression of the Emotions in Man and Animals*, Darwin (1872) argued that emotional expressions are similar in humans and other animals because all animals inherited them from a common ancestor. **Figure 1-6** offers evidence. That people the world over display the same behavior suggests that the trait is inherited.

More on emotions and their expression in Sections 12-6 and 14-3.

3. *Brains and behaviors in complex animals such as humans evolved from simpler animals' brains and behaviors.* Coming up in Section 1-3, we trace the evolution of nervous systems and their increasingly complex repertoires of actions, from a simple netlike arrangement to a multipart nervous system with a brain that controls behavior.

Contemporary Perspectives on Brain and Behavior

Where do modern students of the brain stand on the perspectives of mentalism, dualism, and materialism? In his influential 1949 book *The Organization of Behavior*, psychologist Donald O. Hebb describes the scientific acceptance of materialism in a folksy manner:

> Modern psychology takes completely for granted that behavior and neural function are perfectly correlated, that one is completely caused by the other. There is no separate soul or life force to stick a finger into the brain now and then and make neural cells do what they would not otherwise. (Hebb, 1949, p. iii)

Hebb's claim dovetails with his theory of how the brain produces new behavior. He suggested that learning is enabled by small groups of neurons forming new connections with one another to form a *cell assembly*, which is the substrate for a memory. Cell assemblies interact: one cell assembly becomes connected to another. This linking of cell assemblies is thus the linking of memories, which to Hebb is what produces our complex behavior, including our consciousness of our own and others' actions.

FIGURE 1-6 **An Inherited Behavior** People the world over display the same emotional expressions that they recognize in others—these smiles, for example. This evidence supports Darwin's suggestion that emotional expression is an inherited behavior.

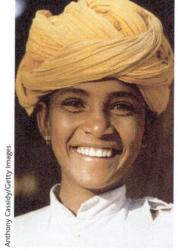

Hebb's argument is materialistic and provides a way of explaining how consciousness is created in terms of the physical properties of the brain. Hebb's explanation of consciousness espouses the philosophical position of *eliminative materialism,* which states that if behavior can be described adequately without recourse to the mind, then the mental explanation should be eliminated. Daniel Dennett (1978) and other philosophers argue that if attributes such as consciousness, pain, and attention can be explained by physical mechanisms, it is unnecessary to appeal to mental explanations.

The Separate Realms of Science and Belief

Materialists, your authors included, continue to use subjective mentalistic words such as *consciousness, pain,* and *attention* to describe complex behaviors. At the same time, they recognize that these words do not describe mental entities. Materialism argues for objective, *measurable* descriptions of behavior that can be referenced to brain activity.

Some people may question materialism's tenet that only the brain is responsible for behavior because they think it denies religion. But materialism is neutral with respect to religion. Many of the world's major religions accept both evolution and the brain's centrality in behavior as important scientific theories. Fred Linge, introduced in Clinical Focus 1-1, has strong religious beliefs, as do the other members of his family. They used their religious strength to aid in his recovery. Yet, despite their religious beliefs, they realize that Linge's brain injury caused his changed behavior and that learning to compensate for his impairments caused his brain function to improve.

Many behavioral scientists hold religious beliefs and see no contradiction between them and their engagement with science. Science is not a belief system but rather a set of procedures designed to allow investigators to confirm answers to a question independently. As outlined in Experiment 1-1, this four-step procedure allows anyone to *replicate,* or repeat, their original conclusions—or find that they cannot.

The four-step experimental procedure is: (1) formulate a theory, (2) make a prediction (hypothesis), (3) test it, (4) confirm or modify the theory.

1-2 Review

Before you continue, check your understanding. Answers to Self-Test appear at the back of the book.

1. The view that behavior is the product of an intangible entity called the mind (psyche) is _____. The notion that the immaterial mind acts through the material brain to produce language and rational behavior is _____. _____, the view that brain function fully accounts for all behavior, guides contemporary research on the brain and behavior.

2. The implication that the brains and behaviors of complex animals such as humans evolved from the brains and behaviors of simpler animals draws on the theory of _____ advanced by _____.

3. The brain demonstrates a remarkable ability to recover, even after severe brain injury, but an injured person may linger in a _____, occasionally able to communicate or to follow simple commands but otherwise not conscious. Those who have such extensive brain damage that no recovery can be expected remain in a _____, alive but unable to communicate or to function independently at even the most basic level.

4. Darwin and Mendel were nineteenth-century contemporaries. Briefly contrast the methods they used to reach their scientific conclusions.

For additional study tools, visit **LaunchPad** at launchpadworks.com

1-3

Evolution of Brains and of Behavior

As some lineages of animals have evolved, their nervous systems and behavior have built up and changed bit by bit. We trace the evolution of the human brain and behavior by describing (1) animals that first developed a nervous system and muscles with

common ancestor Forebear of two or more lineages or family groups; ancestral to both groups.

which to move, (2) how the nervous system grew more complex as the brain evolved to mediate complex behavior, and (3) how the human brain evolved its present complexity, which we cover in the next section.

The popular interpretation of human evolution is that we are descended from apes. Actually, humans *are* apes. Other living apes are not our ancestors, although we are related to them through a **common ancestor**, a forebear from which two or more lineages or family groups arise. To demonstrate the difference, consider the following story.

Two people named Joan Campbell are introduced at a party, and their names provide a rich conversation starter. Although both belong to the Campbell lineage (family line), one Joan is not descended from the other. The two women live in different parts of North America, one in Texas and the other in Ontario, and both their families have been there for many generations.

Nevertheless, after comparing family histories, the two Joans discover that they have ancestors in common. The Texas Campbells are descended from Jeeves Campbell, brother of Matthew Campbell, from whom the Ontario Campbells are descended. Jeeves and Matthew both boarded the same fur-trading ship when it stopped for water in the Orkney Islands north of Scotland before sailing to North America in colonial times.

The Joan Campbells' common ancestors, then, were the mother and father of Jeeves and Matthew. Both the Texas and the Ontario Campbell family lines are descended from this man and woman. If the two Joan Campbells were to compare their genes, they would find similarities that correspond to their common lineage.

In much the same way, humans and other apes are descended from common ancestors. But unlike the Joan Campbells, we do not know exactly who those distant relatives were. By comparing the brain and behavioral characteristics of humans and related animals and by comparing their genes, however, scientists are tracing our lineage back further and further to piece together the origins of our brain and behavior.

Some living animal species display characteristics more similar to those of a common ancestor than do others. For example, in some ways chimpanzees are more similar to the common ancestor of humans and chimpanzees than are modern humans. In the following sections, we trace some major evolutionary events that led to human brains and human behavior by looking at the nervous systems of living animal species and the fossils of extinct animal species.

Origin of Brain Cells and Brains

Earth formed about 4.5 billion years ago, and the first life-forms arose about a billion years later. About 700 million years ago, animals evolved the first brain cells, and by 250 million years ago, the first brain had evolved. A humanlike brain first developed only about 6 million years ago, and our modern human brain has been around for only the past 200,000 years or so.

Although life arose early in our planet's history, brain cells and brains evolved only recently. In evolutionary terms, large, complex brains, such as ours, appeared an eyeblink ago. If you are familiar with the principles of taxonomic classification, which names and orders living organisms according to their evolutionary relationships, read on. If you prefer a brief review before you continue, turn first to The Basics: Classification of Life on pages 16–17.

Evolution of Nervous Systems in Animals

A nervous system is not essential for life. In fact, most organisms, including plants and bacteria, both past and present, have done without one. In animals that do have a nervous system, comparison of a wide variety of species broadly outlines how the nervous system has evolved. We summarize this evolution in the following general steps:

1. *Neurons and muscles.* Brain cells and muscles evolved together, enabling animals to move. Neurons and muscles likely have their origins in single-cell animals such as amoeba that developed numerous ways of moving about, traits that became more specialized in multicellular animals.

2. *Nerve net.* The nervous system representative of evolutionarily older phyla, such as jellyfishes and sea anemones, is extremely simple. It consists of a diffuse **nerve net**, which has no structure that resembles a brain or spinal cord but consists entirely of neurons that receive sensory information and connect directly to other neurons that move muscles. Look again at Figure 1-1 and imagine that the brain and spinal cord have been removed. The human PNS is reminiscent of the nerve net in phylogenetically simpler animals.

3. *Bilateral symmetry.* In more complex animals such as flatworms, the nervous system is more organized, and it features **bilateral symmetry**: the nervous system on one side of the animal mirrors that on the other side. The human nervous system is also bilaterally symmetrical (see Figure 1-1).

4. *Segmentation.* The body of an animal such as an earthworm consists of a series of similar muscular segments. Its nervous system has similar repeating segments. The human spinal cord and brain display such **segmentation**: the vertebrae contain the similar repeating nervous system segments of the spinal cord.

5. *Ganglia.* In still more recently evolved invertebrate phyla, including clams, snails, and octopuses, are clusters of neurons called **ganglia** that resemble primitive brains and function somewhat like them in that they are command centers. In some phyla, *encephalization* (having the ganglia in the head) is distinctive. For example, insects' ganglia are sufficiently large to merit the term *brain*.

6. *Spinal cord.* In relatively highly evolved **chordates**—animals that have both a brain and a spinal cord—a single nervous system pathway connects the brain with sensory receptors and muscles. Chordates get their name from the *notochord*, a flexible rod that runs the length of the back. In humans, the notochord is present only in the embryo; by birth, bony vertebrae encase the spinal cord.

7. *Brain.* The chordate phylum, of which amphibians, reptiles, birds, and mammals are class members, displays the greatest degree of encephalization: a true brain. Of all of the chordates, humans have the largest brain relative to body size, but many other chordates have large brains as well. Although built to a common plan, the brain of each chordate species displays specializations related to the distinctive behaviors of that species.

Chordate Nervous System

A chart called a **cladogram** (from the Greek word *clados*, meaning "branch") displays groups of related organisms as branches on a tree. The cladogram in **Figure 1-7** represents seven of the nine classes to which the approximately 38,500 extant chordate species belong. Wide variation exists among the nervous systems of chordates, but common to all is the basic structural pattern of bilateral symmetry, segmentation, and a spinal cord and brain encased in cartilage or bone.

nerve net Simple nervous system that has no center but consists of neurons that receive sensory information and connect directly to other neurons that move muscles.

bilateral symmetry Body plan in which organs or parts present on both sides of the body are mirror images in appearance. For example, the hands are bilaterally symmetrical, whereas the heart is not.

segmentation Division into a number of parts that are similar; refers to the idea that many animals, including vertebrates, are composed of similarly organized body segments.

ganglia Collection of nerve cells that function somewhat like a brain.

chordate Animal that has both a brain and a spinal cord.

cladogram Phylogenetic tree that branches repeatedly, suggesting a taxonomy of organisms based on the time sequence in which evolutionary branches arise.

Figure 2-30 maps the human spinal cord's segments.

FIGURE 1-7 **Representative Classes of Chordates** This cladogram illustrates evolutionary relationships among animals that have a brain and spinal cord. Brain size increased with the evolution of limbs in Amphibia. Birds and mammals are the most recently evolved chordates, and both classes have large brains relative to body size.

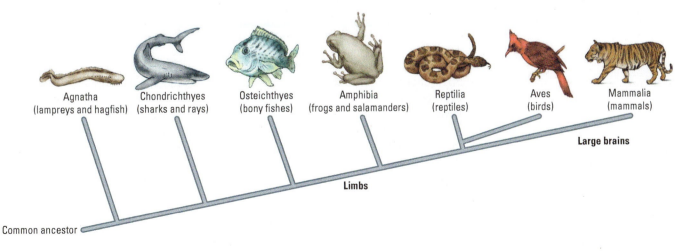

◉ THE BASICS

Classification of Life

Taxonomy is the branch of biology concerned with naming and classifying species by grouping representative organisms according to their common characteristics and their relationships to one another.

As shown in the left column of the Taxonomy of Modern Humans figure, which illustrates the human lineage, the broadest unit of classification is a kingdom, with more subordinate groups being phylum, class, order, family, genus, and species. This taxonomic hierarchy is useful in helping us trace the evolution of brain cells and the brain.

We humans belong to the animal kingdom, the chordate phylum, the mammalian class, the primate order, the great ape family, the genus *Homo*, and the species *sapiens*. Animals are usually identified by their genus and species names. So we humans are called *Homo sapiens sapiens*, meaning "wise, wise human."

The branches in the Cladogram figure, which shows the taxonomy of the animal kingdom, represent the evolutionary sequence (phylogeny) that connects all living organisms. Cladograms are read from left to right: the most recently evolved organism (animal) or trait (muscles and neurons) is farthest to the right.

Of the five kingdoms of living organisms represented in the cladogram, only the one most recently evolved, Animalia, contains species with muscles and nervous systems. It is noteworthy that muscles and nervous systems evolved together to underlie the forms of movement (behavior) that distinguish members of the animal kingdom.

The Evolution of the Nervous System figure shows the taxonomy of the 15 groups, or *phyla*, of Animalia, classified according to increasing complexity of nervous systems and movement. In proceeding to the right from the *nerve net*, we

Taxonomy of Modern Humans

> Taxonomy classifies groups of representative living organisms into increasingly specific, subordinate groups.

Living organisms
Classified in five main kingdoms: Monera (bacteria), Protista (single cells), Plantae (plants), Fungi (fungi), Animalia (animals)

Kingdom: Animals
Characteristics: Neurons and muscles used for locomotion

Phylum: Chordates
Characteristics: Brain and spinal cord

Class: Mammals
Characteristics: Large brains and social behavior

Order: Primates
Characteristics: Visual control of hands

Family: Great apes
Characteristics: Tool use

Genus: Human
Characteristics: Language

Species: Modern human
Characteristics: Complex culture

> Modern humans are the only surviving species of the genus that includes numerous extinct species of humanlike animals.

Research Focus 2-1 elaborates cerebellar function by describing a man born without a cerebellum.

As chordates evolved limbs and new forms of locomotion, their brain became larger. For example, all chordates have a brainstem, but only the birds and mammals have a large forebrain. The evolution of more complex behavior in chordates is closely related to the evolution of the *cerebrum* and *cerebellum*. Their increasing size and complexity in various classes of chordates is illustrated in **Figure 1-8**. These increases accommodate new behaviors, including new forms of locomotion on land, complex movements of the mouth and hands for eating, improved learning ability, and highly organized social behavior.

The cerebrum and the cerebellum are proportionately small and smooth in the earliest evolved classes (e.g., fish, amphibians, and reptiles). In later-evolved chordates,

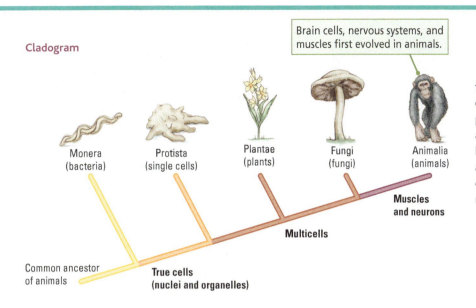

Cladogram

Brain cells, nervous systems, and muscles first evolved in animals.

Monera (bacteria) | Protista (single cells) | Plantae (plants) | Fungi (fungi) | Animalia (animals)

Muscles and neurons

Multicells

Common ancestor of animals

True cells (nuclei and organelles)

find that nervous systems in somewhat more recently evolved phyla, such as flatworms, have more complex structure. These organisms have heads and tails, and their bodies show both *bilateral symmetry* (one half of the body is the mirror image of the other half) and *segmentation* (the body is composed of similarly organized parts). The structure of the human spinal cord resembles this segmented nervous system.

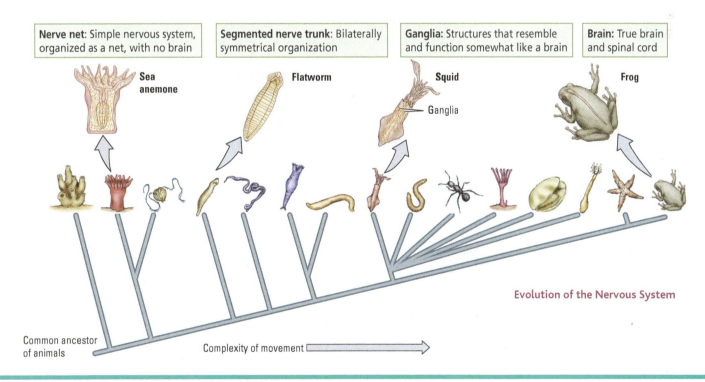

Nerve net: Simple nervous system, organized as a net, with no brain

Segmented nerve trunk: Bilaterally symmetrical organization

Ganglia: Structures that resemble and function somewhat like a brain

Brain: True brain and spinal cord

Sea anemone

Flatworm

Squid

— Ganglia

Frog

Evolution of the Nervous System

Common ancestor of animals

Complexity of movement ⟶

especially the birds and mammals, these structures are much more prominent. In many large-brained mammals, both structures are extensively folded, which greatly increases their surface area while allowing them to fit into a small skull, just as folding a large piece of paper enables it to occupy a small envelope.

Increased size and folding are pronounced in primates, animals with large brains relative to their body size. But relatively large brains with a complex cerebrum and cerebellum have evolved in a number of animal lineages, so humans are neither unique nor special in these respects. As we will describe in the following sections, humans are distinguished in belonging to the large-brained primate lineage and are unique in having the largest, most complex brain in this lineage.

FIGURE 1-8 **Brain Evolution**
The brains of representative chordate species have many structures in common, illustrating a single basic brain plan.

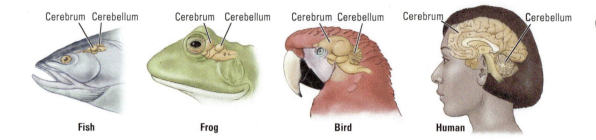

Fish   Frog   Bird   Human

1-3 Review

Before you continue, check your understanding. Answers to Self-Test appear at the back of the book.

1. Because brain cells and muscles evolved only once in the animal kingdom, a similar basic pattern exists in the _____ of all animals.

2. Evolutionary relationships among the nervous systems of animal lineages are classified by increasing complexity, progressing from the simplest _____ to a _____ segmented nervous system to nervous systems controlled by _____ to nervous systems in the phylum _____, which feature a brain and spinal cord.

3. A branching diagram that represents groups of related animals is called a _____.

4. Given that a relatively large brain with a complex cerebrum and cerebellum has evolved in a number of animal lineages, what, if anything, makes the human brain unique?

For additional study tools, visit **LaunchPad** at launchpadworks.com

1-4

Evolution of the Human Brain and Behavior

Anyone can see similarities among humans, apes, and monkeys. Those similarities extend to the brain as well. In this section, we consider how our brain and behaviors link to those of some of our more prominent ancestors. Then we consider the relationship between brain complexity and behavior across species, including human species. We conclude by surveying hypotheses about how the human brain evolved to become so large and the behavior that it mediates so complex. The evolutionary evidence shows that we humans are *specialized* in having an upright posture, making and using tools, and developing language but that we are not *special* because other species also shared these traits, at least to some degree.

Humans: Members of the Primate Order

We humans are members of the primate order, a subcategory of mammals that includes apes, Old World monkeys, New World monkeys, tarsiers, and lemurs (**Figure 1-9**). We are but one of about 275 primate species. Primates have excellent color vision, with the eyes positioned at the front of the face to enhance depth perception. They use their highly developed visual sense to deftly guide their hand movements.

Female primates usually have only one infant per pregnancy, and they spend a great deal more time caring for their young than most other animals do. Primate brains are, on average, larger than those of animals in other mammalian orders, such as rodents (mice, rats, beavers, squirrels) and carnivores (wolves, bears, cats, weasels), and they are larger than the brains of animals in those other orders that have comparable or larger body size.

Humans are members of the great ape family, which includes orangutans, gorillas, and chimpanzees. Apes are arboreal animals with limber shoulders that allow them to brachiate in trees (swing from one handhold to another), a trait retained by humans,

Australian Raymond Dart coined *Australopithecus* in naming the skull of a child he found among fossilized remains from a limestone quarry near Taung, South Africa, in 1924. Choosing so to represent his native land probably was no accident.

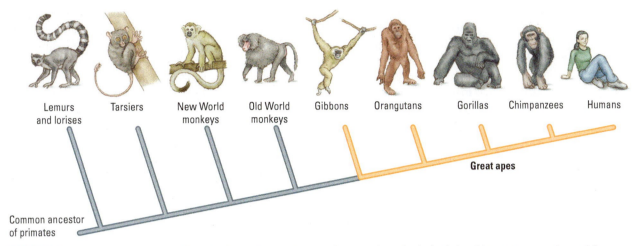

FIGURE 1-9 **Representatives of the Primate Order** This cladogram illustrates hypothetical relationships among members of the primate order. Humans are members of the great ape family. In general, brain size increases across the groupings, with humans having the largest brain of all primates.

who generally do not live in trees these days. Nevertheless, freeing the arms at the shoulder is handy for all sorts of human activities, from traversing monkey bars on the playground to competing in the Olympic hammer toss to raising a hand to ask a question in class. Apes are distinguished as well by their higher intelligence and very large brains—traits that humans exemplify.

Among the apes, we are most closely related to the chimpanzee, having had a common ancestor between 5 million and 10 million years ago. Between that common ancestor and us over the past 5 million years, many **hominids**—primates that walk upright— in our lineage evolved. During most of this time, many hominid species coexisted. At present, however, we are the only surviving hominid species.

Australopithecus: Our Distant Ancestor

One of our hominid ancestors is probably an *Australopithecus* species (from the Latin *austral*, meaning "southern," and the Greek *pithekos*, meaning "ape"). **Figure 1-10** shows reconstructions of the face and body of one such animal, *Australopithecus africanus*. Many species of *Australopithecus* lived, some at the same time, but evidence suggests that this is our common ancestor.

These early hominids were among the first primates to show such human traits as walking upright and using tools. Scientists have deduced their upright posture from the shape of their back, pelvic, knee, and foot bones and from a set of fossilized footprints left by a family of australopiths as they walked through freshly fallen volcanic ash some 3.8 million years ago. These footprints feature impressions of a well-developed arch and an unrotated big toe—more like humans' than other apes'. (Nevertheless, australopiths retained the ability to skillfully climb trees.) The bone structure of their hands evinces tool use (Pickering et al., 2011).

The First Humans

The skull of the first animal to be designated as genus *Homo* (human) was found by Mary and Louis Leakey in the Olduvai Gorge in Tanzania in 1964. The Leakeys named the species *Homo habilis* (handy human) to signify that its members were toolmakers. To date, the earliest member of the genus *Homo*, found in Ethiopia, dates to about 2.8 million years ago. The fossils reveal a jaw and teeth much smaller than in any *Australopithecus* species but characteristic to humans, and their brain was slightly larger than that of *Australopithecus* (Villmoare et al., 2015).

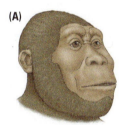

(A)

Australopithecus

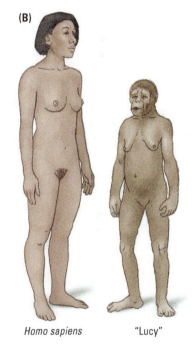

(B)

Homo sapiens   "Lucy"

FIGURE 1-10 **Australopithecus africanus**
(A) The hominid *Australopithecus* walked upright with free hands, as do modern humans, but its brain was about one-third the size of ours and comparable to that of other apes. **(B)** Human and *Australopithecus* figures compared on the basis of the most complete *Australopithecus* skeleton yet found, a young female about 1 meter tall, popularly known as Lucy, who lived 3 million years ago.

hominid General term referring to primates that walk upright, including all forms of humans, living and extinct.

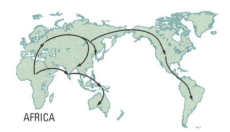

AFRICA

Early humans may have followed such proposed routes out of Africa, first to Asia and Europe, eventually to Australia, and finally to the Americas.

The first humans who spread beyond Africa migrated into Europe and Asia. This species was *Homo erectus* (*upright human*), so named because of the mistaken notion that its predecessor, *H. habilis*, had a stooped posture. *Homo erectus* first shows up in the fossil record about 1.6 million years ago. As shown in **Figure 1-11**, its brain was bigger than that of any preceding hominid, overlapping in size the measurements of present-day human brains. This larger brain likely contributed to its ability to travel and become widely dispersed into Europe and Asia. Because *H. erectus* survived for nearly 2 million years, they may have made many migrations during that time.

The tools made by *H. erectus* were more sophisticated than those made by *H. habilis*, and improved tool use was no doubt enabled by their larger brain. An especially small subspecies of *H. erectus*, about 3 feet tall, was found on the Indonesian island of Flores. Named *Homo floresiensis*, these hominids lived up to about 13,000 years ago (Gordon et al., 2008), which again emphasizes the fact that it is comparatively recently that only one hominid species exists.

A number of *Homo sapiens* species appeared within the past million years; these are collectively referred to as archaic humans. *H. neanderthalis*, named for the Neander Thal (Valley), Germany, where the first Neanderthal skulls were found, were widespread in Europe. As the first fossilized human ancestor to be discovered, Neanderthals have maintained a preeminent place in the study of modern human ancestors. Modern humans, *Homo sapiens sapiens*, appeared about 200,000 years ago, and in Europe where they coexisted with archaic Neanderthals, they interbred until they replaced Neanderthals about 20,000 years ago.

Neanderthals had brains as large as, and perhaps a little larger than, those of modern humans, used similar tools, and wore jewelry and makeup. They lived in family groups similar to modern human ones, made music, cared for their elders, and buried their dead. From these archeological findings, we can infer that Neanderthals probably communicated using language and held religious beliefs.

We do not know how modern humans came to completely replace archaic human species, but perhaps they had advantages in toolmaking, language use, or social organization. Contemporary genetic evidence shows that modern European humans who inherited Neanderthals' genes acquired genes that adapted them to the cold, to novel disease, and possibly to light skin that better absorbs vitamin D (Sankararaman et al.,

FIGURE 1-11 **Increases in Hominid Brain Size** The brain of *Australopithecus* was about the same size as that of living nonhuman apes, but succeeding members of the human lineage display increased brain size. Data from Johanson & Edey, 1981.

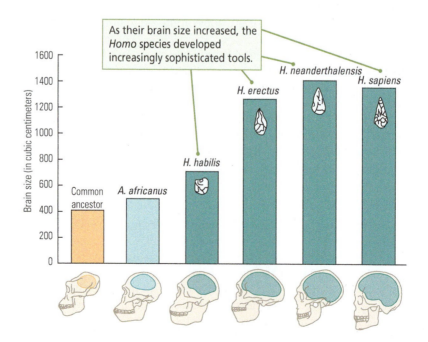

2014). Reconstructions like the one in **Figure 1-12** show how similar to us Neanderthals really were.

One possible human lineage is shown in **Figure 1-13**. A common ancestor gave rise to the *Australopithecus* lineage, and one member of this group gave rise to the *Homo* lineage. The bars in Figure 1-13 are not connected because many more hominid species have been discovered than are shown, and exact direct ancestors are uncertain. The bars overlap because many hominid species coexisted until quite recently.

Relating Brain Size and Behavior

Scientists who study brain evolution often use brain size as a rough measure to explain more complex behavior. But there is more to the story. The number of brain cells is also important, as are the connections that those cells make. Unfortunately, the fossil record provides only skulls from which a measure of brain size can be estimated. In the following section, we will summarize how brain size is compared across species and how it contributes to our understanding of behavior. Then we will describe the importance of brain cell number and of brain cell connections.

Estimating Relative Brain–Body Size

Harry Jerison (1973) describes an index that compares the ratio of brain size to body size across species. He calculates that as body size increases, brain size increases at about two-thirds the increase in body weight. Jerison's underlying assumption is that even if very little is known about an animal's behavior, its brain size could provide some clues to its behavioral complexity. The idea is that species shown to have larger brains must exhibit more complex behavior.

Using the ratio of actual brain size to expected brain size, Jerison developed a quantitative measure, the **encephalization quotient (EQ)**. He defined an average animal (a domestic cat was Jerison's pick) as having an EQ of 1. The diagonal trend line in **Figure 1-14** plots the expected brain–body size ratio of a number of animal species in relation to a trend line representing animals with an EQ of 1. Some species lie below the line: their brain size is smaller than would be expected for an animal of that size. Other species lie above the line: their brain size is larger than would be expected for an animal of that size.

The lower an animal's brain falls relative to the trend line in Figure 1-14, the smaller its EQ; the higher an animal's brain lies relative to the trend line, the larger its EQ. Notice that the rat's brain is a little smaller (lower EQ) and the elephant's brain a little larger (higher EQ) than the ratio predicts. Modern humans, farther above the line than any other animal, have the highest EQ.

Counting Brain Cells

Jerison's EQ provides a rough estimate of comparative brain size, but body size and brain size can vary independently (**Figure 1-15**, top). Some apes, such as the gorillas, are specialized in having large bodies, while others, such as ourselves, are specialized in having large brains.

Counting brain cells is another way to estimate the behavioral capacity of a brain. Consider the roundworm *Caenorhabditis elegans*, which has 959 cells. Of these, 302 are neurons. In contrast, the blue whale—the largest animal that has ever lived, weighing as much as 200 tons—has a brain weighing 15,000 grams (33 lb).

Based on EQs, we would predict that *C. elegans*, with one-third of its body made up of brain cells, has a more complex behavioral repertoire than a blue whale, with 0.01 percent of its body made up of brain cells. But it makes no sense to suggest that a worm's behavior is more complex than a whale's. Counting brain cells provides a better comparison.

Karina Fonseca-Azevedo and her colleagues (Fonseca-Azevedo & Herculano-Houzel, 2012) describe a method of counting brain cells using a counting machine. Not only can they estimate the number of neurons in a brain or a part of the brain, they also can estimate the neurons' *packing density*. For example, two similar-sized brains

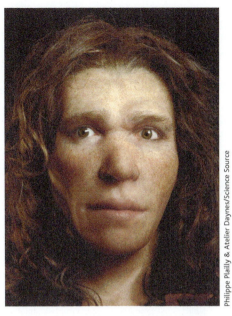

FIGURE 1-12 **Neanderthal Woman** A facial reconstruction by Elisabeth Daynes made from a casting of the skull. The female, whom the discoverers called Pierrette, died a violent death between the ages of 17 and 20. Her 36,000-year-old remains were discovered in western France in 1979, lying near tools from the Neanderthal period. Research Focus 10-1 reports on the discovery of a flute made by Neanderthals.

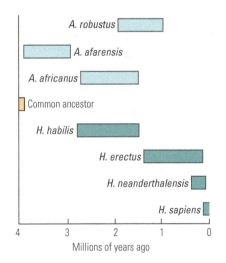

FIGURE 1-13 **Human Origins** The human lineage and a lineage of extinct *Australopithecus* probably arose from a common ancestor about 4 million years ago. The ancestor of the human lineage *Homo* was probably a hominid similar to *A. africanus*.

encephalization quotient (EQ) Jerison's quantitative measure of brain size obtained from the ratio of actual brain size to expected brain size, according to the principle of proper mass, for an animal of a particular body size.

FIGURE 1-14 **Ratios of Brain to Body Size in Common Mammals** As represented logarithmically on this graph, average brain size relative to body weight falls along a diagonal trend line, where you find the cat. Data from Jerison, 1973.

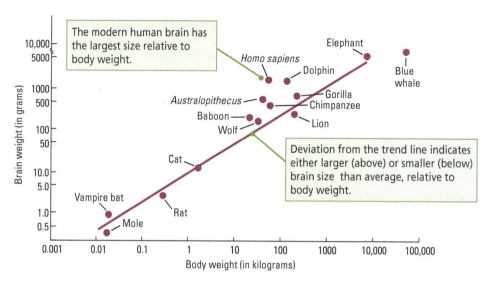

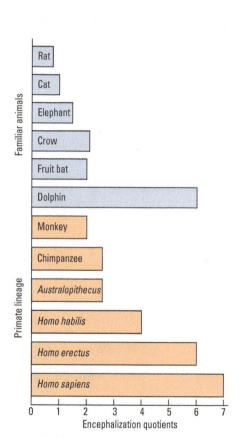

FIGURE 1-15 **Comparing EQs** The EQs of some familiar mammals are ranked at the top of the chart, and members of the primate lineage are ranked at the bottom. Clearly, intelligence is widespread among animals.

could consist of either diffusely distributed large neurons or closely packed small neurons. Using brain cell counts, a blue whale has 30 billion neurons, which is a lot more than the 302 neurons of *C. elegans*, numbers that provide a better explanation of their behaviors than relative size measures.

Fonseca-Azevedo has found that the packing density of neurons is relatively constant in the primate lineage, so EQ and brain cell counts both provide a good comparison of their brain sizes (Figure 1-15, bottom). Knowing that, *Australopithecus* likely had about 50 billion to 60 billion neurons, *Homo habilis* about 60 billion, and *Homo erectus* about 75 billion to 90 billion, whereas modern humans have about 86 billion neurons.

If the number of brain cells is important, does the number or density of cells in different brain regions vary, and is this an additional explanation of behavior variation? It does, and counts of neurons in different regions of the brain provide an answer to a puzzle: Why is the behavior of elephants and dolphins with their very large brains not as complex as human behavior? As detailed in Comparative Focus 1-3, "The Elephant's Brain," pachyderms have an enormous number of neurons, but most are in the cerebellum, an area associated with motor behavior; on the other hand, the number of neurons in the elephant cerebrum, an area associated with cognitive processes, is equivalent to that of chimpanzees. These neuron counts suggest that apes and elephants should have equivalent cognitive abilities, which they do. Furthermore, the dolphin, another animal with a very large brain, has a total of 30 billion neurons, a number similar to the number in chimpanzees—and many fewer than in the smaller human brain—because dolphin neurons are not densely packed. Thus, the behavior of modern humans is complex because of a large brain size with a very large number of densely packed neurons.

The utility of relating neuron number to behavioral complexity is not limited to mammals. Researchers have found that the clever behavior of birds, such as parrots and crows, is related to the larger number of densely packed neurons they have in their cerebrum relative to other birds.

Brain Cell Connections

Brains become larger by the addition of neurons, and the addition of neurons adds disproportionately more connections between those neurons. **Figure 1-16** illustrates one view of how the complexity of the brain evolves as more neurons are added. The first column in the figure uses different colors to illustrate the functions of neurons. Most of the cerebrum of a smaller brain (bottom), such as that of a fish, is devoted to the primary senses and movement. It has neurons for vision, hearing, touch, olfaction, and movement.

The neurons with different functions do not occupy specific regions but have a "salt and pepper" organization. For animals with successively larger brains, the

The Elephant's Brain

The cerebrum and cerebellum have evolved into the human brain's most distinct and largest structures, larger than in any other primate brain. Although the cerebellum appears smaller than the cerebrum physically, its small, tightly packed neurons are four times the number found in the cerebrum (about 68 billion vs. 16 billion), a 4:1 ratio that humans share with all other primates. Typically, the cerebrum is described as mediating cognitive functions, whereas the cerebellum mediates motor function, although in cooperative functions they do share many functions.

African elephants are enormous animals. It is not surprising that they have the largest brain of all terrestrial animals—three times the size of a human's. With such a large brain, why don't elephants share humans' intellectual abilities?

Suzana Herculano-Houzel and her colleagues (2014) made a neuronal count of an African elephant and found that its brain contains three times as many neurons as the human brain (257 billion vs. 86 billion neurons). But remarkably, 251 billion of those neurons (97.5 percent) reside in the elephant's cerebellum.

The elephant's cerebellum contains nearly 45 times as many neurons as its cerebrum. What does this number tell us about the elephant's behavior? An elephant has almost infinite degrees of freedom in the use of its trunk: it can use it to bathe, lift a tree trunk, pick up a peanut, caress a baby, or paint a picture. The vast number of neurons in its cerebellum is probably requisite to controlling the trunk's sensory and motor abilities.

In contrast, the elephant's cerebrum, with twice the mass of that of humans, contains only 5.6 billion neurons, more neurons than most animals can boast but somewhat fewer than the chimpanzees' cerebrum. The elephant's cognitive ability also ranks at about that of a chimp's.

The Herculano-Houzel study offers a conclusion related to the function of the human cerebrum as well. The remarkable cognitive abilities of humans, which exceed those of all other animal species, are best explained by the sheer number of cerebral neurons, which exceed the number found in all other animal species, even those with much larger brains, including elephants.

An African Elephant's Brain In this, the largest brain of all terrestrial animals, both the cerebrum (*left*) and the cerebellum (*right*) are gigantic compared to those of the human brain. But the cerebellum contains 97.5 percent of the neurons. Reproduced or adapted from our websites at http://www.brains.rad.msu.edu and http://brainmuseum.org, supported by the U. S. National Science Foundation.

neurons representing the primary functions aggregate in order to keep their connections short. As their numbers increase, they also begin to form new regions (gray shading). For example, visual pathways to motor regions in a fish direct whole-body movements to guide the fish from one place to another. Visual pathways in a primate not only guide locomotion, they guide control of the arm and hand for reaching. The new function requires both a new region and new connections.

Figure 1-16 also illustrates two kinds of maps that emerge as brains become larger. **Topographic** maps (left) represent the different functional areas—for instance, areas that control vision, hearing, touch, olfaction, and movement. **Connectome** maps (right) represent the connections through which each of these regions influences each other. The evolution of complexity represented by the topographic and connectome maps can be understood by analogous changes that occur as a village grows to become a large city. With growth, a downtown, an industrial area, suburbs, and so forth develop, along with more connecting streets, highways, and freeways. These two different ways of describing the brain are similar to the maps that a computer provides of a city, a scene map of buildings, and a street map of routes. Topographic and connectome descriptions of the brain will be featured throughout this book.

Addition of neurons →

Topographic Map   Connectome Map

FIGURE 1-16 **Evolution of Complexity in the Cerebrum** The first column provides a topographic view of how a brain might change with the addition of neurons. Each color represents a function, such as vision, touch, or hearing. Gray shading represents new areas associated with new functions of the different regions. The second column provides a connectome view of how connections might change as neurons are added as topographic regions separate and become larger.

topographic Representing the different functional areas of the CNS.

connectome All the pathways connecting regions of the CNS.

Why the Hominid Brain Enlarged

The evolution of modern humans—from when humanlike creatures first appeared until humans like us emerged—spans more than 4 million years. This may seem like a long time, but the brain and behavior evolution that occurred in hominids was extremely rapid, given that there was not much change for other animal species over the same time period. What caused these changes? Why did hominids evolve larger brains, and why did their behavior become more complex? Why didn't hominids just remain apes with ape-sized brains?

One hypothesis suggests that numerous drastic climate changes drove adaptation by hominids that led to more complex behavior. Another hypothesis contends that the primate lifestyle favors an increasingly complex nervous system that humans capitalize on. A third links brain growth to brain cooling. And a fourth proposes that a changed rate of maturation favors larger brains. Likely, a combination of all of these and still other factors was influential.

Climate and the Evolving Hominid Brain

Climate changes have driven many physical changes in hominids, ranging from brain changes to the emergence of human culture. Evidence suggests that each new hominid species appeared after climate changes devastated old environments and led to new ones (Tattersall, 2017).

About 8 million years ago, a massive tectonic event (deformation of Earth's crust) produced the Great Rift Valley, which runs through the eastern part of Africa from south to north. The reshaped landmass left a wet jungle climate to the west and a much drier savannah climate to the east. To the west, the apes continued unchanged in their former habitat. But the fossil record shows that in the drier eastern region, apes evolved rapidly into upright hominids in response to the selective environmental pressures that formed their new home.

Thereafter, the climate in East Africa did not remain static. It underwent a number of alterations, with some alterations isolating populations of hominids and others throwing different populations together. The appearance of *Homo habilis* 3 million years ago and the appearance of *Homo erectus* 1 million years ago were associated with these climatic alterations. Climatic changes also track the *disappearance* of other members of the human family. For instance, the warming in Europe that ended the ice age as recently as 30,000 years ago contributed to modern humans prospering and to the Neanderthal and other archaic European and Asiatic human groups disappearing.

What makes *Homo sapiens* the sole survivor? One suggestion is that we modern humans evolved to adapt to change itself and that this adaptability has allowed us to populate every region on Earth (Grove, 2017). The caution is that modern humans have been around only a short time relative to the millions of years that other hominid species survived: our adaptability has yet to be severely tested.

Ape species living in a wetter climate to the west of Africa's Great Rift Valley were cut off from species that evolved into hominids and thus adapted to a drier climate to the east.

The Primate Lifestyle

British anthropologist Robin Dunbar (1998) argues that a primate's social group size, a cornerstone of its lifestyle, is correlated with brain size. His conclusion: the average group size of about 150 favored by modern humans explains their large brains. He cites as evidence that 150 is the estimated group size of hunter-gatherer groups and the average group size of many contemporary institutions—a company in the military, for instance—and coincidentally, the number of people that each of us can gossip about.

Consider how group size might affect the way primates forage for food. Foraging is important for all animals, but while some foraging activities are simple, others are complex. Eating grass or vegetation is an individual pursuit: an animal need only munch and move on. Vegetation eaters such as gorillas do not have especially large brains relative to their body size. In contrast, apes that eat fruit, such as chimpanzees and humans, have relatively large brains.

Katharine Milton (2003) documented the relationship between fruit foraging and larger brains by examining the feeding behavior and brain size of two South American

(New World) monkeys of the same body size. As illustrated in **Figure 1-17**, spider monkeys obtain nearly three-quarters of their nutrients from fruit and have a brain twice as large as that of the howler monkey, which obtains less than half its nutrients from fruit.

What is so special about eating fruit? Fruit harvesting requires good sensory skills such as color vision to see it, good motor skills to reach and manipulate it, good spatial skills to find it, good memory to return to it, and having friends to help find it and ward off competitors. Having a parent who can teach fruit-finding skills and being a good learner are also useful. The payoff in eating fruit is its nutritional value for nourishing a large, energy-dependent brain that uses more than 20 percent of the body's resources. These same skills are useful for obtaining other temporary and perishable types of food, such as those obtained through scavenging, hunting, and gathering.

A neuron's metabolic (energy) cost is estimated as relatively constant across different species but also high relative to that of other types of body cells. So any adaptive advantage to having more neurons must support that energy cost. Fonseca-Azevedo and Herculano-Houzel (2012) suggests that cooking food is a unique contribution to hominid brain development. Gorillas must spend up to 8 hours of each day foraging for vegetation and eating it. Chimps and early hominids, with a more varied diet, could support more neurons provided that they also spent most of their waking time foraging.

The use of fire by *Homo erectus* and later hominids allowed for cooking, which predigests food and thus maximizes caloric gain to the point that much less time need be devoted to foraging. A high degree of male–male, female–female, and female–male cooperation in food gathering and cooking, characteristic of the hominid lifestyle, further supported the evolution of a larger brain.

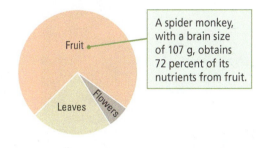

Spider monkey diet

Fruit

Leaves

Flowers

> A spider monkey, with a brain size of 107 g, obtains 72 percent of its nutrients from fruit.

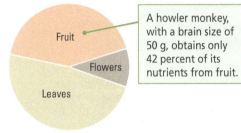

Howler monkey diet

Fruit

Flowers

Leaves

> A howler monkey, with a brain size of 50 g, obtains only 42 percent of its nutrients from fruit.

FIGURE 1-17 **Picky Eaters** Katharine Milton examined the feeding behavior and brain size of two New World monkeys that have the same body size but different brain sizes and diets.

Changes in Hominid Physiology

Cooking food makes it easier to eat. This, in turn, might foster genetic mutations associated with marked size reductions in individual muscle fibers in the face and entire masticatory muscles in hominids (Stedman et al., 2004). The Stedman team speculated that smaller masticatory muscles paved the way for smaller, more delicate bones in the head. Smaller bones in turn allowed for changes in diet and access to more energy-rich food.

Another physiological adaptation may have given a special boost to greater brain size in our human ancestors: changes in the morphology (form) of the skull. Dean Falk (Kunz & Iliadis, 2007) developed the radiator hypothesis from her automobile mechanic's remark that to increase the size of a car's engine, you also have to increase the size of the radiator that cools it. Falk reasoned that if the brain's radiator, the circulating blood, adapted into a more effective cooling system, brain size could increase.

Brain cooling is important because the brain's metabolic activity generates a great deal of heat and is at risk for overheating under conditions of exercise or heat stress. Falk argued that, unlike australopith skulls, *Homo* skulls contain holes through which cranial blood vessels pass. These holes suggest that, compared to earlier hominids, *Homo* species had a much more widely dispersed blood flow from the brain, which would have greatly enhanced brain cooling.

A small jaw distinguishes the earliest Homo *fossils yet discovered.*

Altered Maturation

All animal species' life history can be divided into stages. *Heterochrony* (from the Greek, meaning "different times") is the study of processes that regulate the onset and end-of-life stages and their developmental speed and duration. Several proposals

FIGURE 1-18 **Neoteny** The shape of an adult human's head more closely resembles that of a juvenile chimpanzee's head (*left*) than an adult chimp's head (*right*). This observation leads to the hypothesis that we humans may be neotenic descendants of our more apelike common ancestors.

neoteny Process in which juvenile stages of predecessors become adult features of descendants; idea derived from the observation that more recently evolved species resemble the young of their common ancestors.

suggest that altered heterochronicity accounts for the large human brain and other distinctive human features.

In **neoteny**, juvenile stages of predecessors become adult features of descendants. Neoteny is common in the animal world. Flightless birds are neotenic adult birds, domesticated dogs are neotenic wolves, and sheep are neotenic goats. Many anatomical features link us with the juvenile stages of other primates, including a small face, vaulted cranium, unrotated big toe, upright posture, and primary distribution of hair on the head, armpits, and pubic areas.

Because a human infant's head is large relative to body size, neoteny has also led to adults with proportionally larger bodies and larger skulls to house larger brains. The shape of a baby chimpanzee's head is more similar to the shape of an adult human's head than to an adult chimpanzee's head (**Figure 1-18**). Along with this physical morphology, human adults also retain some behaviors of primate infants, including play, exploration, and intense interest in novelty and learning. The brain processes that support learning thus are retained in adulthood (Zollikofer, 2012).

An alternative view is that the onset and duration of the stages of development change (Workman et al., 2013). Evidence for this idea is that each stage of human development—gestation, infancy, childhood, adulthood—is prolonged relative to such ancestral species as chimpanzees. Prolonged infancy allows the birth and development of more neurons, resulting in a bigger brain. Prolonged childhood enhances learning time; and prolonged adolescence allows for the growth of a bigger body.

The Human Genome

The influences on hominid evolution described above must have been mediated by genetic changes. What were these changes? There is an incomplete data sample for investigating the origins of the hominid *genome* (a catalogue of all of a species' genes) because only the genomes of the apes, archaic humans, and modern humans have been sequenced (i.e., all of the genes have been described). Although apes and modern humans have about 96 percent of their genes in common, each of these genes have many small differences, making it difficult to determine what each difference contributes.

A different approach to understanding the origins of the hominid genome is to ask whether new genes appeared or old genes disappeared in hominids. There are a few such human-specific gene changes (Levchenko et al., 2018). One human-specific gene is SARGP2, a gene that is active when the cerebrum is developing. It plays a role in determining the number of neurons that compose the cerebrum. This gene has mutated, producing duplicate copies in the human genome, three times over the course of human evolution. The mutations are estimated to have occurred about 3.4, 2.4, and 1 million years ago. It is tempting to correlate these mutation events with the jumps in brain size that occurred in *Homo habilis*, *erectus*, and *sapiens*, respectively. It is unlikely the story is as simple as this, however, but the finding encourages a search for other relationships between gene changes and human evolution.

1-4 **Review**

Before you continue, check your understanding. Answers to Self-Test appear at the back of the book.

1. Modern humans share a _____ with the _____, our closest living relative.

2. Modern humans evolved from a _____ lineage that successfully featured _____, _____, and _____, groups in which more than one species existed concurrently.

3. The _____ describes brain size relative to body size, but a complete comparison of different species' brains requires _____.

4. The large human brain evolved in response to a number of pressures and opportunities, including _____, _____, _____, and _____.

5. One hypothesis proposes that *Homo sapiens* has evolved to adapt to change itself. Explain the reasoning behind this hypothesis in a brief paragraph.

For additional study tools, visit **LaunchPad** at launchpadworks.com

1-5

Modern Human Brain Size and Intelligence

In *The Descent of Man*, Charles Darwin detailed the following paradox:

> No one, I presume, doubts the large proportion which the size of man's brain bears to his body, compared to the same proportion in the gorilla or orang, is closely connected with his higher mental powers. . . . On the other hand, no one supposes that the intellect of any two animals or of any two men can be accurately gauged by the cubic contents of their skulls. (Darwin, 1871, p. 37)

Ignoring Darwin, many have tried to tie individual intelligence to gross brain size. If the functional unit of the brain is the brain cell and if larger human brains have more brain cells, does it not follow that brain size and intelligence are related? It depends.

The evolutionary approach we have been using to explain how the large human brain evolved is based on comparisons *between* species. Special care attends the extension of evolutionary principles to physical comparisons *within* species, especially biological comparisons within or among groups of modern humans. In this section, we first illustrate the difficulty of within-species comparisons by considering the complexity of correlating human brain size with intelligence (Deary, 2000). Then we turn to another aspect of studying the brain and behavior in modern humans—the fact that, unlike that of other animals, so much modern human behavior is culturally learned.

Meaning of Human Brain Size Comparisons

Stephen Jay Gould, in his 1981 book *The Mismeasure of Man*, reviews much of the early literature which suggested that brain size and intelligence are related and criticized the research on three counts: brain measurement, correlating brain size and intelligence, and what intelligence is.

First, measuring a person's brain is difficult. If a tape measure is placed around a person's head, factoring out skull thickness is impossible. There is also no agreement about whether volume or weight is a better measure. And no matter which indicator we use, we must consider body size. The human brain varies in weight from about 1000 grams to more than 2000 grams, but people also vary in body mass. To what extent should we factor in body mass in deciding whether a particular brain is large or small? And how should we measure body mass, given that a person's total weight can fluctuate widely over time?

Large differences between the brains of individual people do exist, but the reasons for these differences are numerous and complex. Consider some examples. People may have larger or smaller brain cells. Larger people are likely to have a larger brain than smaller people because they have a larger muscle mass to control. Men have a somewhat larger brain than women, but again men are also proportionately physically larger. Nevertheless, girls mature more quickly than boys, so in adolescence the brain and body size differences may be absent. As people age, they generally lose brain cells, so their brain shrinks.

Neurological diseases associated with aging accelerate the age-related decrease in brain size. Brain injury near the time of birth often results in a dramatic reduction in brain size, even in regions distant from the damage. Stress associated with physical

To find information on specific conditions, consult the Index of Disorders inside the front cover of this book.

Sections 2-1 and 2-6 elaborate on plasticity, Research Focus 8-1 and Section 8-4 on environment and brain development, Section 11-3 on skilled movement, and Section 14-1 on memory.

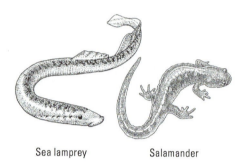

Sea lamprey   Salamander

Figure 15-9 illustrates the profusion of brain networks; Section 15-6 relates network efficiency to intelligence.

Section 15-6 expands on theories of intelligence. Einstein's brain is pictured in Figure 15-20.

or behavioral deprivation in infancy also reduces brain size (Herringa et al., 2013). Neurological disorders associated with a parent's abuse of alcohol or other drugs are associated with conditions such as *fetal alcohol spectrum disorder* (*FASD*), in which the brain can be greatly reduced in size. *Autism spectrum disorder* (*ASD*), a largely genetic condition affecting development, produces a wide variety of brain abnormalities, including either increases or decreases in brain size in different individuals.

Brain size may also increase. For example, just as good nutrition in the early years of life can be associated with larger body size, good nutrition can also be associated with an increase in brain size. The brain's **plasticity**—its ability to change—in response to an enriched environment is associated with growth of existing brain cells and thus an increase in brain size. Furthermore, one way in which the brain stores new skills and memories is to form new connections among brain cells, and these connections in turn contribute to increased brain size.

Finally, we must consider what is meant by intelligence. When we compare behavior across species, we are comparing **species-typical behavior**—behavior displayed by all members of a species. For example, lamprey eels do not have limbs and cannot walk, whereas salamanders do have limbs and can walk: the difference in brain size *between* the two species can be correlated with this trait. When we compare behavior *within* a species, however, we are usually comparing how well one individual performs a certain task in relation to others of the same species—how well one salamander walks relative to how well another salamander walks, for instance.

Early in the twentieth century, Charles Spearman carried out the first formal performance analysis among various tests used to rate intelligence in humans. He found a positive correlation among tests and suggested that a single common factor explained them. Spearman named it *g* for *general intelligence factor*, but it turns out that *g* also varies. Many factors unrelated to inherent ability—among them opportunity, interest level, training, motivation, and health—influence individual performance on a task.

For example, when IQ tests that were given to young adults of one generation are given to the next generation, scores increase by as much as 25 points, a phenomenon called the *Flynn effect* (Flynn, 2012). Taken at face value—though it shouldn't be—the increase suggests that human *g* has risen to such a degree in two generations that most young adults fall in the superior category relative to their grandparents. Obviously, the score change has not been accompanied by a similar increase in brain size. It is more likely that education and other life experiences explain the Flynn effect.

Howard Gardner (2006) proposed that humans have a number of intelligences—verbal, musical, mathematical, social, and so on. Each type of intelligence is dependent on the function of a particular brain region or regions. Hampshire and colleagues (2012), who presented participants with a battery of typical intelligence assessment tests, support Gardner's idea. As participants took the tests, their brain activity was imaged and recorded. The study identified three separate abilities—reasoning, short-term memory, and verbal ability—each associated with a different brain network. The experimenters argue that this finding provides little support for Spearman's *g*. They further suggest that a wider array of assessments would reveal additional intelligence networks.

If you are wondering whether having a larger brain might mean you could study a little less, consider this: the brains of people who are widely considered highly intelligent have been found to vary in size from the low end to the high end of the range for our species. The brain of the brilliant physicist Albert Einstein was average in size.

Acquisition of Culture

The most remarkable thing that our brains have made possible is ever more complex **culture**—learned behaviors passed from generation to generation through teaching and experience (Stout & Hecht, 2017). Most of this culture originated long after our brains evolved.

Cultural growth and adaptation render many contemporary human behaviors distinctly different from those of *Homo sapiens* living 200,000 years ago. Only 30,000 years ago, modern humans made the first artistic relics: elaborate paintings on cave walls and carved ivory and stone figurines. Agriculture appeared still more recently, about 15,000 years ago, and reading and writing were invented only about 7000 years ago.

Most forms of mathematics and many of our skills in using mechanical and digital devices have still more recent origins. Computer programming languages, for example, date to the 1950s. Early *H. sapiens* brains certainly did not evolve to select smartphone apps or imagine traveling to distant planets. Apparently, the things that the human brain did evolve to do contained the elements necessary for adapting to more sophisticated skills.

Alex Mesoudi and his colleagues (2006) suggest that cultural elements, ideas, behaviors, or styles that spread from person to person—called **memes** (after genes, the elements of physical evolution)—can also be studied within an evolutionary framework. They propose that individual differences in brain structure may favor the development of certain memes. Once developed, memes would in turn exert selective pressure on further brain development. For example, chance variations in individuals' brain structure may have favored tool use in some individuals. Tool use proved so beneficial that toolmaking itself exerted selective pressure on a population to favor individuals well skilled in tool fabrication.

Similar arguments can be made with respect to other memes, from language to music, from mathematics to art. Mesoudi's reasoning supports brain science's ongoing expansion into seemingly disparate disciplines, including linguistics, the arts, business, and economics. Studying the human brain, far from examining a body organ's structure, means investigating how it acquires culture and fosters adaptation as the world changes and as the brain changes the world.

Saint Ambrose, who lived in the fourth century, is reportedly the first person who could read silently.

Section 15-3 explores some of psychology's expanding frontiers.

1-5 Review

Before you continue, check your understanding. Answers to Self-Test appear at the back of the book.

1. Behavior that is displayed by all members of a species is called _____.

2. Some modern human behavior is inherent to our nervous system, but far more is learned—passed generation to generation by _____. Ideas, behaviors, or styles called _____ may spread from person to person and culture to culture.

3. Spearman proposed a common intelligence factor he called _____. Gardner supports the idea of _____.

4. Explain the reasoning behind the statement that what is true for evolutionary comparisons across different species may not be true for comparisons within a single species.

For additional study tools, visit **LaunchPad** at launchpadworks.com

plasticity Body's potential for physical or chemical change; enhances its adaptability to environmental change and its ability to compensate for injury. (In the brain and nervous system, this potential is called *neuroplasticity*.)

species-typical behavior Behavior that is characteristic of all members of a species, such as walking in salamanders.

culture Learned behaviors that are passed on from one generation to the next through teaching and imitation.

meme An idea, a behavior, or a style that spreads from person to person within a culture.

Summary

1-1 The Brain in the Twenty-First Century

Studying the brain and behavior leads us to better understand our origins, our human nature, the causes of many behavioral disorders, and the rationale behind treatment for disorders.

The human nervous system is composed of the CNS, which includes the brain and the spinal cord, and the PNS, through which the brain and spinal cord communicate with sensory receptors, with muscles and other tissues, and with the internal organs. The cerebrum and the cerebellum have undergone the most growth in large-brained animal species.

We define behavior as any kind of movement, including mental processes such as thinking and imagining. In animals, behavior is

caused by nervous system activity. Behavioral flexibility and complexity vary greatly across species, as does the nervous system.

For some species, including humans, the brain is the organ that exerts control over behavior. The brain seems to need ongoing sensory and motor stimulation to maintain its intelligent activity.

1-2 Perspectives on Brain and Behavior

Mentalism views behavior as a product of an intangible entity called the mind (psyche); the brain has little importance. Dualism is the notion that the immaterial mind acts through the material brain to produce language and rational behavior, whereas the brain alone is responsible for the "lower" actions that we have in common with other animal species.

Materialism, the view that brain function fully accounts for all behavior—language and reasoning included—guides contemporary research on the brain and behavior. Support for the materialistic view comes from the study of natural selection—the evolutionary theory that behaviors such as human language evolved from the simpler language abilities of human ancestors—and from discoveries about how genes function. Experiments follow the process of science: (1) formulate a theory, (2) generate a question (hypothesis), (3) design a procedure to test it, and (4) evaluate the results to confirm or modify the theory.

After severe TBI, the brain demonstrates a remarkable ability to recover, but after either mild or severe injury, a person can be left with a permanent disability that prevents full recovery to former levels of function. Brain imaging techniques can confirm severe disabilities such as MCS, locked-in syndrome, and PVS.

1-3 Evolution of Brains and of Behavior

Behavioral neuroscientists subscribe to the evolutionary principle that all living organisms are descended from a common ancestor. Brain cells and muscles are quite recent developments in the evolution of life on Earth. Because they evolved only once, a similar basic pattern exists in the nervous systems of all animals.

The nervous systems of some animal lineages have become more complex, with evolution featuring first a nerve net, followed by a bilaterally symmetrical and segmented nervous system, a nervous system controlled by ganglia, and eventually, in chordates, a nervous system featuring a brain and spinal cord.

Mammals are a class of chordates characterized by a large brain relative to body size. Modern humans belong to the primate order, which is distinguished by especially large brains, and to the family of great apes, whose members' limber shoulders allow them to brachiate (hang and swing by the arms).

1-4 Evolution of the Human Brain and Behavior

One of our early hominid ancestors was probably an *Australopithecus*, who lived in Africa several million years ago. It is from an australopith species that *Homo* evolved through species such as *Homo habilis* and *Homo erectus*. Modern humans, *Homo sapiens sapiens*, appeared about 200,000 years ago.

Since *Australopithecus*, the hominid brain has increased in size almost threefold, as has its number of brain cells. The increases were associated with area (topography) and connection (connectome) changes. The EQ describes brain size relative to body size, but a complete comparison of different species' brains requires brain cell counts. Among the factors hypothesized to have stimulated brain evolution in human species are environmental challenges and opportunities, such as climate changes that favored the natural selection of adaptability and more complex behavior patterns. Brain and behavior changes in hominids were mediated by perhaps only a few genes that appeared *de novo* in hominids. Also proposed are lifestyle changes such as social cooperation and cooking food, changes in physiology, and changed maturation rate.

1-5 Modern Human Brain Size and Intelligence

Evolutionary principles learned from studying the brain and behavior *across* species do not easily apply to the brain and behavior *within* a single species, such as *Homo sapiens*. People vary widely in body size, brain size, and, likely, the number of brain cells and the connections between brain cells. Any of these factors can contribute to varying kinds of intelligence, making a simple comparison of brain size and general intelligence unwise.

Recognizing the great extent to which modern human behavior, rather than being inherent in our nervous systems, results from cultural learning and transmission is paramount to understanding how our brains function. Memes may spread from person to person and culture to culture.

Key Terms

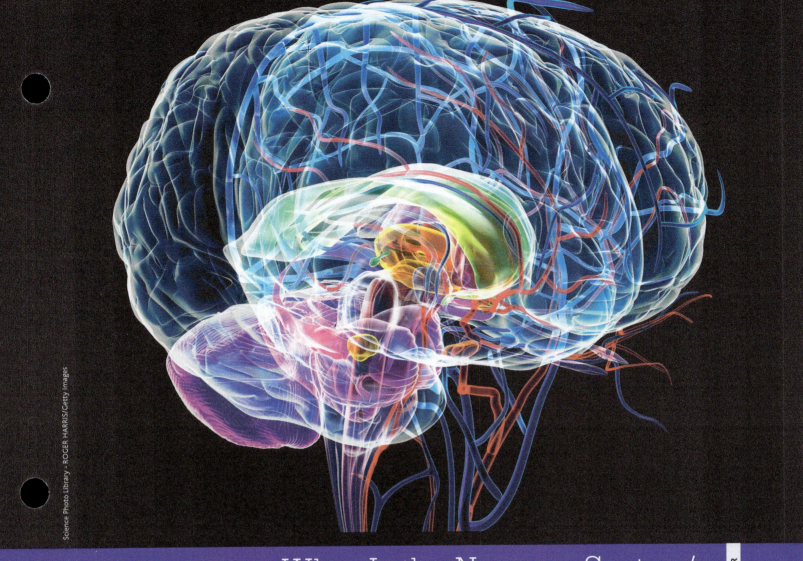

Science Photo Library · ROGER HARRIS/Getty Images

What Is the Nervous System's Functional Anatomy?

CHAPTER 2

Throughout this book, we examine the nervous system with a focus on function—how our brains generate behavior and how, in turn, our behavior influences our brains. In this chapter, we consider the human nervous system's anatomical and functional organization and how its basic components work together to produce behavior. Moreover, we consider how our brains change in the context of plasticity, as illustrated in Research Focus 2-1, Agenesis of the Cerebellum. First, we emphasize the brain's anatomy, and then we elaborate on how the brain works in concert with the rest of the nervous system to produce behavior. This focus on nervous system function and plasticity suggests 10 principles of nervous system organization. We note each principle throughout the chapter and describe all the principles in detail in Section 2-6. These big ideas apply equally to the micro and macro views of the nervous system presented in this chapter and to the broader picture of behavior that emerges in later chapters.

Note that we are using the word *function* two different ways. *Function* can refer to the purpose of the brain—its function is to produce behavior (recall *functionalism* from Chapter 1)—or it can refer to how the brain works, how it functions.

⊚ **RESEARCH FOCUS 2-1**

Agenesis of the Cerebellum

When an adult's brain is damaged, as in *traumatic brain injury*, for example, we see a pattern of behavioral changes that offer insight into brain functions, as described by Fred Linge in Clinical Focus 1-1, Living with Traumatic Brain Injury. Naturally occurring brain injuries rarely remove a single structure completely, leaving the rest of the brain intact. However, *agenesis*, the failure of brain regions to develop, offers researchers a unique window on the brain's organization and function because in rare cases, a complete structure is absent, yet the rest of the brain appears normal.

Historically, the cerebellum was viewed as a motor structure, with the most obvious sign of damage being *ataxia*, a failure of muscular coordination and balance. But the cerebellum's functions are much more extensive than movement control (e.g., Schmahmann, 2010). Adult patients with damage to the cerebellum do have motor disturbances, but they also have cognitive deficits in, for example, abstract thinking and language and in emotional control.

The cerebellum contains the most neurons of any brain region, accounting for 80 percent of the neurons in humans and a whopping 97.5 percent of elephants' neurons—believed to be related to the dexterity of the elephant's trunk. What would happen if the cerebellum failed to develop but the rest of the brain developed apparently normally? We humans would be missing 80 percent of our neurons!

The accompanying images contrast the brain of a person whose brain developed normally (A and B) to the brain of a young man born with agenesis of the cerebellum (C and D). Even lacking 80 percent of his neurons, the young man's behavioral capacities are remarkable, but his behavior is not typical. Now in his thirties, he has an office job and lives alone. He has a distinctive speaking pattern, an awkward gait, and difficulties with balance, as well as deficits in planning and abstract thinking. His social skills and long-term memory are good, though, as is his mastery of routine activities.

Studies of other people with cerebellar agenesis reveal a heterogeneous set of symptoms, but neuropsychological assessments show behavioral deficits reminiscent of people with damage to frontal and parietal cortical regions (e.g., Baumann et al., 2015), even though these cerebral regions are intact. While people with cerebellar agenesis typically have more slowly developing language and motor functions, they show remarkable improvement over time and seem able to compensate for many of their

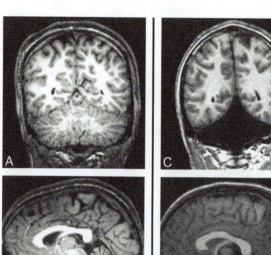
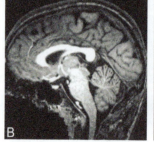
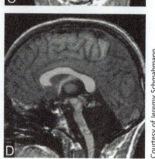

Courtesy of Jeremy Schmahmann

MRI brain scans of a person with a typical cerebellum (A, B) compared to a person with cerebellar agenesis (C, D) of the same age. A and C are viewed in the coronal plane, B and D in the midsagittal plane. For more about this condition, see www.npr.org/blogs/health/2015/03/16/393351760.

symptoms. The individual whose brain you see in images C and D had severe visuomotor spatial disabilities as a child and adolescent, but by age 30 he showed significant improvement (Jeremy D. Schmahmann and Janet C. Sherman, personal communication).

In people with cerebellar agenesis, it is thought that brain plasticity in response to early perturbations allows for compensation as regions of the cerebral cortex begin to function more efficiently. Interestingly, it has been reported that people with cerebellar agenesis appear to have some of the symptoms of *autism* early in life. This observation comports with evidence that dysfunction (rather than absence) of the cerebellum is related to autism (detailed in Clinical Focus 8-2, Autism Spectrum Disorder).

2-1

Overview of Brain Function and Structure

The brain's primary function is to produce *movement*, and collectively this is termed *behavior*. To produce effective behavior, we take in sensory information—such as vision, audition, olfaction, gustation, and somatosensation—as we search, explore, and manipulate our environment. Without stimuli, the brain cannot properly orient the body and direct it to produce appropriate behaviors. The nervous system's sensory organs gather information about the world and convert this information into biological activity that constructs perceptions—what we see, hear, smell, taste, and feel. This subjective reality is essential to carrying out any complex behavior.

When your phone rings, for example, your brain directs your body to reach for it as the nervous system responds to vibrating air molecules by producing the subjective experience of a ringtone. We perceive this stimulus as sound and react to it as if it actually exists, when in fact the ringtone is merely a fabrication of the brain. That fabrication is produced by a chain reaction that takes place when vibrating air molecules hit the eardrum. Without the nervous system, especially the brain, perception of sound does not exist—only the movement of air molecules.

But there is more to hearing a phone's ringtone than vibrating air molecules. Our mental construct of reality is based not only on the sensory information we receive but also on the cognitive processes we might use to interact with that incoming information. Hearing a ringtone when we are expecting a call has a meaning vastly different from its ringing at 3 A.M., when we are not expecting a call.

The subjective reality the brain constructs can be better understood by comparing the sensory realities of two different kinds of animals. You are probably aware that dogs perceive higher-pitched sounds that humans do not perceive. This difference in perception does not mean that a dog's nervous system is better than ours or that our hearing is poorer. Rather, the perceptual world constructed by a dog brain simply differs from the world constructed by human perception. Neither experience is "correct." The difference in subjective experience is due merely to two differently evolved systems for processing sensory stimuli.

When it comes to visual perception, our world is rich with color, whereas dogs see very little color. Human brains and dog brains construct different realities. Subjective differences in brains exist for good reason: they allow different animals to exploit different features in their environments. Dogs use their hearing to detect the movements of prey, such as mice in the grass; early hominids probably used color vision for identifying ripe fruit in trees. Evolution, then, created **adaptations**, equipping each species with a view of the world that helped it survive.

Plastic Patterns of Neural Organization

The brain is *plastic*: neural tissue has the capacity to change in response to the world by changing how it is organized. Just as the brain of the young man profiled in Research Focus 2-1 adapted to cerebellar agenesis, a person blind from birth has enhanced auditory capacities because some of the brain's visual regions have been co-opted for hearing. The brain is also plastic in the sense that connections among neurons in a given functional system are constantly changing in response to experience.

For us to learn and remember anything new, neural circuits must change to represent and store this knowledge. As we learn to play a musical instrument or speak a new language, the particular cortical regions taking part can actually increase in size as they accommodate the new skill. An important aspect of human learning and brain plasticity is related to the development of language and to the expansion of the brain regions related to language. We have learned to read, to calculate, to compose and play music, and to develop the sciences. While the human nervous system evolved long before we

Principle 1: The nervous system produces movement in a perceptual world the brain constructs.

Section 9-1 elaborates on the nature of sensation and perception.

adaptations evolved anatomical/functional features that solved long-standing historical problems.

neuroplasticity The nervous system's potential to physically or chemically modify itself in response to environmental change and to compensate for age-related changes and injury.

phenotypic plasticity An individual's capacity to develop into a range of phenotypes.

Principle 2: Neuroplasticity is the hallmark of nervous system functioning.

Section 1-2 introduces the genotype, phenotype, and epigenetics in an evolutionary context.

FIGURE 2-1 **Phenotypic Plasticity** These two mice are genetically identical but express very different phenotypes because their mothers were fed different supplements when pregnant.

See Figure 1-1 for an anatomical illustration of the human CNS and PNS.

FIGURE 2-2 **Parsing the Nervous System** The nervous system can be conceptualized **(A)** anatomically and **(B)** functionally. The functional approach employed in this book focuses on how the four parts of the nervous system interact.

mastered these achievements, it is still able to learn and remember these new abilities because of brain plasticity.

In turn, culture plays a dominant role in shaping our behavior. Because we drive cars and communicate electronically, we—and our nervous system—are modified in some new ways compared to those of our ancestors who did not engage in these activities. The basis for change in the nervous system is **neuroplasticity**, the nervous system's fundamental potential to physically or chemically modify itself in response to a changing environment and to compensate for age-related changes and injury.

Although it is tempting to see neuroplasticity as a trait unique to animals' nervous systems, it is really part of a larger biological capacity called **phenotypic plasticity**, the individual's capacity to develop a range of *phenotypes*—the characteristics we can see or measure. (See Gilbert & Epel, 2009, for a wonderful discussion of biological plasticity.) For instance, our skin responds to ultraviolet rays by incorporating more melanin, causing it to darken as a protective measure. Stated simply, an individual's *genotype* (genetic makeup) interacts with the environment to elicit a specific phenotype. This phenotype emerges from a large genetic repertoire of possibilities, a phenomenon that in turn results from *epigenetic* influences.

Epigenetic factors do not change genes but rather influence how genes inherited from parents express specific traits. The two mice pictured in **Figure 2-1** appear very different: one is fat, one thin; one has dark fur, the other is light-colored. Yet these mice are clones, genetically identical. They appear so different because their mothers were fed different diets while pregnant. The diet supplements added chemical markers, or epigenetic tags, on specific genes. The tags determine whether the gene is available to influence cells, including neurons, leading to differences in body structure and eating behavior.

Functional Organization of the Nervous System

From an anatomical standpoint, the brain and spinal cord together make up the central nervous system. The nerve fibers radiating out beyond the brain and spinal cord, as well as all the neurons outside the brain and spinal cord, form the peripheral nervous system. **Figure 2-2A** charts this *anatomical* organization. PNS nerves carry sensory information into the CNS and carry motor instructions from the CNS to the body's muscles and tissues, including those that perform such functions as blood circulation and digestion.

Now look at Figure 2-2B. In a *functional* organization, the focus is on how the parts of the system work together. Neurons in the somatic division of the PNS connect through the cranial and spinal nerves to receptors on the body's surface and on its muscles. Somatic neurons gather sensory information for the CNS and convey information from the CNS to move muscles of the head, neck, face, trunk, and limbs. Similarly, the autonomic division of the PNS enables the CNS to govern the workings of your body's internal organs—your heartbeat, urination, pupillary response, and the diaphragm movements that inflate and deflate your lungs. The enteric nervous system,

(A) Anatomical organization

(B) Functional organization

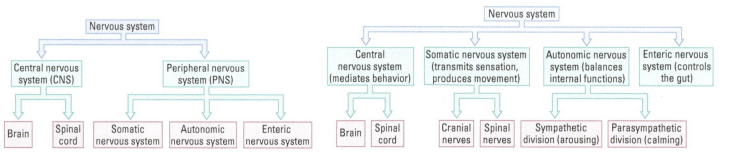

which is often considered part of the autonomic nervous system, controls digestion and stomach contractions.

From a functional standpoint, the major PNS divisions constitute, along with the CNS, an interacting four-part system:

- The CNS includes the brain and the spinal cord—the nervous system core, which mediates behavior.

- The **somatic nervous system (SNS)** includes all the spinal and cranial nerves carrying sensory information to the CNS from the muscles, joints, and skin. It also transmits outgoing motor instructions that produce movement.

- The **autonomic nervous system (ANS)** produces the rest-and-digest response through the *parasympathetic* (calming) *nerves* and its opposite, the fight-or-flight response, or vigorous activity through the *sympathetic* (arousing) *nerves*.

- The **enteric nervous system (ENS)**, formed by a mesh of neurons embedded in the lining of the gut, controls the gut. The ENS can communicate with the CNS via the ANS but mostly operates autonomously.

The directional flow of neural information is important. **Afferent** (incoming) information is sensory, coming into the CNS or one of its parts, whereas **efferent** (outgoing) information is leaving the CNS or one of its parts. When you step on a tack, the afferent sensory signals are transmitted from the body into the brain and then perceived as pain. Efferent signals from the brain cause a motor response: you lift your foot (**Figure 2-3**).

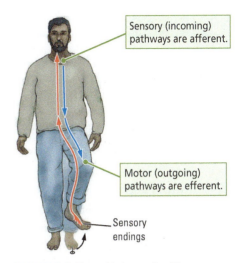

FIGURE 2-3 **Neural Information Flow**

The Brain's Surface Features

When buying a car, people like to look under the hood and examine the engine, the part of the car responsible for its behavior. All that most of us can do is gaze at the maze of tubes, wires, boxes, and fluid reservoirs. What we see makes no sense except in the most general way. We know that the engine somehow generates power to make the car move and to run the sound system, lights, and wipers. But knowing this tells us nothing about what all the many engine parts do.

When it comes to our behavior, the brain is the engine. In many ways, examining a brain for the first time is similar to looking under the hood. We have a vague sense of what the brain does, but most of us have no sense of how its parts accomplish these tasks. We may not even be able to identify those parts. If you are familiar with the anatomical terms and orientations used in drawings and images of brains, read on. If you prefer to review this terminology before you continue, consult The Basics: Finding Your Way Around the Brain.

Protecting the Nervous System

We start our functional overview by opening the hood and observing the brain snug in its home in the skull. The first thing you encounter is not the brain but rather a tough triple-layered protective covering, the **meninges** (**Figure 2-4**). The outer *dura mater* (from Latin, meaning "hard mother") is a tough durable layer of fibrous tissue that is

Spinal reflexes are discussed in detail in Section 11-4 and illustrated in Figure 11-20.

somatic nervous system (SNS) Part of the PNS that includes the cranial and spinal nerves to and from the muscles, joints, and skin, which produce movement, transmit incoming sensory input, and inform the CNS about the position and movement of body parts.

autonomic nervous system (ANS) Part of the PNS that regulates the functioning of internal organs and glands.

enteric nervous system (ENS) Mesh of neurons embedded in the lining of the gut, running from the esophagus through the colon; controls the gut.

afferent Conducting toward a CNS structure.

efferent Conducting away from a CNS structure.

meninges Three layers of protective tissue—dura mater, arachnoid, and pia mater—that encase the brain and spinal cord.

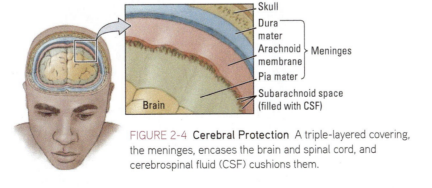

FIGURE 2-4 **Cerebral Protection** A triple-layered covering, the meninges, encases the brain and spinal cord, and cerebrospinal fluid (CSF) cushions them.

◎ THE BASICS

Finding Your Way Around the Brain

When the first anatomists began to examine the brain with the primitive tools of their time, the names they chose for brain regions often manifested their erroneous assumptions about how the brain works. They named one brain region the *gyrus fornicatus* because they thought that it had a role in sexual function, but most of this region actually has nothing to do with sexual activity.

A Wonderland of Nomenclature

As time went on, the assumptions and tools of brain research changed, but naming continued to be haphazard and inconsistent. Many brain structures have several names, and terms are often used interchangeably. This peculiar nomenclature arose because research on the brain and behavior spans several centuries and includes scientists of many nationalities and languages.

Early investigators named structures after objects (the *pulvinar*, for example, was thought to look like a pillow) or ideas (the *limbic system* was thought to be responsible for sexuality and emotions). They used various languages, especially Latin, Greek, and English. More recently, investigators have often used numbers or letters, but even this system lacks coherence because the numbers may be Arabic or Roman and are often used in combination with Greek or Latin letters.

Describing Locations in the Brain

Many names for nervous system structures reflect their anatomical locations with respect to other anatomical structures (for example, the hypothalamus lies below the thalamus), with respect to their relative spatial locations (the lateral ventricles lie lateral to the other ventricles), and with respect to a viewer's perspective (the anterodorsal nucleus of the thalamus is in the front and above the other thalamic nuclei):

- Brain–body orientation illustrates brain structure location from the frame of reference of the human face.

- Spatial orientation illustrates brain structure location in relation to other body parts and body orientation.

Brain–Body Orientation

Structures toward the brain's midline are *medial*; those located toward the sides are *lateral*.

Structures atop the brain or a structure within the brain are *dorsal*.

Anterior is in front; *posterior* is at the back.

Structures toward the bottom of the brain or one of its parts are *ventral*.

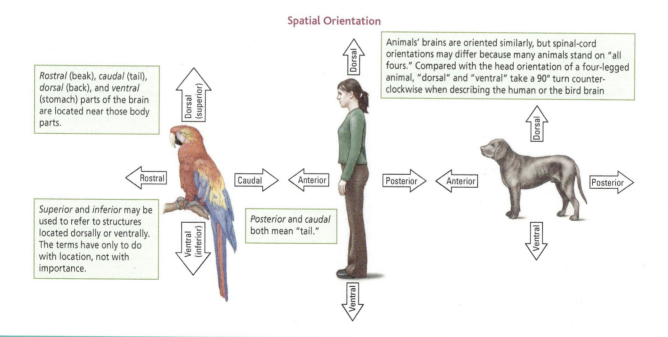

Spatial Orientation

Rostral (beak), *caudal* (tail), *dorsal* (back), and *ventral* (stomach) parts of the brain are located near those body parts.

Superior and *inferior* may be used to refer to structures located dorsally or ventrally. The terms have only to do with location, not with importance.

Posterior and *caudal* both mean "tail."

Animals' brains are oriented similarly, but spinal-cord orientations may differ because many animals stand on "all fours." Compared with the head orientation of a four-legged animal, "dorsal" and "ventral" take a 90° turn counterclockwise when describing the human or the bird brain

- Anatomical orientation illustrates the direction of a cut, or section, through the human brain (part A) from the perspective of a viewer (part B).

These orienting terms are derived from Latin. Consult the accompanying table "Glossary of Anatomical Location and Orientation" for easy reference. It is common practice to combine orienting terms. A structure described as dorsolateral, for example, means that it lies up and to the side, as in the case of the dorsolateral prefrontal cortex.

Finally, the nervous system, like the body, is bilaterally symmetrical: it has a left side and a right side. Structures that lie on the same side are *ipsilateral*; if they lie on opposite sides, they are *contralateral* to each other. Structures that occur in each hemisphere are *bilateral*. Structures that are close to one another are *proximal*; those far from one another are *distal*.

Anatomic Orientation

(A) Plane of section

(B) View of brain

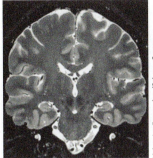

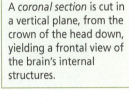

Coronal section

Frontal view

> A *coronal section* is cut in a vertical plane, from the crown of the head down, yielding a frontal view of the brain's internal structures.

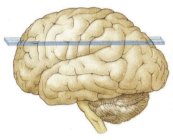

Horizontal section

Dorsal view

> A *horizontal section*, so-called because the view or the cut falls along the horizon, is usually viewed looking down on the brain from above—a dorsal view.

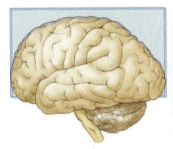

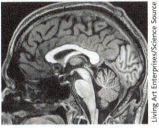

Sagittal section

Medial view

> A *sagittal section* is cut lengthways from front to back and viewed from the side. (Imagine the brain split by an arrow—in Latin, *sagitta*.) Here, a cut in the *midsagittal plane* divides the brain into symmetrical halves, a medial view.

Glossary of Anatomical Location and Orientation

Term	Meaning with respect to the nervous system	Term	Meaning with respect to the nervous system
Anterior	Near or toward the front of the animal or the front of the head (see also *frontal* and *rostral*)	Lateral	Toward the side of the body or brain
Caudal	Near or toward the tail of the animal (see also *posterior*)	Medial	Toward the middle, specifically the body's midline; in reference to brain sections, a side view of the central structures
Coronal	Cut vertically from the crown of the head down; used to reference the plane of a brain section that reveals a frontal view	Posterior	Near or toward the animal's tail (see also *caudal*); for the human spinal cord, at the back
Dorsal	On or toward the back of a four-legged animal (equivalent to posterior for the human spinal cord); in reference to human brain nuclei, above, and to brain sections, viewed from above	Rostral	Toward the beak (front) of the animal (see also *anterior* and *frontal*)
Frontal	Of the front (see also *anterior* and *rostral*); in reference to brain sections, a viewing orientation from the front	Sagittal	Cut lengthways from front to back of the skull to reveal a medial view into the brain from the side; a cut in the midsagittal plane divides the brain into symmetrical halves
Horizontal	Cut along the horizon; used to reference the plane of a brain section that reveals a dorsal view	Superior	Above (see also *dorsal*)
Inferior	Below (see also *ventral*)	Ventral	On or toward the belly of four-legged animals (see also *inferior*); in reference to human brain nuclei, below

Living Art Enterprises/Science Source

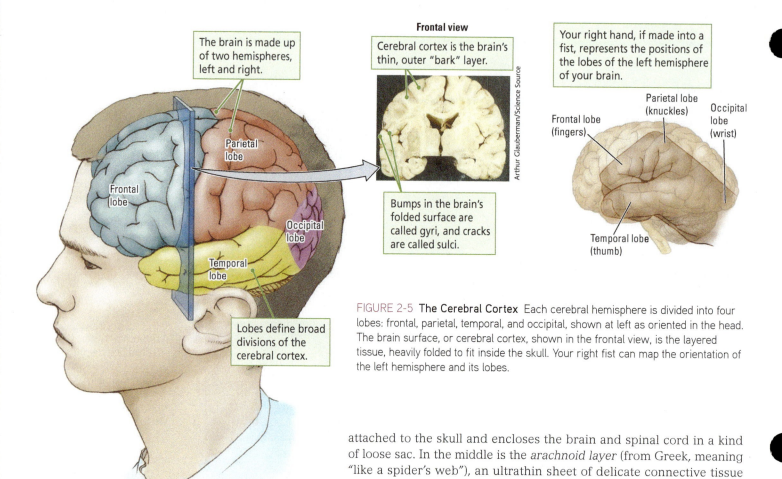

Frontal view

The brain is made up of two hemispheres, left and right.

Cerebral cortex is the brain's thin, outer "bark" layer.

Your right hand, if made into a fist, represents the positions of the lobes of the left hemisphere of your brain.

Parietal lobe (knuckles)

Occipital lobe (wrist)

Frontal lobe (fingers)

Parietal lobe

Arthur Glauberman/Science Source

Frontal lobe

Occipital lobe

Bumps in the brain's folded surface are called gyri, and cracks are called sulci.

Temporal lobe (thumb)

Temporal lobe

Lobes define broad divisions of the cerebral cortex.

FIGURE 2-5 **The Cerebral Cortex** Each cerebral hemisphere is divided into four lobes: frontal, parietal, temporal, and occipital, shown at left as oriented in the head. The brain surface, or cerebral cortex, shown in the frontal view, is the layered tissue, heavily folded to fit inside the skull. Your right fist can map the orientation of the left hemisphere and its lobes.

attached to the skull and encloses the brain and spinal cord in a kind of loose sac. In the middle is the *arachnoid layer* (from Greek, meaning "like a spider's web"), an ultrathin sheet of delicate connective tissue that follows the brain's contours. The inner layer, or *pia mater* (from Latin, meaning "soft mother"), is a moderately tough membrane of connective tissue that clings to the brain's surface.

Between the arachnoid layer and the pia mater flows **cerebrospinal fluid (CSF)**, a colorless solution of sodium, chloride, and other ions. CSF cushions the brain so that it can move or expand slightly without pressing on the skull. The symptoms of meningitis, an infection of the meninges and CSF, are described in Clinical Focus 2-2, Meningitis and Encephalitis.

Cerebral Geography

After removing the meninges, we can examine the brain's surface features, most prominently its two nearly symmetrical left and right hemispheres. **Figure 2-5** diagrams the left hemisphere of a typical human forebrain oriented in the upright human skull. The outer forebrain consists of folded and layered tissue, the **cerebral cortex,** detailed in the frontal view in Figure 2-5. The word *cortex*, Latin for "bark," is apt, considering the cortex's heavily folded surface and its location, covering most of the rest of the brain. Unlike the bark on a tree, however, the brain's folds are not random but rather demarcate its functional cortical zones.

Make a fist with your right hand and hold it up, as shown on the right in Figure 2-5, to represent the positions of the forebrain's broad divisions, or *lobes*, in the skull. Each lobe is simply named for the skull bone it lies beneath:

- Immediately above your thumbnail, your fingers correspond to the location of the **frontal lobe**, which performs the brain's executive functions, such as decision making, and voluntary movement.

- The **parietal lobe** is at the top of the skull, as represented by your knuckles, behind the frontal lobe. Parietal functions include directing our movements toward a goal or to perform a task, such as grasping an object.

cerebrospinal fluid (CSF) Clear solution of sodium, chloride, and other ions that is produced in the ventricles inside the brain and circulates around the brain and spinal cord until it is absorbed beneath the arachnoid layer in the subarachnoid space.

cerebral cortex Heavily folded and layered tissue that is the outer structure of the forebrain; composed of neocortex and allocortex.

frontal lobe Part of the cerebral cortex, which performs the brain's executive functions, such as decision making, and voluntary movement; lies anterior to the central sulcus and beneath the frontal bone of the skull.

parietal lobe Part of the cerebral cortex that directs movements toward a goal or to perform a task, such as grasping an object; lies posterior to the central sulcus and beneath the parietal bone at the top of the skull.

Meningitis and Encephalitis

When harmful viruses or microorganisms, such as bacteria, fungi, and pro- tozoa, invade and multiply in the layers of the meninges, particularly the pia mater and the arachnoid layer, as well as the CSF flowing between them, this leads to *meningitis* (literally "inflammation of the meninges"). In response to the infection, the body produces white blood cells designed to attack and consume these invaders. This inflammatory response increases the pressure within the cranium, which in turn affects the func- tioning of the brain. Unrelieved cranial pressure can lead to delirium and, if the infection progresses, to drowsiness, stupor, coma, and even death.

Usually the earliest symptom of meningitis is severe headache and a stiff neck (cervical rigidity). Head retraction (tilting the head backward) is an extreme form of cervical rigidity. Convulsions, a common symptom in children, indicate that the inflammation is affecting the brain. Meningitis is treated with antibiotics when the cause is microorganisms and sometimes with antiviral drugs for viral infections. Survivors of meningitis can have long-term consequences, such as deafness, epilepsy, hydrocephalus, and cognitive deficits.

Infection of the brain itself is called *encephalitis* (inflammation of the brain). Like meningitis, encephalitis is caused by a number of different invading viruses or microorganisms. Different forms of encephalitis may have different effects on the brain. For example, Rasmussen encephalitis attacks one cerebral hemisphere in children. In most cases, the only effec- tive treatment is radical: *hemispherectomy*, surgical removal of the entire affected hemisphere.

Surprisingly, some young children who lose a hemisphere adapt rather well. They may even complete college, literally with half a brain. But intel- lectual disabilities are a more common outcome of hemispherectomy as a result of encephalitis.

Vaccinations have been proven highly effective as protection against certain types of encephalitis, although many vulnerable populations are

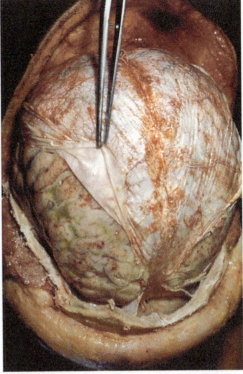

Pus, consisting of dead white blood cells, bacteria with tissue debris, and serum, is visible over the surface of this brain infected with meningitis.

still not being vaccinated. Experts estimate that encephalitis affected 4.3 million people and resulted in 150,000 deaths worldwide in 2015 (GBD 2015 Mortality and Causes of Death Collaborators, 2016).

- The forward-pointing **temporal lobe** lies at the side of the brain below the parietal lobe, in approximately the same place as the thumb on your upraised fist. The temporal lobe includes hearing, language, and musical abilities, as well as facial recognition and emotional processing.

- The area at the back of each hemisphere, near your wrist, constitutes the **occipital lobe,** where visual scene processing begins.

Examining the Brain's Surface from All Angles

As we look at the dorsal view in **Figure 2-6A**, the brain's wrinkled left and right hemi- spheres constitute the cerebrum, which is a major forebrain structure and the most recently expanded feature of the mammalian CNS. Visible from the opposite ventral view in Figure 2-6B are the brainstem, including the wrinkly hemispheres of the smaller *cerebellum* (Latin for "little brain"). Both the cerebrum and the brainstem are visible in the lateral and medial views in Figure 2-6C and D.

Much of the crinkled-up cerebral cortex is invisible from the brain's surface. All we can see are bumps, or **gyri (sing. *gyrus*)**, and cracks, or **sulci (sing. *sulcus*)**. The really deep sulci are called *fissures*. The longitudinal fissure runs between the cerebral hemispheres and the lateral fissure along the sides of the brain. Both are shown in

The brain has several visual-based systems that perform different functions, such as regulating pupil size and providing input to the circadian (day/night cycle) system. *Visual scene* is the visual system that gives rise to our perception of the visual world.

temporal lobe Part of the cerebral cortex that includes hearing, language, musical abilities, facial recognition, and emotional processing; lies below the lateral fissure, beneath the temporal bone at the side of the skull.

occipital lobe Part of the cerebral cortex where visual scene processing begins; the most posterior part of the neocortex, it lies beneath the occipital bone.

gyri (sing. *gyrus*) Small protrusions or bumps formed by the folding of the cerebral cortex.

sulci (sing. *sulcus*) Grooves in brain matter; most are in the neocortex or cerebellum.

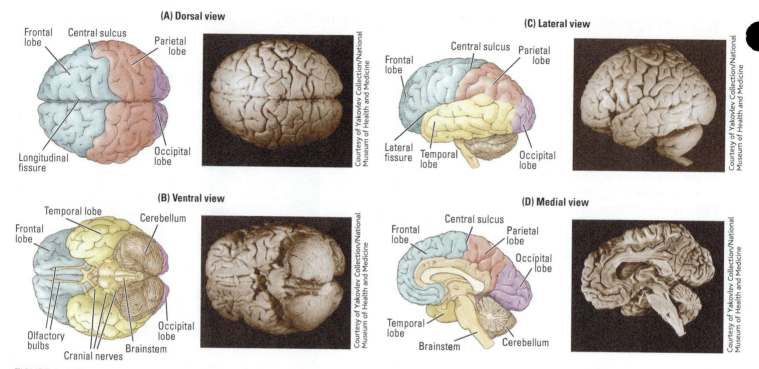

FIGURE 2-6 **Examining the Human Brain** Locations of the lobes of the cerebral hemispheres, shown in dorsal, ventral, lateral, and medial (top, bottom, side, and midline) views, as are the cerebellum, longitudinal and lateral fissures, and the central sulcus.

various views in Figure 2-6, along with the central sulcus that runs from the lateral fissures across the top of the cerebrum.

Looking at the bottom of the brain, the ventral view in Figure 2-6B, we see in the midst of the wrinkled cerebrum and ventral to the cerebellum a smooth, whitish structure with little tubelike protrusions attached. This is the brainstem, the area responsible for critical functions of life, including heart rate, breathing, sleeping, and eating. The tubelike protrusions are the cranial nerves that run to and from the brain as part of the SNS.

Cerebral Circulation

The brain's surface is covered with blood vessels. As with the rest of the body, the arteries feed blood to the brain and send it back through veins to the kidneys and lungs for cleaning and oxygenation. The cerebral arteries emerge from the neck to wrap around the outside of the brainstem, cerebrum, and cerebellum, finally penetrating the brain's surface to nourish its inner regions.

Three major arteries send blood to the cerebrum—the anterior, middle, and posterior cerebral arteries, shown in **Figure 2-7**. Because the brain is highly sensitive to blood loss, a blockage or break in a cerebral artery is likely to lead to the death of the affected region. This condition, known as **stroke,** is the sudden appearance of neurological symptoms as a result of severely reduced blood flow. Because the three cerebral arteries supply different parts of the brain, strokes can disrupt different brain functions, depending on the artery affected.

Because the brain's connections are crossed, stroke in the left hemisphere affects sensation and movement on the right side of the body. The opposite is true for those with strokes in the right hemisphere. Clinical Focus 2-3, Stroke, describes some disruptions that stroke can cause, both to the person who has it and to those who care for stroke survivors.

Principle 3: Many brain circuits are crossed.

The Brain's Internal Features

stroke Sudden appearance of neurological symptoms as a result of severely reduced blood flow.

The simplest way to examine the inside of something is to cut it in half. Of course, the orientation of the cut affects what we see. Consider slicing through a pear. If we cut from side to side, we cut across the core, providing a dorsal view; if we cut from

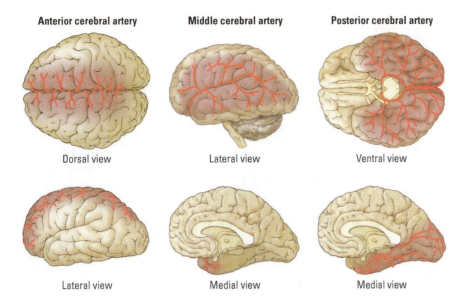

Anterior cerebral artery

Dorsal view

Lateral view

Middle cerebral artery

Lateral view

Medial view

Posterior cerebral artery

Ventral view

Medial view

FIGURE 2-7 **Major Cerebral Arteries** Each of the three major arteries that feed blood to the cerebral hemispheres branches extensively to supply the regions shaded in pink. Section 16-3 elaborates on the effects of stroke and its treatment.

top to bottom, we cut parallel to the core, providing a medial view. Our impression of the inside of a pear is clearly influenced by how we slice it. The same is true of the brain.

Macroscopic Inspection: Regions and Hemispheres

We can reveal the brain's inner features by slicing it parallel to the front of the body, downward through the middle in a coronal section (**Figure 2-8A**). The resulting frontal view, shown in Figure 2-8B, makes immediately apparent that the brain's interior is not homogeneous. Both dark grayish and lighter regions of tissue are visible, and though these regions may not be as distinctive as car engine parts, they nevertheless represent different brain components.

The darker regions are called **gray matter,** largely composed of cell bodies and capillary blood vessels. Within the gray matter, neurons collect and modify information before sending it along. The lighter regions are **white matter,** mostly nerve fibers covered by myelin sheaths that have a high fat content. These fibers produce the white appearance, much as fat droplets in milk make it appear white. White matter fibers form longer-distance connections between and among some of the brain's neurons.

gray matter Areas of the nervous system composed predominantly of neuronal cell bodies that collect and modify information and capillary blood vessels that support this activity.

white matter Areas of the nervous system with fat-rich, myelin-sheathed neuronal axons that form the connections between neurons.

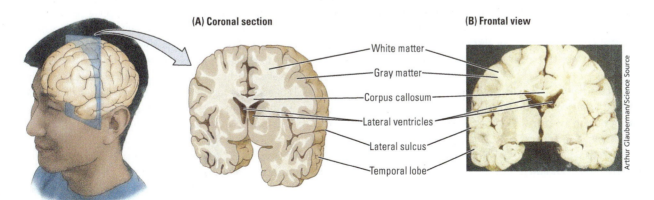

(A) Coronal section

(B) Frontal view

White matter
Gray matter
Corpus callosum
Lateral ventricles
Lateral sulcus
Temporal lobe

Arthur Glauberman/Science Source

FIGURE 2-8 **Coronal Brain Section (A)** The brain is cut down the middle parallel to the front of the body; then a coronal section is viewed at a slight angle. **(B)** This frontal view displays white matter, gray matter, and the lateral ventricles. Visible above the ventricles, a large bundle of whitish fibers, the corpus callosum, joins the hemispheres.

Stroke

Approximately every minute in the United States, someone has a stroke with obvious visible symptoms—that adds up to more than half a million people every year. Worldwide, stroke is the second leading cause of death. Acute symptoms include facial droop, motor weakness in limbs, visual disturbance, speech difficulties, and sudden onset of severe headache.

Even with the best, fastest medical attention, most stroke survivors have some residual motor, sensory, or cognitive deficit. For every 10 people who have a stroke, 2 die, 6 are disabled to varying degrees, and 2 recover to a degree but still have a diminished quality of life (Goyal et al., 2015). Of those who survive, 1 in 10 risk further stroke.

The consequences of stroke are significant for those who have them, as well as for their family and lifestyle. Consider Mr. Anderson, a 45-year-old electrical engineer who took his three children to the movies one Saturday afternoon and collapsed. He had a massive stroke of the middle cerebral artery in his left hemisphere. The stroke has impaired Mr. Anderson's language ever since, and because the brain's connections are crossed, his right-side motor control was affected as well.

Seven years after his stroke, Mr. Anderson remained unable to speak, but he understood simple conversations. Severe difficulties in moving his right leg required him to use a walker. He could not move the fingers of his right hand and so had difficulty feeding himself, among other tasks. Mr. Anderson will probably never return to his engineering career or drive or get around on his own.

Like him, most other stroke survivors require help to perform everyday tasks. Caregivers are often female relatives who give up their own careers and other pursuits. Half of the caregivers develop emotional illness, primarily depression or anxiety or both, in a year or so. Lost income and stroke-related medical bills significantly affect the family's living standard.

We tend to speak of stroke as a single disorder, but there are two major categories of strokes. In the more common *ischemic stroke*, a blood vessel is blocked by either a blood clot, also known as a thrombus, or by some other obstructive material, such as fat, clumps of bacteria, or cancer, called an embolus. *Ischemia* refers to the failure to deliver sufficient oxygen, glucose, and other nutrients for cellular metabolism, as well as the inadequate removal of metabolic waste like carbon dioxide.

The more life-threatening *hemorrhagic stroke* results from a burst vessel bleeding into the brain. While the hemorrhage, like an ischemic stroke, also prevents sufficient delivery and removal of critical molecules, it has the added detriment of exposing neurons directly to the toxic effects of hemoglobin, the gas-carrying molecule in red blood cells that contains high levels of iron.

The hopeful news is that ischemic stroke can be treated acutely with a medication called *tissue plasminogen activator* (t-PA). The body produces t-PA as a natural prevention for excessive clotting. A dosage of t-PA administered within 3 hours of the onset of ischemic symptoms will boost a patient's t-PA levels by about 1000 times above normal, which will facilitate breaking up clots and allow normal blood flow to return to an affected region. Unfortunately, there is no treatment for hemorrhagic stroke, for which the use of clot-busting t-PA would be disastrous.

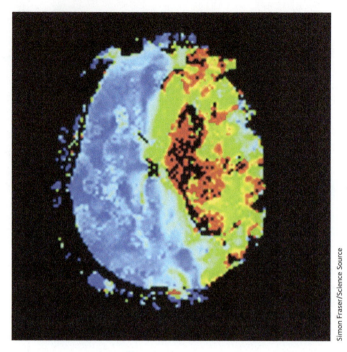

Dorsal view of a brain with a stroke, imaged by computed tomography (CT). The dark area in the right hemisphere has been damaged by the loss of blood flow.

Simon Fraser/Science Source

When patients receive t-PA, the number who make a nearly complete recovery increases by about 25 percent compared with those who receive a placebo (Hatcher & Starr, 2011). In addition, impairments are reduced in the remaining patients who survive the stroke, when the t-PA medication has some effectiveness. Unfortunately, in a small percentage of patients who do not receive any benefit from t-PA, their outcomes are worsened by the treatment. The risk of hemorrhage is about 6 percent in t-PA–treated patients relative to no risk in placebo-treated patients.

Most stroke victims do not visit an emergency room until about 24 hours after symptoms appear—too late for the treatment. Apparently, most people fail to realize that having a stroke requires emergency medical attention.

By taking advantage of developments in neuroimaging, research has shown that it is possible to remove clots from cerebral vessels mechanically (Goyal et al., 2015). This is achieved by using advanced radiographic imaging techniques to guide a long, thin catheter tube with a springlike mechanism on the end, which is inserted into the femoral artery near the groin. The tube is threaded through the body into the brain and right to the clot. The springlike mechanism can either grab the clot or bust it up. These new procedures have expanded the window of benefit to as long as 12 hours after the onset of stroke.

There is also intense interest in developing treatments that stimulate the brain to initiate reparative processes after a patient suffers a stroke. Such treatments are designed to facilitate the patient's functional improvement (see a review by Langhorne et al., 2011).

(A) Lateral view of brain

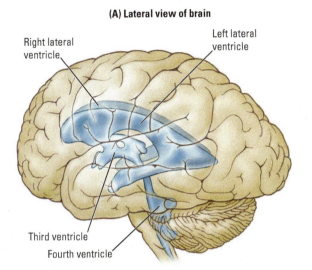

Right lateral ventricle

Left lateral ventricle

Third ventricle

Fourth ventricle

(B) Frontal view of brain

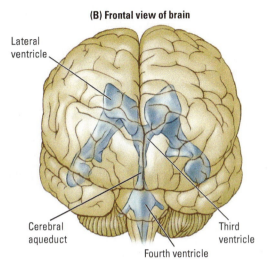

Lateral ventricle

Cerebral aqueduct

Third ventricle

Fourth ventricle

FIGURE 2-9 **Interconnected Cerebral Ventricles** The lateral ventricles are symmetrical, one in each hemisphere. The third and fourth ventricles lie in the brain's midline and connect to the cerebral aqueduct, which runs the length of the spinal cord.

A second feature, apparent at the center of our frontal view in Figure 2-8B, are the lateral **ventricles**—two wing-shaped cavities that contain cerebrospinal fluid. The brain's four ventricles, shown in place in **Figure 2-9**, are filled with CSF made by a network of blood vessels, called the choroid plexus, which lines the ventricles. All four ventricles are connected, so CSF flows from the two lateral ventricles to the third and fourth ventricles, which lie on the brain's midline, and into the *cerebral aqueduct*, a canal that runs down the length of the spinal cord. CSF bathes the brain and circulates to the space between the lower layers of the meninges, where it is absorbed and deposited into the venous bloodstream (see Figure 2-4).

The CSF performs several vital brain functions. The CSF suspends the brain, making it neutrally buoyant so that it acts like it is 1/30 of its actual mass. The CSF also acts as a shock absorber, providing the brain with important protection from mild blows to the head. The chemical content of the CSF is precisely regulated to provide a stable environment for optimal brain function. Slight changes to its chemical composition can cause dizziness and fainting. The brain also produces and distributes about 25 mL of CFS an hour, which accounts for about 1/5 of its total volume. In this way, substances are efficiently delivered to brain cells and waste products cleared away.

Cutting through the brain vertically from front to back produces a sagittal section (**Figure 2-10A**). If we make our cut down the brain's midline—that is, in the midsagittal plane—we divide the cerebrum into its two hemispheres, revealing several distinctive structures in the resulting medial view (Figure 2-10B). One feature is a long band of white matter that runs much of the length of the cerebral hemispheres. This band, the **corpus callosum**, contains about 200 million nerve fibers that join the two hemispheres and allow them to communicate.

Figure 2-10B clearly shows that the neocortex covers the cerebral hemispheres above the corpus callosum; below it are various internal *subcortical regions*. Subcortical regions make intimate reciprocal connections with cortical areas that process sensory, perceptual, cognitive, and motor functions. In this way, when the cortical areas perceive a threat, such as an angry dog, they communicate with subcortical regions that have already begun to increase breathing and heart rate via the sympathetic nervous system. This relation between cortical and subcortical areas illuminates another principle of CNS organization: the concept that redundant and overlapping functions exist at many levels of the nervous system.

If you were to compare medial views of the left and right hemispheres, you would be struck by their symmetry. The brain, in fact, has two of most structures, one on each side, and they are nearly identical. Structural asymmetry in our species can be

ventricles Cavities in the brain that make and contain CSF.

corpus callosum Band of white matter containing about 200 million nerve fibers that connects the two cerebral hemispheres to provide a route for direct communication between them.

Principle 4: The CNS functions on multiple levels.

FIGURE 2-10 **Sagittal Brain Section**
(A) A section in the midsagittal plane separates the hemispheres, allowing **(B)** a medial view of the brain's midline structures, including the subcortical structures that lie ventral to the corpus callosum.

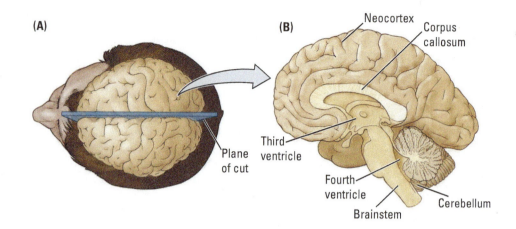

(A)

(B)

Neocortex
Corpus callosum
Third ventricle
Fourth ventricle
Cerebellum
Brainstem
Plane of cut

These neocortical auditory areas are illustrated in Figure 10-13.

Principle 5: The brain is symmetrical and asymmetrical.

Human brains contain about 86 billion neurons and 87 billion glia. Section 3-1 examines their structures and functions in detail.

nuclei (sing. nucleus) A group of neurons forming a cluster that can be identified using special stains.

found in the neocortical auditory areas; in right-handed people, the *planum temporale*, which is responsible for understanding speech, is larger in the left hemisphere, whereas *Heschl's gyrus*, which is responsible for analyzing music, is larger on the right.

The few one-of-a-kind structures, such as the third and fourth ventricles, lie along the brain's midline (see Figure 2-9B). Another one-of-a-kind structure is the pineal gland, which straddles the two hemispheres.

Microscopic Inspection: Cells and Fibers

The brain's fundamental units—its cells—are so small that they can be viewed only with the aid of a microscope. A microscope quickly reveals that the brain has two main types of cells, illustrated in **Figure 2-11**. *Neurons* carry out the brain's communicative and information processing functions, whereas *glial cells* aid and modulate the neurons' activities—for example, by insulating their axons. Both neurons and glia come in many forms, each marked by the work that they do.

We can see the brain's internal structures in even greater detail by dyeing their cells with special stains (**Figure 2-12**). For example, if we use a dye that selectively stains cell bodies, we can see that the neurons in the cortical gray matter lie in layers, revealed by the bands of tissue in Figure 2-12A and C. Each layer contains cells that stain characteristically. Figure 2-12A and B shows that stained subcortical regions are composed of clusters, or **nuclei (sing. nucleus)**, of similar cells.

Although layers and nuclei appear very different, both form functional units in the brain. Whether a particular brain region has layers or nuclei is largely a random product of evolution. By using a stain that selectively dyes neuronal fibers, as shown in Figure 2-12B

FIGURE 2-11 **Brain Cells** Branches emanate from the cell bodies of a prototypical neuron (left) and a glial cell (right). This branching organization increases the cell's surface area. This type of neuron is called a *pyramidal cell* because the cell body is shaped somewhat like a pyramid; the glial cell is called an *astrocyte* because of its star-shaped appearance.

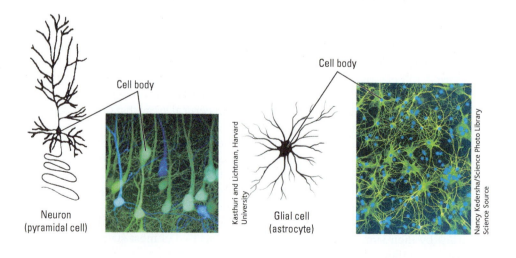

Cell body

Cell body

Neuron (pyramidal cell)

Glial cell (astrocyte)

Kasthuri and Lichtman, Harvard University

Nancy Kedersha/Science Photo Library Science Source

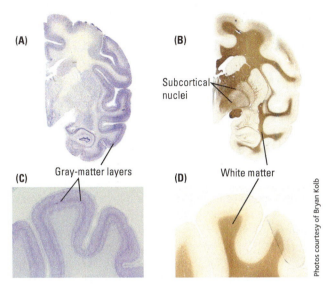

FIGURE 2-12 **Cortical Layers and Glia** Brain sections from the left hemisphere of a monkey (midline is to the left in each image), viewed through a microscope. Cells are stained with **(A and C)** a selective cell body stain for neurons (gray matter) and **(B and D)** a selective fiber stain for insulating glial cells, or *myelin* (white matter). The images reveal very different views of the brain at the macro **(A and B)** and microscopic **(C and D)** levels.

Photos courtesy of Bryan Kolb

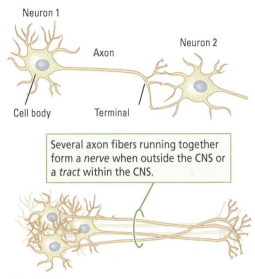

Several axon fibers running together form a *nerve* when outside the CNS or a *tract* within the CNS.

FIGURE 2-13 Neuronal Connections

and D, we can see the borders of the subcortical nuclei more clearly. In addition, we can see that the stained cell bodies lie in regions adjacent to those with most of the fibers.

A key feature of neurons is that they are connected to one another by fibers known as *axons*. When axons run along together, much like the wires that run from a car engine to the dashboard, they form a **nerve** or **tract** (**Figure 2-13**). By convention, a *tract* is a collection of nerve fibers in the brain and spinal cord, whereas bundles of fibers outside the CNS are typically called nerves. Thus, the pathway from the eye to the brain is the optic nerve, whereas the pathway from the cerebral cortex to the spinal cord is the corticospinal tract.

nerve Large collection of axons coursing together *outside* the CNS.

tract Large collection of axons coursing together *in* the CNS.

2-1 Review

Before you continue, check your understanding. Answers to Self-Test appear at the back of the book.

1. The nervous system's function is to produce movement, or _____, in a perceptual world constructed by the _____.

2. The left and right cerebral hemispheres are each divided into four lobes: _____, _____, _____, and _____.

3. The human nervous system has evolved the potential to change, for example, to adapt to changes in the world or to compensate for injury. This attribute is called _____.

4. Neural tissue is of two main types: (1) _____ forms the connections among cells, and (2) _____ collects and processes incoming (afferent) sensory or outgoing (efferent) information.

5. The nerve fibers that lie in the brain form _____. Outside the brain they are called _____.

6. Chart the human nervous system's functional organization.

For additional study tools, visit **LaunchPad** at launchpadworks.com

2-2

The Conserved Pattern of Nervous System Development

The nervous system's basic structural plan is present in developing, embryonic brains, and the striking similarity of the main divisions in embryos as diverse as amphibians and mammals is evident in the earliest stages of development. Because evolution works by tinkering with the developmental programs that give rise to brain structures, simpler and evolutionarily more archaic forms have not been discarded and replaced but rather modified and added to. As a result, all anatomical and functional features of simpler nervous systems are present in and form the base for the most complex nervous systems, including ours.

The bilaterally symmetrical nervous system of simple worms, for example, is common to complex nervous systems. Indeed, we can recognize in humans the spinal cord that constitutes most of the simplest fishes' nervous system. The same is true of the brainstem of more complex fishes, amphibians, and reptiles. The neocortex, although particularly large and complex in humans, is clearly the same organ found in other mammals.

Section 1-3 outlines nervous system evolution, and Section 8-1 covers developmental similarities among humans and other species.

Comparative Brain Evolution

In a vertebrate embryo, the nervous system begins as a sheet of cells. This sheet folds into a hollow tube and develops into three regions—forebrain, midbrain, and hindbrain—which are recognizable as a series of three enlargements at the end of the embryonic spinal cord (**Figure 2-14A**). The adult brain of a fish, an amphibian, or a reptile is roughly equivalent to this three-part brain. The *prosencephalon* (front brain) is responsible for olfaction, the sense of smell; the *mesencephalon* (middle brain) is the seat of vision and hearing; and the *rhombencephalon* (hindbrain) controls movement and balance. The spinal cord is part of the hindbrain.

FIGURE 2-14 **Comparative Brain Evolution and Development** As the mammalian brain has evolved, the forebrain has expanded dramatically.

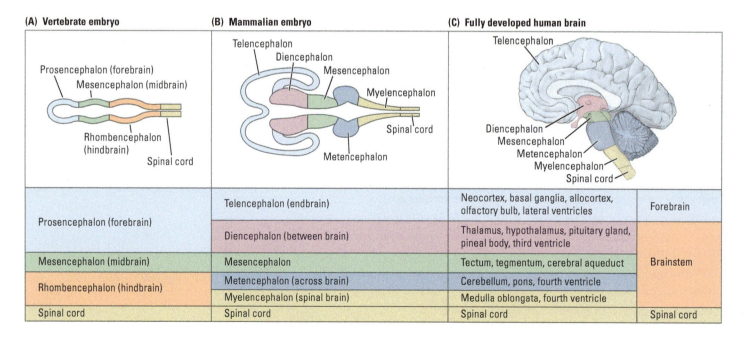

	(A) Vertebrate embryo	(B) Mammalian embryo	(C) Fully developed human brain	
	Prosencephalon (forebrain)	Telencephalon (endbrain)	Neocortex, basal ganglia, allocortex, olfactory bulb, lateral ventricles	Forebrain
		Diencephalon (between brain)	Thalamus, hypothalamus, pituitary gland, pineal body, third ventricle	
	Mesencephalon (midbrain)	Mesencephalon	Tectum, tegmentum, cerebral aqueduct	Brainstem
	Rhombencephalon (hindbrain)	Metencephalon (across brain)	Cerebellum, pons, fourth ventricle	
		Myelencephalon (spinal brain)	Medulla oblongata, fourth ventricle	
	Spinal cord	Spinal cord	Spinal cord	Spinal cord

In mammalian embryos (Figure 2-14B), the prosencephalon develops further to form the subcortical structures known collectively as the *diencephalon* (between brain) and the cerebral hemispheres and cortical areas, or *telencephalon* (endbrain). The mammalian hindbrain develops further into the *metencephalon* (across brain), which includes the cerebellum, and the *myelencephalon* (spinal brain), including the spinal cord.

The human brain is particularly complex, possessing especially large cerebral hemispheres but retaining most other mammalian brain features (Figure 2-14C). Various human cerebral areas necessary to produce language—regions in the frontal, temporal, and parietal lobes—are proportionally larger compared to the brains of other primates. Language is thought to have fostered a novel worldview—in the way we think, reflect on our own thoughts, and imagine.

The Nervous System and Intelligent Behavior

Most behaviors are the product not of a single locus in the brain but rather of many interacting brain areas and levels. These several nervous system regions do not simply replicate function; rather, each region adds a different dimension to the behavior. This hierarchical organization affects virtually every human behavior. Abnormalities associated with brain injury and brain disease that seem bizarre in isolation are but the normal manifestation of parts of a hierarchically organized brain. Our evolutionary history, our developmental history, and our own personal history are integrated at the various anatomical and functional levels of the nervous system.

Principle 6: Brain systems are organized hierarchically and in parallel.

Is the vertebrate nervous system the only path to evolving intelligent behavior? Invertebrate animals, such as the octopus, have traveled on an evolutionary pathway separate from that of vertebrates for over 700 million years. The octopus nervous system, while strikingly different from ours, is complex. Might the octopus learn much as vertebrate animals do?

Italian biologists Graziano Fiorito and Pietro Scotto (1992) placed individuals of *Octopus vulgaris* (the common octopus) in separate tanks, each with an independent water supply, and allowed them to interact visually for 2 hours. As illustrated in the Procedure section of **Experiment 2-1**, the observer octopus watched the demonstrator octopus from an adjacent tank through a transparent wall. The demonstrator was being conditioned to learn that a red ball was associated with a reward, whereas a white ball was associated with a weak electric shock.

As noted in the Results section, the demonstrator animals quickly learned to distinguish between the colored balls. The observers were then placed in isolation. When tested later, they selected the same object the demonstrators had, responded faster than the demonstrators did during their conditioning, and performed the task correctly for 5 days without significant error or further conditioning.

2-2 Review

Before you continue, check your understanding. Answers to Self-Test appear at the back of the book.

1. The brains of vertebrate animals have evolved into three regions: _____, _____, and _____.

2. The functional levels of the nervous system interact, each region contributing different aspects, or dimensions, to produce_____.

3. In a brief paragraph, explain how the evolution of the forebrain in mammals reinforces the principle that the CNS functions on multiple levels.

For additional study tools, visit ⧉ **LaunchPad** at launchpadworks.com

····> **EXPERIMENT 2-1**

Question: Does intelligent behavior require a vertebrate nervous system organization?

Procedure

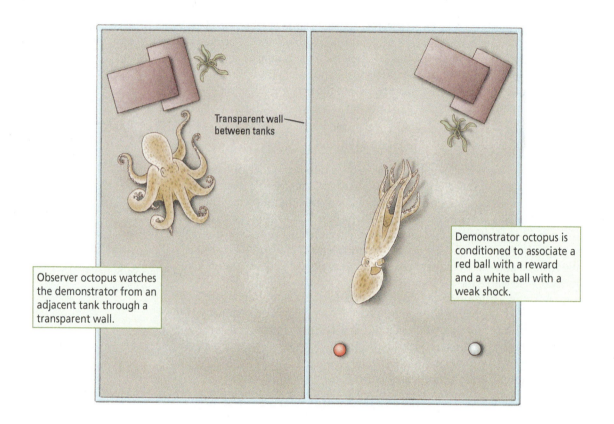

Transparent wall between tanks

Observer octopus watches the demonstrator from an adjacent tank through a transparent wall.

Demonstrator octopus is conditioned to associate a red ball with a reward and a white ball with a weak shock.

Results

1. The demonstrator animal quickly learned to distinguish between the colored balls.

2. When placed in isolation and tested later, the observer animals selected the same object as the demonstrators, responded faster, and performed the task correctly for 5 days without significant error.

Conclusion: Invertebrates display intelligent behavior, such as learning by observation.

Research from Fiorito & Scotto (1992).

2-3

The Central Nervous System: Mediating Behavior

When we look under the hood of a car, we can make some pretty good guesses about what certain parts of a car engine do. For example, the battery must provide electrical power to run the radio and lights, and, because a battery has to be charged, the engine must contain some mechanism for charging it. We can use a similar approach to deduce how the parts of the brain function. The part connected to the optic nerve coming from each eye must have something to do with vision. Structures connected to the auditory nerve coming from each ear must have something to do with hearing.

From such simple observations, we can begin to understand how the brain is organized. The real test comes when analyzing actual brain function: how this seeming jumble of parts produces experiences as complex as human thought. The place to start is the brain's functional anatomy; learning the name of a particular CNS structure is pointless without also learning something about what it does. We focus now on the names and functions of the three major CNS components: spinal cord, brainstem, and forebrain.

Spinal Cord

Although the brain's principal function is to produce movement, ultimately the spinal cord, with its connections to muscles, *executes* most of those body movements, usually following instructions from the brain but at times acting independently via the somatic nervous system. To understand how important the spinal cord is, think of the old saying "running around like a chicken with its head cut off." When a chicken's head is lopped off, the chicken is still capable of running around the barnyard until it collapses from loss of blood. The chicken accomplishes this feat because the spinal cord is acting independently of the brain.

Grasping the spinal cord's complexity is easier once you realize that it is not a single structure but rather a set of segmented switching stations. As detailed in Section 2-4, each spinal segment receives information from a discrete part of the body and sends out commands to that area. Spinal nerves, which are part of the SNS, carry sensory information to the cord from the skin, muscles, and related structures and, in turn, send motor instructions to control each muscle.

You can demonstrate movement controlled by the spinal cord in your own body by tapping your patellar tendon, just below your kneecap (the patella), as shown in **Figure 2-15.** The sensory input causes your lower leg to kick out, and try as you might, it is very hard to prevent the movement. Your brain, in other words, has trouble inhibiting this *spinal reflex:* it is automatic.

Brainstem

The **brainstem** begins where the spinal cord enters the skull and extends upward into the lower areas of the forebrain. The brainstem receives afferent signals coming in from all of the body's senses, and it sends efferent signals out to the spinal cord to control virtually all of the body's movements except the most complex movements of the fingers and toes. The brainstem, then, both creates a sensory world and directs movements.

In some vertebrates, such as frogs, the entire brain is largely equivalent to the mammalian or avian brainstem. And frogs get along quite well, demonstrating that the brainstem is a fairly sophisticated piece of machinery. If we had only a brainstem, we would still be able to construct a world, but it would be a far simpler sensorimotor world, more like the world a frog experiences.

The brainstem, which is responsible for most life-sustaining behavior, can be divided into three regions: hindbrain, midbrain, and diencephalon (which means "between brain," referring to the fact that it borders the brain's upper and lower parts). In fact, the between-brain status of the diencephalon has been controversial: some anatomists place it in the brainstem, and others place it in the forebrain. **Figure 2-16A** illustrates the location of these three brainstem regions under the cerebral hemispheres. Figure 2-16B compares the shape of the brainstem regions to the lower part of your arm when held upright. The hindbrain is long and thick like your forearm, the midbrain is short and compact like your wrist, and the diencephalon at the end is bulbous like a fist.

The hindbrain and midbrain are essentially extensions of the spinal cord; they developed first as vertebrate animals evolved a brain at the anterior end of the body. It makes sense, therefore, that these lower brainstem regions should retain a division between structures having sensory functions and those having motor functions, with sensory structures lying dorsal and motor ones ventral, or in upright humans, posterior and anterior.

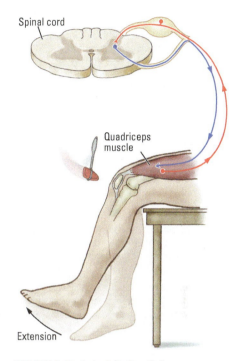

FIGURE 2-15 **Spinal Reflex** Reflexes are explained in Section 11-4.

Here's a trick to help you remember the difference: alphabetically, *afferent* comes before *efferent*; sensory signals enter the brain before an outgoing signal results in a motor response.

brainstem Central structure of the brain (including the hindbrain, midbrain, thalamus, and hypothalamus) that is responsible for most life-sustaining behavior.

Principle 7: Sensory and motor divisions permeate the nervous system.

FIGURE 2-16 **Brainstem Structures (A)** The medial view shows the relationship of the brainstem to the cerebral hemispheres. **(B)** The shapes and relative sizes of the brainstem's three parts are analogous to your fist, wrist, and forearm.

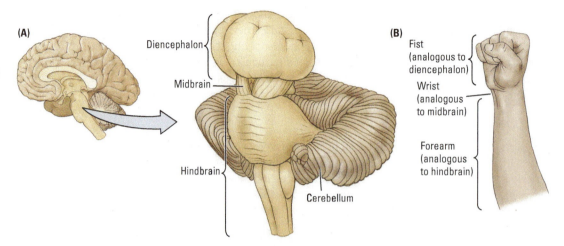

hindbrain Evolutionarily the oldest part of the brain; contains the pons, medulla, reticular formation, and cerebellum, the structures that coordinate and control most voluntary and involuntary movements.

reticular formation Midbrain area in which nuclei and fiber pathways are mixed, producing a netlike appearance; associated with sleep–wake behavior and behavioral arousal.

Each brainstem region performs more than a single task, and each contains various groupings of nuclei that serve various purposes. In fact, all three regions have both sensory and motor functions. However, the hindbrain is especially important in motor functions, the midbrain in sensory functions, and the diencephalon in integrative sensorimotor tasks. Here, we consider the central functions of these three regions; later chapters contain more detailed information about them.

Hindbrain

The **hindbrain** controls motor functions ranging from breathing to balance to fine movements, such as those used in dancing. Its most distinctive structure, and one of the largest in the human brain, is the cerebellum. Its relative size increases with the physical speed and dexterity of a species, as shown in **Figure 2-17A**.

Animals that move relatively slowly (such as a sloth) have a relatively small cerebellum for their body size. Animals that can perform rapid acrobatic movements (such as a hawk or a cat) have a very large cerebellum relative to overall brain size. The human cerebellum, which resembles a cauliflower in the medial view in Figure 2-17B, likewise is important in controlling complex movements. But cerebellar size in humans is also related to cognitive capacity. Relative to other mammals, apes show an expansion of the cerebellum that correlates with increased capacity for planning and executing complex behavioral sequences, including tool use and language (see Barton, 2012).

As we look beyond the cerebellum at the rest of the hindbrain, shown in **Figure 2-18**, we find three subparts: the reticular formation, the pons, and the medulla. Extending the length of the entire brainstem at its core, the **reticular formation** is a netlike mixture of neurons (gray matter) and nerve fibers (white matter). This nerve net

FIGURE 2-17 **The Cerebellum and Movement (A)** Their relatively large cerebellum enables finely coordinated movements such as flying and landing in birds and pouncing on prey in cats. Slow-moving animals such as the sloth have a smaller cerebellum relative to brain size. **(B)** Like the cerebrum, the human cerebellum has left and right hemispheres, an extensively folded cortex with gray and white matter, and subcortical nuclei.

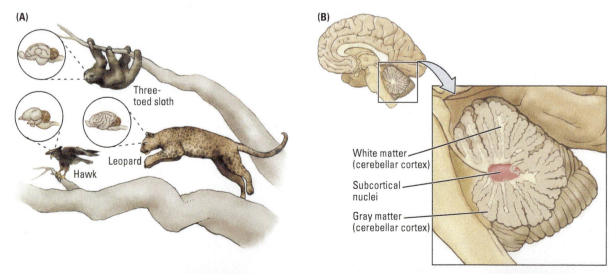

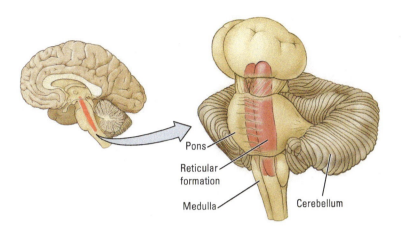

FIGURE 2-18 **Hindbrain** The principal hindbrain structures integrate voluntary and involuntary body movements. The reticular formation is sometimes called the *reticular activating system*.

Pons
Reticular formation
Medulla
Cerebellum

---

midbrain Central part of the brain; contains neural circuits for hearing and seeing as well as for orienting movements.

tectum Roof (area above the ventricle) of the midbrain; its functions are sensory processing, particularly visual and auditory, and the production of orienting movements.

tegmentum Floor (area below the ventricle) of the midbrain; a collection of nuclei with movement-related, species-specific, and pain perception functions.

orienting movement Movement related to sensory inputs, such as turning the head to see the source of a sound.

---

gives the structure the mottled appearance from which its name derives (from Latin *rete*, meaning "net"). The reticular formation's nuclei are localized into small patches along its length. Each has a special function in stimulating the forebrain, such as in waking from sleep.

The *pons* and *medulla* contain substructures that control many vital body movements. Nuclei in the pons receive inputs from the cerebellum and actually form a bridge from it to the rest of the brain (in Latin, *pons* means "bridge"). At the rostral tip of the spinal cord, the medulla's nuclei regulate such vital functions as breathing and the cardiovascular system. For this reason, a blow to the back of the head can kill you: your breathing stops if the hindbrain control centers are injured.

Midbrain

In the **midbrain**, a sensory component called the **tectum** (roof) is dorsal (posterior in upright humans), whereas a motor structure called the **tegmentum** (floor) is ventral (anterior in humans; **Figure 2-19A**). The tectum receives a massive amount of sensory information from the eyes and ears. The optic nerve sends a large bundle of fibers to the *superior colliculus*, whereas the *inferior colliculus* receives much of its input from auditory pathways. The colliculi function not only to process sensory information but also to produce **orienting movements** related to sensory inputs, such as turning your head to see a sound's source.

This orienting behavior is not as simple as it may seem. To produce it, the auditory and visual systems must share a map of the external world so that the ears can tell the eyes where to look. If the auditory and visual maps differed, it would be impossible to use the two together. In fact, the colliculi also have a tactile map. After all, if you want to look at what's making your leg itch, your visual and tactile systems need a common representation of where that place is so you can scratch the itch by moving your arm and hand.

Lying ventral to the tectum, the tegmentum (shown in Figure 2-19B in cross section) is composed of many nuclei, largely with movement-related functions. Several tegmental nuclei control eye movements. The *red nucleus* controls limb movements (and is absent in snakes). The *substantia nigra* connects to the forebrain, a connection especially important in initiating movements. (Clinical Focus 5-2 explains that the symptoms of Parkinson disease are related to the destruction of the substantia nigra.) The *periaqueductal gray matter* (PAG), made up of cell bodies that surround the aqueduct joining the third and fourth ventricles, contains circuits that control species-typical behaviors (e.g., female sexual behavior). These nuclei also play an important role in how opioid drugs can modulate pain.

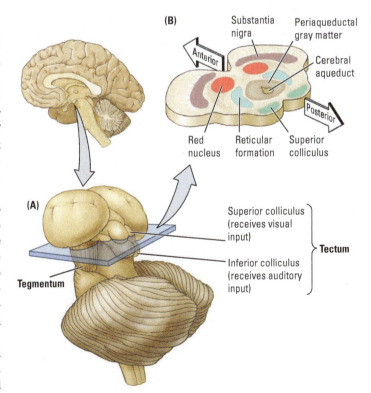

(B) Substantia nigra
Periaqueductal gray matter
Anterior
Cerebral aqueduct
Posterior
Red nucleus
Reticular formation
Superior colliculus

(A)
Tegmentum
Superior colliculus (receives visual input)
Inferior colliculus (receives auditory input)
Tectum

FIGURE 2-19 **Midbrain (A)** Structures in the midbrain are critical for producing orienting movements, species-specific behaviors, and pain perception. **(B)** The tegmentum in cross section, revealing various nuclei. *Colliculus* comes from *collis*, Latin for "hill." The colliculi resemble four little hills on the midbrain's posterior surface.

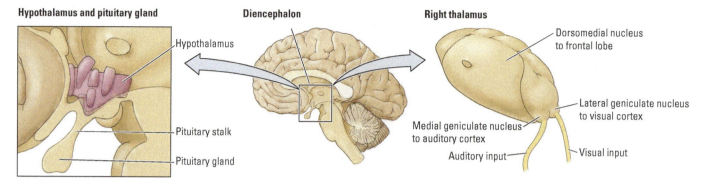

Hypothalamus and pituitary gland

Hypothalamus

Pituitary stalk

Pituitary gland

Diencephalon

Right thalamus

Dorsomedial nucleus to frontal lobe

Lateral geniculate nucleus to visual cortex

Medial geniculate nucleus to auditory cortex

Auditory input

Visual input

FIGURE 2-20 **Diencephalon** The diencephalon (center) is composed of the epithalamus, which includes the pineal gland, the thalamus (shown at right), the hypothalamus (the posterior portion of the pituitary gland, shown at left), and the subthalamus. Thalamic regions connect to discrete cortical regions. Below the thalamus, at the base of the brain, the hypothalamus (in Latin, *hypo* means "below") and pituitary lie above the roof of the mouth. The hypothalamus is composed of many nuclei, each with distinct functions.

Principle 8: The brain divides sensory input for object recognition and movement.

We examine how thalamic sensory nuclei process incoming information in Sections 9-2, 10-2, 11-4, and 12-2 and look at memory pathways in Section 14-3.

---

diencephalon The between brain, which integrates sensory and motor information on its way to the cerebral cortex.

hypothalamus Diencephalon structure that contains many nuclei associated with temperature regulation, eating, drinking, and sexual behavior.

thalamus Diencephalon structure through which information from all sensory systems is organized, integrated, and projected into the appropriate region of the neocortex.

forebrain Evolutionarily the most recent addition to the brain; coordinates advanced cognitive functions such as thinking, planning, and language; contains the allocortex, neocortex, and basal ganglia.

Diencephalon

The **diencephalon**, shown in sagittal section in the center of **Figure 2-20**, integrates sensory and motor information on its way to the cerebral cortex. Its two principal structures are the hypothalamus and the thalamus. The thalamus—one in each hemisphere—lies just to the left of the brainstem's tip, and the hypothalamus (in Latin, *hypo* means "below") lies below the thalamus in each hemisphere.

The **hypothalamus** in each hemisphere lies along the brain's midline; it is composed of about 22 small nuclei and the nerve fiber systems that pass through it. Its critical function is to control the body's production of hormones, accomplished via its interactions with the pituitary gland, shown at left in Figure 2-20. Although it constitutes only about 0.3 percent of the brain's weight, the hypothalamus takes part in nearly all aspects of behavior, including feeding, sleeping, temperature regulation, sexual and emotional behavior, hormone function, and movement. The hypothalamus is organized and functions more or less similarly across mammals. But sex differences have been found in the structures of some of its parts, in some species, probably due to differences between males and females in activities such as sexual behavior and parenting.

The other principal structure of the diencephalon, the **thalamus**, is much larger than the hypothalamus, as are its 20-odd nuclei. Perhaps the most distinctive thalamic function is its role as an organizer and integrator of sensory information traveling to the cerebral cortex from all sensory systems. The optic tract, for example, sends information through a large fiber bundle to a thalamic region called the *lateral geniculate nucleus* (*LGN*), shown at the right tip of the thalamus in Figure 2-20. In turn, the LGN processes some of this information and then sends it to the visual region in the occipital lobe in each hemisphere.

The routes to the thalamus may be indirect. For example, the route for olfaction traverses several synapses before entering the *dorsomedial thalamic nucleus* on its way to the forebrain. This nucleus, which projects to the frontal lobe, performs integrative tasks and thus plays a vital role in attention, planning, abstract thinking, and memory. Analogous sensory regions of the thalamus receive auditory and tactile information, which is subsequently relayed to the respective auditory and tactile cortical regions in each hemisphere. Other thalamic regions have motor functions, as they receive input from those regions where decisions about possible movements are made, and, in turn, relay information to movement planning areas in the neocortex.

Forebrain

The largest and most recently evolved region of the mammalian brain is the **forebrain**. Its major internal and external structures are shown in **Figure 2-21**. Each of its two principal structures has multiple functions. To summarize briefly, the *cerebral cortex* regulates a host of mental activities ranging from perception to planning to emotions and memory; the *basal ganglia* control voluntary movement and also have a role in cognitive functioning.

Extending our analogy between the brainstem and your forearm, imagine that the fist (the diencephalon) is thrust inside a watermelon—the forebrain, with the neocortex as the rind and the allocortex and basal ganglia as the fruit inside. Just as watermelons come in various sizes, so do brains, which in a sense is what evolution has done: the forebrain varies considerably in size across species.

Cerebral Cortex

The forebrain contains the cerebral cortex ("bark") which can be viewed as concentric rings of three-layered cortex, four-layered cortex, and six-layered cortex. For simplicity, we use the name **allocortex** (literally, "other bark") to refer to both the three- and four-layered cortex. Found in the brains of other chordates (including birds, reptiles, and mammals), the allocortex plays a role in controlling motivational and emotional states as well as in certain forms of memory. The six-layered **neocortex** (literally, "new bark") is the tissue visible when we view the brain from the outside, as in Figure 2-5. The more recently expanded neocortex is unique to mammals; its primary function is to construct a perceptual world and respond to that world. Although the neocortex and allocortex have anatomical and functional differences, most neuroscientists usually refer to both types of tissue simply as *cortex*.

Measured by volume, the cortex makes up most of the forebrain, constituting 80 percent of the human brain overall. It is the brain region that has expanded the most in the course of mammalian evolution. The human neocortex has a surface area as large as 2500 square centimeters but a thickness of only 2.3 to 2.8 millimeters, an area equivalent to about four pages of this book. By contrast, a chimpanzee has a cortical area equivalent to about one page. See **Figure 2-22**.

The pattern of sulci and gyri formed by the folding of the neocortex varies across species. Smaller-brained mammals, such as rats and mice, have no sulci or gyri and thus have a smooth, or *lissencephalic*, brain. Larger-brained mammals, including carnivores such as cats, have gyri that form a longitudinal pattern. In primates, the sulci and gyri form a more complex pattern. These *gyrencephalic* brains are the result of a relatively large neocortical sheet repeatedly folded in upon itself so that it fits into the restricted space of the skull.

Allocortex

The allocortex is composed of several distinct three- and four-layer structures that include the hippocampus, part of the amygdala, the cingulate cortex, several structures that make up the olfactory system, and other related areas.

The hippocampus together with its dentate gyrus look astoundingly like a seahorse, and its name comes from the Greek meaning "seahorse" (see the comparison in **Figure 2-23**). It is involved in *consolidation*, the process whereby short-term memories are solidified into long-term memories. Destruction of the hippocampus leads to problems with navigation, finding our way around, as well as difficulties with word finding.

The amygdala (meaning "almond") plays a critical role in anxiety and fear. Removal of the amygdala produces truly startling changes in emotional behavior. A cat with its amygdala removed will wander through a colony of monkeys, completely undisturbed by their hooting and threats. No self-respecting, normally functioning cat would be caught anywhere near such bedlam.

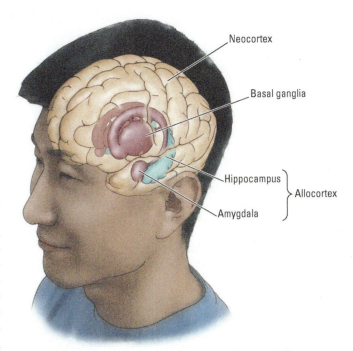

FIGURE 2-21 **Forebrain Structures** The major internal and external forebrain structures integrate sensation, motivation, emotion, and memory to enable such advanced cognitive functions as thinking, planning, and using language.

allocortex Part of the cerebral cortex ("outer bark"), composed of three or four layers; plays a role in controlling motivational and emotional states as well as in certain forms of memory.

neocortex Most recently expanded outer layer ("new bark") of the forebrain, composed of about six layers of gray matter. Its name is a misnomer, as it actually isn't newer because it arose at the same time during evolution as other forms of cortex. It is also called *isocortex* because it is almost always six-layered, with few exceptions.

FIGURE 2-22 **Three Primate Brains** The brains of a Rhesus monkey, chimpanzee, and human, shown here to scale, differ dramatically in size and in surface appearance. With an encephalization quotient of 2.0, the Rhesus monkey's brain is just over one-quarter the size of a human's (EQ 7.0). The chimp's brain, EQ 2.5, is a bit more than one-third as large (see Figure 1-15).

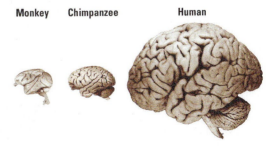

Monkey Chimpanzee Human

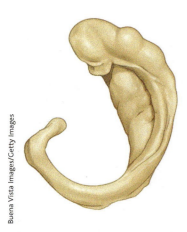 

FIGURE 2-23 **Hippocampi** Dissected human hippocampus (left) named after a seahorse (right).

For more on motivation and emotion, see Sections 12-3 and 12-4; memory, Section 14-3; and brain disorders, Research Focus 16-1 and Section 16-4.

Section 12-2 considers the chemical senses smell and taste in the context of emotional and motivated behavior.

limbic system A conceptual system controlling affective and motivated behaviors and certain forms of memory with key anatomy lying between the neocortex and brainstem; includes the cingulate cortex, amygdala, and hippocampus, among other structures.

The cingulate cortex lies above the corpus callosum, close to the midline. It is involved with emotion formation and processing, learning, and memory, and it is highly influential in linking behavioral outcomes to motivation.

THE CONCEPT OF THE LIMBIC SYSTEM The concept of a **limbic system** has a long and controversial history in neuroscience. In the 1930s, psychiatry was dominated by the theories of Sigmund Freud, who emphasized the roles of sexuality and emotion in human behavior. At the time, the brain regions controlling these behaviors had not yet been identified; coincidentally, the border, or *limbus*, of the brain—that area between the subcortical nuclei of the brainstem and the neocortex, which the astute reader will recognize as allocortex—had no known function. It was a simple step to thinking that perhaps the limbic structures played a central role in sexuality and emotion.

One issue with the limbic system concept is that neuroscientists have never agreed on what anatomical structures should be considered part of it. Another issue is that the original view that the limbic system was the emotional center and the neocortex was the home of cognition doesn't work because cognition depends on acquisition and retention of memories—and the hippocampus, an allocortical structure, plays a primary role in those functions. Thus, several neuroscientists have argued that the term *limbic system* be abandoned because it is obsolete. A more recent view is that specific circuits for specific functions can be traced through several allocortical, neocortical, and brainstem structures.

OLFACTORY SYSTEM At the very front of the brain lie the olfactory bulbs, the organs responsible for detecting odors and providing input to other brain areas responsible for our perception of smell. The olfactory system is unique among human senses, as **Figure 2-24** shows, because it is almost entirely a forebrain structure. The other sensory systems project most of their inputs from the sensory receptors to the midbrain and thalamus. Olfactory input takes a less direct route: the olfactory bulb sends most of its inputs to a specialized region, the *pyriform cortex*, which is also part of the allocortex, on the brain's ventral surface. From there, sensory input progresses to the amygdala and the dorsomedial thalamus (see Figure 2-20, right), which routes it to the frontal cortex.

Smell is one of the first senses to have evolved in animals, yet curiously, the olfactory system lies at the front of the human brain and is considered part of the forebrain (see the ventral view in Figure 2-6B). The olfactory bulbs lie near the olfactory receptors in the

All sorts of behaviors can prove addictive—eating, shopping, sex, video gaming, gambling, even Twitter! How else to explain these Canadian coeds tweeting all bundled up when they could be defrosting on the beach in the Florida sun?

nasal cavity. Although evolution has led to these organs sending their inputs to the pyriform cortex in mammals, their input to the brainstem is more direct in simpler brains.

Compared with the olfactory bulbs of rats, cats, and dogs, which rely more heavily on smell than we do, the human olfactory bulb is relatively small. Nonetheless, it is very sensitive, allowing us to distinguish a surprisingly large number of odors. Smell plays an important role in various aspects of our feeding and sexual behavior.

The **vomeronasal organ (VNO)** contains sensory neurons that detect pheromones, molecules that carry information between individuals of the same species. The axons from these neurons project to the accessory olfactory bulb, which connects to the amygdala and in turn the hypothalamus. The VNO has an important role in reproduction and social behavior in many mammals, but its presence and functionality in humans is controversial.

Neocortical Layers

In the neocortex, six layers of gray matter sit atop the corpus callosum, the white matter structure that is composed of neocortical axons and joins the two cerebral hemispheres. The six layers of the neocortex have distinct characteristics:

- Different layers have different types of cells.
- The cell density varies from layer to layer, ranging from virtually no cells in layer I (the top layer) to very dense cell packing in layer IV (**Figure 2-25**).
- Other differences in appearance are both regional and functional.

These visible differences led neuroanatomists to map the neocortex a century ago. In 1909, Korbinian Brodmann published the map shown in **Figure 2-26**. Based on cytology, the study of cell characteristics, these maps are called **cytoarchitectonic maps**. For example, viewed through a microscope, sensory neocortex in the parietal lobe (shown in red in Figure 2-25) has a large layer IV, and motor cortex in the frontal lobe (shown in blue in Figure 2-25) has a large layer V. Layer IV is afferent; layer V is efferent. It makes sense that a sensory region has a large input layer, whereas a motor region has a large output layer.

Staining neocortical tissue can reveal chemical differences between cells and layers. Some regions are rich in one chemical, others rich in another. These differences presumably relate to functional specialization of different neocortical areas.

The one significant difference between the organization of the neocortex and the organization of other brain parts is its range of connections. Unlike most structures, which connect only to certain brain regions, the neocortex is connected to virtually all other parts of the brain. The neocortex, in other words, is the ultimate meddler. It takes part in everything—a fact that not only makes it difficult to identify specific neocortical functions but also complicates our study of the rest of the brain because we must always consider the neocortex's role in other brain regions.

Consider your perception of clouds. You have no doubt gazed up at clouds on a summer day and imagined sailing ships, elephants, faces, and countless other objects. Although a cloud does not really look like an elephant, you can concoct an image of one if you impose your frontal cortex—that is, your imagination—on the sensory inputs. This kind of cortical activity is *top-down processing* because the top level of the nervous system, the neocortex, is influencing how information is processed in lower regions of the hierarchy—in this case, the midbrain and hindbrain.

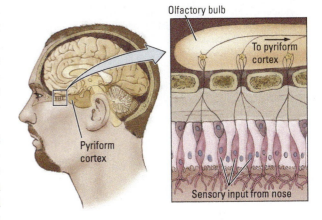

FIGURE 2-24 **Sense of Smell** Our small olfactory bulbs lie at the base of the forebrain, connect to receptor cells that lie in the nasal cavity, and send most of this input to the pyriform cortex en route to the amygdala and thalamus.

vomeronasal organ (VNO) Collection of neurons that detect pheromones; this organ plays a role in reproduction and social behavior in many mammals, though its specific function in humans is disputed.

FIGURE 2-25 **Neocortical Layering** Layer IV is relatively thick in the sensory cortex and relatively thin in the motor cortex. This is because abundant afferent sensory information from the thalamus connects to layer IV. Conversely, layers V and VI are relatively thick in the motor neocortex and thin in the sensory neocortex. Efferent motor information in layer V makes up the corticospinal track, connecting the motor neocortex to the spinal cord to generate movement, and layer VI connects to other cortical areas.

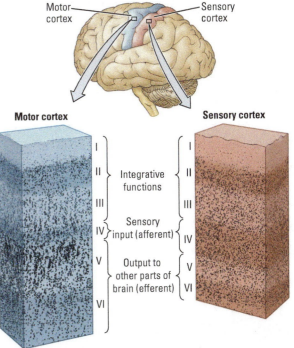

cytoarchitectonic map Map of the neocortex based on the organization, structure, and distribution of the cells.

Cortex is often used as shorthand for the neocortex or neocortical layers. However, cortex may refer to any and all layered structures in the forebrain. In this book, we use the terms *neocortex* and *allocortex* only when making a distinction *between* those structures.

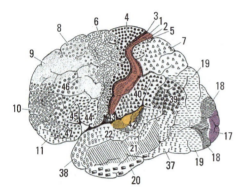

FIGURE 2-26 **Early Brain Map** In his cytoarchitectonic map of the neocortex, Brodmann (1909) defined areas by the organization and characteristics of the cells he examined. The regions shown in color are associated with the simplest sensory perceptions: touch (red), vision (purple), and hearing (orange). As we shall see, the neocortical areas that process sensory information are far more extensive than Brodmann's basic areas.

Principle 9: Brain functions are localized and distributed.

Anatomical features presented in Section 9-2 define occipital lobe boundaries.

The neocortex influences many behaviors besides object perception. It influences our cravings for foods, our lust for things (or people), and how we interpret the meaning of abstract concepts, words, and images. The neocortex ultimately creates our reality, and one reason it serves this function is that it is so well connected.

Cortical Lobes

To review, the human cortex consists of the nearly symmetrical left and right hemispheres, which are separated by the longitudinal fissure, shown at left in **Figure 2-27**. As shown at right, each hemisphere is subdivided into four lobes corresponding to the skull bones overlying them: frontal, parietal, temporal, and occipital. Unfortunately, bone location and brain function are unrelated. As a result, the cortical lobes are rather arbitrarily defined anatomical regions that include many functional zones.

Nevertheless, we can attach some gross functions to each lobe. The frontal lobe is sometimes called the brain's *executive* because it integrates sensory and motor functions, formulates plans of action, and contains the primary motor cortex. The three posterior lobes have sensory functions: the parietal lobe is tactile; the temporal lobe is visual, auditory, and gustatory; and the occipital lobe is visual. We can also predict some effects of injuries to each lobe:

- Individuals with *frontal lobe* injuries may have difficulty organizing and evaluating their ongoing behavior, as well as planning for the future.

- Injuries to the *parietal lobe* make it difficult to identify or locate stimulation on the skin and may contribute to deficits in moving the arms and hands to points in space.

- *Temporal lobe* injuries result in difficulty recognizing sounds, although, unlike people with occipital injuries, those with temporal injury can still recognize that they are hearing something. Temporal lobe injuries can also cause difficulties in processing complex visual information, such as faces.

- People with an injured *occipital lobe* have deficits in processing visual information. Although they may perceive light versus dark, for example, they may be unable to identify either the shape or the color of objects.

Fissures and sulci often establish the boundaries of cortical lobes (Figure 2-27, right). For instance, in humans, the central sulcus and lateral fissure form the boundaries of each frontal lobe, as well as the boundaries of each parietal lobe lying posterior to the central sulcus. The lateral fissure demarcates each temporal lobe, forming its dorsal boundary. The occipital lobes are not so clearly separated from the parietal and temporal lobes because no large fissure marks their boundaries.

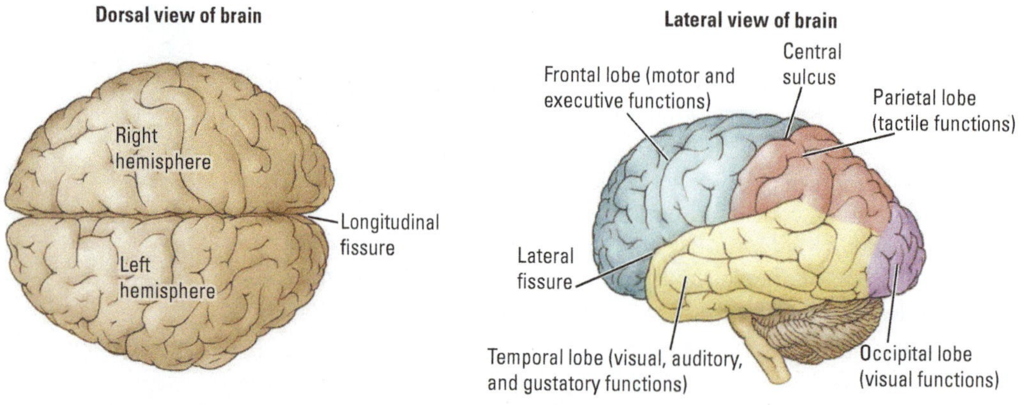

Dorsal view of brain

Right hemisphere

Left hemisphere

Longitudinal fissure

Lateral view of brain

Frontal lobe (motor and executive functions)

Central sulcus

Parietal lobe (tactile functions)

Lateral fissure

Temporal lobe (visual, auditory, and gustatory functions)

Occipital lobe (visual functions)

FIGURE 2-27 **Cortical Boundaries**

Basal Ganglia

The **basal ganglia**, a collection of nuclei that lie in the forebrain just below the white matter of the cortex, consist of three principal structures: the *caudate nucleus*, the *putamen,* and the *globus pallidus*, all shown in **Figure 2-28**. Together with the thalamus and two closely associated nuclei (the substantia nigra and subthalamic nucleus), the basal ganglia form a system that functions primarily to control voluntary movement.

We can observe the functions of the basal ganglia by analyzing the behavior resulting from the many diseases that interfere with their healthy functioning. **Parkinson disease**, a motor system disorder characterized by severe tremors, muscular rigidity, and a reduction in voluntary movement, is among the most common movement disorders among the elderly. People with Parkinsonism take short, shuffling steps; display bent posture; and may need a walker to get around. Many have almost continuous hand tremors and sometimes head tremors as well. Another disorder of the basal ganglia is **Tourette syndrome**, characterized by various motor tics; involuntary vocalizations (sometimes including curse words and grunting sounds); and odd, involuntary body movements, especially of the face and head.

Neither Parkinsonism nor Tourette syndrome is a disorder of *producing* movements, as in paralysis. Rather, they are disorders of *controlling* movements. The basal ganglia, therefore, must play a critical role in controlling and coordinating movement patterns rather than in activating the muscles to move.

basal ganglia Subcortical forebrain nuclei that coordinate voluntary movements of the limbs and body; connected to the thalamus and to the midbrain.

Parkinson disease Disorder of the motor system correlated with a loss of dopamine from the substantia nigra and characterized by tremors, muscular rigidity, and a reduction in voluntary movement.

Tourette syndrome Disorder of the motor system, characterized by involuntary vocalizations (sometimes including curse words and grunting sounds) and odd, involuntary movements of the body, especially of the face and head.

Details on Parkinson disease appear in Clinical Focuses 5-2, 5-3, and 5-4, as well as Sections 11-3 and 16-3. Clinical Focus 11-4 details Tourette syndrome.

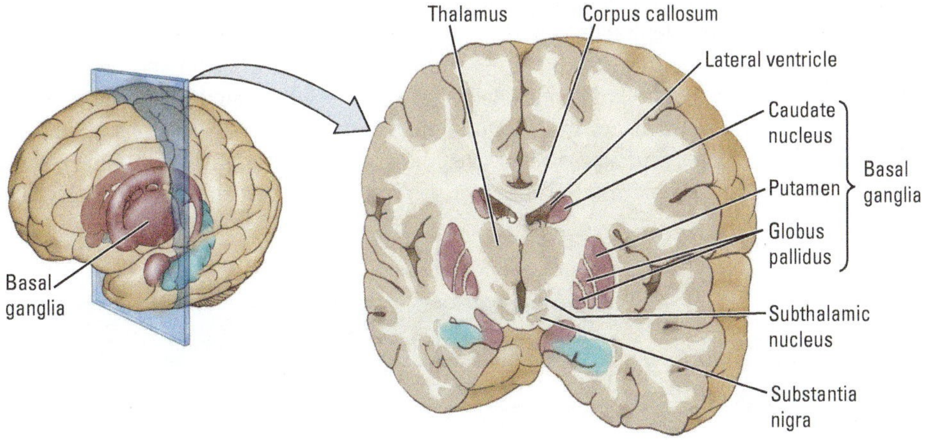

FIGURE 2-28 **Basal Ganglia** A coronal section through the cerebral hemispheres reveals a frontal view of the basal ganglia relative to surrounding forebrain structures. Two associated structures that are likewise instrumental in controlling and coordinating movement, the substantia nigra and subthalamic nucleus, are also shown.

2-3 Review

Before you continue, check your understanding. Answers to Self-Test appear at the back of the book.

1. The three functionally distinct sections of the CNS—spinal cord, brainstem, and forebrain—represent the evolution of multiple_____.

2. The _____ can perceive sensations from the skin and muscles and produce movements independent of the brain.

3. The brainstem includes three functional regions. The _____ is an extension of the spinal cord; the _____ is the first brain region to receive sensory inputs; and the _____ integrates sensory and motor information on its way to the cerebral cortex.

4. The _____ coordinates fine motor movements and various cognitive functions.

5. The forebrain's subcortical regions include the _____, which control voluntary movement, and the _____, which controls mood, motivation, and some forms of memory.

6. The two types of cerebral cortex are the three- and four-layered _____ and the _____, which features six layers that vary in density to perform _____, _____, and _____ functions.

7. Briefly describe the functions performed by the forebrain.

Somatic Nervous System: Transmitting Information

The SNS is monitored and controlled by the CNS—the cranial nerves by the brain and the spinal nerves by the spinal cord segments.

Cranial Nerves

cranial nerves The 12 nerve pairs that control sensory and motor functions of the head, neck, and internal organs.

The linkages provided by the **cranial nerves** between the brain and various parts of the head and neck as well as various internal organs are illustrated and tabulated in **Figure 2-29.** Cranial nerves can have afferent functions, such as sensory inputs to the brain from the eyes, ears, mouth, and nose, or they can have efferent functions, such as motor control of the facial muscles, tongue, and eyes. Some cranial nerves have both sensory and motor functions, such as modulation of both sensation and movement in the face.

The 12 pairs of cranial nerves are known both by their numbers and by their names, as listed in Figure 2-29. One set of 12 controls the left side of the head, whereas the other set controls the right side. This arrangement makes sense for innervating duplicated parts of the head (such as the eyes), but why separate nerves should control the right and left sides of a singular structure (such as the tongue) is not so clear. Yet that is how the cranial nerves work. If you have ever received lidocaine (often called Novocaine) for dental work, you know that when the dentist injects the drug into the gums on one side of your mouth, the same side of your tongue also becomes numb. The rest of the skin and muscles on each side of the head are similarly controlled by cranial nerves located on the same side.

In later chapters, we consider many cranial nerves in detail in discussions on vision, hearing, olfaction, taste, and stress responses. For now, you simply need to know that cranial nerves form part of the SNS, providing inputs to the brain from the head's

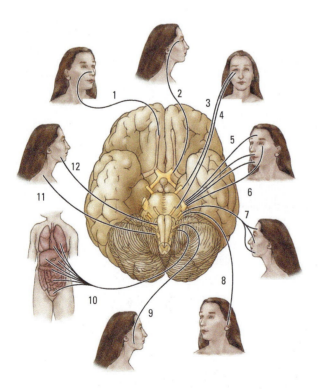

Cranial nerve	Name	Function
1	Olfactory	Smell
2	Optic	Vision
3	Oculomotor	Eye movement
4	Trochlear	Eye movement
5	Trigeminal	Masticatory movements and facial sensation
6	Abducens	Eye movement
7	Facial	Facial movement and sensation
8	Auditory vestibular	Hearing and balance
9	Glossopharyngeal	Tongue and pharynx movement and sensation
10	Vagus	Heart, blood vessels, viscera, movement of larynx and pharynx
11	Spinal accessory	Neck movement
12	Hypoglossal	Tongue movement

FIGURE 2-29 **Cranial Nerves** Each of the 12 pairs of cranial nerves has a different function. A common mnemonic device for learning the order of the cranial nerves is "**O**n **O**ld **O**lympus's **T**owering **T**op, **A** **F**inn and **G**erman **V**iew **S**ome **H**ops." The first letter of each word is, in order, the first letter of the name of each nerve.

sensory organs and muscles and controlling head and facial movements. Some cranial nerves also contribute to maintaining autonomic functions by connecting the brain and internal organs (the vagus, cranial nerve 10) and by influencing other autonomic responses, such as salivation.

Spinal Nerves

The spinal cord lies inside the bony spinal column, which is made up of a series of small bones called **vertebrae (sing. vertebra)**, categorized into five anatomical regions from top to bottom: cervical, thoracic, lumbar, sacral, and coccygeal, as diagrammed in **Figure 2-30A**. You can think of each vertebra in these five groups as a short segment of the spinal column. The corresponding spinal cord segment in each vertebral region functions as that segment's minibrain.

This arrangement may seem a bit odd, but it has a long evolutionary history. Think of a simpler animal, such as a snake. A snake's body is a segmented tube. In that tube is another tube, the spinal cord, which also is segmented. Each of the snake's nervous system segments receives nerve fibers from sensory receptors in the part of the body adjacent to it, and that nervous system segment sends back fibers to the muscles in that body part. Each segment, therefore, works independently.

A complication arises in animals such as humans, whose limbs may originate at one spinal segment level, but, because we stand upright, they extend past other segments of the spinal column. Your shoulders, for example, may begin at C5 (cervical segment 5), but your arms hang down well past the sacral segments. So unlike the snake, which has spinal cord segments that connect to body segments fairly directly adjacent to them, the human body's segments fall schematically into more of a patchwork pattern, as shown in Figure 2-30B. This arrangement makes sense if the arms are extended as they are when we walk on all fours.

Our body segments correspond to spinal cord segments. Each of these body segments is called a **dermatome** (meaning "skin cut"). A dermatome has a sensory nerve to send information from the skin, joints, and muscles to the spinal cord, as well as a motor nerve to control the muscle movements in that particular body segment.

These sensory and motor nerves, known as *spinal* (or *peripheral*) *nerves*, are functionally equivalent to the cranial nerves of the head. Whereas the cranial nerves receive information from sensory receptors in the eyes, ears, facial skin, and so forth, the spinal nerves receive information from sensory receptors in the rest of the body—that is, in the PNS. Similarly, whereas the cranial nerves move the muscles of the eyes, tongue, and face, the peripheral nerves move the muscles of the limbs and trunk.

Somatic Nervous System Connections

Like the CNS, the SNS is bilateral (two-sided). Just as the cranial nerves control functions on the side of the head where they are found, the spinal nerves on the left side of the spinal cord control the left side of the body, and those on the right side of the spinal cord control the body's right side.

Figure 2-31A shows the spinal column in cross section. Look first at the nerve fibers entering its posterior side (in red). These posterior fibers (dorsal in four-legged animals) are afferent: they carry in information from the body's sensory receptors. The fibers gather as they enter a spinal cord segment, and

vertebrae (sing. vertebra) The bones that form the spinal column.

dermatome Body segment corresponding to a segment of the spinal cord.

For the optic nerve, see Section 9-2; auditory nerve, Section 10-2; and olfactory nerve, Section 12-2.

Sections 11-1 and 11-4 review the spinal cord's contributions to movement and to somatosensation.

FIGURE 2-30 **Spinal Segments and Dermatomes (A)** Medial view showing the five spinal cord segments: cervical (C), thoracic (T), lumbar (L), sacral (S), and coccygeal. **(B)** Each segment corresponds to a region of body surface (a dermatome) identified by the segment number (e.g., C5 at the base of the neck and L2 in the lower back).

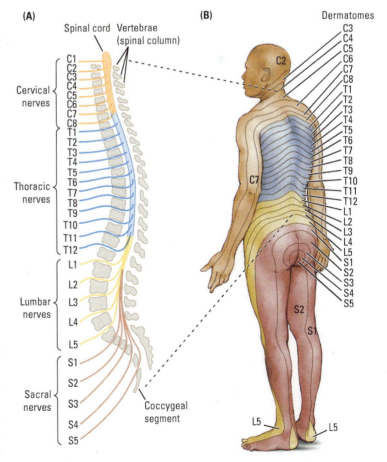

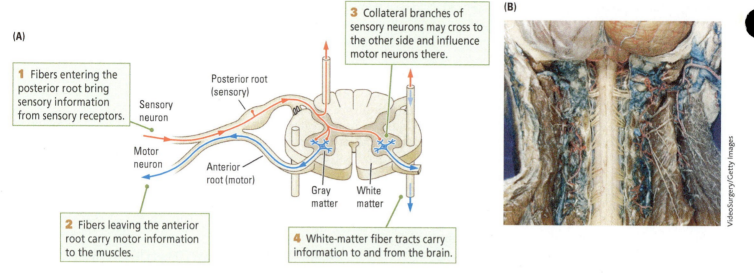

(A)

1 Fibers entering the posterior root bring sensory information from sensory receptors.

3 Collateral branches of sensory neurons may cross to the other side and influence motor neurons there.

(B)

Posterior root (sensory)

Sensory neuron

Motor neuron

Anterior root (motor)

Gray matter

White matter

2 Fibers leaving the anterior root carry motor information to the muscles.

4 White-matter fiber tracts carry information to and from the brain.

VideoSurgery/Getty Images

FIGURE 2-31 Spinal Nerve Connections (A) A cross section of the human spinal cord, viewed from the front. The butterfly-shaped inner regions consist of neural cell bodies (gray matter), and the outer regions consist of nerve tracts (white matter) traveling to and from the brain. **(B)** A posterior view shows the intact human spinal cord exposed.

Sections 11-1 and 11-4 explore spinal cord injuries and treatments; Section 12-3 discusses the link between spinal injury and loss of emotion.

law of Bell and Magendie Sensory fibers are dorsal and motor fibers are ventral.

The law of Bell and Magendie and the condition Bell palsy are both namesakes of Sir Charles Bell—surgeon, neurologist, anatomist, physiologist, artist, and philosophical theologian.

this collection of fibers is called a *posterior root* in humans (dorsal root in four-legged animals).

Fibers leaving the spinal cord's anterior side (in blue) are efferent, carrying information out from the spinal cord to the muscles. They, too, bundle together as they exit the spinal cord and so form an *anterior root* (ventral root in four-legged animals). The outer part of the spinal cord, pictured in Figure 2-31B, consists of white matter, or CNS nerve tracts. These tracts are arranged so that, with some exceptions, posterior tracts are sensory, and anterior tracts are motor. The inner part of the cord, which has a butterfly shape, is gray matter composed largely of cell bodies.

The observation that the posterior/dorsal spinal cord is sensory and the anterior/ventral side is motor in vertebrates, including humans, is one of the nervous system's very few established laws, the **law of Bell and Magendie**. Combined with an understanding of the spinal cord's segmental organization, this law enables neurologists to make accurate inferences about the location of spinal cord damage or disease on the basis of changes in sensation or movement. For instance, if a person has numbness in the fingers of the left hand but can still move the hand fairly normally, one or more of the posterior (dorsal) nerves in spinal cord segments C7 and C8 must be damaged. In contrast, if sensation in the hand is normal but the person cannot move the fingers, the anterior (ventral) roots of the same segments must be damaged. Clinical Focus 2-4, Bell Palsy, further explores the loss of motor function.

Integrating Spinal Functions

So far we have emphasized the spinal cord's segmental organization, but the spinal cord must also somehow coordinate inputs and outputs across different segments. For example, many body movements require coordinating muscles controlled by different segments, just as many sensory experiences require coordinating sensory inputs to different parts of the spinal cord. How is this coordination accomplished? The answer is that the spinal cord segments are interconnected in such a way that adjacent segments can operate together to direct rather complex coordinated movements.

Integrating spinal cord activities does not require the brain's participation, which is why the headless chicken can run around. Still, a close working relationship must exist between the brain and the spinal cord. Otherwise, how could we consciously plan and execute our voluntary actions?

Somehow, information must be relayed back and forth, and examples of this information sharing are numerous. For instance, tactile information from sensory nerves in the skin travels not just to the spinal cord but also to the cerebral cortex through the thalamus. Similarly, the cerebral cortex and other brain structures can control movements through their connections to the spinal cord's anterior roots. So even though the brain and spinal cord can function independently, the two are intimately connected in their CNS functions.

Bell Palsy

C.T. woke up one morning and proceeded with his routine. He sat at the kitchen table in front of the daily newspaper and began to eat his breakfast cereal. The cereal and milk fell out of his mouth. He cleaned it up and tried again with the same result. He then looked in a mirror and discovered the left side of his face was completely paralyzed. He couldn't move his left eyebrow or left smile muscles or any other expressive muscles on the left side of his face. He couldn't wink with the left eye but could close both eyes. Sensation from the left side felt normal, and the sensation and movement of the right side of his face was completely normal. He immediately sought medical attention. C.T., a neuroscientist, figured he had Bell palsy, which his family doctor confirmed.

Bell palsy is diagnosed by exclusion. Many factors can cause facial paralysis, and they need to be ruled out one by one. C.T. underwent blood tests to rule out diabetes and Lyme disease, a neurological exam to rule out stroke, and a CT scan to rule out tumor.

Bell palsy is caused by inflammation of the facial (7th) nerve, probably brought on by a virus or some other inflammatory agent. The 7th nerve travels through the longest boney canal in the body: the fallopian canal. Nerves swell when inflamed, but when constricted by the confines of a boney canal, pressure on the nerve stops them from functioning—hence the paralysis. If the pressure continues unabated for more than 3 weeks, the axons all die. The primary treatment is to reduce inflammation.

For the first 2 weeks after the abrupt onset, C.T. had complete paralysis on the left side of his face. He taped his left eye shut at night to prevent it from drying out and damaging his cornea. His speech was slurred, and he didn't really sound like himself. The muscles of the right side of his face pulled the left side, giving him an asymmetric look (see the accompanying photographs). Eating was a challenge. Drinking was made easy with a straw. At about the 2-week mark, to his great relief, he started to regain some minimal movement in his left eyebrow. As the weeks went by, he was able to move more and more of the left side of his face. By the sixth week, his friends and colleagues said he looked and sounded like himself again, yet he still had about 40% paralysis of the left side.

Bell palsy afflicts about 1 in 65 people at some time in their life. While most people, including C.T., fully recover, a small percentage will have some permanent paralysis, which can profoundly affect their lives. Smiling is an important social signal; when it is impaired, people interpret this as disapproval. This can lead to social isolation, which itself can lead to psychological problems.

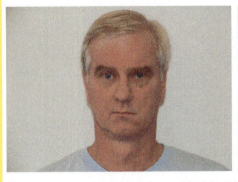
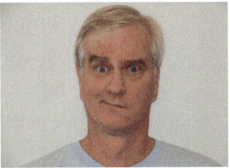
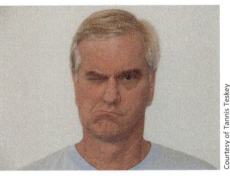

Courtesy of Tannis Teskey

(A) Relaxed face. Strong muscles on the right side of the face pull the nose to the right, while paralyzed muscles on the left side do not pull back. **(B)** An attempt to smile and raise both eyebrows is achieved on the right side of the face but fails on the paralyzed left side. **(C)** An attempt to frown and lower both eyebrows is achieved on the right side of the face but fails on the paralyzed left side.

2-4 Review

Before you continue, check your understanding. Answers to Self-Test appear at the back of the book.

1. Two sets of SNS nerves, the _____ and the _____, receive sensory information or send motor signals to muscles or both.

2. Both sets of SNS nerves are symmetrically organized, and each set controls functions on the _____ side of the body.

3. The cranial nerves have both sensory and motor functions, receiving and sending information to the _____ and to the _____.

4. Define the law of Bell and Magendie and explain why it is important.

For additional study tools, visit 📖 **LaunchPad** at launchpadworks.com

2-5

Autonomic and Enteric Nervous Systems: Visceral Relations

Control of the viscera (internal organs), including the heart, gut, liver, and lungs, requires complex neural systems. Yet the ANS and ENS are hidden partners, functioning in the background as the CNS controls our perceptions and behaviors. If we had to focus consciously on visceral activities, we might do little else. The ANS and ENS interact with the CNS, but each has distinctive anatomy and functions.

ANS: Regulating Internal Functions

Without our conscious awareness, the ANS stays on the job to keep the heart beating, the liver releasing glucose, the pupils of the eyes adjusting to light, and so forth. Without the ANS, which regulates the internal organs and glands via connections through the SNS to the CNS, life would quickly cease. Although learning to exert some conscious control over some of these vegetative activities is possible, such conscious interference is

Section 5-3 explains CNS–ANS communication, Figure 6-22 diagrams the stress response, and Section 16-4 discusses how mood affects reactivity to stress.

FIGURE 2-32 **Autonomic Nervous System** The two ANS pathways exert opposing effects. All fibers connect at "stops" formed by ganglia en route from the CNS to target ANS organs. *Left:* Arousing sympathetic fibers connect to a chain of ganglia near the spinal cord. *Right:* Calming parasympathetic fibers connect to individual ganglia near target organs.

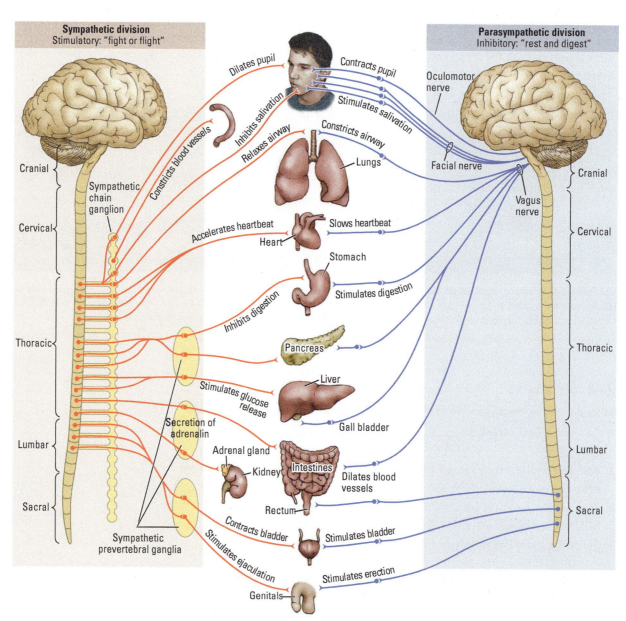

normally unnecessary. An important reason is that the ANS must keep working during sleep, when conscious awareness is off duty. But conscious states, such as stress, can often affect ANS functions, as in the case of a racing or pounding heartbeat. Psychological therapies are often effective in reducing stress if such ANS symptoms persist.

It is tempting to think that the ANS's organization must be pretty simple because it functions outside our conscious awareness. Yet, like the SNS, the ANS also has a surprisingly complex organization. The two ANS divisions work in opposition. The **sympathetic division** arouses the body for action, for example, by stimulating the heart to beat faster and inhibiting digestion when we exert ourselves during exercise or times of stress—the familiar fight-or-flight response. The **parasympathetic division** calms the body down, for example, by slowing the heartbeat and stimulating digestion to allow us to rest and digest after exertion and during quiet times.

Like the SNS, the ANS interacts with the rest of the nervous system, and like the SNS, ANS connections are ipsilateral. Activation of the sympathetic division starts in the thoracic and lumbar spinal cord regions, but the spinal nerves do not directly control the target organs. Rather, the spinal cord is connected to autonomic control centers—collections of neural cells called *ganglia*. The ganglia control the internal organs, and each acts as a minibrain for specific organs.

The sympathetic ganglia are near the spinal cord on each side, forming chains that run parallel to the cord, as illustrated at left in **Figure 2-32** for one set of ganglia. The parasympathetic division also is connected to the spinal cord—specifically, to the sacral region—but the greater part of it derives from three cranial nerves: the vagus nerve, which calms most of the internal organs, and the facial and oculomotor nerves, which control salivation and pupil dilation, respectively (review Figure 2-29). In contrast with the sympathetic division, the parasympathetic division connects with ganglia that are near the target organs, as shown at right in Figure 2-32.

ENS: Controlling the Gut

The ENS is often considered part of the ANS, but it functions largely independently. Digestion is complicated, and evolution has provided this dedicated nervous system to control it. Some scientists have even proposed that the CNS evolved from the gut of very simple organisms.

In fact, the ENS is sometimes called the *second brain* because, like the CNS, it contains a wide range of neuron types, the same chemical transmitters, a profusion of glial cells, and complex integrated neural circuits. Its estimated 200 million to 500 million neurons roughly equals the number in the spinal cord. The gut reacts to a range of hormones and other chemicals with exquisite neural responses. The ENS functions to control bowel motility, secretion, and blood flow to permit fluid and nutrient absorption and to support waste elimination (see Avetisyan et al., 2015). This is no simple task, given the number and balance of nutrients needed to support the body.

ENS neurons are located in a sheet of tissue (*plexus*) lining the esophagus, stomach, small intestine, and colon. As shown in **Figure 2-33**, ENS neurons and glia form ganglia connected by nerve fibers found in two layers of gut tissue. The brain and ENS connect extensively through the ANS, especially via the vagus nerve. Although we are not conscious of our gut "thinking," the ENS sends information directly to the brain—information that affects our mental state—and the brain can modify gut function. Indeed, a growing body of evidence implicates the ENS in many

sympathetic division Part of the autonomic nervous system that arouses the body for action, such as mediating the involuntary fight-or-flight response to alarm by increasing heart rate and blood pressure.

parasympathetic division Part of the autonomic nervous system that acts in opposition to the sympathetic division—for example, preparing the body to rest and digest by reversing the alarm response or stimulating digestion.

Principle 10: The nervous system works by juxtaposing excitation and inhibition.

Section 12-4 expands on how emotions and the ENS interact, Section 12-5 on the ENS and eating.

FIGURE 2-33 **Enteric Nervous System** The ENS is formed by a network of neurons embedded in the lining of the gastrointestinal tract. Congregations of neurons form ganglia that send projections to the ANS and CNS, in part through the vagus nerve (cranial nerve 10), to control gut function.

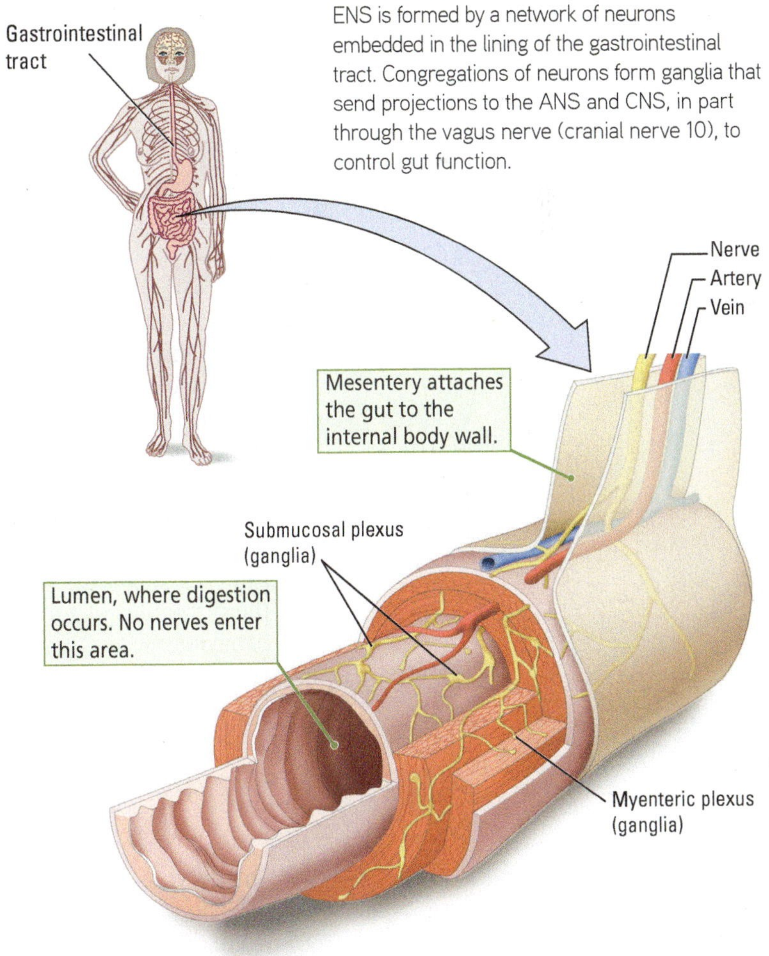

Gastrointestinal tract

Nerve
Artery
Vein

Mesentery attaches the gut to the internal body wall.

Submucosal plexus (ganglia)

Lumen, where digestion occurs. No nerves enter this area.

Myenteric plexus (ganglia)

behavioral disorders, and stress and anxiety commonly modify gut function, leading to such symptoms as nausea and diarrhea.

The ENS interacts with gut bacteria, known collectively as the *microbiome*. About 3.9×10^{13} microbiota populate the adult gut, outnumbering the host cells by a factor of 1.3 (Sender et al., 2016). The microbiota influence nutrient absorption and are a source of neurochemicals that regulate an array of physiological and psychological processes. This relationship has inspired the development of a class of compounds known as *psychobiotics*, live microorganisms used to treat behavioral disorders. Thus, the microbiota can influence both the CNS and ENS, leading to changes in behavior.

2-5 Review

Before you continue, check your understanding. Answers to Self-Test appear at the back of the book.

1. The ANS interacts with the CNS and SNS via sets of autonomic control centers called _____, which act as minibrains to control the internal organs.

2. The _____ division of the ANS arouses the body for action, and the _____ division calms the organs. The two divisions work _____ to allow for quick defensive responses (fight or flight) or to induce a calming (rest and digest) state.

3. Why is the ANS essential to life?

4. The ENS is often called a second brain because of the _____ it contains.

5. The ENS interacts with bacteria that form the_____, which absorbs _____ and produces _____ that can regulate CNS and ENS activity.

6. What are psychobiotics?

For additional study tools, visit **LaunchPad** at launchpadworks.com

Ten Principles of Nervous System Function

Knowing the parts of the nervous system and some general notions about what they do is only the beginning. Learning how the parts work together allows us to proceed to a closer look, in the chapters that follow, at how the brain produces behavior. A deeper appreciation of how the nervous system works also comes with an understanding of the principles of CNS organization and function.

Throughout this chapter, we have identified 10 principles related to the nervous system's functioning. Here we elaborate on each one. As you progress through the book, review these ideas regularly with an eye toward understanding the concept rather than simply memorizing the principle. Soon you will find yourself applying the principles of function as you encounter new information about the brain and behavior.

Principle 1: The Nervous System Produces Movement in a Perceptual World the Brain Constructs

The nervous system's fundamental function is to produce movements that make up behaviors. Movements are not made in a vacuum but are related to sensations, memories, and myriad other forces and factors. Your mental representation of the world depends on the information sent to your brain, your previous experiences, and the neural architecture of your nervous system. People who are color-blind perceive the world very differently from those who perceive color. The perceptual world of people who have perfect pitch differs from that of people without perfect pitch.

Although we tend to think that the world we perceive is what is actually there, individual realities, both between and within species, clearly are mere approximations of what is actually present. The brain of each individual develops in a particular set of environmental circumstances on a plan common to that species. The behavior that the brain produces, in other words, is directly related to the world that the brain has constructed.

Principle 2: Neuroplasticity Is the Hallmark of Nervous System Functioning

Experience alters the brain's organization, and this neuroplasticity is requisite to learning and memory. In fact, the nervous system stores information *only* if neural connections change. Forgetting is presumably due to a loss of the connections that represented the memory.

As Experiment 2-1 on page 48 demonstrates, neuroplasticity is a characteristic not just of the mammalian brain; it is found in the nervous systems of all animals, even the simplest worms. Nonetheless, larger brains have more capacity for change, and thus their neural organization is likely to show more plasticity.

Plasticity can be beneficial in recovering from disorders, such as brain injuries and diseases, as well as in normal aging. Plasticity also allows the brain to compensate for developmental abnormalities, an extreme example being agenesis of brain structures, as discussed in Research Focus 2-1. Although beneficial in such circumstances, neuroplasticity can have drawbacks in the case of extreme stimulation or disease states. Brain analyses of animals given addicting doses of drugs such as cocaine or morphine reveal broad changes in neural connectivity suspected of underlying some maladaptive behaviors related to addiction. Among many other examples of pathological neuroplasticity are those associated with pain, epilepsy, and dementia.

Find details on plasticity and drug addiction in Section 14-4, on feeling and treating pain in Section 11-4, and on epilepsy in Clinical Focus Box 4-1. Section 16-3 details diagnosis and treatment of epilepsy and dementias.

Principle 3: Many Brain Circuits Are Crossed

Most brain inputs and outputs are crossed—that is, they serve the opposite side of the body. Each hemisphere receives sensory stimulation from the opposite (contralateral) side of the body and controls muscles on the contralateral side. Crossed organization explains why people who have a stroke or other damage to the left cerebral hemisphere may have difficulty sensing stimulation to the right side of the body or in moving body parts on the right side. The opposite is true of people whose stroke occurs in the right cerebral hemisphere.

A crossed nervous system must somehow join both sides of the perceptual world together. To do so, innumerable neural connections link the brain's left and right sides. The most prominent connecting cable is the corpus callosum, whose roughly 200 million nerve fibers join the left and right cerebral hemispheres, allowing them to interact.

Four important exceptions to the crossed-circuit principle are olfactory sensation and the somatic, autonomic, and enteric PNS connections. Olfactory information does not cross but rather projects directly into the same (ipsilateral) side of the brain. The cranial and spinal nerves that constitute the SNS are connected ipsilaterally, as are the sympathetic and parasympathetic ANS division connections. Likewise, ipsilateral ENS connections link to the ANS on both sides.

Figure 9-10 illustrates how the human visual system represents the world seen through two eyes as a single perception: both eyes connect with both hemispheres.

Principle 4: The CNS Functions on Multiple Levels

In simple animals, such as worms, the nerve cord essentially constitutes the nervous system. More complex animals, such as fishes, have a brainstem as well, and even more complex animals, like mammals, have also evolved a forebrain. Each new addition to the CNS has added a new level of behavioral complexity without discarding previous levels of control. As animals evolved legs, for example, brain structures simultaneously evolved to move the legs. Later, the development of independent digit movements required even more brainpower. Thus, new brain areas add new levels of nervous system control. The new levels are not autonomous but rather are integrated into existing neural systems as refinements and elaborations of the control that earlier levels provided.

Multiple levels of function can be seen not only in the addition of forebrain areas to refine brainstem control but also in the forebrain itself. As mammals evolved, they developed an increased capacity to represent the world in the cortex, an ability related to the addition of more maps. The new maps are related to the older ones, however, and again are simply an elaboration of the perceived sensory world that existed before.

Principle 5: The Brain Is Symmetrical and Asymmetrical

The left and right hemispheres look like mirror images, but they have some dissimilar features. Cortical asymmetry is essential for integrative tasks, language and body control among them.

Consider speaking. If a language zone existed in both hemispheres, each connected to one side of the mouth, we would actually be able to talk out of both sides of our mouth at once. That would make talking awkward, to say the least. One solution is to locate language control of the mouth on one side of the brain. Organizing the brain in this way allows us to speak with a single voice.

A similar problem arises in controlling body movements in space. We would not want the left and right hemispheres each trying to take us to a different place. Again, if a single brain area controls this sort of spatial processing, problem solved.

Language control is typically situated on the left side, and spatial functions are typically on the right. The brains of many species have such symmetrical and asymmetrical features. In the bird brain, the control of singing is in one hemisphere (usually the left side), as is human language. It is likely that birds and humans evolved the same solution independently—namely, to assign the control to only one side of the brain.

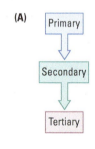

Principle 6: Brain Systems Are Organized Hierarchically and in Parallel

When we consider the multiple levels of CNS function, it becomes apparent that these levels are extensively interconnected to integrate their processing and produce unified perceptions or movements. The nature of neural connectivity leads to the principle that the brain has both serial (or hierarchical) and parallel circuitry.

A hierarchical circuit hooks up a linear series of all regions concerned with a particular function. Consider vision. In a serial system, the information from the eyes goes to regions that detect the simplest properties, such as color or brightness. This information is passed along to another region that determines shape, then to another that measures movement, and so on until at the most complex level the information is understood to be, say, your grandmother. Information therefore flows sequentially from regions that make simpler discriminations to regions that make more complex discriminations in the hierarchy, as illustrated in **Figure 2-34A**.

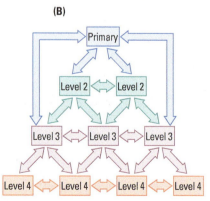

FIGURE 2-34 **Models of Neural Information Processing (A)** Simple hierarchical model of serial cortical processing. **(B)** In a distributed hierarchical processing model, each of several processing streams has multiple levels. Areas at each level interconnect.

However, functionally related brain structures are not always linked linearly. Although the brain has many serial connections, many expected connections are missing. In the visual system, not all cortical regions are connected to one another. The simplest explanation is that the unconnected regions must have widely differing functions.

Parallel circuits operate on a different principle, also illustrated by the visual system. Imagine looking at a car. As we look at a car door, one set of visual pathways processes information about its nature, such as color and shape, whereas another set of pathways processes information about movements such as those necessary to open the door.

These two visual systems are independent of each other, yet they must interact somehow. When you pull open the car door, you do not perceive two different representations—the door's size, shape, and color on the one hand and the opening movements on the other. When you open the door, you have the impression of unity in your conscious experience.

Figure 2-34B illustrates the information flow in such a distributed hierarchy. If you trace the flow from the primary area to levels 2, 3, and 4, you follow the parallel pathways. And while these multiple parallel pathways are also connected to one another, those connections are more selective than connections in a purely serial circuit.

The brain's subsystems are organized into multiple parallel pathways, yet our conscious experiences are unified. As we explore this conundrum throughout the book, keep in mind that your commonsense impressions of how the brain works might not always be correct.

Principle 7: Sensory and Motor Divisions Permeate the Nervous System

The segregation of SNS sensory and motor functions described by the Bell and Magendie law exists throughout the nervous system. Spinal nerves are either sensory or motor. Some cranial nerves are exclusively sensory; some are exclusively motor; and some have two parts, one sensory and one motor, much like spinal nerves serving the skin and muscles.

Review cranial nerve and spinal nerve connections in Figures 2-29 and 2-30.

The lower brainstem regions—hindbrain and midbrain—are essentially extensions of the spinal cord. They retain the spinal cord's division, with sensory structures posterior and motor structures anterior in humans. An important midbrain function is orienting the body to stimuli, which requires sensory input from the midbrain's colliculi (posterior in the human tectum) and motor output, which the tegmentum (anterior) plays a role in controlling. Distinctions between motor and sensory functions become subtler in the forebrain.

Figures 2-16 through 2-20 illustrate brainstem structures.

Distinct sensory nuclei are present in the thalamus, too, although their positions are not segregated, as they are in lower structures. Because all sensory information reaches the forebrain through the thalamus, it is not surprising to find separate nuclei associated with vision, hearing, and touch in this structure. Separate thalamic nuclei also control movements. Other nuclei have neither sensory nor motor functions but rather connect to cortical areas, such as the frontal lobe, that perform more integrative tasks.

Finally, sensory and motor functions are divided in the cortex in two ways:

1. Separate sensory and motor cortical regions process a particular set of sensory inputs, such as vision, hearing, or touch. Others control fine movements of discrete body parts, such as the fingers.

2. The entire cortex is organized around the sensory and motor distinction. As diagrammed in Figure 2-25, layer IV of the cortex always receives sensory inputs, layers V and VI always send motor outputs, and layers I, II, and III integrate sensory and motor operations.

One should keep in mind that sensory and motor systems work together at all levels. For example, the pupil, a motor structure composed of muscles, controls the amount of light that falls on the sensory retina. Also, within muscles a sensory system called the *intrafusal muscle system* detects the amount and rate of change of the *extrafusal muscles*, which actually do the work.

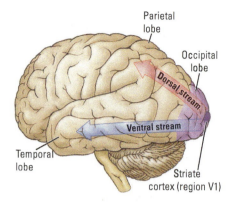

FIGURE 2-35 **Neural Streams** The dorsal and ventral streams mediate vision for action and recognition, respectively.

Sections 9-2 and 9-3 review evidence that led to understanding the visual streams' functions and visual information processing.

Principle 8: The Brain Divides Sensory Input for Object Recognition and Movement

Sensory systems evolved first for influencing movement, not for recognizing things. Simple organisms can detect stimulation such as light and move to or from it. It is not necessary to perceive an object to direct movements toward or away from it. Animals only began to represent their environment as their brains and behaviors became more complex. Animals with complex brains evolved separate systems for recognizing objects and for moving. The human visual systems for visual scene perception and for visually guided movements exemplify this separation well.

Visual information in the cortical circuit travels from the eyes to the thalamus to visual regions of the occipital lobe. From the occipital cortex, the information then diverges along two separate pathways: the *ventral stream*, which leads to the temporal lobe for object identification, and the *dorsal stream*, which goes to the parietal lobe to guide movements relative to objects (**Figure 2-35**). People with ventral stream injuries are blind for object recognition. They cannot distinguish a cup from a spoon. Nevertheless, they shape their hands appropriately when asked to reach for objects that they cannot identify. In contrast, people with dorsal stream injuries can recognize objects, but they make clumsy reaching movements because they do not form appropriate hand postures until they contact objects. Only then do they shape the hand, on the basis of tactile information.

Recognizing that perception for movement and perception for object recognition are independent processes has three important implications for understanding brain organization:

1. The dorsal and ventral visual systems also exemplify parallel information processing in the brain.

2. Although we may think we are aware of our entire sensory world, the sensory analysis required for some movements clearly is not conscious.

3. Unconscious and conscious brain processing underlies an important difference in our cognitive functions. The unconscious movement system is always acting in the present and in response to ongoing sensory input. In contrast, the conscious object recognition system allows us to escape the present and bring to bear information from the past, thus forming the neural basis of enduring memory.

Principle 9: Brain Functions Are Localized and Distributed

A great debate in the early days of brain research was concerned with whether different functions are localized to specific brain regions. Some argued that specific functions are distributed, and no particular region is of prime importance. Others argued for localization, including Paul Broca and Karl Wernicke, who demonstrated decisively that two specific language functions are localized. Broca found that when damage occurs to the ventroposterior region of the frontal lobes, people are unable to produce spoken language. Wernicke found that when damage occurs to a different region, the left posterior superior temporal gyrus, pronounced deficits in language comprehension result. So Broca, Wernicke, and others showed us that particular functions are localized and that there are regions in the brain that are of prime importance, at least in adults.

But does this mean that function is not distributed? Not at all. Consider how particular brain regions operate. Neurons in a specific region receive inputs, make a multitude of internal connections within that region, and then make outputs. Small lesions within a specific region do not necessarily produce any noticeable disruptions. That is because within a brain region, the function is distributed among the neurons that do the information processing; if some neurons are destroyed, the remaining neurons can continue carrying out the function. It is only when the majority of neurons within a specific functional region are destroyed that we see catastrophic failure for the associated function.

Because functions are both localized to specific areas and distributed within those areas, we can see paradoxical effects when certain types of brain damage occur. For instance, complete or nearly complete damage to a fairly localized region can cause irreversible loss of function, whereas widespread but diffuse damage may leave an individual's functional abilities intact. In fact, one characteristic of dementing diseases is that people can endure widespread deterioration of the cortex yet maintain remarkably normal language functions until late stages of the disease. **Alzheimer disease** is a degenerative brain disorder related to aging that first appears as progressive memory loss and only much later develops into generalized dementia.

Alzheimer disease Degenerative brain disorder related to aging that first appears as progressive memory loss and later develops into generalized dementia.

excitation Increase in the activity of a neuron or brain area.

inhibition Decrease in the activity of a neuron or brain area.

For Alzheimer neurochemistry, see Section 5-3; for incidence and possible causes, Section 14-3; and for treatments, Section 16-4.

Principle 10: The Nervous System Works by Juxtaposing Excitation and Inhibition

We have emphasized the brain's role in *making* movements, but we must also recognize that the brain *prevents* movements. To make a directed movement, such as picking up a glass of water, we must refrain from other movements, such as waving the hand back and forth. In producing movement, then, the brain uses both **excitation** (increased neural activity) to produce some action and **inhibition** (decreased neural activity) to prevent other actions.

Brain injury or disease can produce either a *loss* or a *release* of behavior by changing the balance between excitation and inhibition. A brain injury in a region that normally initiates speech may render a person unable to talk—a loss of behavior. A person with an abnormality in a region that inhibits inappropriate language (such as swearing) may be unable to inhibit this form of speech. Such a release of behavior can be seen in some individuals with Tourette syndrome.

Patients with Parkinson disease may have uncontrollable shaking of the hands because the neural system that inhibits such movements has failed. Paradoxically, they often have difficulty initiating movements and appear frozen because they cannot generate the excitation needed to produce deliberate movements.

The juxtaposition of excitation and inhibition, central to the way the brain produces behavior, can also be seen at the level of individual neurons. All neurons evince a spontaneous activity rate that can be either increased (excitation) or decreased (inhibition). Some neurons excite others; some inhibit. Both effects are produced by neuronal communication via specific neurochemicals.

Tourette syndrome and Parkinsonism are dysfunctions of the basal ganglia, which coordinates voluntary movement.

Chapter 3 details nervous system cell structure; Chapter 4, how neurons transmit and integrate information; and Chapter 5, neuronal communication and adaptation.

2-6 Review

Before you continue, check your understanding. Answers to Self-Test appear at the back of the book.

1. Many of the brain's input and output circuits are crossed. In the nervous system, four exceptions to this principle are the_____, the _____, the _____, and the _____.

2. The vertebrate brain has evolved three regions—hindbrain, midbrain, and forebrain—leading to _____ and flexibility in controlling behavior.

3. One aspect of neural activity that resembles the on–off language of digital devices is the juxtaposition of _____ and _____.

4. Explain this statement: Perception is not reality.

For additional study tools, visit 🔲 **LaunchPad** at launchpadworks.com

Summary

2-1 Overview of Brain Function and Structure

The brain's primary function is to produce movements that make up behavior in a perceptual world the brain constructs. This perceptual world is ever-changing. To adapt, the brain must also change, a property referred to as neuroplasticity.

To study how the nervous system works, we abandon the anatomical divisions between the central nervous system and the peripheral nervous system to focus instead on function—on how the CNS interacts with the divisions of the PNS: the somatic, autonomic, and enteric nervous systems.

2-2 The Conserved Pattern of Nervous System Development

The vertebrate nervous system evolved from a relatively simple structure mediating reflexlike behaviors to the complex human brain mediating advanced cognitive processes. To allow for more complex behavior in an increasingly sophisticated perceptual world, archaic forms have not been replaced but rather have been adapted and modified as new structures have evolved.

The principles of nervous system organization and function generalize across the three vertebrate brain regions—hindbrain, midbrain, and forebrain—leading to multiple levels of functioning. The evolution of neural levels of control thus adds flexibility to behavioral control.

2-3 The Central Nervous System: Mediating Behavior

The CNS includes the brain and the spinal cord. The spinal cord receives sensations from the skin and muscles and produces movements independent of the brain. The brain can be divided into the brainstem and forebrain, each made up of hundreds of parts. The brainstem both directs movements and constructs a sensory world through its connections with the sensory systems, spinal cord, and forebrain. The forebrain modifies and elaborates basic sensory and motor functions; regulates cognitive activity, including thought and memory; and ultimately controls movement. The most elaborate parts of the brain, the cerebral cortex and cerebellum, are relatively large in humans.

2-4 Somatic Nervous System: Transmitting Information

The SNS consists of two sets of spinal nerves that enter and leave the spinal column, connecting with muscles, skin, and joints in the body, and the cranial nerves that link the facial muscles and some internal organs to the brain. Both sets of SNS nerves are symmetrical: one set controls each side of the body. Some cranial nerves are sensory, some are motor, and some combine both functions. The spinal cord acts as a minibrain for the peripheral (spinal) nerves that enter and leave its five segments. Each spinal segment works independently, although CNS fibers interconnect them and coordinate their activities.

2-5 Autonomic and Enteric Nervous Systems: Visceral Relations

The ANS controls the body's glands and internal organs and operates largely outside conscious awareness. Its sympathetic (arousing) and parasympathetic (calming) divisions work in opposition. The parasympathetic division directs the organs to rest and digest, whereas the sympathetic division prepares for fight or flight.

The ENS controls the gut over its entire length, from the esophagus to the colon, interacting with the brain via the ANS. ENS activity can affect our behavior and mental state. In turn, the ENS is affected by the microbiome, the roughly 39 trillion bacteria that inhabit our gut.

2-6 Ten Principles of Nervous System Function

Ten principles listed in the right column below form the basis for discussions throughout this book. Understanding them fully will enhance your study of brain and behavior.

Ten Principles of Nervous System Function

1	The nervous system produces movement in a perceptual world the brain constructs.
2	Neuroplasticity is the hallmark of nervous system functioning.
3	Many brain circuits are crossed.
4	The CNS functions on multiple levels.
5	The brain is symmetrical and asymmetrical.
6	Brain systems are organized hierarchically and in parallel.
7	Sensory and motor divisions permeate the nervous system.
8	The brain divides sensory input for object recognition and movement.
9	Brain functions are localized and distributed.
10	The nervous system works by juxtaposing excitation and inhibition.

Key Terms

adaptations, p. 33

afferent, p. 35

allocortex, p. 53

Alzheimer disease, p. 69

autonomic nervous system (ANS), p. 35

basal ganglia, p. 57

brainstem, p. 49

cerebral cortex, p. 38

cerebrospinal fluid (CSF), p. 38

corpus callosum, p. 43

cranial nerves, p. 58

cytoarchitectonic map, p. 56

dermatome, p. 59

diencephalon, p. 52

efferent, p. 35

enteric nervous system (ENS), p. 35

excitation, p. 69

forebrain, p. 52

frontal lobe, p. 38

gray matter, p. 41

gyri (sing. *gyrus*), p. 39

hindbrain, p. 50

hypothalamus, p. 52

inhibition, p. 69

law of Bell and Magendie, p. 60

limbic system, p. 54

meninges, p. 35

midbrain, p. 51

neocortex, p. 53

nerve, p. 45

neuroplasticity, p. 34

nuclei (sing. nucleus), p. 44

occipital lobe, p. 39

orienting movement, p. 51

parasympathetic division, p. 63

parietal lobe, p. 38

Parkinson disease, p. 57

phenotypic plasticity, p. 34

reticular formation, p. 50

somatic nervous system (SNS), p. 35

stroke, p. 40

sulci (sing. *sulcus*), p. 39

sympathetic division, p. 63

tectum, p. 51

tegmentum, p. 51

temporal lobe, p. 39

thalamus, p. 52

Tourette syndrome, p. 57

tract, p. 45

ventricles, p. 43

vertebrae (sing. vertebra), p. 59

vomeronasal organ (VNO), p. 55

white matter, p. 41

Visit **LaunchPad** to access the e-Book, videos, **LearningCurve** adaptive quizzing, flashcards, and more at launchpadworks.com

Lichtman Lab/Harvard University

What Are the Nervous System's Functional Units?

CHAPTER 3

The Beery twins' remarkable story highlights how neuroscientists apply advances in genetics to treat brain disorders. Understanding genes, proteins, and cellular function allows us to understand healthy brain functioning as well.

We begin this chapter by describing nervous system cell structure and function. Brain cells give the nervous system its structure and mediate its moment-to-moment activity, the activity that underlies our behavior. We conclude the chapter by describing Mendelian genetics and the new genetic science of epigenetics that complements Mendel's theory.

3-1
Cells of the Nervous System

The theory that the specialized cell of the nervous system, the *neuron*, is the building block of the nervous system and of our behavior emerged from a controversy between the Italian Camillo Golgi and the Spaniard Santiago Ramón y Cajal. Both men were awarded the Nobel Prize for medicine in 1906, in recognition of their work on the structure of the nervous system.

Imagine that you are Camillo Golgi, at work in your laboratory, staining and examining nervous system tissue. You immerse a thin slice of brain tissue in a solution containing silver nitrate and other chemicals, a technique used at the time to produce black-and-white photographs. A contemporary method, shown in **Figure 3-1A**, produces a color-enhanced microscopic image that resembles the images Golgi saw.

Golgi never revealed just how he came to develop his staining technique.

◎ **RESEARCH FOCUS 3-1**

A Genetic Diagnosis

Fraternal twins Alexis and Noah Beery seemingly acquired cerebral palsy perinatally (at or near birth). They had poor muscle tone and could barely walk. Noah drooled and vomited, and Alexis had tremors. Typically, children with cerebral palsy do not get worse with age, but the twins' condition deteriorated.

In searching the literature for similar cases, their mother, Retta Beery, found a photocopy of a 1991 news report that described a child first diagnosed with cerebral palsy and then found to have a rare condition, dopa-responsive dystonia. (*Dystonia* means "abnormal muscle tone.") It stems from a deficiency of a neurochemical, dopamine, produced by a relatively small cluster of cells in the midbrain.

When Alexis and Noah received a daily dose of L-dopa, a chemical that some brain cells convert to dopamine, they displayed remarkable improvement. "We knew that we were witnessing a miracle," Retta recalls.

A few years later, in 2005, Alexis began to have new symptoms, marked by breathing difficulties. At this time the twins' father, Joe, worked for Life Technologies, a biotech company that makes equipment used for sequencing DNA, the genetic coding molecule found in the nucleus of every cell. Joe arranged for samples of the twins' blood to be sent to the Baylor College of Medicine's DNA sequencing center.

The twins' sequenced genome was compared with that of their parents and close relatives. The analysis showed that the twins had an abnormality in a gene on chromosome 2 for an enzyme that enhances not only dopamine production but also the production of serotonin, another neurochemical made by brainstem cells.

When the twins' doctors added tryptophan, the enzyme that is converted to serotonin, to the L-dopa, both twins showed remarkable

Reeta, Noah, Zach (the twins' brother), Alexis, and Joe at an event promoting the research done by the National Institutes of Health.

Courtesy Retta Beery

improvement. Alexis eventually competed in junior high school track, and Noah played volleyball in the Junior Olympics; both are now in college. This is the first diagnosis established through genome sequencing that led to a treatment success, and it marks the beginning of personalized medicine, diagnosis, and treatment based on a patient's genomic information (Hayes, 2017).

(A)

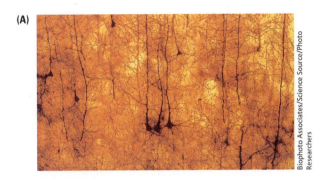

Biophoto Associates/Science Source/Photo Researchers

(B)

Drawing from Ramón y Cajal, 1909–1911.

FIGURE 3-1 **Two Views of a Cell (A)** Tissue preparation revealing human *pyramidal cells* stained using the Golgi technique. **(B)** Cajal's drawing of a single *Purkinje neuron* made from Golgi-stained tissue.

cell body (soma) Core region of the cell containing the nucleus and other organelles for making proteins.

dendrite Branching extension of a neuron's cell membrane; greatly increases the cell's surface area; collects information from other cells.

axon Root, or single fiber, of a neuron that carries messages to other neurons.

The image is beautiful and intriguing, but what do you make of it? To Golgi, this structure suggested that the nervous system is an interconnected network of fibers. He thought that information flowed around this "nerve net," like water running through pipes, and so produced behavior.

Santiago Ramón y Cajal used Golgi's stain to study chick embryos' brain tissue and came to a different conclusion. He assumed that the chick's developing nervous system would be simpler and easier to understand than that of an adult chicken. Figure 3-1B shows an image he rendered from the neural cells using the Golgi stain. Cajal concluded that the nervous system is made up of discrete cells, which begin life as a rather simple structure that becomes more complex with age. When mature, each cell consists of a main body with many extensions projecting from it.

The structure looks something like a plant, with branches coming out the top and roots coming out the bottom. Cajal showed that neurons come in many shapes and sizes and can be distinguished from the glial cells that also made up a large part of brain tissue. Cajal's *neuron theory*—that neurons are the nervous system's functional units—is now accepted. The neuron theory includes the ideas that the interactions between neurons enables behavior and that the more neurons an animal has, the more complex its behavior.

In the century since Golgi and Cajal's pioneering work, scientists have developed many additional staining methods for visualizing neurons, including methods to view living cells that are cultured in a dish with nurturing fluids. They can also implant tiny microscopes, called *endoscopes* or *microendoscopes* (for small microscopes that look into tissue), in the brain to view the structure and activity of its neurons (Belykh et al., 2018). Thus, a wide variety of visualization techniques are used to investigate different problems related to how neurons produce behavior. Subsequent research has also confirmed Golgi's nerve net, a covering called a *perineuronal net* that forms around neurons as they mature (Carulli, 2018). Today, investigators are examining the role of this net in stabilizing the structure of neurons once they mature, in preserving well-learned behavior, and in influencing addictions to drugs and diseases of memory loss that occur as some people age, topics that we will take up in later chapters.

Figure 3-2 shows the three basic subdivisions of a neuron. The core region is called the **cell body**, or **soma** (Greek meaning "body"; the root of words such as *somatic*). A neuron's branching extensions, or **dendrites** (from the Greek for "tree"), collect information from other cells, and its main root is the single **axon** (Greek for "axle"), which carries messages to other neurons. A neuron has only one axon, but most neurons have many dendrites. Some neurons have so many dendrites that they look like a garden hedge, as Cajal's drawing in Figure 3-1B illustrates.

The human nervous system contains 86 billion neurons and 87 billion glial cells that support their function, a ratio of about 1:1 that characterizes the brains of all animals (Herculano-Houzel et al., 2014). Neurons vary greatly in size and shape, but they have a common plan: examining how one neuron works offers insights that can generalized to other neuron types. As you learn to recognize different types of nervous system cells, you will begin to understand how their specialized structures contribute to their functions in your body.

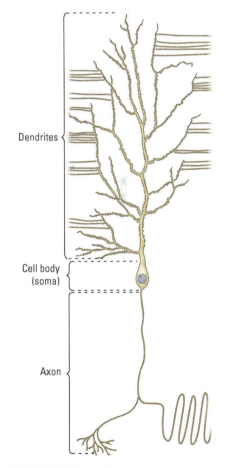

Dendrites

Cell body (soma)

Axon

FIGURE 3-2 **Basic Structure of a Neuron** Dendrites gather information from other neurons, the cell body (soma) integrates the information, and the axon sends the information to other cells. Although a neuron may have many dendrites, it has only one axon.

neural network Functional group of neurons that connects wide areas of the brain and spinal cord.

dendritic spine Protrusion that greatly increases the dendrite's surface area; typical point of dendritic contact with the axons of other cells.

The connectome is introduced in Section 1-4.

Principle 2: Neuroplasticity is the hallmark of nervous system functioning.

Neurons: The Basis of Information Processing

As the information-processing units of the nervous system, neurons acquire information, store it as memory, interpret it, and pass the information along to other neurons to produce behavior. In doing so, they regulate body processes such as breathing, heartbeat, and body temperature, to which we seldom give a thought. Scientists think that neurons work together in groups of many hundreds to many thousands to produce most behavior. It is important, then, to understand not only how neurons function but also how they interconnect and influence one another.

Functional groups of neurons, or **neural networks**, connect wide areas of the brain and spinal cord. The loss of a neuron or two from a network is no more noticeable than the loss of one or two voices from a cheering crowd. It is the crowd that produces the overall sound, not each person. An ongoing effort aims to map the structural connectivity—the physical wiring, or *connectome*—of the entire human brain.

Each neuron's appearance is distinctive, but neurons are also the essence of plasticity. If one views living brain tissue through a microscope, the neurons reveal themselves to be surprisingly active, producing new branches, losing old ones, and making and losing connections with each other as you watch. This dynamic activity underlies both the constancies and the changes in our behavior.

Structure and Function of the Neuron

Figure 3-3 details the external and internal features common to neurons. The cell's surface area is increased immensely by its extensions into dendrites and an axon

FIGURE 3-3 **Major Parts of a Neuron (A)** Typical neuron Golgi-stained to reveal its dendrites and cell body. **(B)** The neuron's basic structures identified. **(C)** An electron micrograph captures the synapse between an axon from another neuron and a dendritic spine. **(D)** High-power light microscopic view inside the cell body. Note the axon hillock at the junction of the soma and axon.

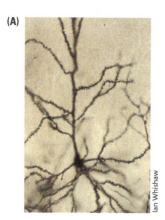

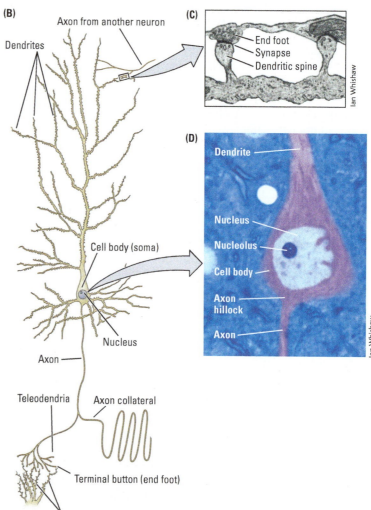

(Figure 3-3A and B). The dendritic area is further increased by many small protrusions called **dendritic spines** (Figure 3-3C). A neuron may have up to 20 dendrites, each dendrite may have one to many branches, and the spines on the branches may number in the thousands. Dendrites collect information from other cells, and the spines are the points of contact with those neurons. The extent of a cell's branches and its spine number correspond to its information-processing capacity.

Each neuron has but a single axon to carry messages to other neurons. The axon begins at one end of the cell body, at an expansion known as the **axon hillock** (little hill), shown in Figure 3-3D. The axon may branch out into one or many **axon collaterals**, which usually emerge from it at right angles, as shown at the bottom of Figure 3-3B.

The axon collaterals may divide into multiple smaller branches (*telodendria*, or end branches). At the end of each telodendrion is a knob called a **terminal button**, or an **end foot**. The terminal button sits very close to but usually does not touch a dendritic spine or some other part of another cell (Figure 3-3C). This near-connection, called a **synapse**, includes the surfaces of the end foot and the neighboring dendritic spine as well as the space between them.

Chapter 4 describes how neurons transmit information; here, we simply generalize about neuronal function by examining shape. Imagine looking down on a river system from an airplane. You see many small streams merging to make creeks, which join to form tributaries, which join to form the main river channel. As the river reaches its delta, it breaks up into many smaller channels again before discharging its contents into the sea.

The general shape of a neuron suggests that it works in a broadly similar way to a river. As illustrated in **Figure 3-4**, the neuron collects information from many sources on its dendrites. It channels the information to its axon, which can send out only a single message over all of its collaterals and telodendria. The synapse is the information transfer site between neurons.

Three Functions of Neurons

Neurons of varying shapes and sizes are structured to perform three specialized functions. **Sensory neurons** (**Figure 3-5A**) conduct information from the sensory receptors in or on the body into the spinal cord and brain. **Interneurons** (Figure 3-5B) associate sensory and motor activity in the CNS, and **motor neurons** (Figure 3-5C) carry information from the brain and spinal cord out to the body's muscles.

SENSORY NEURONS Sensory neurons are structurally the simplest of the three types of neuron. A **bipolar neuron** found in the retina of the eye, for example, has a single short dendrite on one side of its cell body and a single short axon on the other side.

axon hillock Juncture of soma and axon.

axon collateral Branch of an axon.

terminal button (end foot) Knob at the tip of an axon that conveys information to other neurons.

synapse Spatial junction between one neuron and another; forms the information transfer site between neurons.

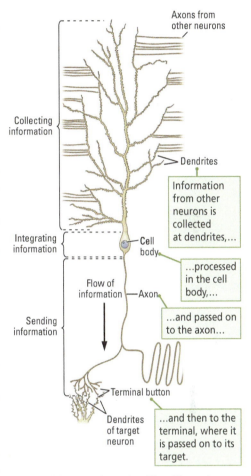

FIGURE 3-4 Information Flow Through a Neuron

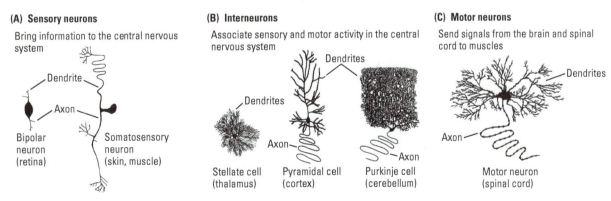

(A) Sensory neurons

Bring information to the central nervous system

Bipolar neuron (retina)

Somatosensory neuron (skin, muscle)

(B) Interneurons

Associate sensory and motor activity in the central nervous system

Stellate cell (thalamus)

Pyramidal cell (cortex)

Purkinje cell (cerebellum)

(C) Motor neurons

Send signals from the brain and spinal cord to muscles

Motor neuron (spinal cord)

FIGURE 3-5 **Neuron Shape and Function (A)** Sensory neurons of many types detect stimulation or collect information and pass it on to **(B)** an interneuron. The multibranched interneuron dendrites collect information from varied sources and link to **(C)** motor neurons, which are distinctively large and which pass on commands to muscles to move. Cells are not drawn to scale.

sensory neuron Cell that detects or carries sensory information into the spinal cord and brain.

interneuron Association cell interposed between a sensory neuron and a motor neuron; in mammals, interneurons constitute most of the brain's neurons.

motor neuron Cell that carries efferent information from the brain and spinal cord to make muscles contract.

bipolar neuron Sensory neuron with one axon and one dendrite.

somatosensory neuron Brain cell that brings sensory information from the body into the spinal cord.

pyramidal cell Distinctively shaped interneuron found in the cerebral cortex.

Purkinje cell Distinctively shaped interneuron found in the cerebellum.

Bipolar neurons transmit afferent (incoming) sensory information from the retina's light receptors to the neurons that carry information into the brain's visual centers.

A bit more structurally complicated is the **somatosensory neuron**, which brings sensory information from the body into the spinal cord, a long distance. Structurally, the somatosensory dendrite connects directly to its axon, so the cell body sits to one side of this long pathway.

INTERNEURONS Also called *association cells* because they link up sensory and motor neurons, interneurons branch extensively to collect information from many sources. A specific type of interneuron, the *stellate* (star-shaped) *cell*, is characteristically small, with many dendrites extending around the cell body. Its axon is difficult to see in the maze of dendrites. One of the main reasons brain sizes vary between species is that there are many more interneurons in larger brains than in smaller brains, giving a correlation between interneuron number and behavioral complexity.

A **pyramidal cell** has a long axon, a pyramid-shaped cell body, and two sets of dendrites. The apical set projects from the cell body apex, the basal set from the base of its cell body. Pyramidal interneurons carry information from the cortex to the rest of the brain and spinal cord. A **Purkinje cell** (named for its discoverer) is a distinctive interneuron with extremely branched dendrites that form a fan shape. It carries information from the cerebellum to the rest of the brain and spinal cord.

MOTOR NEURONS To collect information from many sources, motor neurons have extensive dendritic networks, large cell bodies, and long axons that connect to muscles. Motor neurons reside in the lower brainstem and spinal cord. All efferent (outgoing) neural information must pass through them to reach the muscles.

Neuronal Networks

Sensory neurons collect afferent (incoming) information from the body and connect to interneurons that process the information and pass it on to motor neurons. The motor neurons' efferent connections move muscles and so produce behavior. These three organizational aspects of neurons are thus features of neuronal networks: input, association, and output.

Neurons that project for long distances, such as somatosensory neurons, pyramidal neurons, and motor neurons, are relatively large. In general, neurons with a large cell body have long extensions, whereas neurons with a small cell body, such as stellate interneurons, have short extensions.

Long extensions carry information to distant parts of the nervous system; short extensions are engaged in local processing. For example, the dendrite tips of some somatosensory neurons are in your big toe, whereas the target of their axons is at the base of your brain. These sensory neurons send information over as much as 2 meters—and even farther in very large animals. The axons of some pyramidal neurons must reach from the cortex as far as the lower spinal cord, a distance that can be as long as a meter. The imposing size of this pyramidal cell body therefore accords with the work it must do in providing nutrients and other cellular supplies for its axons and dendrites.

The Language of Neurons: Excitation and Inhibition

Neurons are networkers with elaborate interconnections, but how do they communicate? Simply put, neurons either excite (turn on) or inhibit (turn off) other neurons. Like digital computers, neurons send yes or no signals to one another; the yes signals are excitatory, and the no signals are inhibitory. Each neuron receives up to thousands of excitatory and inhibitory signals every second.

Principle 10: The nervous system works by juxtaposing excitation and inhibition.

James King-Holmes/Science Source

Kike Calvo via AP Images

FIGURE 3-6 **Nervous System Mimics** *Left:* Barbara Webb programmed rules she developed from studying cricket behavior into her Lego cricket robot. *Right:* Social roboticist Heather Knight conducts research on robot body language with her companion, Marilyn Monrobot.

The neuron's response to all those inputs is reasonably democratic: it sums them. A neuron is spurred into action and sends messages to other neurons if its excitatory inputs exceed its inhibitory inputs. If the reverse occurs and inhibitory inputs exceed excitatory inputs, the neuron does not communicate.

By exciting or inhibiting one another, a neuronal network can detect sensory information and "decide" what kind of motor response to make to that information. To confirm whether they understand how an entire neural network produces behavior, scientists might make a model, such as a robot, intended to function in the same way. Robots, after all, engage in goal-oriented actions, just as animals do. A robot's computer must somehow sense the world, coordinate its actions in response, and perform much as an animal's nervous system performs. Researchers construct robotic models to help confirm hypotheses about how the nervous system functions and then use the information derived from this exercise to further refine subsequent robot models to more closely function like an animal's nervous system.

As a result of this two-way modeling, a good deal of robotic intelligence, or *artificial intelligence (AI)*, is based on principles of nervous system function. For example, Barbara Webb's cricket robot, constructed from Lego blocks, wires, and a motor **(Figure 3-6**, left), is designed to mimic a female cricket, which listens for the source of a male's chirping song and travels to it (Reeve et al., 2007). It reflects a beginning step in constructing a more intelligent robot (Figure 3-6, right). **Experiment 3-1** presents another example of the ways that inhibition and excitation might produce a cricket robot's behavior.

Section 4-3 explains how neurons summate excitatory and inhibitory signals.

Five Types of Glial Cells

Glial cells (from the Greek for "glue") are the nervous system's support cells. Although they do not usually transmit information themselves, glial cells help neurons carry out this task, binding them together (some *do* act as glue) and providing support, nutrients, and protection, among other functions.

glial cell Nervous system cell that provides insulation, nutrients, and support and that aids in repairing neurons and eliminating waste products.

···> **EXPERIMENT 3-1**

Question: Can the principles of neural excitation and inhibition control the activity of a simple robot that behaves like a cricket?

Procedure A

In approaching a male, a female cricket must avoid open, well-lit places where a predator could detect her. The female must often choose between competing males, preferring, for example, the male that makes the longest chirps. If we insert sensory neurons between the microphone for sound detection on each side of a hypothetical robot cricket and on the motor on the opposite side, we need only two rules to instruct the female robot to seek out a chirping male cricket:

Rule 1 When a microphone detects a male cricket's song, an excitatory message is sent to the wheel's motors, activating them so the robot moves toward the cricket.

Rule 2 If the chirp is coming from the robot's left or right side, it will be detected as being louder by the microphone on that side, which will make one wheel turn a little faster, ensuring that the robot moves directly toward the sound.

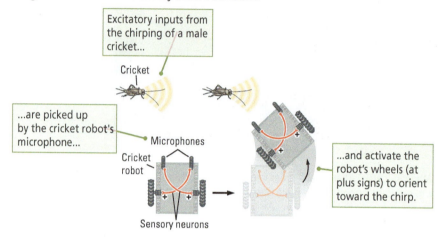

Procedure B

We add two more sensory neurons, coming from photoreceptors on the robot. When activated, these light-detecting sensory neurons inhibit the motor neurons leading to the wheels and prevent the robot from moving toward a male cricket. Now the female cricket robot will move only when it is dark and "safe."

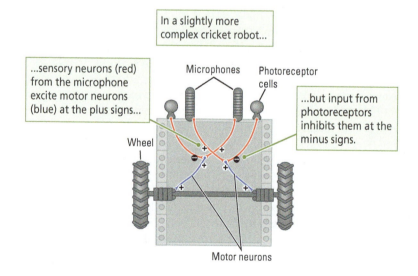

Result

This hypothetical arrangement mimics the functions of sensory and motor neurons and the principle of summating excitatory and inhibitory signals—but with only six neurons and each neuron connected to only one other neuron!

Conclusion

Today, *anthropomimetic robots*, so called because their parts are constructed to mimic the parts of a human body, including its billions of neurons, are being designed to model complex behavior and act as replacements for lost or impaired limbs (Mathews et al., 2017). Entire robots are also being constructed to mimic many aspects of human behavior.

TABLE 3-1 **Types and Functions of Glial Cells**

Type	Appearance	Features and function
Ependymal cell		Small ovoid; secretes cerebrospinal fluid (CSF)
Astrocyte		Star shaped; contributes to neuronal nutrition, support, and repair; contributes to forming blood–brain barrier and to healing scarring after injury
Microglial cell		Small, derived from blood; defensive function to remove dead tissue
Oligodendroglial cell		Forms myelin around CNS axons in brain and spinal cord
Schwann cell		Wraps around peripheral nerves to form myelin

Table 3-1 lists the five major types of glia, along with their characteristic structures and functions.

Glial cells are different from neurons in that most types of glial cells are produced throughout an organism's life, and errors in their replication are a main source of abnormal growths: brain tumors. Clinical Focus 3-2, Brain Tumors, describes the results of such uncontrolled glial cell growth.

Ependymal Cells

On the walls of the ventricles, the fluid-filled cavities inside your brain, are **ependymal cells**, which produce and secrete the cerebrospinal fluid (CSF) that fills the ventricles. CSF is constantly being secreted, and it flows through the ventricles toward the base of the brain, where it is absorbed into the blood vessels. CSF serves several purposes. It acts as a shock absorber when the brain is jarred, carries away waste products, assists the brain in maintaining a constant temperature, and is a source of nutrients for parts of the brain adjacent to the ventricles.

As CSF flows through the ventricles, it passes through some narrow passages, especially from the cerebral aqueduct into the fourth ventricle, which runs through the brainstem. If these passages are fully or partly blocked, fluid flow is restricted. Because CSF is continuously being produced, this blockage causes a buildup of pressure that begins to expand the ventricles, which in turn push on the surrounding brain.

If such a blockage develops in a newborn infant, before the skull bones are fused, the pressure on the brain is conveyed to the skull, and the baby's head swells. This condition, called **hydrocephalus** (literally, "water brain"), can cause severe intellectual impairment and even death. To treat it, doctors insert one end of a tube, called a *shunt*, into the blocked ventricle and the other end into a vein to allow excess CSF to drain into the bloodstream.

Glia form the fatty coverings around neurons—the white matter in brain images such as Figures 2-12B and D.

Figure 2-9 shows the location of the cerebral aqueduct and the four ventricles.

ependymal cell Glial cell that makes and secretes CSF; found on the walls of the brain's ventricles.

hydrocephalus Buildup of fluid pressure in the brain and, in infants, swelling of the head, if the flow of CSF is blocked; can result in intellectual impairment.

⊙ CLINICAL FOCUS 3-2

Brain Tumors

One day while watching a movie in a neuropsychology class, R. J., a 19-year-old college sophomore, collapsed on the floor, displaying symptoms of a seizure. The instructor helped her to the university clinic, where she recovered except for a severe headache. She reported that she had repeated severe headaches.

A few days later, a computed tomography (CT) scan showed a tumor over her left frontal lobe. The tumor was removed surgically, and R. J. returned to classes after an uneventful recovery. Her symptoms have not recurred.

A **tumor** is an uncontrolled growth of new tissue that is independent of surrounding structures. No region of the body is immune, but the brain is a site for more than 120 kinds of tumors. They are a common cause of brain cancer in children.

The incidence of brain tumors in the United States is about 20 per 100,000, according to the Central Brain Tumor Registry of the United States (Ostrom et al., 2016). In adults, brain tumors grow from glia or other supporting cells rather than from neurons, but in infants, tumors may grow from developing neurons. The rate of tumor growth depends on the type of cell affected.

Some tumors are benign, as R. J.'s was, and not likely to recur after removal. Others are malignant, likely to progress and invade other tissue, and apt to recur after removal. Both benign and malignant tumors can pose a risk to life if they develop in sites from which removal is difficult.

The earliest symptoms usually result from increased pressure on surrounding brain structures. They can include headaches, vomiting, mental dullness, changes in sensory and motor abilities, and seizures such as R. J. had. Many symptoms depend on the tumor's location. The three major types of brain tumors are classified according to how they originate:

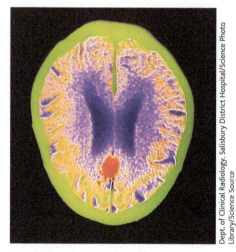

The red area in this false-color CT scan is a meningioma, a noncancerous tumor arising from the meninges, which cover the brain. Large meningiomas may compress the brain but usually do not invade brain tissue.

Dept. of Clinical Radiology, Salisbury District Hospital/Science Photo Library/Science Source

1. *Gliomas* arise from glial cells. They are slow growing, not often malignant, and relatively easy to treat if they arise from astrocytes. Gliomas that arise from the precursor *blast* or *germinal* cells that grow into glia are more often malignant, grow more quickly, and often recur after treatment. U.S. Senator Edward Kennedy was diagnosed with a malignant glioma in 2008 and died a year later. As with R. J., his first symptom was an epileptic seizure.

2. *Meningiomas*, such as R. J.'s, attach to the meninges and so grow entirely outside the brain, as shown in the accompanying CT scan. These tumors are usually encapsulated (contained), and if the tumor is accessible to surgery, chances of recovery are good.

3. *Metastatic tumors* become established when cells from one region of the body transfer to another area (which is what *metastasis* means). Typically, metastatic tumors are present in multiple locations, making treatment difficult. Symptoms of the underlying condition often first appear when the tumor cells reach the brain.

Treatment for brain tumors is usually surgical, and surgery also remains a main diagnostic tool. Chemotherapy is less successful in treating brain tumors than tumors elsewhere in the body because the blood–brain barrier blocks the chemicals' entry into the brain. Radiation therapy (X-ray treatment) is more useful for destroying brain tumor cells but can have negative effects, especially on the developing brain. Alternate treatments currently under investigation include genomic identification of a tumor and its subsequent destruction by targeting its unique genetic composition (Di Lorenzo & Ahluwalia, 2017).

Astroglia

Astrocytes (star-shaped glia, shown in Table 3-1), also called *astroglia*, provide structural support to the CNS. Their extensions attach to blood vessels and to the brain's lining, forming a scaffolding that holds neurons in place. These same extensions provide pathways for certain nutrients to move between blood vessels and neurons. Astrocytes also secrete chemicals that keep neurons healthy and help them heal if injured.

At the same time, astrocytes contribute to the structure of a protective partition between blood vessels and the brain, the **blood–brain barrier**. As shown in **Figure 3-7**, the ends of astrocytes attach to blood vessel cells, causing the vessels to bind tightly together. These tight junctions prevent an array of substances, including many toxins, from entering the brain through the blood vessel walls.

The molecules (smallest units) of these substances are too large to pass between the blood vessel cells unless the blood–brain barrier is somehow compromised. The downside is that many useful drugs, including antibiotics used to treat infections, cannot pass

tumor Mass of new tissue that grows uncontrolled and independent of surrounding structures.

astrocyte Star-shaped glial cell that provides structural support to CNS neurons and transports substances between neurons and blood vessels.

blood–brain barrier Protective partition between blood vessels and the brain formed by tight junctions between the cells that compose blood vessels in the brain; prohibits entry of an array of substances, including toxins, into the brain.

through the blood–brain barrier to enter the brain. As a result, brain infections are difficult to treat. Scientists can bypass the blood–brain barrier and introduce drugs into the brain by inserting small tubes that allow the delivery of a drug directly to a targeted brain region.

Yet another important function of astrocytes is to enhance brain activity. When you engage in any behavior, whether it's reading or running, the neuronal network responsible for that behavior requires more fuel in the form of oxygen and glucose. In response to neuron activity, the blood vessels that supply it expand, allowing greater oxygen- and glucose-carrying blood flow. What triggers the blood vessels to dilate? This is where astrocytes come in. They pass along signals from the neurons to the blood vessels and so contribute to increased blood flow and fuel supply (Kenny et al., 2018).

Astrocytes also contribute to the healing of damaged brain tissue. If the brain is injured by a blow to the head or penetrated by some object, astrocytes form a scar to seal off the damaged area. Although the scar tissue is beneficial in healing the injury, it can also act as a barrier to the regrowth of damaged neurons. One of the many experimental approaches to repairing brain tissue seeks to get the axons and dendrites of CNS neurons to grow around or through a glial scar.

Microglia

Unlike other glial cells, which originate in the brain, **microglia** originate in the blood as an offshoot of the immune system and migrate throughout the nervous system, where they make up about 20 percent of all glial cells. The blood–brain barrier prevents most immune system cells from entering. Instead, microglia play an important part in monitoring and maintaining the health of brain tissue. They identify and attack foreign tissue, as illustrated in **Figure 3-8**. When brain cells are damaged, microglia invade the area to provide *growth factors* that aid in repair.

There are several kinds of microglia, which take different shapes depending on the role they are performing. Microglia engulf any foreign tissue and dead brain cells, an immune process called *phagocytosis*. When full, they take on a distinctive appearance. The stuffed and no-longer-functioning microglia can be detected as small dark bodies, shown in Figure 3-8C, in and near damaged brain regions.

Because microglia are frontline players in protecting the nervous system and removing its waste, considerable research is directed toward the extent to which microglia are involved in protecting the nervous system from disease. A characteristic of Alzheimer disease, a degenerative brain disorder commonly associated with aging, is the deposit of distinctive bodies called *plaques* in regions of damage. Microglia may also play a harmful role, consuming inflamed tissue rather than protecting it. They also interact with astrocytes in brain healing. Although small, as their name suggests, microglia play a mighty role in maintaining the brain's health (Lannes et al., 2017).

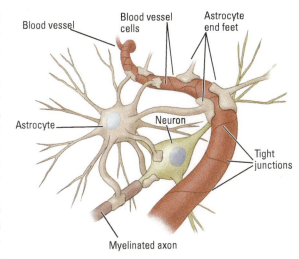

FIGURE 3-7 **Blood–Brain Barrier** Astrocyte processes attach to neurons and to blood vessel cells to stimulate them to form tight junctions and so form the blood–brain barrier. Astrocytes also move nutrients and other chemicals between blood vessels and neurons, support brain structures, and stimulate repair of damaged brain tissue.

Growth factors, described in Section 8-2, are chemicals that stimulate and support brain cell growth, survival, and perhaps even plasticity (see Section 14-4).

microglia Glial cells that originate in the blood, aid in cell repair, and scavenge debris in the nervous system.

For more on understanding and treating Alzheimer disease, see Section 16-3.

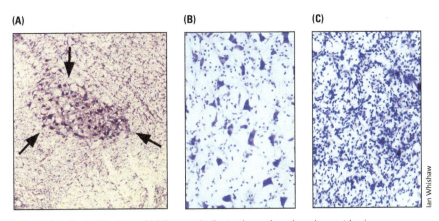

FIGURE 3-8 **Detecting Brain Damage** **(A)** Arrows indicate the red nucleus in a rat brain. **(B)** Close-up of cresyl violet–stained neurons (the large dark bodies) in the healthy red nucleus. **(C)** After exposure to a neurotoxin, only microglia, the small dark objects in the micrograph, survive.

Oligodendroglia and Schwann Cells

Two kinds of glial cells insulate neuronal axons. Like the plastic insulation on electrical wires, **myelin** prevents adjacent neurons from short-circuiting. Myelinated neurons send information much faster than neurons without myelin. Neurons that send messages over long distances quickly, including sensory and motor neurons, are heavily myelinated to increase their messaging speed.

Oligodendroglia myelinate axons in the brain and spinal cord by sending out large, flat branches that enclose and separate adjacent axons. (The prefix *oligo-* means *"few"* and here refers to the fact that these glia have few branches in comparison with astrocytes; see Table 3-1.) **Schwann cells** myelinate axons in the PNS. Each Schwann cell wraps itself repeatedly around a part of an axon, forming a structure somewhat like beads on a string. In addition to myelination, Schwann cells and oligodendroglia contribute to a neuron's nutrition and functioning by absorbing chemicals that the neuron releases and releasing chemicals that the neuron absorbs.

Glial Cells, Disease, and Neuron Repair

The multifaceted relationships among neurons and glia provide insights into nervous system diseases and into brain injury and recovery. The consequences of damage to oligodendroglia and Schwann cells can be as debilitating as damage to neurons themselves. For example, multiple sclerosis (MS), a degenerative nervous system disorder and the most common autoimmune disease, is associated with damage to oligodendroglia that leaves a scar (*sclerosis* means "scar"), rather than myelin, on neurons in nervous system pathways. As a result, information flow along affected nerves is impaired, producing impaired movement and cognitive function.

Glia can also aid in nervous system repair. A deep cut on your body—on your arm or leg, for instance—may cut the axons connecting your spinal cord to muscles and to sensory receptors. Severing of motor neuron axons will render you unable to move the affected part of your body, whereas severing of sensory fibers will result in loss of sensation from that body part. Cessation of both movement and sensation is **paralysis**. Weeks to months after motor and sensory axons are severed, movement and sensation will return. What mediates this recovery?

Both microglia and Schwann cells participate in repairing damage to the peripheral nervous system. When a PNS axon is cut, it degenerates back to the cell body, as shown at the top of **Figure 3-9**. Microglia remove all of the debris left by the dying axon. Meanwhile, the Schwann cells that provided the axon's myelin shrink and divide to form numerous smaller glial cells along the path the axon formerly took. The cell body then sends out axon sprouts that search for and follow the path formed by the Schwann cells.

Eventually, one sprout reaches the intended target and becomes the new axon; all other sprouts retract. The Schwann cells envelop the new axon, forming new myelin and restoring function. In the PNS, then, Schwann cells serve as signposts to guide axons to their appropriate end points. Axons can get lost, however, as sometimes happens after surgeons reattach a severed limb. If axons destined to innervate one finger end up innervating another finger instead, the wrong finger will move when a message is sent along that axon.

When the CNS is damaged—as happens, for example, when the spinal cord is cut— regrowth and repair do not occur, even though the distance that damaged fibers must bridge may be short. That recovery takes place in the PNS but not in the CNS is puzzling. Regrowth in the CNS may not occur in part because as neuronal circuits mature, they become exquisitely tuned to mediate individualized behavior and, in doing so, develop chemical strategies that prevent the proliferation of new cells or the regrowth of existing cells. The oligodendrocytes that myelinate CNS cells do not behave like PNS Schwann cells to encourage brain repair. They may actually play a role in protecting the existing structure of the CNS by inhibiting neuron regrowth (Hirokawa et al., 2017). Understanding how regrowth is inhibited is one approach to finding ways for the damaged CNS to repair itself.

Section 4-2 describes how myelin speeds up the neuron's information flow.

Multiple sclerosis, which is caused by a loss of myelin, is discussed in depth in Clinical Focus 4-2.

Sections 11-1 and 11-4 detail causes of and treatments for spinal cord injury.

myelin Glial coating that surrounds axons in the central and peripheral nervous systems; prevents adjacent neurons from short-circuiting.

oligodendroglia Glial cells in the CNS that myelinate axons.

Schwann cell Glial cell in the PNS that myelinates sensory and motor axons.

paralysis Loss of sensation and movement due to nervous system injury.

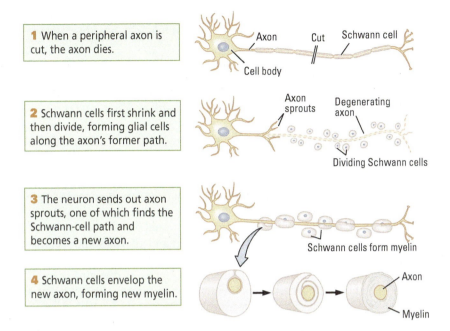

1 When a peripheral axon is cut, the axon dies.

2 Schwann cells first shrink and then divide, forming glial cells along the axon's former path.

3 The neuron sends out axon sprouts, one of which finds the Schwann-cell path and becomes a new axon.

4 Schwann cells envelop the new axon, forming new myelin.

Axon   Cut   Schwann cell
Cell body

Axon sprouts   Degenerating axon
Dividing Schwann cells

Schwann cells form myelin

Axon
Myelin

FIGURE 3-9 **Neuron Repair** Schwann cells aid the regrowth of axons in the somatic nervous system.

3-1 Review

Before you continue, check your understanding. Answers to Self-Test appear at the back of the book.

1. The two classes of nervous system cells are _____ and _____.

2. Neurons, the information-conducting units of the nervous system, act either by _____ or _____ one another through their connecting synapses.

3. The three types of neurons and their characteristic functions are _____, which _____; _____, which _____; and _____, which _____.

4. The five types of glial cells are _____, _____, _____, _____, and _____. Their functions include _____, _____, _____, _____, and _____ neurons.

5. How are robotic models being used to better understand the human nervous system?

For additional study tools, visit **LaunchPad** at launchpadworks.com

Internal Structure of a Cell

What is it about the structure of neurons that generates the remarkable ability to receive, process, store, and send a seemingly limitless amount of information? To answer this question, we must look inside a neuron to see what its components are and understand what they do. Although neurons are minuscule, when we view them with an electron microscope, we find packed inside hundreds of interrelated parts that do the cell's work.

To a large extent, a cell's proteins determine its characteristics and functions. Each cell can manufacture thousands of proteins, which variously take part in building the cell and in communicating with other cells. When memories are formed, proteins are involved; when a neuron malfunctions or contains errors, proteins are involved; and to restore function after brain injury, proteins are involved. In this section, we explain how the different parts of a cell contribute to protein manufacture, describe what a protein is, and detail some functions of proteins.

Water, salts, and ions play prominent parts in the cell's functions, as you will learn in this and the next few chapters. If you already understand the structure of water and you know what a salt is and what ions are, read on. If you prefer a brief chemistry review first, turn to The Basics: Chemistry Review, on pages 88–89.

The Cell as a Factory

We began Section 3-1 by comparing a cell to a miniature factory, with work centers that cooperate to make and ship the cell's products—proteins. To investigate the cell's internal parts—the organelles—and how they function, we begin with a quick overview of the cell's internal structure.

Figure 3-10 displays many external and internal cellular components. A factory's outer wall separates it from the rest of the world and affords some security. Likewise, a cell's double-layered outer wall, or *cell membrane*, separates the cell from its surroundings and allows it to regulate what enters and leaves its domain. The cell membrane envelops the neuron's contents and contributes to forming its cell body, its dendrites and their spines, and its axon and terminals. It thus forms the boundary around a continuous intracellular compartment.

FIGURE 3-10 **Typical Nerve Cell** This view of the outside and inside of a neuron reveals its overall structure and internal organelles and other components.

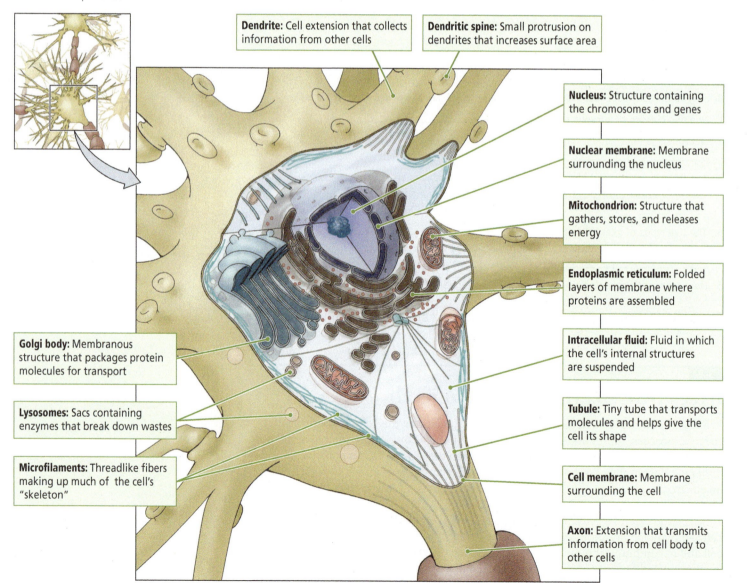

Dendrite: Cell extension that collects information from other cells

Dendritic spine: Small protrusion on dendrites that increases surface area

Nucleus: Structure containing the chromosomes and genes

Nuclear membrane: Membrane surrounding the nucleus

Mitochondrion: Structure that gathers, stores, and releases energy

Endoplasmic reticulum: Folded layers of membrane where proteins are assembled

Intracellular fluid: Fluid in which the cell's internal structures are suspended

Tubule: Tiny tube that transports molecules and helps give the cell its shape

Cell membrane: Membrane surrounding the cell

Axon: Extension that transmits information from cell body to other cells

Golgi body: Membranous structure that packages protein molecules for transport

Lysosomes: Sacs containing enzymes that break down wastes

Microfilaments: Threadlike fibers making up much of the cell's "skeleton"

Very few substances can enter or leave a cell spontaneously because the cell membrane is virtually *impermeable* (impenetrable). Some proteins made by the cell are embedded in the cell membrane, where they facilitate the transport of substances into and out of the cell. These proteins thus serve as the cellular factory's gates.

Although neurons and glia appear to be packed tightly together, like all other cells, they are separated by *extracellular fluid* composed mainly of water, with dissolved salts and many other chemicals. A similar *intracellular fluid* is found inside a cell. What is important is the cell membrane's relative impermeability, which ensures that concentrations of substances inside and outside the cell are different.

In the CNS, the extracellular fluid is CSF.

Within the cell shown in Figure 3-10 are membranes that surround its *organelles*, similar to the work areas demarcated by a factory's interior walls. Each organelle membrane is also relatively impermeable and so concentrates needed chemicals while keeping out unneeded ones.

The prominent *nuclear membrane* surrounds the cell's *nucleus*. Within the nucleus, the genetic blueprints for the cell's proteins are stored, copied, and sent to the "factory floor," the *endoplasmic reticulum* (*ER*). The ER is an extension of the nuclear membrane; here, the cell's protein products are assembled in accordance with instructions from the nucleus. Once those proteins are assembled, many are packaged and sent throughout the cell. The *Golgi bodies* are "mailrooms," where proteins are wrapped, addressed, and shipped.

Other cell components are *tubules* of several kinds. Some (*microfilaments*) reinforce the cell's structure; others aid in the cell's movements. Still others (*microtubules*) form the transportation network that carries proteins to their destinations, much as roads allow a factory's trucks and forklifts to deliver goods to their destinations.

Two other important parts of the cellular factory shown in Figure 3-10 are the *mitochondria* (sing. *mitochondrion*)—the cell's power plants, which supply its energy needs—and *lysosomes*, vesicles that transport incoming nutrients and remove and store waste. Interestingly, more lysosomes are found in old cells than in young ones. Cells apparently have trouble disposing of all their garbage, just as societies do.

Cell Membrane: Barrier and Gatekeeper

The cell membrane separates the intracellular from the extracellular fluid, allowing the cell to function as an independent unit. The membrane's double-layered structure, shown in **Figure 3-11A**, regulates the movement of substances, including water, into

FIGURE 3-11 **Bilayer Cell Membrane Structure (A)** Double-layered cell membrane close up. **(B)** Detail of a phospholipid molecule's polar head and electrically neutral tails. **(C)** Space-filling model shows why the phosphate head's polar regions (positive and negative poles) are hydrophilic, whereas its nonpolar fatty acid tail is hydrophobic.

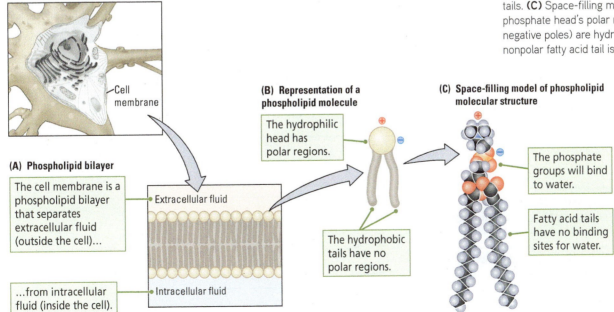

Cell membrane

(A) Phospholipid bilayer

The cell membrane is a phospholipid bilayer that separates extracellular fluid (outside the cell)...

Extracellular fluid

Intracellular fluid

...from intracellular fluid (inside the cell).

(B) Representation of a phospholipid molecule

The hydrophilic head has polar regions.

The hydrophobic tails have no polar regions.

(C) Space-filling model of phospholipid molecular structure

The phosphate groups will bind to water.

Fatty acid tails have no binding sites for water.

◎ THE BASICS

Chemistry Review

The smallest unit of a protein or any other chemical substance is the molecule. Molecules and the even smaller atoms of elements that constitute them are the cellular factory's raw materials.

Elements, Atoms, and Ions

Chemists represent each element, a substance that cannot be broken down into another substance, by a symbol—for example, O for oxygen, C for carbon, and H for hydrogen. The 10 elements listed in the Chemical Composition of the Brain table below constitute virtually the entire makeup of an average living cell. Many other elements are vital to the cell but are present only in minute quantities.

The smallest quantity of an element that retains the properties of that element is an atom. Ordinarily, as shown opposite in part A of the figure Ion Formation, atoms are electrically neutral: their total positive and negative charges are equal.

Atoms of chemically reactive elements such as sodium and chlorine can easily lose or gain negatively charged particles, or electrons. When an atom gives up electrons, it becomes positively charged; when it takes on extra electrons, it becomes negatively charged, as illustrated in part B of Ion Formation. Either way, the charged atom is now an ion. Ions' positive or negative charges allow them to interact. This property is central to cell function.

Chemical Composition of the Brain

Together, oxygen, carbon, and hydrogen account for more than 90 percent of a cell's makeup.

Percentage of weight	Element name, symbol	Atomic structure (not to scale)	Percentage of weight	Element name, symbol	Atomic structure (not to scale)
65.0	Oxygen, O		0.4	Potassium, K	
18.5	Carbon, C				
9.5	Hydrogen, H		0.2	Sulfur, S	
3.5	Nitrogen, N				
1.5	Calcium, Ca		0.2	Sodium, Na	
1.0	Phosphorus, P		0.2	Chlorine, Cl	

Some symbols derive from an element's Latin name—K for *kalium* (Latin for *potassium*) and Na for *natrium* (Latin for *sodium*), for example.

Ions Critical to Neuronal Communication

Ions formed by loss of electrons are represented by an element's symbol followed by one or more plus signs.

Ions formed by gain of electrons are represented by an element's symbol followed by a minus sign.

Na^+	Sodium
K^+	Potassium
Ca^{2+}	Calcium
Cl^-	Chloride

Ion Formation

(A) Atoms

Total positive (+) and negative (–) charges in atoms are equal. The nucleus contains *neutrons* (no charge) and *protons* (positive charge). Orbiting the nucleus are *electrons* (negative charge).

Outer orbit contains 7 electrons

Outer orbit contains 1 electron

Cl atoms have 17 protons and 17 electrons.

Na atoms have 11 protons and 11 electrons.

(B) Ions

The outer orbit gains an electron.

The outer orbit disappears because it lost its only electron.

Charged chloride ion (Cl⁻)

Charged sodium ion (Na⁺)

Chemistry of Water

(A) Water molecule

Two hydrogen atoms share electrons unequally with one oxygen atom, creating a polar water molecule positively charged on the hydrogen end and negatively charged on the oxygen end.

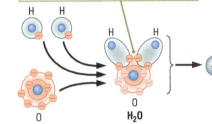

H   H

O

H_2O

(B) Hydrogen bonds

Hydrogen bonds join water molecules to a maximum of four partners.

H^+ and O^{2-} ions in each water molecule are attracted to nearby water molecules.

Because water molecules are polar, they are attracted to other electrically charged substances and to one another. Part B of Chemistry of Water illustrates this attracting force, called a hydrogen bond. Hydrogen bonding enables water to dissolve electrically neutral salt crystals into their component ions. Salts thus cannot retain their shape in water; they dissolve. As illustrated in the figure Salty Water, the polar water molecules muscle their way into the Na^+ and Cl^- lattice, surrounding and separating the ions.

Essentially, it is salty water that bathes our brain cells, provides the medium for their activities, supports their communications, and constitutes the brain's CSF. Sodium chloride and many other dissolved salts, including KCl (potassium chloride) and $CaCl_2$ (calcium chloride) are among the constituents of the brain's salty water.

Molecules: Salts and Water

Salt crystals form bonds via the electrical attraction between ions. The formula for table salt, NaCl (sodium chloride), means that this molecule consists of one sodium ion and one chloride ion. KCl, the formula for the salt potassium chloride, is composed of one potassium ion (K^+) and one chloride ion (Cl^-).

Atoms bind together to form molecules, the smallest units of a substance that contain all of its properties. A water molecule (H_2O) is the smallest unit of water that retains the properties of water. Breaking down water any further would release its component elements, the gases hydrogen and oxygen. The symbol H_2O indicates that a water molecule is the union of two hydrogen atoms and one oxygen atom.

Ionic bonds hold salt molecules together, but the atoms of water molecules share electrons, and electron sharing is not equal: H electrons spend more time orbiting the O atom than orbiting each H atom. As shown in part A of Chemistry of Water, this structure gives the oxygen region of the water molecule a slight negative charge and leaves the hydrogen regions with a slight positive charge. Like atoms, most molecules are electrically neutral, but water is polar: it carries opposite charges on opposite ends.

Salty Water

Negative Cl^- ions attract the positive poles of water molecules. Positive Na^+ ions attract the negative poles of water molecules.

Salt (NaCl)

Water (H_2O)

Polar water molecules surround Na^+ and Cl^- ions in a salt crystal, dissolving it.

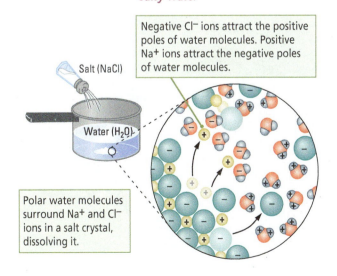

and out of the cell. If too much water enters a cell, it will burst; if too much water leaves a cell, it will shrivel. The cell membrane's structure helps ensure that neither happens.

The cell membrane also regulates the differing concentrations of salts and other chemicals on its inner and outer sides. This regulation is important because, if its concentrations of chemicals are unbalanced, the cell will not function normally. What properties of a cell membrane allow it to regulate water and salt concentrations? One property is its special molecular construction. These molecules, called *phospholipids*, are named for their structure, shown close up in Figure 3-11B.

Figure 3-11C shows a space-filling chemical model of the phospholipid molecule's structure. The molecule has a head containing the element phosphorus (P) bound to some other atoms, and it has two tails, which are lipids, or fat molecules. The head has a polar electrical charge, with a positive charge in one location and a negative charge in another, as do water molecules. The tails consist of hydrogen and carbon atoms that tightly bind to one another by their shared electrons; hence, the fatty tail has no polar regions.

The polar head and the nonpolar tails are the underlying reasons a phospholipid molecule can form cell membranes. The heads are *hydrophilic* (from the Greek *hydro*, meaning "water," and *philia*, meaning "love") and so are attracted to one another and to polar water molecules. The nonpolar lipid tails have no such attraction for water. They are *hydrophobic*, or water hating (from the Greek word *phobia*, meaning "fear").

Quite literally, then, the head of a phospholipid loves water, and the tails hate it. To avoid water, the tails of phospholipid molecules point toward each other, and the hydrophilic heads align with one another and point outward to the watery intracellular and extracellular fluid. In this way, the cell membrane consists of a bilayer (two layers) of phospholipid molecules (see Figure 3-11A).

The bilayer cell membrane is flexible even as it forms a formidable barrier to a wide variety of substances. It is impenetrable to intracellular and extracellular water because polar water molecules cannot pass through the hydrophobic tails on the membrane's interior. Ions in the extracellular and intracellular fluid also cannot penetrate this membrane because they carry charges and thus cannot pass by the polar phospholipid heads. In fact, only a few small molecules, such as oxygen (O_2), carbon dioxide (CO_2), and the sugar glucose, can traverse a phospholipid bilayer.

gene DNA segment that encodes the synthesis of a particular protein.

The Nucleus and Protein Synthesis

In our factory analogy, the nucleus is the cell's executive office, where the blueprints for making proteins are stored, copied, and sent to the factory floor. These blueprints are called **genes**, segments of DNA that encode the synthesis of particular proteins. Genes are contained within the *chromosomes*, the double-helix structures that hold an organism's entire DNA library.

The chromosomes have been likened to books of blueprints. Each chromosome contains thousands of genes. Each gene is the blueprint, or code, for making one protein. The location of the chromosomes in the cell nucleus, the appearance of a chromosome, and the structure of the DNA within a chromosome are shown in **Figure 3-12**.

This static picture of chromosomes does not represent the way they look in living cells. Videos of the cell nucleus show that chromosomes are constantly changing shape and moving in relation to one another, jockeying to occupy the best locations within the nucleus. By changing shape, chromosomes expose different genes to the surrounding fluid, thus allowing the gene to begin the process of making a protein.

A human somatic (body) cell has 23 pairs of chromosomes, or 46 chromosomes in all. (In contrast, there

FIGURE 3-12 **Chromosome** The nerve cell's nucleus contains paired chromosomes of double-stranded DNA molecules bound together by a sequence of nucleotide bases.

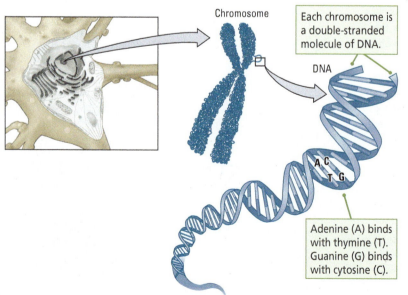

Chromosome

Each chromosome is a double-stranded molecule of DNA.

DNA

A C
T G

Adenine (A) binds with thymine (T). Guanine (G) binds with cytosine (C).

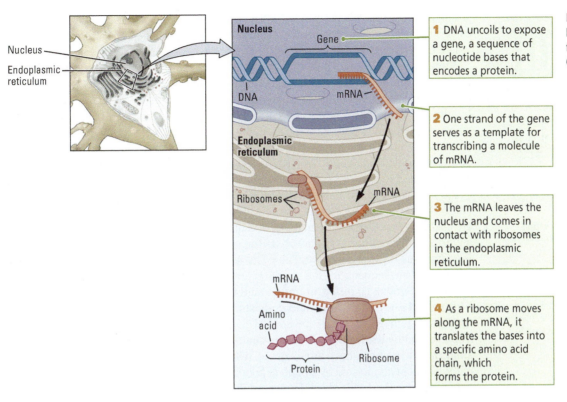

FIGURE 3-13 **Protein Synthesis** Information in a cell flows from DNA to mRNA to protein (peptide chain).

1 DNA uncoils to expose a gene, a sequence of nucleotide bases that encodes a protein.

2 One strand of the gene serves as a template for transcribing a molecule of mRNA.

3 The mRNA leaves the nucleus and comes in contact with ribosomes in the endoplasmic reticulum.

4 As a ribosome moves along the mRNA, it translates the bases into a specific amino acid chain, which forms the protein.

are only 23 chromosomes within a reproductive cell, and they are not paired.) Each chromosome is a double-stranded molecule of *deoxyribonucleic acid* (*DNA*). The two strands of a DNA molecule coil around each other, as shown in Figure 3-12.

Each strand possesses a variable sequence of four *nucleotide bases*, the constituent molecules of the genetic code: *adenine* (A), *thymine* (T), *guanine* (G), and *cytosine* (C). Adenine on one strand always pairs with thymine on the other, whereas guanine on one strand always pairs with cytosine on the other. The two strands of the DNA helix are bound together by the attraction between the two bases in each pair, as illustrated in Figure 3-12. Sequences of hundreds of nucleotide bases within the chromosomes spell out the genetic code. Scientists represent this code by the letters of the nucleotide bases—for example, ATGCCG.

A gene is a segment of a DNA strand. A gene's code is its sequence of thousands of nucleotide bases. Much as a sequence of letters spells out a word, the sequence of ACTG base pairs spells out the order in which *amino acids*, the constituent molecules of proteins, should be assembled to construct a certain protein.

To begin to make a protein, the appropriate gene segment of the DNA strand unwinds to expose its bases. The exposed sequence of nucleotide bases on the DNA strand then serves as a template to attract free-floating molecules called *nucleotides*. The nucleotides attach to the DNA to form a complementary strand of *ribonucleic acid* (*RNA*). The single-stranded nucleic acid molecule then detaches from the DNA and leaves the cell carrying within its structure the code for protein synthesis. This process, called *transcription*, is shown in steps 1 and 2 of **Figure 3-13**. (To transcribe means "to copy," as in copying part of a message you receive in a text.)

In humans, the reproductive cells are the sperm (male) and the egg (female).

Chromosome means "colored body"; chromosomes are so named because they can be readily stained with certain dyes.

The Endoplasmic Reticulum and Protein Manufacture

When RNA is produced through transcription, it forms a chain of bases much like a single strand of DNA, except that the base *uracil* (U) takes the place of thymine. Uracil is attracted to adenine, as is thymine in DNA; otherwise, the base code of RNA and DNA

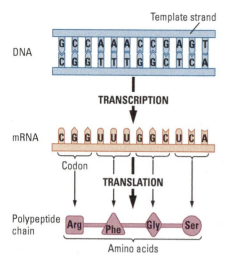

FIGURE 3-14 **Transcription and Translation** In protein synthesis (see Figure 3-13), a particular sequence of nucleotide bases in a strand of DNA (top) is transcribed into mRNA (center). Each sequence of three nucleotide bases in the mRNA strand (a codon) encodes one amino acid. In translation, the amino acids, directed by the codons, link together to form a chain (bottom). The amino acids are tryptophan (Trp), phenylalanine (Phe), glycine (Gly), and serine (Ser).

(A) Amino acid structure

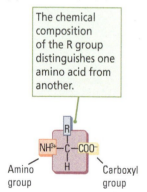

(B) Polypeptide chain

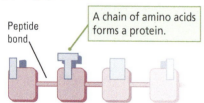

FIGURE 3-15 **Properties of Amino Acids** **(A)** Each amino acid consists of a central carbon atom (C) attached to an amine group (NH^{3+}), a carboxyl group (COO^-), and a distinguishing side chain (R). **(B)** The amino acids are linked by peptide bonds to form a polypeptide chain.

is similar. The transcribed strand of RNA is called *messenger RNA* (mRNA) because it carries the protein code (the message) out of the nucleus to the endoplasmic reticulum, where proteins are manufactured.

Steps 3 and 4 in Figure 3-13 show that the ER consists of membranous sheets folded to form numerous channels. A distinguishing feature of the ER is that it may be studded with *ribosomes*, protein structures that act as catalysts to facilitate the building of proteins. When a mRNA molecule reaches the ER, it passes through a ribosome, where its genetic code is read. In this process of *translation*, a particular sequence of nucleotide bases in the mRNA is transformed into a particular sequence of amino acids. *Transfer RNA* (tRNA) assists in translating nucleotide bases into amino acids.

As shown in **Figure 3-14**, each group of three consecutive nucleotide bases along an mRNA molecule encodes one particular amino acid. These sequences of three bases are called *codons*. For example, the codon uracil, guanine, guanine (UGG) encodes the amino acid tryptophan (Trp), whereas the codon uracil, uracil, uracil (UUU) encodes the amino acid phenylalanine (Phe). The sequence of codons on the mRNA strand determines the sequence of the resulting amino acid chain.

Humans utilize 20 different amino acids, all structurally similar, as illustrated in **Figure 3-15A**. Each amino acid consists of a central carbon atom (C) bound to a hydrogen atom (H), an *amino group* (NH^{3+}), a *carboxyl group* (COO^-), and a *side chain* (represented by the letter R). The side chain varies in chemical composition from one amino acid to another. Each amino group (NH^{3+}) is bound to the carboxyl group (COO^-) of the adjacent amino acid by a *peptide bond*, which gives the amino acid chain its alternative name, *polypeptide chain* (Figure 3-15B).

Just as a remarkable number of words can be made from the 26 letters of the English alphabet, a remarkable number of polypeptide (meaning "many peptides") chains can be made from the 20 amino acids. These amino acids can form 400 (20×20) dipeptides (two-peptide combinations), 8000 ($20 \times 20 \times 20$) tripeptides (three-peptide combinations), and almost countless polypeptides.

In summary, the information flow driven by the genetic code is conceptually quite simple: a gene (a portion of a DNA strand) is transcribed into a strand of mRNA, and ribosomes translate the mRNA into a molecular chain of amino acids, a polypeptide chain, which forms a protein. Thus the sequence of events in building a protein:

$$DNA \rightarrow mRNA \rightarrow protein$$

Proteins: The Cell's Product

A polypeptide chain and a protein are related, but they are not always the same. The relationship is analogous to the relationship between a length of ribbon and a bow that can be made from the ribbon. Long polypeptide chains have a strong tendency to twist into helices (spirals) or to form pleated sheets, which in turn have a strong tendency to fold together to form more complex shapes, as shown in **Figure 3-16**. A **protein** is a folded-up polypeptide chain; its shape is important to the function that it serves.

Any one neuron contains as many as 20,000 genes, and, in principle, these genes can produce as many as 20,000 different protein molecules. The number of proteins that can ultimately be produced by a neuron is far larger than the number of its genes, however. Although each gene codes for one protein, a protein can be cleaved into pieces—by enzymes, for example—or combined with other proteins in a variety of cellular processes to form still other proteins.

A protein's shape and its ability to change shape and to combine with other proteins are central to its function. Proteins can modify the length, shape, and behavior of other proteins and so act as enzymes, proteins that enhance chemical reactions. Proteins embedded in a cell membrane can regulate the flow of substances across the membrane. And proteins can be exported from one cell to another and so act as messenger molecules.

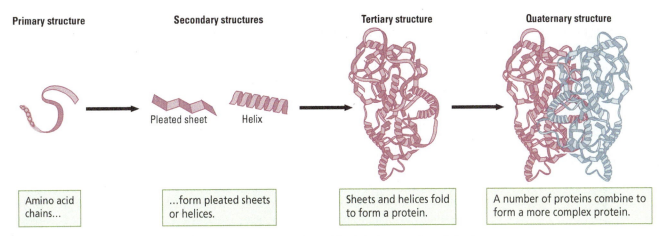

Primary structure   Secondary structures   Tertiary structure   Quaternary structure

Pleated sheet   Helix

| Amino acid chains... | ...form pleated sheets or helices. | Sheets and helices fold to form a protein. | A number of proteins combine to form a more complex protein. |

FIGURE 3-16 **Four Levels of Protein Structure** Whether a polypeptide chain forms a pleated sheet or a helix and what its three-dimensional shape ultimately will be are determined by the amino acid sequence in the primary structure. In rare circumstances, misfolded proteins wreak havoc, as occurs with some prion proteins that are implicated in many degenerative brain diseases, including mad cow disease, wasting diseases in sheep, and possibly Alzheimer and Parkinson disease; see Section 16-3.

Golgi Bodies and Microtubules: Protein Packaging and Shipment

Getting proteins to the right destination is the task of cellular components that package, label, and ship them. These components operate much like a postal or shipping service.

To reach their appropriate destinations, protein molecules that have been synthesized in the cell are wrapped in membranes and marked with addresses to indicate where they are to go. This wrapping and labeling take place in the organelles called Golgi bodies. The packaged proteins are then loaded onto motor molecules that move along the many microtubules radiating through the cell, carrying each protein to its destination. Protein export is illustrated in **Figure 3-17**.

If a protein is destined to remain within the cell, it is unloaded into the intracellular fluid. If it is to be incorporated into the cell membrane, it is carried to the membrane, where it inserts itself. If it is to be exported from the cell, it is usually transferred out in a process called *exocytosis* (meaning "out of the cell"). The membrane, or *vesicle*, in which the protein is wrapped fuses with the cell membrane, and the protein is excreted into the extracellular fluid.

protein Folded-up polypeptide chain that serves a particular function in the body.

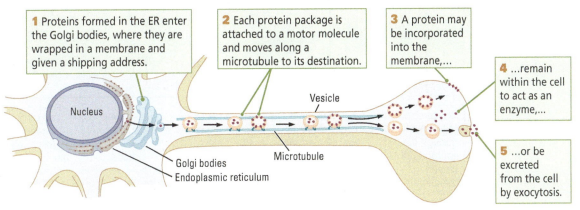

1 Proteins formed in the ER enter the Golgi bodies, where they are wrapped in a membrane and given a shipping address.

2 Each protein package is attached to a motor molecule and moves along a microtubule to its destination.

3 A protein may be incorporated into the membrane,...

4 ...remain within the cell to act as an enzyme,...

5 ...or be excreted from the cell by exocytosis.

Nucleus

Vesicle

Golgi bodies
Endoplasmic reticulum

Microtubule

FIGURE 3-17 **Protein Export** Exporting a protein entails packaging, transporting, and assigning its fate at the destination.

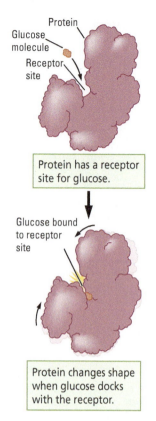

Protein

Glucose
molecule

Receptor
site

**Protein has a receptor
site for glucose.**

Glucose bound
to receptor
site

**Protein changes shape
when glucose docks
with the receptor.**

FIGURE 3-18 **Receptor Binding** When
substances bind to a protein's receptors, the
protein changes shape, which may change its
function.

channel Opening in a protein embedded in the
cell membrane that allows the passage of ions.

gate Protein embedded in a cell membrane
that allows substances to pass through the
membrane on some occasions but not on others.

pump Protein in the cell membrane that actively
transports a substance across the membrane.

Crossing the Cell Membrane: Channels, Gates, and Pumps

Some proteins are embedded in the cell membrane. These proteins serve many functions, including transporting small molecules, such as salts, sugar, and other chemicals, across the membrane. We now consider how three such membrane proteins—channels, gates, and pumps—perform the transport function. In each case, the particular protein's function is an emergent property of its shape.

A protein's shape and its ability to change shape derive from the precise amino acid sequence that composes the protein molecule. Some proteins change shape when other chemicals bind to them; others change shape as a function of temperature; and still others change shape in response to changes in electrical charge. The protein molecule's ability to change shape is analogous to a lock in a door. When a key of the appropriate size and shape is inserted into the lock and turned, the locking device activates and changes shape, allowing the door to be closed or opened.

Such a shape-changing protein is illustrated in **Figure 3-18**. The surface of this protein molecule has a groove, called a *receptor*, analogous to a keyhole. Small molecules, such as glucose, or other proteins can bind to a protein's receptors and cause the protein to change shape. Changes in shape allow the proteins to serve some new function.

Some membrane proteins form **channels** through which substances can pass. Different-sized channels regulate the passage of different-sized substances. **Figure 3-19A** illustrates a protein with a particular shape forming a channel large enough to pass potassium (K^+) but not other ions. Other protein channels allow sodium ions or chloride ions to pass into or out of the cell. Still others allow the passage of various other substances.

Figure 3-19B shows a protein molecule that acts as a **gate** to regulate the passage of substances. Like the protein in Figure 3-18, gates change their shape in response to some trigger. The protein allows substances to pass through when its shape forms a channel and prevents passage when its shape leaves the channel closed.

Changes in protein's shape can also allow it to act as a **pump**. Figure 3-19C shows a protein that changes its shape to pump Na^+ and K^+ across the membrane, exchanging the Na^+ on one side for the K^+ on the other.

Channels, gates, and pumps play an important role in allowing substances to enter and leave a cell. Again, this passage of substances is critical in explaining how neurons send messages. Chapter 4 explores how neurons use electrical activity to communicate.

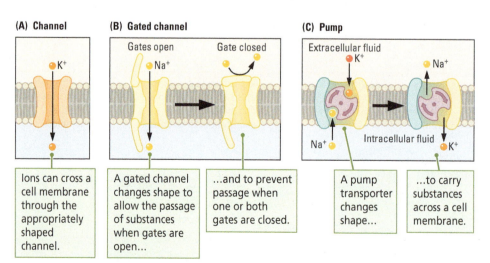

(A) Channel

K^+

Ions can cross a cell membrane through the appropriately shaped channel.

(B) Gated channel

Gates open   Gate closed

Na^+

A gated channel changes shape to allow the passage of substances when gates are open...

...and to prevent passage when one or both gates are closed.

(C) Pump

Extracellular fluid

K^+ Na^+

Na^+ Intracellular fluid K^+

A pump transporter changes shape...

...to carry substances across a cell membrane.

FIGURE 3-19 **Transmembrane Proteins** Channels, gates, and pumps are proteins embedded in the cell membrane.

3-2 Review

Before you continue, check your understanding. Answers to Self-Test appear at the back of the book.

1. The constituent parts of the cell include the _____, _____, _____, _____, _____, and _____.

2. Proteins in the cell membrane serve many functions, including acting at the cell membrane as _____, _____, and _____ to regulate movement of substances across the membrane.

3. The basic sequence of events in building a protein is that _____ makes _____, which in turn makes _____.

4. Once proteins are formed in the _____, they are wrapped in membranes by _____ and transported by _____ to their designated sites in the neuron or its membrane or exported from the cell by _____.

5. Briefly explain how the production of proteins in a cell contributes to behavior.

For additional study tools, visit  **LaunchPad** at launchpadworks.com

3-3

Genes, Cells, and Behavior

Your *genotype* (genetic makeup) influences your physical and behavioral traits, which combine to form your *phenotype* (individual characteristics, including behavioral characteristics). Genetic analysis conducted by the Human Genome Project cataloged the human genome—all 20,000 or so genes in our species—and today individual genomes are routinely sequenced. (Recall the Beery twins in Research Focus 3-1.) James Watson, the co-discoverer of DNA, was the first person to have his genome sequenced.

Researchers have sequencing the genomes of some of our extinct ancestors, including the Neanderthal genome. The genomes of James Watson and the Neanderthal are surprisingly similar, as you'd expect for close hominid relatives. You can have your genome sequenced to reveal many aspects of its coding functions, including your relationship to Neanderthals, if you have European ancestry. The cost is about $100. (Before you decide, you may want to check on any required information sharing with employers and insurers.)

Studying how genes influence our traits is the objective of Mendelian genetics, named for Gregor Mendel, whose research led to the concept of the gene. Studying how the environment influences gene expression is the objective of epigenetics. In this section, we describe how both factors influence our phenotypes.

Mendelian Genetics and the Genetic Code

The nucleus of each human somatic cell contains 23 pairs of chromosomes, or 46 in all. One member of each pair comes from the mother, and the other member comes from the father. The chromosome pairs are numbered from 1 to 23, roughly according to size, with chromosome 1 being the largest (**Figure 3-20**).

Chromosome pairs 1 through 22 are called *autosomes*, and they contain the genes that contribute most to our physical appearance and behavior. The twenty-third pair are the *sex chromosomes*, which contribute to our physical and behavioral sexual characteristics. The two mammalian sex chromosomes are referred to as X and Y, shown at the right in Figure 3-20.

Figure 1-12 shows how a Neanderthal woman might have looked.

FIGURE 3-20 Human Chromosomes
The nucleus of a human cell contains 23 chromosomes derived from the father and 23 from the mother. Sexual characteristics are determined by the twenty-third pair, the X and Y (sex) chromosomes.

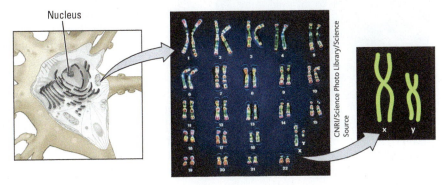

Nucleus

allele Alternative form of a gene; a gene pair contains two alleles.

homozygous Having two identical alleles for a trait.

heterozygous Having two different alleles for the same trait.

mutation Alteration of an allele that yields a different version of its protein.

Ordinarily, female mammals have two X chromosomes, whereas males have an X and a Y. The Y chromosome contains the SRY (sex determining region) gene that makes the SRY protein, which triggers testes development and hence the male phenotype.

Because all but your sex chromosomes are matched pairs, each cell contains two copies of every gene, one inherited from your mother, the other from your father. These two copies of a gene are called **alleles**. The term *matched* here does not necessarily mean identical. The nucleotide sequences in a pair of alleles may be either identical or different. If they are identical, the two alleles are **homozygous** (*homo-* means "the same"). If they are different, the two alleles are **heterozygous** (*hetero-* means "different").

The nucleotide sequence most common in a population is called the *wild-type allele*, whereas a less frequently occurring sequence is called a **mutation**. Any wild-type allele may have a number of mutations—some beneficial, some neutral, and some harmful.

Dominant and Recessive Alleles

If both alleles in a gene pair are homozygous, the two encode the same protein, but if the two alleles in a pair are heterozygous, they encode somewhat different proteins. Three possible outcomes attend the heterozygous condition when these proteins express a physical or behavioral trait: (1) only the allele from the mother may be expressed, (2) only the allele from the father may be expressed, or (3) both alleles may be expressed simultaneously.

A member of a gene pair that is routinely expressed as a trait is called a *dominant* allele; an unexpressed allele is *recessive*. Alleles can vary considerably in their dominance. In complete dominance, only the allele's own trait is expressed in the phenotype. In incomplete dominance, the allele's own trait is expressed only partially. In *codominance*, both the allele's own trait and that of the other allele in the gene pair are expressed completely.

Each gene makes an independent contribution to the offspring's inheritance, even though the contribution may not always be visible in the offspring's phenotype. When paired with a dominant allele, a recessive allele is often not expressed. Still, it can be passed on to future generations and influence their phenotypes when not masked by the influence of some dominant trait.

Genetic Mutations

The mechanism described in Section 3-2 for reproducing genes and passing them on to offspring is fallible. Errors can arise in the nucleotide sequence when reproductive cells make gene copies. The altered alleles are mutations.

A mutation may be as small as a change in a single nucleotide base, called a *single nucleotide polymorphism* (SNP, pronounced "snip"). This one base change results in a change in a codon and a resulting change in one amino acid in a protein. A single amino acid change is a mutation and is often sufficient to alter the protein's function.

Because the average gene has more than 1200 nucleotide bases, an enormous number of SNPs as well as more Complex Losses and changes in bases can occur on a single gene. For example, the *BRCA1* (BReast CAncer) gene, found on chromosome 17, is a caretaker gene that contributes to preventing breast cancer and other cancers in both men and women. More than 1000 mutations of this gene have already been found. Thus, in principle, there are more than 1000 ways in which to have a predisposition to, or increased resistance to, a cancer just from this gene.

A mutation in a nucleotide or the addition of a nucleotide to a gene sequence can be beneficial or disruptive or both. For example, a SNP in which a T base is substituted for an A base in the *HBB* (hemoglobin) gene on chromosome 11 causes *sickle-cell anemia*, a condition in which blood cells take on an abnormal sickle shape. The sickle shape offers some protection against malaria, but sickle cells also have poor oxygen-carrying capacity, which weakens the person who possesses them. Sickle-cell anemia is the most common genetic blood disease, affecting millions of people worldwide, including 80,000 people in the United States.

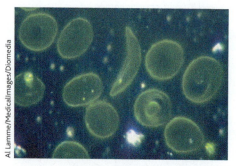

In this micrograph, a sickle cell is surrounded by healthy blood cells.

Al Lamme/MedicalImages/Diomedia

Neuroscientists cannot yet explain human behavior in relation to genes, but we know the severe behavioral consequences of about 2000 genetic abnormalities that affect the nervous system. For example, an error in a gene could produce a protein that should be an ion channel but will not allow the appropriate substance to pass. It may produce a pump that will not pump or a protein that the cell's transportation system refuses to transport.

ACQUIRED GENETIC MUTATIONS The genetic mutations just described may be inherited by offspring from their parents. However, each of us also acquires a surprisingly large number of genetic mutations during our lifetime. These acquired mutations are not inheritable, but they have the potential to affect the behavior of the individual carrier. Some mutations are due to *mitotic* (cell division) errors that occur during our development, and others occur as a cell's DNA engages in its routine activity of producing proteins.

Different mutations may be localized in different parts of the body or brain, or even in individual brain cells. Given that the human brain consists of 86 billion neurons and 87 billion glial cells, all of which arose by cell division from a single cell, it is not surprising that mutations occur. And because most neurons are with us for life and are metabolically active for life, it is not surprising that they can accumulate mutations. Self-generated mutations can feature SNPs or even larger pieces of DNA that escape the mechanisms that normally repair DNA. One analysis of the DNA of single human neurons finds that errors in each neuron accumulate at the rate of one per week. At 1 year of age, a neuron may have up to 300–900 mutations; by 80 years of age, a neuron may have as many as 2000 mutations (Lodato et al., 2018). Do the math: 173 billion brain cells multiplied by up to 2000 mutations per cell is a lot of mutations in a lifetime.

The accumulation of mutations in the brain immediately raises the question of their effects on behavior. While mutations may be beneficial or seemingly neutral to the functioning of the organism that carries them, most mutations likely have negative effects. DNA mutations may contribute to childhood development disorders and could also influence diseases of aging.

In short, we are accustomed to hearing that our genome is inherited from our parents, but it actually gets modified a lot as we develop and age.

Applying Mendel's Principles

Gregor Mendel introduced the concept of dominant and recessive alleles in the nineteenth century, when he studied pea plants. Today, scientists study genetic variation to gain insight into how genes, neurons, and behaviors are linked. This knowledge is directed toward explaining healthy behavior and helping reduce the negative effects of genetic abnormalities, perhaps someday even eliminating them.

Experiment 1-1 describes one of Mendel's experiments.

Allele Disorders That Affect the Brain

Some disorders caused by mutant genes illustrate Mendel's principles of dominant and recessive alleles. One is **Tay-Sachs disease**, caused by a dysfunction in a gene that produces HexA (hexosaminidase A). HexA breaks down a class of lipids (fats) in brain cells. If HexA is nonfunctional, the lipids accumulate in brain cells, resulting in cell damage.

Scientists Warren Tay and Bernard Sachs first described the disorder.

Symptoms usually appear a few months after birth. The baby begins to have seizures, deteriorating eyesight, and degenerating motor and mental abilities. Inevitably, the child dies within a few years. Tay-Sachs mutations appear with high frequency among certain ethnic groups, including Jews of European origin and French Canadians, but the mutation in different populations can be different.

The dysfunctional Tay-Sachs HexA enzyme is caused by a recessive (nonfunctioning) allele of the *HEXA* gene on chromosome 15. Distinctive inheritance patterns result from recessive alleles because two copies (one from the mother and one from the father) are needed for the disorder to develop. A baby can inherit Tay-Sachs disease only when both parents pass on the recessive allele.

Tay-Sachs disease Inherited birth defect caused by the loss of genes that encode the enzyme necessary for breaking down certain fatty substances; appears 4 to 6 months after birth and results in intellectual disability, physical changes, and death by about age 5.

wild type Typical allele (most common in a population).

Huntington disease Hereditary disease characterized by chorea (ceaseless involuntary jerky movements) and progressive dementia, ending in death.

Because both parents have survived to adulthood, both must also possess a corresponding dominant wild-type *HEXA* allele for that particular gene pair. The egg and sperm cells produced by this man and woman will therefore contain a copy of the **wild type**, or the mutation of these two alleles. Which allele is passed on is determined completely by chance.

In any child born of two Tay-Sachs carriers, then, this situation gives rise to three possible gene combinations, as shown in **Figure 3-21A**. The child may have two wild-type alleles, in which case he or she will be spared the disorder and cannot pass it on. The child may have one normal and one Tay-Sachs allele, in which case he or she, like the parents, will be a carrier. Or the child may have two Tay-Sachs alleles, in which case he or she will develop the disease.

The chance of a child of two carriers being normal is 25 percent, the chance of being a carrier is 50 percent, and the chance of having Tay-Sachs disease is 25 percent. If one parent is a Tay-Sachs carrier and the other is normal, any child has a 50–50 chance of being normal or a carrier. Such a couple has no chance of conceiving a baby with Tay-Sachs disease.

The Tay-Sachs allele operates independently of the dominant allele. As a result, it still produces the defective HexA enzyme, so the person who carries it has a higher-than-normal lipid accumulation in the brain. Because this person also has a normal allele that produces a functional enzyme, the abnormal lipid accumulation is not enough to cause Tay-Sachs disease.

A blood test can detect whether a person carries the Tay-Sachs allele. People who find that they are carriers can make informed decisions about conceiving children. If they avoid having children with another Tay-Sachs carrier, none of their children will have the disorder, although some will probably be carriers. Where genetic counseling has been effective, the disease has been eliminated.

The normal dominant allele that a carrier of Tay-Sachs possesses produces enough functional enzyme to enable the brain to operate in a satisfactory way. That would not be the case if the abnormal allele were dominant, however, as happens with the genetic disorder **Huntington disease**. Here, the buildup of an abnormal version of the *huntingtin* protein kills brain cells, especially in the basal ganglia and the cortex. Huntington disease is a landmark disease for neuroscience because it has revealed much about the relationship between a single gene and the nervous system and, perhaps more importantly, because this knowledge can in principle lead to a cure for the disease.

FIGURE 3-21 **Inheritance Patterns**
(A) Recessive condition: If a parent has one mutant allele, the parent will not show symptoms of the disease but will be a carrier. If both parents carry a mutant allele, each of their offspring stands a 25 percent chance of developing the disease. **(B)** Dominant condition: A person with a single allele will develop the disease. If this person mates with a noncarrier, offspring have a 50–50 chance of developing the disease. If both parents are carriers, both will develop the disease, and offspring have a 75 percent chance of developing it.

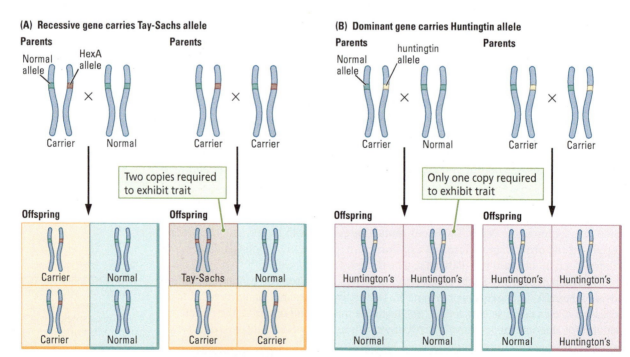

Symptoms can begin at any time from infancy to old age, but they most often start in midlife and include abnormal involuntary movements—which is why the disorder was once called a *chorea* (from the Greek word for "dance"). Other symptoms are memory loss and eventually a complete deterioration of behavior, followed by death. The abnormal *HTT* (huntingtin) allele is dominant, and the recessive allele is normal, so only one defective allele is needed to cause the disease.

Figure 3-21B illustrates the inheritance patterns associated with a dominant allele on chromosome 4 that produces Huntington disease. If one parent carries the defective allele, offspring have a 50 percent chance of inheriting the disorder. If both parents have the defective allele, the chance of inheritance increases to 75 percent. As discussed further in Clinical Focus 3-3, Huntington Disease, because the abnormal *huntingtin* allele usually is not expressed until midlife—that is, usually after the people who possess it have already had children—it is unwittingly passed down even though it is lethal.

As with the allele that causes Tay-Sachs disease, a genetic test can determine whether a person carries the allele that causes Huntington disease. If so, the person can elect not to procreate. A decision not to have children in this case will reduce the incidence of the abnormal *huntingtin* allele in the human gene pool.

CLINICAL FOCUS 3-3

Huntington Disease

Woody Guthrie, whose protest songs made him a spokesperson for farm workers during the Great Depression of the 1930s, is revered as one of the founders of American folk music. His best-known song is "This Land Is Your Land." Singer, songwriter, and recent Nobel Prize winner Bob Dylan was instrumental in reviving Guthrie's popularity in the 1960s. Guthrie's case illustrates much of the history of Huntington disease.

Guthrie died in 1967, after struggling with what was eventually diagnosed as Huntington disease. His mother had died of a similar condition, although her illness was never diagnosed. Two of Guthrie's five children from two marriages developed the disease, and his second wife, Marjorie, became active in promoting its study.

Huntington disease is devastating, characterized by memory impairment; *choreas* (abnormal, uncontrollable movements); and marked changes in personality, eventually leading to nearly total loss of healthy behavioral, emotional, and intellectual functioning. Even before the onset of motor symptoms, Huntington disease impairs *theory of mind*, a person's ability to assess the behavior of others (Eddy & Rickards, 2015).

The symptoms of Huntington disease result from neuronal degeneration in the basal ganglia and cortex. Symptoms can appear at any age but typically start in midlife. In 1983, the *HTT* (huntingtin) gene responsible for forming the abnormal huntingtin protein was found on chromosome 4.

The *HTT* gene has been a source of insights into the transmission of genetic disorders. Part of the gene contains repeats of the base sequence CAG. The CAG codon encodes the amino acid glutamine. If the number of CAG repeats exceeds about 40, then the carrier, with 40 or more glutamine amino acids in the huntingtin protein, has an increased likelihood of Huntington symptoms.

As the number of CAG repeats increases, the onset of symptoms occurs earlier in life, and the disease progresses more rapidly. Typically, non-Europeans have fewer repeats than do Europeans, among whom the disease is more common. The number of repeats can also increase with transmission from the father but not from the mother.

MixPix/Alamy Stock Photo

Woody Guthrie, whose unpublished lyrics and artwork are archived at woodyguthrie.org.

Investigations into why brain cells change in Huntington disease and into potential treatments use transgenic animal models. Mice, rats, and monkeys that have received the *HTT* gene feature the abnormal huntingtin protein and display symptoms of Huntington disease (Stricker-Shaver et al., 2018). Modification of the *HTT* gene using modern genetic engineering is in principle a cure for the disease (Yapijakis, 2017).

Down syndrome Chromosomal abnormality resulting in intellectual impairment and other abnormalities, usually caused by an extra chromosome 21.

Chromosome Abnormalities

Genetic disorders are not caused solely by single defective alleles. Some nervous system disorders are caused by copy number variations—that is, aberrations in a part of a chromosome or even an entire chromosome. Copy number variations are related to a variety of disorders, including autism, schizophrenia, and learning disabilities. Often, though, copy number variation has little obvious consequence or is even beneficial. For example, humans average about 6 copies of the *AMY1* (amylase) gene but may have as many as 15 copies. The gene is an adaptation that improves the ability to digest starchy foods (Mimori et al., 2015).

One condition due to a change in chromosome number in humans is **Down syndrome**, which affects approximately 1 in 700 children. Down syndrome is usually the result of an extra copy of chromosome 21. One parent (usually the mother) passes on to the child two copies of chromosome 21 rather than the normal single chromosome. Combining these two with one chromosome from the other parent yields three chromosome 21s, an abnormal number called a *trisomy* **(Figure 3-22)**.

Although chromosome 21 is the smallest human chromosome, its trisomy can dramatically alter a person's phenotype. People with Down syndrome have characteristic facial features and short stature. They are susceptible to heart defects, respiratory infections, and intellectual impairment. They are prone to developing leukemia and Alzheimer disease. Although people with Down syndrome usually have a shorter-than-normal life span, some live to middle age or beyond. Improved educational opportunities enrich the lives of children with Down syndrome.

Genetic Engineering

Despite advances in understanding gene structure and function, the gap in understanding how genes produce behavior remains wide. To investigate gene structure and behavior relationships, geneticists have invented methods to influence the traits that genes express. This approach collectively defines the science of *genetic engineering*. In its simplest forms, genetic engineering entails manipulating a genome, removing a gene from a genome, or modifying or adding a gene to the genome. Its techniques include selective breeding, cloning, and transgenics.

Selective Breeding

The oldest means of influencing genetic traits is the selective breeding of animals and plants. Beginning with the domestication of wolves into dogs more than 30,000 years

FIGURE 3-22 **Chromosome Aberration** *Left*: Down syndrome, also known as trisomy 21, is caused by an extra chromosome 21 (colored red, bottom row at left). *Right*: Chris Burke, the first person with Down syndrome to play a leading role on a television series—*Life Goes On*, in the 1990s—is now in his fifties and remains an advocate for individuals with Down syndrome. He performs as a lead singer in a band.

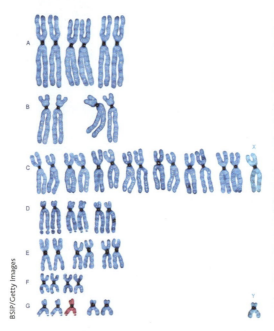

ago, humans have domesticated many animal species by selectively breeding males and females that display particular traits. The selective breeding of dogs, for example, has produced the species with the most diverse traits of all animal species: breeds that can run fast, haul heavy loads, retrieve prey, dig for burrowing animals, climb rocky cliffs in search of sea birds, herd sheep and cattle, or sit on an owner's lap and cuddle. Selective breeding has influenced the dog brain by making it smaller than a wolf's brain but also by giving it a comparatively large number of cortical neurons for a carnivore of its size, which may account for its sociability with humans (Jardim-Messeder et al., 2017).

Maintaining spontaneous mutations is one objective of selective breeding. Using this method, researchers produce whole populations of animals possessing some unusual trait that originally arose as an unexpected mutation in only one individual or in a few animals. In laboratory colonies of mice, for example, multiple spontaneous mutations have been discovered and maintained to produce more than 450 different mouse strains.

Some strains of mice make abnormal movements, such as reeling, staggering, and jumping. Other strains have diseases of the immune system; others are blind or cannot hear. Some mice are smart, some mice are not; some have big brains, some small; and many display distinctive behavioral traits. Some mice are also designed to have neurons that incorporate proteins that produce specialized channels and fluorescent proteins. Some of these fluorescent proteins are so bright that they can be visualized through the skull. If the fluorescence is activated by a metabolic change in a single cell, this cell's activity can be observed through the skull (Iwano et al., 2018). As a result, the neural and genetic bases of the altered behavior in the mice can be studied systematically to understand and treat human disorders.

Cloning

More direct approaches to manipulating the expression of genetic traits include altering early embryonic development. One such method is *cloning*—producing an offspring that is genetically identical to another animal.

To clone an animal, scientists begin with a cell nucleus that contains DNA (usually from a living animal donor), place it in an egg cell from which the nucleus has been removed, and, after stimulating the egg to start dividing, implant the new embryo in the uterus of a female. Because each individual animal that develops from these cells is genetically identical to the donor, clones can be used to preserve valuable traits, to study the relative influences of heredity and environment, or to produce new tissue or organs for transplant to the donor. Dolly, a female sheep, was the first cloned mammal.

Cloning has matured from an experimental manipulation to a commercial enterprise to produce better strains of domestic animals, preserve rare animal species, and even bring back extinct species. The first horse to be cloned was Charmayne James's horse Scamper, the mount she rode to 11 world championships in barrel racing. The first cat to be cloned, shown in **Figure 3-23**, was called Copycat. The first rare species cloned was an Asian gaur, an animal related to the cow. Investigators interested in *de-extinction* propose using preserved cells from species such as the extinct passenger pigeon or from frozen carcasses of the extinct mastodon to clone those animals. (An enclosure to house a de-extinct mastodon has in fact been prepared in Russia.)

Transgenic Techniques

Transgenic technology enables scientists to introduce genes into an embryo or to remove genes from it. In *knock-in technology*, a number of genes or a single gene from one species is added to the genome of another species, passed along, and expressed in subsequent generations of **transgenic animals**. For instance, researchers have introduced into lines of mice, rats, and Rhesus monkeys the human *HTT* gene that causes Huntington disease (Stricker-Shaver et al., 2018). The animals express the abnormal allele and display humanlike Huntington symptoms, allowing investigations into potential treatments for the disease (see Clinical Focus 3-3).

transgenic animal Product of technology in which one or more genes from one species is introduced into the genome of another species to be passed along and expressed in subsequent generations.

Unlike other animals, humans can consent to experimental procedures. Section 7-7 frames debates on the benefits and ethics of conducting research using nonhuman animals.

Sections 7-1 and 7-5 review genetic methods used in neuroscience research.

A team of researchers in Scotland cloned Dolly in 1996. As an adult, she mated and bore a lamb.

FIGURE 3-23 **A Clone and Her Mom** Copycat (left) and Rainbow (right), the cat that donated the cell nucleus for cloning. Although the cats' genomes are identical, their phenotypes, including fur color, differ. One copy of the X chromosome is randomly inactivated in each cell, which explains the color differences. Even clones are subject to phenotypic plasticity: they retain the capacity to develop into more than one phenotype.

Photos used with permission from Texas A&M College of Veterinary Medicine & Biomedical Sciences.

Knockout technology can be used to inactivate a gene, for example, so that a line of laboratory animals fails to express it. The line can then be examined to determine whether the targeted gene is responsible for a specific function or a human disorder and to examine possible therapies. Knockout technology has been used to produce a line of rats that display the emotional and cognitive symptoms of human childhood attention-deficit/hyperactivity disorder in order to explore methods of treatment (Adinolfi et al., 2018).

Gene Modification

A number of new methods for modifying genes involve altering its code, its base pairs. *CRISPR* (Clustered Regularly Interspaced Short Palindromic Repeat, pronounced "crisper") is a new technology that allows for faster and easier modifications of genes. The CRISPR machinery was discovered as part of the immune system of bacteria. A CRISPR RNA base sequence in the bacteria seeks out a matching DNA sequence in the invading virus and cuts the virus DNA, thus inactivating the virus.

The molecular mechanism that identifies an invading virus by its unique DNA sequences can be modified in the laboratory to produce an RNA sequence that can identify specific parts of the DNA in any gene. Using the CRISPR method, the identified gene can be cut, a portion of it deleted, and the deleted portion replaced by another DNA base sequence. This type of gene editing is similar to the way that you edit a sentence with your word processor to delete words, add words, or correct spelling mistakes.

Applications of the CRISPR technology include making plants or animals resistant to viral or bacterial infections, identifying cancer cells (including brain cancer) to kill them, and making animal models to study almost any aspect of behavior, including emotion, memory, and motor behavior. CRISPR technology can in principle also be used to identify genes that are implicated in various diseases, such as the *HTT* gene that causes Huntington disease, and fix the gene. CRISPR technology has been used to study the olfactory behavior of mosquitoes and ants, and it is possible that the genes of these insects can be modified so that they do not identify humans as targets to bite (Vinauger et al., 2018).

For more information on the CRISPR method, see Section 7-1.

Phenotypic Plasticity and the Epigenetic Code

Our genotype is not sufficient to explain our phenotype. We all know that if we expose ourselves to the sun, our skin darkens; if we exercise, our muscles enlarge; if we study, we learn. Our phenotype also changes with our diet and as we age. In short, the extent of phenotypic variation, given the same genotype, is remarkable.

Every individual has a capacity to develop into more than one phenotype. This *phenotypic plasticity* is due in part to the genome's capacity to express a large number of phenotypes and in part to epigenetics, the influence of environment and experience on phenotypic expression.

Seemingly puzzling features in the expression of genomes in relation to phenotypes are illustrated in strains of genetically identical mice, some of which develop a brain with no corpus callosum **(Figure 3-24)**. The absence of this hemispheric connector results from an epigenetic influence on whether the trait is expressed in a particular mouse. It occurs in the embryo at about the time the corpus callosum should form. This lack of *concordance* (incidence of similar behavioral traits) is also observed in patterns of disease incidence in human identical twins, who share the same genome.

The concordance rate between identical twins for a vast array of diseases—including schizophrenia, Alzheimer disease, multiple sclerosis, Crohn disease (a form of inflammatory bowel disease), asthma, diabetes, and prostate cancer—is between 30 and 60 percent. For cleft palate and breast cancer, identical twins' concordance rate is about 10 percent. The expectation from Mendelian genetics is 100 percent concordance. These less-than-perfect concordance rates point to epigenetic factors.

Phenotypic plasticity is in evidence not only in adult organisms but also in cells. In Section 3-1, we described the variety of neurons and glia found in the nervous system.

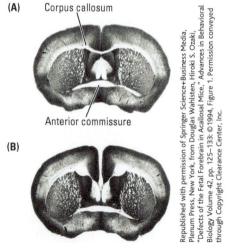

(A) Corpus callosum

Anterior commissure

(B)

Republished with permission of Springer Science+Business Media, Plenum Press, New York, from Douglas Wahlsten, Hiroki S. Ozaki, "Defects of the Fetal Forebrain in Acallosal Mice," Advances in Behavioral Biology Volume 42, pp. 125–133; ©1994, Figure 1. Permission conveyed through Copyright Clearance Center, Inc.

FIGURE 3-24 **Gene Expression** Identical coronal sections through the brains of mice with identical genotypes reveal frontal views of distinctly different phenotypes. **(A)** This mouse had a corpus callosum. **(B)** This mouse did not.

Each of these cells usually has the same genotype. So do the 248 other cell types of our body. How then do they become so different?

The cloned mice shown in Figure 2-1 exemplify phenotypic plasticity.

Applying the Epigenetic Code

The genes expressed in a cell are influenced by factors within the cell and in the cell's environment. Once a fertilized egg begins to divide, each new cell finds itself in a somewhat different environment from that of its parent cell. The cell's environment will determine which genes are expressed and so what kind of tissue it becomes, including what kind of nervous system cell it becomes. Environmental influences do not end at birth, of course. Our environment changes daily throughout our lives, as does its influence on our genes.

Epigenetic mechanisms create phenotypic variation without altering the base pair nucleotide sequence of the genes. Through these mechanisms, experience and the environment can allow a gene to be expressed or prevent its expression. Epigenetics is viewed as a second code; the first code is the genome. Epigenetics describes how a single genetic code produces each somatic cell type, explains how a single genome can code for many phenotypes, and describes how cell functions go astray to produce diseases ranging from cancer to brain dysfunction.

The International Human Epigenome Consortium (IHEC) mandate is to describe the epigenetic code, as the Human Genome Project has described the genetic code.

Epigenetic mechanisms can influence protein production either by blocking a gene to prevent transcription or by unlocking a gene so that it can be transcribed. This is where experiential and environmental influences come into play. To review, each of your chromosomes consists of a long, double-stranded chain of nucleotide bases that forms your DNA. Each gene on a chromosome is a segment of DNA that encodes the synthesis of a particular protein (see Figure 3-13).

Chromosomes are wrapped around supporting molecules of a protein called *histone*. Histone wrapping allows the many yards of a chromosome to be packaged in a small space, as yards of thread are wrapped around a spool. For any gene to be transcribed into messenger RNA, its DNA must be unspooled from the histone. Once unspooled, each gene must be instructed to transcribe mRNA. Then the mRNA must be translated into an amino acid chain that forms the protein. **Figure 3-25** illustrates some ways that each step can be either enabled or blocked:

1. *Histone modification.* DNA may unwrap or be stopped from unwrapping from the histone. At the top of Figure 3-25, a methyl group (CH_3) or other molecule binds to the tails of histones to block DNA from unspooling. The DNA's genes cannot be exposed for transcription with the block in place (left), but the DNA's genes can be opened for transcription (right) if the block is absent or removed.

2. **Gene (DNA) methylation**. Transcription of DNA into mRNA may be enabled or blocked. In Figure 3-25 at center, one or more methyl groups bind to CG base pairs to block transcription.

Methylation dramatically alters gene expression during brain development (see Sections 8-2 and 12-5) and can affect memory and brain plasticity (see Section 14-4).

3. *mRNA modification.* mRNA translation may be enabled or blocked. In Figure 3-25, bottom, noncoding RNA (ncRNA) binds to mRNA, blocking translation.

An environmental influence can either induce or remove one or more blocks, thus allowing the environment to regulate gene expression and influence behavior (Rogers, 2018). It is through these epigenetic mechanisms that cells are instructed to differentiate into various body tissues and that our unique environment and experience induce changes in our brain that make us unique individuals and allow us to learn. Some experientially induced events can also be passed from one generation to the next, as the following classic case study illustrates.

A Case of Inheriting Experience

The idea that traits are passed from parent to child through genes is a cornerstone of Mendelian genetics. Mendel's theory also predicts that individual life experience cannot be inherited. In a now classic report, Lars Olov Bygren and colleagues (Kaati et al., 2007) found, however, that individuals' nutritional experiences can affect their offspring's health.

gene (DNA) methylation Epigenetic process in which a methyl group attaches to the DNA sequence, suppressing or enabling gene expression.

FIGURE 3-25 **Epigenetic Mechanisms**

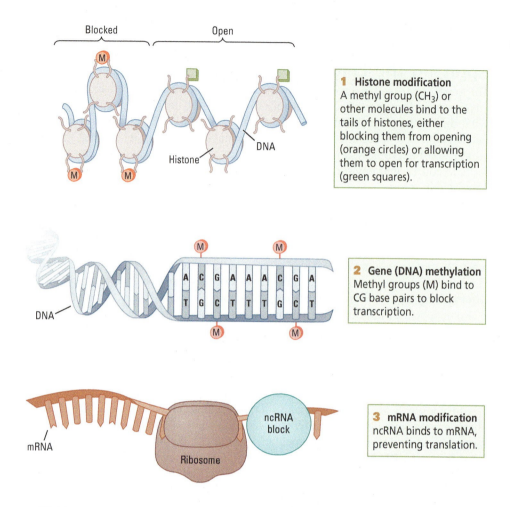

1 Histone modification
A methyl group (CH₃) or other molecules bind to the tails of histones, either blocking them from opening (orange circles) or allowing them to open for transcription (green squares).

2 Gene (DNA) methylation
Methyl groups (M) bind to CG base pairs to block transcription.

3 mRNA modification
ncRNA binds to mRNA, preventing translation.

Section 8-4 examines critical periods, limited time spans during which events have long-lasting influences on development.

The investigators focused on Norrbotten, a sparsely populated northern Swedish region. In the nineteenth century, Norrbotten was virtually isolated from the outside world. If the harvest there was bad, people starved. According to historical records, the years 1800, 1812, 1821, 1836, and 1856 saw total crop failure. The years 1801, 1822, 1828, 1844, and 1863 brought good harvests and abundance.

Bygren and colleagues identified at random individuals who had been subjected to famine or to plenty in the years just before they entered puberty. Then the researchers examined the health records and longevity of these people's children and grandchildren.

The findings seem to defy logic. The descendants of the plenty group had higher rates of cardiovascular disease and diabetes and had a life expectancy more than 7 years shorter than that of the famine group! Notably, these effects were found only in male offspring of males and female offspring of females.

Bygren and colleagues propose that diet during a critical period can modify the genetic expression of sex chromosomes—the Y chromosome in males and the X chromosome in females. Furthermore, this change can be passed on to subsequent generations. Dietary experience in the prepubertal period, just before the onset of sexual maturity, is important: this is the time at which gene expression on the sex chromosomes begins.

Many other studies support the seminal findings of Bygren and his colleagues. Together, this body of research makes a strong argument for epigenetics and for the idea that some epigenetic influences can be passed on for at least a few generations. Evidence that epigenetic influences play a demonstrable role in determining gene expression is highlighting how our experiences shape our brains to influence the individuals we become and how our current environment might influence our descendants' epigenetic inheritance (Guerrero-Bosagna, 2017).

3-3 Review

Before you continue, check your understanding. Answers to Self-Test appear at the back of the book.

1. Each of our _____ chromosome pairs contains thousands of genes, and each gene contains the code for one _____.

2. The genes we receive from our parents may include slightly different _____ of particular genes, which will be expressed in slightly different _____.

3. Abnormalities in a gene, caused by a(n) _____, can result in an abnormally formed protein, hence in abnormal cell function. Chromosome abnormality can result in abnormal functioning of many genes. _____, for example, is caused by an extra copy of chromosome 21, a(n) _____.

4. Tay-Sachs disease results from a(n) _____ allele being expressed; Huntington disease results from the expression of a(n) _____ allele.

5. _____ is a new technology that allows for faster and easier gene modification. Using this method, researchers can identify specific parts of the _____ in any gene, cut it, and replace it with another _____.

6. _____ is an epigenetic mechanism that either enables or blocks transcription.

7. What distinguishes Mendelian genetics from epigenetics?

For additional study tools, visit **LaunchPad** at launchpadworks.com

Summary

3-1 Cells of the Nervous System

The nervous system is composed of two kinds of cells: neurons, which transmit information, and glia, which support neuronal function. Sensory neurons may act as receptors to convey information from the body to the brain, motor neurons command muscles to move, and interneurons link up sensory and motor neuron activities.

Like neurons, glial cells can be grouped by structure and function. Ependymal cells produce CSF. Astrocytes structurally support neurons, help to form the blood–brain barrier, and seal off damaged brain tissue. Microglia aid in brain cell repair and waste removal. Oligodendroglia and Schwann cells myelinate axons in the CNS and in the somatic division of the PNS, respectively.

A neuron is composed of three parts: a cell body, or soma; multiple branching extensions called dendrites, designed to receive information; and a single axon that passes information along to other neurons. Numerous dendritic spines greatly increase a dendrite's surface area. An axon may have branches (axon collaterals), which further divide into telodendria, each ending at a terminal button (end foot). A synapse is the almost-connection between a terminal button and another cell's membrane.

3-2 Internal Structure of a Cell

A surrounding cell membrane protects the cell and regulates what enters and leaves it. Within the cell are a number of organelles, also enclosed in membranes. These compartments include the nucleus (containing the cell's chromosomes and genes), the endoplasmic reticulum (where proteins are manufactured), the mitochondria (where energy is gathered and stored), the Golgi bodies (where protein molecules are packaged for transport), and lysosomes (which break down wastes). A cell also contains a system of tubules (microfilaments) that aid its movements, provide structural support, and act as highways for transporting substances.

To a large extent, the work of cells is carried out by proteins. The nucleus contains chromosomes—long chains of genes, each encoding a specific protein the cell needs. Proteins perform diverse tasks by virtue of their diverse shapes. Some act as enzymes to facilitate chemical reactions; others serve as membrane channels, gates, and pumps; still others are exported for use in other parts of the body.

A gene is a segment of a DNA molecule made up of a sequence of nucleotide bases. Through transcription, a copy of a gene is produced in a strand of messenger RNA. The mRNA travels to the endoplasmic reticulum, where a ribosome moves along the mRNA molecule, translating it into a sequence of amino acids. The resulting amino acid chain is a polypeptide. Polypeptides fold and combine to form protein molecules with distinctive shapes that serve specific purposes in the body.

3-3 Genes, Cells, and Behavior

From each parent, we inherit one of each chromosome in the 23 chromosome pairs that constitute the human genotype. Because all but the sex chromosomes are matched pairs, a cell contains two alleles of every gene. Sometimes the paired alleles are homozygous (the same), and sometimes they are heterozygous (different).

An allele may be dominant and expressed as a trait, recessive and not expressed, or codominant and expressed along with the other allele in the organism's phenotype. One allele of each gene is designated the wild type—the most common in a population—whereas the other alleles are called mutations. A person might inherit any of these alleles from a parent, depending on the parent's genotype.

Genes have the potential to undergo many mutations—of a single base pair, of part of the chromosome, or of the entire chromosome. Mutations can be inherited by offspring from parents, or they can be acquired as we develop and age. Acquired mutations can be localized to different parts of the body, organs (including the brain), or even individual cells. Mutations can be beneficial, harmful, or neutral in their effects on nervous system structure and behavioral function. Genetic research seeks to prevent the expression of genetic and chromosomal abnormalities and to find cures for those that are expressed.

Selective breeding is the oldest form of genetic manipulation. In genetic engineering, an animal's genome is artificially altered. The genetic composition of a cloned animal is identical to that of a parent or sibling. In transgenic animals, a new or altered gene may be added or a gene removed. CRISPR is a relatively new technology in gene modification, faster and easier than previous methods, that allows researchers to identify, cut, and replace specific DNA sequences in the genome.

The genome encodes a range of phenotypes. The phenotype that is eventually produced is determined by epigenetics and further influenced by experience and the environment. Epigenetic mechanisms such as DNA methylation can influence whether genes are transcribed or transcription is blocked without changing the genetic code itself.

Key Terms

allele, p. 96

astrocyte, p. 82

axon, p. 75

axon collateral, p. 77

axon hillock, p. 77

bipolar neuron, p. 78

blood–brain barrier, p. 82

cell body (soma), p. 75

channel, p. 94

dendrite, p. 75

dendritic spine, p. 76

Down syndrome, p. 100

ependymal cell, p. 81

gate, p. 94

gene, p. 90

gene (DNA) methylation, p. 103

glial cell, p. 79

heterozygous, p. 96

homozygous, p. 96

Huntington disease, p. 98

hydrocephalus, p. 81

interneuron, p. 78

microglia, p. 83

motor neuron, p. 78

mutation, p. 96

myelin, p. 84

neural network, p. 76

oligodendroglia, p. 84

paralysis, p. 84

protein, p. 93

pump, p. 94

Purkinje cell, p. 78

pyramidal cell, p. 78

Schwann cell, p. 84

sensory neuron, p. 78

somatosensory neuron, p. 78

synapse, p. 77

Tay-Sachs disease, p. 97

terminal button (end foot), p. 77

transgenic animal, p. 101

tumor, p. 82

wild type, p. 98

Visit **LaunchPad** to access the e-Book, videos, **LearningCurve** adaptive quizzing, flashcards, and more at launchpadworks.com

Bill Diodato/Getty Images

How Do Neurons Use Electrical Signals to Transmit Information?

◎ CLINICAL FOCUS 4-1

Epilepsy

J. D. worked as a disc jockey for a radio station and at parties in his off-hours. One evening, he set up on the back of a truck at a rugby field to emcee a jovial and raucous rugby party. Between musical sets, he made introductions, told jokes, and exchanged toasts.

At about 1 A.M., J. D. suddenly collapsed, making unusual jerky motions, then passed out. He was rushed to a hospital emergency room, where he gradually recovered. The attending physician noted that he was not intoxicated, released him to his friends, and recommended that a series of neurological tests be run the next day. Neuroimaging with state-of-the-art brain scans can usually reveal brain abnormalities (Cendes et al., 2016), but it did not do so in J. D.'s case.

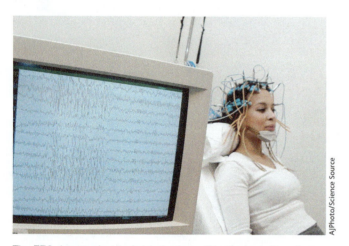

AJPhoto/Science Source

The EEG detects electrical signals given off by the brain in various states of consciousness, as explained in Sections 7-2 and 13-3, Section 16-3 details the diagnosis and treatment of epilepsy.

When the electrical activity in J. D.'s brain was recorded while a strobe light was flashed before his eyes, an *electroencephalogram*, or EEG, displayed a series of abnormal electrical patterns characteristic of epilepsy. The doctor prescribed Dilantin (diphenylhydantoin), an antiseizure drug, and advised J. D. to refrain from drinking alcohol. He was required to give up his driver's license to prevent the possibility of an attack while driving. And he lost his job at the radio station.

After 3 uneventful months, medication was stopped, and J. D.'s driver's license was restored. J. D. convinced the radio station that he could resume work, and subsequently he has remained seizure free.

Epilepsy is a common neurological disease marked by periods of excessive neural synchrony called **electrographic seizures.** The disease is electrical in nature. The brain is normally electrically active; if this activity becomes abnormal, even infrequently, the consequences, including loss of conscious awareness, can be severe.

Electrographic seizures often follow innocuous stimuli—events that would not typically cause seizures in people who do not have epilepsy. The core concept is that the brain of a person with epilepsy has a chronically low seizure threshold and so is subject to recurrent seizures. About 4 in 10 cases of epilepsy have been linked to specific neural causes, among them infections, trauma, tumors, structural abnormalities, or genetic mutations in the proteins that make up ion channels (Bhalla et al., 2011). But that leaves the remaining 60 percent without a clear cause.

If seizures occur repeatedly and cannot be controlled by drug treatment, as occurs in about 30 percent of people with epilepsy, other options may include the high-fat/low-carbohydrate ketogenic diet, deep brain stimulation, and surgical resection of the seizure focus (Rho et al., 2010). Removing this small area of brain tissue may prevent seizures and keep them from spreading to other brain regions.

---

electrographic seizures Abnormal rhythmic neuronal discharges; may be recorded by an electroencephalogram.

Descartes proposed the idea behind dualism—that the nonmaterial mind controls body mechanics; see Section 1-2.

The most reproduced drawing in behavioral neuroscience is nearly 350 years old, predating our understanding of the electrical basis of epilepsy by centuries. Taken from René Descartes's book *Treatise on Man* (1664) and reproduced in **Figure 4-1**, it illustrates the first serious attempt to explain how information travels through the nervous system. Descartes proposed that the carrier of information is cerebrospinal fluid flowing through nerve tubes.

Descartes reasoned that when the fire burns the man's toe, it stretches the skin, which tugs on a nerve tube leading to the brain. In response to the tug, a valve in a brain ventricle opens, and cerebral spinal fluid (CSF) flows down the tube, filling the leg muscles and causing them to contract and pull the toe back from the fire. The flow of fluid through other tubes to other muscles of the body (not shown in Figure 4-1) causes the head to turn toward the painful stimulus and the hand to rub the injured toe.

Descartes's theory was incorrect, yet it is remarkable because he isolated the three basic questions that underlie a behavioral response to stimulation:

1. How do our nerves detect a sensory stimulus and inform the brain about it?

2. How does the brain decide what response to make?

3. How does the brain command muscles to move?

Descartes was trying to explain the very same things that scientists have sought to explain in the intervening centuries. If not by stretched skin tugging on a nerve tube initiating the message, the message must still be initiated somehow. If not by opening valves to initiate the flow of CSF to convey information, the information must still be sent. If not by filling the muscles with fluid that produces movements, the muscles must contract by some other mechanism.

These mechanisms are the subject of this chapter. We examine how neurons convey information from the environment throughout the nervous system and ultimately activate muscles to produce movement. We begin by describing the clues and tools that were first used to explain the nervous system's electrical activity.

4-1

Searching for Electrical Activity in the Nervous System

The first hints about how the nervous system conveys its messages came in the eighteenth century, following the discovery of electricity. Early discoveries about the nature of electricity quickly led to proposals that it plays a role in conducting information in the nervous system. We describe a few milestones that led from this idea to an understanding of how the nervous system really conveys information. If you have a basic understanding of how electricity works and how it is used to stimulate neural tissue, read on. If you prefer to brush up on electricity and electrical stimulation first, turn to The Basics: Electricity and Electrical Stimulation on page 110.

Early Clues That Linked Electricity and Neuronal Activity

In a dramatic demonstration in 1731, Stephen Gray, an amateur scientist, rubbed a rod with a piece of cloth to accumulate electrons on the rod. Then he touched the charged rod to the feet of a boy suspended on a rope and raised a piece of metal foil to the boy's nose. The foil was attracted to the boy's nose, causing it to bend on its approach; as foil and nose touched, electricity passed from the rod through the boy to the foil.

Gray speculated that electricity might be the messenger that spreads information through the nervous system. Two other lines of evidence, drawn from electrical stimulation and electrical recording studies, implicated electrical activity in the nervous system's flow of information.

Electrical Stimulation Studies

When the Italian scientist Luigi Galvani, a contemporary of Gray, observed that frogs' legs hanging on a wire in a market twitched during a lightning storm, he surmised that sparks of electricity from the storm were activating the leg muscles. Investigating this possibility, he found that if an electrical current is applied to an exposed nerve, the muscle connected to that nerve contracts. While it was unclear how the process worked, Galvani had discovered **electrical stimulation**: passing an electrical current from the uninsulated tip of an electrode onto a nerve to produce behavior—a muscular contraction.

Among the many researchers who used Galvani's technique to produce muscle contraction, two mid-nineteenth-century scientists, Gustav Theodor Fritsch and Eduard Hitzig, demonstrated that electrical stimulation of the neocortex causes movement. They studied several animal species, including rabbits and dogs, and may even have stimulated the neocortex of a person whom they were treating for head injuries sustained on a Prussian battlefield. They observed their subjects' arm and leg movements in response to the stimulation of specific parts of the neocortex.

In 1874, Roberts Bartholow, a Cincinnati physician, first described the effects of human brain stimulation. His patient, Mary Rafferty, had a skull defect that exposed

FIGURE 4-1 Descartes's Theory of Information Flow

Print Collector/Getty Images

Gray's experiment resembles accumulating electrons by combing your hair. Hold a piece of paper near the comb, and the paper bends toward it. Negative charges on the comb push negative charges on the paper to its backside, leaving the front side positively charged. Because opposite charges attract, the paper bends toward the comb.

electrical stimulation Passage of an electrical current from the uninsulated tip of an electrode through tissue, resulting in changes in the electrical activity of the tissue.

⊚ THE BASICS

Electricity and Electrical Stimulation

Electricity powers the lights in your home and the batteries that run so many electronic gadgets, from smartphones to electric cars. *Electricity* is the flow of electrons from a body that contains a higher charge (more electrons) to a body that contains a lower charge (fewer electrons). This electron flow can perform work—lighting an unlit bulb, for instance. When biological tissue contains an electrical charge, the charge can be recorded; if living tissue is sensitive to an electrical charge, the tissue can be stimulated.

How Electricity Works

In the Power Source diagram to the right, negatively charged electrons are attracted to the positive pole because opposite charges attract. The electrons on the negative pole have the potential to flow to the positive pole. This *electrical potential*, or electrical charge, is the ability to do work using stored electrical energy.

Electrical potential is measured in *volts*, the difference in charge between the positive and negative poles. These poles are separated by an insulator. Thus, when not connected, the positive and negative poles in a battery, like the poles in each wall socket in your home, hold voltage between the poles.

Electrical Activity in Cells

If the bare tip of an insulated wire, or *electrode*, from each pole of a battery comes into contact with biological tissue, current will flow from the electrode connected to the negative pole into the tissue and from the tissue into the electrode connected to the positive pole. The stimulation comes from the electrode's uninsulated tip. Microelectrodes can record from or stimulate tissue as small as parts of a single living cell.

Electrical stimulation, illustrated in part A of the Studying Electrical Activity in Animal Tissue diagram below, is most effective when administered in brief pulses. A timer in the stimulator turns the current on and off to produce the pulses. In electrical recording, voltage can be displayed by the dial on a voltmeter, a recording device that measures the voltage of a battery or of biological tissue (part B).

Power Source

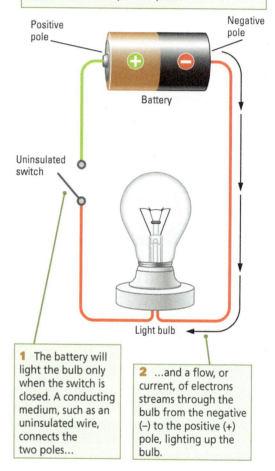

Because electrons carry a negative charge, the negative pole has a higher electrical charge (more electrons) than the positive pole.

Positive pole

Negative pole

Battery

Uninsulated switch

Light bulb

1 The battery will light the bulb only when the switch is closed. A conducting medium, such as an uninsulated wire, connects the two poles…

2 …and a flow, or current, of electrons streams through the bulb from the negative (–) to the positive (+) pole, lighting up the bulb.

Studying Electrical Activity in Animal Tissue

(A) Electrical stimulation

Current leaves the stimulator through a wire lead (red) that attaches to an electrode. From the uninsulated tip of the electrode, the current enters the tissue and stimulates it. The current flows back to the stimulator through a second lead (green) connected to a reference electrode.

1 A stimulating electrode delivers current (electrons) ranging from 2 to 10 millivolts, intensities sufficient to produce a response without damaging cells.

2 The reference electrode contacts a large surface area that spreads out the current and thus does not excite the tissue here.

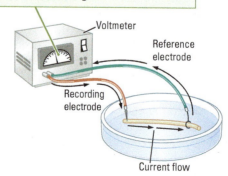

Stimulator

Reference electrode

Stimulating electrode

Uninsulated tip

Nerve

Current flow

(B) Electrical recording

The difference in voltage between the tip of a recording electrode and a reference electrode deflects a needle that indicates the current's voltage.

Voltmeter

Reference electrode

Recording electrode

Current flow

part of her neocortex. Bartholow stimulated her exposed brain tissue to examine the effects. In one of his observations, he wrote:

> Passed an insulated needle into the left posterior lobe so that the non-insulated portion rested entirely in the substance of the brain. The reference was placed in contact with the dura mater. When the circuit was closed, muscular contraction in the right upper and lower extremities ensued. Faint but visible contraction of the left eyelid, and dilation of the pupils, also ensued. Mary complained of a very strong and unpleasant feeling of tingling in both right extremities, especially in the right arm, which she seized with the opposite hand and rubbed vigorously. Notwithstanding the very evident pain from which she suffered, she smiled as if much amused. (Bartholow, 1874)

As you might imagine, Bartholow's report was not well received! The uproar after its publication forced him to leave Cincinnati. Despite his unethical experiment, Bartholow had demonstrated that the brain of a conscious person could be stimulated electrically to produce movement of the body.

Electrical Recording Studies

A less invasive line of evidence that information flow in the brain is partly electrical came from the results of electrical recording experiments. Richard Caton, a physician who lived a century ago, was the first to measure the brain's electrical currents with a sensitive **voltmeter**, a device that measures the flow and the strength of electrical voltage by recording the difference in electrical potential between two bodies. When he placed electrodes on a human subject's skull, Caton reported fluctuations in his voltmeter recordings. Today, this type of brain recording, the **electroencephalogram (EEG),** is a standard tool used for, among other things, monitoring sleep stages and detecting the excessive neural synchrony that characterizes electrographic seizures, as described in Clinical Focus 4-1, Epilepsy.

These pioneering studies provided evidence that neurons send electrical messages, but it would be incorrect to conclude that nerves and tracts carry the kind of electrical current that powers your phone. Hermann von Helmholtz, a nineteenth-century scientist, stimulated a nerve leading to a muscle and measured the time the muscle took to contract. The nerve conducted information at only 30 to 40 meters per second, whereas electricity flows along a wire about a million times faster.

Information flow in the nervous system, then, is much too slow to be a flow of electricity (based on electrons). To explain the electrical signals of a neuron, Julius Bernstein suggested in 1886 that neuronal chemistry (based on ions) produces an electrical charge. He also proposed that the charge could change and thus could act as a signal. Bernstein's idea was that successive waves of electrical change constitute the message conveyed by the neuron.

Moreover, it is not the ions themselves that travel along the axon but rather a *wave* of charge. To understand the difference, consider other kinds of waves. If you drop a stone into a pool of still water, the contact produces a wave that travels away from the site of impact, as shown in **Figure 4-2**. The water itself moves up and down and does not travel away from the impact site. Only the *change in pressure* moves, shifting the height of the water surface and producing the wave effect.

Similarly, when you speak, you induce pressure waves in air, and these waves carry your voice to a listener. If you flick a towel, a wave travels to the other end of the towel. Just as waves through the air send a spoken message, Bernstein's idea was that waves of chemical change travel along an axon to deliver a neuron's message.

Tools for Measuring a Neuron's Electrical Activity

Waves that carry messages in the nervous system are minute and are restricted to the surfaces of neurons. Still, we can produce these waves

voltmeter Device that measures the strength of electrical voltage by recording the difference in electrical potential between two points.

electroencephalogram (EEG) Graph of electrical activity from the brain, which is mainly composed of graded potentials from many neurons.

By the 1960s, the scientific community had established ethical standards for research on human and nonhuman subjects (see Section 7-7). Today, low-intensity and non-damaging brain stimulation is standard in many neurosurgical procedures (see Section 16-3).

Details on these EEG applications appear in Sections 7-2, 13-3, and 16-3.

FIGURE 4-2 **Wave Effect** Waves formed by dropping stones into still water do not entail the water's forward movement but rather pressure differences that change the height of the water surface.

Franklin Kappa/Getty Images

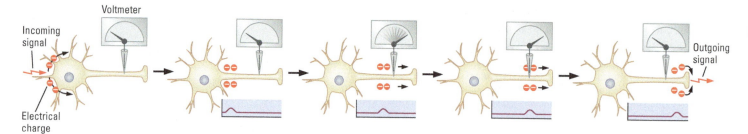

Voltmeter

Incoming signal

Electrical charge

Outgoing signal

FIGURE 4-3 **Wave of Information** Neurons can convey information as a wave, induced by stimulation on the cell body, traveling down the axon to its terminal. A voltmeter detects the wave's passage

using conventional electrical stimulation and measure them using electrical recording techniques to determine how they are produced. When a single axon is stimulated, it produces a wave of excitation. If an electrode connected to a voltmeter is placed on a single axon, as illustrated in **Figure 4-3**, the electrode can detect a change in electrical charge on that axon's membrane as the wave passes.

As simple as this process may seem, recording a wave and determining how it is produced requires a neuron large enough to record, a recording device sensitive enough to detect a tiny electrical impulse, and an electrode small enough to be placed on the surface of a single neuron. The fortuitous discovery of the giant axon of the squid, the invention of the oscilloscope, and the development of microelectrodes met all these requirements.

Giant Axon of the Squid

The neurons of most animals, including humans, are tiny, on the order of 1 to 20 micrometers (µm) in diameter—too small to be seen by the naked eye. The zoologist J. Z. Young, when dissecting the North Atlantic squid *Loligo vulgaris*, noticed that it has giant axons, as large as a millimeter (1000 µm, or about 1/25 inch) in diameter. **Figure 4-4** illustrates *Loligo* and the giant axons leading to its body wall, or mantle, which contracts to propel the squid through the water.

1 micrometer (also called a micron) (µm) = one-millionth of a meter, or one-thousandth of a millimeter (mm).

Measuring only about 1 foot long, *Loligo* is not a giant squid. But its axons are giant, as axons go. Each is formed by the fusion of many smaller axons. Because larger axons send messages faster than smaller axons do, these giant axons allow the squid to jet-propel away from predators.

In 1936, Young suggested to Alan Hodgkin and Andrew Huxley, neuroscientists at Cambridge University in England, that *Loligo*'s axons were large enough to be used for electrical recording studies. They dissected a giant axon out of the squid and kept it

(A)

age fotostock/Alamy Stock Photo

(B)

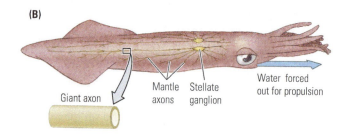

Giant axon

Mantle axons

Stellate ganglion

Water forced out for propulsion

FIGURE 4-4 **Laboratory Specimen (A)** The North Atlantic squid propels itself both with fins and by contracting its mantle to force water out for propulsion. **(B)** The stellate ganglion projects giant axons to contract the squid's mantle.

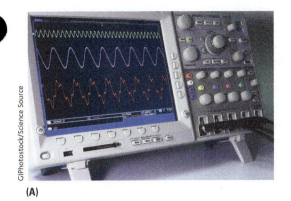

(A)

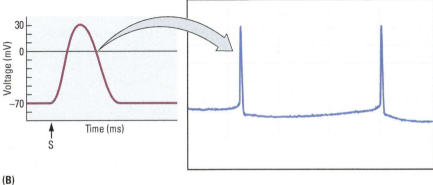

(B)

alive and functioning in a bath of salty liquid that approximated the squid's body fluids. In this way, Hodgkin and Huxley (1939) determined the neuron's ionically based electrical activity. In 1963, they received the Nobel Prize for their accomplishment.

Oscilloscope

Hodgkin and Huxley's experiments were made possible by the invention of the **oscilloscope**, a voltmeter with a screen sensitive enough to display the minuscule electrical signals emanating from a nerve or neuron over time (**Figure 4-5A**). As graphed in Figure 4-5B, the units used when recording the electrical charge from a nerve or neuron are millivolts (mV; 1 mV is one-thousandth of a volt) and milliseconds (ms; 1 ms is one-thousandth of a second). Computers interfaced with recording equipment have largely replaced oscilloscopes.

Microelectrodes

The final device needed to measure a neuron's electrical activity is an electrode small enough to place on or in an axon—a **microelectrode**. A microelectrode can deliver electrical current to a single neuron as well as record from it. One way to create a microelectrode is to etch the tip of a piece of thin wire to a fine point about 1 mm in size and insulate the rest of the wire with a synthetic polymer, like plastic. The tip is placed on or in the neuron, as shown in the left-hand image in **Figure 4-6A**.

A microelectrode can also be made from a thin glass tube tapered to a very fine tip (Figure 4-6A, right image). The tip of a hollow glass microelectrode can be as small as 1 mm. When the glass tube is filled with salty water, a conducting medium through which electrical current can travel, it acts as an electrode. A wire in the salt solution connects the electrode to either a stimulating device or a recording device.

Microelectrodes can record from axons in many ways. The tip of a microelectrode placed on an axon provides an extracellular measure of the electrical current from a tiny part of the axon. The tip of one electrode can be placed on the surface of the axon, and the tip of a second electrode can be inserted into the axon. This technique can be used to measure voltage across the cell membrane.

A still more refined use of a glass microelectrode is to place its tip on the neuron's membrane and apply a little suction until the tip is sealed to a patch of the membrane, as shown in Figure 4-6B. This technique, analogous to placing the end of a soda straw against a piece of plastic wrap and

FIGURE 4-5 Oscilloscope Recording
(A) Basic wave shapes are displayed on a digital oscilloscope, a versatile electronic instrument used to visualize and measure electrical signals as they change. **(B)** On the graph of a trace produced by an oscilloscope, S stands for stimulation. The horizontal axis measures time, and the vertical axis measures voltage. By convention, the axon voltage is represented as negative, in millivolts (mV). On the right, one trace of two action potentials from an individual neuron as displayed on a digital oscilloscope screen.

oscilloscope Specialized device that serves as a sensitive voltmeter, registering changes in voltage over time.

microelectrode A microscopic insulated wire or a saltwater-filled glass tube whose uninsulated tip is used to stimulate or record from neurons.

(A)

To stimulation or recording device

Wire

Insulation

Uninsulated wire tip

Squid axon

Conducting fluid such as salt water

Glass

Open tip

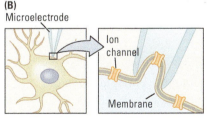

(B)
Microelectrode

Ion channel

Membrane

FIGURE 4-6 Uses of Microelectrodes
(A) A squid axon is larger than the tip of either a wire (left) or a glass (right) microelectrode. Both can be placed on an axon or in it. (Drawings are not to scale.) **(B)** A glass microelectrode can record from only a small area of an axon by suctioning the membrane up onto its tip.

diffusion Movement of ions from an area of higher concentration to an area of lower concentration through random motion.

concentration gradient Difference in the relative abundance of a substance among regions of a container; allows the substance to diffuse from an area of higher concentration to an area of lower concentration.

sucking, allows a recording to be made from only the small patch of membrane sealed to the microelectrode tip.

Using the giant axon of the squid, an oscilloscope, and microelectrodes, Hodgkin and Huxley recorded the electrical voltage on an axon's membrane and learned that the *nerve impulse* is a change in the concentration of specific ions across the cell membrane. The basis of electrical activity in nerves is the movement of intracellular and extracellular ions, which carry positive and negative charges across the cell membrane. We discuss the role of electrical activity in cell functioning in the next section, but first, to understand Hodgkin and Huxley's results, you first need to understand the principles underlying the movement of ions.

How Ion Movement Produces Electrical Charges

The intracellular fluid within a neuron and the extracellular fluid surrounding it contain various ions, including Na^+ (sodium) and K^+ (potassium)—positively charged, as the plus signs indicate—and negatively charged Cl^- (chloride). These fluids also contain numerous protein molecules, most of which hold an overall negative charge (A^-). Positively charged ions are called *cations*, and negatively charged ions, including protein molecules, are called *anions*. Three factors influence the movement of anions and cations into and out of cells: diffusion, concentration gradient, and voltage gradient.

Because molecules move constantly, they tend to spread out from a point of high concentration. This spreading out is **diffusion**. Requiring no additional energy, diffusion results from the random motion of molecules as they move and bounce off one another to gradually disperse in a solution. Diffusion results in a dynamic equilibrium, with a relatively equal number of molecules everywhere in the solution.

Smoke, for example, gradually diffuses through the air in a room until every bit of air contains the same number of smoke molecules. Dye poured into water diffuses in the same way—from its point of contact to every part of the water in the container. Salts placed in water dissolve; their individual ions dissociate and become surrounded by water molecules. The ions and their associated water molecules then diffuse throughout the solution to equilibrium, at which point every part of the container has the same ion concentration.

Concentration gradient describes the relative abundance of a substance in a space. Ions are initially highly concentrated where they enter at the top of a beaker of water, as illustrated in **Figure 4-7**, compared to the bottom of the beaker. As time passes, concentration gradients flow down due to diffusion.

The Basics, on pages 88-89, covers ions. The Salty Water illustration shows how water molecules dissolve salt crystals.

FIGURE 4-7 **Moving to Equilibrium**

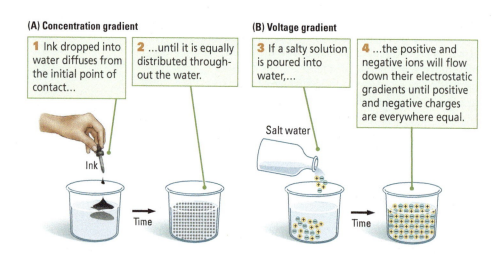

(A) Concentration gradient

1 Ink dropped into water diffuses from the initial point of contact...

2 ...until it is equally distributed throughout the water.

Ink

Time

(B) Voltage gradient

3 If a salty solution is poured into water,...

4 ...the positive and negative ions will flow down their electrostatic gradients until positive and negative charges are everywhere equal.

Salt water

Time

Because ions carry an electrical charge and because like charges repel one another, ion movement can be described by a concentration gradient, the difference in the number of ions between two regions, and a **voltage gradient**, the difference in charge between two regions. Ions move down a voltage gradient from an area of higher charge to an area of lower charge, just as they move down a concentration gradient from an area of higher concentration to an area of lower concentration.

Figure 4-7B illustrates this process. When salt is dissolved in water, the diffusion of its ions can be described either as movement down a concentration gradient (for sodium and chloride ions) or movement down a voltage gradient (for the positive and negative charges). In a container that allows unimpeded movement of ions, the positive and negative charges eventually balance.

A thought experiment will illustrate how a cell membrane influences ion movement. **Figure 4-8A** shows a container of water divided in half by a solid membrane that is impermeable to water and ions. If we place a few grains of table salt (NaCl) in the left half of the container, the salt dissolves. The ions diffuse down their concentration and voltage gradients until the water in the left compartment is in equilibrium.

In the left side of the container, there is no longer a gradient for either sodium or chloride ions because they occur everywhere with the same relative abundance. There are no gradients for these ions on the other side of the container either because the solid membrane prevents the ions from entering that side. But there are concentration and voltage gradients for both sodium and chloride ions *across* the membrane—that is, from the salty side to the freshwater side.

Transmembrane protein molecules embedded in a cell membrane form channels, some with gates, and pumps that allow specific kinds of ions to pass through the membrane. Returning to our thought experiment, we insert a few chloride channels into the membrane that divides the container of water, making the membrane semipermeable—that is, permeable to chloride but not to sodium, as illustrated at the left in Figure 4-8B. Chloride ions will now diffuse through the channels and cross the membrane by moving down their concentration gradient to the side of the container that previously had no chloride ions, shown in the middle of Figure 4-8B. The sodium ions, in contrast, cannot pass through the chloride channels and remain on one side of the cell membrane.

If the only factor affecting the movement of chloride ions were the chloride concentration gradient, the efflux (outflow) of chloride from the salty side to the freshwater side of the container would continue until chloride ions were in equilibrium on both sides. But this is not what happens. Remember that opposite charges attract, so the chloride ions, which carry a negative charge, are attracted to the positively charged sodium ions they left behind. Because they are pulled back toward the sodium ions, the chloride ions cannot diffuse completely. Consequently, the concentration of chloride ions remains somewhat higher in the left side of the container than in the right, as illustrated at the right in Figure 4-8B.

voltage gradient Difference in charge between two regions that allows a flow of current if the two regions are connected.

The cell membrane is an insulator impermeable to salty solutions: dissolved ions, surrounded by water molecules, do not pass through the membrane's hydrophobic tails (review Figure 3-11).

Even though dissolved sodium ions are smaller than chloride ions, they hold water molecules more strongly and thus act like they are bulkier and cannot pass through a narrow chloride channel.

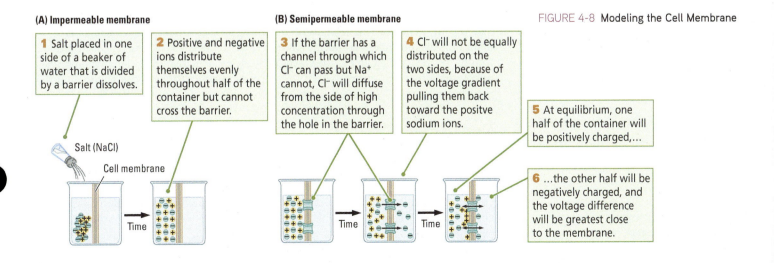

(A) Impermeable membrane

1 Salt placed in one side of a beaker of water that is divided by a barrier dissolves.

2 Positive and negative ions distribute themselves evenly throughout half of the container but cannot cross the barrier.

(B) Semipermeable membrane

3 If the barrier has a channel through which Cl⁻ can pass but Na⁺ cannot, Cl⁻ will diffuse from the side of high concentration through the hole in the barrier.

4 Cl⁻ will not be equally distributed on the two sides, because of the voltage gradient pulling them back toward the positive sodium ions.

5 At equilibrium, one half of the container will be positively charged,...

6 ...the other half will be negatively charged, and the voltage difference will be greatest close to the membrane.

Salt (NaCl)
Cell membrane
Time

FIGURE 4-8 Modeling the Cell Membrane

In other words, the efflux of chloride ions down the chloride concentration gradient is counteracted by the influx (inflow) of chloride ions down the chloride voltage gradient. At some point, an equilibrium is reached: the chloride concentration gradient on the right side of the beaker is balanced by the chloride voltage gradient on the left. In brief:

$$\text{concentration gradient} = \text{voltage gradient}$$

At this equilibrium, the differential concentration of the chloride ions on the two sides of the membrane produces a difference in charge—voltage. The left side of the container is more positively charged because some chloride ions have migrated, leaving a preponderance of positive (Na^+) charges. The right side of the container is more negatively charged because some chloride ions have entered that chamber, where none were before. The charge is highest on the surface of the semipermeable membrane, the area at which positive and negative ions accumulate. Much the same process happens at the semipermeable membranes of real cells.

4-1 Review

Before you continue, check your understanding. Answers to Self-Test appear at the back of the book.

1. Although he was incorrect, _____ was the first to seriously attempt to explain how information travels through the nervous system.

2. Experimental results obtained over hundreds of years from electrical _____ and more recently from electrical _____ implicated electrical activity in the nervous system's flow of information.

3. By the mid-twentieth century, scientists had solved three technical problems in measuring the changes in electrical charge that travel like a wave along an axon's membrane: _____, _____, and _____.

4. The electrical activity of neuronal axons entails the diffusion of ions. Ions may move down a(n) _____ and down a(n) _____.

5. In what three ways does the semipermeable cell membrane affect the movement of ions in the nervous system?

For additional study tools, visit 📖 **LaunchPad** at launchpadworks.com

---

4-2

Electrical Activity at a Membrane

Most biological membranes are semipermeable because they have ion channels embedded within them; we will refer to them simply as membranes. Electrical activity in neurons is the movement of specific ions through channels *across* neuronal membranes. It is this process which allows the waves of electrical activity moving *along* membranes to convey information throughout the nervous system. So how are changes in the movement of ions across neuronal membranes achieved?

Resting Potential

Figure 4-9 shows how the voltage difference is recorded when one microelectrode is placed on the outer surface of an axon's membrane and another is placed on its inner surface. In the absence of stimulation, the difference is about 70 mV. Although the charge on the outside of the membrane is actually positive, by convention it is given a charge of zero. Therefore, the inside of the membrane at rest is −70 mV *relative to* the extracellular side.

Why zero? We are interested in the relative difference, not the actual charge.

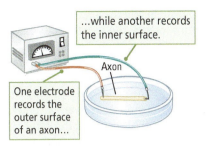

...while another records the inner surface.

Axon

One electrode records the outer surface of an axon...

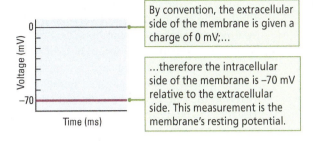

By convention, the extracellular side of the membrane is given a charge of 0 mV;...

...therefore the intracellular side of the membrane is –70 mV relative to the extracellular side. This measurement is the membrane's resting potential.

FIGURE 4-9 **Resting Potential** The electrical charge across a resting cell membrane stores potential energy.

If we were to continue to record for a long time, the charge across the unstimulated membrane would remain much the same. The charge can change, given certain changes in the membrane, but at rest the difference in charge on the inside and outside of the membrane produces an electrical *potential*—the ability to use its stored power, analogous to a charged battery. The charge is thus a store of potential energy called the membrane's **resting potential**.

We might use the term *potential* in the same way to talk about the financial potential of someone who has money in the bank; the person can spend the money at some future time. The resting potential, then, is a store of energy that can be used later. Most of your body's cells have a resting potential, but it is not identical on every axon. Resting potentials vary from −40 to −90 mV, depending on neuronal type and animal species.

Four charged particles take part in producing the resting potential: ions of sodium (Na⁺), potassium (K⁺), chloride (Cl⁻), and large negatively charged protein molecules (A⁻). These are the cations and anions, respectively, defined in Section 4-1. As **Figure 4-10** shows, these charged particles are distributed unequally across the axon's membrane, with more protein anions and potassium ions in the intracellular fluid and more sodium and chloride ions in the extracellular fluid. How do the unequal concentrations arise, and how does each contribute to the resting potential?

Maintaining the Resting Potential

The cell membrane's channels, gates, and pumps maintain the resting potential. **Figure 4-11**, which shows the resting membrane close up, details how these three features contribute to the cell membrane's resting charge:

1. Because the membrane is relatively impermeable to large molecules, the negatively charged proteins (A⁻) remain inside the cell.

2. Ungated potassium and chloride channels allow potassium (K⁺) and chloride (Cl⁻) ions to pass more freely, but gates on sodium channels keep out positively charged sodium ions (Na⁺).

3. Na⁺–K⁺ pumps extrude Na⁺ from the intracellular fluid and inject K⁺.

Inside the Cell

Large protein anions are manufactured inside cells. No membrane channels are large enough to allow these proteins to leave the cell, and their negative charge alone is sufficient to produce transmembrane voltage, or a resting potential. Because most cells in the body manufacture these large, negatively charged protein molecules, most cells have a charge across the cell membrane.

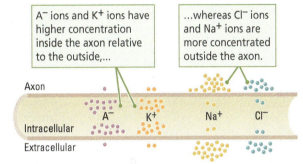

A⁻ ions and K⁺ ions have higher concentration inside the axon relative to the outside,...

...whereas Cl⁻ ions and Na⁺ ions are more concentrated outside the axon.

Axon

Intracellular

A⁻   K⁺   Na⁺   Cl⁻

Extracellular

FIGURE 4-10 **Ion Distribution Across the Resting Membrane** The number of ions distributed across the resting cell membrane is unequal. Protein anions are represented by the label A⁻.

Use this mnemonic to remember which ions are on which side: we put table salt—sodium chloride—on the outside of our food.

resting potential Electrical charge across the insulating cell membrane in the absence of stimulation; a store of potential energy produced by a greater negative charge on the intracellular side relative to the extracellular side.

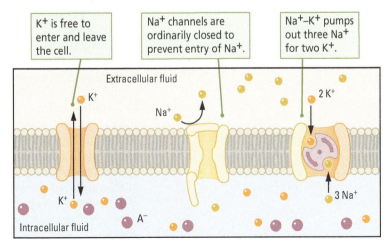

K⁺ is free to enter and leave the cell.

Na⁺ channels are ordinarily closed to prevent entry of Na⁺.

Na⁺–K⁺ pumps out three Na⁺ for two K⁺.

Extracellular fluid

K⁺   Na⁺   2 K⁺

K⁺   A⁻   3 Na⁺

Intracellular fluid

FIGURE 4-11 **Maintaining the Resting Potential** Channels, gates, and pumps in the cell membrane contribute to the transmembrane charge.

To balance the negative charge produced by large protein anions in the intracellular fluid, cells accumulate positively charged potassium ions to the extent that about 20 times as many potassium ions cluster inside the cell as outside it. Potassium ions cross the cell membrane through open potassium channels, as shown in Figure 4-11. With this high concentration of potassium ions inside the cell, however, the potassium concentration gradient across the membrane limits the number of potassium ions entering the cell. In other words, not all the potassium ions that could enter do enter. Because the internal concentration of potassium ions is much higher than the external potassium concentration, potassium ions are drawn out of the cell by the potassium concentration gradient.

A few residual potassium ions on the outside of the membrane are enough to contribute to the charge across the membrane. They add to the net negative charge on the intracellular side of the membrane relative to the extracellular side. You may be wondering whether you read the last sentence correctly. If there are 20 times as many potassium ions inside the cell as there are outside, why should the inside of the membrane have a negative charge? Should not all those potassium ions in the intracellular fluid give the inside of the cell a positive charge instead? No, because not quite enough potassium ions are able to enter the cell to balance the negative charge of the protein anions.

Think of it this way: if the number of potassium ions that could accumulate on the intracellular side of the membrane were unrestricted, the positively charged potassium ions inside would exactly match the negative charges on the intracellular protein anions. There would be no charge across the membrane at all. But the number of potassium ions that accumulate inside the cell is limited because when the intracellular K^+ concentration becomes higher than the extracellular concentration, further potassium ion influx is opposed by its concentration gradient.

Outside the Cell

The equilibrium of the potassium voltage and concentration gradients results in some potassium ions remaining outside the cell. It is necessary to have only a few positively charged potassium ions outside the cell to maintain a negative charge inside the cell. As a result, potassium ions contribute to the charge across the membrane.

Sodium (Na^+) and chloride (Cl^-) ions also take part in producing the resting potential. If positively charged sodium ions were free to move across the membrane, they would diffuse into the cell and eliminate the transmembrane charge produced by the unequal distribution of potassium ions inside and outside the cell. This diffusion does not happen because a gate on the sodium ion channels in the cell membrane is ordinarily closed (see Figure 4-11), blocking the entry of most sodium ions. Still, given enough time, sufficient sodium ions could leak into the cell to neutralize its membrane potential. The cell membrane has a different mechanism to prevent this neutralization.

When sodium ions do leak into the neuron, they are immediately escorted out again by the action of a *sodium–potassium pump,* a protein molecule embedded in the cell membrane. A membrane's many thousands of pumps continually exchange three intracellular sodium ions for two potassium ions, as shown in Figure 4-11. The potassium ions are free to leave the cell through open potassium channels, but closed sodium channels slow the reentry of the sodium ions. In this way, sodium ions are kept out to the extent that about 10 times as many sodium ions reside on the outside of the axon membrane as on its inside. The difference in sodium concentrations also contributes to the membrane's resting potential.

Now consider the chloride ions. Unlike sodium ions, chloride ions move in and out of the cell through open channels in the membrane. The equilibrium point, at which the chloride's concentration gradient equals its voltage gradient, is approximately the same as the membrane's resting potential, so chloride ions ordinarily contribute little to the resting potential. At this equilibrium point, there are about 12 times as many chloride ions outside the cell as inside it.

The cell membrane's semipermeability and the actions of its channels, gates, and pumps thus produce voltage across the cell membrane: its resting potential (**Figure 4-12**).

Graded Potentials

The resting potential provides an energy store that can be used somewhat like the water in a dam: small amounts can be released by opening gates for irrigation or to generate electricity. If the concentration of any of the ions across the unstimulated cell membrane changes, the membrane voltage changes. These **graded potentials** are small voltage fluctuations across the cell membrane.

Stimulating a membrane electrically through a microelectrode mimics the way the membrane's voltage changes to produce a graded potential in the living cell. If the voltage applied to the inside of the membrane is negative, the membrane potential increases in negative charge by a few millivolts. As illustrated in **Figure 4-13A**, it may change from a resting potential of −70 mV to a slightly greater potential of −73 mV.

This change is a **hyperpolarization** because the charge (polarity) of the membrane increases. Conversely, if positive voltage is applied inside the membrane, its potential decreases by a few millivolts. As illustrated in Figure 4-13B, it may change from, say, a resting potential of −70 mV to a slightly lower potential of −65 mV. This change is a **depolarization** because the membrane charge decreases. Graded potentials usually last only a few milliseconds.

Unequal distribution of different ions causes the inside of the axon to be relatively negatively charged.

FIGURE 4-12 **Resting Transmembrane Charge**

graded potential Small voltage fluctuation across the cell membrane.

hyperpolarization Increase in electrical charge across a membrane, usually due to the inward flow of chloride ions or the outward flow of potassium ions.

depolarization Decrease in electrical charge across a membrane, usually due to the inward flow of sodium ions.

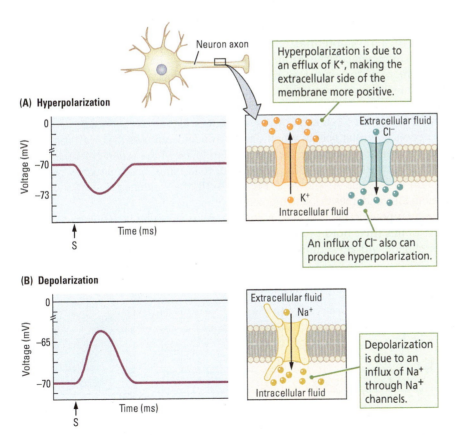

Neuron axon

Hyperpolarization is due to an efflux of K⁺, making the extracellular side of the membrane more positive.

(A) Hyperpolarization

Voltage (mV)

0

−70

−73

Time (ms)

S

Extracellular fluid

Cl⁻

K⁺

Intracellular fluid

An influx of Cl⁻ also can produce hyperpolarization.

(B) Depolarization

Voltage (mV)

0

−65

−70

Time (ms)

S

Extracellular fluid

Na⁺

Intracellular fluid

Depolarization is due to an influx of Na⁺ through Na⁺ channels.

FIGURE 4-13 **Graded Potentials (A)** Stimulation (S) that increases relative membrane voltage produces a hyperpolarizing graded potential. **(B)** Stimulation that decreases relative membrane voltage produces a depolarizing graded potential.

Puffer Fish

Table 6-2 lists a variety of neurotoxins and their sources and summarizes some of their effects.

Hyperpolarization and depolarization typically take place on the soma (cell body) membrane and on neuronal dendrites. These areas contain gated channels that can open and close, thereby changing the membrane potential, as illustrated in Figure 4-13. Three channels—for potassium, chloride, and sodium ions—underlie graded potentials:

1. *Potassium channels.* For the membrane to become hyperpolarized, its extracellular side must become more positive, which can be accomplished with an outward movement, or efflux, of potassium ions. But if potassium channels are ordinarily open, how can the efflux of potassium ions increase? Apparently, even though potassium channels are open, some resistance to the outward flow of potassium ions remains. Reducing this resistance enables hyperpolarization.

2. *Chloride channels.* The membrane can also become hyperpolarized if an influx of chloride ions occurs. Even though chloride ions can pass through the membrane, more ions remain on the outside than on the inside, so a decreased resistance to Cl⁻ flow can result in brief increases of Cl⁻ inside the cell.

3. *Sodium channels.* Depolarization can be produced if normally closed sodium channel gates open to allow an influx of sodium ions.

Evidence that potassium channels have a role in hyperpolarization comes from the fact that the chemical tetraethylammonium (TEA), which blocks potassium channels, also blocks hyperpolarization. The involvement of sodium channels in depolarization is indicated by the fact that the chemical tetrodotoxin (TTX), which blocks sodium channels, also blocks depolarization. The puffer fish, considered a delicacy in some countries, especially Japan, secretes TTX—a potentially deadly poison—to fend off would-be predators. Skill is required to prepare this fish for human consumption. It can be lethal to the guests of careless cooks because its toxin impedes the electrical activity of neurons.

Action Potential

Electrical stimulation of the cell membrane at resting potential produces local graded potentials. An **action potential,** on the other hand, is a brief but very large reversal in an axon membrane's polarity (**Figure 4-14A**) that lasts about 1 ms. The voltage across the membrane suddenly reverses, making the intracellular side positive relative to the extracellular side, then abruptly reverses again to restore the resting potential. Because the action potential is brief, many action potentials can occur within a second, as illustrated in Figures 4-14B and C, where the time scales are compressed.

An action potential occurs when a large concentration of first Na⁺ and then K⁺ crosses the membrane rapidly. The depolarizing phase of the action potential is due to Na⁺ influx, and the hyperpolarizing phase is due to K⁺ efflux. Sodium rushes in and then potassium rushes out. As shown in **Figure 4-15**, the *combined* flow of sodium and potassium ions underlies the action potential.

An action potential is triggered when the cell membrane is depolarized to about –50 mV. At this **threshold potential,** the membrane charge undergoes a remarkable further change with no additional stimulation. The relative voltage of the membrane

action potential Large, brief reversal in the polarity of an axon membrane

threshold potential Voltage on a neural membrane at which an action potential is triggered by the opening of sodium and potassium voltage-activated channels; about –50 mV relative to extracellular surround. Also called *threshold limit*.

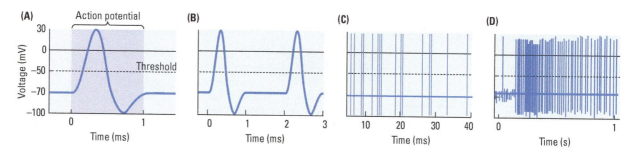

FIGURE 4-14 **Measuring Action Potentials (A)** Phases of a single action potential. The time scales on the horizontal axes are compressed to chart **(B)** each action potential as a discrete event, **(C)** the ability of a membrane to produce many action potentials in a short time, **(D)** and the series of action potentials over the course of 1 second (1000 ms).

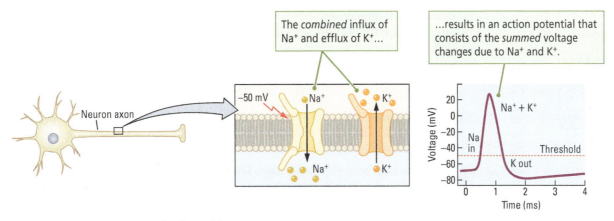

FIGURE 4-15 **Triggering an Action Potential**

drops to zero and continues to depolarize until the charge on the inside of the membrane is as great as +30 mV—a total voltage change of 100 mV. Then the membrane potential reverses again, becoming slightly hyperpolarized—a reversal of a little more than 100 mV. After this second reversal, the membrane slowly returns to its resting potential at –70 mV.

The action potential normally consists of the summed current changes caused first by the inflow of sodium and then by the outflow of potassium on an axon. Experimental results reveal that if an axon membrane is stimulated electrically while the solution surrounding the axon contains the chemical TEA (to block potassium channels), the result is a smaller-than-normal ion flow due entirely to an Na^+ influx. Similarly, if an axon's membrane is stimulated electrically while the solution surrounding the axon contains TTX (to block sodium channels), a slightly different ion flow due entirely to the efflux of K^+ is recorded. **Figure 4-16** illustrates these experimental results, in which the graphs represent *ion flow* rather than voltage change.

Role of Voltage-Activated Ion Channels

What cellular mechanisms underlie the movement of sodium and potassium ions to produce an action potential? The answer is the behavior of a class of gated sodium

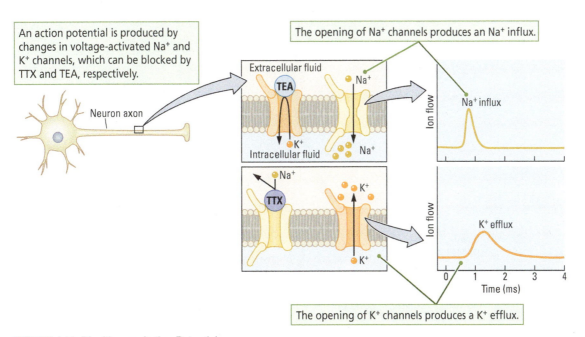

FIGURE 4-16 **Blocking an Action Potential**

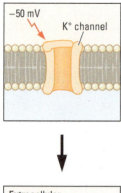

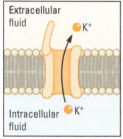

FIGURE 4-17 **Voltage-Activated Potassium Channel**

Exceptions do exist: some CNS neurons discharge during the repolarizing phase.

voltage-activated channel Gated protein channel that opens or closes only at specific membrane voltages.

absolutely refractory The state of an axon in the repolarizing period, during which a new action potential cannot be elicited (with some exceptions) because gate 2 of sodium channels, which are not voltage activated, are closed.

relatively refractory The state of an axon in the later phase of an action potential, during which higher-intensity electrical current is required to produce another action potential; a phase during which potassium channels are still open.

and potassium channels sensitive to the membrane's voltage (**Figure 4-17**). These **voltage-activated channels** are closed when an axon's membrane is at its resting potential: ions cannot pass through them. When the membrane reaches threshold voltage, the configuration of the voltage-activated channels alters: they open briefly, enabling ions to pass through, then close again to restrict ion flow. The sequence of actions is as follows:

1. Both sodium and potassium voltage-activated channels are attuned to the threshold voltage of about –50 mV. If the cell membrane changes to reach this voltage, both types of channels open to allow ion flow across the membrane.

2. The voltage-activated sodium channels respond more quickly than the potassium channels. As a result, the voltage change due to Na⁺ influx takes place slightly before the voltage change due to K⁺ efflux can begin.

3. Sodium channels have two gates. Once the membrane depolarizes to about +30 mV, one of the gates closes. Thus, Na⁺ influx begins quickly and ends quickly.

4. The potassium channels open more slowly than the sodium channels, and they remain open longer. Thus, the efflux of K⁺ reverses the depolarization produced by Na⁺ influx and even hyperpolarizes the membrane.

Action Potentials and Refractory Periods

There is an upper limit to how frequently action potentials occur, and sodium and potassium channels are responsible for it. Stimulation of the axon membrane during the depolarizing phase of the action potential will not produce another action potential. Nor is the axon able to produce another action potential when it is repolarizing. During these times, the membrane is described as being **absolutely refractory**.

If, on the other hand, the axon membrane is stimulated during hyperpolarization, another action potential can be induced, but the second stimulation must be more intense than the first. During this phase, the membrane is **relatively refractory**.

Refractory periods result from the way gates of the voltage-activated sodium and potassium channels open and close. A sodium channel has two gates, and a potassium channel has one gate. **Figure 4-18** illustrates the position of these gates before,

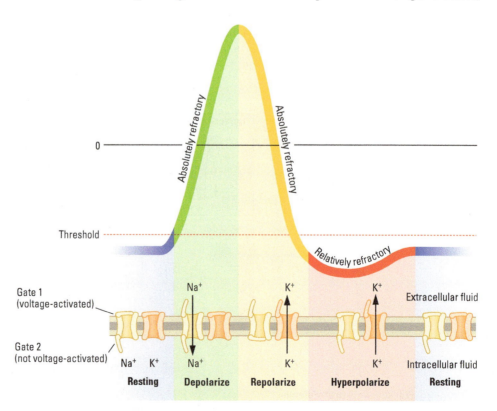

FIGURE 4-18 **Phases of an Action Potential** Initiated by changes in voltage-activated sodium and potassium channels, an action potential begins with a depolarization: gate 1 of the sodium channel opens, and then gate 2 closes. The slower-opening potassium channel gate contributes to repolarization and hyperpolarization until the resting membrane potential is restored.

during, and after the phases of the action potential. We describe changes first in the sodium channels and then in the potassium channels.

During the resting potential, gate 1 of the sodium channel depicted in Figure 4-18 is closed; only gate 2 is open. At the threshold level of stimulation, gate 1 also opens. Gate 2, however, closes very quickly after gate 1 opens. This sequence produces a brief period during which both sodium gates are open. When both gates are open and when gate 2 is closed, the membrane is absolutely refractory.

The opening of the potassium channels repolarizes and eventually hyperpolarizes the cell membrane. The potassium channels open and close more slowly than the sodium channels do. The hyperpolarization produced by a continuing efflux of potassium ions makes it more difficult to depolarize the membrane to the threshold that reopens the gates underlying an action potential. While the membrane is hyperpolarizing, it is relatively refractory.

The changes in polarity that take place during an action potential are analogous to the action of a lever-activated toilet. Pushing the lever slightly produces a slight water flow that stops when the lever is released. This activity is analogous to a graded potential. A harder lever press brings the toilet to threshold and initiates flushing, a response that is out of all proportion to the lever press. This activity is analogous to the action potential.

During the flush, the toilet is absolutely refractory: another flush cannot be induced at this time. During the refilling of the bowl, in contrast, the toilet is relatively refractory, meaning that flushing again is possible but harder. Only after the cycle is over and the toilet is once again at rest can a full flush be produced again.

Nerve Impulse

Suppose you place two recording electrodes at a distance from one another on an axon membrane and then electrically stimulate an area adjacent to one electrode. That electrode would immediately record an action potential. A similar recording would register on the second electrode in a flash. An action potential has arisen near this second electrode also, even though it is some distance from the original point of stimulation.

Is this second action potential simply an echo of the first that passes down the axon? No, it cannot be because the action potential's size and shape are exactly the same at the two electrodes. The second is not just a faint, degraded version of the first but is equal in magnitude. Somehow the full action potential has moved along the axon. This propagation of an action potential along an axon is called a **nerve impulse**.

Why does an action potential move? Remember that the total voltage change during an action potential is 100 mV, far beyond the 20-mV change needed to bring the membrane from its resting state of –70 mV to the action potential threshold level of –50 mV. Consequently, the voltage change on the part of the membrane where an action potential first occurs is large enough to bring adjacent parts of the membrane to a threshold of –50 mV.

When the membrane at an adjacent part of the axon reaches –50 mV, the voltage-activated channels at that location pop open to produce an action potential there as well. This second occurrence, in turn, induces a change in the membrane voltage still farther along the axon, and so on and on, down the axon's length. **Figure 4-19** illustrates this process. The nerve impulse occurs because each action potential propagates another action potential on an adjacent part of the axon membrane. The word *propagate* means "to give birth," and that is exactly what happens. Each successive action potential gives birth to another down the length of the axon.

Because they are propagated by gated ion channels acting on the membrane in their own vicinity, action potentials on a nerve or tract are the same magnitude wherever they occur. An action potential depends

nerve impulse Propagation of an action potential on the membrane of an axon.

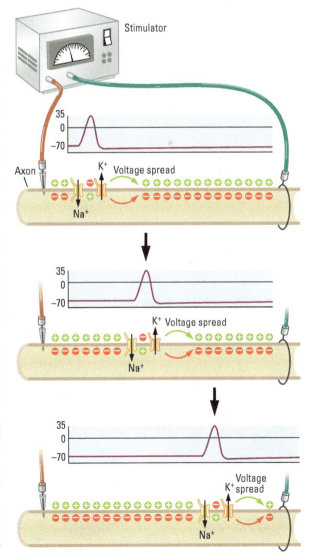

FIGURE 4-19 **Propagating an Action Potential** Voltage sufficient to open Na⁺ and K⁺ channels spreads to adjacent sites of the axon membrane, inducing voltage-activated gates to open. Here, voltage changes are shown on only one side of the membrane.

on energy expended where it occurs, and the same amount of energy is typically expended at every site along the membrane as a nerve impulse is propagated.

As a result, action potentials do not dissipate: an action potential is either generated completely or not generated at all. Action potentials are all-or-none events. As the nerve's impulse, or message, the action potential maintains a constant size and arrives unchanged to every terminal on the nerve that receives it.

Think of the voltage-activated channels along the axon as a series of dominoes. When one falls, it knocks over its neighbor, and so on down the line. There is no decrement in the size of the fall. The last domino travels exactly the same distance and falls just as hard as the first one did.

Essentially, the domino effect happens when voltage-activated channels open. The opening of one channel produces a voltage change that triggers its neighbor to open, just as one domino knocks over the next. The channel-opening response does not grow any weaker as it moves along the axon, and the last channel opens exactly like the first, just as the domino action stays constant to the end of the line.

The Domino Effect

Refractory Periods and Nerve Action

Refractory periods are determined by the position of the gates that mediate ion flow in the voltage-activated channels. This limits the frequency of action potentials to about one every 5 ms. The action potential's refractory phase thus has two practical uses for nerves that are conducting information.

First, the maximum rate at which action potentials can occur is about 200 per second (1 s, or 1000 ms/5 ms limit = 200 action potentials in 1 s). The sensitivity of voltage-activated channels, which varies among kinds of neurons, likewise affects firing frequency.

Second, although an action potential can travel in either direction on an axon, refractory periods prevent it from reversing direction and returning to its point of origin. Refractory periods thus produce a single, discrete impulse that travels away from the initial point of stimulation. When an action potential begins near the cell body, it usually travels down the axon to the terminals.

To return to our domino analogy, once a domino falls, setting it up again takes time. This is its refractory period. Because each domino falls as it knocks down its neighbor, the sequence cannot reverse until the domino is set upright again: the dominos can fall in only one direction. The same principle determines the action potential's direction.

Saltatory Conduction and the Myelin Sheath

Because the giant axons of squid are so large, they can transmit nerve impulses very quickly, much as a large-diameter pipe can rapidly deliver a lot of water. But large axons take up substantial space: a squid cannot accommodate many of them, or its body would be too bulky. For mammals, with our many axons innervating a substantial number of muscles, giant axons are out of the question. Our axons must be extremely slender because our complex movements require a great many of them.

Our largest axons, which run to and from our muscles, are only about 30 μm wide, so the speed with which they convey information should not be especially fast. And yet, like most other vertebrate species, we humans are hardly sluggish creatures. We process information and generate responses with impressive speed. How do we manage to do so if our axons are so thin? The vertebrate nervous system has evolved a solution that has nothing to do with axon size.

Glial cells play a role in speeding nerve impulses in the vertebrate nervous system. Schwann cells in the human peripheral nervous system and oligodendroglia in the central nervous system wrap around some axons, forming the myelin sheath that insulates it (**Figure 4-20**). Action potentials cannot occur where myelin is wrapped around an axon. For one thing, the myelin is an insulating barrier to ionic current

FIGURE 4-20 **Myelination** An axon is insulated by **(A)** oligodendroglia in the CNS and **(B)** Schwann cells in the PNS. Each glial cell is separated by a gap, or node of Ranvier.

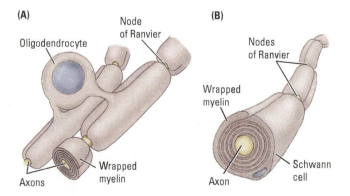

(A)
Oligodendrocyte
Node of Ranvier
Wrapped myelin
Axons

(B)
Nodes of Ranvier
Wrapped myelin
Schwann cell
Axon

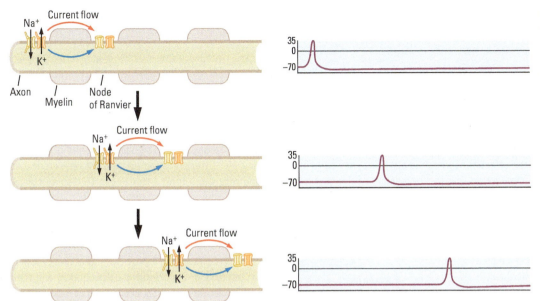

FIGURE 4-21 Saltatory
Conduction Myelinated stretches
of axons are interrupted by nodes
of Ranvier, rich in voltage-activated
channels. In saltatory conduction, the
action potential jumps rapidly from
node to node.

flow. For another, axonal regions that lie under myelin have few channels through which ions can flow, and ion channels are essential to generating an action potential.

But axons are not totally encased in myelin. Unmyelinated gaps between successive glial cell wrappings are richly endowed with voltage-activated channels. These tiny gaps in the myelin sheath, the **nodes of Ranvier**, are sufficiently close to one another that an action potential at one node can open voltage-activated gates at an adjacent node. In this way, a relatively slow action potential jumps quickly from node to node, as shown in **Figure 4-21**. This flow of energy is called **saltatory conduction** (from the Latin verb *saltare*, meaning "to leap").

Myelin has two important consequences for propagating action potentials. First, propagation becomes energetically cheaper, since action potentials regenerate only at the nodes of Ranvier, not along the axon's entire length. Action potential conduction in unmyelinated axons, by contrast, has a significant metabolic energy cost (Crotty et al., 2006). The second consequence is that myelin improves the action potential's conduction speed.

Jumping from node to node speeds the rate at which an action potential can travel along an axon because the current flowing within the axon beneath the myelin sheath travels very fast. While the current moves speedily, the voltage drops quickly over distance. But the nodes of Ranvier are spaced ideally to ensure sufficient voltage at the next node to supersede the threshold potential and thus regenerate the action potential. On larger, myelinated mammalian axons, nerve impulses can travel at a rate as high as 120 meters per second. On smaller, uninsulated axons, they travel only about 30 meters per second.

Spectators at sporting events sometimes initiate a wave that travels around a stadium. Just as one person rises, the next person begins to rise, producing the wave effect. This human wave is like conduction along an unmyelinated axon. Now think of how much faster the wave would complete its circuit around the field if only spectators in the corners rose to produce it. This is analogous to a nerve impulse that travels by jumping from one node of Ranvier to the next. The quick reactions that humans and other mammals are capable of are due in part to this saltatory conduction in their nervous system.

Neurons that send messages over long distances quickly, including sensory and motor neurons, are heavily myelinated. If myelin is damaged, a neuron may be unable to send any messages over its axons. In **multiple sclerosis (MS)**, the myelin formed by oligodendroglia is damaged, which disrupts the functioning of neurons whose axons it encases. Clinical Focus 4-2, Multiple Sclerosis on page 126, describes the course of the disease.

To review glial cell types, appearance, and functions, see Table 3-1.

node of Ranvier The part of an axon that is not covered by myelin.

saltatory conduction Fast propagation of an action potential at successive nodes of Ranvier; *saltatory* means "leaping."

multiple sclerosis (MS) Nervous system disorder resulting from the loss of myelin around axons in the CNS.

CLINICAL FOCUS 4-2

Multiple Sclerosis

One day, J. O., who had just finished university requirements to begin work as an accountant, noticed a slight cloudiness in her right eye. It did not go away when she wiped her eye. Rather, the area grew over the next few days. Her optometrist suggested that she see a neurologist, who diagnosed optic neuritis, an indication that can be a flag for multiple sclerosis (MS).

MS results from a loss of myelin produced by oligodendroglia cells in the CNS (see illustration). It disrupts the affected neurons' ability to propagate action potentials via saltatory conduction. This loss of myelin occurs in patches, and scarring frequently results in the affected areas.

Eventually, a hard scar, or *plaque*, forms at the site of myelin loss, which can be visualized with magnetic resonance imaging (MRI). (MS is called a *sclerosis* from the Greek word meaning "hardness.") Associated with the loss of myelin is impairment of neuron function, which causes the characteristic MS symptoms sensory loss and difficulty in moving.

Fatigue, pain, and depression are commonly associated with MS. Bladder dysfunction, constipation, and sexual dysfunction all complicate it. MS, about twice as common in women as in men, greatly affects a person's emotional, social, and vocational functioning.

Multiple sclerosis is the most common of nearly 80 **autoimmune diseases,** conditions in which the immune system makes antibodies to a person's own body (Rezania et al., 2012). The FDA has approved 15 medications for modifying the course of multiple sclerosis, but it is doubtful that the disease can be fully arrested with current therapies (Reich et al., 2018).

J. O.'s eye cleared over the next few months, and she had no further symptoms until after the birth of her first child 3 years later, when she felt a tingling in her right hand. The tingling spread up her arm, until gradually she lost movement in the arm for 5 months. Then J. O.'s arm movement returned. But 5 years later, after her second child was born, she felt a tin-

gling in her left big toe that spread along the sole of her foot and then up her leg, eventually leading again to loss of movement. J. O. received corticosteroid treatment, which helped, but the condition rebounded when she stopped treatment. Then it subsided and eventually disappeared.

Since then, J. O. has had no major outbreaks of motor impairment, but she reports enormous fatigue, takes long naps daily, and is ready for bed early in the evening. Her sister and a female cousin have experienced similar symptoms, and recently a third sister began to display similar symptoms in middle age, as has J.O.'s daughter, who is in her mid-20s. Furthermore, one of J. O.'s grandmothers had been confined to a wheelchair, but the source of her problem was never determined.

MS is difficult to diagnose. Symptoms usually appear in adulthood; their onset is quite sudden, and their effects can be swift. Initial symptoms may be loss of sensation in the face, limbs, or body or loss of control over movements or loss of both sensation and control. Motor symptoms usually appear first in the hands or feet.

Early symptoms often go into remission and do not appear again for years. In some forms, however, MS progresses rapidly over just a few years until the person is bedridden.

MS is common in the northern-most and southern-most latitudes, so it may be related to a lack of vitamin D, which is produced by the action of sunlight on the skin. The disease may also be related to genetic susceptibility, as is likely in J. O.'s case. Many MS patients take vitamin D_3 and vitamin B_{12}. While MS is the most prevalent chronic inflammatory disease of the CNS, affecting more than 2 million people worldwide (Reich et al., 2018), the underlying cause for the inflammation and loss of myelin is still unknown. It has been suggested that multiple sclerosis may primarily be a degenerative disease that secondarily elicits an autoimmune response (Stys, 2013). Research aimed at solving this problem is important because the answer would likely influence therapeutic approaches.

Normal myelinated nerve fiber

Exposed fiber

Damaged myelin

Nerve affected by MS

4-2 Review

Before you continue, check your understanding. Answers to Self-Test appear at the back of the book.

1. The _____ results from the unequal distribution of _____ inside and outside the cell membrane.

2. Because it is _____ , the cell membrane prevents the efflux of large protein anions and pumps sodium ions out of the cell to maintain a slightly _____ charge in the intracellular fluid relative to the extracellular fluid.

3. For a graded potential to arise, a membrane must be stimulated to the point that the transmembrane charge increases slightly to cause a(n) _____ or decreases slightly to cause a(n) _____ .

4. The voltage change associated with a(n) _____ is sufficiently large to stimulate adjacent parts of the axon membrane to the threshold for propagating it along the length of an axon as a(n) _____ .

5. Briefly explain why nerve impulses travel faster on myelinated axons than on unmyelinated axons.

autoimmune diseases Illness resulting from an abnormal immune response by the body against substances and tissues normally present in the body.

For additional study tools, visit **LaunchPad** at launchpadworks.com

4-3

How Neurons Integrate Information

A neuron's extensive dendritic tree is covered with spines, and through them it can establish more than 50,000 connections from other neurons. A neuron's body, which sits between its dendritic tree and axon, can also receive multiple connections. Nerve impulses traveling from other neurons to each of these synaptic locations bombard the receiving neuron with excitatory and inhibitory inputs.

In the 1950s and 1960s, John C. Eccles (1965) and his students performed experiments that helped answer the question of how the neuron integrates such an enormous array of inputs into a nerve impulse. Rather than record from the giant axon of a squid, Eccles recorded from the cell bodies of large motor neurons in the vertebrate spinal cord. In doing so, he refined the electrical stimulating and recording techniques first developed for studying squid axons (see Section 4-1). Eccles received the Nobel Prize in Physiology or Medicine for his work.

Motor neurons, for example, receive input from multiple sources. A spinal cord motor neuron has an extensive dendritic tree with as many as 20 main branches that subdivide numerous times and are covered with dendritic spines. Input from the skin, joints, muscles, spinal cord, and brain make motor cells ideal for studying how a neuron responds to diverse inputs. Each motor neuron sends its axon directly to a muscle. The motor neuron is the final common pathway the nervous system uses to produce behavior.

Excitatory and Inhibitory Postsynaptic Potentials

To study motor neuron activity, Eccles inserted a microelectrode into a vertebrate's spinal cord until the tip was in or right beside a motor neuron's cell body. He then placed stimulating electrodes on sensory nerve fiber axons entering the spinal cord. By teasing apart the many incoming sensory fibers, he was able to stimulate one nerve fiber at a time.

Experiment 4-1 diagrams the experimental setup Eccles used. As shown at the left in the Procedures section, stimulating some incoming sensory fibers produced a depolarizing graded potential (reduced the charge) on the membrane of the motor neuron to which these fibers were connected. Eccles called these graded potentials **excitatory postsynaptic potentials (EPSPs)**. As graphed on the left side of the Results section, EPSPs reduce (depolarize) the charge on the membrane toward the threshold level and increase the likelihood that an action potential will result.

When Eccles stimulated other incoming sensory fibers, as graphed at the right of the Procedures section, he produced a hyperpolarizing graded potential (increased the charge) on the receiving motor neuron membrane. Eccles called these graded potentials **inhibitory postsynaptic potentials (IPSPs)**. As graphed at the right in the Results section, IPSPs increase the charge on the membrane away from the threshold level and decrease the likelihood that an action potential will result.

Both EPSPs and IPSPs last only a few milliseconds before they decay and the neuron's resting potential is restored. EPSPs are associated with the opening of sodium channels, which allows an influx of sodium ions. IPSPs are associated with the opening of potassium channels, which allows an efflux of potassium ions (or with the opening of chloride channels, which allows an influx of chloride ions).

Although the size of a graded potential is proportional to the intensity of stimulation, an action potential is not produced on the motor neuron's cell body membrane even when an EPSP is strongly excitatory. The reason is simple: the cell body membrane of most neurons does not contain voltage-activated channels. The stimulation must reach the **initial segment**, an area rich in voltage-gated channels, the area near or overlapping the axon hillock, where the action potential begins (Bender & Trussel, 2012).

Figure 2-30A diagrams the human spinal cord in cross section.

You can find several videos online that describe how the initial segment initiates an action potential.

excitatory postsynaptic potential (EPSP) Brief depolarization of a neuron membrane in response to stimulation, making the neuron more likely to produce an action potential.

inhibitory postsynaptic potential (IPSP) Brief hyperpolarization of a neuron membrane in response to stimulation, making the neuron less likely to produce an action potential.

initial segment Area near where the axon meets the cell body that is rich in voltage-gated channels, which generate the action potential.

····> **EXPERIMENT 4-1**

Question: How does stimulating a neuron influence its excitability?

Procedure

Using an oscilloscope, Eccles recorded from the cell body of a motor neuron while stimulating...

Oscilloscope

Stimulate

Stimulate

...an excitatory sensory pathway or...

...an inhibitory sensory pathway.

Excitatory pathway

Inhibitory pathway

Motor neuron

Results

EPSP

IPSP

Stimulating the excitatory pathway produced a membrane depolarization, or excitatory postsynaptic potential (EPSP).

Stimulating the inhibitory pathway produced a membrane hyperpolarization, or inhibitory postsynaptic potential (IPSP).

Voltage (mv)

Time (ms)

S

S

Conclusion: EPSPs increase the likelihood that an action potential will result. IPSPs decrease the likelihood that an action potential will result.

Summation of Inputs

A motor neuron's myriad dendritic spines can each contribute to membrane voltage, via either an EPSP or an IPSP. How do these incoming graded potentials interact at its membrane? What happens if two EPSPs occur in succession? Does it matter if the time between them increases or decreases? What happens when an EPSP and an IPSP arrive together?

Neurons typically receive both excitatory and inhibitory signals simultaneously and, on a moment-to-moment basis, sum up the information they get.

Temporal Summation

If one excitatory pulse is followed some time later by a second excitatory pulse, one EPSP is recorded and then, after a delay, a second identical EPSP is recorded, as shown at the top left in **Figure 4-22**. These two widely spaced EPSPs are independent and do not interact. If the delay between them is shortened so that the two occur in rapid succession, however, a single large EPSP is produced, as shown in the left-center panel of Figure 4-22.

Here, the two excitatory pulses at the same location are summed—added together to produce a larger depolarization of the membrane than either would induce alone. This relationship between two EPSPs occurring close together or even at the same time (bottom-left panel) is called **temporal summation**. The right side of Figure 4-22 illustrates that equivalent results are obtained with IPSPs. Therefore, temporal summation is a property of both EPSPs and IPSPs.

temporal summation Addition of one graded potential to another that occur close in time.

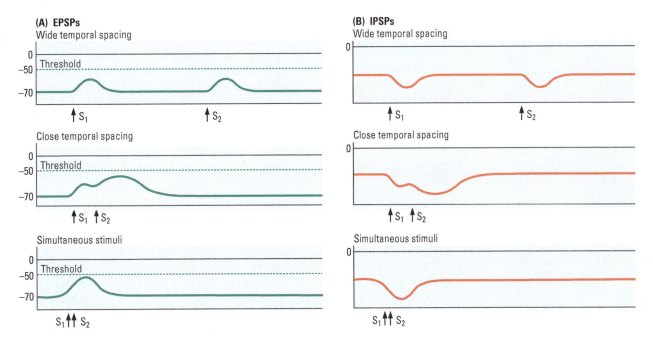

FIGURE 4-22 **Temporal Summation** Stimulation (S_1 and S_2) of two depolarizing pulses separated in time produce two EPSPs similar in size. Pulses close together in time partly sum. Simultaneous EPSPs sum as one large EPSP. Two hyperpolarizing pulses (S_1 and S_2) widely separated in time produce two IPSPs similar in size. Pulses coming fast partly sum. Simultaneous IPSPs sum as one large IPSP.

Spatial Summation

How does physical spacing affect inputs to the cell body membrane? By using two recording electrodes (R_1 and R_2), we can see the effects of spatial relations on the summation of inputs.

If two EPSPs are recorded at the same time but on widely separated parts of the membrane (**Figure 4-23A**), they do not influence one another. If two EPSPs occurring close together in time are also close together on the membrane, however, they sum to form a larger EPSP (Figure 4-23B). This **spatial summation** occurs when two separate inputs are very close to one another both on the cell membrane and in time. Similarly, two IPSPs produced at the same time sum if they occur at approximately the same place and time on the cell body membrane but not if they are widely separated.

spatial summation Addition of one graded potential to another that occur close in space.

Role of Ions in Summation

Summation is a property of both EPSPs and IPSPs in any combination. These interactions make sense when you consider that ion influx and efflux are being summed. The influx of sodium ions accompanying one EPSP is added to the influx of sodium ions accompanying a second EPSP if the two occur close together in time and space. If the two influxes are remote in time or in space or in both, no summation is possible.

The same is true regarding effluxes of potassium ions. When they occur close together in time and space, they sum; when they are far apart in either or both ways, there is no summation. The patterns are identical for an EPSP and an IPSP. The influx of sodium ions associated with the EPSP is added to the efflux of potassium ions associated with the IPSP, and the difference between them is recorded as long

FIGURE 4-23 **Spatial Summation** The process for IPSPs is equivalent to the process for EPSPs.

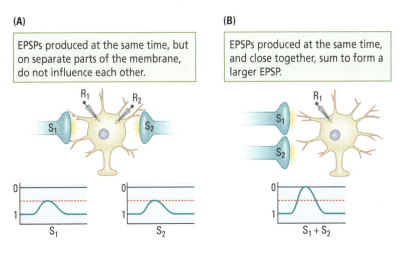

(A) EPSPs produced at the same time, but on separate parts of the membrane, do not influence each other.

(B) EPSPs produced at the same time, and close together, sum to form a larger EPSP.

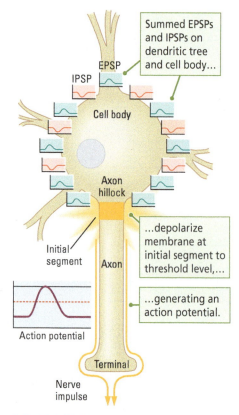

FIGURE 4-24 **Triggering an Action Potential** If the summated graded potentials—the EPSPs and IPSPs—on the dendritic tree and cell body of a neuron charge the membrane to threshold level at the initial segment, an action potential is initiated, and it travels down the axon membrane.

back propagation Reverse movement of an action potential into the soma and dendritic field of a neuron; postulated to play a role in plastic changes that underlie learning.

Principle 2: Neuroplasticity is the hallmark of nervous system functioning.

We explore the neuronal basis of learning in Sections 5-4 and 14-4.

Section 7-1 describes the promise of optogenetics for neuroscience research and for clinical applications.

as they are spatially and temporally close together. If, on the other hand, they are widely separated in time or in space or in both, they do not interact, and there is no summation.

A neuron with thousands of inputs responds no differently from one with only a few inputs; it sums all inputs that are close together in time and space. The cell body membrane, therefore, always indicates the summed influences of multiple temporal and spatial inputs. Therefore, a neuron can be said to analyze its inputs before deciding what to do. The ultimate decision is made at the initial segment, the region on the axon that initiates the action potential.

Voltage-Activated Channels and the Action Potential

Unlike the cell body membrane, the axon is rich in voltage-activated channels, beginning at the initial segment (**Figure 4-24**). These channels, like those on the squid axon, open at a particular membrane voltage. The actual threshold voltage varies with the type of neuron, but to keep things simple, we will stay with a threshold level of −50 mV.

To produce an action potential, the summed graded potentials—the IPSPs and EPSPs—on the cell body membrane must depolarize the membrane at the initial segment to −50 mV. If that threshold voltage is obtained only briefly, voltage-activated channels open, and just one or a few action potentials may occur. If the threshold level is maintained for a longer period, however, action potentials will follow one another in rapid succession, just as quickly as the gates on the voltage-activated channels can reset. Each action potential is then repeatedly propagated to produce a nerve impulse that travels from the initial segment down the length of the axon.

Many neurons have extensive dendritic trees, but dendrites and dendritic branches do not have many voltage-activated channels and ordinarily do not produce action potentials. And distant branches of dendrites may have less influence in producing action potentials initiated at the initial segment than do the more proximal branches of the dendrites. Consequently, inputs close to the initial segment are usually much more influential than those occurring some distance away, and those close to the initial segment are usually inhibitory, creating IPSPs. As in all governments, some inputs have more say than others (Höfflin et al., 2017).

The Versatile Neuron

Dendrites collect information as graded potentials (EPSPs and IPSPs), and the initial segment initiates discrete action potentials delivered to other target cells via the axon. Exceptions to this picture of how a neuron works do exist. For example, some cells in the developing hippocampus can produce additional action potentials, called *giant depolarizing potentials*, when the cell would ordinarily be refractory. It is thought that giant depolarizing potentials aid in developing the brain's neural circuitry (Khalilov et al., 2015).

Because the cell body membrane does not contain voltage-activated channels, a typical neuron does not initiate action potentials on its dendrites. In some neurons, however, voltage-activated channels on dendrites do enable action potentials. The reverse movement of an action potential from the initial segment into the dendritic field of a neuron is called **back propagation**. Back propagation, which signals to the dendritic field that the neuron is sending an action potential over its axon, may play a role in plastic changes in the neuron that underlie learning. For example, back propagation may make the dendritic field refractory to incoming inputs, set the dendritic field to an electrically neutral baseline, or reinforce signals coming in to certain dendrites (Schiess et al., 2016).

The neurons of some nonmammalian species have no dendritic branches. And some ion channels, rather than responding to voltage, respond to light by opening and allowing ions to pass. The many differences among neurons suggest that the nervous system capitalizes on structural and functional modifications to produce adaptive behavior in each species. In research to determine the neuron's specific functions, neuroscientists have incorporated into certain types of neurons ion channels that respond to light, as described in Research Focus 4-3, Optogenetics and Light-Sensitive Ion Channels.

RESEARCH FOCUS 4-3

Optogenetics and Light-Sensitive Ion Channels

Membrane channels that are responsive to light have been discovered in nonmammalian animal species. Using the transgenic technique of **optogenetics**, researchers have successfully introduced light-sensitive channels into a variety of species including worms, fruit flies, and mice.

Optogenetics combines genetics and light to control targeted cells in living tissue. Here, we examine how introducing different light-sensitive channels into a species changes the organism's behavior with one wavelength and reverses them with another wavelength.

One class of light-activated ion channels in the green alga *Chlamydomonas reinhardtii* is channelrhodopsin-2 (ChR2). The ChR2 light-activated channel absorbs blue light and, in doing so, opens briefly to allow the passage of Na^+ and K^+. The resulting depolarization excites the cell to generate action potentials.

Halorhodopsin (NpHR) is a light-driven ion pump, specific for chloride ions and found in phylogenetically ancient bacteria (archaea) known as halobacteria. When illuminated with green-yellow light, the NpHR pumps chloride anions into the cell, hyperpolarizing it and thereby inhibiting its activity.

The behavior of animals with genetically introduced light-sensitive channels has been controlled when their nervous system cells were illuminated with appropriate wavelengths of light. Using optogenetic techniques, light-sensitive channels can be incorporated into specific neural circuits so that light stimulation controls only a subset of neurons.

Stress has both behavioral and hormonal consequences for individuals, which can be transmitted socially to others. Using optogenetic techniques in mice, Sterley and colleagues (2018) *silenced* a specific collection of neurons in the hypothalamus during stress, thus preventing changes to the brain that would normally occur after stress. They then took it one step further and silenced the neurons in a partner mouse of a stressed individual, and the stress did not transfer to the partner. The group next performed the opposite experiment: in the absence of stress, they optogenetically *activated* the same hypothalamic neurons, causing the same changes in the brain as actual stress. They also observed that the partner mouse interacted with the light-activated-stressed individual in the same fashion as they would approach a naturally stressed mouse (Sterley et al., 2018).

The experimental power of optogenetics is unprecedented because we can learn the contribution of specific neuronal types to a behavior or in a disease state. But can optogenetics become a clinical tool to be used in people suffering from a CNS malady such as depression? One major hurdle is that specific viruses are used to transfer the light-activated channels to neurons in localized brain regions, and the usage of viruses in human populations is still fraught with difficulties. There are studies suggesting that impaired vision due to the loss of the light-sensitive cells of the eye could be restored with light-activated channels in surviving retinal neurons (Pan et al., 2015).

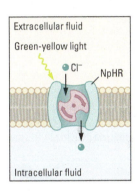

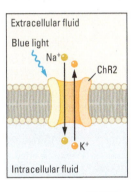

Courtesy of Toni-Lee Sterley and Jaideep Bains

Light-Sensitive Channels

4-3 Review

Before you continue, check your understanding. Answers to Self-Test appear at the back of the book.

1. Graded potentials that decrease the charge on the cell membrane, moving it toward the threshold level, are called _____ because they increase the likelihood that an action potential will occur. Graded potentials that increase the charge on the cell membrane, moving it away from the threshold level, are called _____ because they decrease the likelihood that an action potential will result.

2. EPSPs and IPSPs that occur close together in both _____ and _____ are summed. This is how a neuron _____ the information it receives from other neurons.

3. The membrane of the _____ does not contain voltage-activated ion channels, but if summed inputs excite the _____ to a threshold level, action potentials are triggered and then propagated as they travel along the cell's _____ as a nerve impulse.

4. Explain what happens during back propagation.

For additional study tools, visit **LaunchPad** at launchpadworks.com

optogenetics Transgenic technique that combines genetics and light to excite or inhibit targeted cells in living tissue.

stretch-activated channel Ion channel on a tactile sensory neuron that activates in response to stretching of the membrane, initiating a nerve impulse.

For detail on how sensory receptors transduce external energy into action potentials:
    Hearing, Section 10-1
    Sensation and perception, Section 9-1
    Smell and taste, Section 12-2
    Touch, pain, and balance, Section 11-4
    Vision, Section 9-2

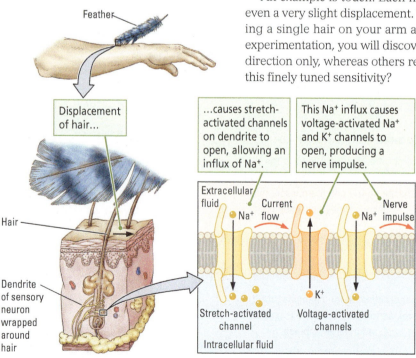

FIGURE 4-25 **Tactile Stimulation** A hair's touch receptor activated by a feather results in a nerve impulse heading to the brain.

4-4

Into the Nervous System and Back Out

The nervous system allows us to respond to afferent (incoming) sensory stimuli by detecting them and sending messages about them to the brain. The brain interprets the information, triggering efferent (outgoing) responses that contract muscles and produce behavior. Until now, we have been dealing only with the middle of this process—how neurons convey information to one another, integrate the information, and generate action potentials. Now we explore the beginning and end of the journey.

To fill in the missing pieces, we explain how a sensory stimulus initiates a nerve impulse and how a nerve impulse produces a muscular contraction. Once again, ion channels are vitally important, but, in muscles, the channels are different from those described so far.

How Sensory Stimuli Produce Action Potentials

We receive information about the world through bodily sensations (touch and balance), auditory sensations (hearing), visual sensations (sight), and chemical sensations (taste and olfaction). Each sensory modality has one or more separate functions. In addition to touch, for example, the body senses include pressure, joint sense, pain, temperature, and itch. Receptors for audition and balance are modified touch receptors. The visual system has receptors for light and for colors. And taste and olfactory senses respond to a plethora of chemical compounds.

Processing all these varied sensory inputs requires a remarkable array of sensory receptors. But in all our sensory systems, the neurons related to these diverse receptors have one thing in common: conduction of information begins at ion channels. Ion channels initiate the chain of events that produces a nerve impulse.

An example is touch. Each hair on the human body allows an individual to detect even a very slight displacement. You can demonstrate this sensitivity yourself by selecting a single hair on your arm and bending it. If you are patient and precise in your experimentation, you will discover that some hairs are sensitive to displacement in one direction only, whereas others respond to displacement in any direction. What enables this finely tuned sensitivity?

The base of each hair is wrapped in a dendrite of a touch neuron. When you bend a hair or otherwise mechanically displace it, the encircling dendrite is stretched (**Figure 4-25**).

The displacement opens **stretch-activated channels** in the dendrite's membrane. When open, these channels allow an influx of sodium ions sufficient to depolarize the dendrite to threshold. At threshold, the voltage-activated sodium and potassium channels initiate a nerve impulse that conveys touch information to your brain.

Other kinds of sensory receptors have similar mechanisms for *transducing* (transforming) the energy of a sensory stimulus into nervous system activity. When displaced, the *hair receptors* that provide information about hearing and balance likewise open stretch-activated channels. In the visual system, photons (light particles) strike opsin proteins in receptors within specialized cells in the eye. The resulting chemical change activates ion channels in *relay neuron* membranes. An odorous molecule in the air that lands on an olfactory receptor and fits itself into a specially shaped compartment opens chemical-activated ion channels. When tissue is damaged, injured cells release chemicals that activate channels on a pain nerve. The point here is that ion channels originate conduction of information in all our sensory systems.

How Nerve Impulses Produce Movement

What happens at the end of the neural journey? After sensory information has traveled to the brain and been interpreted, how does the brain generate output—muscular contractions—as a behavioral response? Behavior, after all, is movement, and for movement to take place, muscles must contract. Motor neurons in the spinal cord are responsible for activating muscles. Without them, movement becomes impossible and muscles atrophy, as described in Clinical Focus 4-4, ALS: Amyotrophic Lateral Sclerosis.

Motor neurons send nerve impulses to synapses on muscle cells. These synapses are instrumental in making the muscle contract. Each motor neuron axon contacts one

Principle 1: The nervous system produces movement in a perceptual world the brain constructs.

◎ **CLINICAL FOCUS 4-4**

ALS: Amyotrophic Lateral Sclerosis

In 1869, French physician Jean-Martin Charcot first described ALS, amyotrophic lateral sclerosis. *Amyotrophic* means "muscle weakness"; *lateral sclerosis* means "hardening of the lateral spinal cord."

In North America, ALS is also known as Lou Gehrig disease. A baseball legend who played for the New York Yankees from 1923 until 1939, Gehrig had set a host of individual records. He was an outstanding hitter, and his incredible durability earned him the nickname The Iron Horse.

Gehrig played on many World Series championship teams, but ALS sapped his strength, forcing him to retire from baseball at age 36. His condition deteriorated rapidly, and he died just 2 years later.

ALS is due primarily to the death of spinal motor neurons, but it can affect brain neurons as well in some instances. It strikes most commonly at age 50 to 75, although its onset can be as early as the teenage years. About 5000 new cases are reported in the United States each year, and roughly 10 percent of people with ALS have a family history of the disorder.

While death often occurs within 5 years of diagnosis, internationally renowned theoretical physicist and cosmologist Stephen Hawking was a notable exception. Diagnosed at age 21, Hawking had a rare early-onset and slowly progressing form of ALS. As a doctoral student at Oxford, he grew increasingly clumsy, and his speech was slightly slurred. In his late twenties, he began to use crutches. In his thirties, his speech deteriorated to the point that only his family and close friends could understand him. In his seventies, and confined to a wheelchair, Hawking, pictured at right, was still able to communicate by using a single cheek muscle attached to a speech-generating device.

ALS typically begins with general weakness, at first in the throat or upper chest and in the arms and legs. Gradually, walking becomes difficult and falling common. ALS does not usually affect any sensory systems, cognitive functions, bowel or bladder control, or even sexual function.

Even as his motor neurons continued to die, Stephen Hawking's mind-blowing advancements continued to enrich our understanding of the universe. Sadly, we lost Stephen Hawking in March 2018.

At present, no cure for ALS exists, although some newly developed drugs appear to slow its progression and offer some hope for future treatments. In 2014, the ALS Ice Bucket Challenge first appeared on YouTube to promote awareness of ALS and encourage donations to research. The Challenge went viral and has been revived every summer since.

Tom Dymond/REX/Shutterstock

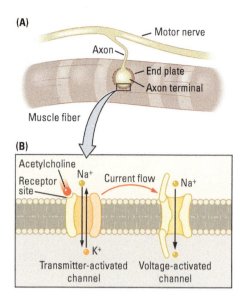

FIGURE 4-26 **Muscle Contraction (A)** When a motor neuron's axon collaterals contact a muscle fiber end plate, **(B)** acetylcholine attaches to receptor sites on the end plate's transmitter-activated channels, opening them. These large membrane channels allow simultaneous influx of Na^+ and efflux of K^+, generating current sufficient to activate voltage-activated channels, triggering action potentials, and causing the muscle to contract.

Sections 5-2 and 5-3 describe the varieties of chemical transmitters and how they function.

FIGURE 4-27 **Myasthenia Gravis** When this patient follows the direction to look up **(1)**, her eyelids quickly become fatigued and droop **(2, 3)**. After a few minutes of rest, her eyelids open normally **(4)**.

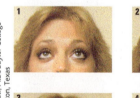

end plate On a muscle, the receptor–ion complex that is activated by the release of the neurotransmitter acetylcholine from the terminal of a motor neuron.

transmitter-activated channel Receptor complex that has both a receptor site for a chemical and a pore through which ions can flow.

or a few synapses with its target muscle (**Figure 4-26A**). The axon terminal contacts a specialized area of the muscle membrane called an **end plate**, where the axon terminal releases the chemical transmitter *acetylcholine*.

Acetylcholine does not enter the muscle but rather attaches to **transmitter-activated channels** on the end plate (Figure 4-26B). When these channels open in response, they allow a flow of Na^+ and K^+ across the muscle membrane sufficient to depolarize the muscle to the threshold for its action potential. Yes, to contract, muscles generate action potentials. At this threshold, adjacent voltage-activated channels open. They in turn produce an action potential on the muscle fiber, as they do in a neuron.

The transmitter-activated channels on muscle end plates are somewhat different from the channels on axons and dendrites. A single end plate channel is larger than two sodium and two potassium channels on a neuron combined. So when its transmitter-activated channels open, they allow both Na^+ influx and K^+ efflux through the same pore. Generating a sufficient depolarization on the end plate to activate neighboring voltage-activated channels on the muscle membrane requires the release of an appropriate amount of acetylcholine.

If the acetylcholine receptors on muscle end plates are blocked, acetylcholine released from the motor neuron cannot properly exert its depolarizing effect. This prevents muscular contraction in conditions such as the autoimmune disease *myasthenia gravis*. In affected individuals, the thymus, an immune system gland that normally produces antibodies that bind to foreign material like viruses, makes antibodies that bind to the acetylcholine receptors on muscles, causing weakness and fatigue (see **Figure 4-27**).

Unlike MS, another autoimmune disease, myasthenia gravis is usually well controlled with treatment, including drugs that suppress the immune system or inhibit acetylcholine breakdown, extending the time the transmitter can act, or by removal of the thymus gland (thymectomy).

The actions of membrane channels can explain a wide range of neural events. Some channels generate the transmembrane charge. Others mediate graded potentials. Still others trigger the action potential. Sensory stimuli activate channels on neurons to initiate a nerve impulse, and the nerve impulse eventually activates channels on motor neurons to produce muscle contractions.

These various channels and their different functions evolved over a long time as new species of animals and their behaviors evolved. We have not described all the different ion channels that neural membranes possess, but you will learn about some additional ones in subsequent chapters.

4-4 Review

Before you continue, check your understanding. Answers to Self-Test appear at the back of the book.

1. Across all sensory systems, the conduction of sensory information that occurs within the neuron begins at the _____.

2. A(n) _____ membrane contains a mechanism for transducing sensory energy into changes in ion channels. In turn, the channels allow ion flow to alter the membrane voltage to the point that _____ channels open, initiating a nerve impulse.

3. Sensory stimuli activate ion channels to initiate a nerve impulse that activates channels on _____ neurons, which in turn contract _____.

4. In myasthenia gravis, a(n) _____ disease, the thymus gland produces antibodies to _____ receptors on muscles, causing weakness and fatigue.

5. Why have so many kinds of ion channels evolved on cell membranes?

For additional study tools, visit 📖 **LaunchPad** at launchpadworks.com

Summary

4-1 Searching for Electrical Activity in the Nervous System

Electrical stimulation studies dating as far back as the eighteenth century show that stimulating a nerve with electrical current induces a muscle contraction. In more recent recording studies, the brain's electrical current, measured using an oscilloscope, shows that electrical activity in the nervous system is continuous.

In the twentieth century, researchers used giant axons of the squid to measure the electrical activity of a single neuron. Using microelectrodes that they could place on or in the cell, they recorded small, rapid electrical changes with an oscilloscope. Today, digital oscilloscopes and computers record these measurements.

A neuron's electrical activity is generated by ions flowing across the cell membrane. Ions flow down a concentration gradient (from an area of relatively high concentration to an area of lower concentration) as well as down a voltage gradient (from an area of relatively high voltage to an area of lower voltage). The opening, closing, and pumping of ion channels in neural cell membranes also affect ion distribution.

4-2 Electrical Activity at a Membrane

Unequal ion distribution on a cell membrane's two sides generates the neuron's resting potential. At rest, the intracellular membrane registers about −70 mV relative to the extracellular side. Negatively charged protein anions are too large to leave the neuron, and the cell membrane actively pumps out positively charged sodium ions. Unequal distributions of potassium cations and chloride anions contribute to the resting potential as well.

Graded potentials, which are short-lived small increases or decreases in transmembrane voltage, result when the neuron is stimulated. Voltage changes affect the membrane's ion channels and in turn change the cross-membrane ion distribution. An increase in transmembrane voltage causes hyperpolarization; a decrease causes depolarization.

An action potential is a brief but large change in axon membrane polarity triggered when the transmembrane voltage drops to a threshold level of about −50 mV. During an action potential, transmembrane voltage suddenly reverses—the intracellular side becomes positive relative to the extracellular side—and abruptly reverses again. Gradually, the resting potential is restored. These membrane changes result from

voltage-activated channels—sodium and potassium channels sensitive to the membrane's voltage.

When an action potential is triggered at the initial segment, it can propagate along the axon as a nerve impulse. Nerve impulses travel more rapidly on myelinated axons because of saltatory conduction: the action potentials leap rapidly between the nodes separating the glial cells that form the axon's myelin sheath.

4-3 How Neurons Integrate Information

Inputs to neurons from other cells can produce both excitatory postsynaptic potentials and inhibitory postsynaptic potentials. The membrane sums their voltages both temporally and spatially to integrate the incoming information. If the summed EPSPs and IPSPs move the membrane voltage at the initial segment to threshold, the axon generates an action potential.

The neuron is a versatile kind of cell. Some species' ion channels respond to light rather than to voltage changes, an attribute that genetic engineers are exploiting. Most of our neurons do not initiate action potentials on the cell body because the cell body membrane does not contain voltage-activated channels. But some voltage-activated channels on dendrites do enable action potentials. Back propagation, the reverse movement of an action potential from the initial segment into the dendritic field of a neuron, may play a role in plastic changes that underlie learning.

4-4 Into the Nervous System and Back Out

Sensory receptor cells convert sensory energy to graded potentials. These changes, in turn, alter transmembrane voltage to trigger an action potential and propagate a nerve impulse that transmits sensory information to relevant parts of the nervous system.

Ion channels come into play to activate muscles as well because the chemical transmitter acetylcholine, released at the axon terminal of a motor neuron, activates channels on the end plate of a muscle cell membrane. The subsequent ion flow depolarizes the muscle cell membrane to the threshold for its action potential. In turn, this depolarization opens voltage-activated channels, producing an action potential on the muscle fiber—hence the muscle contractions that enable movement. In myasthenia gravis, antibodies to the acetylcholine receptor prevent muscle depolarization, which is the basis of weakness and fatigue.

Key Terms

Visit 🎵 **LaunchPad** to access the e-Book, videos, 🎵 **LearningCurve** adaptive quizzing, flashcards, and more at launchpadworks.com

ANDRZEJ WOJCICKI/SCIENCE PHOTO LIBRARY/Getty Images

How Do Neurons Communicate and Adapt?

CHAPTER 5

The Basis of Neural Communication in a Heartbeat

Discoveries about how neurons communicate stem from experiments designed to study what controls an animal's heart rate. As happens with any animal, your heartbeat quickens if you are excited or exercising; if you are resting, it slows. Heart rate changes to match energy expenditure—that is, to meet the body's nutrient and oxygen needs.

Your heartbeat undergoes a dramatic change when you dive beneath water: it slows almost to stopping. This drastic slowing, called diving *bradycardia*, conserves the body's oxygen when you are not breathing. Bradycardia (*brady*, meaning "slow," and *cardia*, meaning "heart") is a useful survival strategy. This energy-conserving response under water is common to many animals. But what controls your heartbeat?

Otto Loewi, a great storyteller, recounted that his classic experiment, which earned him a Nobel Prize in 1936, came to him in a dream. As shown in the Procedure section of Experiment 5-1, Loewi first maintained a frog's heart in a mild saline bath, then electrically stimulated the vagus nerve—the cranial nerve that leads from the brain to the heart. At the same time, he channeled some of the fluid bath from the vessel containing the stimulated heart through a tube to another vessel in which a second heart was immersed but not electrically stimulated.

Loewi recorded both heart rates. His findings are represented in the Results section of Experiment 5-1. The electrical stimulation decreased the rate of the first heart, but more important, the second heartbeat also slowed. This result indicated that the fluid transferred from the first container to the second container carried instructions to slow down.

Where did the message come from originally? Loewi reasoned that a chemical released from the stimulated vagus nerve must have diffused into the fluid bath to influence the second heart. His experiment therefore demonstrated that the vagus nerve contains a chemical that tells the heart to slow its rate.

Loewi subsequently identified the messenger chemical. Later, he also identified a chemical that tells the heart to speed up. The heart adjusts its rate in response to at least two different messages: an excitatory message that says speed up and an inhibitory message that says slow down.

Chris Gomersall/Alamy

Puffins fish by diving underwater, propelling themselves by flapping their short, stubby wings as if flying. During these dives, their heart displays the diving bradycardia response, just as our heart does.

In the preceding chapter, we learned how neurons transmit information as electrical signals: first an action potential is generated and then that impulse flows down an axon to the synapse. In this chapter, first we explain how neurons communicate with one another using excitatory and inhibitory signals. Next, we describe how chemicals carried by one neuron signal receptors on receiving neurons to produce a response. We conclude the chapter by exploring the neural bases of *learning*—that is, how neural synapses adapt physically as a result of an organism's experience.

A Chemical Message

Otto Loewi's successful heartbeat experiment, discussed in Research Focus 5-1, The Basis of Neural Communication in a Heartbeat and diagrammed in **Experiment 5-1**, marked the beginning of research into how chemicals carry information from one neuron to another in the nervous system. Loewi was the first to isolate a chemical messenger. We now know that chemical as **acetylcholine (ACh)**, the same transmitter that activates skeletal muscles, as described in Section 4-4. Yet in Loewi's experiment, ACh acts to *inhibit* heartbeat, to slow it down. It turns out that ACh excites skeletal muscles in the somatic nervous system, causing them to contract, and may either excite or inhibit various internal organs in the autonomic system. How can the same chemical messenger do both? It turns out that the ion channel and its associated receptor, not the molecule itself, determine whether the messenger will be excitatory or inhibitory, which we explore in Section 5-2. And, yes, acetylcholine is the chemical messenger associated with the slowed heartbeat in diving bradycardia.

acetylcholine (ACh) First neurotransmitter discovered in the PNS and CNS; activates skeletal muscles in the SNS; either excites or inhibits internal organs in the ANS.

····> **EXPERIMENT 5-1**

Question: How does a neuron pass on a message?

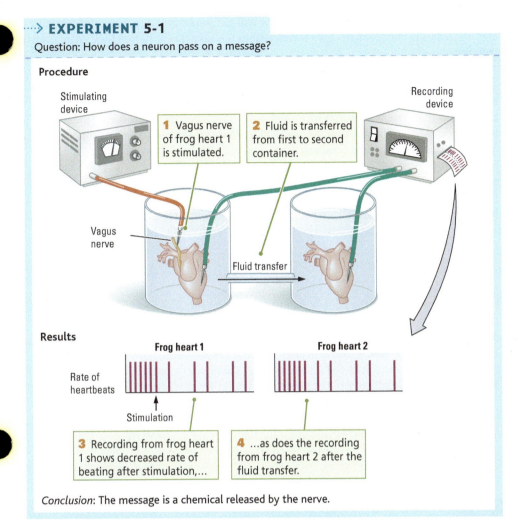

Procedure

Stimulating device

Recording device

1 Vagus nerve of frog heart 1 is stimulated.

2 Fluid is transferred from first to second container.

Vagus nerve

Fluid transfer

Results

Frog heart 1

Frog heart 2

Rate of heartbeats

Stimulation

3 Recording from frog heart 1 shows decreased rate of beating after stimulation,...

4 ...as does the recording from frog heart 2 after the fluid transfer.

Conclusion: The message is a chemical released by the nerve.

epinephrine (EP) Chemical messenger that acts as a neurotransmitter in the CNS and as a hormone to mobilize the body for fight or flight during times of stress; also known as *adrenaline*.

norepinephrine (NE) Neurotransmitter that accelerates heart rate in mammals; found in the brain and in the sympathetic division of the ANS; also known as *noradrenaline*.

neurotransmitter Chemical with an excitatory or inhibitory effect when released by a neuron onto a target.

Acetylcholine (ACh)

Epinephrine (EP)   Norepinephrine (NE)

FIGURE 5-1 **ACh, EP, and NE** Three-dimensional space-filling models contrast the molecular structure of ACh, which inhibits heartbeat, to the structures of EP and NE, which excite the heart in frogs and humans, respectively.

The vagus nerve influences the heart and other internal body processes; see Figure 2-29.

In further experiments modeled on his procedure in Experiment 5-1, Loewi stimulated another nerve to the heart, the accelerator nerve, and heart rate increased. The fluid that bathed the accelerated heart also speeded the beat of a second heart that was not electrically stimulated. Loewi identified the chemical that carries the message to speed up heart rate in frogs as **epinephrine** (**EP**; *epi-*, "above," and *nephron*, "kidney"), also known as *adrenaline*. Adrenaline (Latin) and epinephrine (Greek) are the same substance, produced by the adrenal glands located atop the kidneys. Adrenaline is the name more people know, in part because a drug company used it as a trade name, but epinephrine is common parlance in the science community.

Further experimentation eventually demonstrated that in mammals, the chemical that accelerates heart rate is **norepinephrine** (**NE**; also called *noradrenaline*), a chemical closely related to epinephrine (EP). The results of Loewi's complementary experiments showed that acetylcholine from the vagus nerve inhibits heartbeat, and epinephrine from the accelerator nerve excites it. ACh, EP, and NE molecules are structurally different from each other, as can be seen in **Figure 5-1**, which allows each of them to interact with a specific receptor.

Chemical messengers released by a neuron onto a target to cause an excitatory or inhibitory effect are **neurotransmitters**. Outside the central nervous system, many of the same chemicals, epinephrine among them, circulate in the bloodstream as *hormones*. Under control of the hypothalamus, the pituitary gland releases hormones into the bloodstream to excite or inhibit targets, such as the organs and glands in the autonomic and enteric nervous systems. In part because hormones travel throughout the body to distant targets, their actions are slower than those of CNS neurotransmitters prodded

The role of hormones in the regulation of behavior is explored further in Section 12-4. Section 6-5 explains how hormones influence the brain and behavior.

by the lightning-quick nerve impulse. But the real difference between neurotransmitters and hormones is the distances they travel, within the same body, before they encounter their receptors.

Loewi's discoveries led to the search for more neurotransmitters and their functions. The actual number of transmitters is an open question, with 100 posited as the maximum. The confirmed number is 60, with most of the work being done by 10. Whether a chemical is accepted as a neurotransmitter depends on the extent to which it meets certain criteria. As this chapter unfolds, you will learn those criteria, along with the names and functions of many neurotransmitters. You will also learn how groups of neurons form neurotransmitter systems throughout the brain to modulate, or temper, aspects of behavior. The three Clinical Focus boxes in this chapter tell the fascinating story of how one such neurotransmitter, dopamine, has yielded deep insight into brain function. When depleted in a particular brain area, this neurotransmitter is associated with a specific neurological disorder. The story begins with Clinical Focus 5-2, Parkinson Disease.

Structure of Synapses

Loewi's discovery about the chemical messengers that regulate heart rate was the first of two seminal findings that form the foundation for current understanding of how neurons communicate. The second discovery had to wait until the invention of the electron microscope nearly 30 years later, which allowed researchers to determine that neurotransmitters are packaged into vesicles at the end terminals of axons. When tissue is stained with a substance that reflects electrons, ultrastructural details emerge.

Chemical Synapses

Synaptic structure was first revealed in the 1950s, using electron microscopy. In the center of the micrograph in **Figure 5-2A**, the upper part of the synapse is the axon

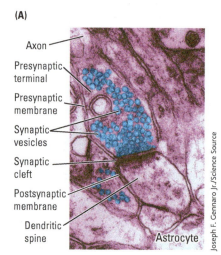

(A)

Axon
Presynaptic terminal
Presynaptic membrane
Synaptic vesicles
Synaptic cleft
Postsynaptic membrane
Dendritic spine

Astrocyte

Joseph F. Gennaro Jr./Science Source

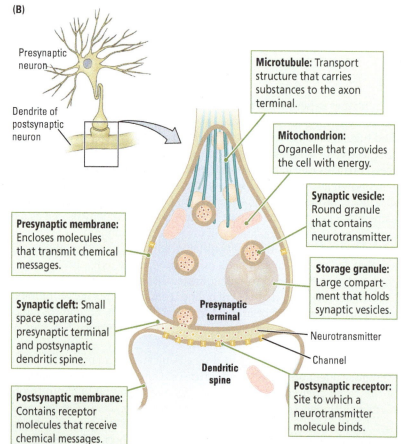

(B)

Presynaptic neuron

Dendrite of postsynaptic neuron

Microtubule: Transport structure that carries substances to the axon terminal.

Mitochondrion: Organelle that provides the cell with energy.

Synaptic vesicle: Round granule that contains neurotransmitter.

Storage granule: Large compartment that holds synaptic vesicles.

Presynaptic membrane: Encloses molecules that transmit chemical messages.

Synaptic cleft: Small space separating presynaptic terminal and postsynaptic dendritic spine.

Presynaptic terminal

Neurotransmitter

Channel

Dendritic spine

Postsynaptic membrane: Contains receptor molecules that receive chemical messages.

Postsynaptic receptor: Site to which a neurotransmitter molecule binds.

FIGURE 5-2 **Chemical Synapse**
(A) Surrounding the central synapse in this electron micrograph are astrocytes, a type of glial cell, axons, dendrites, other synapses, and a synaptic cleft. **(B)** Within a chemical synapse, storage granules hold vesicles containing neurotransmitter that travel to the presynaptic membrane in preparation for release. Neurotransmitter is expelled into the synaptic cleft by exocytosis, crosses the cleft, and binds to receptor proteins on the postsynaptic membrane.

◉ **CLINICAL FOCUS 5-2**

Parkinson Disease

Case VI: The gentleman . . . is seventy-two years of age. . . . About eleven or twelve, or perhaps more, years ago, he first perceived weakness in the left hand and arm, and soon after found the trembling to commence. In about three years afterwards, the right arm became affected in a similar manner: and soon afterwards the convulsive motions affected the whole body and began to interrupt speech. In about three years from that time the legs became affected. (James Parkinson, 1817)

In the 1817 essay from which this case study is taken, British physician James Parkinson reported similar symptoms in six patients, some of whom he had observed only in the streets near his clinic. Shaking was usually the first symptom, and it typically began in a hand. Over a span of years, the shaking spread to include the arm and then other parts of the body.

As the disease progressed, patients had a propensity to lean forward and walk on the balls of their feet. They also tended to run forward to prevent themselves from falling. In the later stages, patients had difficulty eating and swallowing. They drooled, and their bowel movements slowed. Eventually, the patients lost all muscular control and were unable to sleep because of the disruptive tremors.

More than 50 years after James Parkinson's descriptions, French neurologist Jean-Martin Charcot named the condition Parkinson's disease, known today as **Parkinson disease**. Three findings have helped researchers understand its neural basis:

1. In 1919, Constantin Tréatikoff (1974) studied the brains of nine Parkinson patients on autopsy and found that the *substantia nigra*, a small midbrain nucleus, had degenerated. In the brain of one patient who had Parkinsonlike symptoms on only one side of the body, the substantia nigra had degenerated on the side opposite that of the symptoms.

2. Chemical examination of the brains of Parkinson patients showed that disease symptoms appear when the level of **dopamine (DA)**, then a proposed neurotransmitter, was reduced to less than 10 percent of normal in the basal ganglia (Ehringer & Hornykiewicz, 1960/1974).

3. Confirming the role of dopamine in a neural pathway connecting the substantia nigra to the basal ganglia, Urban Ungerstedt found in 1971 that injecting a neurotoxin called 6-hydroxydopamine into rats selectively destroyed these dopamine-containing neurons and produced symptoms of Parkinson disease.

Loss of dopamine-containing substantia nigra neurons has been linked to environmental factors such as insecticides, herbicides, fungicides, flu virus, and toxic drugs. About 10% of people with Parkinson disease have a mutation in one of several specific genes, and it may also be the case

Michael J. Fox gained wide fame as an actor before being diagnosed in 1991, at age 30, with young-onset Parkinson disease. His first book, *Lucky Man*, discusses his first 7 years with the disease, why he went public with his condition, and how he started The Michael J. Fox Foundation and became a leading advocate for research to cure Parkinson disease. His second book, *Always Looking Up: The Adventures of an Incurable Optimist*, describes how he campaigned for stem-cell research as a potential cure.

that people who are susceptible to environmental influences also have a genetic predisposition.

Dopamine itself in other brain areas has been linked not only to motor behavior but also to some forms of learning and to neural structures that mediate reward and addiction. Some Parkinson patients who receive dopaminergic drugs as therapy have become shopaholics or compulsive gamblers, despite showing no such tendencies before treatment.

Treatments for neurological diseases are usually much more effective the earlier they are started, so early detection is important. Joy Milne has an incredible sense of smell that is able to recognize Parkinson disease on the human body. She perceives a "thick musk smell" on people who have Parkinson disease and those yet to be diagnosed—even 10 years before diagnosis. Scientists are working with Joy to help create a diagnostic test for Parkinson disease.

terminal, or end foot; the lower part is the receiving dendrite. The round granular substances in the terminal are the **synaptic vesicles**, which contain neurotransmitter molecules.

Dark patches on the axon terminal membrane are proteins that serve largely as ion channels to signal the release of the transmitters or as pumps to recapture the transmitter after its release. The dark patches on the dendrite consist mainly of receptor molecules also made up of proteins that receive chemical messages. The terminal and

Parkinson disease Motor system disorder correlated with dopamine loss in the substantia nigra; characterized by tremors, muscular rigidity, and reduction in voluntary movement.

dopamine (DA) Amine neurotransmitter involved in coordinating movement, attention, learning, and reinforcing behaviors.

synaptic vesicle Membranous compartment that encloses a fixed number (called a *quantum*) of neurotransmitter molecules.

synaptic cleft Gap separating the neuronal presynaptic membrane from the postsynaptic membrane.

tripartite synapse Functional integration and physical proximity of the presynaptic membrane, postsynaptic membrane, and their intimate association with surrounding astrocytes.

chemical synapse Junction at which messenger molecules are released when stimulated by an action potential.

presynaptic membrane Axon terminal membrane on the transmitter, or output, side of a synapse.

postsynaptic membrane Membrane on the transmitter, or input, side of a synapse.

storage granule Membranous compartment that holds several vesicles containing a neurotransmitter.

anterograde synaptic transmission Process that occurs when a neurotransmitter is released from a presynaptic neuron and binds to a receptor on the postsynaptic neuron.

transporter Protein molecule that pumps substances across a membrane.

The main classes of transmitters are small-molecule, peptide, lipid, gaseous, and ion. We describe each in the next section.

For a refresher on protein export, review Figure 3-17.

the dendrite are separated by a small space, the **synaptic cleft**. The synaptic cleft is central to synapse function because neurotransmitter chemicals must bridge this gap to carry a message from one neuron to the next.

You can also see in the micrograph that the synapse is sandwiched by many surrounding structures, including an astrocyte, other axons and dendritic processes, and other synapses. The surrounding astrocyte contributes to chemical neurotransmission in several ways—by supplying the building blocks for neurotransmitter synthesis, by confining the movement of neurotransmitters to the synapse, and by mopping up excess neurotransmitter molecules, for example. This functional integration and physical proximity of the presynaptic membrane, postsynaptic membrane, and their intimate association with surrounding astrocytes make up what is known as the **tripartite synapse**.

Figure 5-2B details the process of neurotransmission at a **chemical synapse**, the junction where messenger molecules are released from one neuron to interact with the next neuron. Here, the **presynaptic membrane** forms the axon terminal, the **postsynaptic membrane** forms the dendritic spine, and the space between the two is the synaptic cleft. Within the axon terminal are specialized structures, including mitochondria, the organelles that supply the cell's energy needs; **storage granules**, large compartments that hold several synaptic vesicles; and microtubules, which transport substances, including neurotransmitter, to the terminal.

Neurotransmission in Five Steps

Anterograde synaptic transmission is the five-step process of transmitting information across a chemical synapse from the presynaptic side to the postsynaptic neuron (see **Figure 5-3**). In brief:

1. The neurotransmitter is synthesized somewhere inside the neuron.
2. It is packaged and stored within vesicles at the axon terminal.
3. It is transported to the presynaptic membrane and released into the cleft in response to an action potential.
4. It binds to and activates receptors on the postsynaptic membrane.
5. It is degraded or removed, so it will not continue to interact with a receptor and work indefinitely.

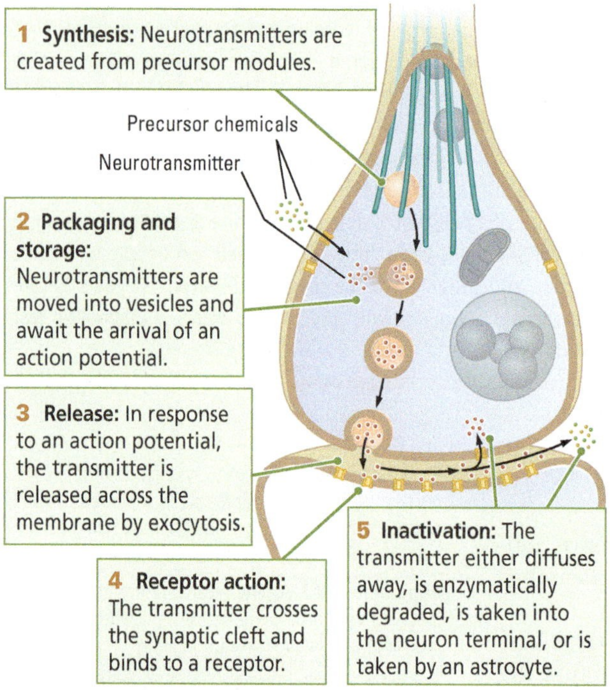

Steps 1 and 2: Neurotransmitter Synthesis, Packaging, and Storage

There are several main classes of transmitters, and they are derived in different ways. The *small-molecule* transmitters are synthesized in the axon terminal from building blocks that are often derived from food. **Transporters** are protein molecules that move substances across cell membranes, and they are responsible for packaging some neurotransmitter classes into vesicles. Mitochondria in the axon terminal provide the energy needed both to synthesize precursor chemicals into the transmitter and to power transporters.

Peptide transmitters are synthesized in the cell body according to instructions in the neuron's DNA, packaged in membranes on the Golgi bodies, and transported on microtubules to the axon terminal. Peptide transmitters may also be manufactured within the presynaptic terminal by ribosomes using mRNA transported to the terminal.

Lipid transmitters cannot be packaged and stored in vesicles, which are composed of lipids, but are rather synthesized "on demand" when an action potential reaches the axon terminal.

Gaseous transmitters are also generated within the cells by enzymes, but they differ from classical signaling molecules in many ways.

1 Synthesis: Neurotransmitters are created from precursor modules.

Precursor chemicals

Neurotransmitter

2 Packaging and storage: Neurotransmitters are moved into vesicles and await the arrival of an action potential.

3 Release: In response to an action potential, the transmitter is released across the membrane by exocytosis.

4 Receptor action: The transmitter crosses the synaptic cleft and binds to a receptor.

5 Inactivation: The transmitter either diffuses away, is enzymatically degraded, is taken into the neuron terminal, or is taken by an astrocyte.

FIGURE 5-3 Anterograde Synaptic Transmission

Although their production is regulated, gaseous transmitters are able to permeate cell membranes and thus are not stored within the cell.

Ion transmitters are not biochemically synthesized. Instead, like all other atoms heavier than helium, they are made in the hearts of dying stars. However, ion transmitters can be packaged and stored in vesicles, usually along with other transmitter types, and then released into the synaptic cleft.

Regardless of their origin, neurotransmitters that are packaged into vesicles can be found in three locations at the axon terminal. Some vesicles are warehoused in granules, some are attached to microfilaments (a type of microtubule; see Figure 5-2B) in the terminal, and still others are attached to the presynaptic membrane. These sites correspond to the steps by which a transmitter is transported from a granule to the membrane, ready to be released into the synaptic cleft.

Step 3: Neurotransmitter Release

Synaptic vesicles loaded with neurotransmitters must dock near release sites on the presynaptic membrane. Then the vesicles are primed to prepare them to fuse rapidly in response to calcium (Ca^{2+}) influx. When an action potential reaches the presynaptic membrane, voltage changes on the membrane set the release process in motion. Calcium cations play a critical role. The presynaptic membrane is rich in voltage-activated calcium channels, and the surrounding extracellular fluid is rich in Ca^{2+}. As illustrated in **Figure 5-4**, the action potential's arrival opens these calcium channels, allowing an influx of calcium ions into the axon terminal.

Primed vesicles quickly fuse with the presynaptic membrane in response to the calcium influx and empty their contents into the synaptic cleft by exocytosis. The vesicles from storage granules and on filaments then move up to replace the vesicles that just emptied their contents.

transmitter-activated receptor Protein that has a binding site for a specific neurotransmitter and is embedded in the membrane of a cell.

ionotropic receptor Embedded membrane protein; acts as (1) a binding site for a neurotransmitter and (2) a pore that regulates ion flow to directly and rapidly change membrane voltage.

metabotropic receptor Embedded membrane protein with a binding site for a neurotransmitter linked to a G protein; can affect other receptors or act with second messengers to affect other cellular processes, including opening a pore.

Step 4: Receptor-Site Activation

After its release from vesicles on the presynaptic membrane, the neurotransmitter diffuses across the synaptic cleft and binds to specialized protein molecules embedded in the postsynaptic membrane. These **transmitter-activated receptors** have binding sites for the transmitter, which we elaborate on in Section 5-3. The properties of the receptors on the postsynaptic membrane determine the effect on the postsynaptic cell. **Ionotropic receptors** are associated with a pore that can open to allow ions to pass through the membrane, rapidly changing membrane voltage in one of two possible ways. These ion channels may allow Na^+ to enter the neuron, depolarizing the postsynaptic membrane, and so have an excitatory action on the postsynaptic neuron. Or they may allow K^+ to leave the neuron or Cl^- to enter the neuron, hyperpolarizing the postsynaptic membrane, and so typically have an inhibitory action on the postsynaptic neuron.

When bound by a transmitter, a second type of receptor, called a **metabotropic receptor**, may initiate intracellular messenger systems; this, in turn, may open an ion channel, thus modulating either excitation or inhibition or influencing other functions of the receiving neuron. (This process is discussed in more detail in Section 5-2.)

In addition to interacting with the postsynaptic membrane's receptors, a neurotransmitter may interact with receptors on the presynaptic membrane: it may influence the cell that just released it. That is, a neurotransmitter may activate presynaptic

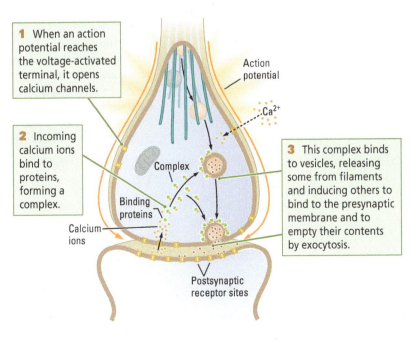

FIGURE 5-4 Neurotransmitter Release

1 When an action potential reaches the voltage-activated terminal, it opens calcium channels.

Action potential

Ca^{2+}

2 Incoming calcium ions bind to proteins, forming a complex.

Complex

Binding proteins

Calcium ions

3 This complex binds to vesicles, releasing some from filaments and inducing others to bind to the presynaptic membrane and to empty their contents by exocytosis.

Postsynaptic receptor sites

autoreceptor Self-receptor in a neuronal membrane; that is, it responds to the same transmitter released by the neuron; part of a negative feedback loop allowing the neuron to adjust its output.

quantum (pl. quanta) Number of neurotransmitter molecules, equivalent to the content of a single synaptic vesicle, that produces a just-observable change in postsynaptic electric potential.

receptors called **autoreceptors** (self-receptors) to receive messages from their own axon terminals. Autoreceptors serve a critical function as part of a negative feedback loop, providing information about whether adjustment to synaptic communication should be made.

How much neurotransmitter is needed to send a message? Bernard Katz was awarded a Nobel Prize in 1970 for providing an answer to this question. While recording electrical activity from the postsynaptic membranes of muscles, he detected small, spontaneous depolarizations now called *miniature postsynaptic potentials*. The potentials varied in size, but each size appeared to be a multiple of the smallest potential.

Katz concluded that the smallest postsynaptic potential is produced by the release of the contents of just one synaptic vesicle. This number of neurotransmitter molecules is called a **quantum (pl. quanta)**. Producing a postsynaptic potential large enough to initiate a postsynaptic action potential requires the simultaneous release of many quanta from the presynaptic cell.

The results of subsequent experiments show that the number of quanta released from the presynaptic membrane in response to a single action potential depends on two factors: (1) the amount of Ca^{2+} that enters the axon terminal in response to the action potential and (2) the number of vesicles docked at the membrane, waiting to be released. Both factors are relevant to synaptic activity during learning, which we consider in Section 5-4.

Step 5: Neurotransmitter Inactivation

Chemical transmission would not be an effective messenger system if a neurotransmitter lingered within the synaptic cleft, continuing to occupy and stimulate receptors. If this happened, the postsynaptic cell could not respond to other messages sent by the presynaptic neuron. Thus, after a neurotransmitter has done its work, it is quickly removed from receptor sites and from the synaptic cleft. Inactivation is accomplished in at least four ways:

1. *Diffusion.* Some of the neurotransmitter simply diffuses away from the synaptic cleft and is no longer available to bind to receptors.

2. *Degradation.* Enzymes in the synaptic cleft break down the transmitter.

3. *Reuptake.* Membrane transporters specific to that transmitter may bring it back into the presynaptic axon terminal for reuse. The by-products of degradation by enzymes also may be taken back into the terminal to be used again in the cell.

Table 3-1 describes astrocytes and other types of glial cells and their functions.

4. *Astrocyte uptake.* Some neurotransmitters are taken up by neighboring astrocytes. Astrocytes can also store certain transmitters for re-export to the axon terminal.

Highlighting the flexibility of synaptic function, an axon terminal has chemical mechanisms that enable it to respond to the frequency of its own use. If the terminal is very active, the amount of neurotransmitter made and stored there increases. If the terminal is not often used, however, enzymes within the terminal buttons may break down excess transmitter. The by-products are then reused or excreted from the neuron. Axon terminals may even send messages to the neuron's cell body, requesting increased supplies of the neurotransmitter or the molecules with which to make it.

Varieties of Synapses

So far, we have considered a generic chemical synapse, with features possessed by most synapses. Synapses vary widely in the nervous system. Each type is specialized in location, structure, function, and target. **Figure 5-5** illustrates this diversity on a single hypothetical neuron.

You have already encountered two kinds of chemical synapses. One is the *axomuscular synapse*, in which an axon synapses with a muscle end plate, releasing acetylcholine. The other synapse familiar to you is the *axodendritic synapse*, detailed in Figure 5-2B, in which the axon terminal of a neuron synapses with a dendrite or dendritic spine of another neuron.

Figure 4-26 shows a schematic view of an axomuscular synapse.

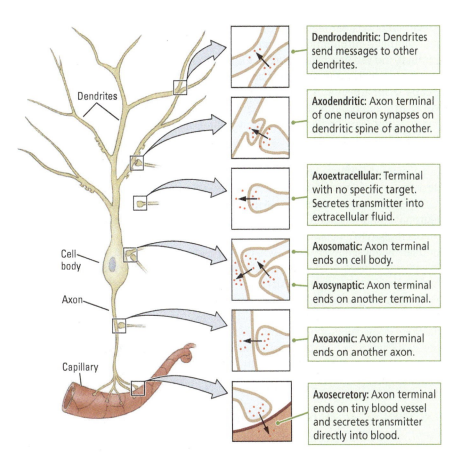

FIGURE 5-5 The Versatile Synapse

Dendrodendritic: Dendrites send messages to other dendrites.

Axodendritic: Axon terminal of one neuron synapses on dendritic spine of another.

Axoextracellular: Terminal with no specific target. Secretes transmitter into extracellular fluid.

Axosomatic: Axon terminal ends on cell body.

Axosynaptic: Axon terminal ends on another terminal.

Axoaxonic: Axon terminal ends on another axon.

Axosecretory: Axon terminal ends on tiny blood vessel and secretes transmitter directly into blood.

gap junction Area of contact between adjacent cells in which connexin proteins in each cell form connecting hemichannels, which, when open, allow ions to pass between the two cells; also called an *electrical synapse*.

Figure 5-5 diagrams axon terminals at the axodendritic synapse, as well as the *axosomatic synapse*, at a cell body; the *axoaxonic synapse*, on another axon; and the *axosynaptic synapse*, on another presynaptic terminal (that is, at the synapse between some other axon and its target). *Axoextracellular synapses* have no specific targets but instead secrete their transmitter chemicals into the extracellular fluid. In the *axosecretory synapse*, a terminal synapses with a tiny blood vessel, a capillary, and secretes its transmitter directly into the blood. Finally, synapses are not limited to axon terminals. Dendrites also may send messages to other dendrites through *dendrodendritic synapses*.

This wide variety of connections makes the synapse a versatile chemical delivery system. Synapses can deliver transmitters to highly specific sites or diffuse locales. Through connections to the dendrites, cell body, or axon of a neuron, transmitters can control the neuron's actions in different ways.

Through axosynaptic connections, they can also exert precise control over another neuron's input to a cell. By excreting transmitters into extracellular fluid or into the blood, axoextracellular and axosecretory synapses can modulate the function of large areas of tissue or even the entire body. Many transmitters secreted by neurons act as hormones circulating in your blood, with widespread influences on your body.

Electrical Synapses

Chemical synapses are the most common synapses in mammalian nervous systems, but they are not the only kind of synapse. Some neurons influence each other electrically through an *electrical synapse*, or gap junction, where two neurons' intracellular fluids or cytoplasm can come into direct contact (**Figure 5-6**). A **gap junction** is formed when connexin proteins in one cell membrane make a *hemichannel* that connects to a hemichannel in an adjacent cell's membrane, allowing ions to pass from one neuron to the other in both directions. Gap junctions constitute a regulated gate between cells because they can either be open or closed.

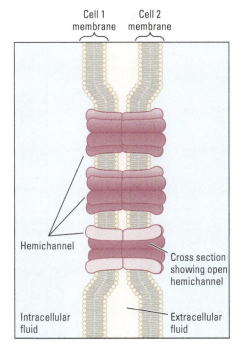

FIGURE 5-6 **Gap Junction** The connexin proteins on adjacent cell membranes connect to form hemichannels, which allow ions to pass between the two neurons.

Gap junctions eliminate the brief delay in information flow—about 5 milliseconds per synapse—of chemical transmission (note the space between the presynaptic terminal and the dendritic spine in Figure 5-2B compared with Figure 5-3). For example, the crayfish's gap junctions activate its tail flick, a response that provides quick escape from a predator. Gap junctions are found in the mammalian brain as well, where in some regions they allow groups of interneurons to synchronize their firing rhythmically. Gap junctions also allow glial cells and neurons to exchange substances (Dere & Zlomuzica, 2012).

Gap junctions also come with some variety. There are different connexin subunits that give rise to different pore sizes, which allows selectivity for specific small molecules. Large biomolecules such as nucleic acids and proteins cannot fit through gap junctions.

Gap junctions further increase the signaling diversity between neurons. Such interneuronal communication may occur via dendrodendritic and axoaxonic gap junctions. Interestingly, gap junctions at axon terminals synapsing on dendrites and cell bodies allow for dual chemical and electrical synaptic transmission. These "mixed synapses" have only recently been discovered, and their functional properties have yet to be determined in the mammalian CNS (Nagy et al., 2017).

If chemical synapses transmit messages more slowly, why do mammals rely on them more than on gap junctions? The answer is that chemical synapses can show plasticity; they can amplify or diminish a signal sent from one neuron to the next; and they can change with experience to alter their signals and thus mediate learning. Gap junctions themselves allow no such plasticity and are built for speed and efficient communication.

Excitatory and Inhibitory Messages

A neurotransmitter can influence a neuron's functioning through a remarkable variety of mechanisms. In its direct actions in influencing a neuron's electrical activity, however, a neurotransmitter acting through its receptors has only one of two immediate effects. It influences transmembrane ion flow either to increase or to decrease the likelihood that the cell with which it comes in contact will produce an action potential. Thus, despite the wide variety of synapses, they all convey messages of only these two types, excitatory or inhibitory. To be precise, neurotransmitters themselves do not determine excitation or inhibition. As noted at the beginning of this section, the ion channel associated with the receptor makes the call.

Excitatory and inhibitory synapses differ in their appearance and are generally located on different parts of the neuron. As shown in **Figure 5-7**, excitatory synapses are typically on the shafts or spines of dendrites, whereas inhibitory synapses are typically on the cell body. Excitatory synapses have round synaptic vesicles; the vesicles in inhibitory synapses are flattened. The material on the presynaptic and postsynaptic membranes is denser in an excitatory synapse than it is in an inhibitory synapse, and the excitatory synaptic cleft is wider. Finally, the active zone on an excitatory synapse is larger than that on an inhibitory synapse.

The differing locations of excitatory and inhibitory synapses divide a neuron into two zones: an excitatory dendritic tree and an inhibitory cell body. Think of excitatory and inhibitory messages as interacting from these two different perspectives. Viewed from an inhibitory perspective, you can picture excitation coming in over the dendrites and spreading past the axon hillock to trigger an action potential at the initial segment. If the message is to be stopped, it is best stopped by inhibiting the cell body close to the initial segment. In this model of excitatory–inhibitory interaction, inhibition blocks excitation by using a "cut 'em off at the pass" strategy.

Another way to conceptualize excitatory–inhibitory interaction is to picture excitation overcoming inhibition. In fact, excitatory synaptic inputs that are farther away from the soma are larger, to counteract the loss of signal that occurs over distance (Magee & Cook, 2000). If the cell body is typically

Each neuron receives thousands of excitatory and inhibitory signals every second. As indicated in **Principle 10:** The nervous system works by juxtaposing excitation and inhibition.

FIGURE 5-7 **Excitatory and Inhibitory Zones** Excitatory synapses typically occupy spines and dendritic shafts on a neuron. Inhibitory synapses are typically found on the cell body.

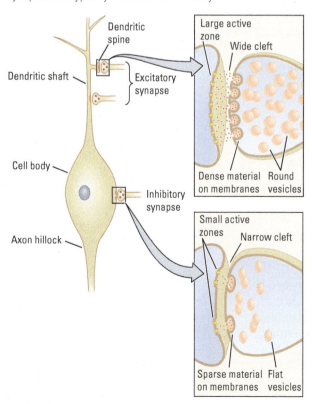

in an inhibited state, the only way to generate an action potential is to reduce cell body inhibition. In this "open the gates" strategy, the excitatory message is like a racehorse ready to run down the track, but first the inhibitory starting gate must be removed.

Behaviors are lost when a disorder prevents excitatory instructions, and they are uncontrollably expressed, or "released," when a disorder prevents inhibitory instructions.

Evolution of Complex Neurotransmission Systems

Considering all the biochemical steps required to get a message across a synapse and the variety of synapses, you might well wonder why—and how—such a complex communication system ever evolved. How did chemical transmitters originate?

To make the origin of chemical secretions for neuronal communication easier to imagine, think about the feeding behaviors of simple single-celled creatures. The earliest unicellular creatures secreted juices onto bacteria to immobilize and prepare them for ingestion. These digestive juices were probably expelled from the cell body by exocytosis: a vacuole or vesicle attached itself to the cell membrane and then opened into the extracellular fluid to discharge its contents. The prey, thus immobilized, was captured through the reverse process of endocytosis.

The exocytosis mechanism for digestion in a single-celled organism is parallel to the release of a neurotransmitter for communication in more complex creatures. Quite possibly, evolution long ago adapted these primordial digestive processes into processes of neural communication in more complex organisms.

5-1 Review

Before you continue, check your understanding. Answers to Self-Test appear at the back of the book.

1. In mammals, the principal form of communication between neurons occurs via _____, even though this structure is slower and more complex than the fused _____.

2. The principal benefit of chemical synapses over electrical synapses is that they can change with _____ to alter their signals and so mediate _____.

3. The nervous system has evolved a variety of synapses:
   _____ between axon terminals and dendrites,
   _____ between axon terminals and cell bodies,
   _____ between axon terminals and muscles,
   _____ between axon terminals and other axons,
   _____ between axon terminals and other synapses.
   A(n) _____ synapse releases chemical transmitters into extracellular fluid, a(n) _____ synapse releases transmitter into the bloodstream as hormones, and a(n) _____ synapse connects dendrites to other dendrites.

4. Excitatory synapses are usually located on a(n) _____, whereas inhibitory synapses are usually located on a(n) _____.

5. Describe the five steps in chemical neurotransmission.

For additional study tools, visit **LaunchPad** at launchpadworks.com

5-2

Varieties of Neurotransmitters and Receptors

Subsequent to Otto Loewi's 1921 discovery that excitatory and inhibitory chemicals control heart rate, many researchers thought that the brain must work under much the same type of dual control. They reasoned that norepinephrine and acetylcholine are the transmitters through which excitatory and inhibitory brain cells worked.

They did not imagine what we know today: the human brain employs a dazzling variety of neurotransmitters and receptors. The neurotransmitters operate in even more versatile ways: some may be excitatory at one location and inhibitory at another, for example, and two or more may team up in a single synapse so that one makes the other more potent. Moreover, each neurotransmitter may interact with several varieties of receptors, each with a somewhat different function.

In this section, you will learn how neurotransmitters are identified and how they fit within broad categories on the basis of their chemical structure. The functional aspects of neurotransmitters interrelate and are intricate, and there is not a simple one-to-one relation between a single neurotransmitter and a single behavior. Furthermore, receptor variety is achieved by the unique combination of protein molecules coming together to form a functional receptor.

Four Criteria for Identifying Neurotransmitters

Among the many thousands of chemicals in the nervous system, which are neurotransmitters? **Figure 5-8** presents four identifying criteria:

1. The transmitter must be synthesized in the neuron or otherwise be present in it.

2. When the neuron is active, the transmitter must be released and produce a response in some target.

3. The same response must be obtained when the transmitter is experimentally placed on the target.

4. A mechanism must exist for removing the transmitter from its site of action after its work is done.

These identifying criteria are fairly easy to apply for examining the somatic nervous system, especially at an accessible nerve–muscle junction with only one main neurotransmitter, acetylcholine. But identifying chemical transmitters in the CNS is not so easy. In the brain and spinal cord, thousands of synapses are packed around every neuron, preventing easy access to any single synapse and its activities. Consequently, multiple techniques, including staining, stimulating, and collecting, are used to identify substances thought to be CNS neurotransmitters. A suspect chemical that has not yet been shown to meet all the criteria is called a *putative* (supposed) *transmitter*.

Researchers trying to identify new CNS neurotransmitters can use microelectrodes to stimulate and record from single neurons. A glass microelectrode is small enough to be placed on specific neuronal targets. It can be filled with a chemical of interest, and when a current is passed through the electrode, the chemical can be ejected into or onto the neuron to mimic neurotransmitter release onto the cell.

Many staining techniques can identify specific chemicals inside the cell. Methods have also been developed for preserving nervous system tissue in a saline bath while experimenters determine how the neurons in the tissue communicate. The use of such living tissue slices simplifies the investigation by allowing the researcher to view a single neuron through a microscope while stimulating it or recording from it.

Acetylcholine was not only the first substance identified as a neurotransmitter but also the first substance identified as a CNS neurotransmitter. A logical argument that predicted its presence even before experimental evidence was gathered greatly facilitated the process. All motor neuron axons leaving the spinal cord use acetylcholine as a transmitter. Each axon has an axon collateral within the spinal cord that synapses on a nearby CNS interneuron. The interneuron, in turn, synapses on the motor neuron's cell body. This circular set of connections, called a *Renshaw loop* (after the researcher who first described it), is shown in **Figure 5-9**.

Because the main axon to the muscle releases acetylcholine, investigators suspected that its axon collateral also might release acetylcholine. For two

Figure 4-6 illustrates the use of a glass microelectrode.

FIGURE 5-8 **Criteria for Identifying Neurotransmitters**

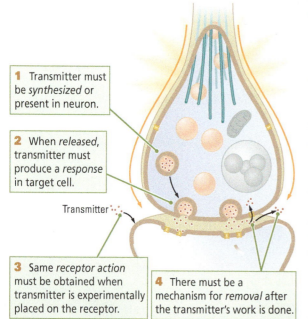

1 Transmitter must be *synthesized* or present in neuron.

2 When *released*, transmitter must produce a *response* in target cell.

Transmitter

3 Same *receptor action* must be obtained when transmitter is experimentally placed on the receptor.

4 There must be a mechanism for *removal* after the transmitter's work is done.

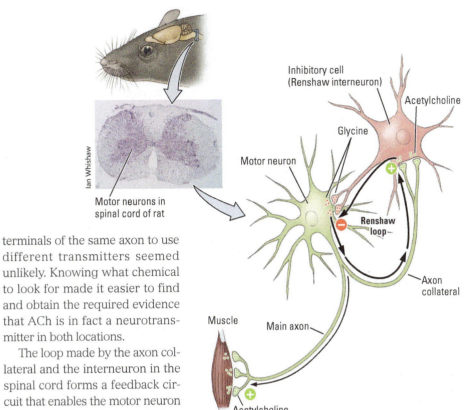

FIGURE 5-9 **Renshaw Loop** Left: Some spinal cord motor neurons project to the rat's forelimb muscles. Right: In a Renshaw loop, the main motor axon (green) projects to a muscle, and its axon collateral remains in the spinal cord to synapse with a Renshaw interneuron (red). The Renshaw interneuron contains the inhibitory transmitter glycine, which acts to prevent motor neuron overexcitation. Both the main motor axon and its collateral terminals contain acetylcholine. When the motor neuron is highly excited, it can modulate its activity level through the Renshaw loop (plus and minus signs).

terminals of the same axon to use different transmitters seemed unlikely. Knowing what chemical to look for made it easier to find and obtain the required evidence that ACh is in fact a neurotransmitter in both locations.

The loop made by the axon collateral and the interneuron in the spinal cord forms a feedback circuit that enables the motor neuron to inhibit itself from overexcitation, should it receive a great many excitatory inputs from other parts of the CNS. Follow the positive and negative signs in Figure 5-9 to see how the Renshaw loop works. If the loop is blocked, as can be done with the toxin strychnine, motor neurons become overactive, producing convulsions that can choke off respiration and so cause death.

The term *neurotransmitter* is used much more broadly now than it was when researchers began to identify these chemicals. Today, the term applies to chemicals that

- Carry a message from the presynaptic membrane of one neuron to another by influencing postsynaptic membrane voltage.
- Change the structure of a synapse.
- Communicate by sending messages in the opposite direction. These *retrograde* (reverse-direction) *messages* influence the release or **reuptake** of transmitters on the presynaptic side.

Classes of Neurotransmitters

We impose some order on the diversity of neurotransmitters by classifying them into groups based on their chemical composition: small-molecule transmitters, peptide transmitters, lipid transmitters, gaseous transmitters, and ion transmitter.

Small-Molecule Transmitters

The quick-acting **small-molecule transmitters**, such as acetylcholine, are typically synthesized from dietary nutrients and packaged ready for use in axon terminals. When a small-molecule transmitter has been released from a terminal button, it can quickly be replaced at the presynaptic membrane.

Because small-molecule transmitters or their main components are derived from the food we eat, diet can influence their abundance and activity in our bodies. This fact is important in the design of drugs that act on the nervous system. Many neuroactive drugs are designed to reach the brain by the same route that small-molecule transmitters or their precursor chemicals follow: the digestive tract.

Table 5-1 lists some of the best-known and most extensively studied small-molecule transmitters. In addition to acetylcholine, four amines (related by a chemical structure

reuptake Inactivation of a neurotransmitter when membrane transporter proteins bring the transmitter back into the presynaptic axon terminal for reuse.

small-molecule transmitter Quick-acting neurotransmitter synthesized in the axon terminal from products derived from the diet.

TABLE 5-1 **Best-Known and Well-Studied Small-Molecule Neurotransmitters**

Acetylcholine (ACh)
Amines
Dopamine (DA)
Norepinephrine (NE, *or* noradrenaline [NA])
Epinephrine (EP, *or* adrenaline)
Serotonin (5-HT)
Amino acids
Glutamate (Glu)
Gamma-aminobutyric acid (GABA)
Glycine (Gly)
Histamine (H)
Purines
Adenosine
Adenosine triphosphate (ATP)

Taking drugs orally is easy and comparatively safe, but not all drugs can traverse the digestive tract. Section 6-1 explains.

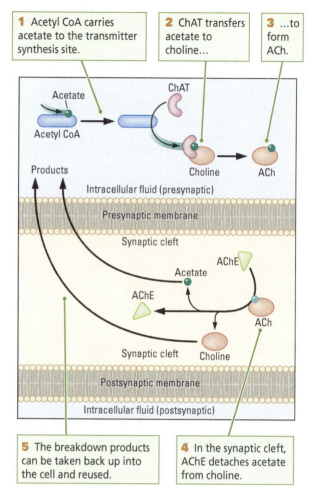

1 Acetyl CoA carries acetate to the transmitter synthesis site.

2 ChAT transfers acetate to choline...

3 ...to form ACh.

5 The breakdown products can be taken back up into the cell and reused.

4 In the synaptic cleft, AChE detaches acetate from choline.

FIGURE 5-10 **Chemistry of Acetylcholine** Two enzymes combine the dietary precursors of ACh within the cell, and a third breaks them down in the synapse for reuptake.

rate-limiting factor Any chemical in limited supply that restricts the pace at which another chemical can be synthesized.

serotonin (5-HT) Amine neurotransmitter; helps to regulate mood and aggression, appetite and arousal, perception of pain, and respiration.

glutamate (Glu) Amino acid neurotransmitter; typically excites neurons.

gamma-aminobutyric acid (GABA) Amino acid neurotransmitter; typically inhibits neurons.

that contains an NH group, or *amine*), four amino acids, and two purines are included in this list.

ACETYLCHOLINE SYNTHESIS Acetylcholine is present at the junction of neurons and muscles, including the heart, as well as in the CNS. **Figure 5-10** illustrates how ACh molecules are synthesized from choline and acetate by two enzymes and then broken down. Choline is among the breakdown products of fats in foods such as egg yolk, avocado, salmon, and olive oil; acetate is a compound found in acidic foods, such as vinegar and lemon juice.

As depicted in Figure 5-10, inside the cell, acetyl coenzyme A (acetyl CoA) carries acetate to the synthesis site, and a second enzyme, choline acetyltransferase (ChAT), transfers the acetate to choline to synthesize acetylcholine. After ACh has been released into the synaptic cleft and diffuses to receptor sites on the postsynaptic membrane, a third enzyme, acetylcholinesterase (AChE), reverses the process, breaking down the transmitter by detaching acetate from choline. The breakdown products can then be taken back into the presynaptic terminal for reuse.

AMINE SYNTHESIS Some transmitters grouped together in Table 5-1 have common biochemical pathways to synthesis and so are related. You are familiar with the amines dopamine (DA), norepinephrine (NE), and epinephrine (EP). To review, DA loss figures in Parkinson disease, EP is the excitatory transmitter at the amphibian heart, and NE is the excitatory transmitter at the mammalian heart.

Figure 5-11 charts the biochemical sequence in which these amines are synthesized. The precursor chemical is tyrosine, an amino acid abundant in food. (Hard cheese and bananas are good sources.) The enzyme tyrosine hydroxylase (enzyme 1 in Figure 5-11) changes tyrosine into L-dopa, which other enzymes convert into dopamine, then norepinephrine, and, finally, epinephrine.

Interestingly, the supply of the enzyme tyrosine hydroxylase is limited. Consequently, so is the rate at which dopamine, norepinephrine, and epinephrine can be produced, regardless of how much tyrosine is present or ingested. This **rate-limiting factor** can be bypassed by the oral administration of L-dopa, which is why L-dopa is a medication used in treating Parkinson disease, as described in Clinical Focus 5-3, Awakening with L-Dopa.

SEROTONIN SYNTHESIS The amine transmitter **serotonin** (5-HT, for 5-hydroxytryptamine) is synthesized from the amino acid L-tryptophan. Tryptophan is abundant in pork, turkey, milk, and bananas, among other foods. Serotonin plays a role in regulating mood and aggression, appetite and arousal, respiration, and pain perception.

AMINO ACID SYNTHESIS Two amino acid transmitters, **glutamate (Glu)** and **gamma-aminobutyric acid (GABA)**, are closely related. GABA is formed by a simple modification of the glutamate molecule, as shown in **Figure 5-12**. These two transmitters are the workhorses of the brain because so many synapses use them.

In the forebrain and cerebellum, glutamate is the main excitatory transmitter, and GABA is the main inhibitory transmitter. Thus, glutamate is a neurotransmitter in excitatory synapses, and GABA is a neurotransmitter in inhibitory synapses. Interestingly, glutamate is widely distributed in CNS neurons, but it becomes a neurotransmitter only if it is appropriately packaged in vesicles in the axon terminal.

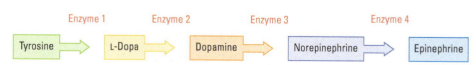

FIGURE 5-11 **Sequential Synthesis of Three Amines** A different enzyme is responsible for each successive molecular modification in this biochemical sequence of amine neurotransmitters. The twins featured in Research Focus 3-1 lack an enzyme that enhances DA production.

Awakening with L-Dopa

He was started on L-dopa in March 1969. The dose was slowly raised to 4.0 mg a day over a period of three weeks without apparently producing any effect. I first discovered that Mr. E. was responding to L-dopa by accident, chancing to go past his room at an unaccustomed time and hearing regular footsteps inside the room. I went in and found Mr. E., who had been chair bound since 1966, walking up and down his room, swinging his arms with considerable vigor, and showing erectness of posture and a brightness of expression completely new to him. When I asked him about the effect, he said with some embarrassment: "Yes! I felt the L-dopa beginning to work three days ago—it was like a wave of energy and strength sweeping through me. I found I could stand and walk by myself, and that I could do everything I needed for myself—but I was afraid that you would see how well I was and discharge me from the hospital." (Sacks, 1976)

In this case history, neurologist Oliver Sacks describes administering L-dopa to a patient who had acquired Parkinsonism as an aftereffect of severe influenza in the 1920s. The relationship between the influenza and the Parkinsonlike symptoms suggests that the flu virus had entered the brain and selectively attacked dopamine neurons in the substantia nigra. By increasing the amount of DA in remaining synapses, L-dopa relieved the patient's symptoms.

Two separate groups of investigators independently gave L-dopa to Parkinson patients beginning in 1961 (Barbeau et al., 1961; Birkmayer & Hornykiewicz, 1961). Both research teams knew that the chemical is catalyzed into dopamine at DA synapses (see Figure 5-11). The L-dopa, it turned out, reduced the patients' muscular rigidity.

This work provided the first demonstration that a neurological condition can be relieved by a drug that aids in increasing the amount of a neurotransmitter. L-Dopa has since become a standard treatment for Parkinson disease. Its effects have been improved by the administration of drugs that prevent L-dopa from being converted to dopamine in the body before it passes through the blood–brain barrier and gets to dopamine neurons in the brain.

L-Dopa is not a cure, however. Parkinson disease still progresses during treatment, and as more and more dopamine synapses are lost, the treatment becomes less and less effective. L-dopa can also produce *dyskinesias*—involuntary, unwanted movements, such as ballistic (throwinglike) or choreic (dancelike) movements. When these side effects eventually become severe, the treatment must be discontinued.

Everett Collection, Inc

The movie *Awakenings* recounts the L-dopa trials conducted by Oliver Sacks and described in his book of the same title.

The amino acid transmitter glycine (Gly) is a much more common inhibitory transmitter in the brainstem and spinal cord, where it acts within the Renshaw loop, for example (review Figure 5-9).

Histidine is an amino acid that serves as the primary biological source of the transmitter **histamine (H)**. Histidine is converted by the enzyme histidine decarboxylase into histamine. Among its many functions, which include control of arousal and of waking, histamine can also cause the constriction of smooth muscles. When activated in allergic reactions, histamine contributes to asthma, a constriction of the airways. You are probably familiar with antihistamine drugs used to treat allergies.

PURINES The purines are synthesized as nucleotides—the kind of molecules that make up DNA and RNA. The purine *adenosine triphosphate* (*ATP*) consists of a molecule of adenine attached to a ribose sugar molecule and three phosphate groups. Removal of the three phosphate groups leaves adenosine, a molecule that plays a central role in promoting sleep, suppressing arousal, and regulating blood flow to various organs through *vasodilation* (the dilation of blood vessels).

```
      COOH              COOH
       |                 |
      CH₂               CH₂
       |                 |
      CH₂               CH₂
       |         →       |
 H₂N—CH            H₂N—CH
       |
      COOH
   Glutamate          GABA
```

FIGURE 5-12 Amino Acid Transmitters Top: Removal of a carboxyl (COOH) group from the bottom of the glutamate molecule produces GABA. Bottom: Their different shapes, illustrated by three-dimensional space-filling models, thus allow these amino acid transmitters to bind to different receptors.

histamine (H) Neurotransmitter that controls arousal and waking; can cause the constriction of smooth muscles; when activated in allergic reactions, constricts airway and contributes to asthma.

neuropeptide Short, multifunctional amino acid chain (fewer than 100 amino acids); acts as a neurotransmitter and can act as a hormone; may contribute to learning.

Section 3-2 includes a detailed description of DNA and RNA and the process of protein synthesis. Figure 3-15 diagrams peptide bonding, and Figure 3-17 diagrams protein export.

Peptide Transmitters

More than 50 short amino acid chains of various lengths (fewer than 100 amino acids) form the families of peptide transmitters, or **neuropeptides**, listed in **Table 5-2**. Synthesized through the translation of mRNA from instructions contained in the neuron's DNA, neuropeptides are multifunctional chains of amino acids that act as neurotransmitters.

TABLE 5-2 **Peptide Neurotransmitters**

Family	Examples
Opioids	Met-enkephalin, dynorphin, beta-endorphin
Neurohypophyseals	Vasopressin, oxytocin
Secretins	Secretin, motilin, glucagon, growth hormone–releasing factor
Insulins	Insulin, insulin growth factors
Gastrins	Gastrin, cholecystokinin
Somatostatins	Somatostatin
Tachykinins	Neurokinin A, neurokinin B, substance P

In some neurons, peptide transmitters are made in the axon terminal, but most are assembled on the neuron's ribosomes, packaged in a membrane by Golgi bodies, and transported by the microtubules to the axon terminals. The entire process of neuropeptide synthesis and transport is relatively slow compared with the nearly ready-made small-molecule neurotransmitters. Consequently, peptide transmitters act slowly and are not replaced quickly.

Neuropeptides, however, perform an enormous range of functions in the nervous system, as might be expected from their large numbers. They act as hormones that respond to stress, enable a mother to bond with her infant, regulate eating and drinking and pleasure and pain, and probably contribute to learning.

Opium, morphine, and related synthetic chemicals such as heroin—long known both to produce euphoria and to reduce pain—mimic the actions of endogenous brain opioid neuropeptides: enkephalins, dynorphins, and endorphins. (The term *enkephalin* derives from the phrase *in the cephalon*, meaning "in the brain or head," whereas the term *endorphin* is a shortened form of "endogenous morphine.")

A part of the amino acid chain in each of these naturally occurring opioid peptides is structurally similar to the others, as illustrated for two of them in **Figure 5-13**. Morphine mimics this part of the chain. The discovery of naturally occurring morphine-like neuropeptides suggested that one or more of them might have analgesic properties and may take part in pain perception. It turns out that beta-endorphin, released in response to exercise and thought to be responsible for runner's high, has many times the analgesic potency of morphine.

Some CNS peptides take part in specific periodic behaviors, each month or each year perhaps. For instance, in a female deer, neuropeptide transmitters act as hormones (luteinizing hormone) that prepare her for the fall mating season. Come winter, a different set of biochemicals facilitates the developing deer fetus. When the mother gives birth in the spring, yet other highly specific neuropeptide hormones—such as oxytocin, which enables her to bond to her fawn, and prolactin, which enables her to nurse—take control.

The same neuropeptides serve similar specific hormonal functions in humans. Others, such as neuropeptide growth hormones, perform far more general functions in regulating growth. Unlike many transmitters that bind to receptors associated with ion channels, neuropeptides are metabotropic and have no direct effects on postsynaptic membrane voltage. Instead, peptide transmitters activate synaptic receptors that indirectly influence cell structure and function. Digestive processes degrade neuropeptide amino acid chains, so they generally cannot be taken orally as drugs, whereas some small-molecule transmitters can.

Met-enkephalin

Leu-enkephalin

FIGURE 5-13 **Opioid Peptides** Parts of the amino acid chains of some neuropeptides that act on brain centers for pleasure and pain are structurally similar and also share similarities to drugs such as morphine, which mimic their functions (see Section 6-2).

Sections 12-3 and 12-6 explain hormonal influence over human motivated and emotional behavior.

Lipid Transmitters

Predominant among the lipid neurotransmitters are the **endocannabinoids** (endogenous cannabinoids), a class of lipid neurotransmitters synthesized at the postsynaptic membrane to act on receptors at the presynaptic membrane. The endocannabinoids include anandamide and 2-AG (2-arachidonoylglycerol), both derived from arachidonic acid, an unsaturated fatty acid. Poultry and eggs are especially good sources. Endocannabinoids participate in a diverse set of physiological and psychological processes that affect appetite, pain, sleep, mood, memory, anxiety, and the stress response. Their scientific history is brief but illustrates how science can progress, punctuated by short steps.

Because endocannabinoids are lipophilic (fat-loving) molecules, they are not soluble in water and are not stored in vesicles. Rather, investigators hypothesize that endocannabinoids are synthesized on demand after a neuron has depolarized and calcium has entered. Calcium activates the enzyme transacylase, the first step in producing anandamide. Once anandamide or 2-AG is synthesized, it diffuses across the synaptic cleft and interacts with its receptor on the presynaptic membrane. Thus, both molecules act as retrograde neurotransmitters, for a time reducing the amount of small-molecule transmitter being released. In this way, the postsynaptic neuron reduces the amount of incoming neural signal.

The CB$_1$ receptor is the target of all cannabinoids, whether generated by the body (endocannabinoids), from plants (phytocannabinoids), or synthetically. Yes, your body is teeming with weed receptors (Scudellari, 2017). CB$_1$ receptors are found at both glutamate and GABA synapses, so cannabinoids act as neuromodulators to inhibit release of glutamate and GABA. Cannabinoids thus dampen both neuronal excitation and inhibition.

Phytocannabinoids are obtained from the hemp plants *Cannabis sativa* and *Cannabis indica*. These plants have been used medically and recreationally for thousands of years, but only recently was an extract from cannabis synthesized. Early in the last century, many constituents of cannabis, including tetrahydrocannabinol (THC) and cannabidiol (CBD), were isolated and their chemical structure determined. In 1967, Yehiel Gaoni and Raphael Mechoulam reported the structure of the THC molecule, the main psychoactive constituent in cannabis. Next, investigators determined how THC is metabolized. (The process is quite slow, which explains why THC can be detected in urine for weeks after cannabis use.)

Research on the physiological and psychological effects of THC in animals and people, which began after its isolation and purification, is ongoing. Twenty-four years after the structure of the THC molecule was determined, the first cannabinoid receptor (CB$_1$) was found. Typically, receptors are activated by endogenous molecules, which motivated researchers to look for endogenous cannabinoids. Four years later, in 1992, anandamide was isolated and its structure determined, but it took another couple decades to figure out that endocannabinoids act as retrograde transmitters (Mechoulam et al., 2014).

Gaseous Transmitters

The gases **nitric oxide (NO)**, **carbon monoxide (CO)**, and **hydrogen sulfide (H$_2$S)** further expand the biochemical strategies that transmitter substances display. As water-soluble gases, they are neither stored in synaptic vesicles nor released from them; instead, the cell synthesizes them on demand. After synthesis, each gas diffuses away, easily crossing the cell membrane and immediately becoming active. Both NO and CO activate metabolic (energy-expending) processes in cells, including processes modulating the production of other neurotransmitters. H$_2$S prevents oxygen from binding in the mitochondria and thus functions to slow down metabolism.

All three gaseous transmitters serve as chemical messengers in many parts of the body. NO and H$_2$S control intestinal wall muscles and dilate blood vessels in active brain regions, allowing these regions to receive more blood. Because NO and H$_2$S also dilate blood vessels in the sexual organs, both are active in producing penile erections. Drugs used to treat erectile dysfunction in men, such as Viagra and Cialis, act by enhancing the chemical pathways influenced by NO. NO does not of itself produce sexual arousal.

Ion Transmitter

Recent evidence has led researchers to classify **zinc** (Zn^{2+}) as a transmitter. As a charged atom, zinc is not biologically synthesized but rather, like all other atoms, was

endocannabinoid Class of lipid neurotransmitters, including anandamide and 2-AG, synthesized at the postsynaptic membrane to act on receptors at the presynaptic membrane; affects appetite, pain, sleep, mood, memory, anxiety, and the stress response.

Fatty acid molecules that contribute to forming the cell membrane likewise are hydrophobic. See Figure 3-11.

Cannabis contains a psychotropic drug discussed in Section 6-2.

nitric oxide (NO) Gaseous neurotransmitter; acts, for example, to dilate blood vessels, aid digestion, and activate cellular metabolism.

carbon monoxide (CO) Gaseous neurotransmitter; activates cellular metabolism.

hydrogen sulfide (H$_2$S) Gaseous neurotransmitter; slows cellular metabolism.

zinc An ion transmitter that is packaged and stored in vesicles and that is then released and interacts with several receptors.

formed by fusion reactions in stars. It is actively transported, packaged into vesicles—usually with another transmitter like glutamate—and released into the synaptic cleft. Zinc interacts with several different receptors to cause biological change. When vesicular zinc becomes dysregulated, cognitive decline associated with age and Alzheimer disease occurs, whereas maintaining zinc homeostasis or correcting it with drug treatment protects cognitive ability (McAllister & Dyck, 2017).

Varieties of Receptors

Each of the two general classes of receptor proteins produces a different effect: one directly changes the postsynaptic membrane's electrical potential, and the other induces cellular change indirectly. A dazzling array of receptor subtypes allows for subtle differences in receptor function.

Two Classes of Receptors

When a neurotransmitter is released from any of the wide varieties of synapses onto a wide variety of targets, as illustrated in Figure 5-6, it crosses the synaptic cleft and binds to a receptor. What happens next depends on the receptor type.

Ionotropic receptors allow ions such as Na^+, K^+, Cl^-, and Ca^{2+} to move across a membrane (the suffix -*tropic* means "moving toward"). As **Figure 5-14** illustrates, an ionotropic receptor has two parts: (1) a binding site for a neurotransmitter and (2) a pore, or channel. When the neurotransmitter attaches to the binding site, the receptor quickly changes shape, either opening the pore and allowing ions to flow through it or closing the pore and blocking the ion flow. Thus, ionotropic receptors bring about rapid changes in membrane voltage and are usually excitatory: they trigger an action potential.

In contrast, a metabotropic receptor has a binding site for a neurotransmitter but lacks its own pore through which ions can flow. Through a series of steps, activated metabotropic receptors indirectly produce changes in nearby membrane-bound ion channels or in the cell's metabolic activity. **Figure 5-15A** shows the first of these two indirect effects. The metabotropic receptor consists of a single protein that spans the cell membrane, its binding site facing the synaptic cleft. Each receptor is coupled to one of a family of guanyl nucleotide–binding proteins, **G proteins** for short, shown on the inner side of the cell membrane in Figure 5-15A. When activated, a G protein binds to other proteins.

A G protein consists of three subunits: alpha, beta, and gamma. (A **subunit** is a protein that assembles with other proteins.) The alpha subunit detaches when a neurotransmitter binds to the G protein's associated metabotropic receptor. The detached alpha subunit can then bind to other proteins within the cell's membrane or its intracellular fluid. If the alpha subunit binds to a nearby ion channel in the membrane, as shown at the bottom of Figure 5-15A, the channel structure changes, modifying the flow of ions through it. If the channel is open, the alpha subunit may close it or, if closed, it may open. Changes in the channel and the ion flow across the membrane influence the membrane's electrical potential.

The binding of a neurotransmitter to a metabotropic receptor can also trigger more complicated cellular reactions, summarized in Figure 5-15B. All these reactions begin when the detached alpha subunit binds to an enzyme. The enzyme in turn activates a **second messenger** (the neurotransmitter being the first messenger) that carries instructions to other cellular structures. As illustrated at the bottom of Figure 5-15B, the second messenger can

- Bind to a membrane-bound channel, causing the channel to change its structure and thus alter ion flow through the membrane

- Initiate a reaction that incorporates intracellular (within the cell) protein molecules into the cell membrane, resulting, for example, in the formation of new ion channels

- Bind to sites on the cell's DNA to initiate or cease the production of specific proteins

Metabotropic receptors also allow for the possibility that a single neurotransmitter's binding to a receptor can activate an escalating sequence of events called an *amplification cascade*. The cascade effect results in many downstream proteins (second

---

Structurally, ionotropic receptors resemble voltage-activated channels, which propagate the action potential. See Figure 4-17.

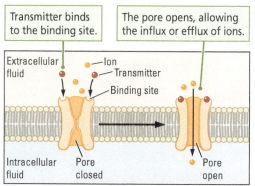

FIGURE 5-14 Ionotropic Receptor When activated, embedded transmitter proteins bring about direct, rapid changes in membrane voltage.

G protein Guanyl nucleotide–binding protein coupled to a metabotropic receptor; when activated, binds to other proteins.

subunit Protein molecule that assembles with other protein molecules.

second messenger Chemical that initiates a biochemical process when activated by a neurotransmitter (the first messenger).

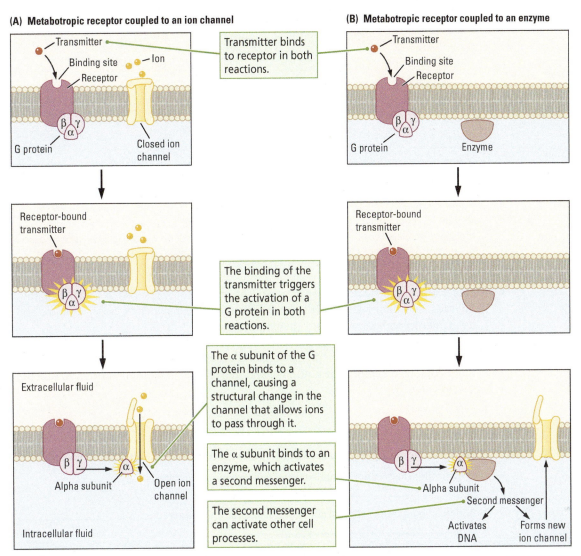

(A) Metabotropic receptor coupled to an ion channel

Transmitter

Binding site — Ion

Receptor

β γ α — G protein

Closed ion channel

Transmitter binds to receptor in both reactions.

Receptor-bound transmitter

β γ α

The binding of the transmitter triggers the activation of a G protein in both reactions.

Extracellular fluid

β γ — α

Alpha subunit   Open ion channel

Intracellular fluid

The α subunit of the G protein binds to a channel, causing a structural change in the channel that allows ions to pass through it.

The α subunit binds to an enzyme, which activates a second messenger.

The second messenger can activate other cell processes.

(B) Metabotropic receptor coupled to an enzyme

Transmitter

Binding site

Receptor

β γ α — G protein   Enzyme

Receptor-bound transmitter

β γ α

β γ — α

Alpha subunit

Second messenger

Activates DNA   Forms new ion channel

FIGURE 5-15 **Metabotropic Receptors**
When activated by a neurotransmitter, embedded membrane receptor proteins trigger associated G proteins, exerting indirect effects **(A)** on nearby ion channels or **(B)** in the cell's metabolic activity.

messengers or channels or both) being either activated or deactivated. Ionotropic receptors do not have such a widespread amplifying effect.

Recall that acetylcholine has an excitatory effect on skeletal muscles, where it activates an ionotropic receptor. Conversely, acetylcholine has an inhibitory effect on the heart rate, where it activates a metabotropic receptor. Furthermore, each transmitter may bind with several different kinds of ionotropic or metabotropic receptors. Elsewhere in the nervous system, for example, ACh activates a wide variety of receptors of either type.

Receptor Subtypes

While there are two general classes of receptors, ionotropic and metabotropic, each neurotransmitter may interact with a number of receptor subtypes specific to that neurotransmitter. Serotonin (5-HT), for instance, has 1 ionotropic receptor subtype (5-HT₃) and 12 subtypes of metabotropic receptors. **Table 5-3** lists the variety of small-molecule neurotransmitter receptor subtypes.

How is this variety achieved? Alternative forms of each subunit can assemble in unique combinations to make a functional receptor. For instance, the functional NMDA receptor, that can act as an ionotropic receptor for glutamate, is always composed of 4 subunits, but a total of 12 distinct subunits are available to come together in various combinations to form the functional receptor. The NMDA receptor can also act as a metabotropic receptor further broadening its function (Weilinger et al., 2016).

Why does the brain contain so many receptor subtypes for each neurotransmitter? The answer seems to be that each subtype has slightly different properties, which

Figure 14-18 diagrams how glutamate and the NMDA receptor function in associative learning.

TABLE 5-3 Small-Molecule Transmitter Receptors

Neurotransmitter	Ionotropic receptors	Metabotropic receptors
Acetylcholine (ACh)	Nicotinic	5 muscarinic*
Dopamine (DA)	—	5 dopamine
GABA	GABAA	GABAB
Glutamate (Glu)	NMDA, AMPA, kainate	7 mGluRs, NMDA
Glycine (Gly)	Glycine, NMDA	—
Histamine (H)	—	3 histamine
Norepinephrine (NE)	—	8 NE alpha and 3 NE beta
Serotonin (5-HT)	5-HT₃	12 5-HT

Peptide neurotransmitters and the lipid neurotransmitters anandamide and 2-AG have specific metabotropic-class receptors. Gaseous neurotransmitters do not have a specific receptor. The ion neurotransmitter zinc has binding sites on several receptor types.

*All metabotropic cholinergic receptors are muscarinic.

confer different activities. These activities can include the presence or absence of binding sites for other molecules, how long a channel remains open or closed, and the ability to interact with intracellular signaling molecules.

It should not be surprising that a brain such as ours, with its incredible complexity, is built on a vast array of units, including copious neurotransmitter types and even more copious receptor types. All this, and more, allows the human brain to function successfully.

5-2 Review

Before you continue, check your understanding. Answers to Self-Test appear at the back of the book.

1. Neurotransmitters are identified using four experimental criteria: _____, _____, _____, and _____.

2. The broad classes of chemically related neurotransmitters are _____, _____, _____, _____, and _____.

3. Acetylcholine is composed of _____ and _____. After release into the synaptic cleft, ACh is broken down by _____, and the products can be recycled.

4. Endocannabinoids are _____ neurotransmitters, made on demand and released from the _____ membrane.

5. Contrast the major characteristics of ionotropic and metabotropic receptors.

For additional study tools, visit 📖 **LaunchPad** at launchpadworks.com

5-3

Neurotransmitter Systems and Behavior

When researchers began to study neurotransmission, they reasoned that any given neuron would contain only one transmitter at all its axon terminals. Newer methods of analysis have revealed that this hypothesis is not strictly accurate. A single neuron may use one transmitter at one synapse and a different transmitter at another synapse. Moreover, different transmitters may coexist in the same terminal or synapse. Neuropeptides have been found to coexist in terminals with small-molecule transmitters, and more than one small-molecule transmitter may be found in a single synapse. In some cases, more than one transmitter is packaged within a single vesicle.

All these findings allow for multiple combinations of neurotransmitters and receptors for them. They caution as well against assuming a simple cause-and-effect relation between a neurotransmitter and a behavior. What are the functions of so many combinations? The answer will likely vary, depending on the behavior that is controlled. Historically, researchers focused on the most abundant transmitter within any given axon terminal and then associated that neurotransmitter with a function or behavior.

We now consider some links between neurotransmitters and behavior. We begin by exploring the three peripheral nervous system divisions: SNS, ANS, and ENS. Then we investigate neurotransmission in the central nervous system.

Neurotransmission in the Somatic Nervous System (SNS)

Motor neurons in the brain and spinal cord send their axons to the body's skeletal muscles, including the muscles of the eyes and face, trunk, limbs, fingers, and toes. Without these SNS neurons, movement would not be possible. Motor neurons are also called **cholinergic neurons** because acetylcholine is their main neurotransmitter. At a skeletal muscle, cholinergic neurons are excitatory, producing muscular contractions.

Just as a single main neurotransmitter serves the SNS, so does a single main receptor, a transmitter-activated ionotropic channel called a *nicotinic acetylcholine receptor* (*nAChr*). As shown in **Figure 5-16**, when ACh binds to this receptor, its pore opens to permit ion flow, thus depolarizing the muscle fiber. The nicotinic receptor pore is large enough to permit the simultaneous efflux of K^+ and influx of Na^+. The molecular structure of nicotine, a chemical found in tobacco, activates the nAChr in the same way that acetylcholine does, which is how this receptor got its name. The molecular structure of nicotine is sufficiently similar to that of ACh that nicotine acts as a mimic, fitting into acetylcholine receptor binding sites.

Acetylcholine is the primary neurotransmitter at skeletal muscles, but other neurotransmitters also occupy these cholinergic axon terminals and are released onto the muscle along with ACh. One is a neuropeptide called calcitonin gene–related peptide (CGRP), which acts through CGRP metabotropic receptors to increase the force with which a muscle contracts.

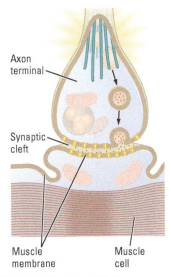

FIGURE 5-16 Nicotinic ACh Receptor
Research from Heuser & Reese, 1977.

Dual Activating Systems of the Autonomic Nervous System (ANS)

The complementary ANS divisions, sympathetic and parasympathetic, regulate the body's internal environment. The sympathetic division rouses the body for action, producing the fight-or-flight response. Heart rate ramps up, and digestive functions ramp down. The parasympathetic division calms the body down, producing an essentially opposite rest-and-digest response. Digestive functions ramp up, heart rate ramps down, and the body is ready to relax.

Figure 5-17 shows the neurochemical organization of the ANS. Both divisions are controlled by acetylcholine neurons that emanate from the CNS at two levels of the spinal cord. The CNS neurons synapse with parasympathetic neurons that also contain acetylcholine and with sympathetic neurons that contain norepinephrine. In other words, cholinergic neurons in the CNS synapse with sympathetic NE neurons to prepare the body's organs for fight or flight. Cholinergic neurons in the CNS synapse with autonomic ACh neurons in the parasympathetic division to prepare the body's organs to rest and digest.

Which type of synapse is excitatory and which inhibitory depends on the particular body organ's receptors. During sympathetic arousal, norepinephrine turns up heart rate and turns down digestive functions because NE receptors on the heart are excitatory, whereas NE receptors on the gut are inhibitory. Similarly, acetylcholine turns down heart rate and turns up digestive functions because its receptors on these organs are reversed: on the heart, inhibitory; on the gut, excitatory. Neurotransmitter activity, excitatory in one location and inhibitory in another, mediates the sympathetic and parasympathetic divisions, forming a complementary autonomic regulating system that maintains the body's internal environment under varying circumstances.

cholinergic neuron Neuron that uses acetylcholine as its main neurotransmitter; *cholinergic* applies to any neuron that uses ACh as its main transmitter.

FIGURE 5-17 **Controlling Biological Functions in the Autonomic Nervous System** The neurotransmitter in all the neurons leaving the spinal cord is acetylcholine. Left: In the sympathetic division, ACh neurons activate autonomic norepinephrine neurons in the sympathetic ganglia. NE stimulates organs required for fight or flight and suppresses activity in organs used to rest and digest. Right: In the parasympathetic division, ACh neurons from the spinal cord activate ACh neurons in the parasympathetic ganglia near their target organs to suppress activity in organs used for fight or flight and to stimulate organs used to rest and digest. To review the ANS divisions and connections in detail, see Figure 2-32.

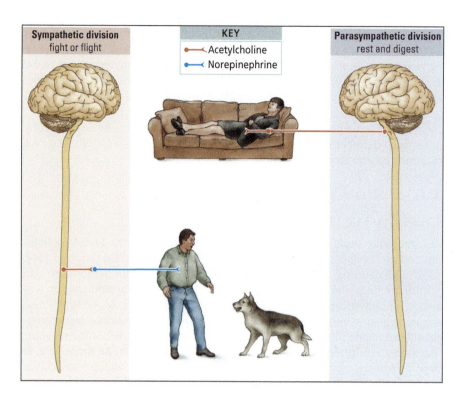

See Section 2-5 for a detailed discussion of the ENS.

Principle 7: Sensory and motor divisions permeate the nervous system.

Enteric Nervous System (ENS) Autonomy

The ENS can act without input from the CNS, which is why it has been called the second brain. It uses the main classes of neurotransmitters—more than 30 transmitters in total. Most of these neurotransmitters are identical to those employed by the CNS. Chief among the small-molecule neurotransmitters used by the enteric nervous system are serotonin and dopamine.

Sensory ENS neurons detect mechanical and chemical conditions in the gastrointestinal system. Via intestinal muscles, motor neurons in the ENS control the mixing of intestinal contents. Secretion of digestive enzymes is also under ENS control.

Four Activating Systems in the Central Nervous System

Just as there is an organization to the neurochemical systems of the PNS, there is an organization of neurochemical systems in the CNS. These systems are remarkably similar across a wide range of animal species, allowing for their identification first in the rat brain and then in the human brain (Hamilton et al., 2010).

For each of the four **activating systems** described here, a relatively small number of neurons grouped together in one or a few brainstem nuclei send axons to widespread CNS regions, suggesting that these nuclei and their terminals help synchronize activity throughout the brain and spinal cord. You can envision an activating system as being analogous to the power supply in a house. The fuse box or breaker box is the source of the power, and from it transmission lines go to each room.

Just as in the ANS, the precise action of the CNS transmitter depends on the brain region that is innervated and on the types of receptors the transmitter acts on at that region. To continue our analogy, the precise activating effect of the power in each room depends on the electrical devices in that room.

Each of four small-molecule transmitters participates in its own neural activating system—the cholinergic, dopaminergic, noradrenergic, and serotonergic systems. **Figure 5-18** locates each system's nuclei, with arrow shafts mapping the axon pathways and arrowheads indicating axon terminal locales.

As summarized on the right in Figure 5-18, each CNS activating system is associated with numerous behaviors. Associations among activating systems, behavior, and brain

activating system Neural pathways that coordinate brain activity through a single neurotransmitter; its cell bodies lie in a brainstem nucleus; axons are distributed through a wide CNS region.

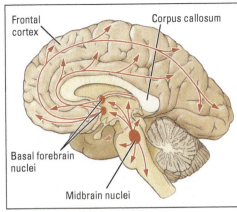

Cholinergic system (acetylcholine)
- Active in maintaining attention and waking EEG pattern.
- Thought to play a role in memory by maintaining neuron excitability.
- Death of cholinergic neurons and decrease in ACh in the neocortex are thought to be related to Alzheimer disease.

FIGURE 5-18 **Major Activating Systems** Each system's cell bodies are gathered into nuclei (shown as ovals) in the brainstem. Their axons project diffusely through the CNS and synapse on target structures. Each activating system is associated with one or more behaviors or diseases.

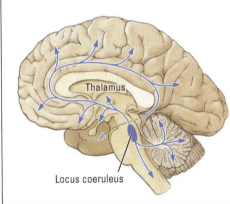

Dopaminergic system (dopamine)
Nigrostriatal pathways (orange projections)
- Active in maintaining normal motor behavior.
- Loss of DA is related to muscle rigidity and dyskinesia in Parkinson disease.

Mesolimbic pathways (purple projections)
- Dopamine release causes repetition of behaviors.
- Thought to be the neurotransmitter system most affected by addictive drugs and behavioral addictions.
- Increases in DA activity may be related to schizophrenia.
- Decreases in DA activity may be related to deficits of attention.

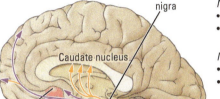

Noradrenergic system (norepinephrine)
- Active in maintaining emotional tone.
- Decreases in NE activity are thought to be related to depression.
- Increases in NE are thought to be related to mania (overexcited behavior).
- Decreased NE activity is associated with hyperactivity and attention-deficit/hyperactivity disorder.

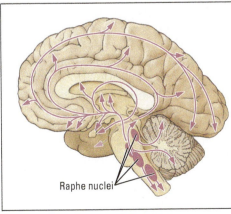

Serotonergic system (serotonin)
- Active in maintaining waking EEG pattern.
- Changes in serotonin activity are related to obsessive-compulsive disorder, tics, and schizophrenia.
- Decreases in serotonin activity are related to depression.
- Abnormalities in brainstem 5-HT neurons are linked to disorders such as sleep apnea and SIDS.

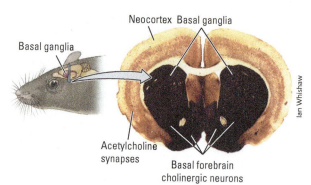

FIGURE 5-19 **Cholinergic Activation** Drawing at left shows the cortical location of the micrograph at right, stained to reveal AChE. Cholinergic neurons in the rat's basal forebrain project to the neocortex, and the darkly stained bands in the cortex show areas rich in cholinergic synapses. The darker central parts of the section, also rich in cholinergic neurons, are the basal ganglia.

Alzheimer disease Degenerative brain disorder related to aging; first appears as progressive memory loss and later develops into generalized dementia.

The EEG detects electrical signals the brain emits during various conscious states; see Sections 7-2 and 13-3.

Focus 14-3 details research on Alzheimer disease. Section 16-3 reviews various causes of and treatments for dementia.

disorders are far less certain. All these relations are subjects of ongoing research. Making definitive correlations between activating systems and behavior or activating systems and a disorder is difficult because the axons of these systems connect to almost every part of the brain and spinal cord. They likely have both specific functions and modulatory roles. We detail some of the documented relationships between the systems and behavior and disorders here and in many subsequent chapters.

Cholinergic System

Figure 5-19 shows in cross section a rat brain stained for the enzyme acetylcholinesterase (AChE), which breaks down ACh in synapses, as diagrammed earlier in Figure 5-10. The darkly stained areas have high AChE concentrations, indicating the presence of cholinergic terminals. AChE permeates the cortex and is especially dense in the basal ganglia. Many of these cholinergic synapses are connections from ACh nuclei in the brainstem, as illustrated in the top panel of Figure 5-18.

The cholinergic system participates in typical waking behavior, attention, and memory. For example, cholinergic neurons take part in producing one form of waking EEG activity. People affected by the degenerative **Alzheimer disease**, which begins with minor forgetfulness, progresses to major memory dysfunction, and later develops into generalized dementia, show a profound loss of cholinergic neurons at autopsy. Two treatment strategies for Alzheimer disease are drugs that either inhibit the enzyme acetylcholinesterase, thereby elevating levels of ACh, or raise the number of nicotinic receptors (Anand et al., 2017). Recall that ACh is synthesized from nutrients in food; thus, the role of diet in maintaining acetylcholine levels also is being investigated.

The brain abnormalities associated with Alzheimer disease are not limited to the cholinergic neurons, however. Autopsies reveal extensive damage to the neocortex and other brain regions. As a result, what role, if any, the cholinergic neurons play in the progress of the disorder is not yet clear. Perhaps their destruction causes degeneration in the cortex or perhaps the cause-and-effect relation is the other way around, with cortical degeneration causing cholinergic cell death. Then, too, the loss of cholinergic neurons is just one of many neural symptoms of Alzheimer disease. This is why drug treatments that prevent cell death are also being developed to slow the progression of Alzheimer disease (Anand et al., 2017).

Dopaminergic System

Figure 5-17 maps the dopaminergic activating system's two distinct pathways. The *nigrostriatal dopaminergic system* plays a major role in coordinating movement. As described throughout this chapter in relation to Parkinsonism, when dopamine neurons in the substantia nigra are lost, the result is a condition of extreme muscular rigidity. Opposing muscles contract at the same time, making it difficult for an affected person to move.

Parkinson patients also exhibit rhythmic tremors, especially of the limbs, which signals a release of formerly inhibited movement. Although the causes of Parkinson disease are not fully known, it can actually be triggered by the ingestion of certain toxic drugs, as described in Clinical Focus 5-4, The Case of the Frozen Addict. Those drugs may act as selective neurotoxins that specifically kill dopamine neurons in the substantia nigra.

Dopamine in the *mesolimbic dopaminergic system* may be the neurotransmitter most affected in addiction—to food, to drugs, and to other behaviors that involve a loss of impulse control. A common feature of addictive behaviors is that stimulating the mesolimbic dopaminergic system enhances

Rhythmic movement helps Parkinson patients restore the balance between neural excitation and inhibition—between the loss and the release of behavior. Some patients participate in a specially designed dance class for people with Parkinson. Participants enjoy the activity and report several benefits.

⊙ **CLINICAL FOCUS 5-4**

The Case of the Frozen Addict

Patient 1: During the first 4 days of July 1982, a 42-year-old man used 4½ grams of a "new synthetic heroin" . . . injected intravenously three or four times daily. . . . The immediate effects were different from heroin, producing an unusual "spacey" high as well as transient visual distortions and hallucinations. (Ballard et al., 1985, p. 949)

Patient 1 was one of seven young adults hospitalized at about the same time in California. All showed symptoms of Parkinson disease that appeared very suddenly after drug injection. They would awake to find themselves "frozen"—only able to move in "slow motion." According to Patient 1, he had to deliberately think through every movement, and described himself as stiff, slow, almost mute, and catatonic. These symptom are extremely unusual in this age group. All who were affected reportedly injected a synthetic heroin that was being sold on the streets in the summer of 1982.

J. William Langston (2008) has recounted when he and colleagues found that the "synthetic heroin" contained a contaminant called MPTP (1-methyl-4-phenyl-1,2,3,6-tetrahydropyridine) that resulted from poor technique during the drug's synthesis. The results of experimental studies in rodents showed that MPTP was not itself responsible for the patients' symptoms but was metabolized into MPP+ (1-methyl-4-phenylpyridinium), a neurotoxin.

The autopsy of one individual who was suspected of having died of MPTP poisoning showed that the brain had selectively lost dopamine neurons in the substantia nigra. The rest of the brain appeared healthy. Injecting MPTP into monkeys, rats, and mice produced similar symptoms and a similar selective loss of dopaminergic neurons in the substantia nigra. Thus, the combined clinical and experimental evidence indicates that a toxin can selectively kill dopamine neurons and that the die-off can induce Parkinson disease.

In 1988, Patient 1 received an experimental treatment at University Hospital in Lund, Sweden. Living dopamine neurons taken from human fetal brains at autopsy were implanted into the caudate nucleus and putamen (Widner et al., 1992). Extensive work with rodents and nonhuman primates in a number of laboratories had demonstrated that fetal neurons, before they develop dendrites and axons, can survive transplantation, mature, and secrete neurotransmitters.

Patient 1 had no serious postoperative complications and was much improved 24 months after the surgery. He could dress and feed himself, visit the bathroom with help, and make trips outside his home. He also responded much better to medication. The accompanying diagrams contrast DA levels in the brain of a Parkinson patient before (left) and 2 years, 4 months after implantation (right).

Transplantation of fetal neurons to treat Parkinson disease typically does not work. Unlike in the case of the frozen addict, Parkinson disease is associated with a continuing, active process that destroys dopaminergic neurons, including transplanted neurons, in the substantia nigra. Because Parkinson disease can affect as many as 20 people per 100,000, scientists continue to experiment with new approaches to transplantation and with genetic approaches for modifying remaining dopamine neurons (Lane et al., 2010).

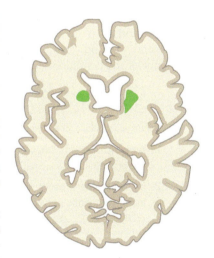

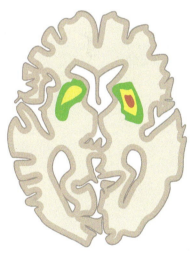

DA levels before fetal DA cell implantation

DA production at 2 years, 4 months after implantation

These diagrams represent PET scans that contrast DA levels in a Parkinson patient's brain before and 28 months after implantation. Research from Widner et al., 1992.

responses to environmental stimuli, thus making those stimuli attractive and rewarding. Indeed, some Parkinson patients who take dopamine receptor agonists as medications show a loss of impulse control that manifests in such behaviors as pathological gambling, hypersexuality, and compulsive shopping (Moore et al., 2014).

Excessive mesolimbic dopaminergic activity has also been proposed to play a role in **schizophrenia**, a behavioral disorder characterized by delusions, hallucinations, disorganized speech, blunted emotion, agitation or immobility, and a host of associated symptoms. Schizophrenia is one of the most common and most debilitating psychiatric disorders, affecting about 1 in 100 people.

Noradrenergic System

Norepinephrine (noradrenaline) may play a part in learning by stimulating neurons to change their structure. Norepinephrine may also facilitate healthy brain development and contribute to organizing movements. A neuron that uses norepinephrine as its transmitter is termed a **noradrenergic neuron** (derived from *adrenaline*, the Latin name for *epinephrine*).

Sections 6-3, 6-4, and 12-1 describe drug effects on the mesolimbic DA system. Sections 6-2 and 7-4 discuss possible causes of schizophrenia, and Section 16-2 discusses its neurobiology.

schizophrenia Behavioral disorder characterized by delusions, hallucinations, disorganized speech, blunted emotion, agitation or immobility, and a host of associated symptoms.

noradrenergic neuron From *adrenaline*, Latin for *epinephrine*; a neuron containing norepinephrine.

major depression Mood disorder characterized by prolonged feelings of worthlessness and guilt, the disruption of normal eating habits, sleep disturbances, a general slowing of behavior, and frequent thoughts of suicide.

mania Disordered mental state of extreme excitement.

obsessive-compulsive disorder (OCD) Behavior characterized by compulsively repeated acts (such as hand washing) and repetitive, often unpleasant, thoughts (obsessions).

Consult the Index of Disorders inside the book's front cover for more information on major depression, mania, ADHD, OCD, sleep apnea, and SIDS.

Behaviors and disorders related to the noradrenergic system concern emotions. Some symptoms of **major depression**—a mood disorder characterized by prolonged feelings of worthlessness and guilt, the disruption of typical eating habits, sleep disturbances, a general slowing of behavior, and frequent thoughts of suicide—may be related to decreased activity of noradrenergic neurons. Conversely, some symptoms of **mania** (excessive excitability) may be related to increased activity in these same neurons. Decreased NE activity has also been associated both with hyperactivity and attention-deficit/hyperactivity disorder (ADHD).

Serotonergic System

The serotonergic activating system maintains a waking EEG in the forebrain when we move and thus participates in wakefulness, as does the cholinergic system. Like norepinephrine, serotonin plays a role in learning, as described in Section 5-4. Some symptoms of depression may be related to decreased activity in serotonin neurons, and drugs commonly used to treat depression act on 5-HT neurons. Consequently, two forms of depression may exist, one related to norepinephrine and another related to serotonin.

Likewise, some research results suggest that various symptoms of schizophrenia also may be related to increases in serotonin activity, which implies that different forms of schizophrenia may exist. Decreased serotonergic activity is related to symptoms observed in **obsessive-compulsive disorder (OCD)**, in which a person has repetitive and often unpleasant thoughts (obsessions) and compulsively repeats acts (such as hand washing). Evidence also points to a link between abnormalities in serotonergic nuclei and conditions such as *sleep apnea* and *sudden infant death syndrome* (*SIDS*).

5-3 Review

Before you continue, check your understanding. Answers to Self-Test appear at the back of the book.

1. Although neurons can contain more than one _____, they are usually identified by the principal _____ in their axon terminals.

2. In the peripheral nervous system, the neurotransmitter at somatic muscles is _____; in the autonomic nervous system, _____ neurons from the spinal cord connect with _____ neurons for parasympathetic activity and with neurons for sympathetic activity.

3. The two principal small-molecule transmitters used by the enteric nervous system are _____ and _____.

4. The four main activating systems of the CNS are _____, _____, _____, and _____.

5. How would you respond to the comment that a behavior is caused solely by a chemical imbalance in the brain?

For additional study tools, visit 🔁 **LaunchPad** at launchpadworks.com

---

5-4

Adaptive Role of Synapses in Learning and Memory

Experiment 2-1 demonstrates observational learning in the octopus and the ubiquity of neuroplasticity.

Among our most cherished abilities are learning and remembering. Neuroplasticity is a requirement for learning and memory and a characteristic of the mammalian brain. In fact, it is a trait of the nervous systems of all animals, even the simplest worms. Larger brains with more synapses are more plastic, however, and thus likely to show more alterations in neural organization.

Alterations in neural organization happen because experience can alter the synapse. Not only are synapses versatile in structure and function, they are plastic: they can change. The synapse, therefore, is the site for the neural basis of **learning**, a relatively persistent or even permanent change in behavior that results from experience.

Donald O. Hebb was not the first to suggest that learning is mediated by structural changes in synapses, but the change that he envisioned in his book *The Organization of Behavior* was novel 70 years ago. Hebb theorized, "When an axon of cell A is near enough to excite a cell B and repeatedly or persistently takes part in firing it, some growth process or metabolic change takes place in one or both cells such that A's efficiency, as one of the cells firing B, is increased" (Hebb, 1949, p. 62). Simply put, cells that fire together wire together. A synapse that physically adapts in this way is called a *Hebb synapse*.

Eric Kandel was awarded a Nobel Prize in 2000 for his descriptions of the synaptic basis of learning in a way that Hebb envisaged: learning in which the conjoint activity of nerve cells serves to link them. Kandel's subject, the marine slug *Aplysia californica*, is an ideal subject for learning experiments. Slightly larger than a softball and lacking a shell, *Aplysia* has roughly 20,000 neurons. Some are quite accessible to researchers, who can isolate and study circuits having relatively few synapses.

When threatened, *Aplysia* defensively withdraws its more vulnerable body parts— the gill (through which it extracts oxygen from the water to breathe) and the siphon (a spout above the gill that excretes seawater and waste). By stroking or shocking the slug's appendages, Kandel and his coworkers (Bailey et al., 2015) produced enduring changes in its defensive behaviors. They used these behavioral responses to study underlying changes in *Aplysia*'s nervous system.

We illustrate the role of synapses in two kinds of learning that Kandel has studied: habituation and sensitization. For humans, both are called *unconscious* because they do not depend on a person's knowing precisely when and how they occur.

Habituation Response

In **habituation**, the response to a stimulus weakens with repeated stimulus presentations. If you are accustomed to living in the country and then move to a city, you might at first find the sounds of traffic and people extremely loud and annoying. With time, however, you stop noticing most of the noise most of the time. You have habituated to it.

Habituation develops with all our senses. We simply become insensitive to the customary background sensations of sound, touch, smell, taste, and even vision. We cease to notice the feel of our clothes sometime after donning them. Most of us aren't aware of the smell of our houseplants (a phenomenon called *nose blindness*), but people who have recently returned from Antarctica report being nearly overwhelmed by it for some time. Tastes can fade over the course of a meal. And if we record the response from photoreceptors to a newly presented light stimulus, they increase their firing rate for some time and then eventually cease firing altogether. In fact, to prevent this form of habituation, our eyes make small, fast random movements, call **saccades**, which continually change the light falling on individual photoreceptors, allowing us to continue to see.

Aplysia habituates to waves in the shallow tidal zone where it lives. These slugs are constantly buffeted by the flow of waves against their body, and they learn that waves are just the background sensations of daily life. They do not flinch and withdraw every time a wave passes over them. They habituate to this stimulus.

A sea slug that is habituated to waves nevertheless remains sensitive to other touch sensations. Prodded with a novel object, it responds by withdrawing its siphon and gill. The animal's reaction to repeated presentations of the same novel stimulus forms the basis for **Experiment 5-2**, studying its habituation response.

Neural Basis of Habituation

The Procedure section of Experiment 5-2 shows the setup for studying what happens to the withdrawal response of *Aplysia*'s gill after repeated stimulation. A gentle jet of water is sprayed on the siphon while gill movement is recorded. If the water jet is presented to *Aplysia*'s siphon as many as 10 times, the gill withdrawal response

Principle 2: Neuroplasticity is the hallmark of nervous system functioning.

Hebb's "cell-assembly" diagram appears at the end of Section 15-1.

Aplysia californica

Section 14-4 investigates the neural bases of brain plasticity in conscious learning and in memory.

learning Relatively persistent or even permanent change in behavior that results from experience.

habituation Learned behavior in which the response to a stimulus weakens with repeated presentations.

saccades Small, fast, random eye movements designed to keep photoreceptors exposed to ever-changing visual stimuli to prevent habituation.

Question: What happens to the gill response after repeated stimulation?

Procedure

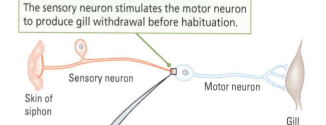

1 Gill withdraws from water jet.

2 Gill no longer withdraws from water jet, demonstrating habituation.

Siphon

After repeated stimulation

Water jet

Results

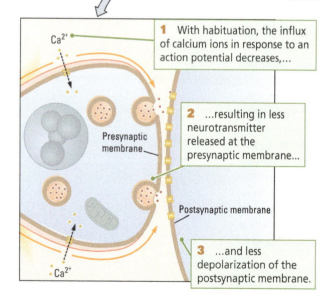

The sensory neuron stimulates the motor neuron to produce gill withdrawal before habituation.

Sensory neuron

Skin of siphon

Motor neuron

Gill muscle

Ca^{2+}

1 With habituation, the influx of calcium ions in response to an action potential decreases,...

Presynaptic membrane

2 ...resulting in less neurotransmitter released at the presynaptic membrane...

Postsynaptic membrane

3 ...and less depolarization of the postsynaptic membrane.

Ca^{2+}

Conclusion: The withdrawal response weakens with repeated presentation of water jet (habituation) due to decreased Ca^{2+} influx and subsequently less neurotransmitter release from the presynaptic axon terminal.

sensitization Learned behavior in which the response to a stimulus strengthens with repeated presentations.

Stress can foster and prolong the effects of PTSD. See Sections 6-5 and 12-6. Section 16-2 covers treatment strategies.

is weaker some minutes later, when the animal is again tested. The decrement in the strength of the withdrawal is habituation, which can last as long as 30 minutes in this case.

The Results section of Experiment 5-2 starts by showing a simple representation of the pathway that mediates *Aplysia's* gill withdrawal response. For purposes of illustration, only 1 sensory neuron, 1 motor neuron, and 1 synapse are shown; in actuality, about 300 neurons may take part in this response. The water jet stimulates the sensory neuron, which in turn stimulates the motor neuron responsible for the gill withdrawal. But exactly where do the changes associated with habituation take place? In the sensory neuron? In the motor neuron? In the synapse between the two?

Habituation does not result from an inability of either the sensory neuron or the motor neuron to produce action potentials. In response to direct electrical stimulation, both the sensory neuron and the motor neuron retain the ability to generate action potentials even after habituation. Electrical recordings from the motor neuron show that as habituation develops, the excitatory postsynaptic potentials (EPSPs) in the motor neuron become smaller.

The most likely way in which these EPSPs decrease in size is that the motor neuron is receiving less neurotransmitter from the sensory neuron across the synapse. And if less neurotransmitter is being received, then the changes accompanying habituation must be taking place in the presynaptic axon terminal of the sensory neuron.

Reduced Sensitivity of Calcium Channels Underlies Habituation

Kandel and his coworkers measured neurotransmitter output from a sensory neuron and verified that less neurotransmitter is in fact released from a habituated neuron than from a nonhabituated one. Recall from Figure 5-4 that neurotransmitter release in response to an action potential requires an influx of calcium ions across the presynaptic membrane. As habituation takes place, that Ca^{2+} influx decreases in response to the voltage changes associated with an action potential. Presumably, with repeated use, voltage-activated calcium channels become less responsive to voltage changes and more resistant to the passage of calcium ions.

The neural basis of habituation lies in the change in presynaptic calcium channels. Its mechanism, which is summarized up close in the Results section of Experiment 5-2, is a reduced sensitivity of calcium channels and a consequent decrease in neurotransmitter release. Thus, habituation can be linked to a specific molecular change, as summarized in the experiment's Conclusion.

Sensitization Response

A sprinter crouched in her starting blocks is often hyperresponsive to the starter's gun: its firing triggers in her a rapid reaction. The stressful, competitive context of the race helps sensitize the sprinter to this sound. **Sensitization**, an enhanced response to some stimulus, is the opposite of habituation. The organism becomes hyperresponsive to a stimulus rather than accustomed to it.

Sensitization occurs within a context. Sudden, novel stimulation heightens our general awareness and often results in larger-than-typical responses to all kinds of stimulation. If a loud noise startles you suddenly, you become much more responsive to other stimuli in your surroundings, including some to which you previously were habituated. In **posttraumatic stress disorder (PTSD)**, physiological arousal related to recurring memories and dreams surrounding a traumatic event persist for months or years after the event. One characteristic of PTSD is a heightened response to stimuli, suggesting that the disorder is in part related to sensitization.

The same thing happens to *Aplysia*. Sudden, novel stimuli can heighten the slug's responsiveness to familiar stimulation. When attacked by a predator, for example, the slug displays heightened responses to many other stimuli in its environment. In the laboratory, a small electric shock to *Aplysia*'s tail mimics a predatory attack and effects sensitization, as illustrated in the Procedure section of **Experiment 5-3**. A single electric shock to the slug's tail enhances its gill withdrawal response for a period that lasts for minutes to hours.

Neural Basis of Sensitization

The neural circuits participating in sensitization differ from those that take part in a habituation response. The Results section of Experiment 5-3 shows the sensory and motor neurons that produce the gill withdrawal response and adds an interneuron that is responsible for sensitization.

An interneuron that receives input from a sensory neuron in *Aplysia*'s tail (and so carries information about the shock) makes an axoaxonic synapse with a sensory neuron in the siphon. The interneuron's axon terminal contains serotonin. Consequently, in response to a tail shock, the tail sensory neuron activates the interneuron, which in turn releases 5-HT onto the axon of the siphon sensory neuron. Information from the siphon still comes through the sensory neuron to activate the motor neuron leading to the gill muscle, but the interneuron's action in releasing 5-HT onto the sensory neuron's presynaptic membrane amplifies the gill withdrawal response.

At the molecular level, shown close up in the Results section of Experiment 5-3, the serotonin released from the interneuron binds to a metabotropic serotonin receptor on the siphon's sensory neuron axon. This binding activates second messengers in the sensory neuron. Specifically, the serotonin receptor is coupled through its G protein to the enzyme adenyl cyclase. This enzyme increases the concentration of second messenger cyclic adenosine monophosphate (cAMP) in the presynaptic membrane of the siphon's sensory neuron.

Through several chemical reactions, cAMP attaches a phosphate molecule (PO_4) to potassium channels, rendering them less responsive. The close-up in Experiment 5-3 sums it up. In response to an action potential traveling down the axon of the siphon's sensory neuron (such as one generated by a touch to the siphon), the potassium channels on that neuron are slower to open. Consequently, K^+ ions cannot repolarize the membrane as quickly as normal, so the action potential lasts longer than it usually would.

Less-Responsive Potassium Channels Underlie Sensitization

The longer-lasting action potential that occurs because potassium channels are slower to open prolongs Ca^{2+} inflow. Ca^{2+} influx is necessary for neurotransmitter release. Thus, greater Ca^{2+} influx results in more neurotransmitter being released from the sensory synapse onto the motor neuron.

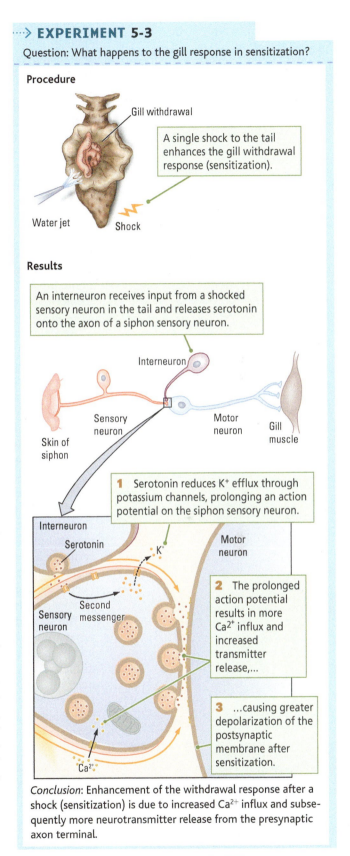

EXPERIMENT 5-3

Question: What happens to the gill response in sensitization?

Procedure

Gill withdrawal

A single shock to the tail enhances the gill withdrawal response (sensitization).

Water jet   Shock

Results

An interneuron receives input from a shocked sensory neuron in the tail and releases serotonin onto the axon of a siphon sensory neuron.

Interneuron

Sensory neuron   Motor neuron   Gill muscle

Skin of siphon

1 Serotonin reduces K^+ efflux through potassium channels, prolonging an action potential on the siphon sensory neuron.

Interneuron
Serotonin

Motor neuron

K^+

Second messenger

Sensory neuron

2 The prolonged action potential results in more Ca^{2+} influx and increased transmitter release,...

3 ...causing greater depolarization of the postsynaptic membrane after sensitization.

Ca^{2+}

Conclusion: Enhancement of the withdrawal response after a shock (sensitization) is due to increased Ca^{2+} influx and subsequently more neurotransmitter release from the presynaptic axon terminal.

posttraumatic stress disorder (PTSD)
Syndrome characterized by physiological arousal associated with recurrent memories and dreams arising from a traumatic event that occurred months or years earlier.

This increased neurotransmitter release produces greater activation of the motor neuron and thus a larger-than-normal gill withdrawal response. If the second messenger cAMP mobilizes more synaptic vesicles, making more neurotransmitter ready for release into the sensory–motor synapse, gill withdrawal may also be enhanced.

Sensitization, then, is the opposite of habituation at the molecular level as well as at the behavioral level. In sensitization, more Ca^{2+} influx results in more transmitter being released, whereas in habituation, less Ca^{2+} influx results in less neurotransmitter being released. The structural basis of cellular memory in these two forms of learning is different, however. In sensitization, the change takes place in potassium channels, whereas in habituation, the change takes place in calcium channels.

Learning as a Change in Synapse Number

Neural changes associated with learning must last long enough to account for a relatively permanent change in an organism's behavior. The changes at synapses described in the preceding sections develop quite quickly, but they do not last indefinitely, as memories often do. How, then, can synapses be responsible for the long-term changes associated with learning and memory?

Repeated stimulation produces habituation and sensitization that can persist for months. Brief training produces short-term learning; longer training periods produce more enduring learning. If you cram for an exam the night before you take it, you might forget the material quickly, but if you study a little each day for a week, your learning may tend to endure. What underlies this more persistent form of learning?

Researchers working with Eric Kandel (Bailey et al., 2015) found that the number and size of sensory synapses change in well-trained, habituated, and sensitized *Aplysia*. Relative to a control neuron, the number and size of synapses decrease in habituated animals and increase in sensitized animals, as represented in **Figure 5-20**. Apparently, synaptic events associated with habituation and sensitization can also trigger processes in the sensory cell that result in the loss or formation of new synapses.

A mechanism through which these processes can take place begins with calcium ions that mobilize second messengers to send instructions to nuclear DNA. The transcription and translation of nuclear DNA in turn initiate structural changes at synapses, including the formation of new synapses and new dendritic spines. Research Focus 5-5, Dendritic Spines: Small but Mighty, summarizes experimental evidence about structural changes in dendritic spines.

The second messenger cAMP plays an important role in carrying instructions regarding these structural changes to nuclear DNA. The evidence for cAMP's involvement comes from studies of the fruit fly *Drosophila*. Two genetic mutations in the fruit fly can produce similar learning deficiencies. Both render the second messenger cAMP inoperative—but in opposite ways. One mutation, called *dunce*, lacks the enzymes necessary to degrade cAMP, so the fruit fly has abnormally high cAMP levels. The other mutation, called *rutabaga*, reduces levels of cAMP below the normal range for *Drosophila* neurons.

FIGURE 5-20 **Physical Basis of Memory**
Relative to a control neuronal connection (left), the number of synapses between *Aplysia*'s sensory neuron and a motor neuron decline as a result of habituation (center) and increase as a result of sensitization (right). Such structural changes may underlie enduring memories.

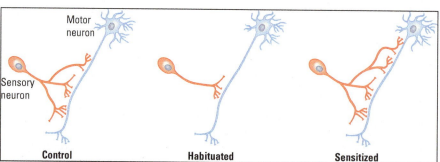
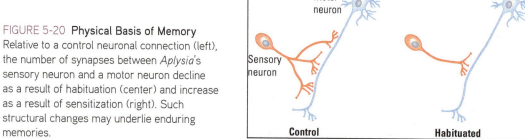

⊙ RESEARCH FOCUS 5-5

Dendritic Spines: Small but Mighty

Dendritic spines, which protrude from the dendrite's shaft, measure about 1 to 3 micrometers (μm, one-millionth of a meter) long and less than 1 μm in diameter. Each neuron can have many thousands of spines. The number of dendritic spines in the human cerebral cortex is estimated at 10^{14}.

Dendritic spines originate in filopodia (from the Latin *file*, for "thread," and the Greek *podium*, for "foot") that bud out of neurons, especially at dendrites. Microscopic observation of dendrites shows that filopodia are constantly emerging and retracting over several seconds.

This budding of filopodia is much more pronounced in developing neurons and in the developing brain (see Figure 8-13). Because filopodia can grow into dendritic spines, their budding suggests that they are searching for contacts from axon terminals to form synapses. When contact is made, some new synapses may have only a short life; others will endure.

A permanent dendritic spine tends to have a large, mushroom-shaped head, giving it a large contact area with a terminal button, and a long stem, giving it an identity apart from that of its dendrite. The heads of spines and the terminals of presynaptic connections form functional compartments that can generate huge electrical potentials and so influence the neuron's electrical messages.

Dendritic spines mediate learning that lasts, including habituation and sensitization. To mediate learning, each spine must be able to act independently, undergoing changes that its neighbors do not undergo.

Examination of dendritic spines in the nervous system shows that some are simple and others complex. The cellular mechanisms that allow synapses to appear on spines and to change shape include microfilaments linked to the membrane receptors, protein transport from the cell body, and the incorporation of nutrients from the extracellular space.

The variety suggests that all this activity changes the appearance of both presynaptic and postsynaptic structures. The illustration summarizes synaptic structures that can be measured and related to learning and behavior and to structural changes that may subserve learning.

Dendritic spines provide the structural basis for our behavior, our individual skills, and our memories (Bosch & Hayashi, 2012). Impairments in forming spines characterize some kinds of mental disability, and the loss of spines is associated with the dementia of Alzheimer disease.

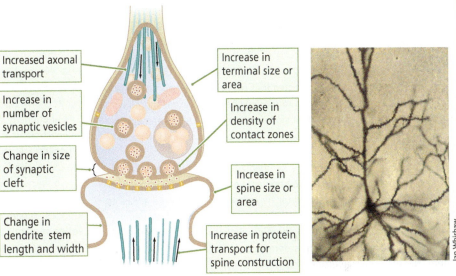

Increased axonal transport

Increase in number of synaptic vesicles

Change in size of synaptic cleft

Change in dendrite stem length and width

Increase in terminal size or area

Increase in density of contact zones

Increase in spine size or area

Increase in protein transport for spine construction

Ian Whishaw

Synaptic structures that may subserve learning.

Significantly, fruit flies with either mutation are impaired in acquiring habituated and sensitized responses because their levels of cAMP cannot be regulated. New synapses seem to be required for learning to take place, and the second messenger cAMP seems to carry instructions to form them. **Figure 5-21** summarizes these research findings.

More lasting habituation and sensitization are mediated by relatively permanent changes in neuronal structure—by fewer or more synaptic connections—and the effects can be difficult to alter. As a result of sensitization, for example, symptoms of PTSD can persist indefinitely.

5-4 Review

Before you continue, check your understanding. Answers to Self-Test appear at the back of the book.

1. Experience alters the _____, the site of the neural basis of _____, a relatively persistent or permanent change in behavior that results from experience.

2. *Aplysia's* synaptic function mediates two basic forms of learning: _____ and _____.

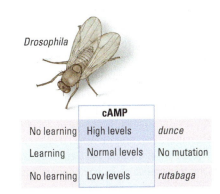

Drosophila

	cAMP	
No learning	High levels	*dunce*
Learning	Normal levels	No mutation
No learning	Low levels	*rutabaga*

FIGURE 5-21 **Genetic Disruption of Learning** Either of two mutations in the fruit fly *Drosophila* inactivates the second messenger cAMP by moving its level either above or below the concentration range the cell can regulate, thus disrupting learning.

3. Changes that accompany habituation take place within the _____ of the _____ neuron, mediated by _____ channels that grow _____ sensitive with use.

4. The sensitization response is amplified by _____ that release serotonin onto the presynaptic membrane of the sensory neuron, changing the sensitivity of presynaptic _____ channels and increasing the influx of _____.

5. One characteristic of _____, defined as physiological arousal related to recurring memories and dreams surrounding a traumatic event that persist for months or years after the event, is a heightened response to stimuli. This suggests that the disorder is in part related to _____.

6. Describe the benefits and/or drawbacks of permanent habituation and sensitization.

For additional study tools, visit **LaunchPad** at launchpadworks.com

Summary

5-1 A Chemical Message

In the 1920s, Otto Loewi suspected that nerves to the heart secrete a chemical that regulates its beat rate. His subsequent experiments with frogs showed that acetylcholine slows heart rate, whereas epinephrine increases it. This observation proved key to understanding the basis of chemical neurotransmission.

The systems for chemically synthesizing an excitatory or inhibitory neurotransmitter are in the presynaptic neuron's axon terminal or its soma, whereas the systems for neurotransmitter storage are in its axon terminal. The receptor systems on which that neurotransmitter acts typically are on the postsynaptic membrane. Such anterograde chemical neurotransmission is dominant in the human nervous system. Nevertheless, neurons also make direct connections with each other through gap junctions, channel-forming proteins that allow direct sharing of ions or nutrients.

The five major stages in the life of a neurotransmitter are (1) synthesis, (2) packaging and storage, (3) release from the axon terminal, (4) action on postsynaptic receptors, and (5) inactivation. After synthesis, the neurotransmitter is transported into synaptic vesicles that are stored near the axon terminal. When an action potential is propagated on the presynaptic membrane, voltage changes set in motion the vesicles' attachment to the presynaptic membrane and neurotransmitter release by exocytosis.

One synaptic vesicle releases a quantum of neurotransmitter into the synaptic cleft, producing a miniature potential on the postsynaptic membrane. Generating an action potential on the postsynaptic cell requires simultaneous release of many quanta of transmitter. After a transmitter has done its work, it is inactivated by such processes as diffusion out of the synaptic cleft, breakdown by enzymes, and reuptake of the transmitter or its components into the axon terminal (or sometimes uptake into astrocytes).

5-2 Varieties of Neurotransmitters and Receptors

Small-molecule transmitters, peptide transmitters, lipid transmitters, gaseous transmitters, and ion transmitters are broad classes for ordering the roughly 100 neurotransmitters that investigators propose might exist. Neurons containing these transmitters make a variety of connections with other neurons, as well as with muscles, blood vessels, and extracellular fluid.

Functionally, neurons can be both excitatory and inhibitory, and they can participate in local circuits or in general brain networks. Excitatory synapses are usually on a dendritic tree, whereas inhibitory synapses are usually on a cell body.

Some neurotransmitters are associated with both ionotropic and metabotropic receptors. An ionotropic receptor quickly and directly induces voltage changes on the postsynaptic cell membrane. Slower-acting metabotropic receptors activate second messengers to indirectly produce changes in the cell's function and structure. A plethora of receptors, formed from combinations of multiple types of proteins called subunits, exist for most transmitters.

5-3 Neurotransmitter Systems and Behavior

Because neurotransmitters are multifunctional, scientists find it impossible to isolate relationships between a single neurotransmitter and a single behavior. Rather, activating systems of neurons that employ the same principal neurotransmitter influence various general aspects of behavior. For instance, acetylcholine, the main neurotransmitter in the SNS, controls movement of the skeletal muscles, whereas acetylcholine and norepinephrine, the main neurotransmitters in the ANS, control the body's internal organs. In the ENS, dopamine and serotonin serve as the main neurotransmitters that regulate the gut's functioning.

The CNS contains not only widely dispersed glutamate and GABA neurons—its main neurotransmitters—but also neural activating systems that employ acetylcholine, norepinephrine, dopamine, or serotonin. All these systems ensure that wide areas of the brain act in concert, and each is associated with various classes of behaviors and disorders.

5-4 Adaptive Role of Synapses in Learning and Memory

Changes in synapses underlie the neural basis of learning and memory. In habituation, a form of learning in which a response weakens as a result of repeated stimulation, calcium channels become less responsive to an action potential. Consequently, less neurotransmitter is released when an action potential is propagated.

In sensitization, a form of learning in which a response strengthens as a result of stimulation, changes in potassium channels prolong the action potential's duration; this results in an increased influx of calcium ions and, consequently, release of more neurotransmitter. With repeated training, new synapses can develop, and both forms of learning can become relatively permanent.

In *Aplysia*, the number of synapses connecting sensory neurons and motor neurons decreases in response to repeated sessions of habituation. Conversely, the number of synapses connecting sensory and motor neurons increases in response to repeated sensitization sessions. These changes in the numbers of synapses and dendritic spines are related to long-term learning.

Key Terms

acetylcholine (ACh), p. 138
activating system, p. 158
Alzheimer disease, p. 160
anterograde synaptic transmission, p. 142
autoreceptor, p. 144
carbon monoxide (CO), p. 153
chemical synapse, p. 142
cholinergic neuron, p. 157
dopamine (DA), p. 141
endocannabinoid, p. 153
epinephrine (EP), p. 139
G protein, p. 154

gamma-aminobutyric acid (GABA), p. 150
gap junction, p. 145
glutamate (Glu), p. 150
habituation, p. 163
histamine (H), p. 151
hydrogen sulfide (H_2S), p. 153
ionotropic receptor, p. 143
learning, p. 163
major depression, p. 162
mania, p. 162
metabotropic receptor, p. 143
neuropeptide, p. 152
neurotransmitter, p. 139

nitric oxide (NO), p. 153
noradrenergic neuron, p. 161
norepinephrine (NE), p. 139
obsessive-compulsive disorder (OCD), p. 162
Parkinson disease, p. 141
postsynaptic membrane, p. 142
posttraumatic stress disorder (PTSD), p. 165
presynaptic membrane, p. 142
quantum (pl. quanta), p. 144
rate-limiting factor, p. 150
reuptake, p. 149
saccades, p. 163

schizophrenia, p. 161
second messenger, p. 154
sensitization, p. 164
serotonin (5-HT), p. 150
small-molecule transmitter, p. 149
storage granule, p. 142
subunit, p. 154
synaptic cleft, p. 142
synaptic vesicle, p. 141
transmitter-activated receptor, p. 143
transporter, p. 142
tripartite synapse, p. 142
zinc, p. 153

Visit 🔁 **LaunchPad** to access the e-Book, videos, 🔁 **LearningCurve** adaptive quizzing, flashcards, and more. launchpadworks.com

Meletios Verras/Getty Images

How Do Drugs and Hormones Influence Brain and Behavior?

◎ **CLINICAL FOCUS** 6-1

Cognitive Enhancement?

Some university and college students take certain psychoactive drugs without a prescription—for example, Adderall obtained through friends or family—to remain alert and focused for extended periods while studying for exams. Indeed, the number of prescriptions for Adderall has fallen, and yet there is an increase in medical problems related to Adderall abuse because the drug is being diverted to those for whom it is not legitimately prescribed. Many college students think stimulants like Adderall and Ritalin are harmless study aids, but misuse can carry serious health risks, including mental health problems, depression, bipolar disorder, incidents of aggressive or hostile behavior, and addiction (Han et al., 2016).

Both Adderall (mainly dextroamphetamine) and Ritalin (methylphenidate) are prescribed as a treatment for **attention-deficit/hyperactivity disorder (ADHD)**, a developmental disorder characterized by core behaviors including impulsivity, hyperactivity, and/or inattention. Methylphenidate and dextroamphetamine are Schedule II drugs, signifying that they carry the potential for abuse and require a prescription when used medically. Their main illicit source is through falsified prescriptions or purchase from someone who has a prescription. Both drugs share the pharmacological properties of amphetamine: prolonging and increasing dopamine levels in the synapse by reversing its transporter (see Section 6-2).

The use of cognitive enhancers is not new. In his classic paper on cocaine, Viennese psychoanalyst Sigmund Freud stated in 1884, "The main use of coca [cocaine] will undoubtedly remain that which the Indians [of Peru] have made of it for centuries . . . to increase the physical capacity of the body." Freud later withdrew his endorsement when he realized that cocaine is addictive.

In 1937, an article in the *American Journal of Psychiatry* reported that a form of amphetamine called Benzedrine improved performance on mental efficiency tests (Bradley, 1937). This information was quickly disseminated among students, who began using the drug as a study aid for examinations. In the 1950s, dextroamphetamine, marketed as Dexedrine, was similarly prescribed for narcolepsy, a sleep disorder, and used illicitly by students as a study aid.

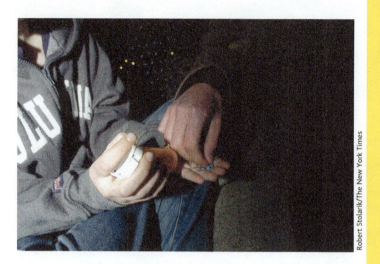

Robert Stolarik/The New York Times

The complex neural effects of amphetamine stimulants center on learning at the synapse by means of habituation and sensitization. With repeated use for nonmedicinal purposes, the drugs can also begin to produce side effects, including sleep disruption, loss of appetite, and headaches. Some people develop cardiovascular abnormalities and/or become addicted to amphetamine.

Treating ADHD with prescription drugs is itself controversial, despite their widespread use for this purpose. According to Aagaard and Hansen (2011), assessing the adverse effects of cognitive enhancement medication is hampered because many participants drop out of studies, and the duration of the studies is short.

Despite the contention that stimulant drugs can improve school and work performance by improving brain function in otherwise healthy individuals, evidence for their effectiveness, other than a transient improvement in motivation, is weak.

---

attention-deficit/hyperactivity disorder (ADHD) Developmental disorder characterized by core behavioral symptoms including impulsivity, hyperactivity, and/or inattention.

psychopharmacology Study of how drugs affect the nervous system and behavior.

Psychopharmacology, the study of how drugs affect the nervous system and behavior, is the subject of this chapter. We begin by looking at the most common ways drugs are administered, the routes they take to reach the central nervous system, and how they are eliminated from the body. We then examine psychoactive drugs based on the primary neurotransmitter system that they interact with. Next, we consider why different people may respond differently to the same dose of a drug and why people may become addicted to drugs. Many principles related to drugs also apply to the action of hormones, the chapter's final topic, which includes a discussion of synthetic steroids that act as hormones.

Before we examine how drugs produce their effects on the brain for good or for ill, we must raise a caution: the sheer number of neurotransmitters, receptors, and possible sites of drug action is astounding. Every drug acts at many sites in the body and brain and affects more than one neurotransmitter system. In other words, every drug has a primary or intended action as well as secondary or unintended actions. Moreover, individual differences—genetic makeup, adverse childhood experiences, sex, age, height, and weight—all influence how drugs affect people. Considering all the variables, psychopharmacological research has made important advances in understanding drug action, but neuroscientists do not know everything there is to know about every drug.

6-1
Principles of Psychopharmacology

Drugs are simply chemical compounds that are administered to bring about some desired change in the body and brain. Drugs are usually used to diagnose, treat, or prevent illness; to relieve mental or physical pain and suffering; or to improve some adverse physiological condition. In this chapter, we focus on **psychoactive drugs**—substances that alter mood, thought, or behavior; are used to manage neuropsychological illness; and may be taken recreationally. We also consider psychoactive drugs that, depending on dose and repeated usage, can act as toxins, producing alterations in behavior, brain damage, or even death.

Drug Routes into the Nervous System

To be effective, a psychoactive drug has to reach its target in the nervous system. The way a drug enters and passes through the body to reach its target is called its *route of administration*. Drugs can be administered orally, inhaled into the lungs, administered rectally in a suppository, absorbed from patches applied to the skin or mucous membranes; or injected into the bloodstream, into a muscle, or even directly into the brain. **Figure 6-1** illustrates some of these routes of drug administration and summarizes the characteristics of drugs that allow them to pass through various barriers to reach their targets.

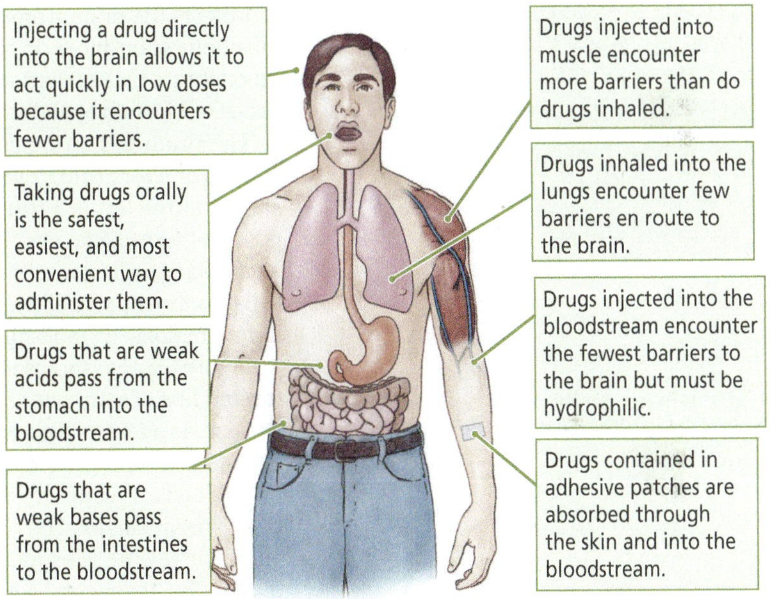

Oral administration is easy and convenient but is nonetheless a complex route. To reach the bloodstream, an ingested drug must first be absorbed through the lining of the stomach or small intestine. Drugs in liquid form are absorbed more readily. Drugs taken in solid form are not absorbed unless the stomach's gastric juices can dissolve them. Some drugs may be destroyed or altered by enzymes in the gastrointestinal tract's microbiome. Whether a drug is an acid or a base also influences its absorption.

Once absorbed by the stomach or intestine, the drug must enter the bloodstream. This leg of the journey requires that the drug have additional properties. Because blood has a high water concentration, the drug must be water-soluble. It is then diluted by the approximately 6 liters of blood that circulate through an adult body. When the drug leaves the bloodstream, the body's roughly 35 liters of extracellular fluid further dilute it.

Our largest organ, the skin, has three cell layers designed to be a protective body coat. Some small-molecule drugs (for example, nicotine in a patch) easily penetrate the skin barrier. Drugs administered as gases or aerosols penetrate the cell linings of the respiratory tract very easily and are absorbed across these membranes into the bloodstream almost immediately after they are inhaled. Thus, they reach the bloodstream by circumventing the barriers in the digestive system or skin. When administered as a gas or in smoke, drugs like nicotine, cocaine, and tetrahydrocannabinol (THC), are similarly absorbed.

Still fewer obstacles confront a drug destined for the brain if that drug is injected directly into the bloodstream. And the fewest obstacles are encountered if a psychoactive drug is injected directly into the brain. This route of administration is normally carried out only by medical professionals in a sterile setting.

With each obstacle eliminated en route to the brain, a drug's dosage can be reduced by a factor of 10. For example, 1 milligram or 1000 micrograms (μg; 1 μg is equal to one-thousandth of a milligram) of amphetamine, a psychomotor stimulant and major component of the drugs described in Clinical Focus 6-1, Cognitive Enhancement?, produces a noticeable behavioral change when ingested orally. If inhaled into the lungs or injected

Figure callouts:

Injecting a drug directly into the brain allows it to act quickly in low doses because it encounters fewer barriers.

Taking drugs orally is the safest, easiest, and most convenient way to administer them.

Drugs that are weak acids pass from the stomach into the bloodstream.

Drugs that are weak bases pass from the intestines to the bloodstream.

Drugs injected into muscle encounter more barriers than do drugs inhaled.

Drugs inhaled into the lungs encounter few barriers en route to the brain.

Drugs injected into the bloodstream encounter the fewest barriers to the brain but must be hydrophilic.

Drugs contained in adhesive patches are absorbed through the skin and into the bloodstream.

FIGURE 6-1 **Routes of Drug Administration**

1000 μg = 1 mg (milligram)

into the blood, circumventing the stomach, a dose of just 100 μg yields the same results. If amphetamine is injected into the cerebrospinal fluid, bypassing both the stomach and the blood, 10 μg is enough to produce an identical outcome, as is merely 1 μg if, rather than being diluted in the cerebrospinal fluid, the drug is applied directly to target neurons.

Drugs that are prepared for inhalation or intravenous injection are much cheaper per dose because the amount required is so much smaller than that needed for an effective oral dose. On the other hand, there are increased risks associated with intravenous injections and direct brain applications under non-sterile conditions, as happens when needles are shared among drug users, because small amounts of blood potentially containing viruses and microorganisms can be passed from one user to another.

Revisiting the Blood–Brain Barrier

The body presents barriers to the internal movement of drugs: cell membranes, capillary walls, and the placenta. The passage of drugs across capillaries in the brain is difficult because the *blood–brain barrier*, the tight junctions between the cells of blood vessels found in the brain, blocks passage of most water-soluble substances. The blood–brain barrier protects the brain's ionic balance and denies many neurochemicals passage into the brain, where they can disrupt communication between neurons. It protects the brain from the effects of many circulating hormones and from toxic and infectious substances. Injury or disease can sometimes compromise the integrity of the blood–brain barrier, letting pathogens through. For the most part, however, the brain is protected from harmful substances.

The brain has a rich capillary network. None of its neurons is farther than about 50 micrometers (μm; 1 μm is equal to one-millionth of a meter) from a capillary. As shown at the left in **Figure 6-2**, brain capillaries (like all other capillaries) are composed of a single layer of *endothelial cells*. In most parts of the body, endothelial cells in capillary walls are not fused, so substances can pass through the clefts between the cells. In most parts of the brain, by contrast, endothelial cell walls are fused to form tight junctions, so molecules of most substances cannot squeeze between them.

Figure 6-2 also shows that the endothelial cells of brain capillaries are surrounded by the end feet of astrocytes attached to and covering most of the capillary wall. Astrocytes provide a route for the exchange of food and waste between capillaries and the brain's extracellular fluid, as well as from there to other cells, shown at the right in Figure 6-2.

The cells of capillary walls in three brain regions, shown in **Figure 6-3**, lack a blood–brain barrier. The pituitary is a source of many hormones secreted into the blood, and their release is triggered in part by other hormones carried to the pituitary by the blood. The absence of a blood–brain barrier in the brainstem's area postrema allows toxic substances in the blood to enter that area and be detected by those neurons, which triggers vomiting to expel any ingested toxins that remain in the stomach.

Figures 4-7 and 4-8 illustrate ion diffusion and concentration and voltage gradients.

Section 13-2 details the pineal gland's pacemaking function.

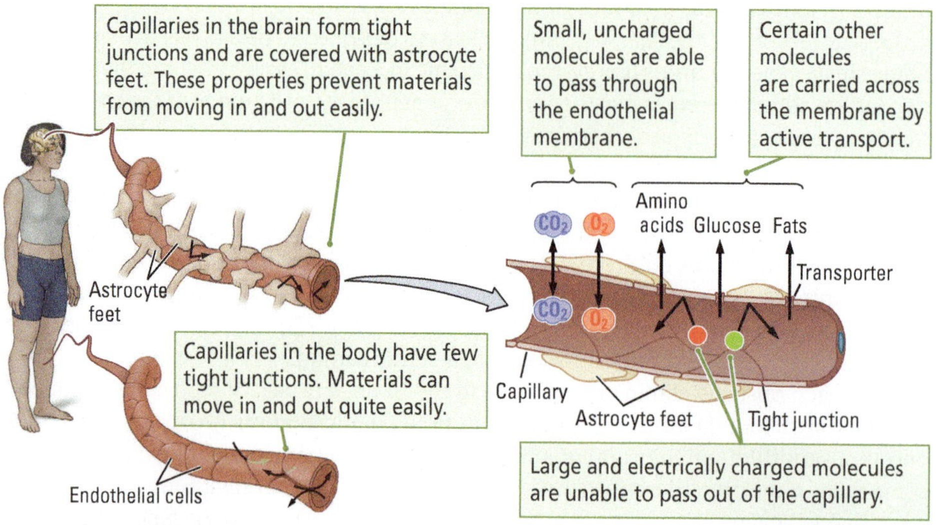

FIGURE 6-2 **Blood–Brain Barrier** Capillaries in most of the body allow for substances to pass between capillary cell membranes, but those in the brain, stimulated by the actions of astrocytes, form the tight junctions of the blood–brain barrier.

Capillaries in the brain form tight junctions and are covered with astrocyte feet. These properties prevent materials from moving in and out easily.

Small, uncharged molecules are able to pass through the endothelial membrane.

Certain other molecules are carried across the membrane by active transport.

Capillaries in the body have few tight junctions. Materials can move in and out quite easily.

Large and electrically charged molecules are unable to pass out of the capillary.

Astrocyte feet

Endothelial cells

Capillary

Amino acids Glucose Fats

Transporter

CO_2 O_2

CO_2 O_2

Astrocyte feet

Tight junction

The pineal gland also lacks a blood–brain barrier, enabling hormones to reach it and modulate the day–night cycles it controls.

To carry out its work, the brain needs, among other substances, oxygen and glucose for fuel and amino acids to build proteins. Fuel molecules reach brain cells from the blood, just as carbon dioxide and other waste products are excreted from brain cells and are carried away by the blood. Molecules of these vital substances cross the blood–brain barrier in two ways:

1. Small molecules, such as oxygen and carbon dioxide, and lipid-soluble molecules can pass through the endothelial membranes.

2. Complex molecules of glucose, amino acids, and other food components are carried across the membrane by active transport systems or ion pumps (transporter proteins specialized to convey a particular substance).

A few psychoactive drug molecules are sufficiently small or have the correct chemical structure to gain access to the CNS. An important property possessed by those few drugs that have CNS effects, then, is an ability to cross the blood–brain barrier.

How the Body Eliminates Drugs

Drugs developed for therapeutic purposes are usually designed not only to have an increased chance of reaching their targets but also to have extended time in the body. Drugs are diluted throughout the body and are often sequestered in fat cells and then released slowly. After a drug is administered, the body begins to break it down through *catabolism*, a process that takes place in several areas of the body, including the kidneys, liver, and the intestines. The body excretes drugs and their metabolites in urine, feces, sweat, breast milk, and exhaled air.

The liver is especially active in catabolizing drugs. This organ houses a family of enzymes involved in drug catabolism, called the *cytochrome P450 enzyme family* (some of which are also present in the gastrointestinal tract microbiome); the liver is capable of breaking down many different drugs into forms more easily excreted from the body. Substances that cannot be catabolized or excreted can build up in the body and become toxic. The metal mercury, for instance, is not easily eliminated and can produce severe neurological effects.

Humans living in modern, industrialized societies consume a large number and enormous quantities of active drugs, which are eliminated from the body, along with their metabolites, and discharged into the environment, usually into water. This situation is highly problematic, as these substances are often reingested by many other animals, including other humans (Brown et al., 2015). Some may affect fertility, development in high-risk groups such as embryos and juveniles, and even the physiology and behavior of adult organisms. The solution is redesigning waste management systems to remove by-products eliminated by humans as well as by other animals (Berninger et al., 2016).

Drug Action at Synapses: Agonists and Antagonists

Most drugs that produce psychoactive effects work by influencing chemical reactions at synapses. To understand how drugs work, we must explore the ways they modify synaptic actions. **Figure 6-4** summarizes the major steps in neurotransmission at a synapse—each a potential site of drug action:

1. *Synthesis* of the neurotransmitter in the cell body, the axon, or the terminal

2. *Packaging* and *storage* of the neurotransmitter in vesicles

3. *Release* of the transmitter from the terminal's presynaptic membrane into the synapse

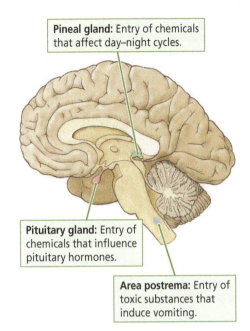

Pineal gland: Entry of chemicals that affect day–night cycles.

Pituitary gland: Entry of chemicals that influence pituitary hormones.

Area postrema: Entry of toxic substances that induce vomiting.

FIGURE 6-3 **Barrier-Free Brain Sites** The pituitary gland is a target for many blood-borne hormones; the pineal gland is a target for hormones that affect circadian rhythms. The area postrema detects and initiates vomiting of noxious substances.

Catabolic processes break down; *anabolic* processes build up.

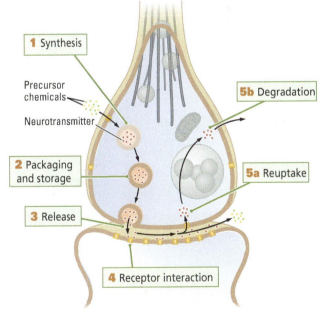

1 Synthesis

Precursor chemicals

Neurotransmitter

2 Packaging and storage

3 Release

4 Receptor interaction

5b Degradation

5a Reuptake

FIGURE 6-4 **Points of Influence** In principle, a drug can modify major chemical processes, any of which result in enhanced or reduced synaptic transmission, depending on the drug's action as an agonist or antagonist.

agonist Substance that enhances neurotransmitter function.

antagonist Substance that blocks neurotransmitter function.

4. *Receptor interaction* in the postsynaptic membrane, as the transmitter acts on an embedded receptor

5a. Inactivation by *reuptake* into the presynaptic terminal for reuse OR

b. Inactivation by enzymatic *degradation* of excess neurotransmitter

Ultimately, a drug that affects any of these synaptic functions either increases or diminishes neurotransmission. Drugs that increase neurotransmission are classified as **agonists**; drugs that decrease neurotransmission are classified as **antagonists**. To illustrate, consider a typical synapse: the acetylcholine synapse between motor neurons and muscles.

An Acetylcholine Synapse: Examples of Drug Action

Figure 6-5 shows how some drugs and toxins act as agonists or antagonists at the acetylcholine (ACh) synapse on skeletal muscles. ACh agonists excite muscles, increasing muscle tone, whereas ACh antagonists inhibit muscles, decreasing muscle tone. Some of these substances may be new to you, but you have probably heard of others. If you know their effects at the ACh synapse, you can understand the relationships between these substances' neurochemical actions and their behavioral effects.

Figure 6-5 includes two toxins that influence ACh release from the axon terminal. Black widow spider venom acts as an agonist by promoting ACh release to excess. A black widow spider bite does not inject enough drug to paralyze a person, though a victim may feel some muscle weakness.

Botulinum toxin, or botulin, is the poisonous agent in improperly processed canned goods. An antagonist, it blocks ACh release, and the effect can last for weeks to months. Severe poisoning can paralyze both movement and breathing and so cause death.

Botulin has medical uses, however. Injected into a muscle, it can selectively paralyze the muscle, making it useful for blocking excessive and enduring muscular twitches or contractions, including the spasms that make movement difficult—such as in people with cerebral palsy. Under the trade name Botox, botulin is also used cosmetically to paralyze facial muscles that cause wrinkling.

Figure 6-5 also shows two drugs that act on ACh receptors. Nicotine's molecular structure is similar enough to that of ACh to allow nicotine to fit into ACh receptors' binding sites, where it causes the associated ion channel to open and therefore acts

Figure 4-26 details the structure and action of ACh at a neuromuscular synapse.

Clinical Focus 11-2 describes the causes and range of outcomes for cerebral palsy.

As illustrated in Section 5-3, a single main receptor serves the sympathetic nervous system: the nicotinic ACh receptor (nAChR).

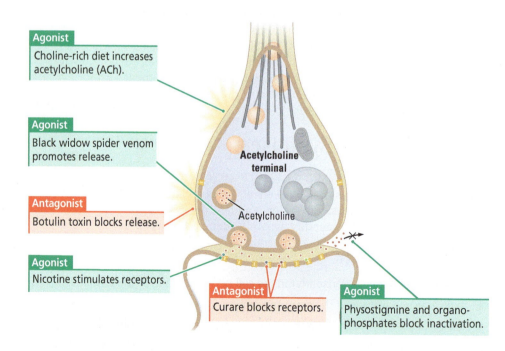

FIGURE 6-5 **Acetylcholine Agonists and Antagonists** Drugs and nutrients can affect ACh transmission by altering its synthesis or release or by binding to the postsynaptic receptor and affecting its breakdown or inactivation.

Agonist
Choline-rich diet increases acetylcholine (ACh).

Agonist
Black widow spider venom promotes release.

Antagonist
Botulin toxin blocks release.

Agonist
Nicotine stimulates receptors.

Acetylcholine terminal

Acetylcholine

Antagonist
Curare blocks receptors.

Agonist
Physostigmine and organo-phosphates block inactivation.

as an agonist. Curare acts as an ACh antagonist by occupying cholinergic receptors, but it does not cause the ion channel to open, and it also prevents ACh from binding to the receptor. Once introduced into the body, curare acts quickly and is cleared from the body in a few minutes. Large doses, however, arrest movement and breathing for a period sufficient to result in death.

Early European explorers of South America discovered that the indigenous peoples living along the Amazon River in South America killed small animals using arrowheads coated with curare prepared from the seeds of a plant. The hunters did not poison themselves when eating the animals because ingested curare cannot pass from the gut into the body. Many curarelike drugs have been synthesized. Some were used to briefly paralyze large animals for examination or tagging for identification. You have probably seen these drugs in action in wildlife videos. Skeletal muscles are more sensitive to curarelike drugs than are respiratory muscles; an appropriate dose paralyzes an animal's movement temporarily but allows it to breathe.

The final drug action shown in Figure 6-5 is that of physostigmine and organophosphate agonists that inhibit acetylcholinesterase (AChE), the enzyme that breaks down ACh, thus increasing the amount available in the synapse. Physostigmine, obtained from an African bean, is also used as a poison by hunters.

Large doses of physostigmine can be toxic because they produce excessive excitation of the neuromuscular synapse, disrupting movement and breathing. In small doses, however, physostigmine is used to treat *myasthenia gravis*, a condition of muscular weakness in which muscle receptors are less than normally responsive to ACh. Physostigmine's action is short lived, lasting only a few minutes or at most a half hour.

Organophosphates bind irreversibly to AChE and consequently allow a toxic buildup of ACh in the synaptic cleft. Many insecticides and chemical weapons are organophosphates. Insects use glutamate as a neurotransmitter at the nerve–muscle junction, but elsewhere in their nervous system, they have nicotinic receptors. Thus, organophosphates poison insects by acting centrally, but they poison chordates by acting peripherally as well. The Chemical Weapons Convention of 1993 banned one potent organophosphate agent, the lethal nerve gas Sarin. That international ban, however, did not restrain the government of Syria, in 2013 and again in 2017, from using Sarin against its own citizens.

Does a drug or toxin that affects neuromuscular synapses also affect ACh synapses in the brain? It depends on whether the substance can cross the blood–brain barrier. Physostigmine and nicotine readily pass the barrier; curare cannot. Nicotine is the psychoactive ingredient in cigarette smoke, and its actions on the brain account for its addictive properties (see Section 6-4). Physostigminelike drugs reportedly have some beneficial effects for memory disorders.

Tolerance

Tolerance is a decreased response to a drug with repeated exposure. Harris Isbell and colleagues (1955) conducted an experiment that, while unethical by today's standards, did suggest how tolerance comes about. The researchers gave volunteers in a prison enough alcohol to initially induce a state of intoxication and then administered additional doses daily over a 13-week period. Yet they found that the participants did not remain drunk for that entire period and had to have their dosage increased.

When the experiment began, the participants showed rapidly rising blood alcohol levels and behavioral signs of intoxication, as shown in the Results section of **Experiment 6-1.** Between the twelfth and twentieth days of alcohol consumption, however, blood alcohol and the signs of intoxication fell, even though the participants increased their alcohol intake. Thereafter, blood alcohol levels and signs of intoxication fluctuated; one did not always correspond to the other. A relatively high blood alcohol level was sometimes associated with a low outward appearance of intoxication. Why?

Figure 5-10 illustrates ACh synthesis and how AChE breaks it down.

In myasthenia gravis, muscle receptors lose their sensitivity to motor neuron messages, as illustrated in Section 4-4.

The Basics: Classification of Life in Section 1-3 charts nervous system evolution in the animal kingdom.

In tolerance, as in habituation, learning takes place when the response to a stimulus weakens with repeated presentations (see Experiment 5-2).

tolerance Decrease in response to a drug with the passage of time.

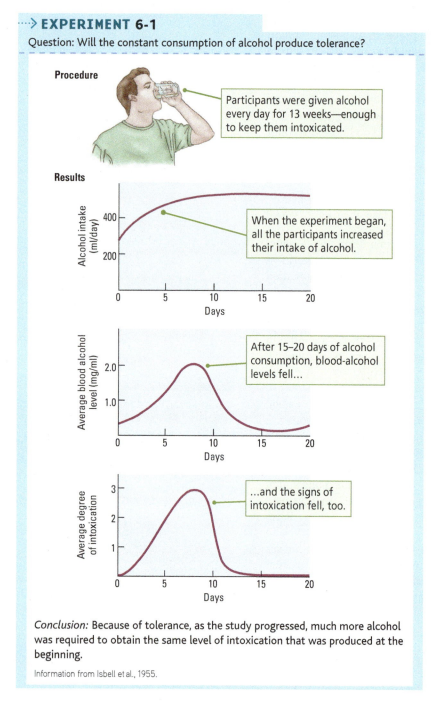

····> EXPERIMENT 6-1

Question: Will the constant consumption of alcohol produce tolerance?

Procedure

Participants were given alcohol every day for 13 weeks—enough to keep them intoxicated.

Results

When the experiment began, all the participants increased their intake of alcohol.

After 15–20 days of alcohol consumption, blood-alcohol levels fell...

...and the signs of intoxication fell, too.

Conclusion: Because of tolerance, as the study progressed, much more alcohol was required to obtain the same level of intoxication that was produced at the beginning.

Information from Isbell et al., 1955.

The three results were the products of three kinds of tolerance, each much more likely to develop with repeated drug use:

1. In *metabolic tolerance*, the number of enzymes needed to break down alcohol in the liver, blood, and brain increases. As a result, any alcohol consumed is metabolized more quickly, so blood alcohol levels fall.

2. In *cellular tolerance*, brain cell activities adjust to minimize the effects of alcohol in the blood. Cellular tolerance can help explain why the behavioral signs of intoxication may be so low despite a relatively high blood alcohol level.

3. *Learned tolerance* explains a drop in outward signs of intoxication. As people learn to cope with the demands of living under the influence of alcohol, they may no longer appear intoxicated.

Does it surprise you that learning plays a role in alcohol tolerance? It has been confirmed in many studies, including a description of the effect first reported by John Wenger and his colleagues (1981). They trained rats to prevent electric foot shocks as they walked on a narrow conveyor belt sliding over an electrified grid. One group of rats received alcohol after training in walking the belt; another group received alcohol before training. A third group received training only, and a fourth group received alcohol only.

After several days' exposure to their respective conditions, all groups received alcohol before a walking test. The rats that had received alcohol before training performed well, whereas those that had received training and alcohol separately performed just as poorly as those that had never had alcohol or those that had not been trained. Despite alcohol intoxication, then, animals can acquire the motor skills needed to balance on a narrow belt. With motor experience, they can learn to compensate for being intoxicated.

Sensitization

Drug tolerance is much more likely to develop with repeated use than with intermittent use, but tolerance does not always follow repeated exposure to a drug. Tolerance resembles habituation in that the response to the drug weakens with repeated presentations. The drug user may have the opposite reaction, *sensitization*—increased responsiveness to successive equal doses. Whereas tolerance generally develops with repeated drug use, sensitization is much more likely to develop with intermittent use.

To demonstrate drug sensitization, Terry Robinson and Jill Becker (1986) isolated rats in observation boxes and recorded their reactions to an injection of amphetamine, which is a dopaminergic agonist. Every 3 or 4 days, the investigators injected the rats and found their motor activities—sniffing, rearing, and walking—more vigorous with each administration of the same drug dose, as graphed in Results 1 of **Experiment 6-2.**

The increased motor activity on successive tests was not due to the animals becoming comfortable with the test situation. Control animals that received no drug failed to display a similar escalation. Administering the drug to rats in their home cages did not

Experiment 5-3 describes sensitization at the level of neurons and synapses. Section 14-4 relates sensitization to neuroplasticity and learned addictions.

···> **EXPERIMENT 6-2**

Question: Does the injection of a drug always produce the same behavior?

Procedure 1

In the Robinson and Becker study, animals were given periodic injections of the same dose of amphetamine. Then the researchers measured the number of times each rat reared in its cage.

Procedure 2

In the Whishaw study, animals were given different numbers of swims after being injected with Flupentixol. Then the researchers measured their speed to escape to a platform in a swimming pool.

Agonist
Amphetamine

Release enhanced

Dopamine

Reuptake transporter blocked

Antagonist
Flupentixol

Receptor blocked

Flupentixol

Results 1

Number of incidents of rearing vs. Number of injections

Results 2

Swimming speed (in cm/sec) vs. Number of trials

Conclusion 1: Sensitization indicated by increased rearing develops with periodic repeated injections.

Conclusion 2: Sensitization depends on the occurrence of a behavior: the swimming speed decreased over time.

Left: Information from Robinson & Becker, 1986. Right: Information from Whishaw et al., 1989.

affect activity in subsequent tests, either. Moreover, the sensitization to amphetamine was enduring. Even when two injections were administered months apart, the animals still showed an escalation of motor behavior. Even a single exposure to amphetamine produced sensitization.

Sensitization is not always characterized by an increase in an elicited behavior but may also manifest as a progressive *decrease* in behavior. Ian Whishaw and his colleagues (1989) administered flupentixol, a drug that blocks dopamine receptors, to rats that had been well trained in a swimming task. As illustrated in Results 2 of Experiment 6-2, the rats' swimming speeds slowed significantly with each successive trial, and eventually the rats stopped swimming altogether. The trial-dependent decrease in swimming was similar whether the trials were massed on the same day or spaced over days or weeks.

The neural basis of sensitization lies in part in changes at the synapse. Studies on the dopamine synapse after sensitization to amphetamine show more dopamine in the synaptic cleft in sensitized animals. Sensitization can be associated with changes in receptor numbers on the postsynaptic membrane, in the rate of transmitter metabolism in the synaptic space, in transmitter reuptake by the presynaptic membrane, and in the number and size of synapses.

Sensitization also has a learned basis. Animals show a change in learned responses to environmental cues as sensitization progresses. Consequently, sensitization is difficult to achieve in an animal tested in its home cage. In the Whishaw group's experiment, administering flupentixol to rats left in their home environment did not influence their performance in subsequent swim tests.

In another study, Sabina Fraioli and her coworkers (1999) gave amphetamine to two groups of rats and recorded the behavioral responses to successive injections. One group of rats lived in the test apparatus, so for that group, home was the test box. The other group was taken out of their home cage and placed in the test box for each day's experimentation. The home group showed no sensitization to amphetamine, whereas the out group displayed robust sensitization.

At least part of the explanation of the home–out effect is that the animals are accustomed to engaging in a certain behavioral repertoire in their home environment, so it is difficult to get them to change their response to home cues even when influenced by a drug. When subjects are away from home, they receive novel out cues, which favor conditioning of new responses.

Sensitization is relevant to understanding some psychopharmacological effects of drugs:

Clinical Focus 8-5 relates the possible origin of schizophrenia and its progress.

1. Many drug therapies, including those for the psychiatric disorder schizophrenia, must be taken for several weeks before they produce beneficial effects. Possibly sensitization underlies the development of these beneficial effects.

2. Sensitization is related to drug dependence. Before a person becomes dependent on or addicted to a drug, he or she must be sensitized by numerous experiences with the drug away from the home environment.

3. Life experiences, especially stressful ones, can produce effects resembling sensitization that prime the nervous system for addiction (Roberts et al., 2015).

6-1 Review

Before you continue, check your understanding. Answers to Self-Test appear at the back of the book.

1. _____, substances that produce changes in behavior by acting on the nervous system, are one subject of _____, the study of how drugs affect the nervous system and behavior.

2. Perhaps the most important obstacle on a psychoactive drug's journey between its entry into the body and its action at a target is the _____, which generally allows only substances needed for nourishment to pass from the capillaries into the _____.

3. Most drugs that have psychoactive effects influence chemical reactions at neuronal _____. Drugs that influence communication between neurons do so by acting either as _____ (increasing the effectiveness of neurotransmission) or as _____ (decreasing the effectiveness of neurotransmission).

4. Behavior may change with the repeated use of a psychoactive drug. These changes include _____ and _____, in which the effect of the drug decreases or increases, respectively, with repeated use.

5. The body eliminates drugs through _____, _____, _____, _____, and _____.

6. Describe briefly how tolerance and sensitization might affect someone who uses cognitive enhancers occasionally (a) at home or (b) at work.

For additional study tools, visit **LaunchPad** at launchpadworks.com

6-2

Psychoactive Drugs

People have been using drugs for therapeutic and recreational reasons likely for as long as there have been, well, people. In fact, our closest relatives, including chimpanzees, bonobos, and gorillas, appear to select and ingest, or topically apply, substances to prevent or reduce the harmful effects of pathogens and toxins—a behavior known as **zoopharmacognosy** (for "animal" + "drug" + "knowing") (Kapadia et al., 2014). Humans have taken this practice a step further by cultivating particular plants and fungi, then extracting, purifying, studying, and synthesizing their psychoactive ingredients—and making a great deal of profit from the enterprise. Over time, we have amassed an enormous catalogue of psychoactive drugs, and there is no question that the templates for these drugs come from the natural world (Campbell, 1996).

Finding a universally acceptable grouping for the psychoactive drugs is virtually impossible. Any system will have a unique set of limitations because drugs with similar chemical structure can have different effects, while drugs with different structure can have similar effects. Furthermore, a single drug acts on many neurochemical systems and has many effects.

A full appreciation of any drug's action requires a multifaceted description, such as can be found in medical compendia. Behavioral descriptions undergo constant review, as illustrated by continuing revisions of the *Diagnostic and Statistical Manual of Mental Disorders* (DSM). Published by the American Psychiatric Association and currently in its fifth edition, the DSM offers a classification system for diagnosing neurological and behavioral disorders, including those caused by drug use. For our purposes, we group psychoactive drugs based on the primary neurotransmitter system that they are known to affect, similarly to the way we organized transmitter systems in Chapter 5. Of course, our grouping system also has limitations. The vast majority of medically prescribed drugs were not created to act on specific neurotransmitter systems; rather, drugs were tested on different patient groups, and specific uses in medical treatments were approved based on analysis of their effectiveness.

Table 6-1 categorizes psychoactive drugs based on their primary neurotransmitter system of action. Each category may contain a few to thousands of chemicals in its subcategories. In the following sections, we highlight drug actions, both on neurochemical systems in the brain and on

zoopharmacognosy Behavior in which non-human animals self-medicate.

TABLE 6-1 **Psychoactive Drugs**

Primary transmitter system	Recreationally used	Medically prescribed (for psychoactive conditions)
Adenosinergic antagonist	caffeine	
Cholinergic agonist	nicotine	tacrine (Cognex)
GABAergic agonists	alcohol	diazepam (Valium), alprazolam (Xanax), clonazepam (Klonopin)
Glutamatergic antagonists	phencyclidine/PCP (angel dust), ketamine (Special K)	memantine (Namenda)
Dopaminergic agonists	cocaine, amphetamine, methamphetamine	dextroamphetamine (Adderall), methylphenidate (Ritalin), L-dopa phenothiazines: chlorpromazine
Dopaminergic antagonists		(Thorazine); butyrophenones: haloperidol (Haldol) clozapine (Clozaril), aripiprazole (Abilify, Aripiprex)
Serotonergic agonists	mescaline (peyote), DMT, psilocybin, lysergic acid diethylamide (LSD), MDMA (Ecstasy)	sertraline (Zoloft), fluoxetine (Prozac), imipramine (Tofranil)
Opioidergic agonists	opium, morphine, heroin	morphine, codeine, oxycodone (Percocet), fentanyl, methadone
Cannabinergic agonists	tetrahydrocannabinol (THC)	THC (Sativex)

synaptic function, and provide some examples. Note that many medically prescribed psychoactive drugs are also recreationally used and abused.

Most psychoactive drugs have three names: chemical, generic, and branded. The chemical name describes a drug's structure; the generic name is nonproprietary and is spelled lowercase; and the proprietary, or brand, name, given by the pharmaceutical company that sells it, is capitalized. Some psychoactive drugs also sport street or club names.

Adenosinergic

We begin with the world's most widely consumed psychoactive drug: caffeine. Caffeine-containing drinks, such as coffee, tea, soft drinks, and "energy drinks," are consumed daily by about 85 percent of adults in the United States. A cup of coffee contains about 100 mg of caffeine; many common soft drinks contain almost as much; and some energy drinks pack as much as 500 mg. You may be using more caffeine than you realize.

Caffeine has a very similar structure to adenosine and binds to adenosine receptors without activating them, thereby blocking the effect of adenosine and thus acting as an adenosine antagonist. Endogenous adenosine induces drowsiness, and caffeine works in opposition to this, making us feel more alert and peppy. Excessive levels can lead to the jitters. But caffeine has other mechanisms of action as well; it inhibits an enzyme that ordinarily breaks down the second messenger, cyclic adenosine monophosphate (cAMP). The resulting increase in cAMP leads to increased glucose production, making more energy available and allowing higher rates of cellular activity. Caffeine also promotes the release of other neurotransmitters, such as dopamine and acetylcholine, which endows caffeine with its stimulant effects that improve reaction time, wakefulness, concentration, and motor coordination (Nehlig, 2010).

Repeated daily intake of caffeine produces a mild form of drug dependence. When the individual stops using caffeine, he or she experiences sleepiness, headache, and irritability. These withdrawal symptoms are avoided by continuing to consume caffeine daily but will fade with time (about 4 to 7 days) if the individual gives up caffeine altogether.

The most well-known source of caffeine is the coffee seed (not a bean) of Coffea plants. But caffeine is also found in the seeds, nuts, leaves, and nectar of a number of other plants native to East Asia and South America.

Why do some plants incorporate caffeine into their tissues? To properly answer this question, we need to consider life from the plants' perspective. Plants face several challenges, such as herbivores, pathogens (like fungi), and attracting pollinators. All of these selective forces, and many others, have shaped plant adaptations; one such adaptation is incorporating toxins such as caffeine into its tissues. Caffeine acts as a natural pesticide, discouraging or killing herbivorous insects and inhibiting the invasion and colonization of pathogenic fungi. Nectar containing caffeine may enhance its rewarding properties in pollinators, such as honeybees, and improve distribution of pollen (Wright et al., 2013). We humans have contributed massively to the success of coffee and tea plants by distributing them widely over our planet, at the expense of native plant and animal species and the local ecology.

Cholinergic

Nicotine is found in the leaves of the tobacco plant, *Nicotiana tabacum*. Like caffeine, it functions as an antiherbivore chemical and was at one time widely used as an insecticide. Nicotine is also found in small amounts in potatoes, tomatoes, and eggplant.

Nicotine's mood-altering effects are unusual in comparison to most drugs. At low doses, nicotine is a stimulant, but at very high doses, it dampens neuronal activity (Wadgave & Nagesh, 2016). Tobacco smokers report feelings of relaxation, sharpness, calmness, and alertness. When smoke from a tobacco cigarette is inhaled, within a few seconds nicotine stimulates acetylcholine nicotinic receptors, which then indirectly causes the release of acetylcholine and several other neurotransmitters, including norepinephrine, epinephrine, arginine vasopressin, serotonin, endorphins, and dopamine. It is the release of dopamine that provides the reinforcing aspect of nicotine.

Nicotine dependence involves both psychological and physical aspects. Smoking cessation leads to heightened anxiety, irritability, craving, inability to feel pleasure, and tremors.

Nicotine is a potentially lethal poison; in fact, the total amount of nicotine in one cigarette, if injected, can be lethal to an inexperienced person. Tolerance develops rapidly, however, and experienced users can withstand much higher levels of the drug. Respiratory diseases, lung cancer, and related negative effects are caused by the harmful chemicals found in tobacco smoke rather than in nicotine itself. This fact has propelled the popularity of vaping, in which nicotine can be inhaled without tobacco smoke. The long-term health effects of e-cigarettes are likely less serious than those of tobacco smoke but are not known.

While smoking is a risk factor for Alzheimer disease, cholinergic agonists are medically prescribed to treat it. Acetylcholinesterase inhibitors, such as tacrine (Cognex), raise ACh levels and may provide a small benefit (Birks et al., 2015), although no medication has been clearly shown to delay or halt the progression of Alzheimer disease.

GABAergic

At low doses, GABAergic agonists reduce anxiety; at medium doses, they sedate; at high doses, they anesthetize or induce coma. At very high doses, they can kill (**Figure 6-6**).

In order to understand how GABAergic agonists work, we must consider the binding sites and channel associated with the GABA$_A$ receptor complex. The GABA$_A$ receptor, illustrated in **Figure 6-7**, contains a site where GABA binds, another separate site where alcohol binds, and still another site where benzodiazepines bind, as well as a chloride ion (Cl⁻) channel.

Excitation of the GABA$_A$ receptor produces an influx of Cl⁻ through its pore. An influx of Cl⁻ increases the concentration of negative charges inside the cell membrane, hyper-polarizing it and making it less likely to propagate an action potential. GABA therefore produces its inhibitory effect by decreasing a neuron's firing rate. Widespread reduction of neuronal firing underlies the behavioral effects of drugs that affect the GABA$_A$ synapse.

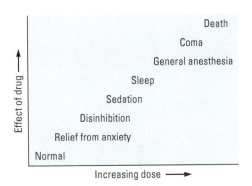

FIGURE 6-6 **Behavioral Continuum of Sedation** Increasing doses of GABAergic agonists affect behavior: low doses reduce anxiety, and very high doses result in death.

GABA is an amino acid. Figure 5-12 shows its chemical structure.

Principle 10: The nervous system works by juxtaposing excitation and inhibition.

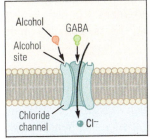

Sedative-hypnotic drugs (alcohol) increase GABA binding, thereby maximizing the time the pore is open.

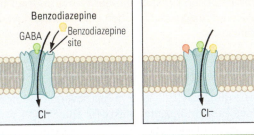

Antianxiety drugs (benzodiazepines) influence the frequency of pore opening.

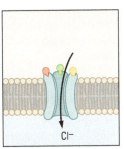

Because their different actions summate, these drugs should not be taken together.

FIGURE 6-7 **Drug Effects at the GABA$_A$ Receptor** These receptors have a binding site for alcohol (left) and a different binding site for benzodiazepines (center). When taken together (right), these two types of drugs can be lethal.

Benzodiazepines are a class of chemicals that include diazepam (Valium), alprozolam (Xanax), and clonazepam (Klonopin) and are medically prescribed to reduce anxiety. Benzodiazepines are often used by people who are having trouble coping with significant physical or mental stress, such as a traumatic accident or a death in the family. They are also used as presurgical relaxation agents and can terminate seizures.

Because the GABA$_A$ receptor has different binding sites for GABA, alcohol, and benzodiazepines, activation of each site promotes an influx of Cl$^-$, but in different ways. The effects of actions at these three sites summate, which is why alcohol and benzodiazepine drugs should not be consumed together. In the United States, combined doses of these drugs reportedly contribute to as many deaths as occur annually from automobile accidents.

A characteristic feature of benzodiazepine drugs is that a user who takes repeated doses develops a tolerance for them. A larger dose is then required to attain the drug's initial effect. Cross-tolerance results when the tolerance for one drug, like benzodiazepines, is carried over to a different member of the drug group. Cross-tolerance also suggests that benzodiazepines and alcohol act on the nervous system in similar ways.

Alcohol (ethyl alcohol, or ethanol) is present in alcoholic beverages and is an extraordinarily popular psychoactive and recreational drug, particularly among college-aged students (see Section 6-3). The fermentation of sugar into alcohol is one of humanity's earliest biotechnologies, dating back at least 9000 years. Alcohol consumption has short-term psychological and physiological effects that depend on several factors, including the amount and concentration of alcohol, the duration over which it is consumed, the amount of food eaten, and the consumer's weight and experience with alcohol. Small amounts of alcohol typically cause an overall improvement in mood and possible euphoria, increased self-confidence and sociability, decreased anxiety, impaired judgment and fine muscle coordination, and a flushing of the face. Medium doses result in lethargy, sedation, balance problems, and blurred vision. High doses lead to profound confusion, slurred speech ("wats da proplem, ossifer?"), staggering, dizziness, and vomiting—an adaptive response to poisoning. Very high doses cause stupor, memory loss, unconsciousness, life-threatening respiratory depression, and inhalation of vomit.

The long-term and frequent consumption of alcohol can lead to increased risk of alcoholism, a condition ruinous to individuals and families, as well as an enormous economic burden; alcoholism costs $249 billion in the United States alone (Sacks et al., 2015). In the United States, about 8 percent of men and 4 percent of women met criteria for alcoholism in 2015 (Substance Abuse and Mental Health Services Administration, 2015). Alcoholics often are malnourished and typically have elevated levels of chronic pancreatitis, liver disease, and cancer. Alcoholism results in damage to the central and peripheral nervous systems, as well as nearly every other system and organ in the body.

Drugs that act on GABA receptors also affect brain development because GABA is one of the substances that regulate brain development. Clinical Focus 6-2, Fetal Alcohol Spectrum Disorder, explores the devastating effects of alcohol on developing fetuses.

Glutamatergic

Glutamate is the main excitatory neurotransmitter in the forebrain and cerebellum. Section 14-4 describes how glutamate and NMDA receptors affect long-term learning.

The glutamatergic system has several receptors, such as NMDA, AMPA, and kainate (see Table 5-3). Antagonists for the NMDA receptor, such as phencyclidine (PCP, or angel dust) and ketamine (Special K), can produce hallucinations and out-of-body experiences. Research indicates that PCP inhibits nicotinic acetylcholine receptors as well as inhibiting dopamine reuptake; therefore, PCP is also a dopaminergic agonist, which may account for some of its psychoactive effects.

Both PCP and ketamine are also known as *dissociative anesthetics*, compounds that produce feelings of detachment—dissociation—from the environment and self because they distort perceptions of sight and sound.

Fetal Alcohol Spectrum Disorder

The term *fetal alcohol syndrome* (FAS) was coined in 1973 to describe a pattern of physical malformation and intellectual disability observed in some children born to alcoholic mothers. It is now called **fetal alcohol spectrum disorder (FASD)** to acknowledge the range of its effects. Children with FASD may have abnormal facial features, such as unusually wide spacing between the eyes. Their brains display a range of abnormalities, from small size with abnormal gyri to abnormal clusters of cells and misaligned cells in the cortex.

Related to these brain abnormalities are certain behavioral symptoms that children with FASD tend to have in common. They display varying degrees of learning disabilities and low intelligence test scores, as well as hyperactivity and other social problems. Individuals with FASD are 19 times as likely to be incarcerated as those without it (Popova et al., 2011).

Numerous studies have attempted to estimate the prevalence of FASD in the United States, with results ranging from under 1% to 10% and possibly higher, but these estimates are likely not generalizable to all communities.

Women who are most at risk for bearing FASD babies are poor and not well educated, their alcohol consumption problems predate pregnancy, and they have little access to prenatal care. It is often difficult to inform these women about the dangers that alcohol poses to a fetus and to encourage them to abstain from drinking alcohol before and during pregnancy.

Alcohol-induced abnormalities can vary from hardly noticeable physical and psychological effects to full-blown FASD. The severity of effects is related to when, how much, and how frequently alcohol is consumed over the course of pregnancy. The effects are worse if alcohol is consumed in the first trimester, a time of organogenesis and the highest levels of DNA synthesis. The risks are exacerbated because many women may not yet realize that they are pregnant at this stage.

Severe FASD is also more likely to coincide with binge drinking, which produces high blood alcohol levels. Other factors related to severe outcomes are poor nutritional health of the mother and the mother's use of other drugs, including nicotine. In addition, alcohol use by mothers and fathers *before* conception can change the methylation status of some genes that contribute to disabilities found on the spectrum (Lee et al., 2015).

A major question related to FASD is how much alcohol is too much to drink during pregnancy. To be completely safe, it is best not to drink alcohol at all in the months preceding as well as during pregnancy. This conclusion is supported by findings that as little as a single drink of alcohol per day during pregnancy can lead to a decrease in children's intelligence test scores.

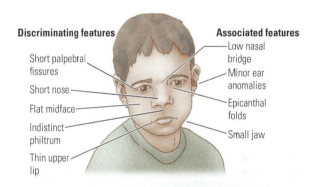

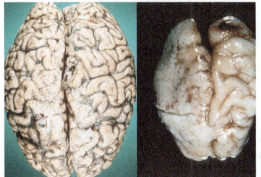

Courtesy of Sterling K. Clarren, M.D., Professor of Pediatrics, University of British Columbia Faculty of Medicine.

(Top) Characteristic facial features that indicate FASD. Effects are not merely physical; many children endure severe intellectual disabilities. (Bottom) The convolutions characteristic of the brain of a healthy child at age 6 weeks (left) are grossly underdeveloped in the brain of a child with FASD (right).

Ketamine is currently medically prescribed for starting and maintaining anesthesia. It induces a trance-like state while providing pain relief, sedation, and memory loss. Ketamine is being tested as a rapid-acting antidepressant and is in phase III clinical trials for use in treating major depressive disorder (Caddy et al., 2014). Its mechanism of action, as a glutamatergic agonist, is very different from those of most modern drugs prescribed to reduce depression, which operate on serotonin and norepinephrine targets (see the Serotonergic section below).

Mematine (Namenda) is an NMDA antagonist that is prescribed in the treatment of Alzheimer disease to prevent neuronal loss.

Dopaminergic

We first consider dopamine agonists that are used recreationally, such as cocaine, amphetamine, and methamphetamine, and agonists that are medically prescribed,

fetal alcohol spectrum disorder (FASD) Range of physical and intellectual impairments observed in some children born to alcoholic parents.

FIGURE 6-8 **Behavioral Stimulant** Cocaine (left) is obtained from the leaves of the coca plant (center). Crack cocaine (right) is chemically altered to form rocks that vaporize when heated at low temperatures.

FIGURE 6-9 **Warning Label** Cocaine was once an ingredient in such invigorating beverages as Coca-Cola.

amphetamine Synthetic compound that increases the neurotransmitter dopamine in the synaptic cleft by reversing the dopamine transporter.

Section 5-1 describes experiments that Otto Loewi performed to identify epinephrine, or adrenaline. Section 7-7 details symptoms and outcomes of ADHD and the search for an animal model of the disease.

such as dextroamphetamine (Adderall), methylphenidate (Ritalin), and L-dopa. We then consider dopamine antagonists that are medically prescribed for schizophrenia and drug-induced psychosis, including chlorpromazine (Thorazine), haloperidol (Haldol), clozapine (Clozaril), and aripiprazole (Abilify, Aripiprex).

Dopamine Agonists

Recreationally used dopaminergic agonists include cocaine, amphetamine, and methamphetamine. Cocaine is purified from leaves of the coca plant (**Figure 6-8**), whereas amphetamine and methamphetamine are synthetically produced.

The indigenous people of Peru have chewed coca leaves through the generations to increase their stamina in the harsh environment and high elevations where they live. Refined cocaine powder can either be sniffed (snorted) or injected. Cocaine users who do not like to inject cocaine intravenously or cannot afford it in powdered form sniff or smoke rocks, or *crack*, a potent, highly concentrated form (shown at right in Figure 6-8). Crack is chemically altered so that it vaporizes at low temperatures, and the vapors are inhaled.

Sigmund Freud (1974) popularized cocaine in the late 1800s as an antidepressant. It was once widely used in soft drinks and wine mixtures promoted as invigorating tonics. It is the origin of the trade name Coca-Cola, which once contained cocaine (**Figure 6-9**). Its addictive properties soon became apparent, however, and it was replaced in these products with caffeine.

Freud also recommended that cocaine be used as a local anesthetic. Cocaine did prove valuable for this purpose, and many derivatives, such as xylocaine (often called Novocain), are used today. These local anesthetic agents reduce a cell's permeability to sodium ions and so reduce nerve conduction.

As **Figure 6-10** shows, **amphetamine** is a dopamine agonist. It prevents dopamine reuptake by reversing the direction of the transporter, allowing dopamine to continue to interact with postsynaptic D_2 receptors.

Amphetamine is a synthetic compound. It was discovered in attempts to synthesize the CNS neurotransmitter epinephrine, which also acts as a hormone to mobilize the body for fight or flight in times of stress (see Figure 6-20 in Section 6-5). Both amphetamine and cocaine are dopamine agonists. Amphetamine acts by reversing the dopamine reuptake transporter, whereas cocaine blocks the transporter. Both leave more dopamine available in the synaptic cleft, but amphetamine also reverses the transporter that typically packages dopamine into vesicles, thus removing dopamine that was already packaged and increasing its abundance in the synaptic terminal. The transporter found on the synaptic terminal then pumps the dopamine previously packaged in vesicles into the synaptic cleft. Thus, amphetamine acts in two different ways to increase the amount of dopamine in synapses, which stimulates dopamine receptors. As noted in Clinical Focus 6-1, amphetamine-based drugs are widely prescribed to treat ADHD.

Benzedrine, a form of amphetamine, was originally used to treat asthma and sold in inhalers as a nonprescription drug through the 1940s. Soon people discovered that they could open the container and ingest its contents to obtain an energizing effect. Amphetamine was widely used in World War II to help troops and pilots stay alert, increase confidence and aggression, and boost morale—a practice that continues today. It was also used among the civilian population to improve wartime workers' productivity. Today, amphetamine is used as a popular weight-loss aid. Many over-the-counter compounds marketed as stimulants or weight-loss aids have amphetaminelike pharmacological actions.

A widely used illegal amphetamine derivative is methamphetamine (also known as meth, speed, crank, smoke, and crystal ice). Lifetime prevalence of methamphetamine use in the U.S. population (the percentage of the population who have used the drug at least once in their lives), once estimated to be as high as 8 percent (Durell et al., 2008), is related to its ease of manufacture in illicit laboratories and to its potency, thus making it a relatively inexpensive yet potentially devastating drug. The process of illicit manufacture makes it difficult to draw conclusions about the effects of methamphetamines compared to the effects of legally synthesized amphetamines.

Amphetamine (Adderall) and methylphenidate (Ritalin) are medically prescribed to treat ADHD, which is characterized by excessive activity and difficulty controlling behavior or paying attention, though many people with ADHD have very long attention spans for tasks they find interesting. The recreational dosage of both drugs is about 50 times higher than the medically prescribed dosage. Chronic recreational use can lead to *psychosis*, a term applied to behavioral disorders characterized by hallucinations (false sensory perceptions), delusions (false beliefs), paranoia, and disordered thoughts, among a host of other symptoms. These symptoms are also observed in individuals diagnosed with *schizophrenia*.

Dopamine Antagonists

The **dopamine hypothesis of schizophrenia** holds that some forms of the disease may be related to excessive dopamine activity—especially in the frontal lobes. If excessive dopamine is a consequence of drug-induced psychosis and some forms of naturally occurring schizophrenia, then dopamine antagonists should ameliorate the symptomology (see Figure 6-10). In fact, the use of dopamine antagonist drugs that preferentially bind to D_2 receptors has improved the functioning of people with schizophrenia. Since 1955, when dopaminergic antagonists (antipsychotic agents, or antipsychotics) were introduced into widespread therapeutic use, resident populations with schizophrenia in state and municipal mental hospitals in the United States have decreased dramatically.

The incidence of schizophrenia is about 1 in every 100, making the success of dopamine antagonists an important therapeutic achievement. Although using dopamine antagonists to treat psychosis makes these mental disorders manageable, it does not constitute a cure. In fact, according to the National Institute on Disability, Independent Living, and Rehabilitation Research, although the number of people in mental institutions remains relatively low, as many as 75 percent of those who are homeless and 50 percent of incarcerated people have mental health issues. According to Human Rights Watch, in 2015 in the United States, 10 times as many mentally ill people were incarcerated as resided in mental institutions.

Dopamine antagonists have been widely used to treat psychosis since the mid-1950s, beginning with the development of what have been called first-generation antipsychotics (FGAs). They include the drug classes phenothiazines (for example, chlorpromazine [Thorazine]) and butyrophenones (haloperidol [Haldol]). FGAs act mainly by blocking the dopamine D_2 receptor, which immediately reduces motor activity and alleviates the excessive agitation of some people with schizophrenia. But because schizophrenia involves more than just D_2 receptors, changes in dopamine synapses

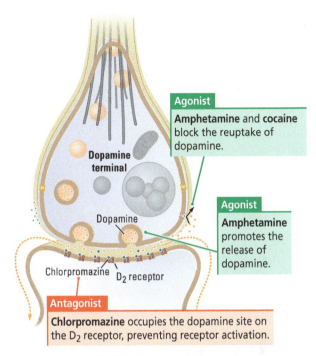

FIGURE 6-10 **Drug Effects at D_2 Receptors** The antipsychotic agent chlorpromazine (Thorazine) can lessen schizophrenia symptoms, and amphetamine or cocaine abuse can produce them. This suggests that schizophrenia may be related, at least in part, to excessive activity at the D_2 receptor.

Psychosis and schizophrenia are described in detail in Section 16-2.

Agonist Amphetamine and cocaine block the reuptake of dopamine.

Agonist Amphetamine promotes the release of dopamine.

Antagonist Chlorpromazine occupies the dopamine site on the D_2 receptor, preventing receptor activation.

dopamine hypothesis of schizophrenia Idea that excess dopamine activity causes symptoms of schizophrenia.

Tardive dyskinesia is discussed further in Section 16-3.

do not completely explain the disorder or the effects of dopaminergic antagonists. Beginning in the 1980s, newer drugs such as clozapine (Clozaril) and several other compounds emerged as second-generation antipsychotics (SGAs). SGAs not only block dopamine D_2 receptors but also block serotonin 5-HT_2 receptors.

The therapeutic actions of D_2 antagonists are not fully understood, and long-term use of these drugs can produce many unwanted side effects, including *tardive dyskinesia* (*TD*). TD is a movement disorder that results in involuntary, repetitive body movements such as grimacing, sticking out the tongue, or smacking the lips, as well as rapid jerking movements or slow writhing movements. Recall that dopamine agonists, such as L-dopa, boost dopamine levels to restore movements in people with Parkinson disease. Thus, dopamine plays a central role in normal movement and mental health and, as discussed in Section 6-3.

Serotonergic

We now consider the serotonergic agonists, but keep in mind that most serotonergic agonists also have adrenergic activity.

Serotonergic agonists are well known for altering perceptions of one's surroundings, feelings, sensations, and images (visual hallucinations), producing what are known as "trips." They were part of the counterculture movement of the 1960s and continue to be used recreationally and spiritually. Some, such as mescaline (peyote; 3,4,5-trimethoxyphenethylamine), DMT (N, N-Dimethyltryptamine), and psilocybin, are found in plants and mushrooms, while others, such as lysergic acid diethylamide (LSD) and MDMA (Ecstasy, XTC; 3,4-Methylenedioxymethamphetamine), are produced synthetically.

In the past century, strong advocates for serotonergic agonists in the United States promoted their use for "mind expansion and personal truth." Mescaline, obtained from the peyote cactus, is legal in the United States for use by Native Americans for spiritual practices. Good trips on serotonergic agonists can be pleasurable and are associated with feelings of joy or euphoria (referred to as a "rush"), disconnection from reality, decreased inhibitions, and the belief that one has extreme mental clarity or superpowers. Bad trips can be associated with irrational fears, panic attacks, paranoia, rapid mood swings, intrusive thoughts of hopelessness, wanting to harm others, and suicidal ideation. Repeated use can lead to problems with sleep, mood, memory, and attention. Currently, these recreationally used drugs are not medically prescribed and are illegal. But there are other serotonergic agonists that are medically prescribed for the treatment of major depression.

Major depression is a mood disorder characterized by prolonged feelings of worthlessness and guilt, disruption of normal eating habits, sleep disturbances such as insomnia, a general slowing of behavior, and frequent thoughts of suicide. At any given time, about 6 percent of the adult U.S. population has major depression, and in the course of a lifetime, 30 percent may have at least one episode that lasts for months or longer. Major depression is diagnosed in twice as many women as men.

Inadequate nutrition, stress from difficult life conditions, acute changes in neuronal function, and damage to brain neurons are among the factors implicated in depression. These factors may be related: nutritional deficiencies may increase vulnerability to stress; stress may change neuronal function; and if unrelieved, altered neuronal function may lead to neuron damage. Section 6-5 offers more information on stress.

Not surprisingly, a number of pharmacological approaches to depression are available. They include normalizing stress hormones, modifying neuronal responses, and stimulating neuronal repair.

major depression Mood disorder characterized by prolonged feelings of worthlessness and guilt, disruption of normal eating habits, insomnia, a general slowing of behavior, and frequent thoughts of suicide.

monoamine oxidase (MAO) inhibitor Drug that blocks the enzyme monoamine oxidase from degrading such neurotransmitters as 5-HT, NE, and DA.

tricyclic Drug, characterized by its three-ring chemical structure, that blocks 5-HT reuptake transporter proteins.

selective serotonin reuptake inhibitor (SSRI) Drug that blocks 5-HT reuptake into the presynaptic terminal and most commonly used to treat depression.

Section 12-4 explores the neural control of emotions and emotional disorders such as depression, and Section 16-2 focuses on its neurobiology and treatments for such disorders.

Medications Used to Treat Depression

Three different types of serotonergic agonist drugs are prescribed for depression: the **monoamine oxidase (MAO) inhibitors**; the **tricyclics**, so called because of their three-ring chemical structure; and the **selective serotonin reuptake inhibitors (SSRIs)**.

The SSRIs lack a three-ring structure but do share some similarities to the tricyclics in their actions.

Drugs prescribed for depression are thought to act by improving chemical neurotransmission at serotonin, noradrenaline (norepinephrine), histamine, and acetylcholine synapses and perhaps at dopamine synapses as well. **Figure 6-11** shows the actions of MAO inhibitors, tricyclics, and SSRIs at a 5-HT synapse, on which most research is focused. These three drugs act as agonists, but they have different mechanisms for increasing serotonin availability.

MAO inhibitors provide for more serotonin release with each action potential by inhibiting monoamine oxidase, an enzyme that breaks down serotonin in the axon terminal. In contrast, the tricyclics and SSRIs block the reuptake transporter that takes serotonin back into the axon terminal. Because the transporter is blocked, serotonin remains in the synaptic cleft, prolonging its action on postsynaptic receptors.

Although these drugs begin to affect synapses very quickly, their antidepressant actions take weeks to develop. One explanation is that these drugs, especially SSRIs, stimulate second messengers in neurons to activate the repair of neurons damaged by stress. Of interest in this respect, one particular SSRI, fluoxetine (Prozac), increases the production of new neurons in the hippocampus, a limbic structure in the temporal lobes. As detailed in Section 6-5, the hippocampus is vulnerable to stress-induced damage, and its restoration by fluoxetine is proposed to underlie one of the drug's antidepressant effects (Hill et al., 2015).

Most people recover from depression within a year of its onset. If depression is left untreated, however, the incidence of suicide among depressed individuals is high, as described in Clinical Focus 6-3, Major Depression. Of all psychological disorders, major depression is one of the most treatable. Cognitive-behavioral therapies are most effective when combined with drug therapies (Comer, 2011).

Despite these successes, about 20 percent of patients with depression fail to respond to antidepressant drugs. Depression can have many causes, including dysfunction in other transmitter systems and even brain damage, such as frontal lobe damage—many of which are not treatable by serotonin agonists. In addition, some people have difficulty tolerating the side effects of antidepressants, which can include increased anxiety, sexual dysfunction, sedation, dry mouth, blurred vision, and memory impairment.

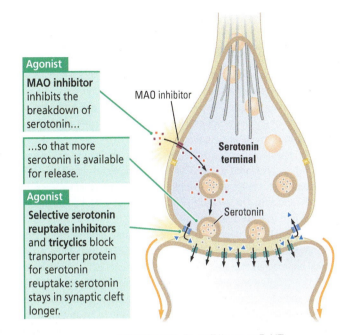

Agonist

MAO inhibitor inhibits the breakdown of serotonin...

...so that more serotonin is available for release.

Agonist

Selective serotonin reuptake inhibitors and **tricyclics** block transporter protein for serotonin reuptake: serotonin stays in synaptic cleft longer.

MAO inhibitor

Serotonin terminal

Serotonin

FIGURE 6-11 **Drug Effects at 5-HT Receptors** Different drugs prescribed to treat depression act on the serotonin synapse in different ways to increase its availability.

Reuptake is part of transmitter inactivation, the last of the five steps of neurotransmission (see Figure 5-3).

Opioidergic

An *opioid* is any endogenous or exogenous compound that binds to opioid receptors to produce morphine-like effects. These psychoactive compounds have sleep-inducing (narcotic) and pain-relieving (analgesic) properties. There are three sources of opioids: isolated (morphine, codeine), altered (heroin, oxycodone), and synthetic (fentanyl, methadone).

Research has identified five classes of opioid peptides: dynorphins, enkephalins, endorphins, endomorphins, and nociceptin. The four receptors on which each opioid peptide binds are the delta, kappa, *mu*, and nociceptin receptors. All opioid peptides and their receptors occur in many CNS regions, as well as in other areas of the body, including the enteric nervous system (ENS). Morphine most closely mimics the endomorphins and binds most selectively to the *mu* receptors.

Opium is a white milky latex extracted from the seed pods of the opium poppy, *Papaver somniferum*, shown at left in **Figure 6-12**. Opium, whose primary active ingredient is morphine, has been used for thousands of years to produce euphoria, analgesia, sleep, and relief from diarrhea and coughing. In 1805, chemist Friedrich Sertürner isolated two chemicals from opium: codeine and morphine. Codeine is

⊚ **CLINICAL FOCUS 6-3**

Major Depression

P. H. was a 53-year-old high school teacher who, although popular with his students, was deriving less and less satisfaction from his work. His marriage was foundering because he was growing apathetic and no longer wanted to socialize or go on vacations. He was having difficulty getting up in the morning and arriving at school on time.

P. H. eventually consulted a physician, complaining of severe chest pains, which he feared signaled an impending heart attack. He informed his doctor that a heart attack would be a welcome relief because it would end his problems. The physician concluded that P. H. had depression and referred him to a psychiatrist.

Since the 1950s, depression has been treated with serotonergic drugs, a variety of *cognitive-behavioral therapies* (*CBTs*), and, when pharmacological approaches fail, electroconvulsive therapy (ECT), in which electrical current is briefly passed through one hemisphere of the brain. The risk of suicide and self-injurious behaviors is high in major depression, especially among depressive adolescents who are resistant to treatment with SSRIs (Asarnow et al., 2011). Even for patients who do respond positively to SSRI treatment, the benefits are usually not observed for the first few weeks of treatment.

The glutamate antagonist ketamine, when given in smaller-than-anesthetic doses, can produce rapid beneficial effects that last for weeks, even in patients who are resistant to SSRI medication (Reinstatler & Youssef, 2015). Ketamine is thus proposed to be useful as an acute treatment for patients with major depression who are at risk for suicide as well as for patients with bipolar depression who are at risk for suicide.

Prompted by complaints from family members that antidepressant drug treatments have caused suicide, especially in children, the U.S. Food and Drug Administration (FDA) has advised physicians to monitor the side effects of SSRIs, including fluoxetine (Prozac), sertraline (Zoloft), and paroxetine (Paxil, Seroxat). Findings from several studies show no difference in the suicide rate between children and adolescents who receive SSRIs and a placebo; in addition, the incidence of suicide after prescriptions were curtailed subsequent to the FDA warning actually increased (Isacsson & Rich, 2014).

---

often an ingredient in prescription cough medicine and pain relievers. The liver has an enzyme that converts it to morphine, although a portion of blond-haired and blue-eyed people lack this enzyme. Morphine, shown at center in Figure 6-12 and named for Morpheus, the Greek god of dreams, alters our perception of pain.

In addition to the natural opioids, semi-synthetic opioids, such as heroin and oxycodone, affect *mu* receptors. Heroin, shown at right in Figure 6-12, is altered from morphine. It is more potent and more fat-soluble than morphine and penetrates the blood–brain barrier more quickly, allowing it to produce very rapid but shorter-acting psychoactive affects. Heroin is a legal drug in some countries but continues to be illegal in others, including the United States.

Synthetic opioids, like fentanyl, are prescribed for clinical use in pain management. All opioids are potently addictive, and abuse of medically prescribed opioids is at a crisis point worldwide. Opioids also may be illegally modified, manufactured, and distributed. People who use opioids can become addicted; some obtain multiple prescriptions and sell them illicitly.

Opioid ingestion produces wide-ranging physiological changes in addition to altering pain perception, including relaxation and sleep, euphoria, and constipation. (And, yes, the use of laxatives to reverse constipation is also on the rise.) Other effects include

FIGURE 6-12 **Potent Poppy** Opium is obtained from the seed pods of the opium poppy (left). Morphine (center) is extracted from opium, and heroin (right) is in turn altered from morphine.

Patrick Field/Getty Images

DEA/Science Source

Bonnie Kamin/PhotoEdit

respiratory depression, which is the primary cause of death of opioid addicts, decreased blood pressure, pupil constriction, hypothermia, drying of secretions (for example, dry mouth), reduced sex drive, and flushed, warm skin.

Repeated opioid use produces tolerance such that within a few weeks, the effective dose may increase tenfold. Thereafter, many desired effects no longer occur. An addicted person cannot simply stop using the drug without adverse effects: severe withdrawal symptoms, physiologically and behaviorally opposite to those produced by the drug, result if drug use is abruptly stopped.

Because opioid use results in both tolerance and sensitization, an opioid user is at constant risk of overdosing. The unreliability of appropriate information on the purity of street forms of opioids contributes to the risk. In the United States and Canada, opioid overdose is currently the number-one cause of death in people under 50 years of age!

Drugs such as *naloxone* (Narcan, Nalone) act as antagonists at opioid receptors. Naloxone is a **competitive inhibitor**: it competes with opioids for neuronal receptors. Because they can enter the brain quickly, competitive inhibitors rapidly block the actions of opioids and so are essential aids in treating opioid overdoses. Many people addicted to opioids carry a competitive inhibitor as a treatment for overdosing. Because they can also be long-acting, competitive inhibitors can be used to treat opioid addiction after the addicted person has recovered from withdrawal symptoms.

Researchers have extensively studied whether opioid peptides produced in the brain can be used as drugs to relieve pain without addictive effects. The answer so far is uncertain, and producing an analgesic that does not produce addiction, which is one of the objectives of pain research, may be difficult to realize. Some countries, like Japan, simply do not treat chronic pain with opioids and are avoiding the opioid crisis. The development of non-opioid pain medications remains an important avenue of research.

Cannabinergic

Tetrahydrocannabinol (THC) is one of 84 cannabinoids and the main psychoactive constituent in cannabis (inappropriately referred to as marijuana), obtained from a couple of species of *Cannabis* plants, shown in **Figure 6-13**. THC alters mood primarily by interacting with the cannabidiol 1 (CB1) receptor found on neurons, and it also binds with the CB2 receptors found on glial cells and in other body tissues. Cannabis has extremely low toxicity—no one has *ever* died of an overdose—but may have a detrimental effect on mood and memory as well as a positive effect on mental overload.

Our body produces two endogenous molecules that bind to CB1 and CB2 receptors: anandamide and 2-AG. Results from numerous lines of research suggest that anandamide reduces anxiety and enhances forgetting. Anandamide may prevent the brain's memory systems from being overwhelmed by all the information to which we are exposed each day.

Evidence points to the usefulness of THC and cannabidiol (CBD), another cannabinoid, as therapeutic agents for a number of disorders. Cannabis relieves nausea and emesis (vomiting) in patients undergoing cancer chemotherapy who are not helped by other treatments and stimulates the appetite in patients with anorexia–cachexia (wasting) syndrome. Cannabis has been found to be helpful for treating chronic pain through mechanisms that appear to be different from those of the opioids. In fact, cannabis reduces the dose of opioids in the treatment of pain.

Cannabis has also proved useful for treating glaucoma (increased pressure in the eye), spastic disorders such as multiple sclerosis, disorders associated with spinal cord injury, and some epilepsy syndromes. Cannabis may also have some neuroprotective properties. Many people self-prescribe cannabis for a wide range of ailments, including PTSD (Roitman et al., 2014).

The term "cold turkey" is a reference to the cold skin that accompanies opioid withdrawal, in which the hair stands up and looks like turkey skin. This effect is opposite the warm skin experience after opioid use.

competitive inhibitor Drug used to treat overdoses and opioid addiction; an example is naloxone, which acts quickly to block opioid action by competing with the opioid for binding sites.

FIGURE 6-13 *Cannabis sativa* A hemp plant, an annual herb, grows over a wide range of altitudes, climates, and soils. Hemp has myriad uses, including in manufacturing rope, cloth, and paper; tetrahydrocannabinol (THC) is the main psychoactive constituent in cannabis.

Marijuana, a Mexican Spanish term with obscure roots, rose in popularity in the early 1900s. The term made the plant sound scary and foreign to White Americans, which fed into a growing racism and xenophobia against Mexicans. Anandamide (from Sanskrit, meaning "*joy*" or "*bliss*") acts on the CB1 receptor that naturally inhibits adenyl cyclase, part of a second messenger system active in sensitization (see Section 5-4).

Synthetic and derived forms of THC have been developed in part to circumvent legal restrictions on its use. Nevertheless, legal restrictions against cannabis and its derivatives hamper scientific investigations into its useful medicinal effects.

6-2 Review

Before you continue, check your understanding. Answers to Self-Test appear at the back of the book.

1. _____, the world's most widely consumed psychoactive drug, binds to _____ receptors but also has other mechanisms of action.

2. Drugs that reduce anxiety and can induce sedation primarily exert their action on the _____ receptor, which through _____ influx hyperpolarizes neurons.

3. Drugs prescribed for depression primarily exert their effect on the _____ergic system.

4. Opioids mimic the action of _____ by binding to the same receptors.

5. Amphetamine stimulates _____, and cocaine blocks _____, at the _____ synapse.

6. On which neurotransmitters do drugs that produce psychotropic effects act?

For additional study tools, visit 🔖 **LaunchPad** at launchpadworks.com

---

6-3

Factors Influencing Individual Responses to Drugs

Specific behaviors often trigger predictable results. You strike the same piano key repeatedly and hear the same note each time. You flick a light switch today, and the bulb glows exactly as it did yesterday. This cause-and-effect consistency does not extend to the effects of psychoactive drugs. Individuals respond to drugs in remarkably different ways at different times.

Behavior on Drugs

Ellen is a healthy, attractive, intelligent 19-year-old university freshman who knows the risks of unprotected sexual intercourse. She learned about HIV and other sexually transmitted infections (STIs) in her high school health class. A seminar about the dangers of unprotected sexual intercourse was part of her college orientation: seniors provided the freshmen in her residence free condoms and safe sex literature. Ellen and her former boyfriend were always careful to use latex condoms during intercourse.

At a homecoming party in her residence hall, Ellen has a great time, drinking and dancing with her friends and meeting new people. She is particularly taken with Brad, a sophomore at her college, and the two of them decide to go back to her room to order a pizza. One thing leads to another, and Ellen and Brad have sexual intercourse without using a condom. The next morning, Ellen wakes up, dismayed and surprised at her behavior and concerned that she may be pregnant or may have contracted an STI. She is terrified that she may develop AIDS (MacDonald et al., 2000).

What happened to Ellen? What is it about drugs, especially alcohol, that makes people sometimes do things they would not ordinarily do? Alcohol is linked to many harmful behaviors that are costly both to individuals and to society. These harmful behaviors include not only unprotected sexual activity but also driving while intoxicated, date rape, spousal or child abuse and other aggressive behaviors, and crime. Among the explanations for the effects of alcohol are disinhibition, learning, and behavioral myopia.

Disinhibition and Impulse Control

An early and still widely held explanation of alcohol's effects is **disinhibition theory**. It holds that alcohol has a selective depressant effect on the cortical brain region that controls judgment while sparing subcortical structures that are responsible for more instinctual behaviors, such as desire. Stated differently, alcohol depresses learned inhibitions based on reasoning and judgment while releasing the "beast" within.

A variation of disinhibition theory argues that the frontal lobes check impulsive behavior. According to this idea, impulse control is impaired after drinking alcohol because of a higher relative sensitivity of the frontal lobes to alcohol. A person may then engage in risky behavior (Hardee et al., 2014).

Proponents of these theories often excuse alcohol-related behavior, saying, for example, "She was too drunk to know better" or "The boys had a few too many and got carried away." Do disinhibition and impulse control explain Ellen's behavior? Not entirely. Ellen had used alcohol in the past and managed to practice safe sex despite its effects. Neither theory explains why her behavior was different on this occasion. If alcohol is a disinhibitor, why is it not *always* so?

Learning

Craig MacAndrew and Robert Edgerton (1969) question disinhibition theory along just these lines in their book *Drunken Comportment*. They cite many instances in which behavior under the influence of alcohol changes from one context to another. People who engage in polite social activity at home when consuming alcohol may become unruly and aggressive when drinking in a bar.

Even behavior at the bar may be inconsistent. Take Joe, for example. While drinking one night at a bar, he acts obnoxious and gets into a fight. On another occasion, he is charming and witty, even preventing a fight between two friends; on a third occasion, he becomes depressed and worries about his problems. MacAndrew and Edgerton also cite examples of cultures in which people are disinhibited when sober only to become inhibited after consuming alcohol, as well as cultures in which people are inhibited when sober and become more inhibited when drinking. What explains all these differences in the effects of alcohol?

MacAndrew and Edgerton suggest that behavior under the effects of alcohol is learned. Learned behavior is specific to culture, group, and setting and can in part explain Ellen's decision to have intercourse with Brad. Where alcohol is used to facilitate social interactions, behavior while intoxicated is a time-out from more conservative rules regarding dating.

Behavioral Myopia

Ellen's lapse in judgment regarding safe sex is more difficult to explain by learning theory. Ellen had never practiced unsafe sex before and had never made it a part of her time-out social activities. So why did she engage in it with Brad?

A different explanation for alcohol-related lapses in judgment, **behavioral myopia** (nearsightedness), is the tendency for people under the influence of (in this case) alcohol to respond to a restricted set of immediate and prominent cues while ignoring more remote cues and possible consequences. Immediate and prominent cues are very strong, obvious, and close at hand (Griffin et al., 2010).

In an altercation, a person with behavioral myopia will be quicker than usual to throw a punch because the fight cue is so strong and immediate. At a raucous party, the myopic drinker will be more eager than usual to join in because the immediate cue of boisterous fun dominates his or her view. Once Ellen and Brad arrived at Ellen's

disinhibition theory Explanation holding that alcohol has a selective depressant effect on the brain's frontal cortex, which controls judgment, while sparing subcortical structures responsible for more instinctual behaviors, such as desire.

behavioral myopia "Nearsighted" behavior displayed under the influence of alcohol, wherein local and immediate cues become prominent; remote cues and consequences are ignored.

room, the sexual cues at the moment were far more immediate than concerns about long-term safety. As a result, Ellen responded to those immediate cues and behaved atypically.

Behavioral myopia can explain many lapses in judgment that lead to risky behavior—such as aggression, date rape, or reckless driving while intoxicated. Individuals who have been drinking may also have poor insight into their level of intoxication: they may believe that they are less impaired than they actually are (Sevincer & Oettingen, 2014).

Addiction and Dependence

B. G., who started smoking when she was 13 years old, has quit many times without success. After successfully abstaining from cigarettes by using a nicotine patch for more than 6 months, B. G. began smoking again. Because the university where she works has a no-smoking policy, she has to leave campus and stand across the street to smoke. Her voice has developed a rasping sound, and she has an almost chronic "cold." She says that she used to enjoy smoking but does not any more. Concern about quitting dominates her thoughts.

B. G. has a drug problem. She is one of the approximately 25 percent of North Americans who smoke. Like B. G., most other smokers realize that it is a health hazard, have experienced unpleasant side effects from it, and have attempted to quit but cannot.

Substance abuse is a pattern of drug use in which people rely on a drug chronically and excessively, allowing it to occupy a central place in their life. In a more advanced state of *substance dependence*, popularly known as **addiction**, people exhibit three characteristics: *escalation, compulsive drug taking,* and *relapse*. Escalation refers to increased drug consumption through increased dose or dosing frequency (Kenny, 2007). Tolerance to the psychoactive effects of the drug cannot explain escalation. Instead, escalation reflects a pathological increase in the motivation to consume a drug (Oleson & Roberts, 2009). Escalation of drug use is a critical factor in the transition from sporadic use to the compulsive and relapsing drug use that characterizes addiction.

Compulsive drug taking is defined as repetitive and persistent drug administration despite negative consequences. It is related to the inability to completely cease taking drugs. Relapse involves the recurrence of compulsive drug use after a period of abstinence. Addictive drug use is marked by inordinate time spent seeking, preparing, and consuming drugs, at the expense of everyday responsibilities, as well as numerous failed attempts at abstinence (Koob et al., 2014).

Drug addicts may also experience unpleasant, sometimes dangerous physical **withdrawal symptoms** if they suddenly stop taking their drug of choice. Symptoms can include muscle aches and cramps, anxiety attacks, sweating, nausea, and even, for some drugs, convulsions and death. Symptoms of alcohol or morphine withdrawal can begin within hours of the last dose and tend to intensify over several days before they subside.

Although B. G. uses nicotine, she is not physically dependent on it. She smokes approximately the same number of cigarettes each day, and she does not suffer severe withdrawal symptoms if she is deprived of cigarettes, although she does display irritability, anxiety, increased appetite, and insomnia. B. G. illustrates that the power of psychological dependence can be as influential as the power of physical dependence.

Many addictive drugs—particularly the dopaminergics, GABAergics, and opioidergics—have a common property: they produce **psychomotor activation** in some part of their dose range. That is, at certain levels of consumption, these drugs make the user feel energetic and in control. This common effect has led to the hypothesis that all abused drugs may act on the same target in the brain:

substance abuse A pattern of drug use in which people rely on a drug chronically and excessively, allowing it to occupy a central place in their life.

addiction A complex brain disorder characterized by escalation, compulsive drug taking, and relapse; called *substance use disorder* per the DSM-5.

withdrawal symptom Physical and psychological behavior displayed by a user when drug use ends.

psychomotor activation Increased behavioral and cognitive activity so that at certain levels of consumption, the drug user feels energetic and in control.

the dopaminergic pathway from the ventral tegmental area to the nucleus accumbens. Drugs of abuse increase dopamine activity in the nucleus accumbens, either directly or indirectly, and drugs that blunt abuse and addiction decrease dopamine activity in the nucleus accumbens.

Risk Factors in Addiction

A number of environmental factors, called *adverse childhood experiences* (ACEs), are associated with an increased risk of drug initiation and drug addiction. ACEs include emotional, physical, and sexual abuse; emotional and physical neglect; mental illness of a household member; witnessing violence against one's mother; substance abuse by a household member; parental separation or divorce; and incarceration of a household member. Each ACE increases the likelihood for early drug initiation by a factor of two to four. Compared to people with 0 ACEs, people with 5 or more ACEs have been found to be 7 to 10 times more likely to report drug use problems and addiction (see **Figure 6-14**).

Data collected over four generations suggests that the effects of these ACEs cannot be accounted for by increased availability of drugs, changing social attitudes toward drugs, or recent massive expenditures and public information campaigns to prevent drug use (Dube et al., 2003). There is some good news here: if you examine Figure 6-14, you will also see that the vast majority (90 percent) of individuals who have experienced five or more ACEs have not become addicted to drugs.

In the population at large, women are about twice as sensitive to drugs as are men, on average, due in part to their smaller size but also to hormonal differences. The long-held general assumption that men are more likely than women to abuse drugs led investigators to neglect researching drug use in women. But the results of more recent research support quite the opposite view: women surpass males in the incidence of addiction to many drugs.

Although the general pattern of drug use is similar in men and women, the sex differences are striking (Becker & Hu, 2008). Women are more likely than men to abuse nicotine, alcohol, cocaine, amphetamine, opioids, cannabinoids, caffeine, and PCP. Women begin to regularly self-administer psychoactive drugs at lower doses than do men, women's use escalates more rapidly, and women are at greater risk for relapse after abstinence.

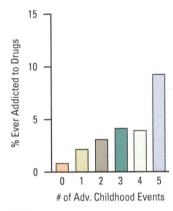

FIGURE 6-14 **ACEs and Drug Addiction** The percentage of individuals with reported drug addiction increases significantly with the addition of each ACE.
Data from Dube et al., 2003.

6-3 Review

Before you continue, check your understanding. Answers to Self-Test appear at the back of the book.

1. _____ is the tendency for people under the influence of a drug to respond to a restricted set of immediate and prominent cues while ignoring more remote cues and possible consequences.

2. _____ is a condition in which people rely on drugs chronically and to excess, whereas _____ is a condition in which people are physically dependent on a drug as well.

3. The evidence that many abused or addictive drugs produce _____, which makes the user feel energetic and in control, suggests that activation in the _____ plays a role in drug abuse and addiction.

4. Common wisdom is incorrect in suggesting that _____ are less likely to abuse drugs than are _____.

5. Why can alcohol-related behavior vary widely in a single individual from time to time?

For additional study tools, visit **LaunchPad** at launchpadworks.com

6-4

Explaining and Treating Drug Abuse

Why do people become addicted to drugs? Early neuropsychological explanations centered on the pleasure associated with natural experiences surrounding sex, chocolate, and catching a fish, as well as the euphoria produced by psychoactive drugs. The pleasurable "rush" would supposedly lead to a variety of impulse control disorders, such as overeating, gambling, and repeated drug taking. But this explanation, known as the *hedonia hypothesis*, has a central problem: the initial pleasurable experience wears off with repeated drug taking and can become quite aversive, yet the user continues to take the drug. (Most of us have witnessed habitual smokers out in the wind and cold having a cigarette.) In other words, over repeated drug exposure, the pleasurable or hedonic experience becomes dissociated from the drug taking. More recent work has shown that there are separate brain circuits for pleasure (liking) and for repeating behaviors (wanting).

Wanting-and-Liking Theory

wanting-and-liking theory Explanation holding that when a drug is associated with certain cues, the cues themselves elicit desire for the drug; also called *incentive sensitization theory*.

To account for the three components of addiction—escalation, compulsive drug taking, and relapse—Terry Robinson and Kent Berridge (2008) proposed the incentive sensitization theory, also called the **wanting-and-liking theory**, because wanting and liking are produced by different brain systems. They define *wanting* as craving, whereas *liking* is the pleasure the drug produces. With repeated use, tolerance for liking develops, and the expression of liking (pleasure) decreases as a consequence (**Figure 6-15**). In contrast, the system that mediates wanting sensitizes, and craving increases.

The first step on the proposed road to drug dependence is the initial experience, when the drug affects a neural system associated with pleasure. At this stage, the user may like the substance—including liking to take it within a given social context. With repeated use, liking the drug may decline from its initial level. At this stage, the user may also begin to show tolerance to the drug's effects and so may begin to increase the dosage to increase liking.

In classical (Pavlovian) conditioning, learning to associate a formerly neutral stimulus (the sound of a bell) with a stimulus (food) elicits an involuntary response (salivation).

With each use, the drug taker increasingly associates the cues related to drug use—be it a hypodermic needle, the room in which the drug is taken, or the people with whom the drug is taken—with the drug-taking experience. The user makes this association because the drug enhances classically conditioned cues associated with drug taking. Eventually, these cues come to possess incentive salience: they induce wanting, or craving, the drug-taking experience.

The neural basis of addiction is proposed to involve multiple brain systems. The decision to take a drug is made in the prefrontal cortex, an area that participates in most daily decisions. When a drug is taken, it activates endogenous opioid systems that are generally related to pleasurable experiences. And wanting drugs may spring from activity in the nucleus accumbens of the dopaminergic activating system.

FIGURE 6-15 **Wanting-and-Liking Theory** With repeated drug use, wanting a drug increases while liking the drug decreases. Wanting (craving) becomes more strongly associated with drug cues, such as lighting a cigarette.

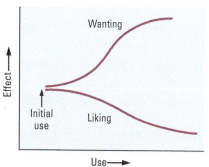

In these mesolimbic pathways, diagrammed in **Figure 6-16**, the axons of dopamine neurons in the midbrain project to structures in the basal ganglia, including the nucleus accumbens, to the frontal cortex, and to the allocortex. When drug takers encounter cues associated with drug taking, this system becomes active, releasing dopamine. Dopamine release is the neural correlate of wanting and the repetition of behavior.

Another brain system may be responsible for conditioning drug-related cues to drug taking. Barry Everitt (2014) proposes that the repeated pairing of drug-related cues to drug taking forms neural associations, or learning, in the dorsal striatum, a region in the basal ganglia consisting of the caudate nucleus and putamen. As the user repeatedly takes the drug, voluntary control gives way to unconscious processes—a habit. The result: drug users lose control of decisions related to drug taking, and the wanting—the voluntary control over drug taking—gives way to the craving of addiction.

Multiple findings align with the wanting-and-liking explanation of drug addiction. Ample evidence confirms that abused drugs and the context in which they are taken initially has a pleasurable effect and that habitual users continue using their drug of choice even when taking it no longer produces any pleasure. Heroin addicts sometimes report that they are miserable: their lives are in ruins, and the drug is not even pleasurable anymore. But they still want it, and they still take it. What's more, desire for the drug often is greatest just when the addicted person is maximally high, not during withdrawal. Finally, cues associated with drug taking—the social situation, the sight of the drug, and drug paraphernalia—strongly influence decisions to take, or continue taking, a drug.

Notwithstanding support for a dopamine basis for addiction, recent research suggests more than one type of addiction. Some rats become readily conditioned to cues associated with reinforcement—for example, a bar that delivers a reward when pressed. Other animals ignore the bar's incentive salience but are attracted to the location where they receive reinforcement. Animals that display the former behavior are termed sign trackers; those in the other group are goal trackers. Sign trackers exposed to addictive drugs appear to attribute incentive salience to drug-associated cues. Their drug wanting is dependent on the brain's dopamine systems. Goal trackers may also become addicted, possibly via different neural systems. Such findings imply at least two types of addiction (Yager et al., 2015).

We can extend wanting-and-liking theory to many life situations. Cues related to sexual activity, food, and even sports can induce wanting, sometimes in the absence of liking. We frequently eat when prompted by the cue of other people eating, even though we may not be hungry and may derive little pleasure from eating at that time. The similarities between exaggerating normal behaviors and drug addiction suggest that they depend on the same learning and brain mechanisms. For this reason, any addiction is extremely difficult to treat.

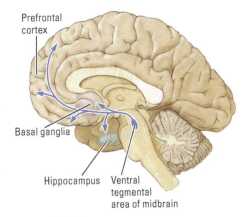

FIGURE 6-16 **Mesolimbic Dopamine Pathways** Axons of neurons in the midbrain ventral tegmentum project to the basal ganglia, including the nucleus accumbens, prefrontal cortex, and hippocampus.

When a rat is placed in an environment where it anticipates a favored food or sex, investigators record dopamine increases in the striatum (see Section 7-5).

People who enjoy high-risk adventure may be genetically predisposed to experiment with drugs, but people with no interest in risk taking are just as likely to use drugs.

Why Doesn't Everyone Become Addicted to Drugs?

Observing that some people are more prone than others to compulsive drug taking, scientists have investigated and found three lines of evidence suggesting a genetic contribution to differences in drug use. First, if a twin abuses alcohol, his or her identical twin (same genotype) is more likely to abuse it than would be a fraternal twins (only some genes in common). Second, people adopted shortly after birth are more likely to abuse alcohol if their biological parents were alcoholic, even though they have had almost no contact with those parents. Third, although most animals do not care for alcohol, selective breeding of mice, rats, and monkeys can produce strains that consume large quantities of it.

Nathan Bilow/Getty Images

Each line of evidence presents problems, however. Perhaps identical twins show greater concordance rates (incidence of similar behavioral traits) for alcohol abuse because their environments are more similar than those of fraternal twins. And perhaps the link between alcoholism in adoptees and their biological parents has to do with nervous system changes due to prenatal exposure to the drug. Finally, the fact that animals can be selectively bred for alcohol consumption does not mean that all human alcoholics have a similar genetic makeup. The evidence for a genetic basis of alcoholism will become compelling only when a gene or set of genes related to alcoholism is found.

Epigenetics offers another complementary explanation of susceptibility to addiction (Hillemacher et al., 2015). Addictive drugs may reduce the transcriptional ability of genes related to voluntary control and increase the transcriptional ability of other genes related to behaviors susceptible to addiction. Epigenetic changes in an individual's gene expression may be relatively permanent and can be passed along, perhaps through the next few generations. For these reasons, epigenetics can account both for the enduring behaviors that support addiction and for the tendency of drug addiction to be inherited.

Less-than-perfect concordance rates between identical twins for diseases ranging from schizophrenia to asthma point to epigenetic inheritance of behaviors by the next generation (see Section 3-3).

Treating Drug Abuse

Figure 6-17 charts the relative incidence of drug use in the United States among people aged 12 and older who reported using at least one psychoactive drug during the preceding year in the National Survey of Drug Use and Health conducted by the National Institute of Drug Use (2016). The two most used drugs, alcohol and tobacco, are legal. The drugs that carry the harshest penalties, cocaine and heroin, are used by far fewer people. But criminalizing drugs clearly is not a solution to drug use or abuse, as illustrated by the widespread use of cannabis, the third most used drug on the chart. In response to its widespread use, several states and Canada have legalized cannabis to some degree, but it remains illegal under U.S. federal law.

Treating drug abuse is difficult in part because legal proscriptions are irrational. In the United States, the Harrison Narcotics Act of 1914 made heroin and a variety of other drugs illegal and made the treatment of addicted people by physicians in their private offices illegal. The Drug Addiction Treatment Act of 2000 partly reversed this prohibition, allowing the treatment of patients but with a number of restrictions. In addition, legal consequences attending drug use vary greatly depending on the drug and the jurisdiction.

From a health standpoint, tobacco has much higher proven health risks than does cannabis. Moderate use of alcohol is likely benign. Moderate use of opioids is likely impossible. Social coercion is useful in reducing tobacco use: witness the marked decline in smoking as a result of prohibitions against smoking in public places. Medical intervention is necessary for the treatment of opioid abusers.

The approaches to treating drug abuse vary depending on the drug. Online and in-person communities associated with self-help and professional groups address the treatment of specific drug addictions. Importantly, because addiction is influenced by conditioning to drug-related cues and by a variety of brain changes, recidivism remains an enduring risk for people who have apparently kicked their habit.

Neuroscience research will continue to lead to better understanding of the neural basis of drug use and to better treatment. The best approach to any drug treatment involves recognizing that addiction is a lifelong problem for most people. Thus, drug addiction must be treated in the same way as chronic behavioral addictions and medical problems—analogous to recognizing that controlling weight with appropriate diet and exercise is a lifelong struggle for many people.

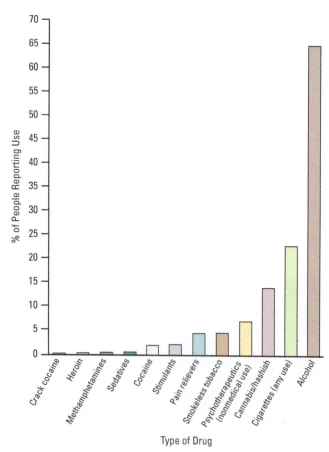

FIGURE 6-17 **Drug Use in the United States in 2016** Results from an annual national survey of Americans aged 12 and older who reported using at least one psychoactive drug during the past year. Percentages for alcohol, tobacco, and marijuana are rounded to the nearest whole numbers.

Data from National Institute of Drug Use, 2016.

Can Drugs Cause Brain Damage?

Many natural substances can act as neurotoxins; **Table 6-2** lists some of them. Ongoing investigations of the neurotoxicity of these substances and other drugs in animal models show that many cause brain damage. Certain drugs of abuse can cause brain damage in humans, but definitive proof is very difficult to obtain. It is difficult to parse other life experiences from drug taking. It is also difficult to obtain the brains of drug users for examination at autopsy. Nevertheless, there is evidence that the developing brain can be particularly sensitive to drug effects, especially in adolescence, a time when drug experimentation is common (Teixeira-Gomes et al., 2015).

In the late 1960s, many reports linked monosodium glutamate (MSG), a salty-tasting, flavor-enhancing food additive, to headaches in some people. In investigating this effect, scientists placed large doses of MSG on cultured neurons, which died. Subsequently, they injected MSG into the brains of experimental animals, where it also killed neurons.

This line of research led to the discovery that many glutamatelike substances, including domoic acid and kainic acid (both toxins in seaweed) and ibotenic acid (found in some poisonous mushrooms), similarly kill neurons (**Figure 6-18**). Some drugs, such as PCP and ketamine, also act as glutamate agonists, leaving open the possibility that at high doses they, too, can cause neuronal death.

Glutamatelike drugs are toxic because they act on glutamate receptors. Glutamate receptor activation results in an influx of Ca^{2+} into the cell, which through second messengers activates a suicide gene leading to apoptosis (cell death). This discovery shows that a drug might be toxic not only because of its general effect on cell function but also as an agent that activates normal cell processes related to apoptosis.

We must add, though, that there is no evidence that moderate consumption of MSG is harmful.

What about the many recreational drugs that affect the nervous system? Are any of them neurotoxic? Sorting out the effects of the drug itself from the effects of other factors related to taking the drug is a major problem. Chronic alcohol use, for instance, can be associated with damage to the thalamus and cortical areas, producing severe memory disorders. Alcohol does not directly cause this damage, though. Alcoholics typically obtain low amounts of thiamine (vitamin B_1) in their diet, and alcohol interferes with the ability of the intestines to absorption of thiamine. Thiamine plays a vital role in maintaining cell membrane structure.

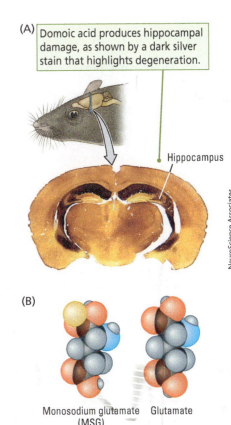

(A) Domoic acid produces hippocampal damage, as shown by a dark silver stain that highlights degeneration.

Hippocampus

NeuroScience Associates

(B)

Monosodium glutamate (MSG) Glutamate

FIGURE 6-18 **Neurotoxicity** **(A)** Domoic acid damage in this rat's hippocampus, and to a lesser extent in many other brain regions, is indicated by the darkest coloring. Domoic acid, a Glu analog and therefore a glutamatergic agonist, is the causative agent in amnesic shellfish poisoning, which can result in permanent short-term memory loss, brain damage, and, in severe cases, death. **(B)** As can be seen here, monosodium glutamate (MSG) and glutamate are nearly identical and have nearly identical properties.

TABLE 6-2 **Some Neurotoxins, Their Sources, and Their Actions**

Substance	Origin	Action
Apamin	Bees and wasps	Blocks Ca^{2+} channels
Botulin	Spoiled food	Blocks ACh release
Caffeine	Coffee seed	Blocks adenosine receptors, blocks Ca^{2+} channels
Colchicine	Crocus plant	Blocks microtubules
Curare	Berry	Blocks ACh receptors
Ibotenic acid	Mushroom	Similar to domoic acid; mimics glutamate
Magnesium	Natural element	Blocks Ca^{2+} channels
Rabies virus	Infected animal	Blocks ACh receptors
Reserpine	Tree	Destroys storage granules
Spider venom	Black widow spider	Stimulates ACh release
Strychnine	Plant	Blocks glycine
Tetrodotoxin	Puffer fish	Blocks membrane permeability to Na^+

Drug-Induced Psychosis

L. V. is 22 years old and has been wandering the halls of a rehabilitation clinic for almost a year. He is either confused or hostile and rarely has lucid moments. L. V. had been using crystal meth during his years as an undergraduate. Just before his final exams in his third year, he had a psychotic attack and since then has been continuously institutionalized.

L. V. grew up with an abusive father and alcoholic mother. As a child, he was artistic and sensitive, and he showed a quiet maturity beyond his years. He had a passion for science fiction and mathematics, and his friends thought he was fun to be around. During his high school years, his family noted long-lasting and recurring periods of silence during which he often withdrew from socialization. L. V. experimented with alcohol, tobacco, cannabis, mushrooms, and cocaine before he found crystal meth (a drug also known as crank or ice), which he would make by combining cold medication, Ritalin, fertilizer, drain cleaner, antifreeze, and Epsom salts.

In low doses, methamphetamine, the active ingredient in crystal meth, elevates mood; increases alertness, concentration, and energy; reduces appetite; and promotes weight loss. At higher doses, it induces psychosis in vulnerable individuals and can cause seizures and brain hemorrhage. Individuals who compulsively take methamphetamine, like L. V., display unpredictable and rapid mood swings, paranoia, hallucinations, delirium, and delusions, often with accompanying violent behavior.

Because methamphetamine is a dopaminergic agonist, it interacts directly with the nucleus accumbens, which can lead to compulsive drug use. Withdrawal symptoms during initial abstinence may persist for months beyond the typical withdrawal period observed for other drugs. Chronic methamphetamine use has a toxic effect on human midbrain dopaminergic neurons and serotonin neurons, leading to reductions in gray-matter volume in several brain regions and adverse changes in markers of metabolic integrity (Krasnova & Cadet, 2009).

A week before L. V.'s psychotic episode, he said he hadn't slept for 2 weeks, and his delusions had escalated. His dank apartment was strewn with drug paraphernalia, soiled bed sheets, and foul odors. There was no food in his apartment, and there hadn't been for some time.

Dopaminergic antagonists are used to treat psychosis, but they are not a cure. Despite treatment, L. V. continues to punch himself in the face, masturbate in public, yell obscenities, and make animal sounds. Doctors see little hope of recovery for him, and the medical profession is seeing a surge in young people who are aggressive and violent due to crystal meth.

Clinical Focus 5-4 reports the chilling case of heroin addicts who developed Parkinson disease after using synthetic heroin laced with a contaminant (MPTP).

Similarly, among the many reports of people with a severe psychiatric disorder subsequent to abusing certain recreational drugs, in most cases determining whether the drug initiated the condition or aggravated an existing problem is difficult. Exactly determining whether the drug itself or some contaminant in it caused a harmful outcome also is difficult. With the increasing sensitivity of brain-imaging studies, however, evidence is increasing that many drugs used recreationally can cause brain damage and cognitive impairments, as discussed in Clinical Focus 6-4, Drug-Induced Psychosis.

The strongest evidence comes from the study of the synthetic amphetamine-like drug MDMA, also called Ecstasy and, in pure powdered form, Molly (Büttner, 2011). Although MDMA is structurally related to amphetamine, it produces hallucinogenic effects and is called a hallucinogenic amphetamine. Findings from animal studies show that doses of MDMA approximating those taken by human users result in the degeneration of very fine serotonergic nerve terminals. In monkeys, significant terminal loss may be permanent. Memory impairments and damage in MDMA users revealed by brain imaging result from similar neuronal damage (Cowan et al., 2008). MDMA may also contain a contaminant called paramethoxymethamphetamine (PMMA). This notoriously toxic amphetamine is often called Dr. Death because the difference between a dose that causes behavioral effects and a dose that causes death is minuscule (Vevelstad et al., 2012). Contamination by unknown compounds can occur in any drug purchased on the street.

The psychoactive properties of cocaine are similar to those of amphetamine, so cocaine also is suspect with respect to brain damage. Cocaine use is related to the blockage of cerebral blood flow and other changes in blood circulation. Brain-imaging studies show that brain regions are reduced in size in cocaine users, suggesting that cocaine use can be toxic to neurons (Liu et al., 2014).

Clinical Focus 7-3 explores the hypothesis that genetic vulnerability predisposes some adolescents to develop psychosis when exposed to cannabis.

THC may trigger psychosis in vulnerable individuals, but there is no evidence that the psychosis is a result of brain damage. Indeed, beyond the therapeutic applications of THC cited in Section 6-2, recent studies suggest that THC may have neuroprotective properties. It can aid brain healing after traumatic brain injury and slow the progression of diseases associated with brain degeneration, including Alzheimer disease and Huntington disease (Nguyen et al., 2014).

6-4 **Review**

Before you continue, check your understanding. Answers to Self-Test appear at the back of the book.

1. The wanting-and-liking theory of addiction suggests that with repeated use, _____ of the drug decreases as a result of _____, while _____ increases as a result of _____.

2. At the neural level, the decision to take a drug is made in the brain's _____. Once taken, the drug activates opioid systems related to pleasurable experiences in the _____. Drug cravings may originate in the _____, and the repeated pairing of drug-related cues and drug taking forms neural associations in the _____ that loosen voluntary control over drug taking.

3. As an alternative to explanations of susceptibility to addiction based on genetic inheritance, _____ can account both for the enduring behaviors that support addiction and for the tendency of drug addiction to be inherited.

4. It is difficult to determine whether recreational drug use causes brain damage in humans because it is difficult to distinguish the effects of _____ from the effects of _____.

5. Briefly describe the basis for a reasonable approach to treating drug addiction.

For additional study tools, visit ✹ **LaunchPad** at launchpadworks.com

6-5

Hormones

Many of the principles related to the interactions of drugs and the body also apply to the certain hormones that act on neuronal receptors. Hormones are secreted by glands in the body and by the brain. Interacting brain and body hormones form feedback loops that regulate their activity. Hormonal influences change across the life span, influencing development and body and brain function (Nugent et al., 2012). In many respects, hormone systems are like neurotransmitter-activating systems except that hormones use the bloodstream as a conveyance. Indeed, many hormones act as neurotransmitters, and many neurotransmitters act as hormones.

Hierarchical Control of Hormones

Many hormones operate in a feedback system that includes the brain and the body. **Figure 6-19** shows how the hypothalamus produces neurohormones that stimulate the pituitary gland to secrete releasing hormones into the circulatory system. The pituitary hormones in turn influence the remaining endocrine glands to release appropriate hormones into the bloodstream to act on various targets in the body and send feedback to the brain about the need for more or less hormone release.

Hormones not only affect body organs but also target virtually all aspects of brain function. Almost every neuron in the brain contains receptors on which various hormones can act. In addition to influencing sex organs and physical appearance, hormones affect neurotransmitter function, especially in neurons that influence sexual development and behavior (Barth et al., 2015). Hormones can influence gene expression by binding to special receptors on or in the cell and then being transported to the nucleus to influence gene transcription. Transcription, in turn, influences the synthesis of proteins needed for a variety of cellular processes. Thus, hormones influence brain and body structure and behavior.

Although many questions remain about how hormones produce or contribute to complex behavior, the diversity of their functions clarifies why the body uses

FIGURE 6-19 Hormonal Hierarchy

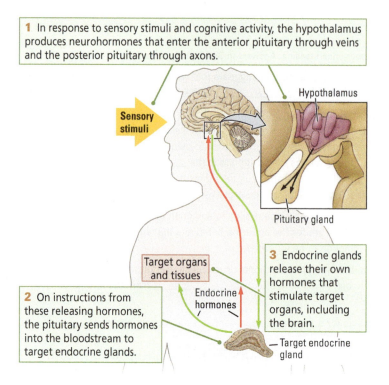

1 In response to sensory stimuli and cognitive activity, the hypothalamus produces neurohormones that enter the anterior pituitary through veins and the posterior pituitary through axons.

Sensory stimuli

Hypothalamus

Pituitary gland

Target organs and tissues

Endocrine hormones

3 Endocrine glands release their own hormones that stimulate target organs, including the brain.

2 On instructions from these releasing hormones, the pituitary sends hormones into the bloodstream to target endocrine glands.

Target endocrine gland

Consult the entry Hormonal Disorders inside the book's front cover for more information.

hormones as messengers: their targets are so widespread that the best possible way of reaching all of them is to travel in the bloodstream, which goes everywhere in the body.

Classes and Functions of Hormones

Hormones can be used as drugs to treat or prevent disease. People take synthetic hormones as replacement therapy if the glands that produce the hormones are removed or malfunction. People also take hormones, especially sex hormones, to counteract the effects of aging, to increase physical strength and endurance, and to gain an advantage in sports. In the human body, as many as 100 hormones are classified chemically as either steroids or peptides.

To refresh your understanding of metabotropic receptors, review Figure 5-15.

Steroid hormones, such as testosterone and cortisol, are synthesized from cholesterol and are lipid (fat) soluble. Steroids diffuse away from their site of synthesis in glands, including the gonads, adrenal cortex, and thyroid. They bind to steroid receptors on the cell membrane or in the cell and frequently act on cellular DNA to influence gene transcription.

Peptide hormones, such as insulin, growth hormone, and the endorphins, are made by cellular DNA in the same way other proteins are made. They influence their target cell's activity by binding to metabotropic receptors on the cell membrane, generating a second messenger that affects the cell's physiology or gene transcription.

steroid hormone Fat-soluble chemical messenger synthesized from cholesterol.

peptide hormone Chemical messenger synthesized by cellular DNA that acts to affect the target cell's physiology.

homeostatic hormone One of a group of hormones that maintain internal metabolic balance and regulate physiological systems in an organism.

gonadal (sex) hormone One of a group of hormones, such as testosterone, that control reproductive functions and bestow sexual appearance and identity as male or female.

Steroid and peptide hormones fall into one of three main functional groups with respect to behavior, and they may function in more than one group:

1. **Homeostatic hormones** maintain a state of internal metabolic balance and regulate physiological systems. Mineralocorticoids (e.g., aldosterone) control both the concentration of water in blood and cells and the levels of sodium, potassium, and calcium in the body, and they promote digestive functions.

2. **Gonadal (sex) hormones** control reproductive functions. They instruct the body to develop as male (testosterone) or female (estrogen); influence sexual behavior

and conception; and, in women, control the menstrual cycle (estrogen and progesterone), birthing of babies, and release of breast milk (prolactin, oxytocin). These hormones, especially oxytocin, influence mother–infant bonding and, in some species, including sheep, are essential for bonding to occur.

3. **Glucocorticoids** (e.g., cortisol and corticosterone), a group of steroid hormones secreted in times of stress, are important in protein and carbohydrate metabolism, as well as in controlling blood sugar levels and cellular absorption of sugar. Hormones activated in psychologically challenging events or emergencies prepare the body to cope by fighting or fleeing.

glucocorticoid One of a group of steroid hormones, such as cortisol, secreted in times of stress; important in protein and carbohydrate metabolism.

anabolic steroid Class of synthetic hormones related to testosterone that have both muscle-building (anabolic) and masculinizing (androgenic) effects; also called *anabolic–androgenic steroid*

Homeostatic Hormones

Homeostatic hormones are essential to life. The body's internal environment must remain within relatively constant parameters for us to function. An appropriate balance of sugars, proteins, carbohydrates, salts, and water is necessary in the blood, in the extracellular compartments of muscles, in the brain and other body structures, and in all cells. The internal environment must be maintained regardless of a person's age, activities, or conscious state. As children or adults, at rest or in strenuous work, when we have overeaten or when we are hungry, to survive we need a relatively constant internal environment.

A typical homeostatic function is controlling blood sugar level. After a meal, digestive processes result in increased glucose in the blood. One group of cells in the pancreas releases insulin, a homeostatic hormone that instructs the enzyme glycogen synthase in liver and muscle cells to start storing glucose in the form of glycogen. The resulting decrease in glucose decreases the stimulation of pancreatic cells so that they stop producing insulin, and glycogen storage stops. When the body needs glucose for energy, another hormone in the liver, glucagon, acts as a countersignal to insulin. Glucagon stimulates another enzyme, glycogen phosphorylase, to initiate glucose release from its glycogen storage site.

Diabetes mellitus is caused by a failure of the pancreatic cells to secrete any or enough insulin. As a result, blood sugar levels can fall (hypoglycemia) or rise (hyperglycemia). In hyperglycemia, blood glucose levels rise because insulin does not instruct body cells to take up glucose. Consequently, cell function, including neuronal function, can fail through glucose starvation, even in the presence of high glucose levels in the blood. Chronic high blood glucose levels cause damage to the eyes, kidneys, nerves, heart, and blood vessels.

In hypoglycemia, inappropriate diet can lead to low blood sugar severe enough to cause fainting. Eric Steen and his coworkers (2005) propose that insulin resistance in brain cells may be related to Alzheimer disease. Hunger and eating are influenced by a number of homeostatic hormones, including leptin and ghrelin. Leptin (from the Greek for "thin"), secreted by adipose (animal fat) tissue, inhibits hunger and so is called the *satiety hormone*. Ghrelin (from the Indio-European *gher*, meaning "to grow"), secreted by the gastrointestinal tract, regulates growth hormones and energy use. Ghrelin also induces hunger. It is secreted when the stomach is empty; secretion stops when the stomach is full. Leptin and ghrelin act on receptors on the same neurons of the arcuate nucleus of the hypothalamus and so contribute to energy homeostasis by managing eating.

Homeostasis comes from the Greek words *stasis* ("standing") and *homeo* ("in the same place"). The homeostatic mechanisms that control regulated behavior are discussed in detail in Section 12-3.

Normal glucose concentration in the bloodstream varies between 80 and 130 mg per 100 milliliters (about 3.3 oz) of blood.

Anabolic–Androgenic Steroids

A class of synthetic hormones related to testosterone, the sex hormone secreted by the testes and responsible for the distinguishing characteristics of the male, has both muscle-building (anabolic) and masculinizing (androgenic) effects. Anabolic–androgenic steroids, commonly known simply as **anabolic steroids**, were synthesized originally to build body mass and enhance endurance. Russian weight lifters were the first to use them, in 1952, to enhance performance and win international competitions.

Synthetic steroid use rapidly spread to other countries and sports, eventually leading to a ban in track and field and then in many other sports, enforced by drug testing. Testing policy has led to a cat-and-mouse game in which new anabolic steroids and new ways of taking them and masking them are devised.

The effects of sex hormones on the brain are detailed in Section 12-5.

Today, the use of anabolic steroids is about equal among athletes and nonathletes. More than 1 million people in the United States have used anabolic steroids not only to enhance athletic performance but also to enhance physique and appearance. Anabolic steroid use in high schools may be as high as 7 percent for males and 3 percent for females.

The use of anabolic steroids carries health risks. Their administration results in the body reducing its manufacture of testosterone, which in turn reduces male fertility and spermatogenesis. Muscle bulk is increased, and so is aggression. Cardiovascular effects include increased risk of heart attack and stroke. Liver and kidney function may be compromised, and the risk of tumors may increase. Male-pattern baldness may be enhanced. Females may have an enlarged clitoris, acne, increased body hair, and a deepened voice.

Anabolic steroids have approved clinical uses. Testosterone replacement is a treatment for hypogonadal males. It is also useful for treating muscle loss subsequent to trauma and for the recovery of muscle mass in malnourished people. In females, anabolic steroids are used to treat endometriosis and fibrocystic disease of the breast.

Glucocorticoids and Stress

Stress is a term borrowed from engineering to describe a process in which an agent exerts a force on an object. Applied to humans and other animals, a stressor is a stimulus that challenges the body's homeostasis and triggers arousal. Stress responses, behavioral as well as physiological, include both arousal and attempts to reduce stress. A stress response can outlast a stress-inducing incident and may even occur in the absence of an obvious stressor. Living with constant stress can be debilitating.

Activating a Stress Response

Surprisingly, the body's response is the same whether a stressor is exciting, sad, or frightening. Robert Sapolsky (2004) uses the vivid image of a hungry lion chasing down a zebra to illustrate the stress response. The chase elicits divergent behavior in the two animals, but their physiological responses are identical. The stress response begins when the body is subjected to a stressor and especially when the brain perceives a stressor and responds with arousal, directed from the brain by the hypothalamus. The response consists of two separate sequences, one fast and the other slow.

THE FAST RESPONSE Shown at left in **Figure 6-20**, the sympathetic division of the ANS is activated to prepare the body and its organs for fight or flight. The parasympathetic division for rest and digest is turned off. The sympathetic division stimulates the medulla on the interior of the adrenal gland to release epinephrine. The epinephrine surge (often called the adrenaline surge, after epinephrine's original name) prepares the body for a sudden burst of activity. Among its many functions, epinephrine stimulates cell metabolism, readying the body's cells for action.

Principle 4: The CNS functions on multiple levels.

THE SLOW RESPONSE As shown at right in Figure 6-20, the slow response is controlled by the steroid cortisol, a glucocorticoid released from the outer layer (cortex) of the adrenal gland. Activating the cortisol pathway takes anywhere from minutes to hours. Cortisol has wide-ranging functions, including turning off all bodily systems not immediately required to deal with a stressor. For example, cortisol turns off insulin so that the liver starts releasing glucose, thus temporarily increasing the body's energy supply. It also shuts down reproductive functions and inhibits the production of growth hormone. In this way, it concentrates the body's energy on dealing with the stress.

Ending a Stress Response

Normally, stress responses are brief. The body mobilizes its resources, deals with the challenge physiologically and behaviorally, and shuts down the stress response. Just as the brain is responsible for turning on the stress reaction, it is also responsible for turning it off. Consider what can happen if the stress response is not shut down:

• The body continues to mobilize energy at the cost of energy storage.

• Proteins are used up, resulting in muscle wasting and fatigue.

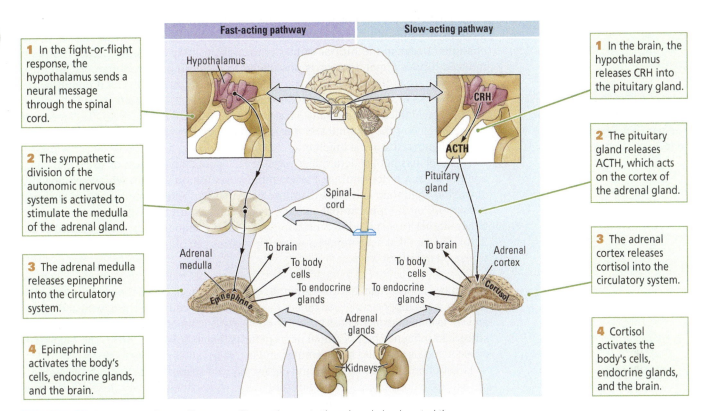

1 In the fight-or-flight response, the hypothalamus sends a neural message through the spinal cord.

2 The sympathetic division of the autonomic nervous system is activated to stimulate the medulla of the adrenal gland.

3 The adrenal medulla releases epinephrine into the circulatory system.

4 Epinephrine activates the body's cells, endocrine glands, and the brain.

1 In the brain, the hypothalamus releases CRH into the pituitary gland.

2 The pituitary gland releases ACTH, which acts on the cortex of the adrenal gland.

3 The adrenal cortex releases cortisol into the circulatory system.

4 Cortisol activates the body's cells, endocrine glands, and the brain.

FIGURE 6-20 **Activating a Stress Response** Two pathways to the adrenal gland control the body's stress response. The fast-acting pathway primes the body immediately for fight or flight. The slow-acting pathway both mobilizes the body's resources to confront a stressor and repairs stress-related damage. CRH, corticotropin-releasing hormone; ACTH, adrenocorticotropic hormone.

- Growth hormone is inhibited, so the body cannot grow.
- The gastrointestinal system remains shut down, reducing the intake and processing of nutrients to replace used resources.
- Reproductive functions are inhibited.
- The immune system is suppressed, contributing to the possibility of infection or disease.

Sapolsky (2005) argues that the hippocampus plays an important role in turning off the stress response. The hippocampus contains a high density of cortisol receptors, and it has axons that project to the hypothalamus. Consequently, the hippocampus is well suited to detecting cortisol in the blood and instructing the hypothalamus to reduce blood cortisol levels.

There may, however, be a more insidious relationship between the hippocampus and blood cortisol levels. Sapolsky observed wild-born vervet monkeys that had become agricultural pests in Kenya and had therefore been trapped and caged. He found that some monkeys sickened and died of a syndrome that appeared to be related to stress. Those that died seemed to have been socially subordinate animals housed with particularly aggressive dominant monkeys. Autopsies showed high rates of gastric ulcers, enlarged adrenal glands, and pronounced hippocampal degeneration. The hippocampal damage may have been due to prolonged high cortisol levels produced by the unremitting stress of being caged with the aggressive monkeys.

Cortisol levels are usually regulated by the hippocampus, but if these levels remain elevated because a stress-inducing situation perpetuates, cortisol eventually damages the hippocampus, reducing its size. The damaged hippocampus is then unable to do its work of reducing the level of cortisol. Thus, a vicious circle is set up in which the hippocampus undergoes progressive degeneration and cortisol levels are not controlled (**Figure 6-21**). Interestingly, other research with rats suggests that following similar stress, the size of the amygdala is increased (Bourgin et al., 2015).

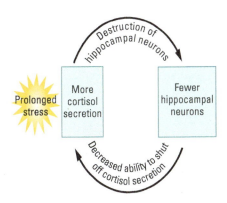

FIGURE 6-21 **Vicious Circle** Unrelieved stress promotes excessive release of cortisol, which damages hippocampal neurons. The damaged neurons cannot detect cortisol and therefore cannot signal the adrenal gland to stop producing it. The resulting feedback loop enhances cortisol secretion, further damaging hippocampal neurons.

PTSD, introduced in Section 5-4 in relation to sensitization, is among the anxiety disorders detailed in Section 12-6. Research Focus 16-1 and Section 16-2 consider treatments.

Because stress response circuits in rats and monkeys are similar to those in humans, it is possible that excessive stress in humans can lead to similar brain changes. Because the hippocampus is thought to play a role in memory, stress-induced hippocampal damage is postulated to result in impaired memory. Because the amygdala is thought to play a role in emotion, stress-induced changes are postulated to result in increased emotional responses. This pattern of behavioral changes resembles posttraumatic stress disorder (PTSD). People with PTSD feel as if they are reliving the trauma, and the accompanying physiological arousal enhances their belief that danger is imminent.

Research has not yet determined whether the cumulative effects of stress can damage the human hippocampus. For example, research on women who were sexually abused in childhood and were diagnosed with PTSD yields some reports of changes in memory or in hippocampal volume, as measured with brain-imaging techniques. Other studies report no differences in abused and nonabused subjects (Landré et al., 2010). The fact that such apparently similar studies can obtain different results can be explained in several ways.

First, the amount of damage to the hippocampus that must occur to produce a stress syndrome is not certain. Second, brain-imaging techniques may not be sensitive to subtle changes in hippocampal cell function or to moderate cell loss. Third, wide individual and environmental differences influence how people respond to stress. Fourth, neonatal stress can influence hippocampal neurogenesis (Lajud & Torner, 2015). The long-term consequence is a smaller hippocampus and increased susceptibility to stress.

Finally, humans are long lived and gather many life experiences that complicate simple extrapolations from a single stressful event. Nevertheless, Patrick McGowan and his colleagues (2009) report that the density of glucocorticoid receptors in the hippocampus of people who committed suicide and had been sexually abused as children was lower than that of both controls and suicide victims who had not been abused.

The decrease in receptors and in glucocorticoid mRNA suggests that childhood abuse induces epigenetic changes in the expression of glucocorticoid genes. The decrease in glucocorticoid receptors presumably renders the hippocampus less able to depress stress responses. The importance of the McGowan study is its suggestion of a mechanism through which stress can influence hippocampal function without necessarily being associated with a decrease in hippocampal volume. This study further underscores the point that stress likely produces many changes in many brain regions. It is unlikely that all these changes have been described or are understood (Clauss et al., 2015).

6-5 Review

Before you continue, check your understanding. Answers to Self-Test appear at the back of the book.

1. The hypothalamus produces _____, which stimulate the _____ to secrete _____ into the circulatory system. Hormone levels circulating in the bloodstream send feedback to the _____.

2. Hormones are classified chemically as _____ or _____.

3. Broadly speaking, _____ hormones regulate metabolic balance, _____ hormones regulate reproduction, and _____ regulate stress.

4. One class of synthetic hormones is _____, which increase _____ and have _____ effects.

5. The stress response has a fast-acting pathway mediated by the release of _____ and a slow-acting pathway mediated by the release of _____.

6. Describe the proposed relationship among stress, cortisol, and the hippocampus.

For additional study tools, visit 📖 **LaunchPad** at launchpadworks.com

Summary

6-1 Principles of Psychopharmacology

Psychoactive drugs—substances that alter mood, thought, or behavior—produce their effects by acting on neuronal receptors or on chemical processes in the nervous system, especially on neurotransmission at synapses. Drugs act either as agonists to stimulate neuronal activity or as antagonists to depress it. Psychopharmacology is the study of drug effects on the brain and behavior.

Drugs can be administered by mouth, by inhalation, by absorption through the skin, rectally by suppository, or by injection. To reach a nervous system target, a psychoactive drug must pass through numerous barriers posed by digestion and dilution, the blood–brain barrier, and cell membranes. Drugs are diluted by body fluids as they pass through successive barriers, are metabolized in the body, and are excreted through sweat glands and in feces, urine, breath, and breast milk.

A common misperception about psychoactive drugs is that they act specifically and consistently, but experience and learning also affect individual responses to drugs. The body and brain may rapidly become tolerant of (habituated to) many drugs, so the dose must increase to produce a constant effect. Alternatively, people may become sensitized to a drug, in which case the same dose produces increasingly strong effects. These forms of learning also contribute to a person's behavior under a drug's influence.

6-2 Psychoactive Drugs

Psychoactive drugs can be organized according to the primary neurotransmitter system they interact with, but all drugs interact with multiple receptor systems. Each group, summarized in Table 6-1 on page 181, contains recreational and medically prescribed drugs—all of which can be abused.

6-3 Factors Influencing Individual Responses to Drugs

A drug does not have a uniform action on every person. Physical differences—in body weight, sex, age, and genetic background—influence a given drug's effects on a given person, as do behaviors, such as learning, and cultural and environmental contexts.

The influence of drugs on behavior varies widely with the situation and as a person learns drug-related behaviors. Behavioral myopia, for example, can influence a person to focus primarily on prominent environmental cues. These cues may encourage the person to act in uncharacteristic ways.

Risk factors for addiction include emotional, physical, and sexual abuse; emotional and physical neglect; having a mentally ill household member; having witnessed violence against mother; substance abuse in the home; parental separation/divorce; and having an incarcerated household member. Women are more sensitive to drugs than men are and may become addicted more quickly and to lower doses of drugs. The incidence of abuse of many kinds of drugs by women equals or exceeds the abuse of those drugs by men.

6-4 Explaining and Treating Drug Abuse

The neural mechanisms implicated in addiction are the same neural systems responsible for wanting and liking more generally. So anyone is likely to be a potential drug abuser. Addiction to drugs involves escalation, compulsive drug taking, and relapse.

Initially, drug taking produces pleasure (liking), but with repeated use the behavior becomes conditioned to associated objects, events, and places. Eventually, the conditioned cues motivate the drug user to seek them out (wanting), which leads to more drug taking. These subjective experiences become associated with prominent cues, and drug seeking promotes craving for the drug. As addiction proceeds, the subjective experience of liking decreases, while wanting increases.

Treatment for addiction varies with the drug. Whatever the treatment approach, success likely depends on permanent lifestyle changes. Considering how many people use tobacco, drink alcohol, use recreational drugs, or abuse prescription drugs, to find someone who has not used a drug when it was available is probably rare. But because of either genetic or epigenetic influences, some people do seem particularly vulnerable to drug abuse and addiction.

Excessive alcohol use can be associated with damage to the thalamus and hypothalamus, but the damage is caused by poor nutrition rather than the direct actions of alcohol. Cocaine can produce brain damage by reducing blood flow or by bleeding into neural tissue. MDMA (Ecstasy) use can result in the loss of fine axon collaterals of serotonergic neurons and associated impairments in cognitive function.

Psychedelic drugs, such as methamphetamine and LSD, can be associated with psychotic behavior. Whether this behavior is due to the drugs' direct effects or to the aggravation of preexisting conditions is not clear.

6-5 Hormones

Steroid and peptide hormones produced by endocrine glands circulate in the bloodstream to affect a wide variety of targets. Interacting to regulate hormone levels is a hierarchy of sensory stimuli and cognitive activity in the brain that stimulates the pituitary gland through the hypothalamus. The pituitary stimulates or inhibits the endocrine glands, which send feedback to the brain via other hormones.

Homeostatic hormones regulate the balance of sugars, proteins, carbohydrates, salts, and other substances in the body. Glucocorticoids are steroid hormones that regulate the body's ability to cope with stress—with arousing and challenging situations.

The hippocampus plays an important role in ending the stress response. Failure to turn off stress responses after a stressor has passed can contribute to susceptibility to PTSD and other psychological and physical diseases. Stress may activate epigenetic changes that modify the expression of genes regulating hormonal responses to stress and may produce brain changes that persist long after the stress-provoking incident has passed.

Synthetic anabolic steroids, used by athletes and nonathletes alike, mimic the effects of testosterone and so increase muscle bulk, stamina, and aggression but can have deleterious side effects.

| Key Terms

addiction, p. 194

agonist, p. 176

amphetamine, p. 186

anabolic steroid, p. 203

antagonist, p. 176

attention-deficit/hyperactivity disorder (ADHD), p. 172

behavioral myopia, p. 193

competitive inhibitor, p. 191

disinhibition theory, p. 193

dopamine hypothesis of schizophrenia, p. 187

fetal alcohol spectrum disorder (FASD), p. 185

glucocorticoid, p. 203

gonadal (sex) hormone, p. 202

homeostatic hormone, p. 202

major depression, p. 188

monoamine oxidase (MAO) inhibitor, p. 188

peptide hormone, p. 202

psychoactive drug, p. 173

psychomotor activation, p. 194

psychopharmacology, p. 172

selective serotonin reuptake inhibitor (SSRI), p. 188

steroid hormone, p. 202

substance abuse, p. 194

tolerance, p. 177

tricyclic, p. 188

wanting-and-liking theory, p. 196

withdrawal symptom, p. 194

zoopharmacognosy, p. 181

Visit LaunchPad to access the e-Book, videos, LearningCurve adaptive quizzing, flashcards, and more at launchpadworks.com

NEIL M. BORDEN/Science Source

Tuning In to Language

The continuing search to understand the organization and operation of the human brain is driven largely by emerging technologies. Over the past decades, neuroscience researchers have developed dramatic new, non-invasive ways to image the brain's activity in people who are awake. One technique, **functional near-infrared spectroscopy (fNIRS)**, gathers light transmitted through cortical tissue to image oxygen consumption in the brain. NIRS, a form of *optical tomography*, is detailed in Section 7-4.

fNIRS allows investigators to measure oxygen consumption as a surrogate marker of neuronal activity in relatively select cortical regions, even in newborn infants. In one study (May et al., 2011), newborns (0–3 days old) wore a mesh cap containing the NIRS apparatus, made up of optical fibers, as they listened to a familiar language as well as unfamiliar languages.

When newborns listened to a familiar language, their brain showed a general increase in oxygenated hemoglobin; when they heard an unfamiliar language, oxygenated hemoglobin decreased overall. But when the babies heard the same sentences played backward, there was no difference in brain response to either language.

The opposing response to familiar and unfamiliar languages demonstrates how prenatal experience shapes the newborn brain's response. This finding leads to many questions. Among them: How does prenatal exposure to language influence later language learning? Do children who are exposed to multiple languages prenatally show better language acquisition than those exposed to just one? How much and at what point in development is prenatal language exposure necessary? Do premature infants show the same results as full-term babies?

Whatever the answers, this study shows that the prenatal brain is tuned in to the language environment into which it will be born.

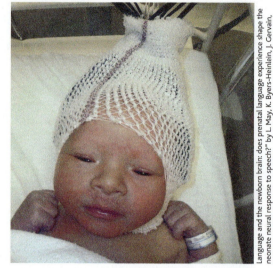

Language and the newborn brain: does prenatal language experience shape the neonate neural response to speech?" by L. May, K. Byers-Heinlein, J. Gervain, and J.F. Werker, 2011. Frontiers in Psychology, 2, 1–9. Image by Judit Gervain.

Newborn with probes placed on the head.

Language and the newborn brain: does prenatal language experience shape the neonate neural response to speech?" by L. May, K. Byers-Heinlein, J. Gervain, and J.F. Werker, 2011. Frontiers in Psychology, 2, 1–9. Photo by Krista Byers-Heinlein

Probe configurations overlaid on schematics of an infant's left and right hemispheres. Red dots indicate light-emitting fibers; blue dots indicate light detectors. The light detectors in the outer strips in both hemispheres sit over regions specialized for language in adults.

The simple, noninvasive nature of fNIRS, described in Research Focus 7-1, Tuning In to Language, likely will yield new insights not only into brain development but also into adult brain function. Over the coming decades, our understanding of the brain–behavior relationship will continue to be driven in large part by new and better technologies, as well as by cleverly exploiting existing ones.

If you lived prior to the twentieth century and were interested in studying how the brain works, you had two obvious choices of how to begin. You could study the behaviors of people who had sustained brain injury or had neurological impairment and then examine their brains after their deaths to determine which parts were responsible for the deficits. Alternatively, you could purposely create lesions in animals and examine how their behaviors changed. Indeed, this was how the relationship between brain and behavior was studied well into the twentieth century.

functional near-infrared spectroscopy (fNIRS) Noninvasive technique that gathers light transmitted through cortical tissue to image oxygen consumption; form of optical tomography.

Although neuroscience techniques used today are highly sophisticated compared to those of the past, the modern approaches share several commonalities with those historically used. Today, we still observe and quantify behavior and aspects of brain function in people with neurological conditions and in a wide variety of animal models. We also manipulate brain function by either increasing or decreasing activity in a highly specific and controlled fashion and then examining the effect of those changes in activity on behavior. The real difference between the historical approaches and those we use today is that we can manipulate and measure the brain with a larger array of tools, many of which are noninvasive and go right down to the molecular level.

Advances in understanding molecular genetics and the analysis of behavior in the early 1950s set the stage for phenomenal advances in neuroscience knowledge. Scientists recognize that new technologies allow for novel insights, lead to more questions, and can dramatically advance their discipline. A large number of prizes, including Nobel Prizes, have been awarded for the development and implementation of new technologies.

Today, brain–behavior analyses combine the efforts of anatomists and geneticists, psychologists and physiologists, chemists and physicists, endocrinologists and neurologists, pharmacologists and psychiatrists, computer scientists and programmers, engineers, and biologists. For aspiring brain researchers in the twenty-first century, the range of available research methods is breathtaking.

We begin this chapter by reviewing how investigators measure behavior in both human and nonhuman subjects and how neuroscientists can manipulate behavior by perturbing the brain. We then consider electrical techniques, including EEG, for recording brain activity; noninvasive procedures, such as fNIRS, that image the brain; and chemical and genetic methods for both manipulating and measuring brain and behavior. After comparing these methods at the chapter's end, we review some issues surrounding the use of nonhuman animals in research.

neuropsychology Study of the relationships between brain function and behavior, especially in humans.

Section 4-1 reviews how EEG enabled investigators to explain electrical activity in the nervous system.

Section 10-4 explores the anatomy of language and music and describes Broca's contributions.

7-1

Measuring and Manipulating Brain and Behavior

During a lecture at a meeting of the Anthropological Society of Paris in 1861, physician Ernest Auburtin argued that language functions are located in the brain's frontal lobes. Five days later, a fellow physician, Paul Broca, observed a brain-injured patient who had lost his speech and was able to say only "tan" and utter a swear word. The patient soon died. Broca and Auburtin examined the man's brain and found the focus of his injury in the left frontal lobe.

By 1863, Broca had collected eight other similar cases and concluded that speech production is located in the third frontal convolution of the left frontal lobe—a region now called *Broca's area*. Broca's findings attracted others to study brain–behavior relationships in patients. The field that developed is what we now call **neuropsychology**, the study of the relationships between brain function and behavior with a particular emphasis on humans. Today, measuring brain and behavior increasingly includes noninvasive imaging, complex neuroanatomical measurement, and sophisticated behavioral analyses.

Early Origins of Behavioral Neuroscience

At the beginning of the twentieth century, the primary tools of neuroanatomy were *histological*: brains were sectioned postmortem, and the tissue (*histo-* in Greek) was

FIGURE 7-1 Staining Cerebral Neurons Viewed through a light microscope, **(A)** a Nissl-stained section of the parietal cortex shows all cell bodies but no cell processes (axons and dendrites). **(B)** At higher magnification, an individual Golgi-stained pyramidal cell from the parietal cortex is visible. The cell body (dark triangular shape at center) and spiny dendrites (A and B) are visible in detail at right. **(C)** The view through an electron microscope shows neuronal synapses in detail. **(D)** Multiple images from a multiphoton microscope are merged to generate a three-dimensional image of living tissue.

Compare Brodmann's map of the cortex, based on staining, shown in Figure 2-26.

(A) Light microscope, low magnification

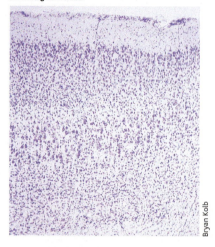

Bryan Kolb

(B) Light microscope, high magnification

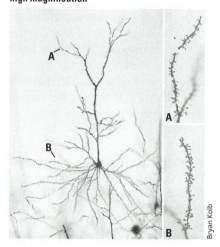

Bryan Kolb

(C) Electron microscope

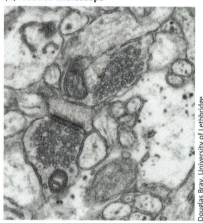

Douglas Bray, University of Lethbridge

(D) Multiphoton microscope

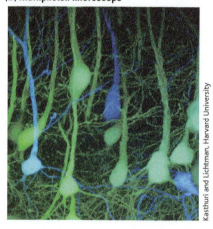

Kasthuri and Lichtman, Harvard University

stained with various dyes. As shown in **Figure 7-1**, there has been progression in microscopy toward greater resolution and specificity and a movement from visualizing dead tissue to living tissue. Scientists can stain sections of brain tissue to identify cell bodies in the brain viewed with a light microscope (shown in panel A), and they can selectively stain individual neurons to reveal their complete structure (panel B). An electron microscope (panel C) makes it possible to view synapses in detail. Multiphoton imaging (panel D) can generate a three-dimensional image of living tissue.

By the dawn of the twentieth century, light microscopic techniques allowed researchers such as Korbinian Brodmann to divide the cerebral cortex into many distinct zones based on the characteristics of neurons in those zones. Investigators presumed that cortical zones had specific functions. Early in the twenty-first century, dozens of techniques had developed for labeling neurons and their connections, as well as glial cells (for one colorful example, see Research Focus 7-2, Brainbow). Today, super-resolution microscopy is also being used to identify the locations of different receptors on the membranes of cells.

Contemporary techniques allow researchers to identify molecular, neurochemical, and morphological (structural) differences among neuronal types and ultimately to relate these characteristics to behavior. We have even miniaturized microscopes to the point where they can be mounted on the head of a mouse. These miniscopes can detect dozens to hundreds of neurons simultaneously by imaging a fluorescent signal activated by the neurons' calcium levels, which indicate firing activity, while the mouse is navigating around an environment (Ghosh et al., 2011).

These techniques for visualizing neurons play a key role in studying the connections between anatomy and behavior, as can be seen in studies of animals trained on various types of learning tasks, such as spatial mazes. Such learning can be correlated with a variety of neuroanatomical changes, such as modifications in the synaptic

RESEARCH FOCUS 7-2

Brainbow: Rainbow Neurons

Were it not for the discovery of stains that can highlight brain cell features, their complexity and connections would remain unknown. Jean Livet (2007) and his colleagues at Harvard University developed a transgenic technique that involves labeling different neurons by highlighting them with distinct colors—a technique called *Brainbow*, a play on the word *rainbow*. (Transgenic techniques are a form of genetic engineering discussed in Section 3-3.)

To mimic the way an LCD or LED monitor produces the full range of colors that the human eye can see by mixing only red, green, and blue, the Brainbow scientists introduced genes that produce cyan (blue), green, and red fluorescent proteins into mice cells. The red gene is obtained from coral, and the blue and green genes are obtained from jellies. (The 2008 Nobel Prize in chemistry was awarded to Roger Tsien, Osamu Shimomura, and Martin Chalfie for their discovery and development of fluorescent proteins in coral and jellies.)

The mice also received a bacterial gene called *Cre*, which activates the color genes inside each cell; due to chance factors, however, the extent to which each gene is activated varies. As the mice develop, the variable expression of the color-coding genes results in cells that fluoresce in at least 100 hues. When viewed through a fluorescent microscope sensitive to these wavelengths, individual brain cells and their connections can be visualized because they have slightly different hues, as illustrated in the accompanying micrographs.

Because individual cells can be visualized, Brainbow offers a way to describe where each neuron sends its processes and how it interconnects with other neurons. You have probably seen an electrical power cord in which the different wires have different colors (black, white, red) that signify what they do and how they should be connected. By visualizing living brain tissue in a dish, Brainbow provides a method for examining changes in neural circuits with the passage of time.

In the future, Brainbow will prove useful for examining populations of cells and their connections—such as which cells are implicated in specific brain diseases. In principle, Brainbow could be turned on at specific times, as an individual ages or solves problems, for example (Rojczyk-Gołębiewska et al., 2015). Yet despite Brainbow's promise, challenges remain. Even the simplest brain contains extraordinary numbers of neurons and fibers. Modifications in Brainbow that restrict visualization to only a few cells and fibers at a time are necessary for their connections to be understood.

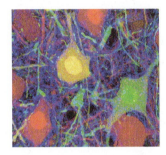
Cell Bodies

Axons

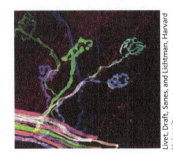
Terminal Buttons

Livet, Draft, Sanes, and Lichtman, Harvard University

organization of cells in specific cortical regions—the visual cortex in animals trained in visually guided mazes is one example—or in the number of newly generated cells that survive in the dentate gyrus, a subregion of the hippocampus. Mammals require this structure for remembering the context in which they encounter information.

Experimental evidence reveals that preventing the growth of new dentate gyrus neurons leads to certain kinds of memory deficits. To test the idea that neurons of the dentate gyrus contribute to object memory formation within a context, researchers tested healthy rats and ADX rats—rats with adrenal glands removed, thus eliminating the hormone corticosterone. Without corticosterone, neurons in the dentate gyrus die.

Procedure 1 in **Experiment 7-1** contrasts the appearance of a healthy rat dentate gyrus (left) and neuronal degeneration in an ADX rat after surgery (right). The behavior of healthy and ADX rats was studied in the object–context mismatch task diagrammed in Procedure 2. During the training phase, the rats were placed in two distinct contexts, A and B, for 10 minutes on each of 2 days. Each context contained a different type of object. On the test day, the rats were placed in either context A or context B but with two different objects—one from that context and a second from the other context.

As noted in the Results section of Experiment 7-1, when healthy rats encounter objects in the correct context, they spend little time investigating because the objects are familiar. If, however, they encounter an object in the wrong context, they are curious and spend about three-quarters of their time investigating, essentially treating the mismatched object as new. But the ADX rats with fewer cells in the dentate gyrus treated the mismatched and in-context objects the same, spending about half of their investigation time with each object.

Another group of ADX rats given treatment known to increase neuron generation in the dentate gyrus—enriched housing and exercise in running wheels—was unimpaired

Corticosterone, a steroid hormone secreted in times of stress, is important in protein and carbohydrate metabolism (see Section 6-5).

⋯→ EXPERIMENT 7-1

Question: Do hippocampal neurons contribute to memory formation?

Procedure 1

Rat hippocampus before (left) and after (right) surgical removal of the adrenal glands. Note fewer neurons resulting from a lack of corticosterone.

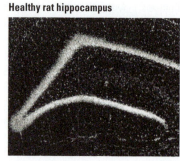

Hippocampus

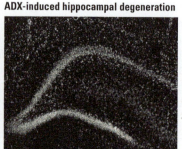

Healthy rat hippocampus

ADX-induced hippocampal degeneration

Courtesy of Dr. Simon Spanswick, Dept. of Psychology, University of Calgary.

Procedure 2

The behavior of healthy rats, ADX rats receiving no treatment, and ADX rats given treatments known to increase neuron generation in the dentate gyrus (enriched housing and exercise in running wheels) was studied in an object–context mismatch task in which two distinct contexts each contained a different type of object.

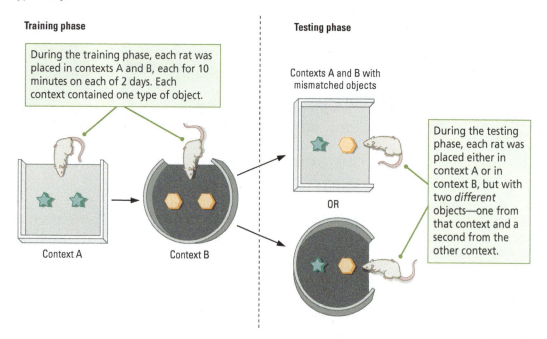

Training phase

During the training phase, each rat was placed in contexts A and B, each for 10 minutes on each of 2 days. Each context contained one type of object.

Context A   Context B

Testing phase

Contexts A and B with mismatched objects

OR

During the testing phase, each rat was placed either in context A or in context B, but with two *different* objects—one from that context and a second from the other context.

Results

Healthy rats investigate the mismatch object more than the object that is in context, but the non-treated ADX rats performed at chance. The ADX rats given enriched housing and exercise in running wheels showed regeneration of dentate granule cells and performed like healthy rats.

The photo at right shows a rat hippocampus. A specific stain was used to identify new neurons in the dentate gyrus, which appear yellow.

Conclusion: Dentate gyrus neurons are necessary for contextual learning.

Courtesy Bryan Kolb

Information from Spanswick & Sutherland, 2010, and Spanswick et al., 2011.

at the object–context mismatch task. Experiment 7-1 concludes that cellular changes in the dentate gyrus and behavioral changes are closely linked: neurons of the dentate gyrus are necessary for contextual learning.

behavioral neuroscience Study of the biological bases of behavior in humans and other animals.

Methods of Behavioral Neuroscience

Behavioral neuroscience—the study of the biological bases of behavior—seeks to understand the brain–behavior relationships in humans and other animals. The object–context mismatch task described in Experiment 7-1 is one of hundreds of different behavioral tests used by neuroscientists in this area. In this section, we describe several neuropsychological tests for humans, as well as some spatial navigation and skilled reaching tasks, including one used with rodents that involves an automated touchscreen apparatus.

A major challenge for behavioral neuroscientists is developing methods for studying both typical and atypical behavior. Measuring behavior in humans and laboratory animals differs in large part because humans speak: investigators can ask them about their symptoms or give them paper-and-pencil and computer-based tests to identify specific symptoms.

Measuring behavior in laboratory animals is more complex. Researchers must learn to speak "ratese" with rat subjects or "monkeyese" with monkeys. In short, researchers must develop ways to enable the animals to reveal their symptoms. The development of the fields of animal learning and *ethology*, the objective study of animal behavior, especially under natural conditions, provided the basis for modern behavioral neuroscience (see Whishaw & Kolb, 2005).

Table 7-3 in Section 7-6 summarizes selected brain measurement techniques, their goals, and examples.

Neuropsychological Testing of Humans

The brain has exquisite control of an amazing array of functions ranging from movement control and sensory perception to memory, emotion, and language. As a consequence, any analysis of behavior must be tailored to the particular function(s) under investigation. Consider the analysis of memory.

People with damage to the temporal lobes often complain of memory disturbance. But memory is not a single function; rather, multiple, independent memory systems exist. We have memory for events, colors, names, places, and motor skills, among other categories, and each must be measured separately. It would be rare indeed for someone to be impaired in *all* forms of memory.

Neuropsychological tests of three distinct forms of memory are illustrated in **Figure 7-2**. The Corsi block-tapping test shown in Figure 7-2A requires participants to observe an experimenter tap a sequence of blocks—blocks 4, 6, 1, 8, 3, for instance. The task is to repeat the sequence correctly. The participant does not see numbers on the blocks but rather must remember the locations of the tapped blocks.

Memory is covered in more detail in Sections 14-1 through 14-3, including a discussion of dissociated memory circuits in Section 14-2.

In this book, we refer to healthy human volunteers in research studies as *participants* and to people that have a brain or behavioral impairment as *patients* or *subjects*.

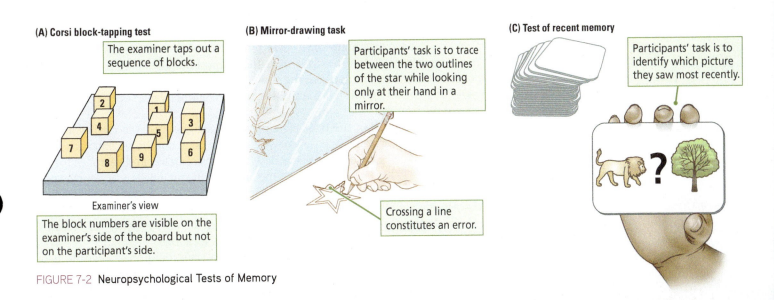

(A) Corsi block-tapping test

The examiner taps out a sequence of blocks.

Examiner's view

The block numbers are visible on the examiner's side of the board but not on the participant's side.

(B) Mirror-drawing task

Participants' task is to trace between the two outlines of the star while looking only at their hand in a mirror.

Crossing a line constitutes an error.

(C) Test of recent memory

Participants' task is to identify which picture they saw most recently.

FIGURE 7-2 Neuropsychological Tests of Memory

Clinical Focus 15-3 compares effects of injuries to particular brain regions on performance of particular neuropsychological tasks.

TABLE 7-1 **Partial List of Rat Behaviors by Category**

Learning and memory
Avoiding
Burying
Discrimination between sensory stimuli
Preferring places
Recognizing objects
Spatial navigating
Species-typical behaviors
Aggression
Caring of young
Circadian activity
Exploring and nose poking
Food hoarding
Food selection and foraging
Grooming and nail trimming
Nest building
Orienting
Playing
Sexual behavior
Social behavior
Vocalizing
Locomotion
Climbing
Jumping
Rearing
Swimming
Turning
Walking, trotting, and running
Skilled movement
Handling food
Pulling string
Walking on beams, posts, rotating rods, ladders
Reflexes
Placing and bracing
Posture and support
Righting
Emotions
Anxiety and fear
Depression
Responses to stress

The Corsi test provides a measure of short-term recall of spatial position, an ability we can call *block span*. The test can be made more difficult by determining the maximum block span of an individual participant (say, 6 blocks) and then adding one (*span + 1*). By definition, the participant will fail on the first presentation but, given the span + 1 repeatedly, will eventually learn it.

Span + 1 identifies a different form of memory from block span. Different types of neurological dysfunction interfere differentially with tasks that superficially appear quite similar. Block span measures the short-term recall of information, whereas the span + 1 task reflects the learning and longer-term memory storage of information.

The *mirror-drawing task* (Figure 7-2B) requires a person to trace a pathway, such as a star, by looking in a mirror. This motor task initially proves difficult because our movements appear backward in the mirror. With practice, participants learn how to accomplish the task accurately, and they show considerable recall of the skill when retested days later. Curiously, patients with certain types of memory problems have no recollection of learning the task on the previous day but nevertheless perform it flawlessly.

In the *recency memory task* (Figure 7-2C), participants are shown a long series of cards, each bearing two stimulus items that are words or pictures. On some trials, a question mark appears between the items. Their task is to indicate whether they have seen the items before and, if so, which item they saw most recently. They might be able to recall that they have seen items before but may be unable to recall which was most recent. Conversely, they might not be able to identify the items as being familiar, but when forced to choose the most recent one, they may be able to identify it correctly.

The latter, counterintuitive result reflects the need for behavioral researchers to develop ingenious ways of identifying memory abilities. It is not enough simply to ask people to recall information verbally, although this too measures a form of memory.

Behavioral Analysis of Rodents

Over the past century, researchers interested in the neural bases of sensation, cognition, memory, emotion, and movement have devised a vast array of mazes and other tests and tasks to determine the neural circuitry underlying specific behaviors in laboratory animals. Rats have very large *behavioral repertoires*, meaning that they display a long list of capabilities, some of which are categorized in **Table 7-1**, that can be independently examined to understand the functional underpinnings of those behaviors.

Figure 7-3 illustrates three tests based on a navigation task devised by Richard Morris (1981). Rats are placed in a large swimming pool with high slippery walls that do not allow the rats to escape. A hidden platform lies just below the water surface. Rats are terrific swimmers, and they quickly navigate around the pool until they bump into the platform. They learn that when they climb onto the platform, they are removed from the pool and returned to their home cage—their preferred place.

In one version of the task, *place learning*, the rat must find the platform from a number of different starting locations in the pool (Figure 7-3A). The only cues available are outside the pool, so the rat must learn the relationship between several cues in the room and the platform's location.

In a second version of the task, *matching-to-place learning*, the rat has already learned that a platform always lies somewhere in the pool, but the rat enters the pool from a different starting location every day. The rat is released and searches for the platform (Figure 7-3B). Once the rat finds the platform, the rat is removed from the pool and, after a brief delay (such as 10 seconds), is released again. The rat's task is to swim directly to the platform. The challenge for the rat in the matching-to-place test is to develop a strategy for finding the platform consistently: it is always in the same location on each trial each day, but each new day brings a new location.

In the *landmark* version of the task, the platform's location is identified by a cue on the pool wall (Figure 7-3C). The platform moves on every trial, but the

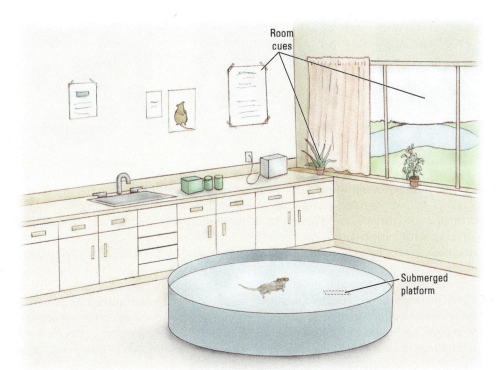

Room cues

Submerged platform

FIGURE 7-3 **Swimming Pool Tasks** General arrangement of the swimming pool used in three visuospatial learning tasks for rats. Red lines in parts A, B, and C mark the rat's swimming path on each trial (T). **(A)** Information from Morris, 1981. **(B)** Information from Whishaw, 1989. **(C)** Information from Kolb & Walkey, 1987.

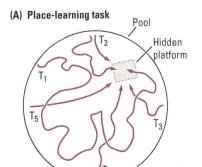

(A) Place-learning task

Pool

Hidden platform

T_2 T_1 T_5 T_3 T_4

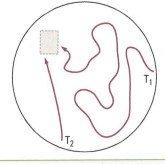

(B) Matching-to-place task

T_1 T_2

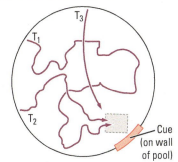

(C) Landmark-learning task

T_3 T_1 T_2

Cue (on wall of pool)

| A rat placed in the pool at various starting locations must learn to find a hidden platform. The rat can do this only by considering the configuration of visual cues in the room—windows, wall decorations, potted plants, and the like. | The rat is again put into the pool at random locations, but the hidden platform is in a new location on each test day. The animal must learn that the location where it finds the platform on the first trial each day is its location for all trials on that day. | The rat must ignore the room cues and learn that only the cue on the wall of the pool signals the location of the platform. The platform and cue are moved on each trial, so the animal is penalized for using room cues to try to solve the problem. |

relationship to the cue is constant. In this task, the brain is learning that the distant cues outside the pool are irrelevant; only the local cue is relevant. Rats with different neurological perturbations are selectively impaired in the three versions of the swimming pool task.

Another type of behavioral analysis in rats is related to movement. A major problem facing people with stroke is a deficit in controlling hand and limb movements. The prevalence of stroke has prompted considerable interest in devising ways to analyze such motor behaviors for the purpose of testing new therapies for facilitating recovery. In one test, rats are trained to reach through a slot to obtain a pellet of sweet food. The movements, which are remarkably similar to the movements people make in a similar task, can be broken down into segments. Investigators can score the segments separately, as they are differentially affected by different types of neurological perturbation.

(A) 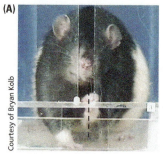 **(B)** 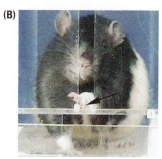 **(C)** 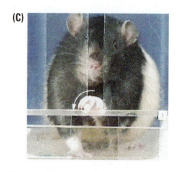 **(D)**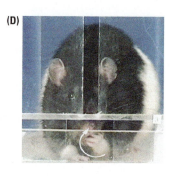

Courtesy of Bryan Kolb

FIGURE 7-4 **Skilled Reaching in Rats** Movement series displayed by rats trained to reach through a narrow vertical slot to obtain a food pellet: **(A)** aim the hand, **(B)** reach over the food, **(C)** grasp the food, **(D)** withdraw and move food to the mouth.

The photo series in **Figure 7-4** details how a rat orients its body to the slot (shown in panel A), puts its hand through the slot (panel B), rotates the hand horizontally to grasp the food (panel C), and rotates the hand vertically and withdraws it to obtain the food (panel D). Primates are not the only animals to make fine digit movements, but because the rat's hand is small and moves so quickly, digit dexterity can be properly observed only during slow-motion video playback.

Tim Bussey, Lisa Saksida, and their colleagues have developed an automated touchscreen platform for cognitive and motivational testing of rodents (**Figure 7-5**). This innovation removes the variation and stress that humans introduce when testing animals. Moreover, it is possible to program the platform to deliver tests that are highly similar to touchscreen tasks used in human cognitive testing (Oomen et al., 2013; Phillips et al., 2018).

Manipulating Brain–Behavior Interactions

A predominant strategy for studying brain–behavior relationships is to manipulate some aspect of brain function and see how behavior changes. Investigators do so to develop hypotheses about how the brain affects behavior and to test those hypotheses.

A second reason to manipulate the brain is to develop animal models of neurological and psychiatric disorders. The general presumption in neurology and psychiatry is that it ought to be possible to restore at least some healthy functioning by pharmacological, behavioral, or other interventions. A major hurdle for developing such treatments is that, like most other new medical treatments, they must be tested in nonhuman subjects first. (In Section 7-7, we take up scientific and ethical issues surrounding the use of animals in research.)

Table 7-2 in Section 7-6 summarizes selected brain manipulation techniques, their goals, and examples.

Brains can be manipulated in various ways, the precise manner depending on the specific research question being asked. Researchers can manipulate the whole animal by exposing it to differing diets, social interactions, exercise, sensory stimulation, and a host of other experiences. For brain manipulation, the principal direct techniques are to inactivate the brain via lesions or with drugs or to activate it with electrical stimulation, drugs, or light.

Behavioral neuroscientists make a manipulation and then measure brain function and behavioral performance. Because a large variety of manipulation techniques and measurement techniques are available to researchers, techniques from these two categories are mixed and matched.

FIGURE 7-5 **Automated Touchscreen Platform for Testing Rodents** Mice or rats are placed in the apparatus and receive a strawberry milkshake reward when they choose the correct visual image by touching the screen.

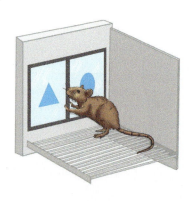 

Courtesy of BrainsCAN and the TCNlab at Western University.

Brain Lesions

The first—and the simplest—technique used for brain manipulation is to ablate (remove or destroy) tissue. Beginning in the 1920s, Karl Lashley, a pioneer of neuroscience research, used *ablation*, and for the next 30 years, he tried to find the site of memory in the brain. He trained monkeys and rats on various mazes and motor tasks and then removed bits of cerebral cortex, with the goal of producing amnesia for specific memories.

To his chagrin, Lashley failed in his quest. He observed instead that memory loss was related to the *amount* of tissue he removed. The conclusion that Lashley reached was that memory is distributed throughout the brain and not located in any single place. Subsequent research strongly indicates that specific brain functions and associated memories are indeed localized to specific brain regions. Ironically, just as Lashley was retiring, William Scoville and Brenda Milner (1957) described a patient from whose brain Scoville had removed both hippocampi as a treatment for epilepsy. The surgery rendered this patient amnesic. During his ablation research, Lashley had never removed the hippocampi because he had no reason to believe the structures had any role in memory. And because the hippocampus is not accessible on the brain's surface, other techniques had to be developed before subcortical lesions could be used.

The solution to accessing subcortical regions is to use a **stereotaxic apparatus**, a device that permits a researcher or a neurosurgeon to target a specific part of the brain for destruction, as shown in **Figure 7-6**. The head is held in a fixed position, and because the location of brain structures is fixed in relationship to the junction of the skull bones, it is possible to visualize a three-dimensional brain map.

Rostral–caudal (front-to-back) measurements correspond to the *y*-axis in Figure 7-6. Dorsal–ventral (top-to-bottom) measurements, the *z*-axis, are made relative to the surface of the brain. Medial–lateral measurements, the *x*-axis, are made relative to the midline junction of the cranial bones. Atlases of the brains of humans and laboratory animals have been constructed from postmortem tissue so that the precise location of any structure can be specified in three-dimensional space.

Consider Parkinsonian tremor, in which the hands can shake so severely that the afflicted person cannot hold a glass of water. The most widely used surgical treatment today is to drill a hole in the skull and, using stereotaxic coordinates obtained for that patient with an MRI (described in detail in Section 7-3), target the globus pallidus. An electrode is then lowered into the globus pallidus, and current is passed through it to destroy the structure and relieve the patient of the tremor. However, a new technique called *high-intensity focused ultrasound* (*HIFU*) can now achieve the same result without the invasive surgery (Quadri et al., 2018). Focused ultrasound uses many individual ultrasonic beams that are all pointed at the same spot in the brain. Each beam passes through tissue with little effect; at the convergent point where all the beams intersect, the energy heats the tissue. Lightly heating the tissue temporarily prevents that part of the brain from working properly, thereby informing the surgeons that their targeting is correct. The tissue heating can then continue until the target is permanently destroyed and the tremor is noninvasively eliminated.

The techniques described so far result in permanent brain damage. With time, the research subject will show **compensation**, the neuroplastic ability to modify behavior from that used prior to the damage. To avoid compensation following permanent lesions, researchers have also developed temporary and reversible lesion techniques such as *regional cooling*, which prevents synaptic transmission. A hollow metal coil is placed next to a neural structure; then chilled fluid is passed through the coil, cooling the brain structure to about 18°C (Lomber & Payne, 1996). When the chilled fluid is removed from the coil, the brain structure quickly warms, and synaptic

stereotaxic apparatus Surgical instrument that permits a researcher or neurosurgeon to target a specific part of the brain.

compensation Following brain damage, the neuroplastic ability to modify behavior from that used prior to the damage.

Both Lashley's work and Scoville and Milner's iconic patient, H. M., are discussed further in Section 14-2.

Review the brain's anatomical locations and orientations in The Basics in Section 2-1.

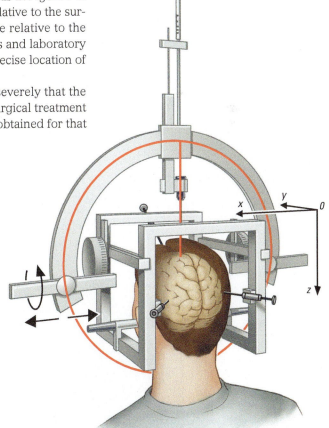

FIGURE 7-6 **Stereotaxic Apparatus** This instrument allows the precise positioning of all brain regions relative to each other and to landmarks on the skull.

Principle 10: The nervous system works by juxtaposing excitation and inhibition.

Read more about Penfield's dramatic discoveries in Sections 10-4 and 11-2.

Figure 12-12 diagrams hypothalamus anatomy. Chapter 12 details its role in motivated, regulatory, sexual, and emotional behavior.

View DBS in place in Figure 1-3.

deep-brain stimulation (DBS) Neurosurgical technique in which electrodes implanted in the brain stimulate a targeted area with a low-voltage electrical current to produce or facilitate behavior.

transcranial magnetic stimulation (TMS) Procedure in which a magnetic coil is placed over the skull to stimulate the underlying brain; used either to induce behavior or to disrupt ongoing behavior.

transmission is restored. Another technique involves local administration of a GABA agonist, which increases local inhibition and in turn prevents the brain structure from communicating with other structures. Degradation of the GABA agonist reverses the local inhibition and restores function.

Brain Stimulation

The brain operates on both electrical and chemical energy, so it is possible to selectively turn brain regions on or off by using electrical or chemical stimulation. Wilder Penfield, in the mid-twentieth century, was the first to use electrical stimulation directly on the human cerebral cortex during neurosurgery. Later researchers used stereotaxic instruments to place an electrode or a cannula in specific brain locations. The objective: enhancing or blocking neuronal activity and observing the behavioral effects.

Perhaps the most dramatic research example comes from stimulating specific regions of the hypothalamus. Rats with electrodes placed in the lateral hypothalamus will eat whenever the stimulation is turned on. If the animals have the opportunity to press a bar that briefly turns on the current, they quickly learn to press the bar to obtain the current, a behavior known as *electrical self-stimulation*. It appears that the stimulation is affecting a neural circuit that involves both eating and pleasure.

Brain stimulation can also be used as a therapy. When the intact cortex adjacent to cortex injured by a stroke is stimulated electrically, for example, it leads to improvement in motor behaviors such as those illustrated in Figure 7-4. Cam Teskey and his colleagues (Brown et al., 2011) successfully restored motor deficits in a rat model of Parkinson disease by electrically stimulating a specific brain nucleus.

Deep-brain stimulation (DBS) is a neurosurgical technique. Electrodes implanted in the brain stimulate a targeted area with continuous pulses of low-voltage electrical current to facilitate behavior. DBS is used with subcortical structures; for example, DBS to the globus pallidus in the basal ganglia of Parkinson patients makes movements smoother, often allowing patients to dramatically reduce their intake of medications. DBS using several neural targets is an approved treatment for obsessive-compulsive disorder. Experimental trials are under way to identify the brain regions optimal for DBS to be used as a treatment for intractable psychiatric disorders such as major depression (Schlaepfer et al., 2013), schizophrenia, and possibly for epilepsy; DBS may also be used as a treatment for stimulating recovery from traumatic brain injury (TBI).

Electrical stimulation of the brain is invasive: holes must be drilled in the skull and an electrode lowered into the brain. Researchers have taken advantage of the relationship between magnetism and electricity to develop a noninvasive technique called **transcranial magnetic stimulation (TMS)**. During a treatment session, a small wire coil is placed adjacent to the skull, as illustrated in **Figure 7-7A**. A high-voltage current pulsed through the coil produces a rapid increase and subsequent decrease

(A)

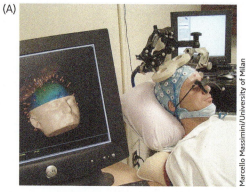

Marcello Massimini/University of Milan

(B)

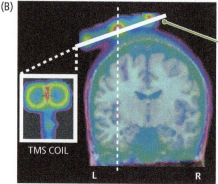

The TMS coil, shown here in a composite MRI and PET scan photograph, interferes with brain function in the adjacent area.

TMS COIL

L   R

Composite MRI and PET scan from Dr. Tomáš Paus, Rotman Research Institute, Baycrest Centre for Geriatric Care

FIGURE 7-7 **Transcranial Magnetic Stimulation (A)** In clinical therapy for depression, TMS influences neural activity in a localized region. **(B)** Composite photo shows how TMS works.

in the magnetic field around the coil. The magnetic field easily passes through the skull and causes a population of neurons in the cerebral cortex to depolarize and fire (Figure 7-7B).

If the motor cortex is stimulated, movement is evoked; or if a movement is in progress, it is disrupted. Similarly, if the visual cortex is stimulated, the participant sees dots of light (*phosphenes*). The effects of brief pulses of TMS do not outlive the stimulation, but *repetitive TMS* (rTMS), or continuous stimulation for up to several minutes, produces more long-lasting effects, including changing function or temporarily inactivating tissue. TMS and rTMS can be used to study brain–behavior relationships in healthy participants, and rTMS has been tested as a potential treatment for a variety of behavioral disorders. A growing body of research also supports its antidepressant actions.

Drug Manipulations

Brain activity can also be stimulated by administration of drugs that pass either into the bloodstream and eventually enter the brain or through an indwelling cannula (illustrated in Figure 7-21 in Section 7-5) that allows direct application of the drugs to specific brain structures. Drugs can influence the activity of specific neurons in specific brain regions. For example, the drug haloperidol, used to treat schizophrenia, reduces dopaminergic neuron function and makes healthy rats dopey and inactive (*hypokinetic*).

In contrast, drugs that increase dopaminergic activity, such as amphetamine, produce *hyperkinetic rats*—rats that are hyperactive. The advantage of administering drugs is that their effects wear off in time as the drugs are metabolized. It thus is possible to study drug effects on learned behaviors, such as skilled reaching (see Figure 7-4) and then to re-examine the behavior after the drug effect wears off.

Claudia Gonzalez and her colleagues (2006) administered nicotine to rats as they learned a skilled reaching task, then studied their later acquisition of a new skilled reaching task. The researchers found that the earlier nicotine-enhanced motor learning impaired the later motor learning. This finding surprised the investigators, but it now appears that repeated exposure to psychomotor stimulants such as amphetamine, cocaine, and nicotine can produce long-term effects on the brain's later plasticity (its ability to change in response to experience), including learning specific tasks.

Genetic Manipulations and Combinations with Light and Drugs

In the past two decades, **synthetic biology**—the design and construction of biological devices, systems, and machines not found in nature—has transformed how neuroscientists manipulate brain cells. Techniques include inserting or deleting a genetic sequence into the genome of a living organism.

A new technique called CRISPR-Cas9 (Clustered Regularly Interspaced Short Palindromic Repeats), one of many CRISPR techniques, was discovered in bacteria for fighting viruses; it serves as an all-purpose tool for cutting the DNA of any cell. Scientists simply provide the bacteria's Cas9 protein with the RNA sequence corresponding to the length of DNA they would like to remove from the subject. In this way, the CRISPR system can be used to silence one or many genes by cutting out those regions in the DNA. Then the DNA's repair machinery can be harnessed to insert a new sequence that replaces the one that was removed.

It is difficult to overestimate the potential impact of CRISPR. As an experimental tool, it can help answer the question: What is the role of this gene or these genes in this behavior? As a therapeutic intervention, it could eventually lead to the elimination of many forms of inherited disease. It could also counter antibiotic-resistant microbes, disable parasites, and improve food security.

Another transgenic technique, **optogenetics**, combines genetics and light to control targeted cells in living tissue. A sequence that codes for a light-sensitive protein associated with an ion channel enables investigators to use light to change the shape (conformation) of the channel.

synthetic biology Design and construction of biological devices, systems, and machines not found in nature.

optogenetics Transgenic technique that combines genetics and light to control targeted cells in living tissue.

Research Focus 16-5 describes use of rTMS to treat depression and other behavioral disorders.

Chapter 6 discusses the influence of drugs on behavior, and Section 6-2 specifically details the effects of the drugs described here, among others.

Section 3-3 explores some techniques in genetic and transgenic engineering.

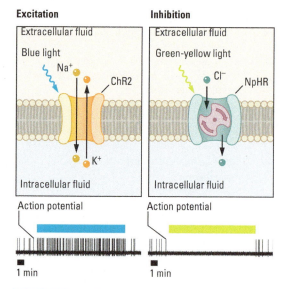

Excitation   **Inhibition**

FIGURE 7-8 **Lighting Up Neurons** Optogenetics allows precise temporal control of cell firing and is rapidly reversible. Specific wavelengths activate light-sensitive proteins expressed in neurons. At bottom left, when blue light illuminates a cell in which ChR2 has been incorporated, its firing rate increases dramatically. At right, when green-yellow light illuminates a cell in which NpHR is incorporated, its firing rate decreases dramatically.

Figure 2-21 diagrams the relative location of the amygdala.

Optogenetics is based on the discovery that light can activate certain proteins that occur naturally and have been inserted into cells of model organisms. For example, *opsins*, proteins derived from microorganisms, combine a light-sensitive domain with an ion channel, as shown in **Figure 7-8**. The first opsin used for the optogenetic technique was channelrhodopsin-2 (ChR2). When ChR2 is expressed in neurons and exposed to blue light, the ion channel opens and immediately depolarizes the neuron, causing excitation. In contrast, stimulation of halorhodopsin (NpHR) with a green-yellow light activates a chloride pump, hyperpolarizing the neuron and causing inhibition. A fiber-optic light can be delivered to selective brain regions such that all genetically modified neurons exposed to the light respond immediately (Haubensak et al., 2010).

Optogenetics has tremendous potential as a research tool. Investigators can insert light-sensitive proteins into specific neuron types, such as pyramidal cells of the CA1 region of the hippocampus, and use light to selectively activate just that cell type. Researchers hail optogenetics for its high spatial and temporal (time) resolution. Ion channels can be placed into specific cell lines and turned on and off on millisecond time scales. Optogenetics also finds application in behavioral studies. For example, the amygdala is a key structure in generating fear in animals; if it is targeted with opsins and then exposed to an inhibitory light, rats immediately show no fear and wander about in a novel open space. As soon as the light is turned off, they scamper back to a safe hiding place.

In the transgenic technique called **chemogenetics**, the inserted synthetic genetic sequence codes for a G protein–coupled receptor engineered to respond exclusively to a synthetic small-molecule "designer drug." Chemogenetics is best known by the acronym *DREADD* (designer receptor exclusively activated by designer drugs). Its principal advantage is that the drug activates only the genetically modified receptors, and the receptors are activated only by the designer drug, not by endogenous molecules (Wess et al., 2013). Thus, specificity is high, but temporal resolution is much lower than with optogenetics because receptors are activated by drugs rather than by light.

7-1 Review

Before you continue, check your understanding. Answers appear at the back of the book.

1. Behavioral neuroscience is the study of relationships between _____ and _____.

2. Anatomical studies rely on techniques such as _____ tissue postmortem or visualizing living tissue using _____.

3. A new innovation in behavioral testing in rodents uses automated _____, which removes the variation and stress that humans introduce when testing animals.

4. Outline the various brain-stimulation methods that either activate or inhibit neural activity.

For additional study tools, visit 📖 **LaunchPad** at launchpadworks.com

---

7-2

Measuring the Brain's Electrical Activity

The brain is always electrically active, even when we sleep. Electrical measures of brain activity are important for studying brain function, for medical diagnosis, and for monitoring the effectiveness of therapies used to treat brain disorders. The four major

chemogenetics Transgenic technique that combines genetics and synthetic drugs to activate targeted cells in living tissue.

techniques for tracking the brain's electrical activity are single-cell recording, electro-encephalography (EEG), event-related potentials (ERPs), and magnetoencephalography (MEG).

In part, these techniques are used to record electrical activity from different parts of neurons. The electrical behavior of cell bodies and dendrites, which give rise to graded potentials, tends to be much more varied and slower than the behavior of axons, which conduct action potentials.

Figure 4-10 diagrams a cell membrane at rest, Figure 4-13 during graded potentials, and Figure 4-15 generating the action potential.

Recording Action Potentials from Single Cells

By the early 1950s, it was becoming possible to record the activity of individual cells by measuring a single neuron's action potentials with fine electrodes inserted into the brain. These microelectrodes can be placed next to cells (*extracellular recording*) or inside cells (*intracellular recording*). Modern extracellular recording techniques make it possible to distinguish the activity of as many as 40 neurons at once. Intracellular recording allows direct study and recording of a single neuron's electrical activity. The two disadvantages of inserting an electrode into a cell are that (1) it can kill the cell, and (2) it cannot be done in awake, freely moving animals. Single-cell recording is therefore confined to neurons grown in a dish or, for short periods (hours), to neurons in living brain slices.

Figure 4-6 illustrates the structure and use of microelectrodes.

We now know from extracellular recordings that cells in the brain's various sensory regions are highly sensitive to specific stimuli. Some cells in the visual system fire vigorously to specific wavelengths of light (a color) or to specific orientations of bars of light (vertical, for example). Other cells in this region respond to more complex patterns, such as faces or hands. Similarly, cells in the auditory system respond to specific sound frequencies (a low or high pitch) or to more complex sound combinations, such as speech (the syllable *ba*, for example).

See, for example, "Seeing Shape" and "Seeing Color" in Section 9-4 and "Processing Language" in Section 10-4.

But certain cells respond to inputs that are rich in information—a fact that reveals much about brain–behavior relationships. John O'Keefe and his colleagues (O'Keefe & Dostrovsky, 1971) showed that neurons in the rat and mouse hippocampus vigorously fire when an animal is in a specific place in the environment. These **place cells**, illustrated in **Figure 7-9**, code the spatial location of the animal and contribute to a spatial map of the world in the brain. The 2014 Nobel Prize in Physiology or Medicine was awarded to John O'Keefe, May-Britt Moser, and Edvard I. Moser "for their discoveries of cells that constitute a positioning system in the brain."

place cells Neurons maximally responsive to specific locations in the world.

Section 13-4 discusses how place cells help store memories.

O'Keefe's group (Cacucci et al., 2008) also demonstrated that, in mice with a genetically engineered mutation that produces deficits in spatial memory, place cells lack specificity: the cells fire to a very broad region of their world. As a result, these mice have difficulty finding their way around, much as human patients with dementia tend to get lost. One reason may be that a change similar to the engineered mutation in mice takes place in human brain cells.

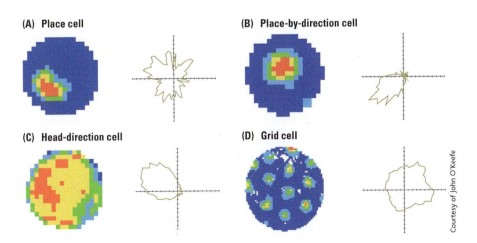

(A) Place cell

(B) Place-by-direction cell

(C) Head-direction cell

(D) Grid cell

Courtesy of John O'Keefe

FIGURE 7-9 **Classes of Spatially Related Cells in the Hippocampal Formation (A and B)** Place cells discharge when a rat is at a spatial location, regardless of its orientation. **(C)** Head-direction cells discharge to indicate where the rat's head points, regardless of its location. **(D)** Grid cells discharge at many locations, forming a virtual grid that is invariant in the face of changes in the rat's direction, movement, or speed. At right in each part, *xy* coordinates indicate the directional selectivity of the cell recorded at left.

1 Electrodes attached to the scalp correspond to specific brain areas...

2 ...to record their electrical activity. This EEG indicates a relaxed person.

FIGURE 7-10 **Recording EEG Waves** EEG is a simple, noninvasive method for recording the brain's electrical activity. EEG waves recorded via computer (see Figure 4-5) can match wave activity to specific brain regions.

electrocorticography (ECoG) Graded potentials recorded with electrodes placed directly on the surface of the brain.

alpha rhythm Regular wave pattern in an electroencephalogram; found in most people when they are relaxed with eyes closed.

Amplitude is a recorded brain wave's height. *Frequency* is the number of brain waves recorded per second.

Section 13-3 describes how EEG measures sleep and dreaming. Clinical Focus 4-1 details epilepsy diagnoses, and Section 16-3 explores treatments.

FIGURE 7-11 **Characteristic EEG Recordings** Brain-wave patterns reflect different states of consciousness in humans. Data from Penfield & Jasper, 1954.

EEG: Recording Graded Potentials from Thousands of Cells

In the early 1930s, Hans Berger discovered that the brain's electrical activity could be recorded simply by placing electrodes on the scalp. In Berger's words, recording these "brain waves" produces an "electrical record from the head"—an electroencephalogram. The EEG measures the summed graded potentials from many thousands of neurons. EEG waves, shown in **Figure 7-10**, are recorded by a computer. In **electrocorticography (ECoG)**, a method used during neurosurgery, electrodes are placed directly on the cerebral cortex.

EEGs reveal some remarkable features of the brain's electrical activity. The EEG recordings in **Figure 7-11** illustrate three of them:

1. EEG changes as behavior changes.

2. An EEG recorded from the cortex displays an array of patterns, some rhythmical.

3. The living brain's electrical activity is never silent, even when a person is asleep or comatose.

When a person is aroused, excited, or even just alert, the EEG pattern has a low amplitude and a fast frequency, as shown in Figure 7-11A. This pattern is typical of an EEG taken from anywhere on the skull of an alert subject—not only humans but other animals, too. In contrast, when a participant is calm and quietly relaxed, especially with eyes closed, the rhythmical brain waves shown in Figure 7-11B often emerge. These **alpha rhythms** are extremely regular, with a frequency of approximately 11 cycles per second and amplitudes that wax and wane as the pattern is recorded. In humans, alpha rhythms are generated in the region of the visual cortex at the back of the brain. If a relaxed person is disturbed, performs mental arithmetic, or opens his or her eyes, the alpha rhythms abruptly stop.

EEG is a sensitive indicator of behaviors beyond simple arousal and relaxation. Parts C, D, and E of Figure 7-11 illustrate EEG changes as a person moves from drowsiness to sleep and finally into deep sleep. EEG rhythms become progressively slower and larger in amplitude. Still slower waves appear during anesthesia, after brain trauma, or when a person is in a coma (shown in Figure 7-11F). Only in brain death does the EEG permanently become a flat line.

These distinctive brain-wave patterns make EEG a reliable tool for monitoring sleep stages, estimating the depth of anesthesia, evaluating the severity of head injury, and searching for brain abnormalities. In epilepsy, for example, brief periods of

(A) Awake or excited

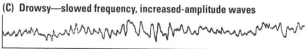

(B) Relaxed, eyes closed, alpha rhythms generated

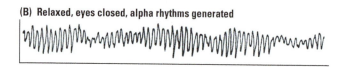

(C) Drowsy—slowed frequency, increased-amplitude waves

(D) Asleep—slower, higher-amplitude waves

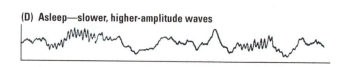

(E) Deep sleep—even slower and higher-amplitude waves

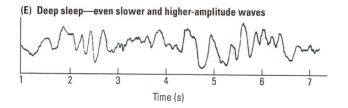

Time (s)

(F) Coma—further slowing

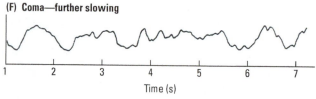

Time (s)

impaired awareness or unresponsiveness and involuntary movements associated with spiking patterns in the EEG characterize electrographic seizures. EEG is an essential tool in the diagnosis of epilepsy and in determining the kind of epilepsy and seizures a person has.

The important point here is that EEG recording provides a useful tool both for research and for diagnosing brain dysfunction. EEG can also be used in combination with the brain-imaging techniques described in Sections 7-3 and 7-4 to provide more accurate identification of the source of the large and highly synchronized EEG waves in epilepsy.

Mapping Brain Function with Event-Related Potentials

Brief changes in an EEG signal in response to a discrete sensory stimulus produce complex electroencephalographic waveforms called **event-related potentials (ERPs)**. ERPs are largely the graded potentials on dendrites that a sensory stimulus triggers. You might think that they should be easy to detect, but they are not.

ERPs are mixed in with so many other electrical signals in the brain that they are difficult to spot just by visually inspecting an EEG record. One way to detect ERPs is to produce the stimulus repeatedly and average the recorded responses. Averaging tends to cancel out any irregular and unrelated electrical activity, leaving in the EEG record only the potentials the stimulus generated.

To clarify this procedure, imagine throwing a small stone into a lake of choppy water. Although the stone produces a splash, the splash is hard to see among all the ripples and waves. Like a splash surrounded by choppy water, an ERP caused by a sensory stimulus is hard to discern from all the other electrical activity around it.

A solution is to throw a number of stones exactly the same size, always hitting the same spot in the water and producing the same splash over and over. If a computer then calculates an average of the water's activity, random wave movements will tend to average one another out, and an observer will see the splashes produced by the stones as clearly as a single stone thrown into a pool of calm water.

Figure 7-12 shows an ERP record (top) that results when a person hears a tone. The EEG record is highly irregular when the tone is first presented. But by averaging more than 100 stimulus presentations, a distinctive wave pattern appears, as shown in the bottom panel of Figure 7-12. This ERP pattern consists of a number of negative (N) and positive (P) waves that occur within a few hundred milliseconds after the stimulus.

The waves are numbered in time sequence. For instance, in Figure 7-12, N_1 is a negative wave occurring about 100 milliseconds after the stimulus, whereas P_2 is a positive wave occurring about 200 milliseconds after the stimulus. (The waves may also be labeled N100 and P200.) Not all these waves are unique to this particular stimulus. Some are common to any auditory stimulus. Other waves, however, correspond to important differences in specific tone. ERPs to spoken words even contain distinctive peaks and patterns that differentiate such similar-sounding words as *cat* and *rat*.

Among the many practical reasons for using ERPs to study the brain is the advantage that this EEG technique is noninvasive. Electrodes are placed on the scalp, not in the brain. Therefore, ERPs can be used to study humans, including those most frequently used participants: college students.

Another advantage is cost. Compared to other techniques, such as brain imaging, EEG and ERP are inexpensive and can be recorded from many brain areas simultaneously by pasting an array of electrodes (sometimes more than 200) onto different parts of the scalp. Because certain brain areas respond only to certain sensory stimuli (for example, auditory areas respond to sounds and visual areas to sights), relative responses at different locations can be used to map brain function.

event-related potential (ERP) Complex electroencephalographic waveform related in time to a specific sensory event.

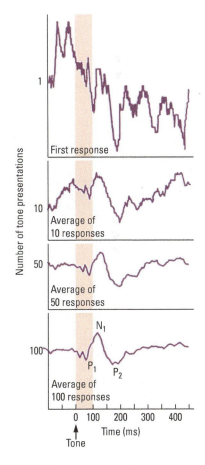

FIGURE 7-12 **Detecting ERPs** In the averaging process for an auditory ERP, a tone is presented at time 0, and EEG activity in response is recorded. After many successive presentations of the tone, the EEG wave sequence develops a distinctive shape that becomes extremely clear after 100 responses are averaged (bottom panel). Positive and negative waves that appear at different times after the stimulus presentation are used for analysis.

⊙ CLINICAL FOCUS 7-3

Mild Head Injury and Depression

When a pallet of boxed tools tipped and part of the load struck his head, B. D., an industrial tool salesman, did not lose consciousness, but he did sustain a serious cut to his scalp and damage to two spinal vertebrae. The attending physician at the hospital emergency room suspected mild concussion but ordered no further neurological workup at the time.

B. D.'s spinal symptoms gradually cleared, but irritability, anxiety, and depression persisted even 2 years later. B. D. was unable to work, and his behavioral changes placed a major strain on his family. His emotional problems led him to withdraw from the world, only worsening his predicament.

While a neuropsychological exam administered to B. D. about 2 years after the injury found his general cognitive ability to be well above average (with an IQ score of 115), he did display significant attentional and short-term memory deficits. A subsequent magnetic resonance image of

his brain failed to find any injury that could explain his symptoms. In fact, B. D.'s serious emotional symptoms are common following mild head injury, even when no other neurological or radiological signs of brain injury present themselves.

One tool for investigating brain functioning in such cases is ERP. Reza and colleagues (2007) compared healthy controls to groups of subjects with mild head injuries, with and without depression. The investigators found that all subjects with head injury displayed a delayed P_3 wave, but only those who were depressed as well also had a delayed N_2 wave. These findings demonstrate that ERP can identify cerebral processing abnormalities in people with depression after mild head injury, even when MRI scans are negative. Such evidence can be critical for people like B. D., who are seeking long-term disability support following what appears to be a mild head injury.

Electrodes attached to the scalp of a research subject are connected to...

Electrodes in geodesic sensor net

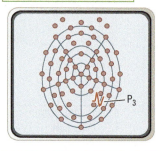

...a computer display of electrical activity, showing a large positive (P_3) wave at the posterior right side of the head.

This electrical activity can be converted into a color representation showing the hot spot for the visual stimulus.

Resting   300 ms after viewing

FIGURE 7-13 **Using ERPs to Image Brain Activity**

Figure 7-13 shows a multiple-recording method that uses 128 electrodes simultaneously to detect ERPs at many cortical sites. Computed averaging techniques reduce the masses of information obtained to simpler comparisons between electrode sites. For example, if the focus of interest is P_3, a positive wave occurring about 300 milliseconds after the stimulus, the computer can display a graph of the skull showing only the amplitude of P_3. A computer can also convert the averages at different sites into a color code, graphically representing the brain regions most responsive to the signal.

ERPs can not only detect which brain areas are processing particular stimuli but can also be used to study the order in which different regions participate. This second use of ERPs is important because we want to know the route that information takes as it travels through the brain. In Figure 7-13, the participant is viewing a picture of a rat that appears repeatedly in the same place on a computer screen. The P_3 recorded from the posterior right side of the head is larger than any other P_3 occurring elsewhere, meaning that this region is a hot spot for processing the visual stimulus. Presumably, this particular participant's right posterior brain is central in decoding the picture of the rat 300 milliseconds after it is presented.

Many other interesting research areas benefit from using ERPs, as described in Clinical Focus 7-3, Mild Head Injury and Depression. ERPs can also be used to study how children learn and process information differently as they mature, as well as how a person with a brain injury compensates for the impairment by using undamaged brain regions. ERPs can even help reveal which brain areas are most sensitive to aging and are therefore most closely related to declining behavioral functions among the elderly. This simple, inexpensive research tool can address all these areas.

Magnetoencephalography

Passing a magnetic field across a wire induces an electrical current in the wire. Conversely, current flowing along a wire induces a magnetic field around the wire. The same is true in the brain. Neural activity, by generating an electrical field, also produces a magnetic field. Although the magnetic field produced by a single neuron is vanishingly small, the field produced by many neurons is sufficiently strong to be recorded on the scalp. The record of this phenomenon, a **magnetoencephalogram (MEG)**, is the magnetic counterpart of the EEG or ERP.

Calculations based on MEG measurements not only describe the electrical activity of neuronal groups but also localize the cell groups generating the measured field in three dimensions. Magnetic waves conducted through living tissue undergo less distortion than electrical signals do, so an MEG can yield a higher resolution than an ERP. A major advantage of MEG over EEG and ERP, then, is the ability of MEG to more precisely identify the source of the activity being recorded. For example, MEG has proved useful in locating the source of epileptic discharges. The disadvantage of MEG is its high cost in comparison with the apparatus used to produce EEGs and ERPs.

7-2 Review

Before you continue, check your understanding. Answers appear at the back of the book.

1. The four major techniques for tracking the brain's electrical activity are _____, _____, _____, and _____.

2. Single-cell recording measures _____ potentials from a single neuron.

3. EEG measures _____ potentials on the cell membrane.

4. Magnetoencephalography measures the _____ and also provides a(n) _____.

5. What is the advantage of EEG techniques over MEG?

For additional study tools, visit **LaunchPad** at launchpadworks.com

magnetoencephalogram (MEG) Magnetic potentials recorded from detectors placed outside the skull.

computed tomography (CT) X-ray technique that produces a static three-dimensional image (called a CT scan) of the brain in cross section.

Anatomical Imaging Techniques: CT and MRI

Until the early 1970s, the only way to actually image the living brain was by using X-rays that produce static images of brain anatomy from one angle. The modern era of brain imaging began in the early 1970s, when Allan Cormack and Godfrey Hounsfield independently developed an X-ray approach now called **computed tomography (CT)**: the *CT scan*. Cormack and Hounsfield both recognized that a narrow X-ray beam could be passed through the same object at many angles, creating many images; the images could then be combined with the use of computing and mathematical techniques to produce a three-dimensional image of the brain. *Tomo-* comes from the Greek word for "section," indicating that tomography yields a picture through a single brain slice.

The CT method resembles the way in which our two eyes (and our brain) work in concert to perceive depth and distance to locate an object in space. The CT scan, however, coordinates many more than two images—roughly analogous to our walking to several vantage points to obtain multiple views. X-ray absorption varies with tissue density. High-density tissue, such as bone, absorbs a lot of radiation. Low-density material, such as ventricular fluid or blood, absorbs little. Neural tissue absorption lies between these extremes. CT scanning software translates these differences in absorption into a brain image in which dark colors indicate low-density regions and light colors indicate high-density regions.

Figure 7-14A shows a typical CT scan. The dense skull forms a white border. The brain's gray-matter density does not differ sufficiently from that of white matter for a CT

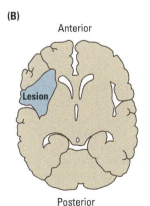
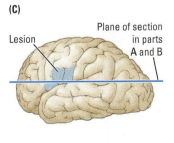

(A) Lesion

(B) Anterior / Lesion / Posterior

(C) Plane of section in parts A and B / Lesion

Neil Borden/Science Source

FIGURE 7-14 **CT Scan and Brain Reconstruction (A)** Dorsal view of a horizontal CT scan of a subject with Broca's aphasia. The dark region at the left anterior is the area of the lesion. **(B)** A schematic representation of the horizontal section, with the area of the lesion shown in blue. **(C)** A reconstruction of the brain, showing a lateral view of the left hemisphere with the lesion shown in blue. Research from Damasio & Damasio, 1989.

scan to distinguish between the two clearly, so the cortex and its underlying white matter show up as a more or less homogeneous gray. Ventricles can be visualized, however, because the fluid in them is far less dense: they, as well as some major fissures in the cortex, are rendered darker in the CT scan. Each point on the image in Figure 7-14A represents about a 1-millimeter-diameter circle of tissue, a resolution sufficient to distinguish two objects about 5 millimeters apart and appropriate for localizing brain tumors and lesions.

The lesion revealed in Figure 7-14A is a damaged region where the presence of fewer neurons and more fluid produces a contrast that appears as a dark area in the CT scan. This subject presented with symptoms of *Broca aphasia*, the inability to speak fluently despite having average comprehension and intact vocal mechanisms. The location of the lesion, in the left frontal cortex (adjacent to the butterfly-shaped lateral ventricles), confirms this diagnosis. Figure 7-14B, a drawing of the same horizontal section, uses color to portray the lesion. Figure 7-14C is a lateral view of the left hemisphere reconstructed from a series of horizontal CT scans and showing the extent of the lesion.

An anatomical alternative to the CT scan, **magnetic resonance imaging (MRI)**, is based on the principle that hydrogen atoms behave like spinning bar magnets in the presence of a magnetic field. The MRI procedure is illustrated in **Figure 7-15**. The dorsal view of the brain portrays density differences among the hydrogen atoms in different neural regions as lighter or darker, depending on density, on the horizontal slice through the head.

Normally, hydrogen atoms point randomly in different directions, but when placed in a large, static magnetic field, they line up in parallel as they orient themselves with respect to the static field's lines of force. In an MRI scanner, radio pulses are applied to a brain whose atoms have been aligned in this manner, and each radio pulse forms a second magnetic field. The second field causes the spinning atoms to deviate from the parallel orientation caused by the static magnetic field to a new orientation.

As each radio pulse ends and the hydrogen atoms realign with the static field, they emit a tiny amount of energy, and a coil detects this realignment. Based on the signals

Section 10-4 delves into aphasias that result from damaged speech areas.

magnetic resonance imaging (MRI) Technique that produces a static three-dimensional brain image by passing a strong magnetic field through the brain, followed by a radio wave, then measuring a radiofrequency signal emitted from hydrogen atoms.

(A)

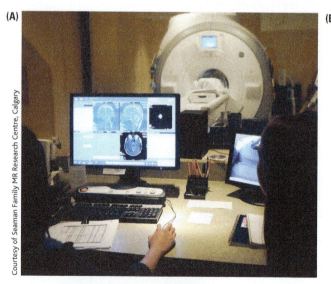

Courtesy of Seaman Family MR Research Centre, Calgary

(B)

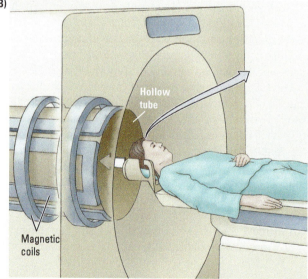

Hollow tube

Magnetic coils

(C)

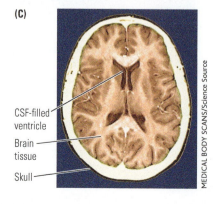

CSF-filled ventricle

Brain tissue

Skull

MEDICAL BODY SCANS/Science Source

FIGURE 7-15 **Magnetic Resonance Imaging (A and B)** The subject is placed in a long metal cylinder that has two sets of magnetic coils arranged at right angles. An additional radiofrequency coil (not shown) surrounds the head, perturbing the static magnetic fields to produce an MRI image of a horizontal section through the head, shown in dorsal view. Electrical currents emitted by wobbling atoms are recorded by MRI to represent different types of tissue—cerebrospinal fluid, brain matter, and bone, for example—as lighter or darker, depending on the density of hydrogen atoms in the tissue, as seen in **(C)**.

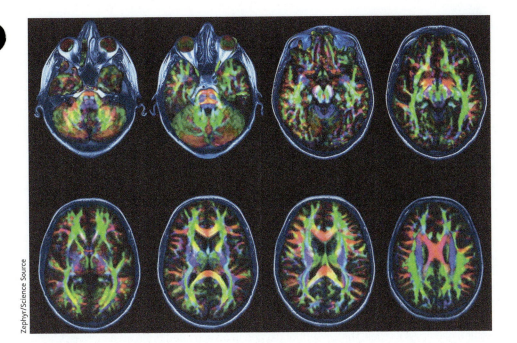

FIGURE 7-16 **Diffusion Tensor Imaging** MRI can measure the diffusion of water molecules in white matter, allowing the visualization of nerve fiber tracts. The front of the brain is at the top in these scans of sections through a healthy brain. The axons are colored according to orientation: fibers running left–right are red, front–back are blue, and up–down are green. Section 15-3 outlines how DTI is helping researchers develop a *brain connectome* to map functional connections in the living brain.

from the coil, a computer re-creates the position of the hydrogen nuclei, producing a magnetic resonance image. Magnetic resonance images may be based on the density of the hydrogen atoms in different brain regions. Areas with high water (H_2O) content (cell body–rich areas), for example, stand out from areas with lower water content (axon-rich areas). Figure 7-15c shows such a magnetic resonance image.

Diffusion tensor imaging (DTI) is an MRI method that detects the directional movements of water molecules to image nerve fiber pathways in the brain. Water can move relatively freely along the axon but less freely across cell membranes. The direction of this water movement is detected by a coil and interpreted by a computer. DTIs can delineate abnormalities in neural pathways. They are also used to identify changes in fiber myelination, such as the damage that leads to myelin loss in multiple sclerosis.

Each scan in the series of DTIs shown in **Figure 7-16** represents a dorsal view at increasing depths through the brain. Although the images appear to show real fibers, DTIs are virtual and based on computer reconstructions of water movement along axons, which should correspond to actual fibers. Nonetheless, DTI easily detects abnormalities such as those that occur in multiple sclerosis, stroke, or concussion, in the imaged fiber pathways and in their myelin sheaths.

Magnetic resonance spectroscopy (MRS) is an MRI method that uses the hydrogen proton signal to determine the concentration of brain metabolites such as *N*-acetylaspartate (NAA) in brain tissue. This measurement is especially useful for detecting persisting abnormalities in brain metabolism in disorders such as concussion.

diffusion tensor imaging (DTI) Magnetic resonance imaging method that can image fiber pathways in the brain by detecting the directional movements of water molecules.

magnetic resonance spectroscopy (MRS) Magnetic resonance imaging method that uses the hydrogen proton signal to determine the concentration of brain metabolites.

Clinical Focus 4-2 describes how myelin loss in MS disrupts neuronal function.

Clinical Focus 16-3 explores the relationship between concussion and degenerative brain disease.

7-3 Review

Before you continue, check your understanding. Answers to Self-Test appear at the back of the book.

1. The principal anatomical brain-imaging methods are _____ and _____.

2. Diffusion tensor imaging identifies _____, whereas magnetic resonance spectroscopy determines _____.

3. In addition to imaging the density of different brain regions, CT and MRI can be used to assess _____.

4. Explain briefly the computed tomography (CT) method of brain imaging.

For additional study tools, visit 🄼 **LaunchPad** at launchpadworks.com

7-4

Functional Brain Imaging

Advances in MRI and computing technologies led to a shift from purely anatomical imaging—which presented a static image of the tissue, as if it were not alive—to functional brain-imaging techniques, which allow investigators to measure the amount of blood flow, oxygen, and glucose usage in the brain as patients or participants solve cognitive problems. When a brain region is active, the amount of blood, oxygen, and glucose flowing to the region increases. It is therefore possible to infer changes in brain activity by measuring either blood flow or levels of the blood's constituents, such as oxygen, glucose, and iron. Three techniques developed from this logic are functional MRI, optical tomography, and positron emission tomography.

Functional Magnetic Resonance Imaging

As neurons become active, they use more oxygen, resulting in a temporary dip in the blood oxygen level. At the same time, active neurons increase blood carbon dioxide levels, which signal blood vessels to dilate, increasing blood flow and bringing more oxygen to the area. Peter Fox and colleagues (Fox & Raichle, 1986) discovered that when human brain activity increases, the extra oxygen produced by increased blood flow actually exceeds the tissue's needs. As a result, the amount of oxygen in an activated brain area increases.

Oxygen is carried on the hemoglobin molecule in red blood cells. Changes in the ratio of oxygen-rich hemoglobin to oxygen-poor hemoglobin alters the blood's magnetic properties because oxygen-rich hemoglobin is less magnetic than oxygen-poor hemoglobin. In 1990, Segi Ogawa and his colleagues showed that MRI could accurately match these changes in magnetic properties to specific brain locations (Ogawa et al., 1990). This process, called **functional magnetic resonance imaging (fMRI)**, signals which areas are displaying changes in activity.

Figure 7-17 shows changes in the fMRI signal in the visual cortex of a person who is being stimulated with light. When the light is turned on, the visual cortex (bottom of the brain images) becomes more active than during baseline (no light). In other words, functional changes in the brain are inferred from increases and decreases in the MRI signal produced by changes in oxygen levels.

functional magnetic resonance imaging (fMRI) Magnetic resonance imaging technique that measures brain activity indirectly by detecting changes associated with blood flow; often used to measure cerebral blood flow during cognitive testing or resting.

FIGURE 7-17 **Imaging Changes in Brain Activity** A functional MRI sequence of a horizontal section at the mid-occipital lobe (bottom of each image) in a normal human brain during visual stimulation. A baseline acquired in darkness (far left) was subtracted from the subsequent images. The participant wore tightly fitting goggles containing light-emitting diodes that were turned on and off as a rapid sequence of scans was obtained over 270 seconds. Note the prominent activity in the visual cortex when the light is on and the rapid cessation of activity when the light is off, all measured in the graph of signal intensity below the images.

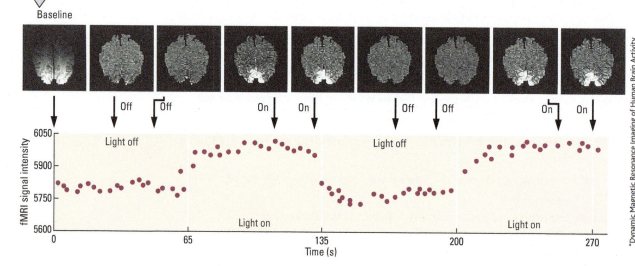

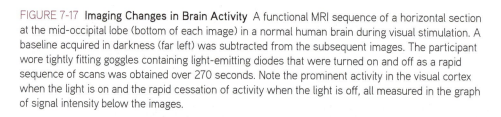

"Dynamic Magnetic Resonance Imaging of Human Brain Activity During Primary Sensory Stimulation," by K. K. Kwong et al., 1992. Proceedings of the National Academy of Sciences (USA), 89, 5678.

When superimposed on MRI-produced anatomical brain images, fMRI changes in activity can be attributed to particular structures. The dense blood vessel supply to the cerebral cortex allows for a spatial resolution of fMRI on the order of 1 millimeter, affording good spatial resolution of the brain activity's source. On the other hand, because changes in blood flow take as long as one-third of a second, the temporal resolution of fMRI is not as precise as that obtained with EEG recordings and ERPs.

Another disadvantage of fMRI is that subjects must lie motionless in a long, noisy tube, an experience that can prove claustrophobic. The confined space and lack of mobility also restrict the types of behavioral experiments that can be performed. Nonetheless, fMRI is a major tool in cognitive neuroscience.

The living brain is always active, and researchers have succeeded in inferring brain function and connectivity by studying fMRI signals when participants are resting—that is, not engaged in any specific task. This signal, **resting-state fMRI (rs-fMRI)**, is collected when participants have their eyes closed or are asked to look at a fixation cross and to keep their eyes open.

The scanner collects brain activity, typically for at least 4-minute blocks. Researchers are attempting to shorten this period by increasing the strength of the static magnetic field and developing more sensitive coils. Statistical analysis of the data entails correlating activity in different brain regions over time. Although rs-fMRI is still in its growth phase, investigators already have identified many consistent networks of brain activity and abnormalities in disease states such as dementia and schizophrenia where patients have trouble with performing cognitive tasks (Takamura & Hanakawa, 2017).

Optical Tomography

Research Focus 7-1, Tuning In to Language, on page 210, describes a brain-imaging study that used functional near-infrared spectroscopy (fNIRS) to investigate newborn infants' responses to language. fNIRS is a form of *optical tomography*, a functional imaging technique that operates on the principle that an object can be reconstructed by gathering light transmitted through it. One requirement is that the object at least partially transmit light. Thus, optical tomography can image soft body tissue, such as that in the breast or the brain.

In fNIRS, reflected infrared light is used to determine blood flow because oxygen-rich hemoglobin and oxygen-poor hemoglobin differ in their absorption spectra. By measuring the blood's light absorption, it is possible to measure the brain's average oxygen consumption. So fNIRS and fMRI measure essentially the same thing but with different tools. In fNIRS, an array of optical transmitter and receiver pairs are fitted across the scalp, as illustrated in **Figure 7-18A**.

Figure 2-7 diagrams the extent of the major cerebral arteries.

resting-state fMRI (rs-fMRI) Magnetic resonance imaging method that measures changes in oxygen when the individual is resting (not engaged in a specific task).

(A)

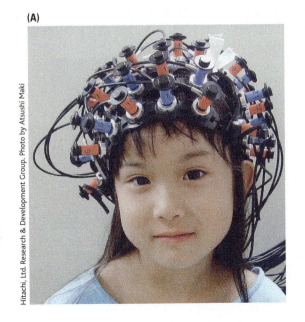

(B)

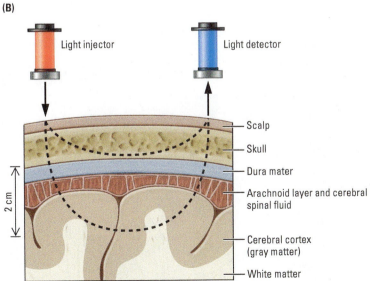

FIGURE 7-18 **How NIRS Works (A)** Light injectors (red) and detectors (blue) are distributed in an array across the head. **(B)** Light injected through the scalp and skull penetrates the brain to a depth of about 2 centimeters. A small fraction of the light is reflected and captured by a detector on the scalp surface. Light is reflected from as deep as 2 centimeters but also from the tissue above it, as illustrated by the banana shape of the curves. Information from Spinney, 2005.

positron emission tomography (PET) Imaging technique that detects changes in blood flow by measuring changes in the uptake of compounds such as oxygen or glucose; used to analyze the metabolic activity of neurons.

Tagged to a glucose molecule, fluorine-18 (^{18}F) acts as a marker for metabolism. The ^{18}F and ^{15}O methods are essentially the same.

FIGURE 7-19 **PET Scanner and Image**
The photo on the left shows a subject lying in a PET scanner, whose design is illustrated in the drawing. In the scan to the right, the bright red and yellow areas are regions of high blood flow.

The obvious advantage of fNIRS is that it is relatively easy to hook up subjects repeatedly and record from them for short periods, from infancy to senescence. The disadvantage is that the light does not penetrate far into the brain, so researchers are restricted to measuring cortical activity (Figure 7-18B). The spatial resolution is also not as good as with other noninvasive methods, although NIRS equipment can now use more than 100 light detectors on the scalp, which allows acceptable spatial resolution in the image. NIRS has been used to differentiate cancerous from noncancerous brain tissue. This advance could potentially lead to safe, extensive surgical removal of brain cancers and improved outcomes (Kut et al., 2015).

Positron Emission Tomography

Researchers use **positron emission tomography (PET)** to study the metabolic activity of brain cells engaged in processing brain functions such as language. PET imaging detects changes in the brain's blood flow by measuring changes in the uptake of compounds such as oxygen and glucose (Posner & Raichle, 1997). A PET camera, like the one shown in **Figure 7-19**, is a doughnut-shaped array of radiation detectors that encircles a person's head. A small amount of water labeled with radioactive molecules is injected into the bloodstream. The person injected with these molecules is in no danger because the molecules used, including the radioactive isotope oxygen-15 (^{15}O), are very unstable. They break down in just a few minutes and are quickly eliminated from the body. (Most of the oxygen in air we breathe is the stable ^{16}O molecule.)

Radioactive ^{15}O molecules release tiny positively charged subatomic particles known as positrons (electrons with a positive charge). Positrons are emitted from an unstable atom because the atom is deficient in neutrons. The positrons are attracted to the negatively charged electrons in the brain, and the collision of the two particles leads to annihilation of both, which produces energy.

This energy, in the form of two photons (a unit of light energy), leaves the head at the speed of light and is detected by the PET camera. The photons leave the head in exactly opposite directions from the site of positron–electron annihilation, so annihilation photon detectors can detect their source, as illustrated in Figure 7-19. A computer identifies the coincident photons and locates the annihilation source to generate the PET image.

The PET system enables blood-flow measurement in the brain because the unstable radioactive molecules accumulate there in direct proportion to the rate of local blood flow. Local blood flow in turn is related to neural activity because potassium ions released from stimulated neurons dilate adjacent blood vessels. The more the blood flow, the higher the radiation counts recorded by the PET camera.

But PET researchers who are studying the link between blood flow and mental activity use a *subtraction procedure*. They subtract the blood-flow pattern when the brain is

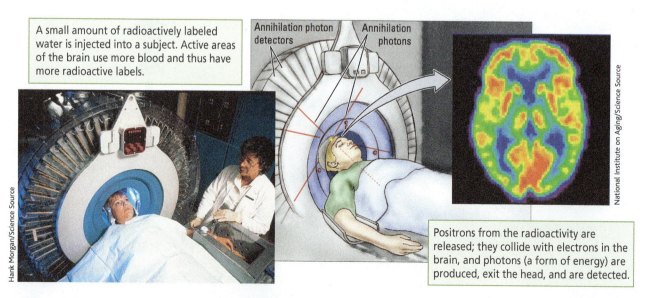

A small amount of radioactively labeled water is injected into a subject. Active areas of the brain use more blood and thus have more radioactive labels.

Annihilation photon detectors   Annihilation photons

Positrons from the radioactivity are released; they collide with electrons in the brain, and photons (a form of energy) are produced, exit the head, and are detected.

Hank Morgan/Science Source

National Institute on Aging/Science Source

in a carefully selected control state from the pattern of blood flow imaged when the subject is engaged in the task under study, as illustrated in the top row of **Figure 7-20**. This subtraction process images the change in blood flow between the two states. The change can be averaged across subjects (middle row) to yield a representative average image difference that reveals which brain areas are selectively active during the task (bottom). PET does not measure local neural activity directly; rather, it infers activity on the assumption that blood flow increases where neuron activity increases.

A significant limitation of PET is that radiochemicals, including the so-called radiopharmaceuticals used in diagnosing human patients, must be prepared in a cyclotron quite close to the scanner because their half-lives are so short that transportation time is a severely limiting factor. Generating these materials is very expensive. Despite the expense, PET has important advantages over other imaging methods:

- PET can detect the decay of literally hundreds of radiochemicals, which allows the mapping of a wide range of brain changes and conditions, including changes in pH, glucose, oxygen, amino acids, neurotransmitters, and proteins.

- PET can detect relative amounts of a given neurotransmitter, the density of neurotransmitter receptors, and metabolic activities associated with learning, brain poisoning, and degenerative processes that might be related to aging.

- PET is widely used to study cognitive function with great success. For example, PET confirms that various brain regions perform different functions.

There are now hybrid scanners for diagnostic imaging, and they come in different combinations, such as PET with CT, PET with MRI, and PET with MRI and EEG. The advantage of these hybrid scanners is that they can acquire high-quality anatomical images and then overlay the functional/metabolic image information, allowing for precise localization that was not available before—all within a single examination.

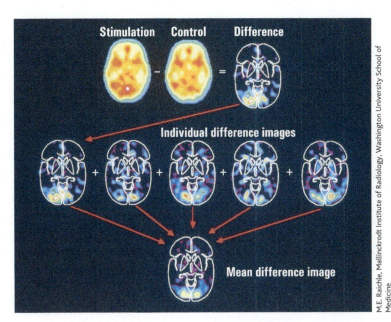

FIGURE 7-20 **The Procedure of Subtraction** In the upper row of scans, the control condition, resting while looking at a static fixation point (control), is subtracted from the experimental condition, looking at a flickering checkerboard (stimulation). The subtraction produces a different scan for each of five experimental subjects, shown in the middle row, but all show increased blood flow in the occipital region. The difference scans are averaged to produce the representative image at the bottom.

7-4 Review

Before you continue, check your understanding. Answers to Self-Test appear at the back of the book.

1. The principal methods of functional brain imaging are _____, _____, and _____.

2. PET uses _____ to measure brain processes and to identify _____ changes in the brain.

3. fMRI and optical imaging measure changes in _____.

4. Why are resting-state measurements useful to researchers?

For additional study tools, visit 🔲 **LaunchPad** at launchpadworks.com

7-5

Chemical and Genetic Measures of Brain and Behavior

Our focus so far has been on how neuroscientists study the individual and collective activity of neurons and how neuronal activity relates to behavior. Neurons are regulated by *genes*, DNA segments that encode the synthesis of particular proteins within cells. Genes control the production of chemicals in a cell, so it is possible to relate

Section 3-1 investigates how neurons function. Section 3-3 relates genes to cell function, genetic engineering, and epigenetic mechanisms.

microdialysis Technique used to determine the chemical constituents of extracellular fluid in freely moving animals.

striatum Caudate nucleus and putamen of the basal ganglia.

cerebral voltammetry Technique used to identify the concentration of specific chemicals in the brain as animals behave freely.

Section 12-7 explores neural effects of rewarding events.

Section 4-1 explains diffusion and concentration gradients in detail.

Section 6-4 investigates why glutamate and similar chemicals can act as neurotoxins.

FIGURE 7-21 **Microdialysis**
Information from Tisdall & Smith, 2006.

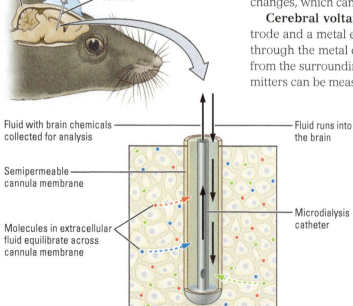

behavior to genes and to chemicals inside and outside the cell. Chemical and genetic approaches require sophisticated technologies that have seen major advances in the past two decades.

Measuring Brain Chemistry

The brain contains a wide mixture of chemicals, ranging from neurotransmitters and hormones to glucose and gases, among many others. Abnormalities in the amounts of these chemicals can cause serious disruptions in behavior. Prime examples are Parkinson disease, characterized by low dopamine levels in the substantia nigra, and depression, correlated with low serotonin and/or noradrenaline production. The simplest way to measure brain chemistry in such diseases is to extract tissue postmortem from affected humans or laboratory animals and undertake traditional biochemical techniques, such as high-performance liquid chromatography (HPLC), to measure specific chemical levels.

Fluctuations in brain chemistry are associated not only with behavioral dysfunction but also with ongoing healthy behavior. For example, research over at least the past 35 years shows that dopamine levels fluctuate in the nucleus accumbens (a structure in the subcortical basal ganglia) in association with stimuli related to rewarding behaviors such as food and sex. Changes in brain chemistry can be measured in freely moving animals using two methods: *cerebral microdialysis* and *cerebral voltammetry*.

Microdialysis, which can determine the chemical constituents of extracellular fluid, is widely used in the laboratory. The technique has found clinical application over the past 15 years. A catheter with a semipermeable membrane at its tip is placed in the brain, as illustrated in **Figure 7-21**. A fluid flows through the cannula and passes along the cell membrane. Simple diffusion drives extracellular molecules across the membrane along their concentration gradient.

Fluid containing the molecules from the brain exits through tubing to be collected for analysis. The fluid is removed at a constant rate so that changes in brain chemistry can be correlated with behavior. For example, if a rat is placed in an environment in which it anticipates sex or a favored food, microdialysis will record an increase in dopamine within the basal ganglia regions of the caudate nucleus and putamen, known as the **striatum**.

Microdialysis is used in some medical centers to monitor chemistry in the injured brain. The effects of TBI or stroke can be worsened by secondary events such as a drastic increase in the neurotransmitter glutamate. Such biochemical changes can lead to irreversible cell damage or death. Physicians use microdialysis to monitor such changes, which can then be treated.

Cerebral voltammetry works on a different principle. A small carbon fiber electrode and a metal electrode are implanted in the brain, and a weak current is passed through the metal electrode. The current causes electrons to be added to or removed from the surrounding chemicals. Changes in extracellular levels of specific neurotransmitters can be measured as they occur.

Because different currents lead to changes in different compounds, it is possible to identify levels of different transmitters, such as serotonin or dopamine, and related chemicals. Voltammetry has the advantage of not requiring the chemical analysis of fluid removed from the brain, as microdialysis does, but it has the disadvantage of being destructive. That is, the chemical measurements require the degradation of one chemical into another, making the technology suitable only for scientific studies in animals. As an example, Wheeler and colleagues used voltammetry to demonstrate that the stress hormone corticosterone induced an increase in the amount of dopamine as well as how long it was detected in the nucleus accumbens (Wheeler et al., 2017). This finding is important because it provides evidence that stress can potentiate the effect of reinforcers.

Measuring Genes in Brain and Behavior

Most human behaviors cannot be explained by genetic inheritance alone, but variations in gene sequences do contribute significantly to brain organization. About 1 in 250 live births are identical twins, people who share an identical genome. Identical twins often have remarkably similar behavioral traits. Twin studies show strong concordance rates that support genetic contributions to drug addiction and other psychiatric disorders. But twin studies also show that environmental factors and life experience must be involved: concordance for most behavioral disorders, such as schizophrenia and depression, is far less than 100 percent. Life experiences act epigenetically to alter gene expression.

Genetic factors can also be studied by comparing people who were adopted early in life and usually would not have a close genetic relationship to their adoptive parents. Here, a high concordance rate for behavioral traits would imply a strong environmental influence on behavior. Ideally, an investigator would be able to study both the adoptive and biological parents to tease out the relative heritability of behavioral traits.

With the development of relatively inexpensive methods of identifying specific genes in people, it is now possible to relate the *alleles* (different forms) of specific genes to behaviors. A gene related to the production of a compound called brain-derived neurotrophic factor (BDNF) is representative. BDNF plays an important role in stimulating neural plasticity, and low levels of BDNF have been found with mood disorders such as depression. The two alleles of this gene are *BDNF Val 66Met* and *BDNF Val 66Val*.

Joshua Bueller and his colleagues (2006) showed that the *Met* allele is associated with an 11 percent reduction in hippocampal volume in healthy participants. Other studies have associated the *Met* allele with poor memory for specific events (*episodic memory*) and a high incidence of dementia later in life. However, the *Val* allele is by no means the better variant: although *Val* carriers have better episodic memory, they also have a higher incidence of neuroticism and anxiety disorders. The two alleles produce different phenotypes because they influence brain structure and functions differently. Other genes that were not measured also differed among Bueller's participants and may have contributed to the observed difference. Research Focus 7-4, Attention-Deficit/Hyperactivity Disorder, gives another example of a common disorder of brain and behavior with a genetic contribution.

Section 8-2 explains how neurotrophic factors (nourishing chemical compounds) support growth and differentiation in developing neurons.

Principle 2: Neuroplasticity is the hallmark of nervous system functioning.

Sections 2-6 and 5-3 introduce factors that contribute to dementias. Clinical Focus 14-3 describes research, and Section 16-3 examines treatments.

Epigenetics: Measuring Gene Expression

An individual's genotype exists in an environmental context fundamental to *gene expression*, the way genes become active or not. While epigenetic factors do not change the DNA sequence, the genes that are expressed can change dramatically in response to environment and experience. Epigenetic changes can persist throughout a lifetime and even across multiple generations.

Changes in gene expression can result from widely ranging experiences, including chronic stress, traumatic events, drugs, culture, and disease. A study by Mario Fraga and his colleagues (2005) stands as a powerful example of gene–experience interactions. The investigators examined epigenetic patterns in 40 pairs of identical twins by measuring two molecular markers related to gene expression.

Although twins' patterns of gene expression were virtually identical when measured in childhood, 50-year-old twins exhibited differences so remarkable as to make them as different epigenetically as young non-twin siblings! The specific cause or causes of such differences are unknown but are thought to be related to lifestyle factors, such as smoking and exercise habits, diet, stressors, drug use, and education, as well as to social experiences, such as marriage and child rearing, among others. The epigenetic drift in the twins supports the findings of less than 100 percent concordance for diseases in identical twins.

See "A Case of Inheriting Experience" in Section 3-3.

Attention-Deficit/Hyperactivity Disorder

Together, attention-deficit/hyperactivity disorder (ADHD) and attention-deficit disorder (ADD) are probably the most common disorders of brain and behavior in children, with an incidence of 4 percent to 10 percent of school-aged children. Although it often goes unrecognized, an estimated 50 percent of children with ADHD still show symptoms in adulthood, where its behaviors are associated with family breakups, substance abuse, and driving accidents.

The neurobiological basis of ADHD and ADD is generally believed to be a dysfunction in the noradrenergic or dopaminergic activating system, especially in the frontal basal ganglia circuitry. Psychomotor stimulants such as Ritalin

In this mainstreamed first-grade classroom, a special education student with ADHD uses the *turtle technique* to cope with frustration and stress.

(methylphenidate) and Adderall (mainly dextroamphetamine) act to increase brain levels of noradrenaline and dopamine and are widely used for treating ADHD. About 70 percent of children show improvement of attention and hyperactivity symptoms with treatment, but there is little evidence that drugs directly improve academic achievement. This is important because about 40 percent of children with ADHD fail to get a high-school diploma, even though many receive special education for their condition.

Stephen Faraone and coworkers (Lecendreux et al., 2015) have challenged a common view that ADHD is a cultural phenomenon reflecting parents' and teachers' tolerance of children's behavior. These investigators conclude that the prevalence of ADHD worldwide is remarkably similar when the same rating criteria are used. Little is known about incidence in developing countries, however. It is entirely possible that the incidence may actually be higher in developing countries, given that the learning environment for children is likely to be less structured than it is in developed nations.

The cause of ADHD is unknown but probably involves dopamine receptors in the forebrain. The most likely areas are the frontal lobe and subcortical basal ganglia. Evidence of reduced brain volumes in these regions in ADHD patients is growing, as is evidence of an increase in the dopamine transporter protein. The dopamine transporter increase would mean that dopamine reuptake into the presynaptic neuron occurs faster than it does in the brains of people without ADHD. The result is a relative decrease in dopamine. Ritalin works by blocking dopamine reuptake.

ADHD is believed to be highly heritable, a conclusion supported by twin studies showing a concordance of about 75 percent in identical twins. Molecular genetic studies have identified at least seven candidate genes, and several of them are related to the dopamine synapse, in particular to the D_4 receptor gene.

The role of epigenetic differences can also be seen across populations. Moshe Szyf, Michael Meaney, and their colleagues (see Szyf et al., 2008) have shown, for instance, that the amount of maternal attention mother rats give to their newborn pups alters the expression of certain genes in the adult hippocampus. These genes are related to the infants' stress response when they are adults. (Maternal attention is measured as the amount and type of mother–infant contact; a difference of up to 6 hours per day can exist between attentive and inattentive mothers.)

A subsequent study by the same group (McGowan et al., 2009) examined epigenetic differences in hippocampal tissue obtained from two groups of humans: (1) suicides with histories of childhood abuse and (2) either suicides with no childhood abuse or controls who died of other causes. The epigenetic changes found in the abused suicide victims parallel those found in the rats with inattentive mothers, again suggesting that early experiences can alter hippocampal organization and function via changes in gene expression.

Experience-dependent changes in gene expression are probably found not only in the hippocampus but throughout the brain as well. For example, Richelle Mychasiuk and colleagues (2011) found that stressing pregnant rats led to wide changes in gene expression in their offspring, in both the frontal cortex and the hippocampus. However, the investigators found virtually no overlap in the altered genes in the two brain regions: the same experience changed different brain regions differently.

Epigenetic studies promise to revolutionize our understanding of gene–brain interactions in healthy brain development and brain function. They will also help researchers develop new treatments for neurological disorders. For example, specific epigenetic changes appear to be related to the ability to make a functional recovery after stroke.

7-5 Review

Before you continue, check your understanding. Answers to Self-Test appear at the back of the book.

1. Concentrations of different chemicals in the brain can be measured in postmortem tissue using a(n) _____ or in vivo using _____ or _____.

2. Gene–environment interactions can be investigated in human populations by comparing _____ of behavioral traits in identical twins and adopted children.

3. The study of genes and behavior focuses on individual differences in _____, whereas the study of epigenetics and behavior examines differences in _____.

4. Describe briefly how epigenetic studies have led to the recognition that life experience and the environment can alter brain function.

For additional study tools, visit ⚓ **LaunchPad** at launchpadworks.com

---

7-6

Comparing Neuroscience Research Methods

We have considered a wide range of research methods for manipulating and measuring brain–behavior interactions. **Tables 7-2** and **7-3** summarize these methods, including goals and examples of each method. How do researchers choose among them all? Their main consideration is their research question. Ultimately, that question is behavioral, but many steps lie along the route to understanding behavior.

TABLE 7-2 Manipulating Brain and Behavior

Method	Experimental goal	Examples
Whole-animal manipulations (Section 7-1)	Determine how an environmental condition affects brain and behavior	Diet, exercise, social interactions, sensory stimulation, drug usage
Brain lesions, permanent (Section 7-1)	Remove or destroy neural tissue to observe behavioral changes	Knife cuts or aspirations, electrolytic lesions, neurotoxic lesions, high-intensity focused ultrasound
Brain lesions, temporary and reversible (Section 7-1)	Short-term silencing of neural tissue to observe behavioral changes	Regional cooling to arrest synaptic transmission, delivery of an agonist for GABA through a cannula to increase local inhibition
Genetic lesions (Sections 3-3; 7-1)	Remove genetic material	Knockout technology, CRISPR
Genetic stimulation (Section 3-3)	Add genetic material	Knock-in technology
Drug manipulations (Section 7-1)	Determine receptor system's role in the CNS	Use drugs to activate (agonists) or inactivate (antagonists) a receptor system
Electrical and magnetic stimulation (Section 7-1)	Excite tissue activity	DBS, TMS
Optogenetics (Section 7-1)	Use light to activate specific ion channels and relate to behavior	Insertion of specific light-sensitive proteins
Chemogenetics (Section 7-1)	Use specific synthetic drugs to activate designer receptors	Insertion of specific G protein–coupled receptors

TABLE 7-3 **Measuring Brain and Behavior**

Method	Experimental goal	Examples
Behavioral analysis (Section 7-1)	Observe behavior; generate tests to allow people and lab animals to demonstrate behavioral capacities	Naturalistic observation; tests, mazes; automated touchscreen platform
Tissue analysis (Section 7-1)	Identify cell types and connections; identify disease states	Stains
Record electrical and magnetic activity (Section 7-2)	Measure action potentials from individual neurons; measure graded potentials to assess coordinated activity of thousands of neurons; measure magnetic fields	Single-cell recording; EEG, ERP; MEG
Anatomical brain imaging (Section 7-3)	Noninvasive examination of brain structures	Miniature microscopes; X-ray; CT; MRI; DTI
Functional brain imaging (Section 7-4)	Measure brain activity as specific behaviors are performed	fMRI; fNIRS; MRS; PET
In vivo chemistry (Section 7-5)	Relate fluctuations in transmitter release to behavior	HPLC; microdialysis, voltammetry
Genetics (Section 7-5)	Determine presence of a gene and its products	DNA, RNA, protein analysis
Epigenetics (Section 7-5)	Discover effect of experience on gene expression, brain, and behavior	Gene expression analysis

Some researchers focus on *morphology* (structure) in postmortem tissue. This approach allows detailed analysis of both macro and micro structure, depending on the method chosen. Identifying brain pathology, as in Parkinson disease, can lead to insights about the causes and nature of a disorder.

Other investigators focus more on the ways neurons generate electrical activity in relationship to behavior or on functional changes in brain activity during specific types of cognitive processing. Both approaches are legitimate: the goal is gaining an understanding of brain–behavior relationships.

But investigators must consider practical issues, too. Temporal resolution (how quickly the measurement or image is obtained); spatial resolution (the accuracy of localization in the brain); and the degree of invasiveness are all pertinent. In addition, it is not feasible to consider MRI-based methods for studies of very young children because they have difficulty remaining absolutely still for long periods.

Similarly, studies of brain-injured patients must take into account factors such as the subject's ability to maintain attention for long periods—during neuropsychological testing or imaging studies, for example. In addition, practical problems such as motor or language impairment may limit the types of methods that researchers can use.

Of course, cost is an ever-present practical consideration. Studying brain and behavior linkages by perturbing the brain is generally less costly than some imaging methods, many of which require expensive machinery. EEG, ERP, and fNIRS are noninvasive and relatively inexpensive to set up (less than $100,000 each). MRI-based methods, MEG, and PET are very expensive (more than $2 million each) and are therefore typically found only in large research centers or hospitals. Similarly, epigenetic studies can be very expensive if investigators consider the entire genome in a large number of biological samples.

7-6 Review

Before you continue, check your understanding. Answers to Self-Test appear at the back of the book.

1. Neuroscience measurements and imaging vary along the dimensions _____, _____, and _____.

2. Relative to the expense of fMRI and PET imaging, noninvasively perturbing the brain using methods such as _____ or administering neuropsychological testing is _____.

3. Catherine is interested in the relationship between dopamine levels in the nucleus accumbens and drug taking. What method(s) could she use to determine this relationship?

For additional study tools, visit 📖 **LaunchPad** at launchpadworks.com

7-7

Using Animals in Brain–Behavior Research

A complete understanding of brain–behavior relationships is limited in part by the ethical constraints placed on experimentation with both humans and nonhuman species. Most countries decide independently which experimental practices are acceptable for humans, for other vertebrates, and for invertebrate species. In general, fewer experimental methods are acceptable for use on humans than are employed on our most closely related primate relatives. Thus, as in most new treatments in medicine, a wide variety of nonhuman species are used to develop and test treatments for human neurological or psychiatric disorders before they are tested on humans.

Although the human and the nonhuman brain have obvious differences with respect to language, the general brain organization across mammalian species is remarkably similar, and the functioning of basic neural circuits in nonhuman mammals appears to generalize to humans. Thus, neuroscientists use widely varying animal species to model human brain diseases as well as to infer typical human brain functioning.

Two important issues surface in use of animal models to develop treatments for brain and behavioral disorders. The first is whether animals actually display neurological diseases in ways similar to humans. The second involves the ethics of using animals in research. We consider each separately.

Benefits of Animal Models of Disease

Some disorders—stroke, for example—seem relatively easy to model in laboratory animals because it is possible to interrupt blood supply to a brain area and induce injury and consequent behavioral change. However, it is far more difficult to determine whether human behavioral disorders can actually be induced in laboratory animals. Consider *attention-deficit/hyperactivity disorder* (*ADHD*), a developmental disorder characterized by the core behavioral symptoms impulsivity, hyperactivity, and/or inattention. The most common issue for children with ADHD is problems at school. Lab animals such as rats and mice do not go to school, so how does one model ADHD in rodents?

ADHD has proved difficult to treat in children, and interest in developing an animal model is high. One way to proceed is to take advantage of the normal variance in the performance of rats on a variety of tests of working memory and cognitive functioning—tests that require attentional processes. The idea is that we can think of ADHD in people or in rats as one extreme on a spectrum of behaviors that are part of a normal distribution in the general population. Many studies show that treating rats with the dopaminergic agonist methylphenidate (Ritalin), a common treatment for children diagnosed with ADHD, actually improves the performance of rats that do poorly on tests requiring attentional processes.

One rat strain, the Kyoto SHR rat, has proved an especially good model for ADHD and is widely used in the lab. The strain presents known abnormalities in prefrontal dopaminergic innervation that correlate with behavioral abnormalities such as hyperactivity. Dopaminergic abnormalities are believed to be one underlying symptom of ADHD in children (as explained in Research Focus 7-4 on page 236). Methylphenidate can reverse behavioral abnormalities, both in children with ADHD and in the SHR rats.

Clinical Focus 6-1 reports on illicit use of prescription ADHD medications to boost performance at school and at work. Section 15-2 explores the nature of attention and disorders that result in deficits of attention.

Animal Welfare and Scientific Experimentation

Using nonhuman animals in scientific research has a long history, but only in the past century have ethical issues surrounding animal research gained considerable attention and laws been instituted. Just as the scientific community has established ethical standards for research on humans, it has also developed regulations governing experimentation on animals. The governments of most developed nations regulate the use of animals in research; most states, territories, and provinces within a country

We present experiments that predate current ethical standards. Bartholow's brain stimulation (Section 4-1) and the volunteers in prison in Experiment 6-1 are examples.

have additional legislation. Universities engaged in research have their own rules governing animal use, as do professional societies of scientists and the journals in which they publish.

Here are four principles used as guidelines in Canada for reviewing experimental and teaching protocols that will use animals:

1. The use of animals in research, teaching, and testing is acceptable only if it promises to contribute to the understanding of environmental principles or issues, fundamental biological principles, or development of knowledge that can reasonably be expected to benefit humans, animals, or the environment.

2. Optimal standards for animal health and care result in enhanced credibility and reproducibility of experimental results.

3. Acceptance of animal use in science critically depends on maintaining public confidence in the mechanisms and processes used to ensure necessary, humane, and justified animal use.

4. Animals are used only if the researcher's best efforts to find an alternative have failed. Researchers who use animals employ the most humane methods on the smallest number of appropriate animals required to obtain valid information.

Legislation concerning the care and use of laboratory animals in the United States is set forth in the Animal Welfare Act, which includes laws passed by Congress in 1966, 1970, 1976, and 1985. Legislation in other countries is similar to that of the United States, and in some European countries, it is much stricter. The U.S. act covers mammals, including rats, mice, cats, dogs, and primates, and birds, but it excludes farm animals that are not used in research. The U.S. Department of Agriculture (USDA) administers the act through inspectors in the Animal Care section of the Animal and Plant Health Inspection Service.

In addition, the Office of Human Research Protections of the National Institutes of Health (NIH) administers the Health Research Extension Act (passed in 1986). The act covers all animal uses conducted or supported by the U.S. Public Health Service and applies to any live vertebrate animal used in research, training, or testing. The act requires that each institution provide acceptable assurance that it meets all minimum regulations and conforms with *The Guide for the Care and Use of Laboratory Animals* (National Research Council, 2011) before conducting any activity that includes animals. The typical method for demonstrating conformance with the guide is to seek voluntary accreditation from the Association for Assessment and Accreditation of Laboratory Animal Care International, a private, nonprofit organization that promotes the humane treatment of animals.

All accredited U.S. and Canadian universities that receive government grant support are required to provide adequate treatment for all vertebrate animals. Reviews and specific protocols for vertebrates, including fish, amphibians, reptiles, birds, and mammals, to be used in research, teaching, or testing are administered through the same process. Anyone using animals in a U.S. or Canadian university submits a protocol to the university's institutional animal care and use committee, composed of researchers, veterinarians, people who have some knowledge of science, and laypeople from the university and the community.

Companies that use animals for research are not required to follow this process. In effect, however, if they do not, they will be unable to publish the results of their research because journals require that research conform to national guidelines on animal care. In addition, discoveries made using animals are not recognized by government agencies that approve drugs for clinical trials with humans if they do not follow the prescribed process. Companies therefore use Good Laboratory Practice (GLP) standards, which are as rigorous as those used by government agencies.

Researchers are to consider alternatives to procedures that may cause more than momentary or slight pain or distress to animals. Most of the attention on alternatives has focused on the use of animals in testing and stems from high public awareness of some tests for pharmacological compounds, especially toxic compounds. In the

United States, the National Institute of Environmental Health Sciences now regulates testing of such compounds.

Despite the legislation related to animal use, some controversy remains over using animals in scientific research. Those at one extreme approve any usage, and those at the other extreme disapprove of using animals for any form of research. Most fall somewhere in between. The debate touches on issues of philosophy, law, morals, custom, and biology.

The issues in this debate are important to researchers in many branches of science who experiment with animals to understand the functions of the human and non-human body, brain, and behavior. They are also important to human and veterinary medicine that can benefit from this research, as well as to people and other animals with diseases or damage to the nervous system. And they are important to those who are philosophically opposed to using animals for work or food. Finally, because you, as a student, encounter many experiments on animals in this book, these issues are important to you as well.

7-7 Review

Before you continue, check your understanding. Answers to Self-Test appear at the back of the book.

1. Laboratory animals can model some disorders, such as stroke, but are less useful for modeling most _____ disorders, such as ADHD, because it is difficult to re-create the human-specific conditions for these disorders.

2. Legislation governing the care and use of laboratory animals used in the United States was set forth in the _____.

3. List some of the reasons for conducting scientific research in animals.

For additional study tools, visit **LaunchPad** at launchpadworks.com

Summary

7-1 Measuring and Manipulating Brain and Behavior

The brain's primary function is to produce behavior, so the fundamental research technique in behavioral neuroscience is to study the direct relationship between brain and behavior. Investigators study healthy humans and other animals as well as human patients and laboratory animals with neurological problems.

Initially, scientists simply observed behavior, but they later developed neuropsychological testing measures designed to study specific functions such as fine movements, memory, and emotion. Today, researchers correlate these behavioral outcomes with anatomical, physiological, chemical, genetic, and other molecular measures of brain organization.

Brain and behavioral relationships can be manipulated by altering brain function, either permanently or temporarily. Permanent changes involve damaging the brain directly by ablation or with neurotoxins that remove or destroy brain tissue. Transient changes in brain activity can be induced either by use of a mild electrical or magnetic current, as in DBS or TMS, or by administration of drugs. The synthetic biology technique CRISPR-Cas9 uses the Cas9 protein in bacteria to cut and replace a sequence of DNA of any cell. Optogenetics, a transgenic technique, employs light-activated ion channels to excite or inhibit targeted cells in living tissue. Chemogenetic stimulation combines designer receptors and synthetic drugs to excite targeted cells in living tissue.

7-2 Measuring the Brain's Electrical Activity

Recordings from single or multiple cells show that neurons fire in specific patterns and that cortical neurons are organized into functional groups that work as coordinated networks. Neurons in sensory areas respond to specific characteristics of stimuli, such as color or pitch. Other neurons, such as place cells in the hippocampal formation, can code for more complex information, such as an object's location in space.

Electroencephalographic or magnetoencephalographic recordings measure electrical or magnetic activity from thousands of neurons at once. EEG can reveal a gross relationship between brain and behavior, as when a person is alert and displays the beta-wave pattern versus when the person is resting or sleeping, indicated by the slower alpha-wave patterns. Event-related potentials, on the other hand, tell us that even though the entire brain is active during waking, certain parts are momentarily much more active than others. ERP records how the location of increased activity changes as information moves from one brain area to another.

EEG and ERP are noninvasive methods that record information from electrodes on the scalp; in the case of MEG, magnetic detectors above the head are used. Electrocorticography, by contrast, records information via electrodes attached directly to the cortex. ECoG and single-cell recording techniques are invasive.

7-3 Anatomical Imaging Techniques: CT and MRI

Computed tomography (CT) and magnetic resonance imaging (MRI) are sensitive to the density of brain structures, ventricles, nuclei, and pathways. CT is a form of three-dimensional X-ray, whereas MRI works on the principle that hydrogen atoms behave like spinning bar magnets in the presence of a magnetic field.

Although CT scans are quicker and less expensive, MRI provides exceptionally clear images, both of nuclei and of fiber pathways in the brain. MRI also indicates that people's brain structure varies widely. Both CT and MRI can be used to assess brain damage from neurological disease or injury, but MRI is more useful as a research tool.

Diffusion tensor imaging is a form of MRI that makes it possible to identify normal or abnormal fiber tracts and myelin in the brain. Magnetic resonance spectroscopy (MRS), another form of MRI, permits practitioners to detect brain metabolites, such as those produced following concussion.

7-4 Functional Brain Imaging

Metabolic imaging shows that any behavior requires the collaboration of widespread neural circuits. Positron emission tomography records blood-flow and other metabolic changes in periods measured in minutes; it requires complex subtraction procedures and the averaging of responses across multiple subjects. Records of blood flow obtained using functional magnetic resonance imaging can be combined with anatomical MRI images to locate changes in an individual brain and to complement ERP results. Resting-state fMRI allows investigators to measure connectivity across brain regions.

Functional near-infrared spectroscopy is the form of optical tomography usually used for functional brain-imaging studies. It works on the principle that an object, including brain tissue, can be reconstructed by gathering light transmitted through the object. fNIRS is much simpler to use than PET or fMRI, but because light does not penetrate very far into the brain, it can be used only to study cortical function.

7-5 Chemical and Genetic Measures of Brain and Behavior

Analysis of changes in both genes and neurochemicals provides insight into the molecular correlates of behavior. Although genes code all the information needed to construct and regulate cells, epigenetic research reveals that the environment and life experience can modify gene expression. Even identical twins, who have an identical genome at birth, in adulthood have widely differing patterns of gene expression and very different brains.

7-6 Comparing Neuroscience Research Methods

The main consideration in neuroscience research is matching the question being posed with the appropriate methodologies to best answer that question. Whatever the approach, the goal is to understand brain–behavior relationships. Tables 7-2 and 7-3 on pages 237 and 238 summarize the manipulations and measurements used in behavioral neuroscience. Among all the practical issues of measurement resolution and invasiveness, cost is often the ultimate consideration.

7-7 Using Animals in Brain–Behavior Research

Understanding brain function in both the healthy brain and the disordered brain often benefits from animal models. Investigators develop animal models to manipulate the brain, to determine how experiential factors and neurological treatments affect brain function.

Because animal subjects cannot protect themselves from abuse, governments and researchers have cooperated to develop ethical guidelines for the use of laboratory animals. These guidelines are designed to ensure that discomfort is minimized, as is the number of animals used for invasive procedures.

▍Key Terms

alpha rhythm, p. 224

behavioral neuroscience, p. 215

cerebral voltammetry, p. 234

chemogenetics, p. 222

compensation, p. 219

computed tomography (CT), p. 227

deep-brain stimulation (DBS), p. 220

diffusion tensor imaging (DTI), p. 229

electrocorticography (ECoG), p. 224

event-related potential (ERP), p. 225

functional magnetic resonance imaging (fMRI), p. 230

functional near-infrared spectroscopy (fNIRS), p. 210

magnetic resonance imaging (MRI), p. 228

magnetic resonance spectroscopy (MRS), p. 229

magnetoencephalogram (MEG), p. 227

microdialysis, p. 234

neuropsychology, p. 211

optogenetics, p. 221

place cells, p. 223

positron emission tomography (PET), p. 232

resting-state fMRI (rs-fMRI), p. 231

stereotaxic apparatus, p. 219

striatum, p. 234

synthetic biology, p. 221

transcranial magnetic stimulation (TMS), p. 220

Visit 📖 **LaunchPad** to access the e-Book, videos, 📖 **LearningCurve** adaptive quizzing, flashcards, and more at launchpadworks.com

Aynur_sib/Getty Images

How Does the Nervous System Develop and Adapt?

Linking Socioeconomic Status to Cortical Development

Nobel Prize–winning American economist James Heckman has argued passionately about one effective strategy for economic growth: investing as early as possible in disadvantaged families promotes optimal development of young children at risk. Heckman notes that children from lower-SES families typically develop gaps in knowledge and ability relative to their more advantaged peers.

These gaps influence health and prosperity, and they persist throughout life. Childhood SES correlates with cognitive development, language, memory, social and emotional processing, and ultimately income and health in adulthood. One reason: early experiences related to SES influence children's cerebral development.

To examine cerebral development, neuroimaging studies visualize differences in brain development that relate to growing up in under-resourced environments. As the brain grows throughout childhood and adolescence, the cortical surface area expands before declining in adulthood (Schnack et al., 2014; also see Figure 8-14). Cortical surface area reflects the amount of neural tissue available for different behaviors and correlates positively with cognitive ability. It should be possible to estimate the effect of early experiences on brain and behavioral development by comparing the cortical surface area and cognitive abilities of people raised in lower- or higher-SES families.

Kimberly Noble and her colleagues (2015) used neuroimaging to investigate the relationship between SES and cortical surface area in more than 1000 participants aged 3 to 20. As shown in the illustration, lower family income, independent of race or sex, was associated with decreased cortical surface area in widespread regions of frontal, temporal, and parietal lobes, the regions shown in red. A follow-up study by the same group found SES moderates patterns of age-related cortical thinning, especially in language-related cortical regions (Piccolo et al., 2016).

The investigators also measured participants' cognitive performance on tests of attention, memory, vocabulary, and reading. The larger the cortical surface area, the better the test outcomes. The negative effects of low SES were especially dramatic at the lower end of the family income spectrum,

especially in families with annual incomes less than $30,000. Follow-up studies by Noble's group have also shown that lower SES is associated with reduced white matter volume and reduced cognitive flexibility, as well as age-related differences in cortical thickness (Ursache & Noble, 2016).

Low SES is associated with poor nutrition, high stress, and insufficient prenatal and infant care. Following on Heckman's thesis, investing in children from low-income families will increase societal health and prosperity because these children can optimize their brain development and realize their developmental potential. Policies aimed toward decreasing poverty can lead to clear improvements in children's cognitive and brain development.

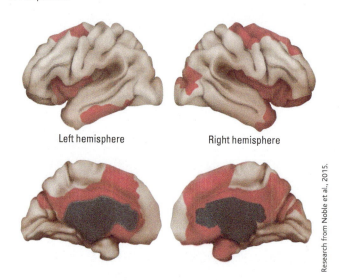

Left hemisphere   Right hemisphere

Research from Noble et al., 2015.

After adjusting for age, sex, race, and parental education, Noble and colleagues associated family income with cortical surface area. Areal brain regions shown in red were significantly smaller in children from low-SES families.

To see how scientists go about studying the interconnected processes of brain and behavioral development, think about all the architectural parallels between how the brain is constructed and how a house is built. House plans are drawn as blueprints; the plans for a brain are encoded in genes. Architects do not specify every detail in a blueprint, nor do genes include every instruction for brain assembly and wiring.

The brain is too complex to be encoded entirely and precisely in genes. This leaves the fate of billions of brain cells partly undecided, especially in regard to the massive undertaking of forming appropriate connections between cells.

If the structure and fate of each brain cell are not specified in advance, what controls brain development? Many factors are at work, and, as with house building, brain development is influenced by the environment in the course of the construction phase and by the quality of the materials. For example, as we saw in Research Focus 8-1, Linking Socioeconomic Status to Cortical Development, living in poverty can compromise children's brain development.

We can shed light on nervous system development by viewing its architecture from different vantage points—structural, functional, and environmental. In this chapter, we consider the neurobiology of development first, explore behavioral correlates of developing brain functions next, and then explore how experiences and environments influence neuroplasticity over the life span.

8-1

Three Perspectives on Brain Development

Brain and behavior develop apace, and scientists thus reason that the two are closely linked. Events that alter behavioral development should similarly alter the brain's structural development and vice versa. As the brain develops, neurons become more and more intricately connected, and these increasingly complex interconnections underlie increasingly complex behaviors. These observations enable neuroscientists to study the relationship between brain and behavioral development from three perspectives:

1. Structural development can be correlated with emerging behaviors.

2. Behavioral development can be predicted by the underlying circuitry that must be emerging.

3. Research can focus on factors such as hormones, injury, or socioeconomic status (SES) that influence both brain structure and behavioral development.

Correlating Emerging Brain Structures with Emerging Behaviors

We can look at the nervous system's structural development and correlate it with the emergence of specific behaviors. For example, the development of certain brain structures links to the motor development of, say, grasping or crawling in infants. As brain structures mature, their functions emerge and develop, as manifested in behaviors we can observe.

Neural structures that develop quickly—the visual system, for instance—exhibit their functions sooner than do structures that develop more slowly, such as those used for speech. Because the human brain continues to develop well into adulthood, some abilities emerge or mature rather late. Some cognitive behaviors controlled by the frontal lobes are among the last to develop. One such behavior, the ability to plan efficiently, is a skill vital to many complexities of life, including organizing daily activities or making travel plans.

The Tower of Hanoi test, illustrated in **Figure 8-1**, shows how planning skills can be measured in the laboratory. The task is to plan how to move colored discs one by one, in the minimum number of moves, from one configuration to another. Most 10-year-olds can solve simple configurations, but more difficult versions of the task, such as that shown in Figure 8-1, cannot be performed efficiently until about age 15 to 17. No surprise, then, that adolescents often appear disorganized: their ability to plan has yet to mature.

Mature adults with acquired frontal lobe injuries also fail to perform well on the Tower of Hanoi test. Such evidence reinforces the idea that children are not miniature adults who simply need to learn the "rules" of adult behavior. A child's brain is vastly different from an adult's, and the brains of children at different ages are not really comparable, either.

GOAL

Move discs on towers below one by one to match goal above.

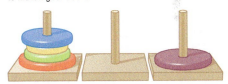

FIGURE 8-1 **Testing Cognitive Development** The Tower of Hanoi is a mathematical puzzle consisting of three rods and several different-sized discs. The task is to match the goal in as few moves as possible, obeying two rules: (1) only one disc may be moved at a time and (2) no disc may be placed on top of a smaller disc.

Correlating Emerging Behaviors with Neural Maturation

We can turn our focus around and scrutinize behavior for the emergence of new abilities, and then we can infer underlying neural maturation. For example, as language emerges in a young child, we expect to find corresponding changes in neural structures that control language. In fact, neuroscientists do find such changes.

At birth, children do not speak, and even extensive training would not enable them to do so because the neural structures that control language production are not yet ready. Thus, as language emerges, the speech-related structures in the brain are undergoing the necessary maturation.

The same reasoning can be applied to frontal lobe development. As frontal lobe structures mature through adolescence and into early adulthood, we look for related changes in behavior. We can also do the reverse: because we observe new abilities emerging in the teenage years and even later, we infer that they must be controlled by late-maturing neural structures and connections.

Identifying Influences on Brain and Behavior

The third approach to developmental interrelations between brain and behavior is to identify and study factors that influence both. From this perspective, the mere emergence of a fully developed brain structure is not enough. We must also know the events that shape how that structure functions and produces behaviors. Some events that influence brain function are sensory experience, injuries, the actions of hormones and genes, and SES.

Logically, if one factor influences behavior, then the brain structures changed by that factor are those responsible for the behavioral outcomes. For example, we might study how the atypical secretion of a hormone affects both a certain brain structure and a certain behavior. We can then infer that because the observed behavior results from the change in brain structure functioning, the structure must typically play some role in controlling the behavior. For example, the presence of testosterone in early development typically occurs only in males and results in changes in the organization and function of specific hypothalamic nuclei. But if the amount of testosterone release is low or if the release occurs at a different developmental time in males, or, alternatively, occurs in females, the structure of the hypothalamus may be altered and, consequently, so may sexual preference and perhaps gender identity.

Section 12-5 offers a detailed discussion of the mechanisms that control nonregulatory behavior, including sexual behavior.

8-1 Review

Before you continue, check your understanding. Answers to Self-Test appear at the back of the book.

1. Structural brain development is correlated with the emergence of _____.

2. Behavioral development predicts the maturation of _____.

3. Three factors that influence brain function are _____, _____, and _____.

4. What important constraint determines when behaviors emerge?

For additional study tools, visit ✖ **LaunchPad** at launchpadworks.com

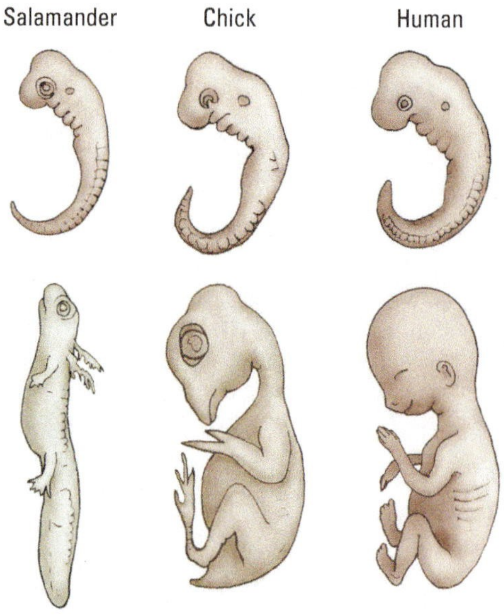

Salamander   Chick   Human

FIGURE 8-2 **Embryos and Evolution** The physical similarity of embryos of different species is striking in the earliest stages of development, as the salamander, chick, and human embryos in the top row show. This similarity led to the conclusion that embryos are not simply miniature versions of adults.

8-2

Neurobiology of Development

Some 2000 years ago, the Roman philosopher Seneca the Younger proposed that a human embryo is an adult in miniature, and thus the task of development is simply to grow bigger. This idea of *preformation* was so appealing that it was widely believed for centuries. Even with the development of the microscope, the appeal of preformation proved so strong that biologists claimed to see microscopic horses in horse semen.

By the mid-1800s, preformation began to lose ground as people realized that embryos look nothing like the adults they become. In fact, it was obvious that embryos of different species more closely resemble one another than their respective parents. The top row of **Figure 8-2** shows the striking similarity among embryos of species as diverse as salamanders, chickens, and humans, each shown in fetal form in the bottom row.

As embryos, all vertebrate species have a similar-looking primitive head, a region with bumps or folds, and a tail. Only as an embryo develops does it acquire the distinctive characteristics of its species. The similarity of young embryos is so great that many nineteenth-century biologists saw it as evidence for Darwin's view that all vertebrates arose from a common ancestor millions of years ago.

The embryonic nervous systems of vertebrates are as similar structurally as their bodies are. **Figure 8-3** details the three-chambered brain of a young vertebrate embryo: forebrain, midbrain, and hindbrain. The remaining neural tube forms the spinal cord. How do these three regions develop? We can trace the events as the embryo matures.

Gross Development of the Human Nervous System

When a sperm fertilizes an egg, the resulting human zygote consists of just a single cell. But this cell soon begins to divide. By the fifteenth day after fertilization, the emerging embryo resembles a fried egg (**Figure 8-4**), a structure formed by several sheets of cells with a raised area in the middle called the *embryonic disc*—essentially the primitive body.

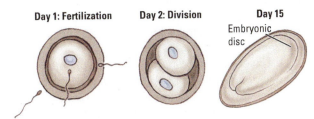

Day 1: Fertilization   Day 2: Division   Day 15
Embryonic disc

FIGURE 8-4 **From Fertilization to Embryo** Development begins at fertilization (day 1), with the formation of the zygote. On day 2, the zygote begins to divide. On day 15, the raised embryonic disc begins to form. Information from Moore, 1988.

By 3 weeks after conception, primitive neural tissue, the **neural plate**, occupies part of the outermost layer of embryonic cells. First, the neural plate folds to form the *neural groove*, detailed in **Figure 8-5**. The neural groove then curls to form the **neural tube**, much as you can curl a flat sheet of paper to make a cylinder.

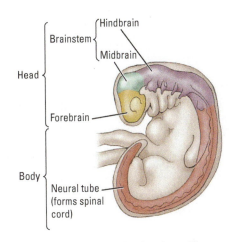

FIGURE 8-3 **Embryonic Vertebrate Nervous System** Forebrain, midbrain, and hindbrain are visible in the human embryo at about 28 days, as is the remaining neural tube, which will form the spinal cord.

Prenatal Stages	
Zygote	Fertilization to 2 weeks
Embryo	2 to 8 weeks
Fetus	9 weeks to birth

neural plate Primitive neural tissue that gives rise to the neural tube.

neural tube Structure in the early stage of brain development from which the brain and spinal cord develop.

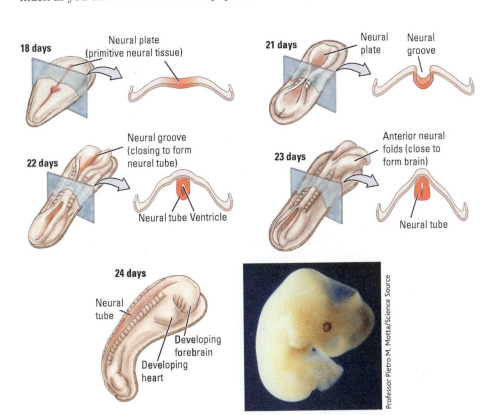

FIGURE 8-5 **Formation of the Neural Tube** A long depression, the neural groove, first forms in the neural plate. By day 21, the primitive brain and neural groove are visible. On day 23, the neural tube is forming as the neural plate collapses inward along the length of the embryo's dorsal surface. The embryo is shown in a photograph at 24 days.

(A) Day 9   **(B) Day 10**   **(C) Day 11**

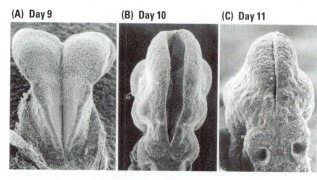

FIGURE 8-6 **Neural Tube Development**
Scanning electron micrographs show the neural tube closing in a mouse embryo. Reproduced with the permission of Prof. Dr. R. E. Poelmann, Dept. Cardiology, Leiden University Medical Center, Leiden University Medical Center, Institute of Biology IBL, University of Leiden, Leiden, The Netherlands.

Gyri and sulci are introduced in Section 2-1.

Adult stem cells that line the subventricular zone also are located in the hippocampus, spinal cord, and retina.

neural stem cell Self-renewing multipotential cell that gives rise to any of the different types of neurons and glia in the nervous system.

subventricular zone Lining of neural stem cells surrounding the ventricles in adults.

progenitor cell (precursor cell) Cell derived from a stem cell that migrates and produces a neuron or a glial cell.

neuroblast Product of a progenitor cell that gives rise to any of the different types of neurons.

glioblast Product of a progenitor cell that gives rise to different types of glial cells.

The cells that form the neural tube can be regarded as the nursery for the rest of the central nervous system. The open region in the tube's center remains open and matures into the brain's ventricles and the spinal canal. The micrographs in **Figure 8-6** show the neural tube closing in a mouse embryo.

The human body and nervous system change rapidly in the ensuing 3 weeks (**Figure 8-7**). By 7 weeks (49 days), the embryo begins to resemble a person. The brain looks distinctly human by about 100 days after conception, but it does not begin to form *gyri* and *sulci* until about 7 months. By the end of the ninth month, the fetal brain has the gross appearance of the adult human brain, but its cellular structure is different.

Origins of Neurons and Glia

As we have noted, the neural tube is the brain's nursery. **Neural stem cells** lining it have an extensive capacity for self-renewal. When a stem cell divides, it produces two stem cells; one dies and the other lives to divide again. This process repeats again and again throughout life. In an adult human, neural stem cells line the ventricles, forming the **subventricular zone**.

If lining the ventricles were all that stem cells did throughout the decades of a human life, they would seem very odd cells to possess. But neural stem cells have a function beyond self-renewal: they give rise to **progenitor cells (precursor cells)**, which also can divide. As shown in **Figure 8-8**, progenitor cells eventually produce nondividing cells known as **neuroblasts** and **glioblasts**. In turn, neuroblasts and glioblasts mature into neurons and glia. Neural stem cells, then, are *multipotent*: they give rise to all the many specialized cell types in the CNS.

Sam Weiss and his colleagues (1996) discovered that stem cells remain capable of producing neurons and glia not just into early adulthood but even in an aging brain. This important discovery implies that neurons that die in an adult brain should be replaceable. But neuroscientists do not yet know how to instruct stem cells to replace them.

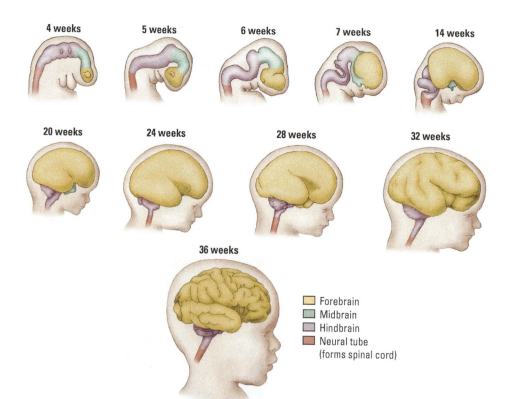

FIGURE 8-7 **Prenatal Brain Development**
The developing human brain undergoes a series of embryonic and fetal stages. You can identify the forebrain, midbrain, and hindbrain by color (review Figure 8-3) as they develop in the course of gestation. At 6 months, the developing forebrain has enveloped the midbrain structures. Research from Cowan, 1979.

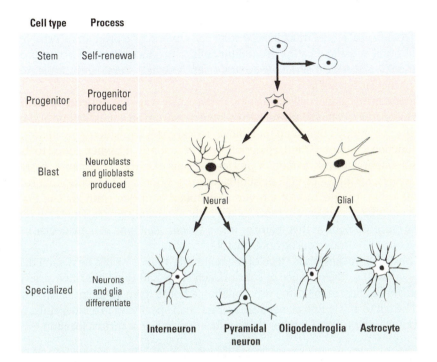

Cell type   **Process**

Stem — Self-renewal

Progenitor — Progenitor produced

Blast — Neuroblasts and glioblasts produced

Neural   Glial

Specialized — Neurons and glia differentiate

Interneuron   Pyramidal neuron   Oligodendroglia   Astrocyte

FIGURE 8-8 **Origin of Brain Cells** Cells in the brain begin as multipotential stem cells, develop into precursor cells, then produce blasts that finally develop into specialized neurons or glia.

One possibility is to make use of signals that the brain typically uses to control stem cell production in adults. For example, the level of the neuropeptide *prolactin* increases when female mice are pregnant and stimulates the fetal brain to produce more neurons. These naturally occurring hormonal signals have been shown to replace lost neurons in brain-injured laboratory animals (see reviews by Bond et al., 2015, and Faiz & Morshead, 2018).

How does a stem cell know to become a neuron rather than a skin cell? In each cell, certain genes are expressed (turned on) by a signal, and those genes then produce a particular cell type. *Gene expression* is a process whereby information from a gene is used in the synthesis of a gene product, such as a protein. You can easily imagine that certain proteins produce skin cells, whereas other proteins produce neurons. Similarly, certain proteins produce one type of neuron, such as pyramidal cells, whereas others might produce granule cells.

The specific signals for gene expression are largely unknown but are probably chemical, and they form the basis of epigenetics. A common epigenetic mechanism that suppresses gene expression during development is *gene methylation*, or *DNA methylation*. In this process, a methyl group (CH_3) attaches to the nucleotide base cytosine lying next to guanine on the DNA sequence. It is relatively simple to quantify gene methylation in different phenotypes, reflecting either an increase or a decrease in overall gene expression.

Methylation alters gene expression dramatically during development. Prenatal stress can reduce gene methylation by 10 percent. This means that prenatally stressed infants express 2000 more genes (of the more than 20,000 in the human genome) than unstressed infants (Mychasiuk et al., 2011). Other epigenetic mechanisms, such as histone modification and mRNA modification, can regulate gene expression, but these mechanisms are more difficult to quantify.

Thus, the chemical environment of a brain cell is different from that of cells elsewhere in the body: different genes in brain cells are activated, producing different proteins and different cell types. The chemical environments needed to trigger cellular differentiation could be produced by the activity of neighboring cells or by chemicals, such as hormones, that are transported in the bloodstream.

Protein synthesis is described in more detail in Section 3-2, and the epigenetic factors influencing gene expression are discussed in Section 3-3.

Figure 3-25 (excerpted below), showing gene methylation, contrasts the mechanisms of histone and mRNA modification to DNA methylation.

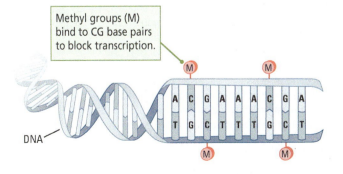

Methyl groups (M) bind to CG base pairs to block transcription.

DNA

neurotrophic factor Chemical compound that supports growth and differentiation in developing neurons and may act to keep certain neurons alive in adulthood.

The differentiation of stem cells into neurons requires a series of gene-activating signals. A chemical signal must induce stem cells to produce progenitor cells; another chemical signal must induce the progenitor cells to produce either neuroblasts or glioblasts. Finally, a chemical signal—perhaps a set of signals—must induce the genes to make a particular type of neuron.

Compounds that signal cells to develop in particular ways are **neurotrophic factors** (*trophic* means "nourishing"). By removing stem cells from an animal's brain and placing those cells in solutions that keep them alive, researchers can study how neurotrophic factors function. One compound, *epidermal growth factor* (EGF), when added to the stem cell culture stimulates production of progenitor cells. Another compound, *basic fibroblast growth factor* (bFGF, or FGF-2), stimulates progenitor cells to produce neuroblasts.

At this point, the destiny of a given neuroblast is undetermined. The blast can become any type of neuron if it receives the right chemical signals. The body relies on a general-purpose neuron that matures into a specific cell type in a particular location when exposed to certain neurotrophic factors.

This flexibility makes brain development simpler than it would be if each different cell type, as well as the number of cells of each type, had to be specified precisely in an organism's genes. In the same way, building a house from all-purpose two-by-fours that can be cut to any length as needed is easier than specifying in a blueprint a precise number of precut pieces of lumber that can be used only in a certain location.

TABLE 8-1 Stages of Brain Development

1. Cell birth (neurogenesis; gliogenesis)
2. Neural migration
3. Cell differentiation
4. Neural maturation (dendrite and axon growth)
5. Synaptogenesis (formation of synapses)
6. Cell death and synaptic pruning
7. Myelogenesis (formation of myelin)

In Research Focus 8-1, investigators used cortical development as a measure of the effects of SES.

Neuronal Growth and Development

The human brain requires approximately 10 billion (10^{10}) cells to form just the cortex that blankets a single hemisphere. This means it must produce about 250,000 neurons per minute at the peak of prenatal brain development. But as **Table 8-1** shows, this rapid formation of neurons (neurogenesis) and glia (gliogenesis) is just the first step in brain growth. These new cells must travel to the correct destination (*migration*), they must differentiate into the right type of neuron or glial cell, and the neurons must then grow dendrites and axons and form synapses.

The brain also prunes unnecessary cells and connections, sculpting itself according to the particular person's experiences and needs. We consider these stages in brain development next, focusing on cortical development, because neuroscientists know more about development of the cortex than of any other area of the human brain. The principles derived from our examination of the cortex, however, apply to neural growth and development in other brain regions as well.

Neuronal Generation, Migration, and Differentiation

Figure 8-9 shows that neurogenesis is largely complete after about 25 weeks of gestation. (Some growth continues until about 5 years of age.) An important exception is the hippocampus, where new neurons continue to develop throughout life.

FIGURE 8-9 **Prenatal Development of the Human Cerebral Cortex** Brain weight and body weight increase rapidly and in proportion. The cortex begins to form about 6 weeks after conception, with neurogenesis largely complete by 25 weeks. Neural migration and cell differentiation begin at about 8 weeks and are largely complete by about 29 weeks. Neuron maturation, including axon and dendrite growth, begins at about 20 weeks and continues until well after birth. Information from Marin-Padilla, 1993.

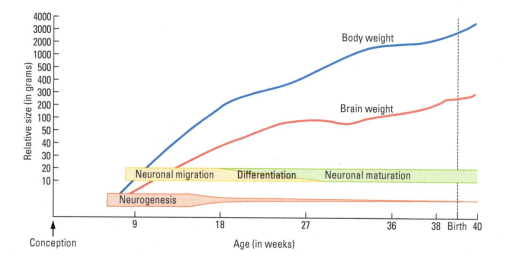

Until after full-term birth, however, the fetal brain is especially delicate and extremely vulnerable to injury, *teratogens* (chemicals that cause malformations), and trauma. Apparently, the developing brain can more easily cope with injury earlier, during neurogenesis, than it can during the later stages of cell migration or cell differentiation, when cell maturation begins (see Table 8-1). One reason may be that once neurogenesis has slowed, it is very hard to start it up again. If neurogenesis is still progressing at a high rate, more neurons can be made to replace injured ones, or perhaps existing neurons can be allocated differently.

The absence of neurogenesis in adulthood, other than in the hippocampus, also explains why adult brain tumors arise from glial cells, which are generated throughout adulthood, rather than from neurons. In contrast, brain tumors in young children are sometimes neuronal, reflecting some lingering neurogenesis.

Cell migration begins shortly after the first neurons are generated and continues for about 6 weeks in the cerebral cortex (and throughout life in the hippocampus). Cell differentiation, in which neuroblasts become specific types of neurons, follows migration. Cell differentiation is essentially complete at birth, although neuron maturation, which includes the growth of dendrites, axons, and synapses, goes on for years and in some parts of the brain may continue throughout adulthood.

The cortex is organized into layers distinctly different from one another in their cellular makeup. How does this arrangement of differentiated areas develop? Neuroscientist Pasko Rakic and his colleagues (e.g., Geschwind & Rakic, 2013) have been finding answers to this question for more than four decades. Apparently, the subventricular zone contains a primitive cortical map that predisposes cells formed in a certain ventricular region to migrate to a certain cortical location. One subventricular region may produce cells destined to migrate to the visual cortex; another might produce cells destined to migrate to the frontal lobes, for example.

How do the migrating cells know where to find these different parts of the cortex? They follow a path made by **radial glial cells**. A glial fiber from each of these path-making cells extends from the subventricular zone to the cortical surface, as illustrated in **Figure 8-10A**. The close-up views in Figures 8-10B and C show that neural cells from a given subventricular region need only follow the glial road to end up in the correct location.

As the brain grows, the glial fibers stretch but still go to the same place. Figure 8-10B also shows a cell moving across the radial glial fibers. Although most cortical neurons follow the radial glial fibers, a small number appear to migrate by seeking some type of chemical signal.

radial glial cell Path-making cell that a migrating neuron follows to its appropriate destination.

Clinical Focus 11-2 describes outcomes resulting from cerebral palsy, caused by brain trauma acquired perinatally.

The hippocampus (see Figure 2-25) is critical to memory (Section 14-3) and vulnerable to stress (Section 6-5).

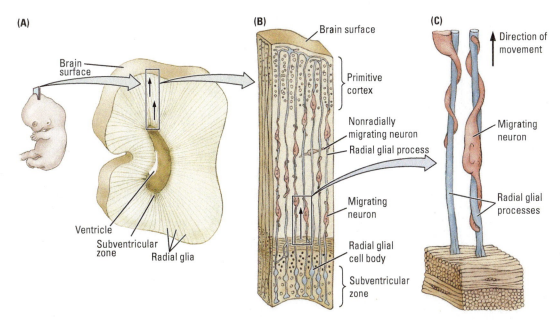

(A)

Brain surface

Ventricle

Subventricular zone

Radial glia

(B)

Brain surface

Primitive cortex

Nonradially migrating neuron

Radial glial process

Migrating neuron

Radial glial cell body

Subventricular zone

(C)

Direction of movement

Migrating neuron

Radial glial processes

FIGURE 8-10 **Neuronal Migration** **(A)** Neuroscientists hypothesize that the cortical map is represented in the subventricular zone. **(B)** Radial glial fibers extend from the subventricular zone to the cortical surface. **(C)** Neurons migrate along the radial glial fibers that take them from the protomap in the subventricular zone to the corresponding region in the cortex. Information from Rakic, 1974.

Figure 2-22 contrasts the sensory and motor cortices' six distinct layers and their functions.

Cortical layers develop from the inside out, much like adding floors to a house. The neurons of innermost layer VI migrate to their locations first, followed by those destined for layer V and so on, as successive waves of neurons pass earlier-arriving neurons to assume progressively more exterior positions in the cortex. And, as with building a house from the ground up, where materials needed to build higher floors must pass through lower floors to get to their destinations, so do the new cells migrate through the lower layers.

To facilitate house construction, each new story has a blueprint-specified dimension, such as 10 feet high. How do neurons determine how thick a cortical layer should be? This is a tough question, especially when you consider that the cortical layers are not all the same thickness.

Local environmental signals—chemicals produced by other cells—likely influence the way cells form layers in the cortex. These intercellular signals progressively restrict the choice of traits a cell can express, as illustrated in **Figure 8-11**. Thus, the emergence of distinct cell types in the brain results not from the unfolding of a specific genetic program but rather from the interaction of genetic instructions, timing, and signals from other cells in the local environment.

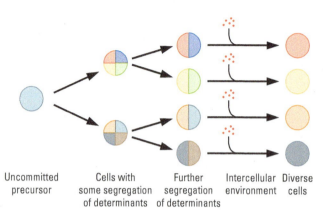

Uncommitted precursor | Cells with some segregation of determinants | Further segregation of determinants | Intercellular environment | Diverse cells

FIGURE 8-11 **Cellular Commitment** As also shown in Figure 8-8, precursor cells have unlimited possibilities, but as they develop, interacting genetic, maturational, and environmental influences increasingly steer them toward developing into a particular cell type.

Neuronal Maturation

After neurons migrate to their destination and differentiate, they begin to mature by first growing dendrites to provide surface area for synapses with other cells and then extending their axons to appropriate targets to initiate synapse formation.

Two events take place in dendrite development: dendritic arborization (branching) and the growth of dendritic spines. As illustrated in **Figure 8-12**, dendrites in newborn babies begin as individual processes protruding from the cell body. In the first 2 years of life, dendrites undergo arborization: They develop increasingly complex extensions that look much like leafless tree branches. The dendritic branches then begin to form spines, where most synapses on dendrites are located.

Although dendritic development begins prenatally in humans, it continues for a long time after birth, as Figure 8-12 shows. Dendritic growth proceeds at a slow rate, on the order of microns (μm, millionths of a meter) per day. Contrast this with the development of axons, which grow on the order of a millimeter per day—about a thousand times faster.

Recall from Section 3-1 that dendrites collect information and that axons transmit information to other neurons.

The disparate developmental rates of axons and dendrites are important because the faster-growing axon can reach its target cell before the cell's dendrites are

FIGURE 8-12 **Neuronal Maturation in Cortical Language Areas** In postnatal cortical differentiation—shown here around Broca's area, which controls speaking—neurons begin with simple dendritic fields that become progressively more complex until a child reaches about 2 years old. Brain maturation thus parallels a behavioral development: the emergence of language. Book: E. Lenneberg. Biological Foundations of Language, New York: Wiley, 1967, pp. 160–161.

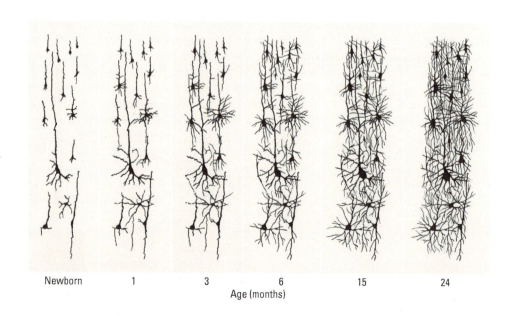

Newborn   1   3   6   15   24

Age (months)

completely formed. Thus, the axon may play a role in dendritic differentiation and ultimately in neuron function—for example, as part of the brain's visual, motor, or language circuitry. Abnormalities in neuronal maturation rate can produce abnormalities in patterns of neural connectivity, as explained in Clinical Focus 8-2, Autism Spectrum Disorder.

autism spectrum disorder (ASD) Range of cognitive symptoms from mild to severe that characterize autism; severe symptoms include greatly impaired social interaction, a bizarre and narrow range of interests, marked abnormalities in language and communication, and fixed, repetitive movements.

◎ CLINICAL FOCUS 8-2

Autism Spectrum Disorder

In the 1940s, Leo Kanner and Hans Asperger first used the term *autism* (from the Greek *autos*, meaning "self") to describe children who seem to live in their own world. Some were classified as intellectually disabled; others seemed to function intellectually.

The contemporary term **autism spectrum disorder (ASD)** accommodates this behavioral range to include children with mild and severe symptoms. Severe symptoms include greatly impaired social interaction, a bizarre and narrow range of interests, marked abnormalities in language and communication, and fixed, repetitive movements.

The autism spectrum includes classic autism and related disorders. *Asperger syndrome*, for example, is distinguished by an obsessive interest in a single topic or object to the exclusion of nearly any other. Children with Asperger are socially awkward and also usually have delayed motor skill development. *Rett syndrome*, characterized by poor expressive language and clumsy hand use, almost exclusively affects girls.

The rate of ASD has been rising over the past four decades, from fewer than 1 person in 2000 in 1980 to the 2016 estimate by the Centers for Disease Control and Prevention that as many as 1 in 68 children has some form of autism. The cause of this increased incidence is uncertain. Suggestions include changes in diagnostic criteria, diagnosis of children at a younger age, and epigenetic influences. Although it knows neither racial nor ethnic nor social boundaries, ASD is four times as prevalent in boys as in girls.

The behavior of many children with ASD is noticeable from birth. To avoid physical contact, these babies arch their backs and pull away from caregivers or grow limp when held. But approximately one-third of children develop typically until somewhere between 1 and 3 years of age, when symptoms of autism emerge.

Perhaps the most recognized characteristics of ASD are failure to interact socially, repetitive rocking or hand flapping, impairments in language development, and resistance to any change in routine. Some children on the autism spectrum are severely impaired; others learn to function quite well. Still others display *savant syndrome*, a narrow range of exceptional abilities such as in music, art, or mathematics, often accompanied by severe cognitive deficits.

The brains of children diagnosed with ASD look remarkably typical. One emerging view is that these brains are characterized by unusual neuronal maturation rates. MRI studies show that at about 6 months of age, the autistic brain's growth rate accelerates to the point that its total volume is 6 percent to 10 percent greater than that of typical children.

Excessive brain volume is especially clear in the amygdala (Nordahl et al., 2012) and in the temporal and frontal lobes, the latter showing greater gray matter volume (see the review by Chen et al., 2011). The subcortical amygdala plays an important role in generating fear, and the social withdrawal component of ASD may be related to the enlarged amygdala.

Accelerated brain growth associated with enlarged regions suggests that connections between cerebral regions are atypical, which would in

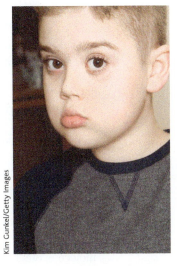 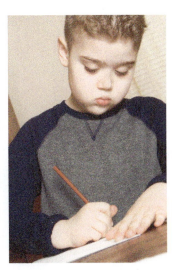

Kim Gunkel/Getty Images

Children with ASD often look typical, but some physical anomalies do characterize the condition. The corners of the mouth may be low compared with the upper lip (left), and the tops of the ears may flop over (right). The ears may be a bit lower than average and have an almost square shape.

turn produce atypical functioning. What leads to such brain development? More than 100 genetic differences have been described in children with ASD, so it is clear that no "autism gene" is at work.

The mechanism that translates genetic irregularities into the autistic brain is unknown but likely includes epigenetic factors that could be prenatal, postnatal, or both. Women who have been exposed to rubella (German measles) in the first trimester of pregnancy have an increased risk of giving birth to a child who develops ASD. Researchers also suspect that industrial toxins can trigger autism, but the cause or causes remain uncertain.

No medical interventions exist for ASD. Behavioral therapies are the most successful, provided they are intense (20 to 40 hours per week) and the therapists are trained practitioners. The earlier interventions begin, the better the prognosis. Neuroscience has so far offered little insight into why behavioral therapies are effective, although in an animal model of autism, Raza and colleagues (2015) showed that tactile stimulation from birth until weaning reverses many morphological abnormalities in cortical neurons, suggesting a possible mechanism.

Autism may appear puzzling because no evolutionary advantage for its symptoms is apparent, but perhaps one exists. Characteristically, children with ASD are overly focused on specific tasks or information. The ability to concentrate on a complex problem for extended periods, it is suggested, is the basis for humankind's development and for cultural advances. But too much of such a good thing may lead to conditions such as ASD.

FIGURE 8-13 **Seeking a Path (A)** At the tip of this axon, nurtured in a culture, a growth cone sends out filopodia seeking specific molecules to guide the axon's direction of growth. **(B)** Filopodia guide the growth cone toward a target cell that is releasing cell adhesion or tropic molecules, represented in the drawing by red dots. Courtesy of Dennis Bray.

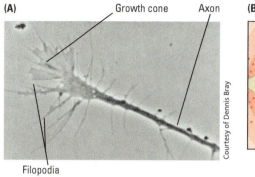

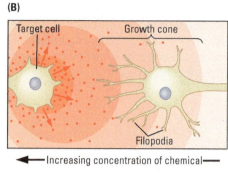

Axon connections present a significant engineering problem for the developing brain. An axon might connect to a cell that is millimeters or even a meter away in the developing brain, and the axon must find its way through complex cellular terrain to get there. Genetic–environmental interaction is at work again, as various molecules that attract or repel the approaching axon tip guide the formation of axonic connections.

Santiago Ramón y Cajal was the first scientist to describe this developmental process a century ago. He called the growing tips of axons **growth cones. Figure 8-13A** shows that as growth cones extend, they send out shoots, analogous to fingers reaching out to find a pen on a cluttered desk. When one shoot, known as a **filopod** (pl. filopodia), reaches an appropriate target, the others follow.

Growth cones are responsive to cues from two types of molecules (Figure 8-13B):

1. **Cell adhesion molecules (CAMs)** are cell-manufactured molecules that either lie on the target cell's surface or are secreted into the intercellular space. Some provide a surface to which growth cones can adhere, hence the name cellular adhesion molecule; others serve to attract or repel growth cones.

2. **Tropic molecules**, produced by the targets that the axons' growth cones are seeking (*tropic* means "moving toward"; pronounced as in *trope*, not *tropical*), essentially tell growth cones to come over here (chemoattractive). They likely also tell other growth cones seeking different targets to keep away (chemorepulsive).

Although Ramón y Cajal predicted their existence more than 100 years ago, tropic molecules have proved difficult to find. The best understood chemoattractive molecules are the **netrins** (from Sanskrit, meaning "to guide"). But the guidance of axon growth also entails telling axons where *not* to go. One class of these chemorepulsive molecules is called the **semaphorins** (Greek for "signal"), which act to prevent axon extension in their vicinity.

Do not confuse *tropic* (guiding) molecules with the *trophic* (nourishing) molecules, discussed earlier, which support neuronal growth.

Synaptic Development

The number of synapses in the human cerebral cortex is staggering, on the order of 10^{14}, or 100,000 trillion. A genetic program that assigns each synapse a specific location could not possibly determine each spot for this huge number. As with all other stages of brain development, only the general outlines of neuronal connections in the brain are likely to be genetically predetermined. The vast array of specific synaptic contacts is then guided into place by a variety of local environmental cues and signals.

A human fetus displays simple synaptic contacts in the fifth gestational month. By the seventh gestational month, synaptic development on the deepest cortical neurons is extensive. After birth, synapse numbers increase rapidly. In the visual cortex, synaptic density almost doubles between ages 2 months and 4 months and then continues to increase until age 1 year. Not all synapses in the developing visual cortex are visually related, however, leading to a phenomenon called *synesthesia*, which is the ability to perceive a sensation of one sense as a sensation of another sense, as when sound leads to a sense of color (see Section 15-5 for a more detailed discussion of this phenomenon).

growth cone Growing tip of an axon.

filopod (pl. filopodia) Process at the end of a developing axon that reaches out to search for a potential target or to sample the intercellular environment.

cell adhesion molecule (CAM) Chemical molecule to which specific cells can adhere, thus aiding in migration.

tropic molecule Signaling molecule that attracts or repels growth cones.

netrin Member of chemoattractive tropic molecules that guide axon growth.

semaphorins Class of chemorepulsive molecules that deflect axons from inappropriate regions.

Cell Death and Synaptic Pruning

To carve statues, sculptors begin with blocks of stone and chisel away the unwanted pieces. The brain does something similar during cell death and synaptic pruning. The chisel in the brain could be a genetic signal, an experience, reproductive hormones, stress, or even SES. The effects of these chisels can be seen in changes in cortical thickness over time, as illustrated in **Figure 8-14**, an atlas of brain images. The cortex actually becomes measurably thinner in a caudal–rostral (back-to-front) gradient, a process that is probably due both to synaptic pruning and to white matter expansion. This expansion stretches the cortex, leading to increased surface area, as illustrated in Research Focus 8-1.

The graph in **Figure 8-15** plots this rise and fall in synaptic density. Pasko Rakic (1974) estimated that at the peak of synapse loss, a person may lose as many as 100,000 per second. Synapse elimination is extensive and prolonged. Peter Huttenlocher (1994) estimated that the process affects 42 percent in the human cortex and, in the prefrontal cortex, it continues into an individual's thirties. We can only wonder what the behavioral consequence of this rapid synaptic loss might be. It is probably no coincidence that children, especially toddlers and adolescents, seem to change moods and behaviors quickly.

How does the brain eliminate excess neurons? The simplest explanation is competition, sometimes referred to as **neural Darwinism**. Charles Darwin believed that one key to evolution is the variation it produces in the traits possessed by a species. Those whose traits are best suited to the local environment are most likely to survive. From a Darwinian perspective, then, more animals are born than can survive to adulthood, and environmental pressures weed out the less fit ones. Similar pressures cause neural Darwinism.

What exactly causes this cellular weeding out in the brain? It turns out that when neurons form synapses, they become somewhat dependent on their targets for survival. In fact, deprived of synaptic targets, neurons eventually die. They die because target cells produce neurotrophic (nourishing) factors absorbed by the axon terminals that function to regulate neuronal survival. *Nerve growth factor* (NGF), for example, is made by cortical cells and absorbed by cholinergic neurons in the basal forebrain.

If many neurons compete for a limited amount of a neurotrophic factor, only some can survive. The death of neurons deprived of a neurotrophic factor is different from the cell death caused by injury or disease. When neurons are deprived of a neurotrophic factor, certain genes seem to be expressed, resulting in a message for the cell to die. This programmed process is called **apoptosis**.

Apoptosis accounts for the death of overabundant neurons, but it does not account for the synaptic pruning from cells that survive. In 1976, French neurobiologist Jean-Pierre Changeux proposed a theory for synapse loss that also is based on competition (Changeux & Danchin, 1976). According to Changeux, synapses persist into adulthood only if they have become members of functional neural networks. If not, they are eventually eliminated from the brain. We can speculate that environmental factors such as hormones, drugs, and experience would influence active neural circuit formation and thus influence synapse stabilization and pruning.

In addition to outright errors in synapse formation that give rise to synaptic pruning, subtler changes in neural circuits may trigger the same process. One such change accounts for the findings of Janet Werker and Richard Tees (1992), who studied the ability of infants to discriminate speech sounds taken from widely disparate languages, such as English, Hindi (from India), and Salish (a Native American language). Their results show that young infants can discriminate speech sounds of different languages without previous experience, but their ability to do so declines in the first year of life. An explanation for this declining ability is that

FIGURE 8-14 **Progressive Changes in Cortical Thickness** MRI scans track the maturation of gray matter in typical development, revealing the length and pattern of maturation from the back of the cortex to the front. Cortical thinning and increased surface area progress together. Courtesy Paul M Thompson/Laboratory of Neuro Imaging, Keck School of Medicine of USC.

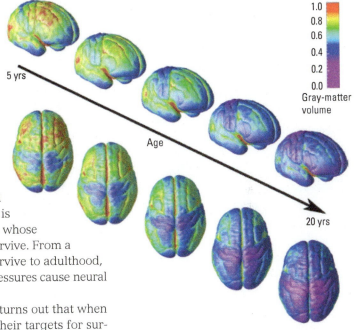

neural Darwinism Hypothesis that the processes of cell death and synaptic pruning are, like natural selection in species, the outcome of competition among neurons for connections and metabolic resources in a neural environment.

apoptosis Genetically programmed cell death.

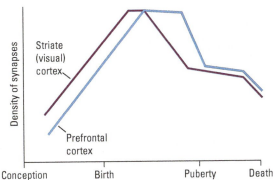

FIGURE 8-15 **Synapse Formation and Pruning** Changes in the relative density of synapses in the human visual cortex and prefrontal cortex (its frontmost part) as a function of age. Data from Bourgeois, 2001.

FIGURE 8-16 **Gray Matter Thickness** Brain maps showing the statistical significance of yearly change in cortical thickness measures taken from MRIs. Shading represents increasing (white) or decreasing (red) cortical thickness.
Research from Sowell, Thompson, & Toga, 2004.

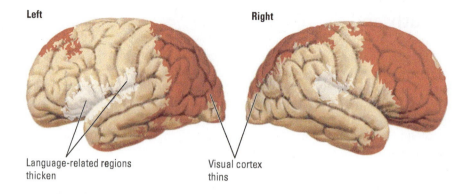

dorsolateral prefrontal cortex (DLPFC) Brodmann areas 9 and 46; makes reciprocal connections with posterior parietal cortex and superior temporal sulcus; responsible for selecting behavior and movement with respect to temporal memory.

default network Brain network of interacting regions of the frontal and parietal lobes that have highly correlated activity.

synapses encoding speech sounds not typically encountered in an infant's daily environment are not active simultaneously with other speech-related synapses. As a result, they are eliminated.

Synaptic pruning may also allow the brain to adapt more flexibly to environmental demands. Human culture is probably the most diverse and complex environment with which any animal must cope. Perhaps the flexibility in cortical organization achieved by the mechanism of selective synaptic pruning is a necessary precondition for successful development in a cultural environment.

Synaptic pruning may also be a precursor related to different perceptions that people develop about the world. Consider, for example, the obvious differences in Eastern and Western philosophies about life, religion, and culture. Given the cultural differences to which people in the East and West are exposed as their brain develops, imagine how different their individual perceptions and cognitions may be. Considered together as a species, however, we humans are far more alike than we are different.

An important and unique characteristic common to all humans is language. As illustrated in Figure 8-14, the cortex generally thins from age 5 to age 20. The sole exception is that major language regions of the cortex actually show an *increase* in gray matter. **Figure 8-16** contrasts the thinning of other cortical regions with the thickening of language-related regions (O'Hare & Sowell, 2008). A different pattern of development for brain regions critical in language processing makes sense, given language's unique role in cognition and the long learning time.

Astrocytes nourish and support neurons; oligodendroglia form myelin in the CNS (see Table 3-1).

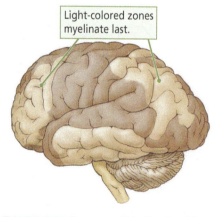

Light-colored zones myelinate last.

FIGURE 8-17 **Progress of Myelination** The fact that the light-colored zones are very late to myelinate led Flechsig to propose that they are qualitatively different in function from those that mature earlier.

Glial Development

Astrocytes and *oligodendrocytes* begin to develop after most neurogenesis is complete and continue to develop throughout life. Radial glial cells form during embryonic development, and most of them differentiate into astrocytes once neural migration along them is complete. Others remain in the subventricular zone and later can give rise to neurons, oligodendrocytes, and more astrocytes (for a review, see Arai & Lo, 2017). Astrocytes play a key role in synaptic pruning during development and contribute to plasticity throughout life (for a review, see Zuchero & Barres, 2015). Oligodendroctyes myelinate axons, which increases the efficiency of axonal function. Consequently, myelination is a useful rough index of cerebral maturation.

In the early 1920s, Paul Flechsig noticed that cortical myelination begins just after birth and continues until at least 18 years of age. He also noticed that some cortical regions were myelinated by age 3 to 4 years, whereas others showed virtually no myelination at that time. **Figure 8-17** shows one of Flechsig's cortical maps with areas shaded according to earlier or later myelination.

Flechsig hypothesized that the earliest-myelinating areas control simple movements or sensory analyses, whereas the latest-myelinating areas control the highest mental functions. MRI analyses of myelin development in the cortex show that white matter thickness largely does correspond to the progress of myelination, confirming

Flechsig's ideas. Myelination continues until at least 20 years of age, as illustrated in **Figure 8-18**, which contrasts total brain volume, gray matter volume, and white matter volume during brain development in females and males.

Unique Aspects of Frontal Lobe Development

The imaging atlas in Figure 8-14 confirms that the frontal lobe is the last brain region to mature. Since the atlas was compiled, neuroscientists have confirmed that frontal lobe maturation extends far beyond its age 20 boundary, including in the **dorsolateral prefrontal cortex (DLPFC)**. The DLPFC, which comprises Brodmann areas 9 and 46, makes reciprocal connections with the posterior parietal cortex and the superior temporal sulcus: it selects behavior and movement with respect to temporal memory. Zdravko Petanjek and colleagues (2011) analyzed synaptic spine density in the DLPFC in a large sample of human brains ranging in age at death from newborn to 91 years.

The analysis confirms that dendritic spine density, a good measure of the number of excitatory synapses, is two to three times greater in children than in adults and that spine density begins to decrease during puberty. The analysis also shows that dendritic spines continue to be eliminated well beyond age 20, stabilizing at the adult level around age 30. Two important correlates attend slow frontal lobe development:

1. *The frontal lobe is especially sensitive to epigenetic influences* (Kolb et al., 2012). In a study of more than 170,000 people, Robert Anda and colleagues (Anda et al., 2006) show that *aversive childhood experiences* (ACEs) such as verbal or physical abuse, a family member's addiction, or loss of a parent are predictive of physical and mental health in middle age. People with two or more ACEs, for example, are 50 times more likely to acquire addictions or attempt suicide. Women with two or more ACEs are 5 times more likely to have been sexually assaulted by age 50. We hypothesize that early aversive experiences promote ACE-related susceptibilities by compromising frontal lobe development.

2. *The trajectory of frontal lobe development correlates with adult intelligence.* Two important features of frontal lobe development are (a) the reduction in cortical thickness and (b) the increase in connectivity between the medial regions of the frontal lobe, the posterior regions of the cingulate cortex, and the lateral regions of the parietal lobe, which together are referred to as the **default network** (see **Figure 8-19**). The trajectory of change in cortical thickness, which continues until late adolescence, and the increased connectivity in the default network, which appears adult-like by about age 13, is related to intelligence. Thus, children who score highest in intelligence show the greatest plastic changes in the frontal lobe over time.

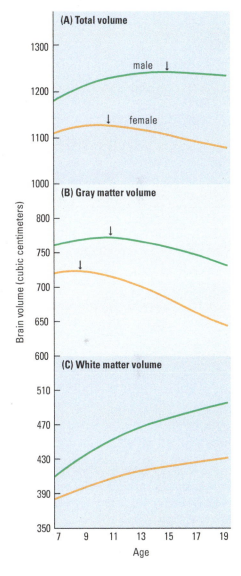

FIGURE 8-18 **Sex Differences in Brain Development** Mean brain volume by age in years for males (green) and females (orange). Arrows above the curves indicate that females show more rapid growth than males, reaching maximum overall volume (**A**) and gray matter volume (**B**) sooner. Decreasing gray matter corresponds to cell and synaptic loss. Increasing white matter volume (**C**) largely corresponds to myelin development. Information from Lenroot et al., 2007.

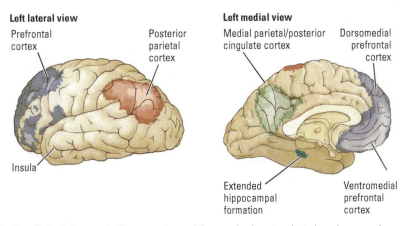

Left lateral view
Prefrontal cortex
Posterior parietal cortex
Insula

Left medial view
Medial parietal/posterior cingulate cortex
Dorsomedial prefrontal cortex
Extended hippocampal formation
Ventromedial prefrontal cortex

FIGURE 8-19 **The Default Network** These regions of the cerebral cortex that show increased connectivity related to intelligence form the default network. Data after Sherman et al., 2014.

Three-dimensional atlases guide researchers to the precise locations of various brain regions (Section 7-1). See Sections 12-4 and 15-3 for more on how the DLPFC functions.

The Adverse Childhood Experience (ACE) Questionnaire is available online, where you can view and answer the questions.

8-2 Review

Before you continue, check your understanding. Answers to Self-Test appear at the back of the book.

1. The central nervous system begins as a sheet of cells, which folds inward to form the _____.

2. The growth of neurons is referred to as _____, whereas formation of glial cells is known as _____.

3. Growth cones are responsive to two types of cues: _____ and _____.

4. The adolescent period is characterized by two ongoing processes of brain maturation: _____ and _____.

5. What is the functional significance of the prolonged development of the frontal lobe?

For additional study tools, visit **LaunchPad** at launchpadworks.com

---

8-3

Using Emerging Behaviors to Infer Neural Maturation

As brain areas mature, a person's behaviors correspond to the functions of the maturing areas. Stated differently, behaviors cannot emerge until the requisite neural machinery has developed. When that machinery is in place, however, related behaviors develop quickly through stages and are shaped significantly by epigenetic factors.

Researchers have studied these interacting changes in the brain and behavior, especially in regard to the emergence of motor skills, language, and problem solving in children. We now explore development in these three areas.

Motor Behaviors

Developing locomotion skills are easy to observe in human infants. At first, babies cannot move about independently, but eventually, they roll over, then crawl, then walk.

Other motor skills develop in less obvious but no less systematic ways. Shortly after birth, infants are capable of flexing their arms in such a way that they can scoop something toward their body, and they can direct a hand, as toward a breast when suckling. Between 1 and 3 months of age, babies also begin to make spontaneous hand and digit movements consisting of almost all the skilled finger movements they will make as an adult—a kind of motor babbling.

These movements at first are directed toward handling parts of their body and their clothes (Wallace & Whishaw, 2003). Only then are reaching movements directed toward objects in space. Tom Twitchell (1965) studied and described how the ability to reach for objects and grasp them progresses in stages, illustrated in **Figure 8-20**.

Between 8 and 11 months, infants' grasping becomes more sophisticated as the pincer grasp, employing the index finger and the thumb, develops. The pincer grasp is significant developmentally: it allows babies to make the very precise finger movements needed to manipulate small objects. What we see, then, is a sequence in the development of grasping: first scooping, then grasping with all the fingers, then grasping with independent finger movements.

If increasingly well-coordinated grasping depends on the emergence of certain neural machinery, anatomical changes in the brain should accompany the emergence of these motor behaviors. Such changes do take place, especially in the development of dendritic arborizations and in fiber connections between neocortex and spinal cord. And a correlation has been found between myelin formation and the ability to grasp (Yakovlev & Lecours, 1967).

A classic symptom of motor cortex damage, detailed in Section 11-1, is permanent loss of the pincer grasp.

FIGURE 8-20 **Development of the Grasping Response of Infants.** Information from Twitchell, 1965.

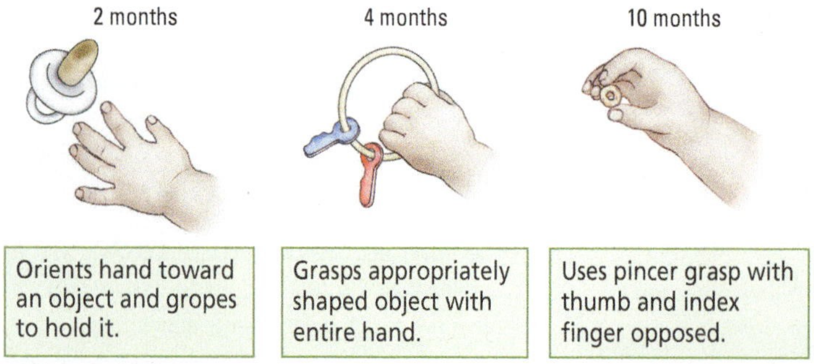

2 months	4 months	10 months
Orients hand toward an object and gropes to hold it.	Grasps appropriately shaped object with entire hand.	Uses pincer grasp with thumb and index finger opposed.

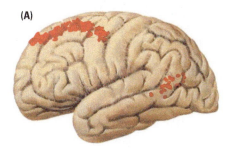
(A)

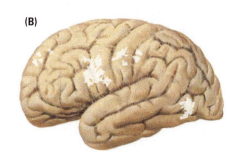
(B)

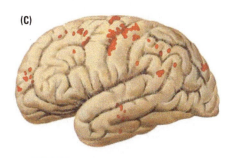
(C)

FIGURE 8-21 **Correlations Between Gray Matter Thickness and Behavior (A)** Red shading corresponds to regions showing significant cortical thinning correlated with improved motor skills. **(B)** White shading corresponds to regions showing significant cortical thickening correlated with improved language skills. **(C)** Red shading shows regions of decreased cortical thickness correlated with improved vocabulary scores. (A) and (B): Research from Lu et al., 2007; (C): Research from Sowell, Thompson, Leonard et al., 2004.

In particular, a group of axons from motor cortex neurons myelinate at about the same time that whole-hand reaching and grasping develop. Another group of motor cortex neurons known to control finger movements myelinates at about the time that the pincer grasp develops. MRI studies of changes in cortical thickness show that increased motor dexterity is associated with decreased cortical thickness in the hand region of the left motor cortex of right-handers (**Figure 8-21A**). It might seem odd that both cortical thinning and thickening can be associated with improved performance, but the reason is straightforward. Thinning partly reflects the pruning of neurons and synapses throughout development, whereas thickening reflects the addition of synapses, along with associated astrocytes and blood vessels related to learning.

We can now make a simple prediction. If specific motor cortex neurons are essential for adult-like grasping movements to emerge, removing those neurons should make an adult's grasping ability similar to a young infant's, which is in fact what happens.

Principle 6: Brain systems are organized hierarchically and in parallel.

Language Development

According to Eric Lenneberg (1967), children reach certain important speech milestones in a fixed sequence and at constant chronological ages. Children start to form a vocabulary by 12 months. Their 5- to 10-word repertoire typically doubles over the next 6 months. By 2 years, vocabulary will range from 200 to 300 words that include mostly everyday objects. In another year, vocabulary approaches 1000 words and begins to include simple sentences. At 6 years, children boast a vocabulary of about 2500 words and can understand more than 20,000 words en route to an adult vocabulary of more than 50,000 words.

Although language skills and motor skills generally develop in parallel, the capacity for language depends on more than the ability to make controlled movements of the mouth, lips, and tongue. Precise movements of the muscles controlling these body parts develop well before children can speak. Furthermore, even when children have sufficient motor skill to articulate most words, their vocabulary does not rocket ahead but rather progresses gradually.

A small proportion of children (about 1 percent) have typical intelligence and motor skill development, yet their speech acquisition is markedly delayed. Such children might not begin to speak in phrases until after age 4, despite an apparently healthy environment and the absence of any obvious neurological signs of brain damage. Because the timing of speech onset appears universal in the remaining 99 percent of children across all cultures, something different has likely taken place in the brain maturation of a child with late language acquisition. The difficulty comes in specifying that difference.

Because the age of language onset is usually between 1 and 2 years and language acquisition is largely complete by age 12, the best strategy for determining the reasons for these differences is to consider how the cortex is different before and after these two milestones. By age 2, cell division and migration are complete in the language zones of the cerebral cortex. The major changes that take place from ages 2 to 12 are in neuronal connectivity and myelination of the speech zones.

Changes in dendritic complexity in speech zones are among the most impressive in the brain. Recall from Figure 8-12 that the axons and dendrites of the speech zone called Broca's area are simple at birth but grow dramatically denser at age 15 to 24 months. This neuronal development correlates with an equally dramatic change in language ability, given that a baby's vocabulary starts to expand rapidly at about age 2.

We can therefore infer that language development may be constrained, at least in part, by the maturing language areas in the cortex. Individual differences in the speed of language acquisition may be accounted for by differences in this neural development. Children with early language ability may have an early-maturing speech zone, whereas this zone may develop later in children with delayed language onset.

Results of MRI studies of the language cortex show that, in contrast with the thinning of motor cortex associated with enhanced dexterity shown in Figure 8-21A, there is a *thickening* of the left inferior frontal cortex areas associated with enhanced phonological processing (understanding speech sounds), as shown in Figure 8-21B. The unique association between cortical thickening and phonological processing is not due to a general relationship between all language functions and cortical thickening, however. Figure 8-21C shows significant thinning of diffuse cortical regions associated with better vocabulary—regions outside the language areas—and vocabulary is one of the best predictors of general intelligence.

Development of Problem-Solving Ability

The first researcher to try to identify discrete stages of cognitive development was psychologist Jean Piaget (1952). He realized that he could infer children's understanding of the world by observing their behavior. For example, a baby who lifts a cloth to retrieve a hidden toy shows an understanding that objects continue to exist even when out of sight. This understanding of *object permanence* is revealed by the behavior of the infant in the top row of photographs in **Figure 8-22**.

An absence of understanding also can be seen in children's behavior, as shown by the actions of the 5-year-old girl in the bottom row of photographs in Figure 8-22. She was shown two identical beakers with identical volumes of liquid, then watched as one beaker's liquid was poured into a shorter, wider beaker. When asked which beaker contained more liquid, she pointed to the taller beaker, not understanding that the amount of liquid remains constant despite the difference in appearance. Children display an understanding of this principle, the *conservation of liquid volume*, at about age 7.

Research Focus 7-1 describes research on newborns' reactions to language.

FIGURE 8-22 **Two Stages of Cognitive Development** The infant shows that she understands object permanence—that things continue to exist when they are out of sight (top). The young girl does not yet understand the principle of conservation of liquid volume. Beakers with identical volumes but different shapes seem to her to hold different amounts of liquid (bottom).

TABLE 8-2 Piaget's Stages of Cognitive Development

Approximate typical age range (yr)	Description of stage	Developmental phenomena
0–2	*I: Sensorimotor* Experiences the world through senses and actions (looking, touching, mouthing)	Object permanence Stranger anxiety
2–6	*II: Preoperational* Represents things with words and images but lacks logical reasoning	Pretend play Egocentrism Language development
7–11	*III: Concrete operational* Thinks logically about concrete events; grasps concrete analogies and performs arithmetical operations	Conservation Mathematical transformations
12+	*IV: Formal operational* Reasons abstractly	Abstract logic Potential for mature moral reasoning

Data from Myers, 2015.

By studying children engaged in such tasks, Piaget concluded that cognitive development is a continuous process. Children's strategies for exploring the world and their understanding of it are constantly changing. These changes are not simply the result of acquiring specific pieces of new knowledge. Rather, at certain points in development, fundamental changes take place in the organization of a child's strategies for learning about the world and for solving problems. With these developing strategies comes new understanding.

Piaget identified four major stages of cognitive development, summarized in **Table 8-2**:

- Stage I is the *sensorimotor* period, from birth to about 18 to 24 months of age. During this time, babies learn to differentiate themselves from the external world, come to realize that objects exist even when out of sight, and gain some understanding of cause and effect.

- Stage II, the *preoperational* period, takes place at age 2 to 6 years. Children gain the ability to form mental representations of things in their world and to represent those things in words and drawings.

- Stage III is the period of *concrete operations*, which typically occurs around 7 to 11 years. Children learn to mentally manipulate ideas about material (concrete) things such as volumes of liquid, dimensions of objects, and arithmetic problems.

- Stage IV, the period of *formal perations*, is attained sometime after age 11. Children are now able to reason in the abstract, not just in concrete terms.

Although there have been many revisions to Piaget's stage theory in the nearly 70 years since it was first proposed, we can still take Piaget's stages as rough approximations of qualitative changes that take place in children's thinking as they grow older, and we can ask what neural changes might underlie them. One place to look for brain changes is in the relative rate of brain growth.

After birth, brain and body do not grow uniformly but rather during irregularly occurring periods commonly called **growth spurts**. In his analysis of ratios of brain weight to body weight, Herman Epstein (1979) found consistent spurts in brain growth between 3 and 10 months (accounting for an increase of 30 percent in brain weight by age 18 months), as well as ages 2 to 4, 6 to 8, 10 to 12, and 14 to 16+ years. The increments in brain weight were about 5 percent to 10 percent in each of these 2-year periods.

Brain growth takes place without a concurrent increase in the number of neurons, so it is most likely due to the growth of glial cells, blood vessels, myelin, and synapses. Although synapses themselves would be unlikely to add much weight to the brain, their growth is accompanied by increased metabolic demands that cause neurons to

growth spurt Sporadic period of sudden growth that lasts for a finite time.

···> **EXPERIMENT 8-1**

Question: In what sequence do the forebrain structures required for learning and memory mature?

Procedure

I. Displacement task

II. Nonmatching-to-sample learning task

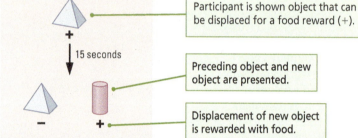

Participant is shown object that can be displaced for a food reward (+).

Preceding object and new object are presented.

Displacement of new object is rewarded with food.

III. Concurrent-discrimination learning task

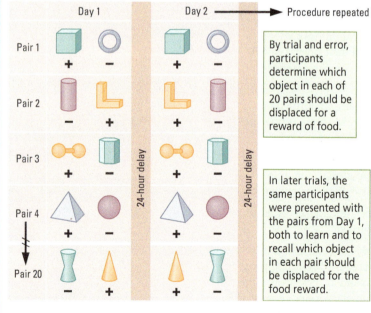

By trial and error, participants determine which object in each of 20 pairs should be displaced for a reward of food.

In later trials, the same participants were presented with the pairs from Day 1, both to learn and to recall which object in each pair should be displaced for the food reward.

Results

Both human and monkey infants learn the concurrent-discrimination task at a younger age than the nonmatching-to-sample task.

Conclusion: Neural structures underlying the concurrent-discrimination task mature sooner than those underlying the nonmatching-to-sample task.

Research from Overman et al., 1992.

become larger, new blood vessels to form, and new astrocytes to be produced for neuronal support and nourishment.

We would expect such an increase in cortical complexity to generate more complex behaviors, so we might predict significant, perhaps qualitative, changes in cognitive function during each growth spurt. The first four brain growth spurts Epstein identified coincide nicely with the four main stages of cognitive development Piaget described. Such correspondence suggests significant alterations in neural functioning with the onset of each cognitive stage.

At the same time, differences in the rate of brain development, or perhaps in the rate at which specific groups of neurons mature, may account for individual differences in the age at which the various cognitive advances identified by Piaget emerge. Although Piaget did not identify a fifth stage of cognitive development in later adolescence, a growth spurt that occurs then implies one.

Growth spurts are superficial measures of changes taking place in the brain. To link them to cognitive development, we need to know at a deeper level what neural events are contributing to brain growth and just where they are taking place. A way to find out is to observe healthy children's attempts to solve specific problems that are diagnostic of damage to discrete brain regions in adults. If children perform a particular task poorly, then whatever brain region regulates that task must not yet be mature. Similarly, if children can perform one task but not another, the tasks apparently require different brain structures, and these structures must mature at different rates.

William Overman and Jocelyne Bachevalier (Overman et al., 1992) used this logic to study the development of forebrain structures required for learning and memory in young children and in monkeys. The Procedure section of **Experiment 8-1** shows the three intelligence test items presented to their participants. The first task was simply to learn to displace an object to obtain a food reward. When participants had learned the *displacement* task, they were trained in two more tasks believed to measure temporal lobe and basal ganglia functioning, respectively.

In the *nonmatching-to-sample* task, participants were shown an object they could displace to receive a food reward. After a brief (15-second) delay, two objects were presented: the first object and a novel object. The participants then had to displace the novel object to obtain the food reward. Nonmatching to sample is thought to measure object recognition, which is a temporal lobe function. The participant can find the food only by recognizing the original object and not choosing it.

In the third task, *concurrent discrimination*, participants were presented with a pair of objects and had to learn that one object in that pair was always associated with a food reward, whereas the other object was never rewarded. The task was made more difficult by sequentially giving partici-pants 20 different object pairs. Each day, they were presented with one trial per pair. Concurrent discrimination is thought to measure trial-and-error learning of specific object information, a function of the basal ganglia.

Healthy adults easily solve both the nonmatching and the concurrent tasks but report that the concurrent task is more difficult because it requires remembering far more information. The key question developmentally is whether there is a difference in the ages at which children (or monkeys) can solve these two tasks.

It turns out that children can solve the concurrent task by about 12 months of age, but not until about 18 months can they solve what most adults believe to be the eas-ier nonmatching task. These results imply that the basal ganglia, the critical area for the concurrent discrimination task, mature more quickly than the temporal lobe, the critical region for the nonmatching-to-sample task.

A Caution about Linking Correlation to Causation

Throughout this section, we have described research results implying that changes in the brain cause changes in behavior. Neuroscientists assert that by looking at behav-ioral development and brain development in parallel, they can make some inferences regarding the causes of behavior. Bear in mind, however, that the fact that two things correlate (take place together) does not prove that one of them *causes* the other.

The correlation–causation problem raises red flags in brain and behavior studies because research in behavioral neuroscience, by its very nature, is often based on cor-relations. For example, knowing that children with a specific neurodevelopmental disor-der were exposed to nicotine in utero does not prove that nicotine caused the disorder, but it does provide a powerful source of insight into the potential cause of the disorder.

8-3 Review

Before you continue, check your understanding. Answers to Self-Test appear at the back of the book.

1. The last stage in motor development in infants is the ability to make _____.

2. Language development is correlated with cortical thinning related to _____ and cortical thickening related to _____.

3. Brain growth spurts correlate with _____.

4. The nonmatching-to-sample task is believed to measure the function of the _____; the concurrent-discrimination learning task is believed to measure the function of the

_____.

5. Describe a major challenge in inferring changes in brain development from the emergence of behaviors.

For additional study tools, visit **Launch**Pad at launchpadworks.com

8-4

Brain Development and the Environment

Developing behaviors are shaped not only by the maturation of brain structures but also by each person's environment and experience. Neuroplasticity suggests that the brain can be molded, at least at the microscopic level. Brains exposed to different envi-ronmental experiences are molded in different ways. For example, culture is an import-ant aspect of the human environment, so culture must help mold the human brain.

Principle 2: Neuroplasticity is the hallmark of nervous system functioning.

Section 1-5 summarizes humanity's acquisition of culture. Section 15-3 discusses the emerging field of social neuroscience.

The Hebb synapse, diagrammed in Section 15-1, illustrates Hebb's predictions about synaptic plasticity. Section 14-4 elaborates his contributions to learning theory.

FIGURE 8-23 **Hebb–Williams Maze** In this version of the maze, a rat is placed in the start box (S) and must learn to find the food in the goal box (G). Investigators can reconfigure the walls of the maze to set new problems. Rats raised in complex environments solve such mazes much faster than do rats raised in standard laboratory cages.

Recall from the previous section that correlation does not prove causation.

We would therefore expect people raised in widely differing cultures to acquire brain structure differences that have lifelong effects on their behavior.

The brain is plastic not only in response to external events but also in response to events within a person's body, including the effects of hormones, injury, and genetic mutations. The developing brain early in life is especially responsive to these internal factors, which in turn alter how the brain responds to external experiences. In this section, we explore a whole range of external and internal environmental influences on brain development. We start with a question: Exactly how does experience alter brain structure?

Experience and Cortical Organization

Researchers can study the effects of experience on the brain and behavior by placing laboratory animals in different environments and observing the results. In one of the earliest such studies, Donald Hebb (1947) took a group of young laboratory rats home and let them grow up in his kitchen. A control group grew up in standard laboratory cages at McGill University.

The home-reared rats had many experiences that the caged rats did not, including being chased with a broom by Hebb's less-than-enthusiastic wife. Subsequently, Hebb gave both groups a rat-specific intelligence test that consisted of learning to solve a series of mazes, collectively known as Hebb–Williams mazes. **Figure 8-23** shows a sample maze. Home-reared rats performed far better on these tasks than caged rats did. Hebb therefore concluded that experience must influence intelligence.

On the basis of his research, Hebb reasoned that people reared in a stimulating environment will maximize their intellectual development, whereas people raised in impoverished or under-resourced environments, such as those described in the SES study in Research Focus 8-1, will not reach their intellectual potential. Although a generalization, Hebb's reasoning seems logical. But how do we define an environment as stimulating or impoverished?

People living in slums typically have few formal educational resources—decidedly not an enriched setting—but that does not mean that the environment offers no cognitive stimulation or challenge. On the contrary, people raised in slums are better adapted for survival in a slum than are people raised in upper-class homes. Does this adaptability make them more intelligent in a certain way? Could it make them more resilient?

On the other hand, slum dwellers may not be well adapted for college life. This is probably closer to what Hebb had in mind when he referred to an impoverished environment as limiting intellectual potential. Indeed, Hebb's logic influenced the development of preschool television programs, such as *Sesame Street*, that offer enrichment for children who would otherwise have little preschool exposure to reading.

At 36 months of age, on average, the vocabulary of children from a low-SES environment is less than one-third that of high-SES children (400 versus 1200 words). This difference grows wider as children develop. It is hypothesized to result from less direct conversation with caregivers and less reading to the children by caregivers. Estimates suggest that by age 4, low-SES children have been exposed to about 30 million fewer words than high-SES children (see review by Kolb & Gibb, 2015)!

The weaker language skills demonstrated by children of low SES is related to the size of cortical language areas as early as age 5 years (Raizada et al., 2008). Patricia Kuhl (2011) makes the important point that SES itself is not the variable that drives the effects on language and brain development. Rather, SES is likely a proxy for the opportunity to learn language, a point that takes us back to James Heckman's thesis in Research Focus 8-1.

Seven decades ago, Hebb's studies used complex stimulating environments, but much simpler experiences can also influence brain development. Tactile stimulation of human infants—such as being held closely, massaged, or stroked—is important not only for bonding with caregivers but also for stimulating brain development. For example, tactile stimulation of premature infants in incubators speeds their growth and allows for quicker release from the hospital. Laboratory studies show that brushing infant rats for 15 minutes 3 times per day for the first 3 weeks of life also speeds up growth and development. The rats show enhanced motor and cognitive skills in adulthood as well. Tactile stimulation also dramatically improves recovery from brain injury incurred early in development.

The idea that early experience can affect later behavior seems sensible enough, but we are left to question why experience should make such a difference. One reason is that experience changes neuronal structure, which is especially evident in the cortex. Neurons in the brains of animals raised in complex environments, such as that shown in **Figure 8-24A**, are larger and richer in synapses than are those of animals reared in barren cages. Compare the neurons in Figure 8-24B. Similarly, 3 weeks of tactile stimulation in infancy increases synapse numbers all over the cortex in adulthood.

Presumably, increased synapse numbers result from increased sensory processing in a complex and stimulating environment. The brains of animals raised in complex settings also display more (and larger) astrocytes. Although complex-rearing studies do not address the effects of human culture directly, making predictions about human development on the basis of their findings is easy. We know that experience can modify the brain, so we can predict that different experiences might modify the brain differently. Take musical training, for example, as Research Focus 8-3, Keeping Brains Young by Making Music, explains.

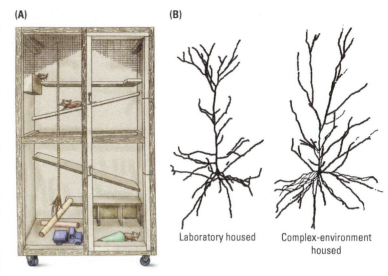

(A) **(B)**

Laboratory housed   Complex-environment housed

FIGURE 8-24 **Enriched Environment, Enhanced Development (A)** A complex environment for a group of about six rats allows the animals to move about and to interact with one another and with toys that are changed weekly. **(B)** Representative neurons from the parietal cortex of a laboratory-caged rat and a complex-environment-housed rat; the latter has about 25 percent more dendritic space for synapses.

Research Focus 5-5 describes some structural changes that neurons undergo as a result of learning.

◎ RESEARCH FOCUS 8-3

Keeping Brains Young by Making Music

Music is a widespread leisure activity that is known to increase brain plasticity and can lead to a wide range of benefits, including enhanced motor skills, increased intelligence, and increased verbal skills—especially when music training begins in childhood. Music is also known to have beneficial rehabilitative effects in stroke patients and those with Parkinson disease. There are now data suggesting that musical training is beneficial in forestalling the effects of aging on the brain (see review by Herholz & Zatorre, 2012). For example, musical practice reduces age-related declines in a variety of cognitive processes, including nonverbal memory and frontal lobe functions.

Lars Rogenmoser and colleagues (2018) used a novel MRI-based procedure known as *BrainAGE* to investigate the impact of musical training on brain maturation. *BrainAGE* is based on a database of structural MRI data that aggregates brain structure across the whole brain to one single value—estimated brain age. Rogenmoser and colleagues found that, compared to amateur or professional musicians, non-musicians exhibited higher *BrainAGE* scores, even in relatively young participants (mean ages of approximately 25 years). Thus, making music early in life appears to modulate the effect of aging on the brain. The *BrainAGE* procedure has applications beyond music. Using this procedure, Katje Franke and colleagues have shown in a series of papers that older estimated brain age is predictive of dementia (see Franke et al., 2014).

Not only does early musical training act to keep the brain young, but music can also be used as a therapy in old brains to make them act like younger brains. You may have noticed that young children often spontaneously break into dance when they hear music. The ability of music to stimulate movement has been used as a therapy to restore behaviors such as walking in patients with Parkinson disease. By hearing, or even mentally remembering, the tune of songs, such patients can move with the music rather than being frozen in place and unable to move.

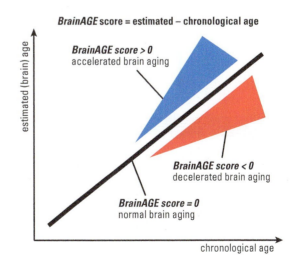

BrainAGE score = estimated – chronological age

BrainAGE score > 0
accelerated brain aging

BrainAGE score < 0
decelerated brain aging

BrainAGE score = 0
normal brain aging

estimated (brain) age

chronological age

Depiction of the *BrainAGE* Concept MRI images of healthy brains at different ages provides a model of normal age-related changes. This graph shows a comparison of new brains with the archived brains to get an estimate of individual brain ages.

chemoaffinity hypothesis Proposal that neurons or their axons and dendrites are drawn toward a signaling chemical that indicates the correct pathway.

Figure 15-12 shows enhanced nerve tract connectivity in people with perfect pitch.

Section 9-2 describes visual system anatomy. Figure 2-19 details midbrain structures.

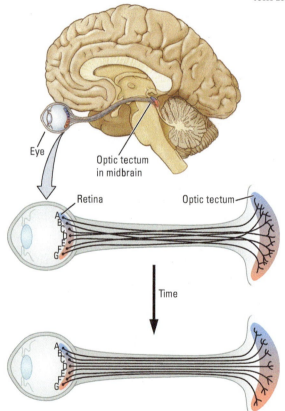

FIGURE 8-25 **Chemoaffinity in the Visual System** Neurons A through G project from the retina to the tectum in the midbrain. The activities of adjacent neurons (C and D, say) are more likely to coincide than are the activities of widely separated neurons such as A and G. As a result, adjacent retinal neurons are more likely to establish permanent synapses on the same tectal neurons. By using chemical signals, axons grow to the approximate location in the tectum (top). The connections become more precise with the passage of time (bottom).

Like early exposure to language during development, early exposure to music alters the brain. Perfect (absolute) pitch, or the ability to re-create a musical note without external reference, is believed to require musical training during an early period, when brain development is most sensitive to this experience. Similarly, adults exposed only to Western music since childhood usually find Eastern music peculiar, even nonmusical, on first encountering it. Not only does early musical training alter brain development, it also acts to enhance healthy brain aging, much like learning a second language early in life. These examples demonstrate that early exposure to music alters neurons in the auditory system (see Levitin & Rogers, 2005).

Such loss of plasticity does not mean that the adult human brain grows fixed and unchangeable. Adults' brains are influenced by exposure to new environments and experiences, although more slowly and less extensively than children's brains are. In fact, evidence reveals that experience affects the brain well into old age—good news for those of us who are no longer children (Kolb et al., 2003). We will return to the discussion of the impact of experience and environment in the context of abnormal brain development in the next section.

Experience and Neural Connectivity

Experience can actually sculpt the brain prenatally, as studies of the developing visual system show clearly. A simple analogy will illustrate the anatomical challenge of connecting the visual receptors in the eyes to the rest of the visual system. Imagine that students in a large lecture hall are each viewing the front of the room (the visual field) through a small cardboard tube, such as an empty paper towel roll. If each student looks directly ahead, he or she will see only a small bit of the total visual field.

Essentially, this is how the photoreceptor neurons in the eyes act. Each cell sees only a small bit of the visual field. The problem is putting all of the bits together to form a complete picture. To do so, analogously to students sitting side by side, receptors that see adjacent views must send their information to adjacent regions in the various parts of the brain's visual system, such as the midbrain. How do they accomplish this feat?

Roger Sperry (1963) suggested the **chemoaffinity hypothesis**, the idea that specific molecules in different cells in various midbrain regions give each cell a distinctive chemical identity. Each cell has an identifiable biochemical label. Presumably, incoming axons seek out a specific chemical, such as the tropic factors discussed in Section 8-2, and consequently land in the correct general midbrain region.

Many experiments have shown this process to take place prenatally as the eye and brain are developing. But the problem is that chemical affinity directs incoming axons only to a general location. To return to our two adjacent retinal cells, how do they now place themselves in precisely the correct position?

Here is where postnatal experience comes in: fine-tuning of neural placement is believed to be activity dependent. Because adjacent receptors tend to be activated at the same time, they tend to form synapses on the same neurons in the midbrain after chemoaffinity has drawn them to a general midbrain region. **Figure 8-25** illustrates this process. Neurons A and G are unlikely to be activated by the same stimulus, so they seldom fire synchronously. Neurons A and B, in contrast, are apt to be activated by the same stimuli, as are B and C. Through this simultaneous activity and with the passage of time, cells eventually line up correctly in the connections they form.

Now consider what happens to axons coming from different eyes. Although the neural inputs from the two eyes may be active simultaneously, neurons in the same eye are more likely to be active together than are cells in different eyes. The net effect is that inputs from the two eyes tend to organize themselves into neural bands, called *columns*, that represent the same region of space in each eye, as shown on the left in **Figure 8-26**. Formation of these segregated cortical columns therefore depends on the patterns of coinciding electrical activity on the incoming axons.

If experience is abnormal—for example, if one eye is covered during a crucial time in development—the neural connections will not be guided appropriately by experience. As shown at the right in Figure 8-26, the effect of suturing one eye closed has the most disruptive effect on cortical organization in kittens between 30 and 60 days after birth. In a child who has a "lazy eye," visual input from that eye does not contribute to fine-tuning the neural connections as it should. So the details of those connections develop abnormally, much as if the eye had been covered. The resulting loss of sharpness in vision is **amblyopia**.

To summarize, an organism's genetic blueprint is vague in regard to exactly which connections in the brain go to exactly which neurons. Experience fine-tunes neural connectivity by modifying those details.

Critical Periods for Experience and Brain Development

The preceding examples of perfect pitch and visual connectivity show that for healthy development, specific sensory experiences occurring at particular times are especially important. A time during which brain development is most sensitive to a specific experience is called either a **critical period** or a *sensitive period*.

The absence of appropriate sensory experience during a critical period may result in abnormal brain development, leading to abnormal behavior that endures even into adulthood. Our colleague Richard Tees offered an analogy to help explain the concept. He pictured the developing animal as a little train traveling past an environmental setting, perhaps the Rocky Mountains. All the windows are closed at the beginning of the journey (prenatal development), but at particular stages of the trip, the windows in certain cars open, exposing the occupants (different parts of the brain) to the outside world. Some windows open to expose the brain to specific sounds, others to certain smells, others to particular sights, and so on.

This exposure affects the brain's development, and the absence of any exposure through an open window severely disturbs that development. As the journey continues, the windows become harder to open, and finally they close permanently. This does not mean that the brain can no longer change, but changes become much harder to induce.

Now imagine two different trains, one headed through the Rocky Mountains and another, the Orient Express, traveling across Eastern Europe. The views from the windows are very different, and the effects on the brain are correspondingly different. In other words, not only is the brain altered by the experiences it has during a critical period, but the particular kinds of experiences encountered matter, too.

An extensively studied example of a behavior occurring during a critical period is the phenomenon of **imprinting**, whereby an animal learns to restrict its social preferences to a specific class of objects, usually the members of its own species. In birds, such as chickens and waterfowl, the critical period for imprinting often comes shortly after hatching. Typically, the first moving object a young hatchling sees is a parent or sibling, so the hatchling's brain appropriately imprints to its own species.

Appropriate imprinting is not inevitable, however. Konrad Lorenz (1970) demonstrated that if the first animal or object that baby goslings encounter is a person, the goslings imprint to that person as though he or she were their mother. **Figure 8-27** shows a flock of goslings that imprinted to Lorenz and followed him wherever he went. Incorrect imprinting has long-term consequences for the hatchlings. They often direct their subsequent sexual behavior toward humans. A Barbary dove that had become imprinted to Lorenz directed its courtship toward his hand and even tried to copulate with the hand if it was held in a certain orientation.

This quick acquisition and its permanent behavioral consequences suggest that during imprinting, the brain makes a rapid change of some kind, probably a structural

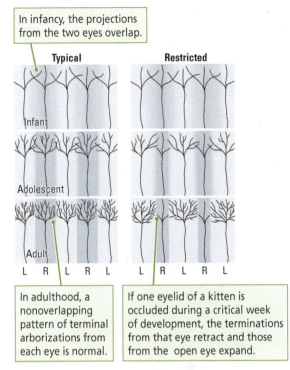

FIGURE 8-26 **Ocular Dominance Columns** Typically in the postnatal development of the cat brain, axons from each eye enter the cortex, where they grow large terminal arborizations. (L, left eye; R, right eye).

In infancy, the projections from the two eyes overlap.

In adulthood, a nonoverlapping pattern of terminal arborizations from each eye is normal.

If one eyelid of a kitten is occluded during a critical week of development, the terminations from that eye retract and those from the open eye expand.

amblyopia Condition in which vision in one eye is reduced as a result of disuse; usually caused by a failure of the two eyes to look in the same direction.

critical period Developmental window during which some event has a long-lasting influence on the brain; also, *sensitive period*.

imprinting Formation of an attachment by an animal to one or more objects or animals at a critical period in development.

FIGURE 8-27 **Strength of Imprinting** Ethologist Konrad Lorenz followed by goslings that imprinted on him. He was the first object that the geese encountered after hatching, so he became their "mother."

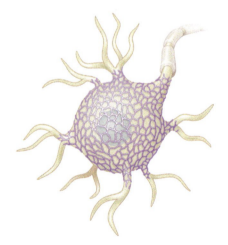

Perineuronal net that covers PV neurons and limits plasticity.

change, given the permanence of the new behavior. Indeed, such a change does happen. Gabriel Horn and his colleagues at Cambridge University (1985) showed that synapses in a specific forebrain region enlarge with imprinting. Thus, imprinting seems a good model for studying brain plasticity during development, in part because the changes are rapid, related to specific experience, and localized in the brain.

But why do critical periods end? Takao Hensch (2017) hypothesizes that two types of *molecular brakes* act in tandem to terminate critical periods. One type of brake is epigenetic and leads to increased expression of certain genes during development, which act to limit plasticity. The second type of brake involves *perineuronal nets*, which are specialized structures in the extracellular matrix that act as a molecular latticework over a neuron (much like the netting that surrounds neuronal cell bodies), such as GABAergic interneurons containing the calcium-binding protein *parvalbumin* (known as PV cells). Perineuronal nets reach maturity at the end of the critical period and can act as a physical barrier to morphological plasticity by blocking the generation of new synapses. There is growing evidence that disruption of perineuronal nets in adulthood can allow a reopening of critical periods. Temporarily removing perineuronal nets on PV cells may provide a promising avenue for the development of brain therapies.

The Adolescent Brain as a Critical Period

There is a growing consensus that adolescence is a period of heightened neural plasticity relative to the juvenile and adult brain (e.g., Fuhrmann et al., 2015). The onset of enhanced plasticity likely coincides with the release of gonadal hormones, but the timing of the reduction in plasticity at the end of adolescence has not been well studied. Several clear brain changes occur during adolescence, including increased production of astrocytes and myelin, decreased cortical thickness, and, most importantly, active changes in connectivity. Connections with the amygdala, striatum, hippocampus, and prefrontal cortex are changing throughout this period. Casey and colleagues (2015) provided an oversimplified illustration (presented in **Figure 8-28**) of the types of changes in prefrontal-subcortical circuitry: the interconnections and their relative strength change with development, providing insight into the emotional, social, and other nonemotional behaviors of adolescents. These studies support the important principle that changes in connectivity must be precise enough for an altered circuit to process information differently and carry out the altered (or new) function.

The fact that adolescence is a critical period for changing neural circuit connectivity is likely adaptive. Considerable learning about the environment, especially the social environment, takes place during this period. But enhanced plasticity also renders the brain vulnerable to a wide range of experiences, such as stress, psychoactive drugs, brain trauma (for example, concussion), and harmful peer relationships, which influence brain organization and function differently in adolescents than

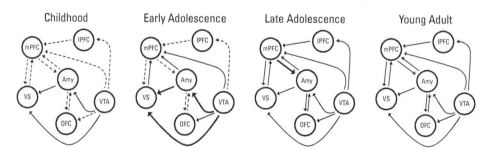

FIGURE 8-28 **Changes in Prefrontal-Subcortical Circuitry** Simplistic illustration of hierarchical age-related changes in connectivity from subcortico-subcortical to cortico-subcortical circuits. Regional changes in connectivity are indicated with dotted and bolded lines. Relative strength of the connections is indicated by the dashed lines (weaker), solid lines (stronger), and bold lines (strongest). Abbreviations: mPFC: medial prefrontal cortex; lPFC: lateral prefrontal cortex; OFC: orbitofrontal cortex; VS: ventral striatum; Amy: amygdala; VTA: ventral tegmental area. Research from Casey et al., 2015.

in adults. It is no accident that many forms of mental illness become apparent in adolescence (e.g., Tottenham & Galvan, 2016).

Hormones and Brain Development

The determination of sex is largely genetic. In mammals, the Y chromosome in males controls the process by which an undifferentiated, primitive gonad develops into testes, as illustrated in **Figure 8-29**. The genitals begin to form in the seventh week after conception, but they appear identical (indifferent) in the two sexes at this early stage. No *sexual dimorphism*, or structural difference, yet exists. The testes subsequently secrete the sex hormone **testosterone**, which stimulates development of male reproductive organs and later, in puberty, the appearance of male secondary sexual characteristics such as facial hair and deepening of the voice.

Gonadal (sex) hormones change the genetic activity of certain cells, most obviously those that form the genitals, but neural cells also respond to them. Regions of the embryonic brain thus also may begin to show sexual dimorphism as testosterone secretion begins, about 60 days after conception. What does sexual differentiation have to do with brain development? Although the answer is largely hormonal, genetic influences contribute, too.

Testosterone stimulates sexual differentiation in male embryos. In its absence, female embryos develop. Prenatal exposure to gonadal hormones shapes male and female brains differently because these hormones activate different genes in the two sexes. Experience, then, affects male and female brains differently. Clearly, genes and experience begin to shape the developing brain very early.

testosterone Sex hormone secreted by the testes and responsible for the distinguishing characteristics of the male.

Section 12-5 detail the actions of gonadal hormones, including testosterone.

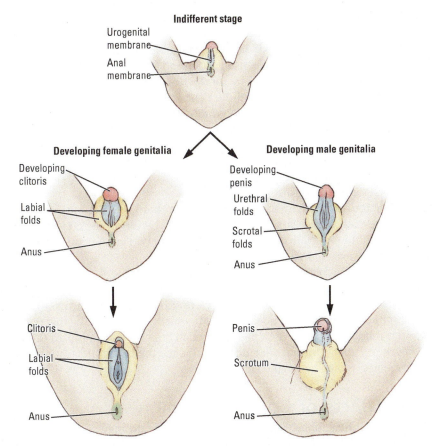

FIGURE 8-29 **Sexual Differentiation in the Human Infant** Early in the indifferent stage, male and female human embryos are identical (top). In the absence of testosterone, female structures emerge (left). In response to testosterone, genitalia begin to develop into male structures at about 60 days (right). Parallel changes take place in the embryonic brain in response to the absence or presence of testosterone.

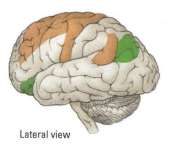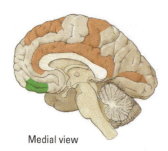

Lateral view   Medial view

FIGURE 8-30 **Sex Differences in Brain Volume** Cerebral areas related to sex differences in the distribution of estrogen (orange) and androgen (green) receptors in the developing brain correspond to areas of relatively larger cerebral volumes in adult women and men. Information from Goldstein et al., 2001.

Gonadal Hormones and Brain Development

Testosterone, the best-known **androgen** (the class of hormones that stimulates or controls masculine characteristics), is released during a brief period of prenatal brain development. Subsequently, it alters the brain much as it alters the sex organs. This process is **masculinization**.

Testosterone does not affect all body organs or all brain regions, but it does affect many brain regions in many ways. It affects the number of neurons formed in certain brain areas, reduces the number of neurons that die, increases cell growth, increases or reduces dendritic branching and synaptic growth, and regulates synaptic activity, among other effects.

Estrogens, the sex hormones responsible for the female's distinguishing characteristics, also influence postnatal brain development. Jill Goldstein and her colleagues found sex differences in the volume of cortical regions known to have differential levels of receptors for testosterone (androgen receptors) and estrogen, respectively, as shown in **Figure 8-30** (Goldstein et al., 2001). Orange areas in the figure are larger in females, and green areas are larger in males. Clearly, a male brain and a female brain are not the same. Hormones alter brain development, and clear sex differences appear in the rate of brain development (see Figure 8-19).

Testosterone's effects on brain development were once believed to be unimportant because this hormone was thought primarily to influence brain regions related to sexual behavior, not regions of higher functions. That belief is false. Testosterone changes cell structure in many cortical regions, with diverse behavioral consequences that include influences on cognitive processes. Although postnatal experiences may influence sex differences in the brain, an MRI study of the brains of newborns by Douglas Dean and his colleagues (2018) has shown that sex differences in brain structure exist at 1 month of life, suggesting that the sex differences emerge in the prenatal period and in the first month of life.

Jocelyne Bachevalier adapted her method, shown in Experiment 8-1, by training infant male and female monkeys in the concurrent discrimination task, as well as in an *object reversal learning task*, in which one object always conceals a food reward, whereas another object never does. After the animal learns this pattern, the reward contingencies are reversed so that the particular object that has always been rewarded is now never rewarded, and the formerly unrewarded object now conceals the reward. When the animal learns this new pattern, the contingencies are reversed again, and so on for five reversals.

Bachevalier found that 2½-month-old male monkeys were superior to female monkeys on the object reversal task, but females did better on the concurrent task. Apparently, the different brain areas required for these two tasks mature at different rates in male and female monkeys.

Bachevalier and her colleague William Overman (Overman et al., 1996) repeated the experiment with children 15 to 30 months old. The results were the same: boys were superior at the object reversal task, and girls were superior at the concurrent task. At 32 to 55 months of age, there was no longer a difference. Presumably, by that point, the brain regions required for both tasks had matured in both boys and girls. At the earlier age, however, gonadal hormones seemed to influence the maturation rate in certain brain regions, just as they had in the baby monkeys.

Lifelong Effects of Gonadal Hormones

Although gonadal hormones' biggest effects on the brain may come during early development, their role is by no means finished in infancy. Both testosterone and estrogen (which females' ovaries produce in large quantities) continue to influence brain structure throughout an animal's life. In fact, removal of the ovaries in middle-aged laboratory rats leads to marked growth of dendrites and glial cells in the cortex. This finding of widespread neural change in the cortex associated with estrogen loss has

androgen Class of hormones that stimulates or controls masculine characteristics.

masculinization Process by which exposure to androgens (male sex hormones) alters the brain, rendering it identifiably male.

estrogen Variety of sex hormones responsible for the distinguishing characteristics of the female.

implications for treating postmenopausal women with hormone replacement therapy, which may reverse the plastic changes.

Gonadal hormones also affect how the brain responds to environmental events. For instance, among rats housed in complex environments, males show more dendritic growth in neurons of the visual cortex than do females (Juraska, 1990). In contrast, females housed in this setting show more dendritic growth in the hippocampus than males do. Apparently, the same experience can affect the male and female brain differently, due to the mediating influence of gonadal hormones.

As females and males develop, then, their brains continue to diverge more and more, much like a fork in a road. After you set out on one path, your direction is forever changed, as the roads increasingly course farther apart.

To summarize, gonadal hormones alter basic neuronal development, shape experience-dependent changes in the brain, and influence neuronal structure throughout our lifetimes. Those who believe that behavioral differences between males and females are solely the result of environmental experiences must consider these neural effects of sex hormones.

In part, it is true that environmental factors exert a major influence. But one reason they do so may be that male and female brains are different to start with. Even the same events experienced by structurally different brains may lead to different effects on those brains. Evidence shows that significant experiences, such as prenatal stress, produce markedly different changes in gene expression in the frontal cortex of male and female rats (Mychasiuk et al., 2011).

Another key question related to hormonal influences on brain development is whether any sex differences in brain organization might be independent of hormonal action. In other words, are differences in the action of sex chromosome genes unrelated to sex hormones? Although little is known about such genetic effects in humans, studies of birds clearly show that genetic effects on brain cells may indeed contribute to sex differentiation.

Songbirds have an especially interesting brain dimorphism: in most species, males sing and females do not. This behavioral difference between the sexes is directly related to a neural birdsong circuit present in males but not in females. Robert Agate and his colleagues (2003) studied the brain of a rare *gynandromorph* zebra finch, shown in **Figure 8-31**. This bird exhibits physical characteristics of both sexes.

Genetic analysis shows that cells on one-half of the bird's brain and body are genetically female and on the other half are genetically male. The two sides of the gynandromorph's body and brain were exposed to the same hormones during prenatal development. Thus, the effect of male and female genes on the birdsong circuit can be examined to determine how the genes and hormones might interact.

If the sex difference in the birdsong circuit were totally related to the presence of hormones prenatally, then the two sides of the brain should be equally masculine or feminine. Agate's results confirm the opposite: the neural song circuit is masculine on the male side of the brain. Only a genetic difference that was at least partly independent of hormonal effects could explain such a structural difference in the brain.

Gut Bacteria and Brain Development

We have emphasized factors that affect CNS development directly, but a less direct route exerts itself via the enteric nervous system. The ENS sends information to the brain that affects our mental state. The brain, in turn, can modify gut function.

An important component of the ENS is the microbiome, the bacteria in the gut with which the ENS interacts. About 10^{14} microbiota populate the adult gut, which means that microbiota outnumber the host body cells by a factor of 10. But in utero, the fetus's gut is sterile. It is only at birth that trillions of microbes from the mother's vaginal and anal fluids, and later from her skin, invade the baby's body and start to grow.

Many neurodevelopmental disorders, including autism, may be related to an atypical microbiome early in life (e.g., Kelly et al., 2017). **Psychobiotics** is a term that refers to the use of live bacteria (probiotics) or compounds that enhance the growth of gut

Details on sexual orientation and gender identity appear in Section 12-5.

FIGURE 8-31 **Gynandromorph** This rare zebra finch has dull female plumage on one side of the body and bright male plumage on the other side. Neural, not gonadal, origin of brain sex differences in a gynandromorphic finch. Agate RJ, Grisham W, Wade J, Mann S, Wingfield J, Schanen C, Palotie A, Arnold AP. Proc Natl Acad Sci U S A. 2003 Apr 15;100(8):4873-8. Copyright(2003) National Academy of Sciences, U.S.A.

Section 2-5 introduces the ENS and microbiome.

psychobiotics Treatment that uses live bacteria (probiotics) or compounds to enhance the growth of gut bacteria (prebiotics).

bacteria (prebiotics) to confer mental health benefits. Although there are not yet many human clinical trials, animal laboratory studies have proven encouraging. For example, a series of studies using a rodent model of early-life stress showed that untreated stressed animals exhibited cognitive deficits in adulthood, whereas animals whose mothers received a probiotic formulation in their drinking water while the pups were nursing displayed no such effects in adulthood (e.g., Cowan et al., 2016). Other studies have shown that certain bacteria can enhance emotional learning and reduce anxiety and the effects of stress (see review by Foster et al., 2017).

8-4 Review

Before you continue, check your understanding. Answers to Self-Test appear at the back of the book.

1. The idea that specific molecules in different cells in various midbrain regions give each cell a distinctive chemical identity is known as the _____.

2. Subnormal visual stimulation to one eye during early development can lead to a loss of acuity, known as _____.

3. The hormone _____ masculinizes the brain during development.

4. The brain's sensitivity to experience is highest during _____.

5. Why do so many mental disorders appear during adolescence?

For additional study tools, visit ⚛ **LaunchPad** at launchpadworks.com

---

8-5

Abnormal Experience and Brain Development

As we have shown, both pre- and postnatal experience and environment play a significant role in modifying brain development. In this section, we discuss how many aversive experiences, as well as injury and exposure to drugs, can lead to abnormal brain development and neurodevelopmental disorders.

Early Life Experience and Brain Development

If complex or enriched experiences early in life can stimulate brain growth and influence later behavior, severely restricted experiences early in life seem likely to retard both brain growth and behavior. To study the effects of such restrictions, Donald Hebb and his colleagues (Clarke et al., 1951) placed young Scottish terriers in the dark with as little stimulation as possible and compared their behavior to that of dogs raised in a typical environment.

When the dogs raised in the barren environment, obviously unethical by today's standards, were later removed from it, their behavior was highly unusual. They showed virtually no reaction to people or other dogs and appeared to have lost any pain sensation. Even sticking pins in them (also unethical) produced no response. When given a dog version of the Hebb–Williams intelligence test for rats, these dogs performed terribly and were unable to learn tasks that dogs raised in more stimulating settings learned easily.

Results of subsequent studies show that depriving young animals of visual input or of maternal contact, specifically, has devastating consequences for their behavioral development and presumably for their brain development. Austin Riesen (1982) and his colleagues extensively studied animals raised in the dark. They found that after early visual deprivation, even though the animals' eyes still work, they may be functionally blind. An absence of visual stimulation results in the atrophy of dendrites on cortical neurons, essentially the opposite of the results observed in the brains of animals raised in complex and stimulating environments.

Not only does the absence of specific sensory inputs adversely affect brain development; so too does the absence of more complex typical experiences. In the 1950s, Harry Harlow (1971) began the first systematic laboratory studies of analogous deprivation in laboratory animals. Harlow showed that infant monkeys raised without maternal (or paternal) contact develop grossly atypical intellectual and social behaviors in adulthood.

Harlow separated baby monkeys from their mothers shortly after birth and raised them in individual cages. Perhaps the most stunning effect occurred in adulthood, when these animals were totally unable to establish normal relations with other animals. Unfortunately, Harlow did not analyze the deprived monkeys' brains. We would predict atrophy of cortical neurons, especially in the frontal lobe regions related to social behavior. Harlow's student Stephen Suomi has found a wide variety of hormonal and neurological abnormalities among motherless monkeys, including epigenetic changes (see the review by Dettmer & Suomi, 2014).

Children who are raised in a barren environment or are abused or neglected are at a serious disadvantage later in life. In the previous section, we discussed the impact of an impoverished environment on the language development of children. Proof is also evident in the hampered intellectual and motor development displayed by children raised in dreadful circumstances, such as those described in Clinical Focus 8-4, Romanian Orphans. Although some argue that children can succeed in school and in life if they really want to, abnormal developmental experiences can clearly alter the brain irrevocably. As a society, we cannot ignore the effects of the environment to which our children are exposed.

Early exposure to stress, including prenatally, also has major effects on a child's later behavior. Stress can alter the expression of certain genes, such as those related to serotonin (5-hydroxytryptamine, or 5-HT) reuptake. Early alteration in serotonin activity can severely alter how the brain responds to stressful experiences later in life.

Stress early in life may predispose people to develop behavioral disorders, such as depression (Tottenham, 2014). Early stress can also leave a lasting imprint on brain structure: the amygdala is enlarged, and the hippocampus is small (Charil et al., 2010). Changes in frontal lobe anatomy have been associated with the development of depressive and anxiety disorders and may be linked to the epigenetic effects described in Section 8-2.

Section 6-5 explains the neurobiology of the stress response. Section 16-2 connects mood and reactivity to stress.

Effects of Adverse Experience on Prenatal Development

As noted in Section 8-4 , brain development can be affected by either parent's experiences before conception or those of the mother or fetus during gestation. Because developmental events change so dramatically and quickly in utero, we should not be surprised that the effects of fetal experiences vary with the precise developmental stage. As a rule, the CNS is especially sensitive during gestational weeks 4 to 8, as the neural tube forms. It remains sensitive through the period of cerebral neurogenesis, which continues until the end of the second trimester. In the previous section, we presented evidence showing how environmental influences can impact an animal's neuronal structure. Work by Robbin Gibb and her colleagues (2014) has also shown that housing pregnant rats in complex environments, as in Figure 8-24A , results in the offspring showing increased dendritic spine density in the cortex, as though the animals had been placed in the environment in adulthood.

As noted, prenatal experiences also can lead to abnormal behavior in children and adults. The consensus is that perinatal adversity, such as gestational stress at or near birth, is a significant risk factor for later behavioral disorders (see Bock et al., 2014). Even events such as stress or drug use that occur *before* conception can lead to epigenetic effects in offspring. Although such effects are usually presumed to come from maternal exposure before conception, increasing evidence from research on humans points to paternal preconception experience also modifying children's brain

◎ **CLINICAL FOCUS 8-4**

Romanian Orphans

In the 1970s, Romania's Communist regime outlawed all forms of birth control and abortion. The natural result was more than 100,000 unwanted children in state-run orphanages. The conditions were appalling.

The children were housed and clothed but given virtually no environmental stimulation. Mostly they were confined to cots with few, if any, playthings and virtually no personal interaction with overworked caregivers, who looked after 20 to 25 children at once. Bathing often consisted of being hosed down with cold water.

After the Communist government fell, the outside world intervened. Hundreds of these children were placed in adoptive homes throughout the world, especially in the United States, Canada, and the United Kingdom. Studies of these severely deprived children on arrival in their new homes document malnourishment, chronic respiratory and intestinal infections, and severe developmental impairments.

A British study by Michael Rutter (1998) and his colleagues assessed the orphans at 2 standard deviations below age-matched children for weight, height, and head circumference (taken as a very rough measure of brain size). Scales of motor and cognitive development assessed most of the children in the impaired range.

The improvement these children showed in the first 2 years after placement in their adoptive homes was nothing short of spectacular. Average height and weight advanced to nearly normal, although head circumference remained below normal. Many tested in the normal range of motor and cognitive development. But a significant number were still considered intellectually impaired. What caused these individual differences in recovery from the past deprivation?

The key factor was age at adoption. Children adopted before 6 months of age did significantly better than those adopted later. In a Canadian study by Elinor Ames (1997), Romanian orphans who were adopted before 4 months of age and then tested at 4½ years of age had an average Stanford–Binet IQ score of 98. Age-matched Canadian controls had an average score of 109. Brain-imaging studies showed that children adopted at an older age had a smaller brain than normal.

Charles Nelson and his colleagues (Berens & Nelson, 2015; Nelson et al., 2007; Smyke et al., 2012) analyzed cognitive and social development as well as event-related potential (ERP) measures in a group of children who had remained in Romania. Whether the children had moved to foster homes or remained in institutions, the studies reveal severe abnormalities at about 4 years of age. The age at adoption was again important, but in the Nelson studies the critical age appears to be before 24 months rather than 6 months, as in the earlier studies.

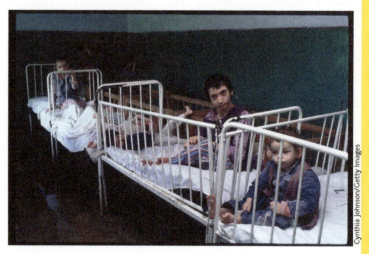

Romanian orphans warehoused in the 1970s and 1980s endured the conditions shown in this photograph. The utter absence of stimuli hampered their normal brain development.

The extent of early deprivation was extreme in the Romanian study, but analysis of children with less extreme periods of institutionalization and subsequent adoption have also shown significant changes in the volume of cerebral structures, especially in the frontal lobe, hippocampus, and amygdala. For example, Hodel et al. (2015) studied a diverse group of post-institutionalized children (ages 12–14) who had entered the United States predominantly from China, Eastern Europe/Russia, and India. These children had been living with their adopted families for an average of about 12 years, but they still exhibited abnormalities in the development of the prefrontal cortex. Hodel's study showed that the prefrontal cortex may be particularly vulnerable to early life adversity.

The inescapable conclusion is that the human brain may be able to recover from a brief period of extreme deprivation in early infancy, but periods longer than 24 months produce significant developmental abnormalities that cannot be overcome completely. The studies of Romanian and other orphans make clear that the developing brain requires stimulation for healthy development. Although the brain may be able to catch up after brief deprivation, severe deprivation lasting many months results in a small brain and associated behavioral abnormalities, especially in cognitive and social skills.

Clinical Focus 6-2 details FASD.

development, perhaps including acquisition of fetal alcohol spectrum disorder (FASD) (e.g., Zuccolo et al., 2016).

In fact, evidence from studies of laboratory animals suggests that the effects of preconception experiences are greater from the father than the mother (e.g., Dias & Ressler, 2014). One explanation is that the preconceptual experiences in males may change the *germline*, which refers to the genetic material of cells that is passed through successive generations. For example, the genetic material in the sperm or egg is part of the germline. The egg cells of adults are not easily changed by experiences because they are formed early in body development in females; but sperm are constantly being renewed, and thus gene expression in sperm is more likely to be altered by experience and passed on to progeny. Yet maternal experience before conception can affect off-spring directly by changing the stress response of the dam, which could in turn alter the offspring's brain development, or by changing the dam's behavior toward her infant(s).

Injury and Brain Development

Into the late 1800s, infants and children were generally believed to show better recovery from brain injury than adults. In the 1930s, Donald Hebb studied children with major birth-related injuries to the frontal lobes and found them to have severe and permanent behavioral abnormalities in adulthood. He concluded that brain damage early in life can alter the brain's subsequent development and actually may be worse than injury later in life.

Have other studies confirmed Hebb's conclusion? Few anatomical studies of humans with early brain injuries exist, but we can make some general predictions from studying laboratory animals. In general, early brain injuries do produce atypical brains, especially at certain critical periods in development.

For humans, the worst time appears to be in the last half of the intrauterine period and the first couple of months after birth. Rats and cats that are injured at a comparable time have a significantly smaller brain than average, and their cortical neurons show general atrophy relative to healthy brains, as illustrated on the left in **Figure 8-32**. Behaviorally, these animals appear cognitively deficient over a wide range of skills.

Injury to the developing brain is not always devastating, however. For example, researchers have known for more than 100 years that children with brain injuries in the first couple of years after birth almost never have the severe language disturbances common to adults with equivalent injuries. Animal studies help explain why.

Whereas damage to the rat brain in the developmental period comparable to the last few months of gestation in humans produces widespread cortical atrophy, damage at a time in rat brain development roughly comparable to ages 6 months to 2 years in humans actually produces more dendritic development in rats (Figure 8-32 at right). Furthermore, these animals show dramatic recovery of functions, which implies that during development the brain has a capacity to compensate for injury. Parallel studies in cats have shown extensive reorganization of cortex-to-cortex connections after early injury to the visual cortex (see the review by Payne & Lomber, 2001).

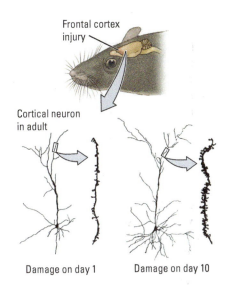

Frontal cortex injury

Cortical neuron in adult

Damage on day 1   Damage on day 10

FIGURE 8-32 **Time-Dependent Effects** Damage to the rat's frontal cortex on the day of birth leads to cortical neurons with simple dendritic fields and sparse growth of spines in the adult (left). In contrast, damage to the frontal cortex at 10 days of age leads to cortical neurons with expanded dendritic fields and denser spines than normal in adults (right). Information from Kolb & Gibb, 1993.

Drugs and Brain Development

The U.S. National Institute on Drug Abuse (NIDA, 2012) estimates that 16 percent of babies born alive in the United States today are exposed to nicotine in utero. Similar statistics on alcohol consumption by pregnant mothers are not available, but the effects of alcohol on the fetus are well documented. Even low doses of commonly prescribed drugs, including antidepressants, antipsychotics, and pain-killers, appear to alter prenatal neuron development in the prefrontal cortex. It manifests after birth in abnormalities in behaviors controlled by the affected regions (see the review by Ross et al., 2015).

NIDA also estimates that 5.5 percent of expectant mothers—approximately 221,000 pregnant women each year in the United States—use an illicit drug at least once in the course of their pregnancy. Among pregnant teenagers aged 15 to 17, that figure climbs to 16 percent, or about 14,000 women. And what about caffeine and nicotine? More than likely, most children were exposed to caffeine (from coffee, tea, cola, energy drinks, and chocolate) in utero and about 16 percent were exposed to nicotine. Laboratory animal studies have shown that prenatal exposure to nicotine alters the brain's response to complex housing: the brain appears less plastic (e.g., Mychasiuk et al., 2014).

The precise effects of prenatal drug intake on brain development are poorly understood, but the overall conclusion from current knowledge is that children with prenatal exposure to a variety of psychoactive drugs have an increased likelihood of later drug use (e.g., Minnes et al., 2014). Although, again, childhood disorders (e.g., learning disabilities and ADHD) are poorly studied, many experts suggest that they may be related

Section 6-3 reviews the prominence of nicotine as a gateway drug. Section 6-4 examines some explanations of and treatments for drug abuse.

Research Focus 7-4 details ADHD, and Clinical Focus 14-1 details dyslexia.

to prenatal exposure to drugs such as nicotine or caffeine or both. As Carl Malanga and Barry Kosofsky (2003) note poignantly, society at large does not yet fully appreciate the impact that prenatal drug exposure can have on the lives of its children.

Other Sources of Abnormal Brain Development

The nervous system need not be damaged by external forces to develop abnormally. Many genetic aberrations are believed to result in abnormalities in brain development and ultimately brain structure. *Spina bifida*, in which the genetic blueprint goes awry and the neural tube does not close completely, leads to an incompletely formed spinal cord. After birth, unless treated with folic acid, children with spina bifida usually have serious motor problems.

Imagine what happens if some genetic aberration causes improper closure of the front end of the neural tube. Because the front end of the neural tube forms the brain (see Figure 8-5), this failure results in gross abnormalities in brain development known as **anencephaly**. Affected infants die soon after birth.

Atypical brain development can be much subtler than anencephaly. For example, if cells do not migrate to their correct locations, and if these mispositioned cells do not subsequently die, they can disrupt brain function and may lead to disorders ranging from seizures to schizophrenia (see review by Guerrini et al., 2007). In a variety of conditions, neurons fail to differentiate normally. In certain cases, neurons fail to produce long dendrites or spines, which results in abnormal brain connectivity and developmental disabilities.

The opposite condition also is possible: neurons continue to make dendrites and form connections with other cells until the neurons are extraordinarily large. The functional consequences of all the newly formed connections can be devastating. Excitatory synapses in the wrong location effectively short-circuit a neuron's function.

Subtle abnormal events also can be devastating—and even terminal. **Sudden infant death syndrome (SIDS)**, the unexplained death while asleep of a seemingly healthy infant less than 1 year old, kills about 2500 babies yearly in the United States alone. Postmortem studies reveal that SIDS victims are more likely than other babies to have a particular gene variation that makes the serotonin transporter unusually efficient. Normally, the serotoninergic system helps to stimulate a respiratory mechanism that responds to high carbon dioxide levels in the blood and acts to expel the gas.

In babies who die of SIDS, serotonin is cleared from the synapse more rapidly than normal. This action makes 5-HT less effective in regulating life-threatening events such as carbon dioxide buildup during sleep. Babies can breathe excessive levels of carbon dioxide that is trapped in their bedding, for example, and suffocate.

In addition to the serotonin transporter abnormality, David Paterson and his colleagues (2006) found an abnormally low occurrence of 5-HT$_{1A}$ receptors in SIDS victims' brains. The researchers found that boys have significantly fewer 5-HT$_{1A}$ receptors than do females, a result consistent with higher SIDS mortality in boys. Hannah Kinney (2009) speculates that the primary defect is increased numbers of 5-HT cells, possibly arising during fetal development and owing to unknown causes, but augmented by adverse prenatal exposure to alcohol, nicotine, and/or other factors. This defect leads to the changes in 5-HT$_{1A}$ receptors.

A curious consequence of abnormal brain development is that behavioral effects may emerge only as the brain matures and the maturing regions begin to play a greater role in behavior. This consequence is true especially of frontal lobe injuries. The frontal lobes continue to develop into early adulthood, and often not until adolescence do the effects of frontal lobe abnormalities become noticeable.

Schizophrenia is a disease characterized by its slow development, usually not becoming obvious until late adolescence. Clinical Focus 8-5, Schizophrenia, relates disease progress and its possible origin.

anencephaly Failure of the forebrain to develop.

sudden infant death syndrome (SIDS) Unexplained death while asleep of a seemingly healthy infant less than 1 year old.

Schizophrenia

When Mrs. T. was 16 years old, she began to experience her first symptom of schizophrenia: a profound feeling that people were staring at her. These bouts of self-consciousness soon forced her to end her public piano performances. Her self-consciousness led to withdrawal, then to fearful delusions that others were speaking about her behind her back, and finally to suspicions that they were plotting to harm her.

At first Mrs. T.'s illness was intermittent, and the return of her intelligence, warmth, and ambition between episodes allowed her to complete several years of college, to marry, and to rear three children. She had to enter a hospital for her illness for the first time at age 28, after the birth of her third child, when she began to hallucinate.

Now, at 45, Mrs. T. is never entirely well. She has seen dinosaurs on the street and live animals in her refrigerator. While hallucinating, she speaks and writes in an incoherent, but almost poetic way. At other times, she is more lucid, but even then the voices she hears sometimes lead her to do dangerous things, such as driving very fast down the highway in the middle of the night, dressed only in a nightgown. . . . At other times and without any apparent stimulus, Mrs. T. has bizarre visual hallucinations. For example, she saw cherubs in the grocery store. These experiences leave her preoccupied, confused, and frightened, unable to perform such everyday tasks as cooking or playing the piano. (Gershon & Rieder, 1992, p. 127)

It has always been easier to identify schizophrenic behavior than to define schizophrenia. Perhaps the one universally accepted criterion for its diagnosis is the absence of other neurological disturbances or affective (mood) disorders that could cause a person to lose touch with reality—a definition by default.

Schizophrenia is generally considered to be a developmental disorder because symptoms usually emerge in adolescence and early adulthood. These symptoms are believed to be a consequence of events occurring early in development and reflect a combination of genetic and environmental effects on brain development. It has been proposed that multiple genes trigger a cascade of neuropathological events, which begin during gestation and progress into adolescence and adulthood, where they are influenced by environmental factors (see review by Rapoport et al., 2012).

Symptoms of schizophrenia vary, suggesting that biological abnormalities also vary from person to person. Most patients appear to stay at a fairly stable level after the first few years of symptoms, with little evidence of a decline in neuropsychological functioning. Symptoms come and go, much as for Mrs. T., but the severity is relatively constant after the first few episodes.

Numerous studies have investigated the brains of schizophrenia patients, both in MRI and CT scans and in autopsies. Although the results vary, most neuroscientists agree that schizophrenic brains weigh less than normal and have enlarged ventricles. Research findings also suggest that brains affected by schizophrenia have smaller frontal lobes (or at least a reduction in the number of neurons in the prefrontal cortex) and thinner parahippocampal gyri. Furthermore, the onset of symptoms appears to be associated with progressive gray matter abnormalities, especially during the early stages of the illness (for a review, see Dietsche et al., 2017).

Joyce Kovelman and Arnold Scheibel (1984) found abnormalities in the orientation of hippocampal neurons in people with schizophrenia. Rather than the consistently parallel orientation of neurons in this region characteristic of healthy brains, schizophrenic brains have a more haphazard organization, as shown in the accompanying drawings.

Pyramidal cell orientation in the hippocampus of **(A)** a healthy brain and **(B)** a schizophrenic brain. Research from Kovelman & Scheibel, 1984.

Hippocampus

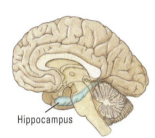

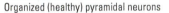

Organized (healthy) pyramidal neurons   Disorganized (schizophrenic) pyramidal neurons

Developmental Disability

Impaired cognitive functioning accompanies abnormal brain development. Impairment may range from mild, allowing an almost normal lifestyle, to severe, requiring constant care. As summarized in **Table 8-3**, such developmental disability can result from chronic malnutrition, genetic abnormalities such as Down syndrome, hormonal abnormalities, brain injury, or neurological disease. Different causes produce different abnormalities in brain organization, but the critical similarity across all types of developmental disability is that the brain is not normal.

Dominique Purpura (1974) conducted one of the few systematic investigations of developmentally disabled children's brains. Purpura used Golgi stain to examine the neurons of children who had died of accident or disease unrelated to the nervous

Section 16-2 describes the schizophrenic brain and Section 5-3 a possible relation to excessive DA or 5-HT activity in that brain.

Figure 3-22 illustrates trisomy, the chromosomal abnormality that causes Down syndrome.

TABLE 8-3 **Causes of Developmental Disability**

Cause	Example mechanism	Example condition
Abnormal embryonic development	Exposure to a toxin	FASD
Birth trauma	Anoxia (oxygen deprivation)	Cerebral palsy
Chronic malnutrition	Abnormal brain development	Kwashiorkor
Drugs (e.g., valproate)	Neural tube defects	Spina bifida ASD
Environmental abnormality	Sensory deprivation	Children in Romanian orphanages
Genetic abnormality	Error of metabolism Chromosomal abnormality	Phenylketonuria Down syndrome
Prenatal disease	Infection	Rubella (German measles) Retardation

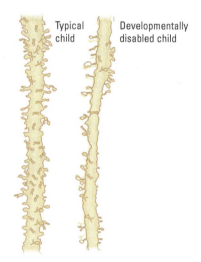

Typical child   Developmentally disabled child

FIGURE 8-33 **Neuronal Contrast**
Representative dendritic branches from cortical neurons in a child of typical intelligence (left) and a developmentally disabled child (right), whose neurons are thinner and have far fewer spines. Information from Purpura, 1974.

system. When he examined the brains of children with various forms of intellectual disability, he found that dendrite growth was stunted and the spines were very sparse relative to dendrites from children of typical intelligence, as illustrated in **Figure 8-33**.

The simpler neuronal structure probably indicates a marked reduction in the number of brain connections, which presumably caused the developmental disability. Variation in both the nature and the extent of neuronal abnormality in different children would lead to different behavioral syndromes. In addition, an abnormality in one system during development can interact with other systems producing new abnormalities. For example, children with recurring ear infections often have delayed hearing development, which in turn can slow language development. Similarly, early stress can alter brain development, which in turn can render the brain sensitive to stressors in adolescence.

How Do Any of Us Develop a Normal Brain?

When we consider the brain's complexity, the less-than-precise process of brain development, and the myriad factors—from SES to gut bacteria—that can influence development, we are left to marvel at how so many of us end up with brains that pass for normal. We all must have had neurons that migrated to wrong locations, made incorrect connections, were exposed to viruses or other harmful substances. If the brain were as fragile as it might seem, to end up with a normal brain would seem to be abnormal.

Apparently, animals have evolved a substantial capacity to repair minor abnormalities in brain development. Most people have developed in the range that we call normal because the human brain's plasticity and regenerative powers overcome minor developmental deviations. By initially overproducing neurons and synapses, the brain gains the capacity to correct errors that might have arisen accidentally.

These same plastic properties later allow us to cope with the ravages of aging. Neurons are dying throughout our lifetime. By age 60, investigators ought to see significant effects from all this cell loss, especially considering the cumulative results of exposure to environmental toxins, drugs, traumatic brain injuries, and other neural perturbations. But this is not what happens.

Although some teenagers may not believe it, relatively few 60-year-olds are demented. By most criteria, the 60-year-old who has been intellectually active throughout adulthood is likely to be much wiser than the 18-year-old whose brain has lost relatively fewer neurons. A 60-year-old chess player will have a record of many more chess matches from which to draw game strategies than would an 18-year-old, for example. Recall, too, that early music or second language experience appears to partly protect the brain from degenerative neural diseases such as dementia.

Clearly, some mechanism must enable us to compensate for loss and minor injury to our brain cells. This capacity for plasticity and change, for learning and adapting, is arguably the most important characteristic of the human brain during development and throughout life.

We return to learning, memory, and neuroplasticity in Chapter 14.

8-5 Review

Before you continue, check your understanding. Answers to Self-Test appear at the back of the book.

1. Brain injuries have an increased potential to produce atypical brains if they occur during _____ periods in development.

2. Postmortem studies have revealed that _____, which is the unexplained death of a sleeping infant, may be linked to a gene variation that makes the serotonin transporter unusually efficient.

3. Riesen's studies on animals raised in the dark show that an absence of _____ stimulation can affect brain development.

4. Explain why, despite the fact that neurons are dying throughout our lifetimes, researchers do not see significant effects from cell loss in the brains of individuals in their fifties and sixties.

5. Why might the effects of preconception experiences be greater from the father than from the mother?

For additional study tools, visit **LaunchPad** at launchpadworks.com

▌Summary

8-1 Three Perspectives on Brain Development

Nervous system development entails more than the unfolding of a genetic blueprint. Development is a complex dance of genetic and environmental events that interact to sculpt the brain to fit within a particular cultural and environmental context. We can approach this dance from three perspectives: (1) correlating emerging brain structures with emerging behaviors, (2) correlating new behaviors with neural maturation, and (3) identifying influences on brain and behavior.

8-2 Neurobiology of Development

Human brain maturation is a long process, lasting as late as age 30. Neurons, the units of brain function, develop a phenotype, migrate, and, as their processes elaborate, establish connections with other neurons even before birth. The developing brain produces many more neurons and connections than it needs and then prunes back in toddlerhood, and again in adolescence and early adulthood, to a stable level maintained by some neurogenesis throughout the life span. Experiences throughout development can trigger epigenetic mechanisms, such as gene methylation, that alter gene expression.

8-3 Using Emerging Behaviors to Infer Neural Maturation

Throughout the world, across the cultural spectrum, from newborn to adult, we all develop through similar behavioral stages. As infants develop physically, motor behaviors emerge in a predictable sequence from gross, poorly directed movements toward objects to controlled pincer grasps to pick up objects as small as pencils by about 11 months. Cognitive behaviors also develop through stages of logic and problem solving. Beginning with Jean Piaget, researchers have identified and characterized four or more distinct stages of cognitive development. Each stage can be identified by specific behavioral tests.

Behaviors emerge as the neural systems that produce them develop. Matching the median timetables of neurodevelopment with observed behavior infers the hierarchical relation between brain structure and brain function. Motor behaviors emerge in synchrony with maturating motor circuits in the cerebral cortex, basal ganglia, and cerebellum, as well as in the connections from these areas to the spinal cord. Similar correlations between emerging behaviors and neuronal development accompany the maturation of cognitive behavior as neural circuits in the frontal and temporal lobes mature in early adulthood.

8-4 Brain Development and the Environment

The brain is most plastic during its development, and neuronal structures and their connections can be molded by various factors throughout development. The brain's sensitivity to factors such as external events, quality of environment, tactile stimulation, drugs, gonadal hormones, stress, and injury varies over time. At critical periods in the course of development, beginning prenatally, different brain regions are particularly sensitive to different events.

8-5 Abnormal Experience and Brain Development

Adverse prenatal and early childhood experiences can have profound effects on brain development and behavior. Prenatal and early life stress can predispose people to develop behavioral disorders, as well as leave a lasting imprint on brain structure. Even parental stress before conception can result in epigenetic effects in the fetus.

Brain perturbations in the course of development from, say, anoxia, trauma, or toxins can alter brain development significantly; can result in severe behavioral abnormalities, including intellectual disability; and may be related to such disorders as ASD or SIDS. Other behavioral disorders emerge in adolescence, a time of prolonged frontal lobe change. Abnormalities affecting one brain system during development can interact with other systems to produce new abnormalities.

The brain has a substantial capacity to repair or correct minor abnormalities, allowing most people to develop normal behavioral repertoires and to maintain brain function throughout life.

Key Terms

amblyopia, p. 267

androgen, p. 270

anencephaly, p. 276

apoptosis, p. 255

autism spectrum disorder (ASD), p. 253

cell adhesion molecule (CAM), p. 254

chemoaffinity hypothesis, p. 266

critical period, p. 267

default network, p. 256

dorsolateral prefrontal cortex (DLPFC), p. 256

estrogen, p. 270

filopod (pl. filopodia), p. 254

glioblast, p. 248

growth cone, p. 254

growth spurt, p. 261

imprinting, p. 267

masculinization, p. 270

netrin, p. 254

neural Darwinism, p. 255

neural plate, p. 247

neural stem cell, p. 248

neural tube, p. 247

neuroblast, p. 248

neurotrophic factor, p. 250

progenitor cell (precursor cell), p. 248

psychobiotics, p. 271

radial glial cell, p. 251

semaphorin, p. 254

subventricular zone, p. 248

sudden infant death syndrome (SIDS), p. 276

testosterone, p. 269

tropic molecule, p. 254

Visit **LaunchPad** to access the e-Book, videos, **LearningCurve** adaptive quizzing, flashcards, and more at launchpadworks.com

How Do We Sense, Perceive, and See the World?

⊙ **CLINICAL FOCUS** 9-1

Migraines and a Case of Blindsight

D. B.'s recurring headaches began at about age 14. A visual aura warned of a headache's approach: an oval area of flashing (scintillating) light would appear just left of center in his field of vision. Over the next few minutes, the oval would enlarge. After about 15 minutes, the flashing light would vanish, and D. B. would be left temporarily blind in the region of the oval.

D. B. described the oval as an opaque white area surrounded by a rim of color. A headache on the right side of his head followed and could persist for as long as 48 hours. D. B. usually fell asleep before that much time elapsed. When he awakened, the headache was gone, and his vision was normal again.

The recurrent headaches D. B. suffered from are called migraines, and they were caused by the dilation of cerebral blood vessels that occurs during an aura. Auras may be auditory, tactile, or visual, and they may result in an inability to move or talk. And just as an aura is usually limited to one side of the visual field, as in D. B.'s case, migraines are usually limited to one side of the head.

Migraines vary in severity, frequency, and duration (left untreated, some may last for hours or even days) and are often accompanied by nausea and vomiting. Migraine is perhaps the most common of all neurological disorders, affecting some 5 to 20 percent of the population at some time in their lives.

D. B.'s attacks continued at intervals of about 6 weeks for 10 years. After one attack, he was left with a small blind spot, or *scotoma*, illustrated in the accompanying photographs. When D. B. was 26 years old, a neurologist found that a collection of abnormal blood vessels at the back of his right occipital lobe was causing the migraine attacks—a most unusual cause.

By the time he was 30, the migraines had begun to interfere with his family life, social life, and job. No drug treatment was effective, and D. B. had the malformed blood vessels surgically removed. The operation relieved his pain and generally improved his life, but a part of his right occipital lobe, deprived of blood, had died. D. B. was blind in the left half of his visual field: as he looks at the world through either eye, he is unable to see anything left of the midline.

Lawrence Weizkrantz (1986) made a remarkable discovery about D. B.'s blindness. D. B. could not identify objects in his blind area but could very accurately tell whether a light had blinked on there and even where the light was. Apparently, D. B.'s brain knew when a light blinked and where it appeared—a phenomenon called *blindsight*, in which his brain knew more than he was aware of consciously. D. B.'s case provides an excellent example of the parallel streams of visual processing in the cortex. His system for processing objects was impaired, but his system for locating objects in space was not.

A similar conclusion comes from the study of patient T. N., who had suffered strokes in each visual cortex, leaving him with clinical blindness over his whole visual field (de Gelder et al., 2008). Like D. B., he retained some unconscious visual abilities, the most impressive being that T. N. could successfully navigate down a long corridor obstructed with objects (a video clip accompanying the de Gelder paper demonstrates this). He claimed not to be aware of the objects and believed he had walked in a straight path down the hallway.

X = Fixation point

As a typical migraine scotoma develops, a person looking at the small white × in the photograph at the far left first sees a small patch of lines. This striped area continues growing outward, leaving an opaque area (scotoma) where the stripes were, almost completely blocking the visual field within 15 to 20 minutes. Normal vision returns shortly thereafter.

As you look at the photographs in Clinical Focus 9-1, Migraines and a Case of Blindsight, you see three people—two women and a man—who appear to be walking and talking on a warm summer day. Trees appear in the background, clearly behind the people. It is tempting to believe that this visual image is transferred whole to the brain, where we see it.

But how could the nervous system do this? There is no viewing screen in the brain. Instead, the nervous system must construct the image from bits of information, such as shape and color. Then the brain must put it all together to form what we perceive as a complete image. The neural reconstruction is not a passive image such as a screen projects. Rather, the brain continuously employs memories, both to interpret moment-to-moment sensory information and to predict the immediate future.

D. B.'s case demonstrates that we are consciously aware of only part of the visual information our brain is processing. This *selective awareness* is an important working principle behind human sensation and perception. Weizkrantz, a world-renowned visual neuroscientist at Oxford University, detected it in the visual system only because of D. B.'s injury.

The ability to lose conscious visual perception while retaining unconscious vision, as D. B. did, leads us to the chapter's central question: How do we see the world? We are in fact unaware of much of the sensory processing that takes place in the neural pathways for vision, hearing, touch, taste, and smell. All our senses convert energy into neural activity that has meaning for us. We begin this chapter with a general summary of sensation and perception that explores how this energy conversion takes place. We next look at visual system anatomy and consider the connections between the eyes and the sections of the brain that process visual information.

Turning to the perceptual experience of sight, we focus on how neurons respond to visual input and enable the brain to perceive features such as color, shape, and movement. At the chapter's end, we explore vision's culmination: understanding what we see. How do we infuse light energy with meaning to grasp the content of written words or to see the beauty in a painting? Read on.

Vision is this chapter's main topic; hearing is Chapter 10's. Section 11-4 covers body senses and balance. Section 12-2 explains smell and taste.

9-1

Nature of Sensation and Perception

We naturally presume that our sensory experiences tell us what is "real" in our environment, but our sensory experience can deceive us; two people looking at the same image can see very different things. We may believe that we see, hear, touch, smell, and taste real things in a real world. In fact, the only input our brain receives from the "real" world is a series of action potentials that originate from energy that is transduced by our sensory receptors and passed along to the neurons that form our various sensory pathways.

Although we experience visual and body sensations as fundamentally different from one another, the action potentials produced in these two sensory systems are similar, as are the neurons themselves. Neuroscientists understand how neurons can turn energy, such as light waves, into nerve impulses. They also know the pathways those nerve impulses travel to reach the brain. But they do not know how we end up perceiving one set of nerve impulses as what the world looks like and another set as what we are hearing.

Our sensory systems appear to be extremely diverse: vision, audition, touch, taste, and olfaction seem at first to have little in common. Although our perceptions and behaviors in relation to them differ, each sensory system is organized on a similar hierarchical plan. We now consider the features common to the sensory systems—receptors, neural relays between receptor and neocortex, sensory coding and representation, and perception.

Sensory Receptors

Sensory receptor neurons are specialized to transduce (convert) environmental energy—light, for example—into neural activity. If we put flour into a sieve and shake it, the more finely milled particles fall through the holes, whereas the coarser particles and lumps do not. Sensory receptors are designed to respond only to a narrow band of energy—analogous to particles of certain sizes—such as the specific wavelengths of electromagnetic energy that form the basis of our vision. Each sensory system's receptors are specialized to filter a different form of energy:

- For vision, the photoreceptors in the retina convert light energy into chemical energy, which is in turn converted into action potentials. (Section 4-2 gives a detailed discussion of action potentials.)

- In the auditory system, air pressure waves are first converted into mechanical energy, which activates the auditory receptors that produce action potentials in auditory receptor neurons.

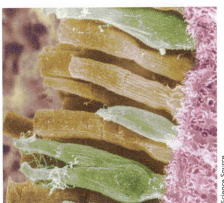

Science Source

Vision begins in the photoreceptor cells, the rods and cones shown here. Section 9-2 details how they work.

receptive field Region of sensory space (for example, skin surface) in which a stimulus modifies a receptor's activity.

- In the somatosensory system, mechanical energy activates receptors sensitive to touch, pressure, or pain. These somatosensory receptors in turn generate action potentials in somatosensory receptor neurons.

- For taste and olfaction, various chemical molecules in the air or in food fit themselves into receptors of various shapes to activate action potentials in the respective receptor neurons.

Were our visual receptors somewhat different, we would be able to see in the ultraviolet range as well as the visible parts of the electromagnetic spectrum, as honeybees and butterflies can. The same can be said of our other sensory receptors: receptors in the human ear respond to a wide range of sound waves, but elephants and bats can hear and produce sounds far below and above, respectively, the range humans can hear. Different species are specialized to respond to different aspects of sensory inputs.

In a sense, our pet dogs have "superhuman" powers: they can detect trace odors; hear low-range sounds, as elephants do; and see in the dark. But we have our own "super" powers because, like most other primates, we have superior color vision. In a way, the dog world is olfactory, and ours is color. Thus, for each species and its individual members, sensory systems filter the inputs to produce an idiosyncratic representation of reality.

An animal's perception of the world depends on its nervous system's complexity and organization.

Receptive Fields

Every sensory receptor organ and cell has a **receptive field**, a specific part of the world to which it responds. If you fix your eyes on a point directly in front of you, for example, what you see of the world is the scope of your eyes' receptive field. If you close one eye, the visual world shrinks. What the open eye sees is the receptive field for that eye.

Each photoreceptor cell (out of about 120 million) in the eye points in a slightly different direction and so has a unique receptive field. You can grasp the conceptual utility of the receptive field by considering that the brain uses information from each sensory receptor's receptive field not only to identify sensory information but also to contrast the information each receptor field is providing.

Receptive fields not only sample sensory information but also help locate events in space. Because adjacent receptive fields may overlap, the contrast between their responses to events help us localize sensations. This spatial dimension of sensory information produces cortical patterns and maps that form each person's sensory reality.

Principle 1: The nervous system produces movement in a perceptual world the brain constructs.

Receptor Density and Sensitivity

Sensory receptors are not evenly distributed across the body or its organs. For example, visual receptors are more numerous in the center of our visual field than toward the edges. This difference explains why our vision is sharper in the center than at the periphery. Similarly, tactile receptors on the fingers are numerous compared with those on the arm; as a result, fingers can discriminate touch remarkably well, whereas the arm cannot. Thus, the density of receptors is related to sensory sensitivity.

In addition to the density of our receptors, our sensory systems use different types of receptors to enhance our perceptual experience. For instance, the visual system uses different sets of receptors to respond to light and color. Color photoreceptors are small and densely packed to make sensitive color discriminations in bright light. Receptors for black–white vision are larger and more scattered, but their sensitivity to light—say, a lighted match at a distance of 2 miles on a dark night—is truly remarkable.

Differences in density and sensitivity of sensory receptors determine many animals' special abilities—dogs' excellent olfactory ability and the excellent tactile ability of raccoons' digits. Variations in receptor density in the human auditory receptor organ may explain such abilities as perfect pitch, displayed by some musicians.

Craig Lovell/Eagle Visions Photography/Alamy Stock Photo

Section 10-4 explains how we perceive music.

Neural Relays

All receptors connect to the cortex through a sequence of intervening neurons. The number of these neural relays varies across different sensory systems. For example, one route for vision passes from the retina to the thalamus to the first area of visual cortex (called V1), and then to other visual cortical regions. For audition, input from the auditory receptors in the ear goes to the hindbrain, midbrain, thalamus, and finally the cortex.

Sensory information is modified at each stage in the relay, allowing each region to construct different aspects of the sensory experience. In the visual system, each of our two eyes has a separate view of the world. The information from the two views is combined in the thalamus such that the input from the left side or right side of each field is superimposed to produce two visual fields, one for the left and one for the right. At the next stage in the relay, V1, the brain begins to separate different aspects of the visual input such as shape and color. There is also a second visual pathway that goes from the retina to the superior colliculus and then to the thalamus and cortex. This pathway is involved in the perception of movement.

Neural relays also allow sensory systems to interact. A dramatic effect of sensory interaction is the visual modification of sound. If a person hears a speech syllable such as *ba* while observing someone who is articulating *ga*, the listener hears not the actual sound *ba* but a hybrid sound, *da*. The viewed lip movements modify the listener's auditory perception.

This interaction effect is potent: it highlights the fact that a speaker's facial gestures influence our perception of speech sounds. As Roy Hamilton and his colleagues (2006) described, synchrony of gestures and sounds is an important aspect of language acquisition. The difficulty of learning a foreign language can relate to the difficulty of blending a speaker's articulation movements with the sounds the speaker produces.

Sensory Coding and Representation

After it has been transduced, all information from all sensory systems is encoded by action potentials that travel along nerves until they enter the spinal cord or brain. From there the action potentials travel on nerve tracts within the central nervous system. Every bundle carries the same kind of signal. How do action potentials encode different sensations? (How does vision differ from touch?) How do they encode the features of particular sensations? (How does purple differ from blue?)

Parts of these questions seem easy to answer; others pose a fundamental challenge to neuroscience. The presence of a stimulus can be encoded by an increase or a decrease in a neuron's discharge rate, and the amount of increase or decrease can encode stimulus intensity. As detailed in Section 9-4, qualitative visual changes, such as from red to green, can be encoded by activity in different neurons or even by different levels of discharge in the same neuron. (For example, more activity might signify redder, while less activity might signify greener.)

What is less clear is how we perceive such sensations as vision, touch, sound, and smell as different from one another. Part of the explanation is that each sensation is processed in its own distinct cortical region. Also, we learn through experience to distinguish them. In addition, each sensory system has a preferential link with certain movements, constituting a separate wiring that helps keep each system distinct at all levels of neural organization. For instance, the sudden appearance of an object, such as a ball, produces withdrawal responses to avoid being struck, even though we may not know what we are avoiding until other regions can analyze the details.

The distinctions among the sensory systems, however, are not always clear: some people hear in color or identify smells by how the smells sound to them. This mixing of the senses is called *synesthesia*. Anyone who has shivered when hearing a piece of music or cringed at the noise fingernails make when scraping a blackboard has "felt" sound.

In most mammals, the neocortex represents the sensory field of each modality— vision, hearing, touch, smell, or taste—as a spatially organized neural representation of the external world. This **topographic map** is a neural–spatial representation of the body or of the areas of the sensory world perceived by a sensory organ. All mammals have at least one primary cortical area for each sensory system, such as V1. Additional

topographic map Spatially organized neural representation of the external world.

Principle 6: Brain systems are organized hierarchically and in parallel.

The process by which sensory information produces action potentials is described in Section 4-4.

Section 15-6 details synesthesia.

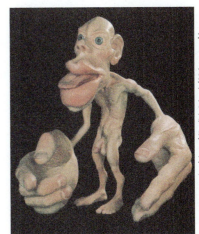

Sensory Homunculus (plaster)/English School, (20th century)/ NATURAL HISTORY MUSEUM, LONDON/Natural History Museum, London, UK/Bridgeman Images.

This curious figure reflects the topographic map in the sensorimotor cortex. Disproportionately large areas control the body parts we use to make the most-skilled movements. See Sections 11-2 and 11-5.

(A)

(B)

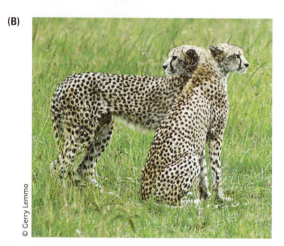

© Gerry Lemmo

FIGURE 9-1 **Perceptual Illusions (A)** Edgar Rubin's ambiguous reversible image can be perceived as a vase or as two faces. **(B)** Likewise ambiguous in the photo, each cheetah's head can be perceived as belonging to either cheetah's body.

areas are usually referred to as *secondary* because most of the information that reaches these areas is relayed through the primary area. Each additional representation is probably dedicated to encoding one specific aspect of the sensory modality. For vision, different additional representational areas may take part in perceiving color, movement, and form.

Perception

Compared with the richness of actual sensation, our description of sensory neuroanatomy and function is bound to seem sterile. **Sensation** is far more than the simple registration of physical stimuli from the environment by the sensory organs. Our sensory impressions are affected by the context in which they take place, by our emotional state, and by our past. All these factors contribute to **perception**, the subjective experience of sensation—how we interpret what we sense.

Evidence that perception is more than sensation lies in the fact that different people transform the same sensory stimulation into totally different perceptions. A classic demonstration of this fact uses an ambiguous image such as the well-known Rubin's vase shown in **Figure 9-1A**. This image may be perceived either as a vase or as two faces. If you fix your eyes on the center of the picture, the two perceptions may alternate, even though the sensory stimulation remains constant.

Similarly, the photograph of two cheetahs in Figure 9-1B is ambiguous. Which head goes with which cheetah? As with the Rubin's vase, the two perceptions may alternate. Such ambiguous images and illusions demonstrate the workings of complex perceptual phenomena and enlighten our insight into our cognitive processes.

9-1 Review

Before you continue, check your understanding. Answers to Self-Test appear at the back of the book.

1. _____ are energy filters that transduce incoming physical energy into neural activity.

2. _____ fields locate sensory events. Receptor _____ determines sensitivity to sensory stimulation.

3. We distinguish one sensory modality from another by its target in the _____.

4. Sensation registers physical stimuli from the environment by the sensory organs. Perception is the _____ experience of sensation.

5. How is the anatomical organization similar for each sense?

For additional study tools, visit 📖 **LaunchPad** at launchpadworks.com

---

9-2

The Visual System's Functional Anatomy

Our primary sensory experience is visual. Far more of the human brain is dedicated to vision than to any other sense. Understanding the visual system's organization, then, is key to understanding human brain function. To build this understanding, we begin by following the routes that visual information takes into and within the brain. This exercise is a bit like traveling a road to discover where it goes. As you trace the route, keep in mind the photographs in Clinical Focus 9-1 and what the different levels of the visual system are doing to capture those images in the brain.

sensation Registration by the sensory organs of physical stimuli from the environment.

perception Subjective interpretation of sensations by the brain.

Structure of the Retina

Light energy travels from the outside world through the pupil and into the eye, where it strikes a light-sensitive surface, the **retina**, at the back of the eye (**Figure 9-2**). From this stimulation of **photoreceptor** cells on the retina, we begin to construct a visual world. If you are familiar with the properties of the electromagnetic spectrum and with the structure of the eye, read on. To refresh your knowledge of these topics, read The Basics: Visible Light and the Structure of the Eye before you continue.

Figure 9-2 includes a photograph of the retina, which is composed of photoreceptors beneath a layer of neurons connected to them. The neurons lie in front of the photoreceptor cells, but they do not prevent incoming light from being absorbed by those receptors because the neurons are transparent and the photoreceptors are extremely sensitive to light.

Together, the photoreceptor cells and the retinal neurons perform some amazing functions. They translate light into action potentials, discriminate wavelengths so that we can distinguish colors, and work in a range of light intensities from bright to dim. These cells afford visual precision sufficient for us to see a human hair lying on the page of this book from a distance of 18 inches.

As in a camera, the image of objects projected onto the retina is upside down and backward. This flip-flopped orientation poses no problem for the brain. Remember that the brain is constructing the outside world, so it does not really care how the image is oriented initially. In fact, the brain can make adjustments regardless of the orientation of the images that it receives.

If for several days you were to wear glasses that invert visual images, the world would first appear upside down but then would suddenly appear right side up again because your brain would correct the distortion (Held, 1968). Curiously, upon removing

retina Light-sensitive surface at the back of the eye consisting of neurons and photoreceptor cells.

photoreceptor Specialized retinal neuron that transduces light into neural activity.

Virtually all retinal neurons are insensitive to light and thus are unaffected by light passing through them en route to the light-sensitive photoreceptors.

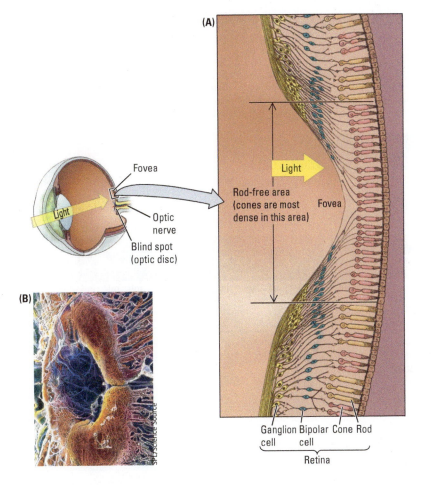

FIGURE 9-2 **Central Focus** This cross section through the retina **(A)** shows the depression at the fovea—also shown in the scanning electron micrograph **(B)**—where photoreceptors are packed most densely and where our vision is clearest.

◎ THE BASICS

Visible Light and the Structure of the Eye

The brain's visual system analyzes visible light—the part of the electromagnetic (EM) spectrum that the human eye evolved to capture and focus.

Light: The Stimulus for Vision

Light can enter the eye directly from a source that produces it (such as a lamp or the sun) or indirectly after reflecting from a surface (such as the pages of a book or the surface of water). As illustrated in the accompanying Electromagnetic Spectrum diagram, not all light waves are the same length, and only a sliver of the EM spectrum is visible to us. If our photoreceptors could detect light in the shorter ultraviolet or longer infrared wavelengths, we would see additional colors.

Structure of the Eye

The range of light visible to humans is constrained not by the properties of light waves but rather by the properties of our visual receptors. How do photoreceptor cells in the retina absorb light energy and initiate the processes leading to vision? The diagram How the Eye Works illustrates the eye's structure and shows how its design captures and focuses light.

Optical Errors of Refraction

A web of muscles adjusts the shape of the eye's lens to bend light to greater or lesser degrees, which allows near or far images to be focused on the retina. When images are not properly focused, we need corrective lenses.

The eye, like a camera, works correctly only when sufficient light passes through the lens and is focused on the receptor surface—the retina in the eye or the light-sensitive material in the camera. If the focal point of the light falls slightly in front of the receptor surface or slightly behind it, a refractive error causes objects to appear blurry. Refractive errors in the eye are of two basic types, diagrammed in Refractive Errors.

Myopia (nearsightedness) afflicts about 50 percent of young people in the developed world. Hyperopia (farsightedness) is a less common refractive error, but as people age, the lens loses its elasticity and consequently becomes unable to refract light from nearby objects correctly. This form of hyperopia, called presbyopia (old-sightedness), is so common that you rarely find people older than 50 who do not need glasses to see up close, especially for reading.

It is also common to see young children wearing corrective lenses. The incidence of myopia in the United States has doubled in the past 40 years, to about 42 percent. It is even higher in Northern Europe (50 percent) and Asia (50 percent to 80 percent). Two factors probably account for the increase. First, more young people are attending school longer and thus are doing more close-up work, especially reading; close-up work strains the eye muscles. Second, people are spending less and less time outdoors in bright light. Bright light makes the pupil contract, which improves visual depth of field; your eyes focus better. Children should probably spend at least 2 hours each day outside in bright light. Consider that myopia is less common in countries such as Australia (17 percent), where bright light is plentiful.

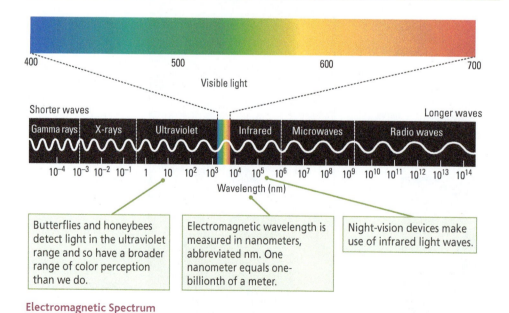

The electromagnetic energy visible to humans varies in wavelength from about 400 to 700 nanometers. We perceive the shortest visible wavelengths as deep purple. As wavelength increases, perceived color morphs from violet to blue to green to yellow, orange, and red: the colors of the rainbow.

Visible light

400   500   600   700

Shorter waves   Longer waves

Gamma rays | X-rays | Ultraviolet | Infrared | Microwaves | Radio waves

10^{-4} 10^{-3} 10^{-2} 10^{-1} 1 10 10^2 10^3 10^4 10^5 10^6 10^7 10^8 10^9 10^{10} 10^{11} 10^{12} 10^{13} 10^{14}

Wavelength (nm)

Butterflies and honeybees detect light in the ultraviolet range and so have a broader range of color perception than we do.

Electromagnetic wavelength is measured in nanometers, abbreviated nm. One nanometer equals one-billionth of a meter.

Night-vision devices make use of infrared light waves.

Electromagnetic Spectrum

How the Eye Works

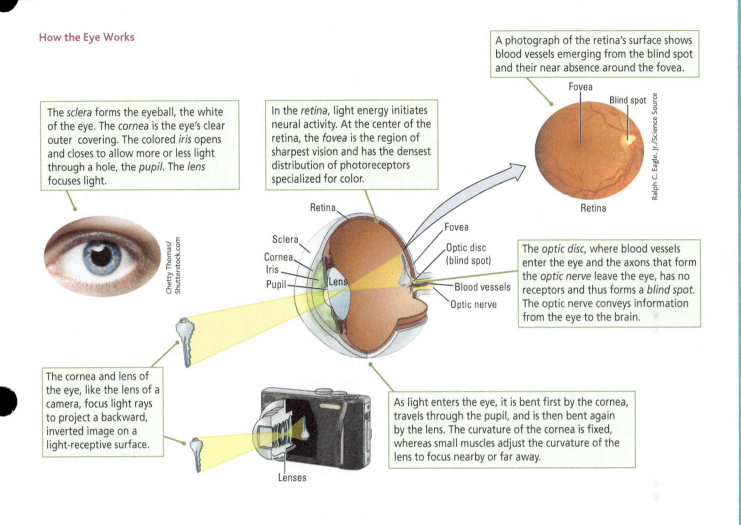

The *sclera* forms the eyeball, the white of the eye. The *cornea* is the eye's clear outer covering. The colored *iris* opens and closes to allow more or less light through a hole, the *pupil*. The *lens* focuses light.

In the *retina*, light energy initiates neural activity. At the center of the retina, the *fovea* is the region of sharpest vision and has the densest distribution of photoreceptors specialized for color.

A photograph of the retina's surface shows blood vessels emerging from the blind spot and their near absence around the fovea.

Fovea
Blind spot
Retina

Ralph C. Eagle, Jr./Science Source

Chetty Thomas/Shutterstock.com

Retina
Sclera
Cornea
Iris
Pupil
Lens

Fovea
Optic disc (blind spot)
Blood vessels
Optic nerve

The *optic disc*, where blood vessels enter the eye and the axons that form the *optic nerve* leave the eye, has no receptors and thus forms a *blind spot*. The optic nerve conveys information from the eye to the brain.

The cornea and lens of the eye, like the lens of a camera, focus light rays to project a backward, inverted image on a light-receptive surface.

Lenses

As light enters the eye, it is bent first by the cornea, travels through the pupil, and is then bent again by the lens. The curvature of the cornea is fixed, whereas small muscles adjust the curvature of the lens to focus nearby or far away.

Refractive Errors

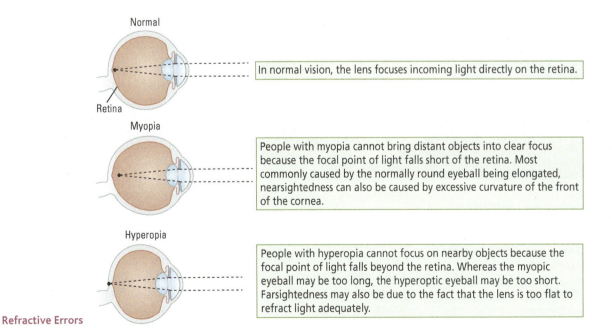

Normal
Retina

In normal vision, the lens focuses incoming light directly on the retina.

Myopia

People with myopia cannot bring distant objects into clear focus because the focal point of light falls short of the retina. Most commonly caused by the normally round eyeball being elongated, nearsightedness can also be caused by excessive curvature of the front of the cornea.

Hyperopia

People with hyperopia cannot focus on nearby objects because the focal point of light falls beyond the retina. Whereas the myopic eyeball may be too long, the hyperoptic eyeball may be too short. Farsightedness may also be due to the fact that the lens is too flat to refract light adequately.

FIGURE 9-3 **Acuity Across the Visual Field** Focus on the star in the middle of the chart to understand the relative sizes of letters legible in the central field of vision compared with the peripheral field.

FIGURE 9-4 **Find Your Blind Spot** Hold this book about 12 inches away from your face. Shut your left eye and look at the cross with your right eye. Slowly bring the page toward you until the red spot in the center of the yellow disc disappears and the entire disc appears yellow. The red spot is now in your blind spot. Your brain replaces the area with the surrounding yellow to fill in the image. Turn the book upside down to test your left eye.

the glasses, the world would temporarily seem upside down once again because your brain at first would be unaware that you had tricked it again. Eventually, though, your brain would solve this puzzle, too, and the world would flip back to the correct orientation.

Fovea

Try this experiment. Focus on the print at the left edge of this page. The words will be clearly legible. Now, while holding your eyes still, try to read the words on the right side of the page. It will be very difficult, even impossible, even though you can see that words are there.

The lesson is that our vision is better in the center of the visual field than at the margins, or *periphery*. Letters at the periphery must be much larger than those in the center for us to see them as well. **Figure 9-3** shows how much larger. The difference is partly due to the fact that photoreceptors are more densely packed at the center of the retina, in a region known as the **fovea**. Figure 9-2 shows that the retinal surface is depressed at the fovea. This depression is formed because many optic nerve fibers skirt the fovea to facilitate light access to its receptors.

Blind Spot

Now try another experiment. Stand with your head over a tabletop and hold a pencil in your hand. Close one eye. Stare at the edge of the tabletop nearest you. Now hold the pencil in a horizontal position with the eraser on the table. Beginning at a point approximately below your nose, move the pencil slowly along the table in the direction of the open eye.

When you have moved the pencil about 6 inches, the eraser will vanish. You have found your **blind spot**, a small area of the retina also known as the *optic disc*. This is the area where blood vessels enter and exit the eye and where fibers leading from retinal neurons form the optic nerve, which goes to the brain. There are therefore no photoreceptors in this part of the retina. You can use **Figure 9-4** to demonstrate the blind spot in another way.

Fortunately, your visual system solves the blind spot problem: your optic disc is in a different location in each eye. The optic disc is lateral to the fovea in each eye, which means that it is to the left of the fovea in the left eye and to the right of the fovea in the right eye. Because the two eyes' visual fields overlap, the right eye can see the left eye's blind spot and vice versa.

Using both eyes together, then, you can see the whole visual world. For people blind in one eye, the sightless eye cannot compensate for the blind spot in the functioning eye. Still, the visual system compensates for the blind spot in several other ways, so these people have no sense of a hole in their field of vision.

The blind spot is of particular importance in neurology. It allows neurologists to indirectly view the condition of the optic nerve while providing a window on events in the brain. If intracranial pressure increases, as occurs with a tumor or brain abscess (an infection), the optic disc swells, leading to *papilledema* (swollen disc). The swelling occurs in part because, like all other neural tissue, the optic nerve is surrounded by cerebrospinal fluid (CSF). Pressure inside the cranium can displace CSF around the optic nerve, causing swelling at the optic disc.

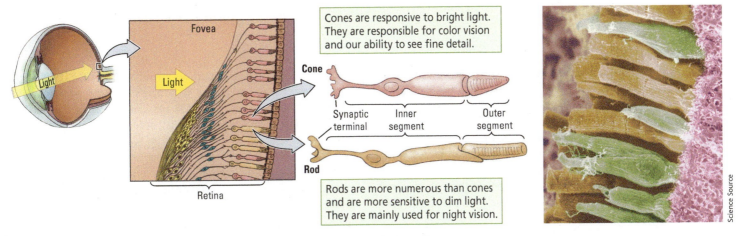

> Cones are responsive to bright light. They are responsible for color vision and our ability to see fine detail.

> Rods are more numerous than cones and are more sensitive to dim light. They are mainly used for night vision.

FIGURE 9-5 **Photoreceptor Cells** Rods and cones are tubelike structures, as the scanning electron micrograph at right shows. They differ especially in the outer segment that contains the light-absorbing visual pigment. Rods are especially sensitive to broad-spectrum luminance and cones to particular wavelengths of light.

Another cause of papilledema is inflammation of the optic nerve itself, a condition known as *optic neuritis*. Whatever the cause, a person with a swollen optic disc usually loses vision due to pressure on the optic nerve. If the swelling is a result of optic neuritis, probably the most common neurological visual disorder, the prognosis for recovery is good.

Photoreceptors

The retina's photoreceptor cells convert light energy first into chemical energy and then into neural activity. Light striking a photoreceptor triggers a series of chemical reactions that lead to a change in membrane potential (electrical charge), which in turn leads to a change in the release of neurotransmitters onto nearby neurons.

The eye contains two types of image-forming photoreceptors: rods and cones, shown in **Figure 9-5**, which differ in many ways. Structurally, rods are longer than cones and cylindrical at one end, whereas cones have a tapered end. **Rods** are more numerous than cones; are sensitive to low levels of brightness (luminance), especially in dim light; and function mainly for night vision (see Clinical Focus 9-2, Visual Illuminance). **Cones** do not respond to dim light, but they are highly responsive to bright light. Cones mediate both color vision and our ability to see fine detail (visual acuity).

Rods and cones are unevenly distributed over the retina. The fovea has only cones, but their density drops dramatically beyond the fovea. For this reason, our vision is not so sharp at the edges of the visual field, as demonstrated in Figure 9-3.

A final difference between rods and cones is in their light-absorbing pigments. All rods have the same pigment, whereas each cone has one of three pigments. These four pigments, one in the rods and three in the cones, form the basis for our vision.

As shown on the spectrum in **Figure 9-6**, the three cone pigments absorb light across a range of visible frequencies, but each is most responsive to a small range of wavelengths—short (bluish light), medium (greenish light), and long (reddish light). As you can see on the background spectrum in Figure 9-6, however, if you were to look at lights with wavelengths of 419, 531, and 559 nanometers (nm), they would not appear blue, green, and red but rather blue-green, yellow-green, and orange. Remember, though, that you are looking at the

fovea Central region of the retina specialized for high visual acuity; its receptive fields are at the center of the eye's visual field.

blind spot Retinal region where axons forming the optic nerve leave the eye and where blood vessels enter and leave; has no photoreceptors and is thus said to be blind.

rod Photoreceptor specialized for functioning at low light levels.

cone Photoreceptor specialized for color and high visual acuity.

A nanometer (nm) is one-billionth of a meter.

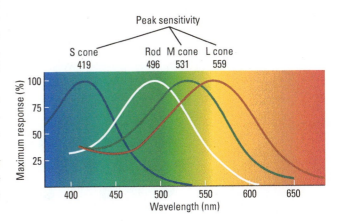

FIGURE 9-6 **Range and Peak Sensitivity** Our color perception corresponds to the summed activity of the three cone types: S cones, M cones, and L cones (for short, medium, and long wavelengths). Each type is most sensitive to a narrow range of the visible spectrum. Rods (white curve) prefer a range of wavelengths centered on 496 nm but do not contribute to our color perception. Rod activity is not summed with the cones in the color vision system.

◎ **CLINICAL FOCUS 9-2**

Visual Illuminance

The eye, like a camera, works correctly only when sufficient light passes through the lens and is focused on the receptor surface—the retina of the eye or the light-sensitive surface in the camera. Too little light entering the eye or the camera produces a problem of *visual illuminance*, in which objects are too dim and it is hard to see any image at all. The reason objects appear blurry in low illuminance is likely that we are mostly using rods, which provide a less sharp image.

Visual illuminance is typically a complication of aging eyes. It cannot be cured by corrective lenses. As we age, the eye's lens and cornea allow less light through, so less light strikes the retina. Don Kline (1994) estimated that between ages 20 and 40, people's ability to see in dim light drops by 50 percent—and over each additional 20 years, by a further 50 percent. As a result, seeing in dim light becomes increasingly difficult, especially at night.

The only way to compensate for visual illuminance is to increase lighting. Night vision is especially problematic. Not surprisingly, statistics show a marked drop in the number of people who drive at night in each successive decade after age 40.

These photographs represent the typical drop in luminance between age 20 (left) and age 60 (right).

lights with all three of your cone types and that each cone pigment responds to light across a range of frequencies, not just to its frequency of maximum absorption.

Both the presence of three cone receptor types and their relative numbers and distribution across the retina contribute to our perception of color. As **Figure 9-7** shows, the three cone types are distributed more or less randomly across the retina, making our ability to perceive different colors fairly constant across the visual field. The numbers of red and green cones are approximately equal, but blue cones are fewer. As a result, we are not as sensitive to wavelengths in the blue part of the visible spectrum as we are to red and green wavelengths.

Other species that have color vision similar to humans' also have three types of cones with three color pigments. Because of slight variations in these pigments, however, the exact frequencies of maximum absorption differ among species. For humans, the exact frequencies are not identical with the numbers given earlier, which are an average across mammals. They are actually 426 and 530 nm for the blue and green cones, respectively, and 552 or 557 nm for the red cone. The two peak sensitivity levels of red cones represent the two variants that humans have evolved. The difference in these two red cones appears minuscule, but it does make a functional difference in some human females' color perception.

The gene for the red cone is carried on the X chromosome. Males have only one X chromosome, so they have only one of these genes and only one type of red cone. The situation is more complicated for females, who possess two X chromosomes. Although most women have only one type of red cone, those who have both are more sensitive than the rest of us to color differences at the red end of the spectrum. We could say that women who have both red cone types have a slightly rosier view of the world: their color

FIGURE 9-7 **Retinal Receptors** The retinal mosaic of rods and three cone types. This diagram represents the distribution near the fovea, where cones outnumber rods. Red and green cones outnumber blue ones.

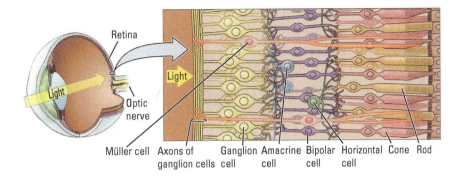

FIGURE 9-8 **Retinal Cells** Neurons in the retina—bipolar, horizontal, amacrine, and ganglion cells—form two layers moving outward from the rods and cones at the retinal surface. Light must pass through both transparent neuron layers to reach the photoreceptors. Müller cells run from the front of the retina to the back.

receptors construct a world with a richer range of red experiences. But they also have to contend with seemingly peculiar color coordination by others.

Types of Retinal Neurons

Photoreceptors are connected to two layers of retinal neurons. In the progression from the rods and cones toward the brain shown in **Figure 9-8**, the first layer contains three cell types: *bipolar, horizontal,* and *amacrine.* Horizontal cells link photoreceptors with bipolar cells, whereas amacrine cells link bipolar cells with cells in the second neural layer, the **retinal ganglion cells (RGCs)**. RGC axons collect in a bundle at the optic disc and leave the eye to form the optic nerve. RGCs are especially sensitive to increased intraocular pressure, which can lead to blindness (see Clinical Focus 9-3, Glaucoma).

Retinal ganglion cells fall into two major categories, called M and P cells in the primate retina. The designations derive from the distinctly different cell populations in the visual thalamus to which these two classes of RGCs send their axons. As shown in **Figure 9-9**, one population consists of **magnocellular cells** (hence M); the other consists of **parvocellular cells** (hence P). The larger M cells receive their input primarily from rods and so are sensitive to light but not to color; the smaller P cells receive their input primarily from cones and so are sensitive to color.

M cells are found throughout the retina, including the periphery, where we are sensitive to movement but not to color or fine detail. P cells are found largely in the region of the fovea, where we are sensitive to color and fine details. As we follow the ganglion cell axons into the brain, you will see that these two categories of RGCs maintain their distinctiveness throughout the visual pathways.

retinal ganglion cell (RGC) One of a group of retinal neurons with axons that give rise to the optic nerve.

magnocellular (M) cell Large visual system neuron sensitive to moving stimuli.

parvocellular (P) cell Small visual system neuron sensitive to differences in form and color.

In Latin, *magno* means "large," and *parvo* means "small."

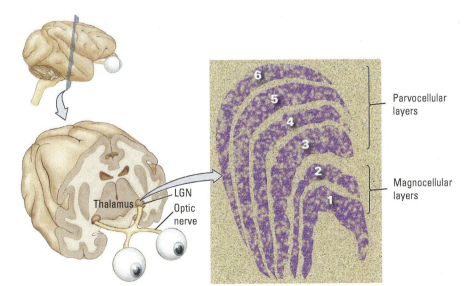

FIGURE 9-9 **Visual Thalamus** The optic nerves connect with the lateral geniculate nucleus of the thalamus. The LGN has six layers: two magnocellular layers, which receive input mainly from rods, and four parvocellular layers, which receive input mainly from cones.

◉ CLINICAL FOCUS 9-3

Glaucoma

Glaucoma, a group of eye diseases damaging the optic nerve, is the most common cause of irreversible blindness and a prime target for research to restore vision. The optic nerve begins with the axons of the retinal ganglion cells (RGCs), and if they are dead or dysfunctional, vision is impossible. Thus, the clinical goal with glaucoma is to repair or replace RGCs after injury. One challenge is that RGC axons do not spontaneously regenerate after injury, and when the RGCs die, they are not replaced. Given the prevalence of this type of blindness, the U.S. National Eye Institute's primary research goal is to discover ways to repair RGCs and their connections into the brain.

One strategy for restoring vision is to stimulate RGCs to regenerate axons. Andrew Huberman and his colleagues (Lim et al., 2016) used both genetic and visual stimulation to enhance neural activity in the RGCs of mice with severed RGC axons. They activated a common growth-inducing mechanism in cells, called the *mTOR signaling pathway*, while at the same time repeatedly exposing the eye to high-contrast black-and-white images. This procedure stimulated the RGCs to re-establish many of the lost connections to their correct targets and allow a partial restoration of vision. The authors believe that the next step is to provide additional sources of increasing neural activity in the RGCs to enhance regeneration and restore more visual capacity.

A second strategy for vision restoration is to replace RGCs by transplanting healthy RGCs from recently deceased donors. Studies in rats have shown that transplanted RGCs thrive, respond to light signals, and extend axons into the brain to reach usual targets (Venugoplalan et al., 2016). Although this procedure is not quite ready to head to the clinic, it appears to offer a clinically viable strategy for curing blindness related to RGC death.

Not all blindness originating in the eye is related directly to lost RGCs, however. If photoreceptors are dysfunctioning or dying, as happens in retinitis pigmentosa (RP), blindness will also occur. Several possible therapies are under active investigation. One is to implant prosthetic devices into the eye to convert light to electrical signals and then pass it on to RGCs. Another option is to introduce light-sensitive ion-gated channels to repair the receptors. Preliminary results in humans and nonhuman primates suggest that this type of approach can stimulate recovery of the ability to read words.

Another possibility is based on independent parallel work by two different research groups on mouse models of RP, in which experimenters used CRISPR to reprogram genes expressed in rods, leading to an increase in conelike cells, with restoration of visual function (Yu et al., 2017; Zhu et al., 2017). Taken together, these reparative strategies alone or in combination offer a realistic possibility for visual restoration (see review by Laha et al., 2017).

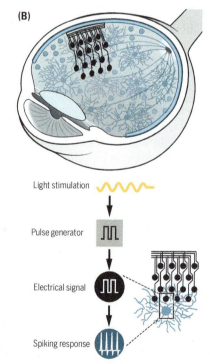

(A)

Allogeneic transplantation
RGCs from healthy eyes into host eyes may represent a viable strategy for curing irreversible forms of blindness

Site of optic nerve damage

Transplanted donor RGCs → Intrinsic signals drive initial neurite and axonal outgrowth → Complete integration into retina and axon grows into optic nerve

(B)

Light stimulation

Pulse generator

Electrical signal

Spiking response

Two Potential Treatments to Restore Vision (A) Healthy RPGs can be injected into a damaged eye to potentially restore lost vision. **(B)** A prosthetic device implanted in the eye can convert light to electrical signals and then pass it on to RGCs. Republished with permission of American Association for the Advancement of Science, from Bireswar Laha, Ben K. Stafford, Andrew D. Huberman, "Regenerating optic pathways from the eye to the brain." *Science*, 2017, June 9;356(6342):1031-1034, Figures 3,4. Permission conveyed through Copyright Clearance Center, Inc.

The retina also has special glial cells in the retina called *Müller cells* that span from the retina's inner membrane at the front to the photoreceptors at the back of the retina and act as optical fibers, channeling light to the buried photoreceptors (see Figure 9-8).

Although the primary function of the eye is to form images, the eye also acts to collect information on ambient light intensity. A tiny subset of retinal ganglion cells (around 1 percent) contain melanopsin, a light-sensitive protein, and thus form a third type of photoreceptor in the eye. These photoreceptors function to synchronize circadian rhythms, regulate pupil size, and regulate melatonin release.

optic chiasm Junction of the optic nerves, one from each eye, at which the axons from the nasal halves of the retinas cross to the brain's opposite side.

Circadian rhythms are discussed in more detail in Chapter 13.

Visual Pathways

RGCs form the optic nerve, the road into the brain. This road forks off to several places. The destinations of these branches give us clues to what the brain is doing with visual input and how the brain constructs our visual world.

Crossing the Optic Chiasm

We begin with the optic nerves, one exiting from each eye. Just before entering the brain, the optic nerves partly cross, forming the **optic chiasm**.

About half the fibers from each eye cross in such a way that the left half of each optic nerve goes to the left side of the brain, and the right half goes to the brain's right side, as diagrammed in **Figure 9-10**. The medial path of each retina, the *nasal retina*, crosses to the opposite side; the lateral path, the *temporal retina*, travels straight back on the same side. Because light that falls on the right half of each retina actually comes from the left side of the visual field, information from the left visual field goes to the brain's right hemisphere, and information from the right visual field goes to the left hemisphere. Thus, half of each retina's visual field is represented on each side of the brain.

The optic chiasm gets its name from the shape of the Greek letter chi (X, pronounced "kai").

By connecting both eyes with both hemispheres, our visual system represents the world seen through two eyes as a single perception.

Principle 3: Many brain circuits are crossed.

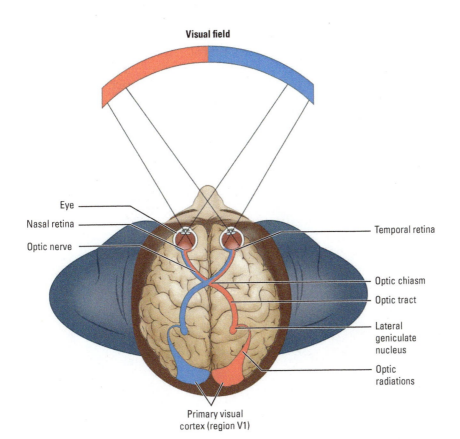

FIGURE 9-10 **Crossing the Optic Chiasm** This dorsal view shows the visual pathway from each eye to the primary visual cortex of each hemisphere. Information from the right side of the visual field (blue) moves from the two left halves of the retinas, ending in the left hemisphere. Information from the left side of the visual field (red) hits the right halves of the retinas and travels to the right side of the brain.

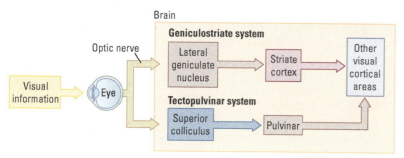

FIGURE 9-11 **Main Visual Pathways into the Brain** The optic nerve follows (1) the geniculostriate path to the primary visual cortex and (2) the tectopulvinar path to the temporal and parietal lobes. (The LGN of the thalamus is part of the diencephalon, shown in Figure 2-20; the superior colliculus in the tectum is part of the midbrain, shown in Figure 2-19.)

Figure 13-7 maps the retinohypothalamic tract into the SCN.

geniculostriate system Projections from the retina to the lateral geniculate nucleus to the visual cortex.

striate cortex Primary visual cortex (V1) in the occipital lobe; shows stripes (striations) on staining.

tectopulvinar system Projections from the retina to the superior colliculus to the pulvinar (thalamus) to the parietal and temporal visual areas.

retinohypothalamic tract Neural route formed by axons of photosensitive retinal ganglion cells (pRGCs) from the retina to the suprachiasmatic nucleus; allows light to entrain the SCN's rhythmic activity.

Three Routes to the Visual Brain

Two main pathways lead to the visual cortex in the occipital lobe: the geniculostriate pathway for processing the object's image and the tectopulvinar pathway for directing rapid eye movements. Another smaller pathway tracks into the hypothalamus.

GENICULOSTRIATE SYSTEM On entering the brain, the RGC axons separate, forming two distinct pathways, as shown in **Figure 9-11**. All of the P ganglion axons and some of the M ganglion axons form a pathway called the **geniculostriate system**. This pathway goes from the retina to the lateral geniculate nucleus (LGN) of the thalamus and then to layer IV of the primary visual cortex in the occipital lobe.

When stained, the primary visual cortex shows a broad stripe across it in layer IV and so is known as the **striate** (striped) **cortex** (**Figure 9-12**). The geniculostriate system therefore bridges the thalamus (geniculate) and the striate cortex. From the striate cortex, the axon pathway divides. One route goes to vision-related regions of the parietal lobe, and another route goes to vision-related regions of the temporal lobe.

TECTOPULVINAR SYSTEM The second pathway leading from the eye is formed by the axons of the remaining M ganglion cells. These cells send their axons to the midbrain's superior colliculus, which sends connections to the pulvinar region of the thalamus. This pathway is therefore known as the **tectopulvinar system** because it runs from the eye through the midbrain tectum to the pulvinar (see Figure 9-11). The pulvinar sends connections to the parietal and temporal lobes, bypassing the occipital visual areas.

RETINOHYPOTHALAMIC TRACT Between 1 percent and 3 percent of RGCs are unique in that they are *photosensitive*: they act as photoreceptors. These *pRGCs*, which contain the pigment melanopsin, absorb blue light at a wavelength (between 460 and 480 nm) different from the wavelengths of rods or cones (see Figure 9-6). Axons of pRGCs form a small third visual pathway, the **retinohypothalamic tract**.

The retinohypothalamic tract synapses in the tiny suprachiasmatic nucleus (SCN) in the hypothalamus, next to the optic chiasm. Photosensitive RGCs participate both in regulating circadian rhythms and in the pupillary reflex that expands and contracts the pupil in response to the amount of light falling on the retina. Farhan Zaidi and colleagues (2007) studied two profoundly blind subjects who lack functional rods and cones. The researchers found that stimulation with 480-nm (blue) light increases alertness and appears to play some rudimentary role in visual awareness.

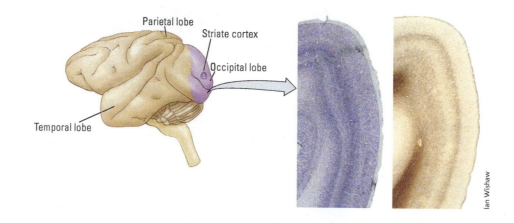

FIGURE 9-12 **Striate Cortex** Area V1 is also called the *striate cortex* because sections appear striated (striped) when stained with either a cell body stain (left) or a myelin stain (right). The sections shown here come from a rhesus monkey's brain.

Ian Wishaw

Dorsal and Ventral Visual Streams

The geniculostriate and tectopulvinar pathways extend into the visual brain. Each eventually leads to either the parietal lobe or the temporal lobe. Our next task is to determine the role each lobe plays in building our visual world. As we look at the photographs in Clinical Focus 9-1, we can identify objects, and we can point to them. Identifying and pointing are different functions.

Having identified the temporal lobe and parietal lobe visual pathways, researchers went looking for their possible functions. Why would evolution produce two different destinations for these neural pathways? Each route must produce visual knowledge for a different purpose.

David Milner and Mel Goodale (2006) proposed that these two purposes are to identify a stimulus (the *what* function) and to control movement to or away from the stimulus (the *how* function). This *what–how* distinction came from an analysis of the routes that visual information takes when it leaves the striate cortex. **Figure 9-13** shows the two distinct visual pathways that originate in the striate cortex, one progressing to the temporal lobe and the other to the parietal lobe. The pathway to the temporal lobe is the **ventral stream**, whereas the pathway to the parietal lobe is the **dorsal stream**.

Both the geniculostriate and the tectopulvinar pathways contribute to the dorsal and ventral streams. To understand how the two streams function, we return to the details of how visual input from the eyes contributes to them.

Geniculostriate Pathway

The RGC fibers from the two eyes distribute their connections to the two lateral geniculate nuclei (left and right) of the thalamus. At first glance, this appears to be an unusual arrangement. As shown in Figure 9-10, the fibers from the left half of each retina go to the left LGN; those from the right half of each retina go to the right LGN. But the fibers from each eye do not go to exactly the same LGN location.

Each LGN has six layers, and the projections from the two eyes go to different layers, as illustrated in anatomical context in Figure 9-9 and diagrammed in **Figure 9-14**. Layers 2, 3, and 5 receive fibers from the ipsilateral eye (the eye on the same side), whereas layers 1, 4, and 6 receive fibers from the contralateral eye (the eye on the opposite side). This arrangement provides for combining the information from the two eyes as well as for segregating the information from the P and M ganglion cells.

Axons from the P cells go only to layers 3 through 6 (the parvocellular layers), whereas axons from the M cells go only to layers 1 and 2 (the magnocellular layers). Because the P cells are responsive to color and fine detail, LGN layers 3 through 6 must be processing information about color and form. In contrast, the M cells mostly process information about movement, so layers 1 and 2 must deal with movement.

Just as there are six layers in the thalamic LGN (numbered 1 through 6), there are also six layers in the striate cortex (numbered I through VI). That there happen to be six layers in each location is an accident of evolution found in all primate brains. Let us now see where these LGN cells from the thalamus send their connections within the visual cortex.

Layer IV is the main afferent (incoming) layer of the cortex. In the visual cortex, layer IV has several sublayers, two of which are known as IVCα and IVCβ. LGN layers 1 and 2 go to IVCα, and layers 3 through 6 go to IVCβ. A distinction between the P and M functions thus continues in the striate cortex.

As illustrated in **Figure 9-15**, input from the two eyes also remains separated in the cortex. The input from the ipsilaterally and contralaterally connected parts of the LGN go to adjacent

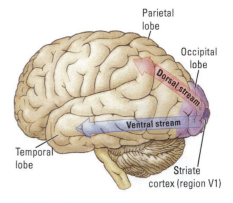

FIGURE 9-13 **Visual Streaming** Information travels from the occipital visual areas to the parietal and temporal lobes, forming the dorsal (*how*) and ventral (*what*) streams, respectively.

Principle 8: The brain divides sensory input for object recognition and movement.

ventral stream Visual processing pathway from V1 to the temporal lobe for object identification and perceiving related movements.

dorsal stream Visual processing pathway from V1 to the parietal lobe; guides movements relative to objects.

Figure 2-25 maps layers I through VI in the primary motor and sensory cortices.

FIGURE 9-14 **Geniculostriate Pathway**

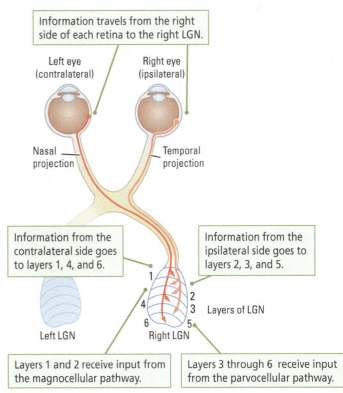

Information travels from the right side of each retina to the right LGN.

Left eye (contralateral)   Right eye (ipsilateral)

Nasal projection   Temporal projection

Information from the contralateral side goes to layers 1, 4, and 6.

Information from the ipsilateral side goes to layers 2, 3, and 5.

Layers of LGN

Left LGN   Right LGN

Layers 1 and 2 receive input from the magnocellular pathway.

Layers 3 through 6 receive input from the parvocellular pathway.

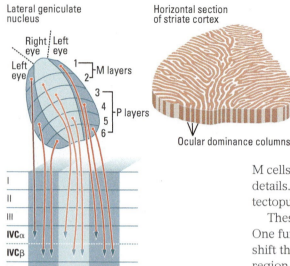

Lateral geniculate nucleus

Horizontal section of striate cortex

Right / Left eye / eye

Left eye

1 ⎤
2 ⎦ M layers

3
4 ⎤ P layers
5
6

Ocular dominance columns

I
II
III
IVCα
IVCβ
V
VI

Cortical visual area 1

FIGURE 9-15 **Maintaining Separate Visual Input** Left: Information from the eyes is segregated by layers in the LGN, which maintains this segregation in its projections from the thalamus to the primary visual cortex. Information from each eye travels to adjacent regions in cortical layer IV. Right: A horizontal plane through striate cortex shows a zebralike effect of alternating left and right eye regions.

Many textbooks emphasize the *how* pathway as a *where* function. Because *where* is both a property of *what* a stimulus is and a cue for *how* to control movement, we use Milner and Goodale's *what–how* distinction.

Every mammal has at least one primary cortical area for each sensory system. The primary area relays most information that reaches secondary areas.

strips of occipital cortex. These strips, which are about 0.5 mm across, are known as **cortical columns**.

In summary, P and M retinal ganglion cells send separate pathways to the thalamus, and this segregation continues in the striate cortex. The left and right eyes also send separate pathways to the thalamus; these pathways, too, remain segregated in the striate cortex.

Tectopulvinar Pathway

To review, magnocellular (M) RGCs found throughout the retina receive input primarily from the rods and so are sensitive to light but not to color. M cells in the periphery of the retina are sensitive to movement but not to color or fine details. In the brain, some M cells join P cells to form the geniculostriate pathway. The tectopulvinar pathway is formed by the axons of the remaining M cells.

These M cells send their axons to the superior colliculus in the midbrain's tectum. One function of the tectum is to produce orienting movements—to detect stimuli and shift the eyes toward them. The superior colliculus sends connections to the pulvinar region of the thalamus. The medial pulvinar sends connections to the parietal lobe, and the lateral pulvinar sends connections to the temporal lobe. One type of information that these connections are conveying is related to *where*. *Where* is important in both the *what* and *how* visual streams.

The *where* function of the tectopulvinar system is useful in understanding D. B.'s blindsight, described in Clinical Focus 9-1. His geniculostriate system was disrupted by surgery, but his tectopulvinar system was not, which allowed him to identify the location of stimuli (*where*) that he could not identify (*what*).

Occipital Cortex

Our route down the visual pathways has led us from the retina all the way back to the occipital lobe and into the parietal and temporal lobes. Now we explore how visual information proceeds from the striate cortex through the rest of the occipital lobe to the dorsal and ventral streams.

As shown in **Figure 9-16**, the occipital lobe is composed of at least six visual regions: V1, V2, V3, V3A, V4, and V5. As noted earlier, V1 is the striate cortex; this is the **primary visual cortex**. The remaining occipital visual areas form the **extrastriate (secondary visual) cortex**, with each region processing specific features of visual information. Because each occipital region has a unique cytoarchitecture (cellular structure) and unique inputs and outputs, we can infer that each must be doing something different from the others.

As shown in Figures 9-12 and 9-15, a remarkable feature of region V1 is its striations—its distinctly visible layers. When Margaret Wong-Riley and her colleagues (1993) stained region VI for the enzyme cytochrome oxidase, which has a role in cell

cortical column Anatomic organization that represents a functional unit six cortical layers deep and approximately 0.5 mm square, perpendicular to the cortical surface.

primary visual cortex (V1) Striate cortex in the occipital lobe that receives input from the lateral geniculate nucleus.

extrastriate (secondary visual) cortex (V2–V5) Visual cortical areas in the occipital lobe outside the striate cortex.

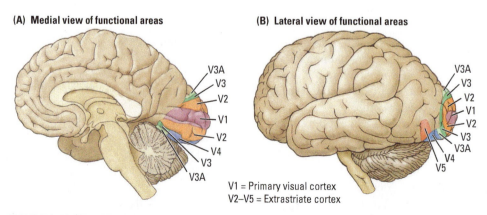

(A) Medial view of functional areas

V3A
V3
V2
V1
V2
V4
V3
V3A

(B) Lateral view of functional areas

V3A
V3
V2
V1
V2
V3
V3A
V4
V5

V1 = Primary visual cortex
V2–V5 = Extrastriate cortex

FIGURE 9-16 **Visual Regions of the Occipital Lobe**

metabolism, they found an unexpected heterogeneity. So they sectioned the V1 layers in such a way that each cortical layer was in one plane of section, much like peeling off the layers of an onion and laying them flat on a table. The surface of each flattened layer can then be viewed from above.

The heterogeneous cytochrome staining now appears as random blobs in the V1 layers, as diagrammed in **Figure 9-17**. These darkened regions have in fact become known as **blobs**, and the less-dark regions separating them are known as *interblobs*. Blobs and interblobs serve different functions. Neurons in the blobs take part in color perception; neurons in the interblobs participate in perception of form and motion. Within region V1, then, input arriving from the P cell and M cell pathways of the geniculostriate system is segregated into three separate types of information: color, form, and motion.

All three types of information move from region V1 to the adjoining region V2. Here, the color, form, and motion inputs remain segregated, again seen through the pattern of cytochrome oxidase staining. But as Figure 9-17 shows, the staining pattern in region V2 differs from that in region V1. Region V2 has a pattern of thick and thin stripes intermixed with pale zones. The thick stripes receive input from the movement-sensitive neurons in region V1; the thin stripes receive input from V1's color-sensitive neurons; and the pale zones receive input from V1's form-sensitive neurons.

As charted in **Figure 9-18**, the visual pathways proceed from region V2 to the other occipital regions and then to the parietal and temporal lobes, forming the dorsal and ventral streams. Although many parietal and temporal regions take part, the major ones are region G in the parietal lobe (thus called region PG) and region E in the temporal lobe (thus called region TE).

The simple records of color, form, and motion from the occipital regions are assembled in the dorsal and ventral streams to produce a rich, unified visual world of complex objects (such as faces and paintings) and complex skills (such as bike riding and ball catching). We can think of the complex representations of the dorsal and ventral streams as consisting of *how* functions and *what* functions. *How* is looking at, reaching for, and grasping; *what* is the spoon.

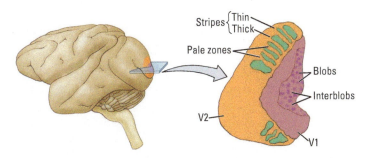

FIGURE 9-17 **Heterogeneous Layering** Blobs in region V1 and stripes in region V2 are illustrated in this drawing of a flattened section through the visual cortex of a monkey. The blobs and stripes are revealed by a special stain for cytochrome oxidase, a marker for mitochondria, the organelles in cells that gather, store, and release energy.

blob Region in V1 that contains color-sensitive neurons, as revealed by staining for cytochrome oxidase.

Vision Beyond the Occipital Cortex

Visual processing that begins in the occipital cortex continues via the ventral and dorsal streams into the temporal and parietal visual cortex. Each region has multiple areas

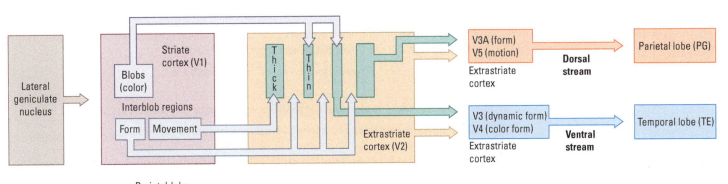

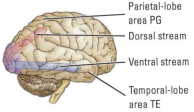

Parietal-lobe area PG
Dorsal stream
Ventral stream
Temporal-lobe area TE

FIGURE 9-18 **Charting the Visual Streams** The dorsal stream, which controls visual action (top), begins in region V1 and flows through V2 to the other occipital areas and finally to the parietal cortex, ending in area PG. The ventral stream, which controls object recognition (bottom), begins in region V1 and flows through V2 to the other occipital areas and finally to the temporal cortex, ending in area TE. Information from the blobs and interblobs in V1 flows to the thick, thin, and pale zones of V2 and then to regions V3 and V4 to form the ventral stream. Information in the thick and pale zones goes to regions V3A and V5 to form the dorsal stream.

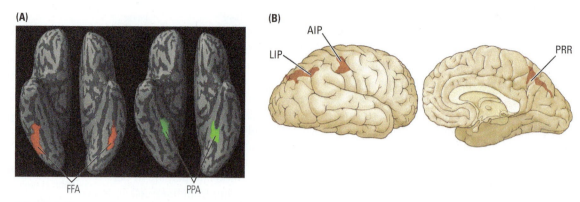

FIGURE 9-19 **Vision Beyond the Occipital Cortex (A)** In the temporal lobe, the fusiform face area (FFA) processes faces, and the parahippocampal place area (PPA) processes scenes. **(B)** In the parietal lobe, the lateral intraparietal area (LIP) contributes to eye movements; the anterior intraparietal area (AIP) is involved in visual control of grasping; and the parietal reach region (PRR) participates in visually guided reaching. Republished with permission of the American Association for the Advancement of Science, from Hasson, U., Y. Nir, I. Levy, G. Fuhrmann, and R. Malach. Inter subject synchronization of cortical activity during natural vision. Science 303:1634–1640, 2004, permission conveyed through Copyright Clearance Center, Inc.

specialized for specific visual functions. For example, **Figure 9-19A** shows two regions on the ventral surface of the temporal lobes. One is specialized for recognizing faces (fusiform face area [FFA]) and the other for analyzing landmarks such as buildings or trees (parahippocampal place area [PPA]). As we gaze at the photographs in Clinical Focus 9-1, then, the three faces activate the FFA, and the trees engage the PPA. Figure 9-19B shows three regions in the parietal lobe related to eye movements (lateral intraparietal area [LIP]) and visual control of grasping (anterior intraparietal area [AIP]). The parietal reach region (PRR) has a role in visually guided reaching movements.

Damage to these regions can produce surprisingly specific deficits. For example, damage to the FFA leads to **facial agnosia**, or *prosopagnosia*, a condition in which an individual cannot recognize faces. We saw one patient with prosopagnosia so severe that she could not recognize her identical twin sister's face. Curiously, her other visual functions seemed to be normal.

Agnosia means "not knowing." Section 15-7 ties conditions like agnosia to the search for a neural basis of consciousness.

9-2 Review

Before you continue, check your understanding. Answers to Self-Test appear at the back of the book.

1. Neurons that project into the brain from the retina and form the optic nerve are called
   _____.

2. _____ retinal ganglion cells receive input mostly from cones and carry information about color and fine detail, whereas _____ retinal ganglion cells receive input mostly from rods and carry information about light but not color.

3. The two major pathways from the retina into the brain are _____ and
   _____.

4. Damage to the fusiform face area in the temporal lobe can produce _____.

5. Contrast the paths and functions of the dorsal and ventral streams.

For additional study tools, visit 🅼 **LaunchPad** at launchpadworks.com

9-3

Location in the Visual World

facial agnosia Face blindness—the inability to recognize faces; also called *prosopagnosia*.

visual field Region of the visual world seen by the eyes.

As we move about from place to place, we encounter objects in specific locations. If we had no awareness of location, the world would be a bewildering mass of visual information. The next leg of our journey down the neural roads traces how the brain constructs a spatial map. In Clinical Focus 9-1, each of the photographs has a left and a right, an up and a down. All these elements must be coded separately in the brain.

Neural coding of location begins in the retina and is maintained throughout all visual pathways. To understand how this spatial coding is accomplished, imagine your visual world as seen by your two eyes. Imagine the large red and blue rectangles in **Figure 9-20** as a wall. Focus your gaze on the black cross in the middle of the wall.

The part of the wall that you can see without moving your head is your **visual field**. It can be divided into two halves, the left and right visual fields, by drawing a vertical line through the middle of the black cross. Now recall from Figure 9-10 that the left half of each retina looks at the right side of the visual field, whereas the right half of each retina looks at the visual field's left side. Thus, input from the right visual field goes to the left hemisphere, and input from the left visual field goes to the right hemisphere.

Therefore, the brain can easily determine whether visual information lies to the left or right of center. If input goes to the left hemisphere, the source must be in the right visual field; if input goes to the right hemisphere, the source must be in the left visual field. This arrangement tells you nothing about the precise location of an object in the left or right side of the visual field, however. To understand how precise spatial localization is accomplished, we must return to the retinal ganglion cells.

Coding Location in the Retina

Look again at Figure 9-8, and you can see that each RGC receives input through bipolar cells from several photoreceptors. In the 1950s, Stephen Kuffler, a pioneer in visual system physiology, made an important discovery about how photoreceptors and retinal ganglion cells are linked (Kuffler, 1952). By shining small spots of light on the receptors, he found that each ganglion cell responds to stimulation on just a small circular patch of the retina—the ganglion cell's receptive field.

A ganglion cell's receptive field is therefore the retinal region on which it is possible to influence that cell's firing. Stated differently, the receptive field represents the outer world as seen by a single cell. Each RGC sees only a small bit of the world, much as you would if you looked through a narrow cardboard tube. The visual field is composed of thousands of such receptive fields.

Now let us consider how receptive fields enable the visual system to interpret an object's location. Imagine that the retina is flattened like a piece of paper. When a tiny light shines on different parts of the retina, different ganglion cells respond. For example, when a light shines on the top-left corner of the flattened retina, a particular RGC responds because that light is in its receptive field. Similarly, when a light shines on the top-right corner, a different RGC responds.

By using this information, we determine the location of a light on the retina by the ganglion cell it activates. Another location device determines where the light must be coming from in order to hit a particular place on the retina. Light coming from above hits the bottom of the retina after passing through the eye's lens, and light from below hits the top of the retina. Information at the top of the visual field stimulates ganglion cells on the bottom of the retina; information at the bottom of the field stimulates ganglion cells on the top of the retina.

Location in the Lateral Geniculate Nucleus and Region V1

Now consider the connection from the ganglion cells to the lateral geniculate nucleus. In contrast to the retina, the LGN is not a thin sheet; it is shaped more like a sausage. We can compare it to a stack of sausage slices, with each slice representing a layer of cells.

Figure 9-21 shows how the connections from the retina to the LGN can represent location. A retinal ganglion cell that responds to light in the top-left region of the retina

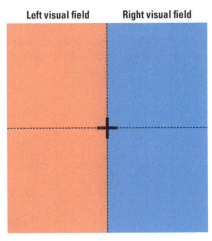

Left visual field | **Right visual field**

FIGURE 9-20 **Visual-Field Demonstration** As you focus on the cross at center, information to the left of this focal point forms the left visual field (red) and travels to the right hemisphere. Information to the right of the focal point forms the right visual field (blue) and travels to the left hemisphere. The visual field can be split horizontally as well: information above the focal point is in the upper visual field, and that below the focal point is in the lower visual field.

Like a camera lens, the lens in the eye focuses light rays to project a backward, inverted image on a light-receptive surface (see the diagram How the Eye Works in The Basics).

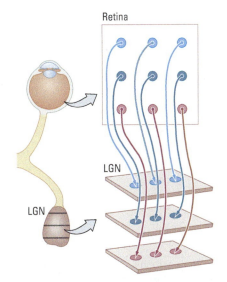

FIGURE 9-21 **Receptive-Field Projection** Information from a receptive field in the retina retains its spatial relation when sent to the lateral geniculate nucleus. Information at the top of the visual field goes to the top of the LGN; information from the bottom of the visual field goes to the bottom of the LGN; and information from the left or right goes to the left or right of the LGN, respectively.

FIGURE 9-22 **Topographic Organization of Region V1** The fovea sends information to a disproportionately large part of the occipital cortex, which is why visual acuity is best in the central part of the visual field.

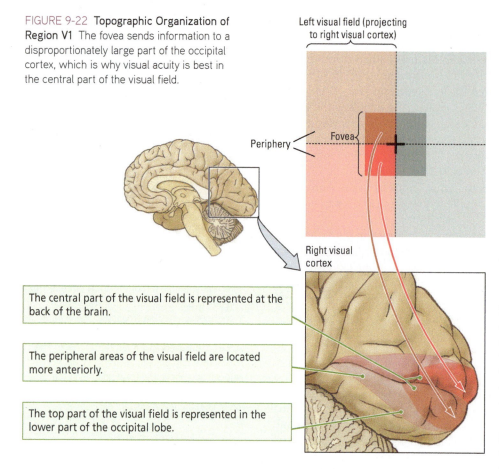

Left visual field (projecting to right visual cortex)

Periphery

Fovea

Right visual cortex

The central part of the visual field is represented at the back of the brain.

The peripheral areas of the visual field are located more anteriorly.

The top part of the visual field is represented in the lower part of the occipital lobe.

connects to the left side of the first slice. A retinal ganglion cell that responds to light in the bottom-right region of the retina connects to the right side of the last slice. In this way, the location of left–right and top–bottom information is maintained in the LGN.

Like the ganglion cells, each LGN cell has a receptive field—the region of the retina that influences its activity. If two adjacent retinal ganglion cells synapse on a single LGN cell, the receptive field of that LGN cell will be the sum of the two ganglion cells' receptive fields. As a result, the receptive fields of LGN cells are bigger than those of RGCs.

The LGN projection to the striate cortex (region V1) also maintains spatial information. As each LGN cell, representing a particular place, projects to region V1, a spatially organized neural representation—a topographic map—is produced in the cortex. As illustrated in **Figure 9-22**, this representation is essentially a map of the visual world.

The central part of the visual field is represented at the back of the brain, whereas the periphery is represented more anteriorly. The upper part of the visual field is represented at the bottom of region V1 and the lower part at the top of V1. The other regions of the visual cortex (such as V3, V4, and V5) have topographic maps similar to that of V1. Thus, the V1 neurons must project to the other regions in an orderly manner, just as the LGN neurons project to region V1 in an orderly way.

Within each visual cortical area, each neuron's receptive field corresponds to the part of the retina to which the neuron is connected. As a rule of thumb, cells in the cortex have much larger receptive fields than do RGCs. This large field size means that the receptive field of a cortical neuron must be composed of the receptive fields of many RGCs, as illustrated in **Figure 9-23**.

One additional wrinkle pertains to the organization of topographic maps. Harry Jerison (1973) proposed the principle of proper mass, which states that the amount of neural tissue responsible for a particular function is proportional to the amount of neural processing that function requires. The more complex a function is, the larger a specific region performing that function must be. The visual cortex provides some good examples.

You can see in Figure 9-22 that not all parts of the visual field are equally represented in region V1. The small central part of the visual field seen by the fovea is represented by a larger area in the cortex than the visual field's periphery, even though the periphery covers a much larger area. In accord with Jerison's principle, we would predict more processing of foveal information than of peripheral information in region V1. This prediction makes intuitive sense because we can see more clearly in the center of the visual field than at the periphery (see Figure 9-3). In other words, sensory areas that have more cortical representation provide a more detailed construct of the external world.

In Figure 1-14, we apply Jerison's ideas to relative differences in overall brain size across mammals.

FIGURE 9-23 **Receptive-Field Hierarchy**

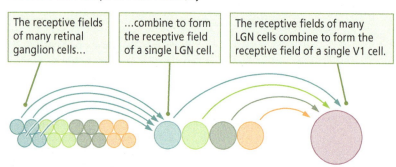

The receptive fields of many retinal ganglion cells...

...combine to form the receptive field of a single LGN cell.

The receptive fields of many LGN cells combine to form the receptive field of a single V1 cell.

Visual Corpus Callosum

Topographic mapping based on neuronal receptive fields is an effective way for the brain to code object location. But if the left visual field is represented in the right cerebral hemisphere and the right visual field is represented in the left cerebral hemisphere, how are the two halves of the visual field ultimately merged into a unified representation? After all, we have the subjective impression not of two independent visual fields but rather of a single, continuous field of vision.

The answer to how this unity is accomplished lies in the corpus callosum, which binds the two sides of the visual field together at the midline. Until the 1950s, its function was largely a mystery. Physicians had occasionally cut the corpus callosum to control severe epilepsy or to reach a very deep tumor, but patients did not appear much affected by this surgery. The corpus callosum clearly linked the two hemispheres of the brain, but exactly which parts were connected was not yet known.

We now realize that the corpus callosum connects only certain brain structures. As shown in **Figure 9-24**, the frontal lobes have many callosal connections, but the occipital lobes have almost none. If you think about it, there is no reason for a neuron in the visual cortex that is looking at one place in the visual field to be concerned with what another neuron in the opposite hemisphere is looking at in another part of the visual field.

Cells that lie along the midline of the visual field are an exception, however. These cells look at adjacent places in the visual field, one slightly to the left of center and one slightly to the right. Callosal connections between such cells zip the two visual fields together by combining their receptive fields to overlap at the midline. The two fields thus become one.

9-3 Review

Before you continue, check your understanding. Answers to Self-Test appear at the back of the book.

1. The visual field is composed of thousands of small _____ of the ganglion cells.

2. List four types of cells that have visual receptive fields: _____, _____, _____, and _____.

3. Inputs to different parts of cortical region V1 from different parts of the retina essentially form a(n) _____ of the visual world within the brain.

4. The two sides of the visual world are bound together as one perception by the _____.

5. How does Jerison's principle of proper mass apply to the visual system?

For additional study tools, visit **LaunchPad** at launchpadworks.com

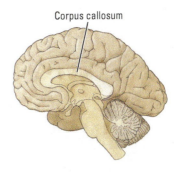

Section 15-4 describes the revelations learned from studying split-brain patients, whose corpus callosa have been severed.

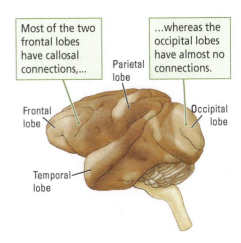

FIGURE 9-24 **Callosal Connections** Darker areas show regions of the rhesus monkey cortex that receive projections from the opposite hemisphere through the corpus callosum.

9-4

Neuronal Activity

Individual neurons make up the visual system pathways. By studying how these cells behave when their receptive fields are stimulated, we can begin to understand how the brain processes the features of the visual world beyond the location of a light. We first examine how neurons in the ventral stream respond to objects' shapes and colors and then briefly consider how neurons in the dorsal stream direct vision for action.

Seeing Shape

Imagine a microelectrode placed near a neuron somewhere in the visual pathway from retina to cortex. The microelectrode is recording changes in the neuron's firing rate. This cell occasionally fires spontaneously, producing action potentials with each discharge. Assume that the neuron discharges, on average, once every 0.08 second. Each action potential is brief, on the order of 1 millisecond.

Figure 4-6 diagrams how microelectrodes work.

(A) Baseline (12 per second)

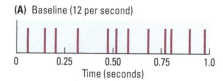

(B) Excitation

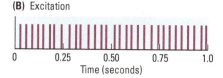

(C) Inhibition

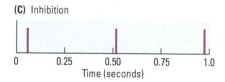

FIGURE 9-25 **Recording Neuronal Stimulation** Each action potential is represented by a spike. **(A)** In a 1-second period at this neuron's baseline firing rate, 12 spikes were recorded. **(B)** A firing rate over baseline signals excitation. **(C)** A firing rate under baseline signals inhibition.

Principle 10: The nervous system works by juxtaposing excitation and inhibition.

FIGURE 9-26 **On–Off Receptivity (A)** In the receptive field of an RGC with an on-center and off-surround, a spot of light shining on the center excites the neuron, but a spot of light in the surround inhibits it. When the light in the surround is turned off, firing rate increases briefly—an offset response. A light shining in both the center and the surround (periphery) would produce a weak increase in firing. **(B)** In the receptive field of an RGC with an off-center and on-surround, light in the center produces inhibition, light on the surround produces excitation, and light across the entire field produces weak inhibition.

If we plot action potentials spanning 1 second, we see only spikes in the record because the action potentials are so brief. **Figure 9-25A** is a single cell recording of 12 spikes in the span of 1 second. If the firing rate of this cell increases, we see more spikes (Figure 9-25B). If the firing rate decreases, we see fewer spikes (Figure 9-25C). The increase in firing is the result of neuronal excitation, whereas the decrease indicates inhibition. Excitation and inhibition, of course, are the principal information transfer mechanisms in the nervous system.

Now suppose we present a stimulus to the neuron by illuminating its receptive field in the retina, perhaps by shining a light on a blank screen within the cell's visual field. We might place before the eye a straight line positioned at a 45° angle. The cell could respond to this stimulus either by increasing or decreasing its firing rate. In either case, we would conclude that the cell is generating information about the line.

The same cell could show excitation to one stimulus, inhibition to another stimulus, and no reaction at all to a third. The cell could be excited by lines oriented 45° to the left and inhibited by lines oriented 45° to the right. Similarly, the cell could be excited by stimulation in one part of its receptive field (such as the center) and inhibited by stimulation in another part (such as the periphery).

Finally, we might find that the cell's response to a particular stimulus is selective. Such a cell would indicate the importance of the stimulus to the animal. For instance, the cell might be excited when a stimulus is presented with food but inhibited when the same stimulus is presented alone. In each case, the cell is selectively sensitive to characteristics in the visual world.

Neurons at each level of the visual system have distinctly different characteristics and functions. Our goal is not to look at each neuron type but rather to consider generally how some typical neurons at each level differ from one another in their contributions to processing shape. We focus on neurons in three areas: the ganglion cell layer of the retina, the primary visual cortex, and the temporal cortex.

Processing in RGCs

Neurons in the retina do not detect shape because their receptive fields are minuscule dots. Each retinal ganglion cell responds only to the presence or absence of light in its receptive field, not to shape. Shape is constructed by processes in the cortex from the information that those ganglion cells pass on about events in their receptive fields.

The receptive field of a ganglion cell has a concentric circle arrangement, as illustrated in **Figure 9-26A**. A spot of light falling in the receptive field's central circle excites some of these cells, whereas a spot of light falling in the receptive field's

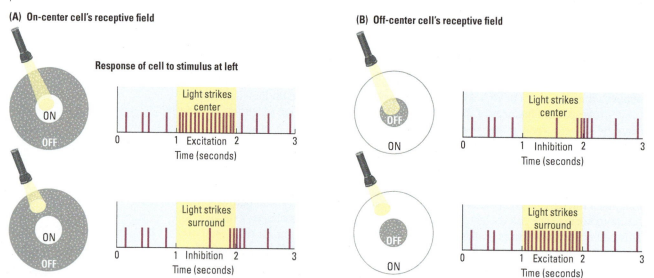

(A) On-center cell's receptive field

Response of cell to stimulus at left

ON
OFF

Light strikes center

0   1   Excitation   2   3
Time (seconds)

ON
OFF

Light strikes surround

0   1   Inhibition   2   3
Time (seconds)

(B) Off-center cell's receptive field

OFF
ON

Light strikes center

0   1   Inhibition   2   3
Time (seconds)

OFF
ON

Light strikes surround

0   1   Excitation   2   3
Time (seconds)

surrounding area (periphery) inhibits the cell. A spot of light falling across the entire receptive field weakly increases the cell's firing rate.

This type of neuron is called an *on-center cell*. Other RGCs, called *off-center cells*, have the opposite arrangement, with light in the center of the receptive field inhibiting, light in the surrounding area exciting, and light across the entire field producing weak inhibition (Figure 9-26B). The on–off arrangement of RGC receptive fields makes these cells especially responsive to tiny spots of light.

This description of ganglion cell receptive fields might mislead you into thinking that they form a mosaic of discrete little circles on the retina. In fact, neighboring retinal ganglion cells receive their inputs from an overlapping set of photoreceptors. As a result, their receptive fields overlap, as illustrated in **Figure 9-27**. In this way, a small spot of light shining on the retina is likely to produce activity in both on-center and off-center RGCs.

How can on-center and off-center ganglion cells tell the brain anything about shape? The answer is that a ganglion cell tells the brain about the amount of light hitting a certain spot on the retina compared with the average amount of light falling on the surrounding retinal region. This comparison is known as **luminance contrast**. *Luminance* is the amount of visible light reflected to the eye from a surface, and *contrast* is the difference in luminance between adjacent parts of that surface. The photographs in Clinical Focus 9-1 show us two clear differences in luminance contrast. On the left, the woman's pink top contrasts sharply with her black slacks, but the sleeve on the right contrasts far less with the background. It does not appear as bright.

To understand how luminance contrast tells the brain about shape, consider the hypothetical population of on-center ganglion cells represented in **Figure 9-28**. Their receptive fields are distributed across the retinal image of a light–dark edge. Some of the ganglion cells' receptive fields are in the dark area, others are in the light area, and still others' fields straddle the edge of the light.

The ganglion cells with receptive fields in the dark or light areas are least affected because they receive either no stimulation or stimulation of both the excitatory and inhibitory regions of their receptive fields. The ganglion cells most affected by the stimulus are those lying along the edge. Ganglion cell B is inhibited because the light falls mostly on its inhibitory surrounding area; ganglion cell D is excited because its entire excitatory center is stimulated, but only part of its inhibitory surround is.

Consequently, information transmitted from retinal ganglion cells to the visual areas in the brain does not give equal weight to all visual field regions. Rather, it emphasizes regions containing differences in luminance—areas along the edges. So RGCs are really sending signals about edges, and edges form shapes.

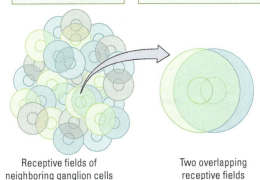

| The receptive fields of retinal ganglion cells overlap extensively,... | ...so any two adjacent fields look at almost the same part of the world. |

Receptive fields of neighboring ganglion cells

Two overlapping receptive fields

FIGURE 9-27 **Overlapping Receptive Fields**

luminance contrast Amount of light an object reflects relative to its surroundings.

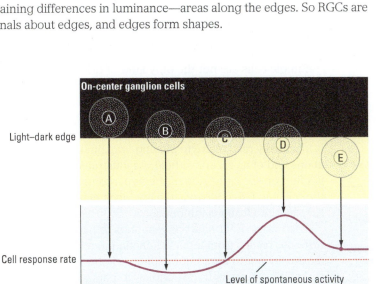

FIGURE 9-28 **Activity at the Margins** Responses of a hypothetical population of on-center ganglion cells whose receptive fields (A–E) are distributed across a light–dark edge. The activity of the cells along the edge is most affected relative to those away from the edge. Information from Purves et al., 1997.

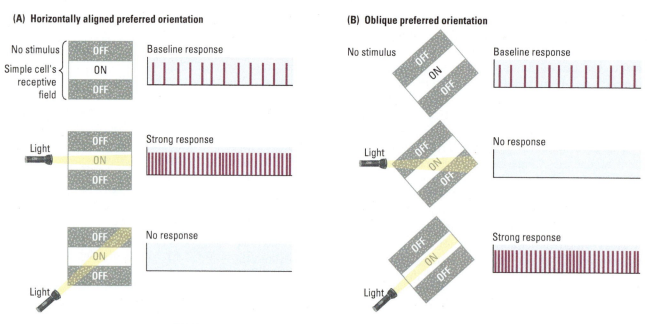

(A) Horizontally aligned preferred orientation

No stimulus — Simple cell's receptive field — OFF / ON / OFF — Baseline response

Light — OFF / ON / OFF — Strong response

OFF / ON / OFF — No response — Light

(B) Oblique preferred orientation

No stimulus — OFF / ON / OFF — Baseline response

Light — OFF / ON / OFF — No response

OFF / ON / OFF — Strong response — Light

FIGURE 9-29 **Typical Receptive Fields for Simple V1 Cells** Simple cells respond to a bar of light in a particular orientation, such as **(A)** horizontal or **(B)** oblique. The position of the bar in the visual field is important because the cell either responds (ON) or does not respond (OFF) to light in adjacent visual field regions.

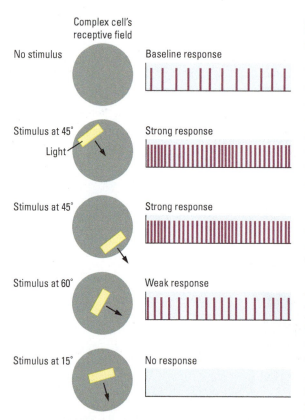

Complex cell's receptive field

No stimulus — Baseline response

Stimulus at 45° — Light — Strong response

Stimulus at 45° — Strong response

Stimulus at 60° — Weak response

Stimulus at 15° — No response

FIGURE 9-30 **Receptive Field of a Complex Cell** Unlike a simple cell's on–off response pattern, a complex cell in V1 shows the same response throughout its circular receptive field, responding best to bars of light moving at a particular angle. The response is reduced or absent with the bar of light at other orientations.

Processing Shape in the Primary Visual Cortex

Now consider cells in region V1 that receive their visual inputs from LGN cells, which in turn receive theirs from retinal ganglion cells. As you read on, think about how these cortical cells are responding to the Clinical Focus 9-1 photographs. Because each V1 cell receives input from multiple RGCs, the receptive fields of the V1 neurons are much larger than those of retinal neurons. Consequently, V1 cells respond to stimuli more complex than simply light on or light off. In particular, these cells are maximally excited by bars of light oriented in a particular direction rather than by spots of light. These V1 cells are therefore called *orientation detectors*.

Like the ganglion cells, some orientation detectors have an on–off receptive-field arrangement, but the arrangement is rectangular rather than circular. Visual cortex cells with this property are known as *simple cells*. Typical receptive fields for simple cells in V1 are shown in **Figure 9-29**.

Simple cells are not the only kind of orientation detector in the primary visual cortex; several functionally distinct types of neurons populate region V1. For instance, the receptive fields of *complex cells*, such as those in **Figure 9-30**, are maximally excited by bars of light moving in a particular direction through the visual field. A *hypercomplex cell*, like a complex cell, is maximally responsive to moving bars but also has a strong inhibitory area at one end of its receptive field. As illustrated in **Figure 9-31**, a bar of light landing on the right side of the hypercomplex cell's receptive field excites the cell; but if, for example, the bar lands mainly on the inhibitory area to the left, the cell's firing is inhibited.

Each class of V1 neurons responds to bars of light in some way, yet this response results from input originating in retinal ganglion cells that respond maximally not to bars but to spots of light. How does this conversion from responding to spots to responding to bars take place? An example will help explain the process.

A thin bar of light falls on the retinal photoreceptors, striking the receptive fields of perhaps dozens of retinal ganglion cells. The input to a V1 neuron comes from a group of ganglion cells that happen to be aligned in a row, as in **Figure 9-32**. That V1 neuron is activated (or inhibited) only when a bar of light hitting the retina strikes that particular row of ganglion cells. If the bar of light shines at a slightly different angle, only some of the retinal ganglion cells in the row are activated, so the V1 neuron is excited only weakly.

Figure 9-32 illustrates the connection between light striking the retina in a certain pattern and the activation of a simple cell in the primary visual cortex, one that responds to a bar of light in a particular orientation. Using the same logic, we can also diagram the retinal receptive fields of complex or hypercomplex V1 neurons.

A characteristic of cortical structure is that the neurons are organized into functional columns. The connectivity pattern in a column is vertical: inputs arrive in layer IV and then connect with cells in the other layers. **Figure 9-33** shows such a column, a 0.5-mm-diameter strip of cortex that includes representative neurons and their connections.

Neurons within a cortical column have similar functions. For example, **Figure 9-34A** shows that neurons within the same column respond to lines oriented in the same direction. Adjacent columns house cells responsive to different line orientations. Figure 9-34B shows the cortical columns of input coming from each eye, discussed earlier, called **ocular dominance columns**. So V1 has orientation columns housing neurons of similar sensitivity, as well as ocular dominance columns with input from one eye or the other.

Processing Shape in the Temporal Cortex

Consider neurons along the ventral stream in temporal lobe region TE. Rather than being responsive to spots or bars of light, TE neurons are maximally excited by complex visual stimuli, such as faces (see Figure 9-19A) or hands, and can be remarkably

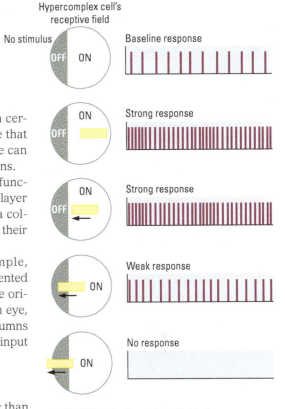

FIGURE 9-31 **Receptive Field of a Hypercomplex Cell** A hypercomplex cell in V1 responds to a moving bar of light in a particular orientation (e.g., horizontal) anywhere in the excitatory (ON) part of its receptive field. If most of the bar extends into the inhibitory area (OFF), however, the response is inhibited.

ocular dominance column Functional column in the visual cortex maximally responsive to information coming from one eye.

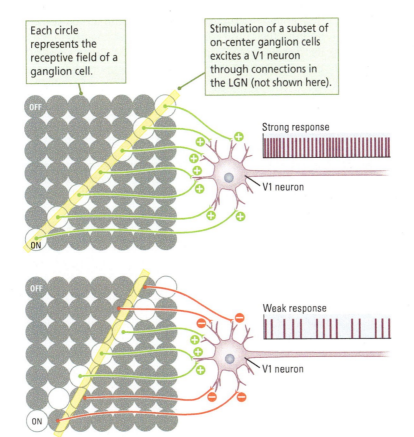

FIGURE 9-32 **V1 Receptivity** A V1 cell responds to a row of ganglion cells in a particular orientation on the retina. The bar of light strongly activates a row of ganglion cells, each connected through the LGN to a V1 neuron. The activity of this V1 neuron is most affected by a bar of light at a 45° angle.

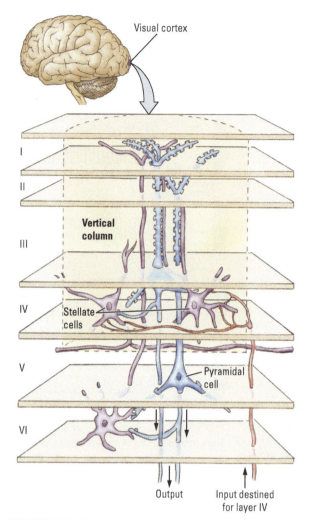

Visual cortex

I

II

**Vertical
column**

III

IV   Stellate
cells

V   Pyramidal
                               cell

VI

Output   Input destined
              for layer IV

FIGURE 9-33 **Neural Circuit in a Column in the Visual Cortex**
In this three-dimensional view, sensory inputs enter the cortical
column at layer VI (bottom) and terminate on stellate cells in
layer IV that synapse with pyramidal cells in layers III and V.
The information flow is vertical. Axons of the pyramidal cells
leave the column to join other columns or structures. Information
from Szentagothai, 1975.

specific in their responsiveness. They may be responsive to particular faces
seen head-on, to faces viewed in profile, to the posture of the head, or even
to particular facial expressions.

How far does this specialized responsiveness extend? Would it be practical to have visual neurons in the temporal cortex specialized to respond
to every conceivable feature of objects? Keiji Tanaka (1993) approached this
question by presenting monkeys with many three-dimensional representations of animals and plants to find stimuli that are effective in activating
particular neurons of the inferior temporal cortex.

Having identified stimuli that were especially effective, such as faces or
hands, he then wondered which specific features of those stimuli are critical to stimulating the neurons. Tanaka found that most neurons in area TE
require rather complex features for their activation. These features include
a combination of characteristics such as orientation, size, color, and texture. Furthermore, neurons with similar but not identical responsiveness
to particular features tend to cluster in columns, as shown in **Figure 9-35**.

Apparently, then, an object is represented not by the activity of a single
neuron but rather by the activity of many neurons with slightly varying
stimulus specificities. These neurons are grouped in a column. This finding
is important because it provides an explanation for *stimulus equivalence*—
recognizing an object as remaining the same despite being viewed from
different orientations.

Think of how the representation of objects by multiple neurons in a column can produce stimulus equivalence. If each neuron in the column module varies slightly in regard to the features to which it responds but the
effective stimuli largely overlap, the effect of small changes in incoming
visual images will be minimized, and we will continue to perceive an object
as itself.

The stimulus specificity of neurons in the inferior temporal cortex in
monkeys shows remarkable neuroplasticity. If monkeys are trained to
discriminate particular shapes to obtain a food reward, not only do they
improve their discriminatory ability but neurons in the temporal lobe modify their preferred stimuli to fire maximally to some of the stimuli used in
training. This result shows that the temporal lobe's role in visual processing is not determined genetically but is instead subject to experience, even
in adults.

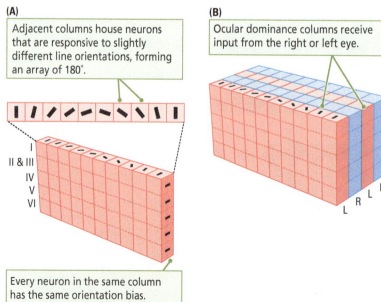

(A)
Adjacent columns house neurons
that are responsive to slightly
different line orientations, forming
an array of 180°.

I
II & III
IV
V
VI

Every neuron in the same column
has the same orientation bias.

(B)
Ocular dominance columns receive
input from the right or left eye.

L R L R
   L R

FIGURE 9-34 Organization of Functional
Columns in V1

We can speculate that this neuroplastic characteristic evolved because it allows the visual system to adapt to a changing visual environment. Think of how different the demands on your visual recognition abilities are when you move from a dense forest to a treeless plain to a city street. The visual neurons of your temporal cortex can adapt to these differences (Tanaka, 1993). In addition, experience-dependent visual neurons ensure that people can identify visual stimuli that were never encountered as the human brain evolved.

The preferred stimuli of neurons in the primary visual cortex are not modified by experience. This implies that the stimulus preferences of V1 neurons are genetically programmed. Regardless, the functions of the V1 neurons underlie the more complex and flexible characteristics of the inferior temporal cortex neurons.

Seeing Color

Scientists have long wondered why—and how—we see a world so rich in color. One hypothesis on the *why* is that color vision evolved first in the great apes, specifically in apes that eat fruit. Chimpanzees and humans are members of this family. Over their evolution, both species have faced plentiful competition for ripe fruits—from other animals, insects, and each other. Scientists suspect that color vision gave the great apes a competitive evolutionary advantage.

An explanation of how color vision works has its roots in the Renaissance, 600 years ago in Italy. Painters of the time discovered that they could obtain the entire range of colors in the visual world by mixing only three colors of paint (red, blue, and yellow). This is the process of *subtractive color mixing* shown in **Figure 9-36A**.

We now know that such trichromatic color mixing is a property of the cones in the retina. Subtractive color mixing works by removing light from the mix. This is why matte black surfaces reflect no light: the darker the color, the less light it contains.

Conversely, *additive color mixing* increases light to make color (Figure 9-36B). The lighter the color, the more light it contains, which is why a white surface reflects the entire visible spectrum. Unlike those of paint, the primary colors of light are red, blue, and green. Light of different wavelengths stimulates the three cone receptor types in different ways. It is the ratio of activity of these three receptor types that forms our impressions of colors.

Trichromatic Theory

According to the **trichromatic theory**, the color we see—say, blue at short 400-nm wavelengths, green at medium 500 nm, and red at long 600 nm—is determined by the relative responses of the corresponding cone types (see Figure 9-6). If all three types are equally active, we see white.

Trichromatic theory predicts that if we lack one cone receptor type, we cannot process as many colors as we could with all three. This is exactly what happens when a person is born with only two cone types. The colors this person cannot perceive depend on which receptor type is missing, as illustrated in Research Focus 9-4, Color-Deficient Vision.

The mere presence of cones in an animal's retina does not mean that the animal has color vision as we know it. It simply

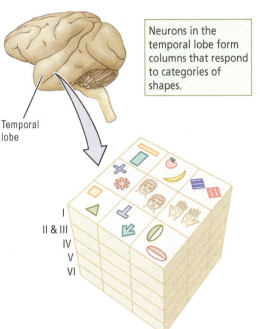

Neurons in the temporal lobe form columns that respond to categories of shapes.

Temporal lobe

FIGURE 9-35 **Columnar Organization of Area TE** Neurons with similar but slightly different pattern selectivity cluster in vertical columns, perpendicular to the cortical surface.

Principle 2: Neuroplasticity is the hallmark of nervous system functioning.

Changes in a neuron's preferred stimulus reflect changes in its sensitivity to particular features.

Section 1-4 recounts several ideas on how the primate lifestyle, including diet, encouraged the evolution of complex nervous systems.

trichromatic theory Explanation of color vision based on the coding of three primary colors: red, green, and blue.

(A)

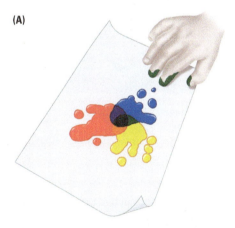

(B)

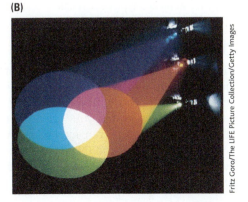

Fritz Goro/The LIFE Picture Collection/Getty Images

FIGURE 9-36 **Color Mixing (A)** Subtractive color mixing absorbs light waves that we see as red, blue, or yellow. When all visible wavelengths are absorbed, we see black. **(B)** Additive color mixing reflects light waves that we see as red, blue, and green. When all visible wavelengths are reflected, we see white.

Color-Deficient Vision

Most people's retinas contain three cone types; these people have trichromatic vision. But some people are missing one or more cone types and are thus often mistakenly said to be color-blind—mistakenly because people who have two types of cones still can distinguish lots of colors, though not as many as people with three cones.

To have no color vision at all, one would have to have only one type of photoreceptor, rods. This is a rare occurrence, but we do have a friend who has no concept of color. It has led to a lifetime of practical jokes because others (especially his wife) must choose properly color-coordinated clothes for him to wear.

The complete lack of red cones leads to a condition called *protanopia*; the lack of green cones is *deuteranopia*; the lack of blue cones is *tritanopia*. The frequency of each condition is about 1 percent in men and 0.01 percent in women. Having fewer cones of one type, most commonly the green cone, also is possible. This condition afflicts about 5 percent of men and 0.4 percent of women.

The illustration provides a simple approximation, compared with trichromats (left), of what people with protanopia (center) or deuteranopia (right) see. Individuals with protanopia and deuteranopia still see plenty of color, but that color is significantly different from the color that trichromats see. Many domestic animals (dogs, cats, and horses among them) have deuteranopia, which actually gives them an advantage in seeing objects that would appear camouflaged to trichromats. In fact, military forces often use humans with deuteranopia to help see through camouflage.

There is no cure for color blindness, but there are new treatments in which people wear glasses that change the wavelength of light entering the eye, allowing the wearers to perceive color as it is seen by people with normal vision. Although the potential benefit of this treatment has received widespread coverage in mainstream media, thus far there have been no randomized clinical trials, only numerous testimonials. To date, there are two companies manufacturing the glasses (see colormax.org and enchroma.com).

Image as viewed by a trichromat observer

Protanopia: image as viewed by an observer lacking red cones

Deuteranopia: image as viewed by an observer lacking green cones

Dr. Terrace L. Waggoner/www.ColorVisionTesting.com

means that the animal has photoreceptors that are particularly sensitive to light. Many animals lack color vision as we know it, but the only animal with eyes known to have no cones at all is a type of fish called a skate. A key feature of primate color vision is the processing of color in V1 and V4.

Opponent Processes

Although the beginning of color perception in the cones follows the trichromatic model, succeeding levels of color processing use a different strategy. Try staring first at the red and blue box in **Figure 9-37** for about 30 seconds and then at the white box next to it. When you shift your gaze to the white surface, you will see an afterimage in the colors opposite to red and blue—green and yellow. Conversely, if you stare at a green and yellow box and then shift to white, you will see a red and blue afterimage. Such afterimages lead to the sense that there are actually four basic colors (red, green, yellow, and blue).

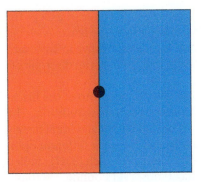 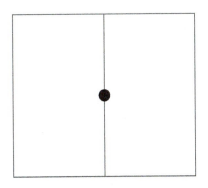

FIGURE 9-37 **Demonstrating Opposing Color Pairs** Stare at the rectangle on the left for about 30 seconds. Then stare at the white box on the right. You will see an afterimage of green on the red side and of yellow on the blue side.

opponent process Explanation of color vision that emphasizes the importance of the apparently opposing color pairs: red versus green and blue versus yellow.

color constancy Phenomenon whereby an object's perceived color tends to remain constant relative to other colors, regardless of changes in illumination.

A characteristic of RGCs explains the two opposing pairs of four basic colors. Remember that RGCs have an on–off and center–surround organization. Stimulation to the center of the cell's receptive field is either excitatory (in some cells) or inhibitory (in other cells), whereas stimulation to the periphery of the receptive field is opposite (see Figure 9-26).

This arrangement can be adapted to produce color-opponent cells. If one wavelength of light produced excitation and another inhibition, cells would evolve that are excited by red and inhibited by green (or vice versa), as would cells that are excited by blue and inhibited by yellow (or vice versa). Red–green and blue–yellow would therefore be linked to each other as color opposites, or opponents.

In fact, about 60 percent of human retinal ganglion cells are color-sensitive in this way, with the center responsive to one wavelength and the surrounding area to another. The most common **opponent-process** pairing, shown in **Figure 9-38**, is medium-wavelength (green) versus long-wavelength (red), but we also have blue versus yellow RGCs. Most likely, opponent-process cells evolved to enhance the relatively small differences in spectral absorption among the three cone types.

Cortical neurons in region V1 also respond to color in an opponent-process manner reminiscent of retinal ganglion cells. Recall that color inputs in the primary visual cortex go to the blobs that appear in sections stained for cytochrome oxidase (see Figure 9-17). These blobs are where the color-sensitive cells are located.

Figure 9-39 models how the color-sensitive cells in the blobs are inserted amid the orientation-sensitive and ocular dominance columns. The primary visual cortex thus appears to be organized into modules that include ocular dominance and orientation-sensitive columns as well as blobs. Think of V1 as being composed of several thousand modules, each analyzing color and contour for a particular visual region. This organization allows the primary visual cortex to perform several functions concurrently.

How do neurons in the visual system beyond V1 process color? You have already learned that cells in region V4 respond to color, but in contrast with the cells in region V1, these V4 cells do not respond to particular wavelengths. Rather, they are responsive to different perceived colors, with the center of the field being excited by a certain color and the surrounding area being inhibited.

Speculation swirls about the function of these V4 cells. One idea is that they are important for **color constancy**, the property of perception whereby colors appear to remain the same relative to one another despite changes in light. For instance, were you to look at a bowl of fruit through light-green glasses, the fruit would take on a greenish tinge, but bananas would still

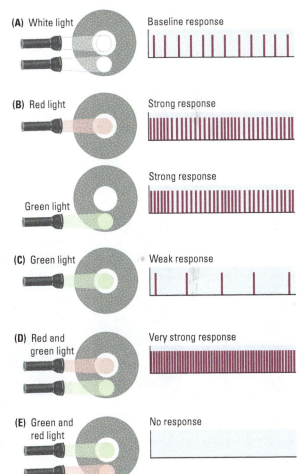

FIGURE 9-38 **Opponent-Color Contrast Response**
(A) A red–green color-sensitive RGC responds weakly to white light on its center and surround because red and green cones absorb white light to similar extents, so their inputs cancel out. **(B)** The cell responds strongly to a spot of red light in its center as well as to red's paired wavelength, green, in the surround. **(C)** It is strongly inhibited by a small spot of green in its center. **(D)** The RGC responds very strongly to simultaneous illumination of the center with red and the surround with green. **(E)** It is completely inhibited by the simultaneous illumination of the center with green and the surround with red.

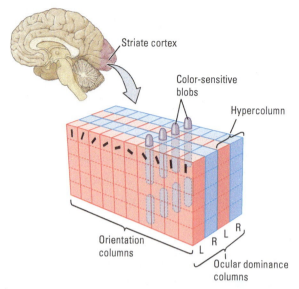

FIGURE 9-39 **V1 Modules** A model of striate cortex showing the orientation-sensitive columns, ocular dominance columns, and color-sensitive blobs as composed of two hypercolumns. Each consists of a full set (red and blue) of orientation-sensitive columns spanning 180° of preferred angle as well as a pair of blobs. All cells in the hypercolumn share the same receptive field.

look yellow relative to red apples. If you removed all the fruit except the bananas and looked at them through the tinted glasses, the bananas would appear green because the color you perceive is isolated relative to any other. Monkeys with V4 lesions lose color constancy, though they can discriminate different color wavelengths.

In February 2015, Celia Bleasdale took a cell phone photo of the black-and-blue dress she intended to wear to her daughter's wedding. The image, now referred to as "The Dress," was posted online and immediately went viral because different observers expressed radically different opinions of the color scheme (see **Figure 9-40**). Pascal Wallisch (2017) studied this phenomenon by surveying about 13,000 observers online. He found that observers' unconscious assumptions about the source of the illumination of the dress influenced their color perception. People who believed the dress to be illuminated with artificial incandescent light saw the dress as blue, whereas people who believed the dress was photographed in daylight saw the dress as gold. Our assumptions are a necessary component of the human visual system's color constancy. *The Dress* not only provides an example of color constancy but also shows how our color perception is idiosyncratic.

Neuronal Activity in the Dorsal Stream

A striking characteristic of many cells in the visual areas of the parietal cortex is that they are virtually silent to visual stimulation when a person is under anesthesia. This is true of neurons in the posterior parietal regions of the dorsal stream. In contrast, cells in the visual temporal cortex do respond to visual stimulation when a person is anesthetized.

The silence on the part of neurons in the posterior parietal cortex under anesthesia makes sense if their role is to process visual information for action. In the absence of action when a person is unconscious, there is no need for processing. Hence, the cells are inactive.

Cells in the dorsal stream are of many types, their details varying with the nature of the movement in which a particular cell takes part. One interesting cell category processes the visual appearance of an object to be grasped. If a monkey is going to pick up an apple, for instance, these cells respond even when the monkey is only looking at the apple. The cells do not respond when the monkey encounters the same apple if no movement is to be made.

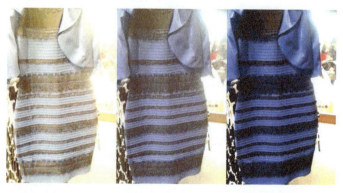

FIGURE 9-40 **Color Constancy** Depending on the viewer, the dress in the center photo is perceived as either white and gold or blue and black. The image is color-balanced, at left, to show the dress as white and gold; at right, as blue and black. What color is the original?

These dorsal stream cells also respond if the monkey merely watches another monkey making movements to pick up the apple. Apparently, the cells have some understanding of what is happening in the external world. But that understanding is always related to action performed with respect to visually perceived objects. These cells led David Milner and Mel Goodale (2006) to conclude that the dorsal stream is a *how* visual system, as described in Section 9-3.

But the dorsal stream may actually have a greater role in shape perception than previously thought. Recent fMRI studies have shown that the dorsal pathway can also perceive and process objects, although studies of patients show that it cannot do this without the presence of the ventral stream (Freud et al., 2017). It is still not known exactly what role the dorsal stream plays in object perception, but the results suggest that shape processing may be more distributed than previously believed. This will likely be a lively area of research in the coming years.

The blue and black dress at right is the original.

9-4 Review

Before you continue, check your understanding. Answers to Self-Test appear at the back of the book.

1. Neurons in the primary visual cortex respond to properties of shapes, especially to _____ oriented in a certain direction.

2. Recognition of complex visual stimuli such as faces is completed in the _____ lobe.

3. The idea that the color we see is determined by the relative responses of the three cone types in the retina is called _____.

4. Retinal ganglion cells mediate color vision by _____ processes.

5. Describe the opponent process in the retinal ganglion cells.

For additional study tools, visit 🌀 **LaunchPad** at launchpadworks.com

homonymous hemianopia Blindness of the entire left or right visual field.

quadrantanopia Blindness of one quadrant of the visual field.

scotoma Small blind spot in the visual field caused by migraine or by a small lesion of the visual cortex.

The Visual Brain in Action

Anatomical and physiological studies of brain systems leave one key question unanswered: How do all of the cells in these systems act together to produce a particular function? One way to answer this question is to evaluate what happens when parts of the visual system are dysfunctional. Then we can see how these parts contribute to the workings of the whole. We use this strategy to examine the neuropsychology of vision—the study of the visual brain in action.

Injury to the Visual Pathway Leading to the Cortex

What happens when parts of the visual pathway leading from the eye to the cortex are injured? For instance, destruction of the retina or optic nerve of one eye produces *monocular blindness*, the loss of sight in that eye. Partial destruction of the retina or optic nerve produces a partial loss of sight in one eye, restricted to the visual field region that has severed connections to the brain.

Injuries to the visual pathway beyond the eye also produce blindness. For example, complete cuts of the optic tract, the LGN, or cortical region V1 result in **homonymous hemianopia**, blindness of one entire side of the visual field, as shown in **Figure 9-41A**. We encountered this syndrome in Clinical Focus 9-1, the story of D. B.'s lesion in region V1. Should a lesion in one of these areas be partial, as is often the case, the result is **quadrantanopia**, destruction of only a part of the visual field, illustrated in Figure 9-41B. Note that injuries affecting vision are rarely localized to gray matter but also include white matter, leading to disconnection of different brain regions.

Figure 9-41C shows that small lesions in V1 often produce small blind spots, or **scotomas**, in the visual field. Clinical Focus 9-1 observes that scotomas can be a warning symptom for migraine sufferers. But brain-injured people are often totally unaware of them. One reason is that the eyes are usually moving.

FIGURE 9-41 **Consequences of Lesions in Region V1** The shaded areas indicate regions of visual loss. **(A)** A complete lesion of V1 in the left hemisphere results in hemianopia affecting the right visual field. **(B)** A large lesion of the lower lip of the calcarine fissure produces quadrantanopia that affects most of the upper right visual quadrant. **(C)** A smaller lesion of the lower lip of the calcarine fissure results in a smaller scotoma.

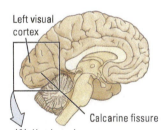

Left visual cortex

Calcarine fissure

(A) Hemianopia

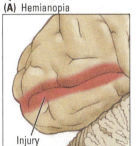

Injury

(B) Quadrantanopia

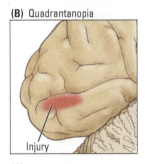

Injury

(C) Scotoma

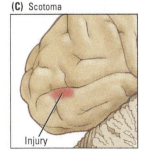

Injury

Left visual field   Right visual field

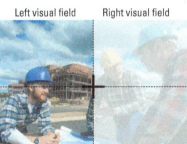

Glowimages/Getty Images

visual-form agnosia Inability to recognize objects or drawings of objects.

We make tiny, involuntary eye movements almost constantly. Because of this usually constant eye motion, called *nystagmus,* a scotoma moves about the visual field, allowing the intact brain regions to perceive all the information in that field. If the eyes are temporarily held still, the visual system actually compensates for a scotoma through pattern completion—filling in the hole, so to speak—so that the people and objects in the visual world are perceived as whole. The result: a seemingly normal set of perceptions.

The visual system may cover up a scotoma so successfully that its presence can be demonstrated to the patient only by tricking the visual system. The trick is to place an object entirely within the scotoma and, without allowing the patient to shift gaze, asking what the object is. If the patient reports seeing nothing, to confirm the existence of a blind area, the examiner moves the object out of the scotoma so that it suddenly appears in the intact region of the visual field.

This technique is similar to demonstrating the presence of the blind spot that is due to the optic disc (as in Figure 9-4). When a person is looking at an object with only one eye, the brain compensates for the scotoma in the same way as for the optic disc's blind spot. As a result, the person does not notice the scotoma.

Thus, the type of blindness offers clues about where in the visual pathway the cause of the problem lies. If the loss of vision is in one eye only, the problem must be in that eye or its optic nerve; if the vision loss affects both eyes, the problem most likely is in the brain. Many people have difficulty understanding why a person with damage to the visual cortex has difficulty with both eyes. They fail to realize that the visual field, not the eye, is represented in the brain.

Beyond region V1, the nature of visual loss caused by injury is considerably more complex. It is also very different in the ventral and dorsal streams. We therefore look at each pathway separately.

Injury to the *What* Pathway

We have encountered an example of damage to the *what* pathway: the case of D. B. in Clinical Focus 9-1. He appeared to be blind in his affected visual field but could point to the location of blinking lights in that field, suggesting that some part of his visual system was working. An even more dramatic example of ventral stream injury comes from the case of D. F., a 35-year-old woman who, while taking a shower, was poisoned by carbon monoxide (CO) from a faulty gas-fueled water heater. The length of her exposure is unclear, but when her roommate found her, the shower was running cold. CO poisoning can cause several kinds of neurological damage, and the result for D. F. was an extensive lesion of the lateral occipital region, including cortical tissue in the ventral visual pathway.

D. F.'s principal deficit was **visual-form agnosia**, an inability to recognize objects, real or drawn (see Farah, 1990). Not only was D. F. unable to recognize objects, especially line drawings of objects, but she could neither estimate their size and orientation nor draw copies of them. Likewise, as **Figure 9-42** illustrates, patient J. W., who suffered occipital damage similar to D. F., also fails to recognize or copy simple drawings.

Clearly, D. F.'s lesion interfered with her ventral stream *what* pathway. Remarkably, despite her inability to identify objects or to estimate their size and orientation, D. F. retained the capacity, illustrated in **Figure 9-43**, to appropriately shape her hand when reaching out to grasp something. Goodale, Milner, and their research colleagues (1991) studied D. F. extensively for years and devised a way to demonstrate D. F.'s skill at reaching for objects.

The middle column in **Figure 9-44** shows the grasp patterns of a control participant (S. H.) when she picks up something irregularly shaped. S. H. grasps the object along whichever of the two axes makes it easier to pick up. When D. F. is presented with the same task, shown in the left-hand column, she is as good as S. H. at placing her index finger and thumb on appropriately opposed grasp points.

Clearly, D. F. remains able to use the structural features of objects to control her visually guided grasping movements, even though she is unable to interpret these same features. This result demonstrates once more that we are consciously aware of

Original   J. W.'s copy

FIGURE 9-42 **Injury to the Ventral Stream** J. W. survived a severe heart attack while exercising. As a result, he suffered anoxia (loss of oxygen) and ensuing occipital damage. Subsequently, he was unable to recognize the simple line drawings on the left and copied them poorly (right).

Section 9-2 describes damage to the temporal lobe area that causes facial agnosia.

FIGURE 9-43 **Visual Guidance** You may consciously reach for an object such as a pen or a mug, but your hand forms the appropriate posture automatically, without your conscious awareness. Figure 11-1 details this type of sequentially organized movement.

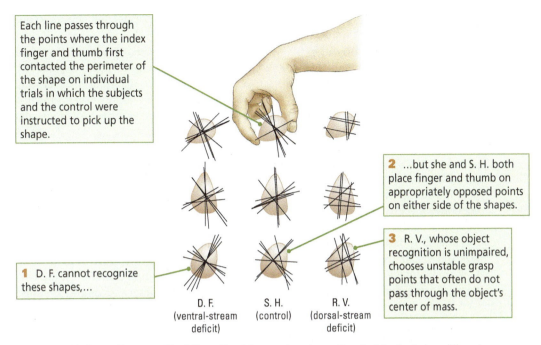

Each line passes through the points where the index finger and thumb first contacted the perimeter of the shape on individual trials in which the subjects and the control were instructed to pick up the shape.

2 ...but she and S. H. both place finger and thumb on appropriately opposed points on either side of the shapes.

3 R. V., whose object recognition is unimpaired, chooses unstable grasp points that often do not pass through the object's center of mass.

1 D. F. cannot recognize these shapes,...

D. F.
(ventral-stream deficit)

S. H.
(control)

R. V.
(dorsal-stream deficit)

FIGURE 9-44 **Grasp Patterns** The Milner–Goodale experiments confirm that the brain has different systems for visual object recognition and visual guidance of movement.
Information from Milner & Goodale, 2006.

only a small part of the sensory processing that goes on in the brain. Furthermore, D. F.'s ability to use structural features of objects for guiding movement but not for perceiving shapes again shows us that the brain has separate systems for each type of visual operation.

D. F.'s lesion is quite far back in the ventral visual pathway. More anterior lesions produce other deficits, depending on the exact location. For example, J. I., described by Oliver Sacks and Robert Wasserman (1987), was an artist who developed complete color deficiency due to a cortical lesion presumed to be in region V4. His principal symptom was *achromatopsia*, or color agnosia. He saw the world in black and white, but despite his inability to distinguish any colors whatsoever, J. I.'s vision appeared otherwise unaffected.

Similarly, L. M., a woman described by Josef Zihl and his colleagues (1983), lost her ability to detect movement after suffering a lesion presumed to be in region V5. In her case, objects either vanished when they moved or appeared frozen despite their movement. L. M. had particular difficulty pouring tea into a cup because the fluid appeared to be frozen in midair. Yet she could read, write, and recognize objects, and she appeared to have normal form vision—until objects moved.

These varied cases demonstrate that cortical injuries in the ventral stream all somehow interfere with determining what things are or are like or are doing. In each case, the symptoms are somewhat different, however, which is thought to be indicative of damage to different subregions or substreams of the ventral visual pathway.

Injury to the *How* Pathway

Early in the twentieth century, R. Bálint (1909) described a rather peculiar set of visual symptoms associated with a bilateral parietal lesion. The patient had full visual fields and could recognize, use, and name objects, pictures, and colors normally. But he had a severe deficit in visually guided reaching, even though he could still make accurate movements directed toward his own body (presumably guided by tactile feedback from his joints). Bálint called this syndrome **optic ataxia**.

Since Bálint's time, many descriptions of optic ataxia associated with parietal injury have been recorded. Goodale has studied several such patients, one of whom is a woman identified as R. V. (Milner & Goodale, 2006). In contrast with patient D. F.'s visual

Section 11-4 details the somatic senses, including proprioception, or body awareness.

optic ataxia Deficit in the visual control of reaching and other movements.

form agnosia, R. V.'s perception of drawings and objects was normal, but she could not guide her hand to reach for objects.

The rightmost column in Figure 9-44 shows that, when asked to pick up the same irregularly shaped objects that D. F. could grasp normally, R. V. often failed to place her fingers on the appropriate grasp points, even though she could distinguish the objects easily. In other words, although R. V.'s perception of an object's features was normal for the task of describing that object, her perception was not normal for the task of visually guiding her hand to reach for the object.

To summarize, people with damage to the parietal cortex in the dorsal visual stream can see perfectly well, yet they cannot accurately guide their movements on the basis of visual information. Guidance of movement is the dorsal stream's function. In contrast, people with damage to the ventral stream cannot perceive objects because object perception is a ventral stream function. Yet these same people can guide their movements to objects on the basis of visual information.

Patients with dorsal stream damage, like R. V., have intact ventral streams that analyze the visual characteristics of objects. Patients with ventral stream damage, like D. F., have intact dorsal streams that visually direct movements. Comparing the two types of cases enables us to infer the visual functions of the dorsal and ventral streams.

9-5 Review

Before you continue, check your understanding. Answers to Self-Test appear at the back of the book.

1. Complete cuts of the optic tract, LGN, or V1 produce _____.

2. Small lesions of V1 produce small blind spots called _____.

3. Destruction of the retina or the optic nerve of one eye produces _____.

4. The effect of severe deficits in visually guided reaching is called _____.

5. Contrast the effects of injury to the dorsal stream and the effects of injury to the ventral stream.

For additional study tools, visit **⚏ LaunchPad** at launchpadworks.com

| Summary

9-1 Nature of Sensation and Perception

Sensory systems allow animals, including ourselves, to adapt. Animals adapted to different environments vary widely in their sensory abilities. What is distinctive about humans is the extent to which we can transform sensations into perceptual information to mediate aspects of language, music, and culture. For each sense, mammals represent the world in topographic maps that form neural–spatial representations in the cortex.

9-2 The Visual System's Functional Anatomy

Like all other sensory systems, vision begins with receptor neurons. The visual photoreceptors (rods and cones) at the back of the eye in the retina transduce the physical energy of light waves into neural activity.

Rods are sensitive to dim light. Cones, which are sensitive to bright light, mediate color vision. Each of the three cone types is maximally sensitive to a different wavelength—short, medium, or long. We see these wavelengths, respectively, as the colors blue, green, or red; thus the short, medium, and long cone receptors often are referred to as blue, green, and red receptors.

Retinal ganglion cells receive input from photoreceptors through bipolar cells and send out their axons from the retinas to form the optic nerve. P ganglion cells receive input mostly from cones and convey information about color and fine detail. M cells receive input from rods and convey information about luminance and movement but not color.

The optic nerve forms two distinct major routes into the brain. The geniculostriate pathway synapses first in the thalamic LGN nucleus and then in V1. The tectopulvinar pathway synapses first in the midbrain's tectum (superior colliculus), then in the pulvinar of the thalamus, and finally in the temporal and parietal visual cortex areas. A few optic nerve fibers also form the retinohypothalamic tract, which functions in part to control circadian rhythms.

Among the visual regions in the occipital cortex, V1 and V2 carry out multiple functions; the remaining regions (V3, V3A, V4, and V5) are specialized. Visual information flows from the thalamus to V1 and V2 and then divides to form the visual stream pathways. The unconscious dorsal stream aids in guiding movements visually, whereas the conscious ventral stream aids in visual object perception.

9-3 Location in the Visual World

At each step along the visual pathways, neuronal activities are distinctly different; it is the summed neural activity in all regions that produces our visual experience. Each functional column in the cortical visual regions is about 0.5 mm in diameter and extends to the depth of the cortex. The visual system cortical columns are specialized for processes such as analyzing line orientation or comparing similar shapes as complex as faces.

9-4 Neuronal Activity

Neurons in the ventral stream are selective for aspects of shape. Those in the visual cortex are maximally responsive to lines of different orientations. Upstream, cells in the inferior temporal cortex are responsive to shapes—some abstract—and, in other cases, to concrete forms as complex as hands or faces.

Cones in the retina are maximally responsive to different light wavelengths, roughly corresponding to colors we perceive as green, blue, and red. At the next level, RGCs' center-surround organization facilitates their opponent-process function: the cells are excited by one hue and inhibited by another, as, for example, red versus green or blue versus yellow.

Color-sensitive cells in V1, located in the blobs, also have opponent-process properties. Cells in region V4 respond to colors that we perceive rather than to particular visible light wavelengths. Both the luminance and the color of nearby objects influence the colors we perceive.

9-5 The Visual Brain in Action

Upon entering the brain, information from the left and right visual fields proceeds on the optic nerve to the brain's right and left sides, respectively. As a result of these contralateral connections, damage to the visual areas on one side of the brain results in visual disturbance in both eyes because half of each retina's visual field is represented on each side of the brain.

Specific visual functions are localized to different brain regions, so local damage results in the loss of a particular function. Damage to region V4 produces a loss of color constancy, for example; damage to regions in the parietal cortex inhibits the contralateral hand's grasping ability.

As summarized in the illustration, the visual streams perform distinct functions: (A) object recognition (the *what*) in the ventral stream and (B) visual action (the *how*) in the dorsal stream. We are largely unconscious of the ongoing online analyses of the dorsal stream that allow us to make accurate movements in relation to objects.

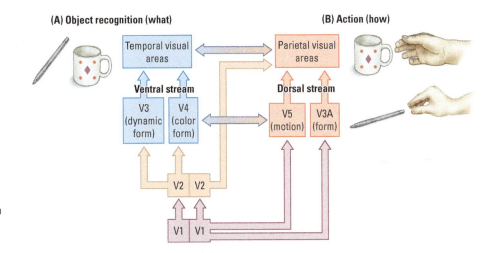

(A) The ventral stream begins in V1 and flows through V2 to V3 and V4, and then into the temporal visual areas. (B) The dorsal stream begins in V1 and flows through V5 and V3A to the posterior parietal visual areas. Double-headed arrows show information flow between the two streams—between recognition and action, perception and behavior.

| Key Terms

blind spot, p. 291

blob, p. 299

color constancy, p. 311

cone, p. 291

cortical column, p. 298

dorsal stream, p. 297

extrastriate (secondary visual) cortex (V2–V5), p. 298

facial agnosia, p. 300

fovea, p. 291

geniculostriate system, p. 296

homonymous hemianopia, p. 313

luminance contrast, p. 305

magnocellular (M) cell, p. 293

ocular dominance column, p. 307

opponent process, p. 311

optic ataxia, p. 315

optic chiasm, p. 295

parvocellular (P) cell, p. 293

perception, p. 286

photoreceptor, p. 287

primary visual cortex (V1), p. 298

quadrantanopia, p. 313

receptive field, p. 284

retina, p. 287

retinal ganglion cell (RGC), p. 293

retinohypothalamic tract, p. 296

rod, p. 291

scotoma, p. 313

sensation, p. 286

striate cortex, p. 296

tectopulvinar system, p. 296

topographic map, p. 285

trichromatic theory, p. 309

ventral stream, p. 297

visual field, p. 300

visual-form agnosia, p. 314

How Do We Hear, Speak, and Make Music?

CHAPTER **10**

SCIENCE PHOTO LIBRARY/Science Source

Evolution of Language and Music

The finding that modern humans (*Homo sapiens*) made music early on implies that music has been important in our recent evolution. Behavioral scientists have shown that music is as central to our social and emotional lives as language.

Thomas Geissmann (2001) noted that among most of the 26 species of singing primates, males and females sing duets. All singing primates are monogamous, suggesting that singing may somehow relate to sexual behaviors. Music may also play a role in primates' parenting behaviors.

The human brain is specialized for analyzing certain aspects of music in the right temporal lobe, which complements the left temporal lobe's specialization for analyzing aspects of speech. Did music and spoken language evolve simultaneously in our species? Possibly.

Neanderthals (*Homo neanderthalensis*) have long fascinated researchers. The species originated about 300,000 years ago and disappeared about 30,000 years ago. During some of that time, they coexisted in Europe and the Middle East with *Homo sapiens*, whom they resembled in many ways because they shared a common ancestor. In some locales, the two species may have shared resources and tools.

Researchers long hypothesized that Neanderthal culture was significantly less developed than that of early modern humans. Yet Neanderthals had a brain as large as or larger than that of *Homo sapiens*, with whom they appear to have shared many cultural similarities. Neanderthals buried their dead with artifacts, which implies that they held spiritual beliefs, but we have no conclusive evidence that they made visual art. In contrast, *Homo sapiens* began painting on cave walls some 30,000 years ago, near the end of the Neanderthal era. Anatomically, some skeletal analyses of the larynx suggest that Neanderthals' articulated language ability was less well developed than that of their *Homo sapien* contemporaries. However, it appears that Neanderthals made music.

The accompanying photo shows a bone flute found in 1995 by Ivan Turk, a paleontologist at the Slovenian Academy of Sciences in Ljubljana. Turk was excavating a cave in northern Slovenia that had been used by Neanderthals as a hunting camp. Buried in the cave among a cache of stone tools was the leg bone of a young bear that looks as if it was fashioned into a flute.

The bone has holes aligned along one side that could not have been made by gnawing animals. Rather, the holes' spacing resembles positions found on a modern flute. But the bone flute is at least 43,000 years old— perhaps as old as 82,000 years. All the evidence suggests that Neanderthals, not modern humans, made the instrument.

Bob Fink, a musicologist, analyzed the flute's musical qualities. He found that an eight-note scale similar to a do-re-mi scale could be played on the flute; but compared with the scale most familiar in European music, one note was slightly off. That "blue" note, a staple of jazz, is standard in musical scales throughout Africa and India today.

The similarity between Neanderthal and contemporary musical scales encourages us to speculate about the brain that conceived this ancient flute. Like modern humans, Neanderthals probably had complementary hemispheric specialization for language and music. This may have contributed to the two species cohabitating and to interbreeding that led to 1 to 4 percent of alleles being of Neanderthal origin in humans whose lineages, in the past 30,000 years, come from outside Africa.

Ancient Bone Flute The hole alignment in this piece of bear femur, found in a cave in northern Slovenia, suggests that Neanderthals made a flute from the bone and made music with the flute.

Archive of the Institute of Archaeology ZRC SAZU, photo: Marko Zaplatil

Language and music are universal among humans. The oral language of every known culture follows similar basic structural rules, and people in all cultures make and enjoy music. Music and language allow us both to organize and to interact socially. Like music, language probably improves parenting. People who can communicate their intentions to one another and to their children presumably are better parents.

Language is the use of complex systems of communication and includes syntax (innate grammar). Although the processing and production of certain forms of language may involve specific sensory and motor systems for input and output, language itself is independent of the route of sensory input and structures of motor output. For instance, sign language uses visual input and motor output using the hands and arms, whereas spoken language uses auditory input and motor output using the vocal cords. In this chapter, however, we focus on *vocalization* (spoken language or speech) and *audition* (perceiving sounds).

Humans' capacities for spoken language and music are linked conceptually because both are based on sound. Understanding how and why we engage in speech and music is this chapter's goal. We first examine the physical energy that we perceive as sound and then how the human ear and nervous system detect and interpret sound. We next examine the complementary neuroanatomy of human language and music processing. Finally, we investigate how two other species, birds and whales, interpret and utilize auditory stimuli.

sound wave Mechanical displacement of molecules caused by changing pressure that possesses the physical properties of frequency, amplitude, and complexity. Also referred to as a *compression wave.*

frequency Number of cycles a wave completes in a given time.

10-1
Sound Waves: Stimulus for Audition

Just as what we see is the brain's construct, so is what we experience as sound. Without a brain, sight and sound do not exist. When you strike a tuning fork, the energy of its vibrating prongs displaces adjacent air molecules. **Figure 10-1** shows how, as one prong moves to the left, air molecules to the left compress (grow more dense) and air molecules to the right become more rarefied (grow less dense). The opposite happens when the prong moves to the right. The undulating energy generated by this displacement of molecules causes *compression waves* of changing air pressure to emanate from the fork. These **sound waves** move through compressible media—air, water, ground—but not through the vacuum of outer space.

The top graph in **Figure 10-2** represents waves of changing air pressure emanating from a tuning fork by plotting air molecule density against time at a single point. The bottom graph shows how the energy from the right-hand prong of the tuning fork moves to make the air pressure changes associated with a single cycle. A *cycle* is one complete peak and valley on the graph—the change from one maximum or minimum air pressure level of the sound wave to the next maximum or minimum level, respectively.

Physical Properties of Sound Waves

Light is electromagnetic energy we see; sound is mechanical energy we hear. Sound wave energy has three physical attributes—*frequency*, *amplitude*, and *complexity*—produced by the displacement of air molecules and summarized in **Figure 10-3**. The auditory system analyzes each property separately, just as the visual system analyzes color and form separately.

Sound Wave Frequency

Sound waves in air travel at a fixed speed of 1100 feet (343 meters) per second and more than four times faster in water, but sound energy varies in wavelength. **Frequency** is the number of cycles a wave completes in a given amount of time. Sound wave

Principle 1: The nervous system produces movement in a perceptual world the brain constructs.

Section 9-4 explains how we see shapes and colors.

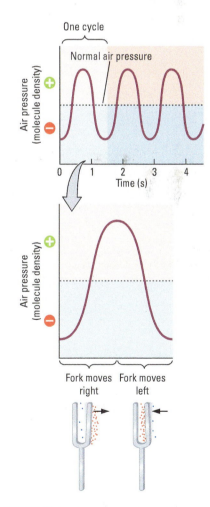

FIGURE 10-2 **Visualizing a Sound Wave** Air molecule density plotted against time at a single point relative to the tuning fork's right prong. Physicists call the resulting cyclical waves *sine waves.*

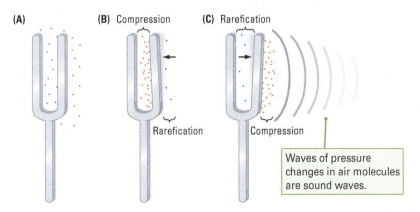

FIGURE 10-1 **How a Tuning Fork Produces Sound Waves (A)** The fork is still, and air molecules are distributed randomly. **(B)** When struck, the fork's right arm moves to the left; air on the leading edge compresses, and air on the trailing edge rarefies. **(C)** As the arm rebounds, air to the right compresses, and air to the left rarefies.

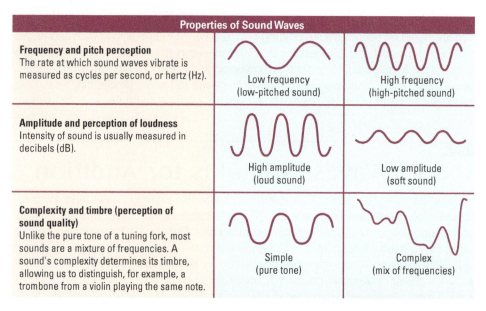

Properties of Sound Waves		
Frequency and pitch perception The rate at which sound waves vibrate is measured as cycles per second, or hertz (Hz).	Low frequency (low-pitched sound)	High frequency (high-pitched sound)
Amplitude and perception of loudness Intensity of sound is usually measured in decibels (dB).	High amplitude (loud sound)	Low amplitude (soft sound)
Complexity and timbre (perception of sound quality) Unlike the pure tone of a tuning fork, most sounds are a mixture of frequencies. A sound's complexity determines its timbre, allowing us to distinguish, for example, a trombone from a violin playing the same note.	Simple (pure tone)	Complex (mix of frequencies)

FIGURE 10-3 **Physical Dimensions of Sound Waves** The frequency, amplitude, and complexity of sound wave sensations correspond to the perceptual dimensions of pitch, loudness, and timbre.

frequencies are measured in cycles per second, called **hertz (Hz)**, in honor of physicist Heinrich Rudolph Hertz.

One hertz is 1 cycle per second, 50 hertz is 50 cycles per second, 6000 hertz is 6000 cycles per second, and so on. Sounds we perceive as low pitched have fewer wave frequencies (fewer cycles per second), whereas sounds that we perceive as high pitched have more wave frequencies (many cycles per second), as shown in the top panel of Figure 10-3.

Just as we can perceive light only at visible wavelengths, we can perceive sound waves only in the limited range of frequencies plotted in **Figure 10-4**. Healthy young adult humans' hearing range is from about 20 to 20,000 hertz. Many animals communicate with sound: their auditory system is designed to interpret their species-typical sounds. After all, what is the point in making complicated songs or calls if other members of your species cannot hear and interpret them?

The range of sound wave frequencies heard by different species varies extensively. Some (such as frogs and birds) have a rather narrow hearing range; others (such as dogs, whales, and humans) have a broad range. Some species use extremely high frequencies (bats go as high as 115 kilohertz, as indicated in Figure 10-4); others (fish, for example) use the low range.

The auditory systems of whales and dolphins are responsive to a remarkably wide range of sound waves. Characteristics at the extremes of these frequencies allow marine mammals to use them in different ways. Very low-frequency sound waves travel long distances in water. Whales produce them for underwater communication over hundreds of miles. High-frequency sound waves echo and form the basis of sonar. Dolphins produce them in bursts and listen for the echoes that bounce back from objects. The echoes help the dolphins to navigate and locate prey.

Differences in sound wave frequencies become differences in pitch when heard. Each note in a musical scale must have a different frequency because each has a different pitch. Middle C on the piano, for instance, has a frequency of 264 hertz.

Most people can discriminate between one musical note and another, but some can actually name any note they hear (A, B flat, C sharp, and so forth). This *perfect* (or *absolute*) *pitch* runs in families, suggesting a genetic influence. On the side of experience, most people who develop perfect pitch also receive musical training in matching pitch to note from an early age.

hertz (Hz) Measure of sound wave frequency (repetition rate); 1 hertz equals 1 cycle per second.

Section 8-4 suggests a critical period in brain development most sensitive to musical training. Figure 15-12 shows enhanced connectivity in people with perfect pitch.

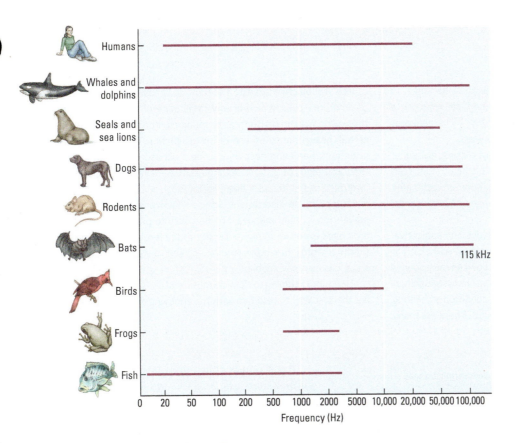

FIGURE 10-4 **Hearing Ranges among Animals** Frogs and birds hear a relatively narrow range of frequencies; the ranges for whales and dolphins are extensive, as is that for dogs. Humans' hearing range is broad, yet we do not perceive many sound frequencies at both the extreme upper and extreme lower ranges that other animals can both make and hear.

Sound Wave Amplitude

Sound waves vary not only in frequency, which causes differences in perceived pitch, but also in **amplitude** (strength), which causes differences in perceived *intensity*, or *loudness*. If you hit a tuning fork lightly, it produces a tone with a frequency of, say, 264 hertz (middle C). If you hit it harder, the frequency remains 264 hertz, but you also transfer more energy into the vibrating prong, increasing its amplitude.

The fork now moves farther left and right but at the same frequency. Increased air molecule compression intensifies the energy in a sound wave, which amplifies the sound (makes it louder). Differences in amplitude are graphed by increasing the height of a sound wave, as shown in the middle panel of Figure 10-3.

Sound wave amplitude is usually measured in **decibels (dB)**, the strength of a sound relative to the threshold of human hearing as a standard, pegged at 0 decibels (**Figure 10-5**). Typical speech sounds, for example, measure about 40 decibels. Sounds that register more than about 70 decibels we perceive as loud; those of less than about 20 decibels we perceive as soft, or quiet, like a person whispering.

The human nervous system evolved to be sensitive to soft sounds and so is actually blown away by extremely loud ones. People regularly damage their hearing through exposure to very loud sounds (such as rifle fire at close range) or even by prolonged exposure to sounds that are only relatively loud (such as at a live concert). Prolonged exposure to sounds louder than 100 decibels is likely to damage our hearing. Clinical Focus 10-2, Tinnitus, describes a common condition that may result from such damage.

amplitude Stimulus intensity; in audition, roughly equivalent to loudness, graphed by the increasing height of a sound wave.

decibel (dB) Measure of the relative physical intensity of sounds.

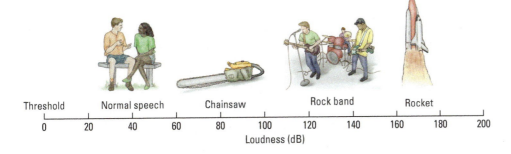

FIGURE 10-5 **Sound Intensity**

CLINICAL FOCUS 10-2

Tinnitus

As a young man, J. E. spent a great deal of time at the rifle range. In fact, he fired 200 rounds a month for years. He did not wear appropriate noise attenuators to dampen the sound. Now in his 70s, J. E. experiences *tinnitus*—ringing in the ears—and has for the past 15 years.

Tinnitus is described as a ringing, whining, whistling, clicking, hissing, or roaring, and it may be soft or loud, low pitched or high pitched. Tinnitus can be intermittent or it can be continuous, as in J. E.'s case. Tinnitus is estimated to affect about 10 to 15 percent of people under the age of 40 worldwide; its prevalence doubles with advanced age.

There are two broad categories of tinnitus: objective and subjective. *Objective tinnitus* may be the result of actual sound produced within the ear. For instance, muscle spasms around the middle ear or blood flow can cause sounds that some individuals can detect, which they report as an annoying tinnitus.

Subjective tinnitus, the more common form, is a condition of hearing a sound in the absence of an external auditory stimulus. There are many causes of subjective tinnitus. The most common is noise-induced damage to inner hair cells, which is why rates of tinnitus are very high among those who work in high-intensity sound environments such as war zones, certain heavy industries, and music production. Other causes include ear infections, head and neck injuries, and exposure to certain drugs. More than 260 medications—including aspirin—have been reported to cause intermittent tinnitus as a side effect.

At present, no medications provide effective treatment for tinnitus, and prevention is recommended. The best way to prevent tinnitus is to avoid prolonged exposure to high-intensity sound levels of 70 decibels or higher (in other words, *turn down your music*) and to wear ear plugs when those situations are unavoidable.

J. E. enjoys listening to classical music and finds that auditory distractions are the best way to help him with the annoying effects of tinnitus.

FIGURE 10-6 **Breaking Down a Complex Tone** The waveform of a single note (top) from Don Byron's clarinet and the simple sound waves—the fundamental frequency (middle) and overtones (bottom)—that make up the complex tone.

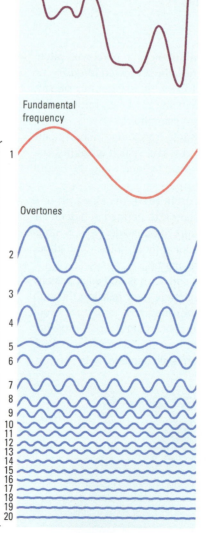

Waveform from clarinet

Fundamental frequency

Simple waves that make up the sound of a clarinet

Overtones

Craig Lovell/Eagle Visions Photography/Alamy

Rock bands routinely play music that registers higher than 120 decibels and sometimes as high as 135 decibels. Adrian Drake-Lee (1992) found that rock musicians had a significant loss of sensitivity to sound waves, especially at about 6000 hertz. After a typical 90-minute concert, this loss was temporarily far worse; as much as a 40-fold increase in sound pressure was needed to reach a musician's hearing threshold. But rock concerts are not the only music venue that can damage hearing. There are also reports that symphony orchestras also produce dangerously high sound levels and that hearing loss is common among symphony musicians (Teie, 1998). Similarly, prolonged listening through headphones or earbuds to music played loudly on personal music players is responsible for significant hearing loss in many young people (Daniel, 2007).

Sound Wave Complexity

Sounds with a single frequency wave are *pure tones*, much like those that emanate from a tuning fork or pitch pipe, but most sounds mix wave frequencies together in combinations called *complex tones*. To better understand the blended nature of a complex tone, picture a clarinetist, such as Don Byron in **Figure 10-6**, playing a steady note. The upper graph in Figure 10-6 represents the sound wave a clarinet produces.

The waveform pattern is more complex than the simple, regular waves visualized in Figures 10-2 or 10-3. Even when a musician plays a single note, the instrument is making a complex tone. Using a mathematical technique known as Fourier analysis, we can break down this complex tone into its many component pure tones, the numbered waves traced at the bottom of Figure 10-6.

The *fundamental frequency* (wave 1) is the rate at which the complex waveform pattern repeats. Waves 2 through 20 are *overtones*, a set of higher-frequency sound waves that vibrate at whole-number (integer) multiples of the fundamental frequency. Different musical instruments sound unique because they produce overtones of different amplitudes. Among the clarinet's overtones, represented by the heights of the blue waves in Figure 10-6, wave 5 is low amplitude, whereas wave 2 is high amplitude.

As primary colors blend into nearly infinite variety, so pure tones blend into complex tones. Complex tones emanate from musical instruments, from the human voice, from birdsong, and from machines or repetitive mechanisms that make rhythmic buzzing or humming sounds. A key feature of complex tones, besides being made up of two or more pure tones, is *periodicity*: the fundamental frequency repeats at regular intervals. Sounds that are aperiodic, or random, we call *noise*.

Perception of Sound

Visualize what happens when you toss a pebble into a pond. Waves of water emanate from the point where the pebble enters the water. These waves produce no audible sound. But if your skin were able to convert the water wave energy (sensation) into neural activity that stimulated your auditory system, you would hear the waves when you placed your hand in the rippling water (perception). When you removed your hand, the sound would stop.

The pebble hitting the water is much like a tree falling to the ground, and the waves that emanate from the pebble's entry point are like the air pressure waves that emanate from the place where the tree strikes the ground. The frequency of the waves determines the pitch of the sound heard by the brain, whereas the height (amplitude) of the waves determines the sound's loudness.

Our sensitivity to sound waves is extraordinary. At the threshold of human hearing, we can detect the displacement of air molecules of about 10 picometers. We are rarely in an environment where we can detect such a small air pressure change: there is usually too much background noise. A quiet, rural setting is probably as close as we ever get to an environment suitable for testing the acuteness of our hearing. The next time you visit the countryside, take note of the sounds you can hear. If there is no sound competition, you can often hear a single car engine miles away.

1 picometer = one-trillionth of a meter

In addition to detecting minute changes in air pressure, the auditory system is also adept at simultaneously perceiving different sounds. As you read this chapter, you can differentiate all sorts of sounds around you—traffic on the street, people talking next door, your air conditioner humming, footsteps in the hall. As you listen to music, you detect the sounds of different instruments and voices.

You can perceive more than one sound simultaneously because each frequency of change in air pressure (each different sound wave) stimulates different neurons in your auditory system. Sound perception is only the beginning of your auditory experience. Your brain interprets sounds to obtain information about events in your environment, and it analyzes a sound's meaning. Your use of sound to communicate with other people through both spoken language and music clearly illustrates these processes.

Properties of Spoken Language and Music as Sounds

Language and music differ from other auditory sensations in fundamental ways. Both convey meaning and evoke emotion. Analyzing meaning in sound is a considerably more complex behavior than simply detecting a sound and identifying it. The brain has evolved systems that analyze sounds for meaning: speech in the left temporal lobe and music in the right.

Infants are receptive to speech and musical cues before they have any obvious utility, which suggests both the innate presence of these skills and the effects of prenatal experiences. Humans have an amazing capacity for learning and remembering linguistic and musical information. We are capable of learning a vocabulary of tens of

Music classes for infants have been shown to benefit their development.

thousands of words, often in many spoken languages, and a capacity for recognizing thousands of songs.

Language facilitates and expands communication. We can organize our complex perceptual worlds by categorizing information with words. We can tell others what we think and know and imagine. Imagine the efficiency that gestures and language added to the cooperative food hunting and gathering behaviors of early humans.

All these benefits of language seem obvious, but the benefits of music may seem less straightforward. In fact, music helps us to regulate our own emotions and to affect the emotions of others. After all, when do people most commonly make music? We sing and play music to communicate with infants and put children to sleep. We play music to enhance social interactions and gatherings and romance. We use music to bolster group identification—school songs and national anthems are examples. Music as we know it might be unique to humans. Studies of nonhumans provide little evidence for preferences for music over other sounds.

Another characteristic that distinguishes speech and musical sounds from other auditory inputs is their delivery speed. Nonspeech and nonmusical noise produced at a rate of about 5 segments per second is perceived as a buzz. (A sound segment is a distinct unit of sound.) Normal speed for speech is on the order of 8 to 10 segments per second, and we are capable of understanding speech at nearly 30 segments per second. Speech perception at these higher rates is astounding because the input speed far exceeds the auditory system's ability to transmit all the speech segments as separate pieces of information.

Properties of Language

Experience listening to a particular language helps the brain analyze rapid speech, which is one reason people who are speaking languages unfamiliar to you often seem to be talking incredibly fast. Your brain does not know where the foreign words end and begin, so they seem to run together in a rapid-fire stream.

A unique characteristic of our perception of speech sounds is our tendency to hear variations of a sound as if they were identical, even though the sound varies considerably from one context to another. For instance, the English letter *d* is pronounced differently in the words *deep*, *deck*, and *duke*, yet a listener perceives the pronunciations to be the same *d* sound.

The auditory system must therefore have a mechanism for categorizing sounds as being the same despite small differences in pronunciation. Experience must affect this mechanism because different languages categorize speech sounds differently. A major obstacle to mastering a foreign language after age 10 is the difficulty of learning which sound categories are treated as equivalent.

> Auditory constancy is reminiscent of the visual system's capacity for color constancy; see Section 9-4.

Properties of Music

As with other sounds, the subjective properties that people perceive in musical sounds differ from one another. One subjective property is *loudness*, the magnitude of a sound as judged by a person. Loudness is related to the amplitude of a sound wave measured in decibels, but loudness is also subjective. What is very loud music for one person may be only moderately loud for another, whereas music that seems soft to one listener may not seem at all soft to someone else. Your perception of loudness also changes with context. After you've slowed down from driving fast on a highway, for example, your car's music system seems louder. The reduction in road noise alters your perception of the music's loudness.

Another subjective property of musical sounds is *pitch*, the position of each tone on a musical scale, as judged by the listener. Although pitch is clearly related to sound wave frequency, there is more to it than that. Consider the note middle C as played on a piano. This note can be described as a pattern of sound frequencies, as is the clarinet note in Figure 10-6.

Like the note played on the piano, any musical note is defined by its fundamental frequency—the lowest frequency of the sound wave pattern, or the rate at which the overall pattern repeats. For middle C, the fundamental frequency is 264 hertz, and the sound waves for notes C, E, and G, as measured by a spectrograph, are shown in **Figure 10-7**. Notice that by convention, sound wave spectrographs are measured in kilohertz (kHz), or thousands of hertz. Thus, if we look at the fundamental frequency for middle C, it is the first large wave on the left, at 0.264 kilohertz. The fundamental frequencies for E and G are 0.330 and 0.392 kilohertz, respectively.

An important feature of the human brain's analysis of music is that any pure note, like middle C, is perceived as being the same note whether it is played on a piano or on a guitar, even though the sounds of these instruments differ widely. The right temporal lobe extracts pitch from sound, whether the sound is speech or music. In speech, pitch contributes to the perceived melodic tone of a voice, or **prosody**.

A final property of musical sound is *quality*, or *timbre* (pronounced "TAM-ber"), the perceived characteristics that distinguish a particular sound from all others of similar pitch and loudness. We can easily distinguish the timbre of a violin from that of a trombone, even if both instruments are playing the same note at the same loudness. The quality of their sounds differs.

10-1 Review

Before you continue, check your understanding. Answers to Self-Test appear at the back of the book.

1. The physical stimulus for audition, produced by changes in _____, is a form of mechanical energy converted in the ear to neural activity.

2. Sound waves have three physical attributes: _____, _____, and _____.

3. Four properties of musical sounds are _____, _____, _____, and _____.

4. Sound is processed in the _____ lobes.

5. What distinguishes speech and musical sounds from other auditory inputs?

For additional study tools, visit 📖 **LaunchPad** at launchpadworks.com

10-2

Functional Anatomy of the Auditory System

To understand how the nervous system analyzes sound waves, we begin by tracing the pathway sound energy takes to and through the brain. The ear collects sound waves from the surrounding air and converts their mechanical energy to electrochemical neural energy, which begins a long route through the brainstem to the auditory cortex.

Before we can trace the journey from ear to cortex, we must ask what the auditory system is designed to do. Because sound waves have the properties frequency, amplitude, and complexity, we can predict that the auditory system is structured to decode these properties. Most animals can tell where a sound comes from, so some mechanism must locate sound waves in space. Finally, many animals, including humans, not only analyze sounds for meaning but also make sounds. Because the properties of the sounds an animal produces fall within the range of the ones that it hears, we can infer that the neural systems for sound production and analysis must be closely related.

In humans, the evolution of sound-processing systems for both language and music was accompanied by enhancement of specialized cortical regions, especially in the temporal lobes. In fact, a major difference between the human cortex and the monkey cortex is a marked expansion of auditory areas in humans (see **Figure 10-8**).

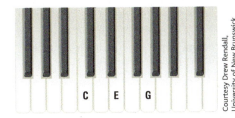

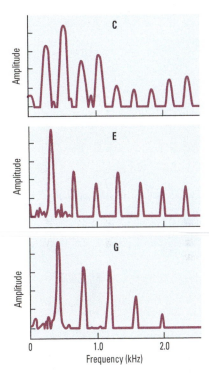

FIGURE 10-7 **Fundamental Frequencies of Piano Notes** Waveforms of the notes C, E, and G, as played on a piano and recorded on a spectrograph. The first wave in each graph is the fundamental frequency; the secondary waves are the overtones.

prosody Melodic tone of the speaking voice.

FIGURE 10-8 **Monkey and Human Cortical Regions**

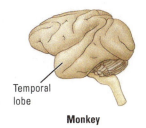

Temporal lobe

Monkey

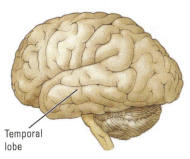

Temporal lobe

Human

ossicle Bone of the middle ear; includes hammer, anvil, and stirrup.

cochlea Inner ear structure containing the auditory receptor cells.

Structure of the Ear

The ear is a biological masterpiece in three acts: outer ear, middle ear, and inner ear, all illustrated in **Figure 10-9**.

Processing Sound Waves

Both the *pinna,* the funnel-like external structure of the outer ear, and the external ear canal, which extends a short distance from the pinna inside the head, are made of cartilage and flesh. The pinna is designed to catch sound waves in the surrounding environment and deflect them into the external ear canal. To enhance sound detection when we want to hear better, we often cup a hand around the pinna.

Because it narrows from the pinna, the external canal amplifies sound waves and directs them to the *eardrum* at its inner end. When sound waves strike the eardrum, it vibrates, the rate of vibration varying with the frequency of the waves. On the inner side of the eardrum, as depicted in Figure 10-9, is the middle ear, an air-filled chamber that contains the three smallest bones in the human body, connected in a series.

Cochlea actually means "snail shell" in Latin.

These three **ossicles** are called the *hammer,* the *anvil,* and the *stirrup* because of their distinctive shapes. The ossicles attach the eardrum to the *oval window,* an opening in the bony casing of the **cochlea**, the inner ear structure that contains the auditory receptor cells. These receptor cells and the cells that support them are collectively called the *organ of Corti,* shown in detail in Figure 10-9.

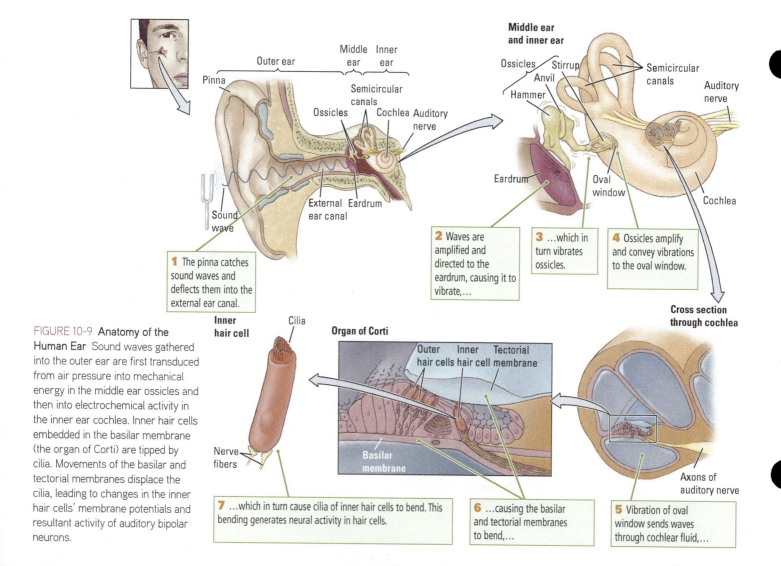

FIGURE 10-9 **Anatomy of the Human Ear** Sound waves gathered into the outer ear are first transduced from air pressure into mechanical energy in the middle ear ossicles and then into electrochemical activity in the inner ear cochlea. Inner hair cells embedded in the basilar membrane (the organ of Corti) are tipped by cilia. Movements of the basilar and tectorial membranes displace the cilia, leading to changes in the inner hair cells' membrane potentials and resultant activity of auditory bipolar neurons.

1 The pinna catches sound waves and deflects them into the external ear canal.

2 Waves are amplified and directed to the eardrum, causing it to vibrate,…

3 …which in turn vibrates ossicles.

4 Ossicles amplify and convey vibrations to the oval window.

5 Vibration of oval window sends waves through cochlear fluid,…

6 …causing the basilar and tectorial membranes to bend,…

7 …which in turn cause cilia of inner hair cells to bend. This bending generates neural activity in hair cells.

When sound waves vibrate the eardrum, the vibrations are transmitted to the ossicles. The leverlike action of the ossicles amplifies the vibrations and conveys them to the membrane that covers the cochlea's oval window. As Figure 10-9 shows, the cochlea coils around itself and looks a bit like a snail shell. Inside its bony exterior, the cochlea is hollow, as the cross-sectional drawing reveals.

The hollow cochlear compartments are filled with lymphatic fluid, and floating in its midst is the thin **basilar membrane**. Embedded in a part of the basilar membrane are outer and inner **hair cells**. At the tip of each hair cell are several filaments called *cilia*, and the cilia of the outer hair cells are embedded in the overlying *tectorial membrane*. The inner hair cells loosely contact this tectorial membrane.

Pressure from the stirrup on the oval window makes the cochlear fluid move because a second membranous window in the cochlea (the *round window*) bulges outward as the stirrup presses inward on the oval window. In a chain reaction, the waves traveling through the cochlear fluid bend the basilar and tectorial membranes, and the bending membranes stimulate the cilia at the tips of the outer and inner hair cells.

basilar membrane Receptor surface in the cochlea that transduces sound waves into neural activity.

hair cell Specialized neurons in the cochlea tipped by cilia; when stimulated by waves in the cochlear fluid, the cilia bend and generate graded potentials in inner hair cells, the auditory receptor cells.

Transducing Sound Waves into Neural Impulses

How does the conversion of sound waves into neural activity code the various properties of sound that we perceive? In the late 1800s, Hermann von Helmholtz proposed that sound waves of different frequencies cause different parts of the basilar membrane to resonate. Von Helmholtz was partly correct. Actually, all parts of the basilar membrane bend in response to incoming waves of any frequency. The key is *where* the peak displacement takes place (**Figure 10-10**).

This solution to the coding puzzle was determined in 1960, when George von Békésy observed the basilar membrane directly. He saw a traveling wave moving along the membrane all the way from the oval window to the membrane's apex. The coiled cochlea in Figure 10-10A maps the frequencies to which each part of the basilar membrane is most responsive. When the oval window vibrates in response to the vibrations of the ossicles, shown beside the uncoiled membrane in Figure 10-10B, it generates waves that travel through the cochlear fluid. Békésy placed little grains of silver along the basilar membrane and watched them jump in different places to different frequencies of incoming waves. Higher wave frequencies caused maximum peaks of displacement near the base of the basilar membrane; lower wave frequencies caused maximum displacement peaks near the membrane's apex.

As a rough analogy, consider what happens when you shake a rope. If you shake it quickly, the waves in the rope are small and short, and the peak of activity remains close to the base—the hand holding the rope. But if you shake the rope slowly, with a broader movement, the longer waves reach their peak farther along the rope—toward the apex. The key point is that, although both rapid and slow shakes produce movement along the entire length of the rope, the point of maximum displacement depends on whether the wave movements are rapid or slow.

This same response pattern holds for the basilar membrane and sound wave frequency. All sound waves cause some displacement along the entire length of the membrane, but the amount of displacement at any point varies with the frequency of the sound wave. In the human cochlea, shown uncoiling in Figure 10-10A, the basilar membrane near the

FIGURE 10-10 **Anatomy of the Cochlea** **(A)** The basilar membrane is maximally responsive to frequencies mapped as the cochlea uncoils. **(B)** Sound waves of different frequencies produce maximal displacement of the basilar membrane (shown uncoiled) at different locations.

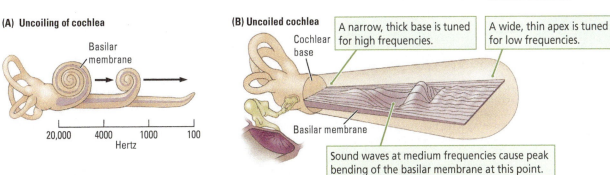

(A) Uncoiling of cochlea

Basilar membrane

20,000   4000   1000   100
Hertz

(B) Uncoiled cochlea

Cochlear base

Basilar membrane

A narrow, thick base is tuned for high frequencies.

A wide, thin apex is tuned for low frequencies.

Sound waves at medium frequencies cause peak bending of the basilar membrane at this point.

otoacoustic emissions Spontaneous or evoked sound waves produced within the ear by the cochlea that escape from the ear.

medial geniculate nucleus Major thalamic region concerned with audition.

primary auditory cortex (area A1) Asymmetrical structures within Heschl's gyrus in the temporal lobes; receives input from the ventral region of the medial geniculate nucleus.

Principle 7: Sensory and motor divisions permeate the nervous system.

FIGURE 10-11 **Transducing Waves into Neural Activity** Movement of the basilar membrane produces a shearing force in the cochlear fluid that bends the cilia, leading to the opening or closing of calcium channels in the outer hair cells. An influx of calcium ions leads the inner hair cells to release neurotransmitter, stimulating increased action potentials in auditory neurons.

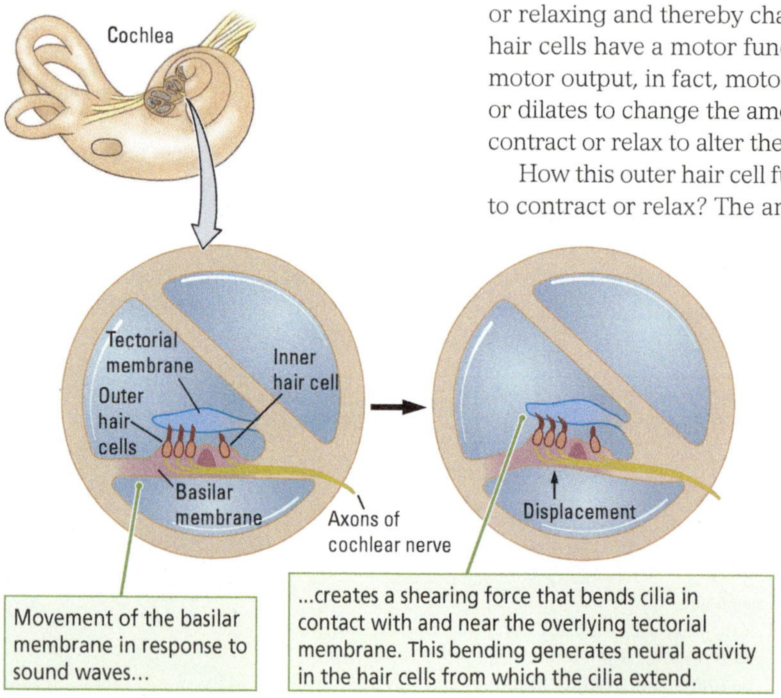

oval window is maximally affected by frequencies as high as about 20,000 hertz, the upper limit of our hearing range. The most effective frequencies at the membrane's apex register less than 100 hertz, closer to our lower limit of about 20 hertz (see Figure 10-4).

Intermediate frequencies maximally displace points on the basilar membrane between its ends, as shown in Figure 10-10B. When a wave of a certain frequency travels down the basilar membrane, hair cells at the point of peak displacement are stimulated, resulting in a maximal neural response in those cells. An incoming signal composed of many frequencies causes several points along the basilar membrane to vibrate, exciting hair cells at all these points.

Not surprisingly, the basilar membrane is much more sensitive to changes in frequency than is the rope in our analogy because the basilar membrane varies in thickness along its entire length. It is narrow and thick at the base, near the oval window, and wider and thinner at its tightly coiled apex. The combination of varying width and thickness enhances the effect of small frequency differences. As a result, the cochlear receptors can code small differences in sound wave frequency as neural impulses.

Auditory Receptors

Two kinds of hair cells transform sound waves into neural activity. Figure 10-9 (bottom left) shows the anatomy of the inner hair cells; **Figure 10-11** illustrates how sound waves stimulate them. A young person's cochlea has about 12,000 outer and 3500 inner hair cells. The numbers fall off with age. Only the inner hair cells act as auditory receptors, and their numbers are small, considering how many different sounds we can hear. As diagrammed in Figure 10-11, both outer and inner hair cells are anchored in the basilar membrane. The tips of the cilia of outer hair cells are attached to the overlying tectorial membrane, but the cilia of the inner hair cells only loosely touch that membrane. Nevertheless, the movement of the basilar and tectorial membranes causes the cochlear fluid to flow past the cilia of the inner hair cells, bending them back and forth.

Animals with intact outer hair cells but no inner hair cells are effectively deaf. That is, they can perceive only very loud, low-frequency sounds via the somatosensory system. You may have experienced this feeling when a subwoofer or a passing truck caused vibrations in your chest. Inner hair cells can be destroyed by prolonged exposure to intense sound pressure waves, infections, diseases, or certain chemicals and drugs. Inner hair cells do not regenerate in mammals; thus, once your inner hair cells have died, hearing loss is permanent.

Outer hair cells function by sharpening the cochlea's resolving power, contracting or relaxing and thereby changing tectorial membrane stiffness. That's right: the outer hair cells have a motor function. While we typically think of sensory input preceding motor output, in fact, motor systems can influence sensory input. The pupil contracts or dilates to change the amount of light that falls on the retina, and the outer hair cells contract or relax to alter the physical stimulus detected by the inner hair cells.

How this outer hair cell function is controlled is puzzling. What stimulates these cells to contract or relax? The answer seems to be that through connections with axons in the auditory nerve, the outer hair cells send a message to the brainstem auditory areas and receive a reply that causes the cells to alter tension on the tectorial membrane. In this way, the brain helps the hair cells construct an auditory world. The outer cells are also part of a mechanism that modulates auditory nerve firing, especially in response to intense sound pressure waves and thus offers some protection against their damaging effects.

A final question remains: How does movement of the inner hair cell cilia alter neural activity? The neurons of the auditory nerve have a spontaneous baseline rate of firing action potentials, and this rate is changed by the amount of neurotransmitter the hair cells release. It turns out that movement of the cilia changes the inner hair cell's polarization and its rate of neurotransmitter release. Inner hair

Cochlea

Tectorial membrane

Inner hair cell

Outer hair cells

Basilar membrane

Axons of cochlear nerve

Displacement

Movement of the basilar membrane in response to sound waves...

...creates a shearing force that bends cilia in contact with and near the overlying tectorial membrane. This bending generates neural activity in the hair cells from which the cilia extend.

Otoacoustic Emissions

While the ear is exquisitely designed to amplify and convert sound waves into action potentials, it is unique among the sensory organs. The ear also *produces* the physical stimulus it is designed to detect! A healthy cochlea produces sound waves called **otoacoustic emissions**.

The cochlea acts as an amplifier. The outer hair cells amplify sound waves, providing an energy source that enhances cochlear sensitivity and frequency selectivity. Not all the energy the cochlea generates is dissipated within it. Some escapes toward the middle ear, which works efficiently in both directions, thus setting the eardrum in motion. The eardrum then acts as a loudspeaker, radiating sound waves—the otoacoustic emissions—out of the ear.

Sensitive microphones placed in the external ear canal can detect both types of otoacoustic emissions: spontaneous and evoked. As the name implies, *spontaneous otoacoustic emissions* occur without external stimulation. *Evoked otoacoustic emissions* are generated in response to sound waves, and they are useful for assessing hearing impairments.

A simple, noninvasive test can detect and evaluate evoked otoacoustic emissions, and this test is particularly useful with newborns and children who are too young to take conventional hearing tests. A small speaker and microphone are inserted into the ear. The speaker emits a click sound, and the microphone detects the resulting evoked emission without damaging the delicate workings of the inner ear. Missing or abnormal evoked emissions predict a hearing deficit. Many wealthy countries now sponsor universal programs to test the hearing of all newborn babies using otoacoustic emissions.

Otoacoustic emissions serve a useful purpose, but even so, they play no direct role in hearing. They are considered an *epiphenomenon*—a secondary phenomenon that occurs in parallel with or above (*epi*) a primary phenomenon.

---

cells continuously leak calcium, and this leakage causes a small but steady amount of neurotransmitter release into the synapse. Movement of the cilia in one direction results in depolarization: calcium channels open and release more neurotransmitter onto the dendrites of the cells that form the auditory nerve, generating more nerve impulses. Movement of the cilia in the other direction hyperpolarizes the cell membrane, and transmitter release decreases, thus decreasing activity in auditory neurons.

Inner hair cells are amazingly sensitive to the movement of their cilia. A movement of only about 0.3 nm is sufficient to allow sound wave detection—that's about the diameter of a large atom! Such sensitivity helps to explain why our hearing is so incredibly sensitive. Research Focus 10-3, Otoacoustic Emissions, describes a consequence of cochlear function.

Section 4-2 reviews phases of the action potential and its propagation as a nerve impulse.

Principle 10: The nervous system works by juxtaposing excitation and inhibition.

Figure 2-29 lists and locates the cranial nerves, and in its caption is a mnemonic for remembering them in order.

Pathways to the Auditory Cortex

Inner hair cells in the organ of Corti synapse with neighboring bipolar cells, the axons that form the auditory (cochlear) nerve. The auditory nerve in turn forms part of the eighth cranial nerve, the auditory vestibular nerve that governs hearing and balance. Whereas ganglion cells in the eye receive inputs from many receptor cells, bipolar cells in the ear receive input from but a single inner hair cell receptor.

Cochlear-nerve axons enter the brainstem at the level of the medulla and synapse in the cochlear nucleus, which has ventral and dorsal subdivisions. Two nearby structures in the hindbrain (brainstem), the superior olive (a nucleus in the olivary complex) and the trapezoid body, receive connections from the cochlear nucleus, as charted in **Figure 10-12**. Projections from the cochlear nucleus connect with cells on the same side of the brain, as well as with cells on the opposite side. This arrangement mixes the inputs from the two ears to form a single sound perception.

Both the cochlear nucleus and the superior olive send projections to the inferior colliculus in the dorsal midbrain. Two distinct pathways emerge from the inferior colliculus, coursing to the **medial geniculate nucleus** in the thalamus. The ventral region of the medial geniculate nucleus projects to the **primary auditory cortex (area A1)**, whereas the dorsal region projects to the auditory cortical regions adjacent to area A1.

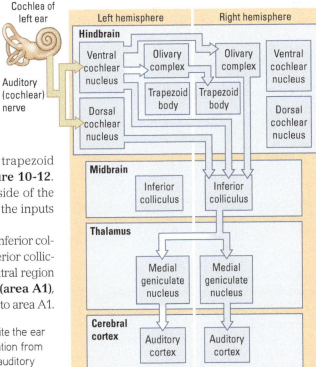

FIGURE 10-12 **Auditory Pathways** Auditory inputs cross to the hemisphere opposite the ear in the hindbrain and midbrain, then recross in the thalamus. In this way, the information from each ear reaches both hemispheres. Multiple nuclei process inputs en route to the auditory cortex, charted here for the left ear.

Seeing with Sound

As detailed in Section 10-5, **echolocation**, the ability to use sound to locate objects in space, has been extensively studied in species such as bats and dolphins. But it was reported more than 50 years ago that some blind people also echolocate.

More recently, anecdotal reports have surfaced of blind people around the world navigating using clicks made with their tongues and mouths and then listening to the returning echoes. Congenitally blind people can ride a bicycle down a street filled with silent obstacles such as parked cars. But how do they do this, and what part of the brain enables it?

Behavioral studies of blind people reveal that echolocators make short, spectrally broad clicks by moving the tongue backward and downward from the roof of the mouth directly behind the teeth. Skilled echolocators can identify properties of objects such as position, distance, size, shape, and texture (Teng & Whitney, 2011).

Thaler and colleagues (2011) used fMRI to investigate the neural basis of this ability. They studied two blind echolocation experts and compared brain activity for sounds that contained both clicks and returning echoes with brain activity for control sounds that did not contain the echoes. The investigators found that the participants use echolocation to localize objects in the environment. More importantly, these individuals are able to use echolocation to perceive the shape, motion, and even identity of objects!

When the blind participants listened to recordings of their echolocation clicks and echoes compared to silence, both the auditory cortex and the primary visual cortex showed activity. Sighted controls showed activation only in the auditory cortex. Remarkably, when the investigators compared the brain activity

of the controls to recordings that contained echoes versus those that did not, the auditory activity disappeared. By contrast, as illustrated in the figure, the blind echolocators showed activity only in the visual cortex when sounds with and without echoes were compared. Sighted controls (findings not indicated) showed no activity in either the visual or auditory cortex in this comparison.

These results suggest that blind echolocation experts process click–echo information using brain regions typically devoted to vision. Thaler and his colleagues propose that the primary visual cortex is performing a spatial computation using information from the auditory cortex.

More immediately, the study suggests that echolocation could be taught to blind and visually impaired people to provide them increased independence in their daily lives.

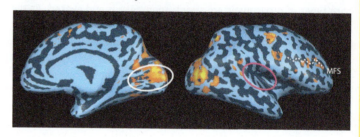

Seeing with Sound When cortical activation for sound with and without echoes is imaged in a blind echolocator, only the visual cortex shows activation (left) relative to the auditory cortex (right). Research from Thaler et al., 2011. Neural correlates of Natural Human echolocation in Early and Late Blind Echolocation Experts. PLoS ONE, 6, (5)e20162. doi:10.1371/journal.pone.0020162

Analogous to the two distinct visual pathways—the ventral stream for object recognition and the dorsal stream for visual control of movement—a similar distinction exists in the auditory cortex (Romanski et al., 1999). Just as we can identify objects by their sound characteristics, we can direct our movements by the sound we hear. The role of sound in guiding movement is less familiar to sight-dominated people than it is to those who are blind. Nevertheless, the ability exists in us all. Imagine waking up in the dark and reaching to pick up a ringing telephone or to turn off an alarm clock. Your hand automatically forms the appropriate shape in response to the sound you have heard. That sound guides your movements much as visual images can guide them.

Relatively little is known about the what–how auditory pathways in the cortex. One auditory pathway appears to continue through the temporal lobe, much like the ventral visual pathway, and plays a role in identifying auditory stimuli. A second auditory pathway apparently goes to the posterior parietal region, where it forms a dorsal route for the auditory control of movement. It appears as well that auditory information can gain access to the visual cortex, as illustrated in Research Focus 10-4, Seeing with Sound.

Figure 9-11 maps the visual pathways through the brain.

Auditory Cortex

In humans, the primary auditory cortex (A1) lies within Heschl's gyrus, surrounded by secondary cortical areas (A2), as shown in **Figure 10-13A**. The secondary cortex lying behind Heschl's gyrus is called the *planum temporale* (Latin for *temporal plane*).

In right-handed people, the planum temporale is larger on the left than it is on the right side of the brain, whereas Heschl's gyrus is larger on the right side than on the left. The cortex of the left planum forms a speech zone known as **Wernicke's area** (the posterior speech zone), whereas the cortex of the larger right-hemisphere Heschl's gyrus has a special role in analyzing music.

echolocation The ability to use sound to locate objects in space.

Wernicke's area Secondary auditory cortex (planum temporale) lying behind Heschl's gyrus at the rear of the left temporal lobe; regulates language comprehension. Also known as the *posterior speech zone.*

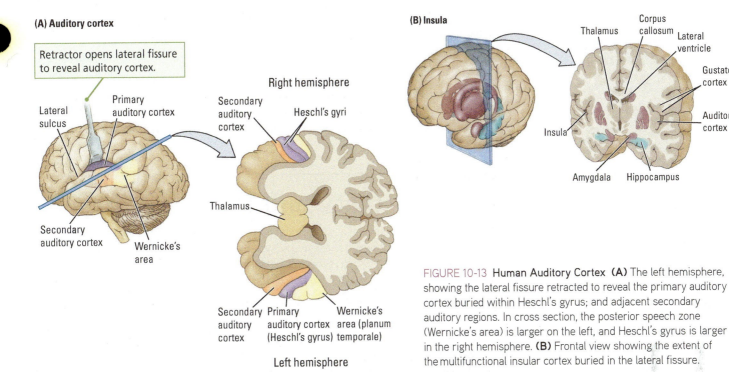

FIGURE 10-13 **Human Auditory Cortex** **(A)** The left hemisphere, showing the lateral fissure retracted to reveal the primary auditory cortex buried within Heschl's gyrus; and adjacent secondary auditory regions. In cross section, the posterior speech zone (Wernicke's area) is larger on the left, and Heschl's gyrus is larger in the right hemisphere. **(B)** Frontal view showing the extent of the multifunctional insular cortex buried in the lateral fissure.

These hemispheric differences mean that the auditory cortex is anatomically and functionally asymmetrical. Although cerebral asymmetry is not unique to the auditory system, it is most obvious here because auditory analysis of speech takes place only in the left hemisphere of right-handed people. About 70 percent of left-handed people have the same anatomical asymmetries as right-handers, an indication that speech organization is not strictly related to hand preference. Language, including speech and other functions such as reading and writing, is asymmetrical as well, although the right hemisphere also contributes to these broader functions.

The remaining 30 percent of left-handers fall into two distinct groups. The organization in about half of these people is opposite that of right-handers. The other half have some idiosyncratic bilateral speech representation. That is, about 15 percent of all left-handed people have some speech functions in one hemisphere and some in the other hemisphere.

Localization of language on one side of the brain is an example of **lateralization**. Note here that, in neuroanatomy, if one hemisphere is specialized for one type of analysis, the other hemisphere has a complementary function: for example, the left hemisphere is specialized for language, and the right hemisphere appears to be lateralized for music.

The temporal lobe sulci enfold a volume of cortical tissue far more extensive than the auditory cortex (Figure 10-13B). Buried in the lateral fissure, cortical tissue called the **insula** contains not only lateralized regions related to language but also areas controlling taste perception (the gustatory cortex) and areas linked to the neural structures underlying social cognition. As you might expect, injury to the insula can produce such diverse deficits as disturbance of both language and taste.

lateralization Localization of function primarily on one side of the brain.

insula Multifunctional cortical tissue located within the lateral fissure; contains language and taste perception–related regions and neural structures underlying social cognition.

Principle 5: The brain is symmetrical and asymmetrical.

10-2 Review

Before you continue, check your understanding. Answers to Self-Test appear at the back of the book.

1. Incoming sound wave energy vibrates the eardrum, which in turn vibrates the _____.

2. The auditory receptors are the _____, found in the _____.

3. The motion of cochlear fluid causes displacement of the _____ and _____ membranes.

4. The axons of bipolar cells from the cochlea form the _____ nerve, which is part of the _____ cranial nerve.

5. The auditory nerve originating in the cochlea projects to various nuclei in the brainstem; then it projects to the _____ in the midbrain and the _____ in the thalamus.

6. Describe the asymmetrical structure and functions of the auditory cortex.

For additional study tools, visit 🅜 **LaunchPad** at launchpadworks.com

---

Neural Activity and Hearing

We now turn to the neuronal activity in the auditory system that produces our perception of sound. Neurons at different levels in this system serve different functions. To get an idea of what individual hair cells and cortical neurons do, we consider how the auditory system codes sound wave energy so that we perceive pitch, loudness, location, and pattern.

Hearing Pitch

Recall that perception of pitch corresponds to the frequency (repetition rate) of sound waves measured in hertz (cycles per second). Hair cells in the cochlea code frequency as a function of their location on the basilar membrane. In this **tonotopic representation**, hair cell cilia at the base of the cochlea are maximally displaced by high-frequency waves, which we hear as high-pitched sounds; those at the apex are displaced the most by low-frequency waves, which we hear as low-pitched sounds. Because each bipolar-cell axon that forms the cochlear nerve is connected to only one inner hair cell, the bipolar cells convey information about the spot on the basilar membrane, from apex to base, that is being stimulated.

Recordings from single fibers in the cochlear nerve reveal that although each axon transmits information about only a small part of the auditory spectrum, each cell does respond to a range of sound wave frequencies—if the wave is sufficiently loud. That is, each hair cell is maximally responsive to a particular frequency and also responds to nearby frequencies, but the sound wave's amplitude must be greater (louder) for those nearby frequencies to excite the receptor's membrane potential.

We can plot this range of hair cell responses to different frequencies at different amplitudes as a tuning curve. As graphed in **Figure 10-14**, each hair cell receptor is maximally sensitive to a particular wavelength but still responds somewhat to nearby wavelengths.

Bipolar cell axons in the cochlea project to the cochlear nucleus in an orderly manner (see Figure 10-12). Axons entering from the base of the cochlea connect with one location; those entering from the middle connect to another location; and those entering from the apex connect to yet another. Thus, the basilar membrane's tonotopic representation is reproduced in the hindbrain cochlear nucleus.

This systematic representation is maintained throughout the auditory pathways and into the primary auditory cortex. **Figure 10-15** shows the distribution of projections from the base and apex of the cochlea across area A1. Similar tonotopic maps can be constructed for each level of the auditory system.

This systematic auditory organization has enabled the development of **cochlear implants**—electronic devices surgically inserted in the inner ear that serve as

Tonotopic literally means "of a tone place."

Individual hair cells and photoreceptors (see Figure 9-5) maximally respond to their preferred frequency but also respond to a range of frequencies within their sensory domains.

tonotopic representation In audition, structural organization for processing of sound waves from lower to higher frequencies.

cochlear implant Electronic device implanted surgically into the inner ear to transduce sound waves to neural activity and allow a deaf person to hear.

FIGURE 10-14 **Tuning Curves** Graphs plotted by the sound wave frequency and amplitude energy required to increase the firing rates of two axons in the cochlear nerve. The lowest point on each tuning curve is the frequency to which that hair cell is most sensitive. The curve at left is centered on a frequency of 1000 Hz, the midrange of human hearing; the curve at right is centered on a frequency of 10,000 Hz, in the high range.

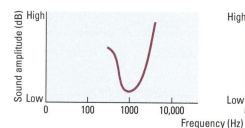

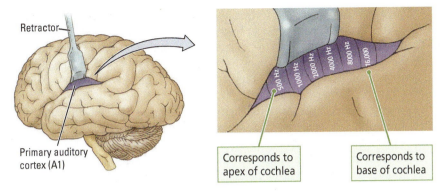

Retractor

Primary auditory
cortex (A1)

Corresponds to
apex of cochlea

Corresponds to
base of cochlea

FIGURE 10-15 **Tonotopic Representation
of Area A1** A retractor holds the lateral
fissure open to reveal the underlying primary
auditory cortex. The anterior end of area
A1 corresponds to the apex of the cochlea,
hence low frequencies. The posterior end
corresponds to the base of the cochlea, hence
high frequencies.

prostheses to allow deaf people to hear (see Loeb, 1990). Cochlear implants are not a
cure for deafness but rather are a hearing substitute. In **Figure 10-16**, a miniature
microphonelike processor secured to the skull detects the component frequencies of
incoming sound waves and sends them to the appropriate places on the basilar membrane through tiny wires. The nervous system does not distinguish between stimulation coming from this artificial device and stimulation coming through the middle ear.

As long as appropriate signals go to the correct locations on the basilar membrane,
the brain will hear. Cochlear implants work well, allowing the deaf to detect even the
fluctuating pitches of speech. Their success corroborates the tonotopic representation
of pitch in the basilar membrane.

Even so, the quality of sound that cochlear implants create is impoverished relative to
natural hearing. Adults who lose their hearing and then get cochlear implants describe
the sounds as "computerized" and "weird." Many people with implants find music
unpleasant and difficult to listen to. Graeme Clark (2015) developed a prototype high-fi-
delity cochlear implant with 50 electrodes to increase basilar membrane stimulation. His
goal is to achieve better music perception and enhanced ability to discern specific voices
in noisy rooms. No matter what the person's age, a shorter time span between the hearing
loss and treatment can lead to better hearing: early intervention can lead to better results.

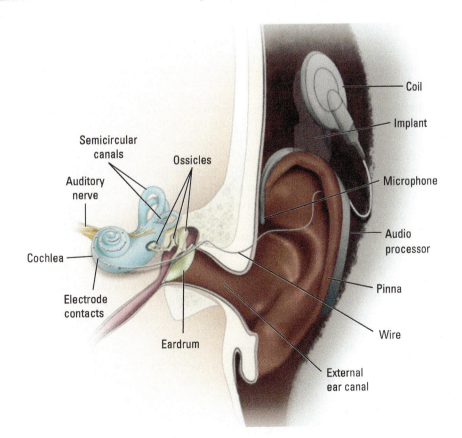

Semicircular
canals

Auditory
nerve

Ossicles

Cochlea

Electrode
contacts

Eardrum

External
ear canal

Coil

Implant

Microphone

Audio
processor

Pinna

Wire

FIGURE 10-16 **Tonotopic Technology**
A cochlear implant captures incoming sound
wave stimulation via a microphone worn
behind the ear. An audio processor converts
the frequencies into electric current and
stimulates the correct locations on the basilar
membrane.

One minor difficulty with frequency detection is that the human cochlea does not respond in a tonotopic manner to frequencies below about 200 hertz, yet we can hear frequencies as low as 20 hertz. At its apex, all the cells respond to movement of the basilar membrane, but they do so in proportion to the frequency of the incoming wave (see Figure 10-10B). Higher rates of bipolar cell firing signal a higher frequency, whereas lower rates of firing signal a lower frequency.

Why the cochlea uses a different system to distinguish pitch within this range of very low-frequency sound waves is not clear. It probably has to do with the physical limitations of the basilar membrane. Discriminating among low-frequency sound waves is vital to animals such as elephants and whales, which depend on these frequencies to communicate. These species most likely have more neurons at the apex of the basilar membrane than we humans have.

Detecting Loudness

The simplest way for cochlear (bipolar) cells to indicate sound wave intensity is to fire at a higher rate when amplitude is greater, which is exactly what happens. More intense air pressure changes produce more intense basilar membrane vibrations and therefore greater shearing of the cilia. Increased shearing leads to more neurotransmitter being released onto bipolar cells. As a result, the bipolar axons fire more frequently, telling the auditory system that the sound is getting louder.

Detecting Location

Psychologist Albert Bregman devised a visual analogy to describe what the auditory system is doing when it detects sound location:

> Imagine a game played at the side of a lake. Two small channels are dug, side by side, leading away from the lake, and the lake water is allowed to fill them up. Partway up each channel, a cork floats, moving up and down with the waves. You stand with your back to the lake and are allowed to look only at the two floating corks. Then you are asked questions about what is happening on the lake. Are there two motorboats on the lake or only one? Is the nearer one going from left to right or right to left? Is the wind blowing? Did something heavy fall into the water? You must answer these questions just by looking at the two corks. This would seem to be an impossible task. Yet consider an exactly analogous problem. As you sit in a room, a lake of air surrounds you. Running off this lake, into your head, are two small channels—your ear canals. At the end of each is a membrane (the ear drum) that acts like the floating corks in the channels running off the lake, moving in and out with the sound waves that hit it. Just as the game at the lakeside offered no information about the happenings on the lake except for the movements of the corks, the sound-producing events in the room can be known by your brain only through the vibrations of your two eardrums. (Bregman, 2005, p. 35)

We estimate the location of a sound both by taking cues derived from one ear and by comparing cues received at both ears. The fact that each cochlear nerve synapses on both sides of the brain provides mechanisms for locating a sound source. In one mechanism, neurons in the brainstem compute the difference in a sound wave's arrival time at each ear—the *interaural time difference* (ITD). Differences in arrival time need not be large to be detected. If two sounds presented through earphones are separated in time by as little as 10 microseconds, the listener will perceive that a single sound came from the leading ear.

This computation of left-ear–right-ear arrival times is carried out in the medial part of the superior olivary complex (see Figure 10-12). Because these hindbrain cells receive inputs from each ear, they can compare exactly when the signal from each ear reaches them.

Figure 10-17 shows how sound waves originating on the left reach the left ear slightly before they reach the right ear. As the sound source moves from the side of the head toward the middle, a person has greater and greater difficulty locating it: the ITD becomes smaller and smaller until there is no difference at all. When we detect no difference, we infer that the sound is either directly in front of us or directly behind us. To locate it, we turn our head, making the sound waves strike one

FIGURE 10-17 **Locating a Sound** Compression waves originating on the left side of the body reach the left ear slightly before reaching the right. The ITD is small, but the auditory system can discriminate it and fuse the dual stimuli so that we perceive a single, clear sound coming from the left. Horizontal orienting is *azimuth detection;* vertical orienting is *elevation detection.*

Extra distance that sound must travel to reach the right ear.

Art Wolfe/Getty Images

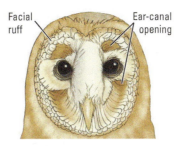

Facial ruff

Ear-canal opening

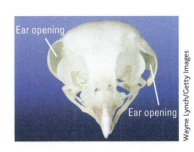

Ear opening

Ear opening

Wayne Lynch/Getty Images

FIGURE 10-18 **Hunting by Ear** Left: In the dark, a barn owl aligns its talons with the body axis of the mouse it is about to catch. Center: The owl's facial ruff collects and funnels sound waves into ear canal openings through tightly feathered troughs above and below the eyes. The owl's left ear is more sensitive to sound waves from the left and below because the ear canal is higher on the left side, and the trough is tilted down. The right-side ear canal is lower, and the trough tilts up, making the right ear more sensitive to sound waves from the right and above. Right: The boreal owl's asymmetric skull produces a similar auditory asymmetry. Information from Knudsen, 1981.

ear sooner. We have a similar problem distinguishing between sounds directly above and below us. Again, we solve the problem by tilting our head, thus causing the sound waves to strike one ear before the other.

Another mechanism used by the auditory system to detect the source of a sound is the sound's relative loudness on the left and the right—the *interaural intensity difference* (IID). The head acts as an obstacle to higher-frequency sound waves, which do not easily bend around the head. As a result, higher-frequency waves on one side of the head are louder than on the other. The lateral part of the superior olive and the trapezoid body detect this difference. Again, sound waves coming from directly in front or behind or from directly above or below require the same solution: tilting or turning the head.

Head tilting and turning take time, which is important for animals, such as owls, that hunt using sound. Owls need to know the location of a sound simultaneously in at least two directions—right or left and above or below. Owls, like humans, can orient in the horizontal plane to sound waves by using ITD. In addition, the owl's ears have evolved to detect the relative loudness of sound waves in the vertical plane. As diagrammed in **Figure 10-18**, owls' ears are slightly displaced vertically. This solution allows owls to hunt entirely by sound in the dark. Bad news for mice.

Detecting Patterns in Sound

Perceiving sound wave patterns as meaningful units, such as units of music and speech, is fundamental to human auditory analysis. Because music perception and language perception are lateralized in the right and left temporal lobes, respectively, we can guess that neurons in the right and left temporal cortex take part in pattern recognition and analysis of both auditory experiences. Studying the activities of individual auditory neurons in humans is not easy, however, because there is no noninvasive way to do so.

Most of what neuroscientists know comes from studies of how individual neurons respond in nonhuman primates. Both human and nonhuman primates have a ventral and dorsal cortical pathway for audition. Neurons in the ventral pathway decode spectrally complex sounds—which some investigators refer to as *auditory object recognition*—including the meaning of speech sounds for people and species-typical vocalizations in monkeys (for a review, see Rauschecker, 2012). Less is known about the properties of neurons in the dorsal auditory stream, but this path clearly has a role in integrating auditory and somatosensory information to control speech production. We could call it *audition for action*.

Audition for action parallels unconscious, visually guided movements by the dorsal stream; see Figure 9-18.

10-3 Review

Before you continue, check your understanding. Answers to Self-Test appear at the back of the book.

1. Bipolar neurons in the cochlea form _____ representations that code sound wave frequencies.

2. Loudness is indicated by the firing rate of cells in the _____.

3. Detecting the location of a sound is a function of neurons in the _____ and _____ of the brainstem.

4. The function of the dorsal auditory pathway can be described as _____.

5. Explain how the brain detects a sound's location.

For additional study tools, visit ♒ **LaunchPad** at launchpadworks.com

---

10-4

Anatomy of Language and Music

This chapter began with the evolutionary implications of discovering a flute made by Neanderthals (see Research Focus 10-1, Evolution of Language and Music). That Neanderthals made flutes implies not only that they made music but also that they processed musical sound wave patterns. In our brain, musical ability is generally a right-hemisphere specialization complementary to language ability, and it is lateralized to the left hemisphere in most people.

No one knows whether these complementary systems evolved together in the hominid brain, but it is highly likely. Language and music abilities are highly developed in the modern human brain. Although little is known about how each is processed at the cellular level, electrical stimulation and recording as well as blood-flow imaging studies yield important insights into the cortical regions that process them. We investigate such studies next, focusing first on how the brain processes language.

Section 7-4 surveys functional brain-imaging methods; Section 7-2 reviews methods for measuring the brain's electrical activity.

Processing Language

An estimated 5000 to 7000 human languages are spoken in the world today, and many more have gone extinct in past millennia. Researchers have wondered whether the brain has a single system for understanding and producing any language, regardless of its structure, or whether disparate languages, such as English and Japanese, are processed differently. To answer this question, it helps to analyze languages to determine just how fundamentally similar they are, despite their obvious differences.

Uniformity of Language Structure

Foreign languages often seem impossibly complex to those who do not speak them. Their sounds alone may seem odd and difficult to make. To a native English speaker, for instance, certain languages, such as Japanese, probably sound especially melodic and almost without obvious consonants, whereas European languages, such as German or Dutch, may sound heavily guttural with many consonants.

Even within such related languages as Spanish, Italian, and French, marked differences can make learning one of them challenging, even if the student already knows another. Yet as real as all these linguistic differences may be, they are superficial. The similarities among human languages, although not immediately apparent, are actually far more fundamental than their differences.

Noam Chomsky (1965) is usually credited as the first linguist to stress similarities over differences in human language structure. In a series of books and papers written over more than a half-century, Chomsky has made a sweeping claim, as have researchers such as Steven Pinker (1997). They argue that all languages have common structural characteristics stemming from a genetically determined constraint, and these common characteristics form the basis of universal grammar theory. Humans, apparently, have a built-in capacity for learning and using language, just as we have for walking upright.

Chomsky was greeted with deep skepticism when he first proposed this idea in the 1960s, but it has since become clear that the capacity for human language is indeed genetic. An obvious piece of evidence: language is universal in human populations. All people everywhere use language.

The complexity of a language is unrelated to its culture's technological complexity. The languages of technologically unsophisticated peoples are every bit as complex and elegant as the languages of postindustrial cultures. The English of Shakespeare's time is neither inferior nor superior to today's English; it is just different.

Another piece of evidence that Chomsky adherents cite for the genetic basis of human language is that humans learn language early in life and seemingly without effort. By about 12 months of age, children everywhere have started to speak words. By 18 months, they are combining words, and by age 3 years, they have a rich language capability.

> A one-year-old's 5- to 10-word vocabulary doubles in the next 6 months and by 36 months mushrooms to 1000 words; see Section 8-3.

Perhaps the most amazing thing about language development is that children are not formally taught the structure of their language, just as they are not taught to crawl or walk. They just do it. As toddlers, they are not painstakingly instructed in the rules of grammar. In fact, their early errors—sentences such as "I goed to the zoo"—are seldom even corrected by adults. Yet children master language rapidly. They also acquire language through a series of stages that are remarkably similar across cultures. Indeed, the process of language acquisition plays an important role in Chomsky's theory of its innateness—which is not to say that language development is not influenced by experience.

At the most basic level, children learn the language or languages that they hear spoken. In an English household, they learn English; in a Japanese home, Japanese. They also pick up the language structure—the vocabulary and grammar—of the people around them, even though that structure can vary from one speaker to another. Children go through a sensitive period for language acquisition, probably from about 1 to 6 years of age. If they are not exposed to language throughout this critical period, their language skills are severely compromised. If children learn two languages simultaneously, the two share the same part of Broca's area. In fact, their neural representations overlap (Kim et al., 1997).

> Section 15-1 discusses the connection between language and human thought, and Section 15-4 explores the areas of the brain involved in language processing.

Both its universality and natural acquisition favor the theory for a genetic basis of human language. A third piece of evidence is the many basic structural elements common to all languages. Granted, every language has its own particular grammatical rules that specify exactly how various parts of speech are positioned in a sentence (syntax), how words are inflected to convey different meanings, and so forth. But an overarching set of rules also applies to all human languages, and the first rule is that there *are* rules.

For instance, all languages employ parts of speech that we call subjects, verbs, and direct objects. Consider the sentence *Jane ate the apple*. *Jane* is the subject, *ate* is the verb, and *apple* is the direct object. Syntax is not specified by any universal rule but rather is a characteristic of the particular language. In English, syntactical order (usually) is subject, verb, object; in Japanese, the order is subject, object, verb; in Gaelic, the order is verb, subject, object. Nonetheless, all these languages have both syntax and grammar.

The existence of these two structural pillars in all human languages is seen in the phenomenon of *creolization*—the development of a new language from what was formerly a rudimentary language, or *pidgin*. In one example of creolization from Queensland of northeastern Australia, Pacific Islanders speaking numerous different languages were sent to work together on plantations. These laborers began to develop a pidgin, drawing vocabulary primarily from English but also from German, Malay, Portuguese, and their own Austronesian languages.

This English-based pidgin evolved into Tok Pisin, which is now one of the three official languages of Papua New Guinea, is spoken by 6 million people, and is crowding out other languages in that region. The pidgin had a crude syntax (word order) but lacked a formal

Broca's area Anterior left-hemisphere speech area that functions with the motor cortex to produce movements needed for speaking.

aphasia Inability to speak or comprehend language despite the presence of normal comprehension and intact vocal mechanisms. *Broca's aphasia* is the inability to speak fluently despite the presence of normal comprehension and intact vocal mechanisms. *Wernicke's aphasia* is the inability to understand or to produce meaningful language even though word production remains intact.

Principle 9: Brain functions are localized and distributed.

Section 7-1 links Broca's observations to his contributions to neuropsychology.

grammatical structure. The children of the laborers who invented this pidgin grew up with caretakers who spoke only pidgin to them. Yet within a generation, these children had developed their own creole, a language complete with a formal syntax and grammar.

Clearly, the pidgin invented of necessity by adults was not a learnable language for children. Their innate biology shaped a new language similar in basic structure to all other human languages. Creolized languages seem to evolve in a similar way, even though the base languages are different. This phenomenon is possible only because there is an innate biological component to language development.

Localizing Language in the Brain

By the mid-1800s, it had become clear that language functions were at least partly localized not just within the left hemisphere but to specific areas there. Clues that led to this conclusion began to emerge early in the nineteenth century, when neurologists observed patients with frontal lobe injuries who had language difficulties.

Then, in 1861, physician Paul Broca confirmed that certain language functions are localized in the left hemisphere. Broca concluded, on the basis of several postmortem examinations, that language is localized in the left frontal lobe, in a region just anterior to the central fissure. A person with damage in this area is unable to speak despite having both an intact vocal apparatus and normal language comprehension. The confirmation of **Broca's area** was significant because it triggered the idea that the left and right hemispheres might have different functions.

Other neurologists of the time believed that Broca's area might be only one of several left-hemisphere regions that control language. In particular, they suspected a relation between hearing and speech. Proving this suspicion correct, Karl Wernicke later described patients who had difficulty comprehending language after injury to the posterior region of the left temporal lobe, identified as Wernicke's area in **Figure 10-19**.

In Section 10-2, we identified Wernicke's area as a speech zone (see Figure 10-13A). Damage to any speech area produces some form of **aphasia**, the general term for any inability to comprehend or produce language, despite the presence of otherwise normal comprehension and intact vocal mechanisms. At one extreme, people who suffer *Wernicke's aphasia* can speak fluently, but their language is confused and makes little sense, as if they have no idea what they are saying. At the other extreme, a person with *Broca's aphasia* cannot speak despite having normal comprehension and intact physiology.

Wernicke went on to propose a model, diagrammed in Figure 10-19A, for how the two language areas of the left hemisphere interact to produce speech. He theorized that images of words are encoded by their sounds and stored in the left posterior temporal cortex. When we hear a word that matches one of those sound images, we recognize it, which is how Wernicke's area contributes to speech comprehension.

FIGURE 10-19 **Neurology of Language** **(A)** In Wernicke's model of speech recognition, stored sound images are matched to spoken words in the left posterior temporal cortex, shown in red. **(B)** Speech is produced through the connection that the arcuate fasciculus makes between Wernicke's area and Broca's area.

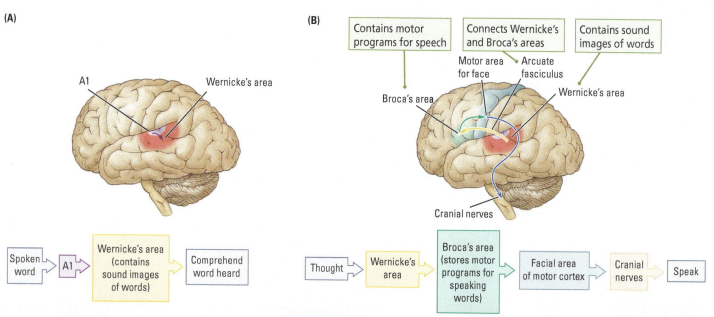

To *speak* words, Broca's area in the left frontal lobe must come into play because the motor program to produce each word is stored in this area. Messages travel to Broca's area from Wernicke's area through the *arcuate fasciculus*, a fiber pathway that connects the two regions. Broca's area in turn controls articulation of words by the vocal apparatus, as diagrammed in Figure 10-19B.

Wernicke's model provided a simple explanation both for the existence of two major language areas in the brain and for the contribution each area makes to the control of language. But the model was based on postmortem examinations of patients with brain lesions that were often extensive. Not until neurosurgeon Wilder Penfield's pioneering brain stimulation studies, begun in the 1930s, were the left hemisphere language areas clearly and accurately mapped.

Auditory and Speech Zones Mapped Using Brain Stimulation

Among Penfield's discoveries are that Broca's area is not the independent site of speech production, and Wernicke's area is not the independent site of language comprehension. Electrical stimulation of either region disrupts both processes.

Penfield took advantage of the chance to map the brain's auditory and language areas when he operated on patients undergoing elective surgery to treat epilepsy that was unresponsive to antiseizure medication. The goal of this surgery is to remove tissues where the abnormal discharges are initiated without damaging the areas responsible for linguistic ability or vital sensory or motor functioning. To determine the locations of these critical regions, Penfield used a weak electrical current to stimulate the brain surface. By monitoring the patient's responses during stimulation in different locations, Penfield could map brain functions over the entire exposed cortex.

Typically, two neurosurgeons perform the operation under local anesthesia applied to the skin, skull, and dura mater, as a neurologist analyzes the electroencephalogram in an adjacent room. Patients, who are awake, are asked to contribute during the procedure, and the effects of brain stimulation in specific regions can be determined in detail and mapped. Penfield (shown operating in **Figure 10-20A**) placed tiny numbered tickets on different parts of the brain's surface where the patient noted that stimulation had

Section 7-1 describes brain stimulation techniques used in neuroscience research.

FIGURE 10-20 **Mapping Cortical Functions (A)** Neurosurgery for eligible epilepsy patients who failed to respond to antiseizure medications. The patient is fully conscious, lying on his right side, and kept comfortable with local anesthesia. Wilder Penfield stimulates discrete cortical areas in the patient's exposed left hemisphere. In the background, a neurologist monitors an EEG recorded from each stimulated area to help identify the epileptogenic focus. The anesthetist (seated) observes the patient's responses to the cortical stimulation. **(B)** A drawing overlies a photograph of the patient's exposed brain. The numbered tickets identify points Penfield stimulated to map the cortex in this patient's brain. At points 26, 27, and 28, a stimulating electrode disrupted speech. Point 26 presumably is in Broca's area, 27 is the motor cortex facial control area, and 28 is in Wernicke's area.

(A)

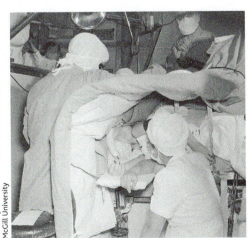

Courtesy Penfield Archive, Montreal Neurological Institute, McGill University

(B)

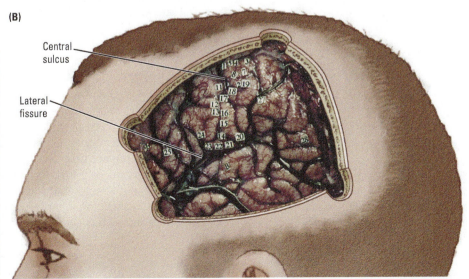

Central sulcus

Lateral fissure

supplementary speech area Speech production region on the left frontal lobe dorsal surface.

produced some noticeable sensation or effect, and he eventually produced the cortical map shown in Figure 10-20B.

When Penfield stimulated the auditory cortex, patients often reported hearing such sounds as a ringing that sounded like a doorbell, a buzzing noise, or a sound like birds chirping. This result is consistent with later single-cell recordings from the auditory cortex in nonhuman primates. Findings in these later studies showed that the auditory cortex participates in pattern recognition.

Penfield also found that stimulation in area A1 seemed to produce simple tones—ringing sounds, and so forth—whereas stimulation in the adjacent auditory cortex (Wernicke's area) was more apt to cause some interpretation of a sound—ascription of a buzzing sound to a familiar source such as a cricket, for instance. There was no difference in the effects of stimulation of the left or right auditory cortex, and the patients heard no words when the brain was stimulated.

Sometimes, however, stimulation of the auditory cortex produced effects other than sound perceptions. Stimulation of one area, for example, might cause a patient to feel deaf, whereas stimulation of another area might produce a distortion of sounds actually being heard. As one patient exclaimed after a certain region had been stimulated, "Everything you said was mixed up!"

Penfield was most interested in the effects of brain stimulation not on simple sound wave processing but on language. He and later researchers used electrical stimulation to identify four important cortical regions that underlie speech production and comprehension. The two classic regions—Broca's area and Wernicke's area—are left-hemisphere regions. Located on both sides of the brain are the other two major language use regions: the dorsal area of the frontal lobes and the areas of the motor and somatosensory cortex that control facial, tongue, and throat muscles and sensations. Although the effects on speech vary depending on the region, stimulating any of them disrupts speech in some way.

Clearly, much of the left hemisphere takes part in audition. **Figure 10-21** shows the areas that Penfield found engaged in some way in processing language. In fact, Penfield mapped cortical language areas in two ways, first by disrupting speech and then by eliciting speech. Not surprisingly, damage to any speech area produces some form of aphasia.

DISRUPTING SPEECH Penfield expected that electrical current might disrupt ongoing speech by effectively short-circuiting the brain. To test his hypothesis, he stimulated different cortical regions while the patient was speaking. In fact, the speech disruptions took several forms, including slurring, word confusion, and difficulty finding the right word. Such aphasias are detailed in Clinical Focus 10-5, Left-Hemisphere Dysfunction.

Electrical stimulation of the **supplementary speech area** on the dorsal surface of the frontal lobe (shown in Figure 10-21) can even stop ongoing speech completely, a reaction that Penfield called *speech arrest*. Stimulation of other cortical regions far removed from the temporal and frontal speech areas has no effect on ongoing speech, with the exception of motor cortex regions (shown in Figure 10-21) that control facial movements. This exception makes sense because talking requires movement of facial, tongue, and throat muscles.

ELICITING SPEECH The second way Penfield mapped language areas was to stimulate the cortex when a patient was not speaking. Here, the goal was to see if stimulation caused the person to utter a speech sound. Penfield did not expect to trigger coherent speech; cortical electrical stimulation is not physiologically normal and so probably would not produce actual words or word combinations. His expectation was borne out.

Stimulation of regions on both sides of the brain—for example, the supplementary speech areas—produces a sustained vowel cry, such as *Oooh* or *Eee*. Stimulation of the facial areas in the motor and somatosensory cortices produces some vocalization related to mouth and tongue movements. Stimulation outside these speech-related zones produces no such effects.

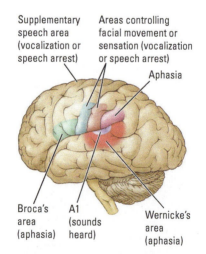

Supplementary speech area (vocalization or speech arrest)

Areas controlling facial movement or sensation (vocalization or speech arrest)

Aphasia

Broca's area (aphasia)

A1 (sounds heard)

Wernicke's area (aphasia)

FIGURE 10-21 **Cortical Regions That Control Language** This map, based on Penfield's extensive study, summarizes the left-hemisphere areas where direct stimulation may disrupt speech or elicit vocalization.
Information from Penfield & Roberts, 1956.

Left-Hemisphere Dysfunction

Susan S., a 25-year-old college graduate and mother of two, had epilepsy. When she had a seizure, which was almost every day, she lost consciousness for a short period, during which she often engaged in repetitive behaviors, such as rocking back and forth.

Medication can usually control such seizures, but the drugs were ineffective for Susan. The attacks disrupted her life: they prevented her from driving and restricted the types of jobs she could hold. So Susan decided to undergo neurosurgery to remove the region of abnormal brain tissue that was causing the seizures.

The procedure has a high success rate. Susan's surgery entailed removal of a part of the left temporal lobe, including most of the cortex in front of the auditory areas. Although it may seem a substantial amount of the brain to cut away, the excised tissue is usually abnormal, so any negative consequences typically are minor.

After the surgery, Susan did well for a few days; then she started to have unexpected and unusual

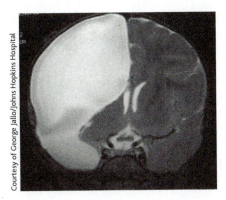

Courtesy of George Jallo/Johns Hopkins Hospital

Postoperative MRI of a patient who has lost most of the left hemisphere.

complications that resulted in the loss of the remainder of her left temporal lobe, including the auditory cortex and Wernicke's area. The extent of lost brain tissue resembles that shown in the accompanying MRI.

Susan no longer understood language, except to respond to the sound of her name and to speak just one phrase: I love you. Susan was also unable to read, showing no sign that she could even recognize her own name in writing.

To find ways to communicate with Susan, one of your authors tried humming nursery rhymes to her. She immediately recognized them and could say the words. He also discovered that her singing skill was well within the normal range, and she had a considerable repertoire of songs.

Susan did not seem able to learn new songs, however, and she did not understand messages that were sung to her. Apparently, Susan's musical repertoire was stored and controlled independently of her language system.

Auditory Cortex Mapped by Positron Emission Tomography

To study the metabolic activity of brain cells engaged in tasks such as processing language, researchers use PET, a brain-imaging technique that detects changes in brain blood flow. Among the many PET studies of auditory stimulation, a series conducted by Robert Zatorre and his colleagues (1992, 1996) serves as a good example. These researchers hypothesized that simple auditory stimulation, such as bursts of noise, are analyzed by area A1, whereas more complex auditory stimulation, such as speech syllables, are analyzed in adjacent secondary auditory areas.

The researchers also hypothesized that performing a discrimination task for speech sounds would selectively activate left-hemisphere regions. This selective activation is exactly what they found. **Figure 10-22A** shows increased activity in the primary auditory cortex in response to bursts of noise, whereas secondary auditory areas are activated by speech syllables (Figure 10-22B and C).

Both types of stimuli produced responses in both hemispheres but with greater activation in the left hemisphere for the speech syllables. These results imply that area A1 analyzes all incoming auditory signals, speech and nonspeech, whereas the secondary

Section 7-4 details procedures used to obtain a PET scan.

FIGURE 10-22 **Cortical Activation in Language-Related Tasks (A)** Passively listening to noise bursts activates the primary auditory cortex. **(B)** Listening to words activates the posterior speech zone, including Wernicke's area. **(C)** Making a phonetic discrimination activates the frontal region, including Broca's area.

(A) Listening to bursts of noise

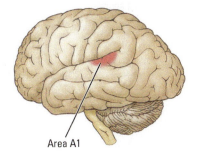

Area A1

(B) Listening to words

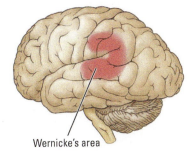

Wernicke's area

(C) Discriminating speech sounds

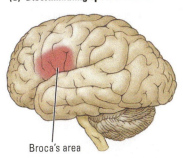

Broca's area

auditory areas are responsible for some higher-order signal processing required for analyzing language sound patterns.

As Figure 10-22C shows, the speech sound discrimination task yielded an intriguing additional result: Broca's area in the left hemisphere was also activated. The involvement of this frontal lobe region during auditory analysis may seem surprising. In Wernicke's model, Broca's area is considered the storage area for motor programs needed to produce words. It is not usually a region thought of as a site of speech sound discrimination.

A possible explanation is that to determine that the *g* in *bag* and the *g* in *pig* are the same speech sound, the auditory stimulus must be related to how the sound is actually articulated. That is, speech sound perception requires a match with the motor behaviors associated with making the sound.

This role for Broca's area in speech analysis is confirmed further when investigators ask people to determine whether a stimulus is a word or a nonword (for example, *tid* versus *tin* or *gan* versus *tan*). In this type of study, information about how the words are articulated is irrelevant, and Broca's area need not be recruited. Imaging reveals that Broca's area is not activated.

Processing Music

Although Penfield did not study the effect of brain stimulation on musical analysis, many researchers study musical processing in brain-damaged patients. Collectively, the results of these studies confirm that musical processing is in fact largely a right-hemisphere specialization, just as language processing is largely a left-hemisphere one.

Localizing Music in the Brain

A famous patient, the French composer Maurice Ravel (1875–1937), provides an excellent example of right-hemisphere predominance for music processing. *Boléro* is perhaps Ravel's best-known work. At the peak of his career, Ravel developed aphasia as a result of a previously undiagnosed degenerative brain disorder exacerbated by a severe blow to the head followed a few months later by a left-hemisphere stroke. Yet many of his musical skills remained intact post-stroke because they were localized to the right hemisphere. He could still recognize melodies, pick up tiny mistakes in music he heard, and even judge the tuning of pianos. His music perception was largely intact.

Skills that had to do with producing music, however, were among those destroyed. Ravel could no longer recognize written music, play the piano, or compose. This dissociation of music perception and music production may parallel the dissociation of speech comprehension and speech production in language. Apparently, the left hemisphere plays at least some role in certain aspects of music processing, especially those that have to do with making music.

To find out more about how the brain carries out the perceptual side of music processing, Zatorre and his colleagues (1994) conducted PET studies. When participants listened simply to bursts of noise, Heschl's gyrus became activated (**Figure 10-23A**), but perception of melody triggers major activation in the right-hemisphere auditory cortex lying in front of Heschl's gyrus (Figure 10-23B), as well as minor activation in the same left-hemisphere region (not shown).

FIGURE 10-23 **Cortical Activation in Music-Related Tasks** **(A)** Passively listening to bursts of noise activates Heschl's gyrus. **(B)** Listening to a melody activates the secondary auditory cortex. **(C)** Making relative pitch judgments about two notes in each melody activates a right frontal lobe area.

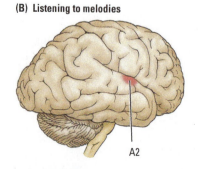

(A) Listening to bursts of noise

Heschl's gyrus

(B) Listening to melodies

A2

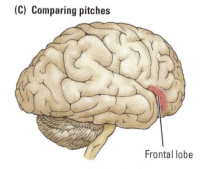

(C) Comparing pitches

Frontal lobe

The Brain's Music System

Nonmusicians enjoy music and have musical ability. Musicians show an enormous range of ability: some have perfect pitch and some do not, for example. About 4 percent of the population is tone deaf. Their difficulties, characterized as **amusia**—an inability to distinguish between musical notes—are lifelong.

Robert Zatorre and his colleagues (Bermudez et al., 2009; Hyde et al., 2007) used MRI to look at differences among the brains of musicians, nonmusicians, and amusics. MRIs of the left and right hemispheres show that the cortical thickness is greater in dorsolateral frontal and superior temporal regions in musicians than in nonmusicians. Curiously, musicians with perfect pitch have thinner cortex in the posterior part of the dorsolateral frontal lobe. Thinner appears to be better for some music skills.

Compared to nonmusicians, then, musicians with thicker-than-normal cortex must have enhanced neural networks in the right-hemisphere frontal–temporal system linked to performing musical tasks. But thicker-than-normal cortex can bestow both advantage and impairment.

Analysis of amusic participants' brains showed thicker cortex in the right frontal area and in the right auditory cortex regions. Some abnormality in neuronal migration during brain development is likely to have led to an excess of neurons in the right frontal–temporal music pathway of the amusics, and their impaired music cognition resulted.

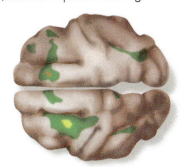

Right hemisphere

Left hemisphere

Compared to nonmusicians and amusics, musicians' thicker cortex, shown in the green, yellow, and red areas, contributes to performance. Research Focus 14-5 describes how playing music can affect sensorimotor maps in the cortex. Research from Bermudez et al., 2009.

In another test, participants listened to the same melodies. The investigators asked them to indicate whether the pitch of the second note was higher or lower than that of the first note. During this task, which necessitates short-term memory of what was just heard, blood flow in the right frontal lobe increased (Figure 10-23C). As with language, then, the frontal lobe plays a role in auditory analysis when short-term memory is required. People with enhanced or impaired musical abilities show differences in frontal lobe organization, as demonstrated in Research Focus 10-6, The Brain's Music System.

As noted earlier, the capacity for language is innate. Sandra Trehub and her colleagues (1999) showed that music may be innate as well, as we hypothesized at the beginning of the chapter. Trehub found that infants show learning preferences for musical scales versus random notes. Like adults, children are sensitive to musical errors, presumably because they are biased for perceiving regularity in rhythms. Thus, it appears that the brain is prepared at birth for hearing both music and language, and presumably it selectively attends to these auditory signals.

Music as Therapy

The power of music to engage the brain has led to its use as a therapeutic tool for brain dysfunctions. The best evidence of its effectiveness lies in studies of motor disorders such as stroke and Parkinson disease (Johansson, 2012). Listening to rhythm activates the motor and premotor cortex and can improve gait and arm training after stroke. Musical experience reportedly also enhances the ability to discriminate speech sounds and to distinguish speech from background noise in patients with aphasia.

Music therapy also appears to be a useful complement to more traditional therapies, especially when there are problems with mood, such as in depression or brain injury. This may prove important in the treatment of stroke and traumatic brain injury, with which depression is a common complication in recovery. Music therapy also has positive effects following major surgery, both in adults and children, by reducing both their pain perception and the amount of pain medication they use (Sunitha Suresh et al., 2015). With all these applications, perhaps researchers will decide to use noninvasive imaging to determine which brain areas music therapy recruits.

amusia Tone deafness—inability to distinguish between musical notes.

The brain may be tuned prenatally to the language it will hear at birth; see Research Focus 7-1.

Parkinson patients step to the beat of music to improve their gait length and walking speed.

Sections 16-1 and 16-3 revisit music therapy.

10-4 Review

Before you continue, check your understanding. Answers to Self-Test appear at the back of the book.

1. The human auditory system has complementary specialization for the perception of sounds: left for _____ and right for _____.

2. The three frontal lobe regions that participate in producing language are _____, _____, and _____.

3. _____ area identifies speech syllables and words and stores their representations in that location.

4. _____ area matches speech sounds to the motor programs necessary to articulate them.

5. At one end of the spectrum for musical ability are people with _____, and at the other are people who are _____.

6. What evidence supports the idea that language is innate?

For additional study tools, visit **LaunchPad** at launchpadworks.com

---

10-5

Auditory Communication in Nonhuman Species

Sound has survival value. You will appreciate this if you've ever narrowly escaped becoming an accident statistic by crossing a busy intersection on foot while listening to music or talking on a cell phone. Audition is as important a sense to many other animals as vision is to humans. In addition, humans and many other animals communicate with members of their species by using sound.

Here, we consider just two types of auditory communication in nonhumans: birdsong and whale songs. Each provides a model for understanding different aspects of brain–behavior relations in which the auditory system plays a role.

Birdsong

Of about 8500 living bird species, about half are considered songbirds. Birdsong has many functions, including attracting mates (usually employed by males), demarcating territories, and announcing location or even just presence.

Parallels Between Birdsong and Language

Figure 10-24 shows sound wave spectrograms for the songs of male white-crowned sparrows that live in three localities near San Francisco. These songs differ markedly from region to region, much as dialects of the same human language vary. The differences stem from the fact that song development in young birds is influenced not just by genes but also by early experience and learning. Young birds that have good tutors can acquire more elaborate songs than can other members of their species (Marler, 1991).

These gene–experience interactions are the result of epigenetic mechanisms. For example, brain areas that control singing in adult song sparrows show altered gene expression in spring as the breeding—and singing—season begins (Thompson et al., 2012). Birdsong and human language have broad similarities beyond regional variation. Both appear to be innate yet are sculpted

FIGURE 10-24 **Birdsong Dialects** The songs of male white-crowned sparrows recorded in three locales around San Francisco Bay are similar, but sound wave spectrograms reveal that the dialects differ. Like humans, birds acquire regional dialects. Information from Marler, 1991.

White-crowned sparrow

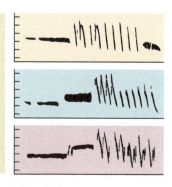

by experience. Humans seem to have a basic template for language that is programmed into the brain, and experience adds a variety of specific structural forms to this template. If a young bird is not exposed to song until it is a juvenile and then listens to recordings of birdsongs of various species, the young bird shows a general preference for its own species' song. This preference must mean that each bird has a species-specific song template in the brain. As with human language, experience modifies the details of this birdsong template.

Another broad similarity between birdsong and human language is the great diversity. Among birds, diversity is apparent in the sheer number of songs that some species possess. Though species such as the white-crowned sparrow have but a single song, others, like the marsh wren, can have as many as 150.

The number of syllables in birdsong also varies greatly, ranging from 30 for the canary to about 2000 for the brown thrasher. Similarly, modern human languages vary significantly in the type and number of elements they employ. The number of meaningful patterns in speech sounds in human languages ranges from about 15 for some Polynesian languages to about 100 for some dialects spoken in the Caucasus Mountains. English has 24.

A final broad similarity between birdsong and human language lies in how they develop. In many bird species, song development is heavily influenced by experience during a critical period, just as language development is in humans. Birds also go through stages in song development, just as humans go through stages in language development. Hatchlings make noises that attract their parents' attention, usually for feeding, and human babies emit cries to signal hunger, among other things.

The fledgling begins to make noises that Charles Darwin compared to the prespeech babbling of human infants. These noises, called *subsong*, are variable in structure, low in volume, and often produced as the bird appears to doze. Presumably, subsong, like human babbling, is practice for the later development of adult communication after the bird has left the nest.

As a young bird matures, it starts to produce sound wave patterns that contain recognizable bits of the adult song. Finally, the adult song emerges. In most species, the adult song remains remarkably stable, although a few species, such as canaries, can develop a new song every year to replace the previous year's song.

Neurobiology of Birdsong

The neurobiology of birdsong is a topic of intense research, partly because it provides an excellent model of brain changes that accompany learning and partly because it offers insight into how sex hormones influence behavior. In the 1970s, Fernando Nottebohm and his colleagues first identified the major structures controlling birdsong, illustrated in **Figure 10-25** (Nottebohm & Arnold, 1976). The largest structures are the higher vocal control center (HVC) and the nucleus *robustus archistriatalis* (RA). The axons of the HVC connect to the RA, which in turn sends axons to the twelfth cranial nerve. This nerve controls the muscles of the *syrinx*, the structure that actually produces the song.

The HVC and RA have several important characteristics, including some that are similar to auditory functions in humans:

- The structures are asymmetrical in some bird species, with those in the left hemisphere larger than those on the right. In many cases, this asymmetry is similar to the lateralized control of language in humans: if the left-hemisphere pathways are damaged, the bird stops singing, but similar injury in the right hemisphere has no effect on song.

- Birdsong structures are sexually dimorphic: they are much larger in males than in females. In male canaries, the structures are five times as large as in the female. This sex difference is due to the hormone testosterone in males. Injection of testosterone into female birds causes the song-controlling nuclei to increase in size. The rare gynandromorph zebra finch shown in Figure 8-31 exhibits physical characteristics of both sexes.

- The size of the birdsong-controlling nuclei is related to singing skill. Unusually talented singers among male canaries tend to have larger HVCs and RAs than do less gifted singers.

FIGURE 10-25 **Avian Neuroanatomy** Lateral view of the canary brain shows several left-hemisphere nuclei that control song learning. Two that are necessary both for adult singing and for learning the song are the higher vocal control center (HVC) and the nucleus robustus archistriatalis (RA). Other regions necessary for learning the song during development but not required for adult singing include the dorsal archistriatum (Ad), the lateral magnocellular nucleus of the anterior neostriatum (LMAN), area X of the avian striatum, and the medial dorsolateral nucleus of the thalamus (DLM).

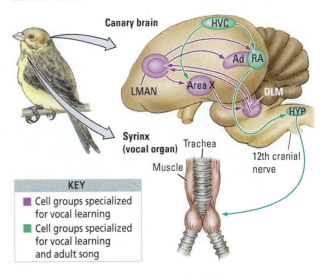

Canary brain
HVC
Ad RA
Area X
LMAN
DLM
HYP
Syrinx (vocal organ) Trachea
Muscle
12th cranial nerve

KEY
- Cell groups specialized for vocal learning
- Cell groups specialized for vocal learning and adult song

- The HVC and RA contain cells that produce birdsong as well as cells responsive to hearing song, especially the song of a bird's own species.

The same structures therefore play a role in both song production and song perception. This avian neural anatomy is comparable to the overlapping roles of Broca's and Wernicke's areas in language perception and production in humans.

Whale Songs

Analog radio stations transmit their signals in one of two forms: amplitude modulation (AM) and frequency modulation (FM). Both forms transmit information as variations in electromagnetic waves, but AM works by varying the amplitude (intensity) of the signal, whereas FM works by varying the frequency (pitch). Each system has pros and cons. AM, which was first successfully carried out in the mid-1870s, is cheaper and can be transmitted over longer distances. FM, developed in the 1930s, is less prone to interference than AM, but is impacted by physical barriers, such as mountains and buildings.

Variations in amplitude and frequency are not just the tools of radio broadcast. We use them in our normal speech. Cetaceans (whales, dolphins, and porpoises) have also evolved to use a variety of AM and FM sounds for several different communication purposes. Living in the oceans presents certain challenges. For instance, vision and smell are limited because of the way suspended particulates scatter light and odorous molecules diffuse more slowly than they would in air. But water also presents an advantage: sound travels more than four times faster in water than in air.

The humpbacked whale's songs are composed of a set of predictable and regular sounds that bear striking similarities to human musical traditions. They have been described as being probably the most complex songs in the animal kingdom. Whale songs may aid in mate selection, social bonding, navigation, and individual identification. Researchers wonder if whales sometimes sing purely for aesthetic enjoyment.

Whale songs follow a distinct hierarchical structure, like a set of nested matryoshka dolls. Base units are composed of single uninterrupted emissions that last for a few seconds and contain frequency or amplitude modulation. Frequencies vary from 20 hertz to 24 kilohertz, and a spectrogram representation reveals the pulsed nature of the FM sounds, as seen in **Figure 10-26**. A collection of base units makes up a phrase, and

FIGURE 10-26 **Spectrogram Representation of Humpback Whale Song** This spectrogram (a representation of a spectrum of sound) shows the frequency (top) and amplitude (bottom) of a humpback whale (pictured) song. Both the frequency and amplitude indicate the pulsed nature of the song, as phrases are repeated over and over.

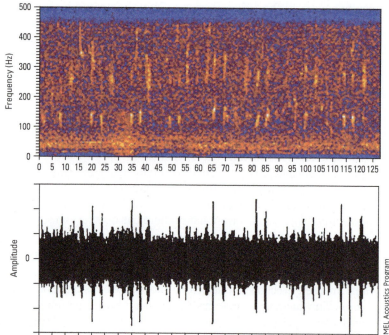

when a phrase is repeated over and over, it becomes a theme. A set of themes is a song, and a song can last up to half an hour. This length of song is impressive and is likely related to cetaceans' extraordinary ability to remember long strings of information—strings about 10 times longer than the average human can remember.

Whales sharing an area that can be as large as an entire ocean basin sing virtually the same song. The song itself is constantly changing over time, and it appears that old combinations are not reused. Whale songs are no longer being transmitted as far as they once were, due to the increase in ambient noise pollution that humans are creating with large-scale ocean shipping; this interference is fracturing the whale communities that share the same song.

10-5 Review

Before you continue, check your understanding. Answers to Self-Test appear at the back of the book.

1. Song development in young birds is influenced both by genes and by early experience and learning, interactions indicative of _____.

2. In many bird species, the control of song in the brain is lateralized to the _____ hemisphere.

3. A(n) _____ representation can display the pulsed nature of whale songs.

4. What does the presence of dialects in birdsong in the same species demonstrate?

For additional study tools, visit **LaunchPad** at launchpadworks.com

| Summary

Although we often take language and music for granted, both play central roles in our mental lives and in our social lives. Language and music provide ways to communicate with other people—and with ourselves. They facilitate social identification, parenting, and cultural transmission.

10-1 Sound Waves: Stimulus for Audition

The stimulus for the auditory system is the mechanical energy of sound waves that results from changes in air pressure. The ear transduces three fundamental physical qualities of sound wave energy: frequency (repetition rate), amplitude (size), and complexity. Perceptually, neural networks translate these energies into the pitch, loudness, and timbre of the sounds we hear.

10-2 Functional Anatomy of the Auditory System

Beginning in the ear, mechanical and electrochemical systems combine to transform sound waves into auditory perceptions—what we hear. Changes in air pressure are conveyed in a mechanical chain reaction from the eardrum to the bones of the middle ear to the oval window of the cochlea and the cochlear fluid that lies behind it in the inner ear. Movements of the cochlear fluid produce movements in specific regions of the basilar membrane, leading to changes in the electrochemical activity of the auditory receptors, the inner hair cells on the basilar membrane that send neural impulses through the auditory nerve into the brain.

10-3 Neural Activity and Hearing

The basilar membrane has a tonotopic organization. High-frequency sound waves maximally stimulate hair cells at the base, whereas low-frequency sound waves maximally stimulate hair cells at the apex, enabling cochlear neurons to code sound frequencies.

Tonotopic organization analyzes sound waves at all levels of the auditory system, which also detects both amplitude and location. The firing rate of cochlear neurons codes sound amplitude, with louder sounds producing higher firing rates than softer sounds do. Location is detected by structures in the brainstem that compute differences in the arrival times and loudness of a sound in the two ears.

Cochlear hair cells synapse with bipolar neurons that form the cochlear nerve, which in turn forms part of the eighth cranial nerve. The cochlear nerve takes auditory information to three structures in the hindbrain: the cochlear nucleus, the superior olive, and the trapezoid body. Cells in these areas are sensitive to differences in both sound wave intensity and arrival times at the two ears. In this way, they enable the brain to locate a sound.

The auditory pathway continues from the hindbrain areas to the inferior colliculus of the midbrain, then to the medial geniculate nucleus in the thalamus, and finally to the auditory cortex. As for vision, dorsal and ventral pathways exist in the auditory cortex: one for pattern recognition and the other for controlling movements in auditory space. Cells in the cortex are responsive to specific sound categories, such as species–specific communication.

10-4 Anatomy of Language and Music

Despite differences in the patterns and structures of speech sounds, all human languages have the same basic foundation: syntax and grammar, which implies an innate template for creating language. Auditory areas of the left hemisphere cortex play a special role in analyzing language-related information, whereas those in the right hemisphere play a special role in analyzing music-related information. The right temporal lobe also analyzes prosody, the melodic qualities of speech.

Among several left-hemisphere language-processing areas, Wernicke's area identifies speech syllables and words and so is critically engaged in speech comprehension. Broca's area matches speech sound patterns to the motor behaviors necessary to make them and so plays a major role in speech production. Broca's area also discriminates between closely related speech sounds. Aphasia is an inability to speak (Broca's aphasia) or to comprehend language (Wernicke's aphasia), despite the presence of normal cognition and intact vocal mechanisms.

Auditory analysis of music draws more on right-hemisphere activity than on the left-hemisphere activity. In addition, music production is not localized to the right hemisphere; it recruits the left hemisphere as well. Music perception engages both the right temporal and frontal regions.

The power of music to engage both right- and left-hemisphere activity makes it a powerful tool for engaging an injured or dysfunctioning brain. Music therapy is playing an increasingly important role in treatment.

10-5 Auditory Communication in Nonhuman Species

Nonhuman animals have evolved specialized auditory structures and behaviors. Regions of songbirds' brains are specialized for producing and comprehending song. In many species, these regions are lateralized to the left hemisphere, analogous in a way to how language areas are lateralized to the left hemisphere in most humans. Similarities in the development of song in birds and the development of language in humans, as well as similarities in the neural mechanisms underlying both the production and the perception of birdsong and language, are striking. Whales sing by modulating both amplitude and frequency, much as human do in vocal communication.

Key Terms

aphasia, p. 340

amplitude, p. 323

amusia, p. 345

basilar membrane, p. 329

Broca's area, p. 340

cochlea, p. 328

cochlear implant, p. 334

decibel (dB), p. 323

echolocation, p. 332

frequency, p. 321

hair cell, p. 329

hertz (Hz), p. 322

insula, p. 333

lateralization, p. 333

medial geniculate nucleus, p. 330

ossicle, p. 328

otoacoustic emissions, p. 330

primary auditory cortex (area A1), p. 330

prosody, p. 327

sound wave, p. 321

supplementary speech area, p. 342

tonotopic representation, p. 334

Wernicke's area, p. 332

Visit 🅼 **LaunchPad** to access the e-Book, videos, 🅼 **LearningCurve** adaptive quizzing, flashcards, and more at launchpadworks.com

Tim Gainey / Alamy Stock Photo

How Does the Nervous System Respond to Stimulation and Produce Movement?

CHAPTER **11**

◉ **RESEARCH FOCUS 11-1**

Neuroprosthetics

Most of us seamlessly control the approximately 650 muscles that move our bodies. But if the motor neurons that control those muscles no longer connect to them, as happens in amyotrophic lateral sclerosis (ALS, or Lou Gehrig disease), then movement becomes impossible, and eventually even breathing may cease.

This happened to Scott Mackler, a neuroscientist and marathon runner, who developed ALS in his late 30s. Dependent on a respirator to breathe, he developed *locked-in syndrome*: Mackler lost virtually all ability to communicate.

ALS has no cure, and death often occurs within 5 years of diagnosis. Yet Scott Mackler beat the odds: he survived for 17 years before he died in 2013, at age 55. Mackler beat locked-in syndrome, too, by learning to translate his mental activity into movement. He returned to work at the University of Pennsylvania, stayed in touch with family and friends, and even gave an interview to CBS's *60 Minutes* in 2008.

Mackler was a pioneer in *brain–computer interface* (*BCI*) technology. BCIs employ the brain's electrical signals to direct computer-controlled devices. **Neuroprosthetics** is a field that focuses on development of computer-assisted devices, such as BCIs, to replace lost biological function.

A *computer–brain interface* (*CBI*) employs electrical signals from a computer to instruct the brain. Cochlear implants that deliver sound-related signals to the inner ear to allow hearing are an example. *Brain–computer–brain interfaces* (*BCBIs*) combine the BCI and CBI approaches, enabling the brain to command robotic devices that provide sensory feedback to the brain.

In 2008, Mackler's BCI took up to 20 seconds to execute a single command. Advances in computer technology promise to make communication much faster and more versatile in the future (Lazarou et al., 2018).

BCBIs command robotic hands to grasp objects while tactile receptors on the robot are delivering touch and other sensory information to the user. BCBIs now also control exoskeletal devices that reach and walk and return touch, body position, and balance information to guide movement.

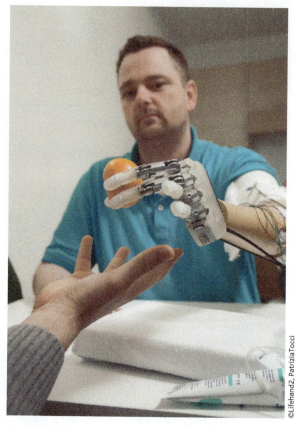

Brain–computer–brain interfaces such as the robotic limb shown here enable the brain to command robotic devices that provide sensory feedback.

In essence, BCBIs use variations in CNS activity to generate signals to interact with machines.

---

neuroprosthetics Field that develops computer-assisted devices to replace lost biological function.

Section 1-1 offers a simple definition of behavior: any movement in a living organism.

We begin here with movement and end with sensation. Section 4-4 begins with sensation and ends with movement.

Movement is a defining feature of animals, and this chapter explores how the nervous system produces movement. The somatosensory system, which includes fine touch, pressure, pain, temperature, and balance, is more closely related to movement than are the other senses, which is why we will describe *somatosensation* in this chapter.

At the level of the spinal cord, somatosensory information contributes to motor reflexes. In the brainstem, somatosensation contributes to movement timing and control. In the cerebrum, somatosensation contributes to complex voluntary movements. Indeed, for many functions, the other senses work through the somatosensory system to produce movement. If the motor system is a vehicle and the somatosensory system is the driver, the other sensory systems act like backseat drivers. A brief summary of the interactions between the motor system and somatosensation is given in The Basics: Relating the Somatosensory and Motor Systems.

11-1

Hierarchical and Parallel Movement Control

Getting from decisions to movements involves most of our nervous system. **Figure 11-1** illustrates the stepwise sequence your CNS performs in the seemingly simple act of directing your hand to pick up a cup. Once you decide to pick it up, you visually inspect the cup to determine what part to grasp. The visual cortex relays this information through the cortical somatosensory regions to the motor regions that plan and initiate the movement. Only then does the brain send instructions to the spinal cord segments that control your arm and hand muscles. The brain's role in this relationship is demonstrated by the functioning of neuroprosthetic devices, which are described in Research Focus 11-1.

As you grasp the cup's handle, information from sensory receptors in your fingers aids in adjusting your grip and sends information back through the spinal cord to the somatosensory cortex and from there to the motor cortex to confirm that you are holding the cup. Other brain regions also participate in controlling the movement. The sub-cortical basal ganglia help to produce the appropriate amount of force for grasping the cup handle, while in the brainstem, the cerebellum helps to regulate the movement's timing and accuracy.

Clearly, the movement required to pick up a cup involves widespread CNS regions. These regions are hieratically arranged. Forebrain areas involved in deciding to pick up the cup must act through lower functional areas, the brainstem and spinal cord. There must also be some parallel organization within these brain areas because you can do other things, such as speaking or singing, at the same time that you pick up a cup. Finally, there must also be some independence in the function of these brain regions. Once you have made the decision to pick up the cup, most of the movement happens without conscious control. Few of us can describe the sequence of actions or produce an accurate pantomime of the movements we make to actually grasp a cup, although we have performed the action thousands of times (Kuntz et al., 2018). To understand how these CNS regions work together to produce decisions and movements, we now consider the major components of the motor system, starting with the forebrain.

Principle 1: The nervous system produces movement in a perceptual world the brain constructs.

For now, remember that the entire sensorimotor system is organized hierarchically. When you reach the chapter's end, review Figure 11-1 to reinforce what you've learned.

Principle 4: The CNS functions on multiple levels.

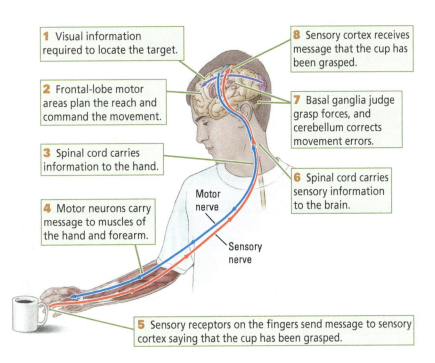

1 Visual information required to locate the target.

2 Frontal-lobe motor areas plan the reach and command the movement.

3 Spinal cord carries information to the hand.

4 Motor neurons carry message to muscles of the hand and forearm.

Motor nerve

Sensory nerve

8 Sensory cortex receives message that the cup has been grasped.

7 Basal ganglia judge grasp forces, and cerebellum corrects movement errors.

6 Spinal cord carries sensory information to the brain.

5 Sensory receptors on the fingers send message to sensory cortex saying that the cup has been grasped.

FIGURE 11-1 Sequentially Organized Movement

354   CHAPTER 11 • HOW DOES THE NERVOUS SYSTEM RESPOND TO STIMULATION AND PRODUCE MOVEMENT?

◎ THE BASICS

Relating the Somatosensory and Motor Systems

The intimate relationship between the motor and somatosensory systems is apparent in their close anatomical relationships. *Afferent* somatosensory information travels from the body inward via the somatic nervous system. Movement information travels out of the central nervous system via a parallel *efferent* motor system.

As diagrammed in the accompanying Information Flow figure, when you step on a tack, the sensory signals transmitted by the SNS from the body through the spinal cord and into the brain are afferent. Efferent signals from the CNS trigger a motor response: you lift your foot.

The spinal cord connects the somatosensory and motor systems throughout the CNS. The figure below, Connections Between the Nerves and the Spine, shows the spinal cord in cross section. In the outer part, which consists of white matter, posterior tracts are sensory and anterior tracts are motor, with some exceptions. The inner cord is gray matter composed largely of cell bodies and shaped like a butterfly.

SNS nerves entering the spinal cord's posterior side carry information inward from the body's sensory receptors and merge into a posterior root as the fibers enter a spinal cord segment of the CNS. Fibers leaving the spinal cord's anterior side carry information out from the spinal cord to the muscles. They, too, bundle together as the fibers exit the spinal cord, forming an *anterior root*. (Bundles of nerve fibers within the CNS are called tracts; outside the CNS they are called *nerves*.)

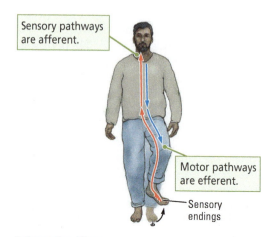

Information Flow

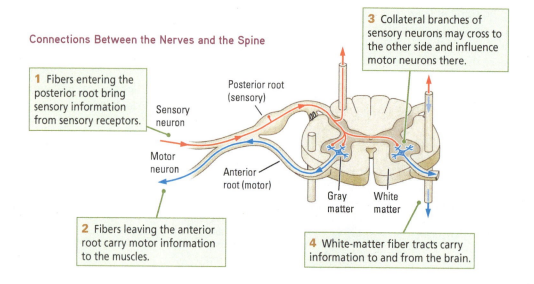

Connections Between the Nerves and the Spine

1 Fibers entering the posterior root bring sensory information from sensory receptors.

Sensory neuron

Posterior root (sensory)

3 Collateral branches of sensory neurons may cross to the other side and influence motor neurons there.

Motor neuron

Anterior root (motor)

Gray matter   White matter

2 Fibers leaving the anterior root carry motor information to the muscles.

4 White-matter fiber tracts carry information to and from the brain.

Forebrain: Initiating Movement

Complex movements consist of many acts. Consider playing basketball. At every moment, players must make decisions and perform actions. Dribble, pass, and shoot are different movement categories, and each can be performed in many ways. Skilled players choose among the categories effortlessly and blend them together seemingly without thought.

An early explanation for control of such complex movements centered on feedback: after we act, we wait for feedback about how well the action has succeeded,

The spinal cord lies within a series of small bones called *vertebrae*, categorized into the five anatomical regions diagrammed in the Spinal Segments and Dermatomes figure. Each spinal segment corresponds to a region of body surface called a *dermatome* (literally, "skin cut"), shown on the right. From top to bottom, the cervical, thoracic, lumbar, sacral, and coccygeal regions are identified by spinal segment number: C5 (cervical segment 5) at the base of the neck, for example, and L2 (lumbar segment 2) in the lower back.

Body and nervous system segmentation has a long evolutionary history that can be seen in spineless worms as well as in vertebrates. The cervical and lumbar dermatomes represent the human forelimbs and

hind limbs. Their arrangement is sequential if you imagine a human on all fours.

The Layering in the Neocortex diagram plumbs the depths of the primary motor cortex (shown in blue) and adjacent sensory (red) cortical regions. Viewed through a microscope, the six cortical layers differ in appearance, characteristics, and functions. Layer IV is relatively thick in the sensory cortex but relatively thin in the motor cortex. Layer V is relatively thick in the motor cortex and relatively thin in the sensory cortex. Cortical layer IV is afferent and layer V is efferent, and this makes sense: sensory regions have a large input layer, and motor regions have a large output layer.

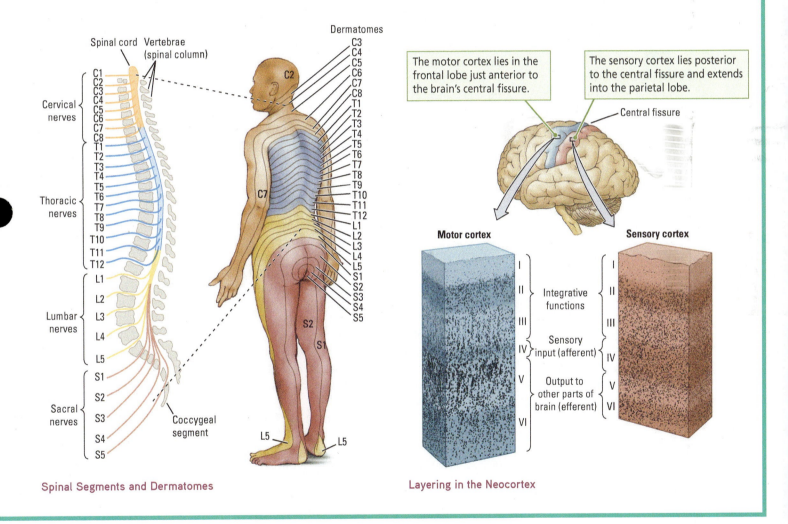

Spinal Segments and Dermatomes

Layering in the Neocortex

then make the next movement. The pioneering neuroscience researcher Karl Lashley (1951), in the article "The Problem of Serial Order in Behavior," found fault with this explanation.

Lashley realized that we perform skilled movements too quickly to rely on feedback about one movement before shaping the next. The time required to receive feedback about the first movement combined with the time needed to develop a plan for the subsequent movement and send a corresponding message to muscles is simply too long for effective action. Lashley argued that movements must be performed as **motor sequences**, with the next sequence held in readiness while the ongoing one is under way.

Lashley experimented for three decades to find the location of memory in the brain. He failed.

motor sequence Movement modules preprogrammed by the brain and produced as a unit.

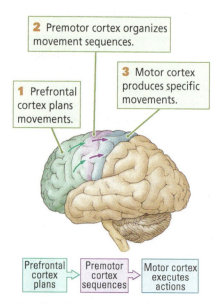

2 Premotor cortex organizes movement sequences.

3 Motor cortex produces specific movements.

1 Prefrontal cortex plans movements.

| Prefrontal cortex plans | → | Premotor cortex sequences | → | Motor cortex executes actions |

FIGURE 11-2 **Initiating a Motor Sequence**

Sections 12-6 and 15-2 explore cognitive deficits caused by frontal lobe injury.

Principle 6: Brain circuits process information hierarchically and in parallel.

All complex behaviors, including speaking, playing piano, and playing basketball, require selecting and executing movements as sequences. Most of our motor learning involves mastering sequences of action. As one sequence is being executed, the next sequence is being prepared to follow the first smoothly. The act of speaking illustrates this activity. When people use complex rather than simple word sequences, they are more likely to pause and make *umm* and *ahh* sounds, suggesting that it is taking them more time than usual to organize their speech sequences.

Initiating a Motor Sequence

Each frontal lobe is divided into several regions, including the three illustrated in **Figure 11-2**. From front to back, they are prefrontal cortex, premotor cortex, and primary motor cortex. These regions act hierarchically and in parallel.

PREFRONTAL CORTEX Atop the hierarchy, the prefrontal cortex (PFC) plans our behavior. Deciding to get up at a certain hour to arrive at work on time, choosing to stop at the library to return a book, even identifying whether a behavior is right or wrong and whether it should be performed at all are examples of PFC functions. The PFC does not specify the precise movements to be made; it simply makes a decision on which goal to select. Humans with PFC injury often break social and legal rules not because they do not know the rules or the consequences of breaking them but because their decision making is faulty.

PREMOTOR CORTEX To bring a plan to completion, the prefrontal cortex sends instructions to the premotor cortex, which produces movements coordinating many body parts. If the premotor cortex is damaged, sequences cannot be coordinated and goals cannot be accomplished. For example, the monkey on the right in **Figure 11-3** has a lesion in the dorsal premotor cortex. The monkey has been given the task of extracting a piece of food wedged in a hole in a table (Brinkman, 1984).

The monkey simply pushes the food with a finger. The food drops to the floor and is lost. To succeed at the task, the monkey should catch the food by holding a palm beneath the hole as the food is being pushed out. But this brain-injured animal is unable to make the two complementary movements together. It can push the food with a finger or extend an open palm, but it cannot coordinate the action of its two hands, as the healthy monkey on the left can.

PRIMARY MOTOR CORTEX The primary motor cortex (area M1) specializes in producing focal skilled movements, such as those involving our arms, hands, and mouth. To understand its role, consider the rich array of movements we can use to grasp objects. We can hold them in one hand, with two hands, or between a hand and another part of the body, for example.

In using the pincer grip (**Figure 11-4A**), we hold an object between the thumb and index finger. We can also perform many precision grips using the thumb and one or more of our other fingers in opposition. Precision grips not only enable us to pick up small objects easily but also allow us to use the objects with considerable skill.

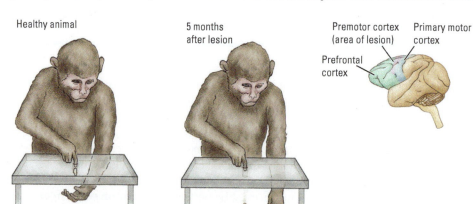

Healthy animal

5 months after lesion

Premotor cortex (area of lesion)   Primary motor cortex

Prefrontal cortex

FIGURE 11-3 **Premotor Control** On a task requiring both hands, the healthy monkey can push the peanut out of a hole with one hand and catch it in the other, but 5 months after receiving a lesion of the premotor cortex, the brain-injured monkey cannot do this.
Information from Brinkman, 1984.

In contrast, when using a whole-hand grip, also called a power grip (Figure 11-4B), we hold an object with all our fingers and with more power but less precise skill.

People with damage to area M1 have difficulty performing reaching movements and shaping their fingers correctly to perform various hand grasps. They also have difficulty talking and performing many skilled hand, arm, and trunk movements, such as bringing their hand to their mouth to feed themselves (Wolbrecht et al, 2018).

(A) Pincer grip

(B) Whole-hand grip

FIGURE 11-4 **Getting a Grip** In a pincer grip **(A)**, an object is held between the thumb and index finger. In a power, or whole-hand, grip **(B)**, the entire hand holds the object. Figure 8-20 illustrates the development of grasping responses in infants, from the whole-hand grip to the pincer grip.

Experimental Evidence for Hierarchical and Parallel Movement Control

The frontal lobe regions in each hemisphere that plan, coordinate, and execute different kinds of movements are hierarchically related, but each region can also act with some independence. Hierarchical organization is illustrated when the prefrontal cortex formulates a plan of action and then instructs the premotor cortex to organize the appropriate movement sequence, which the primary motor cortex executes. Parallel organization is illustrated by the fact that we can make a variety of plans and make whole-body or discrete movements, independently of each other. Parallel organization is also illustrated by the fact that we use these brain regions to form a wide range of plans and body movements, suggesting that different subregions and sub-pathways are involved in different aspects of motor behavior. **Figure 11-5** shows the brain regions that were active as the participants in one study performed various tasks (Roland, 1993).

As the participants use a finger to push a lever, increased blood flow is limited to the primary somatosensory and primary motor cortex (Figure 11-5A). As the participants execute a sequence of finger movements, blood flow also increases in the premotor cortex (Figure 11-5B). And as the participants use a finger to trace their way through a maze, a task that requires coordinated movements in relationship to a goal, blood flow increases in the prefrontal cortex as well (Figure 11-5C). Notice that as the participants were performing these tasks, relative blood flow increased most in the regions taking part in the required movements rather than throughout the frontal lobe.

Section 7-4 describes imaging methods that record and measure blood flow in the brain.

Brainstem: Species-Typical Movement

In a series of studies, the neuroscientist Walter Hess (1957) found that the brainstem controls species-typical behaviors, which are actions displayed by every member of a species—such as the pecking of a robin, the hissing of a cat, or the breaching of a whale. Species-typical movements, then, are mainly innate and organized by brainstem neurons. Hess developed the technique of implanting electrodes into the brains of cats

Section 1-5 introduces species-typical behavior, noting that evolutionary principles apply *across* species but not to individuals *within* a species.

(A) Simple movement

Blood flow increases in hand area of primary somatosensory and primary motor cortex when participants use a finger to push a lever.

Motor cortex | Sensory cortex

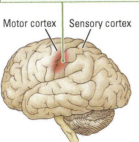

(B) Movement sequence

Blood flow increases in premotor cortex when participants perform a sequence of movements.

Dorsal premotor cortex

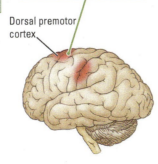

(C) Complex movement

When participants use a finger to find a route through a maze, blood flow also increases in prefrontal, temporal, and parietal cortex.

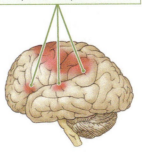

FIGURE 11-5 **Hierarchical Movement Control in the Brain** Research from Roland, 1993.

····> **EXPERIMENT 11-1**

Question: What are the effects of brainstem stimulation under different conditions?

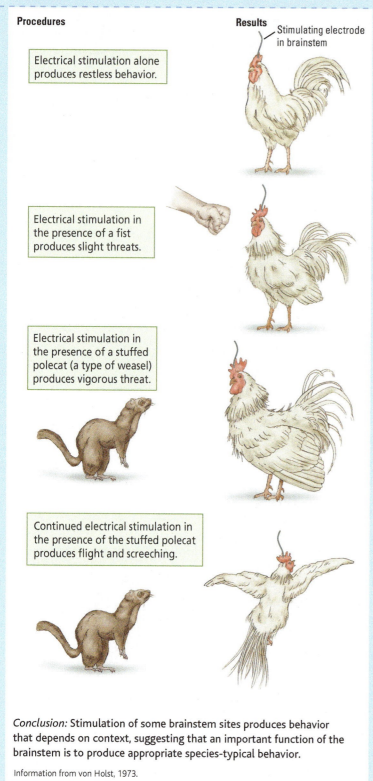

Procedures

Electrical stimulation alone produces restless behavior.

Electrical stimulation in the presence of a fist produces slight threats.

Electrical stimulation in the presence of a stuffed polecat (a type of weasel) produces vigorous threat.

Continued electrical stimulation in the presence of the stuffed polecat produces flight and screeching.

Results

Stimulating electrode in brainstem

Conclusion: Stimulation of some brainstem sites produces behavior that depends on context, suggesting that an important function of the brainstem is to produce appropriate species-typical behavior.

Information from von Holst, 1973.

and other animals and cementing them in place. These electrodes could then be attached to stimulating leads in the freely moving animal without causing it much discomfort.

By stimulating the brainstem, Hess elicited the innate movements that the animal might be expected to make. A resting cat could be induced to suddenly leap up with an arched back and erect hair as though frightened, for example, by an approaching dog. The elicited movements began abruptly when the stimulating current was turned on and ended equally abruptly when it was turned off. An animal performed such species-typical behaviors in a subdued manner when the stimulating current was low and displayed increased vigor as the stimulating current was turned up.

The actions varied depending on the brainstem site that was stimulated. Stimulating some sites produced head turning; others, walking or running; and still others, displays of aggression or fear. The animal's response to a particular stimulus could be modified accordingly. For instance, when shown a stuffed toy, a cat responded to electrical stimulation of some brainstem sites by stalking it and responded to stimulation of other sites by showing fear and withdrawing.

Hess's experiments have been confirmed and expanded on by other researchers using many animal species. **Experiment 11-1** shows the effects of brainstem stimulation on a chicken under various conditions (von Holst, 1973). Notice the effect of context: how the stimulated neural site interacts both with the object presented and with the stimulation's duration.

With stimulation at a certain site alone, the chicken displays only restless behavior. When a fist is displayed, the same stimulation elicits slightly threatening behavior. When the display switches from a fist to a stuffed polecat, the chicken responds with vigorous threats. Finally, with continued stimulation in the presence of the polecat, the chicken flees, screeching.

Such experiments show that producing complex patterns of adaptive behavior is an important brainstem function. These adaptive patterns include movements used in eating and drinking and in sexual behavior. Animals can be induced to display survival-related behaviors when certain brainstem areas are stimulated. An animal can even be induced to eat nonfood objects, such as chips of wood, if the part of the brainstem that triggers chewing is stimulated.

Grooming illustrates how the brainstem coordinates complex action patterns (Kalueff et al., 2016). A grooming rat sits back on its haunches, licks its paws, wipes its nose with its paws, wipes its paws across its face, and finally turns to lick the fur on its body. These movements are always performed in the same order, from the face to the shoulders and then toward the rear of the body.

The next time you dry off after a shower or swimming, note the grooming sequence you use. Humans' grooming pattern is very similar to the one rats use.

In addition to controlling grooming, the brainstem is also important for maintaining posture, standing upright, coordinating limb movements, swimming and walking, and making nests. The effects of damage to brainstem regions that organize many adaptive movements can be seen in the effects of **locked-in syndrome**, similar to those Scott Mackler experienced in connection with ALS (see Research Focus 11-1; also see Section 1-1). A patient with locked-in syndrome is aware and awake but cannot move or communicate verbally because nearly all voluntary muscles except those of the eyes are completely paralyzed.

The effects of brainstem damage on behavior can also be seen in **cerebral palsy (CP)**, a disorder primarily of motor function, in which making voluntary movements becomes difficult, while many aspects of conscious behavior controlled by the cortex may remain intact. CP is often caused by brainstem trauma before or shortly after birth. As described in Clinical Focus 11-2, Cerebral Palsy, trauma leading to cerebral palsy can sometimes happen in early infancy as well.

locked-in syndrome Condition in which a patient is aware and awake but cannot move or communicate verbally because of complete paralysis of all voluntary muscles except the eyes.

cerebral palsy (CP) Group of disorders that result from brain damage acquired perinatally (at or near birth).

Clinical Focus 4-4 details ALS.

Cerebral Palsy

E. S. had a cold and infection when he was about 6 months old. Subsequently, he had great difficulty coordinating his movements. As he grew up, his hands and legs were almost useless, and his speech was extremely difficult to understand. E. S. was considered intellectually disabled and spent most of his childhood in a custodial school.

When E. S. was 13 years old, the school bought a computer. One teacher attempted to teach E. S. to use it by pushing the keys with a pencil held in his mouth. Within a few weeks, the teacher realized that E. S. could communicate and complete school assignments on the computer. He eventually received a motorized wheelchair that he could control with finger movements of his right hand.

Assisted by the computer and the wheelchair, E. S. attended college, where he became a student leader. He graduated with a degree in psychology, became a social worker, and now works with children with cerebral palsy.

William Little, an English physician, first noticed in 1853 that difficult or abnormal births could lead to later motor difficulties in children. The disorder that Little described was cerebral palsy (also called *Little disease*), a group of disorders that result from brain damage acquired perinatally (at or near birth). Cerebral palsy is common, with an incidence estimated to be 1.5 in every 1000 births. Among babies who weigh less than 2.5 kilograms (5.5 pounds) at birth, the incidence is higher—about 10 in 1000.

The most common causes of cerebral palsy are birth injury, especially due to *anoxia* (lack of oxygen), and genetic defects. Anoxia may result from a defect in the placenta, the organ that allows oxygen and nutrients to pass from mother to child in utero, or it may be caused by a tangled umbilical cord that reduces the oxygen supply to the infant during birth. Other causes include infections, hydrocephalus, seizures, and prematurity. All may produce a defect in the immature brain before, during, or just after birth.

Children with cerebral palsy may appear healthy in the first few months of life, but as the nervous system develops, motor disturbances become noticeable. Common symptoms include spasticity, an exaggerated contraction of muscles when they are stretched; dyskinesia, involuntary extraneous movements such as tremors and uncontrollable jerky twists (athetoid movements); and rigidity, or resistance to passive movement. The affected person may be confined to a wheelchair.

To examine the relationship between brain development and susceptibility to brain injury, investigators can use an MRI-derived baby connectome that maps a baby's changing brain connections during development. This connectome gives a comprehensive map of the structural connectivity (the physical wiring) of the baby's brain. The baby connectome can reveal developmental abnormalities in brain connections, such as those indicative of cerebral palsy, at very early ages, thus expanding the time window to initiate therapeutic strategies (Ballester-Plané et al., 2017).

Courtesy of The Medical University of South Carolina

Many people with cerebral palsy have successful professional careers, including Dr. John Melville, who operates his wheel chair with finger movements of his right hand.

Christopher Reeve (left) portraying Superman in 1984 and (right) in 2004, 9 years after his spinal cord injury.

Scratch reflex

Spinal Cord: Executing Movement

The late actor Christopher Reeve, who portrayed Superman in three 1980s films, was thrown from a horse during a riding competition in 1995. Reeve's spinal cord was severed near its upper end, at the C1–C2 level (see the Spinal Segments and Dermatomes figure in The Basics). The injury left Reeve's brain intact and functioning, and it left his remaining spinal cord intact and functioning, too, but his brain and spinal cord were no longer connected.

Other than head movements and slight movement in his shoulders, Reeve's body was completely paralyzed. He was even unable to breathe without assistance. A century earlier, such a severe injury would have been fatal, but modern and timely medical treatment helped Reeve to survive—and even act in and direct more films—for nearly a decade.

A cut to the cervical region of the spinal cord, such as Christopher Reeve endured, entails paralysis and loss of sensation in the arms and legs, a condition called **quadriplegia**. If the cut is below the cervical nerves, **paraplegia** results: paralysis and loss of sensation are confined to the legs and lower body, as described in Clinical Focus 11-3, Spinal Cord Injury. Christopher Reeve and his late wife Dana founded the Christopher and Dana Reeve Foundation for spinal cord research. It is dedicated to improving the life and function of people with spinal cord–injuries, as well as to searching for cures for spinal cord injury.

Far from being only a relay between the body and brain, the spinal cord contains complex motor programs. A spinal cord patient can walk on a conveyor belt if the body is supported. Indeed, Christopher Reeve was able to walk in a swimming pool, where his body was supported by water.

When a spinal cord injury patient's leg is moved backward on a conveyor belt, causing the foot to lose support, the limb reflexively lifts off the belt and swings forward underneath the body. As the foot touches the surface of the belt again, tactile receptors initiate the reflex that causes the foot to push against the surface and support the body's weight. In this way, several spinal reflexes work together to facilitate the complex movement of walking. Walking's reflexive organization can even be obtained in a premature or newborn baby: when held upright, the baby will perform stepping movements.

Among the complex reflexes observed in other vertebrates is the **scratch reflex**. Here, an animal reflexively scratches a part of its body in response to a stimulus from the body surface. The complexity of the scratch reflex is revealed in the movement's accuracy. Absent the brain's direction, the tip of a limb (usually a hind limb in a quadruped) can be correctly directed to the irritated body part. Typically, itching is the sensation that elicits scratching; it is likely that the sensory receptors on the skin that produce itch evolved for detecting parasites and other foreign objects. We return to itching sensations in Section 11-4.

In humans and other animals whose spinal cord is severed, spinal reflexes still function, even though the spinal cord is cut off from communication with the brain. As a result, the paralyzed limbs may display spontaneous movements or spasms. But the brain can no longer guide the timing of these movements. Consequently, reflexes related to bladder and bowel control may have to be artificially stimulated by caregivers.

quadriplegia Paralysis of the legs and arms due to spinal cord injury.

paraplegia Paralysis of the legs due to spinal cord injury.

scratch reflex Automatic response in which an animal's hind limb reaches to remove a stimulus from the surface of its body.

⊙ CLINICAL FOCUS 11-3

Spinal Cord Injury

Each year, about 11,000 people in the United States and 1000 people in Canada undergo spinal cord injury (as reported by the Foundation for Spinal Cord Injury). Nearly 40 percent of these injuries occur in traffic accidents, and another 40 percent occur as a result of falls. Often the spinal cord is completely severed, leaving an individual with no sensation or movement from the site of the cut downward.

Although 12,000 annual spinal cord injuries may seem like a large number, it is small relative to the number of people in the United States and Canada who undergo other kinds of nervous system damage each year. To increase public awareness of their condition and promote research into possible treatments, some, like Canadian Rick Hansen, have been especially active.

Hansen's paraplegia resulted from a lower thoracic spinal injury in 1975. Twelve years later, to raise public awareness of the potential of people with disabilities and raise money for a spinal cord injury fund, he wheeled himself 40,000 kilometers around the world. The fund contributes to rehabilitation, wheelchair sports, and public awareness programs. It now sponsors the Blusson Spinal Cord Centre in Vancouver, Canada, the largest institution in the world dedicated to spinal cord research, housing over 300 investigators.

Spinal cord injury is usually due to trauma to the cord that results in a number of secondary degenerative processes that increase the size of the lesion. Thereafter, the formation of scar tissue, a cavity, and cysts block communication between the two severed sides. Research on spinal cord injury is directed at minimizing the acute changes that take place after the insult, devising ways to facilitate neural communication across the injury and improving mobility and home care.

Nanotechnology, the science of making and using molecular-sized tools, holds promise for decreasing the acute effects of spinal injury and restoring function. Nanotechnology works with substances between 1 and 100 nanometers (nm) in size. (A nanometer is one-billionth, or 10^{-9}, of a meter.)

Nanotubes or nanovesicles can be engineered to transport drugs, RNA, or new stem cells into the area of injury, where they can arrest degenerative changes and help form neural bridges across the injury. Nanotubes that can carry chemicals or conduct electrical impulses can be threaded into the injury through blood vessels and then into the very small capillaries within the spinal cord. They can also be injected as molecules that self-assemble into scaffolding or tubes when they reach a target area.

Nanoscaffolding, introduced into the injury to form a bridge, can aid the regrowth of axons across the injury. Nanoaxons can be introduced into the region of injury to synapse with neurons on both sides of the injury and to carry messages across the injury. Nanovesicles, small capsules that contain drugs such as nerve growth factors, can be injected to sites of injury to promote cell growth. Because they are small, nano-medicinal substances can interface with spinal cord cells on both sides of an injury (Dalamagkas et al., 2018).

Stacy Pearsall/Getty Images

11-1 Review

Before you continue, check your understanding. Answers to Self-Test appear at the back of the book.

1. The CNS regions and pathways involved in motor control display both a(n) _____ and a(n) _____ arrangement.

2. The _____ cortex plans movements, the _____ cortex organizes movement sequences to carry out the plan, and the _____ cortex executes precise movements.

3. The _____ is responsible for species-typical movements, for survival-related actions, and for posture and walking.

4. In addition to serving as a pathway between the brain and the rest of the body, the _____ independently produces reflexive movements.

5. Explain what happens when the brain is disconnected from the spinal cord and why.

For additional study tools, visit 📖 **LaunchPad** at launchpadworks.com

homunculus Representation of the human body in the sensory or motor cortex; also any topographical representation of the body by a neural area.

Section 4-1 describes the milestones that led to understanding how the nervous system uses electrical charge to convey information.

Figure 10-20 shows Penfield using brain stimulation to map the cortex.

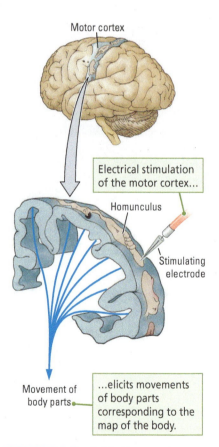

FIGURE 11-6 **Penfield's Homunculus** Movements are topographically organized in M1. Stimulation of dorsal medial regions produces movements in the lower limbs. Stimulation in ventral regions of the cortex produces movements in the upper body, hands, and face.

11-2

Motor System Organization

Although we humans tend to rely primarily on our hands for manipulating objects, we can learn to handle things with other body parts, such as the mouth or a foot, if we have to. Some people without arms become proficient at using a foot for writing or painting or even for driving. What properties of the motor system allow such versatility in carrying out skilled movements? In this section, we examine first the organization of the motor cortex, and then the descending pathways from the motor cortex to the brainstem and spinal cord, and finally the motor neurons that in turn connect with the body's muscles.

Motor Cortex

In 1870, two physicians, Gustav Fritsch and Eduard Hitzig, discovered that they could electrically stimulate the neocortex of an anesthetized dog to produce movements of the mouth, limbs, and paws on the opposite side of the dog's body. They provided the first direct evidence that the neocortex controls movement. Later researchers confirmed the finding with a variety of animal subjects, including rats, monkeys, and apes.

Based on this research background, beginning in the 1930s Wilder Penfield (Penfield & Boldrey, 1958) used electrical stimulation and the effects it produced to map the cortices of conscious human patients who were about to undergo elective neurosurgery. Penfield used his stimulation results to assist in surgery, but because he was stimulating the brain, he kept the intensity and duration of the stimulation to a minimum; consequently, the movements that he produced in his patients were mainly brief twitches. In Section 10-4, we discussed Penfield's work identifying the auditory and speech zones in the cortex.

Mapping the Motor Cortex

Penfield summarized his results by drawing cartoons of body parts to represent the areas of the motor cortex that produce movement in those parts. The result was a **homunculus** (pl. *homunculi*; Latin for "little person") spread out across the primary motor cortex, as illustrated in **Figure 11-6**. Because the body is symmetrical, an equivalent motor homunculus is discernible in the primary motor cortex of each hemisphere, and each motor cortex mainly controls movement in the opposite side of the body. Penfield also identified another, smaller motor homunculus in the dorsal premotor area of each frontal lobe, a region sometimes referred to as the *supplementary motor cortex*.

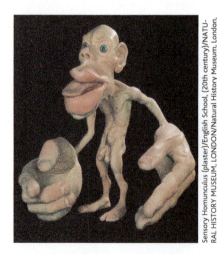

FIGURE 11-7 **Homuncular Human** An artist's representation illustrates the disproportionate areas of the sensory and motor cortices that control different body parts.

Sensory Homunculus (plaster)/English School, (20th century)/NATURAL HISTORY MUSEUM, LONDON/Natural History Museum, London, UK/Bridgeman Images

The striking feature of the homunculus shown in **Figure 11-7** is the relative sizes of the brain regions associated with specific body parts compared with the sizes of actual parts of the human body. The homuncular human has huge hands with an especially large thumb and large lips and tongue. By contrast, the trunk, arms, and legs—most of the area of a real body—are small.

These distortions illustrate that extensive areas of M1 allow precise regulation of the hands, fingers, lips, and tongue (see Figure 11-6). Body areas over which we have relatively little motor control, such as the trunk, have a much smaller representation in the motor cortex.

The homunculus as laid out across the motor cortex is discontinuous—arranged differently from those of an actual body. The cortical area that produces eye movements is in front of the homunculus head on the motor cortex (see the top drawing in Figure 11-6), and the head is oriented with the chin up and the forehead down (bottom drawing). The tongue is below the forehead.

Modeling Movement

The motor homunculus shows at a glance that relatively large areas of the brain control the body parts we use to make the most skilled movements—our hands, mouth, and eyes. This makes it useful for understanding M1's **topographic organization** (functional layout). Debate over how the motor areas represented by Penfield's homunculus might produce movement has been considerable.

An early idea was that each part of the homunculus controls muscles in that part of the body. Information from other cortical regions could be sent to the motor homunculus, and neurons in the appropriate part of the homunculus could then activate body muscles required for producing the movement. If you wanted to pick up a coin, for example, messages from the M1 finger area would instruct the fingers.

More recent experiments using longer durations of electrical stimulation than those used by Penfield suggest that the motor cortex represents not muscles but rather a repertoire of fundamental movement categories (Graziano, 2009). The drawings in **Figure 11-8** illustrate several movement categories produced by longer-duration stimulation; these movements closely resemble those usually used by a monkey. They include (A) ascend, descend, or jump, (B) reach to clasp, (C) defensive posture or expression, (D) hand movement toward the mouth, (E) masticate (chew) or lick, (F) hand movement in central space, and (G) hand movement in distal space. Notice that this map shows that whole-body movements are elicited from the premotor cortex, and more precise hand and mouth movements are elicited from M1. All these movements occur only when the electrical stimulation lasts long enough for the movement to take place.

Each observed movement has the same end, regardless of the starting location of a monkey's limb or its other ongoing behavior. Electrical stimulation that results in the

topographic organization Neural spatial representation of the body or areas of the sensory world perceived by a sensory organ.

FIGURE 11-8 **Natural Movement Categories** Movement categories evoked by electrical stimulation of the monkey cortex and the primary motor and premotor regions from which the categories were elicited. Research from Aflalo & Graziano, 2007.

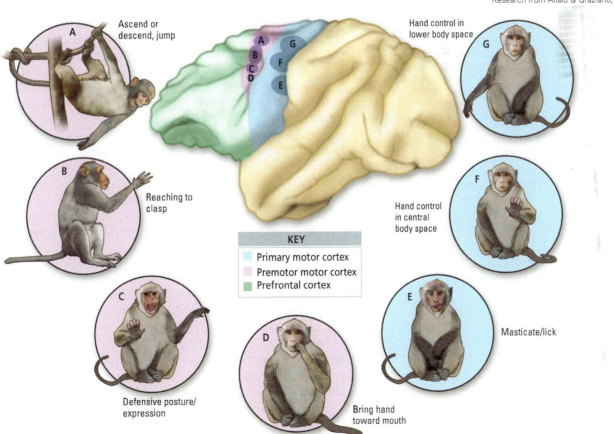

Ascend or descend, jump

Hand control in lower body space

Reaching to clasp

Hand control in central body space

Defensive posture/ expression

Bring hand toward mouth

Masticate/lick

KEY
- Primary motor cortex
- Premotor motor cortex
- Prefrontal cortex

····> **EXPERIMENT 11-2**

Question: How does the motor cortex take part in the control of movement?

Procedure

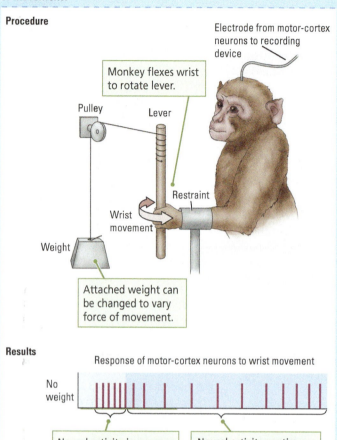

Electrode from motor-cortex neurons to recording device

Monkey flexes wrist to rotate lever.

Pulley

Lever

Restraint

Wrist movement

Weight

Attached weight can be changed to vary force of movement.

Results

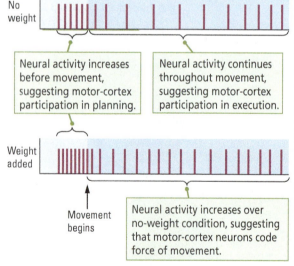

Response of motor-cortex neurons to wrist movement

No weight

Neural activity increases before movement, suggesting motor-cortex participation in planning.

Neural activity continues throughout movement, suggesting motor-cortex participation in execution.

Weight added

Movement begins

Neural activity increases over no-weight condition, suggesting that motor-cortex neurons code force of movement.

Conclusion: The motor cortex takes part in planning movement, executing movement, and adjusting the force and duration of a movement.

Research from Evarts, 1968.

Section 4-4 details the process by which neural activity produces movement.

position-point theory Idea that the motor cortex allows an appropriate body part to be moved to a point in space.

hand coming to the mouth always recruits the hand. If a weight is attached to the monkey's arm, the evoked movement compensates for the added load.

But categorized movements are inflexible: when an obstacle is placed between the hand and the mouth, the hand hits the obstacle. If stimulation continues after the hand has reached the mouth, the hand remains there for the duration of the stimulation. Furthermore, broad movement categories—for example, reaching—cluster together on the motor cortex, but reaching directed to different parts of space is elicited from slightly different cortical points in the topographic reaching map. One explanation of these results is the **position-point theory**, which states that the motor cortex has a map of where parts of the body can be in space so that when a part of the cortex is stimulated, the associated part of the body moves to the appropriate spatial position, regardless of its starting position.

MRI studies on human subjects suggest that the human motor cortex, like the monkey motor cortex, is also organized in terms of functional movement categories (Meier et al., 2008). The motor cortex maps appear to represent basic types of movements that learning and practice can modify. In other words, the motor cortex encodes not muscle twitches but a lexicon, or dictionary, of movements. As with words and sentences, these few movements used in different combinations produce all the movements you are capable of, even in activities as complex as playing basketball.

Motor Cortex and Skilled Movement

In a study designed to investigate how neurons in the motor cortex control movement, Edward Evarts (1968) used the simple procedure illustrated in **Experiment 11-2**. He trained a monkey to flex its wrist to move a bar. Different weights could be attached to the bar. An electrode implanted in the wrist region of the monkey's motor cortex recorded the activity of neurons there.

Evarts discovered that the neurons began to discharge even before the monkey began the movement, as shown in the Results section of Experiment 11-2. Thus, these neurons take part in planning the movement as well as initiating it. The neurons continued to discharge as the wrist moved, confirming that they also play a role in *producing* the movement. Finally, the neurons discharged at a higher rate when the bar was loaded with a weight. This finding shows that motor cortex neurons increase a movement's force by increasing their firing rate and its duration, as stated in the experiment's Conclusion.

Evarts's findings also reveal that the motor cortex has a role in specifying the end point of a movement. Motor cortex neurons in the wrist might have discharged when the monkey flexed its wrist inward but not when the wrist was extended back to its starting position. These on–off neuronal responses are a simple way of coding a desired final position of a movement. In short, not only does Evarts's experiment support the position-point theory, it also shows that movements made to a point in space take into account environmental contingencies, such as whether the limb has to move a load in getting to its destination.

The activity of motor neurons in freely moving monkeys suggests that the neurons, depending on their location, move the body or parts of the body to specific positions (Aflalo & Graziano, 2007). For example, if some neurons are very active when a hand is moved to a specific location, they are progressively less active when the hand is moved away from that position. Thus, the neurons in the motor cortex regions illustrated in Figure 11-8 are responsible for configuring movements that achieve the same end point produced when those same neurons are electrically stimulated.

An interesting study by Schieber (2011) suggests that the same motor cortex neurons involved in planning a movement are also involved in withholding a movement on instruction and in mental imagery. Motor neurons may display subthreshold activity, which is activity not strong enough to produce a movement, suggesting that the neurons may be thinking about the movement or imagining it. Subthreshold activity has been harnessed to allow motor cortex neurons to control brain–computer interfaces while not producing overt movement in the subject (see Research Focus 11-1).

Plasticity in the Motor Cortex

An intimate relationship connects the activity of M1 neurons with movement of the body. The studies just described show that flexibility is part of the relationship. Flexibility underlies another property of the motor cortex: its plasticity, which contributes both to motor learning and to recovery after the motor cortex is damaged, as the following example explains.

A study by Randy Nudo and his coworkers (1996), summarized in the Procedure section of **Experiment 11-3**, illustrates change due to cortical damage. These researchers

Section 14-4 explores how motor maps change in response to learning.

Clinical Focus 2-3 describes motor disruptions that stroke causes; Section 16-3 reviews stroke treatments.

····> **EXPERIMENT 11-3**

Question: What is the effect of rehabilitation on the cortical representation of the forelimb after brain damage?

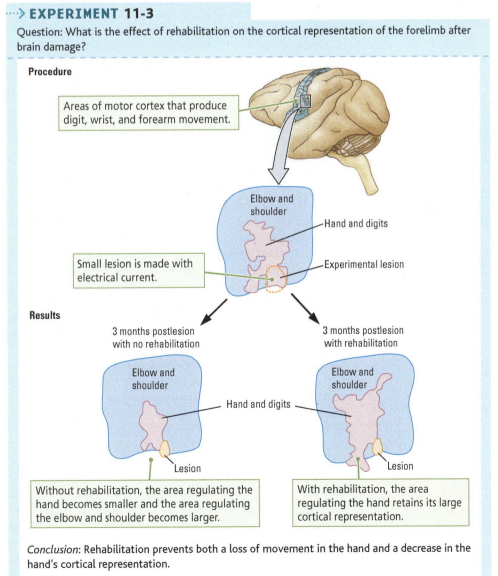

Procedure

Areas of motor cortex that produce digit, wrist, and forearm movement.

Elbow and shoulder

Hand and digits

Small lesion is made with electrical current.

Experimental lesion

Results

3 months postlesion with no rehabilitation

3 months postlesion with rehabilitation

Elbow and shoulder

Hand and digits

Elbow and shoulder

Lesion

Lesion

Without rehabilitation, the area regulating the hand becomes smaller and the area regulating the elbow and shoulder becomes larger.

With rehabilitation, the area regulating the hand retains its large cortical representation.

Conclusion: Rehabilitation prevents both a loss of movement in the hand and a decrease in the hand's cortical representation.

Research Nudo et al., 1996.

constraint-induced therapy Procedure in which restraint of a healthy limb forces a patient to use an impaired limb to enhance recovery of function.

corticospinal tract Bundle of nerve fibers directly connecting the cerebral cortex to the spinal cord, branching at the brainstem into an opposite-side lateral tract that informs movement of limbs and digits and a same-side anterior tract that informs movement of the trunk; also called *pyramidal tract.*

Section 7-1 describes ablation techniques used by neuroscience researchers to manipulate the brain.

FIGURE 11-9 **Left-Hemisphere Corticospinal Tract** Nerve fibers descend from the left-hemisphere motor cortex to the brainstem, where the tract branches into the spinal cord. The lateral tract crosses the brainstem's midline, descending into the right side of the spinal cord to move limb and digit muscles on the body's right side. The anterior tract remains on the left side to move muscles at the body's midline.

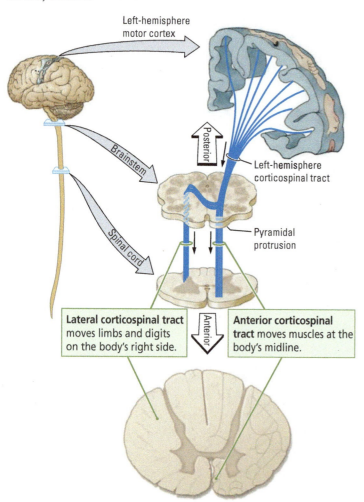

mapped the motor cortices of monkeys to identify the hand and digit areas. They then surgically removed a small part of the cortex that represents the digit area. After undergoing this electrolytic lesion, the monkeys used the affected hand much less, relying mainly on the good hand.

When the researchers stimulated the cortex of the monkeys 3 months later, the animals were unable to produce many lower-arm movements—including movements of the wrist, hand, and digits—that they had produced prior to the lesion. Much of the area representing the hand and lower arm had disappeared from the animals' cortical maps. The shoulder, upper arm, and elbow areas had spread out to take up what had formerly been space representing the hand and digits. The Results section of Experiment 11-3 shows this topographic change.

The experimenters wondered whether the change could have been prevented had they forced the monkeys to use the affected arm. To find out, they used the same procedure on other monkeys, except that during the postsurgery period, they forced the animals to rely on the bad arm by binding the good arm in a sling.

When the experimenters re-examined these monkeys' motor maps 3 months later, they found that the hand and digit area retained its larger size. Even though no neural activity occurred in the spot with the lesion, the monkeys had gained some function in the digits that used to be connected to the damaged spot. Apparently, the remaining cortical digit area was now controlling the movement of these fingers.

Most likely, plasticity is promoted in the formation of new connections and the strengthening of existing connections among different parts of the motor homunculus. Humans who have had a stroke to the motor cortex also display plasticity-mediated recovery. They may at first be completely unable to use their contralateral forelimb, but with time and practice, they may recover a great deal of movement.

As Nudo's monkey experiment illustrates, one way to enhance recovery is to restrain the good limb. **Constraint-induced therapy,** which forces use of the affected limb, is a major therapy for stroke-induced limb paralysis. Its effectiveness depends on frustration of the good limb, which promotes a concerted effort to use the bad limb and promotes neural plasticity (Gillick et al, 2018).

Corticospinal Tracts

The main efferent pathways from the motor cortex to the brainstem to the spinal cord are the **corticospinal tracts.** The axons from these tracts originate mainly in motor cortex layer V pyramidal cells but also extend from the premotor cortex and the sensory cortex (see the Layering in the Neocortex diagram in The Basics). The axons descend into the brainstem, sending collaterals to numerous brainstem nuclei, and eventually emerge on the brainstem's ventral surface, where they form a large bump on each side. These bumps, or pyramids, give the corticospinal tracts their alternative name, the *pyramidal tracts.* These tracts are organized such that the parts that control finger, hand, and arm movements cross from the cortex of one hemisphere to the opposite side of the spinal cord, and the parts that control trunk and shoulder movements do not cross.

The corticospinal axons cross at the pyramids. Some axons descending from the left hemisphere cross over to the right side of the spinal cord. Likewise, some axons descending from the right hemisphere cross over to the left side of the spinal cord. The remaining axons stay on their original side. This division produces two corticospinal tracts, a *lateral corticospinal tract* that is crossed and a *ventral corticospinal tract* that is uncrossed. **Figure 11-9** illustrates the origin of the corticospinal tracts in the left-hemisphere cortex, their division in the brainstem, and their routes as they descend into the spinal cord as two spinal cord tracts.

Motor Neurons

Within the spinal cord, corticospinal fibers make synaptic connections with both interneurons and motor neurons. The interneurons are involved in organizing complex movements, such as movements involving many joints. In addition to whole-body movements such as walking or jumping, the motor neurons can also produce more fractionated movements, such as those used for grasping objects with a hand or the fingers. The motor neurons also carry all nervous system commands out to the muscles. The cross section of a spinal cord in **Figure 11-10** shows the locations of the interneurons and the motor neurons of the spinal cord.

Spinal cord motor neurons are located in the anterior part of the spinal cord, the anterior horns, which jut out from the anterior part of the spinal cord. The anterior horns contain both kinds of motor neurons. Interneurons lie just medial to the motor neurons and project onto them. The motor neurons send their axons to the body muscles. The fibers from the corticospinal tracts make synaptic connections with both the interneurons and the motor neurons, but the motor neurons carry all nervous system commands to the muscles.

Figure 11-10 shows that a homunculus of the body is represented in the spinal cord. The more lateral motor neurons project to muscles that control the fingers and hands, whereas intermediate motor neurons project to muscles that control the arms. The most medial motor neurons project to muscles that control the body's shoulders and trunk. Axons of the lateral corticospinal tract connect mainly with the lateral interneurons and motor neurons, and axons of the anterior corticospinal tract connect mainly to the medial interneurons and motor neurons.

To visualize how the cortical regions responsible for different movements relate to the motor neuron homunculus in the spinal cord, look again at Figure 11-9. Place your finger on the index finger region of the motor homunculus on the left side of the brain. If you trace the axons of the cortical neurons downward, your route takes you through the brainstem, across its midline, and down the right lateral corticospinal tract.

The journey ends at the interneurons and motor neurons in the most lateral region of the spinal cord's right anterior horn—the horn on the opposite (contralateral) side of the nervous system from which you began. Following the axons of these motor neurons, you find that they synapse on muscles that move the right index finger.

If you repeat the procedure by tracing the pathway from the trunk area of the motor homunculus, near the top on the left side of the brain, you follow the same route through the upper part of the brainstem. You do not cross over to the opposite side, however. Instead, you descend into the spinal cord on the left side, the same (ipsilateral) side of the nervous system on which you began, eventually ending up in the most medial interneurons and motor neurons of the left side's anterior horn. (At this point, some of these axons also cross over to the other side of the spinal cord.) Thus, if you follow these motor neuron axons, you end up at their synapses with the muscles that move the trunk on both sides of the body.

This visualization can help you remember the routes taken by motor system axons. The limb regions of the motor homunculus contribute most of their fibers to the lateral corticospinal tract, the fibers that cross over to the opposite side of the spinal cord. They activate motor circuits that move the arm, hand, leg, and foot on the opposite side of the body. In contrast, the trunk regions of the motor homunculus contribute their

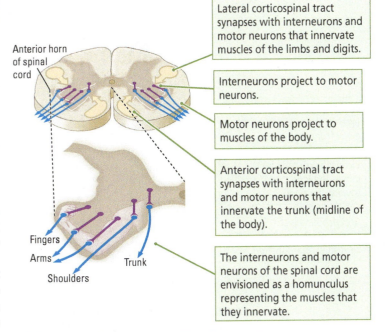

Lateral corticospinal tract synapses with interneurons and motor neurons that innervate muscles of the limbs and digits.

Interneurons project to motor neurons.

Motor neurons project to muscles of the body.

Anterior corticospinal tract synapses with interneurons and motor neurons that innervate the trunk (midline of the body).

The interneurons and motor neurons of the spinal cord are envisioned as a homunculus representing the muscles that they innervate.

Anterior horn of spinal cord

Fingers
Arms
Shoulders
Trunk

FIGURE 11-10 **Motor Tract Organization** Interneurons and motor neurons in the left and right anterior spinal cord tracts are topographically arranged: the more lateral neurons innervate more distal parts of the limbs (those farther from the midline), and the more medial neurons innervate more proximal body muscles (those closer to the midline).

If you are right-handed, the neurons your brain is using to carry out this task are the same neurons that you are tracing.

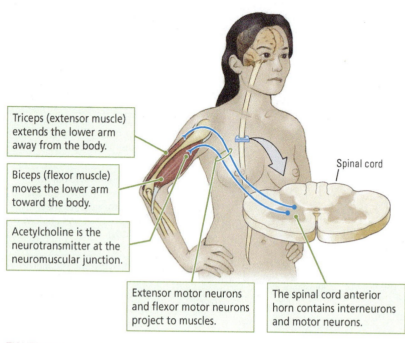

Triceps (extensor muscle) extends the lower arm away from the body.

Biceps (flexor muscle) moves the lower arm toward the body.

Acetylcholine is the neurotransmitter at the neuromuscular junction.

Spinal cord

Extensor motor neurons and flexor motor neurons project to muscles.

The spinal cord anterior horn contains interneurons and motor neurons.

FIGURE 11-11 **Coordinating Muscle Movement**

fibers to the anterior corticospinal tract. Only a few of these fibers cross, close to their termination in the spinal cord; most control the trunk and limbs on the same side of the body.

Remember that the motor cortex is organized in terms of functional movement categories, such as reaching or climbing (see Figure 11-8). A similar template in the spinal cord ensures that instructions from the motor cortex are reproduced faithfully. Presumably, lateral interneurons produce acts of reaching or bringing the hand to the mouth, and the medial interneurons and motor neurons produce whole-body movements, including walking. Recall that a spinal cord isolated from the brain by a cut is still capable of many kinds of movements, and it is able to do so because the movements are organized by its interneurons and motor neurons.

In addition to the corticospinal pathways, about 24 other pathways from the brainstem to the spinal cord carry instructions, such as information related to posture and balance (see Section 11-4), and they control the enteric nervous system as well as portions of the sympathetic division of the ANS. Remember that for all these functions, the motor neurons are the final common path.

Control of Muscles

Spinal cord motor neurons synapse on the muscles that control body movements. For example, the biceps and triceps of the upper arm control movement of the lower arm. Limb muscles are arranged in pairs, as shown in **Figure 11-11**. One member of a pair, the extensor, moves (extends) the limb away from the trunk. The other member of the pair, the flexor, moves (flexes) the limb in toward the trunk. Experiment 11-2 demonstrates the on–off responses of cortical motor neurons, depending on whether the flexor or extensor muscle is being used.

Figure 4-26 illustrates ACh action at a motor neuron–muscle junction.

Connections between spinal cord interneurons and motor neurons ensure that the muscles work together so that when one muscle contracts, the other relaxes. Thus, the spinal cord interneurons and motor neurons not only relay instructions from the brain but also, through their connections, cooperatively organize the movement of many muscles. As you know, the neurotransmitter at the motor neuron–muscle junction is acetylcholine.

11-2 Review

Before you continue, check your understanding. Answers to Self-Test appear at the back of the book.

1. The _____ organization of the motor cortex is represented by a(n) _____, in which parts of the body that are capable of the most skilled movements (especially the mouth, fingers, and thumbs) are regulated by _____ cortical regions.

2. _____ theory states that the motor cortex has a map of where body parts can be in space, such that when a part of the cortex is stimulated, the associated body part moves to an appropriate special position.

3. Many corticospinal-tract fibers cross to the opposite side of the spinal cord to form the _____ tracts; some stay on the same side to form the _____ tracts.

4. The anterior corticospinal tracts carry instructions for _____ movements, whereas the lateral corticospinal tracts carry instructions for _____ and _____ movements.

5. Motor neuron axons in the spinal cord carry instructions to _____ that are arranged in pairs. One _____ a limb; the other _____ the limb.

6. What does the plan of movements in the motor cortex, as revealed by electrical stimulation, tell us about the brain's representation of movement?

For additional study tools, visit ♛ **Launch**Pad at launchpadworks.com

11-3

Basal Ganglia, Cerebellum, and Movement

The main evidence that the basal ganglia and the cerebellum perform motor functions is that damage to either structure impairs movement. Both have extensive connections with the motor cortex, which further suggests their participation in movement. After an overview of each structure's anatomy, we look at some symptoms that arise after damage to the basal ganglia or the cerebellum. Then we consider the roles each structure plays in controlling movement.

Basal Ganglia and the Force of Movement

The neocortex connects extensively with the basal ganglia, a collection of nuclei lying just beneath the cortex, as illustrated in **Figure 11-12**. One function of the basal ganglia is to modulate the activity of cortical motor systems. In doing so, they participate in a wide range of functions, including association or habit learning, motivation, and emotion, as well as motor control.

Anatomy of the Basal Ganglia

Among the nuclei forming the basal ganglia are the *caudate nucleus* and the *putamen*, which together form the *striatum* (meaning "striped body" and named for the fibers, including corticospinal fibers, running through it), and the subthalamic nucleus and globus pallidus. As shown in Figure 11-12, the prominent striatum extends as a tail (*caudate* means "having a tail") into the temporal lobe, ending in the amygdala. With respect to functions of the neocortex, there are three main basal ganglia connections:

1. All areas of the neocortex project to the basal ganglia.

2. The basal ganglia project to the motor cortex via relays in the thalamus.

3. The basal ganglia receive connections from the dopamine cells of the midbrain substantia nigra over the nigrostriatal pathway and also project to the substantia nigra.

Through these connections, the basal ganglia form reciprocal circuits, or loops, connecting all cortical regions to the motor cortex. Other loops connect the basal ganglia and substantia nigra, allowing the substantia nigra to modulate the subcortical–motor cortex loops. Separate loops likely participate in selecting and producing skilled movements for learned actions and emotional expression. Some of these loops' functions are revealed in behavioral deficits that follow damage to the basal ganglia.

How the Basal Ganglia Control Movement Force

Two types of movement disorders—in many ways opposites—result from basal ganglia damage. If cells of the caudate putamen are damaged, unwanted writhing and

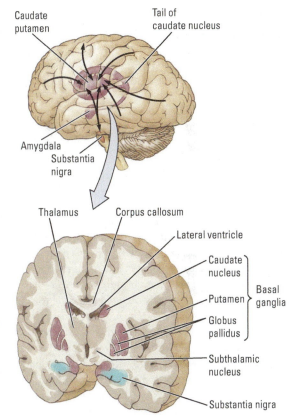

FIGURE 11-12 **Basal Ganglia Connections** The caudate putamen in the basal ganglia connects to the amygdala through the tail of the caudate nucleus. The lateral see-through view shows the basal ganglia relative to surrounding structures, including the substantia nigra, with which it shares reciprocal connections. The basal ganglia receive input from most regions of the cortex and send input into the frontal lobes through the subthalamic nucleus.

Figure 5-18 traces the nigrostriatal pathways in the dopaminergic activating system and highlights their importance for maintaining healthy motor behavior.

Clinical Focus 3-3 describes the genetic basis of Huntington disease.

Detailed coverage of Parkinson disease and its treatment appears in Chapters 5, 7, and 16.

hyperkinetic symptom Excessive involuntary movement, as seen in Tourette syndrome.

hypokinetic symptom Paucity of movement, as seen in Parkinson disease.

twitching movements called *dyskinesias* result. In Huntington disease, for example, characterized by involuntary, exaggerated, and disjointed movements, striatal cells are destroyed. Other involuntary movements related to striatal damage are the unwanted tics and vocalizations peculiar to the topic of Clinical Focus 11-4, Tourette Syndrome.

In addition to causing involuntary movements, or **hyperkinetic symptoms**, as just described, basal ganglia damage can result in a loss of control over motor ability, or **hypokinetic symptoms** that feature rigidity and difficulty initiating and producing voluntary movements. Parkinson disease is marked by hypokinetic symptoms caused by the loss of dopamine cells in the substantia nigra that project into the basal ganglia.

The fact that either hyperkinetic or hypokinetic symptoms arise after to basal ganglia damage suggests that one function of these nuclei is regulating movement force. The idea is that hyperkinetic disorders such as Huntington disease result from errors of too much force and so result in excessive movement. Hypokinetic disorders such as Parkinson disease result from errors of too little force and so result in insufficient movement.

In support of these ideas, in studies involving a reaching task, Huntington subjects reached using too much force, thus seemingly flinging a limb. Parkinson subjects reached with too little force, thus producing slowed movement (Moisello et al., 2011).

◎ CLINICAL FOCUS 11-4

Tourette Syndrome

The neurological disorder Tourette syndrome (TS) was first described in 1885 by Georges Gilles de la Tourette, a French neurologist, who described the symptoms as they appeared in one of his patients. When she was 7, Miss D. was afflicted with convulsive movements of the hands and arms. These abnormal tics frequently occurred when she tried to write, causing her to make poorly formed letters. After a tic, her movements were well controlled until another convulsive movement occurred. At first, she was thought to be acting out, and she was reprimanded. Eventually it became clear that the movements were involuntary. The movements involved the shoulders and the neck and were accompanied by facial grimaces. By the time she was 26, the tics began to include her speech, and she made strange cries and said words that made no sense.

The statistical incidence of Tourette syndrome is about 1 in 1000 people. TS affects all racial groups and seems to be hereditary, and the age range of onset is 2 to 25 years.

The most frequent symptoms of Tourette syndrome are involuntary tics and complex movements, such as hitting, lunging, or jumping. People with TS may also emit sudden cries and other vocalizations or may inexplicably utter words that do not make sense in the context, including *coprolalia* (uttering vulgar words) and swearing.

Tourette syndrome is thought to reflect an abnormality of the basal ganglia, especially in the right hemisphere, because its symptoms can be controlled with haloperidol, an antipsychotic drug that blocks dopamine synapses in the basal ganglia. Understanding the neural cause is difficult because the condition may be part of a group of disorders that include tics and hyperactivity and that vary widely in their symptoms (Riva et al., 2018).

The urge to make involuntary movements and vocalizations may be similar to behaviors that have an urge-to-action feature, such as the contagious yawning and stretching that often occur after others are observed to display the same behavior. Much of our learning occurs as a result of copying others; frequently, speech habits, mannerisms, and the styles of others can be quickly and unconsciously adopted. This idea has led researchers to suggest that the compulsion associated with conditions such as Tourette syndrome results from activity in brain systems that mediate normal learning by imitation (Brown et al., 2017).

YinYang/E+/Getty Images

We frequently yawn after we see others yawn. The urge-to-action featured in contagious yawning may reflect the activity of neural systems normally devoted to learning by imitation. The urge-to-action symptoms associated with Tourette syndrome may reflect abnormal activity in these neural systems that likely include the basal ganglia.

An MRI study of basal ganglia activity in healthy participants who, for a small monetary reward, considered how much force to apply in a gripping task, showed more basal ganglia activity when they contemplated using a more forceful grip and less activity when contemplating a less forceful grip. Together, these studies suggest that the basal ganglia play a role not just in producing force but also in computing the effortful costs of making movements (Fisher et al., 2017).

What features of the reciprocal basal ganglia loops allow for selecting movements or modulating movement force? The *volume control* theory holds that the basal ganglia can influence whether movement occurs. As illustrated in **Figure 11-13**, a pathway (green) from the thalamus to the cortex to the spinal cord produces movement. The globus pallidus (red) can inhibit this pathway at the level of the thalamus.

The globus pallidus is controlled by two basal ganglia pathways, one indirect and one direct. If the globus pallidus is excited, it in turn inhibits the thalamus and blocks movement. If it is inhibited, motor cortex circuits that include the thalamus are able to produce movement. Thus, the globus pallidus thus acts like a volume control. If it is turned down, movement can occur; if it is turned up, movement is blocked. This model proposes that diseases of the basal ganglia affecting its "volume control" function impair movement so that it is either excessive or slowed. This model also suggests that it is through this volume control mechanism that we make choices, selecting goals that we think may benefit us while rejecting less optimal options (Hikosaka et al., 2018).

The idea that the globus pallidus acts like a volume control is the basis for several treatments for Parkinson disease. Consistent with the volume control theory, recordings made from globus pallidus cells of Parkinson disease patients shows that their activity is excessive, and likely accounts for the patients' difficulty in moving. If the globus pallidus or the subthalamic nucleus (a relay in the indirect pathway) is partially surgically destroyed in these Parkinson patients, muscular rigidity is reduced, and normal movement is improved. Similarly, deep brain stimulation (DBS) of the globus pallidus inactivates it, freeing movement.

Interestingly, impairments in the application of force may underlie motor disorders of skilled movements such as writer's cramp, drumming cramp, and gaming keyboard cramp—impairments in hand movement, called *selective dystonias*, that stem from engaging in repetitive tasks. One such impairment, the yips, is distorted execution of skilled movements by professional athletes. For example, the yips may end the career of a professional golfer by ruining the player's swing (van Wensen & van de Warrenburg, 2018).

Another structure in the basal ganglia, the nucleus accumbens, is also called the ventral striatum because it is the most ventral basal ganglia nucleus. The nucleus accumbens receives projections from dopamine cells of the ventral tegmental area, a nucleus just medial to the substantia nigra in the midbrain. Called the mesolimbic dopamine (DA) pathway (see **Figure 11-14**), it is part of a loop that aids our perception of cues signaling reward and is related to drug addiction, a topic discussed in Chapter 6.

Cerebellum and Movement Skill

Musicians have a saying: "Miss a day of practice and you're okay, miss two days and you notice, miss three days and the world notices." Apparently, changes take place in the brain when we practice or neglect to practice a motor skill. The cerebellum may be the affected component of the motor system. Whether the skill is playing a musical instrument, pitching a baseball, or texting, the cerebellum is critical for acquiring and maintaining motor skills.

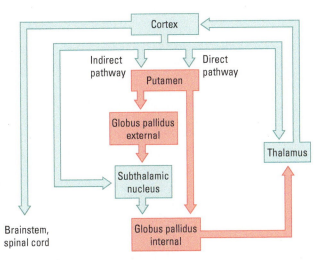

FIGURE 11-13 **Regulating Movement Force** Two pathways in the basal ganglia modulate movements produced in the cortex. Green pathways are excitatory; red are inhibitory. The indirect pathway excites the globus pallidus internal, whereas the direct pathway has an inhibitory effect. If activity in the indirect pathway dominates, the thalamus shuts down, and the cortex is unable to produce movement. If direct-pathway activity dominates, the thalamus can become overactive, amplifying movement. Information from Alexander & Crutcher, 1990.

Figure 1-3 shows electrodes implanted in the brain for DBS.

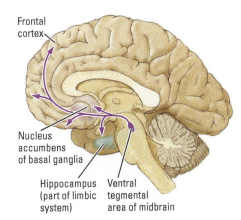

FIGURE 11-14 **Mesolimbic DA Pathway** The mesolimbic DA pathway (purple projections from ventral tegmentum) is a substrate not only of reward but of addictive behavior as well. See Section 6-4.

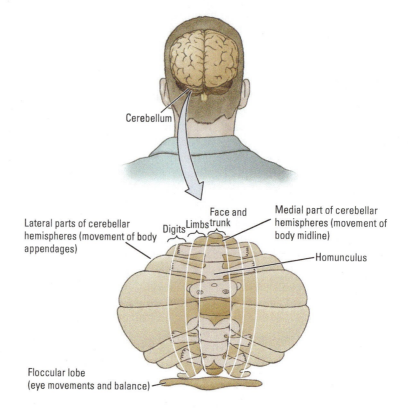

FIGURE 11-15 **Cerebellar Homunculus** The cerebellar hemispheres control body movements, and the flocculus controls eye movements and balance. In the cerebellum's topographical organization, relatively medial parts represent the body's midline, and relatively lateral parts represent the limbs and digits.

The elephant's cerebellum, by contrast, contains 97.5 percent of its neurons. Details in Comparative Focus 1-3.

Anatomy of the Cerebellum

The cerebellum sits atop the brainstem, clearly visible just behind the cerebrum, and like the cerebrum, it is divided into two hemispheres (**Figure 11-15**). A small lobe, the flocculus, projects from its ventral, or inferior, surface. The cerebellum makes up about 10 percent of the mammalian brain, but it contains about four times as many neurons as does the cortex and is distinctive in having many more folds than does the cerebral cortex.

As Figure 11-15 shows, the cerebellum can be divided into several regions, each specialized for an aspect of motor control. At its base, the flocculus receives projections from the middle ear vestibular system (described in Section 11-4) and takes part in controlling balance. Many projections from the flocculus go to the spinal cord and to the motor nuclei that control eye movements.

Just as the motor cortex has a homuncular organization and multiple homunculi, the cerebellar hemispheres have at least two, as shown in Figure 11-15. The medial part of each homunculus controls the face and the body's midline. The more lateral parts connect to motor cortex areas associated with movements of the limbs, hands, feet, and digits. Pathways from the cerebellar hemispheres project to nuclei at the interface of the cerebellum and spinal cord. These in turn project to other brain regions, including the motor cortex.

To summarize the cerebellum's topographic organization, the trunk of the homunculus is represented in its central part; the limbs and digits are represented in the lateral parts. Tumors or damage to midline areas of the cerebellum disrupt balance, eye movement, upright posture, and walking but do not substantially disrupt other movements, such as reaching, grasping, and using the fingers. A person with medial damage to the cerebellum may, when lying down, show few symptoms. Damage to lateral parts of the cerebellum disrupts arm, hand, and finger movements much more than movements of the body's trunk.

The arrangement and connections of the cerebellum are built to a common plan. The cerebellar cortex consists of three layers of cells, with the distinctive Purkinje cells forming the second layer. Purkinje cells are the output cells of the cerebellum. This plan suggests that the cerebellum has a common function with respect to its control over other motor system regions.

Ramón y Cajal's drawing of a Purkinje cell, circa 1900.

How the Cerebellum Improves Movement Control

Attempts to understand how the cerebellum controls movement have focused on movement timing. The cerebellum can time movement through its connections with each region of the neocortex, such that different regions of the cerebellum participate in the timing of different behaviors. We have a great deal of difficulty producing two different movements at the same time—for example, tapping our head with one hand and making a circular movement on the chest with the other hand. If we synchronize the rhythm of the two movements, the action is much easier. Such synchronization of the timing of movements may be a function of the cerebellum.

Tom Thach (2007), in an intriguing experiment, illustrates how the cerebellum times movements to keep them accurate. Control participants and subjects with cerebellar damage threw darts at a target, as shown in the Procedure section of **Experiment 11-4**. After a number of throws that allowed them to become reasonably accurate, both groups donned glasses containing wedge-shaped prisms that displaced the apparent location of the target to the left. Now when they threw a dart, it landed to the left of the intended target.

····> **EXPERIMENT 11-4**

Question: Does the cerebellum help make adjustments required to keep movements accurate?

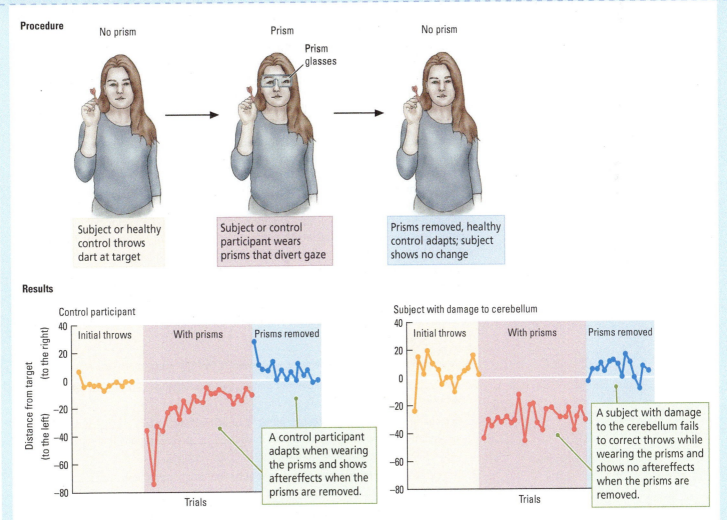

Procedure

No prism — Prism — No prism

Prism glasses

Subject or healthy control throws dart at target

Subject or control participant wears prisms that divert gaze

Prisms removed, healthy control adapts; subject shows no change

Results

Control participant

Distance from target (to the right) / (to the left)

Initial throws — With prisms — Prisms removed

A control participant adapts when wearing the prisms and shows aftereffects when the prisms are removed.

Trials

Subject with damage to cerebellum

Initial throws — With prisms — Prisms removed

A subject with damage to the cerebellum fails to correct throws while wearing the prisms and shows no aftereffects when the prisms are removed.

Trials

Conclusion: Many movements we make depend on moment-to-moment learning and adjustments made by the cerebellum.

Information from Thach et al., 1992.

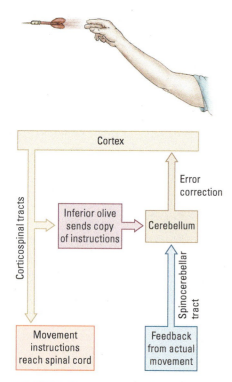

FIGURE 11-16 **Intention, Action, and Feedback** By comparing the message for the intended movement with the movement that was actually performed, the cerebellum sends an error message to the cortex to improve the accuracy of a subsequent movement.

Both groups showed this initial distortion in aim. But then came an important difference, graphed in the Results section of Experiment 11-4. When controls saw the dart miss the mark, they adjusted each successive throw until reasonable accuracy was restored. In contrast, subjects with cerebellar damage could not correct for this error. Time after time, they missed the target far to the left.

Next, the controls removed the prism glasses and threw a few more darts. Again, a significant difference emerged. The first dart thrown by each participant was much too far to the right (due to the previous adjustment they had learned to make), but soon each one adjusted once again until his or her former accuracy was regained.

In contrast, subjects with damage to the cerebellum showed no aftereffects of wearing the prisms; they had never compensated for the glasses to begin with. This experiment suggests that many movements we make—whether throwing a dart, organizing a movement sequence to shoot a basketball, or even timing our social and emotional behaviors—depend on moment-to-moment adjustments made by the cerebellum (Guell et al., 2018).

To better understand how the cerebellum improves motor skills by timing movements, consider the model charted in **Figure 11-16**. Imagine throwing a dart. You aim at the bull's-eye, throw the dart, and find that it misses the board completely. You aim again, this time adjusting your throw to correct for the original error. The model illustrates that there are actually two versions of your action: (1) the movement you intended to make and (2) the actual movement, as recorded by sensory receptors in your arm and shoulder. If you carry out the intended movement successfully, you need make no correction on your next try. But if you miss, and you frequently will, an adjustment is called for.

The model illustrates that the cortex sends instructions to the spinal cord to throw a dart at the target. A copy of the same instructions is sent to the cerebellum through the *inferior olive*, a nucleus in the brainstem that projects to the cerebellum. Then, when you throw the dart, the sensory receptors in your arm and shoulder code the actual movement you make and send a message about it back to the cerebellum through the spinocerebellar tract. The cerebellum now has information about both versions of the movement—what you intended to do and what you actually did—and can calculate the error and inform the cortex about how to correct the movement. When you next throw a dart, you incorporate the correction into your throw. If the cerebellum is damaged, the ability to correct errors by comparing intended and actual movements is impaired (Therrien & Bastian, 2015).

We can imagine that all of our behavior, even our social behavior, involves a learning process that is similar to dart throwing. We experiment to gauge the effect of our actions on others and, depending on the outcome, we modify our future behavior. The impairments in social skills in autism spectrum disorder may be related to reduced experimentation with social skills (Casartelli et al., 2017).

11-3 Review

Before you continue, check your understanding. Answers to Self-Test appear at the back of the book.

1. The _____ contribute to motor control by adjusting the _____ associated with each movement.

2. Damage to the basal ganglia results either in unwanted involuntary _____ movements (too much force exerted) or in such _____ rigidity that movements are difficult to perform (too little force exerted).

3. The cerebellum contributes to motor control by improving movement _____ and the learning of motor _____.

4. Describe how the cerebellum improves execution of motor skills.

For additional study tools, visit **LaunchPad** at launchpadworks.com

11-4

Somatosensory System Receptors and Pathways

The motor system produces movement, but without sensation, movement would lack direction and would quickly become impaired. The somatosensory system is indispensable for this guidance. The body senses tell us about the physical contact we make with the world, as well as how successful our physical interactions with the world are.

Somatic sensation is unique among sensory systems. It is distributed throughout the body, not localized in the head, as are vision, hearing, taste, and smell. Somatosensory receptors in the skin, muscles, and internal organs, including the circulatory system, feature specialized dendritic attachments on sensory neurons—or the dendrites themselves are the sensory receptors. Somatosensory neurons convey information to the spinal cord and brain. Only one part of the system is confined to a single organ. The inner ear houses the vestibular system, which contributes to our sensations of balance and head movement.

In considering the motor system, we started at the cortex and followed the motor pathways out to the spinal cord (review Figures 11-9 and 11-10). This efferent route follows the outward flow of neural instructions regarding movement. As we explore the somatosensory system, we proceed in the opposite direction because afferent sensory information flows inward, from the body's sensory receptors through sensory pathways in the spinal cord to the cortex.

Principle 7: Sensory and motor divisions permeate the nervous system.

Somatosensory Receptors and Perception

Our body is covered with somatosensory receptors, including body hair, which is attached to the dendrites of sensory neurons. Many receptor types are embedded in surface skin, in deeper layers of the skin, and in muscles, tendons, and joints. Some receptors consist simply of a sensory neuron dendrite. Others are specialized capsules or connective tissue surrounding a dendrite, and still others include a dendrite attached to the base of a hair.

The density of somatosensory receptors varies greatly throughout the body and determines sensitivity to stimulation. Body parts that are highly sensitive to touch—including the hands, feet, lips, and tongue—have far more sensory receptors than less sensitive body parts—the arms, back, and legs.

Humans have two kinds of skin, hairy skin and glabrous skin. **Glabrous skin**, which includes the lips, tongue, and palms of the hands and feet, is hairless and exquisitely sensitive to a wide range of stimuli. It covers the body parts that we use to explore objects.

The skin's touch sensitivity can be measured with a two-point sensitivity test. By touching the skin with two sharp points simultaneously, we can observe how close together the points can be placed while still being detected by the participant as two points rather than one. On glabrous skin, we can detect the two points when they are as close as 3 millimeters apart.

On hairy skin, two-point sensitivity is weaker by a factor of about 10. The two points seem to merge into one below a separation distance ranging from 2 to 5 cm, depending on the exact body part tested. You can confirm these differences in sensitivity on your own body by touching two sharp pencil points to a palm and to a forearm, varying the distances between the two points. Be sure not to look as you touch each surface.

Two-point sensitivity test

Classifying Somatosensory Receptors

The varied types of somatosensory receptors in the human body may total as many as 20 or more, but they can all be classified into the three functional groupings, illustrated in **Figure 11-17**: perceptions of irritation, pressure, or movement.

glabrous skin Skin that does not have hair follicles but contains larger numbers of sensory receptors than do hairy skin areas.

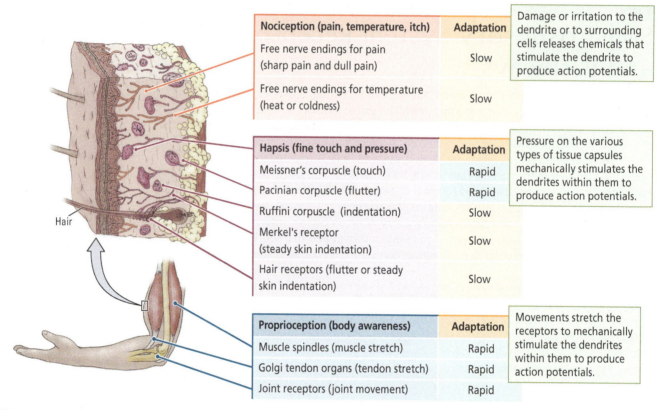

Nociception (pain, temperature, itch)	Adaptation	Damage or irritation to the dendrite or to surrounding cells releases chemicals that stimulate the dendrite to produce action potentials.
Free nerve endings for pain (sharp pain and dull pain)	Slow	
Free nerve endings for temperature (heat or coldness)	Slow	

Hapsis (fine touch and pressure)	Adaptation	Pressure on the various types of tissue capsules mechanically stimulates the dendrites within them to produce action potentials.
Meissner's corpuscle (touch)	Rapid	
Pacinian corpuscle (flutter)	Rapid	
Ruffini corpuscle (indentation)	Slow	
Merkel's receptor (steady skin indentation)	Slow	
Hair receptors (flutter or steady skin indentation)	Slow	

Proprioception (body awareness)	Adaptation	Movements stretch the receptors to mechanically stimulate the dendrites within them to produce action potentials.
Muscle spindles (muscle stretch)	Rapid	
Golgi tendon organs (tendon stretch)	Rapid	
Joint receptors (joint movement)	Rapid	

FIGURE 11-17 **Somatosensory Receptors** Perceptions derived from the body senses of nociception, hapsis, and proprioception depend on various receptors in various parts of the skin, muscles, joints, and tendons.

Figure 4-25 illustrates the cellular processes at work in a sensory neuron dendrite when a touch receptor is activated.

nociception Perception of pain, temperature, and itch.

hapsis Perceptual ability to discriminate objects on the basis of touch.

proprioception Perception of the position and movement of the body, limbs, and head.

rapidly adapting receptor Body sensory receptor that responds briefly to the onset of a stimulus on the body.

IRRITATION Nociception is the perception of pain, temperature, or itch. Most nociceptors are free nerve endings, the tips of sensory neuron dendrites, as diagrammed at the top of Figure 11-17. When damaged or irritated, these endings secrete chemicals, usually peptides, that stimulate the nerve to produce an action potential. The action potential then conveys a message about pain, temperature, or itch to the central nervous system.

PRESSURE Hapsis (from the Greek for "touch") is the ability to discriminate objects on the basis of touch. Haptic receptors enable us to perceive fine touch and pressure and to identify objects that we touch and grasp. Haptic receptors occupy both superficial and deep skin layers and are attached to body hairs as well.

As diagrammed in the center of Figure 11-17, haptic receptors consist of a dendrite attached to a hair, to connective tissue, or to a dendrite encased in a capsule of tissue. Mechanical stimulation of the hair, tissue, or capsule activates touch-sensitive Na^+ ion channels on the dendrite, which in turn initiate an action potential. Differences in the tissue forming the capsule determine the kinds of mechanical energy transduced by the haptic receptor to the nerve. For example, pressure that squeezes the capsule of a Pacinian corpuscle is the necessary stimulus for initiating an action potential conveying pressure information. Displacement of a hair is a necessary stimulus for initiating action potentials conveying some other types of touch information.

MOVEMENT Proprioception, or body awareness, is the perception of body location and movement. Proprioceptors are encapsulated nerve endings that are sensitive to the stretch of muscles and tendons and the movement of joints. In the Golgi tendon organ shown at the bottom of Figure 11-17, for instance, an action potential is triggered when the tendon moves, stretching the receptor attached to it.

Duration of Receptor Response

Somatosensory receptors are specialized to tell us when a sensory event occurs, when it stops occurring, and/or whether it is still occurring. Information about when a stimulus occurs is handled mainly by **rapidly adapting receptors**, which activate neurons when stimulation begins and when it ends. As shown in Figure 11-17, haptic receptors that respond to touch (Meissner corpuscles), to fluttering sensations (Pacinian corpuscles), and to vibration (Ruffini corpuscles) are all rapidly adapting receptors.

In contrast, **slowly adapting receptors** activate neurons as long as a sensory event is present: they detect whether a stimulus is still occurring. For instance, after you have put on an article of clothing and become accustomed to how it feels, only slowly adapting haptic receptors (such as Merkel receptors and hair receptors) remain active.

The difference between a rapidly adapting receptor and a slowly adapting receptor rests on two factors: how the receptor is stimulated and how the ion channels in the membrane of its dendrite respond to mechanical stimulation. The stimulation may be sharp or cold, fluttery or deep, a stretch or a swerve.

Posterior Root Ganglion Neurons

The dendrites that carry somatosensory information into the CNS belong to neurons whose cell body is just outside the spinal cord in posterior root ganglia. Their axons enter the spinal cord. As illustrated in **Figure 11-18**, such a posterior root ganglion neuron contains a single long dendrite. Only the tip is responsive to sensory stimulation. This dendrite is continuous with the neuron's axon, which enters the spinal cord. The somatosensory cell body sits to one side of this long pathway.

Every spinal cord segment is flanked by a posterior root ganglion that contains many types of neurons. Each type responds to a particular kind of somatosensory information. Within the spinal cord, the axons of posterior root ganglion neurons may synapse with other neurons or continue to the brain or do both.

The axons of posterior root ganglion neurons vary in diameter and myelination. These structural features are related to the kind of information the neurons carry. Proprioceptive information (location and movement) and haptic information (touch and pressure) are carried by posterior root ganglion neurons that have large, well-myelinated axons. Nociceptive information (pain, temperature, itch) is mainly carried by posterior root ganglion neurons that have smaller axons with little or no myelin.

Because of their size and myelination, the larger neurons carry information faster than the smaller neurons do. One possible reason proprioceptive and haptic neurons are designed to carry messages quickly is that their information requires rapid response. Imagine that you've touched a hot stove. A myelinated pain fiber activates and instructs the hand to withdraw quickly. A nonmyelinated pain fiber, less hurried, will let you know for some time afterward that your finger has been burned.

slowly adapting receptor Body sensory receptor that responds as long as a sensory stimulus is on the body.

Myelin is the fatty coating around axons, formed by glial cells, that speeds neurotransmission. See Section 3-1.

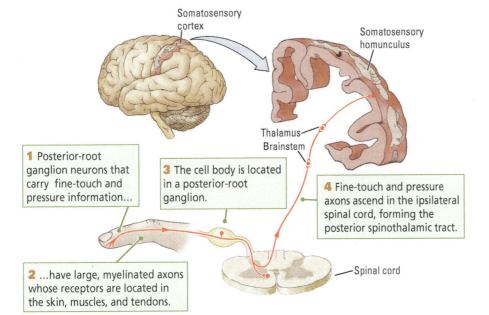

1 Posterior-root ganglion neurons that carry fine-touch and pressure information...

2 ...have large, myelinated axons whose receptors are located in the skin, muscles, and tendons.

3 The cell body is located in a posterior-root ganglion.

4 Fine-touch and pressure axons ascend in the ipsilateral spinal cord, forming the posterior spinothalamic tract.

Somatosensory cortex

Somatosensory homunculus

Thalamus
Brainstem

Spinal cord

FIGURE 11-18 **Haptic Neuron of the Posterior Root Ganglion** The dendrite and axon of this neuron of the posterior root ganglion, which are contiguous, carry sensory information from the skin to the CNS. These large, myelinated ganglionic axons travel up the spinal cord to the brain in the posterior column, whereas the small axons synapse with neurons whose axons cross the spinal cord and ascend on the other side (shown in Figure 11-20).

deafferentation Loss of incoming sensory input, usually due to damage to sensory fibers; also loss of any afferent input to a structure.

Disruption of Posterior Root Ganglion Function

We can support the claim that sensory information is essential for movement by describing what happens when posterior root ganglion cells do not function. A clue comes from a visit to the dentist. If you have ever had the area around a tooth numbed for dental work, you have felt the strange effect of losing sensation on one side of your face. Not only do you lose pain perception but you also seem to lose the ability to move your facial muscles properly, making it awkward to talk and smile and downright dangerous to chew. Similarly, if your mouth or hands become terribly cold, disrupting receptor function, talking or making hand movements becomes difficult. So even though only the sensory nerves are blocked, movement is affected as well.

In much the same way, sensory nerve damage affects both sensory perceptions and motor abilities. John Rothwell and his colleagues (1982) described a patient, G. O., who had undergone **deafferentation** (had lost afferent sensory fibers) because of a disease that destroyed somatosensory posterior root ganglion neurons. G. O. received no sensory input from his hands. He could not, for example, feel when his hand was holding something.

However, G. O. could still accurately produce a range of finger movements, and he could outline figures in the air even with his eyes closed. He could also move his thumb accurately through different distances and at different speeds, judge weights, and match movement force. Nevertheless, his hands were relatively useless to him in daily life. Although G. O. could drive his old car, he was unable to learn to drive a new one. He was also unable to write, fasten shirt buttons, or hold a cup.

G. O. began movements quite normally, but as he proceeded, the movement patterns gradually fell apart, ending in failure. Part of G. O.'s difficulties lay in maintaining muscle force for any time. When he tried to carry a suitcase, he would quickly drop it unless he continually looked down to confirm that he was carrying it. Clearly, although only G. O.'s sensory neurons were damaged, he also had severe motor disability, including inability to learn new motor skills, and a cognitive disability in learning new motor skills.

Disruption of Body Awareness

Oliver Sacks's research informed scientific understanding of conditions as diverse as Parkinson disease (Clinical Focus 5-3 and Section 16-3), ventral visual stream injury (Section 9-5), and thinking (Section 15-1).

Movement abnormalities also result from more selective damage to neurons that carry proprioceptive information about body location and movement. Neurologist Oliver Sacks (1998) gives a dramatic example in his description of a patient, Christina, whose proprioceptive sensory fibers throughout her body were damaged after she took megadoses of vitamin B₆. Christina was left with little ability to control her movements and spent most of each day lying prone. Here is how she describes what a loss of proprioception means:

> "What I must do then," she said slowly, "is use vision, use my eyes, in every situation where I used—what do you call it?—proprioception before. I've already noticed," she added, musingly, "that I may lose my arms. I think they are in one place, and I find they're in another. This proprioception is like the eyes of the body, the way the body sees itself. And if it goes, as it's gone with me, it's like the body's blind. My body can't see itself if it's lost its eyes, right? So I have to watch it—be its eyes." (Sacks, 1998, p. 46)

Clearly, Christina's motor system is intact, but with no sense of where in space her body is and what it is doing, she is almost completely immobilized. Jonathan Cole (1995) described the now classic case of Ian Waterman, who lost proprioception after a presumed viral infection at age 19. He is the only person to have learned how to move again, and this relearning took years. All his regained movement was mediated by vision; if he lost focus or closed his eyes, he would collapse. He managed to replace the "eyes of his body" with visual control of his movements.

Somatosensory Pathways to the Brain

As the axons of somatosensory neurons enter the CNS in the spinal cord, they divide, forming two pathways to the brain. The haptic-proprioceptive axons for touch and

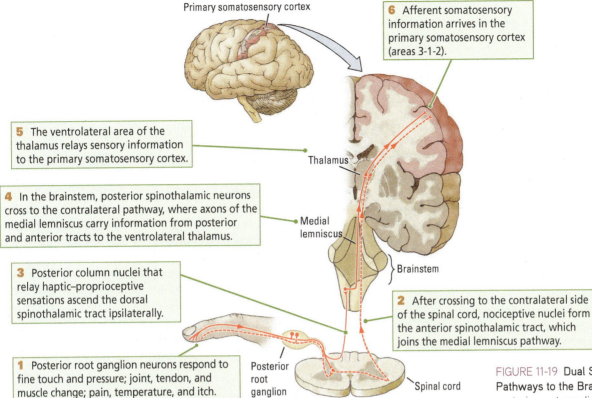

Primary somatosensory cortex

6 Afferent somatosensory information arrives in the primary somatosensory cortex (areas 3-1-2).

5 The ventrolateral area of the thalamus relays sensory information to the primary somatosensory cortex.

Thalamus

4 In the brainstem, posterior spinothalamic neurons cross to the contralateral pathway, where axons of the medial lemniscus carry information from posterior and anterior tracts to the ventrolateral thalamus.

Medial lemniscus

Brainstem

3 Posterior column nuclei that relay haptic–proprioceptive sensations ascend the dorsal spinothalamic tract ipsilaterally.

2 After crossing to the contralateral side of the spinal cord, nociceptive nuclei form the anterior spinothalamic tract, which joins the medial lemniscus pathway.

1 Posterior root ganglion neurons respond to fine touch and pressure; joint, tendon, and muscle change; pain, temperature, and itch.

Posterior root ganglion

Spinal cord

FIGURE 11-19 **Dual Somatosensory Pathways to the Brain** As neurons from the posterior root ganglia enter the spinal cord, the two somatosensory pathways to the brain diverge.

body awareness ascend the spinal cord ipsilaterally, whereas nociceptive (pain, temperature, itch) nerve fibers synapse with neurons whose axons cross immediately to the contralateral side of the spinal cord before ascending to the brain. **Figure 11-19** shows these two routes through the spinal cord. The posterior haptic-proprioceptive pathway is shown as a solid red line and the anterior nociceptive pathway as a dashed red line.

Ipsilateral connections lie on the side of the body on which they enter; contralateral connections lie on the side opposite.

The Posterior Spinothalamic Tract

Haptic-proprioceptive axons, which lie in the posterior portion of the spinal cord, form the **posterior spinothalamic tract**. These axons for fine touch and pressure synapse in the posterior column nuclei at the base of the brain. As shown in Figure 11-19, axons of neurons in the posterior column nuclei cross to the other side of the brainstem and ascend as part of a pathway called the medial lemniscus (*lemniscus* is Greek for "ribbon" or "band").

These posterior column axons synapse in the **ventrolateral thalamus**, the part of the thalamus that sends afferent information about body senses on to the somatosensory cortex. Although ventrolateral thalamic neurons send most of their axons to the somatosensory cortex, some do go to the motor cortex. Thus, three relay neurons are required to carry haptic-proprioceptive information from a receptor to the cortex: posterior root ganglia neurons, posterior column nuclei neurons, and thalamic neurons. Because posterior column neurons cross to the opposite hemisphere, each hemisphere perceives the opposite side of the somatosensory world.

Principle 3: Many brain circuits are crossed.

The Anterior Spinothalamic Tract

Most nociceptive axons take a different route to the brain. As shown in Figure 11-19, they first synapse with neurons in the anterior part of the spinal cord's gray matter, and, in turn, these neurons send their axons across to the other side of the spinal cord. There, these axons form the **anterior spinothalamic tract**, which carries afferent information about pain, temperature, and itch to the thalamus. This tract joins the medial lemniscus in the brainstem to continue on to the ventrolateral thalamus.

posterior spinothalamic tract Pathway that carries fine-touch and pressure fibers toward the brain.

ventrolateral thalamus Part of the thalamus that carries information about body senses to the somatosensory cortex.

anterior spinothalamic tract Pathway from the spinal cord to the thalamus that carries information about pain and temperature toward the brain.

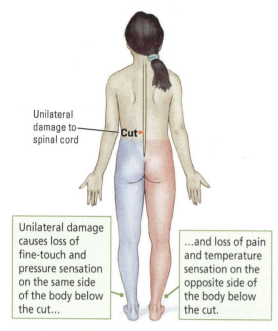

Unilateral damage to spinal cord — Cut

Unilateral damage causes loss of fine-touch and pressure sensation on the same side of the body below the cut...

...and loss of pain and temperature sensation on the opposite side of the body below the cut.

FIGURE 11-20 Effects of Unilateral Damage to the Somatosensory System

The thalamic neurons project to the somatosensory cortex. So again, conveying information from a pain or temperature receptor to the cortex requires three groups of relay neurons: posterior root neurons, spinal cord gray matter neurons, and ventrolateral thalamic neurons.

Effects of Unilateral Somatosensory System Damage

Unilateral damage dissociates the functions of the two somatosensory pathways—haptic-proprioceptive and nociceptive. Because these pathways enter the spinal cord together, separate in the spinal cord, and finally join up again in the brainstem, unilateral damage to the system results in distinctive sensory losses, depending on the site of injury.

Damage to the posterior roots produces global somatosensory deficits in a particular part of the body. In contrast, as illustrated in **Figure 11-20**, after unilateral spinal cord injury, loss of hapsis and proprioception occurs unilaterally, to the side of the body below where the damage occurred. Loss of nociception also occurs unilaterally, but to the opposite side of the body, below where the damage occurred. Unilateral damage at the points where the pathways merge in the brainstem, thalamus, and cortex again affects hapsis, proprioception, and nociception together, with all symptoms occurring on the opposite side of the body.

Spinal Reflexes

Not only do somatosensory nerve fibers convey information to the cortex, they also participate in behaviors mediated by the spinal cord and brainstem. Spinal cord somatosensory axons, even those ascending the posterior columns, give off axon collaterals, with each somatosensory neuron making synapses with interneurons and motor neurons on both sides of the spinal cord. The circuits made between sensory neurons and muscles through these connections mediate spinal reflexes.

The simplest spinal reflex is formed by a single synapse between a sensory neuron and a motor neuron. **Figure 11-21** illustrates such a **monosynaptic reflex**, the knee jerk. It affects the quadriceps muscle of the thigh, which is anchored to the leg bone by the patellar tendon. When the lower leg hangs free and this tendon is tapped with a

monosynaptic reflex Reflex requiring one synapse between sensory input and movement.

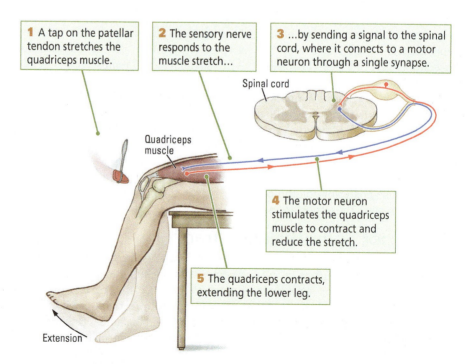

1 A tap on the patellar tendon stretches the quadriceps muscle.

2 The sensory nerve responds to the muscle stretch...

3 ...by sending a signal to the spinal cord, where it connects to a motor neuron through a single synapse.

Spinal cord

Quadriceps muscle

4 The motor neuron stimulates the quadriceps muscle to contract and reduce the stretch.

5 The quadriceps contracts, extending the lower leg.

Extension

FIGURE 11-21 Monosynaptic Reflex

small hammer, the quadriceps muscle is stretched, activating the stretch-sensitive sensory receptors embedded in it.

The sensory receptors then send a signal to the spinal cord through sensory neurons that synapse with motor neurons projecting to the same thigh muscle. The discharge from the motor neurons stimulates the muscle, causing it to contract to resist the stretch. Because the tap is brief, the stimulation is over before the motor message arrives, and the muscle contracts even though it is no longer stretched. This contraction pulls the leg up, producing the knee jerk reflex.

This simplest of reflexes entails monosynaptic connections between single sensory neurons and single motor neurons. Somatosensory neurons receiving information from the skin make much more complex connections with both interneurons and motor neurons. These multisynaptic connections are responsible for more complex spinal movements, such as those involved in standing and walking, actions that include many muscles on both sides of the body.

Feeling and Treating Pain

As many as 30 percent of physician visits involve pain symptoms, as do 50 percent of emergency room visits. People have pain as a result of acute injuries such as broken bones, chronic conditions such as cancer and arthritis, and everyday conditions such as stiff muscles from exercising. Women have pain during menstruation, pregnancy, and childbirth. The incidence of living with pain increases as people age, and for many people, pain is a constant companion.

Perceiving Pain

People can experience *central pain* in a part of the body that is not obviously injured. One type of central pain is *phantom limb pain*. As described in Research Focus 11-5, Phantom Limb Pain, phantom sensations are felt in a limb that has been lost—hence the term.

Although people in pain would happily dispense with it, pain is necessary: the rare person born without pain receptors develops body deformities because of failure to adjust posture and may receive acute injuries because of failure to avoid harm.

Pain perception results from synthesizing a plethora of sensory information. There may be as many as eight kinds of pain fibers, judging from the peptides and other chemicals released by these nerves when irritated or damaged. Some of these chemicals irritate surrounding tissue, stimulating it to release other chemicals to stimulate blood flow and to stimulate the pain fibers themselves. These reactions contribute to pain, redness, and swelling at the site of an injury.

Consider itch. We may feel itchy and consequently scratch a foreign object on our body. We also frequently feel itch in the absence of an obvious stimulus. Some drugs, including opioids, enhance itch sensations in the absence of a physical stimulus at the itchy body part.

Haptic information also contributes to pain perception. For example, people can accurately report the location and characteristics of various kinds of pain, but in the absence of fine-touch and pressure information, pain is more difficult to identify and localize.

The anterior spinothalamic tract, illustrated in Figure 11-19, is the main pain pathway to the brain, but as many as four other pathways may carry pain information from the spinal cord to the brain. These pathways are both crossed and uncrossed and project to the reticular formation of the midbrain, where they produce arousal; to the amygdala, where they produce emotional responses typically associated with pain; and to the hypothalamus, where they activate hormonal and cardiovascular responses.

The existence of multiple pain pathways in the spinal cord makes it difficult to treat chronic pain, even by selectively cutting the anterior spinothalamic tract—one radical procedure used to control chronic pain. It is likely that each pain pathway has its own function, whether for sensation, arousal, emotional responses, or other physiological responses.

Phantom Limb Pain

Up to 80 percent of people who have had a limb amputated also endure phantom limb phenomena, including pain and other sensations and motor phantoms, such as phantom movement and cramps (Kern et al., 2009). Phantom sensations and movements are illusions that originate in the brain.

Various techniques used to minimize phantom limb pain include drug-based pain management with opioids and the injection of pain medications into the spinal cord. An innovative method devised by V. S. Ramachandran and D. Rogers-Ramachandran (1996) assists the patient in setting up a counterillusion that the limb is intact and is providing normal sensory input to the brain.

Ramachandran devised a mirror box into which a person who has lost an arm inserts the intact arm and then observes its reflection in the mirror. The reflection suggests that the missing arm is present and can be controlled, as shown in the illustration. (Note that the walls of the box in this illustration have been removed to show the hidden arm.) The perception of the limb as intact counteracts phantom pain and cramps.

Inspired by Ramachandran's mirror box, researchers have developed other illusions to suggest that a missing limb is present and can be controlled. One method involves using virtual reality goggles. Another uses the so-called rubber limb phenomenon to produce the illusion that a missing limb is present. To induce this phenomenon, the stump of the amputated limb is stimulated tactually while the subject observes a prosthetic limb being touched.

All of the illusions lessen phantom limb pain and cramps by suggesting that a normal limb is present. Using similar logic, Hellman and associates (2015) suggest the possibility of developing neuroprosthetic limbs that provide their users sensory information to alleviate phantoms.

Alessandria and colleagues (2011) wanted to determine whether phantom limbs and their associated sensations also occur during dreaming.

They awoke sleeping amputees during R-sleep (rapid eye movement sleep) and asked them to recount their dreams. In none of the dreams did the participants remember having any amputated limb or phantom limb sensations.

One explanation of phantom limb pain is that we retain a brain representation of our body that persists after the loss of a limb. This interpretation is complicated by reports of supernumerary phantom limbs—the illusion of having an extra limb—and of people who report an alien limb—that is, they deny that one of their limbs belongs to them.

Responding to Pain

Neuronal circuits in the spinal cord allow haptic-proprioceptive and nociceptive pathways to interact. These interactions may be responsible for our puzzling and variable responses to pain. For example, people who are engaged in combat or intense athletic competition may receive a serious physical injury but start to feel the pain only much later.

A friend of ours was attacked by a grizzly bear while hiking and received 200 stitches to bind his wounds. When friends asked if it hurt to be bitten by a grizzly bear, he surprisingly answered no, explaining, "I had read the week before about someone who was killed and eaten by a grizzly bear. So I was thinking that this bear was going to eat me unless I got away. I did not have time for pain. I was fighting for my life. It was not until the next day that I started feeling pain."

The primacy of our friend's fear over his pain is related to the stress he was under. Not feeling pain in a fight-or-flight situation is obviously adaptive, as this story illustrates, and may be related to the activation of endogenous opioid peptides. Treatments for pain include opioid drugs (such as morphine), acupuncture (which entails the rapid vibration of needles embedded in the skin), and simply rubbing the area surrounding the injury. Psychological factors interact with pain treatments, and most studies on pain management find that placebos can be as effective as actual treatments.

To explain both the perception of pain and how it can be suppressed in so many ways, Ronald Melzack and Patrick Wall (1965) proposed the gate theory of pain,

Section 6-2 notes similarities between the brain's endogenous opioids and opioid analgesic drugs.

which has had enduring appeal. According to the theory, activities in different sensory pathways play off against each other and so determine whether and how much pain is perceived as a result of an injury. According to the gate theory, haptic-proprioceptive stimulation can reduce pain perception, whereas the absence of such stimulation can increase pain perception through interactions at a pain gate.

The **pain gate**, illustrated in **Figure 11-22**, consists of a haptic-proprioceptive fiber that conveys fine touch and pressure information and a nociceptive fiber that conducts pain information. Each fiber synapses with the same interneuron. Collaterals from the haptic-proprioceptive pathway excite the interneuron, whereas collaterals from the nociceptive pathway inhibit it. The interneuron, in turn, inhibits a neuron that relays pain information from the spinal cord to the brain. Consequently, when the haptic-proprioceptive pathway is active, the interneuron is stimulated, inhibiting the secondary pain neuron, and the interneuron acts as a gate, reducing the pain sensation.

Treating Pain

Gate theory helps explain how many pain treatments work (Foster et al., 2015). When you stub your toe, for instance, you feel pain because the pain pathway to the brain is open. If you then rub your toe, pain is reduced. Rubbing activates the haptic-proprioceptive pathway and reduces the information flow in the pain pathway because the pain gate partly closes, relieving the pain by crowding it out.

Similarly, a variety of pain treatments, including massage, warm water immersion, and acupuncture, may produce pain-relieving effects by selectively activating haptic and proprioceptive fibers relative to pain fibers, thus closing the pain gate. For acupuncture, vibrating needles on different body points presumably activate fine-touch and pressure fibers. The pain gate model may also explain why opioid drugs influence pain. The interneuron that is the gate uses an endogenous opioid as an inhibitory neurotransmitter. Thus, opioids relieve pain by mimicking the actions of the endogenous opioid neurotransmitter of the interneuron.

One of the most successful pain treatments is injecting small amounts of morphine under the dura mater, the outer layer of the meninges. This epidural anesthesia is mediated by the action of morphine on interneurons in the spinal cord. Although morphine is a highly useful pain treatment, its effects lessen with continued use. This form of habituation may be related to changes that take place on the postsynaptic receptors of pain neurons in the spinal cord and brain.

Gate theory also suggests an explanation for the pins-and-needles effect we feel after sitting too long in one position. Loss of oxygen from reduced blood flow first deactivates the large myelinated axons that carry touch and pressure information, leaving the small unmyelinated fibers that carry pain and temperature messages unaffected. As a result, ungated sensory information flows in the pain and temperature pathway, leading to the pins-and-needles sensation.

Neural circuits resembling pain gates may be located in the brainstem and cortex as well as the spinal cord. These gates help explain how cognition and emotion influence pain and how other approaches to pain relief work. For example, researchers have found that feelings of severe pain can be lessened when people can shift their attention from the pain to other stimuli. Dentists have long used this technique by giving their patients something soothing to watch or listen to during procedures.

The brain can also influence the pain signal it receives from the spinal cord. The cell bodies of **periaqueductal gray matter (PAG)** neurons, shown in **Figure 11-23**, surround the cerebral aqueduct connecting the third and fourth ventricles. Electrical stimulation of the PAG is effective in suppressing pain. Neurons in the PAG produce their pain-suppressing effect by exciting pathways (including serotonergic and noradrenergic pathways) in the brainstem that project to the spinal cord. There, they inhibit neurons that form the ascending pain pathways. Activation in these inhibitory circuits in part explains why pain sensation and perception ease

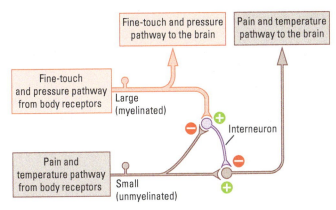

FIGURE 11-22 **Pain Gate** A spinal cord interneuron receives excitatory input (plus signs) from the fine-touch and pressure pathway; and inhibitory input (minus signs) from the pain and temperature pathway. The interneuron's relative activity then determines whether pain and temperature information ascends to the brain. Information from Melzack, 1973.

pain gate Hypothetical neural circuit in which activity in fine-touch and pressure pathways diminishes the activity in pain and temperature pathways.

periaqueductal gray matter (PAG) Nuclei in the midbrain that surround the cerebral aqueduct joining the third and fourth ventricles; PAG neurons contain circuits for species-typical behaviors (e.g., female sexual behavior) and play an important role in the modulation of pain.

Figure 2-4 diagrams the triple-layered meninges encasing the brain and spinal cord.

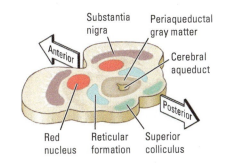

FIGURE 11-23 **PAG** The PAG is one nucleus in the midbrain's tegmentum (floor), shown here in cross section.

DBS is pictured in Figure 1-3.

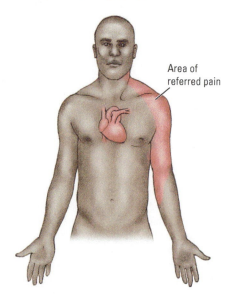

FIGURE 11-24 **Referred Pain** During a heart attack, pain from receptors in the heart is commonly felt in the left shoulder and upper arm, especially in men.

Vestibular hair cells work on the same principles as cochlear hair cells, which mediate hearing. See Section 10-2.

Cranial nerve 8 conveys both hearing and balance information to the brain. See Figure 2-29.

during sleep. Deep brain stimulation of the PAG by implanted microelectrodes is one way of treating pain that is resistant to all other therapies, including treatment with opioid drugs.

Many internal organs, including the heart, kidneys, and blood vessels, have pain receptors, but the ganglion neurons carrying information from these receptors do not have their own pathway to the brain. Instead, they synapse with spinal cord neurons that receive nociceptive information from the body's surface. Consequently, the spinal cord neurons that relay pain and temperature messages to the brain receive two sets of signals: one from the body's surface and the other from the internal organs.

These spinal cord neurons cannot distinguish the two sets of signals—nor can we. As a result, pain in body organs is felt as **referred pain** coming from the body surface. For example, pain in the heart associated with a heart attack is felt as pain in the left shoulder and upper arm (**Figure 11-24**). Pain in the stomach is felt as pain in the midline of the trunk; pain in the kidneys is felt as pain in the lower back. Pain in blood vessels in the head is felt as diffuse pain that we call a headache. (Remember that the brain has no pain receptors.)

Vestibular System and Balance

The only localized part of the somatosensory system, the **vestibular system**, consists of two organs, one in each inner ear. As **Figure 11-25A** shows, each vestibular organ consists of two groups of receptors: the three semicircular canals form one group, and the otolith organs—the utricle and the saccule—form the other group. These vestibular receptors do two jobs: (1) the semicircular canals detect head rotatory movements, and (2) the otoliths sense the body's relationship to gravity and linear acceleration.

In Figure 11-25A, the semicircular canals are oriented in three planes that correspond to the three dimensions in which we move through space. Each canal furnishes information about movement in its particular plane. The semicircular canals are filled with a fluid called endolymph. Immersed in the endolymph is a set of hair cells.

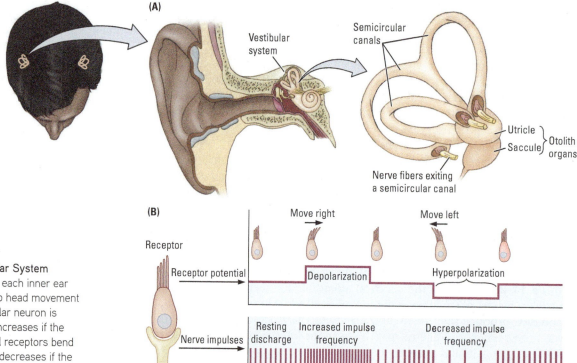

FIGURE 11-25 **The Vestibular System**
(A) The vestibular organs in each inner ear contain hair cells sensitive to head movement and to gravity. **(B)** A vestibular neuron is normally active. Its activity increases if the cilia at the tips of its hair cell receptors bend in one direction, but activity decreases if the receptors bend in the opposite direction.

When the head moves, the endolymph also moves, pushing against the hair cells and bending the cilia at their tips. The force of the bending is converted into receptor potentials in the hair cells that send action potentials over auditory vestibular nerve axons to the brain. These axons are normally quite active: bending the cilia in one direction increases receptor potentials, consequently increasing vestibular nerve axon activity; bending them in the other direction decreases vestibular afferent axon activity. These responses are diagrammed in Figure 11-25B. Typically, when the head turns in one direction, the receptor message on that side of the body increases neuronal firing. The message on the body's opposite side leads to decreased firing.

The utricle and saccule lie stacked just beneath the semicircular canals, as shown at the right in Figure 11-25A. These organs also contain hair cells, but the receptors are embedded in a gelatinous substance that contains otoconia (sing. otoconium), small crystals of the salt calcium carbonate. When you tilt your head, the gelatin and otoconia press against the hair cells, bending them. The mechanical action of the hair bending modulates the rate of action potentials in vestibular afferent axons that convey messages about the head's position in three-dimensional space.

The receptors in the vestibular system tell us about our location relative to gravity, about acceleration and deceleration of our movements, and about changes in movement direction. They also allow us to ignore the otherwise destabilizing influence that our movements might have on us. When you are standing on a moving bus, for example, even slight movements of the vehicle could potentially throw you off balance, but they do not. Similarly, when you move, you easily avoid tipping over, despite the constant shifting of your body weight. Your vestibular system enables your stability.

To demonstrate the role of vestibular receptors in helping you compensate for your own movements, try this experiment. Hold your hand in front of your eyes and shake it. Your hand appears blurry. Now shake your head instead of your hand, and the hand remains in focus. Compensatory signals from your vestibular system allow you to see the hand as stable, even though you are moving around.

Vertigo (from the Latin for "spinning"), a sensation of spinning when one is not moving, is a dysfunction of the inner ear that can be accompanied by nausea as well as difficulty maintaining balance while walking. A common way to induce vertigo is to spin, as children do when playing. Vertigo can also occur from looking down from a height or looking up at a tall object, or even as one is simply standing up or sitting down. One intoxicating effect of alcohol is vertigo. **Ménière disease**, named after a French physician, is a disorder of the inner ear resulting in vertigo and loss of balance (Nevoux et al., 2018).

referred pain Pain that arises in one of the internal organs but is felt on the surface of the body.

vestibular system Somatosensory system comprising a set of receptors in each inner ear that respond to body position and to movement of the head.

Ménière disease Disorder of the middle ear resulting in vertigo and loss of balance.

11-4 Review

Before you continue, check your understanding. Answers to Self-Test appear at the back of the book.

1. Body senses contribute to the perception of _____ (touch and pressure), _____ (location and movement), and _____ (temperature, pain, itch).

2. Haptic-proprioceptive information is carried into the CNS by the _____ spinothalamic tract; nociceptive information is carried in by the _____ spinothalamic tract.

3. The two tracts interact in the spinal cord to regulate pain perception via a(n) _____.

4. In the midbrain, the _____ suppresses pain by activating neuromodulatory circuits that inhibit pain pathways.

5. The only localized somatosensory system is the _____ system, which helps us maintain _____ by signaling information about the head's position and our movement through space.

6. Explain how proprioception acts as the "eyes of the body."

For additional study tools, visit **LaunchPad** at launchpadworks.com

11-5

Exploring the Somatosensory Cortex

Somatosensory neurons do more than convey sensation to the brain: they enable us to perceive things that we describe as pleasant or unpleasant, the shape and texture of objects, the effort required to complete tasks, and even our spatial environment. They also play a central role in movement. **Figure 11-26** illustrates the two main somatosensory areas in the cortex.

The primary somatosensory cortex (SI), which receives projections fom the thalamus, consists of Brodmann areas 3–1–2 (shaded red in Figure 11-26). The primary somatosensory cortex begins to construct perceptions from somatosensory information. It mainly consists of the postcentral gyrus in the parietal lobe, just behind the central fissure. Thus, SI lies adjacent to the primary motor cortex, on the other side of the central fissure in the frontal lobe.

The secondary somatosensory cortex (SII; Brodmann areas 5 and 7, shaded green and purple in Figure 11-26) is located in the parietal lobe just behind SI. SII is involved in combining the somatosensory system with information from the visual and auditory systems.

Korbinian Brodmann numbered these areas more than a century ago on his map of the cortex (see Figure 2-26).

FIGURE 11-26 **Somatosensory Cortex** Stimulation of the primary somatosensory cortex in the parietal lobe produces sensations that are referred to appropriate body parts. Information from the primary somatosensory cortex travels to the secondary somatosensory cortex for further perceptual analysis.

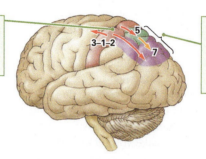

Primary somatosensory cortex (3-1-2) receives sensory information from the body.

Secondary somatosensory cortex (5, 7) receives sensory information from the primary somatosensory cortex.

Somatosensory Homunculus

In his studies of human patients undergoing brain surgery, Wilder Penfield electrically stimulated the somatosensory cortex and recorded patients' responses. Stimulation at sites mainly in the primary somatosensory cortex elicited sensations in the foot; stimulation of other sites produced sensations in a hand, the trunk, or the face. By mapping these responses, Penfield was able to construct a somatosensory homunculus in the cortex, shown in **Figure 11-27A**. The sensory homunculus looks nearly identical to the motor homunculus shown in Figure 11-6 in that the most sensitive areas of the body are accorded relatively large cortical areas.

Using smaller electrodes and more precise recording techniques in monkeys, Jon Kaas (1987) found that Penfield's homunculus could be subdivided into a series of thinner homunculi. When Kaas stimulated sensory receptors on the body and recorded the activity of cells in the sensory cortex, he found that the somatosensory cortex comprises four representations of the body. Each is associated with a class of sensory receptors.

The progression of these representations across SI from front to back is shown in Figure 11-27B. Area 3a cells are responsive to muscle receptors; area 3b cells are responsive to slow-responding skin receptors. Area 1 cells are responsive to rapidly adapting skin receptors, and area 2 cells are responsive to deep tissue pressure and joint receptors. In another study, Hiroshi Asanuma (1989) and his coworkers found a fifth sensory representation in the motor cortex (area 4) in which cells respond to muscle and joint receptors.

Perceptions constructed from elementary sensations depend on combining the sensations. This combining takes place as areas 3a and 3b project onto area 1, which in turn projects onto area 2. Whereas a cell in area 3a or 3b may respond to activity in only a certain area on a certain finger, for example, cells in area 1 may respond to similar information from a number of fingers.

At the next level of synthesis, cells in area 2 respond to stimulation in a number of locations on a number of fingers, as well as to stimulation from different kinds of

(A) Penfield's single-homunculus model

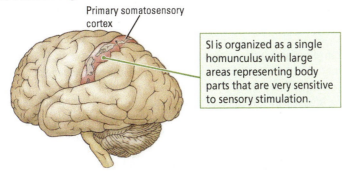

Primary somatosensory cortex

SI is organized as a single homunculus with large areas representing body parts that are very sensitive to sensory stimulation.

FIGURE 11-27 Two Models of the Primary Somatosensory Cortex

(B) Four-homunculus model

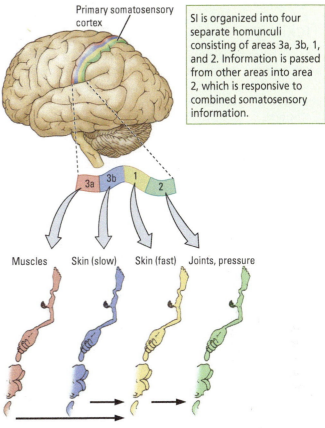

Primary somatosensory cortex

SI is organized into four separate homunculi consisting of areas 3a, 3b, 1, and 2. Information is passed from other areas into area 2, which is responsive to combined somatosensory information.

3a   3b   1   2

Muscles   Skin (slow)   Skin (fast)   Joints, pressure

somatosensory receptors. Thus, area 2 contains multimodal neurons responsive to force, orientation, and direction of movement. We perceive all these properties when we hold an object in our hands and manipulate it.

With each successive information relay, both the size of the pertinent receptive fields and the synthesis of somatosensory modalities increase. The segregation of sensory neuron types at the level of the cortex is likely the basis for our ability to distinguish among different kinds of sensory stimuli coming from different sources. For example, we distinguish between tactile stimulation on the surface of the skin, which is usually produced by some external agent, and stimulation coming from muscles, tendons, and joints, which is usually produced by our own movements.

At the same time, we perceive the combined sensory properties of a stimulus. For instance, when we manipulate an object, we know the object both by its sensory properties, such as temperature and texture, and by the movements we make as we handle it. Thus, SI provides for somatosensory synthesis, too. The tickle sensation seems rooted in an other-versus-us somatosensory distinction, as described in Research Focus 11-6, Tickling.

See Section 9-1 for details on receptive fields.

Research by Vernon Mountcastle (1978) shows that cells in the SI are arranged in functional columns running from layer I to layer VI, similar to the functional columns found in the visual cortex. Every cell in a functional somatosensory cortical column responds to a single class of receptors. Some columns are activated by rapidly adapting skin receptors, others by slowly adapting skin receptors, still others by pressure receptors, and so forth. All neurons in a functional column receive information from the same local skin area. In this way, neurons lying within a column seem to be an elementary functional unit of the somatosensory cortex.

Figure 9-33 shows functional column organization in V1.

Secondary Somatosensory Cortex

The *secondary somatosensory cortex* (SII) not only receives somatosensory information from the SI, it also receives information from the visual cortex and auditory cortex. In studies using monkeys, electrical stimulation of the SII produces movements that resemble the movements produced by electrical stimulation of the motor cortex. Stimulation of the more dorsal regions of the SII produce whole-body movements resembling jumping and climbing; stimulation of the more ventral regions of the SII produce movements of reaching to points around the body or to the mouth. This topographic arrangement of movement in the SII is not only similar to the topographic arrangement of movement in the motor cortex, its anatomy indicates that there are neural connections between the functional zones of the SII and the motor cortex.

The connections between somatosensory cortex and motor cortex suggest that movement begins in somatosensory cortex. But what is the precise contribution of

Tickling

Everyone knows the effects and consequences of tickling. The perception is a curious mixture of pleasant and unpleasant sensations. The two kinds of tickling are *kinismesis*, the sensation from a light caress, and *gargalesis*, the pleasurable effect of hard rhythmic probing.

The tickle sensation is felt not only by humans but also by other primates and by cats, rats, and probably most other mammals. Play in rats is associated with 50-kilohertz vocalizations, and tickling body regions that are targets of the rats' own play also elicits 50-kilohertz vocalizations (LaFollette et al., 2017).

Tickling is rewarding because people and animals solicit tickles from others. They even enjoy observing others being tickled. Using a robot and brain imaging techniques, Sarah Blakemore and her colleagues (1998) explained why we cannot tickle ourselves.

Blakemore had participants deliver two kinds of identical tactile stimuli to the palms of their hand. In one condition, the stimulus was predictable and in the other a robot introduced an unpredictable delay in the stimulus. Only the unpredictable stimulus was perceived as a tickle. Thus, it is not the stimulation itself but its unpredictability that accounts for the tickle perception. This is why we cannot tickle ourselves: we know what we are doing. Windt and associates (2015), using a self-report method, found that during lucid dreams, the self–other distinction is absent: people do dream that they tickle themselves.

One interesting feature of tickling is the distinctive laughter it evokes. This laughter can be identified by sonograms (sound analysis), and people can distinguish tickle-related laughter from other forms of laughter. In mother–child interactions, tickling laughter may serve to strengthen social bonds (Ishijima & Negayama, 2017).

Intrigued by findings that all apes appear to laugh during tickling, Ross and coworkers (2010) compared tickle-related laughter in apes and found that human laughter is more similar to chimpanzee laughter than to the laughter of gorillas and other apes. We humans thus have inherited from our common ape ancestors both a susceptibility to tickling and laughter.

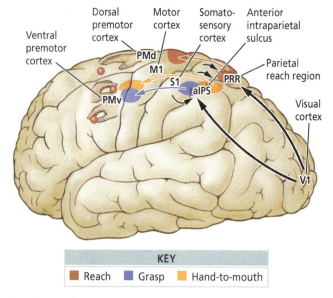

Oksana Kuzmina/Shutterstock.com

KEY
■ Reach ■ Grasp ■ Hand-to-mouth

FIGURE 11-28 **Multiple channels for eating** Eating a food item such as an apple requires three channels: A reach channel (red) takes the hand to the apple, a grasp channel (purple) shapes the fingers to grasp the apple, and a hand-to-mouth channel (orange) brings the apple to the mouth. The reach and grasp actions are performed under visual guidance.

the somatosensory cortex? A likely explanation is that our visual and auditory cortices identify the spatial locations of objects in our surroundings with which we might interact. This information is sent to the somatosensory parietal cortex, which identifies the body part that we might use to interact with objects at that location. This information is then sent to the motor cortex, which performs the movement.

An example of this type of movement arrangement is illustrated in **Figure 11-28**. This figure shows three pathways, or channels: a dorsal channel for reaching, a ventral channel for grasping, and, between the two, a channel for bringing the hand to the mouth. The channels for reaching and grasping receive connections from the visual cortex; the channel for hand-to-mouth movement does not. When we reach for a food item such as an apple, the reach channel directs our hand to the spatial location of the apple, the grasp channel shapes our fingers to appropriately grasp it, and the hand-to-mouth channel brings it to our mouth. The hand-to-mouth channel does not require visual information because our somatosensory system can identify that we are holding an apple, it knows where the mouth is, and it can arrange transport of the apple to our mouth (Karl et al., 2018). As this example demonstrates, our movements are synthetized using a smaller number of building-block movements, such as those illustrated in Figure 11-8. These building blocks are like words that can be arranged in different ways to produce different sentences.

Effects of Somatosensory Cortex Damage

Damage to the SI impairs the ability to make even simple sensory discriminations and movements. Suzanne Corkin and her coworkers (1970) demonstrated this effect by examining patients with cortical lesions that included most of areas 3–1–2 in one hemisphere. The researchers mapped the primary sensory cortex of each of these patients before they underwent elective surgery for removal of a carefully defined piece of that cortex, including the hand area. The patients' sensory and motor skills in both hands were tested on three occasions: before the surgery, shortly after the surgery, and almost a year afterward.

The tests included pressure sensitivity, two-point touch discrimination, position sense (reporting the direction in which a finger was being moved), and haptic sense (using touch to identify objects, such as a pencil, a coin, eyeglasses, and so forth). For all the sensory abilities tested, the surgical lesions produced a severe and seemingly permanent deficit in the contralateral hand. Sensory thresholds, proprioception, and hapsis were all greatly impaired.

Nevertheless, like the motor cortex, the somatosensory cortex is plastic. Plasticity is illustrated by the reorganization of the somatosensory cortex after deafferentation. Tim Pons and his coworkers (1991) reported a dramatic change in the somatosensory maps of monkeys in which the ganglion cells projecting to the spinal cord for one arm had been cut, deafferentating the limb, a number of years earlier. The researchers had wanted to develop an animal model of damage to sensory nerves that could offer insight into human injuries, but they were interrupted by a legal dispute with an animal advocacy group. Years later, as the health of the animals declined, a court injunction allowed the mapping experiment to be conducted.

Section 7-7 considers debates over using laboratory animals in brain–behavior research.

Pons and his coworkers discovered that the area of somatosensory cortex that had formerly represented the arm no longer did so. Light touches on a monkey's lower face now activated cells in what had formerly been the cortical arm region. As illustrated in **Figure 11-29**, the cortical facial area had expanded by as much as 10 to 14 millimeters, virtually doubling its original size by entering the arm area.

(A) Control monkey

This area of the somatosensory cortex represents the arm and face.

This normal pattern is illustrated by a normal face.

Leg
Trunk
Arm
Face

(B) Deafferentated monkey

The area of the somatosensory cortex that formerly represented the arm has been taken over by expansion of the face area.

This expansion is illustrated by an elongated face.

Leg
Trunk
Face

FIGURE 11-29 **Somatosensory Plasticity** Information from Pons et al., 1991.

This massive change was completely unexpected. The stimulus–response patterns associated with the expanded facial area of the cortex appeared indistinguishable from those associated with the original facial area. Furthermore, the trunk area, which bounded the other side of the cortical arm area, did not expand into the vacated arm area. A possible explanation of the expansion of the face area is that this monkey began to use its mouth to compensate for many of the movements that were the responsibility of its hand before deafferentation.

Figure 14-23 diagrams this phenomenon.

Somatosensory Cortex and Complex Movement

How are our abilities to move and to interpret stimulation on the body related? As we have described, the somatosensory cortex makes an important contribution to movement. Damage to the secondary somatosensory cortex does not disrupt the plans for making movements, but it does disrupt how the movements are performed, leaving their execution fragmented and confused. This inability to complete a plan of action accurately—to make a voluntary movement—is called **apraxia**. The following case highlights its symptoms:

Apraxia derives from the Greek words for "no" and "action."

> A woman with a biparietal lesion [damage on the left- and right-hemisphere secondary somatosensory cortex] had worked for years as a fish-filleter. With the development of her symptoms, she began to experience difficulty in carrying on with her job. She did not seem to know what to do with her knife. She would stick the point in the head of a fish, start the first stroke, and then come to a stop. In her own mind she knew how to fillet fish, but yet she could not execute the maneuver. The foreman accused her of being drunk and sent her home for mutilating fish.
>
> The same patient also showed another unusual phenomenon that might possibly be apraxic in nature. She could never finish an undertaking. She would begin a job, drop it, start another, abandon that one, and within a short while would have four or five uncompleted tasks on her hands. This would cause her to do such inappropriate actions as putting the sugar bowl in the refrigerator, and the coffeepot inside the oven. (Critchley, 1953, pp. 158–159)

apraxia Inability to make voluntary movements in the absence of paralysis or other motor or sensory impairment, especially an inability to make proper use of an object.

The somatosensory cortex contributes to movement by participating in both the dorsal and ventral visual streams. The dorsal action stream works without conscious awareness, so that we automatically shape a hand as we reach to grasp a cup (recall Figure 11-1). Within this stream, a number of channels specify the movements—reaching, manipulating, bringing a cup to the mouth—and perform these responses not only to somatosensory information but also to visual and auditory information. The ventral perceptual stream, in contrast, works with conscious awareness for perception—that an object is a cup, it contains water, and we are thirsty.

As **Figure 11-30** illustrates, the dorsal stream projects to the secondary somatosensory cortex and then to the frontal cortex. In this way, it integrates visual information with somatosensory information to produce movements appropriately to targets, as in reaching for a cup.

The secondary somatosensory area contributes perceptual information to the ventral stream by providing conscious haptic information about object identity and completed movements. From this information the frontal cortex can imagine the consequence of a movement and select the actions that appropriately follow from those already completed.

The different contributions of the dorsal stream and the ventral stream to movement are illustrated in the difference in movement displayed by people when they make a real action of reaching for a food item to eat it compared to when they pantomime the same movement. The pantomime movement is not as precise as the real movement, but its communicative value is just as accurate: observers understand what a person means when he or she pantomimes a reaching-to-eat movement (van Nispen et al., 2018).

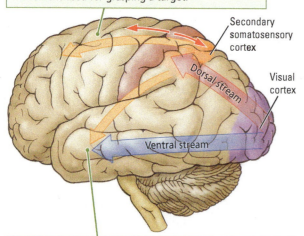

Information from the secondary somatosensory cortex contributes to the dorsal stream by specifying the movement used for grasping a target.

Secondary somatosensory cortex

Dorsal stream

Visual cortex

Ventral stream

Information from the secondary somatosensory cortex contributes to the ventral stream by providing information about objects' size, shape, and texture.

FIGURE 11-30 **Visual Aid** Section 9-4 explains how visual information from the dorsal and ventral streams contributes to movement.

11-5 Review

Before you continue, check your understanding. Answers to Self-Test appear at the back of the book.

1. The _____ somatosensory cortex (SI), arranged as a series of homunculi, feeds information to the _____ somatosensory cortex (SII), which also receives information from the _____ cortex and _____ cortex.

2. Damage to the secondary somatosensory cortex produces _____, an inability to complete a series of movements.

3. The somatosensory cortex provides information to the _____ stream to produce unconscious movements and also provides information to the _____ stream for conscious recognition of objects.

4. Explain briefly why we can't tickle ourselves.

For additional study tools, visit **LaunchPad** at launchpadworks.com

Summary

In the nervous system, the somatosensory and motor systems are inter-related at all levels. At the level of the spinal cord, sensory information contributes to motor reflexes; in the brainstem, sensory information contributes to complex regulatory movements. At the level of the neo-cortex, sensory information represents the sizes, shapes, and positions of objects and records just-completed movements.

11-1 Hierarchical and Parallel Movement Control

Movement is organized hierarchically, using the entire nervous system (review Figure 11-1). The forebrain plans, organizes, and initiates movements, whereas the brainstem coordinates regulatory functions, such as eating and drinking, and controls neural mechanisms that maintain posture and produce locomotion. Many reflexes are organized at the level of the spinal cord and occur without the brain's involvement.

11-2 Motor System Organization

Maps produced by stimulating the primary motor cortex show that it is organized topographically as a homunculus, with different cortical areas capable of producing different movements. Motor cortex neurons initiate movement, produce movement, control movement force, and indicate movement direction. Disuse of a limb, as might result from a motor cortex injury, results in shrinkage of the limb's cortical representation. This shrinkage can be prevented, however, if the limb can be forced into use, as in constraint-induced therapy.

Two corticospinal pathways emerge from the motor cortex to the spinal cord. Lateral corticospinal axons project from cortical areas that control arm and hand movements. The lateral tract crosses from the contralateral brain hemisphere to form synapses with spinal inter-neurons and motor neurons located laterally in the spinal cord, and on the side opposite the brain hemisphere where the lateral tract formed. Anterior corticospinal tract axons project from the cortical motor regions that produce whole-body movements. The anterior tract synapses with interneurons and motor neurons located medially and ipsilaterally in the spinal cord.

Spinal cord interneurons and motor neurons also are topographically organized: lateral motor neurons project to digit, hand, and arm muscles to produce arm and hand movements, and medial motor neurons project to trunk muscles and mediate whole-body movements, including locomotion.

11-3 Basal Ganglia, Cerebellum, and Movement

Movement abnormalities result from damage to the basal ganglia or to the cerebellum. Both structures participate in movement control by modulating the movements initiated by the cortex. The basal ganglia regulate force; the cerebellum maintains accuracy and participates in learning.

11-4 Somatosensory System Receptors and Pathways

Distributed throughout the body, the somatosensory system consists of more than 20 types of specialized sensory neurons and receptors, each sensitive to a particular form of mechanical energy. Located in posterior dorsal root ganglia, each of these neurons carries sensory information into the spinal cord and the brain.

Neurons carrying proprioceptive (location and movement) information and haptic (touch and pressure) information have axons that ascend the spinal cord as the posterior spinothalamic tract. These fibers synapse in the posterior column nuclei at the base of the brain. From there, axons cross to the other side of the brainstem to form the medial lemniscus, which ascends to the ventrolateral thalamus. Most of the ventrolateral thalamus cells project to the somatosensory cortex.

Nociceptive (pain, temperature, and itch) posterior root ganglion neurons synapse on entering the spinal cord. Their relay neurons cross the spinal cord to ascend to the thalamus as the anterior spinothalamic tract.

Because the two somatosensory pathways take somewhat different routes, unilateral spinal cord damage impairs proprioception and hapsis ipsilaterally, below the site of injury, and impairs nociception contralaterally below the site.

11-5 Exploring the Somatosensory Cortex

The somatosensory system is represented topographically in parietal areas 3-1-2. The most sensitive body parts are accorded the largest somatosensory regions, as befits the body parts most capable of fine movements.

A number of sensory homunculi represent various sensory modalities, and these regions are hierarchically organized. If sensory input from anywhere in the body is cut off from the cortex by damage to sensory fibers, adjacent functional sensory cortex can expand into the now-unoccupied region.

The somatosensory cortex is composed of two main areas: the primary somatosensory cortex (SI), which receives projections from the thalamus and begins to construct perceptions of somatosensory information, and the secondary somatosensory cortex (SII), which is involved in combining the somatosensory system with information from the visual and auditory systems. Through the dorsal visual stream, the somatosensory cortex contributes to directing hand and body movements to visual targets. The somatosensory cortex also contributes to the ventral visual stream to produce perception of external objects, through which we can imagine the consequences of our movements.

| Key Terms

anterior spinothalamic tract, p. 379

apraxia, p. 390

cerebral palsy (CP), p. 359

constraint-induced therapy, p. 366

corticospinal tract, p. 366

deafferentation, p. 378

glabrous skin, p. 375

hapsis, p. 376

homunculus, p. 362

hyperkinetic symptom, p. 370

hypokinetic symptom, p. 370

locked-in syndrome, p. 359

Ménière disease, p. 385

monosynaptic reflex, p. 380

motor sequence, p. 355

neuroprosthetics, p. 352

nociception, p. 376

pain gate, p. 383

paraplegia, p. 360

periaqueductal gray matter (PAG), p. 383

position-point theory, p. 364

posterior spinothalamic tract, p. 379

proprioception, p. 376

quadriplegia, p. 360

rapidly adapting receptor, p. 376

referred pain, p. 385

scratch reflex, p. 360

slowly adapting receptor, p. 377

topographic organization, p. 363

ventrolateral thalamus, p. 379

vestibular system, p. 385

Visit 🔖 **LaunchPad** to access the e-Book, videos, 🔖 **LearningCurve** adaptive quizzing, flashcards, and more at launchpadworks.com

Kerkez/Getty Images

What Causes Emotional and Motivated Behavior?

CHAPTER 12

◉ **RESEARCH FOCUS 12-1**

The Pain of Rejection

We use words like *sorrow*, *grief*, and *heartbreak* to describe a loss. Loss evokes painful feelings, and the loss or absence of contact that comes with social rejection leads to hurt feelings. Several investigators have attempted to discover whether physically painful and emotionally hurtful feelings are manifested in the same neural regions.

Physical pain (say, hot or cold stimuli) is easy to inflict, but inducing equivalently severe emotional, or affective, pain is more difficult. Ethan Kross and colleagues (2011) performed an experiment that may have succeeded in balancing participants' degree of emotional and physical pain. Using fMRI, they scanned 40 people who had recently gone through an unwanted breakup. To compare brain activation, the participants viewed two photographs: one of their ex-partner, to evoke negative emotion, and the other of a same-gender friend with whom the participant shared a pleasant time at about the time of the breakup. The picture order was randomized across participants.

Emotional cue phrases associated with each photograph directed the participants to focus on a specific experience they shared with each person. The physical stimulus employed by the researchers, which was administered in a separate session, was either painfully hot or painless warm stimulation of participants' forearms.

The research question is Do physical pain and social pain have a common neuroanatomical basis? The results, shown in the illustration, reveal that four regions respond to both types of pain: the insula, dorsal anterior cingulate cortex (dACC), somatosensory thalamus, and secondary somatosensory cortex (SII). The conclusion: social rejection hurts in much the same way that physical pain hurts.

Previous studies, including those of Eisenberger and colleagues (2003, 2006), showed anterior cingulate activity during the experience of both physical and emotional pain. But Kross's results also showed activity in cortical somatosensory regions related to physical pain. The results imaged by Kross and colleagues suggest that the brain systems underlying emotional reactions to social rejection may have developed by co-opting brain circuits that support the affective component of physical pain. We hasten to point out, however, that the overlapping activity in brain regions does not rule out unique neural components of emotional experiences. Certainly our subjective experiences are unique (e.g., Kragel et al., 2018).

Another insight from the Kross study is that normalizing the activity of these brain regions probably provides a basis for both physical and mental restorative processes. Seeing the similarity in brain activation during social pain and physical pain helps us understand why social support can reduce physical pain, much as it soothes emotional pain.

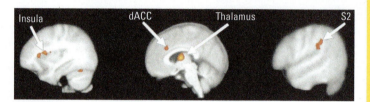

Overlapping Social Rejection and Physical Pain These fMRIs are the result of averaging scans from 40 participants to image the brain's response to physical or emotional pain. We see activation in the insula, dorsal anterior cingulate cortex (dACC), somatosensory thalamus, and/or secondary somatosensory cortex (SII). Research from E. Kross, M.G. Berman, W. Mischel, E.E. Smith, & T.D. Water, "Social rejection shares somatosensory representations with physical pain", 2011, Proceedings of the National Academy of Sciences (USA), 108, 6270–6275.

Knowing that the brain makes emotional experience real—more than mere metaphors of *hurt* or *pain*—how do we incorporate our thoughts and reasons for behaving as we do? Clearly, our subjective feelings and thoughts influence our actions. The cognitive interpretations of subjective experiences are **emotions**—anger, fear, sadness, jealousy, embarrassment, joy. These interpretations can operate outside our immediate awareness.

This chapter begins by exploring the causes of behavior. Sensory stimulation, neural circuits, hormones, and reward are primary factors in behavior. We focus both on emotion and on the underlying reasons for behaviors that seem purposeful and goal directed (in other words, "motivated"). Like emotion, motivated behavior is both inferred and subjective, and it can occur without awareness or intent. It includes both regulatory behaviors (such as eating), which are essential for survival, and nonregulatory behaviors (such as curiosity), which are not required to meet an animal's basic needs.

Research on the neuroanatomy responsible for emotional and motivated behavior focuses on a neural circuit formed by the hypothalamus, the frontal lobes, and the structures associated with the limbic system. But behavior is influenced as much by the interaction of our social and natural environments and by evolution as it is by biology. To explain how all these interactions affect the brain's control of behavior, we concentrate on two specific examples: eating and sexual activity. Our exploration leads us to revisit the idea of reward, which is key to explaining emotional and motivated behaviors.

emotion Cognitive interpretation of subjective experiences that can influence thought and behavior.

12-1

Identifying the Causes of Behavior

We may think that the most obvious explanation for our behavior is simply that we act in a state of free will: we do what we want to, and we always have a choice. But free will is not a likely cause of behavior.

Consider Roger. We first met 25-year-old Roger in the admissions ward of a large mental hospital when he approached us and asked if we had any snacks. We had chewing gum, which he accepted eagerly. We thought little about this encounter until 10 minutes later, when we noticed Roger eating the flowers from the stems in a vase on a table. A nurse took the vase away but said little to Roger.

Later, as we wandered about the ward, we encountered a worker replacing linoleum floor tiles. Roger was watching the worker, and as he did, he dipped his finger into the pot of gluing compound and licked the glue from his finger, as if he were sampling honey from a jar. When we asked Roger what he was doing, he said that he was really hungry and that this stuff was not too bad. It reminded him of peanut butter.

One of us tasted the glue and concluded that it did not taste like peanut butter— it tasted awful. Roger was undeterred. We alerted a nurse, who quickly removed him from the glue. Later, we saw him eating flowers from another bouquet.

Neurological testing revealed that a tumor had invaded Roger's hypothalamus at the base of his brain. He was indeed hungry all the time and in all likelihood could consume more than 20,000 calories a day if allowed to do so.

Would you say that Roger was exercising free will regarding his appetite and food preferences? Probably not. Roger seemed compelled to eat whatever he could find, driven by a ravenous hunger. The nervous system, not an act of free will, produced this behavior and undoubtedly produces many others.

If free will does not adequately explain why we act as we do, what does? One obvious answer is that we do things that we find rewarding. Rewarding experiences must activate brain circuits that make us feel good. Consider the example of prey killing by domestic cats.

One frustrating thing about being a cat owner is that even well-fed cats kill small animals, such as birds and mice. Most people are not much bothered when their cats kill mice: they view mice as a nuisance. But birds are different. People enjoy watching birds in their yard and garden. Many cat owners wonder why their pets keep killing birds.

To provide an answer, we look to the activities of neural circuits. Cats must have a brain circuit that controls prey killing. When this circuit is active, a cat makes an "appropriate" kill. Viewed in an evolutionary context, it makes sense for cats to have such a circuit: in the days when doting humans did not keep cats as pets, cats did not have food dishes that were regularly filled.

Why does this prey-killing circuit become active when a cat does not need food? One explanation is that, to secure survival, the activity of circuits like the prey-killing circuit is in some way rewarding—it makes the cat feel good. As a result, the cat will engage often in the pleasure-producing behavior. This helps to guarantee that the cat will usually not go hungry.

In the wild, after all, a cat that did not like killing would probably be dead. In the 1960s, Steve Glickman and Bernard Schiff (1967) first proposed the idea that behaviors such as prey killing are rewarding. We return to reward in Section 12-7 because it is important in understanding the causes of behavior.

Many people find watching and sharing cute cat videos rewarding: it makes them feel good, and they do it often.

Behavior for Brain Maintenance

Some experiences are rewarding; others are aversive, again because brain circuits are activated to produce behaviors that reduce the aversive experience. One example is the brain's inherent need for stimulation.

Psychologists Robert Butler and Harry Harlow (1954) conducted a series of studies in which they placed rhesus monkeys in a dimly lit room with a small door that could be

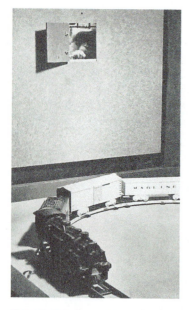

FIGURE 12-1 **Brain Maintenance** Monkeys quickly learn to solve puzzles or perform other tricks to gain access to a door that looks out from their dimly lit quarters into an adjacent room. A toy train is a strong visual incentive for the monkey peeking through the door; a bowl of fruit is less rewarding. University of Wisconsin; "Persistence of Visual Exploration in Monkeys," by R. A. Butler and H. F. Harlow, 1954, Journal of Comparative and Physiological Psychology, 47, p. 260.

opened to view an adjoining room. As shown in **Figure 12-1**, the researchers could vary the stimuli in the adjoining room so that the monkeys could view different objects or animals each time they opened the door.

Monkeys in these conditions spent a lot of time opening the door and viewing whatever was on display, such as toy trains circling a track. The monkeys were even willing to perform various tasks just for an opportunity to look through the door. The longer they were deprived of a chance to look, the more time they spent looking when finally given the opportunity.

The Butler and Harlow experiments show that in the absence of stimulation, the brain will seek it out.

Neural Circuits and Behavior

Researchers have identified brain circuits for "reward" and discovered that these circuits can modulate to increase or decrease activity. Researchers studying the rewarding properties of sexual activity in males, for example, found that a man's frequency of copulation correlates with his levels of **androgens** (hormones related to masculine characteristics). Unusually high androgen levels are related to ultrahigh sexual interest; abnormally low androgen levels are linked to low sexual interest or perhaps no interest at all. The brain circuits are more difficult to activate in the absence of androgens.

Another way to modulate reward circuits comes via our chemical senses, smell and taste. The odor of a mouse can stimulate hunting in cats, whereas the odor of a cat will drive mice into hiding. Similarly, the smell from a bakery can make us hungry, whereas foul odors can reduce the rewarding value of our favorite foods. Although we tend to view the chemical senses as relatively minor in our daily lives, they are central to motivated and emotional behavior.

Understanding the neural basis for motivated behavior has wide application. For instance, we can say that Roger had a voracious and indiscriminate appetite either because the brain circuits that initiate eating were excessively active or because the circuits that terminate eating were inactive. Similarly, we can say that Harlow and Butler's monkeys were interested in opening the door because the neural circuits that respond to sensory inputs were abnormally underactive. So the main reason for a particular thought, feeling, or action lies in what is going on in brain circuits.

Evolutionary Influences on Behavior

An understanding of brain circuits can help us understand the causes of behavior, but we are still left with the question Why? One evolutionary explanation of behavior hinges on the concept of **innate releasing mechanisms (IRMs)**, activators for inborn adaptive responses that aid an animal's survival. IRMs help an animal to feed, reproduce, and escape predators. The concept is best understood by analyzing its parts.

IRMs are present from birth rather than acquired through experience, as the term *innate* implies. These mechanisms have proved adaptive and therefore have been maintained in the genome of the species. The term *releasing* indicates that IRMs act as triggers for behaviors set in motion by internal programs.

Let us return to prey killing by cats. The cat's brain must have a built-in mechanism that triggers stalking and killing in response to a stimulus such as a bird or a mouse. A cat must also have a built-in mechanism that triggers mating behavior in the presence of a suitable cat of the opposite sex. Not all cat behaviors are due to IRMs, but you probably can think of other innate releasing mechanisms that cats possess—arching and hissing on encountering a threat, for example. For all these IRMs, the animal's brain must have a set of norms against which it can match stimuli to trigger an appropriate response.

androgen Hormones related to masculine characteristics and that play a role in levels of sexual interest.

innate releasing mechanism (IRM) Hypothetical mechanism that detects specific sensory stimuli and directs an organism to take a particular action.

An experiment by Bryan Kolb and Arthur Nonneman (1975) suggests the existence of such innate, internalized norms. The researchers allowed a litter of 6-week-old kittens to play in a room and become familiar with it. After this adjustment period, they introduced a two-dimensional image of an adult cat in a Halloween posture, as shown in **Figure 12-2A**, and a "Picasso" control version, as shown in Figure 12-2B.

The kittens responded to the Halloween cat image with raised fur, arched backs, and bared teeth, all signs of being threatened by the image of the adult cat. Some even hissed at the model. These kittens had no experience with any adult cat except their mother, and there was no reason to believe that she had ever shown them this behavior. The Picasso cat evoked no response. Some sort of template of this posture must be prewired in the kitten brain. Seeing the model that matched this preexisting template automatically triggered a threat response. This innate trigger is an IRM.

The IRM concept also applies to humans. In one study, Tiffany Field and her colleagues (1982) asked an adult to display to young infants various exaggerated facial expressions, such as happiness, sadness, and surprise. As **Figure 12-3** shows, the babies responded with very much the same expressions the adults displayed. These newborns were too young to be imitating the adult faces intentionally. Rather, babies must innately match these facial expressions to internal templates, in turn triggering some prewired program to reproduce the expressions in their own faces. Such an IRM would have adaptive value if these facial expressions serve as important social signals for humans.

Evidence for a prewired motor program related to facial expressions also comes from study of congenitally blind children, who spontaneously produce the very same facial expressions that sighted people do, even though they have never seen them in others. IRMs are prewired into the brain, but experience can modify them. Our cat Hunter's stalking skills were not inherited fully developed at birth but rather matured functionally as she grew older. The same is true of many human IRMs, such as those for responding to sexually arousing stimuli.

Different cultures may emphasize different stimuli as arousing. Even within a single culture, what different people find sexually stimulating varies. Nonetheless, some human attributes are universally sexually arousing. For most human males, an example is the hip-to-waist ratio of human females: women with a hip-to-waist ratio of .70 are curvy and considered ideal across cultures. This ratio is probably part of an IRM.

The IRM concept can be related to the Darwinian view of nervous system evolution. Natural selection favors behaviors that prove adaptive for an organism, and these behaviors are passed on to future generations. Because behavior patterns are produced by the activity of neurons in the brain, the natural selection of specific behaviors is really the selection of particular brain circuits.

Animals that survive long enough to reproduce and have healthy offspring are more likely to pass on their brain circuit genes than are animals with traits that make them less likely to survive and successfully reproduce. Thus, feral cats adept at stalking prey or responding fiercely to threats are more likely to survive and produce many offspring, passing on their adaptive brain circuits and behaviors to their young. In humans, the ideal hip-to-waist ratio in women appears to be an indicator of health and fertility and is likely related to longevity and increased fecundity. In this way, evolution comes to select traits that become widespread in the species over time.

The Darwinian view seems straightforward when we consider how cats evolved brain circuits for stalking prey or responding to threats. Similarly, the connection between hip-to-waist ratio and successful child rearing may appear sensible

(A)

(B)

Courtesy of Arthur Nonneman and Bryan Kolb

FIGURE 12-2 **Innate Releasing Mechanism in Cats** **(A)** Displaying the Halloween cat image stimulates defensive responses in cats—raised fur, arched backs, and bared teeth. This behavior appears at about 6 weeks of age in kittens who have never seen such a posture before. **(B)** The scrambled "Picasso cat" evokes no response at all.

FIGURE 12-3 **Innate Releasing Mechanism in Humans** Facial expressions made by young infants in response to expressions made by the experimenter. Republished with permission of the American Association for the Advancement of Science, from M Field, R Woodson, R Greenberg, D Cohen,"Discrimination and imitation of facial expression by neonates", Science 8 October 1982: Vol. 218 no. 4568 pp. 179-181, Figure 1. Permission conveyed through Copyright Clearance Center, Inc.

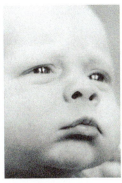

evolutionary psychology Discipline that seeks to apply principles of natural selection to understand the causes of human behavior.

reinforcer In operant conditioning, any event that strengthens the behavior it follows.

Section 1-2 reviews Darwin's theory, materialism, and contemporary perspectives on brain and behavior.

Section 15-5 posits a genetic explanation for the evolution of sex-related cognitive differences.

for humans, but the evolutionary influence is less obvious when applied to complex human behaviors. Why, for instance, have humans evolved the behavior of killing other humans? At first glance, it seems counterproductive to the survival of the human species. Why has it endured? For an answer, we turn to **evolutionary psychology**, the field that applies principles of natural selection to explanations of human behavior.

Evolutionary psychologists assume that any behavior, including homicide, occurs because natural selection has favored the neural circuits that produce it. When two men fight a duel, one commonsense explanation might be that they are fighting over grievances. But evolutionary psychologists would instead ask Why is a behavior pattern that risks people's lives sustained in a population? Their answer: fights are about social status.

Men who fought and won duels passed on their genes to future generations. Through time, therefore, the traits associated with successful dueling—strength, aggression, agility—became more prevalent among humans, as did dueling. Martin Daly and Margot Wilson (1988) extended this evolutionary analysis to further account for homicide. In their view, homicide may endure in our society despite its severe punishment because it is related to behaviors that were adaptive in the human past.

David Buss (2014) has examined patterns of mate selection across thousands of participants from 37 cultures, seeking to identify factors beyond culture that influence mate selection. His conclusions after nearly 30 years of study are that women around the world value dependability, stability, education, and intelligence in a long-term mate. Men, however, value good looks, health, and a desire for home and children more than women do.

Older men and younger women are most likely to exhibit a mutually desired set of traits, which leads to a universal tendency for age differences between mates. On average, older men are more stable, dependable, and educated than younger men, and younger women are healthier and able to have more children than older women. Although the idea is controversial, Buss argues that these preferences are a product of natural selection in a Stone Age environment, when women and men would have faced different daily problems and thus would have developed separate adaptations related to mating.

Evolutionary theory cannot account for all human behavior, perhaps not even homicide or mate selection. By casting an evolutionary perspective on the neurological bases of behavior, though, evolutionary psychologists can generate intriguing hypotheses about how natural selection might have shaped the brain and behavior.

Environmental Influences on Behavior

Many psychologists have emphasized learning as a cause of behavior. No one would question that we modify our behavior as we learn, but the noted behaviorist B. F. Skinner (1938) went much further. He believed that behaviors are selected by environmental factors.

Skinner's argument is simple. Certain events function as rewards, or **reinforcers**. When a reinforcing event follows a particular response, similar responses are more likely to occur. Skinner argued that reinforcement can be manipulated to encourage the display of complex behaviors.

The power of experience to shape behavior by pairing stimuli and rewards is typified by one of Skinner's experiments. A pigeon is placed in a box that has a small disc on one wall (the stimulus). If the pigeon pecks at the disc (the response), a food tray opens, and the pigeon can feed (the reinforcement or reward). The pigeon quickly learns the association between the stimulus and the response, especially if the disc has a small spot on it. It pecks at the spot, and within minutes it has mastered the response needed to receive a reward.

Now the response requirement can be made more complex. The pigeon might be required to turn 360 degrees before pecking the disc to gain the reward. The pigeon can learn this response, too. Other contingencies might then be added, making the

Skinner box

response requirements even more complex. For instance, the pigeon might be trained to turn in a clockwise circle if the disc is green, to turn in a counterclockwise circle if the disc is red, and to scratch at the floor if the disc is yellow.

If you suddenly came across this complex behavior in a pigeon, you would probably be astounded. But if you understood the experience that had shaped the bird's behavior, you would understand its cause. The rewards offered to the pigeon altered its behavior: its responses were controlled by the color of the disc on the wall.

Skinner extended behavioral analysis to include actions of all sorts—behaviors that at first do not appear easily explained. For instance, he argued that understanding a person's reinforcement history could account for various phobias. Someone who once was terrified by a turbulent plane ride thereafter avoids air travel and manifests a phobia of flying. The avoidance of flying is rewarding because it lowers the person's anxiety level, which then maintains the phobic behavior.

Skinner also argued against the commonly held view that much of human behavior is under our own control. From Skinner's perspective, free will is an illusion because behavior is controlled not by the organism but rather by the environment, through experience. Yet what is the experience actually doing? Increasing evidence suggests that epigenetic changes regulate changes in memory circuits. Skinner was not studying the brain directly, but it is becoming clear that epigenetics supports his perspective. We learn many complex behaviors through changes in memory-related genes that act to modify neural circuits (see the review by Day & Sweatt, 2011).

The environment does not always change the brain. A case in point can be seen again in pigeons. A pigeon in a Skinner box can quickly learn to peck a disc to receive a bit of food, but it cannot learn to peck a disc to escape from a mild electric shock to its feet. Why not? Although the same simple pecking behavior is being rewarded, apparently the pigeon's brain is not prewired for this second kind of association. The bird is prepared genetically to make the first association, for food, but not prepared for the second. This makes adaptive sense: typically, a pigeon flies away from noxious situations.

John Garcia and R. A. Koelling (1966) were the first psychologists to demonstrate the specific nature of this range of behavior–consequence associations that animals are able to learn. Garcia observed that farmers in the western United States are constantly shooting at coyotes for attacking lambs, yet despite the painful consequences, the coyotes never seem to learn to stop killing lambs in favor of safer prey. The reason, Garcia speculated, is that a coyote's brain is not prewired to make this kind of association.

So Garcia proposed an alternative to deter coyotes from killing lambs—an association that a coyote's brain is prepared to make: the connection between eating something that makes one sick and avoiding that food in the future. Garcia gave the coyotes a poisoned lamb carcass, which sickened but did not kill them. With only one pairing of lamb and illness, most coyotes learned not to eat sheep for the rest of their lives.

Many humans have similarly acquired food aversions because a certain food's taste—especially a novel taste—was subsequently paired with illness. This **learned taste aversion** is acquired even when the food eaten is in fact unrelated to the later illness. As long as the taste and the nausea are paired in time, the brain is prewired to connect them.

One of us ate his first Caesar salad the night before coming down with a stomach flu. A year later, he was offered another Caesar salad and, to his amazement, felt ill just at the smell of it. Even though he knew that the salad had not caused his earlier illness, he nonetheless had formed an association between the novel flavor and the illness. This strong and rapid *associative learning* makes adaptive sense. Having a brain that is prepared to make a connection between a novel taste and subsequent illness helps an animal avoid poisonous foods and so aids in its survival. A curious aspect of taste aversion learning is that we are unaware of having formed the association until we encounter the taste and/or smell again.

The fact that the nervous system is often prewired to make certain associations but not others has led to the concept of **preparedness** in learning theories. Preparedness

learned taste aversion Acquired association between a specific taste or odor and illness; leads to an aversion to foods that have the taste or odor.

preparedness Predisposition to respond to certain stimuli differently from other stimuli.

Epigenetic mechanisms mediate synaptic plasticity, especially in learning and memory. See Section 14-4.

Section 14-4 has more on how our brains are wired to link unrelated stimuli.

can help account for some complex behaviors. For example, if two rats are paired in a small box and exposed to a mild electric shock, they will immediately fight with one another, even though neither was responsible for the shock. Apparently, the rat brain is predisposed to associate injury with nearby objects or other animals. The extent to which we might extend this idea to explain such human behaviors as bigotry and racism is an interesting topic to ponder.

12-1 Review

Before you continue, check your understanding. Answers to Self-Test appear at the back of the book.

1. Glickman and Schiff first proposed the idea that animals engage in prey-killing behaviors, such as when a cat kills a bird, because these behaviors are _____.

2. One reason animals get bored and seek new activities is to maintain brain _____.

3. A man's frequency of copulation correlates with his _____.

4. The brain of a species is prewired to produce _____ to specific sensory stimuli selected by evolution to prompt certain associations between events.

5. Why is free will inadequate to explain why we do the things we do?

For additional study tools, visit 🎮 **LaunchPad** at launchpadworks.com

The Chemical Senses

Chemical reactions are central to nervous system activity, and *chemosignals* (chemical signals) play a central role in motivated and emotional behavior. Mammals identify group members by odor; mark their territory with urine and other odorants; identify favorite and forbidden foods by taste; and form associations among odors, tastes, and emotional events.

Olfaction

Olfaction is the most puzzling sensory system. We can discriminate thousands of odors, yet we have great difficulty finding words to describe what we smell. We may like or dislike smells or compare one smell to another, but we lack a vocabulary for olfactory perceptions.

Wine experts rely on olfaction to tell them about wines, but they must learn to use smell to do so. Training courses in wine sniffing typically run a full day each week for a year, and most participants have great difficulty passing the final test. This degree of difficulty contrasts with that of vision and audition, senses designed to analyze the specific qualities of sensory input, such as pitch in audition or color in vision. Olfaction seems designed to discriminate whether information is safe or familiar—is the smell from an edible food? from a friend or a stranger?—or to identify a signal, perhaps from a receptive mate.

Receptors for Smell

Conceptually, identifying chemosignals is similar to identifying other sensory stimuli (light, sound, touch), but rather than converting physical energy such as light or sound waves into receptor potentials, scent interacts with chemical receptors. This constant chemical interaction must be tough on the receptors: in contrast with receptors for light, sound, and touch, chemical receptors are constantly being replaced. The life of an olfactory receptor neuron is about 60 days.

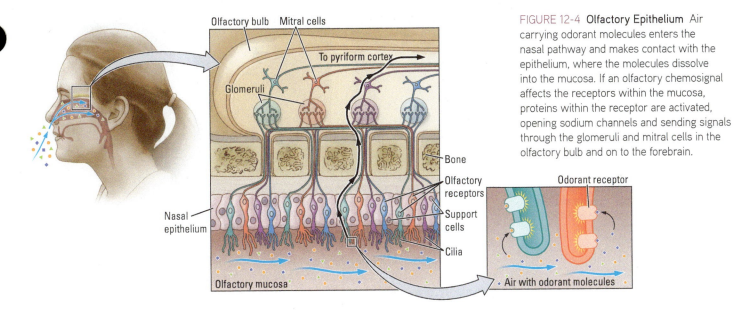

FIGURE 12-4 **Olfactory Epithelium** Air carrying odorant molecules enters the nasal pathway and makes contact with the epithelium, where the molecules dissolve into the mucosa. If an olfactory chemosignal affects the receptors within the mucosa, proteins within the receptor are activated, opening sodium channels and sending signals through the glomeruli and mitral cells in the olfactory bulb and on to the forebrain.

The receptor surface for olfaction, illustrated in **Figure 12-4**, is the *olfactory epithelium* in the nasal cavity. The epithelium is composed of receptor cells and support cells. Each receptor cell sends a process ending in 10 to 20 cilia into a mucous layer, the *olfactory mucosa*. Chemicals in the air we breathe dissolve in the mucosa to interact with the cilia. If an olfactory chemosignal affects the receptors, metabotropic activation of a specific G protein leads to an opening of sodium channels and a change in membrane potential.

The epithelial receptor surface varies widely across species. In humans, this area is estimated to range from 2 to 4 square centimeters; in dogs, about 18 square centimeters; and in cats, about 21 square centimeters. No wonder our sensitivity to odors is less acute than that of dogs and cats: they have 10 times as much receptor area as humans have! Roughly analogous to the tuning characteristics of cells in the auditory system, olfactory receptor neurons in vertebrates do not respond to specific odors but rather to a range of odors.

How are we able to smell many different odors despite having a small number of receptor types? The simplest explanation is that any given odorant stimulates a unique pattern of receptors, and the summed activity or pattern of activity produces our perception of a particular odor. Analogously, the visual system enables us to identify several million colors with only three receptor types in the retina; the summed activity of the three cones leads to our richly colored life.

A fundamental difference, however, is that the olfactory system is estimated to contain about 400 kinds of receptors, compared with just 4 (rods plus the cones) in the visual system. Some researchers propose that humans can discriminate up to 1 trillion smells. At present, the true number is unknown but is likely more than commonly believed (Gerkin & Castro, 2015).

Olfactory Pathways

Olfactory receptor cells project to the olfactory bulb, ending in ball-like tufts of dendrites—the *glomeruli* shown in Figure 12-4—where they form synapses with the dendrites of *mitral cells*. Mitral cells send their axons from the olfactory bulb to the broad range of forebrain areas summarized in **Figure 12-5**. Many olfactory targets, such as the amygdala and pyriform cortex, have no connection *through* the thalamus, as do other sensory systems. However, a thalamic connection (to the dorsomedial nucleus) does project to the **orbitofrontal cortex (OFC)**, the prefrontal area behind the eye sockets (the orbits). In Section 12-6, we explain the central role of the OFC in emotional behaviors.

Figure 5-15A illustrates activity in such a metabotropic receptor.

orbitofrontal cortex (OFC) Prefrontal cortex behind the eye sockets (the *orbits*); receives projections from the dorsomedial nucleus of the thalamus; central to a variety of emotional and social behaviors, including eating; also called *orbital frontal cortex*.

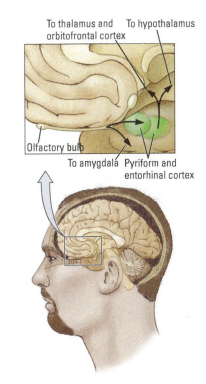

FIGURE 12-5 **Olfactory Pathways**

FIGURE 12-6 **Response to Pheromones** Left: A cat sniffs a urine-soaked cotton ball. Center: It raises its upper lip to close off the nasal passages. Right: It follows with the full gape response characteristic of flehmen, a behavior mediated by the accessory olfactory system.

Courtesy Bryan Kolb and Arthur Nonneman

pheromone Odorant biochemical released by one animal that acts as a chemosignal and can affect the physiology or behavior of another animal.

Accessory Olfactory System

A unique class of odorants is **pheromones**, biochemicals released by one animal that act as chemosignals and can affect the physiology or behavior of another animal of the same species.

Pheromones are unique odors. In most mammals (though perhaps not in humans), they are detected by a special olfactory receptor system, the *vomeronasal organ*, which is made up of a small group of sensory receptors connected by a duct to the nasal passage. The receptor cells in the vomeronasal organ send their axons to the accessory olfactory bulb, which lies adjacent to the main olfactory bulb; this connects primarily with the amygdala and hypothalamus, via which it probably plays a role in reproductive and social behavior.

It is likely that the vomeronasal organ participates in the analysis of pheromones, such as those in urine or sweat. You may have seen horses or cats engage in a behavior known as *flehmen*, illustrated in **Figure 12-6**. When exposed to novel urine from a cat or human, cats raise their upper lip to close off the nasal passages and suck air into the mouth. The air flows through the duct on the roof of the mouth en route to the vomeronasal organ.

Human Olfactory Processing

Our ability to distinguish a surprisingly large number of odors upends the common misperception that humans have a miserable sense of smell relative to other mammals. Still, our threshold for detecting many smells is certainly inferior to that of our pet dogs, cats, and horses. Yet humans have a surprisingly acute sensitivity to behaviorally significant smells, and data from a variety of sources indicate a vital link between human olfaction and the ability to maintain a social life.

The compound delta 4,16-androstadien-3-one (*androstadienone*), a natural component of human sweat, plays a unique role in communication between humans. There is growing evidence that people can identify their own odor, the odor of kin versus not-kin, and the odor of friends versus strangers with an accuracy well above chance (e.g., Olsson et al., 2006). Yet there does not appear to be a functional vomeronasal organ in humans. How are these social odors perceived? Tom Hummer and colleagues (2017) used fMRI to examine the effect of androstadienone on the brain's response to emotional images (relative to neutral images) of participants who were exposed to the odor versus no odor. They found increased activity in the right dorsolateral prefrontal and orbital prefrontal regions, especially when the images were positive. Another study provides evidence that smelling a stranger's odor activates the amygdala and insular cortex, similar to activation observed for fearsome visual stimuli, such as masked or fearsome faces (Lundstrom et al., 2008).

The insula contains regions related to language, taste perception, and social cognition.

Gustation

Research reveals significant differences in taste preferences both between and within species. Humans and rats like sucrose and saccharin solutions, but dogs reject saccharin, and cats are indifferent to both, inasmuch as they do not detect sweetness at all. The failure of cats to taste sweetness may not be surprising: they are pure carnivores, and nothing that they normally eat is sweet.

Within the human species, clear differences in taste thresholds and preferences are obvious. An example is the preference for or dislike of bitter tastes—the flavor of brussels sprouts, for instance. People tend to love them or hate them. Linda Bartoshuk (2000) showed absolute differences among adults: some perceive certain tastes as very bitter, whereas others are indifferent to them. Presumably, the latter group is more tolerant of brussels sprouts.

Sensitivity to bitterness is related to genetic differences in the ability to detect a specific bitter chemical (6-n-propylthiouracil, or PROP). PROP bitterness associates with allelic variation in the taste receptor gene TAS2R38. People able to detect minute quantities of PROP find the taste extremely bitter; they are sometimes called *supertasters*. Those who do not taste PROP as very bitter are *nontasters*. The advantage of being a supertaster is that many bitter "foods" are poisonous. The disadvantage is that supertasters avoid many nutritious fruits and vegetables, such as grapefruit, that they find too bitter.

Differences in taste thresholds also emerge as we age. Children are much more responsive to taste than adults and are often intolerant of spicy foods because they have more taste receptors than adults have. It is estimated that by age 20, humans have lost at least 50 percent of their taste receptors. No wonder children and adults have different food preferences.

Receptors for Taste

Taste receptors are found in taste buds on the tongue, under the tongue, on the soft palate on the roof of the mouth, on the sides of the mouth, and at the back of the mouth on the nasopharynx. Each of the five taste receptor types responds to a different chemical component in food. The four most familiar are sweet, sour, salty, and bitter. The fifth type, called the *umami* (meaning "savory" in Japanese) receptor, is especially sensitive to glutamate. Although it was once widely believed that different regions of the tongue are responsible for each of the five basic tastes, we now know that the five taste receptors are found all over the tongue.

Taste receptors are grouped into taste buds, each containing several, if not all, receptor types, as illustrated in **Figure 12-7**. Gustatory stimuli interact with the receptor tips, the *microvilli*, to open ion channels, leading to changes in membrane potential. At its base, the taste bud contacts the branches of afferent cranial nerve 7 (facial), 9 (glossopharyngeal), or 10 (vagus).

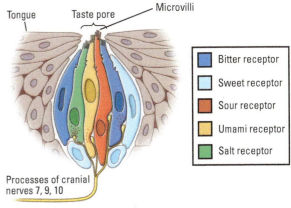

FIGURE 12-7 **Anatomy of a Taste Bud**
Information from Smith & Shepherd, 2003.

Gustatory Pathways

Cranial nerves 7, 9, and 10 form the main gustatory nerve, the *solitary tract*. On entering the brainstem, the tract splits, as illustrated in **Figure 12-8**. One route (traced in red) travels through the posterior medulla to the ventroposterior medial nucleus of the thalamus. This nucleus in turn sends out two pathways, one to the primary somatosensory cortex (SI) and the other to the primary gustatory cortex of the insula, a region just rostral to the secondary somatosensory cortex (SII).

The gustatory region in the insula is dedicated to taste, whereas SI is also responsive to tactile information and is probably responsible for our reactions to a food's texture. The gustatory cortex sends a projection to the orbital frontal cortex. Neuroimaging studies suggest that the mixture of olfactory and gustatory input in the orbital cortex gives rise to our perception of flavor. It is believed that the insula identifies the nature and intensity of flavors, whereas the orbital frontal cortex evaluates the affective properties of tastes. Ambience, including music and light, also affects this region of orbital cortex, increasing blood flow and so enhancing our experience of flavor.

The second pathway from the gustatory nerve (shown in blue in Figure 12-8) projects via the nucleus of the solitary tract in the brainstem to the hypothalamus and amygdala. Researchers hypothesize that these inputs somehow play a part in eating, possibly evaluating the pleasantness and strength of flavors.

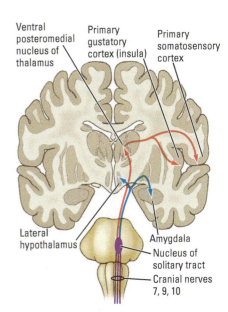

FIGURE 12-8 **Gustatory Pathways**

12-2 Review

Before you continue, check your understanding. Answers to Self-Test appear at the back of the book.

1. The receptor surface for olfaction is the _____.

2. Olfactory and gustatory pathways pass through the thalamus and merge in an area behind the eye sockets known as the _____.

3. Chemosignals that affect the behavior of another animal are called _____.

4. The perception of bitterness is related to both the _____ and the number of _____.

5. What role does olfactory processing play in humans' social behavior?

For additional study tools, visit 🅼 **LaunchPad** at launchpadworks.com

Section 6-5 explores hormonal regulation of homeostatic mechanisms.

12-3

Neuroanatomy of Motivated Behavior

Motivation refers to an internal state that acts to initiate or energize behavior (from the Latin *motivus*, meaning "a moving cause"). The neural circuits that control motivated behavior encompass regions at all levels of the brain, but the critical neural structure in producing motivated behavior is the hypothalamus. The hypothalamus receives projections from all major subdivisions of the nervous system and functions to integrate diverse adaptive behaviors. It is not an individual brain region but rather is composed of smaller neural units devoted to specific functions.

In his epic review, Larry Swanson (2000) concluded that the hypothalamus is an integrative center of a larger "behavioral control column" (or network) controlled by the cerebral hemispheres. This behavioral column is composed of a rostral brainstem region devoted to social (including reproductive and defensive) behaviors and ingestion (eating and drinking), as well as a more caudal region extending into other brainstem areas related to exploration and foraging behaviors, such as the substantia nigra and ventral tegmentum. These functions are modulated by the cerebral hemispheres through descending pathways from the cerebral cortex, striatum, and pallidum. The hypothalamus acts to organize these cerebral inputs and produce feedback loops that regulate cerebral information to orchestrate homeostasis and motivated behaviors; it also ensures that the cerebral regions are aroused and online when needed. In addition, outputs from the hypothalamus project to the pituitary to control the release of a broad range of hormones.

In **Figure 12-9**, the neck of a funnel represents the hypothalamus, and the cerebral hemispheres form the funnel's rim. To produce behavior, the hypothalamus sends axons to other brainstem circuits—but not all behavior is controlled via the funnel to the hypothalamus. Many other routes to the brainstem and spinal cord bypass the hypothalamus, among them projections from the motor cortex to the brainstem and spinal cord. Thus, it is primarily motivated behaviors that require hypothalamic involvement.

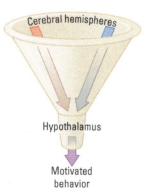

FIGURE 12-9 **Funneling Signals** In this model, many inputs from the cerebral hemispheres funnel through the hypothalamus, which sends its axons to control brainstem circuits that produce motivated behaviors.

Regulatory and Nonregulatory Behavior

Animals seek mates, food, or sensory stimulation because of brain activity, but we talk about such behavior as being motivated. Motivated behaviors are not something in the brain that we can point to, however. Rather, motivations are inferences we make about why an animal, humans included, engages in a particular behavior. The two general classes of motivated behaviors are regulatory and nonregulatory. In this section, we explore both categories before exploring the neuroanatomy of motivation.

Regulatory Behaviors

Regulatory behaviors—behaviors motivated by an organism's survival—are controlled by **homeostatic mechanisms**. By analogy, consider a house whose thermostat is set at 18 degrees Celsius (°C). When the temperature falls below a certain tolerable range (say, to 16°C), the thermostat turns on the furnace. When the temperature rises above a certain tolerable level (say, 20°C), the thermostat turns on the air conditioner.

Human body temperature is controlled in a somewhat similar manner by a thermostat in the hypothalamus that holds internal temperature at about 37°C, a temperature referred to as a *set point*. Even slight variations cause us to engage in various behaviors to regain the set point. For example, when body temperature drops slightly, neural circuits that increase body temperature turn on. These neural circuits might induce an involuntary response such as shivering or a seemingly voluntary behavior such as moving closer to a heat source. Conversely, if body temperature rises slightly, we sweat or move to a cooler place.

Similar mechanisms control many other homeostatic processes, including the amount of water in the body, the balance of dietary nutrients, and the blood sugar level. Control of many such homeostatic systems is quite complex, requiring both neural and hormonal mechanisms. In some way, however, all of the body's homeostatic systems involve hypothalamic activity.

Imagine that specific cells are especially sensitive to temperature. When they are cool, they become very active; when they are warm, they become less active. These cells could function as a thermostat, telling the body when it is too cool or too warm. A similar set of cells could serve as a glucostat, controlling the level of sugar in the blood, or as a hydrostat, controlling the amount of water in the body. In fact, the body's real homeostatic mechanisms are slightly more complex than this imagined one, but they work on the same general principle.

Mechanisms to hold constant various conditions such as temperature have evolved because the body, including the brain, is a chemical soup in which thousands of reactions are taking place all the time. Maintaining constant temperature is critical. When temperature changes, even by 2°C, the rates at which chemical reactions take place change.

Such fluctuations might be tolerable, within certain limits, if all the reaction times changed to the same extent. But they do not. Consequently, an increase of 2°C might increase one reaction by 10 percent and another by only 2 percent. Such uneven changes would wreak havoc with finely tuned body processes such as metabolism and the workings of neurons.

A similar logic applies to maintaining homeostasis in other body systems. For instance, cells require certain concentrations of water, salt, and glucose to function properly. Wild fluctuations in the concentrations cause a gross disturbance of metabolic balance and eventually biological disaster.

Nonregulatory Behaviors

Unlike regulatory behaviors, such as eating or drinking, **nonregulatory behaviors** are neither required to meet the basic survival needs of an animal nor controlled by homeostatic mechanisms (see table to the right). Thus, nonregulatory behaviors include everything else we do—from sexual intercourse to parenting to such curiosity-driven activities as conducting psychology experiments.

Some certain nonregulatory behaviors, such as sexual intercourse, do involve the hypothalamus, but most of them probably do not. Rather, such behaviors entail a variety of forebrain structures, especially the frontal lobes. Presumably, as the forebrain evolved and enlarged, so did our range of nonregulatory behaviors.

Activities of the Hypothalamic Circuit

The hypothalamus maintains homeostasis by acting on both the endocrine system and the autonomic nervous system (ANS) to regulate our internal environment. The hypothalamus also influences the behaviors selected by the rest of the brain, especially by

regulatory behavior Behavior motivated to meet an animal's survival needs.

homeostatic mechanism Process that maintains critical body functions within a narrow, fixed range.

nonregulatory behavior Behavior unnecessary to an animal's basic survival needs.

Categories of Motivated Behavior

Some regulatory behaviors
Internal body temperature maintenance
Eating and drinking
Salt consumption
Waste elimination

Some nonregulatory behaviors
Sex
Parenting
Aggression
Food preference
Curiosity
Reading

FIGURE 12-10 **Nuclei and Regions of the Hypothalamus** **(A)** Medial view shows the relationship between the hypothalamic nuclei and the rest of the brain. **(B)** Frontal view shows the relative positions of the hypothalamus, thalamus, and—in the midline between the left and right hemispheres—the third ventricle. Note the three principal hypothalamic regions: periventricular, lateral, and medial.

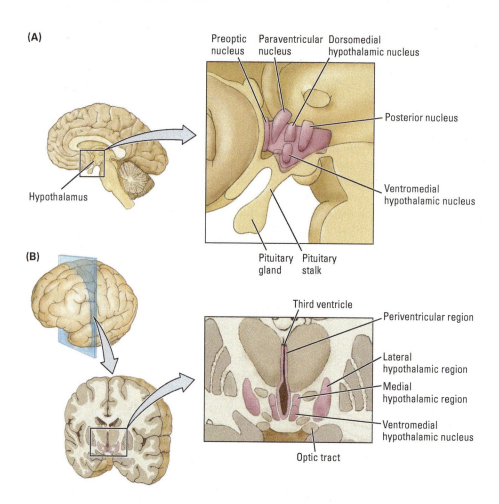

pituitary gland Endocrine gland attached to the bottom of the hypothalamus; its secretions control the activities of many other endocrine glands; associated with biological rhythms.

medial forebrain bundle (MFB) Tract that connects brainstem structures with various parts of the limbic system; forms the activating projections that run from the brainstem to the basal ganglia and frontal cortex.

Figure 2-32 diagrams ANS pathways and connections.

Sections 6-2 and 6-4 elaborate on dopamine's importance in experiences related to drug use.

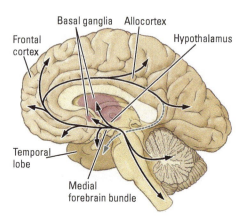

FIGURE 12-11 **Medial Forebrain Bundle** The activating projections that run from the brainstem to the basal ganglia and frontal cortex are major components of the MFB, a primary pathway for fibers connecting various parts of the limbic system with the brainstem.

the cerebral hemispheres. Although it constitutes less than 1 percent of the human brain's volume, the hypothalamus controls an amazing variety of motivated behaviors, ranging from heart rate to eating and sexual activity.

Hypothalamic Involvement in Hormone Secretions

A principal function of the hypothalamus is to control the **pituitary gland**, which is attached to it by a stalk (**Figure 12-10A**). Figure 12-10B diagrams the anatomic location of the hypothalamus in each hemisphere, with the thalamus above and the optic tracts just lateral.

We can divide the hypothalamus into three regions, lateral, medial, and periventricular, as illustrated in the frontal view in Figure 12-10B. The lateral hypothalamus, composed both of nuclei and of nerve tracts running up and down the brain, connects the lower brainstem to the forebrain. The principal tract, shown in **Figure 12-11**, is the **medial forebrain bundle (MFB)**.

The MFB connects brainstem structures with various parts of the limbic system and forms the activating projections that run from the brainstem to the basal ganglia and frontal cortex. Fibers that ascend from the dopamine- and noradrenaline-containing cells of the lower brainstem form a significant part of the MFB. The dopamine-containing MFB fibers contribute to the control of many motivated behaviors, including eating and sex. They also contribute to pathological behaviors, such as addiction and impulsivity.

Each hypothalamic nucleus is anatomically distinct, and most have multiple functions, in part because the cells in each nucleus contain a different mix of peptide neurotransmitters. Each peptide participates in different behaviors. For instance, transmitters in the cells in the paraventricular nucleus may be vasopressin, oxytocin, or various combinations of other peptides (such as enkephalin and neurotensin). When peptide neurotransmitters act, we may experience a range of feelings such as well-being (endorphins) or

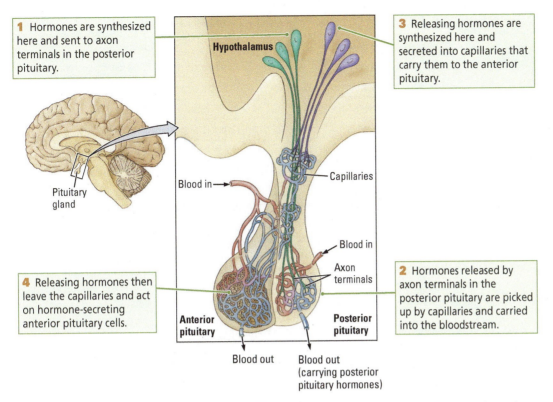

1 Hormones are synthesized here and sent to axon terminals in the posterior pituitary.

3 Releasing hormones are synthesized here and secreted into capillaries that carry them to the anterior pituitary.

Hypothalamus

Pituitary gland

Blood in →

Capillaries

← Blood in

Axon terminals

4 Releasing hormones then leave the capillaries and act on hormone-secreting anterior pituitary cells.

2 Hormones released by axon terminals in the posterior pituitary are picked up by capillaries and carried into the bloodstream.

Anterior pituitary

Posterior pituitary

Blood out

Blood out (carrying posterior pituitary hormones)

FIGURE 12-12 **Hypothalamus and Pituitary Gland** The anterior pituitary is connected to the hypothalamus by a system of blood vessels that carry hormones from the hypothalamus to the pituitary. The posterior pituitary receives input from axons of hypothalamic neurons. Both regions respond to hypothalamic input by producing hormones that travel in the bloodstream to stimulate target organs.

attachment (oxytocin and vasopressin). For example, oxytocin is released during intimate moments such as nurturing behavior, hugging, or sex, and thus is sometimes known as the bonding hormone.

The production of various neuropeptides hints at the special relationship between the hypothalamus and the pituitary. The pituitary consists of distinct anterior and posterior glands, as shown in **Figure 12-12**. The posterior pituitary is composed of neural tissue and is essentially a continuation of the hypothalamus.

Neurons in the hypothalamus make peptides (for example, oxytocin and vasopressin) that are transported down their axons to terminals lying in the posterior pituitary. If these neurons become active, they send action potentials to the terminals to release the peptides stored there. But rather than affecting another neuron, as occurs at most synapses, capillaries (tiny blood vessels) in the posterior pituitary's rich vascular bed pick up these peptides.

The peptides then enter the bloodstream, which carries them to distant targets, where they exert their effects. Vasopressin, for example, affects water resorption by the kidneys, and oxytocin controls both uterine contractions and the ejection of milk by mammary glands in the breasts. Peptides can have multiple functions, depending on where their receptors are. Thus, oxytocin not only controls milk ejection in females but also performs a more general role in several forms of affiliative behavior, including parental care, grooming, and sexual behavior in both men and women (Insel & Fernald, 2004).

The glandular tissue of the anterior pituitary, by contrast, synthesizes various hormones. The major hormones and their functions are listed in **Table 12-1**. The hypothalamus controls the release of these anterior pituitary hormones by producing **releasing hormones**, peptides that act to increase or decrease hormone release. Releasing hormones, which are produced by hypothalamic cell bodies, are secreted into capillaries that transport them to the anterior pituitary, as Figure 12-12 shows.

Section 5-2 reviews the structures and functions of peptide neurotransmitters.

releasing hormone Peptide released by the hypothalamus that increases or decreases hormone release from the anterior pituitary.

TABLE 12-1 Major Hormones Produced by the Anterior Pituitary

Hormone	Function
Adrenocorticotrophic hormone (ACTH)	Controls secretions of the adrenal cortex
Thyroid-stimulating hormone (TSH)	Controls secretions of the thyroid gland
Follicle-stimulating hormone (FSH)	Controls secretions of the gonads
Luteinizing hormone (LH)	Controls secretions of the gonads
Prolactin	Controls secretions of the mammary glands
Growth hormone (GH)	Promotes growth throughout the body

A releasing hormone can either stimulate or inhibit the release of an anterior pituitary hormone. For example, the anterior pituitary produces the hormone prolactin, but its release is controlled by a prolactin-releasing factor and a prolactin release–inhibiting factor, both synthesized in the hypothalamus. Hormone release by the anterior pituitary in turn provides the brain a means for controlling what is taking place in many other parts of the body. Three factors control hypothalamic hormone-related activity: feedback loops, neural regulation, and experience-based responses.

FEEDBACK LOOPS When the level of, say, thyroid hormone is low, the hypothalamus releases thyroid-stimulating hormone–releasing hormone (TSH-releasing hormone), which stimulates the anterior pituitary to release TSH. TSH then acts on the thyroid gland to secrete more thyroid hormone.

Receptors in the hypothalamus detect the thyroid hormone level. When that level rises, the hypothalamus lessens its secretion of TSH-releasing hormone. This type of system is essentially a form of homeostatic control that works as a feedback mechanism, a system in which a neural or hormonal loop regulates the initiation of neural activity or hormone release, as illustrated in **Figure 12-13A**.

The hypothalamus initiates a cascade of events that culminates in hormone secretion, but it pays attention to how much hormone is released. When a certain level is reached, it stops its hormone-stimulating signals. Thus, the feedback mechanism in the hypothalamus maintains a fairly constant circulating level of certain hormones.

NEURAL CONTROL Hormonal activities of the hypothalamus necessitate regulation by other brain structures, largely in the cerebral hemispheres. Figure 12-13B diagrams this neural control in relationship to the effects of oxytocin released from the hypothalamus by the paraventricular nucleus, which lies within the periventricular region illustrated in Figure 12-10. As stated earlier, one function of oxytocin is to stimulate cells of the mammary glands to release milk. As shown in Figure 12-13B, when an infant suckles

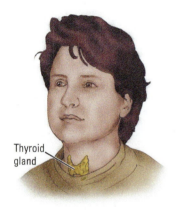

Thyroid gland

FIGURE 12-13 **Hypothalamic Controls** **(A)** Releasing hormones from the hypothalamus stimulate the anterior pituitary to release hormones. The pituitary hormones stimulate target organs, such as the thyroid and adrenal glands, to release their hormones. In the feedback loop, those hormones in turn influence the hypothalamus to decrease its secretion of the releasing hormones. **(B)** In the milk letdown response, oxytocin released from the hypothalamus stimulates the mammary glands to release milk. Milk letdown is enhanced by infant-related stimuli and inhibited by maternal anxiety.

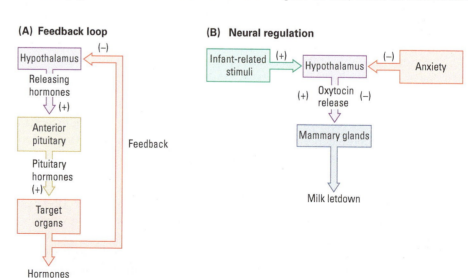

(A) Feedback loop

Hypothalamus → Releasing hormones (+) → Anterior pituitary → Pituitary hormones (+) → Target organs → Hormones

(−) Feedback

(B) Neural regulation

Infant-related stimuli (+) → Hypothalamus ← (−) Anxiety

(+) Oxytocin release (−) → Mammary glands → Milk letdown

the breast, the tactile stimulation causes hypothalamic cells to release oxytocin, which stimulates milk letdown. In this way, the oxytocin cells participate in a fairly simple reflex that is both neural and hormonal.

Other stimuli can influence oxytocin release, however, which is where control by other brain structures comes in. For example, the sight, sound, or even thought of her baby can trigger a lactating mother to eject milk. Conversely, as diagrammed in Figure 12-13B, feelings of anxiety in a lactating woman can inhibit milk ejection. These excitatory and inhibitory influences exerted by cognitive activity imply that the cortex can influence neurons in the periventricular region. It is likely that projections from the frontal lobes to the hypothalamus perform this role.

EXPERIENTIAL RESPONSES A third control on the hormonal activities of the hypothalamus is the brain's responses to experience: neurons in the hypothalamus undergo structural and biochemical changes just as cells in other brain regions do. In other words, hypothalamic neurons are like neurons elsewhere in the brain in that they can be changed by heavy demands on them.

Principle 2: Neuroplasticity is the hallmark of nervous system functioning.

Such changes in hypothalamic neurons can affect hormone output. For instance, when a woman is lactating, the cells producing oxytocin increase in size to promote oxytocin release and meet the increasing demands of a growing infant for more milk. Through this control, which is mediated by experience, a mother provides her baby with sufficient milk over time. Thus, we can see that both the neural regulation and the environmental demands can influence a single system (in this case, oxytocin and milk letdown) in different ways.

Hypothalamic Involvement in Generating Behavior

Not only does the hypothalamus control hormone systems, but it is also central in generating behavior. This function was first demonstrated by studies in which stimulating electrodes were placed in the hypothalamus of various animals, ranging from chickens to rats and cats. When a small electric current was delivered through a wire electrode, an animal suddenly engaged in some complex behavior—eating, drinking, or digging; displaying fear, attack, predatory, or reproductive behavior. The specific behavior exhibited depended on which site was stimulated. All of the behaviors were smooth, well integrated, and indistinguishable from typically occurring ones. Furthermore, all were goal directed.

The onset and termination of these behaviors depended entirely on hypothalamic stimulation. For example, if an electrode in a certain location elicited eating behavior, the animal ate as soon as the stimulation was turned on and continued to eat until the stimulation was turned off. If the food was removed, however, the animal would not eat but might engage in other behaviors, such as drinking. Recall that Roger, profiled in Section 12-1, ate continuously if foodlike materials were present, corresponding to the continuous hypothalamic activity caused by a tumor.

Figure 12-14 illustrates the effect of stimulation at a site that elicits digging. When no current is delivered, the animal sits quietly. When the current is turned on, the

FIGURE 12-14 **Generating Behavior** When rats receive electrical stimulation to the hypothalamus, they produce goal-directed behaviors. This rat is stimulated to dig when and only when the electricity is on and when sawdust is present. If the sawdust is removed (not shown), there is no digging.

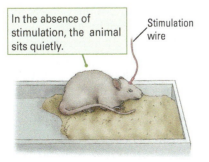

In the absence of stimulation, the animal sits quietly.

Stimulation wire

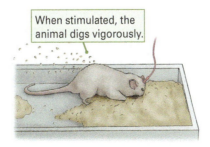

When stimulated, the animal digs vigorously.

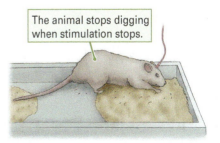

The animal stops digging when stimulation stops.

animal vigorously digs in the sawdust; when the current is turned off, the animal stops digging. If the sawdust is removed, the animal does not dig.

Two more important characteristics of behaviors generated by hypothalamic stimulation are related to (1) survival and (2) reward. Animals apparently find the stimulation of these behaviors pleasant, as suggested by the fact that they willingly expend effort, such as pressing a bar, to trigger the stimulation. Recall that cats kill birds and mice because the act of stalking and killing prey is rewarding to them. Similarly, we can hypothesize that animals eat because eating is rewarding, drink because drinking is rewarding, and mate because mating is rewarding.

12-3 Review

Before you continue, check your understanding. Answers to Self-Test appear at the back of the book.

1. The two types of motivated behaviors are _____ behaviors, which maintain homeostasis, and _____ behaviors, encompassing basically all other behaviors.

2. The brain's homeostat for many functions is found in the _____.

3. The anterior pituitary gland produces _____.

4. Explain how the hypothalamus acts as a integrative center for the behavioral control column.

For additional study tools, visit **≈ LaunchPad** at launchpadworks.com

---

12-4

Control of Regulatory Behavior

The two distinctly different types of motivated behaviors described in Section 12-3 are *regulatory* behaviors, which maintain vital body system balance, or homeostasis; and *nonregulatory* behaviors, those not controlled by a homeostatic mechanism—basically all other behaviors. We focus here on the control of two regulatory behaviors in humans—eating and fluid intake. In the next section, we explore control of human sexual behavior, a nonregulatory behavior that is of enormous significance to humans.

Controlling Eating

Eating entails far more than sustenance alone. We must eat and drink to live, but we also derive great pleasure from these acts. For many people, eating is a focus of daily life, not just for survival, but also for its centrality to social activities such as get-togethers with family and friends or business meetings, and even to group identification (gourmet, vegetarian, snack food junkie, dieter, and so on).

Control over eating is a source of frustration and even grief for many people in the developed world. In 2000, the World Health Organization identified **obesity**, the excessive accumulation of body fat, as a worldwide epidemic. The United States is a case in point. From 1990 to 2017, the proportion of overweight people increased from about 50 percent to 70 percent of the population. The proportion of people considered obese increased from about 12 percent in 1990 to 38 percent in 2016, and the Centers for Disease Control and Prevention predicts that it will rise to 42 percent by 2030.

The increasing numbers of overweight and obese children and adults persist despite a substantial decrease in fat intake in American diets. What behaviors might cause persistent weight gain in the postindustrial world? One clue is found in history. Until the mid-twentieth century, much of our food was only seasonally available. In a world with uncertain food availability, it makes sense for the body to store excess calories in the form of fat to be used later, when food is scarce. Throughout history, and in many cultures today, plumpness was and is desirable as a standard of beauty and a sign of health and wealth.

obesity Excessive accumulation of body fat.

⊙ CLINICAL FOCUS 12-2

Diets and Rhythms

Among the wide range of diets and weight-loss strategies on the market, none has stopped the obesity epidemic facing the developed world. Overall, studies on the effectiveness of different diets show that although people generally lose weight in the first months or year, they usually gain it back, and in many cases weight increases over the baseline. The failure of diets to control weight suggests that we may need a different approach to weight control.

One challenge in developing obesity interventions is that little is known about the cognitive regulation of eating-related behaviors. Much is known about the role of molecules, cells, and even brain areas in the control of eating, but it is not yet clear how these elements all work together. It has become clear over the past decade, however, that rhythms in brain activity (known as oscillations) act to integrate diverse brain regions (see, for example, Buzaki, 2011). Oscillations can be measured at many levels, ranging from membrane potentials to EEG. Diffuse brain circuits can work together to produce behavior simply by being in phase and oscillating at the same rhythms.

Marta Carus-Cadavieco and colleagues (2017) asked whether the dissociation between food-seeking behavior and metabolic needs leading to obesity could be related to brain oscillations in a diffuse eating system. Using an impressive range of electrophysiological, optogenetic, and molecular techniques in mice, they were able to show that a gamma

rhythm (30–80 Hz) originating in the prefrontal cortex tied together the lateral septum and lateral hypothalamus to direct food seeking and eating. Optogenetic stimulation could either drive or reduce food-seeking behavior through effects on neurons in the lateral hypothalamus (see the accompanying figure).

The prefrontal cortex sends projections to the lateral septum, which send inhibitory inputs to eating-related neurons in the lateral hypothalamus. This pathway interacts via gamma rhythms to modulate eating.
(Research from Narayanan & DiLeone, 2017.)

This work demonstrates a mechanism whereby cognitive activity can control eating. Although prefrontal rhythms are well known to synchronize cortical networks in humans, it was not known that they could also affect subcortical networks. Because gamma activity can be measured by scalp EEG, it may be possible to monitor how modulation of the prefrontal-driven oscillatory rhythms coordinate the eating network, which could lead to direct interventions to regulate body weight.

In postindustrial societies, people often eat as though food will be scarce, even though it is continuously and easily available. The failure to burn off the extra calories by exercising results in weight gain and health risks. Compounding the problem, the development of electronic media, which began roughly in the 1980s, has led to a more sedentary lifestyle than was common in previous generations.

The human control system for eating has multiple neurobiological inputs, including cognitive factors such as thinking about food and the association between environmental cues and the act of eating. The constant pairing of such cues with eating—for example, snacking paired with studying or television viewing—can result in the cues alone becoming a motivation, an incentive to eat. We return to this phenomenon in the discussion of reward and addiction in Section 12-7.

About half of the U.S. population has dieted at some point in their life. At any given time, at least 25 percent report that they are currently on a diet. For insight into a different approach to weight control, see Clinical Focus 12-2, Diets and Rhythms.

Eating disorders entail being either overweight or underweight. **Anorexia nervosa** is an eating disorder with a huge cognitive component: self-image. A person's body image is highly distorted in anorexia. This misperception leads to an exaggerated concern with being overweight. That concern spirals to excessive dieting, compulsive exercising, and severe, potentially life-threatening weight loss. Anorexia is especially prevalent among adolescent girls.

The neurobiological control of eating behavior in humans is not a simple process. The multiple inputs to the human control system for eating come from three major sources: the cognitive factors already introduced, the hypothalamus, and the digestive system.

Digestive System and Control of Eating

Digestion is controlled by the enteric nervous system (ENS). As illustrated in **Figure 12-15**, the digestive tract begins in the mouth and ends at the anus. As food travels through the tract, the digestive system extracts three types of nutrients: lipids (fats),

anorexia nervosa Exaggerated concern with being overweight that leads to inadequate food intake and often excessive exercising; can lead to severe weight loss and even starvation.

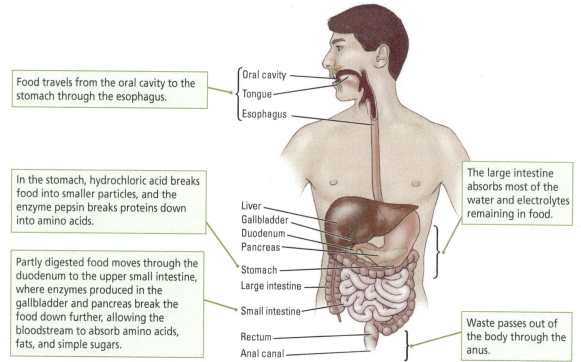

Food travels from the oral cavity to the stomach through the esophagus.

Oral cavity
Tongue
Esophagus

In the stomach, hydrochloric acid breaks food into smaller particles, and the enzyme pepsin breaks proteins down into amino acids.

The large intestine absorbs most of the water and electrolytes remaining in food.

Liver
Gallbladder
Duodenum
Pancreas
Stomach
Large intestine
Small intestine

Partly digested food moves through the duodenum to the upper small intestine, where enzymes produced in the gallbladder and pancreas break the food down further, allowing the bloodstream to absorb amino acids, fats, and simple sugars.

Rectum
Anal canal

Waste passes out of the body through the anus.

FIGURE 12-15 **The Digestive System**

Figure 2-33 diagrams the inner workings of the ENS and Section 5-3 describes the main neurotransmitters it employs.

amino acids (the building blocks of proteins), and glucose (sugar). Each nutrient is a specialized energy reserve. Because we require varying amounts of these reserves, depending on what we are doing, the body has detector cells to keep track of the level of each nutrient in the bloodstream.

Glucose is the body's primary fuel and virtually the only energy source for the brain. Because the brain requires glucose even when the digestive tract is empty, the liver acts as a short-term reservoir of glycogen, a starch that acts as an inert form of glucose. When blood sugar levels fall, as when we are sleeping, detector cells tell the liver to convert glycogen into glucose for release into the bloodstream.

Thus, the digestive system functions mainly to break down food, and the body needs to be apprised of how this breakdown is proceeding. Feedback mechanisms provide such information. When food reaches the intestines, it interacts with receptors in the ENS to trigger the release of at least 10 different peptide hormones, including cholecystokinin (CCK), glucagonlike peptide 1 (GLP-1), and peptide YY (PYY). Each peptide hormone, by virtue of its release as food, is absorbed and acts as a satiation or satiety signal that inhibits food intake. For example, when CCK is infused into an animal's hypothalamus, the animal's appetite diminishes.

Hypothalamus and Control of Eating

Eating is influenced by hormones, including insulin, growth hormone, and sex steroids, that stimulate and inhibit eating and also aid in converting nutrients into fat and fat into glucose. The hypothalamus, which controls hormone systems, is the key brain structure in eating as well as in satiety.

Section 6-5 reviews the major categories of hormones and how they work.

Investigation into how the hypothalamus controls eating began in the early 1950s, when researchers discovered that damage to the lateral hypothalamus in rats caused the animals to stop eating, a symptom known as **aphagia** (in Greek, *phagein* means "to eat"). In contrast, damage to the ventromedial hypothalamus (VMH) caused the animals to overeat—thus displaying **hyperphagia**. A VMH-lesioned rat that overate to the point of obesity is shown in the Procedure section of **Experiment 12-1**. The Results section reveals that the VMH-lesioned rat weighed more than 1 kilogram, three times the weight of her healthy sister, at 340 grams.

aphagia Failure to eat; may be due to an unwillingness to eat or to motor difficulties, especially with swallowing.

hyperphagia Overeating that leads to significant weight gain.

The researchers also found that electrical stimulation of the lateral hypothalamus elicits eating, whereas stimulation of the ventromedial hypothalamus inhibits eating.

The opposing effects of injury and stimulation to these two regions led to the idea that the lateral hypothalamus signals turn on eating, whereas the VMH signals turn off eating. This model quickly proved too simplistic.

Not only does the lateral hypothalamus contain cell bodies, but fiber bundles also pass through it. Damage to either the cell bodies or the fibers can produce aphagia. Similarly, damage to fibers passing through the VMH often causes injury as well to the paraventricular nucleus of the hypothalamus (review Figure 12-10A). But the role of the hypothalamus in controlling eating involves more than the activities of its lateral and ventromedial structures alone.

In fact, another hypothalamic region, the arcuate nucleus, contains two major classes of neurons, one that initiates eating (e.g., neurons expressing genes for neuropeptide Y) and one that reduces eating behavior, the principal transmitter being α-melanocyte–stimulating hormone (α-MSH). Changes in hormone levels reflecting glucose (insulin) and lipid (leptin) levels in the blood act to stimulate either the first class, which initiates eating, or the second class, which acts to inhibit eating. Neurons of the arcuate nucleus also connect to the paraventricular nucleus. Damage to this region produces hyperphagia, as noted in the case of Roger at the beginning of this chapter.

The summed activity of all such hypothalamic neurons constitutes a complex homeostat that controls eating. **Figure 12-16** shows that this homeostat receives inputs from three sources: the enteric nervous system (such as information about blood glucose levels), the hormone systems (such as information about the level of appetite-diminishing CCK), and parts of the brain that process cognitive factors. We turn to these cognitive factors next.

Cognitive Control of Eating

Pleasure and its absence are cognitive factors in controlling eating. Just thinking about a favorite food can make many of us feel hungry. The cognitive aspect to eating includes not only images of food that we pull from memory but also external sensations, especially food-related sights and smells. Learned associations, such as the taste aversions discussed in Section 12-1, are also related to eating.

Neural control of the cognitive factors important for controlling eating in humans probably originates in multiple brain regions. Two structures are clearly important: the amygdala and the orbital prefrontal cortex. Damage to the amygdala alters food preferences and abolishes taste aversion learning. These effects are probably related to the amygdala's efferent connections to the hypothalamus.

The amygdala's role in regulating species-typical behaviors is well established, but the role of the orbital PFC is more difficult to pin down. Rats and monkeys with damage to the orbital cortex lose weight, in part because they eat less. Humans with orbital injuries are invariably slim, but we know of no formal studies on their eating habits. The orbital prefrontal cortex receives projections from the olfactory bulb, and cells in this region respond to smells. Because odors influence the taste of foods, it is likely that damage to the orbital cortex decreases eating due to diminished sensory responses to food odor and perhaps to taste.

An additional cognitive factor in the control of eating is the pleasure we derive from it, especially from eating foods with certain tastes. Think chocolate. What pleasure is and how the brain produces it are discussed in Section 12-7 in the context of reward.

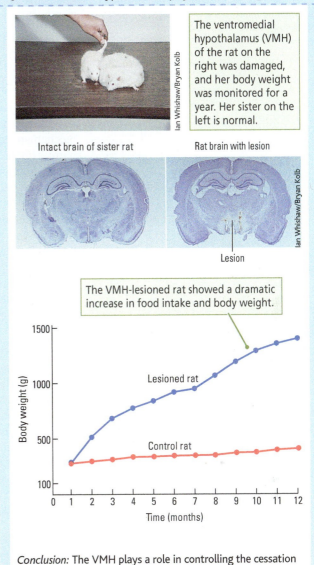

EXPERIMENT 12-1

Question: Does the hypothalamus play a role in eating?

The ventromedial hypothalamus (VMH) of the rat on the right was damaged, and her body weight was monitored for a year. Her sister on the left is normal.

Intact brain of sister rat   Rat brain with lesion

Lesion

The VMH-lesioned rat showed a dramatic increase in food intake and body weight.

Body weight (g) vs *Time (months)*

Lesioned rat

Control rat

Conclusion: The VMH plays a role in controlling the cessation of eating. Damage to the VMH results in prolonged and dramatic weight gain.

FIGURE 12-16 Modeling Control of Eating

osmotic thirst Thirst that results from a high concentration of dissolved chemicals, or *solutes*, in body fluids.

hypovolemic thirst Thirst produced by a loss of overall fluid volume from the body.

Randy Seeley and Stephen Woods (2003) noted that in spite of contemporary problems with weight gain, adult mammals do a masterful job of matching their caloric intake to caloric expenditure. Consider that a typical man eats 900,000 calories per year. To gain just 1 extra pound he would need to eat 4000 calories more than he burned in that year. This increase amounts to only 11 calories per day, equivalent to a single potato chip. But people rarely eat just one chip.

Controlling Drinking

The human body is 70 percent water; dissolved in that water are chemicals that participate in the hundreds of reactions necessary for bodily functions. Essential homeostatic mechanisms control water levels (and hence chemical concentrations) within rather narrow limits. The rate of a chemical reaction is partly determined by the concentration of the participating chemicals.

As with eating, we drink for many reasons. We consume certain beverages—such as coffee, wine, beer, or juice—for an energy boost or to relax, as part of social activities, or just because they taste good. We drink water for its health benefits, to help wash down a meal, or to intensify the flavor of dry foods. On a hot day, we drink water because we are thirsty, presumably because we become dehydrated through sweating and evaporation.

These examples illustrate the two kinds of thirst. **Osmotic thirst** results from increased concentrations of dissolved chemicals, known as solutes, in the body fluids. **Hypovolemic thirst** results from a loss of overall fluid volume from the body.

Osmotic Thirst

Solutes inside and outside cells are ideally concentrated for the body's chemical reactions. Maintaining this concentration requires a kind of homeostat, much like the mechanism that controls body temperature. Deviations from the ideal solute concentration activate systems to reestablish it.

When we eat salty foods, such as potato chips, the salt (NaCl) spreads through the blood and enters the extracellular fluid between our cells. This shifts the solute concentration away from the ideal. Receptors in the hypothalamus along the third ventricle detect the altered solute concentration and relay the message "too salty" to various hypothalamic areas that in turn stimulate us to drink. Other messages are sent to the kidneys to reduce water excretion.

Turning to sugar-sweetened beverages to quench thirst from eating salty foods increases the likelihood of weight gain.

WATER INTOXICATION Eating too much leads to obesity. What happens when we drink too much water? Our kidneys are efficient at processing water, but if we drink a large volume all at once, the kidneys cannot keep up.

The result is a condition called water intoxication. Body tissues swell with the excess fluid, essentially drowning the cells in fresh water. At the same time, the relative concentration of sodium drops, leading to an electrolyte imbalance.

Water intoxication can produce widely ranging symptoms, from irregular heartbeat to headache. In severe cases, people may show motor disorganization, as though they are drunk. The most likely way for an adult to develop water intoxication is to sweat heavily, by running a marathon in hot weather, for example, and then drink too much water without added electrolytes.

Hypovolemic Thirst

Unlike osmotic thirst, hypovolemic thirst arises when the total volume of body fluids declines, motivating us to drink more and replenish those fluids. In contrast with osmotic thirst, however, hypovolemic thirst encourages us to choose something other than water because water would dilute the solute concentration in the blood. Rather, we prefer to drink flavored beverages that contain salts and other nutrients, such as fruit juices or milk.

Hypovolemic thirst and its satiation are controlled by a hypothalamic circuit different from the one that controls osmotic thirst. When fluid volume drops, the kidneys send a hormone signal (angiotensin) that stimulates midline hypothalamic neurons. These neurons, in turn, stimulate drinking.

12-4 Review

Before you continue, check your understanding. Answers to Self-Test appear at the back of the book.

1. The three main hypothalamic regions that control eating are the _____, _____, and _____.

2. Digestion is controlled by the _____ nervous system.

3. _____ thirst results from an increase in the concentration of dissolved chemicals; _____ thirst results from a decline in the total volume of body fluids.

4. Describe the cognitive factors in the control of eating.

For additional study tools, visit **LaunchPad** at launchpadworks.com

---

12-5

Sexual Differences and Sexual Behavior

Individuals must eat and drink continually to survive. This is the essence of regulatory behavior. But notwithstanding procreation, which is essential to the survival of the species, sexual behavior is nonregulatory; it is not essential for an individual organism's survival. This fact does nothing to diminish the importance of sexual behavior. But before we discuss sexual behavior, we first look at sexual differentiation.

Margaret McCarthy and colleagues (2017) have identified 10 concepts that are consistent with the established evidence and form the foundation for our understanding of sexual differentiation (see **Table 12-2**). We summarize these 10 concepts next and recommend the McCarthy review for an in-depth discussion.

TABLE 12-2 **Ten Things We Know About Sexual Differentiation**

1. Hormones cause sex differences by acting during development as well as in adulthood.
2. There are sex differences in behavior.
3. There are sex differences in physiology.
4. There are sex differences in disease susceptibility.
5. There are sex differences in neural and glial structure and neural connectivity.
6. There are sex differences in neurochemistry.
7. Androgens and estrogens play a role in sexual differentiation in the brain.
8. Sex chromosome complement contributes to sexual differentiation.
9. Sex differences are context dependent.
10. Sexual differentiation depends on four key processes: neurogenesis, cell migration, cell death, and the differentiation of neural circuits.

Data Source: McCarthy et al., 2017.

Sexual Differentiation of the Brain

Charles Phoenix and colleagues (1959) first showed that hormones have two general effects on brain organization: during development gonadal hormones *organize* the brain, and in adulthood they *activate* many sex-specific behaviors, such as mating behaviors. We return to this concept in more detail below, but many other behaviors show sex differences as well (for a more extensive discussion, see Kolb & Whishaw, 2015). Perhaps the best-known sex difference in humans is the female advantage in verbal fluency, which is apparent in young children. When asked to write down words beginning with a particular letter in five minutes, females typically produce at least 10% more words than males. Karson Kung and colleagues (2016) found that higher levels of salivary testosterone at 1–3 months are related to a smaller expressive vocabulary measured at 18–30 months.

Perhaps the clearest example of sex differences involves spatial behavior (see Section 15-5 for a more extensive discussion). A male advantage in spatial navigation is found not only in humans but also in most other mammals that have been studied. Male rodents typically can navigate larger territories and are better at solving problems, such as the Morris Water Task (see Figure 7-3A), in which the solution requires the mental construction of a configuration of the room cues. But if room cues must be ignored, such as in the landmark task (see Figure 7-3C), females perform better. Therefore, a major difference is seen in the *strategy* used by each sex rather than in the spatial cognitive *ability* of each sex. This strategy difference alerts us to the fact that sex differences are context dependent. In another example, the wording of instructions on a test can influence outcome by altering the strategy typically used by one sex or the other.

It is important to note as well that sex differences in behavior are not absolute; the differences tend to be about 1 standard deviation apart. Thus, when male rats solve the Morris Water Task faster than females, it is not because females are unable to do the task; rather, females are slower to learn the correct strategy—and vice versa for the landmark task.

Sex differences in physiology can also be seen in statistics for neurological diseases, and especially for neurodevelopmental disorders, which are more common in boys. This male bias is striking because these early-onset disorders are less likely to have experiential causes but rather reflect pre- or postnatal differences in brain development. For adult-onset disorders, sex differences vary by disease. For example, females have a higher incidence of Alzheimer disease (1.5 to 3 times greater), after accounting for the sex difference in life expectancy, whereas males have a higher incidence of Parkinson disease (1.5 times greater).

Sex differences in behavior, physiology, and neurological disorders likely reflect sex differences in the brain. There is an extensive literature showing sex differences in brain structure—both in the size of different brain regions and in the structure of neurons, glia, and connections—as well as in the details of neurochemistry (see Kolb & Whishaw, 2015; McCarthy et al., 2017; Ritchie et al., 2018). For example, the amygdala is larger in males, and the language areas are larger in females. Differences in connectivity are reflected in the observation that females have greater interhemispheric connections and males have greater intrahemispheric connections. Finally, sex differences in neurotransmitter and neurotransmitter receptor expression are seen throughout the brain.

See Section 15-5 for further discussion of sex differences in cognitive organization.

Sexual differentiation is also directly related to sex chromosomes. This can be seen most clearly in females, who typically have two X chromosomes. Normally, one of the X chromosomes is largely silenced, but about 15% of the genes escape inactivation. Therefore, female cells have a double dose of some genes, which creates epigenetic effects that influence gene expression (see Arnold et al., 2016, for a review).

Finally, McCarthy and her colleagues note that it is important to recognize that sexual differentiation of any trait must be due to effects on the basic processes of brain development (see Table 8-1), namely neurogenesis, cell migration, cell death, and the differentiation of neural circuits by neuronal differentiation and maturation. Determining how hormonal or genetic factors differentially affect these processes in female or male brains has proven difficult because of the complexity (see McCarthy et al., 2017, for an extensive discussion).

Effects of Sex Hormones on the Brain

With McCarthy's foundational concepts in mind, we now turn to a discussion of hormones as they relate to sex-related behavior. During the fetal stage of prenatal development, a male's Y chromosome controls the differentiation of embryonic gonad tissue into testes, which secrete testosterone. This process is an organizing effect of gonadal hormones. Testosterone masculinizes both the sex organs and the brain during development. A major organizing effect of gonadal hormones on the brain is in the hypothalamus, especially the preoptic area of the medial hypothalamus. Organizing effects also operate in other nervous system regions, notably the amygdala, the prefrontal cortex, and the spinal cord.

Gonadal hormones produce enzymes necessary for epigenetic changes such as gene methylation. One action of steroid hormones is to methylate brain regions. For example, estrogen methylates the preoptic area of females, leading to the suppression of male characteristics. Growing evidence indicates that increased environmental levels of compounds, such as agricultural pesticides, can interfere with hormone activity, resulting in multigenerational epigenetic effects (see, for example, McCarthy et al., 2009). These effects may be linked to anxiety levels and obesity and possibly to the organizational effects of gonadal hormones.

Sex-related differences in the nervous system make sense behaviorally. After all, animal courtship rituals differ between the sexes, as do copulatory behaviors, with females typically engaging in sexually receptive responses and males in mounting ones. Producing these sex differences in behaviors depends on the action of gonadal hormones on the brain during development and in adulthood.

Hormonal actions on the adult brain are referred to as **activating effects**, in contrast with developmental **organizing effects**. Next we consider both types of effects.

Organizing Effects of Sex Hormones

During fetal development, a male's testes produce male hormones, the androgens. In the developing rat, androgens are produced during the last week of fetal development and the first week after birth. The androgens produced at this time greatly alter both neural structures and later behavior. For example, a male rat's hypothalamus and prefrontal cortex differ structurally from those of both female rats and of males that were not exposed to androgens during development.

Male rats with little exposure to the androgen testosterone during development behave like genetically female rats in adulthood. If given estrogen and progesterone, they become sexually receptive and display typical female behaviors when mounted by males. Male rats castrated in adulthood do not act in this way.

Sexual dimorphism, the differential development of brain areas in the two sexes, arises from a complex series of steps. Cells in the brain produce aromatase, an enzyme that converts testosterone into estradiol, one of the class of female sex hormones called estrogens. That is, when males produce testosterone, the brain converts it to an estrogen. Thus, a female hormone, estradiol, actually masculinizes the male brain.

Females are not masculinized by the presence of estrogens because fetuses of both sexes produce a liver enzyme (alpha fetoprotein) that binds to estrogen, rendering it incapable of entering neurons. Testosterone is unaffected by alpha fetoprotein: it enters neurons and is converted into estradiol.

The organizing effects of testosterone are clearly illustrated in the preoptic area of the hypothalamus (see Figure 12-10A), which plays a critical role in male rats' copulatory behavior. Comparing this area in males and females, Roger Gorski (1984) and his colleagues found a nucleus about five times as large in males as in females. Significantly, manipulating gonadal hormones during development can alter the sexual dimorphism of the preoptic area. Castrating male rats at birth leads to a smaller preoptic area; treating infant females with testosterone enlarges it.

The organizing effects of gonadal hormones are more difficult to study in humans. It is known that alpha fetoprotein, a fetal protein, is less effective in blocking estrogen in humans, indicating that human fetuses of both sexes are exposed to estrogen. This finding suggests that androgens may play a more central role in sexual differentiation in humans. The direct role of androgens can be seen in the studies by John Money and Anke Ehrhardt (1972). Clinical Focus 12-3, Androgen Insensitivity Syndrome and Androgenital Syndrome, describes this role.

activating effects Hormonal actions that influence activities in the adult brain.

organizing effects Hormonal actions that influence the organizational development of the fetal brain.

sexual dimorphism Differential development of brain areas in the two sexes.

The case study in Section 3-3 describes such epigenetic inheritance.

Section 8-4 explains organizing influences of gonadal hormones and critical periods in brain development.

⊙ CLINICAL FOCUS 12-3

Androgen Insensitivity Syndrome and the Androgenital Syndrome

After the testes have formed in a male fetus, sexual development depends on the actions of testicular hormones. Studying people with *androgen insensitivity syndrome* makes this dependence crystal clear. In this syndrome, an XY (genetic male) fetus produces androgens, but the body cannot respond to them.

Because androgen insensitivity syndrome does not affect estrogen receptors, these people are still responsive to estrogen produced by both the adrenal glands and the testes. As a result, they develop female secondary sexual characteristics during puberty, even without additional hormone treatment. A person with androgen insensitivity syndrome is therefore a genetic male who develops a female phenotype—that is, appears to be female, as shown in the photograph on the left.

If no Y chromosome is present to induce the growth of testes, an XX (genetic female) fetus develops ovaries and becomes a female. If the adrenal glands of either the mother or the infant produces an excessive amount of androgens, however, exposure of the female fetus to them produces *androgenital syndrome* (*congenital adrenal hyperplasia*).

The effects vary, depending on when the androgens are produced and on the level of exposure. In extreme cases, the clitoris enlarges until it can be mistaken for a small penis, as shown in the photograph on the right.

In less severe cases, no gross change in genital structure develops, but there is a behavioral effect: these girls show a high degree of tomboyishness. In early childhood, they identify with boys and prefer boys' clothes, toys, and games. One explanation for this behavioral effect is that the developing brain is masculinized, which changes later behavior.

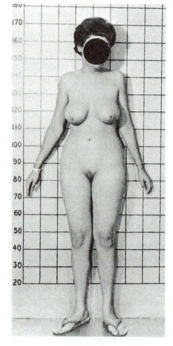
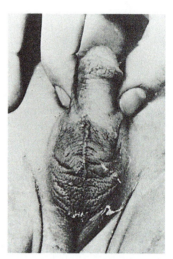

Left: In androgen insensitivity syndrome, a genetic male (XY) is insensitive to gonadal androgens but remains sensitive to estrogens, which leads to the development of a female phenotype. Right: In congenital adrenal hyperplasia, a genetic female (XX) is exposed to androgens produced by the adrenal gland embryonically, which leads to the partial development of male external genitalia. Reprinted from Man and Woman, Boy and Girl by John Money and Anke A. Ehrhardt (1972)/John's Hopkin's University Press, Baltimore.

Activating Effects of Sex Hormones

The sexual behavior of both males and females depends on the actions of gonadal hormones on the adult brain. In most vertebrate species, female sexual behavior varies in the course of an estrous cycle, during which the levels of ovarian hormones fluctuate. The rat's estrous cycle is about 4 days long, with sexual receptivity occurring only in the few hours during which the production of the ovarian hormones estrogen and progesterone peaks. These ovarian hormones alter brain activity, which in turn alters behavior. In female rats, various chemicals released after mating inhibit further mating behavior.

The activating effect of ovarian hormones can be seen clearly in hippocampal cells. **Figure 12-17** compares hippocampal pyramidal neurons taken from female rats at two points in the estrous cycle: one when estrogen levels are high and the other when they are low. When estrogen levels are high, more dendritic spines and presumably more synapses emerge. These neural differences during the estrous cycle are all the more remarkable when we consider that cells in the female hippocampus are continually changing their connections to other cells every 4 days throughout the animal's adulthood.

In males, testosterone activates sexual behavior in two distinct ways. First, testosterone's actions on the amygdala are related to the motivation to seek sexual activity. Second, the actions of testosterone on the hypothalamus are needed to produce copulatory behavior. We look at both processes next.

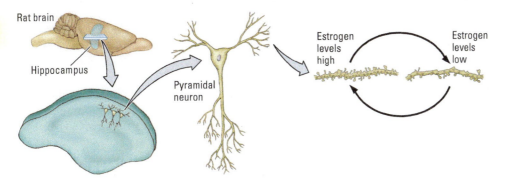

FIGURE 12-17 **Hormonal Effects**
A comparison of the dendrites of hippocampal pyramidal neurons at high and low levels of estrogen in the rat's (4-day) estrous cycle reveals far fewer dendritic spines in the low period. Information from Woolley et al., 1990.

Neural Control of Sexual Behavior

The hypothalamus is the critical structure involved in controlling copulatory behaviors in both male and female mammals. The ventromedial hypothalamus controls the female mating posture, which in quadrupedal animals is called *lordosis*: arching the back and elevating the rump while the female otherwise remains quite still. Damage to the VMH abolishes lordosis. The role of the VMH is probably twofold: it controls the neural circuit that produces lordosis, and it influences hormonal changes in the female during coitus.

In males, neural control of sexual behavior is somewhat more complex. The medial preoptic area, which is larger in males than in females, controls copulation. Damage to this area greatly disrupts mating performance, whereas its electrical stimulation activates mating, provided that testosterone is circulating in the bloodstream. Curiously, although destruction of the medial preoptic area stops male mammals from mating, they continue to show interest in receptive females. For instance, monkeys with lesions in the medial preoptic area will not mate with receptive females, but they will masturbate while watching females from across the room.

Barry Everitt (1990) designed an ingenious apparatus that allows male rats to press a bar to obtain access to receptive females. After males were trained to use this apparatus, shown in **Figure 12-18**, lesions were made in their medial preoptic areas. Immediately, their sexual behavior changed: they would still press the bar to obtain access to females but would no longer mate with them.

Apparently, the medial preoptic area controls mating but not sexual motivation. The brain structure responsible for motivation appears to be the amygdala. When Everitt trained male rats in the apparatus and then lesioned their amygdala, they would no longer press the bar to gain access to receptive females, but they would mate with receptive females provided to them.

It is not practical to discriminate small hypothalamic nuclei in fMRI studies of humans. Studies have shown a bilateral increase in hypothalamic activity when men view erotic video clips but not when they view sports video clips. The degree of sexual arousal is related to the increase in hypothalamic activity (e.g., Brunetti et al., 2008).

In summary, the hypothalamus controls copulatory behavior in both male and female mammals. In males, the amygdala influences sexual motivation, and it probably plays a key role in female sexual motivation as well, especially among females of species, such as humans, whose sexual activity is not tied to fluctuations in ovarian hormones.

Sexual Orientation, Sexual Identity, and Brain Organization

Does **sexual orientation**—a person's sexual attraction to the opposite sex or to the same sex or to both sexes—have a neural basis? Sexual orientation appears to be determined during early development, influenced by genetics and by epigenetic factors during prenatal brain development. No solid evidence points to any postnatal experience directing sexual orientation.

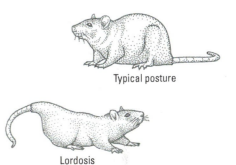

Typical posture

Lordosis

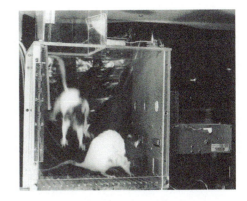

FIGURE 12-18 **Studying Sexual Motivation and Mating** In this experiment, a male rat must press the bar 10 times to gain access to a receptive female who drops in through a trapdoor. The copulatory behavior of the male rat illustrates mating behavior, whereas the bar pressing for access to a female rat illustrates sexual motivation. Photo courtesy of Barry J. Everitt, Department of Experimental Psychology and the MRC-Wellcome Behavioural and Clinical Neuroscience Institute, University of Cambridge.

sexual orientation A person's pattern of sexual attraction—to the opposite sex or to the same sex or to both sexes.

gender identity The degree to which a person feels male or female.

transgender Possessing personal characteristics that transcend traditional gender boundaries and corresponding sexual norms; a person's belief that he or she was born the wrong sex.

Indeed, it appears virtually impossible to change a person's sexual orientation. Lesbian couples commonly rear heterosexual children, and no evidence supports the notion that homosexuality is a lifestyle choice or that it is an effect of social learning (Bao & Swaab, 2011). The place to look for differences, therefore, is in the brains of people who identify themselves as heterosexual or homosexual.

Like rats, humans have sex-related differences in the structure of the hypothalamus and amygdala. Several hypothalamic nuclei are two to three times larger in males (for a review, see McCarthy et al., 2017). Sexual differentiation of the brain results from the effect of testosterone and is complete by birth.

But sex differences in the brain are not simply a matter of hormones. Epigenetics plays a role, too, beginning early in development. In females, for example, one of the two X chromosomes is largely silenced, but not all its genes are silenced, thereby providing a basis for sex differences. Furthermore, emerging evidence suggests that sex differences in the hypothalamus result from differences in gene methylation (again, see McCarthy et al., 2017).

Among homosexuals, variations in epigenetic effects could lead to differences in the architecture and function of the hypothalamus. Differences in the hypothalamus of heterosexual and homosexual men suggest that homosexual men form, in effect, a third sex because their hypothalamus differs from that of both females and heterosexual males.

Architectural and functional differences in the hypothalamus may form a basis for the spectrum of **gender identity**—a person's degree of feeling male or female. People who view themselves as **transgender**, whose personal characteristics transcend traditional gender boundaries and corresponding sexual norms, believe they were born the wrong sex. Their desire to live as a member of the other sex can be so strong that they undergo gender reassignment.

Several biological factors appear to influence the likelihood of transgender identity—chromosomal abnormalities, polymorphisms of the genes for the estrogen and androgen receptors, atypical gonadal hormone levels, prenatal exposure to certain anticonvulsants, and immune system activity directed toward the Y chromosome. These factors are hypothesized to lead to changes in the architecture and function of brain structures, especially the hypothalamus, which match transgender people's identities even while their sex organs do not (Bao & Swaab, 2011).

More evidence favoring a neural basis for gender identity, including transgender identity, is offered in Section 15-5.

Cognitive Influences on Sexual Behavior

People think about sex, dream about sex, make plans about sex. These behaviors may include activity in the amygdala or the hypothalamus, but they must certainly also include the cortex. This is not to say that the cortex is essential for sexual motivation and copulation, however.

In studies of rats whose entire cortex has been removed, both males and females still engage in sexual activity, although the males are somewhat clumsy. Nevertheless, the cortex must play a role in certain aspects of sexual behavior. For instance, imagery about sexual activity must include activity in the cortical ventral visual pathway. And thinking about sexual activity and planning for it must require frontal lobe participation.

As you might expect, these aspects of sexual behavior are not easily studied in rats, and they remain uncharted waters in research on humans. However, changes in the sexual behavior of people with frontal lobe injury are well documented. For example, the wife of a man who 5 years earlier had a small tumor removed from the medial frontal region complained that since the operation, she and her husband had no sexual contact whatever. He was simply not interested, even though they were both still in their twenties. The husband said that he no longer had sexual fantasies or sexual dreams, and although he still loved his wife, he did not have any sexual urges toward her or anyone else. Such cases clearly indicate that the human cortex is important in controlling sexual behaviors. The exact nature of its role remains poorly understood.

12-5 Review

Before you continue, check your understanding. Answers to Self-Test appear at the back of the book.

1. The key brain structures in the control of sexual behavior are the _____ and the _____.

2. The two types of effects that hormones exert on the brain are _____ and _____.

3. The brain structure responsible for mating in males is the _____, whereas the structure responsible for sexual motivation is _____.

4. Describe why sex differences in the brain are not simply a matter of hormones.

For additional study tools, visit **LaunchPad** at launchpadworks.com

12-6

The Neural Control of Emotion

The study of emotion dates back to the late nineteenth century, but there is still little consensus over exactly how to define emotion (see reviews by Kringelbach & Phillips, 2014; Levenson et al., 2017). Opposing theoretical positions hinder agreement on even basic concepts, such as whether emotions are discrete (anger, love, sadness, and so on) or dimensional (positive to negative). Most people can agree that emotions are central to human life, but we should note that emotions are not restricted to humans (see review by Anderson & Adolphs, 2014). A horse that is expecting alfalfa for dinner will turn up its nose at grass hay and may stomp its front feet and toss its head. Two dogs that are in competition for attention may snap at one another. In fact, it has even been proposed that flies show emotion.

Many neuroscientists are moving to the position that rational decision making actually depends on accurate emotional processing. Neurological patients who can no longer process emotional information are characterized by poor judgment in a variety of situations (see Bechara, 2017). It is becoming clear that the control of emotions includes more than just the brainstem; rather, it is related to activity in both cortical and subcortical regions.

Emotion, like motivation, is intangible: it is an inferred state. But the importance of emotion to our everyday lives is hard to exaggerate. Emotion can motivate us. It inspires artistic expression, for example, from poetry to filmmaking to painting. Many people enjoy the arts simply because they evoke emotions. And while people find certain emotions pleasant, severe and prolonged negative emotions, especially anxiety and depression, can develop into clinical disorders.

To explore the neural basis of emotions, we must first specify the types of behavior we want to explain. Think of a recent emotional experience. Perhaps you had a serious disagreement with a close friend or were recently engaged to be married. These experiences often include autonomic responses such as rapid breathing, sweating, and dry mouth. Emotions may also entail strong subjective feelings that we label as anger, fear, or love, among others. Finally, emotions typically entail thoughts or plans related to the experience itself and may take the form of replaying conversations and events in your mind, anticipating what you might say or do differently in the future.

These three forms of emotional experience suggest the influence of different neural systems. The autonomic component must include the hypothalamus and associated structures, as well as the enteric nervous system (the neurons in the gut). The components of subjective feelings are more difficult to localize but clearly include the amygdala and probably parts of the frontal lobes. And thoughts and plans are likely to be cortical.

A major challenge in identifying the neural correlates of emotion lies with the problem that emotion words, such as *anger* or *love*, are not the emotion. In a thoughtful review, Kagan (2018) notes that just because many languages contain words that are approximate synonyms of the English terms *happy*, *surprise*, *anger*, *fear*, *disgust*, *sad*, and so on does not mean that these named states are related to specific brain activity. Emotions occur in context, and brain activity is strongly influenced by context. To further complicate our understanding, measures of brain activity related to emotion normally are made using fMRI—and this is most certainly not a normal context for emotional experiences.

In the past few years, there have been several attempts to correlate specific patterns of brain activity with emotion words. As Kagan points out, however, no emotion word—when stripped of information about context, the nature of the agent inducing the emotion (fear of an upcoming exam, for example), the origin of the change in feeling, and the basis for inferring the emotion—has been linked to a particular brain state (see Clark-Polner et al., 2017, for more discussion). Rather, emotions are more likely to be related to diffuse networks (see Dubois et al., 2017, for more on this). Before considering where these networks might be found, we look briefly at theories of emotion.

Theories of Emotion

Three general theoretical models have emerged over the past century. The first model, labeled as *constructivist theory*, suggests that the brain interprets physiological changes (such as trembling and rapid heartbeat) as an emotion. This perspective implies that the brain (most likely the cortex) produces a cognitive response to autonomic information. That response varies with the context in which the autonomic arousal occurs, including the effects on the gut via the ENS. In cases of extreme autonomic activity, serotonin release surges in the gut, which can lead to diarrhea and cramping. If we are frightened by a movie, we feel a weaker, shorter-lived emotion than if we are frightened by a real-life encounter with a gang of muggers. Variations of this perspective have gone by many terms, beginning with the *James–Lange theory*, named for its originators, but all assume that the brain concocts a story to explain bodily reactions.

Two lines of evidence support the James–Lange theory and similar points of view. One is that the same autonomic responses can accompany different emotions. That is, particular emotions are not tied to unique autonomic changes. This line of evidence leaves room for interpreting what a particular pattern of arousal means, even though particular physiological changes may suggest only a limited range of possibilities. The physiological changes experienced during fear and happiness are unlikely to be confused.

The second line of evidence supporting the view that physiological changes are the starting point for emotions comes from people with reduced information about their own autonomic arousal, due, for example, to spinal cord injury. Spinal injury results in a decrease in perceived emotion, and its severity depends on how much sensory input is lost. **Figure 12-19** illustrates this relationship. People with the greatest loss of sensory input, which occurs with injuries at the uppermost end of the spinal cord, also have the greatest loss of emotional intensity. In contrast, people with injuries to the lower end of the spinal cord retain most of their visceral input and have essentially typical emotional reactions.

The second type of emotional theory is *appraisal theory* (for a review see Moors et al., 2013). Contemporary versions of appraisal theory define emotions as processes rather than states. They view emotional episodes as the activity of several biological subsystems or components: (1) an appraisal component in which there is an evaluation of the context; (2) somatic components (physiologic effects); (3) a behavioral component; and (4) a feeling component, which includes a subjective experience or feeling. Rather than process specific emotions in specific regions (such as the amygdala for fear), the appraisal component involves an extensive neural network that processes various aspects of the appraisal.

Some versions of appraisal theory also propose that emotions are dependent on an affective core, or pleasure system, that gives affective tone to emotion and interacts with appraisals (see Kringelbach & Berridge, 2017). Thus, emotions are ranked along dimensions of pleasant/unpleasant and aroused/not aroused (see Anderson &

After Christopher Reeve's spinal cord was severed at the cervical level (high), his emotions may have been blunted, but his motivation clearly remained intact. See Section 11-1.

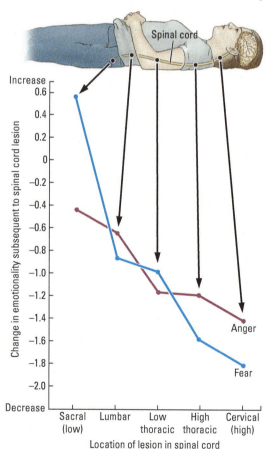

FIGURE 12-19 **Losing Emotion** Spinal cord injury blunts the emotional experience. Loss of emotionality is greatest when the lesion is high on the spine. Information from Beatty, 1995.

Adolphs, 2014) (see **Figure 12-20**). We return to pleasure in our discussion of reward in Section 12-7.

Although not a formal model like the first two theories, a general *neuropsychological theory of emotion* proposes that emotional control is asymmetrical. Given that there are significant asymmetries in the control of a variety of cognitive functions, this theory suggests that related emotional systems must also be lateralized.

This idea can be traced back to at least the 1930s, when clinicians noticed that patients with large left and right hemisphere injuries suffered starkly different changes in emotional behavior. Typically, left hemisphere lesions produce fearfulness and depression, and right hemisphere lesions are associated with emotional indifference. Given that a patient with a large left-hemisphere injury presumably has an intact right hemisphere, researchers reasoned that the observed behaviors of a left hemisphere–injured patient must reflect the activity of the right hemisphere. This observation led to the conclusion that the right hemisphere plays a major role in producing strong emotions, especially emotions regarded as negative, such as fear and anger. Because the left hemisphere has a major role in language, it has been suggested that cognitive appraisals include the left hemisphere, whereas the right hemisphere's role is more automatic. In other words, the right hemisphere *generates* emotional feelings, and the left hemisphere *interprets* those feelings.

We must note that although there is considerable evidence for asymmetric control of emotional behavior, there is a danger in overemphasizing laterality at the expense of diminishing the bilateral role of regions such as the prefrontal cortex, anterior cingulate cortex, and amygdala (for an extensive review, see Kolb & Whishaw, 2015). In many ways, the role of cerebral *site* (for example, prefrontal cortex) is far greater than cerebral *side*.

Emotion and the Limbic Circuit

It was not until the early part of the twentieth century that physiologists began to study the relationship among autonomic, endocrine, and hormonal factors and inferred emotional states. Paul Broca, impressed by the development of brain structures that seemed to ring around the brainstem in amphibians and reptiles, described these structures as the *limbic lobe*.

Although the limbic lobe concept is vague, the idea continues to have heuristic value, and today it is referred to as the *limbic system*, even though it is not a single system. The structures are formed from a primitive three- and four-layered cortex (known as the allocortex), which lies adjacent to the six-layered neocortex. In mammals, the allocortex encompasses the cingulate (meaning "girdle") gyrus and the hippocampal formation, as shown in **Figure 12-21**. The hippocampal formation includes the **hippocampus**—an allocortical structure important in species-typical behaviors, memory, and spatial navigation and vulnerable to the effects of stress—and the *parahippocampal cortex* adjacent to it.

FIGURE 12-20 **Two-Dimensional Space of Emotion** Emotions are rated on this grid as ranging from pleasant to unpleasant and varying in arousal (intensity). Research from: Anderson & Adolphs, 2014.

Cerebral asymmetry in cognitive functions is discussed in Chapter 15.

hippocampus From the Greek word for *seahorse*; distinctive allocortical structure lying in the medial temporal lobe; participates in species-typical behaviors, memory, and spatial navigation and is vulnerable to the effects of stress.

The limbic circuit derives its name from the Latin *limbus*, meaning "border."

The allocortex is found in the brains of mammals and other chordates, especially birds and reptiles. See Section 2-3 for more details.

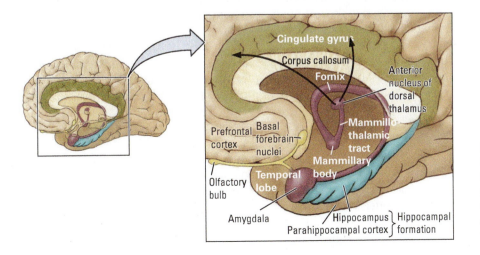

FIGURE 12-21 **Broca's Concept of the Limbic System** Encircling the brainstem, the limbic system as described by Broca consists of the cingulate gyrus and hippocampal formation (the hippocampus and parahippocampal cortex), the amygdala, the mammillothalamic tract, and the anterior thalamus.

(A)

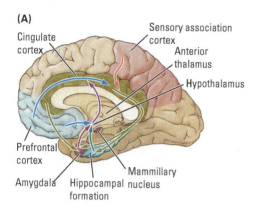

(B)

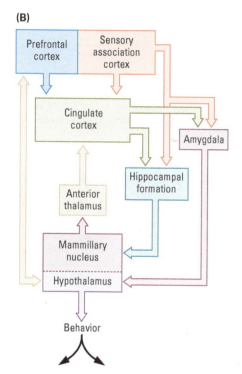

(C)

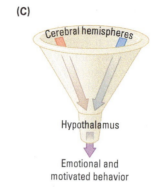

FIGURE 12-22 **Limbic System (A)** In this contemporary conception of the limbic system, an interconnected network of structures—the Papez circuit—controls emotional expression. **(B)** A schematic representation, coded to brain areas shown in part A by color, charts the limbic system's major connections. **(C)** A reminder that parts A and B can be conceptualized as part of a funnel rim of outputs that, through the hypothalamus, produce emotional and motivated behavior.

Section 15-2 elaborates on multisensory integration and the binding problem.

amygdala The part of the brain that participates in species-typical behaviors, emotion, and emotional memory. From the Greek word for *almond*, reflecting the general shape in the medial temporal lobe.

Organization of the Limbic Circuit

As anatomists began to study the limbic structures, connections to the hypothalamus became evident. It also became apparent that the limbic system has a role in emotion. For instance, in the 1930s, James Papez observed that people with rabies display radically abnormal emotional behavior, and postmortem examinations showed that the rabies had selectively attacked the hippocampus. (Definitive proof of rabies still requires postmortem hippocampal examination.)

Papez concluded from his observations that the limbic lobe and associated subcortical structures provide the neural basis of emotion. He proposed a neural circuit, traced in **Figure 12-22A**, now known as the *Papez circuit*, whereby emotion could reach consciousness, presumed at that time to reside in the cerebral cortex. In 1949, Paul MacLean expanded Papez's concept of the limbic circuit to include the amygdala and prefrontal cortex. Figures 12-21 and 12-22A show the amygdala lying adjacent to the hippocampus in the temporal lobe, with the prefrontal cortex lying just anterior.

Figure 12-22B charts the limbic circuit schematically. The hippocampus, amygdala, and prefrontal cortex all connect with the hypothalamus. The mammillary nucleus of the hypothalamus connects to the anterior thalamus, which in turn connects with the cingulate cortex. The cingulate cortex completes the circuit by connecting with the hippocampal formation, amygdala, and prefrontal cortex. This anatomical arrangement can be compared to the funnel in Figure 12-22C, which shows the hypothalamus as the spout leading to motivated and emotional behavior.

There is now little doubt that most structures associated with the concept of a limbic system, especially the amygdala and hypothalamus, take part in emotional behaviors, as detailed later in this section. But most limbic structures perform important roles in various motivated behaviors as well, especially in motivating species-typical behaviors such as eating and sexual activity.

Amygdala

Named for the Greek word for "almond" because of its shape, the **amygdala** consists of three principal subdivisions: the corticomedial area, the basolateral area, and the central area. Like the hypothalamus, the amygdala receives inputs from all sensory systems. But in contrast with the hypothalamic neurons, more complex stimuli are necessary to excite amygdalar neurons. Indeed, many amygdalar neurons are *multimodal*: they respond to more than one sensory modality. In fact, some respond to the entire sensory array: sight, sound, touch, taste, and smell. These amygdalar cells must shape a rather complex image of the sensory world.

The amygdala sends connections primarily to the hypothalamus and the brainstem, where it influences neural activity associated with emotions and species-typical behavior. For example, when the amygdala of a person with epilepsy is electrically stimulated before brain surgery, that person becomes fearful and anxious. We observed a woman who responded with increased respiration and heart rate, saying that she felt as if something bad was going to happen, although she could not specify what.

Amygdala stimulation can also induce eating and drinking. We observed a man who drank water every time the stimulation was turned on. (There happened to be a pitcher of water on the table next to him.) Within 20 minutes, he had consumed about 2 liters of water. When asked if he was thirsty, he said, "No, not really. I just feel like drinking."

The role of the amygdala in emotion can be seen most clearly in monkeys whose amygdalae have been removed. In 1939, Heinrich Klüver and Paul Bucy reported an extraordinary result, now known as **Klüver–Bucy syndrome**, that followed removal of the amygdala and anterior temporal cortex of monkeys. The principal symptoms included the following:

1. Tameness and loss of fear

2. Indiscriminate dietary behavior (eating many types of formerly rejected foods)

3. Greatly increased autoerotic, homosexual, and heterosexual activity with inappropriate object choice (e.g., the sexual mounting of chairs)

4. Tendency to attend to and react to every visual stimulus

5. Tendency to examine all objects by mouth

6. Visual agnosia, an inability to recognize objects or drawings of objects

Visual agnosia results from damage to the ventral visual stream in the temporal lobe, but the other symptoms are related to the amygdalectomy. Tameness and loss of fear are especially striking. Monkeys that normally show a strong aversion to stimuli such as snakes show no fear of them whatsoever. In fact, amygdalectomized monkeys may pick up live snakes and even put them in their mouths.

Although Klüver–Bucy syndrome is not common in humans—because bilateral temporal lobectomies are rare—its symptoms can be seen in people with certain forms of encephalitis, a brain infection. In some cases, encephalitis centered on the base of the brain can damage both temporal lobes and produce many Klüver–Bucy symptoms, including especially indiscriminate sexual behavior and the tendency to examine objects by mouth.

The amygdala's role in Klüver–Bucy syndrome points to its central role in emotion. So does its electrical stimulation, which produces an autonomic response (such as increased blood pressure and arousal) as well as a feeling of fear. Fear produced by the brain in the absence of an obvious threat may seem odd, but fear is basic to species' survival. To improve their chances of surviving, most organisms using fear as a stimulus minimize their contact with dangerous animals, objects, and places and maximize their contact with safe things.

Awareness of danger and of safety has both an innate component and a learned component, as Joe LeDoux (2014) emphasized. The innate component, much as in the IRMs described in Section 12-1, is the automatic processing of species-relevant sensory information—inputs from the visual, auditory, and olfactory systems. The importance of olfactory inputs is not obvious to humans; our senses are dominated by vision. But olfactory information connects directly to the amygdala in the human brain (see Figure 12-21). For many other animals, olfactory cues predominate.

A rat that has never encountered a ferret shows an immediate fear response to the odor of ferret. Other novel odors (such as peppermint or coffee) do not produce an innate fear reaction in the rat. The innate response triggers in the rat an autonomic activation that stimulates conscious awareness of danger.

In contrast, the learned component of fear consists of the avoidance of specific animals, places, and objects that the organism has come to associate with danger. The organism is not born with this avoidance behavior prewired. In a similar way, animals learn to increase contact with environmental stimuli that they associate with positive outcomes, such as food or sexual activity or, in the laboratory, drugs. Damage to the amygdala interferes with all these behaviors. The animal loses not only its innate fears but also its acquired fears of and preferences for certain environmental stimuli.

To summarize, the survival of a species requires a functioning amygdala. The amygdala influences autonomic and hormonal responses through its connections to the hypothalamus. It influences our conscious awareness of the positive and negative consequences of events and objects through its connections to the prefrontal cortex.

Klüver–Bucy syndrome Behavioral syndrome, characterized especially by hypersexuality, that results from bilateral injury to the temporal lobe.

Chapter 9 describes varieties of visual-form agnosia in a range of case studies.

Clinical Focus 2-2 examines some causes and symptoms of encephalitis.

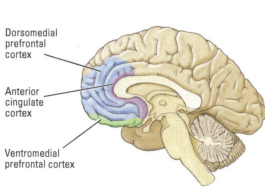

(A) Lateral view

Dorsolateral prefrontal cortex   Premotor cortex   Motor cortex   Central sulcus

Prefrontal cortex

Orbitofrontal cortex

(B) Ventral view

Ventromedial prefrontal cortex   Orbitofrontal cortex

(C) Medial view

Dorsomedial prefrontal cortex

Anterior cingulate cortex

Ventromedial prefrontal cortex

FIGURE 12-23 **Gross Subdivisions of the Frontal Lobe and Prefrontal Cortex**

Figure 11-2 charts the hierarchy of frontal lobe regions with regard to movement. Section 11-2 discusses the functions of the motor and premotor regions.

Prefrontal literally means "in front of the front."

Section 16-2 elaborates on the causes of and treatments for schizophrenia.

Prefrontal Cortex

The prefrontal cortex is a large area made up of several functionally distinct regions mapped in **Figure 12-23A**.

The general areas of the prefrontal cortex are the dorsolateral region; the orbitofrontal cortex (OFC), also shown from a ventral aspect in Figure 12-23B; and the ventromedial PFC. The anterior cingulate cortex (ACC), shown in Figure 12-23C, is closely associated with the PFC although not strictly part of it.

The prefrontal cortex contributes to specifying the goals toward which movement should be directed. It controls the processes by which we select movements appropriate to the particular time and context. This selection may be cued by internal information, such as memory and emotion, or it may be made in response to context (environmental information).

Like the amygdala, the frontal lobes receive highly processed information from all sensory areas, and many neurons in the prefrontal cortex, like those in the amygdala, are multimodal. As shown in **Figure 12-24**, the prefrontal cortex receives input via connections from the amygdala, dorsomedial thalamus, sensory association cortex, posterior parietal cortex, and dopaminergic cells of the ventral tegmental area.

Dopaminergic input is important for regulating how prefrontal neurons react to stimuli, including emotional ones. Abnormalities in this dopaminergic projection may account for some disorders, including schizophrenia, in which people evince little emotional reaction to typically arousing stimuli.

Figure 12-24 also shows the areas to which the prefrontal cortex sends connections—its output. The inferior prefrontal region projects axons to the amygdala and the

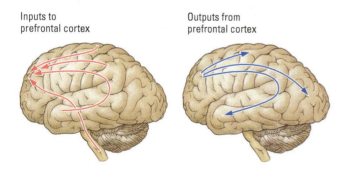

Inputs to prefrontal cortex

Outputs from prefrontal cortex

FIGURE 12-24 **Prefrontal Connections** The PFC receives inputs (red arrows in the anatomical illustration) and sends outputs (blue arrows in the illustration) to the areas charted on the diagram to the right.

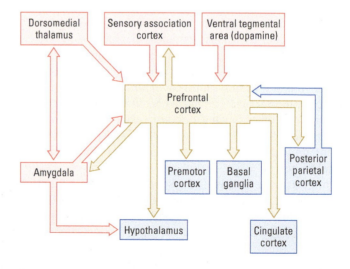

hypothalamus in particular. These PFC axons provide a route for influencing the ANS and ENS, which control changes in blood pressure, respiration, and other internal processes, especially those related to emotions. The dorsolateral prefrontal region sends its connections primarily to the sensory association cortex, posterior parietal cortex, cingulate cortex, basal ganglia, and premotor cortex and plays a larger role in cognitive behaviors than in emotional behaviors.

One overall function of the prefrontal cortex is to select behaviors appropriate to the particular time and place, cued either by internal information or environmental context. Disruption to this selection function can be seen in people with injury to the dorsolateral frontal lobe (see Figure 12-23A). They become overly dependent on environmental cues to determine their behavior. Like small children, they can be easily distracted by what they see or hear. We have all experienced a loss of concentration to some extent, but for a patient with frontal lobe damage, the problem is exaggerated and persistent. Because the person becomes so absorbed in irrelevant stimuli, he or she cannot act on internalized information most of the time.

A good example is J. C., in whom bilateral damage to the dorsolateral prefrontal cortex resulted from having a tumor removed. J. C. would lie in bed most of the day, fixated on television programs. He was aware of his wife's opinion of this behavior, but only the sound of the garage door opening when she returned home from work in the evening would stimulate him into action. Getting out of bed was controlled by this specific environmental cue; without it, he seemed to lack motivation. Television completely distracted him from acting on internal knowledge of things that he could or should do.

Adapting behavior appropriately to the environmental context also is a PFC function. Most people readily change their behavior to match the situation at hand. We behave one way with our parents, another with our friends, another with our children, and yet another with our coworkers. Each set of people constitutes a different context, and we shift our behaviors accordingly. Our tone of voice, our use of slang or profanity, and the content of our conversations are quite different in different contexts.

Even among our peers we act differently, depending on who is present. We may be relaxed in the presence of some people and ill at ease with others. It is therefore no accident that the size of the frontal lobes is related to species' sociability. Social behavior is extremely rich in contextual information, and humans are highly social animals.

Controlling behavior in context requires detailed sensory information, which is conveyed from all sensory regions to the frontal lobes. This sensory input includes not only information from the external world but also internal information from the ANS. People with damage to the orbital prefrontal cortex, as is common in traumatic brain injuries (TBIs), have difficulty adapting their behavior to the context, especially the social context. Consequently, they often make social gaffes.

In summary, the role of the frontal lobes in selecting behaviors is important for considering what causes behavior. The frontal lobes act much like a composer, but instead of selecting notes and instruments, they select our actions. Not surprisingly, the frontal lobes are sometimes described as housing the brain's executive functions. To grasp the full extent of frontal lobe control of behavior, see Clinical Focus 12-4, Agenesis of the Frontal Lobe.

Prefrontal Cortex and Emotional Behavior

At about the same time that Klüver and Bucy began studying their monkeys, Carlyle Jacobsen was studying the effects of frontal lobotomy on the cognitive capacities of two chimpanzees. A frontal lobotomy, which involves inserting a sharp instrument into the frontal lobes and moving it back and forth to disconnect the lobes from the rest of the brain, destroys substantial brain tissue.

In 1936, Jacobsen reported that one of the chimps was particularly neurotic before being subjected to this procedure. She became more relaxed afterward. Incredibly, a leading Portuguese neurologist of the time, Egas Moniz, seized on this observation as a treatment for behavioral disorders in humans; thus, the frontal lobotomy was initiated as the first technique of **psychosurgery**, or neurosurgery intended to alter behavior.

Section 15-2 expands on the role of prefrontal regions in cognition.

PFC output influences movement (Section 11-1), memory (Section 14-3), and cognition (Section 15-2).

Clinical Focus 1-1 and Section 1-1 recount behavioral effects of TBI; Section 14-5 details recovery; Section 16-3 explores TBI symptoms and treatments.

Section 15-2 considers the frontal lobes and the executive function of planning.

psychosurgery Any neurosurgical technique intended to alter behavior.

⊙ **CLINICAL FOCUS** 12-4

Agenesis of the Frontal Lobes

The role of the frontal lobes in motivated behavior is perhaps best understood by looking at J. P.'s case, described in detail by Stafford Ackerly (1964). Born in December 1914, J. P. was a problem child. Early on, he became a wanderer. Police officers would find him miles from home, as he had no fear of being lost. Severe whippings by his father did not deter him.

J. P.'s behavioral problems continued and expanded as he grew older, and by adolescence, he was constantly in trouble. Yet J. P. also had a positive side. When he started school, his first-grade teacher was so impressed with his polite manners that she began writing a letter to his parents to compliment them on having such a well-mannered child who was such a good influence in the class.

As she was composing the letter, she looked up to find J. P. exposing himself to the class and masturbating. This juxtaposition of polite manners and odd behavior characterized J. P.'s conduct throughout his life. At one moment he was charming; at the next, he was engaged in socially unacceptable behavior.

J. P. developed no close friendships with people of either sex, in large part because of his repeated incidents of public masturbation, stealing, excessive boastfulness, and wandering. He was a person of average intelligence who seemed unaffected by the consequences of his behavior. Police officers, teachers, and neighbors all ascribed intention to J. P.'s behavior: all believed that he was willfully misbehaving and blamed his parents for not enforcing sufficiently strict discipline.

Perhaps as a result, not until he was 19 years old was J. P.'s true condition detected. To prevent him from serving a prison term for repeated automobile theft, a lawyer suggested that J. P. undergo psychiatric evaluation. The psychiatrist who examined him ordered an X-ray (the only brain scan available at the time). The image revealed that J. P. lacked a right frontal lobe, and his left frontal lobe was about 50 percent the normal size. It is almost certain that his frontal lobes simply failed to develop.

Failure of a structure to develop is known as *agenesis*; J. P.'s condition was agenesis of the frontal lobes. His case offers an unusual opportunity to study the role of the frontal lobes in motivated behavior.

Clearly, J. P. lacked the bag of mental tricks that most people use to come to terms with the world. Normally, behavior is affected both by its past consequences and by current environmental input. J. P. did not seem much influenced by either factor. As a result, the world was simply too much for him. He always acted childlike and was unable to formulate plans or to inhibit many of his behaviors. He acted on impulse. At home, he was prone to aggressive outbursts about small matters, especially with regard to his mother.

Curiously, J. P. seemed completely unaware of his life situation. Even though the rest of his brain was working fairly well—his IQ score was in the normal range, and his language skills were very good—the rest of his brain was unable to compensate for the absence of frontal lobes.

It was later refined by Walter Freeman to become the transorbital leukotomy illustrated in **Figure 12-25**.

The use of psychosurgery grew rapidly in the 1950s. In North America alone, nearly 40,000 people received frontal lobotomies as a treatment for psychiatric disorders. Not until the 1960s was any systematic research conducted into the effects of frontal lesions on social and emotional behavior. By that time, the frontal lobotomy had virtually vanished as a "treatment." We now know that prefrontal lesions in various species, including humans, severely impact social and emotional behavior.

Agnes is a case in point. We met Agnes at the same psychiatric hospital where we met Roger (whose indiscriminate eating we described in Section 12-1). At the time, Agnes, a 57-year-old woman, was visiting one of the nurses. She had, however, once been a patient.

The first thing we noticed about Agnes was that she exhibited no outward sign of emotion. She showed virtually no facial expression. Agnes had been subjected to a procedure known as a *frontal leukotomy* because her husband, an oil tycoon, felt that she was too gregarious. Evidently, he felt that her "loose lips" were a detriment to his business dealings. He convinced two psychiatrists that she would benefit from psychosurgery, and her life was changed forever.

To perform a leukotomy, as illustrated in Figure 12-25, a surgeon uses a special knife called a leukotome to sever the connections of a region of the orbitofrontal cortex (see Figure 12-22). In our conversations with Agnes, we quickly discovered her considerable insight into the changes brought about by the leukotomy. In particular, she indicated that she no longer had any feelings about things or most people, although, curiously, she was attached to her dog. She said that she often just felt empty and much like a zombie.

Agnes's only moment of real happiness in the 30 years since her operation was the sudden death of her husband, whom she blamed for ruining her life. Unfortunately,

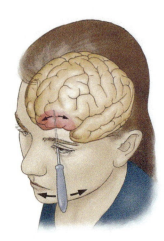

FIGURE 12-25 **Transorbital Leukotomy** In this procedure, a leukotome is inserted through the bone of the eye socket to disconnect the orbitofrontal cortex from the rest of the brain.

Agnes squandered her dead husband's considerable wealth as a consequence of her inability to plan or organize. This inability, we have seen, is another symptom of prefrontal injury.

The orbitofrontal area has direct connections with the amygdala and hypothalamus. Stimulating it can produce autonomic responses, and, as we saw in Agnes, damage to the orbital region can produce severe personality change characterized by apathy and loss of initiative or drive. The orbital cortex is probably responsible for the conscious awareness of emotional states produced by the rest of the limbic system, especially the amygdala.

Agnes's loss of facial expression is also typical of frontal lobe damage. In fact, people with frontal lobe injuries and people who have schizophrenia or autism spectrum disorder (ASD) are usually impaired at both producing and perceiving facial expressions, including a wide range of expressions found in all human cultures—happiness, sadness, fear, anger, disgust, and surprise. As with J. P.'s frontal lobe agenesis, described in Clinical Focus 12-4, it is difficult to imagine how such people can function effectively in our highly social world without being able to express their own emotions or to recognize those of others.

While facial expression is a key to recognizing emotion, so is tone of voice, or *prosody*. Patients with damage to the frontal lobe are devoid of prosody, both in their own conversations and in understanding the prosody of others. The lost ability to comprehend or produce emotional expression in both faces and language partly explains those patients' apathy. In some ways, they are similar to spinal cord patients who have lost autonomic feedback and so can no longer feel the arousal associated with emotion. These patients can no longer either read emotion in other people's faces and voices or express it in their own.

As noted earlier, there is growing evidence that emotion is linked to decision making, and the ventromedial prefrontal cortex (vmPFC) plays a key role in that process. Patients with damage to the vmPFC develop severe deficits in personal and social decision making, despite having largely preserved intellectual abilities (see Bechara, 2017). It is hypothesized that the vmPFC has a role in accessing visceral (internal) information that is related to the value (pleasant, unpleasant) of objects in the world. Noninvasive imaging studies (fMRI) have also shown that changes in the activity of the vmPFC result in changes in the subjective pleasantness of experiences with food, drugs, music, and sexual orgasm (see Berridge & Kringelbach, 2015). It is important to note, however, that imaging studies show a more extensive network of increased activity, including in the anterior cingulate cortex, the insular cortex, and subcortical regions such as the amygdala and striatum. We return to these regions in our discussion of reward in Section 12-7.

Emotional Disorders

Major depression, a highly disruptive emotional disorder, is characterized by some or all the following: prolonged feelings of worthlessness and guilt, disruption of normal eating habits, sleep disturbances, a general slowing of behavior, and frequent thoughts of suicide. A depressed person feels severely despondent for a long time. Major depression has become increasingly common in the past 50 years, and it affects about 6 percent of the population at any given time.

Depression has a genetic component. It not only runs in families but also frequently tends to occur in both members of a pair of identical twins. The genetic component in depression implies a biological abnormality, but the cause remains unknown. Neuroscience researchers' interest in the role of epigenetic changes in depression, however, is increasing. One hypothesis is that early life stress may produce epigenetic changes in the prefrontal cortex (see the review by Schroeder et al., 2010).

Excessive anxiety is an even more common emotional problem than depression. Anxiety disorders, including posttraumatic stress disorder (PTSD), phobias, generalized anxiety disorder, panic disorder, and obsessive-compulsive disorder (OCD), are estimated

ASD is the topic of Clinical Focus 8-2; schizophrenia is the topic of Clinical Focus 8-5.

The insular cortex is visible in the fMRI from Research Focus 12-1 and is diagrammed in Figure 10-13.

Major depression, detailed in Clinical Focus 6-3, is among the most treatable psychological disorders. Cognitive and intrapersonal therapies are as effective as drugs. See Sections 16-2 and 16-3.

⊙ CLINICAL FOCUS 12-5

Anxiety Disorders

Animals typically become anxious at times of obvious danger. But anxiety disorders are different. They are characterized by intense feelings of fear or anxiety inappropriate for the circumstances. People with an anxiety disorder have persistent and unrealistic worries about impending misfortune. They also tend to have multiple physical symptoms attributable to hyperactivity of the sympathetic nervous system.

G. B.'s case is a good example. He was a 36-year-old man with two college degrees who began to have severe spells initially diagnosed as a heart condition. He would begin to breathe heavily, sweat, develop heart palpitations, and sometimes feel pains in his chest and arms. During these attacks, he was unable to communicate coherently and would lie helpless on the floor until an ambulance arrived to take him to an emergency room.

Extensive medical testing and multiple attacks over about 2 years eventually led to the diagnosis of **generalized anxiety disorder**. Like most of the rest of the 5 percent of the U.S. population who have a generalized anxiety disorder at some point in their life, G. B. was unaware that he was overly anxious. The cause of generalized anxiety is difficult to pinpoint, but one likely explanation is related to the cumulative effects of general stress.

Although G. B. appeared outwardly calm most of the time, he had been a prodemocracy activist in communist Poland, a dangerous position. Because of the dangers, he and his family eventually escaped from Poland to Turkey, and from there they went to Canada. G. B. may have had continuing worries about the repercussions of his political activities—worries (and stress) that eventually found expression in generalized anxiety attacks.

The most common and least disabling types of anxiety disorders are **phobias**. A phobia pertains to a clearly defined, dreaded object (such as spiders or snakes) or situation (such as enclosed spaces or crowds). Most people have a mild aversion to some types of stimuli. Such aversion becomes a phobia only when a person's feelings about a disliked stimulus lead to overwhelming fear and anxiety.

The incidence of disabling phobias—those that are serious enough to interfere with living well—is surprisingly high, estimated to affect at least 1 in 10 people. Most people with a phobia control the emotional reaction by avoiding what they dread. Others face their fears in controlled settings, with the goal of overcoming them.

Panic disorder, another form of anxiety disorder, has an estimated incidence on the order of 3 percent of the population. Symptoms include recurrent attacks of intense terror that begin without warning and without any apparent relationship to external circumstances. A panic attack usually lasts only a few minutes, but the experience is always terrifying. Sudden activation of the sympathetic nervous system leads to sweating, a wildly beating heart, and trembling.

Although panic attacks may occur only occasionally, the victim's dread of another episode may be continual. Consequently, many people with panic disorder also have *agoraphobia*, a fear of public places or situations in which help might not be available. This phobia makes some sense because a person with a panic disorder may feel particularly vulnerable about the possibility of having an attack in a public place.

Freud believed that anxiety disorders are psychological in origin and treatable with talking therapies in which people confront their fears. Today, cognitive-behavioral therapies serve this purpose. A behavioral therapy called *mindfulness*, a form of meditation, is proving effective in treating anxiety disorders. Its effectiveness is correlated with suppressed activity in the anterior cingulate region (Garrison et al., 2015). The effect is greater in trained as opposed to novice meditators, which supports the value of mindfulness training programs.

Pharmacologically, anxiety disorders are most effectively treated with benzodiazepines such as diazepam (Valium), the best known. Alprazolam (Xanax) is the most commonly prescribed drug for panic attacks. Benzodiazepines act by augmenting GABA's inhibitory effect and are believed to exert a major influence on neurons in the amygdala.

Whether treatments are behavioral, pharmacological, or both, the general goal is to normalize brain activity.

---

generalized anxiety disorder Persistently high levels of anxiety often accompanied by maladaptive behaviors to reduce anxiety; thought to be caused by chronic stress.

phobia Fear of a clearly defined object or situation.

panic disorder Recurrent attacks of intense terror that come on without warning and without any apparent relationship to external circumstances.

Figure 6-7 illustrates the action of antianxiety agents at the GABA$_A$ receptor.

Section 16-2 further explores anxiety disorders and reviews treatments.

to affect 18 percent to 30 percent of the population. As described in Clinical Focus 12-5, Anxiety Disorders, symptoms include persistent fears and worries in the absence of any direct threat, usually accompanied by various physiological stress reactions, such as rapid heartbeat, nausea, and breathing difficulty.

As with depression, the root cause of anxiety disorders is unknown, but the effectiveness of the drug treatments described in Clinical Focus 12-5 implies a biological basis. The most widely prescribed anxiolytic (antianxiety) drugs are the benzodiazepines, such as Valium, Librium, and Xanax. Why would the brain have a mechanism for benzodiazepine action? It certainly did not evolve to allow us to take Valium. Probably this mechanism is part of a system that both increases and reduces anxiety levels. The mechanism for raising anxiety seems to entail a compound known as diazepam-binding inhibitor, which appears to bind antagonistically with the GABA$_A$ receptor, increasing anxiety.

Increased anxiety can be beneficial, especially if we are drowsy and need to be alert to deal with a crisis. Impairment of this survival mechanism or the one that reduces anxiety can cause serious emotional problems, even anxiety disorders.

12-6 Review

Before you continue, check your understanding. Answers to Self-Test appear at the back of the book.

1. The three types of theories of emotion are _____, _____, and
   _____.

2. Three key brain regions involved in emotions are _____, _____, and
   _____.

3. The studies of two chimpanzees with large frontal lobe lesions led to the development of what psychiatric treatment?

4. Describe the symptoms of Klüver–Bucy syndrome.

For additional study tools, visit 🅼 **LaunchPad** at launchpadworks.com

12-7

Reward

Throughout this chapter, we have concluded repeatedly that animals engage in a wide range of voluntary behaviors because those behaviors are rewarding. That is, these behaviors increase the activity in neural circuits that function to maintain an animal's contact with certain environmental stimuli, either in the present or in the future. Presumably, the animal perceives the activity of these circuits as pleasant. This conclusion would explain why reward can help maintain not only adaptive behaviors, such as eating and sexual activity, but also potentially nonadaptive behaviors, such as drug addiction. After all, evolution would not have prepared the brain specifically for the eventual development of psychoactive drugs.

The Reward System

To understand the neural circuitry of pleasure and reward, we should recognize that rewards are not a single thing but rather involve several different components. The English word *hedonic*, derived from the Greek word for "pleasure," today refers to many types of pleasure, including sensory, cognitive, social, aesthetic, and moral. *Anhedonia* refers to the lack of pleasure, which can result from a breakdown in the reward system. Kent Berridge and Terry Robinson (2003) emphasize that reward has three main components: (1) *learning* about rewards and the cues that predict their availability; (2) *motivation* for these rewards and the cues associated with them ("wanting" the reward); and (3) *affective* (hedonic) responses to the actual pleasure of rewards ("liking" the reward). A challenge for neuroscience is to understand how brain mechanisms generate each of these components. Consider why we increase contact with a stimulus such as chocolate. Three independent factors are at work: our knowledge of where chocolate might be, our desire to eat the chocolate (wanting), and the pleasurable effect of eating the chocolate (liking). Where do these events occur in the brain?

The first clue to the presence of a reward system in the brain came with an accidental discovery by James Olds and Peter Milner in 1954. They found that rats would perform behaviors such as pressing a bar to administer a brief burst of electrical stimulation to specific sites in their brain. This phenomenon is called *intracranial self-stimulation*, or *brain stimulation reward*.

Typically, rats will press a lever hundreds or even thousands of times per hour to obtain this brain stimulation, stopping only when they are exhausted. Why would animals engage in such behavior when it has absolutely no survival value to them or to their species? The simplest explanation is that the brain stimulation is activating the system underlying reward. Stimulation along the MFB tract activates fibers that form the ascending pathways from dopamine-producing cells of the midbrain tegmentum, shown in **Figure 12-26**. This mesolimbic dopamine pathway sends

Robinson and Berridge's wanting-and-liking theory of addiction includes a multipart reward system; see Section 6-4.

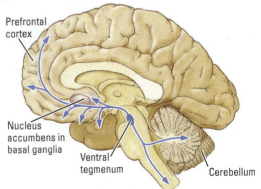

FIGURE 12-26 **Mesolimbic Dopamine System** Axons emanating from the ventral tegmentum (blue arrows) project diffusely through the brain. Dopamine release in these mesolimbic pathways has a role in feelings of reward and pleasure. The nucleus accumbens is a critical structure in this reward system.

Section 7-1 describes how electrical stimulation works both as a treatment and as a research tool.

terminals to sites that include especially the nucleus accumbens in the basal ganglia and the prefrontal cortex.

It was initially hypothesized that the brain stimulation appeared to be activating the mesolimbic dopamine pathway, which sends terminals to sites that include especially the nucleus accumbens in the basal ganglia and the prefrontal cortex. Blocking dopamine with drugs such as neuroleptics appear to take the pleasure out of normally rewarding events such as self-stimulation and amphetamine, leading Roy Wise (1980) to propose that dopamine synapses represent a place where sensory inputs are translated into hedonic messages that we experience as pleasure. Thus was born the well-known idea that dopamine is the pleasure transmitter. Unfortunately, the idea is wrong. Wise himself has since admitted this, but the idea remains in the public's imagination.

Perhaps the first clear indication that dopamine is not the pleasure molecule came from earlier studies by Berridge and Robinson (1998). Berridge had been using facial expression in rats and people to measure how pleasurable or unpleasurable tastes were. As shown in **Figure 12-27**, exposure to palatable tastes (chocolate) elicits hedonic reactions in humans, such as licking the fingers and lips. In contrast, exposure to unpleasant tastes such as something overly salty elicits negative reactions such as grimacing, spitting, or wiping the mouth with the back of the hand. Rats, too, show distinctive positive and negative responses to pleasant and unpleasant tastes.

Now consider rats with lesions of the ascending dopaminergic pathway to the forebrain. These rats do not eat. Is it simply that they do not desire to eat (a loss of wanting), or has food become aversive to them (a loss of liking)? By watching the facial expressions and body movements after food is squirted into the mouth of a rat that otherwise refuses to eat, we can tell to what extent a loss of liking is a factor in the animal's food rejection. Interestingly, rats that do not eat after receiving lesions to the dopamine pathway act as though they still like food.

Next, consider a rat with a self-stimulation electrode in the lateral hypothalamus. This rat will often eat heartily while the stimulation is on. The obvious inference is that the food must taste good—presumably even better than usual. But what happens if we squirt food into the rat's mouth and observe its behavior when the stimulation is on versus when it is off?

If the brain stimulation primes eating by evoking pleasurable sensations, we would expect the animal to be more positive in its facial and body reactions to foods when the stimulation is turned on. In fact, the opposite occurs. During stimulation, rats react more aversively to tastes such as sugar and salt than when stimulation is off. Apparently, the stimulation increases wanting but not liking.

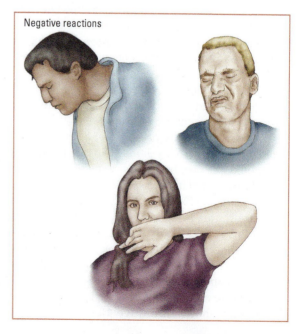

FIGURE 12-27 **Human Reactions to Taste** Sucrose and other palatable tastes elicit positive (hedonic) reactions, including licking the fingers and the lips. Quinine and other unpleasant tastes elicit negative (aversive) reactions, including spitting, expressing distaste, and wiping the mouth with the back of the hand. Information from Berridge, 1996.

Such experiments show that what appears to be a single event—reward—is actually composed of at least two independent processes. Just as our visual system independently processes *what* and *how* information in separate streams, our reward system appears to process wanting and liking independently. Reward is not a single phenomenon any more than perception or memory is.

Mapping Pleasure in the Brain

Although the experiences of different pleasures (for example, delicious foods, romantic gestures, listening to music) may seem very different from each other, neuroimaging studies suggest that they all activate surprisingly similar brain circuitry in regions of the prefrontal cortex, anterior cingulate cortex, and insula, as well as subcortical limbic structures such as the nucleus accumbens, ventral pallidum, and amygdala (for details see Berridge & Kringelbach, 2015). Although there is overlap between the wanting and liking systems, wanting is generated by a large distributed brain system dominated by dopamine projections, especially to the striatum and prefrontal cortex. In contrast, liking is generated by a smaller set of hedonic hotspots within the limbic circuitry, shown in **Figure 12-28**.

From this perspective, we can see that dopamine is the neurotransmitter related to wanting, but what is the neurotransmitter(s) related to liking? Berridge and his colleagues have identified small regions in the nucleus accumbens and associated ventral pallidum and ventromedial orbitofrontal cortex and insula, as well as a site in the hindbrain dorsal pons, that contribute to hedonic functions and are known to contribute to taste and pain. Each of these hotspots uses opioid (natural heroin-like transmitters) and endocannabinoid (natural marijuana-type neurotransmitters)—but never dopamine—to amplify liking (pleasure) reactions. These hedonic hotspots are relatively small in each region, but they appear to act together as a unified system to enhance pleasure. The intensity of pleasure is believed to be related to the number of regions simultaneously activated.

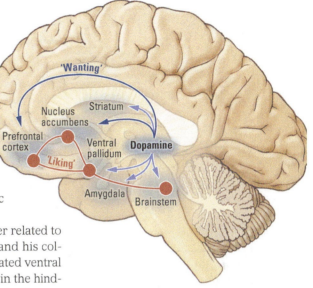

FIGURE 12-28 Liking and Wanting Systems in the Brain Wanting is mediated by an extensive brain system including dopamine projections (the blue arrows), whereas liking is mediated by a more restricted brain system of small hedonic hotspots (red). Research from Berridge & Robinson, 2016.

Pleasure Electrodes?

Pleasure is not merely a sensation or thought but is best conceived of as an additional "hedonic gloss," which creates the pleasure-versus-displeasure affect (see review by Kringelbach & Berridge, 2017). The hedonic gloss of objects or events is generated in the brain by activity in networks of hedonic hotspots (pleasure) or coldspots (displeasure). Berridge and his colleagues have identified these regions in the rodent nucleus accumbens and ventral pallidum, the adjacent insula in the cortex, and orbitofrontal cortex through direct neurochemical or optogenetic manipulation generating positive or negative changes in "liking" reactions to tastes (see details in Berridge & Kringelbach, 2015).

Recall that the active search for a pleasure center in the brain was initiated, at least in part, by Olds and Milner's discovery that rats would press a bar to get an electrical current to the brain. Although we now know that the current was evoking wanting, not pleasure, the question remains: Could stimulation of hotspots actually induce pleasure, and, more importantly, could stimulation be used to reverse states of *anhedonia*, such as depression? Studies of the effects of deep brain stimulation in humans in the 1970s were claimed to have shown feelings of pleasure, but a review of this work by Berridge and Kringelbach (2015) suggests that there is no evidence that patients actually acknowledged this effect.

Nonetheless, in the past decade deep brain stimulation has developed as a therapeutic technique for a wide range of conditions, including chronic pain, depression, and Parkinson disease. Stimulation of the nucleus accumbens of humans has been reported to induce sudden feelings of "wanting" to do something, but there is as yet no convincing evidence that such stimulation can produce "liking" (pleasure). There are clearly technical issues: electrodes would need to be targeted at a hotspot without also stimulating an adjacent cold spot, which would produce a mixed response. There is, however, growing evidence that stimulation of the nucleus accumbens or prefrontal cortex can provide relief from anxiety or depression, which can have a significant positive impact on people's lives.

12-7 Review

Before you continue, check your understanding. Answers to Self-Test appear at the back of the book.

1. Animals engage in voluntary behaviors because the behaviors are _____.

2. Neural circuits maintain contact with rewarding environmental stimuli in the present or in the future through _____ and _____ subsystems.

3. The neurotransmitter hypothesized to be related to reward is _____, and the neurotransmitters hypothesized to be related to liking are _____ and _____.

4. What is intracranial self-stimulation, and what does it tell us about the brain's reward system?

For additional study tools, visit ⚏ **LaunchPad** at launchpadworks.com

Summary

12-1 Identifying the Causes of Behavior

Our inner subjective feelings (emotions) and goal-directed thoughts (motivations) influence how we behave and adapt as individuals and as a species. Emotion and motivation are inferred states that can escape conscious awareness or intent and that make the case for free will difficult to argue.

Biologically, reward motivates animals to engage in behavior. Aversive circumstances prompt brain circuits to produce behaviors that will reduce those circumstances. The brain inherently needs stimulation. In its absence, the brain will seek it out.

Sensory stimulation leads to hormone activity and to dopamine activity in the brainstem. Neural circuits organized in the brainstem control species-typical behaviors, such as mouse killing by cats and singing by birds. These brainstem circuits manifest their evolutionary advantage: they are rewarding. Rewarding behavior motivates living beings. When animals disengage from behaviors that motivate their species, they go extinct.

Behavior is controlled by its consequences as well as by its biology. Consequences may affect the evolution of a species or the behavior of an individual. Behaviors selected by evolution are often triggered by innate releasing mechanisms (IRMs). Behaviors selected only in an individual animal are shaped by that animal's environment and are learned.

12-2 The Chemical Senses

In the olfactory and gustatory senses, chemical neuroreceptors in the nose and tongue interact with chemosignals, leading to neural activity in cranial nerve 1 for olfaction and cranial nerves 7, 9, and 10 for taste. The cranial nerves enter the brainstem and, through a series of synapses, pass into the forebrain. Smell and taste inputs merge in the orbitofrontal cortex to produce our perception of flavor.

12-3 Neuroanatomy of Motivated Behavior

The neural structures that initiate emotional and motivated behaviors are the hypothalamus, pituitary gland, amygdala, dopaminergic and noradrenergic activating pathways from nuclei in the lower brainstem, and frontal lobes.

The experience of both emotion and motivation is controlled by activity in the ANS, hypothalamus, and forebrain, especially the amygdala and frontal cortex. Emotional and motivated behavior may be unconscious responses to internal or external stimuli controlled either by the activity of innate releasing mechanisms or by cognitive responses to events or thoughts.

12-4 Control of Regulatory Behavior

The two distinctly different types of motivated behaviors are (1) regulatory (homeostatic) behaviors that maintain vital body system balance and (2) nonregulatory behaviors, which are basically all nonreflexive behaviors and behaviors not controlled by a homeostatic mechanism. Eating and drinking are regulatory behaviors controlled by the interaction of the digestive and hormonal systems, the enteric nervous system, and the hypothalamic and cortical circuits. Osmotic thirst results from increased concentrations of dissolved chemicals, known as solutes, in the body fluids. Hypovolemic thirst results from a loss of overall fluid volume from the body.

12-5 Sexual Differences and Sexual Behavior

Sexual differentiation results from an organizing effect of gonadal hormones and sex chromosomes during development. Sexual differentiation results in sexually dimorphic brain structures and behavior. Gonadal hormones also affect brain and behavior through activating effects later in life.

Copulatory behavior is controlled by the hypothalamus (ventrome-dial hypothalamus in females and the preoptic area in males). Sexual activity is a nonregulatory behavior motivated by the amygdala. Sexual orientation (a person's attraction to the opposite or same sex) and gender identity (a person's feeling of being male or female) are related to the organization of the hypothalamus. Differences in hypothalamic organization are likely related to epigenetic effects in early development.

12-6 The Neural Control of Emotion

Emotion is an inferred state that is difficult to define. We consider three models of emotion. Constructivist theories argue that the brain produces a cognitive response to autonomic states. Appraisal theories define emotional episodes as processes rather than states. Emotions result from an evaluation of context, including somatic components, which lead to a subjective feeling. Neuropsychological theories emphasize asymmetrical cerebral control of emotions.

Emotions are not found in a single place in the brain but rather are distributed in limbic and frontal lobe structures, especially the amygdala and prefrontal cortex. Emotional disorders, such as depression and anxiety, are believed to result from dysfunction in these structures.

12-7 Reward

Survival depends on maximizing contact with some environmental stimuli and minimizing contact with others. The reward mechanism controls this differential. Two independent features of reward are wanting and liking. The wanting component is thought to be controlled by dopaminergic activating systems, whereas the liking component is thought to be controlled by opioid and endocannabinoid systems. The wanting system is generated by a large distributed brain system dominated by dopamine projections found especially in striatal and prefrontal regions. The liking system is distributed by a smaller localized set of hedonic hotspots in the striatum and brainstem.

| Key Terms

activating effects, p. 417
amygdala, p. 424
androgen, p. 396
anorexia nervosa, p. 411
aphagia, p. 412
emotion, p. 394
evolutionary psychology, p. 398
gender identity, p. 420
generalized anxiety disorder, p. 430

hippocampus, p. 423
homeostatic mechanism, p. 405
hyperphagia, p. 412
hypovolemic thirst, p. 414
innate releasing mechanism (IRM), p. 396
Klüver–Bucy syndrome, p. 425
learned taste aversion, p. 399
medial forebrain bundle (MFB), p. 406

nonregulatory behavior, p. 405
obesity, p. 410
orbitofrontal cortex (OFC), p. 401
organizing effects, p. 417
osmotic thirst, p. 414
panic disorder, p. 430
pheromone, p. 402
phobia, p. 430
pituitary gland, p. 406

preparedness, p. 399
psychosurgery, p. 427
regulatory behavior, p. 405
reinforcer, p. 398
releasing hormone, p. 407
sexual dimorphism, p. 417
sexual orientation, p. 419
transgender, p. 420

Visit **LaunchPad** to access the e-Book, videos, **LearningCurve** adaptive quizzing, flashcards, and more at launchpadworks.com

Why Do We Sleep and Dream?

CHAPTER **13**

Doing the Right Thing at the Right Time

We have all heard this advice: Maintaining regular sleeping and eating habits contributes to good health. Scientific evidence supports this good advice.

We humans are **diurnal animals** (from the Latin *dies*, meaning "day"): we are active during daylight and we sleep when it is dark. This day-and-night rhythm is our **circadian rhythm**, and it regulates not only our sleep but other behaviors such as eating times. Many other animals have a similar circadian rhythm.

Today our environment allows us to intrude on our circadian rhythm in two ways. Artificial lighting allows us to extend our waking hours well into the night and into sleep time. Handy food sources—often easily metabolized high-calorie foods—allow us to eat whenever we want.

Together these intrusions into our natural circadian rhythm contribute to a combination of medical disorders known as **metabolic syndrome** that collectively increase the risk of developing sleep disorders, cardiovascular disease, and diabetes (Lajoie et al., 2015).

The roots of metabolic syndrome may lie in disruptions of our **biological clocks**, the neural systems that regulate our circadian behavior. We likely have two clocks: One that controls sleep–waking and another that controls the functioning of body organs related to feeding, such as the liver, pancreas, and gut. The clock that controls sleep–waking responds to light, whereas the clock that controls feeding responds to eating.

The activity of these two clocks is reciprocal: disrupting one disrupts the other.

Irregular sleep and meal schedules thus change the synchrony of biological clocks. Metabolic rate, plasma glucose, and pancreatic insulin secretion can slow down or speed up at inappropriate times, contributing to obesity and diabetes. Prevention and treatment for obesity and diabetes can include doing the right thing at the right time when it comes to sleep schedules and mealtimes.

Daniel Schoenen / LOOK-foto/Getty Images

Our daily rhythms of sleeping and waking, feeding, exercising, and social interaction are rhythmical over days and years. Other animals share these daily activities and also migrate, hibernate, and shed or grow feathers or fur as the seasons change. In this chapter, we answer questions related to these daily and seasonal rhythms, including how the brain produces biological rhythms, why sleep evolved, and what neural mechanisms regulate sleeping, waking, and sleep-related disorders.

13-1

A Clock for All Seasons

We first consider biological rhythms and then present evidence that some rhythms are produced by a biological clock. Because environmental cues are not always consistent, we examine how our biological clock helps us interpret environmental cues in an adaptive way. We will also consider evidence for health consequences when behavior comes into conflict with our biological clock.

Biological Rhythms

Biorhythms are cyclical changes in behavior or bodily functions. They have their origins in the first unicellular organisms and are a feature of all living organisms today.

diurnal animal Organism that is active chiefly during daylight.

circadian rhythm Day–night rhythm.

metabolic syndrome Combinations of medical disorders, including obesity and insulin abnormalities, that collectively increase the risk of developing cardiovascular disease and diabetes.

biological clock Neural system that times behavior by producing biorhythms.

biorhythm A natural rhythm in behavior or bodily process.

Ashima Narain/Getty Images

Why Do We Sleep and Dream?   CHAPTER 13

Doing the Right Thing at the Right Time

We have all heard this advice: Maintaining regular sleeping and eating habits contributes to good health. Scientific evidence supports this good advice.

We humans are **diurnal animals** (from the Latin *dies*, meaning "day"): we are active during daylight and we sleep when it is dark. This day-and-night rhythm is our **circadian rhythm**, and it regulates not only our sleep but other behaviors such as eating times. Many other animals have a similar circadian rhythm.

Today our environment allows us to intrude on our circadian rhythm in two ways. Artificial lighting allows us to extend our waking hours well into the night and into sleep time. Handy food sources—often easily metabolized high-calorie foods—allow us to eat whenever we want.

Together these intrusions into our natural circadian rhythm contribute to a combination of medical disorders known as **metabolic syndrome** that collectively increase the risk of developing sleep disorders, cardiovascular disease, and diabetes (Lajoie et al., 2015).

The roots of metabolic syndrome may lie in disruptions of our **biological clocks**, the neural systems that regulate our circadian behavior. We likely have two clocks: One that controls sleep–waking and another that controls the functioning of body organs related to feeding, such as the liver, pancreas, and gut. The clock that controls sleep–waking responds to light, whereas the clock that controls feeding responds to eating.

The activity of these two clocks is reciprocal: disrupting one disrupts the other.

Irregular sleep and meal schedules thus change the synchrony of biological clocks. Metabolic rate, plasma glucose, and pancreatic insulin secretion can slow down or speed up at inappropriate times, contributing to obesity and diabetes. Prevention and treatment for obesity and diabetes can include doing the right thing at the right time when it comes to sleep schedules and mealtimes.

Daniel Schoenen / LOOK-foto/Getty Images

Our daily rhythms of sleeping and waking, feeding, exercising, and social interaction are rhythmical over days and years. Other animals share these daily activities and also migrate, hibernate, and shed or grow feathers or fur as the seasons change. In this chapter, we answer questions related to these daily and seasonal rhythms, including how the brain produces biological rhythms, why sleep evolved, and what neural mechanisms regulate sleeping, waking, and sleep-related disorders.

diurnal animal Organism that is active chiefly during daylight.

circadian rhythm Day–night rhythm.

metabolic syndrome Combinations of medical disorders, including obesity and insulin abnormalities, that collectively increase the risk of developing cardiovascular disease and diabetes.

biological clock Neural system that times behavior by producing biorhythms.

biorhythm A natural rhythm in behavior or bodily process.

13-1

A Clock for All Seasons

We first consider biological rhythms and then present evidence that some rhythms are produced by a biological clock. Because environmental cues are not always consistent, we examine how our biological clock helps us interpret environmental cues in an adaptive way. We will also consider evidence for health consequences when behavior comes into conflict with our biological clock.

Biological Rhythms

Biorhythms are cyclical changes in behavior or bodily functions. They have their origins in the first unicellular organisms and are a feature of all living organisms today.

Every cyclical activity has a **period**, the time required to complete one cycle of activity. Biorhythms are defined by their periods.

A variety of different biorhythms regulate an organism's behaviors and functions. *Circannual rhythms* have a period of about a year. Many animals' migratory and mating cycles are circannual. Other biorhythms have monthly or seasonal periods greater than a day but less than a year. These are *infradian rhythms*. The menstrual cycle and associated hormonal changes of human females, with an average period of about 28 days, is an infradian biorhythm. The menstrual cycle is linked to the cycle of the moon and thus also referred to as a *circalunar cycle* (Amariei et al., 2014). *Circadian rhythms* have a daily period, as exemplified by the human sleep–waking cycle; many other biological functions share this rhythm. *Ultradian rhythms* have a period of less than a day. Our eating behavior, which takes place about every 90 minutes to 2 hours, including snacking, is one example.

period Time required to complete an activity cycle.

In Latin, *circa* means "around," *annum* means "year," and *dies* means "day."

Biological rhythm	Time frame	Example
Circannual	Yearly	Migratory cycles of birds
Infradian	More than a day	Human menstrual cycle
Circadian	Daily	Human sleep–wake cycle
Ultradian	Less than a day	Human eating cycles

The Origin of Biorhythms

Biorhythms are a feature of most animals and plants, including unicellular organisms, but how they evolved is unclear. What is clear is that they help living things adapt to the cyclical changes that take place in the environment as a result of Earth's rotation and orbit in relation to the sun.

Because the Earth's axis is tilted slightly, as it makes its annual orbit around the sun, the North and South Poles incline slightly toward the sun for part of the year and slightly away from it for the rest of the year (see **Figure 13-1**). Regions near the equator undergo little change in day and night length over the course of a year, but the magnitude of the day–night changes increases as distance from the equator increases. As the Southern Hemisphere inclines toward the sun, its inhabitants experience longer days and shorter nights; inhabitants in the Northern Hemisphere experience shorter days and longer nights. This relationship reverses as the year progresses.

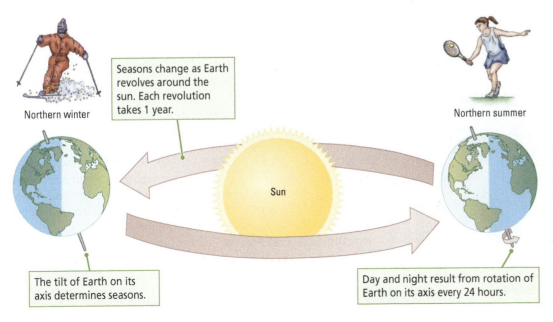

Northern winter

Seasons change as Earth revolves around the sun. Each revolution takes 1 year.

Sun

Northern summer

The tilt of Earth on its axis determines seasons.

Day and night result from rotation of Earth on its axis every 24 hours.

FIGURE 13-1 **Origins of Biorhythms** Each point on Earth between the Arctic and Antarctic Circles faces the sun for part of its daily rotation cycle (daytime) and faces away from the sun for the other part (nighttime). Seasonal changes in temperature and in the amount of daylight result from the tilt of Earth's axis during its annual revolution around the sun.

Circadian comes from the Latin *circa*, meaning "around" and *diem*, meaning "day."

A circadian biorhythm allows an organism to make adjustments to day and night changes and to the relative lengthening and shortening of day and night at the latitude at which it lives. A circannual biorhythm helps an animal adapt to the environmental changes that occur over a year, especially if it lives in northern and southern climates.

Adding to the challenges posed by daily and seasonal changes, many animals do not stay at the same latitude. Migration requires adaption to the changes in the length of the day and night, climate, and food availability. In the following sections, we will first describe how some biorhythms help us adapt to daily changes, and then we will describe how the same biorhythms interact with other, shorter and longer biorhythms.

Circadian Rhythms

Just as human waking and sleep behavior have a circadian rhythm, so also do pulse rate, blood pressure, body temperature, rate of cell division, blood cell count, alertness, urine composition, metabolic rate, sexual drive, feeding behavior, responsiveness to medications, cognitive ability, and emotions. The activity of nearly every cell in our bodies produces a circadian rhythm.

Circadian rhythms are not unique to animals. Plants display rhythmic behavior exemplified by species whose leaves or flowers open during the day and close at night. Even unicellular algae and fungi display rhythmic behaviors related to the passage of the day. Some animals, including lizards and crabs, change color in a rhythmic pattern. The Florida chameleon, for example, turns green at night, whereas its coloration matches its environment during the day. In short, almost every living organism and every living cell displays circadian rhythms (Bosler et al., 2015).

THE ENDOGENOUS ORIGIN OF CIRCADIAN RHYTHMS Circadian rhythms are produced by an endogenous (internal) mechanism referred to as a biological clock. The existence of a biological clock was first recognized in 1729 by the geologist Jean Jacques d'Ortous de Mairan (see Raven et al., 1992). In an experiment similar to the one illustrated in the Procedure section of **Experiment 13-1**, de Mairan isolated a plant from daily light, dark, and temperature cues. He noted that the rhythmic movements of its leaves seen over a light–dark cycle continued when it was isolated, as graphed in the Results section of the experiment.

What concerned investigators who came after de Mairan was the possibility that some undetected external cue stimulates the plant's rhythmic behavior. Such cues could include changes in temperature, in electromagnetic fields, and even in the intensity of cosmic rays from outer space. But further experiments showed that daily fluctuations are *endogenous*—they come from within the plant. Thus, the plant must have a biological clock.

Similar experiments show that almost all organisms, including humans, have circadian clocks that synchronize behavior to the temporal passage of a day and make predictions about tomorrow. A circadian clock signals that if daylight lasts for a given time today, it will last for about the same time tomorrow. A circadian clock allows us to anticipate events and prepare for them both physiologically and cognitively. And unless external factors get in the way, a circadian clock regulates feeding times, sleeping times, and metabolic activity as appropriate to day–night cycles. Circadian clocks also produce epigenetic effects: they influence gene expression in every cell in the body (Gaucher et al., 2018).

···▷ **EXPERIMENT 13-1**

Question: Is plant movement exogenous or endogenous?

Procedure

The movements of the plant's leaves are recorded in constant dim light.

A pen attached to a leaf is moved when the leaf moves,...

Revolving drum

Pen

Results

...producing a record of the movement.

Leaf up

Leaf down

Bryan Kolb/Ian Whishaw

Conclusion: Movement of the plant is endogenous. It is caused by an internal clock that matches the temporal passage of a real day.

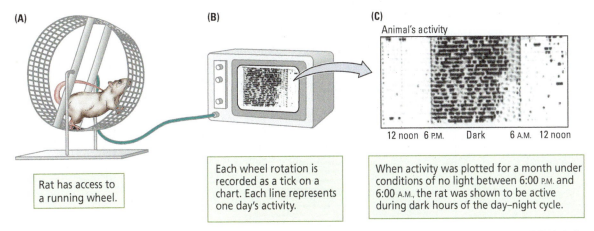

(A)

Rat has access to a running wheel.

(B)

Each wheel rotation is recorded as a tick on a chart. Each line represents one day's activity.

(C)

Animal's activity

12 noon   6 P.M.   Dark   6 A.M.   12 noon

When activity was plotted for a month under conditions of no light between 6:00 P.M. and 6:00 A.M., the rat was shown to be active during dark hours of the day–night cycle.

FIGURE 13-2 **Recording the Daily Activity Cycle of a Rat** Data from Richter, 1965.

MEASURING CIRCADIAN RHYTHMS Although the existence of the endogenous circadian clock was demonstrated nearly 300 years ago, detailed study of biorhythms had to await the development of electrical and computer-based timing devices. Behavioral analysis requires a method for counting behavioral events, as well as a method for displaying those events in a meaningful way. For example, rat behavior was first measured by giving the animal access to a running wheel for exercise (**Figure 13-2A**).

A computer records each turn of the wheel and displays the result (Figure 13-2B). Because rats are nocturnal, sleeping during light hours and becoming active during dark hours, their wheel running takes place in the dark. If each day's activity is plotted under the preceding day's activity in a column, we observe a pattern—a cycle of activity over time. A glance at the pattern reveals when and how active the animal is (Figure 13-2C). Electronic innovations that place movement sensors in smart watches and smartphones are now used to measure the circadian activity of human participants.

Free-Running Rhythms

The fact that a behavior appears to be rhythmic does not mean that it is ruled only by a biological clock. Animals may postpone migrations as long as food supplies last. They adjust their circadian activities in response to the availability of food, the presence of predators, and competition from other members of their own species. We humans obviously change our daily activities in response to seasonal changes, work schedules, and play opportunities. Therefore, whether a rhythmic behavior is produced by a biological clock and the extent to which it is controlled by a biological clock must be demonstrated experimentally.

To determine whether a rhythm is produced by a biological clock, researchers can conduct one of a number of tests in which they manipulate conditions. A test may be given (1) in continuous light, (2) in light of varying brightness, (3) in continuous darkness, (4) by light choice of the participant, or (5) with eating, activity, and sleep times all regulated. Each treatment yields a slightly different insight into the period of the biological clock.

Aschoff (1978) first demonstrated that the human sleep–waking rhythm is governed by a biological clock that has a preferred period. He and his coworkers allowed participants to select their light–dark cycle and studied them in an underground bunker, where no cues signaled when day began or ended. The participants selected the periods when they were active and when they slept, and they turned the lights on and off at will. In short, they selected the length of their own day and night.

Measures of ongoing behavior and recording of sleep periods with sensors on the beds revealed that the participants continued to show daily sleep–activity rhythms. This finding confirms that humans have an endogenous biological clock that governs sleep–waking behavior. **Figure 13-3** shows, however, that the biorhythm is different when compared with biorhythms before and after isolation. Although the period of the participants' sleep–wake cycles approximated 24 hours before and after

FIGURE 13-3 **Free-Running Rhythm in a Human** The record for days 1 through 3 shows the daily sleep period under typical day–night conditions. The record for days 4 through 20 shows the free-running rhythm that developed while this participant was isolated in a bunker and allowed to control day and night lengths. The daily activity period shifts from 24 hours to 25.9 hours. On days 21 through 25, the period returns to 24 hours as the participant is again exposed to a natural light–dark cycle. Data from Hobson, 1989.

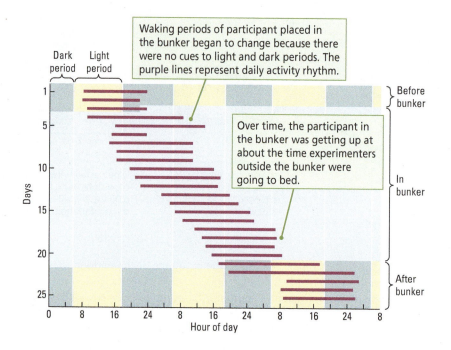

the test, during the test the cycles lengthened to about 25 to 27 hours, depending on the person.

The participants chose to go to bed 1 to 2 hours later every "night." Soon they were getting up at about the time the experimenters outside the bunker were going to bed. Clearly, the participants were displaying their own cycle. This cycle is called a **free-running rhythm**, one that has a period of the body's own devising.

Subsequent research suggests the human free-running rhythm is not as long as that described by Aschoff. Because the participants controlled the lights in their environment, the light affected the apparent phase of their rhythm by advancing the length of time they stayed up each day. When light, eating times, temperature, and sleep times are added into the experiment to more closely regulate behavior, the average human free-running period is about 24.1 to 24.2 hours (Phillips et al., 2011).

The period of free-running rhythms also depends on the light-related biology of a species. When hamsters, a nocturnal species, are tested in constant darkness, their free-running periods are a little shorter than 24 hours; when they are tested in constant light, their free-running periods are a little longer than 24 hours. In the constant darkness test with two closely related species, rats have a cycle that expands slightly, and mice have a cycle that contracts slightly. As **Figure 13-4** shows, the opposite free-running periods can be found in some diurnal animals (Binkley, 1990). When sparrows, diurnal birds, are tested in constant darkness, their free-running periods are a little longer than 24 hours; when they are tested in constant light, their free-running periods are a little shorter than 24 hours. Thus, period length for any species or condition requires explicit experimental verification.

Zeitgebers

The daily cycle of light and dark varies with latitude and with the seasons. To be useful, the biological clock must keep to a time that predicts actual changes in the day–night cycle. If free-running rhythms are not exactly 24 hours, how does a biological clock that is set to a circadian rhythm keep accurate time? The free-running period suggests that the biological clock is like a slightly defective clock and eventually provides times that are inaccurate by hours and so is useless.

If we reset an errant clock each day, however—say, when we awaken—it provides useful information. Aschoff realized that when their participants in the bunker were again exposed to regular light cues, their circadian period was reset. Aschoff

free-running rhythm Rhythm of the body's own devising in the absence of all external cues.

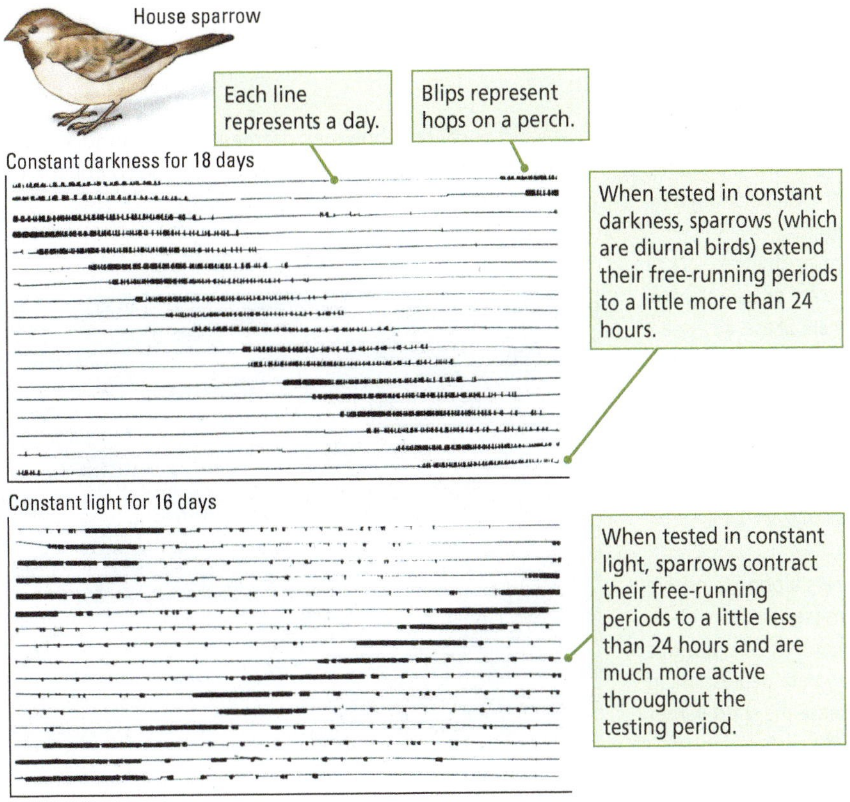

House sparrow

Each line represents a day.

Blips represent hops on a perch.

Constant darkness for 18 days

When tested in constant darkness, sparrows (which are diurnal birds) extend their free-running periods to a little more than 24 hours.

Constant light for 16 days

When tested in constant light, sparrows contract their free-running periods to a little less than 24 hours and are much more active throughout the testing period.

FIGURE 13-4 **Free-Running Rhythms of a Diurnal Animal** Data from Binkley, 1990.

and his team called a clock-setting cue a **Zeitgeber** (German for "time giver"). From the results of many experiments, we know that light is the most potent Zeitgeber for many animals, including humans.

Entraining a Circadian Rhythm

When a Zeitgeber resets a biorhythm, the rhythm is said to be **entrained**. Clinical Focus 13-2, Seasonal Affective Disorder, explains light's importance in entraining circadian rhythms. When its biological clock is entrained, an animal is able to organize its daily schedule, including when to eat, exercise, and sleep. For some animals that live in polar regions, the constant light of summer and the constant dark of winter exceed their clock's capacity to adjust; for those animals, the clock turns off. The light Zeitgeber is most effective for humans at both sunrise and sunset. There are many nonphotic Zeitgebers, however, including ambient temperature, activity, mealtimes, work, and social events that can in some circumstances entrain the circadian rhythm if the event occurs at the same time each day.

DISRUPTING THE CIRCADIAN RHYTHM When we stay up late in artificial light, sleep late some days, and get up early by using an alarm clock on other days, we disrupt our circadian rhythm. **Light pollution**, the extent to which artificial lighting floods our workplaces, homes, and environment, also disrupts the circadian rhythm. Light pollution has increased with the use of LED (light-emitting diode) lights, in which blue wavelengths are not filtered (see Clinical Focus 13-2). Disruptions of the circadian rhythm account for inconsistent behavior associated with accidents, daytime fatigue, alterations in emotional states, obesity, diabetes, and other disorders characteristic of metabolic syndrome, described in Clinical Focus 13-1, Doing the Right Thing at the Right Time. In addition, humans display many of these same symptoms in coping with more northern and southern latitudes, due in part to the reduced effectiveness of prolonged light or dark to synchronize the circadian rhythm (Jagannath et al., 2017).

Zeitgeber Environmental event that entrains biological rhythms; German for "time giver."

entrain To determine or modify the period of a biorhythm.

light pollution Exposure to artificial light that changes activity patterns and so disrupts circadian rhythms.

Seasonal Affective Disorder

One explanation of *seasonal affective disorder* (*SAD*), a form of depression displayed by as many as 10 percent of people who live in northern latitudes, is that low levels of sunlight in winter do not entrain the circadian rhythm. Consequently, a person's circadian rhythm is disrupted.

Because people vary in the duration of their free-running rhythms, lack of entrainment affects individuals differently. Some people are phase-retarded, with desired sleep time coming earlier each day; some are phase-advanced, with desired sleep time coming later each day. Zhang and colleagues (2016) have described variants in the Period gene, one of the genes that is involved in timing the circadian cycle, which may be related to the susceptibility to display SAD and the phase-advanced feature of the circadian rhythm. By preparing mice with the Period gene knocked out, these researchers produced mice with a depressive phenotype. Such findings support an association between altered circadian rhythms and depression.

Because a class of retinal ganglion cells that express a photosensitive pigment called *melanopsin* are responsive to blue light (see Section 13-2), it has been proposed that exposure to bright white light that contains this blue frequency can reset the circadian clock and ameliorate depression. In this treatment, called *phototherapy*, the idea is to increase the short winter photoperiod by exposing a person to artificial bright light in the morning or both morning and evening (Mårtensson et al., 2015). Typical room lighting is not bright enough.

A word of caution, however: decreased exposure to sunlight in winter can result in vitamin D deficiency, which may also contribute to depression (Kerr et al., 2015).

During the polar night in northern Norway, schoolchildren take light treatment to combat SAD.

Entrainment works best if the adjustment made to the biological clock is not too large. People who work night shifts are often subject to huge adjustments, especially when they work the graveyard shift (typically 11:00 P.M. to 7:00 A.M.), the period when they would normally sleep. Study results show that adapting to such a change is difficult and stressful, and it increases susceptibility to disease by altering immune system rhythms (Paganelli et al., 2018). Compared with people who have a regular daytime work schedule, people who work night shifts and switch between work and nonwork schedules have a higher incidence of metabolic syndrome. Thus, shift workers benefit from vigilance in maintaining good sleep habits and diet and in exercising to minimize other risk factors for metabolic syndrome. Adaptations to shift work fare better if people first work the swing shift (typically 3:00 P.M. to 11:00 P.M.) for a time before beginning the graveyard shift.

Long-distance air travel—say from North America to Europe or Asia—also demands large and difficult time adjustments. For example, travelers flying east from New York to Paris begin their first day in Europe just when their biological clock is signaling that it is time for sleep (**Figure 13-5**). The difference between a person's circadian rhythm and the daylight cycle in a new environment can produce the disorientation and fatigue of **jet lag**.

The west-to-east traveler generally has a more difficult adjustment than does the east-to-west traveler, who needs to stay up only a little longer than usual. The occasional traveler may cope with jet lag quite well, by managing jet lag with sleep on arrival or shortly after. The brain's biological clock resets in a day, and other body organs follow after about a week. For frequent travelers and flight crews, resetting is not so easy. Persistent asynchronous rhythms generated by jet lag are associated with altered sleep and temperature rhythms, fatigue, stress, and even reduced success by sports teams traveling more than 3 hours from west to east (Diekman & Bose, 2018).

jet lag Fatigue and disorientation resulting from rapid travel through time zones and exposure to a changed light–dark cycle.

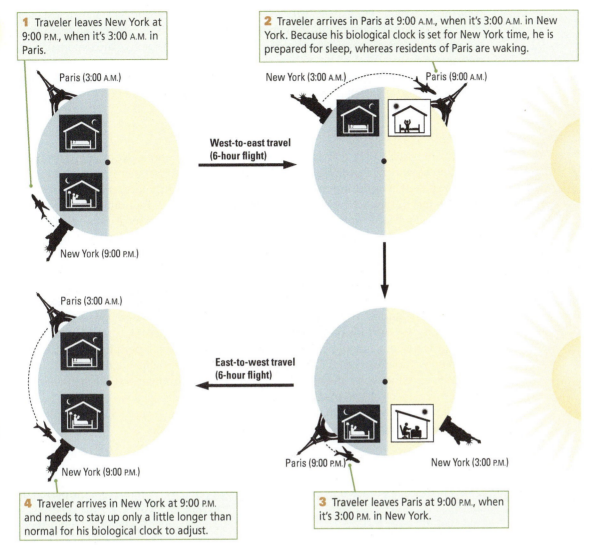

1 Traveler leaves New York at 9:00 P.M., when it's 3:00 A.M. in Paris.

2 Traveler arrives in Paris at 9:00 A.M., when it's 3:00 A.M. in New York. Because his biological clock is set for New York time, he is prepared for sleep, whereas residents of Paris are waking.

Paris (3:00 A.M.)

New York (3:00 A.M.)   Paris (9:00 A.M.)

West-to-east travel (6-hour flight)

New York (9:00 P.M.)

Paris (3:00 A.M.)

East-to-west travel (6-hour flight)

New York (9:00 P.M.)

Paris (9:00 P.M.)   New York (3:00 P.M.)

4 Traveler arrives in New York at 9:00 P.M. and needs to stay up only a little longer than normal for his biological clock to adjust.

3 Traveler leaves Paris at 9:00 P.M., when it's 3:00 P.M. in New York.

FIGURE 13-5 Jet Lag Disruption in the entrainment of a person's biological clock is undoubtedly more pronounced in west-to-east jet travel because the disruption in the person's circadian rhythm is dramatic. On the return journey, the traveler's biological clock has a much easier adjustment to make.

13-1 Review

Before you continue, check your understanding. Answers to Self-Test appear at the back of the book.

1. Many behaviors occur in a rhythmic pattern in relationship to time. These biorhythms may display a yearly, or _____, cycle or a daily, or _____, cycle.

2. Although biological clocks keep fairly good time, their _____ rhythms may be slightly shorter or longer than 24 hours unless they are reset each day by _____.

3. _____ and _____ can disrupt circadian rhythms.

4. Explain why the circadian rhythm is important.

For additional study tools, visit **LaunchPad** at launchpadworks.com

13-2

The Suprachiasmatic Biological Clock

Curt Richter was the first researcher who attempted to locate biological clocks in the brain. In the 1930s, he captured wild rats and tested them in activity wheels. He found that the rats ran, ate, and drank when the lights were off and were relatively quiescent when the lights

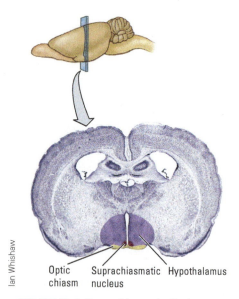

Ian Whishaw

| Optic | Suprachiasmatic | Hypothalamus |
| chiasm | nucleus | |

FIGURE 13-6 Suprachiasmatic Nucleus in a Rat Brain

were on. By ablating brain tissue with electric current, Richter found that animals lost their circadian rhythm after damage to the hypothalamus (Richter, 1965). Subsequently, by making much more discrete lesions, experimenters found that a region of the hypothalamus, the suprachiasmatic nucleus (SCN), acts as the master biological clock (Honma, 2018). The SCN is named for its location just above (*supra-*) the optic chiasm, where the optic tracts cross at the base of the hypothalamus, as shown in **Figure 13-6**.

Suprachiasmatic Rhythms

Evidence for the SCN's role as a CNS biological clock comes from many sources, including the loss of rhythmical eating, drinking, and exercise after brain damage; the activity of SCN cells during light phases of the cycle; and the presence of a pathway from the eye to the SCN. Although the SCN is considered the brain's master clock, two other neural structures, the intergeniculate leaflet and the pineal gland, also have a clocklike role in controlling behavior. Furthermore, nearly every cell in the body can be rhythmical; each can have its own clock.

Evidence supporting the idea that something other than the SCN can act as a clock includes the observation that feeding behavior in rats retains a timed occurrence after SCN removal. Animals without an SCN can still display anticipatory behavior—becoming active in relation to scheduled mealtimes—and can organize related behaviors, including memory for food locations, in relationship to mealtimes. How this anticipatory behavior is timed is not known, but it may be influenced by a peripheral clock in the liver, adipose tissue, or gut (Fadda et al., 2018). In addition, scheduled feeding activity can act as a Zeitgeber for the main SCN clock. That is, a regular feeding schedule can entrain the SCN clock and many other body organs and cells, and an irregular feeding schedule can be disruptive. In all other respects, however, the suprachiasmatic nucleus acts as the master clock, setting the time for all the other clocks.

Keeping Time

If SCN neurons are isolated from one another, each remains rhythmic, but the period of some cells differs from that of other cells. Thus, rhythmic activity is a property of SCN cells, yet the timing of the rhythm must depend on groups of cells that synchronize their activity in relationship to each other. Their entrainment depends on external inputs, however.

The SCN receives information about light through the retinohypothalamic tract, a pathway from the retina to the SCN (**Figure 13-7**). The main source of the retinohypothalamic tract signal does not come from the rods and cones, however, but from specialized retinal ganglion cells (RGCs). These RGCs contain the photosensitive pigment *melanopsin*, which is sensitive to wavelengths of blue light (about 460 to 480 nm).

The existence of light-sensitive retinal ganglion cells that are involved in entraining the circadian rhythm explains the continued presence of an entrained rhythm in people who are blind as a result of retinal degeneration that destroys the rods and cones (Zaidi et al., 2007). Even so, melanopsin-containing RGCs also receive inputs from cones and rods. Cones can influence the activity of RGCs in bright daylight, and rods can influence their activity in dim light. Artificial light from LED lights can have a stronger blue-light component than more old-fashioned lights, making this form of light a potent source of light

FIGURE 13-7 The Retinohypothalamic Tract and the SCN

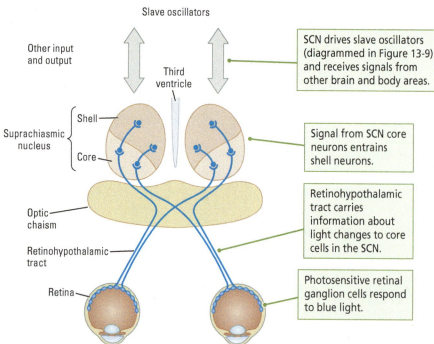

Slave oscillators

Other input and output

Third ventricle

Suprachiasmic nucleus
- Shell
- Core

Optic chaism

Retinohypothalamic tract

Retina

SCN drives slave oscillators (diagrammed in Figure 13-9) and receives signals from other brain and body areas.

Signal from SCN core neurons entrains shell neurons.

Retinohypothalamic tract carries information about light changes to core cells in the SCN.

Photosensitive retinal ganglion cells respond to blue light.

pollution. One solution to this unwanted stimulation is to filter out blue light by using filters that give light a yellow appearance; such filters are now options on computers and cell phones.

Melanopsin-containing photosensitive RGCs are distributed across the retina, and in humans they make up between 1 percent and 3 percent of all RGCs. Their axons inner-vate the SCN bilaterally. Melanopsin-containing ganglion cells use glutamate as their primary neurotransmitter but also contain two cotransmitters: substance P and pituitary adenylate cyclase–activating polypeptide (PACAP). When stimulated by light, melanop-sin-containing RGCs are excited, and in turn they excite cells in the SCN.

As illustrated in Figure 13-7, the SCN consists of two parts, a more ven-trally located *core* and a more dorsally located *shell*. The retinohypothalamic tract activates the core cells. Core neurons are not rhythmic, but they entrain the shell neurons, which are rhythmic.

In addition to receiving retinohypothalamic input, the SCN receives pro-jections from other brain regions, including the intergeniculate leaflet in the thalamus and the raphe nucleus, which is the nonspecific serotonergic-activating system of the brainstem. The terminal regions of these inputs to the SCN display variations, suggesting that various portions of the shell and the core have somewhat different functions.

As described above, the SCN's circadian rhythm is usually entrained by morning and evening light, but it can also be entrained or disrupted by sudden changes in lighting, by arousal, by moving about, and by feeding. These influences differ from the light entrainment provided over the retino-hypothalamic tract. The intergeniculate leaflet and the raphe nucleus are pathways through which nonphotic events can influence the SCN rhythm (Cain et al., 2007).

Immortal Time

The endogenous rhythm of SCN cells is not learned. When animals are raised in constant darkness, their behavior is still rhythmic. In experiments in which animals have been maintained without entraining cues for a num-ber of generations, each generation continues to display rhythmic behavior. Even if the mother has received an SCN lesion so that her behavior is not rhythmic, her offspring's behavior is rhythmic.

Evidence supporting the idea that suprachiasmatic cells are genetically programmed for rhythmicity comes from studies performed in Canada by Martin Ralph and his colleagues with the use of transplantation techniques (Ralph & Lehman, 1991). **Figure 13-8** illustrates the experiment.

As reflected in the top chart, hamsters are tested in constant dim light or in constant darkness to establish their free-running rhythms. They then receive a suprachiasmatic lesion followed by another test to show that the lesion has abolished their rhythmicity (center chart). Finally, the hamsters receive trans-plants of suprachiasmatic cells obtained from hamster embryos. About 60 days later, the hamsters again show rhythmic activity, demonstrating that the transplanted cells have been integrated into the host brain and have reestablished rhythmic behavior (bottom chart). Follow-up studies show that the rhythms of many, but not all, body organs also show restored rhythmic activity following the suprachiasmatic transplant.

What Ticks?

Molecular research shows that the circadian rhythm involves a feedback loop. Two different proteins are first made from DNA instructions. Once made, they combine. The combined protein, called a **dimer** (for two proteins), then inhibits the genes that made its original constituent proteins. Next, the dimer degrades, and the process begins anew. Research Focus 13-3, Synchronizing Biorhythms at the Molecular Level, describes this feedback loop in mammals. Just as the back-and-forth swing of a pendu-lum makes a grandfather clock tick, the increase and decrease in protein synthesis once each day produce the cellular rhythm.

Section 9-2 traces three main routes from the retina to the visual brain. Figure 9-8 diagrams the retina's cellular structure.

Glutamate is the main excitatory neurotransmitter in the CNS.

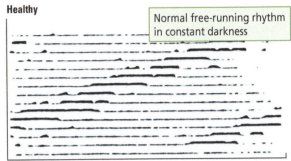

Healthy

Normal free-running rhythm in constant darkness

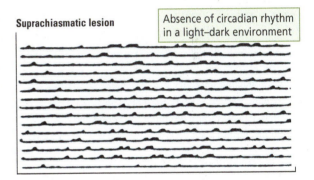

Suprachiasmatic lesion

Absence of circadian rhythm in a light–dark environment

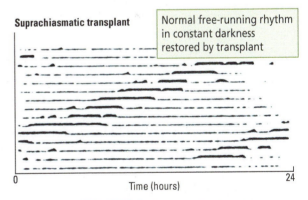

Suprachiasmatic transplant

Normal free-running rhythm in constant darkness restored by transplant

0   Time (hours)   24

FIGURE 13-8 **Circadian Rhythms Restored by Neural Transplantation** Information from Ralph & Lehman, 1991.

dimer Two proteins combined into one.

Figure 3-13 diagrams the process of protein synthesis.

◎ RESEARCH FOCUS 13-3

Synchronizing Biorhythms at the Molecular Level

In 2017, American researchers Jeffrey C. Hall, Michael Rosbash, and Michael W. Young were awarded the Nobel Prize in Physiology or Medicine for their contributions to our understanding of the human biological clock and their description of the molecular change by which the clock keeps time to regulate our circadian rhythm.

The timing mechanism in the suprachiasmatic nucleus (SCN), the brain's master clock, resides in each individual cell that has a circadian rhythm, as well as in most of the body's other cells. The cell's main clock mechanism is a *transcription-translation-inhibition-feedback loop* that paces the clock over a 24-hour period. The complete clockwork in the feedback loop involves as many as 10 genes and their protein products. Its sequence, mapped in the illustration, follows:

STEP 1: TRANSCRIPTION In the cell nucleus, one of three *Period* genes (*Per1,* * *Per2, Per3*) and one of two *Cryptochrome* genes (*Cry1, Cry2*) are transcribed into the appropriate *Per or Cry* mRNA.

STEP 2: TRANSLATION Ribosomes in the endoplasmic reticulum translate these mRNAs into the appropriate PER† and CRY proteins. In the extranuclear fluid, the two proteins come together to form a dimer, or two-protein combination of PERCRY.

STEP 3: INHIBITION The PERCRY dimer enters the cell nucleus, where it binds to and inhibits the Enhancer box (Ebox), a part of the DNA that activates transcription of the *Period* and *Cryptochrome* genes. The result of this inhibition is that *Per* and *Cry* are no longer produced.

*Gene and mRNA names are italicized.
†PROTEIN names are capitalized.

STEP 4: DECAY After it plays its inhibitory role, the PERCRY dimer decays. When this occurs, the *Per* and *Cry* genes resume expression, and the 24-hour cycle begins anew.

This sequence of gene turn-on followed by gene turn-off occurs in an inexorable daily loop.

Mutations in any circadian gene can lead to circadian alterations, including absence of a biorhythm or an altered biorhythm. For example, alleles of *Period 1* and *Period 2* genes determine chronotype—whether an individual will be early to bed and early to rise or late to bed and late to rise. The search for therapies for clock disorders includes looking for small molecules that can act as drugs to reset biorhythms disrupted by jet lag, shift work, and epigenetic and inherited gene irregularities.

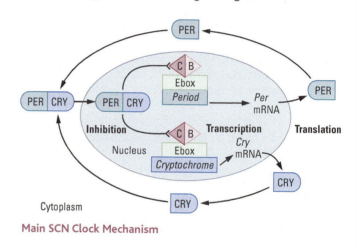

Main SCN Clock Mechanism

Pacemaking Circadian Rhythms

The SCN itself is not directly responsible for producing behavior. After it has been damaged, drinking and eating, sleeping, and wakefulness still occur—though they no longer occur at appropriate times.

An explanation for how the SCN controls biological rhythms is illustrated in **Figure 13-9**. Light entrains the SCN, and the SCN in turn drives a number of slave oscillators. Each slave oscillator is responsible for the rhythmic occurrence of one activity. In other words, drinking, eating, body temperature, and sleeping are each produced by a separate slave oscillator.

FIGURE 13-9 Circadian Timing System Organization

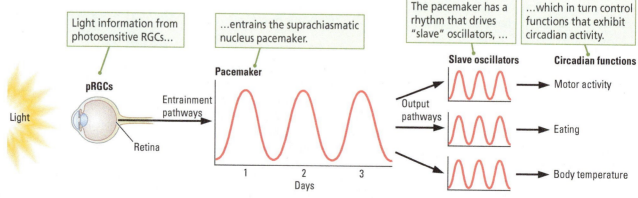

The SCN clock entrains slave oscillators through a remarkable array of pathways. SCN neurons send axonal connections to nuclei close by in the hypothalamus and thalamus. The SCN connects with pituitary endocrine neurons. The SCN also sends indirect messages to autonomic neurons in the spinal cord to inhibit the pineal gland from producing the hormone **melatonin**, which influences daily and seasonal biorhythms. SCN cells themselves release hormones. Thus, through multiple pathways, the SCN exerts its control on the entire body.

An illustration of the SCN's widespread effects is its control of two hormones, melatonin and glucocorticoids. The SCN controls the release of melatonin from the pineal gland so that melatonin circulates during the dark phase of the circadian cycle. It also controls the release of glucocorticoids from the adrenal glands so that they circulate during the light phase of the circadian cycle.

Melatonin promotes sleep and activates the parasympathetic rest-and-digest system, as well as other physiological events in the body. Glucocorticoids mobilize glucose for cellular activity to support arousal responses in the sympathetic system. These two hormones will entrain body organs that have receptors for them, and most organs do. Thus, melatonin promotes rest activities during the dark portion of the circadian cycle, and glucocorticoids promote arousal activities during the light portions of the circadian cycle. Their actions explain in part why it is difficult to sleep during the day and difficult to stay awake at night. The role of melatonin as a slave oscillator in part explains its use as a drug for regulating sleep (Zwart et al., 2018).

melatonin Hormone secreted by the pineal gland during the dark phase of the day–night cycle; influences daily and seasonal biorhythms.

Figure 12-12 diagrams how the pituitary gland works.

Figure 2-32 diagrams the autonomic nervous system. Section 6-5 describes how glucocorticoids affect the body and brain.

Pacemaking Circannual Rhythms

The suprachiasmatic nucleus controls circannual rhythms as well. Russel Reiter (1980) first illustrated this form of pacemaking in hamsters. Hamsters are summertime (long-day) breeders. As the days lengthen in springtime, the gonads of male hamsters grow and release hormones that stimulate sexual behavior. As the days shorten in the winter, the gonads shrink, the amount of the hormones they produce decreases, and the males lose interest in sex.

During the dark phase of the day–night cycle, the pineal gland secretes melatonin; during the light phase, it does not. **Figure 13-10** shows that when a male hamster's melatonin level is low, the gonads enlarge, and when the level is high, the gonads shrink. The SCN thus controls the pineal gland's sway over the gonads.

During the long daylight period of the circadian cycle, the SCN inhibits melatonin secretion by the pineal gland. As the days become shorter, the melatonin release increases. When the daylight period is shorter than 12 hours, melatonin release time becomes sufficient to inhibit the hamster's gonads, and they shrink. Melatonin also influences the testes of short-day breeders, such as sheep and deer, that mate in the fall and

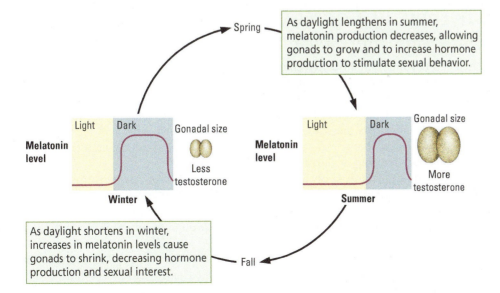

FIGURE 13-10 **Hamster's Circannual Pacemaker** Information from Reiter, 1980.

early winter. Melatonin's effect on reproductive behavior in these species is the reverse of that in the hamster: reproductive activities begin as melatonin release increases. There is no evidence that a melatonin cycle influences the gonads of human males.

In his classic book *Biological Clocks in Medicine and Psychiatry*, Curt Richter (1965) hypothesized that many physical and behavioral disorders might be caused by shocks, either physical or environmental, that upset the timing of biological clocks. For example, the record of psychotic episodes of the English writer Mary Lamb, illustrated in **Figure 13-11**, is one of many rhythmic records that Richter thought represented the action of an abnormally functioning biological clock. Richter noted that because disorders are now treated, often with drugs, rhythmic patterns may be muted and so are harder to detect.

FIGURE 13-11 **Dysfunctional Clock?** Attacks of mental illness displayed by the English writer Mary Lamb through her adult life appear to have had a cyclical component. Such observations would be difficult to obtain today because the drugs used to treat psychiatric disorders can mask disordered biorhythms. Information from Richter, 1965.

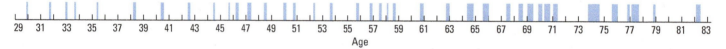

Chronotypes

Across human populations, and within other animal species, individuals show variation in their circadian activities. These distinctive patterns of behavior are referred to as **chronotypes** ("time types"). Some people are early to bed and early to rise and are energetic in the morning. Other people are late to rise and late to bed and are energetic in the evening. These "lark" and "owl" chronotypes are likely produced by differences in SCN neurons and the genes that influence the clock in those neurons. A large number of genes contribute to the function of the mammalian biological clock, and alleles of these genes are associated with chronotypes. In hamsters and mice, mutant gene variations produce chronotypes with circadian periods as varied as 24, 20, or 17 hours (Monecke et al., 2011).

Comparative studies of the free-running rhythms of African Americans and European Americans show that the former have shorter free-running periods. Genetic studies suggest that small changes in about 10 genes influence the chronotypes of these populations (Putilov et al., 2017). Presumably, these genetic differences allowed the clocks of the ancestral African populations living closer to the equator to synchronize with the more equal day and night length. Similar genetic forces allowed the ancestral European populations in northern latitudes to synchronize with the more variable day and night length. As genetic analysis becomes less expensive, the study of the genes underlying chronotypes is providing new insights into individual differences in our biological clocks and into the relationships between chronotypes and disease.

Rhythms of Cognitive and Emotional Behavior

Circadian rhythms can influence emotional experience, learning and retention, decision making, and motivation. Numerous studies have addressed the *time-of-day* question, such as the best time of day to learn and to work. Unfortunately, many of these studies predate the discovery of chronotypes and the understanding that any population of participants may include a significant number of larks and owls. Furthermore, we now understand that chronotype changes with age: many people shift from being adolescent owls to being old larks.

Now the question is, does chronotype influence the time-of-day performance of an individual? Gale and Martyn (1998) tested Benjamin Franklin's maxim "early to bed and early to rise make a man healthy, wealthy, and wise" in a large population of British participants aged over 65; they did not find that one group was any healthier, wealthier, or wiser than the other.

In a review of a large number of cognitive and performance measures, Schmidt and colleagues (2012) did come to some conclusions about performance and time of day.

chronotype Time type; individual variations in circadian activity.

First, synchrony between time of day and chronotype is a dominant effect: morning people do better in the morning, and evening people do better in the evening. Second, highly practiced behaviors are not influenced much by time-of-day effects. Third, some large differences between young and old people related to performance and time of day are likely related to chronotype. Finally, a weakness in studies of time-of-day effects is that they depend on self-reports of chronotype. More rigorous studies will depend on determining chronogenotype—that is, which chronotype allele people have.

A different question related to time of day and learning is *time stamping*: Is memory for learned items better when test–retest is given at the same time of the circadian cycle? Much everyday behavior is synchronized with circadian period. Animals have a variety of needs for food, water, and sleep, and it is adaptive for them to know when these resources become available. If food is available on a schedule, animals display anticipatory behaviors, becoming active as the feeding time arrives, for example. Other anticipatory events include salivation, intestinal activity, and sensations of hunger. Anticipatory activity might also include recalling events related to the timing of feeding and food location. Many cognitive activities can occur in the absence of the SCN, but it is adaptive for them to occur at the right time and place. SCN activity enables this. As animals age, their ability to associate appropriate activity with appropriate time declines, impairing their daily schedule, an effect that might in part account for poor scheduling and sleep in some older humans (Mulder et al., 2015). In athletics, there is a strong home advantage for many sports, and it is likely that the advantage stems from a time-of-day effect in which competition fits into a home daily schedule better than an away schedule.

Studies also find that the circadian period influences emotional behavior. A time-of-day effect may account for some of our emotional responses to daily events, independent of the events themselves. An interesting example is fear. Nighttime fear is common, but is it the dark or the nighttime circadian rhythm that accounts for heightened emotion? By independently varying lighting conditions and test times during the circadian cycle, Li and colleagues (2015) found heightened emotional responses to stimuli at night, independent of ambient lighting. Thus, the cycle, not just darkness, contributes to emotional responding. Apparently, at least two factors explain why horror movies watched at night are scary: the movie's content and the time-of-day effect.

13-2 Review

Before you continue, check your understanding. Answers to Self-Test appear at the back of the book.

1. Biological rhythms are timed by internal biological clocks. The master clock is the
   _____.

2. Light cues entrain the suprachiasmatic nucleus to control daily rhythms via the
   _____ tract, which receives information via _____ cells.

3. Pacemaking produced by the SCN is a product of its _____ cells, which activate slave oscillators via both _____ signals and _____ connections.

4. Why should mealtimes occur at the same time of day each day?

For additional study tools, visit **LaunchPad** at launchpadworks.com

13-3

Sleep Stages and Dreaming

Waking behavior encompasses periods when we are physically active or inactive, and so does sleep. Our sleeping behavior consists of periods of rest, napping, long bouts of sleep, and the many things we do during sleep, including snoring, dreaming, thrashing about, even sleepwalking. In this section, we describe some sleeping and dreaming behaviors and the neural processes underlying them.

Recommended Sleep Duration by Age

Age	Sleep time (hours)
Newborn up to 3 months	14–17
Infant under 1 year	12–15
Toddler up to 3 years	11–14
Preschool	10–13
Elementary-school age	9–11
Adolescent	8–10
Adult	7–9
Adult 65 years and older	7–8

Source: Information from National Sleep Foundation.

Measuring How Long We Sleep

One measure of sleeping and waking behavior is *self-report*: people record in a diary when they wake and when they retire to sleep. These diaries show both optimal average sleep durations and considerable variation in sleep–waking behavior. An optimal sleep time of 7 to 8 hours per night is a popular adage, but many exceptions exist. People sleep more when they are young, after engaging in physical activity, or when pregnant. Some people are long sleepers; some are short sleepers. Numerous genetic mutations have been identified in people displaying very short sleep durations—as short as 1 hour. Some people nap for a brief period in the daytime; others never nap. Variations in sleeping times are normal, and napping normally is best if it is short in duration (less than 20 min), happens earlier in the day to avoid disrupting nighttime sleep, and occurs at scheduled times of day.

Measuring Sleep

Laboratory sleep studies allow researchers to measure sleep accurately and to record physiological changes associated with sleep. Miniaturized sleep-measuring technology and data compression now allow laboratory methods to be extended into the home (Lan et al., 2015). Measuring sleep requires recording at least three electrical body signals: brain activity, muscle activity, and eye movement. **Figure 13-12** illustrates a typical polygraph setup in a sleep laboratory and the commonly used measures that define sleep.

Electrodes pasted onto standard locations on the skull's surface yield an electro-encephalogram (EEG), a record of brain-wave activity. Electrodes placed on neck muscles provide an electromyogram (EMG), a record of muscle activity. Electrodes located near the eyes provide an electrooculogram (EOG), a record of eye movements. Body temperature, circulating hormones, and blood glucose levels provide additional measures of sleep.

(A) Electroencephalogram (EEG)

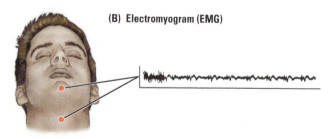

FIGURE 13-12 **Sleep Laboratory Setup** Electronic equipment records readouts from electrodes attached to the sleeper. **(A)** EEG made from a point on the skull relative to a neutral point on the ear. **(B)** EMG made between two muscles, such as those on the chin and throat. **(C)** EOG made between the eye and a neutral point on the ear.

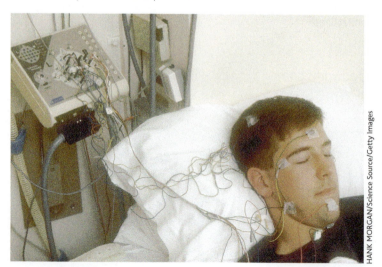

HANK MORGAN/Science Source/Getty Images

(B) Electromyogram (EMG)

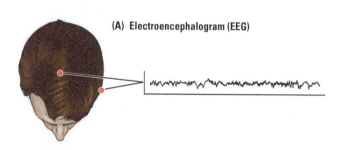

(C) Electrooculogram (EOG)

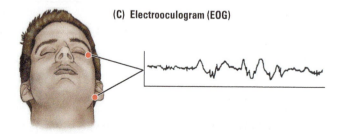

Stages of Waking and Sleeping

Sleep, like waking, is not a unitary state but encompasses a number of stages. The EEG recording shows distinct patterns of brain-wave activity for states categorized as awake, relaxed, drowsy, sleep, deep sleep, and dreaming (see **Figure 13-13**). Sleep consists of periods when a sleeper is relatively still and periods when the mouth, fingers, and toes twitch. This behavior is readily observed in household pets and bed partners. In 1955, Eugene Aserinsky and Nathaniel Kleitman (Lamberg, 2003) observed that this twitching is periodic and is also associated with rapid eye movements (REMs) and an awake pattern in the EEG record. Since their report, the conventional classification has been to refer to this state of sleep as **REM sleep (R-sleep)** and to refer to other sleep states as **non-REM (NREM) sleep (N-sleep)**. Consistent with this designation, the American Association of Sleep Medicine provides a five-point classification of sleep based on EEG patterns that incorporates the R-sleep/N-sleep distinction:

- W—Waking
- N1—NREM stage 1
- N2—NREM stage 2
- N3—NREM stage 3
- R—REM

REM sleep (R-sleep) Faster brain-wave pattern displayed by the neocortical EEG record during sleep.

non-REM sleep (N-sleep) Slow-wave sleep associated with rhythms having slower waves with larger amplitude.

Figure 7-10 diagrams EEG patterns that reflect a range of sleep/waking states in humans.

W-Waking

50 µV

1 sec

N1-Sleep

Theta waves

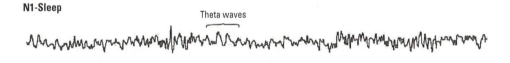

N2-Sleep

Sleep Spindle

K Complex —

N3-Sleep

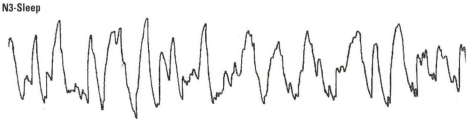

R-Sleep

Sawtooth Waves   Sawtooth Waves

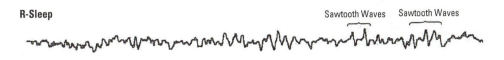

FIGURE 13-13 **EEG Sleep Patterns**
The EEG patterns of the neocortex are the basis for defining stages of waking and sleep.
Information modified from Kelley, 1991.

Excited–beta rhythm

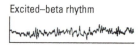

Relaxed, eyes closed–alpha rhythm

Deep sleep–delta rhythm

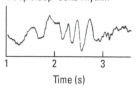

1   2   3
Time (s)

beta rhythm Fast brain-wave activity pattern associated with a waking EEG.

alpha rhythm Large, extremely regular brain waves with a frequency ranging from 7 to 11 Hz.

delta rhythm Slow brain-wave activity pattern associated with deep sleep.

atonia Reduced muscle tone; condition of maximally low muscle inactivity produced by motor neuron inhibition.

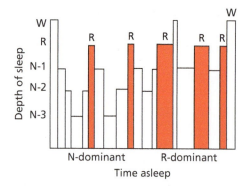

FIGURE 13-14 **A Hypnogram** Over a typical night's sleep, a person undergoes several sleep state changes in roughly 90-minute periods. N-sleep dominates the early sleep periods, and R-sleep dominates later sleep. The duration of each sleep stage is reflected in the thickness of each bar, which is color-coded to the corresponding stage. The depth of each stage is graphed as the relative height of the bar. Information from Kelley, 1991.

W (Waking) State

The W state represents behavior varying from alert wakefulness to drowsiness. When a person is awake, the EEG pattern consists of small-amplitude (height) waves with a fast frequency (repetition period). This pattern, the **beta rhythm**, is defined by a frequency of 15 to 30 Hz (times per second). The pattern is also called *fast-wave activity-activated EEG*, or *waking EEG*. Associated with waking, the EMG is active, and the EOG indicates that the eyes move.

When awake people relax and close their eyes, they may produce the **alpha rhythm** (see the associated marginal traces). These are large, extremely regular brain waves with a frequency ranging from 7 to 11 Hz. Humans generate alpha rhythms in the region of the visual cortex at the back of the brain, and the rhythms abruptly stop if a relaxed person is disturbed or opens his or her eyes. Not everyone displays alpha rhythms, and some people display them much more strongly than others.

N1 Sleep

The behavioral state of a person in N1 is sleep onset. The EEG indicates that beta-wave activity gives way to low-amplitude, mixed-frequency activity, including 4- to 7-Hz theta-wave activity. Concurrently, the EMG remains somewhat active, as the muscles have tone, and the EOG typically indicates that the eyes can be rolling.

N2 Sleep

A person in N2 is asleep. In this behavioral state, a person continues to produce theta waves but also produces periodic *sleep spindles* (brief runs of 11- to 16-Hz rhythmic waves) and *K-complexes*, well-defined sharp waves followed by slow waves, all lasting for about a half-second.

N3 Sleep

N3 is deep sleep. A person in this behavioral state is difficult to arouse, groggy when aroused, and quick to go back to sleep when undisturbed. The EEG is characterized by larger-amplitude, slow EEG waves called **delta rhythms**. Still, the EMG indicates muscle activity, signifying that the muscles retain tone, although the EOG indicates that the eyes do not move.

R-Sleep (REM)

R-sleep consists of periods when a sleeper is relatively still and periods when the eyes display REMs, as indicated by the EOG, and the mouth, fingers, and toes twitch. Other than these movements, the EMG indicates that muscles are inactive, a condition termed **atonia** (Greek via Latin, meaning "without tone"). The EEG displays a beta rhythm similar to that displayed in the W stage and N1 stage.

Other Sleep-Related and Waking-Related Activities

Although electrophysiological measures define the sleep stages, many other bodily and physiological events are associated with waking and sleep stages. Measures of metabolic activity, such as body temperature, generally decline during sleep. Breathing and heart rate provide further insights into waking and sleeping. The sleeper's behaviors—tossing and turning, moaning and laughing—also occur during specific sleep stages. Taken together, these measures yield insights into the many causes and symptoms of normal sleep and disturbed sleep.

A Typical Night's Sleep

Figure 13-14 illustrates a hypnogram (sleep graph, also called a *somnogram*) of one participant cycling through the various sleep stages in the course of a night's sleep. Notice that the depth of sleep, as indicated by a progression from N1 through N3, changes several times through the night and that each of these progressions is followed by an R-sleep stage. This N–R sequence lasts approximately 90 minutes and occurs five times in the course of the participant's sleep period. The labels indicating R-sleep in Figure 13-14 tell us that the sleep stage durations roughly divide sleep into two parts: the first is dominated by N-sleep and the second dominated by R-sleep.

A person's duration of R-sleep varies at different times of life and changes dramatically over the life span. Periods of R-sleep are high in infancy; they increase during growth spurts, in conjunction with physical exertion, and during pregnancy. **Figure 13-15** shows that most people sleep less as they grow older. In the first 2 years of life, R-sleep makes up nearly half of sleep time, but it declines proportionately until in middle age it constitutes little more than 10 percent of sleep time.

Contrasting N-Sleep and R-Sleep

Although sleep seems like an inactive period, a remarkable range of activity takes place during sleep. Events associated with N-sleep and R-sleep, for example, are dramatically different, not only in physiological measures but also in such behavioral events as cognition, memory storage, and sleep disorders.

During N-sleep, body temperature declines, heart rate and blood flow decrease, body weight decreases from water loss in perspiration, and growth hormone levels increase. N-sleep is also the time when we toss and turn in bed, pull on the covers, and engage in other movements. (For an extreme example, see Clinical Focus 13-4, Restless Legs Syndrome.) If we talk in our sleep or grind our teeth, we do so during N-sleep. If we flail, banging an arm or kicking a foot, we usually do so in N-sleep. Some people even get up and walk around, and this sleepwalking takes place during N-sleep. All this activity during our so-called resting state is remarkable! We maintain muscle tone during N-sleep and can sleep in a variety of postures, including standing up, sitting (as might occur during a nap in a lecture), or in any of several reclining positions.

R-sleep is no less eventful than N-sleep. During R-sleep, mechanisms that regulate body temperature stop working, and body temperature moves toward room temperature. You may wake up from R-sleep feeling cold or hot (or because you are cold or hot), depending on the temperature of the room, because your body has drifted toward room temperature during an R-sleep period. During portions of R-sleep, eyes move; toes, fingers, and mouths twitch; and males have penile erections. Still, we are paralyzed, as indicated by atonia. This absence of muscle tone is the result of inhibitory signals sent from the brainstem to motor neurons in the spinal cord that command movement. In the sleep lab, atonia is recorded on an electromyogram as the absence of muscle activity (see Figure 13-12B).

Posture is not completely lost during N-sleep. At the onset of R-sleep, an animal usually subsides into a sprawled position as muscle paralysis sets in. **Figure 13-16** illustrates the sleep postures of a horse. Horses can sleep while standing up by locking their knee joints, and they can sleep while lying down with their head held slightly up. At these times, they are in N-sleep; when completely sprawled out, they are in R-sleep.

One explanation for the twitching of eyes, face, and distal parts of the limbs in R-sleep is that such movements help to maintain blood flow in those parts of the body. Another explanation is that the brain is developing coordinated movements and tuning the neural circuits that support those movements—an activity especially important to infants, who have not yet developed full motor control (Blumberg, 2015).

Dreaming

Vivid dreaming occurs during R-sleep. This remarkable relationship was discovered by William Dement and Nathaniel Kleitman in 1957 (Dement, 1972). When participants were awakened from R-sleep, they reported that they had been having vivid dreams. In contrast, participants who were aroused from N-sleep were less likely to report that they had been dreaming, and the dreams they did report were less vivid. The technique of electrical recording from a sleeping participant in a sleep laboratory made it possible to identify sleep states and any associated dreaming.

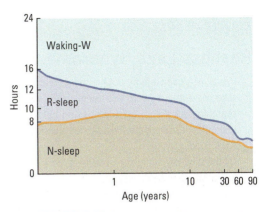

FIGURE 13-15 **Sleeping and Waking over the Life Span** The amount of time humans spend sleeping decreases with age. The proportion of R-sleep is especially high in the first few years of life. Information from Roffward et al., 1966.

FIGURE 13-16 **Nap Time** Horses usually seek open, sunny areas for a brief sleep. I. Q. W.'s horse Lady Jones illustrates three sleep postures. *Top:* N-sleep, standing with legs locked and head down. *Center:* N-sleep, lying down with head up. *Bottom:* R-sleep, in which all postural and muscle tone is lost.

Courtesy of Ian Whishaw

● CLINICAL FOCUS 13-4

Restless Legs Syndrome

I've always been a fairly untalented sleeper. Even as a child, it would take me some time to fall asleep, and I would often roll around searching for a comfortable position before going under. But my real difficulties with sleeping did not manifest themselves until early adulthood. . . .

Initially, my symptoms consisted of a mild tingling in my legs. It caused me to be fidgety and made it hard to fall asleep. Eventually, I went through a number of days without much sleep and reached a point where I simply could not function. I went to a doctor who prescribed a small course of sleeping medication (a benzodiazepine). I was able to get good sleep and my sleep cycle seemed to get back on track. Over the next decade I had periodic bouts of tingling in my legs which caused me to be fidgety and interfered with sleep. As time passed, the bouts occurred with increasing frequency and the symptoms became more noticeable and uncomfortable. I would simply suffer through these bouts, sleeping poorly and paying the consequences. . . .

Being a student, I did not have a regular doctor. Unfortunately, most physicians I met did not know about restless legs syndrome, or RLS, and thought I was "drug seeking" or merely stressed out. I received a variety of patronizing responses and found these experiences insulting and demeaning. . . .

When I took my current position, I started seeing a doctor on a regular basis, and experimented with better medications. By this time, my sleep was being seriously affected by RLS. The sensations in my legs were something like a combination of an ache in my muscles (much like one gets after exercising) and an electrical, tingling sensation. They would be briefly relieved with movement, such as stretching, rubbing, contracting my muscles, or changing position, but would return within seconds. In fact, my wife says my cycle is about 13 to 15 seconds between movements. I do this either when awake or during sleep. Trying not to move greatly increases the discomfort—much like trying to not scratch a very bad itch. The symptoms get worse in the evening and at night. Most nights, I have trouble falling asleep. Other nights, I wake up after an hour or so and then have trouble going back under. . . .

I am very up front about the fact that I have RLS. In fact, whenever I teach the topic of sleep and sleep disorders in my brain and behavior classes, I always make some time to talk about my experiences with RLS. Occasionally, students approach me with their own difficulties, and I try to provide them with information and resources. (Stuart Hall, Ph.D., University of Montana)

Envision/Getty Images

Restless legs syndrome (RLS) is a disorder in which people experience unpleasant sensations in the legs, described as creeping, crawling, tingling, pulling, or painful, often accompanied by periodic leg movements. One or both legs may be affected, and sometimes the arms may also be affected. RLS affects around 5 percent of the population, more commonly women than men. In mild cases, massage, exercise, stretching, and hot baths may be helpful. For more severe cases, patients can restrict their intake of caffeine and take benzodiazepines to help them get to sleep.

RLS is difficult to treat (Wijemanne & Jankovic, 2015). L-Dopa, a drug used to treat Parkinson disease, is frequently used as a treatment. RLS has been associated with poor iron uptake, especially in the substantia nigra, and some people have been helped by iron supplements. One focus of research into RLS is to improve iron absorption by the brain.

How often do we dream? People's reports on their dreaming behavior once suggested that some people dream, whereas others never dream. Waking participants during R-sleep periods shows that everyone dreams, that we dream several times each night, and that dreams last longer as a sleep session progresses. Those who claimed not to dream obviously forget what their dreams were—perhaps because they do not wake up during a dream or immediately afterward, which allows subsequent N-sleep activity to erase the memory of the dream. It could also be that the neural systems that store our daily memories are not fully active during R-sleep. Or perhaps, just as we don't remember much of each day's waking events because they are not important, we conclude that some dreams are not worth remembering. As far as anyone has been able to tell, there is no deleterious consequence for not remembering dreams.

Common wisdom once suggested that dreams last but an instant. By waking people up at different intervals after the onset of R-sleep and matching the reported dream content to the previous duration of R-sleep, research has shown that dreams take place in real time. An action that a person performs in a dream lasts about as long as it would take to perform while awake. Why does it sometimes appear that a dream takes place in a moment? It is likely that time shrinking is a product of remembering a dream, just as time shrinking is a feature of our recall of other memories.

What We Dream about

Past explanations of dreaming have ranged from messages from the gods to indigestion. The first modern treatment of dreams was made by the founder of psychoanalysis, Sigmund Freud, in *The Interpretation of Dreams*, published in 1900. In Freud's report, and others like it, dreams are selected for discussion because they have some interesting features. There is, however, no way to know that this way of selecting dreams is representative of the range of dreams that a person may have.

We briefly consider Freud's theory because it remains popular in psychoanalysis and in the arts and is representative of other psychoanalytical theories of dreams. Freud suggested that the function of dreams is the symbolic fulfillment of unconscious wishes—specifically sexual wishes. He further proposed that dreams have two levels of meaning. The *manifest content* of a dream is a series of often bizarre, loosely connected images and actions. The *latent content* of the dream contains its true meaning. Certain images, called *phallic symbols*, reflect sexual events. As interpreted by a psychoanalyst, the symbolic events of a dream provide a coherent account of the dreamer's unconscious wishes.

Freud provided a method for interpreting manifest symbols and reconstructing the latent content of dreams. For example, he pointed out that a dream usually begins with an incident from the previous day, incorporates childhood experiences, and includes ongoing unfulfilled wishes. He also identified several types of dreams, such as those that deal with childhood events, anxiety, and wish fulfillment. The latent content of the dream was important to Freud and other psychoanalysts in clinical practice because interpretation of dreams was proposed to offer insight into a patient's problems.

Other psychoanalysts, unhappy with Freud's emphasis on sex, developed their own dream interpretation systems. The psychoanalyst Carl Jung, a contemporary of Freud, proposed that dream symbolism signifies distant human memories long since lost to conscious awareness. Jung proposed that dreams allow the dreamer to relive the history of the human race—our "collective unconscious." As more theories of dream interpretation develope, their central weakness becomes apparent: there is no way to know which interpretation is correct.

Experimental analysis indicates that most dreams are related to events that have happened quite recently and concern ongoing problems. Colors of objects, symbols, and emotional content most often relate to events taking place in a person's recent waking period. Calvin Hall and his colleagues (1982) documented more than 10,000 dreams of healthy people and found that more than 64 percent are associated with sadness, anxiety, or anger. Only about 18 percent are happy. Hostile acts against the dreamer outnumber friendly acts by more than 2 to 1. Freud's theory notwithstanding, only about 1 percent of dreams include content that seems related to sexual feelings or acts. Subsequent studies of the content of dreams have shown that about 80 percent are dreams about the recent past and only about 20 percent reference events that are more than a year old. Dreams are also age-appropriate; for example, adolescent males tend to have dreams that include more aggression than older males.

The two contemporary explanations of dream content are polar opposites: one sees no meaning in dreams, while the other sees the content of dreams as reflecting biologically adaptive coping mechanisms. The first approach is bottom-up: the person has

Figure 16-1 presents a contemporary take on Freud's model of the mind.

a dream, and then either the dreamer or a dream interpreter analyzes it. The second approach is top-down: the dreamer creates the dream (Foulkes & Domhoff, 2014).

Dreams as Meaningless Brain Activity

In his bottom-up approach, J. Allan Hobson's (2004) *activation–synthesis theory* states that during a dream, the cortex is bombarded by signals from the brainstem, and these signals produce the pattern of waking EEG. In response to this excitation, some parts of the cortex generate images, actions, and emotions from personal memory stores. In the absence of external verification, these dream events are fragmented and bizarre and reveal nothing more than that the cortex is activated.

Hobson proposes, on the basis of PET imaging, that part of the frontal cortex is less active in dreaming than in waking. The frontal cortex controls working memory for recent events and attention. The dreamer thus cannot remember and link dream events as they take place because monitoring by the frontal cortex is required for these functions. On waking, the dreamer may attempt to come up with a story line for these fragmented meaningless images. In Hobson's theory, dreams are personal in that memories and experiences are activated, but they have no intrinsic meaning.

Chapter 14 describes the extent of frontal cortex involvement in memory. Attention is discussed in detail in Section 15-2.

Dreams as a Coping Strategy

Antti Revonsuo uses content analysis to argue that dreams are biologically adaptive in that they lead to enhanced coping strategies for threatening life events (Valli & Revonsuo, 2009). The evolutionary aspect of this top-down approach, or *coping theory*, is that enhanced performance is especially important for people whose environment typically includes dangerous events that constitute extreme threats to reproductive success. Dreams provide the dreamer with strategies for dealing with problems, even without the dreamer having to remember the dream. Revonsuo notes people seldom dream about reading, writing, and calculating, even if these behaviors occupy much of their day.

Dream threats are the same events that are threatening in waking life (**Figure 13-17**). For example, animals and strange men who could be characterized as enemies figure prominently in dreams.

In contrast with the threat interpretation of dreams, Malcolm-Smith and her colleagues (2012) report that approach behavior occurs more frequently in dreams than does avoidance behavior. They therefore suggest that reward-seeking behavior is as likely to represent a dream's latent content as avoidance behavior.

An extension of the top-down approach to dream interpretation is that people are problem solvers when awake, and problem solving continues during sleep (Edwards et al., 2013). Have you ever been advised to "sleep on it," and did that prove to be good advice?

Part of the challenge in studying dreams is that they occur throughout our sleep–waking behavior. Dreams occur during N-sleep but not as vividly as in R-sleep. We can have dreamlike experiences just as we drop off to sleep, as our ongoing thoughts seem to disintegrate into hallucinations. Sometimes we are aware of our dreams as we

FIGURE 13-17 **Dream Content** Terrifying visions that may persist even after awakening from a frightening dream as represented in *The Night*, by Swiss painter Ferdinand Hodler. *The Night*, by Ferdinand Hodler (1853–1918). Oil on canvas 116 × 299 cm. Kunstmuseum, Bern, Switzerland.

Erich Lessing / Art Resource, NY

dream, a phenomenon called *lucid dreaming*. People who have vivid dreamlike experiences when awake are said to be hallucinating. And, of course, we daydream when awake. Eric Klinger (1990) argues that daydreams are ordinary and often fun, with little of the turmoil of REM dreams, and so seem the true opposite of night dreams.

Clearly, much about dreams is not understood. Very young children spend a lot of time in R-sleep yet do not report complex dreams filled with emotion and conflict. Children may experience brief frightening dreams called *night terrors* during N-sleep. Night terrors can be so vivid that the child continues to experience the dream and the fear after awaking. A 4-year-old child suddenly woke up screaming that she was covered in ants. It took hours for her father to convince her that her experience was not real and that she could go back to bed. Only reassurance from a sleep expert later convinced the father that nothing was amiss with his daughter and that night terrors are common among young children (Carter et al., 2014).

13-3 Review

Before you continue, check your understanding. Answers to Self-Test appear at the back of the book.

1. The five-point classification of sleep based on EEG patterns divides sleep into
   _____, _____, _____, _____, and _____.

2. A polygraph can be used to record three common measures of sleep. R-sleep is characterized by eye movement, as recorded by the _____; atonia, recorded by the _____; and waking activity, recorded by the _____.

3. Sleepers experience about _____ R-sleep periods each night, with the duration of each period getting _____ as sleep progresses.

4. What major factor makes interpreting dreams difficult?

For additional study tools, visit **LaunchPad** at launchpadworks.com

13-4

What Does Sleep Accomplish?

Sleep is not a passive process that results from a decrease in sensory stimulation. Findings from sensory deprivation research reveal that when participants are isolated in quiet bedrooms, they spend less time asleep, not more. Sleep does not set in for lack of anything better to do. Here, we consider three contemporary explanations for sleep: as adaptive, as restorative, and as supportive of memory.

Sleep as a Biological Adaptation

Many lines of evidence argue that sleep is a biologically adaptive behavior influenced by the way a species has evolved to interact with its environment. Sleep serves as an energy-conserving strategy for coping in times when food is scarce. If the food that a species eats has a high nutrient value, that species can spend less time foraging and more time sleeping. Whether a species is predator or prey also influences its sleep behavior. A predator can sleep at its ease; the prey's sleep time is reduced because it must remain alert and ready to fight or flee at unpredictable times (**Figure 13-18**). Strictly nocturnal or diurnal animals are likely to sleep when they cannot travel easily. Dement (1972) proposed this colloquially: "We sleep to keep from bumping into things in the dark."

Figure 13-19 charts the average sleep times of some common mammals. Herbivores, including donkeys, horses, and cows, spend a long time collecting enough food to sustain themselves. Long awake time and relatively short sleep time for them is adaptive. Because they are also prey, long awake time and less sleep time is also adaptive, as they watch for predators. Carnivores, including domestic cats and dogs, eat nutrient-rich foods and usually consume most of a day's or even a week's food at

FIGURE 13-18 **Do Not Disturb** Biological theories of sleep suggest that it is an energy-conserving strategy that serves other functions as well, such as staying safe through the night.

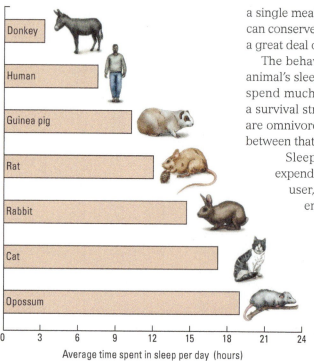

FIGURE 13-19 **Average Sleep Time** Sleep time is affected both by the amount of time different species require to obtain food and by the risk of predation.

---

basic rest–activity cycle (BRAC) Recurring cycle of temporal packets (about 90-minute periods in humans), during which an animal's level of arousal waxes and wanes.

a single meal. Because they do not need to eat constantly and because by resting they can conserve energy, and because they are not at great risk of predation, a lifestyle with a great deal of sleep is adaptive.

The behavior of some animals does appear odd, however, so understanding any animal's sleep behavior requires understanding its natural history. Opossums, which spend much of their time asleep, may have specialized in energy conservation as a survival strategy. We humans are average among species in our sleep time. As we are omnivores and not subject to overwhelming predation, our sleep is intermediate between that of herbivores and carnivores.

Sleep can contribute to energy conservation because energy is not being expended in moving the body or supporting posture. The brain is a major energy user, and switching off the brain during sleep, especially N-sleep, conserves energy. The decline in body temperature during sleep decreases the body's metabolism, as exemplified by animals that display extreme decreases in body temperature characteristic of hibernation.

The Basic Rest–Activity Cycle

A good explanation of sleep must account not only for sleep but also for N-sleep and R-sleep. Before the discovery of R-sleep, Kleitman suggested that animals have a **basic rest–activity cycle (BRAC)** that for humans lasts about 90 minutes (see Dement, 1972). Kleitman based his hypothesis on the observation that human infants have frequent feeding periods between which they sleep.

As illustrated in **Figure 13-20**, the behavior of adult humans does suggest that activity and rest are organized into 90-minute temporal packets. School classes, work periods, exercise sessions, mealtimes, coffee breaks, and snack times appear to be divided into intervals of 90 minutes or so. The later discovery that R-sleep occurs at intervals of about 90 minutes suggests that it too can be considered a continuation into sleep of the 90-minute BRAC rhythm. This hypothesis assumes that periods of eating are periods of high brain activity, just as are periods of R-sleep.

Kleitman proposed that the BRAC rhythm is so fundamental that it cannot be turned off. Accordingly, for a night's sleep to be uninterrupted by periodic waking (and perhaps snacking), the body is paralyzed, and only the brain is active. An analogy: rather than turning off a fuel-powered car's engine when you're stopped at a red light, you apply the brakes to keep the idling car from moving. For R-sleep, the atonia that paralyzes movement is the brakes.

Sleep as a Restorative Process

In Macbeth's description of sleep, Shakespeare illustrates in words the idea that sleep has restorative properties:

Sleep that knits up the ravell'd sleave of care,
The death of each day's life, sore labour's bath,
Balm of hurt minds, great nature's second course,
Chief nourisher in life's feast.

—Act II, scene 2

FIGURE 13-20 **Behavioral Rhythms** Our behavior is dominated by a basic rest–activity cycle (red), through which our activity levels change in the course of the day, and by an N-sleep–R-sleep cycle (purple) during the night.

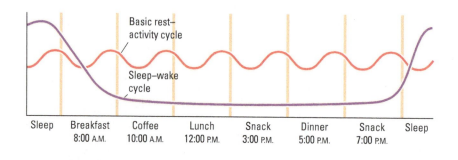

Sleep Deprivation Studies

We can understand the idea of sleep as restorative from our personal perspective. Toward the end of the day we grow tired, and when we awaken from sleep, we are refreshed. If we do not get enough sleep, we become irritable. One hypothesis of sleep as restorative proposes that the chemical events that provide energy to cells are reduced during waking and replenished during sleep.

Even so, fatigue and alertness may simply be aspects of the circadian rhythm and have nothing at all to do with wear and tear on the body or depletion of its essential resources. To evaluate whether sleep is essential for bodily processes, investigators have conducted sleep deprivation studies. These studies have not clearly identified any essential function for sleep but rather point to multiple physiological and cognitive functions altered by various degrees of sleep deprivation (Elliott et al., 2014).

Sleep researcher William Dement participated as an observer in one case study on sleep deprivation that illustrates this point. In 1965, as part of a science fair project, a high school student named Randy Gardner planned to break the world record of 260 hours (almost 11 days) of consecutive wakefulness with the help of two classmates who would keep him awake. Gardner did break the record, and then he slept for 14 hours and reported no ill effects. It is worth noting, however, that there are individual differences in the negative consequences of sleep deprivation (Van Dongen et al., 2004). Given concerns about the deleterious effects that sleep deprivation has on health, Guinness World Records no longer records wakefulness records.

Dement reported that Gardner hallucinated and had cognitive and memory lapses during his period of sleep deprivation. These negative effects did not last. Reviews of sleep deprivation research are consistent in concluding that limited periods of sleep deprivation produce no marked physiological alterations.

Reoccurring brief sleep deprivation and irregular sleep do have adverse physiological consequences, however, in that they are associated with poorer cognitive performance. Performance on tasks that require attention declines as a function of hours of sleep deprivation. Sleep deprivation figures in accidents at work and on the road. Sleep deprivation deficit does not manifest itself in an inability to do a task because sleep-deprived participants can perform even very complex tasks; rather, the deficit is in maintaining sustained attention. Irregular sleep can also contribute to metabolic syndrome, described in Clinical Focus 13-1.

A confounding factor in evaluating sleep-deprived participants is that they take **microsleeps**, brief sleep periods lasting up to a few seconds. During microsleep, participants may remain sitting or standing, but their eyelids droop briefly, and they become less responsive to external stimuli. If you have driven a car while tired, you may have had a microsleep and awakened just in time to prevent yourself from driving off the road—or worse.

R-Sleep Deprivation

Some studies have focused on the selective benefits of R-sleep. To deprive a participant of R-sleep, researchers allow participants to sleep but awaken them as R-sleep begins. R-sleep deprivation has two effects. Participants show an increased tendency to enter R-sleep in subsequent sleep sessions, so awakenings must become more and more frequent. After R-sleep deprivation, participants experience R-sleep rebound, showing more than the usual amount of R-sleep in the first available sleep session.

Because most sleep studies are of relatively brief duration, capturing potential long-term physiological changes that may take place during or after sleep deprivation remains elusive. The consequences of sleep deprivation may become apparent only some time after an experimental manipulation has taken place. Furthermore, gross assessment of behavior may be less adequate for documenting the effects of sleep deprivation than more focal physiological and behavioral assessments. For example, some evidence suggests that R-sleep deprivation weakens the immune system, decreasing resistance to infections and other disease (Lungato et al., 2015). Rodent studies suggest that R-sleep deprivation reduces neurogenesis, especially in the

microsleep Brief sleep period lasting a second or so.

hippocampus, thus impairing memory processes and weakening resistance to stress (Kreutzmann et al., 2015).

Two kinds of observations, however, argue against effects of prolonged or even complete R-sleep deprivation in some circumstances. Virtually all antidepressant drugs, including MAO inhibitors, tricyclic antidepressants, and SSRIs, suppress R-sleep either partly or completely. The clinical effectiveness of these drugs may in fact derive from their R-sleep suppressant effects (Wilson & Argyropoulos, 2005). Nevertheless, about 6 percent of people on antidepressants display *R-sleep behavioral disorder*, characterized by agitated movements, as if the sleeper were acting out dreams (see Section 13-6). This symptom suggests that some aspects of R-sleep are resistant to the R-sleep suppressing effects of the drug, at least for some people (Postuma et al., 2013).

In several reported cases, lower-brainstem damage seems to have resulted in a complete loss of R-sleep. For example, patients with brainstem lesions reportedly remained ambulatory and verbally communicative, and they appeared to live quite satisfactorily without R-sleep (Osorio & Daroff, 1980).

Sleep for Memory Storage

The suggestion that sleep plays a role in memory dates back over a century, and in the interval, a lot has changed with respect to our understanding of memory and sleep. Investigators now know of two general categories of memory. *Episodic memory* includes conscious information, such as our autobiographical memories and knowledge of facts. *Implicit memory* includes unconscious processes, such as motor skills. Within these categories, specific types of memory include spatial, emotional, verbal, and even immune system memory. As described earlier in this chapter, we also know that during the various stages of sleep, many EEG and neuronal events, biochemical events, and genetic events take place. For example, within each of the four stages of sleep, a number of EEG rhythms indicate that underlying neuronal activity changes during different sleep/waking states. In addition, although it is conventional to define sleep on the basis of cortical EEG activity, the rest of the brain is also affected by sleeping. Thus, the central challenge for sleep-related memory research lies in associating the complexity of memory with the complexity of brain metabolic and genetic events (Rasch & Born, 2013).

Investigators also know that storing memory takes time. The simplest example is the effects of massed versus spaced training: learning is much better when it is spaced over time. Optimal spacing of learning may be an inter-training interval in which some sleep occurs, either a nap or a night's sleep, between training sessions. Substantial experimental evidence indicates that both naps and a night's sleep are followed by improved memory.

Memory is proposed to have at least three phases: labile, storage, and recall. During the initial *labile phase*, as a memory is encoded, it is fragile and must compete with existing memories and the addition of new memories. Thus, associated with the activities of waking, memory is at risk for being abolished. The *storage phase* forges a relatively permanent representation of the memory; it depends on biochemical and genetic activities that underlie structural changes in the nervous system. These structural changes may be better formed in the relative quietness—that is, in sleep. The *recall phase* puts the memory to work at some future time and also integrates it into existing memory stores. Replay during sleep may accomplish this objective as well.

Research on the role of sleep in memory focuses on the latter two processes, storage and recall, and is conducted within the framework of three theories: multiple process, sequential process, and storage process. *Multiple process theories* propose that different kinds of memory are stored during different sleep states. For example, explicit memory for facts and autobiographical events is stored during N-sleep, whereas motor memory is stored during R-sleep. *Sequential process theories* propose that different features of memory are improved in different ways during different sleep states; for example, a memory is first refined in N-sleep and then stored in R-sleep. *Storage process theories*

Section 6-2 reviews the full spectrum of psychoactive drugs, including those used to treat depression.

Section 14-1 expands on the workings of explicit and implicit memory systems.

propose that brain regions that handle different kinds of memory during waking continue to do so during sleep.

Each theory of memory and sleep has generated a great deal of research, so it might be useful to consider a theory concerning the way that sleep can assist memory formation.

The Synaptic Homeostasis Theory of Sleep and Memory

The *synaptic homeostasis memory theory of sleep* is both a theory of why we sleep and a theory of how we store memory. The theory is based on the idea that sleep allows synapses that have been active during waking to return to a relatively quiet state during sleep (Tononi & Cirelli, 2016). Synaptic activity is the major consumer of the brain's energy, and synaptic activity is high during waking activities (Lucas et al., 2018). Not only do daytime events call upon a lot of synaptic activity, but all this activity changes synapses and begins to use up their plasticity—their ability to undergo further change. During sleep, the slow electrical waves, especially the 4- to 7-Hz theta waves of N1-sleep and N2-sleep, allow synaptic activity to shift to a resting or homeostatic energy-conserving state. In this state, synapses can return to the state in which they are more plastic and so are available to be engaged during the next waking period.

Principle 2: Neuroplasticity is the hallmark of nervous system functioning.

As an analogy, consider your own working space: during the day, you take out books, move paper around, and perhaps even accumulate some dishes or wrappings from snacks. If left in this condition each day, your working space would quickly become unusable. But if you clean up after each working day, it is ready to be used the next day. According to the theory, this is what the brain is doing during sleep: cleaning up.

The memory storage component of the theory is that some synapses, especially those that have recently been involved in a new learning experience, are more meta-bolically active than other synapses and take longer to return to a resting state. Because these synapses are more active than surrounding synapses in N-sleep, they are in an optimal condition to undergo structural changes without interference. It is these structural changes that represent new memory.

The homeostatic theory is supported by experiments showing that access to N-sleep soon after learning improves memory and that interference with the slow-wave activity associated with N-sleep disrupts memory formation. Presumably, the neural circuits that support different kinds of learning undergo similar synaptic homeostatic changes that underlie the more permanent memories.

N-Sleep and Explicit Memory

Using an experimental method, Gerrard and colleagues (2008) find that, when a rat is in a certain location in an environment, many hippocampal cells fire. These **place cells** are relatively inactive until the rat passes through that place again. Recordings from as many as 100 cells at the same time in three conditions—during N-sleep prior to food search, during a food search task, and during N-sleep after a food search—show that during the food search, the activity of some place cells becomes correlated. During the rats' subsequent periods of N-sleep, the correlations recur (**Figure 13-21**).

Figure 7-9 shows the classes of place cells and their directional selectivity.

This result suggests that the memory of the previous food-searching experience is being replayed and thus stored during N-sleep. In pursuing the idea that memory for places is stored during sleep, one research group identified neuronal firing of hippocampal cells in awake animals in relationship to a specific location in a maze. Then during sleep, they provided rewarding brain stimulation whenever that neuronal firing pattern occurred. In a subsequent test in the maze, the reinforced animals showed a preference for the target location. The experiments had produced an episodic memory for that place as the animals slept (de Lavilléon et al., 2015).

R-Sleep and Implicit Memory

To determine whether humans' dreams are related to memory, Pierre Maquet and his coworkers in Belgium (2000) trained participants on a serial reaction task.

place cell Hippocampal neuron maximally responsive to specific locations in the world.

FIGURE 13-21 **Neural Replay?** Hippocampal cell activity suggests that rats dream about their experiences. Dots on the periphery of the circles represent the activity of 42 hippocampal cells recorded at the same time during (left) N-sleep before a food-searching task, (center) the food-searching task, and (right) N-sleep after the task. No strong correlations among cells emerged during the N-sleep that preceded the food search, but correlations were strong among cells during the food search and during the subsequent slow-wave sleep. Information from Wilson & McNaughton, 1994.

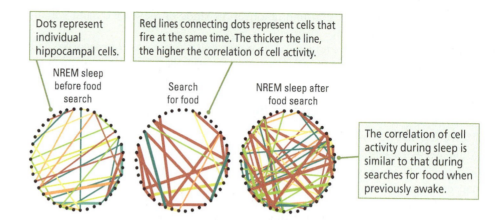

Dots represent individual hippocampal cells.

Red lines connecting dots represent cells that fire at the same time. The thicker the line, the higher the correlation of cell activity.

NREM sleep before food search

Search for food

NREM sleep after food search

The correlation of cell activity during sleep is similar to that during searches for food when previously awake.

The investigators observed regional blood flow in the brain with PET scans during training and during R-sleep on the subsequent night. The participants faced a computer screen displaying six positional markers and were instructed to push one of six keys when a corresponding positional marker was illuminated. They did not know that the illumination sequence was predetermined. This exemplifies an implicit memory task in which a motor skill is mastered.

As training progressed, the investigators could tell that participants were learning because their reaction times improved during trials in which a positional marker was correlated with a preceding marker. On PET scan measures of brain activation, a similar pattern of neocortical activation appeared during task acquisition and during R-sleep (**Figure 13-22**). On the basis of this result, Maquet and coworkers suggested first that the participants were dreaming about their learning experience and second that replay during R-sleep strengthened the task memory. Research in which participants are given a language task that contains hidden rules finds that sleep also strengthens this implicit rule learning (Batterink et al., 2014). Thus, the conclusion is that rule learning in both motor and cognitive domains is strengthened during sleep, including R-sleep.

Storing Memories During Sleep

Although evidence shows that memory strengthens during sleep, it is less clear whether the neural and molecular changes that support sleep memory storage are similar or different from those that store memory during wakefulness. Researchers are addressing this question in innovative animal models of sleep. Nelini and coworkers (2012) studied spatial memory formation in chicks, a species in which such memories are stored mainly in the right hemisphere. Chickens, like many other bird species, alternate sleep in each hemisphere, and the researchers showed that after a learning experience, the right hemisphere displayed more sleep than did the left hemisphere. Birds' selectivity in hemispheric sleep opens up the possibility of comparing plastic changes between the hemispheres as a way of understanding genetic, biochemical, and plastic changes associated with memory formation.

The fruit fly Drosophila also offers insights into the effects of sleep on memory and on plasticity. Dissel and colleagues (2015) identified a variety of mutations that disrupt memory formation and plasticity and found that the memory disruptions decrease

Principle 5: The brain is symmetrical and asymmetrical.

Reaction-time task

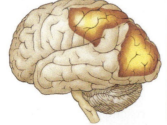

Participants are trained on a reaction-time task, and brain activity is recorded with PET.

REM sleep that night

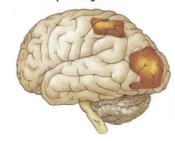

Participants display a similar pattern of brain activity during subsequent REM sleep.

FIGURE 13-22 **Do We Store Implicit Memories During R-Sleep?** Information from Maquet et al., 2000.

after sleep. Slight increases in ambient temperature put one mutant strain of fly to sleep, which greatly aided the research. For this strain, a learning task can be followed by various sleep doses induced by manipulating room temperature. A finding of this research is that the same neurons that enhance memory also are the ones that induce sleep. This finding suggests a causal link between memory and sleep: *Drosophila* sleep to remember! Generalizing this finding to humans suggests that learning will make us want to sleep as well.

13-4 Review

Before you continue, check your understanding. Answers to Self-Test appear at the back of the book.

1. Three contemporary explanations for sleep propose that it is a(n) _____ adaption, a(n) _____ process, or an aid in storing _____.

2. _____ memory is associated with N-sleep, and _____ memory is associated with R-sleep.

3. In rats performing a spatial task, correlations develop between _____ firing in the hippocampus that is then replayed in _____ sleep.

4. When you are sleep deprived, you are more likely to slip into a(n) _____ for a few seconds.

5. Describe a difficulty in relating memory formation to sleep.

For additional study tools, visit **LaunchPad** at launchpadworks.com

13-5
Neural Bases of Sleep

The idea that the brain contains a sleep-inducing substance has long been suggested as an explanation of sleep. This idea is reinforced by the fact that a variety of chemical agents induce sleep. Such substances include sedative-hypnotics and morphine. Our understanding of circadian rhythms suggests, however, that changes in many neuro-chemicals and hormones and the metabolic activity of most of the body's cells produce our sleep–waking cycles.

The hormone melatonin, secreted from the pineal gland during the dark phase of the light–dark cycle, causes sleepiness. A synthetic form can be taken as a sleep aid, so melatonin might be thought to be the sleep-producing substance. But sleep survives the removal of the pineal gland. Melatonin and many other chemical substances may contribute to sleep, not cause it (see Research Focus 13-3).

Some observations suggest that it is not a circulating bloodstream compound that produces sleep. In dolphins and birds, only one brain hemisphere sleeps at a time. This ability presumably allows an animal's other hemisphere to remain behaviorally alert. It suggests that sleep is produced by the action of some brain region within each hemisphere. Were a circulating chemical the cause of sleep, both hemispheres would sleep at the same time because they share a common circulatory system.

In this section, we consider the neural mechanisms that regulate sleep. First, we examine evidence that the activity of a slave oscillator of the suprachiasmatic nucleus produces sleep (see Figure 13-7). Second, we look at evidence that a number of brain-stem nuclei control the various events associated with sleep, with different areas associated with N-sleep and R-sleep.

Reticular Activating System and Sleep

A pioneering experiment by Giuseppe Moruzzi and Horace Magoun (1949) began to answer the question of which brain areas regulate sleep. The experimenters were recording the cortical EEG from anesthetized cats while electrically stimulating the

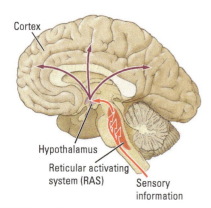

FIGURE 13-23 Sleep–Wake Controller The reticular activating system (RAS), a region at the center of the brainstem, contains a mixture of cell bodies and fiber pathways. RAS stimulation produces a waking EEG, whereas damaging it produces a slow-wave sleeplike EEG.

reticular activating system (RAS) Large reticulum (mixture of cell nuclei and nerve fibers) that runs through the center of the brainstem; associated with sleep–wake behavior and behavioral arousal; also called the *reticular formation.*

coma Prolonged state of deep unconsciousness resembling sleep.

Figure 5-18 summarizes the major neural activating systems and their functions.

Figure 6-5 shows agonist action at the ACh synapse.

FIGURE 13-24 Brain Activators Basal forebrain ACh neurons produce an activated EEG pattern when a rat is alert but immobile. The 5-HT raphe neurons of the midbrain produce an activated EEG pattern when the rat moves.

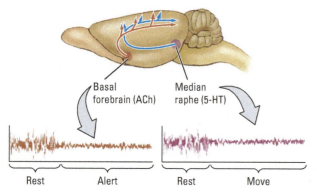

cats' brainstem. They were surprised to find that, in response to the electrical stimulation, large, slow waves typical of anesthesia are replaced by the low-voltage fast-wave beta EEG typical of waking.

The waking EEG activity outlasted the stimulation period, demonstrating that the effect was not due to the online activity of neurons in the region of the stimulating electrode but could be maintained by these neurons independent of the stimulation. During the "waking period," the anesthetized cat did not become behaviorally aroused, but its cortical EEG appeared to indicate that it was awake. In a normally sleeping cat, the same stimulation did lead to waking.

Subsequent experiments show that a waking EEG and waking behavior can be induced from a large neural area running through the center of the brainstem. Anatomically, this area is composed of a mixture of cell nuclei and nerve fibers that form a reticulum (meaning *net*). Moruzzi and Magoun named this brainstem area the **reticular activating system (RAS)** and proposed that it is responsible for sleep–waking behavior. **Figure 13-23** diagrams the location of the RAS.

If someone disturbs you when you are asleep, you usually wake up. To explain that this experimentally induced effect did not result simply from similar sensory stimulation, Moruzzi and Magoun cut the brainstem just behind the RAS, severing its incoming sensory pathways. RAS stimulation still produced a desynchronized EEG, showing that the RAS is the source of waking. It follows that normal waking up occurs because the RAS becomes active.

The idea that the brainstem participates in waking behavior helps explain why brainstem damage can result in **coma**, a prolonged state of deep unconsciousness resembling sleep. In one well-publicized case, after taking a minor tranquilizer and having a few drinks at a birthday party, a 21-year-old woman named Karen Ann Quinlan sustained RAS damage that left her comatose (Quinlan & Quinlan, 1977). She was hospitalized, placed on a respirator to support breathing, and fed by tubes. Her family fought a protracted legal battle to have her removed from life support, a battle they finally won before the Supreme Court of New Jersey. Even after she was removed from the respirator, however, Karen Ann lived for 10 more years with artificial feeding in a perpetual coma.

Neural Basis of EEG Changes Associated with Waking

Research built on the pioneering studies of the RAS has since revealed that many neural systems in the brainstem play a role in sleeping and waking behavior. Case Vanderwolf (Vanderwolf, 2002) showed that at least two brainstem systems influence waking EEG. **Figure 13-24** illustrates their locations in the rat brain.

The basal forebrain contains large cholinergic cells. These neurons secrete acetylcholine (ACh) from their terminals onto cortical neurons to stimulate a waking beta-rhythm EEG. This activity is usually associated with alert but immobile behavior such as behavior that occurs in association with paying attention. The midbrain structure the median raphe contains serotonin (5-HT) neurons, whose axons also project diffusely to the cortex, where they also stimulate cortical cells to produce a beta EEG. This activity is usually associated with movement such as walking.

Although the two pathways produce similar patterns of waking EEG activity, their relationships to behavior differ. If the activity of the cholinergic projection is blocked by drugs or by lesions to the cells of the basal forebrain, the waking EEG normally recorded from an immobile rat is replaced by EEG activity resembling that of N-sleep. Only if the rat walks or is otherwise active is a waking EEG obtained from the cortex. These findings, graphed in Figure 13-24, suggest that the cholinergic EEG is responsible for waking associated with being alert yet still, whereas the serotonergic activation is responsible for the waking EEG associated with movement.

Neither the basal forebrain system nor the median raphe system is responsible for behavior. In fact, if both structures are pharmacologically or surgically destroyed, a rat can still stand and walk around. Its EEG, however, permanently resembles that of a sleeping animal.

As long as one activating system is producing a waking EEG, rats can learn simple tasks. But if both systems are destroyed, an animal, while still able to walk around, is no longer able to learn or display intelligent behavior. In a sense, the cortex is like a house in which the lights are powered by two separate sources: both must fail for the house to be left in darkness, but if at least one source is operating, the lights stay on.

These experimental results suggest that the RAS produces its arousal effects by influencing activity in these two pathways, which then produce EEG events associated with waking. In humans, the basal forebrain and median raphe likely produce the same two desynchronized EEG patterns that they produce in rats. Consequently, when we are alert and still, cholinergic neurons are active; when we move, serotonin neurons are also active.

Perhaps when you have felt sleepy—say, in a class or behind the wheel of a car—you may have been able to wake yourself up by moving, such as by shaking your head or stretching. Presumably, while sitting still, your arousal level decreased as your cholinergic neurons became inactive. When you moved, activating your serotonergic neurons restored your arousal level. When we enter sleep, both cholinergic and serotonergic neurons become less active, allowing slow waves to emanate from the cortex.

Neural Basis of R-Sleep

Barbara Jones (1993) and her colleagues described a group of cholinergic neurons known as the **peribrachial area** that contributes to R-sleep. This area is located in the dorsal brainstem just anterior to the cerebellum (**Figure 13-25**). Jones selectively destroyed peribrachial cells by spraying them with the neurotoxin kainic acid. She found that R-sleep was drastically reduced. This result suggests that the peribrachial area contributes to R-sleep and R-sleep–related behaviors.

The peribrachial area extends into a more ventrally located nucleus called the **medial pontine reticular formation (MPRF)**, shown in Figure 13-25. Lesions of the MPRF also abolish R-sleep, and injections of cholinergic agonists (drugs that act like ACh) into this region induce R-sleep. If both the peribrachial area and the MPRF take part in producing R-sleep, how do other events related to R-sleep—including a waking EEG, rapid eye movements (REMs), and atonia—take place? **Figure 13-26** charts an explanation, showing how other R-sleep-related activities are induced:

- The peribrachial area initiates R-sleep by activating the MPRF.

- The MPRF sends projections to excite basal forebrain cholinergic neurons, and they activate the EEG recorded from the cortex.

- The MPRF also excites brainstem motor nuclei to produce rapid eye movements and other twitches.

- The atonia of R-sleep is produced by the MPRF through a pathway that sends input to the subcoerulear nucleus located just behind it.

- The subcoerulear nucleus excites the magnocellular nucleus of the medulla, which sends projections to the spinal motor neurons to inhibit them so that paralysis is achieved during the R-sleep period.

In support of this neural arrangement, Michel Jouvet (1972) observed that cats with lesions in the subcoerulear nucleus display a remarkable behavior when they enter R-sleep. Rather than stretching out in the atonia that typically accompanies R-sleep, the cats stood up, looked around, and made movements of catching an imaginary mouse or running from an imaginary threat. Apparently, if cats with damage to this brain region dream about catching mice or escaping from a threat, they act out their dreams. We revisit Jouvet's phenomenon in the next section, which describes sleep disorders.

peribrachial area Cholinergic nucleus in the dorsal brainstem having a role in R-sleep behaviors; projects to medial pontine reticular formation.

medial pontine reticular formation (MPRF) Nucleus in the pons that participates in R-sleep.

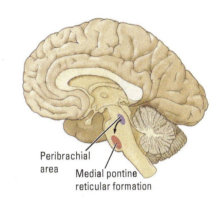

Peribrachial area

Medial pontine reticular formation

FIGURE 13-25 Brainstem Nuclei Responsible for R-Sleep Damage to either the peribrachial area or the medial pontine formation reduces or abolishes R-sleep.

Principle 10: The nervous system works by juxtaposing excitation and inhibition.

FIGURE 13-26 Neural Control of R-Sleep

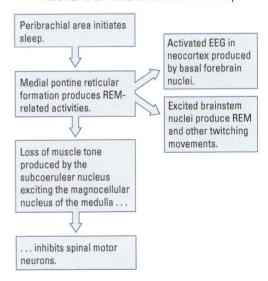

Peribrachial area initiates sleep.

Medial pontine reticular formation produces REM-related activities.

Activated EEG in neocortex produced by basal forebrain nuclei.

Excited brainstem nuclei produce REM and other twitching movements.

Loss of muscle tone produced by the subcoerulear nucleus exciting the magnocellular nucleus of the medulla . . .

. . . inhibits spinal motor neurons.

13-5 Review

Before you continue, check your understanding. Answers to Self-Test appear at the back of the book.

1. The _____ in the central region of the brainstem is associated with sleep–walking behavior.

2. Damage to the RAS produces _____.

3. The peribrachial area and the MPRF, through activating pathways to the neocortex and spinal cord, are responsible for producing events associated with _____ sleep.

4. Cats with lesions to the _____ nucleus act out their dreams.

5. If you nod off to sleep at an inappropriate or inconvenient time, why does moving awaken you?

For additional study tools, visit 📖 **LaunchPad** at launchpadworks.com

13-6

Disorders of Sleep

Occasional sleep disturbances are annoying and may impair performance the following day. About 15 percent of people complain of ongoing sleep problems; an additional 20 percent complain of occasional sleep problems. As people age, the incidence of complaints increases.

An early classification of sleep disorders listed at least 81 separate disorders. Currently, the *International Classification of Sleep Disorders* lists six categories of sleep disorders (Sateia, 2014). Some disorders produce symptoms of **insomnia**, which is a difficulty or inability to fall asleep or experience sleep that is satisfying. Others produce daytime sleepiness. Still others produce symptoms of **hypersomnia**, a difficulty in waking up or staying awake or being excessively tired while awake. There are many causes of these sleep-related conditions, some of which are due to disruption of the neural circuits that regulate sleep and waking and some of which are caused indirectly by lifetime events. The following sections describe only some of these disorders in order to illustrate key features of the organization of our sleep.

Inability to Sleep

Insomnia is a descriptive term for the inability to fall asleep or stay asleep, or to experience satisfactory sleep. It is a symptom of a number of sleep conditions. Our understanding of insomnia is complicated by the wide variation among people in how much time they spend asleep (Kay & Buysse, 2017). Some short sleepers may think they should sleep more, and some long sleepers may think they should sleep less. Yet the sleeping pattern may be appropriate for each. In other cases, the sleep cycle may be advanced, so that an individual falls asleep later and later, or the sleep cycle may be shortened, so that an individual wakes up earlier and earlier. Both conditions can be periodic or consistent and are disruptive to daytime schedules.

People's sleep is also disrupted by lifestyle choices such as those described in Clinical Focus 13-1. Staying up late, for example, may set a person's circadian rhythm forward, encouraging a cascade of late sleep followed by staying up still later. Indoor and outdoor light pollution contributes to sleep disorders by disrupting circadian rhythms. Some sleep problems are brought on by shift work or by jet lag, as described in Section 13-1. Other common causes of sleep disorders are stress, long work hours, and an irregular lifestyle. Just worrying about insomnia is estimated to play a major role in 15 percent of cases.

Depressed people may sleep too little. Anxiety and depression account for about 35 percent of insomnias. Quantitative differences also exist in depressed patients' sleep because they enter R-sleep very quickly, as do people who are sleep deprived.

insomnia Symptom of a number of disorders characterized by an inability to fall asleep or stay asleep.

hypersomnia Disorder of falling asleep at inappropriate times, or a difficulty staying awake.

Insomnia is brought on by sedative-hypnotic drugs, including barbiturates, sodium amytal, and many other tranquilizers. These sleeping pills do help people get to sleep, but the person is likely to feel groggy and tired the next day, which defeats the purpose of taking the drug. Although sleeping pills promote N-sleep, they deprive the user of R-sleep. In addition, people develop tolerance to these medications, become dependent on them, and display rebound insomnia when they stop taking them. A person then may increase the dose each time the drug fails to produce the desired effect. The syndrome in which patients unsuccessfully attempt to sleep by increasing their drug dosage is called *drug dependence insomnia*.

Fatal familial insomnia is an almost complete inability to sleep. As its name implies, this condition contributes to death after a number of months. The disease occurs in midlife and is cause by a gene mutation of the *PRNP* gene on chromosome 20, which expresses the protein that is or becomes a causative prion. The mutation causes a misfolding of the protein, resulting in cascading effects that include brain cell death. Fatal familial insomnia is associated with a number of symptoms, including panic attacks, paranoia, phobias, weight loss, and eventual dementia. It is rare and though there is no treatment, a mouse model of the condition has been created to study the disease and search for treatments.

For more about prion disorders, see Section 16-3.

Section 6-1 presents theories of drug tolerance and dependence.

Inability to Stay Awake

Daytime sleepiness can have many causes, including poor sleep habits, disruptions to the circadian cycle, and jet lag. J. S. reported that sleeping in class was a chronic problem. Not only did he sleep in class, he fell asleep whenever he tried to study. He even fell asleep at the dinner table and in other inappropriate locations. His sleeping problem made getting through high school challenging and was making it difficult for J. S. to pass his college courses.

J. S. often fell asleep while sitting still, and his sleeping bouts consisted of brief spurts of N-sleep lasting 5 to 10 minutes. This pattern is similar to napping and to dozing in class after a late night but is distinguishable by its frequency and disruptive effect. J. S. eventually discussed the problem with his physician and received a prescription for Ritalin, an amphetaminelike drug that stimulates dopamine transmission. The treatment proved helpful.

Clinical Focus 6-1 explores amphetamine use for cognitive enhancement. Research Focus 7-4 describes how Ritalin mitigates symptoms of ADHD.

Sleep clinic studies of people with excessive daytime sleepiness have resulted in a surprising discovery concerning one cause of the condition: **sleep apnea**, an inability to breathe during sleep. Clinical Focus 13-5, Sleep Apnea, describes a person who spent all night, every night, waking up to breathe. This nighttime behavior left him extremely tired and caused him to nod off in the daytime. Being overweight is one contributor to sleep apnea as an overweight individual's respiratory pathway may be constricted. Sleep apnea can also have central causes in the neural circuits that regulate respiration. It has been suggested that sudden infant death, a condition in which a sleeping child inexplicitly dies, might be caused by sleep apnea.

Apnea from Latin *a*, for "not," and *pnea*, for "breathing."

Sleeping beauty syndrome, also called *Kleine–Levin syndrome*, is a very rare condition that usually afflicts adolescent males and in which the sufferer has recurring bouts of excessive sleeping. A single sleep episode may last from 15 hours to more than 20 hours. Periods of excessive sleeping may last for a week or more, interspersed with periods in which sleep has a more normal duration. Some sufferers may experience an increased urge to eat and hypersexuality when awake. There is no obvious cause for the condition and no effective treatment.

Narcolepsy derives from the Greek words for "numbness" and "to be seized."

Narcolepsy

Narcolepsy is a rare but striking condition with symptoms that can include sleep paralysis, cataplexy, and hypnagogic hallucinations and excessive daytime sleepiness, whether or not the person has had a full night's sleep. Sufferers also report mental cloudiness, lack of energy and concentration, memory lapses, a depressed mood, and sometimes extreme exhaustion. Whereas a usual sleep pattern involves periods of N-sleep before R-sleep, people with narcolepsy immediately go into R-sleep.

sleep apnea Inability to breathe during sleep, causing a sleeper to wake up to breathe.

sleeping beauty syndrome A rare condition in which the sufferer has recurring bouts of excessive sleeping.

narcolepsy A rare condition with symptoms that can include sleep paralysis and cataplexy.

⦿ CLINICAL FOCUS 13-5

Sleep Apnea

The first time I went to a doctor for my insomnia, I was twenty-five—that was about thirty years ago. I explained to the doctor that I couldn't sleep; I had trouble falling asleep, I woke up many, many times during the night, and I was tired and sleepy all day long. As I explained my problem to him, he smiled and nodded. Inwardly, this attitude infuriated me—he couldn't possibly understand what I was going through. He asked me one or two questions: Had any close friend or relative died recently? Was I having any trouble in my job or at home? When I answered no, he shrugged his shoulders and reached for his prescription pad. Since that first occasion I have seen I don't know how many doctors, but none could help me. I've been given hundreds of different pills—to put me to sleep at night, to keep me awake in the daytime, to calm me down, to pep me up—have even been psychoanalyzed. But still I cannot sleep at night. (quoted in Dement, 1972, p. 73)

When this patient entered the Stanford University Sleep Disorders Clinic in 1972, recording electrodes monitored his brain, muscle, eye, and breathing activity while he slept.

The attending researchers were amazed to find that he had to wake up to breathe. They observed that he would go more than a minute without breathing before he woke up, gasped for breath, and returned to sleep. Then the sequence began again.

Sleep apnea may be produced by a CNS problem, such as weak neural command to the respiratory muscles in the case of *central sleep apnea*, or it may be caused by collapse or blockage of the upper airway in the case of *obstructive sleep apnea*. When people with sleep apnea stop breathing, they either wake up completely and have difficulty getting back to sleep or they partially awaken repeatedly throughout the night to gasp for breath.

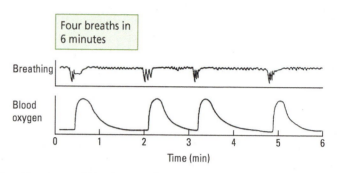

Breathing rate and blood oxygen level recorded during R-sleep, when muscle tone is ordinarily low, from a person with sleep apnea. Blood oxygen increased after each breath and then continued to fall until another breath was taken. This person inhaled only 4 times in the 6-minute period; a healthy sleeper would breathe more than 60 times in the same interval.

Sleep apnea affects people of all ages and both sexes, and 30 percent of those older than 65 may have some form of it. Sleep apnea can even occur in children; it may be related to some cases of *sudden infant death syndrome* (*SIDS*), or crib death, in which otherwise healthy infants inexplicably die in their sleep. Obstructive sleep apnea is more common among overweight people and those who snore, two conditions in which airflow is restricted.

Treatments for sleep apnea include weight loss, a face mask to deliver negative pressure to open the airway, an appliance to expand the upper airway, and, as a last resort, surgery. Untreated sleep apnea can cause high blood pressure and other cardiovascular disease, memory problems, weight gain, impotence, headaches, and brain damage due to oxygen insufficiency (Corrêa et al., 2015).

In **sleep paralysis**, both atonia and dreaming can occur when a person is just falling asleep or waking up. Sleep paralysis is a symptom of narcolepsy, but non-narcoleptic people commonly experience it as well. L. M., a college senior, recounted the following incident: She had just gone to sleep when her roommate came into their room. L. M. woke up and intended to ask her roommate if she wanted to go skating the next morning but found herself unable to speak. She tried to turn her head to follow her roommate's movements across the room but found that she was paralyzed. She had the terrifying feeling that some creature was hiding in the bathroom waiting for her roommate. She tried to cry out but produced only harsh gurgling noises. In response to these peculiar noises, the roommate knocked her out of her paralysis by hitting her with a pillow.

Sleep paralysis is common. In informal class surveys, almost one-third of students report having had such an experience. The atonia is typically accompanied by dread or fear. It seems likely that in sleep paralysis, around the time of sleep onset or offset, a person is partially in R-sleep. He or she is dreaming, atonia has occurred, but the sleeper remains "awake." When sleep paralysis occurs as a person wakes up, the paralysis and dreaming characteristic may be due to an R-sleep episode that has not completely ended.

Cataplexy is atonia of R-sleep that occurs when a person is awake and active. The person loses muscle tone and gradually, or even quickly, falls to the floor, atonic.

sleep paralysis Atonia and dreaming that occur when a person is awake, usually just falling asleep or waking up.

cataplexy State of atonia, as in R-sleep, occurring while a person is awake and active; linked to strong emotional stimulation.

The collapse can be so sudden that injury is a risk. Cataplexy can be triggered by excitement or laughing. While in an atonic condition, the person sees imaginary creatures or hears imaginary voices, which are referred to as **hypnagogic hallucinations**. People who fall into a state of cataplexy with these hypnagogic hallucinations give every appearance of having fallen into R-sleep while remaining "awake."

Narcolepsy can have a genetic basis. In 1970, William Dement was given a litter of Doberman Pinscher dogs and later a litter of Labrador Retrievers. These dogs displayed cataplexy. The disease is transmitted as a recessive trait: to develop it, a dog must inherit the gene from both its mother and its father. The descendants of those dogs, and others who have been found to have the condition, provide animal models for investigating the neural basis of the disease as well as its treatment.

Jerome Siegel (2004) investigated the cause of narcolepsy in dogs. He found that neurons in the subcoerulear nucleus of the brainstem become inactive and neurons in the magnocellular nucleus of the medulla become active during attacks of cataplexy, just as they do during R-sleep. On the basis of anatomical examinations of the brains of narcoleptic dogs, Siegel also found that there was neuronal loss in the hypothalamus and amygdala.

This line of investigation led to the discovery that a subset of these affected neurons produces a peptide neurotransmitter called *orexin* (also called *hypocretin*) that serves as a signaling molecule to maintain wakefulness. Orexin cells, which are located in the hypothalamus, send projections to many other brain regions. In this respect, their organization is similar to nonspecific activating systems using acetylcholine and serotonin; orexin cells also activate these systems. Orexin cells, through the wide distribution of their projections to other brain areas, play a role in maintaining waking (Mieda, 2017).

To test the idea that orexin loss is related to narcolepsy, investigators have developed mice that lack the gene related to orexin production. When these mice become active, such as at feeding time, they collapse into cataplexy, supporting the idea that an orexin system contributes to waking behavior. In addition to genetic causes, another proposed cause of narcolepsy in humans is an autoimmune reaction: the immune system attacks and kills orexin cells.

R-Sleep Behavioral Disorder

In Section 13-5, we described the experiment in which Jouvet reported that cats with lesions to the subcoerulear region of the brainstem entered R-sleep without accompanying atonia and so apparently acted out their dreams. R-sleep behavioral disorder (R-sleep without atonia) is a condition similar to the one described by Jouvet but is reported in people who have either a genetic basis or a neurological cause associated with aging. People who display R-sleep behavioral disorder behave as though they are acting out their dreams (Mahowald & Schenck, 2015). Schenk and his colleagues (Schenck et al., 1986) describe the behavior of a 67-year-old patient who had a dream in which someone was shooting at him from a ridge. In his dream, he decided to crawl behind the ridge to shoot back. When he awoke, he found he was kneeling alongside the bed with his arms extended as if holding a rifle and ready to shoot.

In the dream, the patient saw vivid images but heard nothing and felt afraid. Although many patients have described such experiences, most are elderly and suffer from brain injury or other brain-related disorders. R-sleep behavioral disorder can be treated with benzodiazepines, antianxiety drugs that block R-sleep.

hypnagogic hallucination Dreamlike event occurring as sleep begins or while a person is in a state of cataplexy.

The word *cataplexy* comes from the Greek word *kataplessein*, meaning "to strike down." *Hypnagogic* comes from the Greek *hypnos*, meaning "sleep," and *agogos*, for "leading into."

Figure 3-21 explains inheritance patterns for genetic disorders.

Section 3-3 investigates knockout technology and other genetic engineering techniques.

13-6 Review

Before you continue, check your understanding. Answers to Self-Test appear at the back of the book.

1. Disorders of N-sleep include _____, in which a person has difficulty falling asleep at night, and _____, in which a person falls asleep involuntarily in the daytime.

2. Treating insomnia with sleeping pills, usually sedative-hypnotics, may cause _____: progressively higher doses must be taken to achieve sleep.

3. Disorders of R-sleep include _____, in which a person awakens but cannot move and is afraid, and _____, in which a person may lose all muscle tone and collapse while awake.

4. People who act out their dreams, a condition termed _____, may have damage to the _____ nucleus.

5. Explain the role that orexin cells play in maintaining activity during waking.

For additional study tools, visit ▟ **LaunchPad** at launchpadworks.com

13-7

What Does Sleep Tell Us about Consciousness?

René Descartes conceived his idea of a mind through a lucid dream, one in which a person has some consciousness and can report on, or even direct, the events of a dream. He dreamed that he was interpreting the dream as it occurred. Later, when awake, he reasoned that if he could think and analyze a dream while asleep, his mind must function during both waking and sleeping. He proposed that the mind must therefore be independent of the body that undergoes sleeping and waking transitions. Contemporary fMRI studies suggest that lucid dreaming is especially common in people who display high levels of prefrontal cortex activity in Brodmann's areas 9 and 10 (Filevich et al., 2015).

As described in preceding sections, what we colloquially refer to as waking comprises at least three states. First, alert consciousness without accompanying movement is associated with cholinergic system activity. Second, consciousness with movement is associated with additional serotonergic system activity. Third, the peptide orexin also plays a role in maintaining waking activity.

Similarly, sleep consists of N-sleep and R-sleep phases. N-sleep entails three stages, indicated by characteristic features of the EEG (see Figure 13-12A). R-sleep periods consist of at least two stages, one in which small twitching movements and REMs occur and intervening periods in which twitching and REMs are absent.

R-sleep neurobehavioral events can also occur relatively independently. Sleepers may awake to find themselves in a condition of sleep paralysis, during which they experience the hallucinations and fear that are common in dreams. People who are awake may fall into a state of cataplexy: they are conscious of being awake during the atonia and visual and emotional features of dreams. Both are conditions in which neural centers in the brainstem produce loss of muscle tone in the absence of a sleep state.

Sleep researcher J. Allan Hobson reported his peculiar symptoms after a brainstem stroke (Hobson, 2002). For the first 10 days after the stroke, he had complete insomnia, experiencing neither N-sleep nor R-sleep. Whenever he closed his eyes, however, he did have visual hallucinations that had a dreamlike quality. This experience suggested that eye closure is sufficient to produce the visual components of R-sleep but with neither loss of consciousness nor atonia. Hobson eventually recovered typical sleeping patterns, and the hallucinations stopped.

Beyond teaching us that the neural basis of consciousness is complex, the study of sleep states and dreaming may help explain some psychiatric and drug-induced conditions. For example, visual and auditory hallucinations are among the symptoms of schizophrenia. Are these hallucinations dream events that occur unexpectedly during waking? Many people who take hallucinogenic drugs such as LSD report experiencing visual hallucinations. Does the drug initiate visual features of dreams? People who have panic attacks suffer from very real fright that has no obvious cause. Are they experiencing the fear attacks that commonly occur during sleep paralysis and cataplexy?

Section 1-2 recounts how Descartes chose the pineal gland as the seat of the mind.

What the study of sleep tells us about consciousness is that a remarkable number of variations of conscious states exist. Some are associated with what we usually term waking and sleeping, and these variations can mix together to produce a range of odd conditions. When it comes to consciousness, there is far more to sleeping and waking than just sleeping and waking.

Section 15-7 explores the neural basis of consciousness and ideas about why humans are conscious.

Summary

13-1 A Clock for All Seasons

Biorhythms are cyclical behavior patterns of varying length displayed by animals, plants, and even single-celled organisms. Biorhythms displayed by mammals include, among others, circadian (daily) rhythms and circannual (yearly) rhythms. In the absence of environmental cues, circadian rhythms are free-running, lasting a little more or a little less than their usual period of about 24 hours, depending on the individual organism or the environmental conditions. Cues called Zeitgebers reset biological clocks to a 24-hour rhythm. Circadian rhythms allow us to synchronize our behavior with our body's metabolic processes—so that we are hungry and at optimal times. Environmental intrusions into our natural circadian rhythm, from artificial lighting to jet lag, contribute to metabolic syndrome. Biological clocks produce epigenetic effects: they regulate gene expression in every cell in the body.

13-2 The Suprachiasmatic Biological Clock

A biological clock is a neural structure responsible for producing rhythmic behavior. Our master biological clock is the suprachiasmatic nucleus (SCN). The SCN is responsible for circadian rhythms; it has its own free-running rhythm with a period of a little more than 24 hours. Stimuli from the environment, especially sunrise and sunset, as well as meals or exercise, entrain the free-running rhythm so that its period approximates 24 hours. Across human populations, and within other animal species, individuals show variation in their circadian activities; these distinctive patterns are referred to as chronotypes.

SCN neurons are active in the daytime and inactive at night. These neurons retain their rhythmicity when disconnected from other brain structures, when removed from the brain and cultured in a dish, and after culture in a dish for many generations. When reimplanted in a brain without an SCN, they restore the animal's circadian rhythms. Aspects of neuronal circadian rhythms, including their period, are under genetic and epigenetic control.

13-3 Sleep Stages and Dreaming

Sleep events are measured by recording the brain's activity to produce an electroencephalogram (EEG), muscular activity to produce an electromyogram (EMG), and eye movements to produce an electrooculogram (EOG).

A typical night's sleep, as indicated by physiological measures, consists of stages that take place in cycles over the course of the night. During R-sleep (for rapid eye movement, or REM, sleep), the EEG displays a waking pattern, and the sleeper displays rapid eye movements. Sleep stages in which the EEG has a slower rhythm are called N-sleep (for non-REM sleep) stages.

Intervals of N-sleep and R-sleep alternate four or five times each night. The duration of N-sleep periods is longer earlier in sleep, whereas the duration of R-sleep periods is longer in the later part of sleep. These intervals also vary with age.

A sleeper in N-sleep has muscle tone, may toss and turn, and has dreams that are not especially vivid. A sleeper in R-sleep has vivid dreams in real time but has no muscle tone and so is paralyzed. Dream duration coincides with the duration of the R-period.

The activation–synthesis hypothesis proposes that dreams are not meaningful but are merely a by-product of the brain's state of excitation during R-sleep. The coping hypothesis suggests that dreaming evolved as a mechanism to deal with challenges and fears posed by life.

13-4 What Does Sleep Accomplish?

Several theories of sleep have been advanced, but the main proposition is that sleep is a biological adaptation that conserves energy. Sleep is suggested as a restorative process that fixes wear and tear in the brain and body, including synapses. Sleep also organizes and stores memories.

13-5 Neural Bases of Sleep

Separate neural regions are responsible for N-sleep and R-sleep. The reticular activating system (RAS), located in the central brainstem, is responsible for N-sleep. If the RAS is stimulated, a sleeper awakes; if it is damaged, a person may enter a coma.

The peribrachial area and the medial pontine reticular formation in the brainstem are responsible for R-sleep. If these areas are damaged, R-sleep may no longer occur. Pathways projecting from these areas to the cortex produce the cortical activation of R-sleep, and those projecting to the brainstem produce the muscular paralysis of R-sleep.

13-6 Disorders of Sleep

Disorders of N-sleep include insomnia (the inability to sleep), hypersomnia (difficulty staying awake), and narcolepsy (inconveniently falling asleep in the daytime). Sedative-hypnotics used to induce sleep may induce drug dependence insomnia, a sleep disorder in which progressively larger doses are required to produce sleep.

Disorders of R-sleep include sleep paralysis, in which a person awakens but remains unable to move and sometimes feels fear and dread. In cataplexy, caused by a loss of orexin cells in the brain, a person collapses into a state of paralysis while awake. At the same time, the person may have hypnagogic hallucinations similar to dreaming. In R-sleep behavioral disorder, a sleeping person acts out dreams.

13-7 What Does Sleep Tell Us about Consciousness?

Sleep research provides insight into consciousness by revealing many kinds of waking and sleeping. Just as the events of wakefulness intrude into sleep, the events of sleep can intrude into wakefulness. The array of conditions thus produced demonstrates that consciousness is not a unitary state.

Key Terms

alpha rhythm, p. 454

atonia, p. 454

basic rest–activity cycle (BRAC), p. 460

beta rhythm, p. 454

biological clock, p. 438

biorhythm, p. 438

cataplexy, p. 470

chronotype, p. 450

circadian rhythm, p. 438

coma, p. 466

delta rhythm, p. 454

dimer, p. 447

diurnal animal, p. 438

entrain, p. 443

free-running rhythm, p. 442

hypersomnia, p. 468

hypnagogic hallucination, p. 471

insomnia, p. 468

jet lag, p. 444

light pollution, p. 443

medial pontine reticular formation (MPRF), p. 467

melatonin, p. 449

metabolic syndrome, p. 438

microsleep, p. 461

narcolepsy, p. 469

non-REM sleep (N-sleep), p. 453

peribrachial area, p. 467

period, p. 439

place cell, p. 463

REM sleep (R-sleep), p. 453

reticular activating system (RAS), p. 466

sleep apnea, p. 469

sleep paralysis, p. 470

sleeping beauty syndrome, p. 469

Zeitgeber, p. 443

Visit **LaunchPad** to access the e-Book, videos, **LearningCurve** adaptive quizzing, flashcards, and more launchpadworks.com

RUSSELL KIGHTLEY/SCIENCE PHOTO LIBRARY/Getty Images

How Do We Learn and Remember?

CHAPTER 14

Remediating Dyslexia

Dyslexia, impairment in learning to read and write, may be the most common learning disability. Children with dyslexia (from Greek words suggesting "bad" and "reading") have difficulties in reading, writing, spelling, and phonological processing, which is the discrimination of phonemes (units of sound in speech) in language. These learning difficulties are not accounted for by mental age, sight defects, or insufficient schooling. Estimates of the prevalence of dyslexia in the United States range from 5 to 17 percent, making it a common problem.

For many years, the general consensus was that dyslexia is chiefly a phonological deficit, which led researchers to focus on auditory processing and the auditory system, especially the thalamus and auditory cortex. Over the past decade, however, a shift toward viewing developmental disorders as multidimensional has led to growing interest in the role of extended cortical networks and cortical connectivity (see, for example, Kronbichler & Kronbichler, 2018).

Brain-imaging studies have shown that, relative to the brains of healthy participants, activity in the brains of people with dyslexia is reduced in the left temporoparietal, occipitotemporal, and inferior frontal cortex (see review by Martin et al., 2016). The reduced temporoparietal activity is associated with deficits in auditory processing. The reduced occipitotemporal activity occurs largely in the visual word-form area (VWFA), which is believed to be responsible for rapid word recognition. The reduced inferior frontal activity occurs in the inferior frontal gyrus, a large region that includes the anterior speech zone known as Broca's area.

The reduced activity in these brain regions results in inconsistent neural processing of sound, which is hypothesized to reflect the large variability in auditory processing common in children with dyslexia (Tallal, 2012). Children who perform most poorly on auditory discrimination tasks tend to develop poor reading skills. A variety of training programs have been devised to stimulate plasticity in the reading-related brain systems, and many have proven effective in improving attention, listening, and reading skills. These programs range from musical training and neuroplasticity-based auditory training designed to improve dynamic auditory processing to the use of speech that has been computer modified to enhance the various aspects

of the rapidly changing acoustic components of ongoing speech. For example, Jane Hornickel and colleagues (2012) used assistive listening devices with their dyslexic subjects for a year to enhance acoustic clarity and attention. The program reduced the variability of neurophysiological responses to sound, and this result has been linked to improved reading and phonological awareness.

One study used fMRI to investigate the effectiveness of a remedial treatment program based on the assumption that the fundamental problem in learning disabilities lies in auditory processing, specifically of language sounds (Temple et al., 2003). Remediation involves learning to make increasingly difficult sound discriminations, such as distinguishing *ba* from *da*.

When the sounds are spoken slowly, discriminating between them is easy; but as they grow briefer and occur more quickly, discrimination becomes more difficult. The representative fMRIs shown here reveal decreased activation in many brain regions in untreated dyslexic children compared with typical children. With training, dyslexic readers can normalize their brain activity and, presumably, its connectivity.

The extent of increased brain activation in the language-related regions (circled in the images) correlates to the amount of increased brain activation overall. The results suggest that the remedial treatment improves brain function in regions associated with phonological processing and also produces compensatory activation in related brain regions.

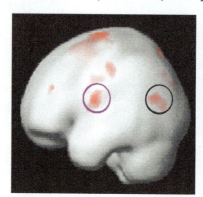

Typical-reading children while rhyming

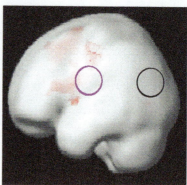

Dyslexic-reading children while rhyming (before remediation)

Regions of the frontal and temporoparietal cortex that showed decreased activation in children with untreated dyslexia. From Temple et al., 2003.

"Neural Deficits in Children with Dyslexia Ameliorated by Behavioral Remediation: Evidence from Functional MRI," by E. Temple, G. K. Deutsch, R. A. Poldrack, S. L. Miller, P. Tallal, M. M. Merzenich, and J. D. E. Gabrieli, 2003, *Proceedings of the National Academy of Sciences (USA)* 100, pp. 2860–2865.

---

dyslexia Impairment in learning to read and write; probably the most common learning disability.

Principle 2: Neuroplasticity is the hallmark of nervous system functioning.

The brain is plastic. It changes throughout life, allowing us to modify our behavior, to adapt and learn, and to remember. If we reflect on our own lives, we can easily compile a list of experiences that must change the brain: profound changes during development, acquisition of culture, learning a new language or a new game, and the ability to cope with the neurodegeneration of aging and to accommodate neurological injury or disease at any age.

Learning is common to all these experiences. Understanding how the brain supports learning is fundamental in neuroscience. At the level of the neuron, synapses change with experience—learning new information, for example. But how are learning-related changes organized in the brain to support memory? One research strategy is to investigate neuronal changes that support the learning of specific types of information by describing changes in cells exposed to specific sensory experiences. Another strategy is to examine neural changes related to a range of experiences, including learning and memory, electrical brain stimulation, chemical influences, and brain injury. This chapter reviews both types of studies, but first, we establish what we mean by learning and memory and how both are tested.

Connecting Learning and Memory

Learning is a relatively permanent change in an organism's behavior as a result of experience (see, for example, the learning programs described in Clinical Focus 14-1, Remediating Dyslexia). **Memory** is the ability to recall or recognize previous experience. Memory thus implies a mental representation of a previous experience. This representation is thought to be the product of a physical trace, or *engram*, of the memory in the brain (for a history of the term *engram*, see Josselyn et al., 2017). Neuroscientists have shown that the engram results from physical changes in the brain, both at synapses and in the nucleus of neurons.

At the macro level, we infer what we know about learning and memory formation from behavioral changes, not by observing the brain directly. Studying learning and memory therefore requires behavioral measures that evaluate how these changes come about. We begin here by reviewing how learning and memory researchers study animals in the laboratory. The results suggest, in a general way, how the brain organizes its learning and memory systems.

Studying Learning and Memory in the Laboratory

A challenge for psychologists studying memory in laboratory animals (or people) is to get subjects to reveal what they remember. For humans, investigators tend to use either paper-and-pencil or computer-based tests. But because non-human laboratory animals do not speak or write, investigators must devise ways for a subject to show its knowledge. Different non-human species "talk" to us in different ways, so the test choice must match each species' capabilities.

Mazes or swimming pools are typically used to study rats because rats live in tunnels and near water. Monkey studies take advantage of monkeys' sharp vision and avid curiosity by requiring them to look under objects for food or to watch television monitors. With birds, natural behaviors such as singing are used.

Two classic traditions for training animals to talk to investigators emerged a century ago. These diverse approaches are based on the work of Edward Thorndike (1898) in the United States and on experiments conducted by Ivan Pavlov in Russia beginning in the 1890s.

Pavlovian Conditioning

Early in the twentieth century, Ivan Pavlov, a Russian physiologist, discovered that when a food reward accompanies some stimulus, such as a tone, dogs learn to associate the stimulus with the food. Then whenever they hear the tone, they salivate even though no food is present. This type of learning has many names, including **Pavlovian conditioning**, *respondent conditioning*, and *classical conditioning*, and many studies document its characteristics.

A key feature of Pavlovian conditioning is that animals learn to associate two stimuli (such as the presentation of the food and the tone) and to communicate to us that they have learned it by giving the same response (salivation) to both stimuli. Pet owners know that to a cat or dog, the sound of a can being opened is a clear stimulus for food. Two forms of Pavlovian conditioning are common in experiments today: eyeblink conditioning and fear conditioning. Each is associated with neural circuits in discrete brain regions; thus both are especially useful.

Eyeblink conditioning has been used to study Pavlovian learning in rabbits and people (**Figure 14-1**). In these studies, a tone (or some other stimulus) is associated

learning Relatively permanent change in an organism's behavior as a result of experience.

memory Ability to recall or recognize previous experience.

Pavlovian conditioning Learning achieved when a neutral stimulus (such as a tone) comes to elicit a response after its repeated pairing with some event (such as delivery of food); also called *classical conditioning* or *respondent conditioning*.

eyeblink conditioning Experimental technique in which subjects learn to pair a formerly neutral stimulus with a defensive blinking response.

Figure 7-3 samples swimming pool tests for rats; Experiment 15-1, monkeys' perceptual threshold; and Clinical Focus 15-3, the effects of brain injuries on humans' cognitive performance.

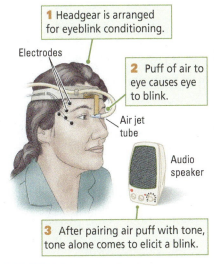

1 Headgear is arranged for eyeblink conditioning.

Electrodes

2 Puff of air to eye causes eye to blink.

Air jet tube

Audio speaker

3 After pairing air puff with tone, tone alone comes to elicit a blink.

FIGURE 14-1 **Eyeblink Conditioning** Neural circuits in the cerebellum mediate this form of stimulus–response learning.

Question: Does an animal learn the association between emotional experience and environmental stimuli?

Procedure and Results

Rat receives mild electrical shock in combination with tone.

Tone plus shock

Later →

If a light is presented alone later, rat ignores it.

Light only— no tone

Later →

Rat freezes in fear when tone alone sounds.

Tone only

Conclusion: The rat has learned an association between the tone and the shock, which produces a fear response. Circuits that include the amygdala take part in this learning process.

In the cerebellum, the flocculus controls eye movements; see Figure 11-15.

conditioned stimulus (CS) In Pavlovian conditioning, an originally neutral stimulus that, after association with an unconditioned stimulus (UCS), triggers a conditioned response (CR).

unconditioned stimulus (UCS) A stimulus that naturally and automatically (unconditionally) triggers an unconditioned response (UCR).

unconditioned response (UCR) Unlearned, naturally occurring response to an unconditioned stimulus (UCS), such as salivation when food is in the mouth.

conditioned response (CR) In Pavlovian conditioning, the learned response to a formerly neutral conditioned stimulus (CS).

fear conditioning Conditioned emotional response between a neutral stimulus and an unpleasant event, such as a shock, that results in a learned association.

with a painless puff of air to the participant's eye. The tone is the **conditioned stimulus (CS)** that comes to elicit a blink produced initially by the air puff. The air puff is the **unconditioned stimulus (UCS)** because blinking is the normal reaction—the **unconditioned response (UCR)**—to a puff of air. The participant communicates having learned that the signal stimulus predicts the puff by blinking in response to the signal (the CS) alone—a **conditioned response (CR)**. The circuits in the cerebellum that mediate such Pavlovian learning are designed to pair motor responses with environmental events. Eyeblink conditioning experiments take advantage of this biological predisposition.

In **fear conditioning**, an unpleasant but harmless stimulus is used to elicit an emotional response: fear. A rat or other animal is placed in a box. A mild but unpleasant electric current, approximating a spark of static electricity, can be passed through the grid floor. As shown in **Experiment 14-1**, a tone (the CS) is presented just before a brief, unexpected mild electric shock. When the tone is presented later without the shock, the animal acts afraid, becoming motionless and perhaps urinating in anticipation of the shock. A novel stimulus, perhaps a light, presented in the same environment has little effect. Thus, the animal communicates that it has learned the association between the tone and the shock.

Because the CR is emotional, circuits of the amygdala rather than the cerebellum mediate fear conditioning. Although both eyeblink and fear conditioning are Pavlovian, different brain areas mediate the learning.

FIGURE 14-2 Thorndike's Puzzle Box

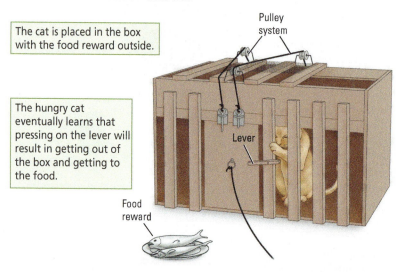

The cat is placed in the box with the food reward outside.

Pulley system

The hungry cat eventually learns that pressing on the lever will result in getting out of the box and getting to the food.

Lever

Food reward

Operant Conditioning

In the United States, Edward Thorndike (1898) began a second tradition for studying learning and memory. Thorndike was interested in how animals solve problems. In one series of experiments, he placed a cat in a box with a plate of fish outside it (**Figure 14-2**). The only way for the hungry cat to get to the fish was to figure out how to get out of the box.

The solution was to press on a lever to activate a system of pulleys that opened the box door. The cat gradually learned that its actions had consequences: on the initial trial, the cat touched the releasing mechanism only by chance as it restlessly paced inside the box. The cat apparently learned that something it had done opened the door, and it tended to repeat its behaviors from just before the door opened. After a few trials, the cat took just seconds to get the door open to devour the fish.

Later studies by B. F. Skinner (e.g., 1938) used a similar strategy of *reinforcement* to train rats to press bars or pigeons to peck keys to obtain food. Just as Thorndike's cats learned to escape his puzzle boxes, many animals learn to press the bar or peck the key simply if they are placed in the apparatus and allowed to discover the response that obtains the reward. Thorndike called this type of learning *instrumental conditioning*, but it is more commonly known as **operant conditioning**. The animal demonstrates that it has learned the association between its actions and the consequences by performing the task faster.

The variety of operant associations is staggering: we learn constantly to associate our behavior with its consequences. It is no surprise, then, that operant learning is not localized to any particular brain circuit. The necessary circuits vary with the task requirements. For example, olfactory tasks involve olfactory-related structures like the orbitofrontal cortex and amygdala, spatial tasks recruit the hippocampus, and motor tasks require the basal ganglia.

Two Categories of Memory

Humans present a distinct challenge to researchers studying memory because much of our learning is verbal. Psychologists have studied human memory since the mid-1800s, but only in the past few decades have cognitive psychologists developed sophisticated measures of learning and memory for neuropsychological investigations. Two such measures help distinguish between two categories of memory in humans.

In one kind of task, one group of participants reads a list of words, such as *spring*, *winter*, *car*, and *boat*. Another group reads a list consisting of the words *trip*, *tumble*, *run*, and *sun*. All the participants are then asked to define a series of words. One is *fall*.

The word *fall* has multiple meanings, including the season and a tumble. People who have just read the word list containing names of seasons are likely to give the meaning as *autumn*; those who have read the second list, containing action words, typically give the meaning as *tumble*. Some form of unconscious (and unintentional) learning takes place as the participants read the word lists. This unconscious learning is also known as **priming**, which occurs when exposure to a stimulus influences a response to a later stimulus.

This task measures **implicit memory**: participants demonstrate knowledge—a skill, conditioned response, or recall of events on prompting—but cannot explicitly retrieve the information. People with **amnesia**, a partial or total loss of memory, perform at normal levels on tests of implicit memory. The amnesic person has no recollection of having read the word list yet acts as though some neural circuit has been influenced by it. In amnesia, a *dissociation*—a disconnect—occurs between the memory of the unconscious (or implicit) learning and **explicit memory**, conscious recollections of training, such as the name of the person in charge of the training or the layout of the training room. Nonamnesic people can retrieve an explicit memory and indicate that they know the retrieved item is correct.

This implicit–explicit distinction is not restricted to verbal learning; it is true of visual learning and motor learning as well. For example, when people are shown the top panel of the Gollin figure test in **Figure 14-3** and asked what it shows, they are unlikely to identify an image. They are then presented with a succession of more nearly complete sketches until they can identify the picture. When control participants and amnesics are later shown the same sketch, both groups identify the figure sooner than they could the first time. Even though the amnesic subjects may not recall having seen the sketches before, they behave as though they have.

To measure implicit motor skills learning, a person learns a skill, such as the pursuit rotor task shown in **Figure 14-4**. A small metal disc moves in a circular pattern on a turntable that also is moving. The task is to hold a stylus on the small disc as it spins. This task is not as easy as it looks, especially when the turntable is moving quickly. Nonetheless, with an hour's practice, most people become

operant conditioning Learning procedure in which the consequences (such as obtaining a reward) of a particular behavior (such as pressing a bar) increase or decrease the probability of the behavior occurring again; also called *instrumental conditioning*.

priming Using a stimulus to sensitize the nervous system to a later presentation of the same or a similar stimulus.

implicit memory Unconscious memory: subjects can demonstrate knowledge, such as a skill, conditioned response, or recall of events on prompting but cannot explicitly retrieve the information.

amnesia Partial or total loss of memory.

explicit memory Conscious memory: subjects can retrieve an item and indicate that they know the retrieved item is the correct one.

FIGURE 14-3 **Gollin Figure Test** Participants are shown a series of drawings in sequence, from least to most clear, and asked to identify the image. Most people must see several panels before they can identify the image. On a retention test some time later, however, participants identify the image sooner than they did on the first test, indicating some form of memory for the image. Amnesic subjects also show improvement on this test, even though they do not recall having taken it.

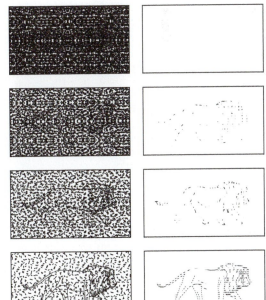

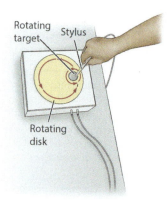

FIGURE 14-4 Pursuit-Rotor Task The participant must keep the stylus in contact with a metal disc moving in a circular pattern on a turntable while also rotating in a circular pattern. Although the task is difficult, most people show significant improvement after brief training. Given a second test at some later time, both participants and amnesics show task retention, but typically the amnesics do not recall having learned it before.

declarative memory Ability to recount what one knows, to detail the time, place, and circumstances of events; often lost in amnesia.

procedural memory Ability to recall a movement sequence or how to perform some act or behavior.

learning set Rules of the game; implicit understanding of how a problem can be solved with a rule that can be applied in many different situations.

TABLE 14-1 Differentiating Two Memory Categories

Terms that describe conscious memory	Terms that describe unconscious memory
Explicit	Implicit
Declarative	Nondeclarative
Fact	Skill
Memory	Habit
Knowing that	Knowing how
Locale	Taxon
Conscious recollection	Skills
Elaboration	Integration
Memory with record	Memory without record
Autobiographical	Perceptual
Representational	Dispositional
Episodic	Procedural
Semantic	Nonassociative
Working	Reference

Note: This paired list of terms differentiates conscious from unconscious forms of memory. It will help you relate other memory discussions to the one in this book, which favors the explicit–implicit distinction.

reasonably proficient. Presented with the same task a week later, both controls and amnesics take less time to perform it. Here, too, the amnesics fail to recall having performed the task before.

The distinction between tests of implicit memory and explicit memory is consistent and therefore must offer a key to how the brain stores information. Some theorists make subtle distinctions between the implicit–explicit dichotomy we use and other terminologies for categorizing unconscious and conscious memory. Many researchers prefer to distinguish between **declarative memory**, the specific contents of specific experiences that can be verbally recalled (times, places, or circumstances), and **procedural memory**, the ability to perform a task. As applied to humans, there is little practical difference.

Table 14-1 lists commonly used dichotomies, the general distinction being that one memory category requires recalling specific information, whereas the other refers to knowledge of which we are not consciously aware. We can include Pavlovian conditioning and Thorndike's and Skinner's operant learning in this analysis, too: all are forms of implicit learning.

Nonspeaking animals can display explicit memory. One of your authors owned a cat that loved to play with a little ball. One day, as the cat watched, the ball was temporarily put on a high shelf to keep it away from an inquisitive toddler. For weeks afterward, the cat sat and stared at the shelf where the ball had been placed, even though the ball was not visible—an example of explicit memory.

Animals also display explicit memory when they learn psychological tasks. Rats can be trained to find highly palatable food in a new location in a large compound each day. The task is to go to the most recent location. This piece of information is explicit and demonstrably can be forgotten. Suppose a rat trained to find food in a particular location in a small arena is given several trials with the food at a new location and then retested an hour, a day, 3 days, or a week later. The rat has no difficulty with an hour's delay or perhaps even a day's. Some rats are flawless at 3 days, but most have forgotten the location by the time a week has elapsed. Instead, they wander around looking for the food. This behavior illustrates their implicit memory of the **learning set**, the rules of the game—an implicit understanding of how a problem can be solved with a rule that can be applied in many situations—here, that a desired food can be found with a certain search strategy.

What Makes Explicit and Implicit Memory Different?

One reason explicit and implicit memories differ is that the set of neural structures that houses each type is different. Another reason they differ is that the brain processes explicit and implicit information differently.

Encoding and Processing Memories

Before information is processed, it must be changed into a form that can be stored in the brain, a process referred to as *encoding*. There are many types of encoding. For example, visual encoding is the storage of visual sensory information, such as the position of an object in a room. Semantic encoding is the storage of input that has a particular meaning and becomes part of one's knowledge of the world, such as knowing that London is in England. The process of encoding is not yet well understood, but it appears to include modification of synapses, creation of new synapses, changes in gene expression, and modification of, or creation of, proteins.

Implicit information is encoded in much the same way it is perceived: it can be described as data-driven, or bottom-up, processing. The idea is that information enters the brain through sensory receptors and then is processed in a series of subcortical and cortical regions. For instance, visual information about an object moves from the photoreceptors (the bottom) to the thalamus, occipital cortex, and then through the ventral stream to the temporal lobe (the top), where the object is recognized.

Explicit memory, in contrast, depends on conceptually driven, or top-down, processing: the person reorganizes the data. If you were searching for a particular object—say, your keys—you would ignore other objects. This process is top down because circuits in the temporal lobe (the top) form an image (keys) that influences how incoming visual information (the bottom) is processed and, in turn, greatly influences information recall later.

Because a person has a relatively passive role in encoding implicit memory, he or she has difficulty recalling the memory spontaneously but recalls it more easily with priming by the original stimulus or some feature of it. Because a person plays an active role in processing information explicitly, internal cues (such as related memories) used in processing can also be used to initiate spontaneous recall.

Findings from studies of eyewitness testimony demonstrate the active nature of explicit memory recall—as well as its fallibility (e.g., Loftus, 1997). In a typical experiment, participants view a video clip of an accident in which a car collides with another car stopped at an intersection. One group is asked to estimate how fast the moving car was going when it "smashed" into the other car. A second group is asked how fast the car was going when it "bumped" into the other car.

Later questioning indicates that the memory of how fast the moving car was going is biased by the instruction: participants looking at "smashing" cars estimate faster speeds than do participants looking at "bumping" cars. The instruction actually causes the information to be processed differently. In both cases, participants were certain their memories were accurate.

Other experiments show that implicit memory also is fallible. For example, participants are read the following list of words: *sweet, chocolate, shoe, table, candy, horse, car, cake, coffee, wall, book, cookie, hat*. After a few minutes' delay, they hear a second list of words that includes some from the first list and some that are new. Participants are asked to identify which words were included in the first list and to indicate how certain they are of the identification.

One of the words in the second list is *sugar*. Most participants are certain that *sugar* was in the first list. Although other sweet things were included, *sugar* was not. This demonstration is intriguing because it shows how easily we can form false memories and defend their veracity with certainty.

Although we can distinguish memories generally as implicit or explicit, the brain does not process all implicit or all explicit memories in the same way. Memories can be divided according to categories that differ from those listed in Table 14-1. For instance, we can make a distinction between memories for different types of sensory information.

Different neural areas process visual and auditory information, so it is reasonable to assume that auditory memories are encoded in brain regions different from the regions that encode visual memories. We can also make a distinction between information stored in *short-term memory* and information held in *long-term memory*, as illustrated in **Figure 14-5**. In short-term memory, information—such as the final score of a playoff game or the combination of your friend's bike lock—is held in memory only briefly, for a few minutes at most, and then discarded. In long-term memory, information—such as your own bike lock's combination—is held in memory indefinitely, perhaps for a lifetime. Long-term memory is more complex and includes different types of explicit memory as well as implicit memory and emotional memory.

The frontal lobes are central in short-term memory, whereas the temporal lobe is central in long-term storage of verbal information. The crucial point is that no single place in the nervous system can be identified as *the* location for memory or learning. Virtually the entire nervous system can be changed by experience, but different parts of an experience change different parts of the nervous system. One challenge for the experimenter is to devise ways of manipulating experience to demonstrate change in different parts of the brain.

FIGURE 14-5 Multiple Memory Systems The broadest classification of memory distinguishes transient *short-term memory* for recent sensory, motor, or cognitive information from relatively permanent *long-term memory*. Conscious, long-term memories may be *explicit*—events and facts that you can spontaneously recall—and either *episodic*, for personal experiences (your first day at school), or *semantic*, for facts (England is in Europe). *Implicit*, nonconscious memories (say, riding a bicycle) consist of learned skills, conditioned responses, and events recalled on prompting. *Emotional memory* for the affective properties of stimuli or events (your first kiss) is vivid and has characteristics of implicit and explicit memories.

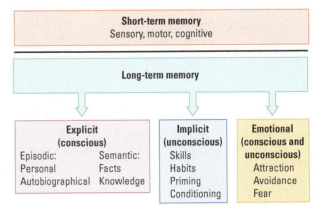

Short-term memory		
Sensory, motor, cognitive		

Long-term memory		

Explicit (conscious)		Implicit (unconscious)	Emotional (conscious and unconscious)
Episodic: Personal Autobiographical	Semantic: Facts Knowledge	Skills Habits Priming Conditioning	Attraction Avoidance Fear

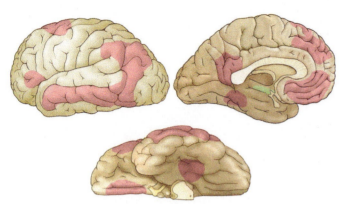

FIGURE 14-6 **Semantic Memory System**
The various components of the semantic memory system found in the left hemisphere are shown in red. Research from Binder et al., 2009.

Storing Memories

Over the past two decades, hundreds of noninvasive imaging studies have looked for the engram of semantic memories, which include our knowledge about the world. Jeffrey Binder and his colleagues (2009) performed a meta-analysis of 120 fMRI semantic memory studies. They found a distinct network comprising seven different left-hemisphere regions, including regions of the parietal lobe, temporal lobe, prefrontal cortex, and posterior cingulate cortex (see **Figure 14-6**). Not all regions are active at once when a semantic memory is stored, but subregions are likely to be relatively specialized for specific object characteristics (such as color or shape) or types of knowledge (such as names or places).

This extensive network is similar to what is known as the *default network*, which is the network of regions active when participants are resting rather than engaged in specific cognitive tasks. Given the similarity in the semantic memory and default network, it appears that semantic processing constitutes a large component of the cognitive activity that occurs during passive states. In the resting state, the semantic system is operating on the internal stores of knowledge to "make sense" of all the new information. Binder and his colleagues note that these regions are more extensive than those described for nonhuman primates and may explain uniquely human capacities to use language productively, plan, solve problems, and create technological and cultural artifacts.

What Is Special about Personal Memories?

One aspect of explicit memory unique to each of us is our personal, or *autobiographical*, memory. This **episodic memory** includes not only a record of events (episodes) that took place but also a record of our presence and role in the events. Our personal experiences form the basis of who we are and the rules by which we live. That is, we have memories not only for events but also for their context at a particular time in a particular place. We thus gain a concept of time and a sense of our personal role in a changing world.

There has been a long-standing question concerning how and where autobiographical memories are stored in the brain, but the current consensus is that the key regions involved in this process are the ventromedial prefrontal cortex (vmPFC) and hippocampus, and the pathways between them. Heidi Bonnici and Eleanor Maguire conducted a series of clever fMRI studies to examine this question. In an initial fMRI study, Bonnici and her colleagues (2012) asked participants to recall three personal episodes that were 2 weeks old and compared the recall to episodes that were 10 years old. The goal was to determine if the patterns of brain activity could be used to predict which of the memories was being recalled by the participant. The results showed that, although the discriminability in the hippocampus was similar for the old and new memories, discriminability in the prefrontal cortex was much poorer for the new memories; this suggested that the memories were not yet strongly represented there.

In the second study, 2 years later, the authors tested the same participants on the same memories, which were now 2 and 12 years old (Bonnici & Maguire, 2018). There was no change in the hippocampal results, but the discriminability in the prefrontal activity was now similar for the newer and older memories, suggesting that the memory representations were now equally strong for both. Thus, there was a change in the engram in the prefrontal cortex over the 2 years, but the hippocampus remained stable.

Imagine what would happen if you lost your personal memories. You would still recall events but would be unable to see your role in them. People with frontal lobe injuries sometimes exhibit such symptoms, as illustrated in a case described by Endel Tulving (2002).

episodic memory Autobiographical memory for events pegged to specific place and time contexts.

K. C. suffered a serious traumatic brain injury in a motorcycle accident that produced multiple cortical and subcortical lesions. Remarkably, K. C.'s cognitive abilities were intact and indistinguishable from those of most typical healthy adults. He played chess and the organ, and his short-term memory was intact. He knew who he was and when his birthday was, the names of schools he had attended, and the location of his family's cottage. Recalling facts, figures, dates, and times posed no difficulty for K. C.

What K. C. could no longer do was to recall any personally experienced events. This episodic autobiographical amnesia covered his entire life from birth. He knew facts about himself but had no memory for events that included him personally. For example, K. C. could recall going to school and the knowledge he had gained there, but he could not describe an event that took place in school that specifically included him.

Hippocampal injury is also associated with poor episodic memory. Cornelia McCormick and colleagues (2018) compared autobiographical memory and brain activity in patients with temporal lobe epilepsy (including unilateral hippocampal injury) and in controls. The patients showed reduced hippocampal activity during episodic memory retrieval, which was associated with impaired episodic memory. Curiously, they also showed increased vmPFC activity during memory retrieval, presumably as a result of partial compensation for the hippocampal dysfunction.

Just as some people exhibit poor autobiographical memory, a rare group displays *highly superior autobiographical memory* (*HSAM*) (LePort et al., 2012). These people display virtually complete recall for events in their lives, usually beginning around age 10, and can often describe any episode, including the day of the week and date that it occurred. They can even recall the weather that day, as well as social and public events. Brain imaging of those who display HSAM shows increased gray matter in the temporal and parietal lobes and increased size in the fiber projection between the temporal and frontal lobes.

Lawrence Patihis and colleagues (2013) wondered if HSAM individuals might also be immune to memory distortion, such as the false memories described earlier. The investigators found that HSAM individuals are as likely as other participants to develop false memories. Whatever the source of their extraordinary autobiographical memory, it does not prevent the sort of memory distortions the rest of us experience. The source of HSAM has only begun to be explored but does not appear to reflect superior cognitive functioning. And though HSAM individuals show superior personal memories, their memory of personal memories described by other people shows no signs of elevated performance. Their ability appears to require an experience that is part of their personal narrative (LePort et al., 2017).

14-1 Review

Before you continue, check your understanding. Answers to Self-Test appear at the back of the book.

1. An organism learns that some stimulus is paired with a reward. This is _____ conditioning.

2. After learning that consequences follow its behavior, an organism modifies its behavior. This is _____ conditioning.

3. Information that is unconsciously learned forms _____ memory, whereas specific factual information forms _____ memory.

4. _____ memory is autobiographical and unique to each person.

5. Where is memory stored in the brain?

For additional study tools, visit 🔶 **LaunchPad** at launchpadworks.com

Brain lesions are an ablation technique—the first and simplest brain manipulation; see Section 7-1.

14-2

Dissociating Memory Circuits

Beginning in the 1920s and continuing until the early 1950s, American psychologist Karl Lashley searched in vain for the neural circuits underlying memories. Lashley's working hypothesis was that memories must be represented in the perceptual and motor circuitry used in problem solving. To find that circuitry, he investigated the ways laboratory rats and monkeys learn specific tasks for food reward. He believed that if he either removed bits of this circuitry or disconnected it from the rest of the brain, amnesia should result.

In fact, neither ablation procedure produced amnesia. Lashley found instead that the severity of memory disturbance was related to the *size* of the lesion rather than to its location. After searching for 30 years, Lashley concluded that he had failed to find the location of a memory trace, although he believed that he knew where it was *not* located (Lashley, 1960).

Disconnecting Explicit Memory

Neurosurgeon William Scoville discovered serendipitously what Lashley's studies had not predicted. Scoville was attempting to rid people of seizures by removing the abnormal brain tissue that caused them. In August 1953, he performed a bilateral medial temporal lobe removal on a young man, Henry Molaison (H. M.), whose severe epilepsy could not be controlled by medication. H. M.'s seizures originated in the medial temporal lobe region, so Scoville bilaterally removed much of the hippocampal formation, along with some of the amygdala and adjacent neocortical structures. The procedure left the more lateral temporal lobe tissue intact. As shown in **Figure 14-7**, removal specifically included the anterior part of the hippocampus, the amygdala, and adjacent cortex.

The behavioral symptoms Scoville noted after the surgery were completely unexpected. He invited Brenda Milner (Milner et al., 1968) to study H. M. Milner had been studying memory difficulties in patients with unilateral temporal lobe removals for the treatment of epilepsy. She and her colleagues worked with H. M. for more than 50 years, making his the most studied case in neuroscience (see, for example, Corkin, 2002). H. M. died in 2008. (For an engaging history of Case H. M., see Dittrich, 2016.)

H. M.'s most remarkable symptom was severe amnesia: he was unable to recall anything that had happened since his surgery in 1953. H. M. retained an above-average IQ score (118 on the Wechsler Adult Intelligence Scale; 100 is average), and he performed at normal on perceptual tests. His recall of events from his childhood and school days was intact. Socially, H. M. was well mannered, and he engaged in sophisticated conversations. He had, however, no recall for recent events. H. M. lacked any explicit memory.

In one study by Suzanne Corkin (2002), H. M. was given a tray of hospital food, which he ate. A few minutes later, he was given another tray. He did not recall having eaten the first meal and proceeded to eat another. A third tray was brought, and this time he ate only the dessert, explaining that he did not seem to be very hungry.

To understand the implications and severity of H. M.'s condition, one need only consider a few events in his postsurgical life. His father died, but H. M. continued to ask where his father was, only to experience anew the grief of learning that his father had passed away. (Eventually, H. M. stopped asking about his father, suggesting that some type of learning had taken place.)

FIGURE 14-7 **Extent of H. M.'s Surgery** H. M.'s right-hemisphere lesion is highlighted in the brain viewed ventrally. The lesion runs along the wall of the medial temporal lobe. The left side of the brain has been left intact to show the relative location of the medial temporal structures. Parts A, B, and C, based on MRI scans, depict a series of coronal sections of H. M.'s brain. Research from Corkin et al., 1997.

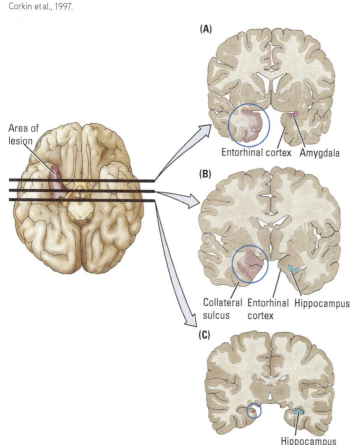

Area of lesion

(A) Entorhinal cortex   Amygdala

(B) Collateral sulcus   Entorhinal cortex   Hippocampus

(C) Hippocampus

⊚ CLINICAL FOCUS 14-2

Patient Boswell's Amnesia

At the age of 48, Boswell developed herpes simplex encephalitis, a brain infection. He had completed 13 years of schooling and had worked for nearly 30 years in newspaper advertising. By all accounts a normal, well-adjusted person, Boswell was successful in his profession.

Boswell recovered from the acute symptoms, including seizures and a 3-day coma. His intelligence postdisease was low average, probably due to neurological damage caused by the infection. Nonetheless, his speech and language remained typical in every respect, and he showed no perceptual or movement deficits. Boswell was left with a severe amnesic syndrome, however. If he heard a short paragraph and was asked to describe its main points, he routinely scored zero. He could only guess the day's date and was unable even to guess the year. When asked what city he was in, he simply guessed.

Boswell did know his place of birth, however, and could correctly recall his birth date about half the time. In sum, Boswell had severe amnesia for events both before and after his encephalitis. Like H. M., he showed implicit memory on tests such as the pursuit rotor task.

Antonio Damasio and his colleagues (1989) have investigated Boswell's amnesia extensively, and his brain pathology is now well documented. The critical damage, diagrammed in the adjoining illustration, is bilateral destruction of the medial temporal regions and a loss of the basal forebrain and the posterior part of the orbitofrontal cortex. In addition, Boswell lost the insular cortex from the lateral fissure (not visible in the illustration).

Boswell's sensory and motor cortices are intact, as are his basal ganglia, but his injury is more extensive than H. M.'s. Like H. M., he has no new memories. Unlike H. M., he also has a severe loss of access to

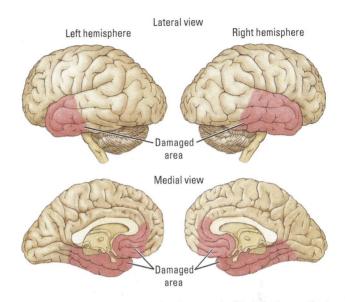

Since recovering from a herpes simplex encephalitis infection, patient Boswell has had great difficulty remembering events before and after his illness. Areas of damage in the medial temporal region, basal forebrain, and posterior orbitofrontal cortex are highlighted in red. Compare the figure above to Figure 14-6.

old information, probably due to his insular and prefrontal injuries. Nonetheless, again like H. M.'s, Boswell's procedural memory is intact, illustrating the dissociation between neural circuits underlying explicit and implicit forms of memory.

Similarly, in the hospital, he typically asked the nurses, with many apologies, to tell him where he was and how he had come to be there. He remarked on one occasion, "Every day is alone in itself, whatever enjoyment I've had and whatever sorrow I've had." He perceived his surroundings but could not comprehend his situation because he did not remember what had gone before.

Formal tests of H. M.'s memory showed, as you would expect, no recall for specific information just presented. In contrast, his implicit memory performance was nearly intact. He performed at normal on tests such as the incomplete figure and pursuit rotor tasks, illustrated in Figures 14-3 and 14-4, respectively. While his implicit memory system must have been intact, the systems crucial to explicit memory were missing or dysfunctional. Yet H. M. recognized faces, including his own, and he recognized that he aged. Face recognition depends on the parahippocampal gyrus, which was partly intact on H. M.'s right side. Clinical Focus 14-2, Patient Boswell's Amnesia, describes a case similar to H. M.'s.

Prosopagnosia, an inability to recognize faces, and other visual form agnosias are discussed in Chapter 9.

Disconnecting Implicit Memory

Among the reasons Lashley's research did not find a syndrome like that shown by H. M., the two most important are that Lashley did not damage the medial temporal regions. Nor did he use tests of explicit memory, so his animal subjects would not have shown H. M.'s deficits. Rather, Lashley's tests were mostly measures of implicit memory, with which H. M. had no problems.

The following case illustrates that Lashley probably should have been looking in the basal ganglia for the deficits that his implicit memory tests revealed. The basal ganglia

Clinical Focus features 5-2, 5-3, and 5-4 and Section 7-1 detail aspects of Parkinson disease. Section 16-3 reviews treatments.

play a central role in motor control. Among the compelling examples of implicit memory is motor learning—such as that related to driving and playing musical instruments or online games.

J. K. was above average in intelligence and worked as a petroleum engineer for 45 years. In his mid-seventies, he began to show symptoms of Parkinson disease, in which the projections from the dopaminergic cells of the brainstem to the basal ganglia die. At about age 78, J. K.'s memory difficulties started.

Curiously, his memory disturbance was related to tasks J. K. had performed his whole life. On one occasion, he stood at his bedroom door, frustrated by his inability to recall how to turn on the lights. "I must be crazy," he remarked. "I've done this all my life and now I can't remember how to do it!" On another occasion, he was seen trying to turn off the radio with the television remote control. This time he explained, "I don't recall how to turn off the radio so I thought I would try this thing!"

J. K.'s clear implicit memory deficit contrasts sharply with his awareness of daily events. He recalled explicit events as well as most men his age and spoke intelligently on issues of the day that he had just read about. Once when two of us visited him, one of us entered the room first, and he immediately asked where the other was, even though it had been 2 weeks since we told him that we would be coming to visit.

This intact long-term memory is vastly different from H. M.'s situation: he would not have remembered that anybody was coming even 5 minutes after being told. Because Parkinson disease primarily affects the basal ganglia, J. K.'s deficit in implicit memory was probably related to his basal ganglia dysfunction.

14-2 Review

Before you continue, check your understanding. Answers to Self-Test appear at the back of the book.

1. Based on the case of H. M., we can conclude that the structures involved in explicit memory include the _____, the _____, and adjacent cortex.

2. Implicit memory deficits in patients with Parkinson disease demonstrate that a major structure in implicit memory is the _____.

3. What is the main difference between the Lashley and Milner studies?

For additional study tools, visit 🌊 **LaunchPad** at launchpadworks.com

---

14-3

Neural Systems Underlying Explicit and Implicit Memories

Findings from laboratory studies, largely on rats and monkeys, have reproduced the symptoms of patients such as H. M. and J. K. by injuring the animals' medial temporal regions and basal ganglia, respectively. Other structures, most notably in the frontal and temporal lobes, also participate in certain types of explicit memory. We now consider the systems for explicit and implicit memory separately.

Neural Circuit for Explicit Memories

The hippocampus participates in species-specific behaviors, spatial navigation, and memory; it is also vulnerable to stress.

The dramatic amnesic syndrome discovered in H. M. in the 1950s led investigators to focus on the hippocampus, at the time regarded as a large brain structure, in search of a function. But H. M. had other damaged structures, too, and the initial focus on the hippocampus as the location of explicit memory processing turned out to be misguided.

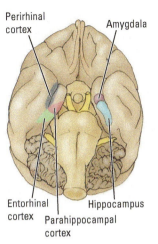

Perirhinal cortex

Amygdala

Entorhinal cortex

Hippocampus

Parahippocampal cortex

FIGURE 14-8 **Medial Temporal Structures** Ventral view of the rhesus macaque monkey brain. Left side: The medial temporal regions. Each plays a distinct role in processing sensory information for memory storage. Right side: The hippocampus and amygdala are not directly visible from the brain surface; they lie within the cortical regions illustrated on the left. All these structures are present on both sides of the brain.

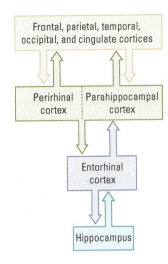

Frontal, parietal, temporal, occipital, and cingulate cortices

Perirhinal cortex | Parahippocampal cortex

Entorhinal cortex

Hippocampus

FIGURE 14-9 **Reciprocal Medial Temporal Connections** Flow of input from the sensory cortices: first to the parahippocampal and perirhinal regions, then to the entorhinal cortex, and finally to the hippocampus. The hippocampus feeds back to the medial temporal regions and then to the neocortical sensory regions.

After decades of anatomical and behavioral studies sorted out the complexities, consensus on the anatomy of explicit memory coalesced by the mid-1990s. The primary structures for explicit memory include the medial temporal region, the prefrontal cortex, and structures closely related to them.

The macaque monkey's medial temporal region shares many anatomical similarities with the same region in the human brain. In addition to the hippocampus and amygdala, three medial temporal areas, illustrated in **Figure 14-8**, take part in explicit memory: lying adjacent to the hippocampus are the **entorhinal cortex**, the **parahippocampal cortex**, and the **perirhinal cortex**. A sequential arrangement of two-way connections, charted in **Figure 14-9**, projects from the major cortical regions into the perirhinal and parahippocampal cortices, which in turn project to the entorhinal cortex and then to the hippocampus.

The prominent cortical input to the perirhinal region is from the visual ventral stream coursing through the temporal lobe. The perirhinal region is thus a prime candidate location for visual object memory. Similarly, the parahippocampal cortex receives strong input from parietal regions believed to take part in visuospatial processing and likely participates in **visuospatial memory**—using visual information to recall an object's location in space.

Because both the perirhinal and the parahippocampal regions project to the entorhinal cortex, this region probably participates in more integrative memory functions. The entorhinal cortex is in fact the first area to show cell death in Alzheimer disease, a neurocognitive disorder characterized by severe deficits in explicit memory (see Clinical Focus 14-3, Alzheimer Disease).

One implication of the anatomical organization shown in Figure 14-9 is that the parahippocampal and perirhinal cortices act together as a gateway into the entorhinal cortex and hippocampus. Although this is a widely accepted perspective, it ignores the extensive connections between the prefrontal cortex and the hippocampus (for an extensive discussion, see Murray et al., 2017). We return to the prefontal–hippocampal interaction in memory shortly.

The Hippocampus and Spatial Memory

We are left with a conundrum. If the hippocampus is not the key structure in explicit memory, even as it receives the entorhinal connections, what does it do? John O'Keefe and Lynn Nadel were the first to advance the idea, in 1978, that the hippocampus is probably engaged in visuospatial memory processes required for places, such as recalling an object's location.

Certainly both laboratory animals and human patients with selective hippocampal injury have severe deficits in various forms of spatial memory. Similarly, monkeys with

Consult sources published before 1995, and you may find explanations for memory far different from this chapter's (see Gazzaniga, 2000).

In Greek, *para* means "beside"; *rhino* means "nose." The perirhinal cortex lies beside the rhinal sulcus on the bottom of the brain.

Section 9-2 traces visual pathways in detail.

Section 16-3 elaborates on Alzheimer and other neurocognitive disorders and on prion theory.

entorhinal cortex Cortex located on the medial temporal lobe surface; provides a major route for neocortical input to the hippocampal formation; often degenerates in Alzheimer disease.

parahippocampal cortex Cortex located along the dorsal medial temporal lobe surface.

perirhinal cortex Cortex lying next to the rhinal fissure on the ventral surface of the brain.

visuospatial memory Use of visual information to recall an object's location in space.

⊙ CLINICAL FOCUS 14-3

Alzheimer Disease

In the 1880s, it was noted that the brain may undergo atrophy with aging, but the reason was not specifically described until the German physician Alois Alzheimer published a landmark study in 1906. Alzheimer described a set of behavioral symptoms and associated neuropathology in a 51-year-old woman who was demented. The cellular structure of her neocortex and allocortex showed various abnormalities.

An estimated 5.7 million people in the United States have Alzheimer disease, although the only certain diagnostic test remains postmortem examination of cerebral tissue. The disease progresses slowly, and many people with Alzheimer disease probably die of other causes before the cognitive symptoms incapacitate them.

We knew of a physics professor who continued to work until, when he was nearly 80, he died of a heart attack. Postmortem examination of his brain revealed significant Alzheimer pathology. His colleagues had attributed the professor's slipping memory to "old-timer's" disease.

The cause of Alzheimer disease remains unknown, although it has been variously attributed to genetic predisposition, abnormal levels of trace elements (e.g., aluminum), immune reactions, slow viruses, and *prions* (abnormal, infectious forms of proteins). Two principal neuronal changes take place in Alzheimer disease:

1. *Loss of cholinergic cells in the basal forebrain.* One treatment for Alzheimer disease, therefore, is medication that increases acetylcholine levels in the forebrain. An example is Exelon, which is the trade name for rivastigmine, a cholinergic agonist that appears to provide temporary relief from the progression of the disease and is available both orally and as a skin patch.

2. *Development of neuritic plaques in the cerebral cortex.* A **neuritic plaque** consists of a central core of homogeneous protein material (*amyloid*) surrounded by degenerative cellular fragments. The plaques are not distributed evenly throughout the cortex but are concentrated especially in temporal lobe areas related to memory. Neuritic plaques are often associated with another abnormality, neurofibrillary tangles, which are paired helical filaments found in both the cerebral cortex and the hippocampus. The prion paradigm holds that misfolded tau proteins, illustrated here, which have the ability to self-propagate, cause

many age-related neurodegenerative diseases (Walker & Jucker, 2015). Researchers are conducting clinical trials on new drugs that act either to find and neutralize misfolded proteins or as immunizing agents, to prevent protein misfolding (Wisniewski & Goni, 2015).

Cortical neurons begin to deteriorate as the cholinergic loss, plaques, and tangles develop. The first cells to die are in the entorhinal cortex (see Figure 14-8). Significant memory disturbance ensues.

A controversial idea emerging from stroke neurologists is that dementia may reflect a chronic cerebrovascular condition: marginal high blood pressure. Marginal elevations in blood pressure can lead to cerebral microbleeds, especially in white matter. Years or even decades of tiny bleeds would eventually lead to increasingly disturbed cognition. This may first appear as *mild cognitive impairment* (*MCI*) that slowly progresses with cumulative microbleeds (see Arvanitakis et al., 2018).

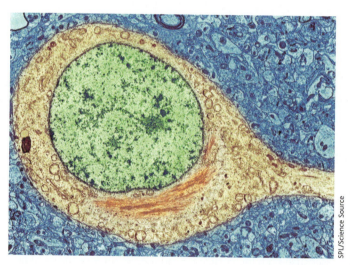

SPL/Science Source

The red area (bottom right) near the cell nucleus in this false-color brain cell from a person with Alzheimer disease represents a neurofibrillary tangle of misfolded tau proteins.

---

neuritic plaque Area of incomplete necrosis (dead tissue) consisting of a central protein core (amyloid) surrounded by degenerative cellular fragments; often seen in the cortex of people with neurocognitive disorders such as Alzheimer disease.

Section 1-4 explains the encephalization quotient, an index of ratios of brain to body size. EQs allow comparisons of the relative brain sizes of different species.

hippocampal lesions have difficulty learning the locations of objects (*visuospatial learning*), as can be demonstrated in tasks such as the ones illustrated in **Figure 14-10**.

Monkeys are trained to displace objects to obtain a food reward (Figure 14-10A), then given one of two tasks. In the *visual-recognition task* (Figure 14-10B), the animal displaces a sample object for the food reward. After a short delay, the animal is presented with two objects. One is novel. The task is to learn to displace the novel object for the food reward. This task tests explicit visual object memory. Monkeys with perirhinal lesions are impaired at the task.

In the *object-position task* (Figure 14-10C) the monkey is shown one object to be displaced for a food reward. Then the monkey is shown the same object along with a second, identical one. The task is to learn to displace the object that is in the same position as it was in the initial presentation. Monkeys with hippocampal lesions are selectively impaired at this task.

From these results, we would predict that a species with an especially good spatial memory should have bigger hippocampi than do species with a poorer spatial memory. David Sherry and his colleagues (1992) tested this hypothesis in birds.

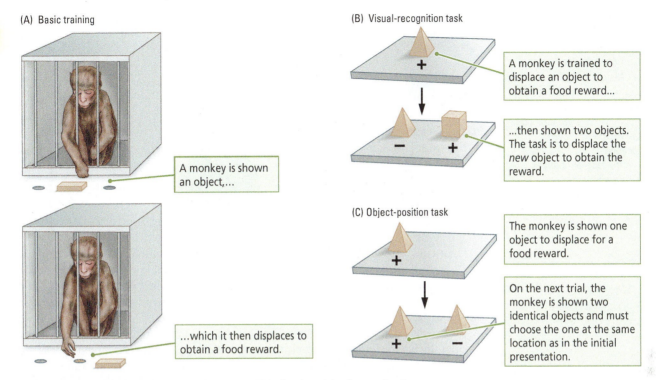

(A) Basic training

A monkey is shown an object,...

...which it then displaces to obtain a food reward.

(B) Visual-recognition task

A monkey is trained to displace an object to obtain a food reward...

...then shown two objects. The task is to displace the *new* object to obtain the reward.

(C) Object-position task

The monkey is shown one object to displace for a food reward.

On the next trial, the monkey is shown two identical objects and must choose the one at the same location as in the initial presentation.

FIGURE 14-10 **Two Memory Tasks for Monkeys (A)** In "basic training," a monkey learns to displace an object to obtain a food reward. In **(B)** and **(C)**, the plus and minus signs indicate whether the object (1) is or (2) is not associated with food.

Many species of birds are *cachers*: they harvest sunflower seeds and other favored foods and hide (cache) them to eat later. Some birds can find hundreds of items they have cached. To evaluate whether the hippocampus plays a role in this activity, Sherry and his coworkers measured hippocampal size in closely related bird species, only one of which is a food cacher. As shown in **Figure 14-11**, the hippocampal formation is larger in birds that cache food than in birds that do not. In fact, the hippocampi of food-storing birds are more than twice as large as expected for birds of their brain size and body weight.

Sherry found a similar relationship when he compared different species of food-storing rodents. Merriam's kangaroo rats, rodents that store food throughout their territory, have larger hippocampi than bannertail kangaroo rats, which store food only in their burrow. Hippocampal size, both in birds and in mammals, appears to be related to the cognitive demands of two highly spatial activities: foraging for food and storing food.

One prediction we might make based on the Sherry experiments is that people who have a job with high spatial demands have large hippocampi. Taxi drivers in London fit this category. Successful candidates for a cab driver's license in London must demonstrate that they know the location of every street in that huge and ancient city. Using MRI, Eleanor Maguire and her colleagues (2000) found the posterior region of the hippocampus in London taxi drivers to be significantly larger than the same region in the control participants. This finding presumably explains why a select few pass a spatial memory test that most of us would fail miserably.

Spatial Cells in the Hippocampal Formation

Given the role of the hippocampus in spatial behavior, we might predict that individual cells would code spatial information. They do. Three classes of spatially related cells have been identified in the rat and mouse hippocampus (**Figure 14-12**). Together they form an internal GPS, a neural global positioning system. That is, neurons vigorously fire when an animal is in a specific place in the environment. In 2014, John O'Keefe, Edvard Moser, and May-Britt Moser were awarded the Nobel Prize in Physiology or Medicine for this discovery.

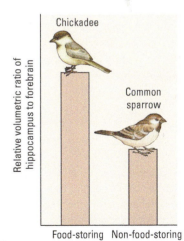

Chickadee

Common sparrow

Relative volumetric ratio of hippocampus to forebrain

Food-storing   Non-food-storing

FIGURE 14-11 **Inferring Spatial Memory** This graph relates hippocampal volume to forebrain volume in food-storing (left) and non-food-storing (right) families of songbirds. Birds that cache food, such as the black-capped chickadee, have hippocampi about twice as large as those of birds, such as the sparrow, that are not cachers. Data from Sherry et al., 1992.

FIGURE 14-12 **Classes of Spatially Related Cells in the Hippocampal Formation** At right in each part, X–Y coordinates indicate the directional selectivity of the cell recorded at left. **(A** and **B)** Place cells discharge when a rat is at a spatial location, regardless of its orientation. **(C)** Head direction cells discharge when the rat's head points in a given direction, regardless of its location. **(D)** Grid cells discharge at many locations, forming a virtual grid that is invariant in the face of changes in the rat's direction, movement, or speed.
Research from O'Keefe, 2006.

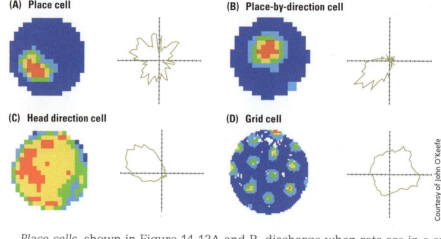

(A) Place cell

(B) Place-by-direction cell

(C) Head direction cell

(D) Grid cell

Courtesy of John O'Keefe

Place cells, shown in Figure 14-12A and B, discharge when rats are in a spatial location, regardless of its orientation. *Head direction cells* (Figure 14-12C) discharge whenever a rat's head points in a particular direction. *Grid cells* (Figure 14-12D) discharge at many locations, forming a virtual grid invariant to changes in the rat's direction, movement, or speed.

These cells are not localized to the hippocampus but are found within a network that includes the hippocampus as its central structure. Place cells and head direction cells are located in the hippocampus and closely related structures. Grid cells are found in the entorhinal cortex, a major afferent route into the hippocampus (see Figure 14-9). Taken together, we can envision the place cell system as indicating where things are in the world, the grid system indicating how big our present navigating environment is, and the head direction and grid systems telling us where we ourselves are in the environment.

Reciprocal Connections for Explicit Memory

The temporal lobe pathway of explicit memory is reciprocal: connections from the neocortex run to the entorhinal cortex and then back to the neocortex (see Figure 14-9). Reciprocal connections have two benefits:

1. Signals from the medial temporal regions back to the cortical sensory regions keep the sensory experience alive in the brain: the neural record of an experience outlasts the actual experience.

2. The pathway back to the neocortex keeps it apprised of information being processed in the medial temporal regions.

Although we have focused on the medial temporal regions, other structures are also important in explicit memory. People with frontal lobe injuries are not amnesic like H. M. or J. K., but they do have difficulties with memory for the temporal (time) order of events. Imagine being shown a series of photographs and asked to remember them. A few minutes later, you are asked whether you recognize two photographs and, if so, to indicate which one you saw first.

H. M. would not remember the photographs. People with frontal lobe injuries would recall having seen the photographs but would have difficulty recalling which one they had seen more recently. The frontal lobe's role in explicit memory clearly is subtler than that of the medial temporal lobe.

The basal ganglia systems that take part in implicit memory do not feed back to the cortex, which helps explain the unconscious nature of implicit memory.

THE FRONTAL LOBE AND SHORT-TERM MEMORY All sensory systems in the brain send information to the frontal lobe, as do the medial temporal regions. This information is not used for direct sensory analysis, so it must have another purpose. In general, the frontal lobe appears to participate in many forms of short-term memory.

Joaquin Fuster (e.g., Fuster et al., 2000) studied single-cell activity in the frontal lobe during short-term memory tasks. For instance, if monkeys are shown an object that they must remember for a short time before being allowed to make a response, neurons in the prefrontal cortex show sustained firing during the delay. Consider the tests illustrated in **Figure 14-13**:

- In the general design for each test, a monkey is shown a light (the cue); after a delay, it must make a response to get a reward.

- In the *delayed-response task*, the monkey is shown two lights in the choice test and must choose the one that is in the same location as the cue.

- In the *delayed-alternation task*, the monkey is again shown two lights in the choice tests but now must choose the light that is *not* in the same location as the cue.

- In the *delayed matching-to-sample task*, the monkey is shown, say, a red light, and then, after a delay, a red light and a green light. The task is to choose the red light, regardless of its new location.

Fuster found that in each task, certain cells in the prefrontal cortex fire throughout the delay. Animals that have not learned the task show no such cell activity. Curiously, if a trained animal makes an error, its cellular activity corresponds: the cells stop responding before the error occurs. They have "forgotten" the cue.

TRACING THE EXPLICIT MEMORY CIRCUIT People who have chronically abused alcohol can develop an explicit memory disturbance known as **Korsakoff syndrome**. In some cases, severe deficits in explicit memory extend to implicit memory as well. Korsakoff syndrome is caused by a thiamine (vitamin B₁) deficiency that kills cells in the medial part of the diencephalon—the between brain at the top of the brainstem—including the medial thalamus and mammillary bodies in the hypothalamus. In 80 percent of Korsakoff patients, the frontal lobes show atrophy (loss of cells). The memory disturbance is probably so severe because the damage includes not only forebrain but also brainstem structures (see Clinical Focus 14-4, Korsakoff Syndrome).

Mortimer Mishkin and his colleagues (Mishkin, 1982; Murray, 2000) proposed a neural circuit for explicit memory that incorporates the evidence from both humans and laboratory animals with injuries to the temporal and frontal lobes. **Figure 14-14** presents a modified version of the Mishkin model. Anatomically (Figure 14-14A), it includes not only the frontal and temporal lobes but also the medial thalamus, implicated in Korsakoff syndrome, and the basal forebrain–activating systems implicated in Alzheimer disease. Figure 14-14B charts the information flow:

- Sensory and motor neocortical areas send their connections to the medial temporal regions, which are in turn connected to the medial thalamus and prefrontal cortex.

- Basal forebrain structures are hypothesized to play a role in maintaining appropriate activity levels in other forebrain structures so that they can process information.

- The temporal lobe structures and prefrontal cortex are hypothesized to be central to long-term explicit memory formation.

- The prefrontal cortex is central to maintaining temporary (short-term) explicit memories as well as memory for the recency (chronological order) of explicit events.

Consolidation of Explicit Memories

Amnesia often appears to be time dependent. H. M. could not form new explicit memories but appeared to have had good recall of facts and events from periods long before his surgery, including his childhood. Such findings led to the idea that the medial temporal region could *not* be the ultimate storage site for long-term memories but that the neocortex was the more likely site (for a review, see Squire et al., 2015).

This idea led to the hypothesis that the hippocampus *consolidates* new memories, a process that makes them permanent. In **consolidation**, or stabilizing a memory trace after learning, memories move from the hippocampus to diffuse neocortical regions. Once they move, hippocampal involvement is no longer needed.

In the following tests, a monkey is shown a light, which is the cue, and then it makes a response after a delay.

Delayed-response task: The monkey must choose the light that is in the same location as the cue.

Delayed-alternation task: The monkey must choose the light that is not in the same location as the cue.

Delayed matching-to-sample task: The monkey must choose the light that is the same color as the cue.

FIGURE 14-13 **Testing Short-Term Memory** A monkey performing a short-term memory task responds by pressing the disc to get a fruit juice reward (top). The correct disc varies, depending on the task requirements (bottom). (For each task, an arrowhead shows the correct choice.) Information from Fuster, 1995.

The brain's activating systems, shown in Figure 14-14, are described in detail in Section 13-5.

Korsakoff syndrome Permanent loss of the ability to learn new information (anterograde amnesia) and to retrieve old information (retrograde amnesia) caused by diencephalic damage resulting from chronic alcoholism or malnutrition that produces a vitamin B₁ deficiency.

consolidation Process of stabilizing a memory trace after learning.

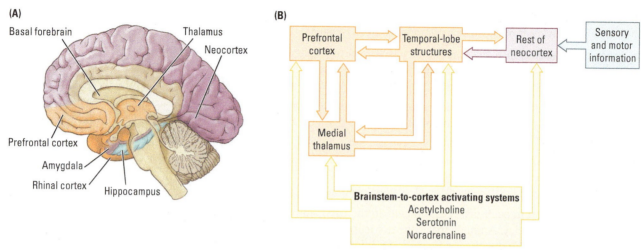

(A)

Basal forebrain

Thalamus

Neocortex

Prefrontal cortex

Amygdala

Rhinal cortex

Hippocampus

(B)

Prefrontal cortex

Temporal-lobe structures

Rest of neocortex

Sensory and motor information

Medial thalamus

Brainstem-to-cortex activating systems
Acetylcholine
Serotonin
Noradrenaline

FIGURE 14-14 **Reciprocal Neural Circuit Proposed for Explicit Memory (A)** General neuroanatomical areas controlling explicit memory. **(B)** The information flow begins on the right with inputs from the sensory and motor systems, which are not considered part of the explicit memory circuit.

It is not clear how memories are moved, however, or how long it takes. Robert Sutherland and his colleagues (2010) propose a model of consolidation called the *distributed reinstatement theory*. In their model, a learning episode rapidly produces a stored memory representation that is strong in the hippocampus but weak elsewhere. The memory is replayed on the time scale of hours or days after the learning, leading to enhanced representations outside the hippocampus. Each repetition of the learning—that is, each practice—progressively enhances the nonhippocampal memory representation. Then, if the hippocampus is extensively damaged, the memory remains.

Memory is not constant over time. When people get misleading information about events they have experienced, for example, their later recall of those events often is modified. Indeed, this process contributes to the notorious unreliability of eyewitness testimony. (Do you remember the "smashing" and "bumping" car collisions from Section 14-1?) The fact that memories appear to be changeable seems to fly in the face of the consolidation concept, which presumes that once consolidated, memories are fixed.

One solution to this conundrum suggests that whenever a memory is replayed in the mind, it is open to further consolidation, or **reconsolidation**, the process of restabilizing a memory trace after the memory is revisited. Interest in this idea has been intense, and although the final story is yet to be written, it appears that reconsolidation does occur, at least for some types of memories. One problem with reconsolidation, however, is that memories can be altered if the context of the reconsolidation is changed. The technique of always using the same space when studying probably decreases the likelihood of memory changes in reconsolidation.

One way to think of the process is to see memory consolidation as never-ending: new information is constantly being integrated into existing memory networks (for a review, see McKenzie & Eichenbaum, 2011). After all, we frequently recall memories, rehash them, and integrate them with new events. Our memories are not laid on a tabula rasa but must be interwoven into a lifetime of memories.

One implication of reconsolidation is that it ought to be possible to erase negative memories by using amnesic agents when the memory is revisited. This idea has important implications for reducing or eliminating the effects of strong emotional experiences, such as those seen in posttraumatic stress disorder (PTSD). One promising agent is the inert gas xenon, which has been used in humans as a fast-acting anesthetic and has been shown to erase memories during reconsolidation in a rat model of PTSD (Meloni et al., 2014).

Section 5-4 links sensitization to PTSD. Sections 6-5 and 12-6 document how stress fosters and prolongs its effects, and Research Focus 16-1 covers treatments.

Neural Circuit for Implicit Memories

Hypothesizing that the basal ganglia are central to implicit memory, Mishkin and his colleagues proposed a neural circuit for implicit memories (Mishkin, 1982; Mishkin

reconsolidation Process of restabilizing a memory trace after the memory is revisited.

Korsakoff Syndrome

Over the long term, alcoholism, especially when accompanied by malnutrition, obliterates memory. When 62-year-old Joe R. was hospitalized, his family complained that his memory had become abysmal. His intelligence was in the average range, and he had no obvious sensory or motor difficulties. Nevertheless, he could not say why he was in the hospital and usually stated that he was actually in a hotel.

When asked what he had done the previous night, Joe R. typically said that he "went to the Legion for a few beers with the boys." Although he had, in fact, been in the hospital, it was a sensible response because going to the Legion is what he had done on most nights in the preceding 30 years.

Joe R. was not certain what he had done for a living but believed he had been a butcher. In fact, he had been a truck driver for a local delivery firm. His son was a butcher, however, so once again his story related to something in his life.

Joe's memory for immediate events was little better. On one occasion, we asked him to remember having met us; then we left the room. On our return 2 or 3 minutes later, he had no recollection of ever having met us or of having taken psychological tests that we had administered.

Joe R. had Korsakoff syndrome. Sergei Korsakoff was a Russian physician who in the 1880s first called attention to a syndrome that accompanies chronic alcoholism. The most obvious symptom is severe memory loss, including amnesia for both information learned in the past (**retrograde amnesia**) and information learned since the onset of the memory disturbance (**anterograde amnesia**).

One unique characteristic of the amnesic syndrome in Korsakoff patients is that they tend to make up stories about past events rather than admit that they do not remember. These stories are generally plausible, like those Joe R. told, because they are based on actual experiences.

Curiously, Korsakoff patients have little insight into their memory disturbance and are generally indifferent to suggestions that they have a memory problem. Such patients are generally apathetic to what's going on around them, too. Joe R. was often seen watching television when the set was turned off.

The cause of Korsakoff syndrome is a thiamine (vitamin B₁) deficiency resulting from poor diet and prolonged intake of large quantities of alcohol. (In addition to a "few beers with the boys," Joe R. had a long history of drinking a 26-ounce bottle of rum every day.) The thiamine deficiency results in the death of cells in the midline diencephalon, including especially the medial regions of the thalamus and the mammillary bodies of the hypothalamus.

Most Korsakoff patients also show cortical atrophy, especially in the frontal lobe. With the appearance of Korsakoff symptoms, which can happen suddenly, prognosis is poor. Only about 20 percent of patients show much recovery after a year on a vitamin B₁–enriched diet. Joe R. had shown no recovery after several years and spent the final 15 years of his life in a hospital setting.

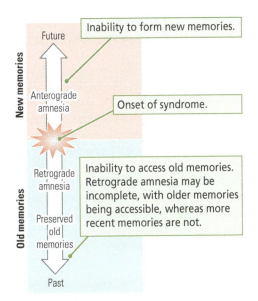

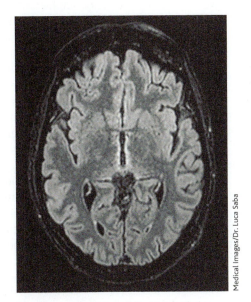

MRI scan from a Korsakoff patient showing degeneration along the middle region of the diencephalon (light area).

et al., 1997). As **Figure 14-15** shows, the basal ganglia receive input from the entire neocortex and send projections first to the ventral thalamus and then to the premotor cortex. The basal ganglia also receive widely and densely distributed projections from dopamine-producing cells in the substantia nigra. Dopamine appears necessary for basal ganglia circuits to function and may indirectly participate in implicit memory formation.

retrograde amnesia Inability to remember events that took place before the onset of amnesia.

anterograde amnesia Inability to remember events subsequent to a disturbance of the brain such as head trauma, electroconvulsive shock, or neurodegenerative disease.

(A)

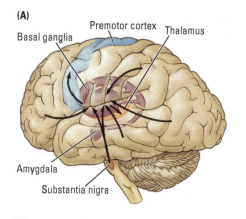

(B)

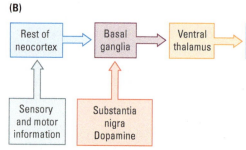

FIGURE 14-15 **Unidirectional Neural Circuit Proposed for Implicit Memory** **(A)** Anatomical areas controlling implicit memory. **(B)** Circuit diagram showing the one-way flow of implicit information, beginning with inputs from the sensory and motor systems not considered part of the memory circuit.

emotional memory Memory for the affective properties of stimuli or events.

Section 12-6 details the amygdala's influence on emotional behavior. Clinical Focus 12-5 describes panic and other anxiety disorders.

The ANS monitors and controls life support functions (Figure 2-32); the ENS controls the gut (Figure 2-33). Section 11-4 reviews the PAG's role in pain perception.

The connection from the cortex to the basal ganglia in the implicit memory system flows in only one direction. Most of the neocortex receives no direct information regarding activities in the basal ganglia. Mishkin believes that this unidirectional flow accounts for the unconscious nature of implicit memories. For memories to be conscious, the neocortical regions involved must receive feedback, as they do in the explicit memory system Mishkin and colleagues proposed (see Figure 14-14).

Mishkin's models show why people with basal ganglia dysfunction, as occurs in Parkinson disease, have implicit memory deficits. People with frontal or temporal lobe injuries, by contrast, have relatively good implicit memories, even as they may have profound explicit memory disturbances. Some people with Alzheimer disease can play games expertly, even with no recollection of having played them before. Daniel Schacter (1983) wrote of a golfer with Alzheimer disease whose medial temporal system was severely compromised by the disease but whose basal ganglia were unaffected. Despite this golfer's explicit knowledge impairment, as indexed by his inability to find balls he had shot or to remember how many strokes he had made on each hole, the man retained his ability to play the game.

Neural Circuit for Emotional Memories

Whether **emotional memory** for the affective properties of stimuli or events is implicit or explicit is not altogether clear. It could be both. Certainly, people can react with fear to specific stimuli they can identify, and we have seen that they can also fear situations for which they do not seem to have specific memories. Panic disorder is a common pathology of emotional memory. People show marked anxiety but cannot identify a specific cause. Emotional memory has a unique anatomical component: the amygdala, which mediates fear conditioning (see Experiment 14-1) and seems to evoke our feelings of anxiety toward stimuli that by themselves would not typically produce fear.

Emotional memory has been studied most thoroughly in fear conditioning by pairing unpleasant stimuli, such as foot shock, with a tone. Michael Davis (1992) and Joseph LeDoux (1995) used fear conditioning to demonstrate that the amygdala is critical to emotional memory. Damage to the amygdala abolishes emotional memory but has little effect on implicit or explicit memory.

The amygdala has close connections with medial temporal cortical structures as well as with the rest of the cortex. It also sends projections to brainstem structures that control autonomic responses such as blood pressure and heart rate; to the hypothalamus, which controls hormonal systems; to the periaqueductal gray matter (PAG), which affects pain perception; and to the enteric nervous system (ENS). The amygdala hooks in to the implicit memory system through its connections with the basal ganglia (**Figure 14-16**).

Fear is not the only aspect of emotional memory the amygdala codes, as a study of severely demented patients by Bob Sainsbury and Marjorie Coristine (1986) illustrates. The patients were believed to have severe cortical abnormalities but intact amygdalar functioning. The researchers first established that the patients' ability to recognize photographs of close relatives was severely impaired.

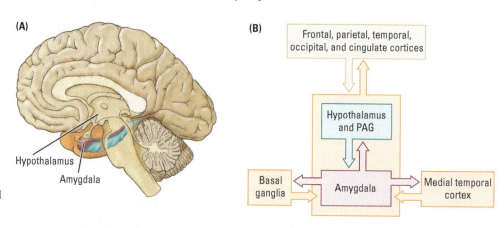

FIGURE 14-16 **Neural Circuit Proposed for Emotional Memory (A)** The amygdala is the key structure in emotional memory. **(B)** Circuit diagram showing information flow in emotional memory.

The patients were then shown four photographs, one depicting a relative (either a sibling or a child) who had visited in the past 2 weeks and the other three depicting complete strangers. The task was to identify the person whom they liked better than the other three. Although the subjects were unaware that they knew anyone depicted in the photographs, they consistently preferred pictures of their relatives. This result suggests that although the explicit, and probably the implicit, memory of the relative was gone, each patient's emotional memory guided his or her preference.

We tend to remember emotionally arousing experiences vividly, a fact confirmed by findings from both animal and human studies. James McGaugh (2004) concluded that emotionally significant experiences, pleasant and unpleasant, must activate hormonal and brain systems that act to stamp in these vivid memories.

McGaugh noted that many neural systems probably take part, but the basolateral part of the amygdala is critical. The general idea is that emotionally driven hormonal and neurochemical activating systems (probably cholinergic and noradrenergic) stimulate the amygdala. The amygdala in turn modulates the laying down of emotional memory circuits in the rest of the brain, especially in the medial temporal and prefrontal regions and in the basal ganglia. We would not expect people with amygdala damage to have vivid memory for emotion-laden events, and they do not (Cahill et al., 1995).

Figure 5-18 traces neural activating system connections. Section 6-5 explains how hormones work.

Evolution of Memory Systems

Elizabeth Murray, Steven Wise, and Kim Graham (2017) published a proposal on the organization of memory systems that differs dramatically from those described above. They suggest that several memory systems arose during evolution to exploit specific opportunities at particular times and places; they contend that this exploitation led to radical changes in cerebral anatomy and function. They further argue that virtually all cortical areas are involved in memory, with different regions using specialized neural networks. This idea is not radically different from what we discussed above (see Figure 14-8, for example), but it does include more regions than are usually suggested. Murray and colleagues' more radical proposal is that with the large expansion of the human brain, and especially prefrontal regions and the related connections with the hippocampal region, the human explicit memory system not only encodes experiences but embeds them in time and in our concept of self. Thus, we perceive ourselves to be participating in an ongoing chain of events, and when we retrieve memories, we experience them from the perspective of a participant or an observer. The authors argue that this way of experiencing and encoding memory is *true explicit memory* and is unique to humans.

Note that Figures 14-14 and 14-15 include boxes for the "Rest of neocortex" in the proposed neural circuit for explicit and implicit memory.

The result of this significant change in cerebral anatomy is the emergence of the many unique cognitive abilities that humans possess, including language. A full accounting of this proposal is beyond the scope of this chapter, but one can predict that over the next decade, it will generate considerable academic discussion and research. The authors foresee this in their statement: "Readers who view the cortex of other mammals as replicas in miniature or amalgams of primate areas will find our principal thesis unpalatable, to say the least."

14-3 Review

Before you continue, check your understanding. Answers to Self-Test appear at the back of the book.

1. The two key structures for explicit memory are the _____ and the _____.

2. A system consisting of the basal ganglia and neocortex forms the neural basis of the _____ memory system.

3. The _____ and associated structures form the neural basis for emotional memory.

4. The progressive stabilization of memories is known as _____.

5. Why do we remember emotionally arousing experiences so vividly?

For additional study tools, visit **LaunchPad** at launchpadworks.com

14-4

Structural Basis of Brain Plasticity

We have encountered three categories of memory—explicit, implicit, and emotional—and their underlying brain circuits. Next, we consider how the neurons in these circuits change to allow us to consolidate and store memories. The consensus among neuroscientists is that the changes take place at the synapse, in part simply because that is where neurons influence one another. This idea dates to 1928, when the Spanish anatomist Santiago Ramón y Cajal suggested that learning might produce prolonged morphological (structural) changes in the efficiency of synapses activated in the learning process. Cajal's idea turned out to be easier to propose than to study.

Researchers still encounter a major challenge as they investigate Cajal's suggestion because it is not clear where in the brain to look for synaptic changes that might correlate with memory for a specific stimulus. The task is formidable. Imagine trying to find the exact location of the neurons responsible for storing your grandmother's name. You would face a similar challenge in trying to pinpoint the neurons responsible for the memory of an object in a monkey's brain as the monkey performs the visual recognition task illustrated in Figure 14-10B.

One approach to finding memory's neuronal correlates aims first to determine that synaptic changes do correlate with memory in the mammalian brain; second, to localize the synaptic changes to specific neural pathways; and third, to analyze the synaptic changes themselves. This section reviews studies that begin to show how experience correlates with synaptic changes related to memory. We first consider a strategy based on neuronal physiology and experience. We then look at gross neural changes that correlate with select experiences. These range from potentially good—living in enriched environments and learning specific tasks—to probably bad—chronic administration of trophic factors, hormones, and addictive drugs. These diverse experiences modify the brain's general synaptic organization in a strikingly similar manner.

Long-Term Potentiation

Findings from studies of behavioral *habituation* (a weakened response to a stimulus) and *sensitization* (a strengthened response) in the sea slug *Aplysia* show that physical changes in synapses do underlie learning. Adaptive synapses in the mammalian brain participate in **associative learning**, a response elicited by linking unrelated stimuli together—by learning that A goes with B.

Learned associations are a common type of explicit memory; examples include associating a face with a person, an odor with a food, or a sound with a musical instrument. The phenomenon underlying associative learning entails an enduring neural change in a postsynaptic cell after an excitatory signal, or EPSP, from the presynaptic cell crosses the synaptic gap.

Both the relatively simple circuitry of the hippocampus and the ease of recording postsynaptic potentials there make this brain structure ideal for studying the neural basis of associative learning. In 1973, Timothy Bliss and Terje Lømø demonstrated that repeated electrical stimulation of the pathway entering the hippocampus progressively increases EPSP size as recorded from hippocampal cells. The enhancement in the size of these graded field potentials lasts several hours to weeks or even longer. Bliss and Lømø called it **long-term potentiation (LTP)**, a long-lasting increase in synaptic effectiveness after high-frequency stimulation.

Figure 14-17A illustrates the experimental procedure for obtaining LTP. The presynaptic neuron is stimulated electrically, and the electrical activity the stimulation produces is recorded from the postsynaptic neuron. The readout in Figure 14-17A shows the EPSP produced by a single pulse of electrical stimulation. In a typical experiment, many test stimuli are given to estimate the size of the induced EPSP. Then a strong burst of stimulation, consisting of a few hundred pulses of electrical current per second, is administered (Figure 14-17B). The test pulse is then given again. The increased amplitude of the EPSP endures for as long as 90 minutes after the high-frequency burst: LTP has taken place.

Cajal's neuron theory—that the neuron is the nervous system's functional unit—is now universally accepted, including the idea that these discrete cells' interactions enable behavior. Cajal's work is discussed in detail in Section 3-1.

Experiment 5-2 explains habituation at the neuronal level; Experiment 5-3 describes sensitization.

Postsynaptic potentials increase (excitatory/ EPSP) or decrease (inhibitory/IPSP) the probability that an action potential will occur. See Experiment 4-1.

---

associative learning Linkage of two or more unrelated stimuli to elicit a behavioral response.

long-term potentiation (LTP) Long-lasting increase in synaptic effectiveness after high-frequency stimulation.

(A)

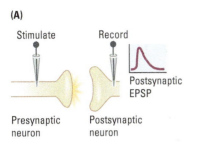

Stimulate   Record

Postsynaptic EPSP

Presynaptic neuron   Postsynaptic neuron

(B)

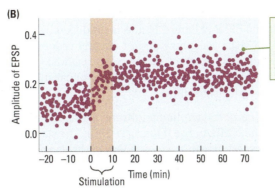

Each dot represents EPSP amplitude in response to one weak test stimulation.

FIGURE 14-17 **Recording Long-Term Potentiation (A)** Experimenters stimulate the presynaptic neuron with a test pulse and record the EPSP from the postsynaptic neuron. **(B)** After an intense stimulation period, the amplitude of the EPSP produced by the test pulse increases: LTP has taken place.

For the EPSP to increase in size, more neurotransmitter must be released from the presynaptic membrane, or the postsynaptic membrane must become more sensitive to the same amount of transmitter, or both changes must take place.

Increased transmitter release can result from enhanced calcium influx into the presynaptic terminal, which begins a chain of events leading to enhanced glutamate release. It can also be increased by the production of diffusible postsynaptic retrograde messengers that modify transmitter release. The precise mechanism of the retrograde messengering is not clear, but gases such as carbon monoxide and nitric oxide have been proposed. In addition, both ionotropic and metabotropic receptors at the presynaptic terminals can modulate LTP.

The discovery of LTP led to a revolution in thinking about how memories are stored. As investigators varied the stimulation that produced LTP, they discovered its opposite. Instead of using high-frequency stimulation (e.g., 100 Hz), they used low-frequency stimulation (e.g., 5 Hz) and recorded a *decrease* in EPSP size, termed **long-term depression (LTD)**. If LTP is a mechanism for creating memories, perhaps LTD is a mechanism for clearing out old memories.

If LTP and LTD form a basis for understanding synaptic changes underlying memory, two predictions follow. First, when animals learn problems, we should see enhanced LTP in the recruited pathways. Second, LTP should produce enduring changes in synaptic morphology that resemble those seen in memory. Both predictions appear to be true.

The original studies of LTP concentrated on excitatory glutamate synapses. Glutamate is released from the presynaptic neuron and acts on two different types of receptors on the postsynaptic membrane, the NMDA and AMPA receptors, as shown in **Figure 14-18A**. AMPA receptors ordinarily mediate responses produced when glutamate is released from a presynaptic membrane. They allow sodium ions (Na⁺) to

Deep brain stimulation used for severely depressed subjects induces a change, similar to LTP, which appears to increase brain plasticity; see Section 16-3.

long-term depression (LTD) Long-lasting decrease in synaptic effectiveness after low-frequency electrical stimulation.

FIGURE 14-18 **Lasting Effects of Glutamate** Enhanced glutamate prompts a neurochemical cascade that underlies synaptic change and LTP.

(A) Weak electrical stimulation

Because the NMDA receptor pore is blocked by a magnesium ion, release of glutamate by a weak electrical stimulation activates only the AMPA receptor.

(B) Strong electrical stimulation (depolarizing EPSP)

A strong electrical stimulation can depolarize the postsynaptic membrane sufficiently that the magnesium ion is removed from the NMDA receptor pore.

(C) Weak electrical stimulation

Now glutamate, released by weak stimulation, can activate the NMDA receptor to allow Ca²⁺ influx, which, through a second messenger, increases the function or number of AMPA receptors or both.

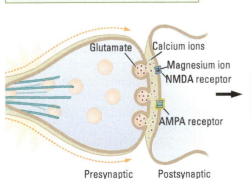

Glutamate   Calcium ions

Magnesium ion
NMDA receptor

AMPA receptor

Presynaptic neuron   Postsynaptic neuron

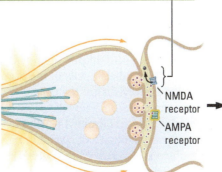

NMDA receptor

AMPA receptor

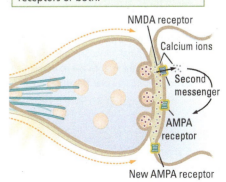

NMDA receptor

Calcium ions

Second messenger

AMPA receptor

New AMPA receptor

NMDA is shorthand for N-methyl-D-aspartate; AMPA stands for alpha-amino-3-hydroxy-5-methylisoxazole-4-propionic acid.

enter, depolarizing and thus exciting the postsynaptic membrane. The initial amplitude of the EPSP in Figure 14-17A is produced by this AMPA receptor action.

NMDA receptors do not usually respond to glutamate because their pores are blocked by magnesium ions (Mg^{2+}). NMDA receptors are doubly gated ion channels that can open to allow the passage of calcium ions if two events take place at approximately the same time:

1. The postsynaptic membrane is depolarized, displacing the magnesium ion from the NMDA pore (Figure 14-18B). The strong electrical stimulation delivered by the experimenter serves as a way of displacing magnesium.

2. NMDA receptors are activated by glutamate from the presynaptic membrane (Figure 14-18C).

With the doubly gated NMDA channels open, calcium ions enter the postsynaptic neuron and act through second messengers to initiate the cascade of events associated with LTP. These events include increased responsiveness of AMPA receptors to glutamate, formation of new AMPA receptors, and even retrograde messages to the presynaptic terminal to enhance glutamate release. One or more of these actions produces the final EPSP amplitude in Figure 14-17B.

Although the studies generated by the Bliss and Lømø discoveries have focused on excitatory synapses, experiments on inhibitory GABA interneurons demonstrate phenomena similar to LTP and LTD, labeled *LTPi* and *LTDi*. This discovery was a surprise. At the time, it was generally believed that inhibitory neurons were not plastic, but they definitely are. It appears that plasticity of GABAergic (inhibitory) synapses plays some fundamental role in modulating networks of excitatory neurons.

Studying LTP mechanisms highlights neuroscientists' uncertainty over where plastic changes are located. Our discussion emphasizes postsynaptic changes, but a strong case can be made that key presynaptic changes are at work, too (e.g., MacDougall & Fine, 2014). In general, plasticity likely requires change on both sides of the synapse. The presynaptic side, by virtue of being activated first, may prove key in the early phases of synaptic changes.

Measuring Synaptic Change

In principle, experience could change the brain in either of two ways: by modifying existing circuitry or by creating novel circuitry. In actuality, the plastic brain uses both strategies.

Modifying Existing Circuits

The simplest way to find synaptic change is to look for gross changes in the morphology of dendrites. Essentially, dendritic spines are extensions of the neuron membrane that allow more space for synapses. Cells that have few or no dendrites have limited space for inputs, whereas cells with complex dendritic protrusions may have space for tens of thousands of inputs.

So more dendrites means more connections. Change in dendritic structure, therefore, implies change in synaptic organization. In complex neurons, such as pyramidal cells, 95 percent of synapses are on the dendrites. Measuring the extent of dendritic changes allows us to infer synaptic change.

Dendritic shape is highly changeable. Dale Purves and his colleagues (Purves & Voyvodic, 1987) labeled cells in the dorsal root ganglia of living mice with a dye that allowed them to visualize the cells' dendrites. When they examined the same cells at intervals ranging from a few days to weeks, they identified obvious qualitative changes in dendritic extent (**Figure 14-19**). We can assume that new dendritic branches have new synapses and that lost branches mean lost synapses.

An obvious lesson from the Purves studies is that neuronal morphology is not static: neurons change their structure in response to changing experiences. As they search for neural correlates of memory, researchers can take advantage of this changeability

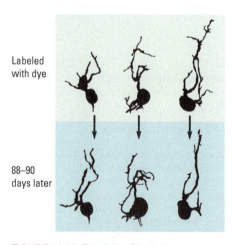

Labeled with dye

88–90 days later

FIGURE 14-19 **Dendritic Plasticity** Reconstructions of parts of the dendrites from three mouse spinal ganglion cells after 3 months evince changes in both the extension and the retraction of particular dendritic branches. Information from Purves & Voyvodic, 1987.

Figure 3-5 shows how dendrites branch from three types of neurons.

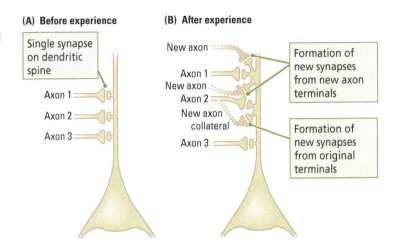

(A) Before experience

Single synapse on dendritic spine

Axon 1
Axon 2
Axon 3

(B) After experience

New axon
Axon 1
New axon
Axon 2
New axon collateral
Axon 3

Formation of new synapses from new axon terminals

Formation of new synapses from original terminals

(C) Various observed shapes of new dendritic spines

FIGURE 14-20 **Effects of Experience on Dendrites (A)** Three inputs to a pyramidal cell dendrite. Each axon forms a synapse with a different dendritic spine. **(B)** In forming multiple spine heads, either the original axons can divide and innervate two spine heads, or new axons or axon collaterals (dotted outlines) can innervate the new spine heads. **(C)** Single dendritic spines may sprout multiple synapses.

by studying variations in dendritic morphology that are correlated with specific experiences, such as learning some task.

What do changes in dendritic morphology reveal? Let us consider a given neuron that generates more synaptic space. The new synapses can provide either additional contacts between neurons that were already connected with that neuron or contacts between neurons not formerly connected. **Figure 14-20** illustrates examples of these distinct synapse types.

New synapses can result either from the growth of new axon terminals or from the formation of synapses along axons as they pass by dendrites (Figure 14-20A and B). In both cases, new synapses correspond to changes in local or regional circuitry rather than to the development of new connections between distant parts of the brain. Forming new connections between widely separated brain regions would be difficult in a fully grown brain: the dense plexus of cells, fibers, and blood vessels blocks the way.

Research Focus 5-5 diagrams how dendritic spines form and explains why they provide the structural basis for behavior.

Creating Novel Circuits

Only 30 years ago, the general assumption was that the mammalian brain does not generate new neurons in adulthood. The unexpected discovery in the 1970s that the brains of songbirds such as canaries grow new neurons to produce songs in the mating season led researchers to reconsider this assumption. They found that the adult mammalian brain is also capable of generating new neurons.

This discovery emerged from directly injecting animals with a compound—bromodeoxyuridine (BrdU)—that is taken up by cells when they divide to produce new cells, including neurons. When the compound is injected into adult rats, dividing cells incorporate it into their DNA. In later analysis, a specific stain can identify the new neurons.

The BrdU technique yielded considerable evidence that the mammalian brain, including the primate brain, can generate neurons destined for the olfactory bulb, the hippocampal formation, and possibly even the frontal and temporal lobe neocortex (Eriksson et al., 1998; Gould et al., 1999). The reason is not yet clear, but adult neurogenesis may enhance brain plasticity, particularly in processes underlying learning and memory. Elizabeth Gould and her colleagues (1999) showed, for example, that generation of new neurons in the hippocampus is enhanced when animals learn explicit memory tasks.

Experience appears to increase the generation of these new neurons. A fascinating demonstration of experience driving neurogenesis comes from a study by Katherine Woollett and Eleanor Maguire (2011). We noted in Section 14-3 that London taxi drivers, who must learn the locations of and pass an exam on central London's roughly 25,000 irregular streets, have larger-than-normal volume in their hippocampal posterior region. The investigators wanted to determine whether the increase resulted from taking a 4-year course to pass the exam or was already present when the candidate drivers started the course.

Section 10-5 discusses the neurobiology of birdsong.

Experiment 7-1 confirms the hypothesis that hippocampal neurons contribute to memory formation.

Woollett and Maguire recorded structural MRIs from the would-be taxi drivers before and after training and then compared the trainees who qualified ($n = 39$) with those who failed ($n = 20$). The MRIs showed that hippocampal volume increased in the qualifiers. Those who failed showed no changes. Woollett and Maguire later showed that when taxi drivers retired, the hippocampal volume decreased, indicating that the changes were related to use.

Enriched Experience and Plasticity

Section 8-4 details Hebb's first enrichment exercise—and his wife's reaction.

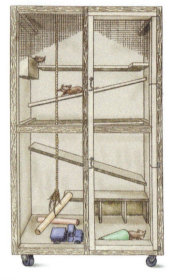

FIGURE 14-21 **Enriched Enclosure for Rats**

One way to stimulate animals' brains is to house the animals in environments that provide sensory or motor experience. Donald Hebb (1947, 1949) took laboratory rats home and gave them the run of his kitchen. After an interval, Hebb compared these "enriched" rats with a group that had remained caged in his laboratory at McGill University: he trained both groups to solve various mazes. The enriched animals performed better, and Hebb concluded that one effect of the enriched experience is to enhance later learning. This important conclusion laid the foundation for the U.S. Head Start programs, which provide healthy, enriched academic experiences for preschool-aged children living in under-resourced environments.

Subsequent investigators have opted for a more constrained enriched enclosure. For example, in our own studies, we place groups of about six rats in enclosures (see **Figure 14-21**). The enclosures give animals a rich social experience as well as extensive sensory and motor experience. The most obvious consequence is increased brain weight—on the order of 10 percent relative to cage-reared animals—even though the "enriched" rats typically weigh less, in part because they get more exercise.

The key question is What is responsible for the increased brain weight? A comprehensive series of studies by Anita Sirevaag and William Greenough (1988) used light- and electron-microscopic techniques to analyze 36 aspects of cortical synaptic, cellular, and vascular morphology in rats raised either in a cage or in a complex environment. The simple conclusion: in response to differential experiences, a coordinated change occurs not only in dendritic extent but also in glial, vascular, and metabolic processes (**Figure 14-22**).

Animals with enriched experience have more synapses per neuron, as well as more astrocytes, more blood capillaries, and higher mitochondrial volumes. Clearly, when the brain changes in response to experience, the expected neural changes take place, and adjustments in the metabolic requirements of the now larger neurons take place as well.

Gerd Kempermann and his colleagues (1998) sought to determine whether experience actually alters the number of neurons in the brain. To test this idea, they compared neuronal generation in the hippocampi of mice housed in a complex environment with that of mice reared in a laboratory cage. They located the number of new neurons by injecting the animals with BrdU several times while they were living in complex housing.

The new neurons generated in the brain during the experiment incorporated the BrdU. When the researchers later looked at the hippocampi, they found more new neurons in the complex-housed rats than in the caged rats. Although the investigators did not look in other parts of the brain, such as the olfactory bulb, we can reasonably expect that similar changes took place in other neural structures. This result is exciting because it implies that experience not only can alter existing circuitry but also can influence neurogenesis and thus new circuitry.

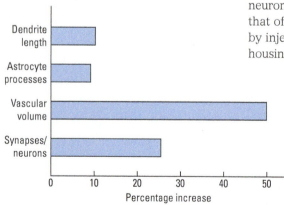

FIGURE 14-22 **Consequences of Enrichment** Cortical changes that occur in response to experience are found not only in neurons but also in astrocytes and vasculature. Data from Turner & Greenough, 1985; Sirevaag & Greenough, 1987; and Kolb et al., 2003.

Sensory or Motor Training and Plasticity

Studies showing neuronal change in animals housed in a complex environment demonstrate that large areas of the brain can change with such experience. This finding leads us to ask whether specific experiences produce synaptic changes in localized cerebral regions. One way to approach this question is to give animals specific experiences and then see how their brains have changed. Another way is to look at the brains of people who have had a lifetime of some particular experience. We consider each research strategy separately.

Manipulating Experience Experimentally

Fen-Lei Chang and William Greenough (1982) conducted perhaps the most convincing manipulated-experience study. They took advantage of the fact that the laboratory rat's visual pathways are about 90 percent crossed. That is, about 90 percent of connections from the left eye to the cortex project through the right thalamus to the right hemisphere and vice versa for the right eye.

Chang and Greenough placed a patch over one eye of each rat and then trained the animals in a maze. The visual cortex of only one eye received input about the maze, but their two hemispheres' auditory, olfactory, tactile, and motor regions were equally active as the animals explored. A comparison of the neurons in each hemisphere revealed that those in the visual cortex of the trained hemisphere had more extensive dendrites. Because the hemispheres did not differ in other respects, the researchers concluded that some feature associated with encoding, processing, or storage of visual input from training was responsible for forming new synapses.

Randy Nudo and his colleagues (1997) conducted complementary studies, mapping the motor cortex of monkeys. They noted striking individual differences in topography. The investigators speculated that individual variability might be due to each monkey's experiences up to the time at which the cortical map was derived. To test this idea directly, Nudo and colleagues trained two groups of squirrel monkeys to retrieve banana-flavored food pellets from either a small food well or a large one. The monkeys from the first group were able to insert their entire hand into the large well, but the monkeys from the second group were able to fit only one or two fingers into the small well, as illustrated in the Procedures section of **Experiment 14-2**.

Researchers allowed the monkeys from each group to make the same number of finger flexions to retrieve the food. They charted each group's success over a 2-week period (after about 12,000 flexions total). The monkeys trained on the small well improved with practice, making fewer finger flexions per food retrieval as training proceeded. Maps of forelimb movements, shown in the Results section, were produced by microelectrode stimulation of the cortex. The maps show systematic changes in the animals trained on the small but not on the large well. Presumably, these changes result from the more demanding motor requirements of the small-well condition. The results demonstrate that learning new motor skills, not simply repetitive motor use, shapes the functional topography of the motor cortex.

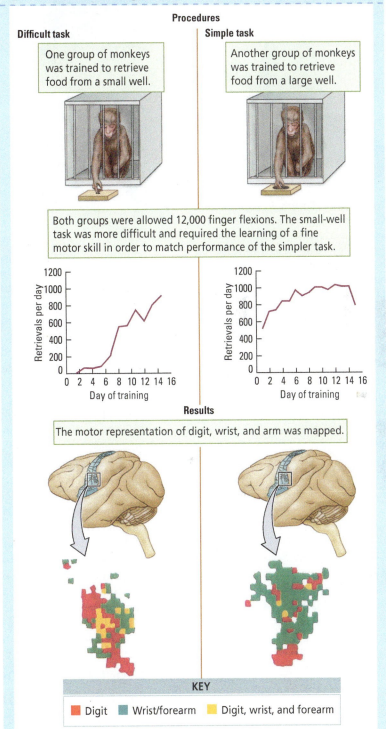

EXPERIMENT 14-2

Question: Does the learning of a fine motor skill alter the cortical motor map?

Procedures

Difficult task

One group of monkeys was trained to retrieve food from a small well.

Simple task

Another group of monkeys was trained to retrieve food from a large well.

Both groups were allowed 12,000 finger flexions. The small-well task was more difficult and required the learning of a fine motor skill in order to match performance of the simpler task.

Results

The motor representation of digit, wrist, and arm was mapped.

KEY

■ Digit   ■ Wrist/forearm   ■ Digit, wrist, and forearm

Conclusion: The digit representation in the brain of the animal with the more difficult task is larger, corresponding to the neuronal changes necessary for the acquired skill.

Information from Nudo et al., 1997.

In humans, only about half the optic fibers cross. Figure 9-10 diagrams the pathways.

(A)

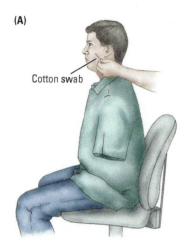

Cotton swab

(B)

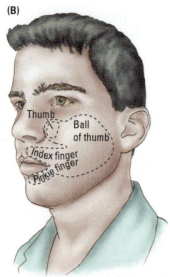

Thumb

Ball of thumb

Index finger

Pinkie finger

FIGURE 14-23 **Cortical Reorganization**
When a hand amputee's face is stroked
lightly with a cotton swab **(A)**, the person
experiences the stroke as a light touch on
the missing hand **(B)** as well as a touch to
the face. The deafferented cortex forms a
representation of the amputated hand on
the face. As in the normal somatosensory
homunculus, the thumb is disproportionately
large. Information from Ramachandran, 1993.

Research Focus 11-5 recounts
Ramachandran's therapy for minimizing
phantom limb pain.

Sections 10-4 and 15-3 discuss the benefits
of music for the brain. Section 16-1 describes
music as therapy for neurological disorders,
including Parkinson disease.

Most studies demonstrating plasticity in the motor cortex have been performed with laboratory animals whose
cortex was mapped by microelectrode stimulation. Today,
imaging techniques such as transcranial magnetic stimulation (TMS) and functional magnetic resonance imaging
(fMRI) make it possible to show parallel results in humans
who have special motor skills. For example, right-handed
musicians who play stringed instruments show an
increased cortical representation of the fingers of the left
hand and Braille readers an increased cortical representation of the reading finger.

Thus, the functional organization of the motor cortex is
altered by skilled use in humans. It can also be altered by
chronic injury in humans and laboratory animals. Jon Kaas
(2000) showed that when the sensory nerves in one limb
are severed in monkeys, large-scale changes in somatosensory maps ensue. In particular, in the absence of input,
the relevant part of the cortex no longer responds to limb
stimulation, which is not surprising. But this cortex does not remain inactive. Rather,
the deafferented cortex begins to respond to input from other body parts. The region
that formerly responded to hand stimulation now responds to stimulation on the face, a
cortical area normally adjacent to the hand area.

Similar results can be found in the cortical maps of people who have had a limb
amputated. For example, Vilayanur Ramachandran (1993) found that when a hand
amputee's face is brushed lightly with a cotton swab, the person has a sensation of
the amputated hand being touched. **Figure 14-23** illustrates the rough map of the
hand that Ramachandran was actually able to chart on the face. The likely explanation
is that the face area in the motor cortex has expanded to occupy the deafferented limb
cortex, but the brain circuitry still responds to the cortical activity as representing input
from the limb. This response may explain the phantom limb pain often experienced by
amputees.

The idea that experience can alter cortical maps can be demonstrated with other
experiences. For instance, if animals are trained to make certain digit movements over
and over again, the cortical representation of those digits expands at the expense of
the remaining motor areas. Similarly, if animals are trained extensively to discriminate
among different sensory stimuli such as tones, the auditory cortical areas responding
to those stimuli increase in size.

As described in Research Focus 14-5, Movement, Learning, and Neuroplasticity, one
effect of musical training is to alter the motor representations of the digits used to play
different instruments. We can speculate that musical training probably alters the auditory representations of specific sound frequencies as well. Both changes are essentially
forms of memory, and the underlying synaptic changes likely take place on the appropriate sensory or motor cortical maps.

Experience-Dependent Change
in the Human Brain

According to Ramachandran's amputee study, the human brain appears to change with
altered experience. But this study did not examine neuronal change directly; it inferred
neuronal change from behavior. The only way to examine synaptic change directly is
to look directly at brain tissue. In living humans, this is not an option, but the brains of
people who have died of something other than neurological causes can be examined so
that the structure of their cortical neurons can be related to their experiences.

One way to approach this idea is to look for a relationship between neuronal structure and education. Arnold Scheibel and his colleagues conducted many such studies

Movement, Learning, and Neuroplasticity

Many lines of research show that practicing a motor skill—playing a musical instrument, for instance—induces changes in the cortical somatosensory and motor maps. The mental maps generally become larger, at least for the finger and hand representations.

Presumably, musical skill improves with practice, but are other abilities enhanced, too? Patrick Ragert and colleagues (2003) showed that professional pianists have not only better motor skills in their fingers but enhanced somatosensory perception as well.

When the researchers measured the ability to detect subtle sensory stimulation of the fingertips, they found that the pianists were more sensitive than controls. They also found that the enhanced tactile sensitivity was related to the hours per day that the musicians spent practicing.

The investigators then asked whether the enhanced perceptual ability precluded further improvement in the musicians. Surprisingly, when both the musicians and controls were given a 3-hour training session designed to improve tactile sensitivity, the musicians showed more improvement than did the controls. Again, the extent of improvement correlated with daily practice time.

This result implies that well-practiced musicians not only learn to play music but also develop a greater capacity for learning. Rather than use up all the available synapses, they gain the capacity to make even more.

Not all motor learning is good, however. Many musicians develop *focal hand dystonia*—abnormal finger and hand positions, cramps, and difficulty

emreogan/Getty Images

coordinating hand and finger movements. Dystonia can be so disabling that some musicians must give up their occupation.

Typically, dystonia afflicts musicians who practice trying to make perfect finger movements on their instruments. Musicians at high risk include string players, who receive vibratory stimulation at their fingertips. The constant practice has been suggested to lead not only to improved musical ability but also to distorted or disordered cortical motor maps. Synchronous activation of the digits by the vibration leads to this unwanted side effect.

Victor Candia and colleagues (2003) reasoned that musicians' dystonia was probably an example of disordered learning and could be treated by retuning the motor map. The investigators used magnetoencephalography (MEG) to measure changes in sensory-evoked magnetic fields in the cortex.

At the beginning of the study, the musicians with dystonia had a disordered motor map: the finger areas overlapped one another. In training, each subject used a hand splint tailored to his or her hand. The splint immobilized different fingers while the subjects independently moved the others.

After 8 days of training for about 2 hours per day, the subjects showed marked alleviation in the dystonic symptoms, and the neuroimaging showed a normalization of the cortical map, with distinct finger areas. Thus, training reversed the learned changes in the motor map and treated the dystonia. The musicians had actually learned a disorder, and they were able to unlearn it.

---

in the 1990s (e.g., Jacobs & Scheibel, 1993; Jacobs et al., 1993). In one, they found a relationship between dendrite size in Wernicke's area and level of education. In the brains of college-educated deceased people, the cortical neurons from this language area had more dendritic branches than did those from people with a high-school education, which, in turn, had more dendritic material than did those from people with less education. The general conclusion is that education increases neuron complexity, but it is also possible that people who have more dendrites may be more likely to go to college—a hypothesis that is not easy to test.

Another way to look at the relationship between neurons in Wernicke's area and behavior is to take advantage of the now well-documented observation that, on average, females' verbal abilities are superior to those of males. When Scheibel and his colleagues examined the structure of neurons in Wernicke's area, they found that females do have more extensive dendritic branching there than males do.

Finally, these investigators took a slightly different approach to the link between experience and neuronal morphology. They began with two hypotheses. First, they suggested a relationship between the complexity of dendritic branching and the nature of the computational tasks performed by a brain area.

Wernicke's area contributes to speech and to language comprehension; see Figure 10-19.

Figure 15-17 diagrams tasks that consistently show, on average, that females' verbal fluency surpasses males' and that males outperform females on spatial reasoning tasks.

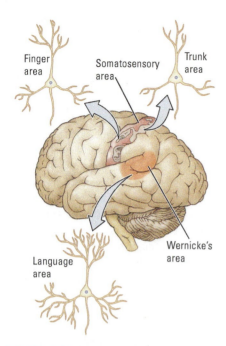

Finger area
Somatosensory area
Trunk area
Language area
Wernicke's area

FIGURE 14-24 Experience and Neuronal Complexity Confirmation of Scheibel's hypothesis that cell complexity is related to the computational demands required of the cell. Neurons that represent the body's trunk area have relatively less computational demand than do cells representing the finger region. In turn, cells engaged in higher cognitive functions (such as language, as in Wernicke's area) have greater computational demand than do those engaged in finger functions.

Figure 3-25 illustrates two aspects of methylation: histone and DNA modification.

See Figure 12-4 for a refresher on anatomy related to olfaction.

To test this hypothesis, they examined the dendritic structure of neurons in different cortical regions that handle different computational tasks. For example, when they compared the structure of neurons corresponding to the somatosensory representation of the trunk with those for the fingers, they found the latter to have more complex cells (**Figure 14-24**). They reasoned that the somatosensory inputs from receptive fields on the chest wall would constitute less of a computational challenge to cortical neurons than would those from the fingers and that the neurons representing the chest would therefore be less complex.

The group's second hypothesis was that dendritic branching in all regions is subject to experience-dependent change. The researchers hypothesized that predominant life experience (e.g., occupation) should, as a result, alter dendritic structure. Although they did not test this hypothesis directly, they did make an interesting observation. In their study comparing cells in the trunk area, in the finger area, and in the supramarginal gyrus—a parietal lobe region associated with higher cognitive processes (thinking)—they found curious individual differences.

For instance, especially large differences in trunk and finger neurons appeared in the brains of people who had a high level of finger dexterity maintained over long periods (say, career word processors). In contrast, no difference between trunk and finger neurons was found in sales representatives. Remember that Scheibel and colleagues conducted their research before portable electronic devices entered the workplace; we would not expect a good deal of specialized finger use among sales reps of that time and thus would see less complex demands on their finger neurons.

In summary, although the studies showing a relationship between experience and neuronal structure in humans depend on correlations rather than actual experiments, the findings are consistent with those observed in experimental studies of other species. We are thus led to the general conclusion that specific experiences can produce localized changes in the synaptic organization of the brain and that such changes form the structural basis of memory.

Epigenetics of Memory

An enigma in the search for neural mechanisms underlying memory is the fact that whereas memories remain stable over time, all cells are constantly undergoing molecular turnover. The simplest explanation for this is epigenetic: specific sites in the DNA of neurons involved in specific memories might exist in either a methylated or a nonmethylated state.

Courtney Miller and colleagues (2010) tested this idea directly by measuring methylation in the hippocampi of rats that underwent contextual fear conditioning (see Experiment 14-1). They showed that fear conditioning is associated with rapid methylation, but if they pharmacologically blocked methylation, there was no memory. The investigators conclude that epigenetic mechanisms mediate synaptic plasticity broadly—but especially in learning and memory. One implication of these results is that cognitive disorders, including memory defects, could result from aberrant epigenetic modifications (for a review, see Day et al., 2015).

There is also evidence that memory-related epigenetic changes can be transmitted to later generations. Brian Dias and colleagues (2015) trained male mice in an olfactory fear conditioning paradigm in which a specific odor was paired with mild footshock. The mice with this training developed more olfactory neurons responsive to the odor and more axons into the olfactory glomeruli. These changes in the olfactory bulb were also observed in the offspring and grand-offspring even though the younger mice had never been conditioned. Inheritance was associated with decreased DNA methylation around the specific olfactory receptor gene in the sperm of the original males and their offspring. Other studies have shown that early traumatic stress alters small non-coding RNAs in sperm, and this is related to behavioral and metabolic alterations in offspring (see, for example, Gapp et al., 2014). Together, these studies suggest that epigenetic changes related to experiences may contribute to the inheritance of phenotypes across generations.

Plasticity, Hormones, Trophic Factors, and Drugs

The news media often report that psychoactive drugs can damage your brain. Some drugs certainly do act as toxins and can selectively kill brain regions, but a more accurate description of drug action is that they *change* the brain. Although not many studies have looked at drug-induced morphological changes, evidence reveals that some compounds can greatly change the brain's synaptic organization. These compounds include hormones, neurotrophic factors, and psychoactive drugs. We briefly consider each category.

Hormones and Plasticity

Levels of circulating hormones are critical both in determining brain structure and in eliciting certain behaviors in adulthood. Although the structural effects of hormones were once believed to be expressed only in the course of development, current belief is that adult neurons also can respond to hormonal manipulations with dramatic structural changes. Here we consider the actions of gonadal hormones and stress hormones.

Research findings have established that structural differences in cortical neurons of male and female rats depend on gonadal hormones. More surprising, perhaps, is that gonadal hormones continue to influence cell structure and behavior in adulthood. Elizabeth Hampson and Doreen Kimura (1988) showed that women's performance on various cognitive tasks changes throughout the menstrual cycle as their estrogen levels fluctuate.

Changes in estrogen level appear to alter the structure of neurons and astrocytes in the neocortex and hippocampus, which probably accounts for at least part of the performance fluctuation. **Figure 14-25** illustrates changes in dendritic spines in the hippocampal cells of female rats at different phases of their 4-day estrous cycle. As the estrogen level rises, the number of synapses rises; as the estrogen level drops, the number of synapses declines.

Curiously, estrogen's influence on cell structure may differ in the hippocampus and neocortex. Jane Stewart found, for example, that when the ovaries of middle-aged female rats are removed, estrogen levels drop sharply, producing increased numbers of spines on pyramidal cells throughout the neocortex but decreased spine density in the hippocampus (Stewart & Kolb, 1994). How these synaptic changes might influence processes such as memory is not immediately obvious, but the question is reasonable, especially because menopausal women also experience sharp drops in estrogen levels and a corresponding decline in verbal memory ability.

This question is also relevant to middle-aged men, who show a slow decline in testosterone levels that correlates with a drop in spatial ability. Rats that are gonadectomized in adulthood show increased cortical spine density, much like the ovariectomized females. Although we do not know how this change relates to spatial behavior, a reasonable supposition is that testosterone levels might influence spatial memory throughout life.

When the body is stressed, the pituitary gland produces adrenocorticotrophic hormone (ACTH), which stimulates the adrenal cortex to produce steroid hormones, the *glucocorticoids*. Important in protein and carbohydrate metabolism, control of sugar levels in the blood, and absorption of sugar by cells, glucocorticoids have many actions on the body, including the brain. Robert Sapolsky (1992) proposed that glucocorticoids can sometimes be neurotoxic. In particular, he found that with prolonged stress, glucocorticoids appear to kill hippocampal cells.

Elizabeth Gould and her colleagues (1998) showed that even brief periods of stress can reduce the number of new granule cells produced in the hippocampi of monkeys, presumably through the actions of stress hormones. Evidence of neuron death and reduced neuron generation in the hippocampus has obvious implications for animal behavior, especially for processes such as spatial memory. Finally, Richelle Mychasiuk

Section 6-5 explains the classes, functions, and control that hormones exert; Section 8-4, their organizing effects during development; Section 12-5, their activating effects in adulthood.

Estrogen levels high

Estrogen levels low

FIGURE 14-25 Hormones and Neuroplasticity Sections of dendrites from hippocampal cells during times of high and low estrogen levels during the rat's 4-day estrous cycle reveal many more dendritic spines when estrogen levels are high. Information from Woolley et al., 1990.

Figure 6-20 illustrates the body's stress response.

and her colleagues (2016) showed that stress has contrasting epigenetic effects in the hippocampus and prefrontal cortex, with virtually no overlap between males and females.

In sum, hormones can alter the brain's synaptic organization and even the number of neurons in the brain. Little is known today about the behavioral consequences of such changes. It is likely that hormones can alter the course of plastic changes in the brain, possibly through epigenetic mechanisms.

Neurotrophic Factors and Plasticity

Section 8-2 explains how neurotrophic factors send these signals.

Neurotrophic factors, chemical compounds listed in **Table 14-2** that signal stem cells to develop into neurons or glia, also act to reorganize neural circuits. The first, **nerve growth factor (NGF)**, was discovered in the peripheral nervous system more than a generation ago. NGF is trophic (nourishing) in the sense that it stimulates neurons to grow dendrites and synapses and in some cases promotes neuronal survival.

A Hebb synapse—one that changes with use so that learning takes place—hypothetically employs just such a mechanism; see Section 5-4.

Trophic factors produced in the brain by neurons and glia can affect neurons both through cell membrane receptors and by actually entering the neuron to act internally on its operation. Trophic factors may be released postsynaptically, for example, to act as signals that can influence the presynaptic cell. Experience stimulates their production, so neurotrophic factors have been proposed as agents of synaptic change. For example, brain-derived neurotrophic factor (BDNF) increases when animals solve specific problems such as mazes. This finding has led to speculation that BDNF release may enhance such plastic changes as the growth of dendrites and synapses.

Although many researchers would like to conclude that BDNF has a role in learning, this conclusion does not necessarily follow. When animals solve mazes, their behavior differs from their behavior when they remain in cages. So we must first demonstrate that changes in BDNF, NGF, or any trophic factor are actually related to forming new synapses. Nevertheless, if we assume that trophic factors do act as synaptic change agents, then we should be able to use increased trophic factor activity during learning as a marker for where to look for changed synapses associated with learning and memory.

TABLE 14-2 **Molecules Exhibiting Neurotrophic Activities**

Proteins initially characterized as neurotrophic factors
Nerve growth factor (NGF)
Brain-derived neurotrophic factor (BDNF)
Neurotrophin 3 (NT-3)
Ciliary neurotrophic factor (CNTF)
Growth factors with neurotrophic activity
Fibroblast growth factor, acidic (aFGF *or* FGF-1)
Fibroblast growth factor, basic (bFGF *or* FGF-2)
Epidermal growth factor (EGF)
Insulinlike growth factor (ILGF)
Transforming growth factor (TGF)
Lymphokines (interleukin 1, 3, 6 or IL-1, IL-3, IL-6)
Protease nexin I, II
Cholinergic neuronal differentiation factor

Psychoactive Drugs and Plasticity

Many people regularly use the stimulant caffeine, and some use more stimulating psychoactive drugs, such as nicotine, amphetamine, or cocaine. The long-term consequences of abusing psychoactive drugs are now well documented, but the question of *why* these drugs cause problems remains to be answered. One explanation for the behavioral changes associated with chronic psychoactive drug abuse is that the drugs change the brain.

One experimental demonstration of these changes is *drug-induced behavioral sensitization*, often referred to as simply **behavioral sensitization**, the progressive increase in behavioral actions in response to repeated administration of a drug. Behaviors increase even when the amount given in each dose does not change. Behavioral sensitization occurs with most psychoactive drugs, including amphetamine, cocaine, morphine, and nicotine.

Section 5-4 details experiments conducted on *Aplysia*.

The sea slug *Aplysia* becomes more sensitive to a stimulus after repeated exposure. Psychoactive drugs appear to have a parallel action: they lead to increased behavioral sensitivity to their actions. For example, a rat given a small dose of amphetamine may show increased activity. When the rat is given the same dose of amphetamine on subsequent occasions, the increase in activity is progressively larger. If no drug is given for weeks or even months and then amphetamine is given in the same dose as before, behavioral sensitization picks up where it left off and continues to progress. Some long-lasting change must have taken place in the brain in response to the drug. Drug-induced behavioral sensitization can therefore be viewed as a memory for a particular drug.

nerve growth factor (NGF) Neurotrophic factor that stimulates neurons to grow dendrites and synapses and in some cases promotes the survival of neurons.

behavioral sensitization Escalating behavioral response to the repeated administration of a psychomotor stimulant such as amphetamine, cocaine, or nicotine; also called *drug-induced behavioral sensitization*.

The parallel between drug-induced behavioral sensitization and other forms of memory leads us to ask if the changes in the brain after behavioral sensitization are similar to those found after other forms of learning. They are. For instance, there is evidence of increased numbers of receptors at synapses and of more synapses in sensitized animals.

In a series of studies, Terry Robinson and his colleagues found dramatic increases in dendritic growth and spine density in rats sensitized to amphetamine, cocaine, or nicotine relative to rats that received injections of a saline solution (Robinson & Kolb, 2004). **Experiment 14-3** compares the effects of amphetamine and saline treatments on cells in the nucleus accumbens in the basal ganglia. Neurons in amphetamine-treated brains have more dendritic branches and increased spine density. Repeated exposure to psychoactive stimulants thus alters the structure of brain cells. These changes in turn may be related to learned addictions.

These plastic changes were not found throughout the brain. Rather, they were localized to regions such as the prefrontal cortex and nucleus accumbens that receive a large dopamine projection. (Recall from Section 6-4 that dopamine is believed to factor significantly in the wanting aspect of drug use.) Other psychoactive drugs also appear to alter neuronal structure. THC (an active component of cannabis), morphine, and certain antidepressants change dendritic length and spine density, although in ways different from those of stimulants. Morphine, for example, reduces dendritic length and spine density in the nucleus accumbens and prefrontal cortex (Robinson & Kolb, 2004).

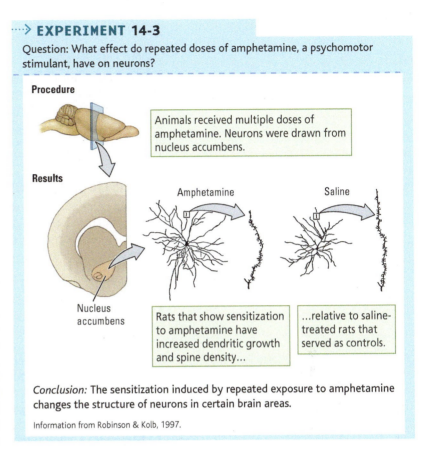

> **EXPERIMENT 14-3**

Question: What effect do repeated doses of amphetamine, a psychomotor stimulant, have on neurons?

Procedure

Animals received multiple doses of amphetamine. Neurons were drawn from nucleus accumbens.

Results

Amphetamine

Saline

Nucleus accumbens

Rats that show sensitization to amphetamine have increased dendritic growth and spine density...

...relative to saline-treated rats that served as controls.

Conclusion: The sensitization induced by repeated exposure to amphetamine changes the structure of neurons in certain brain areas.

Information from Robinson & Kolb, 1997.

What do drug-induced changes in synaptic organization mean for later experience-dependent plasticity? If rats are given amphetamine, cocaine, nicotine, or THC for 2 weeks before being placed in a complex environment, the expected increases in dendritic length and spine density in the cortex do not happen (see Kolb et al., 2003; Kolb et al., 2018). This is not because the brain can no longer change: giving the animals additional drug doses can still produce change. Rather, something about prior drug exposure alters the way in which the brain later responds to experience.

Why prior drug exposure has this effect is as yet unknown, but obviously drug taking can have long-term effects on brain plasticity. One possible explanation is epigenetic. Giving animals repeated doses of amphetamine or nicotine decreases methylation in both the prefrontal cortex and the nucleus accumbens, and decreased methylation is related to drug- and region-specific increases in gene expression (Mychasiuk et al., 2013). These epigenetic changes may render the synapses less able to change in response to later experiences.

Chapter 6 details the influence of drugs on the brain and behavior.

Some Guiding Principles of Brain Plasticity

Brain plasticity will continue as a fundamental concept underlying research into brain–behavior relationships through the coming decades. Some basic rules have emerged to guide this research (see Kolb & Gibb, 2014, for more details). Here we list seven.

1. Behavioral Change Reflects Brain Change

The brain's primary function is to produce behavior, but behavior is not static. We learn and remember, we think new thoughts or visualize new images, and we change throughout life. All these processes require changes in neural networks. Whenever neural networks change, behavior, including mental behavior, also changes. A corollary is especially important as neuroscientists search for treatments for brain injuries or behavioral disorders: *to change behavior, we must change the brain.*

2. All Nervous Systems Are Plastic in the Same General Way

Even the simplest animals, such as the roundworm *C. elegans*, can show simple learning that correlates with neuronal plasticity. The molecular details may differ between simple and complex systems, but the principles of neuroplasticity appear to be conserved across both simple and complex animals. This conservation allows more studies of neural plasticity among a wider range of animal species than in most other areas of neuroscience.

Investigators study neuroplasticity in species ranging from worms and insects to fish, birds, and mammals.

3. Plastic Changes Are Age Specific

The brain responds to the same experiences differently at different ages—and especially during development. The prefrontal cortex is late to mature, for example, so the same experience affects this region differently in infancy than it does in adolescence and on throughout life.

Section 8-4 traces how brain organization details change rapidly—and sometimes critically—during development.

4. Prenatal Events Can Influence Brain Plasticity Throughout Life

Prenatal experiences can alter brain organization. Potentially negative experiences, such as prenatal exposure to recreational or prescription drugs, and positive experiences, such as tactile stimulation of the mother's skin, may alter gene expression or induce other epigenetic effects that produce enduring effects on brain organization. Even paternal or maternal experiences before conception can alter later offsprings' brain development and organization.

Section 8-4 recounts benefits of tactile stimulation; Clinical Focus 8-2, epigenetic factors in the autism spectrum; Clinical Focus 6-2, the tragedy of fetal alcohol spectrum disorder.

5. Plastic Changes Are Brain-Region Dependent

Although we are tempted to expect plastic changes in neuronal networks to be fairly general, it is becoming clear that many experience-dependent changes are highly specific. We saw this specificity in the effects of psychoactive drugs on the prefrontal cortex but not on other cortical regions. Not only do drugs selectively change the prefrontal cortex, but the dorsolateral and orbital prefrontal areas also show opposite changes; the precise changes varying with the particular drug. For example, stimulants such as amphetamine increase spine density in the dorsolateral region but decrease it in the orbital region.

Figure 12-23 diagrams these prefrontal regions.

6. Experience-Dependent Changes Interact

Metaplasticity is a property of a lifetime's interaction among different plastic changes in the brain. As an animal travels through life, infinite experiences can alter its brain organization. A lifetime's experiences might interact. Housing animals in complex environments produces profound changes in their neural network organization, but prior exposure to psychoactive drugs completely blocks the enrichment effect. Conversely, although complex housing does not block drug effects, enrichment markedly attenuates them. Prenatal events can affect later drug effects: prenatal tactile stimulation of the mother, for example, reduces the later effects of psychoactive drugs on the offspring.

7. Plasticity Has Pros and Cons

We have mainly emphasized the neuroplastic changes that can support improved motor and cognitive function. But, as noted for the effects of psychoactive drugs, plastic changes in neural networks can also interfere with behavior. Drug addicts whose prefrontal cortex has been altered are prone to poor judgment in their personal life. People who have posttraumatic stress disorder show altered blood flow in the amygdala and cingulate cortex. That's the bad news.

The good news is that by encouraging plastic changes that reverse these prefrontal alterations, we can treat or even eliminate some prefrontal disorders. For instance, age-related neurocognitive disorder is related to synaptic loss that various forms of cognitive therapy can reverse (e.g., Mahncke et al., 2006).

metaplasticity Interaction among different plastic changes in the brain.

14-4 Review

Before you continue, check your understanding. Answers to Self-Test appear at the back of the book.

1. Repeated high-frequency stimulation of excitatory neurons leads to the phenomenon of _____, whereas repeated low-frequency stimulation leads to _____.

2. LTPi and LTDi are found in _____ neurons.

3. Structural changes underlying memory include changes in both _____ and the _____.

4. Learning complex spatial information has been linked to increased gray matter in the _____.

5. The progressive increase in behavioral actions in response to repeated administration of a drug is called _____.

6. How can plastic changes in the brain produce adverse effects?

For additional study tools, visit 📖 **LaunchPad** at launchpadworks.com

---

Recovery from Brain Injury

The nervous system appears conservative in its use of mechanisms related to behavioral change. If neuroscientists wish to change the brain, as after injury or disease, then they should look for treatments that will produce plastic changes related to learning, memory, and other behaviors.

Recall that H. M. failed to recover his lost memory capacities, even after 55 years of practice in trying to remember information. Relearning simply was not possible for H. M. He had lost the requisite neural structures. But other people do show some recovery.

A common assumption might suggest that the recovery process after brain trauma requires the injured person to relearn lost skills, whether walking, talking, or using the fingers. But what exactly does recovery entail? Partial recovery of function is common after brain injury, but a person with brain trauma or brain disease has lost neurons. The brain may be missing structures critical for relearning or remembering.

Donna's Experience with Traumatic Brain Injury

Donna started dancing when she was 4 years old, and she was a natural. By the time she finished high school, she had the training and skill necessary to apprentice with and later join a major dance company. Donna remembers vividly the day she was chosen to dance a leading role in *The Nutcracker*. She had marveled at the costumes as she watched the popular Christmas ballet as a child, and now she would dance in those costumes!

The births of two children interrupted her career as a dancer, but Donna never lost the interest. In 1968, when both her children were in school, she began dancing again with a local company. To her amazement, she could still perform most of the movements, although she was rusty on the choreography of the classical dances that she had once memorized so meticulously. Nonetheless, she quickly relearned. In retrospect, she should not have been so surprised because she had always had an excellent memory.

One evening in 1990, while on a bicycle ride, a drunk driver struck Donna. She was wearing a helmet but received a brain-damaging blow to the head—a **traumatic brain injury (TBI)**. She was comatose for several weeks. As she regained consciousness, she was confused and had difficulty talking to and understanding others. Her memory was

traumatic brain injury (TBI) Damage to the brain that results from a blow to the head.

Clinical Focus 1-1 and Section 1-1 introduce consequences of and treatments for TBI, which we elaborate here and in Section 16-3.

very poor; spatial disorientation meant she often got lost; she endured various motor disturbances; and she had difficulty recognizing anyone except her family and closest friends.

Over the ensuing 10 months, Donna regained most of her motor abilities and language skills, and her spatial abilities improved significantly. Nonetheless, she was short-tempered and easily frustrated by the slowness of her recovery, symptoms typical of people with brain trauma. She suffered periods of depression.

Donna also found herself prone to inexplicable surges of panic when doing simple things. On one occasion early in her rehabilitation, she was shopping in a large super-market and became overwhelmed by the number of salad dressing choices. She ran from the store, and only after she sat outside and calmed herself could she go back inside to continue shopping.

Two years later, Donna was dancing once again, but she found learning and remembering new steps difficult. Her emotions were still unstable, which put a strain on her family, but her episodes of frustration and temper outbursts grew far less frequent.

A year later, they were gone, and her life was not obviously different from that of other middle-aged women.

Even so, some cognitive changes persisted. Donna seemed unable to remember the names or faces of new people she met. She lost concentration if background distractions such as a television or a radio playing intruded. She could not dance as she had before her injury, but she did work at it diligently. Her balance on sudden turns gave her the most difficulty. Rather than risk falling, she retired from her life's first love.

Donna's case demonstrates the human brain's capacity for continuously changing its structure and ultimately its function throughout a lifetime. From what we have explored in this chapter, we can identify three ways in which Donna could recover from her brain injury: she could learn new ways to solve problems, she could reorganize the brain to do more with less, and she could generate new neurons to produce new neural circuits. We briefly examine each possibility.

The brains of these dancers change in response to new experiences and new abilities. After her accident, Donna's brain had to change to allow her to regain her lost abilities, but she never recovered the ability that these young women have to learn new dances.

Three-Legged Cat Solution

A cat that loses a leg quickly learns to compensate for the missing limb and once again become mobile. It shows recovery of function: the limb is gone, but behavior has changed to compensate. This simplest solution to recovery from brain injury is thus called the *three-legged cat solution*.

A similar explanation can account for many instances of apparent recovery of function after TBI. Imagine a right-handed person has a stroke that costs her the use of her right hand and arm. Unable to write with the affected limb, she switches to her left hand. Such behavioral compensation presupposes that some nervous system changes underlie this new skill.

New-Circuit Solution

A second way to recover from brain damage is for the brain to form new connections that allow it to do more with less. This change is most easily accomplished by processes similar to those we considered for other forms of plasticity. The brain changes its neural connections to overcome the loss.

Without some intervention, recovery from most brain injuries is relatively modest. Recovery can increase significantly if the person engages in behavioral, pharmacological, or brain-stimulation therapy that encourages the brain to make new connections.

Behavioral therapy—such as speech therapy, physiotherapy, and music therapy—presumably increases brain activity, which facilitates neural changes. In a pharmacological intervention, the patient takes a drug, such as nerve growth factor (NGF), known to influence brain plasticity. When NGF is given to animals with stroke damage to the motor cortex, their motor functions improve (**Experiment 14-4**). The behavioral changes correlate with a dramatic increase in dendritic branching and spine

···→ **EXPERIMENT 14-4**

Question: Does nerve growth factor stimulate recovery from stroke, influence neural structure, or both?

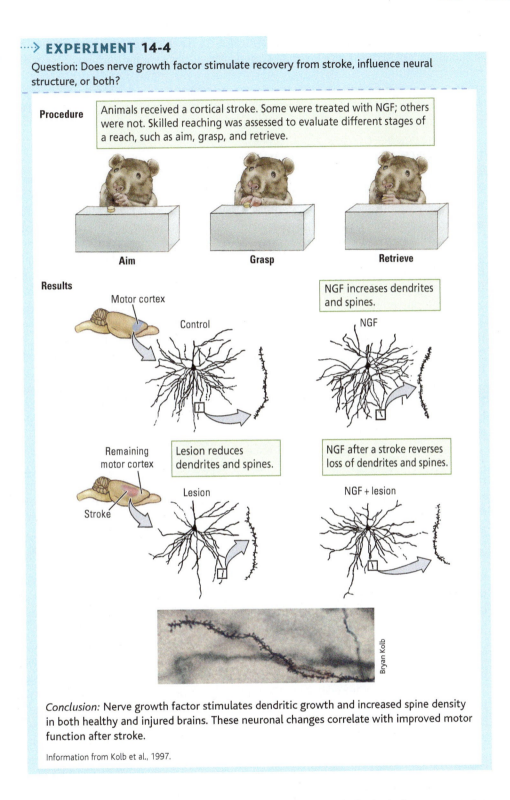

Procedure | Animals received a cortical stroke. Some were treated with NGF; others were not. Skilled reaching was assessed to evaluate different stages of a reach, such as aim, grasp, and retrieve.

Aim   Grasp   Retrieve

Results

Motor cortex

Control

NGF increases dendrites and spines.

NGF

Remaining motor cortex

Lesion reduces dendrites and spines.

Lesion

NGF after a stroke reverses loss of dendrites and spines.

NGF + lesion

Stroke

Bryan Kolb

Conclusion: Nerve growth factor stimulates dendritic growth and increased spine density in both healthy and injured brains. These neuronal changes correlate with improved motor function after stroke.

Information from Kolb et al., 1997.

density in the remaining intact motor regions. The morphological changes correlate with improved motor functions, such as reaching with the forelimb to obtain food, as illustrated in Experiment 14-2 (Kolb et al., 1997). But because brain tissue is still missing, recovery is by no means complete.

In principle, we might expect that any drug that stimulates the growth of new connections would help people recover from brain injury. However, neural growth must occur in brain regions that can influence a lost function. A drug that stimulates synaptic growth on cells in the visual cortex, for example, would not enhance recovery of hand use. The visual neurons play no direct role in moving the hand.

epidermal growth factor (EGF) Neurotrophic factor; stimulates the subventricular zone to generate cells that migrate into the striatum and eventually differentiate into neurons and glia.

Clinical Focus 5-4 recounts a successful case of fetal stem cell transplantation.

The striatum, a region in the basal ganglia, includes the caudate nucleus and putamen.

Even in adults, neural stem cells line the subventricular zone, which is diagrammed in Figure 8-10A.

A third strategy to generate new neural circuits is to use either deep brain stimulation (DBS) or direct electrical stimulation of perilesional regions. The goal of electrical stimulation is to directly increase activity in remaining parts of specific damaged neural networks. In DBS, it is to put the brain into a more plastic (trainable) state so that rehabilitation therapies work better. Both strategies are in preliminary clinical trials.

Lost Neuron Replacement Solution

The third way a patient like Donna could pursue recovery is to generate new neurons to produce new neural circuits. The idea that brain tissue could be transplanted from one animal to another goes back a century. Tissue transplanted from fetal brains will grow and form some connections in the new brain, but, unfortunately, in contrast with transplanted hearts or livers, transplanted brain tissue functions poorly. The procedure seems most suited to conditions in which a small number of functional cells are required, as in the replacement of dopamine-producing cells in Parkinson disease or in the replacement of suprachiasmatic cells to restore circadian rhythms.

By 2004, dopamine-producing cells had been surgically transplanted into the striata of many Parkinson patients. Although the disease has not been reversed, some patients, especially younger ones, have shown functional gains that justify the procedure. Nonetheless, ethical issues will remain as long as the tissue is taken from aborted human fetuses.

Adult stem cells offer a second way to replace lost neurons. Investigators know that the brain is capable of making neurons in adulthood. The challenge is to get the brain to do so after an injury. Brent Reynolds and Sam Weiss (1992) made the first breakthrough in this research.

Cells lining the ventricles of adult mice were removed and placed in a culture medium. The researchers demonstrated that if the correct trophic factors are added, the cells begin to divide and can produce new neurons and glia. Furthermore, if the trophic factors—particularly **epidermal growth factor (EGF)**—are infused into the ventricle of a living animal, the subventricular zone generates cells that migrate into the striatum and eventually differentiate into neurons and glia.

In principle, it ought to be possible to use trophic factors to stimulate the subventricular zone to generate new cells in the injured brain. If these new cells were to migrate to the site of injury and essentially regenerate the lost area, as shown in **Figure 14-26**, then it might be possible to restore at least some lost function. Not all lost behaviors could be restored, however, because the new neurons would have to establish the same connections with the rest of the brain that the lost neurons once had.

This task would be daunting: connections would have to be formed in an adult brain that already has billions of connections. Nonetheless, such a treatment might someday be feasible, and preclinical laboratory trials are promising. Cocktails of trophic factors are effective in stimulating neurogenesis in the subventricular zone after brain injury. For example, shown at left in Figure 14-26, animals first received ischemic injuries (strokes), then received intraventricular infusions of trophic factors for 14 days. New cells migrated to the site of injury, as shown at right in Figure 14-26, and many of them differentiated into immature neurons.

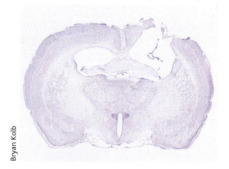
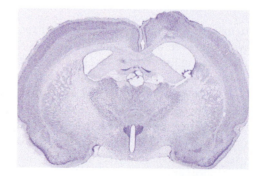

FIGURE 14-26 **Stem Cells Do the Trick** Left: After cortical stroke—damage is visible at upper right—infusion of epidermal growth factor into a rat's lateral ventricle induced neurogenesis in the subventricular zone. Right: The stem cells migrated to the site of injury and filled in the damaged area. The cytological organization is, however, abnormal.

Bryan Kolb

Although they did not integrate well into the existing brain, the new cells influenced behavior and led to functional improvement (Kolb et al., 2007). The mechanism of influence is poorly understood. The new neurons apparently had some trophic influence on the surrounding uninjured cortex. Preliminary clinical trials with humans are under way and so far show no ill effects in volunteers.

14-5 Review

Before you continue, check your understanding. Answers to Self-Test appear at the back of the book.

1. Three ways to compensate for the loss of neurons are _____, _____, and _____.

2. Two ways of using electrical stimulation to enhance postinjury recovery are _____ and _____.

3. Endogenous stem cells can be recruited to enhance functional improvement by using _____ factors.

4. What is the lesson of the three-legged cat?

For additional study tools, visit **LaunchPad** at launchpadworks.com

|Summary

14-1 Connecting Learning and Memory

Learning is a change in an organism's behavior as a result of experience. Memory is the ability to recall or recognize previous experience. For more than a century, laboratory studies using animals have uncovered two diverse types of learning: Pavlovian (or classical) and operant (or instrumental).

The two basic types of memory are implicit (unconscious) and explicit (conscious). Episodic memory includes not only a record of events (episodes) that occurred but also our presence there and our role in the events. The frontal lobe likely plays a unique role in this autobiographical memory.

14-2 Dissociating Memory Circuits

Multiple subsystems control different aspects of memory within the explicit and implicit systems. People with damaged explicit memory circuits have impaired recall for facts and events. People with damaged implicit memory circuits are impaired in their recall and/or performance of skills and habits.

14-3 Neural Systems Underlying Explicit and Implicit Memories

The neural circuits underlying implicit and explicit memory are distinctly different: the reciprocal system for explicit memory includes medial temporal structures; the unidirectional system for implicit memory includes the basal ganglia. Emotional memory has characteristics of both implicit and explicit memory. Neural circuits for emotional memory also are unique in that they include the amygdala. Figure 14-5 summarizes broad categories within these multiple memory systems.

For memories to become established in the brain—the process of consolidation—experiences must change neural connections, and these changes must become relatively permanent. When memories are revisited, neural connectivity can become less fixed, allowing for the neural networks and thus the memory to be modified, a process called reconsolidation.

14-4 Structural Basis of Brain Plasticity

The brain has the capacity for structural change, and structural change presumably underlies functional change. The brain changes structure in two fundamental ways in response to experience.

First, existing neural circuits change largely by modifying synaptic connections. One proposed mechanism of synaptic change is long-term potentiation (LTP), reflected in modification of EPSPs following learning.

Second, novel neural circuits form both by forging new connections among existing neurons and by generating new neurons. Generating new neurons in the hippocampus is one mechanism for establishing novel circuits. A likely mechanism for maintaining synaptic changes is epigenetic: specific sites in the neuronal DNA in modified circuits can exist in either methylated or unmethylated states.

Neuronal activity is key to brain plasticity: through it, synapses form and change. Neuronal activity can be induced by general or specific experience as well as by electrical or chemical stimulation. Chemical stimulation may range from hormones and neurotrophic compounds to psychoactive drugs.

Much of the brain is capable of plastic change with experience. Different experiences lead to changes in different neural systems. The following table summarizes seven principles that guide research about brain plasticity and behavior.

Some Guiding Principles of Brain Plasticity
1. Behavioral change reflects brain change.
2. All nervous systems are plastic in the same general way.
3. Plastic changes are age specific.
4. Prenatal events can influence brain plasticity throughout life.
5. Plastic changes are brain-region dependent.
6. Experience-dependent changes interact.
7. Plasticity has pros and cons.

14-5 Recovery from Brain Injury

Plastic changes after brain injury parallel those seen when the brain changes with experience. Changes related to recovery do not always occur spontaneously, however; rather, they must be stimulated by behavioral training, by the effects of psychoactive drugs or neurotrophic factors, or by electrical brain stimulation. The key to stimulating recovery from brain injury is to increase the plastic changes underlying the recovery.

Key Terms

amnesia, p. 479

anterograde amnesia, p. 493

associative learning, p. 496

behavioral sensitization, p. 506

conditioned response (CR), p. 478

conditioned stimulus (CS), p. 478

consolidation, p. 491

declarative memory, p. 480

dyslexia, p. 476

emotional memory, p. 494

entorhinal cortex, p. 487

epidermal growth factor (EGF), p. 512

episodic memory, p. 482

explicit memory, p. 479

eyeblink conditioning, p. 477

fear conditioning, p. 478

implicit memory, p. 479

Korsakoff syndrome, p. 491

learning, p. 477

learning set, p. 480

long-term depression (LTD), p. 497

long-term potentiation (LTP), p. 496

memory, p. 477

metaplasticity, p. 508

nerve growth factor (NGF), p. 506

neuritic plaque, p. 488

operant conditioning, p. 479

parahippocampal cortex, p. 487

Pavlovian conditioning, p. 477

perirhinal cortex, p. 487

priming, p. 479

procedural memory, p. 480

reconsolidation, p. 492

retrograde amnesia, p. 493

traumatic brain injury (TBI), p. 509

unconditioned response (UCR), p. 478

unconditioned stimulus (UCS), p. 478

visuospatial memory, p. 487

Visit **LaunchPad** to access the e-Book, videos, **LearningCurve** adaptive quizzing, flashcards, and more launchpadworks.com

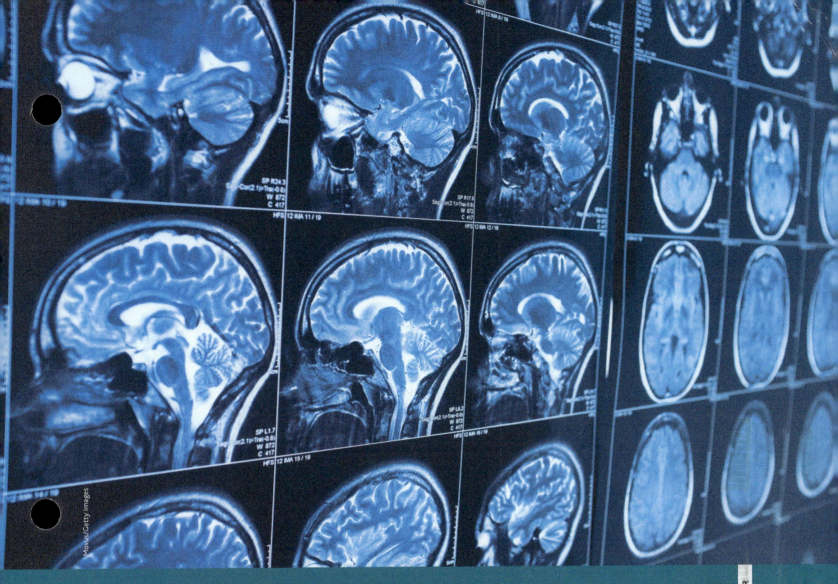

Movus/Getty Images

How Does the Brain Think?

CHAPTER **15**

Split Brain

Epileptic seizures may begin in a restricted region of one brain hemisphere and spread through the fibers of the corpus callosum to the corresponding location in the opposite hemisphere. To prevent the spread of seizures that cannot be controlled through medication, neurosurgeons sometimes sever the 200 million nerve fibers of the corpus callosum. The procedure is medically beneficial for many people with epilepsy, leaving them virtually seizure free, with only minimal effects on their everyday behavior. In special circumstances, however, the aftereffects of a severed corpus callosum become more readily apparent, as extensive psychological testing by Roger Sperry, Michael Gazzaniga, and their colleagues has demonstrated (Gazzaniga, 1970; Sperry, 1968). We note that although this procedure is seldom used today, the study of patients by these investigators has provided unique and important insights into brain function.

On close inspection, such split-brain patients reveal a unique behavioral syndrome that offers insight into the nature of cerebral asymmetry. Cortical asymmetry is essential for such integrative tasks as language and body control.

One split-brain participant was presented with several blocks. Each block had two red sides, two white sides, and two half-red and half-white sides, as illustrated. The task was to arrange the blocks to form patterns identical with those shown on cards.

When the subject used his right hand to perform the task, he had great difficulty. His movements were slow and hesitant. In contrast, when he

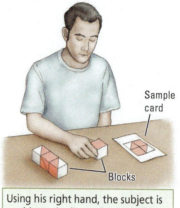

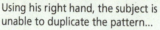

Using his right hand, the subject is unable to duplicate the pattern...

...but with his left hand, the split-brain patient performs the task correctly.

In this experiment, a split-brain patient's task is to arrange a set of blocks to match the pattern shown on the card. Information from Gazzaniga et al., 1999.

performed the task with his left hand, his solutions were not only accurate but also quick and decisive.

Findings from studies of other split-brain patients have shown that, as tasks of this sort become more difficult, left-hand superiority increases. Participants whose brain is intact perform equally well with either hand, indicating the intact connection between the two hemispheres. But in split-brain subjects, each hemisphere works on its own.

Apparently, the right hemisphere, which controls the left hand, has visuospatial capabilities that the left hemisphere does not.

Studies of split-brain patients reveal that the left and right cerebral hemispheres engage in fundamentally different types of thinking. Typically, however, we are unaware of these brain asymmetries. In this chapter, we examine the neural systems and subsystems that control thinking. In the mammalian brain, these systems are in the cortex.

Our first task is to define the mental processes we wish to study—to ask What is the nature of thought? Then we consider the cortical regions—for vision, audition, movement, and associative function—that play major roles in thinking. We examine how these cortical connections are organized into such systems and subsystems as the dorsal and ventral visual streams and how neuroscientists study them.

Next, we explore the brain's asymmetrical organization and delve deeper into split-brain phenomena. Another distinguishing feature of human thought is the different ways in which individual people think. We consider several sources of these differences, including those related to gender and to what we call intelligence. Finally, we address consciousness and how it may relate to the neural control of thought.

15-1

The Nature of Thought

Studying abstract mental processes such as thought, language, memory, emotion, and motivation is tricky. They cannot be seen but can only be inferred from behavior and are best thought of as **psychological constructs**, ideas that result from a set of impressions. The mind constructs an idea as being real, even though it is not tangible.

psychological construct Idea or set of impressions that some mental ability exists as an entity; memory, language, and emotion are examples.

We run into trouble when we try to locate constructs such as thought or memory in the brain. That we have words for these constructs does not mean that the brain is organized around them. Indeed, it is not. For instance, although people talk about memory as a unitary thing, the brain neither treats memory as unitary nor localizes it in one particular place. The many forms of memory are each treated differently by widely distributed brain circuits. The psychological construct of memory that we think of as being a single thing turns out not to be unitary at all.

To assume a neurological basis for psychological constructs such as memory and thought is risky, but we certainly should not give up searching for where and how the brain produces them. After all, thought, memory, emotion, motivation, and other such constructs are the most interesting activities the brain performs.

Psychologists typically use the term **cognition** (knowing) to describe thought processes—that is, how we come to know about the world. For behavioral neuroscientists, cognition usually entails the ability to pay attention to stimuli (whether external or internal), to identify stimuli, and to plan meaningful responses to them. External stimuli cue neural activity in our sensory receptors. Internal stimuli can spring from the autonomic nervous system (ANS) as well as from neural processes—from constructs such as memory and motivation.

cognition Act or process of knowing or coming to know; in psychology, refers to thought processes; in behavioral neuroscience, refers to identification and planned response to stimuli.

syntax Sets of rules for putting together words; proposed to be unique to human language.

Section 14-1 details types of memory, Section 14-4 how neuroplasticity contributes to memory processing and storage.

Characteristics of Human Thought

Human cognition is widely believed to have unique characteristics. For one, human thought is verbal, whereas the thought of other animals is nonverbal. Language is presumed to give humans an edge in thinking, and in some ways it does:

- Language provides the brain a means of categorizing information. It allows us to easily group together objects, actions, and events that have common factors.

- Language provides a means of organizing time, especially future time. It enables us to plan our behavior around time (say, Monday at 3 P.M.) in ways that nonverbal animals cannot.

- Perhaps most importantly, human language has **syntax**—sets of rules for putting together words to create meaningful utterances.

Neuroscientists have generally assumed that modern language is a recent phenomenon restricted to modern humans beginning about 100,000 years ago (see Chomsky, 2010). Recently, evidence has emerged to suggest that Neanderthals also had language and that the common ancestor of modern humans and Neanderthals had this capacity some 500,000 years ago (Dediu & Levinson, 2013). If this view is correct, the authors propose, present-day linguistic diversity could contain traces of the languages spoken by other human forms such as Neanderthals.

Linguists argue that although other nonhuman animals, such as chimpanzees, can use and recognize vocalizations (about three dozen for chimps), they do not rearrange these sounds to produce new meanings. Linguists maintain that this lack of syntax makes chimpanzee language literal and inflexible, although it can still be quite complex, as seen in the chimp Kanzi discussed in Comparative Focus 1-2, The Speaking Brain. Human language, in contrast, has enormous flexibility that enables us to talk about virtually any topic, even highly abstract topics like psychological constructs. In this way, our thinking is carried beyond a rigid here and now.

Neurologist Oliver Sacks illustrated the importance of syntax to human thinking in his description of Joseph, an 11-year-old deaf boy who was raised without sign language for his first 10 years and so was never exposed to syntax. According to Sacks:

The appearance of human language correlates with a dramatic brain size increase; see Section 2-3. Section 10-4 explains foundations underlying all languages.

> Joseph saw, distinguished, used; he had no problems with perceptual categorization or generalization, but he could not, it seemed, go much beyond this, hold abstract ideas in mind, reflect, play, plan. He seemed completely literal—unable to juggle images or hypotheses or possibilities, unable to enter an imaginative or figurative realm. . . . He seemed, like an animal, or an infant, to be stuck in the present, to be confined to literal and immediate perception. (Sacks, 1989, p. 40)

Language, including syntax, develops innately in children because the human brain is programmed to use words in a form of universal grammar. But in the absence of words—either spoken or signed—no grammar can develop. Without the linguistic flexibility that grammar allows, it is difficult for "higher-level" thought to emerge. Syntax, in other words, influences the very nature of our thinking. But we would be remiss if we did not acknowledge that chimpanzees are capable of remarkable cognitive abilities (for example, see Dolins et al., 2014).

In addition to arranging words in syntactical patterns, the human brain has a passion for stringing together events, movements, and thoughts. We combine musical notes into melodies, movements into dance, images into videos. We design elaborate rules for games and governments. It seems reasonable to conclude that the human brain is organized to chain together events, movements, and thoughts. Syntax is merely one example.

We do not know how this propensity to string things together evolved, but one possibility is natural selection: stringing movements together into sequences is highly adaptive. It would allow for building houses or weaving threads into cloth, for instance.

William Calvin (1996) proposed that the motor sequences most important to ancient humans were those used in hunting. Throwing a rock or a spear at a moving target is a complex act that requires much planning. Sudden ballistic movements, such as throwing, last less than one-eighth of a second and cannot be corrected by feedback. The brain has to plan every detail and then spit out the details as a smooth-flowing sequence.

Figure 11-2 diagrams the frontal lobe hierarchy that initiates motor sequences.

Today, a football quarterback does exactly this when he throws a football to a receiver running a zigzag pattern to elude a defender. A skilled quarterback can hit the target on virtually every throw, stringing movements together rapidly in a continuous sequence, with no pauses or gaps. This skill is uniquely human. Chimpanzees can throw, but no chimpanzee could learn to throw a ball to hit a target moving in a zigzag pattern.

The human predisposition to sequence movements may have encouraged language development. Spoken language, after all, is a sequence of movements involving the throat, tongue, and mouth muscles. Viewed in this way, language is the by-product of a brain that was already predisposed to operate by stringing together movements, events, or even ideas.

A critical characteristic of human motor sequencing is our ability to create novel sequences with ease. We constantly produce new sentences. Composers and choreographers earn their living making new music and dance sequences. Novel movement or thought sequences are a product of the frontal lobe. People with frontal lobe damage have difficulty generating novel solutions to problems. They are described as lacking imagination. The frontal lobes are critical not only for organizing behavior but also for organizing thinking. One major difference between the human brain and other primates' brains is the size of the frontal lobes.

Neural Units of Thought

What exactly goes on within the brain to produce what we call thinking? Is thought an attribute exclusive to humans? Before you answer, consider the mental feats of Alex the parrot, profiled in Comparative Focus 15-2, Animal Intelligence.

Alex's cognitive abilities are unexpected in a bird. In the past 40 years, the intellectual capacities of chimpanzees and dolphins have provoked great interest, but Alex's mental life appears to have been just as rich as the mental life of those two large-brained mammals.

The fact that birds are capable of thought is a clue to the neural basis of thought. A logical presumption may be that thinking, which humans are so good at, must be due to some special property of the massive human neocortex. But birds do not possess a neocortex. Rather, they evolved specific brain nuclei that function much as the layers of the human cortex do. This organizational difference in the forebrain of birds and mammals implies that thinking must be an activity of complex neural circuits, not of some particular brain region.

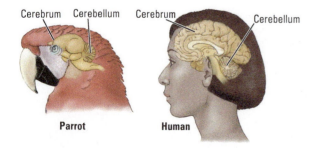

Cerebrum Cerebellum Cerebrum Cerebellum

Parrot **Human**

COMPARATIVE FOCUS 15-2

Animal Intelligence

Intelligent animals think. We all know that parrots can talk, but most of us assume that no real thought lies behind their words. An African grey parrot named Alex proved otherwise. Irene Pepperberg, pictured here with Alex and another subject, studied his ability to think and use language for more than three decades (Pepperberg, 1990, 1999, 2006).

A typical session with Alex and Pepperberg proceeded roughly as follows (Mukerjee, 1996): Pepperberg would show Alex a tray with four corks. "How many?" she would ask. "Four," Alex would reply. She then might show him a metal key and a green plastic one.

"What toy?"

"Key."

"How many?"

"Two."

"What's different?"

"Color."

Alex did not just have a vocabulary: words had meaning to him. He correctly applied English labels to numerous colors (red, green, blue, yellow, gray, purple, orange), shapes (two-, three-, four-, five-, six-cornered), and materials (cork, wood, rawhide, rock, paper, chalk, wool). He also labeled various items made of metal (chain, key, grate, tray, toy truck), wood (clothespin, block), and plastic or paper (cup, box).

Most surprisingly, Alex used words to identify, request, and refuse items. He responded to questions about abstract ideas, such as the color, shape, material, relative size, and quantity of more than 100 objects.

Alex's thinking was often quite complex. Presented with a tray that contained seven items—a circular rose-colored piece of rawhide, a piece of purple wool, a three-cornered purple key, a four-cornered yellow piece of rawhide, a five-cornered orange piece of rawhide, a six-cornered purple piece of rawhide, and a purple metal box—and then asked, "What shape is the purple hide?" Alex would answer correctly, "Six-corner."

To come up with this answer, Alex had to comprehend the question, locate the correct object of the correct color, determine the answer to the question about the object's shape, and encode his answer into an appropriate verbal response. This task was not easy. After all, four objects were pieces of rawhide, and three objects were purple.

The African grey parrot Alex, shown here with Irene Pepperberg and a sampling of the items he could count, describe, and answer questions about. Alex died in 2007 at the age of 31.

Alex could not respond just to one attribute. Rather, he had to combine the concepts of rawhide and purple and find the object that possessed them both. Then he had to figure out the object's shape. Clearly, considerable mental processing was required, but Alex succeeded at such tasks time and again.

Alex also demonstrated that he understood what he said. If he requested one object and was presented with another, he was likely to say no and repeat his original request. In fact, when given incorrect objects on numerous occasions in formal testing, he said no and repeated his request 72 percent of the time, said no without repeating his request 18 percent of the time, and made a new request the other 10 percent of the time.

These responses suggest that Alex's requests led to an expectation in his mind. He knew what he was asking for, and he expected to get it.

The idea of neural circuits is the essence of Donald Hebb's (1949) concept that **cell assemblies** (networks of neurons) represent objects or ideas, and the interplay among the networks results in complex mental activity such as cognition. Connections among neurons are not random but rather are organized into systems and subsystems. Thinking must result from the activity of these complex neural circuits. One way to identify their role is to consider how individual neurons respond during cognitive activity.

William Newsome and his colleagues (1995) took this approach in training monkeys to identify apparent motion in a set of moving dots on a television screen. The Procedure section of **Experiment 15-1** shows how the researchers varied the difficulty of the task by manipulating the number of dots that moved in the same direction. If all the dots move in the same direction, perceiving the whole array as moving is very easy. If only a small percentage of the dots move in the same direction, however, perceiving apparent motion in that direction is much more difficult.

In fact, a threshold number of dots moving together is required to make directional motion apparent. If too few dots are moving in the same direction, the viewer gets

cell assembly Hypothetical group of neurons that become functionally connected via common sensory inputs; proposed by Hebb as the basis of perception, memory, and thought.

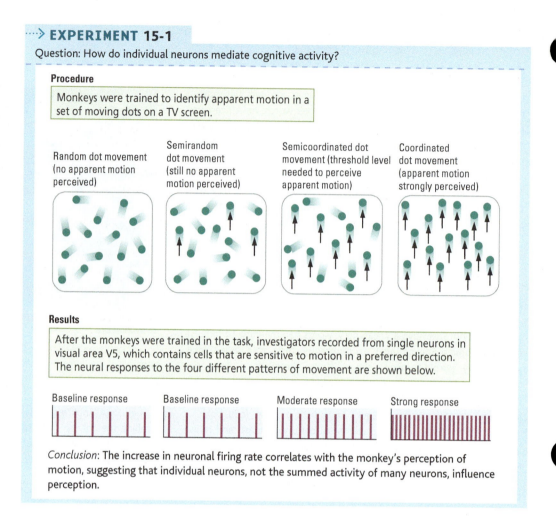

····> **EXPERIMENT 15-1**

Question: How do individual neurons mediate cognitive activity?

Procedure

Monkeys were trained to identify apparent motion in a set of moving dots on a TV screen.

Random dot movement (no apparent motion perceived)

Semirandom dot movement (still no apparent motion perceived)

Semicoordinated dot movement (threshold level needed to perceive apparent motion)

Coordinated dot movement (apparent motion strongly perceived)

Results

After the monkeys were trained in the task, investigators recorded from single neurons in visual area V5, which contains cells that are sensitive to motion in a preferred direction. The neural responses to the four different patterns of movement are shown below.

Baseline response

Baseline response

Moderate response

Strong response

Conclusion: The increase in neuronal firing rate correlates with the monkey's perception of motion, suggesting that individual neurons, not the summed activity of many neurons, influence perception.

an impression of random movement. Apparently, on the basis of the proportion of dots moving in the same direction, the brain concludes whether dots are moving in a consistent direction.

After the monkeys were trained in the task, the investigators recorded from single neurons in visual area V5, which contains cells sensitive to movement in a preferred direction. When vertical movement crosses its receptive field, a neuron that is sensitive to vertical motion responds with a vigorous burst of action potentials. But just as the observer has a threshold for perceiving coherent motion in one direction, so too does the neuron. If at some point the random activity of the dots increases to a level that obscures movement in a neuron's preferred direction, the neuron will stop responding because it does not detect any consistent pattern.

So how does the activity of any given neuron correlate with the perceptual threshold for apparent motion? On the one hand, if our perception of apparent motion results from the summed activity of many dozens or even thousands of neurons, little correlation would exist between the activity of any one neuron and the perception. On the other hand, if individual neurons influence our perception of apparent motion, then a strong correlation would exist between the activity of a single cell and the perception.

The results of Experiment 15-1 are unequivocal: the sensitivity of individual neurons is very similar to the perceptual sensitivity of the monkeys to apparent motion. As shown in the Results section, if individual neurons failed to respond to the stimulus, the monkeys behaved as if they did not perceive any apparent motion.

This finding is curious. Given the large number of V5 neurons, it seems logical that perceptual decisions are based on the responses of a large pool of neurons.

Figure 9-16 locates visual regions V1 through V5 in the occipital lobe.

Figures 9-33 to 9-35 diagram functional columns in occipital and temporal cortices.

The loss of a few neurons in V5 is unlikely to have much effect on the perception of movement, but recall the case of L. M. in Chapter 9, who had a large injury to V5 and lost her ability to see movement.

Still, Hebb's idea of a cell assembly—an ensemble of neurons that represents a complex concept (see **Figure 15-1**)—suggests some way of converging the inputs of individual neurons to arrive at a consensus. Here, the neuronal ensemble represents a sensory event (apparent motion) that the activity of the ensemble detects. Cell assemblies could be distributed over fairly large regions of the brain, or they could be confined to smaller areas, such as cortical columns.

Via computer modeling, cognitive scientists have demonstrated the capacity of cell assembly circuits to perform sophisticated statistical computations. Other complex tasks, such as Alex the parrot's ability to detect an object's color, also are believed to entail neuronal ensembles. Cell assemblies provide the basis for cognition. Different ensembles come together, much like words in language, to produce coherent thoughts.

What do individual neurons contribute to a cell assembly? Each acts as a computational unit. As Experiment 15-1 shows, even one solitary neuron can fire on its own if its summed inputs indicate that movement is taking place. Neurons are the only elements in the brain that combine evidence to generate knowledge. They are the foundation of cognitive processes and of thought. The combination of individual neurons into novel neural networks produces complex mental representations—ideas, for instance.

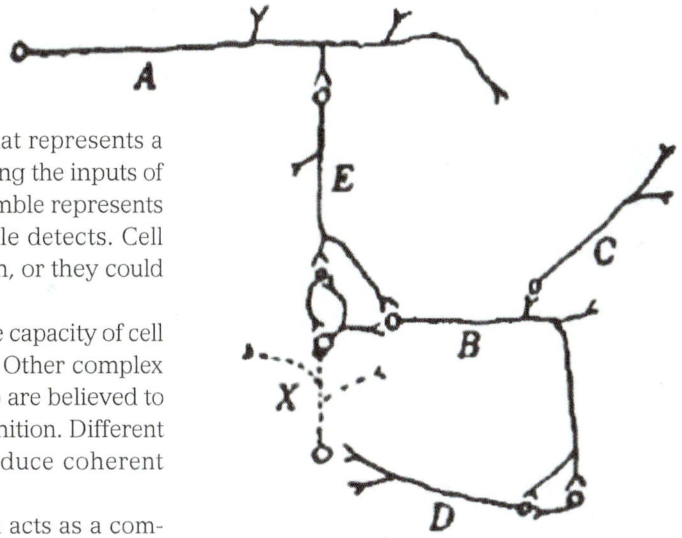

FIGURE 15-1 Hebb's Cell Assembly
"Cells that fire together wire together."
Reprinted with permission from Taylor and Francis Group, LLC Books from D. O. Hebb, "The Organization of Behavior" Copyright 1949, 2002, Figure 9, p. 71. Permission conveyed through Copyright Clearance Center, Inc.

15-1 Review

Before you continue, check your understanding. Answers to Self-Test appear at the back of the book.

1. Cognition, or thought, entails the abilities of _____, _____, and _____ stimuli.

2. Unlike in other animals, humans have the added advantage of _____, which adds _____ to thought.

3. The _____ is the basic unit of thought production.

4. Describe the most important way in which human thought differs from thinking in other animals.

For additional study tools, visit 🔊 **LaunchPad** at launchpadworks.com

association cortex Neocortex outside primary sensory and motor cortices; functions to produce cognition.

15-2

Cognition and the Association Cortex

Altogether, the primary sensory and motor cortical regions occupy about one-third of the neocortex (**Figure 15-2**). The remaining two-thirds, located in the frontal, temporal, parietal, and occipital lobes, is referred to generally as the **association cortex**. It functions to produce cognition.

A fundamental difference between the association cortex and primary sensory and motor areas is that the association cortex has a distinctive pattern of connections. A major source of input to all cortical areas is the thalamus, which rests atop the brainstem. The primary sensory cortex receives inputs from thalamic nuclei that receive information from the body's sense organs. But inputs to the association cortex come from thalamic areas that receive their inputs from other cortical regions. As a result, inputs to the association cortex are already highly

FIGURE 15-2 Cortical Functions Lateral view of the left hemisphere and medial view of the right hemisphere, showing the primary motor and sensory areas. All remaining cortical areas are collectively referred to as the association cortex, which functions in thinking.

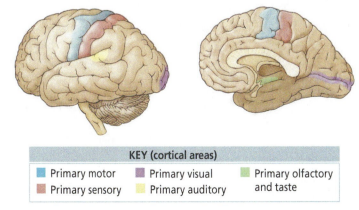

KEY (cortical areas)		
■ Primary motor	■ Primary visual	■ Primary olfactory and taste
■ Primary sensory	■ Primary auditory	

(A) Lateral view

Dorsolateral prefrontal cortex

Orbital prefrontal cortex

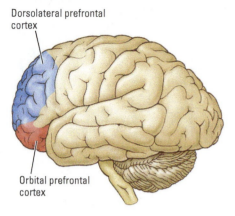

(B) Medial view

Dorsomedial prefrontal cortex

Anterior cingulate cortex

Ventromedial prefrontal cortex

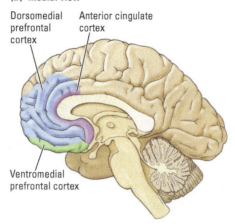

FIGURE 15-3 **Prefrontal Association Cortex** Lateral view of the brain's left hemisphere **(A)** and medial view of the right hemisphere **(B)** represent regions of the prefrontal cortex (PFC) in relationship to the associated anterior cingulate allocortex, shown in (B).

processed. So this information must be fundamentally different from the raw information reaching the primary sensory and motor cortex. The association regions contain knowledge either about our external or internal world or about movements.

Due to the close relationship to the visual and auditory sensory regions, the temporal association regions tend to produce cognition related to visual and auditory processing. Similarly, the parietal cortex is closely related to somatosensation and movement control. In contrast, the frontal cortex coordinates information coming from the parietal and temporal association regions with information coming from subcortical regions.

As diagrammed in **Figure 15-3**, the multiple subdivisions of the *prefrontal cortex (PFC)* encompass its dorsal, lateral, orbital, and medial regions. Activity in each prefrontal region is associated with the types of cognitive processing that we describe throughout this chapter. An additional frontal lobe region shown in Figure 15-3 is the anterior cingulate cortex (ACC). Although the ACC was once believed only to play a role in emotion, it is becoming clear that it functions as an interface between emotion and cognition.

To understand the types of knowledge that the association areas contain, we next consider discrete cognitive behaviors and then trace these behaviors to different parts of the association cortex.

Knowledge about Objects

Visualize a milk carton sitting on a counter directly in front of you. What do you see? Now imagine moving the carton a few inches off to one side as you continue to stare directly ahead. What do you see now? Next, imagine that you tilt the carton toward yourself at a 45° angle. Again, what do you see? Probably you answered that you saw the same thing in each situation: a rectangular box with lettering on it.

Intuitively, you feel that the brain must see the object much as you have perceived it. The brain's seeing, however, is more compartmentalized than are your perceptions. Compartmentalization is revealed in people with damage to various regions of the occipital cortex, many of whom lose one particular aspect of visual perception. For instance, those with damage to visual area V4 can no longer perceive color, whereas those with damage to area V5 can no longer see movement (when the milk carton moves, it becomes invisible to them).

Moreover, your perception of the milk carton's consistently rectangular shape does not always match the forms your visual system is processing. When you tip the carton toward you, you still perceive it as rectangular, even though it is no longer presenting a rectangular shape to your eyes. Your brain has somehow ignored the change in information about shape that your retinas have sent it and concluded that this object, no matter its apparent shape, remains the same milk carton.

There is more to your conception of the milk carton than merely perceiving and processing its physical characteristics. You also know what a milk carton is, what it contains, and where you can get one. The knowledge about milk cartons that you have acquired is represented in the temporal association cortex, which forms the ventral stream of visual processing. If the temporal association regions are destroyed, a person loses visual knowledge not only about milk cartons but also about all other objects. The person becomes *agnosic* (unknowing).

Knowledge about objects includes even more than how they look and what they are used for. It depends on what will be done with the information—how to pick up the milk carton, for example. Knowledge of *what* things are is temporal; knowledge of *how* to grasp the object is parietal (**Figure 15-4**).

Principle 8: The brain divides sensory input for object recognition and movement.

Section 9-5 recounts cases illustrative of various visual-form agnosias.

Parietal lobe

Occipital lobe

Dorsal stream

Ventral stream

Temporal lobe

Striate cortex (region V1)

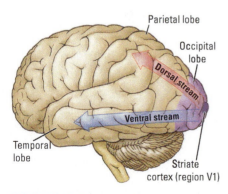

FIGURE 15-4 **Streaming Visual Information** The dorsal visual stream mediates vision for action. The ventral stream mediates vision for object recognition.

Multisensory Integration

Our knowledge about the world comes through multisensory channels. When we see and hear a barking dog, the visual information and auditory information fit together seamlessly. How do all our neural systems and functional levels combine to afford us a unified conscious experience?

Philosophers, impressed with this integrative capacity, identified the **binding problem**, which asks how the brain ties its single and varied sensory and motor events together into a unified perception or behavior. It is gradually becoming clear how the brain binds up our perceptions and how this ability is gradually acquired in postnatal life (see the review by Stein & Rowland, 2011).

One solution to the sensory integration aspect of the binding problem lies in multimodal regions of the association cortex—that is, regions populated by neurons that respond to information from more than one sensory modality, as illustrated in **Figure 15-5**. Investigators presume that multimodal regions combine characteristics of stimuli across different senses when we encounter them separately or together. For example, the fact that we can visually identify objects that we have only touched implies a common perceptual system linking the visual and somatic circuits. Section 15-5 describes the condition known as *synesthesia*, in which stimulation from one sensory modality (for example, taste) concurrently induces the experience of a different modality (touch).

Spatial Cognition

Spatial cognition refers to our knowledge about the environment that allows us to determine where we and objects in our environment are, how to go from one place to another, how to interpret our spatial world, and how to communicate about space (for an extensive discussion, see Waller & Nadel, 2013). There are multiple ways to conceptualize space, including the distinction between body, grasping, distal, and cognitive space (see **Figure 15-6A**); allocentric (object-to-object) and egocentric (self-to-object) space (Figure 15-6B); and a more abstract cognitive space (Figure 15-6C).

Imagine going for a walk in an unfamiliar park. Rather than walking around in circles, you proceed in an organized, systematic way. You also need to find your way back. These abilities require a representation of the physical environment in your mind's eye.

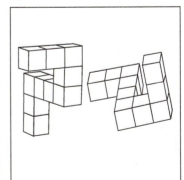

FIGURE 15-5 **Multisensory Areas in the Monkey Cortex** Color-coded areas represent regions where anatomical data and/or electrical stimulation demonstrate multisensory interactions. Dashed lines represent multimodal areas revealed when sulci are opened. Information from Ghanzanfar & Schroeder, 2006.

The senses of smell and taste combine to produce the experience of flavor; see Section 12-2.

binding problem Philosophical question focused on how the brain ties single and varied sensory and motor events together into a unified perception or behavior.

(A)

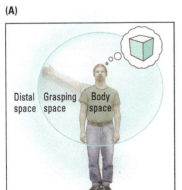

(B) Spatial Reference Frames

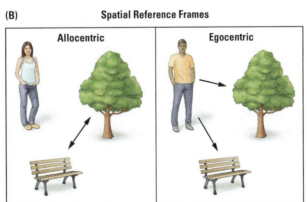

(C)

FIGURE 15-6 **Ways to Conceptualize Space** Space, both external and mental, can be related to the body (panel A). (After Kolb & Whishaw, 2015) The location of objects can be represented in egocentric and allocentric spatial reference frames (panel B). (After Proulx et al., 2016). The same figure can be oriented differently in space (panel C).

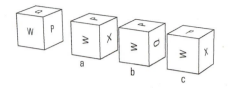

FIGURE 15-7 **Mental Manipulation**
Try this sample test item used to measure spatial orientation. Compare the three cubes on the right with the one on the left. No letter appears on more than one face of a given cube. Which cube—a, b, or c—could be a different view of the cube on the left? The correct answer is at the bottom of the page.

Principle 4: The CNS functions on multiple levels.

Section 1-3 traces nervous system evolution across the animal kingdom.

At some time during the walk, let's say that you are uncertain of where you are—a common problem. One solution is to make a mental image of your route, complete with various landmarks and turns. It is a small step from mentally manipulating these kinds of navigational landmarks and movements to manipulating other kinds of images in your mind. Thus, the ability to mentally manipulate visual images seems likely to have arisen in parallel with the ability to navigate in space.

The evolution of skill in mental manipulation is also closely tied to the evolution of physical movements. It is likely that animals first moved using whole-body movements (the swimming motion of a fish), then developed coordinated limb movements (quadrupedal walking), and finally mastered discrete limb movements, such as a human arm reaching out. As the guidance strategies for controlling movements became more sophisticated, cognitive abilities evolved to support the guidance systems.

It seems unlikely that more sophisticated cognitive abilities evolved on their own. Why would a fish, say, be able to manipulate an object in its mind that it could not manipulate in the real world? But a human, who can manipulate objects by hand, should be able to imagine such manipulations. Once the brain can manipulate objects that are physically present, it seems a small step to manipulating imagined objects—to solve problems like the one depicted in **Figure 15-7**. The ability to manipulate an object in the mind's eye probably flows from the ability to manipulate tangible objects with the hands.

Research findings provide clues to the brain regions participating in various aspects of spatial cognition. For instance, the dorsal stream in the parietal lobes is central in controlling vision for action. Humans make discrete limb movements to points in space, so a reasonable supposition is that the dorsal stream's evolutionary development provided a neural basis for such spatial cognitive skills as mentally rotating objects. By tracing the evolutionary development of the human brain, we find that the parietal association regions expanded considerably more in humans than in other primates. This expanded brain region functions in part to perform the complex spatial operations just discussed. Humans have a capacity for building that far exceeds that of our nearest relative, the chimpanzee. Perhaps our increased capacity for building and manipulating objects played heavily into our developing cognitive spatial abilities.

Deficits of Spatial Behavior

Evidence gathered over the past 60 years indicates that the posterior parietal cortex has a special role in spatial behavior because patients with right posterior parietal lesions show a variety of spatial deficits. One example is topographic disorientation, an inability to find one's way in relationship to salient environmental cues, even in familiar environments. There are multiple forms of *topographic disorientation*, including *egocentric disorientation*, which is a difficulty perceiving relative locations of objects with respect to the self. In his fascinating account of a Russian World War II soldier with a bullet wound to his parietal cortex, Alexander Luria (1972) describes how the man got off at a bus stop in sight of his apartment building but had to ask for directions to the building. Other patients are reported to be unable to set a course to a specific location, even though they are able to recognize landmarks and their own location in relationship to landmarks. They essentially have "no sense of direction." Further examples of spatial deficits include an inability to mentally manipulate objects, like those shown in Figures 15-6C and 15-7.

Deficits in spatial behavior are seen not only after posterior parietal lesions but also after damage to posterior cingulate cortex and medial temporal regions (see Kolb & Whishaw, 2015, for details). Given that the parietal cortex forms the major component of the dorsal stream, it would not be surprising to discover that the dorsal stream is involved in many aspects of spatial cognition. Patients with bilateral injuries to the posterior parietal cortex may show Balint syndrome, a serious disturbance of spatial processing that includes deficits in directing eye gaze peripherally and in comprehending the spatial features of a familiar object. These patients are unable to judge the location of objects in space, estimate distance, discriminate length and size, or evaluate depth

The answer to the mental manipulation in Figure 15-7 is *a*.

and thickness. As a result, they run into objects when walking and have difficulty reading and counting scattered objects.

An extensive literature implicates the temporal cortex, and especially medial temporal regions, in spatial behavior. Both the dorsal and ventral streams converge on the hippocampus, and, as described in Section 14-3 there are several classes of spatially tuned cells in the hippocampal formation (see Figure 14-12). There is also a relationship between the size of the posterior hippocampal region and spatial navigation skills in humans. Taxi drivers in London, England, have larger posterior hippocampal regions than bus drivers, who navigate a fixed route; and fMRI studies show greater activation of the posterior hippocampal region of taxi drivers when they play a video game in which they virtually navigate around London (see the review by Woollett et al., 2009). Curiously, when the taxi drivers retire, their hippocampi shrink over time, suggesting that navigation expertise results in structural changes that reverse with disuse.

Attention

Imagine that you're meeting some friends at a football game. You search for them as you meander through the crowd in the stadium. Suddenly, you hear one friend's distinctive laugh and turn to scan in that direction. You see your group and rush to join them.

This everyday experience demonstrates the nature of **attention**, selective narrowing or focusing of awareness to part of the sensory environment or to a class of stimuli. Even as sounds, smells, feelings, and sights bombard you, you still can detect a familiar laugh or spot a familiar face: you can direct your attention. We can attend selectively to thoughts as well as to sensory stimuli. Who hasn't at some time been so preoccupied with a thought as to exclude all else from mind? Attention can similarly be directed inward as well as outward.

Selective Attention

As with many other inferred mental processes, studying the neural basis of attention is challenging. Research with monkeys trained to attend to particular locations or visual stimuli, however, has identified neurons in the cortex and midbrain that show enhanced firing rates to particular locations or visual stimuli. Significantly, the same stimulus can activate a neuron at one time but not at another, depending on the monkey's learned focus of attention.

James Moran and Robert Desimone (1985) trained monkeys to hold a bar while gazing at a fixation point on a screen. A sample stimulus (a vertical red bar) appeared briefly at one location in the visual field, followed about 500 milliseconds later by a test stimulus at the same location (see **Figure 15-8**). When the test stimulus was identical with the initial sample stimulus, an animal was rewarded if it immediately released the bar.

Each animal was trained to attend to stimuli presented in one particular area of the visual field and to ignore stimuli in any other area. In this way, the same visual stimulus could be presented to different regions of a neuron's receptive field to test whether the cell's response varied with stimulus location.

As the animals performed the task, the researchers recorded neurons firing in visual area V4. These neurons are sensitive to color and form, and different neurons respond to different combinations of the two variables (such as a red vertical bar or a green horizontal bar). Visual stimuli were presented either in the correct location for a reward or in an incorrect location for no reward.

Before training, the neurons responded to all stimuli regardless of location. The results of the experiment showed that after training neurons responded only when a visual stimulus was in the reward location; the neurons would not respond when the same stimulus was presented in a no-reward location. This finding tells us that attending to specific parts of the sensory world is a property of single neurons: more evidence that the neuron is the computational unit of cognition.

attention Narrowing or focusing awareness to a part of the sensory environment or to a class of stimuli.

Fixation point   Stimulus

FIGURE 15-8 **Selective Attention**

contralateral neglect Ignoring a part of the body or world on the side opposite (contralateral to) that of a brain injury.

extinction In neurology, neglect of information on one side of the body when presented simultaneously with similar information on the other side of the body.

Damage to the parietal association cortex described here differs from the loss of proprioception following damage to the neurons that carry sensory information to the cortex, as described in Section 11-4.

FIGURE 15-9 **Testing for Extinction** A stroke patient who shows neglect for information presented to his left visual field responds differently depending on whether objects in the left and right visual fields are similar or different.

When shown two identical objects

Patient's right visual field

Patient's left visual field

Patient sees only the object in his right visual field.

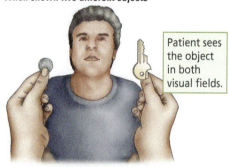

When shown two different objects

Patient sees the object in both visual fields.

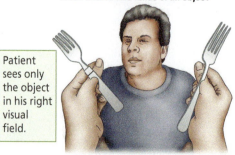

When shown two kinds of an object

Patient sees only the object in his right visual field.

Deficits of Attention

Attention is probably a property of neurons throughout the brain, with some regions playing more prominent roles than others. The frontal lobes, for instance, are central in attention. People with frontal lobe injuries tend to become overly focused on environmental stimuli. They seem to selectively direct attention to an excessive degree or to have difficulty shifting attention. Studies of these people suggest that the frontal association cortex controls the ability to direct attention flexibly to where it is needed. Indeed, planning, a key frontal lobe function, requires this ability.

That the parietal association cortex is key in other aspects of attention is perhaps best illustrated by the attention deficit referred to as *neglect*. Neglect occurs when a brain-injured person ignores sensory information that should be considered important. Usually, the condition affects only one side of the body and is called **contralateral neglect**. We observed a dog that had developed a right-hemisphere tumor and ate only the food on the right side of its dish, ignoring the food on the left side. Neglect is a fascinating symptom because often no damage to sensory pathways accompanies it. Rather, neglect is a failure of attention.

People with damage to the parietal association cortex of the right hemisphere may have particularly severe neglect of objects or events in the left side of their world. For example, one man dressed only the right side of his body, shaved only the right side of his face, and read only the right side of a page (if you can call that reading). He could move his left limbs spontaneously, but when asked to raise both arms, he would raise only the right. When pressed, he could be induced to raise the left arm, but he quickly dropped it to his side again.

As people with contralateral neglect begin to recover, they show another interesting symptom. They neglect information on one side of the body when it is simultaneously presented with similar information on the other side of the body. **Figure 15-9** shows a common clinical test for this symptom, called **extinction**.

In an extinction test, the patient is asked to keep his or her eyes fixed on the examiner's face and to report objects presented in one or both sides of the visual field. When presented with a single object, such as a fork, to one side or the other, the patient orients himself or herself toward the appropriate side of the visual field, so we know that he or she cannot be blind on either side. But now suppose that two forks are presented, one on the left and one on the right. The patient ignores the fork on the left and reports the one on the right. When asked about the left side, the patient is quite certain that nothing appeared there and that only one fork was presented, on the right.

Perhaps the most curious aspect of neglect is that people who have it fail to pay attention not only to one side of the physical world around them but also to one side of the world represented in their mind. We studied one woman who had complete neglect for everything on her left side. She complained that she could not use her kitchen because she could never remember the location of anything on her left.

We asked her to imagine standing at the kitchen door and to describe what was in the various drawers on her right and left. She could not recall anything on her left. We then asked her to imagine walking to the end of the kitchen and turning around. We again asked her what was on her right, the side of the kitchen that had previously been on her left. She broke into a big smile and tears ran down her face as she realized that she now knew what was on that side of the room. All she had to do was reorient her body in her mind's eye. She later wrote and thanked us for changing her life, because she was now able to cook again. Clearly, neglect can exist in the mind as well as in the physical world.

Although complete contralateral neglect is usually associated with parietal lobe injury, specific forms of neglect can arise from other injuries. Ralph Adolphs and his colleagues (2005) describe the case of S. M., a woman with bilateral amygdala damage who could not recognize fear in faces. On further study, the reason was discovered: S. M. failed to look at the eyes when she looked at faces; instead, she looked at other facial features, such as the nose. Because fear is most clearly identified in the eyes, not the nose, she did not identify the emotion. When she was specifically instructed to look at the eyes, her recognition of fear became entirely normal. Thus, the amygdala plays a role in directing attention to the eyes to identify facial expressions.

Planning

At noon on a Friday, a friend proposes that she and you go to a nearby city for the weekend to attend a concert. She will pick you up at 6 P.M., and you will drive there together.

Because you are completely unprepared for this invitation and because you are going to be busy until 4 P.M., you must rush home and get organized. En route, you stop at a fast food restaurant so that you won't be hungry on the 2-hour drive. You also need cash, so you head to the nearest ATM. When you get home, you grab various pieces of clothing appropriate for the concert and the trip. You also pack your toiletries. You somehow manage to get ready by 6 P.M., when your friend arrives.

Although the task of getting ready in a hurry may make us a bit harried, most of us can manage it. People with frontal lobe injury cannot. To learn why, let's consider what the task requires:

1. To plan your behavior, you must select from many options. What do you need to take with you? Cash? Which ATM is closest, and what is the quickest route to it? Are you hungry? What is the fastest way to get food on a Friday afternoon?

2. In view of your time constraint, you have to ignore irrelevant stimuli. If you pass a sign advertising a sale in your favorite store, for instance, you have to ignore it and persist with the task at hand.

3. You have to keep track of what you have done already, a requirement that is especially important while you are packing. You do not want to forget anything or pack duplicates. You do not want to take four pairs of shoes but no toothbrush.

The task's general requirements can be described as the temporal (time) organization of behavior. You are planning what you need to do and when you need to do it. Temporal planning is the general function of the frontal lobes, especially the prefrontal cortex.

But to plan, you also need to recognize objects (an occipital and temporal lobe function) and to make appropriate movements with respect to them (a parietal lobe function). You can therefore think of the frontal lobes as acting like an orchestra conductor. The frontal lobes make and read a motor plan to organize behavior in space and time—a kind of score, analogous to the musical score a conductor uses. People with frontal lobe injuries are simply unable to organize their behavior.

Performance on the Wisconsin Card Sorting Test exemplifies the deficits frontal lobe injury causes. **Figure 15-10** shows the testing materials. The subject is presented with four stimulus cards bearing designs that differ in color, form, and number of elements, thus setting up three possible sorting categories. The subject must sort a deck of cards into piles in front of the various stimulus cards, depending on the sorting category called for. But the correct sorting category is never stated. The subject is simply told after placing each card whether the choice is correct or incorrect, and he or she must figure out the new solution based only on this feedback.

In one trial, for example, the first correct sorting category is color. After the subject has sorted a number of cards by color, the correct solution switches, without warning, to form. When the subject has started to sort by form, the correct solution again changes unexpectedly, this time to the number of items on each card. The sorting rule later becomes color again, and so on, with each change in rule being unannounced.

Shifting response strategies is particularly difficult for people with frontal lobe lesions: they may continue responding to the original stimulus (color) for as many as 100 cards until the test ends. This pattern, known as **perseveration**, is the tendency to emit repeatedly the same verbal or motor response to varied stimuli.

perseveration Tendency to emit repeatedly the same verbal or motor response to varied stimuli.

FIGURE 15-10 **Wisconsin Card Sorting Test** The participant receives a deck of cards containing multiple copies of those represented here and is presented with a row of four cards selected from among them. The task is to place each card in the pile under the appropriate card in the row, sorting by one of three possible categories. Participants are never explicitly told what the correct sorting category is—color, number, or form. They are told only whether their responses are correct or incorrect. After subjects have begun sorting by one category, the tester unexpectedly changes to another category.

Frontal lobe subjects may even comment that they know that color is no longer the correct category, but they continue to sort by color. One stated: "Form is probably the correct solution now so this [sorting by color] will be wrong, and this will be wrong, and wrong again." Despite knowing the correct sorting category, the frontal lobe patient cannot shift behavior in response to the new external information.

Imitation and Understanding

In all communication—verbal and nonverbal—the sender and receiver must share an understanding of what matters. If a person speaks a word or makes a gesture, another person will understand only if he or she interprets it correctly. To accomplish this coordination in communication, the processes of producing and perceiving a message must share a common representation in the sender's and the receiver's brains.

How do both sender and receiver of a potentially ambiguous gesture, such as a raised hand or a faint smile, achieve a common understanding? Giacomo Rizzolatti and his colleagues proposed an answer (Rizzolatti, 2007; Rizzolatti & Craighero, 2004). In monkeys' frontal lobes, they identified neurons that discharge while movements of the hand or mouth or both are occurring. These neural discharges do not precede the movements but instead occur in synchrony with them. But it takes time for a neural message to go from a frontal lobe to a hand, so we would predict that, if these cells are controlling the movements, they will discharge *before* the movements take place. The cells must therefore be recording a movement that is taking place.

In the course of his studies in the 1990s, Rizzolatti made the serendipitous discovery that many "movement" neurons located in the inferior frontal and posterior parietal cortex discharge when a monkey sees other monkeys make the same movements. They also discharge when the monkey sees the experimenter make the movements. Rizzolatti called them **mirror neurons**, and the name stuck. The researchers proposed that mirror neurons represent actions—one's own or those of others. Such neural representations could be used both for imitating others' actions and for understanding their meanings, thus enabling appropriate responses. Mirror neurons therefore could provide the link between the sender and the receiver of a communication.

Rizzolatti and his colleagues used PET to look for these same neuron populations in humans. Participants were asked to watch a movement, to make the same movement, or to imagine the movement. Each condition activated a region of the lateral frontal lobe in the left hemisphere, including Broca's area. Taken together with the results of the monkey studies, this finding suggests that primates have a fundamental mechanism for recognizing action. People apparently recognize others' actions because the neural patterns produced when they observe those actions are similar to those produced when they themselves make the same actions.

In the early 2000s, mirror neurons were hypothesized to be the basis of *understanding* actions rather than merely recognizing them. This possibility had profound implications and led to propositions that mirror neurons are the basis of speech and language, empathy, social cognition, theory of mind—even civilization! Dysfunction of the mirror neuron system was proposed as a basis for disorders, such as the broken mirror hypothesis of autism (Ramachandran & Oberman, 2006). The lure of mirror neurons spread well beyond neuroscience and into the popular media: mirror neurons became widely perceived as being among the most important neuroscience discoveries in the past generation.

Within a few years, cracks began to show in the mirror. Gregory Hickok (2014) has argued that mirror neurons do not make actions understandable, but they do refine movement control. Hickok and others suggest that mirror neurons do not "understand" action, but rather their function arises from an association between executing an action and the self-observation of the action.

Thus, the neurons learn to mirror. But why? One possible benefit is that because the actions of others are relevant to one's own actions, having a system to link others' perceived actions with one's own appropriate actions is adaptive. An extension of this idea is that mirror neurons are activated after an action is understood by other brain regions as a way to make predictions about future actions (Hickok, 2013). In this view,

mirror neuron Cell in the primate premotor and parietal cortex that fires when an individual observes an action taken by another individual.

mirror neurons simply reflect the fact that the brain understands actions (Csibra, 2007). The advantage of this type of mirror system is that with this knowledge, we can make movements more quickly and more accurately.

15-2 Review

Before you continue, check your understanding. Answers to Self-Test appear at the back of the book.

1. The association cortex contains _____ and functions to produce _____.

2. As a general rule, the _____ lobes generate knowledge about objects, whereas the _____ lobes produce various forms of spatial cognition.

3. The frontal lobes function not only to make movements but also to _____ and to _____.

4. _____ neurons in the frontal and parietal lobes represent actions—one's own or those of others.

5. Describe the function of multimodal cortex.

For additional study tools, visit ⚏ **LaunchPad** at launchpadworks.com

---

15-3

Expanding Frontiers of Cognitive Neuroscience

Sophisticated noninvasive stimulation and recording techniques for measuring the brain's electrical activity and noninvasive brain-imaging methods led to the emergence of a new field in studying brain and behavior: **cognitive neuroscience**, the field that studies the neural bases of cognition. Cognitive neuroscience focuses on high-tech research methods but continues to rely on the decidedly low-tech tools of neuropsychological assessment—behavioral tests that compare the effects of brain injuries on performing particular tasks. Clinical Focus 15-3, Neuropsychological Assessment, illustrates its benefits.

Sophisticated imaging techniques are helping cognitive neuroscientists map the human brain. Imaging methods assist social psychologists in discovering how the brain mediates social interactions and aid economists in discovering how the brain makes decisions, as discussed later in this section.

Mapping the Brain

Among the great scientific challenges of the twenty-first century, mapping the human **brain connectome** may be the most intriguing. Toward this end, the U.S. National Institutes of Health (NIH) awarded grants totaling $40 million to map the complete structural and functional fiber pathway connections of the human brain in vivo. Researchers participating in the Human Connectome Project (HCP) are combining diffusion tensor imaging (DTI) and functional connectivity magnetic resonance imaging (fcMRI) to plot these connections in the living human brain. By the end of 2016, HCP investigators had completed scanning 1200 healthy adults' brains, including 300 twin pairs.

The first step in the mapping was to identify an accurate parcellation of the cerebral cortex. Researchers have been constructing brain maps for over 100 years, but the number of distinct areas varies from about 50 to 200, depending on the method of analysis. The HCP investigators used a machine learning classifier of more than 500 brains to parcel the cortex into 180 areas whose presence could be detected in about 97 percent of new HCP participants (Glasser et al., 2016). This parcellation will enable substantially improved structural and functional studies of the human cerebral cortex.

In addition to these efforts, an explosion of studies outside the HCP also seeks to describe specific processes and disorders using mapping technology. For example, in

For more on the HCP, including connectome images, go to www.humanconnectomeproject.org. *National Geographic* published an accessible article in February 2014.

---

cognitive neuroscience Study of the neural bases of cognition.

brain connectome Map of the complete structural and functional fiber pathways of the human brain in vivo.

◎ CLINICAL FOCUS 15-3

Neuropsychological Assessment

In this high-tech age of PET, fMRI, and ERP, low-tech behavioral assessment endures as among the best, simplest, and most economical ways to measure cognitive function.

To illustrate the nature and power of neuropsychological assessment, we compared the performance of three patients on an array of tests selected from among those used in a complete neuropsychological assessment. The five tests presented here measure verbal and visual memory, verbal fluency, abstract reasoning, and reading. Performance was compared with that of a healthy control participant.

In the delayed memory tests—one verbal, the other visual—the patients and the control were read a list of words and two short stories. They were also shown a series of simple drawings. Their task: repeat the words and stories immediately after hearing them and draw the simple figures.

Half an hour later, without warning, they were asked to perform the tasks again. Their performance on these tests yielded the delayed verbal and visual memory scores listed in the table.

In the delayed verbal fluency test, patients and control had 5 minutes to write down as many words as they could think of that start with the letter *s*, excluding numbers and people's names. Then came the Wisconsin Card Sorting Test, which assesses abstract reasoning (see Figure 15-10). Finally, all were given a reading test.

Subjects' Scores

Test	Control	J. N.	E. B.	J. W.
Delayed verbal memory	17	9*	16	16
Delayed visual memory	12	14	8*	12
Verbal fluency	62	62	66	35*
Card-sorting errors	9	10	12	56*
Reading	15	21	22	17

*Atypically poor score.

The first patient, J. N., was a 28-year-old man who had developed a tumor in the anterior and medial left temporal lobe. His preoperative psychological tests showed superior intelligence scores. His only significant deficits appeared on tests of verbal memory.

When we saw J. N. a year after surgery that successfully removed the tumor, he had returned to his job as a personnel manager. His intelligence was still superior, but as the score summary shows, he was impaired on the delayed verbal memory test, recalling only about 50 percent as much as the control and other subjects.

The second patient, E. B., was a college senior majoring in psychology. An aneurysm in her right temporal lobe had burst due to a bulge in the artery. The anterior part of that lobe had been removed. E. B. was of above-average intelligence and completed her undergraduate degree with good grades. Her score on the delayed visual memory test, just over half the scores of the other test-takers, clearly showed her residual deficit.

The third patient, also of above-average intelligence, was J. W., a 42-year-old police detective who had a college degree. A benign tumor had been removed from his left frontal lobe.

We saw J. W. 10 years after his surgery. He was still on the police force but working a desk job. His verbal fluency was markedly reduced, as was his ability to solve the card-sorting task. His reading skill, however, was unimpaired. This was also true of the other patients.

Two principles emerge from the results of these three neuropsychological assessments:

1. *Brain functions are localized.* Damage to different brain regions produces different symptoms.

2. *Brain organization is asymmetrical.* Left-hemisphere damage preferentially affects verbal functions; right-hemisphere damage preferentially affects nonverbal functions.

---

a review, Roser Sala-Llonch and colleagues (2015) report that as people age, they show reduced functional connectivity compared to young adults. The investigators hypothesize that this finding could explain age-related cognitive changes.

Using fMRI in Brain Mapping

The functional correlations MRI (fcMRI) technique uses resting-state fMRI (rs-fMRI) to measure functional correlations between brain regions. Pooling rs-fMRI data across thousands of healthy young adults makes it possible to identify consistent patterns of connectivity, or nerve tracts, in the brain. Utilizing rs-fMRI data from 1000 participants, Thomas Yeo and colleagues (2011) parcellated the human cerebral cortex into the 17 networks illustrated in **Figure 15-11**.

The cerebral cortex is made up of primary sensory and motor networks, as well as the multiple, large-scale networks that form the association cortex. The sensory and motor networks are largely local: adjacent areas tend to show strong functional coupling with one another. In Figure 15-11, the turquoise and blue/gray regions in the somatosensory and motor cortex and the purple region in the visual cortex illustrate these couplings.

In contrast, the association networks include areas distributed throughout the prefrontal, parietal, anterior temporal, and midline regions. In Figure 15-11, the distributed yellow regions show prefrontal–posterior parietal connectivity. Some distributed networks, shown in light red, include temporal, posterior parietal, and prefrontal regions.

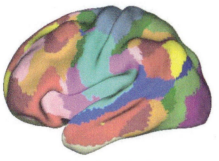
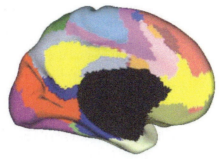

Left hemisphere, lateral view   **Left hemisphere, Medial view**

FIGURE 15-11 **Parcellation of Cerebral Cortical Networks** An estimate of 17 cortical networks based on fcMRI data from 1000 participants. Each color represents a network. Some, such as the blue auditory areas in the temporal lobe, are localized; others are widely distributed, such as the yellow regions, which reveal prefrontal–posterior parietal connectivity. Republished with permission of the American Physiological Society from B. T. T. Yeo, F. M. Fienen, J. Sepulcre, M. R. Sabuncu, D. Lashkari, et al., "The Organization of the Human Cerebral Cortex Estimated by Intrinsic Functional Connectivity," 2011, Journal of Neurophysiology, 106, pp. 1125–1165. Permission conveyed through Copyright Clearance Center, Inc.

Unlike DTI, fcMRI does not measure static anatomical connectivity but rather uses temporal (time-based) correlations between neurophysiological activities in different regions to infer functional connectivity. One obvious direction of investigations based on fcMRI is searching for individual phenotypic variations. Such mapping will allow examination of specific traits (such as musical ability) or psychiatric diagnoses (see the review by Kelly et al., 2012).

Tractography Using Diffusion Tensor Imaging

DTI studies provide results, often called *tractography*, that complement the networks mapped by fcMRI. Tractography measures actual neuroanatomical pathways that can be related to specific traits. Traditional postmortem tract tracing was performed on single brains. Today, tractography can be performed quickly on many living brains, and measurements can be made simultaneously in the entire brain. This advance allows researchers to correlate specific behavioral traits with specific patterns of connectivity.

Psyche Loui and her colleagues (2011) were interested in the neural basis of perfect (or absolute) pitch—the ability not only to discriminate among musical notes but also to name any note heard. Perfect pitch is rare among humans but is shared by people with remarkable musical talents. Think Mozart. Development of perfect pitch is sensitive to early experiences, including musical training and exposure to tonal languages such as Japanese.

Loui's team studied musicians, with and without absolute pitch, who were matched in gender, age, handedness, ethnicity, IQ score, and years of musical training. Participants were given a test of pitch-labeling that allowed the researchers to place the musicians with absolute pitch into two categories: more accurate and less accurate. The less accurate group was superior to participants without absolute pitch, who could not accurately identify the note.

The investigators hypothesized that absolute pitch could be related to increased connectivity in brain regions that process sounds. They used DTI to reconstruct white-matter tracts connecting two temporal cortex regions involved in auditory processing, the superior and middle temporal gyri, and regions not involved in auditory processing (corticospinal tract). The results, reproduced in **Figure 15-12**, show that people with absolute pitch have greater connectivity in temporal lobe regions responsible for pitch perception than do people without it. The effect is largest in people in the more accurate group.

FIGURE 15-12 **Tractography of Temporal Lobe Auditory Circuits** Color overlaid on DTI images demonstrates tracts between the superior temporal gyrus and middle temporal gyrus in three individuals. Participants A and B had more accurate and less accurate perfect pitch, respectively; Case C did not. The tracts that connect the regions in the left hemisphere (orange) are larger in participants A and B than in C. Tracts colored purple connect the regions in the right hemisphere. Copyright © 2011, Massachusetts Institute of Technology. Loui, P., Li, H. C., Hohmann, A., & Schlaug, G. (2011). Enhanced Connectivity in Absolute Pitch Musicians: A Model of Hyperconnectivity. Journal of Cognitive Neuroscience 23(4), 1015-1026. Permission conveyed through Copyright Clearance Center, Inc.

(A) More accurate perfect pitch   **(B) Less accurate perfect pitch**   **(C) Lacking perfect pitch**

Left hemisphere   Right hemisphere   Left hemisphere   Right hemisphere   Left hemisphere   Right hemisphere

hyperconnectivity Increased local connections between two related brain regions.

social neuroscience Interdisciplinary field that seeks to understand how the brain mediates social interactions.

theory of mind Ability to attribute mental states to others.

Research Focus 2-1 describes the effects of cerebellar agenesis.

Although enhanced connectivity appears in both hemispheres of the musicians, when the investigators correlated performance on a test of absolute pitch with tract volume, only left-hemisphere tract volume predicted performance. It appears that having more local connections, or **hyperconnectivity**, in the left hemisphere is responsible for absolute pitch.

It is tempting to speculate that other exceptional talents, such as creativity, might be related to hyperconnectivity in cerebral regions. Conversely, we can speculate that reduced structural and functional connectivity is related to cognitive impairments acquired after brain injuries and/or neurodevelopmental and psychiatric disorders.

Cognition and the Cerebellum

So far, we have emphasized the role of the neocortex in cognitive functions, in part because of its marked expansion in size and neuron numbers in primate brains. Yet the human cerebellum accounts for 80 percent of the brain's neurons. The cerebellum has long been known to play a central role in motor control and motor learning, but the concurrent evolution of neocortex, cerebellum, and cognitive complexity in primates suggests that the cerebellum may play a larger role in cognitive processes than investigators have appreciated (e.g., Barton, 2012).

The extensive neocortex–cerebellum interconnections include prefrontal cortex, Broca's area, and neocortical regions that have sensory or perceptual functions. Thus, the cerebellum appears to be critical in producing fine movements and perception, but some executive function also may be associated with working memory, attention, language, music, and decision-making processes (Baumann et al., 2015). No single coherent model of cerebellar activity in cognition has emerged, partly because researchers interested in cognitive functions have neglected the cerebellum for decades. Only recently has research pointed to the role the cerebellum may play in emotion and mood disorders (for example, Adamaszek et al., 2017).

Undoubtedly, the coming decade will deliver an abundance of new information, allowing for a better-informed model of cerebellar functions in cognition.

Social Neuroscience

By combining cognitive neuroscience tools, especially functional neuroimaging, with abstract constructs from social psychology, **social neuroscience** seeks to understand how the brain mediates social interactions. Matthew Lieberman (2007) identified broad themes that attempt to encompass all cognitive processes involved in understanding and interacting with others and in understanding ourselves.

Understanding Others

Animals' minds and experiences are not open to direct inspection. We infer animals' minds in part by observing their behaviors and, in the case of humans, by listening to their words. In doing so, we may develop a **theory of mind (ToM)**, the attribution of mental states to others. Theory of mind includes an understanding that others may have feelings and beliefs different from our own. This broader understanding has led some investigators to conclude that theory of mind may be uniquely human. But many researchers who study apes strongly believe that other primates, too, possess a theory of mind.

Many fMRI studies over the past decade suggest that the brain region believed to be most closely associated with ToM is the dorsolateral prefrontal cortex (see Figure 15-3). Human prefrontal regions are disproportionately large compared to other mammals, after correcting for brain size, but other primates also have large prefrontal regions. The anatomy supports the likelihood that apes also possess a theory of mind.

The capacity to understand others can also be inferred from the presence of empathy. For example, when participants watch videos of others smelling disgusting odors, they report a feeling of disgust. Lieberman and his colleagues (Rameson et al., 2012) used fMRI to assess the neural correlates of empathy by asking participants to empathize with sad images. Empathy correlated with increased activity in the medial prefrontal region, suggesting that the area is critical for empathic experience.

Although the original studies on ToM focused on humans, there is a growing literature suggesting that many other animals may have a form of ToM, although this view has attracted some skeptics (for example, see the review by Heyes, 2015). Nonetheless, experimental methods have been developed to examine the degree of understanding that one animal can gain by observing the intention, gaze, perspective, or knowledge of another. Some studies claim that apes and some monkeys show ToM, as do dogs and corvid birds (jays, crows, ravens) and parrots (for example, Bugnar et al., 2016; Maginnity & Grace, 2014).

Understanding Oneself

Not only are we humans aware of others' intentions, but we also have a sense of self. Humans, as well as some apes, dolphins, elephants, pigs, and magpies, have the ability to recognize themselves in a mirror; human infants demonstrate this ability by about 21 months of age. Studies using fMRI show that when we recognize our own face versus the faces of familiar others, brain activity increases in the right lateral prefrontal cortex and in the lateral parietal cortex. The parietal cortex activation is thought to reflect the body's recognition of what itself feels like.

But self-recognition is only the beginning of understanding oneself. People also have a self-concept that includes beliefs about their own personal traits (such as kind and intelligent). When participants are asked to determine whether trait words or sentences are self-descriptive, brain activity in medial prefrontal regions increases.

Self-Regulation

Self-regulation is the ability to control emotions and impulses as a means of achieving long-term goals. We may wish to yell at the professor because an exam was unfair, but most of us recognize that this action will not be productive. Dynamic imaging studies again reveal that prefrontal regions are critical in social cognition—in this case in self-regulation.

Children are often poor self-regulators, which probably reflects slow development of the prefrontal regions responsible for impulse control. A uniquely human ability of self-regulation is to put feelings into words, a strategy that allows us to control emotional outbursts. Curiously, such verbal labeling is associated with increased activity in the right lateral prefrontal regions but *not* in the left.

Section 8-2 describes unique aspects of frontal lobe development that extend beyond childhood—up to age 30.

Not only can humans control their emotions, they also have expectations about how a stimulus might feel (for example, an injection by syringe). Our expectations can alter the actual feeling of an event. It is common for people to say "ouch" when they do something like stub a toe, even if they actually feel no pain. Nobukatsu Sawamoto and colleagues (2000) found that when participants expect pain, activity increases in the anterior cingulate cortex (see Figure 15-3B), a region associated with pain perception, even if the stimulus turns out not to be painful. In a recent review of more than 10,000 fMRI studies, Matthew Lieberman and Naomi Eisenberger (2015) conclude that the best description of the function of the anterior cingulate cortex is related to pain processing.

Feeling and treating physical pain is a topic in Section 11-4. Research Focus 12-1 reports on emotional pain.

Living in a Social World:
Social Cognition and Brain Activity

We spend much of our waking time interacting with others socially. In a sense, our understanding of our self and our social interactions link together into a single mental action. One important aspect of this behavior includes forming attitudes and beliefs about ourselves and about others. When we express attitudes (including prejudices) toward ideas or human groups, brain imaging shows activation in prefrontal, anterior cingulate, and lateral parietal regions.

Similarly, social cognitions that run the gamut from understanding ourselves to understanding others are clearly associated with activation of specific brain regions, especially prefrontal regions. The obvious conclusion is that prefrontal activity

neuroeconomics Interdisciplinary field that seeks to understand how the brain makes decisions.

produces our social cognitions, just as activity in visual regions produces our visual perceptions. But this conclusion has proven controversial, in part because of the nature of the analysis of fMRI data and because the high cost of fMRI experiments is a factor in both determining the number of participants in a study and limiting the feasibility of replication studies.

The ability to replicate studies is central to the scientific method and is rarely done in fMRI studies (see further discussion in Poldrack et al., 2017). However, in the past few years, several meta-analyses combining studies from many locations have provided greater validity to the conclusions; recall the 10,000 pain and anterior cingulate studies reviewed earlier in this chapter.

Neuroeconomics

Leonard Mlodinow's wonderful 2009 book *The Drunkard's Walk: How Randomness Rules Our Lives* offers many everyday examples.

Historically, economics was a discipline based on the "rational actor," which involves the belief that people make rational decisions. In the real world, people often make decisions based on assumption or intuition, as is common in gambling. Why don't people always make rational decisions?

The cerebral processes underlying human decision making are not easily inferred from behavioral studies. But investigators in the field of **neuroeconomics**, which combines ideas from economics, psychology, and neuroscience, attempt to explain those processes by studying patterns of brain activity as people make decisions in real time. The general assumption among neuroeconomists is that two neural decision pathways influence our choices. One is deliberate, slow, rule-driven, and emotionally neutral; it acts as a *reflective system*. The other pathway—fast, automatic, emotionally biased—forms a *reflexive system*.

Figure 6-16 maps the dopaminergic pathways associated with reward.

If people must make quick decisions they believe will provide immediate gain, widespread activity appears in the dopaminergic reward system. This includes the ventromedial prefrontal cortex and ventral striatum (nucleus accumbens): the reflexive pathway. If slower, deliberative decisions are possible, activity is greater in the lateral prefrontal, medial temporal, and posterior parietal cortex, the areas that form the reflective pathway.

Neuroeconomists are looking to identify patterns of neural activity in everyday decision making, patterns that may help account for how people make decisions about their finances, social relations, and other personal choices. Although most neuroeconomic studies to date have used fMRI, in principle these studies could also use other noninvasive imaging technologies. Epigenetic factors probably contribute to developing the balance between the reflective and reflexive systems in individuals. Epigenetic studies therefore may help explain why many people make decisions that are not in their long-term best interest.

Because of predictions that all mammals will have similar reflective and reflexive decision systems and because all animals make decisions, the neural bases of decision processes in nonhumans undoubtedly will receive more study in the future.

15-3 Review

Before you continue, check your understanding. Answers to Self-Test appear at the back of the book.

1. Noninvasive imaging techniques enable cognitive psychologists to investigate the neural bases of thought in the "normal" brain, leading to the field called _____.

2. By using imaging methods such as DTI and fcMRI, researchers are developing a _____, a map of the complete structural and functional fiber pathway connections in the living human brain.

3. The formerly unappreciated role of the _____ in cognition is now attracting researchers' attention.

4. Social neuroscience is an interdisciplinary field that seeks to understand how the brain mediates _____.

5. Our attribution of mental states to others is known as _____.

6. Neuroeconomics seeks to understand the neural bases of _____.

7. List four general themes of social neuroscience research.

For additional study tools, visit **LaunchPad** at launchpadworks.com

15-4

Cerebral Asymmetry in Thinking

Fundamental to behavioral neuroscience was the finding by Paul Broca and his contemporaries in the mid-1800s that language is lateralized to the brain's left hemisphere. But the implications of lateralized brain functions were not fully understood until the 1960s, when Roger Sperry (1968) and his colleagues began to study people who, as described in Research Focus 15-1, had undergone surgical separation of the two hemispheres as a treatment for intractable epilepsy. It soon became apparent that the cerebral hemispheres are more functionally specialized than researchers had previously realized. Before considering how the brain's two sides cooperate in generating cognitive activity, we look at the anatomical differences between the left and right hemispheres. Note that although the cerebral asymmetry of most left-handers is similar to that of right-handers, about one-third have a somewhat different organization, which is beyond the scope of this discussion (for details see Kolb & Whishaw, 2015).

Seizing on Sperry's findings, the 1980s saw an avalanche of self-help books about "left-brained" and "right-brained" people. The theories espoused in these books largely ignored functions shared by both hemispheres, and the novelty eventually wore off, but the concept of cerebral asymmetry remains important to understanding how the human brain thinks.

Anatomical Asymmetry

Building on Broca's findings, investigators have learned how the language- and music-related areas of the left and right temporal lobes differ anatomically. In particular, the primary auditory area is larger on the right, whereas the secondary auditory areas are larger on the left in most people. Other brain regions also are asymmetrical.

Principle 5: The brain is symmetrical and asymmetrical.

Figure 15-13 shows that the lateral fissure, which partly separates the temporal and parietal lobes, has a sharper upward course in the right hemisphere relative to the left. As a result, the posterior right temporal lobe is larger than the same region on the left, as is the left parietal lobe relative to the right.

Among the anatomical asymmetries in the frontal lobes, the region of sensorimotor cortex representing the face is larger in the left hemisphere than in the right, a difference that presumably corresponds to the left hemisphere's special role in talking. Broca's area is organized differently on the left and the right. The area visible on the brain's surface is about one-third larger on the right than on the left, whereas the cortical area buried in the sulci of Broca's area is greater on the left than on the right.

Not only do these gross anatomical differences exist, but so too do hemispheric differences in the details of their cellular and neurochemical structures. For example, neurons in Broca's area on the left have larger dendritic fields than do corresponding neurons on the right. The discovery of structural asymmetries tells us little about the reasons for such differences, but there are clear correlations with differences in cognitive processing by the brain's two sides.

Although many anatomical asymmetries in the human brain are related to language, brain asymmetries are not unique to humans. Most, if not all, mammals have asymmetries, as do many bird species. The functions of cerebral asymmetry therefore cannot be limited to language processing. Rather, human language likely evolved after the brain became asymmetrical. Language simply took advantage of processes, including the development of mirror neurons, that had already been lateralized by natural selection in earlier members of the human lineage.

FIGURE 15-13 **Cerebral Asymmetry** The lateral fissure takes a flatter course in the left hemisphere than in the right. As a result, the posterior right temporal lobe is larger than the same region on the left side, and the inferior parietal region is larger on the left than on the right.

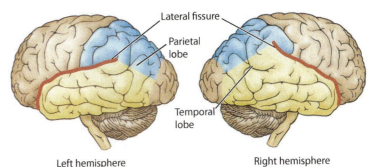

Lateral fissure

Parietal lobe

Temporal lobe

Left hemisphere

Right hemisphere

(A) Participant G. H.

Injury to this area of the right hemisphere caused difficulties in copying drawings, assembling puzzles, and finding the way around a familiar city.

(B) Participant M. M.

Injury to this area of the left hemisphere caused difficulties in language, copying movements, reading, and generating names of objects or animals.

FIGURE 15-14 **Contrasting Parietal Lobe Injuries**

Functional Asymmetry in Neurological Patients

The specialized functions of the cerebral hemispheres become obvious in people with damage to the left or right side of the brain. To see these functional differences clearly, compare the cases of G. H. and M. M.

Right Parietal Damage

When G. H. was 5 years old, as he was hiking with his family, a large rock rolled off an embankment and hit him on the head. He was unconscious for a few minutes and had a severe headache for a few days but quickly recovered. Around age 18, however, he started having seizures. Neurosurgical investigation revealed that G. H. had had a right posterior parietal injury from the rock accident. **Figure 15-14A** shows the area affected. After surgery to remove this area, G. H. had weakness on the left side of his body and showed contralateral neglect. But these symptoms lessened fairly quickly, and a month after the surgery, they had completely cleared.

Nevertheless, G. H. had chronic difficulties in copying drawings; 4 years after the surgery, he still performed this task at about the level of a 6-year-old. He also had trouble assembling puzzles, a pastime he had enjoyed before the surgery. When asked to perform mental manipulations like the one in Figure 15-7, he became very frustrated and refused to continue. G. H. also had difficulty finding his way around familiar places. The landmarks he had used to guide his travels before the surgery no longer worked for him. G. H. now has to learn street names and use a verbal strategy to go from one place to another.

Left Parietal Damage

Meningioma is imaged in Clinical Focus 3-2.

M. M.'s difficulties were quite different from G. H.'s. A meningioma had placed considerable pressure on the left parietal region. The tumor was surgically removed when M. M. was 16 years old. It had damaged the area shown in Figure 15-14B.

After the surgery, M. M. had various problems, including *aphasia*, impaired language use. The condition lessened over time: a year after the surgery, M. M. spoke fluently. Unfortunately, other difficulties persisted. In solving arithmetic problems, in reading, and even in simply calling objects or animals by name, M. M. performed at about a 6-year-old level. She had no difficulty making movements spontaneously, but when asked to copy a series of arm movements, such as those diagrammed in **Figure 15-15**, she had great difficulty. She could not figure out how to make her arm move to match the example. A general impairment in making voluntary movements in the absence of paralysis or a muscular disorder is a symptom of *apraxia*, the inability to complete a plan of action accurately.

Section 10-4 describes how left-hemisphere damage causes aphasias. Section 11-5 explains how somatosensory cortex damage contributes to apraxia.

Lessons from Patients G. H. and M. M.

What can we learn about brain function by comparing G. H. and M. M.? Their lesions were in approximately the same location but in opposite hemispheres, and their symptoms were very different.

Judging from G. H.'s difficulties, the right hemisphere contributes to controlling spatial skills, such as drawing, assembling puzzles, and navigating in space. In contrast, M. M.'s condition reveals that the left hemisphere seems to contribute to controlling language functions and cognitive tasks related to schoolwork—namely, reading and arithmetic. In addition, the left hemisphere's role in controlling voluntary movement sequences differs from the right hemisphere's role.

Series 1

Series 2

FIGURE 15-15 **Two Arm Movement Series**
Subjects observe the tester perform each
sequence and then copy it as accurately as
they can. People with left-hemisphere injury,
especially in the posterior parietal region, are
impaired at copying such movements.

dichotic listening Experimental procedure
for simultaneously presenting a different
auditory input to each ear through stereophonic
earphones.

To some extent, then, the left and right hemispheres think about different types of
information. The question is whether these functional differences can be observed in
a healthy brain.

Functional Asymmetry in the Healthy Brain

In the course of studying the auditory capacity of people with temporal lobe lesion, Doreen
Kimura (1967) found something unexpected. She presented her control participants with
two strings of digits, one played into each ear, a procedure known as **dichotic listening**.
The task was to recall as many digits as possible.

Kimura found that the controls recalled more digits presented to the right ear
than to the left. This result is surprising because the auditory system crosses repeatedly, beginning in the midbrain. Nonetheless, information coming from the right
ear seems to have preferential access to the left (speaking) hemisphere.

In a later study, Kimura (1973) played two pieces of music for participants, one
to each ear. She then gave the participants a multiple-choice test, playing four bits
from musical selections and asking the participants to pick out the bits they had
heard before. In this test, she found that participants were more likely to recall the
music played to the left ear than to the right. This result implies that the left ear has
preferential access to the right (musical) hemisphere.

The demonstration of this functional asymmetry in the healthy brain provoked
much interest in the 1970s, leading to demonstrations of functional asymmetries
in the visual and tactile systems as well. Consider the visual system. If we fixate on
a target, such as a dot positioned straight ahead, all the information to the left of
the dot goes to the right hemisphere, and all the information to the right of the dot
goes to the left hemisphere, as shown in **Figure 15-16**.

If information is presented for a relatively long time—say, 1 second—we can easily
report what was in each visual field. If, however, the presentation is brief—say, only
40 milliseconds—then the task is considerably harder. This situation reveals a brain
asymmetry.

Words presented briefly to the right visual field and hence sent to the left
hemisphere are more easily reported than are words presented briefly to the
left visual field. Similarly, if complex geometric patterns or faces are shown
briefly, those presented to the left visual field and hence sent to the right hemisphere are more accurately reported than are those presented to the right
visual field.

FIGURE 15-16 **Visual Pathways to the
Hemispheres** When fixating at a point,
each eye sees both visual fields but sends
information about the right visual field only
to the left hemisphere. Information about
the left visual field proceeds only to the right
hemisphere. In healthy participants given short
exposures to stimuli (well under 1 second), the
left hemisphere is more accurate at perceiving
words, whereas the right hemisphere is more
accurate at perceiving objects, including faces.

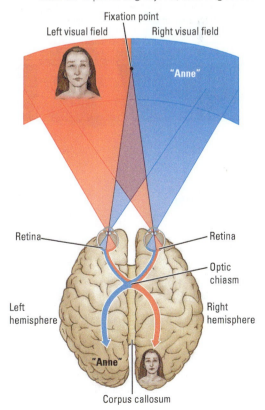

Apparently, the hemispheres not only think about different types of information, they also process information differently. The left hemisphere seems biased toward processing language-related information, whereas the right hemisphere seems biased toward processing nonverbal, and especially spatial, information.

A word of caution: although asymmetry studies are fascinating, what they tell us about the differences between the hemispheres is not entirely clear. They tell us *something* is different, but it is a broad leap to conclude that the hemispheres house entirely different skill sets. The hemispheres have many common functions, such as controlling movement in the contralateral hand and processing sensory information through the thalamus. Still, differences in the hemispheres' cognitive operations do exist. We can better understand these differences by studying split-brain patients, whose cerebral hemispheres have been surgically separated for medical treatment.

Functional Asymmetry in the Split Brain

Before considering the details of split-brain studies, let us review what we already know about cerebral asymmetry. First, the left hemisphere talks; the right hemisphere does not. Second, as demonstrated in Research Focus 15-1 (page 516), the right hemisphere performs better than the left on certain nonverbal tasks, especially those that engage visuospatial skills.

But how does a severed corpus callosum affect how the brain thinks? After the corpus callosum has been cut, the hemispheres have no way of communicating with one another. The left and right hemispheres are therefore free to think about different things. In a sense, a split-brain patient has two brains.

One way to test the hemispheres' cognitive functions in a split-brain patient takes advantage of the fact that, in a healthy brain, information in the left visual field goes to the right hemisphere, and information in the right field goes to the left hemisphere (see Figure 15-16). With the corpus callosum cut, however, information presented to one side of the brain has no way of traveling to the other side. It can be processed only in the hemisphere that receives it.

Experiments 15-2 and **15-3** show some basic testing procedures based on this dichotomy. The split-brain subject fixates on the dot in the center of the screen while information is presented to the left or right visual field. The person must respond with the left hand (controlled by the right hemisphere), with the right hand (controlled by the left hemisphere), or verbally (also a left-hemisphere function). In this way, researchers can observe what each hemisphere knows and what it is capable of doing.

As illustrated in Experiment 15-2, a picture—say, of a spoon—might be flashed and the subject asked to state what he or she sees. If the picture is presented to the right visual field, the person will answer, "Spoon." If the picture is presented to the left visual field, however, the person will say, "I see nothing." The subject responds in this way for two reasons:

1. The right hemisphere (which receives the visual input) does not talk, so it cannot respond verbally, even though it sees the spoon in the left visual field.

2. The left hemisphere does talk, but it does not see the spoon, so it answers—quite correctly, from its own perspective—that nothing was presented.

Now suppose the task changes, as shown in Experiment 15-3A. If the picture of a spoon is still presented to the left visual field, but the subject

---

····> **EXPERIMENT 15-2**

Question: Will severing the corpus callosum affect the way in which the brain responds?

Procedure

The split-brain subject fixates on the dot in the center of the screen while an image is projected to the left or right visual field. He is asked to identify verbally what he sees.

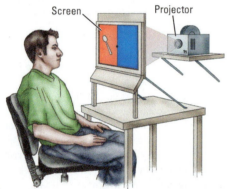

Results

If the spoon is presented to the right visual field, the subject answers, "Spoon."

If the spoon is presented to the left visual field, the subject answers, "I see nothing."

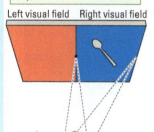  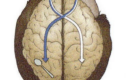

Left visual field   Right visual field   Left visual field   Right visual field

Severed corpus callosum

Conclusion: When the left hemisphere, which can speak, sees the spoon in the right visual field, the subject responds correctly. When the right hemisphere, which cannot speak, sees the spoon in the left visual field, the subject does not respond.

┄┄▷ EXPERIMENT 15-3

(A) Question: How can the right hemisphere of a split-brain subject show that it knows information?

(B) Question: What happens if both hemispheres are asked to respond to competing information?

Procedure

The split-brain participant is asked to use his left hand to pick out the object shown on the screen to the left visual field (right hemisphere).

Procedure

Each visual field is shown a different object—a spoon to the left and a pencil to the right. The split-brain participant is asked to use both hands to pick up the object seen.

Results

The participant chooses the spoon with his left hand because the right hemisphere sees the spoon and controls the left hand. If the right hand is forced to choose, it will do so by chance because no stimulus is shown to the left hemisphere.

Results

In this case, the right and left hands do not agree. They may each pick up a different object, or the right hand may prevent the left hand from performing the task.

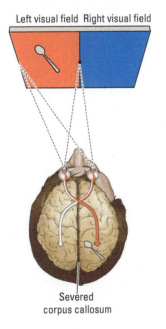

Left visual field Right visual field

Severed
corpus callosum

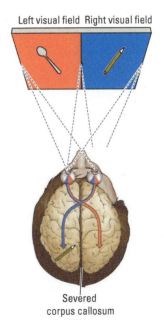

Left visual field Right visual field

Severed
corpus callosum

Conclusion: Each hemisphere is capable of responding independently. The left hemisphere may dominate in a competition, even if the response is not verbal.

now is asked to use the left hand to pick out the object shown on the screen, the left hand (controlled by the right hemisphere, which sees the spoon) readily picks out the correct object. Can the right hand also choose correctly? No, because it is controlled by the left hemisphere, which cannot see the spoon. If the person in this situation is forced to select an object with the right hand, the left hemisphere does so at random.

Now let's consider an interesting twist (see Experiment 15-3B), in which each hemisphere is shown a different object—say, a spoon to the right hemisphere and a pencil to the left. The subject is asked to use both hands to pick out "the object." The problem here is that the right and left hands do not agree. While the left hand tries to pick up the spoon, the right hand tries to pick up the pencil or tries to prevent the left hand from picking up the spoon.

This conflict between the hemispheres can be seen in the everyday behavior of some split-brain subjects. One woman, P. O. V., reported frequent interhemispheric competition for at least 3 years after her surgery. "I open the closet door. I know what I want to wear. But as I reach for something with my right hand, my left comes up and takes something different. I can't put it down if it's in my left hand. I have to call my daughter."

We know from Experiment 15-2 that the left hemisphere is capable of using language, and Research Focus 15-1 reveals that the right hemisphere has visuospatial capabilities that the left hemisphere does not. Although findings from half a century of studying split-brain patients show that the hemispheres process information differently, another word of caution is needed. There is more functional overlap between the hemispheres than was at first suspected. The right hemisphere, for instance, does have some language functions, and the left hemisphere does have some spatial abilities. Nonetheless, the two undoubtedly are different.

Explaining Cerebral Asymmetry

Various hypotheses propose to explain hemispheric differences. One idea, that the left hemisphere is important in controlling fine movements, dates back a century. Recall M. M., the meningioma patient with left parietal lobe damage and apraxia (see Figure 15-14B). Although the apraxia subsided, she was left with chronic trouble copying movements.

Perhaps one reason that the left hemisphere has a role in language is that speaking requires fine motor movements of the mouth and tongue. Significantly, damage to the language-related areas of the left hemisphere almost always interferes with both language and movement, whether the person speaks or signs. Reading Braille, a tactile writing system that renders characters in combinations of small bumps, however, may not be so affected by left-hemisphere lesions. Most people prefer to use the left hand to read Braille, which essentially consists of spatial patterns, and processes related to reading Braille may therefore reside in the right hemisphere.

That said, another clue that the left hemisphere's specialization for language may be related to its special role in controlling fine movements comes from investigating where the brain processes certain parts of speech. Recall that cognitive systems for representing abstract concepts likely are related to systems that produce more concrete behaviors. Consequently, we might expect that the left hemisphere would participate in forming concepts related to fine movements.

Concepts that describe movements are the parts of speech we call *verbs*. A fundamental difference between left- and right-hemisphere language abilities is that verbs seem to be processed only in the left hemisphere, whereas nouns are processed in both hemispheres. In other words, not only does the left hemisphere specialize in producing actions, it also produces mental representations of actions in the form of words.

If the left hemisphere excels at language because it is better at controlling fine movements, what is the basis of the right hemisphere's abilities? One idea is that the right hemisphere specializes in controlling movements in space. In a sense, this role elaborates the functions of the dorsal visual stream (diagrammed in Figure 15-4).

Once again, we can propose a link between movement at a concrete level and movement at a more abstract level. If the right hemisphere is producing movements in space, then it is also likely to produce mental images of such movements. We would therefore predict impairment of right-hemisphere patients' ability both to think about and to make spatially guided movements. And they are thus impaired.

Bear in mind, however, that theories about the reasons for hemispheric asymmetry are highly speculative. The brain has evolved to produce movement and to construct a sensory reality, so the observed asymmetry must somehow relate to these overriding functions. That is, more recently evolved functions, such as language, likely are exten-

Principle 1: The nervous system produces movement in a perceptual world the brain constructs.

sions of preexisting functions. So the fact that language is represented asymmetrically does not mean that the brain is asymmetrical because of language. After all, other species that do not talk have asymmetrical brains.

Left Hemisphere, Language, and Thought

As we end our examination of brain asymmetry, consider one more provocative idea. Michael Gazzaniga (1992) proposed that the left hemisphere's superior language skills are important for understanding the differences between humans' and other animals' thinking. He called the speaking hemisphere the *interpreter*. The following experiment, using split-brain patients as subjects, illustrates what Gazzaniga meant.

Each hemisphere is shown a picture of a match followed by a picture of a piece of wood, for example. Another set of pictures is then shown. The task is to pick from this set a third picture that has an inferred relationship to the first two. In this example, the third related picture might be a bonfire. The right hemisphere is incapable of making the inference that a match struck and held to a piece of wood could start a bonfire, whereas the left hemisphere easily arrives at this interpretation.

An analogous task uses words. One hemisphere or the other might be shown the words *pin* and *finger* and then asked to pick out a third word related to the other two. In this case, the correct answer might be *bleed*.

The right hemisphere cannot make this connection. Although it has enough language ability to pick out close synonyms for *pin* and *finger* (*needle* and *thumb*, respectively), it cannot make the inference that pricking a finger with a pin will result in bleeding.

Again, the left hemisphere has no difficulty with this task. Apparently, the left hemisphere's language capability gives it a capacity for interpretation that the right hemisphere lacks. One reason may be that language serves to label and express the computations of other cognitive systems.

Gazzaniga goes even further. He suggests that the evolution of left-hemisphere language abilities makes humans a "believing" species: humans can make inferences and have beliefs about sensory events. By contrast, Alex, the African grey parrot profiled in Comparative Focus 15-2, would not have been able to make inferences or hold beliefs because he did not have a system analogous to our left-hemisphere language system. Alex could use language but could not make inferences about sensory events with language.

Gazzaniga's idea is intriguing. It implies a fundamental difference in the nature of cerebral asymmetry—and therefore in the nature of cognition—that exists between humans and other animals because of the nature of human language. We return to this idea in Section 15-7.

15-4 Review

Before you continue, check your understanding. Answers to Self-Test appear at the back of the book.

1. The right hemisphere plays a role in _____ and _____.

2. The left hemisphere plays a role in _____ and _____.

3. The split brain results from severing the _____.

4. Why does it matter that the two cerebral hemispheres process information differently?

For additional study tools, visit 📖 **Launch**Pad at launchpadworks.com

15-5

Variations in Cognitive Organization

No two brains are identical. Some differences are genetically determined; others result from plastic changes caused, for example, by experience and learning or epigenetic factors. Some brain differences are idiosyncratic (unique to a particular person); many

(A) Spatial relation–type task

Participants were asked to draw a line to indicate waterline in tipped glass.

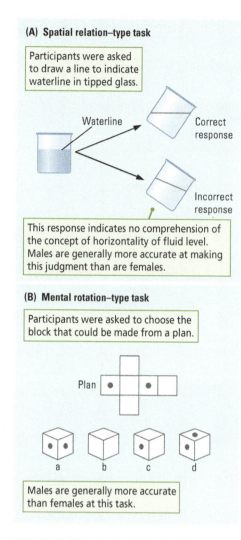

Waterline → Correct response

Incorrect response

This response indicates no comprehension of the concept of horizontality of fluid level. Males are generally more accurate at making this judgment than are females.

(B) Mental rotation–type task

Participants were asked to choose the block that could be made from a plan.

Plan

a   b   c   d

Males are generally more accurate than females at this task.

(C) Short-term-memory–type task

Participants were asked to fill in the empty boxes with the appropriate symbols from the top row.

1	2	3	4	5	6	7	8	9
○	//	□	△	×	>	∩	⬡	|||

2	8	3	2	1	4	2	3	5	9	2	1	7	3	6

9	7	2	3	1	4	6	1	9	7	4	3	1	6	8

When given a larger number of boxes to fill in and a time limit, females complete from 10 to 20 percent more items than males do.

(D) Verbal fluency–type task

Participants were asked to fill in each blank to form words that make a sentence.

1. F_____ M_____ A_____ J_____

2. C_____ B_____ E_____ S_____

3. D_____ I_____ J_____ K_____

Females are generally faster at this type of test than males are.

FIGURE 15-17 **Tasks That Reliably Show Sex-Related Cognitive Differences**

others are systematic and common to whole categories of people. In this section, we consider two systematic variations in brain organization—those related to sex and handedness—and one idiosyncratic variation, the fascinating sensory phenomenon called *synesthesia*.

Sex Differences in Cognitive Organization

The idea that men and women think differently probably originated with the first men and women. Science backs it up. Books, including one by Doreen Kimura (1999), present persuasive evidence for marked differences between men's and women's performance on many cognitive tests. As illustrated in **Figure 15-17**, paper-and-pencil tests consistently show that, on average, females have better verbal fluency than males, whereas males do better on tests of spatial reasoning. Our focus here is on how such differences relate to the brain.

Neural Bases of Sex Differences

Considerable evidence points to sex differences, both in the brain's gross cerebral structure and at a neuronal level. Jill Goldstein and her colleagues (2001) conducted a large MRI study of sexual dimorphism in the human brain. They found that women have larger volumes of dorsal prefrontal and associated paralimbic regions, whereas men have larger volumes of more ventral prefrontal regions (**Figure 15-18**). (Brain size is related to body size, and on average, male brains are bigger than female brains, so the investigators corrected for size.)

A more recent study of more than 5000 brains shows a fairly similar pattern of differences when corrected for brain size. In addition, this study shows a striking difference in the pattern of intrahemispheric connections (Ritchie et al., 2018). Not only is the general pattern different, but women have more dispersed connections within white matter than men do. Finally, researchers show that for all measures, there was considerable overlap between the sexes (~50 percent), and males had much higher variability.

FIGURE 15-18 **Sex Differences in Brain Volume** Women's brain volume in prefrontal and medial paralimbic regions (orange) is significantly higher than men's. Men have larger relative volumes in the medial and orbitofrontal cortex and the angular gyrus (green). Orange areas correspond to regions that have high levels of estrogen receptors during development, green to regions high in androgen receptors during development. Information from Goldstein et al., 2001.

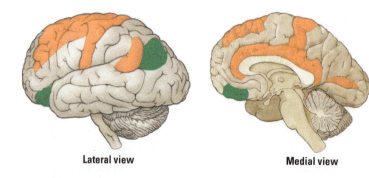

Lateral view   Medial view

Another way to measure sex differences is in cortical thickness, independent of volume. **Figure 15-19** shows that relative to men, women have increased cortical gray matter concentration in many cortical regions. Men's gray matter concentration, by contrast, is more uniform across the cortex. The MRI studies represented in Figures 15-18 and 15-19 thus point to differences between men's and women's cortical organization.

Sex differences in neuronal structure also exist. Gonadal hormones influence the structure of neurons in the prefrontal cortices of rats (Kolb & Stewart, 1991). The cells in one prefrontal region, located along the midline, have larger dendritic fields (and presumably more synapses) in males than in females, as shown in the top row of **Figure 15-20**. In contrast, the cells in the orbitofrontal region have larger dendritic fields (and presumably more synapses) in females than in males, as shown in the bottom row. These sex differences are not found in rats that have had their testes or ovaries removed at birth. Presumably, sex hormones somehow change the brain's organization and, ultimately, its cognitive processing.

Stewart and Kolb (1994) found that the presence or absence of gonadal hormones affects the brain in adulthood as well as in early development. In this study, which focused on how hormones affect recovery from brain damage, middle-aged female rats' ovaries were removed. On examining the brains of these rats and those of control rats some months later, researchers observed that the cortical neurons of the rats whose ovaries had been removed—especially the prefrontal neurons—had undergone structural changes. The cells had grown 30 percent more dendrites, and their spine density increased compared with the control rats' cells. Clearly, gonadal hormones can affect the brain's neuronal structure at any point in an animal's life.

An additional way to consider the neural basis of sex differences is to look at the effects of cortical injury in men and women. If sex differences exist in the neural organization of cognitive processing, differences in the effects of cortical injury in the two sexes should appear. Doreen Kimura (1999) conducted this kind of study and showed that the pattern of cerebral organization within each hemisphere may in fact differ between the sexes.

Investigating people who had a cortical stroke in adulthood, Kimura tried to match the location and extent of injury in her male and female subjects. She found that men and women were almost equally likely to be aphasic subsequent to left-hemisphere lesions of some kind. But men were more likely to be aphasic and apraxic after damage to the left posterior cortex, whereas women were far more likely to be aphasic and apraxic after lesions to the left frontal cortex.

These results, summarized in **Figure 15-21**, suggest a sex difference in intrahemispheric organization, a conclusion supported by a later study (**Figure 15-22**) using diffusion tensor analysis of brain networks in more than 900 participants. The population, comprising nearly equal numbers of each sex, showed that females have greater interhemispheric connectivity, whereas males' intrahemispheric connectivity is greater (Ingalhalikar et al., 2014).

Evidence strongly favors a neural basis for gender identity, including transgender identity. Georg Kranz and colleagues (2014) used diffusion tensor analysis to compare brain networks of female-to-male and male-to-female transsexuals with those of gender-typical females and males. The imaging replicated the distinctly different pattern of hemispheric connectivity in gender-typical females and males. The pattern of connectivity in transsexuals, however, falls halfway between that of females and that of males.

That is, DTIs of the white matter microstructure of transgender females and males falls halfway between those of gender-typical females and males. The investigators take these patterns as evidence that neural white matter microstructure is influenced by the hormonal environment during late prenatal and early postnatal brain development. This is the time, they hypothesize, that determines gender identity. But genital differentiation is determined earlier in development. The timing difference thus makes a genital–gender mismatch possible.

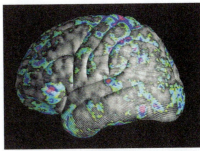

Left hemisphere

FIGURE 15-19 **Sex Differences in Gray Matter Concentration** Women show increased gray matter concentration in the cortical regions shown in color on this MRI. Gray-shaded regions are not statistically different in males and females. Courtesy Dr. Arthur Toga, Laboratory of Neuro Imaging at USC.

Section 12-5 describes the gender identity spectrum.

FIGURE 15-20 **Sex Differences in Neuronal Architecture** In the frontal cortices of male and female rats, cells in the midline frontal region (top two drawings) are more complex in males than in females, whereas the opposite is true of the orbitofrontal region (bottom two drawings).

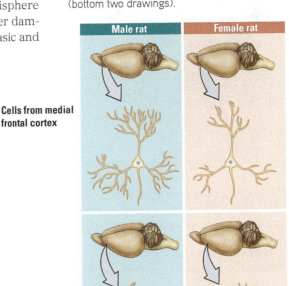

Cells from medial frontal cortex

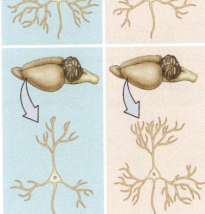

Cells from orbito-frontal region

FIGURE 15-21 **Evidence for Sex Differences in Cortical Organization** Apraxia and aphasia are associated with frontal damage to the left hemisphere in women and with posterior damage in men. Information from Kimura, 1999.

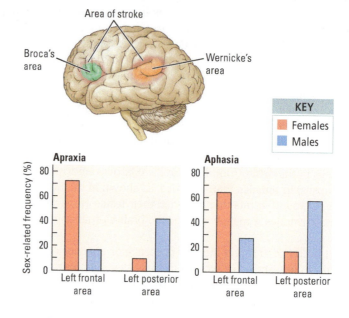

(A) Male brain

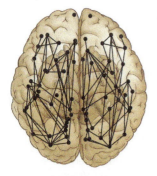

(B) Female brain

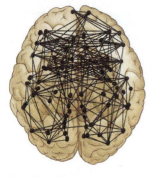

FIGURE 15-22 **Sex Differences in the Connectome** DTI analysis of brain networks in these dorsal views reveals greater intrahemispheric connections in males **(A)** and greater interhemispheric connections in females **(B)**. Information from Ingalhalikar et al., 2014.

Evolution of Sex-Related Cognitive Differences

Although gonadal hormones have taken center stage in explaining sex differences in cognitive function, we are still left to question how these differences arose. To answer this question, we must look back at human evolution. Mothers pass their genes to both sons and daughters, and fathers do the same. Ultimately then, males and females of a species have virtually all their genes in common.

The only way a gene can affect one sex preferentially is for the animal's gonadal hormones to influence the gene's activities. Gonadal hormones are in turn determined by the presence or absence of the Y chromosome, which carries a gene called the *testes-determining factor (TDF)*. TDF stimulates the body to produce testes, which then manufacture androgens, which in turn influence other genes' activities.

Like other body organs, the brain is a potential target of natural selection. We should therefore expect to find sex-related differences in the brain whenever the sexes differ in the adaptive problems they have faced in their species' evolution. Aggressive behavior is a good example. Males in most mammalian species typically are more physically aggressive than females. This trait presumably improved males' reproductive success by selecting against individuals with lesser aggressiveness. Producing higher levels of aggression entails male hormones. We know from studies of nonhuman species that aggression is related directly to the presence of androgens and to their effects on gene expression, both during brain development and later in life. In this case, therefore, natural selection has worked on gonadal hormone levels to favor aggressiveness in males.

Explaining sex-related differences in cognitive processes, such as language or spatial skills, is more speculative than explaining sex-related differences in aggressive behavior. Nevertheless, some hypotheses come to mind. We can imagine, for instance, that in the history of mammalian evolution, males have tended to range over larger territories than have females. This behavior requires spatial abilities, so evolution would have favored these skills in males.

Support for this hypothesis comes from comparing spatial problem solving in males of closely related mammalian species—species in which the males range over large territories versus species in which the males' range is not extensive. Pine voles, for example, have a restricted range and no sex-related difference in range, whereas meadow voles have a range about 20 times as large as that of pine voles, and male meadow voles range more widely than the females.

Meadow voles display far superior spatial skills compared to pine voles. A sex difference in spatial ability among meadow voles favors males, but pine voles have no such sex difference. The hippocampus is implicated in spatial navigation skills. Significantly, the hippocampus is larger in meadow voles than in pine voles, and it is larger in male meadow voles than in females (Gaulin, 1992). A similar logic could help explain sex-related differences in spatial abilities between human males and females (see Figure 15-17).

Explanations of sex-related differences in language skills are also speculative. One hypothesis holds that if males were hunters and often away from home, home-based females formed social groups selectively favored to develop tools—language, for example—for social interactions. We might also argue that females with superior fine motor skills (such as foraging for food and making clothing and baskets) had a selective advantage. The relationship between language and fine motor skills may have favored enhanced language capacities in females.

Although such speculations are interesting, they are not testable. We will probably never know with certainty why sex-related differences in brain organization developed.

Handedness and Cognitive Organization

Nearly everyone prefers one hand to the other for writing or throwing a ball. Most people prefer the right hand. In fact, left-handedness has historically been viewed as odd. But it is not rare. An estimated 10 percent of the human population worldwide is left-handed. This proportion represents only the number of people who write with the left hand. When broader criteria are used to determine left-handedness, estimates range from 10 percent to 30 percent of the population.

Because the left hemisphere controls the right hand, the general assumption is that right-handedness is somehow related to the presence of speech in the left hemisp If this were so, language would be located in the right hemisphere of left-handed peo ple. This hypothesis is easily tested, and it turns out to be false.

In the course of preparing patients with epilepsy for surgery to remove the abnormal tissue causing their seizures, Ted Rasmussen and Brenda Milner (1977) injected the left or right hemisphere with sodium amobarbital. This drug produces a short-acting anesthesia of the entire hemisphere, making it possible to determine where speech originates. As described in Clinical Focus 15-4, Sodium Amobarbital Test, if a person becomes aphasic when the drug is injected into the left hemisphere but not when the drug is injected into the right, then speech must reside in that person's left hemisphere.

Rasmussen and Milner found that in virtually all right-handed people, speech was localized in the left hemisphere, but the reverse was not true for left-handed people. About 70 percent of left-handers also had speech in the left hemisphere. Of the remaining 30 percent, about half had speech in the right hemisphere and half had speech in both hemispheres. Findings from neuroanatomical studies have subsequently shown that left-handers with speech in the left hemisphere have asymmetries similar to those of right-handers. By contrast, in left-handers with speech originating in the right hemisphere or in both hemispheres—known as **anomalous speech representation**— the anatomical symmetry is reversed or absent.

Sandra Witelson and Charlie Goldsmith (1991) examined whether any other gross differences in the brain structure of right- and left-handers might exist. One possibility is that the connectivity of the cerebral hemispheres may differ. To test this idea, the investigators studied the hand preference of terminally ill subjects on a variety of one-handed tasks. They later performed postmortem studies of these patients' brains, paying particular attention to the size of the corpus callosum. They found that the callosal cross-sectional area was 11 percent greater in left-handed and ambidextrous (little or no hand preference) people than in right-handed people.

Whether this enlarged callosum is due to a greater number of fibers, to thicker fibers, or to more myelin remains to be seen. If the larger corpus callosum is due to

anomalous speech representation Condition in which a person's speech zones are located in the right hemisphere or in both hemispheres.

◎ **CLINICAL FOCUS 15-4**

Sodium Amobarbital Test

Guy, a 32-year-old lawyer, had a vascular malformation over the region corresponding to the posterior speech zone. The malformation was beginning to cause neurological symptoms, including seizures. The ideal surgical treatment was removal of the abnormal vessels.

The complication with this surgery is that removing vessels sitting over the posterior speech zone poses a serious risk of permanent aphasia. Because Guy was left-handed, his speech areas could be in the right hemisphere. If so, the surgical risk would be much lower.

To achieve certainty in such doubtful cases, Jun Wada and Ted Rasmussen (1960) pioneered the technique of injecting sodium amobarbital, a barbiturate, into the carotid artery to briefly anesthetize the ipsilateral hemisphere. (Injections are now usually made through a catheter inserted into the femoral artery.) The procedure enables an unequivocal localization of speech because injection into the speech hemisphere results in speech arrest lasting as long as several minutes. As speech returns, it is characterized by aphasic errors.

Injection into the nonspeaking hemisphere may produce no or only brief speech arrest. The amobarbital procedure has the advantage of allowing each hemisphere to be studied separately in the functional absence of the other (anesthetized) hemisphere. Because the period of anesthesia lasts several minutes, a variety of functions, including memory and movement, can be studied to determine a hemisphere's capabilities.

The sodium amobarbital test is always performed bilaterally, with the second cerebral hemisphere being injected several days after the first one to make sure no residual drug effect lingers. In the brief

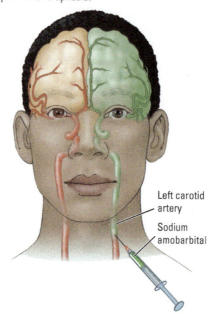

Left carotid artery

Sodium amobarbital

To avoid damaging speech zones in patients about to undergo brain surgery, surgeons inject sodium amobarbital into the carotid artery. The drug anesthetizes the hemisphere where it is injected (here, green), allowing the surgeon to determine whether that hemisphere is dominant for speech.

period of drug action, the patient is given a series of simple tasks requiring the use of language, memory, and object recognition. To test speech, the patient is asked to name some common objects presented in quick succession, to count, to recite the days of the week forward and backward, and to spell simple words.

If the injected hemisphere is nondominant for speech, the patient may continue to carry out the verbal tasks, although there is often a period as long as 30 seconds during which he or she appears confused and is silent but can resume speech with urging. When the injected hemisphere is dominant for speech, the patient typically stops talking and remains completely aphasic until recovery from the anesthesia is well along, somewhere in the range of 4 to 10 minutes.

Guy was found to have speech in the left hemisphere. During the test of his left hemisphere, he could not talk. Later, he said that when he was asked about a particular object, he wondered just what the question meant. When he finally had some vague idea, he had no idea what the answer was or how to say anything. By then he realized that he had been asked all sorts of other questions to which he had also not responded.

When asked which objects he had been shown, he said he had no idea. However, when given an array of objects and asked to choose with his left hand, he identified the objects by pointing because his nonspeaking right hemisphere controlled that hand. In contrast, his speaking left hemisphere had no memory of the objects: it had been asleep.

---

synesthesia Ability to perceive a stimulus of one sense as the sensation of a different sense, as when sound produces a sensation of color; literally, *feeling together*.

Musician–composer Stevie Wonder is a synesthete, as were music legends Duke Ellington and Franz Liszt, Nobel Prize–winning physicist Richard Feynman, and novelist Vladimir Nabokov (and his son).

more fibers, the difference would be on the order of 25 million more fibers. Presumably, such a difference would have major implications for the organization of cognitive processing in left- and right-handers.

Synesthesia

Some variations in brain organization are idiosyncratic rather than systematic. **Synesthesia** is an individual's capacity to join sensory experiences across sensory modalities. Examples include the ability to hear colors or taste shapes. Edward Hubbard (2007) estimated the incidence of synesthesia at about 1 in 23 people, although for most it likely is limited in scope.

Sensory blendings may be difficult to imagine. How can sounds or letters possibly produce colors? Studies of synesthetes show that the same stimuli always elicit the same experiences for them. The most common form of synesthesia is colored hearing. For many synesthetes, this means hearing both speech and music in color—perceiving a visual mélange of colored shapes, movement, and scintillation. The fact that colored hearing is more common than other types of synesthesia is curious.

The five primary senses (vision, hearing, touch, taste, and smell) all generate synesthetic pairings. Most, however, are in one direction. For instance, whereas synesthetes may see colors when they hear, they do not hear sounds in colors. Furthermore, some sensory combinations occur rarely, if at all. In particular, taste or smell rarely triggers a synesthetic response.

Because each case is idiosyncratic, synesthesia's neurological basis is difficult to investigate. Few studies have related it directly to brain function or brain organization, and different people may experience it for different reasons. Various hypotheses have been advanced to account for synesthesia, such as extraordinary neural connections between the sensory regions being related in a particular synesthete; increased activity in the frontal lobe multimodal cortex, which receives inputs from more than one sensory area; or particular sensory inputs that elicit unusual patterns of cerebral activation. The condition may at least partly be determined by genes influencing brain development. Whatever the explanation, when it comes to certain sensory inputs, the brain of a synesthete certainly works differently from other people's brains.

15-5 Review

Before you continue, check your understanding. Answers to Self-Test appear at the back of the book.

1. The two major contributors to organizational differences in individual brains are _____ and _____.

2. Differences in the cerebral organization of thinking are probably related to differences in the _____ that underlie different types of cognitive processing.

3. People who experience certain sensations in more than one sensory modality are said to have _____.

4. What roles do gonadal hormones play in brain organization and function?

For additional study tools, visit **LaunchPad** at launchpadworks.com

---

15-6

Intelligence

Intelligence exerts a major influence on anyone's thinking ability. It is easy to identify in people and even easy to observe in other animals. Yet intelligence is not at all easy to define. Despite a century of study, researchers have not yet reached agreement on what intelligence entails. We therefore begin this section by reviewing some hypotheses of intelligence.

Concept of General Intelligence

In the 1920s, Charles Spearman proposed that although different kinds of intelligence may exist, there is also an underlying general intelligence, which he called the g factor. Consider for a moment what a general intelligence factor might mean for the brain. Presumably, brains with high or low g would have some general difference in brain architecture—perhaps in gyral patterns, cytoarchitectonics, vascular patterns, or neurochemistry, for example.

Cytoarchitectonics refers to brain cell organization, structure, and distribution.

The difference in g could not be something as simple as size because human brain size (which varies from about 1000 to 2000 grams) correlates poorly with intelligence. Another possibility is that g is related to special cerebral connectivity or even to the ratio of neurons to glia. Still another possibility is that g is related to the activation of specific brain regions, possibly in the frontal lobe (Duncan et al., 2000; Gray & Thompson, 2004).

Section 1-5 reveals fallacies inherent in correlating human brain size with intelligence.

The results of preliminary studies of Albert Einstein's brain implied that cerebral connectivity and ratio of glia to neuron may be important. Sandra Witelson and her

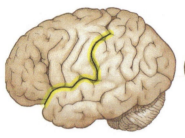

FIGURE 15-23 **Einstein's Brain** The lateral fissure of Einstein's brain takes an exaggerated upward course relative to its course in typical brains, essentially fusing the posterior temporal regions with the inferior parietal regions (compare this image to the typical lateral fissure shown in Figure 15-13). The arrow in each hemisphere indicates Einstein's ascending lateral fissure as it runs into the postcentral sulcus.

colleagues (Witelson et al., 1999) found that although Einstein's brain is the same size and weight as the average male brain, its lateral fissure is short, and both the left and the right lateral fissures take a particularly striking upward deflection (**Figure 15-23**). This arrangement essentially fuses the inferior parietal area with the posterior temporal area.

The inferior parietal cortex has a role in mathematical reasoning, so it is tempting to speculate that Einstein's mathematical abilities were related to neural rearrangements in this area.

But another important difference may distinguish Einstein's brain. Marion Diamond and her colleagues (1985) looked at its glia-to-neuron ratio versus the mean for a control population. They found that Einstein's ratio in the inferior parietal cortex was higher than average: each neuron in this region had an unusually high number of glial cells supporting it.

The glia-to-neuron ratio was not unusually high in any other cortical areas of Einstein's brain measured by these researchers. Possibly, then, certain types of intelligence could be related to differences in cell structure in localized brain regions. But even if this hypothesis proves correct, it offers little neural evidence in favor of a general intelligence factor.

One possibility is that g is related to the brain's language processes because language ability qualitatively changes the nature of cognitive processing in humans. So perhaps people with very good language skills also have an advantage in general thinking ability.

Many other hypotheses on intelligence have been set forth since Spearman's, all following from the general idea that there are distinct forms of intelligence that should be dissociable. The idea of multiple human intelligences should not be surprising, given the varied cognitive operations the human brain can perform. To date, however, such theories have not considered the anatomy and function of the brain directly, and, although they are often favored by educators, they have not been rigorously tested scientifically.

Divergent and Convergent Intelligence

One clear difference between lesions in the parietal and temporal lobes and lesions in the frontal lobes is in the way they affect performance on standardized intelligence tests. Posterior lesions produce reliable and often large decreases in intelligence test scores, whereas frontal lesions do not. This is puzzling. If frontal lobe damage does not diminish a person's intelligence test score, why do people with this kind of damage often do irrational things, such as failing to go to work or keep appointments? The answer lies in the difference between two kinds of intelligence.

According to J. P. Guilford (1967), traditional intelligence tests measure **convergent thinking**—applying knowledge and reasoning skills to narrow the range of possible solutions to a problem and then zeroing in on one correct answer. Typical intelligence test items using vocabulary words, arithmetic problems, puzzles, block designs, and so forth all require convergent thinking. They demand a single correct answer that can be easily scored.

In contrast, **divergent thinking** reaches outward from conventional knowledge and reasoning skills to explore new, more unconventional solutions to problems. Divergent thinking assumes a variety of possible approaches and answers to a question rather than a single "correct" solution. A task that requires divergent thinking might ask you to list all the possible uses you can imagine for a coat hanger.

Clearly, a person who is very good at divergent thinking might not necessarily be good at convergent thinking and vice versa. The distinction is useful because it helps us to understand the effects of brain injury on thought. Frontal lobe injury is believed to interfere with divergent thinking. The convergent thinking measured by standardized IQ tests is often impaired in people with damage to the temporal and parietal lobes.

Injury to the left parietal lobe in particular causes devastating impairment in the ability to perform cognitive processes related to academic work. People with this kind of

convergent thinking Form of thinking that searches for a single answer to a question (such as $2 + 2 = ?$); contrasts with divergent thinking.

divergent thinking Form of thinking that searches for multiple solutions to a problem (how many ways can a pen be used?); contrasts with convergent thinking.

injury may be aphasic, alexic (having difficulty understanding and processing written words), and apraxic. Many have severe deficits in arithmetic ability. All such impairments would interfere with school performance and performance at most jobs.

Patient M. M., discussed in Section 15-4, had left parietal lobe injury and was unable to return to school. In contrast with people like M. M., those with frontal lobe injuries that spare Broca's language area seldom have deficits in reading, writing, or arithmetic—tasks associated with convergent thinking. And they show no decrement in standardized IQ tests. C. C.'s case provides a good example.

C. C. had a meningioma along the midline between the frontal lobes. Extracting it required removal of brain tissue from both hemispheres. Before his surgery, C. C. was a prominent lawyer. Afterward, although he still had a superior IQ and superior memory, he was unable to work, in part because he no longer had any imagination. He could not generate the novel solutions to legal problems that had characterized his career before the surgery. Thus, both M. M. and C. C. had problems that prevented them from working, but their problems differed because their injuries affected different kinds of thinking.

Intelligence, Heredity, Epigenetics, and the Synapse

Donald Hebb proposed another way to categorize human intelligence. Like Guilford, Hebb thought of people as having two forms, which he called intelligence A and intelligence B. Unlike Guilford's convergent–divergent dichotomy, Hebb's **intelligence A** refers to innate intellectual potential, which is highly heritable: it has a strong genetic component. **Intelligence B** is observed intelligence, which is influenced by experience as well as other factors, such as disease, injury, or exposure to environmental toxins, especially during development.

Hebb (1980) understood that experience can influence brain cell structure significantly. In his view, experiences influence brain development, and thus observed intelligence, because they alter the brain's synaptic organization. It follows that appropriate postnatal experiences can enhance development of intelligence B in people with lower-than-average intelligence A, whereas a poor or under-resourced environment can hinder the development of intelligence B in people with higher-than-average intelligence A. The task is to identify a good environment and a bad environment so as to stimulate people to reach their highest potential intelligence.

One implication of Hebb's view of intelligence is that the brain's synaptic organization is key. Synaptic organization is partly directed by a person's genes, but it is also affected by epigenetic factors. Variations in the experiences to which people are exposed, coupled with variations in genetic patterns, undoubtedly contribute to the individual differences in intelligence that we observe—both quantitative (as measured by IQ tests) and qualitative (as seen in special abilities such as mathematics).

How Smart Brains Differ

A seminal review by Rex Jung and Richard Haier (2007) compares 37 neuroimaging studies of intelligence and concludes that differences in intelligence are linked to structural and functional variations in the lateral prefrontal cortex, medial prefrontal cortex, posterior parietal cortex, and sensory areas in the occipital and temporal lobes. The authors recognize that these regions are connected by white matter tracts and propose that these regions form a network, which they call the Parieto-Frontal Integration Theory of intelligence (P-FIT) model, that underlies intelligence. In the decade following this proposal, there has been significant methodological improvements in imaging technology, but the general consensus remains that a parieto-frontal network forms the basis of intelligence and that individual differences in intelligence are related to structural and functional differences in these regions (for a review, see Haier, 2017).

More recently, Ulrike Basten and colleagues (2015) have modified the P-FIT model to differentiate between functional (brain activation in fMRI) and structural (amount of

intelligence A Hebb's term for innate intellectual potential, which is highly heritable and cannot be measured directly.

intelligence B Hebb's term for observed intelligence, influenced by experience and other factors in the course of development; measured by intelligence tests.

Review Research Focus 8-1. Section 8-4 recounts Hebb's pioneering work on the importance of enriched environments in early childhood education.

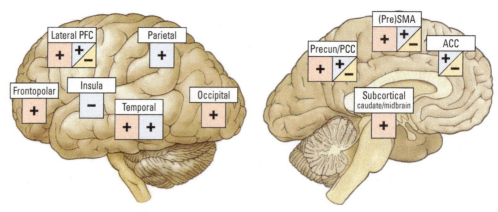

FIGURE 15-24 **The Brain Bases of Intelligence** A meta-analysis of structural MRIs (pink) and fMRIs (gray/yellow) collected during cognitive tasks found clusters of regions showing positive (+) or negative (−) associations between intelligence and brain activation.

(A)

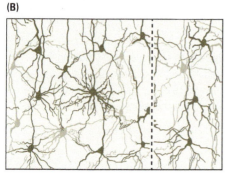

(B)

FIGURE 15-25 **Neurite Density** Panel A shows the high neurite density and dendritic arborization correlated with lower intelligence. Panel B shows the comparatively lower density and arborization correlated with higher intelligence. Higher-intelligence individuals have a larger cortical volume and more neurons, which is indicated by the dotted line.

gray matter in MRI) correlates of intelligence. This new version also identifies both positive and negative associations between intelligence and brain activation. Thus, higher intelligence is associated with increased activation in some regions and reduced activation in others (see **Figure 15-24**). Furthermore, the authors' analysis extends the network to include insular cortex, posterior cingulate cortex, and subcortical structures. They note, however, that we do not yet know how differences in intelligence arise from these differences, nor can we be certain that the differences between brains appears *because* of differences in intelligence rather being the cause of the differences.

Differences in regions in the P-FIT model can also be seen at the microstructural level. Erhan Genc and colleagues (2018) combined an advanced diffusion tensor imaging with a culturally neutral reasoning test. They measured all 180 areas from the Human Connectome Project and confirmed the positive association between intelligence and the volume of cerebral cortex. In addition, they found that specific microstructural properties are associated with intelligence, especially the cortical regions in the parietal-frontal network. Cortical gray matter is mostly composed of neurites (dendrites and axons); because these structures restrict the movement of water molecules, it is possible to estimate neurite density and orientation.

The results showed that neurite density is negatively correlated with intelligence (see **Figure 15-25**). At first glance, this appears counterintuitive because it means that less is better; but recall that, during brain maturation, synapses are overproduced and then pruned, making the brain more efficient. Conditions in which pruning is reduced, such as Down syndrome, result in less efficient cerebral processing and lower intelligence. Thus, this study shows that human intelligence is related to brain structure in two different ways. First, bigger brains with more neurons are associated with higher intelligence. And second, higher intelligence is associated with sparsely and well-organized dendritic arbor, which increases processing speed and network efficiency.

15-6 Review

Before you continue, check your understanding. Answers to Self-Test appear at the back of the book.

1. Different concepts of intelligence include Spearman's _____, Guilford's concepts of _____ and _____ thinking, Hebb's _____ and _____, and the _____ Theory of Intelligence.

2. Intelligence is likely related to the brain's _____ organization as well as to its _____ efficiency.

3. Evidence that Hebb's intelligence A can be altered by experience to produce intelligence B is evidence of _____ influences on brain organization.

4. How might intelligence be related to brain organization and function?

For additional study tools, visit ≋ **LaunchPad** at launchpadworks.com

Consciousness

Our conscious experience is familiar and intimate yet remains largely a mysterious product of the brain. Everyone has an idea of what it means to be conscious, but like thinking and intelligence, consciousness is easier to identify than to define. Definitions range from a mere manifestation of complex thought processes to more slippery notions that see it as the subjective experience of awareness, or the "inner self."

Despite the difficulty of defining consciousness, scientists generally agree that it is a process—not a thing—that emerges as information is sorted out. For example, vision involves the interplay among sensory receptors, pathways to the brainstem and cortex, and processing in multiple brain regions. Our visual experience is not the result of any specific region; it is an emergent property that gives us an integrated percept. Consciousness allows us to combine such integrated information from multiple brain systems, such as those associated with sensory perception, emotion, thinking, and so on.

Why Are We Conscious?

Countless people, including neuroscience researchers, have wondered why we experience **consciousness**, the mind's level of responsiveness to impressions made by the senses. The simplest explanation is that consciousness provides an adaptive advantage. Either our construct of the sensory world or our selection of behavior is enhanced by being conscious. Consider visual consciousness.

According to Francis Crick and Christof Koch (1998), an animal such as a frog acts a bit like a zombie when it responds to visual input. Frogs respond to small, preylike objects by snapping and to large, looming objects by jumping. These responses are controlled by different visual systems and are best thought of as reflexive rather than conscious. And these visual systems work well for the frog. So why would humans need to add consciousness? Crick and Koch suggest that reflexive systems are fine when their number is limited, but as their numbers grow, reflexive arrangements become inefficient, especially when two or more systems conflict. As the amount of information about an event increases, it becomes advantageous to produce a single complex representation and make it available for a sufficient time to the parts of the brain—such as the frontal lobes—that choose among many possible action plans. This sustained, complex representation is consciousness.

Of course, to survive we must retain the ability to respond quickly and unconsciously when we need to. This reflexive ability exists alongside our ability to process information consciously. The ventral visual stream is conscious, but the dorsal stream, which acts more rapidly, is not. Athletes model the unconscious action of the online dorsal stream. To hit a baseball or tennis ball traveling at more than 100 miles per hour requires athletes to swing before they are consciously aware of actually seeing the ball. Conscious awareness of the ball comes just after hitting it.

In a series of experiments, Marc Jeannerod and his colleagues (Castiello et al., 1991) found a similar dissociation between behavior and awareness in healthy volunteers as they make grasping movements. **Experiment 15-4** illustrates a representative experiment. Participants were required to grasp one of three rods as quickly as possible. A light on a rod indicated it to be the correct target rod on any given trial.

On some trials, unknown to the participants, the light jumped from one target to another. Participants were asked to report whether such a jump had occurred. As shown in the Results section of the experiment, although participants were able to make the trajectory correction, they were sometimes actually grasping the correct target before they were aware the light had changed.

On some trials, the extent of dissociation between motor and vocal responses was so great that, to their surprise, participants grasped the target some 300 milliseconds before they emitted the vocal response. As with baseball players, their conscious awareness of the stimulus event occurred only after their movements took place. No thought was required to make the movement, just as frogs catch flies without having to think about it.

···❯ **EXPERIMENT 15-4**

Question: Can people alter their movements without conscious awareness?

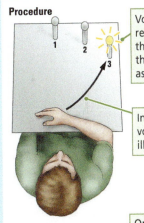

Procedure

Volunteers were required to move their hands and grasp the illuminated rod as quickly as possible.

In this trial, the volunteer reaches for illuminated rod 3.

Results

On some trials, the light jumps from one target to another,...

... causing the volunteer to correct his trajectory. Most participants found that they were actually grasping the new target before they were aware that the light had jumped.

Conclusion: It is possible to dissociate behavior and conscious awareness.

Research from Frith et al., 1999.

Unconscious movements are different from those consciously directed toward a specific object, as when we reach into a bowl of jellybeans to select a candy of a certain color. In this case, we must be aware of all the different colors surrounding the color we want. Here the conscious ventral stream is needed to discriminate among particular stimuli and respond differentially to them. Consciousness, then, allows us to select behaviors that correspond to an understanding of the nuances of sensory inputs.

What Is the Neural Basis of Consciousness?

Consciousness must be related in some way to neural system activity, particularly in the forebrain. One way to investigate these systems is to contrast two kinds of neurological conditions.

In the first condition, a person lacks conscious awareness of some subset of information, even though he or she processes that information unconsciously. Examples include blindsight, visual form agnosia, implicit learning in amnesia, and contralateral neglect (discussed in Section 15-2). Another example is obsessive-compulsive disorder, in which people persist in some checking behavior—to see that the stove is off or the door is locked—even though they have already checked many times.

All these phenomena show that stimuli can be highly processed by the brain without entering conscious awareness. This is quite different from the second neurological condition, in which people are consciously aware of stimuli that are not actually there. Examples include phantom limbs and the hallucinations of schizophrenia. In both, consciousness of specific events, such as pain in a missing limb or hearing voices, exists even though these events clearly are not "real."

We can draw two conclusions from these contrasting conditions. First, the representation of a visual object or event is likely to be distributed over many parts of the visual system and probably over parts of the frontal lobes as well. Damage to different areas not only produces different specific symptoms, such as agnosia or neglect, but can also produce a specific loss of visual consciousness. Disordered functioning can induce faulty consciousness, such as hallucinations. Second, because visual consciousness can be lost, it follows that parts of the neural circuit must produce this awareness. But how does this work? Over the past decade, several theories of the neural basis of consciousness have been proposed. We will briefly consider three in order to give a flavor of the nature of these theories.

First, Antonio Damasio (2012) proposed an *evolutionary theory*. He argues that early organisms were simple, without a real nervous system. As organisms became more complex, with more and more cells, a nervous system developed to coordinate the activity of these cells. Neurons emerged and came to be responsible for the organization of the other cells, followed by the emergence of a sense of internal state, or *interoception*, and a sense of external state, or *exteroception*. As nervous systems became more complex to meet the needs of increasingly complex organisms, there was a development of incentives—namely, the ability to choose advantageous opportunities. A reward system developed to maximize incentives, as did an alerting system (the reticular activating system) to activate other systems.

This development led to the evolution of emotions, again to maximize opportunities for survival. Sensory systems became more complex, and as the cerebral cortex evolved and expanded in mammals, the number of cerebral maps of the external world expanded—again to maximize incentives. Damasio posits that "mind" emerges from the expansion of maps, which again was advantageous, and that maps began to "feel" like something with a representation of the physical and social environments that an individual inhabited. This mind led to a sense of "self," which Damasio proposes as the emergence of consciousness.

Next, a group of theories that we collectively call *information integration theory* defines consciousness as the ability to integrate information (see Thagard & Stewart, 2014). Every action capable of choosing among alternatives generates information, which is integrated to the extent that it becomes a system above and beyond its inputs. Thus, the information generated by the system as a whole is greater than information

Clinical Focus 9-1 describes blindsight, Section 9-5, visual agnosias, Section 14-2, implicit learning in amnesia, and Section 16-3, OCD.

Research Focus 11-5 outlines phantom limb pain, Figure 14-23, how amputation remaps the cortex, and Clinical Focus 8-5, brain abnormalities in schizophrenia.

generated by its independent parts, and consciousness emerges. It follows that more complex brains will generate more information and that consciousness increases. Unique among consciousness theories, some information integration theories go on to suggest that as computers become better at integrating information, they will become conscious without a brain.

A third type of theory, the *semantic pointer competition (SPC) theory* (see Thagard & Stewart, 2014), proposes that consciousness results from three mechanisms: (1) representation of the world by firing patterns in neural populations; (2) binding of representations into more complex representations called semantic pointers; and (3) competition among semantic pointers to capture the most salient aspects of an organism's current state. In short, consciousness is a neural process emerging from complex neural networks. The central idea is the concept of a *semantic pointer*, which is a special kind of neural representation that can operate as an integrator of sensory, motor, and emotional representations, and also, in the case of humans, verbal representations.

For example, a person's neural concept of chocolate has multiple sensory representations (such as sweetness, texture, flavor), motor representations (such as reaching, grasping, and chewing), emotional representations (rewarding properties of chocolate), and possibly verbal representations ("It has a lot of calories"). The simpler representations are thus bound together into a more compact form suitable for manipulation. Semantic pointers do not by themselves explain consciousness, however. Countless neural representations of our experiences are being formed all the time, and they are in competition for our attention. Our qualitative experiences—all the sensations, feelings, and thoughts that we are aware of—result from competition among the semantic pointers, and this experience is consciousness.

We can see from this brief overview that there are competing explanations of why consciousness has emerged. It may make other adaptive processes (emotion, attention, learning) more effective, or it might be a side effect of complex neural processes of information integration or semantic pointer competition. But we are still left with the question of whether some brain areas are central to consciousness. We restrict our discussion here to the mammalian brain but recognize that other animals (especially birds) are likely to have consciousness.

The general consensus holds that the neural basis of consciousness has two distinct dimensions: (1) the level of consciousness (arousal/wakefulness), which is related to the activity of ascending activating systems of the brainstem, and (2) the content of consciousness, which is related to the connections between the thalamus and the cortex (the thalamocortical system). Our focus here is on the *content* of consciousness because, although arousal is necessary for consciousness, it is not sufficient. Brain-injured patients in a "vegetative" state may exhibit unresponsive wakefulness for years, with no obvious signs of conscious content.

Over the past decade, imaging studies have provided some clues, but also controversy, as to the key regions related to the content of consciousness (for a review, see Storm et al., 2017). There is considerable literature suggesting that parieto-frontal networks, such as the default network, are essential to consciousness; but lesion, stimulation, and imaging studies are pointing to the junction of the parietal, temporal, and occipital areas (sometimes referred to as the *temporal-parietal junction* [TPJ]) as a "hot zone" for consciousness. In particular, it appears that activity (or inactivity) in different regions is associated with differing experiential contents. For example, activity in the fusiform face area is related to face perception, and people with injuries to the fusiform face area will be "unconscious" of faces. We can anticipate that developments in noninvasive imaging techniques and studies will be key to better understanding the neural correlates of consciousness in the coming decade.

15-7 Review

Before you continue, check your understanding. Answers to Self-Test appear at the back of the book.

1. _____ is the mind's level of responsiveness to impressions made by the senses.

2. The _____ is conscious, but the dorsal stream, which acts more rapidly, is not.

3. The neural representation that integrates sensory, motor, emotional, and verbal representations is known as _____.

4. Briefly describe the three theories of the neural basis of consciousness covered in this section.

For additional study tools, visit 📖 **LaunchPad** at launchpadworks.com

Summary

15-1 The Nature of Thought

The complex processes we call thinking, or cognition, are products of both human and nonhuman brain activity. We use such words as *language* and *memory* to describe cognitive operations, but these concepts are abstract psychological constructs—merely inferred and not found in discrete places in the brain. They exist but have no physical form.

The brain carries out multiple cognitive operations—perception, action for perception, imagery, planning, spatial cognition, and attention. Each requires widespread activity in many cortical areas. The unit of cognition, however, is the neuron.

15-2 Cognition and the Association Cortex

The brain's association cortex includes medial, dorsal, and orbital subdivisions of the prefrontal cortex, the posterior parietal cortex, and anterior regions of the temporal lobe. Cell assemblies in the association cortex specifically take part in most forms of cognition.

The frontal lobes not only plan, organize, and initiate movements but also organize our behavior over time (temporally). As a general rule, the temporal lobes generate knowledge about objects, whereas the parietal lobes produce varied forms of spatial cognition. Neurons in both the temporal lobes and the parietal lobes contribute to our ability to selectively attend to sensory information.

Regions in the frontal and parietal lobes contain mirror neurons that represent actions—one's own or those of others. Such neural representations could be used both for imitating others' actions and for moving more quickly and more accurately. A significant area of the cortex is multisensory, allowing the brain to combine characteristics of stimuli across sensory modalities, whether we encounter the stimuli together or separately.

15-3 Expanding Frontiers of Cognitive Neuroscience

Neuropsychological studies that began in the late 1800s to examine the behavioral capacities of people and laboratory animals with localized brain injuries did not allow investigators to study "normal" brains. Today, noninvasive brain recording systems and imaging techniques further the field of cognitive neuroscience, which studies the neural basis of cognition by measuring brain activity while healthy participants engage in cognitive tasks.

An important step in identifying the neural bases of cognition is mapping cortical connections for the brain connectome. Two promising imaging tools are functional connectivity magnetic resonance imaging (fcMRI) and tractography using diffusion tensor imaging (DTI).

The cerebellum, which houses 80 percent of the human brain's neurons, was long believed to have primarily motor functions. Emerging data, however, reveal cerebellar involvement in a wide range of cognitive functions as well.

Social neuroscience, a field that combines cognitive neuroscience with social psychology, explores how we understand others' intentions by constructing a theory of mind (ToM). Social neuroscience also investigates how we develop attitudes, beliefs, and a sense of self. Using noninvasive imaging techniques such as fMRI, researchers have shown that social cognition primarily involves activity in the prefrontal cortex.

Neuroeconomics combines psychology, neuroscience, and economics in seeking to understand human decision making. fMRI studies reveal two decision-making pathways. One is slow and reflective, involving diffuse regions of association cortex. The other is quick and reflexive, involving the dopaminergic reward system.

15-4 Cerebral Asymmetry in Thinking

Cognitive operations are organized asymmetrically in the left and right cerebral hemispheres: the two hemispheres carry out complementary functions. The most obvious functional difference is language, typically housed in the left hemisphere.

Cerebral asymmetry, manifested in anatomical differences between the two hemispheres, can be inferred from the differential effects of injury to opposite sides of the brain. Asymmetry can also be seen in the healthy brain and in the brain that is surgically split to relieve intractable epilepsy. Various syndromes result from association cortex injury, among them agnosia, apraxia, aphasia, and amnesia. Each includes the loss or disturbance of some cognitive function.

15-5 Variations in Cognitive Organization

Unique brains produce unique thought patterns. Marked variations in brain organization among individuals are exhibited in idiosyncratic capacities such as synesthesia. Systematic differences in cognition exist as well, manifested in the performance of females and males on cognitive tests, especially on tests of spatial and verbal behavior.

Sex differences in cognition result from the action of gonadal hormones on cortical organization, possibly on the architecture of cortical neurons, and ultimately on neural networks. Female and male cerebral hemispheres exhibit marked differences in anatomical organization.

Right- and left-handers also differ in hemispheric organization. Left-handers constitute at least three distinct groups. In one, speech appears to reside in the left hemisphere, as it does in right-handers. The other two groups have anomalous speech representation, either in the right hemisphere or in both hemispheres. The reasons for these organizational differences remain unknown.

15-6 Intelligence

Intelligence is easy to spot but difficult to define. Obvious differences exist across as well as within species, and we find varied forms of intelligence among humans within our own culture and in other cultures. Intelligence is unrelated to differences in brain size within a species or to any obvious gross structural differences among members of the species. Intelligence may be related to synaptic organization and processing efficiency. A review by Jung and Haier conclude that differences in intelligence are linked to structural and functional variations in certain cortical brain regions; they propose the Parieto-Frontal Integration Theory of intelligence (P-FIT) based on their model.

15-7 Consciousness

Consciousness, the mind's level of responsiveness to impressions made by the senses, emerges from the complexity of the nervous system. We discuss three theories, or groups of theories, that seek to explain how consciousness emerged: it may make other adaptive processes (emotion, attention, learning) more effective, or it might be a side effect of complex neural processes of information integration or semantic pointer competition. Developments in noninvasive imaging techniques and studies will be key to better understanding the neural correlates of consciousness.

Key Terms

anomalous speech representation, p. 545

association cortex, p. 521

attention, p. 525

binding problem, p. 523

brain connectome, p. 529

cell assembly, p. 519

cognition, p. 517

cognitive neuroscience, p. 529

consciousness, p. 551

contralateral neglect, p. 526

convergent thinking, p. 548

dichotic listening, p. 537

divergent thinking, p. 548

extinction, p. 526

hyperconnectivity, p. 532

intelligence A, p. 549

intelligence B, p. 549

mirror neuron, p. 528

neuroeconomics, p. 534

perseveration, p. 527

psychological construct, p. 516

social neuroscience, p. 532

synesthesia, p. 546

syntax, p. 517

theory of mind, p. 532

Visit ⧉ **LaunchPad** to access the e-book, videos, ⧉ **LearningCurve** adaptive quizzing, flashcards, and more at launchpadworks.com

What Happens When the
Brain Misbehaves?

CHAPTER **16**

◎ **RESEARCH FOCUS 16-1**

Posttraumatic Stress Disorder

Life is filled with stress. Routinely, we cope. But some events are physically threatening and emotionally shattering and have long-term consequences. For about 10% of people, flashbacks, disturbing dreams, and persistent thoughts can interfere with daily activities long after physical danger has passed. These symptoms can lead to emotional numbness and a diagnosis of **posttraumatic stress disorder, or PTSD** (Daskalakis et al., 2018).

Traumatic events that may trigger PTSD include violent assault, natural or human-caused disaster, accident, and war, as well as the stresses of certain types of work. For example, veterans of the conflicts in Iraq and Afghanistan—many not directly exposed to combat—developed symptoms of PTSD, including intrusive, unwanted thoughts related to stressful events, negative thoughts and mood, and altered arousal and reactivity responses. These same effects can occur for people who encounter trauma as firefighters, police officers, and medical workers. The prevalence of this condition has spurred intense interest in understanding its neural basis and identifying new treatments.

One beneficial therapy, though it may sound counterintuitive, is to relive a traumatic event. In **virtual reality (VR) exposure therapy**, a controlled virtual immersion environment combines realistic street scenes, sounds, and odors that allow people to relive traumatic events (Norr et al., 2018). The Virtual Iraq and Afghanistan Simulation is customized for war veterans to start with benign events—such as children playing—and gradually add increasingly stressful components, culminating in such traumatic events as a roadside bomb exploding in the virtual space around an armored personnel carrier, illustrated here. VR exposure therapy is also

Courtesy Albert "Skip" Rizzo, Ph.D., USC-ICT

used *prior* to stress exposure for soldiers, police officers, firefighters, and other first responders as a means of preventing PTSD.

Many unknowns related to PTSD remain, including whether virtual reality treatment is the best treatment for everyone and whether counseling or having social support are as effective for others. There is also interest in why many people do *not* develop PTSD following extremely stressful events, as well as in the extent to which PTSD is associated with other health events, including previous stressors, diabetes, and head trauma (Horn & Feder, 2018). That said, assessment and treatment options for most of those who endure PTSD are poor: more than half of people, for example, receive no assessment or treatment.

posttraumatic stress disorder (PTSD) Syndrome characterized by physiological arousal brought on by recurring memories and dreams related to a traumatic event for months or years after the event.

virtual reality (VR) exposure therapy Controlled virtual immersion environment that, by allowing individuals to relive traumatic events, gradually desensitizes them to stress.

Understanding of PTSD illustrates how thinking on the brain's role in health can evolve. Largely as a result of symptoms displayed by returning Vietnam War veterans, in 1980 the DSM-III introduced PTSD as a mental disorder. Other investigators then pointed out similarities in symptoms among war veterans, rape victims, people subjected to accidents and natural disasters, and people who encountered trauma as a result of their occupations.

The many discussions of behavioral disorders and diseases presented throughout this book serve both to illustrate the brain's organization and functioning and to describe how knowledge about brain function contributes to our understanding and treatment of brain disorder and disease. Our focus in this chapter is the central role of the brain in diagnosis and treatment.

16-1

Multidisciplinary Contributions to Brain and Behavior

A prominent feature of PTSD diagnosis is that a traumatic external agent, rather than internal causes, is influential in producing the characteristic set of behavioral symptoms described in Research Focus 16-1, Posttraumatic Stress Disorder. Neuroscientists now recognize that the brain also contributes to PTSD and that trauma can result in epigenetic effects that can be transmitted to subsequent generations (Youssef et al., 2018). Furthermore, many people who are subjected to traumatic external agents do not go on to display PTSD. Clearly, multiple factors are relevant to understanding PTSD.

Consider a different condition, **phenylketonuria (PKU)**, in which apparently healthy newborn babies begin to develop an array of puzzling symptoms that lead to severe physical and cognitive disability. They develop a musty odor in the breath, skin, or urine, and they begin to have skin rashes and seizures. With time, their development is delayed, they become hyperactive, and they develop emotional, social, and intellectual problems and psychiatric disorders.

As complex as the condition may appear, a single brain abnormality can explain everything about it and its treatment. PKU is the most common inherited metabolic disease, an autosomal recessive disorder affecting more than 10,000 newborns each year globally. PKU results from a defect in the gene for phenylalanine hydroxylase (PAH), an enzyme that breaks down the amino acid phenylalanine. Phenylalanine is a precursor molecule for a number of other amines, including tyrosine, norepinephrine, and dopamine. PKU is related not to the presence of the phenylalanine but to excessive amounts of phenylalanine. An abnormality in PAH can be caused by more than 1000 different naturally occurring mutations in the PAH gene. To inherit PKU, both parents must carry a defective PHA gene. The recessive condition can in some circumstances confer resistance to certain fungal toxins.

PKU can be treated by restricting dietary intake of phenylalanine—foods high in protein, including beef, fish, cheese, and soy. A strict diet in infancy prevents brain damage, and controlled diet throughout life ensures protection. Expectant mothers who have had PKU might provide an in utero environment with high phenylalanine levels, and this too can be controlled if the mother restricts her dietary intake of phenylalanine. Several drugs to reduce phenylalanine levels are in development, including drugs that substitute an enzyme that acts like PHA to break down phenylalanine (Zong et al., 2018).

As the examples of PTSD and PKU illustrate, brain and behavior research, diagnosis, and treatment are multidisciplinary. One way to summarize methods of studying links between brain and behavior is to consider them from the macro level of the whole organism down to the molecular level of neuronal excitation and inhibition. Behavioral studies by their nature investigate the whole organism, but understanding the whole organism requires understanding its parts—its cells, its chemistry, and its genes.

Molecular biology offers neuroscientists varied approaches to studying behavior. Scientists can breed strains of animals, such as fruit flies, fish, or mice, with either a gene knocked out (deleted or inactivated) or a gene inserted. Techniques in molecular biology are used both to create animal models of human disorders and to generate treatments. Variations on this technology include methods for turning genes on or off for periods of time. What is clear from this research is that the genes related to disordered behavior in fruit flies, fish, and mice are largely the same as those related to similar disordered behavior in people.

Today, brain-imaging techniques allow behavioral neuroscientists to describe structures and pathways in an individual brain and the changes it undergoes during development, learning, and after damage—all without directly accessing the brain. Understanding the brain's structure and function leads to the understanding that individual brains differ—why, for example, one person may have PTSD or any other disorder, whereas another person in similar circumstances does not.

Clinical Neuroscience

Before we delve into the discussion of brain disorders, let's first review the professional landscape of those who study and treat them. A large number of professionals are involved in diagnosing and providing therapy for behavioral disorders. For example, psychologists deal with problems at the level of behavior, psychiatrists deal with problems related to brain dysfunction, and neurologists deal with problems related to nervous system damage. Psychologists likely have Ph.D.s, and psychiatrists and neurologists have degrees in medicine; all have special training in some aspect of treatment, belong to professional societies, and are licensed to provide their services.

phenylketonuria (PKU) Behavioral disorder caused by elevated levels of the amino acid phenylalanine in the blood and resulting from a defect in the gene for the enzyme phenylalanine hydroxylase; the major symptom is severe developmental disability.

Chapter 7 surveys research methods ranging from single-cell recordings to functional brain imaging.

Section 3-3 reviews genetics, genetic engineering, and epigenetic mechanisms; Section 7-5 explores techniques for measuring genetic and epigenetic influences.

Sections 7-3 and 7-4 discuss anatomical and functional imaging techniques.

clinical neuroscience Specialty in the field of neuroscience that focuses on the diagnosis and treatment of diseases and disorders affecting the brain and central nervous system.

The professional character of health care is reflected in the years of education health-care workers require, the complexity of services that health-care providers give, and the licensing required for health-care workers to receive financial compensation from health-care insurance companies or governments. When loved ones develop brain disorders, family members usually become the primary caregivers and, as such, join practitioners as participants because they and their loved ones are those most affected.

Behavioral disorders—traditionally classified as social, psychological, psychiatric, or neurological—reflect the assessment and treatment roles different professional groups play. As our understanding of brain function increases, the lines between behavioral disorders are blurring. Increasingly, practitioners are synthesizing their insights into a unified understanding of mind and brain, a **clinical neuroscience** that views the brain as the ultimate source of behavior and analyzes the diseases and disorders that affect it.

With this understanding of the multidisciplinary nature of brain and behavior in mind, we will now survey behavioral, psychiatric, and neurological disorders in the following sections. In each section, we examine how disorders are classified, treated, and distributed in the population and review established and emerging treatments.

Behavioral Disorders

We know that the brain is complex. We do not yet understand all its parts and their functions, nor do we yet know how the brain produces mind, a sense of well-being, and a sense of self. Still, significant advances have led to the realization that, while under some circumstances the brain copes competently with life's challenges, under other circumstances, it is not up to the task.

To illustrate progress in studying brain and behavior over the past century, let's contrast the theories of Sigmund Freud with present-day views. The underlying tenet of Freud's approach is that our motivations are largely hidden away in our unconscious mind. Freud posited that a repressive force actively withholds our sexual and aggressive motivations from conscious awareness. He believed that mental illness resulted from the failure of the repressive processes.

Freud proposed the three components of mind illustrated in **Figure 16-1A**:

1. Primitive functions, including the "instinctual drives" of sex and aggression, arise from the *id*, the part of the mind that Freud thought operated on an unconscious level.

2. The rational part of the mind he called the *ego*, the part of the mind that operates at the conscious level.

3. The *superego* aspect of mind acts to repress the id and to mediate ongoing interactions between the ego and the id.

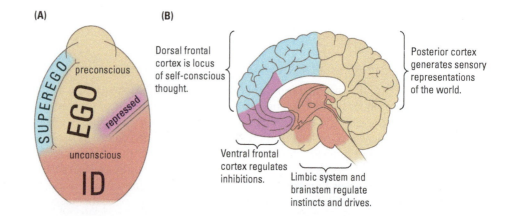

FIGURE 16-1 **Mind Models (A)** Freud based his model of the mind, drawn in 1933, solely on clinical observations (color added). **(B)** In a contemporary brain imaging and lesioning studies map, the brainstem and limbic system correlate with Freud's depiction of the id, the ventral frontal and posterior cortex with the ego, and the dorsal frontal cortex with the superego. Information from a drawing by Mark Solms and Oliver Turnbull (2002).

For Freudians, abnormal behaviors result from the emergence of unconscious drives into voluntary conscious behavior. The aim of *psychoanalysis*, the original talk therapy, is to trace symptoms to their unconscious roots and thus expose them to rational judgment.

By the 1970s, scientific studies of the brain had rendered the whole notion of id, ego, and superego antiquated. Nevertheless, some resemblance between Freud's theory and modern brain theory is apparent (Figure 16-1B). The limbic system and brainstem have properties akin to those of the id: they produce emotional and motivated behavior, including the will to survive and to reproduce. The posterior and the dorsolateral frontal cortices have properties akin to those of the ego: they allow us to learn and to solve everyday problems. The prefrontal neocortex has properties akin to those of the superego, enabling us to be aware of others and to learn to follow social norms.

We now recognize that the brain is composed of hundreds of interacting structures, not just three. We also know that the functions of these brain parts depend upon ongoing expression of genes, interactions of myriad chemicals, and functioning and connections of glia and neurons. Finally, we understand that behavioral disorders can be caused by genetic abnormalities, abnormalities in nervous system development over the life span, and environmental and epigenetic effects that modulate genetic and developmental expression. Nevertheless, as abundantly displayed in earlier chapters and in agreement with Freud, many processes underlying our functions are unconscious: they operate outside our awareness.

Diagnosing Behavioral Disorders

The National Institute of Mental Health (NIMH) estimates that, in a given year, about 1 in 4 people in the United States has a diagnosable behavioral disorder, and nearly half of the population does over their lifetime. Only a minority receive treatment of any kind, and even fewer receive treatment from a mental health specialist. Large-scale surveys of neurological disorders show a similar pattern of prevalence. Together, behavioral, psychiatric, and neurological disorders are the leading cause of disability after age 15.

The contrast between PTSD and PKU described at the beginning of this section illustrates the difficulties in understanding behavioral disorders. Both conditions present with an array of symptoms that seem equally complex. For PTSD, the complexity remains; but for PKU, the explanation is simple, and there is an effective treatment.

Knowledge about behavioral disorders is hampered by the subjective nature of behavior. Most diagnostic information gathered about a patient's behavior comes from both the patient and the caregivers and family members who know the subject and are often better diagnosticians than professionals who have limited interactions with the subject (Sacrey et al., 2015). Nevertheless, people are often not objective observers of their own behaviors or those of a loved one. We tend to be selective in noticing and reporting symptoms. If we believe someone has a memory problem, for example, we often notice memory lapses that we might ordinarily ignore.

Nor are we often specific in identifying symptoms. Simply identifying a memory problem is not sufficient. Treatment requires knowing exactly what type of memory deficit underlies a problem. Losses of memory for words, places, or habits—each has different underlying pathologies and brain systems.

Sections 14-2 and 14-3 explain a range of memory deficits.

Just as patients and their loved ones make diagnosis difficult, so too do diagnosticians. Behavioral information about patients may be interpreted differently by general physicians, psychiatrists, neurologists, psychologists, social workers, and others. Evaluators with different conceptual biases shape and filter the questions they ask and the information they gather.

Classifying Behavioral Disorders

Classification systems have a long history in science, and their purpose is to gain insights into biological processes and to generate theories to explain those processes. Many classification systems have been developed to explain psychological, psychiatric, and neurological disorders; indeed, each of these professional groups has its own classification system, which is frequently revised in light of new

TABLE 16-1 **Summary of DSM-5 Diagnostic Classification of Disorders**

Diagnostic category
Neurodevelopmental disorders
Schizophrenia spectrum and other psychiatric disorders
Bipolar and related disorders
Depressive disorders
Anxiety disorders
Obsessive-compulsive and related disorders
Trauma- and stressor-related disorders
Dissociative disorders
Somatic symptom disorder and related disorders
Feeding and eating disorders
Elimination disorders
Sleep–wake disorders
Sexual dysfunctions
Gender dysphoria
Disruptive, impulse-control, and conduct disorders
Substance-related and addictive disorders
Neurocognitive disorders
Personality disorders

Source: Information from American Psychiatric Association, 2013.

Diagnostic and Statistical Manual of Mental Disorders (DSM) The American Psychiatric Association's classification system for psychiatric disorders.

TABLE 16-2 **PKU: RDoC Pathogenesis of a Behavioral Disorder**

Level of analysis	Known information
Genes	Inborn metabolism error; recessive defective gene (autosomal) with about 1000 variants
Molecules	Conversion of phenylalanine to tyrosine impaired, elevating levels of phenylalanine and its metabolites in the blood, which occurs before and after birth
Cells	Decrease in neuron size and dendritic length; lowered spine density; reduced glutamine activity
Circuits	Decreased lamination
Physiological behavior	Reduced enzyme activity; intellectual impairment with an onset that varies with the gene abnormality; slow growth; seizure; abnormal EEG
Self-report	IQ score below 50 (in 95 percent of patients); significant loss of meaningful life and productivity if untreated
Treatment	Dietary intake of phenylalanine restricted; enzyme substitution

knowledge. The World Health Organization has developed an extensive classification of diseases, *The International Classification of Diseases*. This classification is used by many countries to compile statistical data related to health. Although it provides an extensive overview of disease, it is not primarily directed toward disease diagnosis and treatment.

The first set of criteria for diagnoses in behavior was developed in 1972. Since that time, two parallel sets of criteria have gained prominence. The best known, and probably the most widely used classification, is the American Psychiatric Association's **Diagnostic and Statistical Manual of Mental Disorders (DSM)**, now in its fifth edition, DSM-5. The intent of this system is to aid diagnosis and treatment. **Table 16-1** outlines the classification scheme for behavioral disorders in the DSM-5.

The other classification system, launched by NIMH, is the *Research Domain Criteria* (RDoC; pronounced "R doc"). With this classification system, NIMH is looking to transform behavioral diagnoses by incorporating genetics, imaging, and cognitive science, among other levels of information. The DSM begins from the premise that labeling a condition will lead to understanding the condition and treating it. The RDoC begins from the premise that understanding basic biological function will lead to understanding malfunction and its treatment.

According to the NIMH, "the RDoC framework is centered around dimensional psychological constructs (or concepts) relevant to human behavior and mental disorders, as measured using multiple methodologies and as studied within the contexts of developmental trajectories and environmental influences." These constructs relate to specific characteristics of brain functionality and RDoC uses various molecular, physiological, genetic, behavioral, and neurobiological measures ("units of analysis")—for example, genetic testing, surveys, and brain imaging—to describe and study these constructs and the connections between them. **Table 16-2** lists some of what we know about PKU using RDoC units of analysis: genes, molecules, cells, circuits, and so on. Note that the underlying problem becomes less apparent with the procession of entries in the table. In fact, it is not possible to predict the specific biochemical abnormality from information at the neurological, behavioral, or social level—exactly where the most accessible information resides.

The different approaches that underlie the DSM and the RDoC will be familiar to you. Throughout this book, we have described the function of the brain in terms of systems for movement, motivation, memory, and so on. This is the approach taken by the RDoC classification. To aid in our description of each system, we have detailed malfunctions characterized by abnormal conditions that could be associated with the given system. This is the approach taken by the DSM-5. For example, our discussion of the motor systems includes a description of Parkinson disease, and our discussion of memory systems includes a description of Alzheimer disease.

Classification systems, such as *taxonomy*—the branch of biology that groups organisms according to their common characteristics and relationships—have advanced our knowledge of brain structure and function. Likewise, classifications of behavioral disorders produced by the behavioral sciences have advanced our understanding of the role of the brain in behavioral disorders. Yet all classification systems have limitations. The DSM-5 is arbitrary and unavoidably dependent on prevailing cultural views. Naming disorders or systems is problematic as well. The term *idiot* once designated a person with a low IQ score. When the term became pejorative, it was replaced with the term *retarded*. That term is now pejorative as well, and the DSM-5 uses the term *intellectually disabled*.

Another criticism is epitomized by the statement "just because you name a disorder does not mean it exists." In a sense, Emily Dickinson expresses this idea in the opening line of her poem "Much Madness": "Much Madness is divinest Sense—To a discerning Eye."

The RDoC classification of behaviors receives less criticism than does the DSM-5, but that may be because fewer people use it. One criticism of the RDoC is that it represents only one view of the organization of normal behavior and is therefore subjective. Combining behavioral diagnoses with genetic analysis and neuroimaging may move practitioners beyond symptom checklists and to objective medical diagnoses. Although imaging analyses help target problems with the brain, current imaging techniques do not detect all brain pathology. In addition, the relevant criterion when assessing the effects of a gene is not whether the gene is present or absent but whether it is or is not expressed. The challenge in using the RDoC approach lies in improving current techniques and developing new ones that can identify subtler nervous system abnormalities.

The Basics in Section 1-3 provides an overview of taxonomy.

If all behavioral disorders could be analyzed as readily as PKU, neuroscience research could quickly yield cures for each of them. For PKU, the distinctive smell detected by one mother in her baby's urine was the first link in a chain of discoveries that led to the identification of elevated phenylalanine. Many disorders do not result from a single genetic abnormality, however, and the causes of most disorders remain conjectural. The major problem remains: diagnosis of a disability is based mainly on behavioral symptoms, and behavioral symptoms give few clues to specific neurochemical or neurostructural causes.

Causes of Disordered Behavior

Neuroscientists presume that abnormal brain functioning results in disordered behavior. In a general sense, there are at least six general causes of abnormal brain function:

1. *Genetic errors* in which a single gene may cause a disorder (as in Huntington disease) or a constellation of genes may be involved (as with schizophrenia).

2. *Epigenetic mechanisms* at work prenatally, later in life, and even in succeeding generations. Most of our genes are continually active, and our behavior and our environment can modify their activity.

3. *Progressive cell death* resulting from neurodegenerative causes (as in Parkinson or Alzheimer disease). In some cases, a single abnormal protein can initiate a cascade of events that result in progressive cell death.

4. *Rapid cell death* (as in stroke or traumatic brain injury), in which the circulatory system is interrupted or the brain is concussed or penetrated.

5. *Loss of neural function and connections* seen in disorders such as multiple sclerosis and myasthenia gravis, in which, for example, an individual's own immune system attacks neural elements.

6. *Life stress*, including inadequate developmental opportunities, poor nutrition, and PTSD.

At the microscopic level is genetic error, such as that responsible for Tay-Sachs disease and Huntington disease. Intermediate categories include one-time events, such as infections, injuries, and toxins. At the macro level, nutrition, stress, and negative experience are prominent actors. Of course, many of these factors interact. Genetic vulnerability to stress, infection, or pollution may be the immediate cause of some disorders. In other cases, no direct genetic predisposition is needed: disordered behavior arises strictly from epigenetic factors, such as stress and negative experiences, which influence gene expression and function.

Table 16-3 lists some likely causal categories underlying behavioral disorders.

TABLE 16-3 **Some Causes of Selected Behavioral Disorders**

Cause	Disorder
Genetic error	Tay-Sachs disease
Hormonal	Androgenital syndrome
Developmental	Autism
Infection	Encephalitis
Injury	Traumatic brain injury
Toxins	MPTP poisoning
Poor nutrition	Korsakoff syndrome
Stress	Anxiety disorders, PTSD
Negative experience	Developmental delays

Clinical Focus 3-3 describes the genetic basis of Huntington disease; Clinical Focus 5-2, neural degeneration in Parkinson disease; Clinical Focus 2-3, symptoms and aftereffects of stroke; and Clinical Focus 4-2, myelin breakdown in MS.

The Index of Disorders on the inside cover lists all the behavioral disorders discussed in this book, but they constitute a mere fraction of the total number of known disorders.

Treating Behavioral Disorders

Treatments for behavioral disorders need not be direct biological or medical interventions. Just as the brain can alter behavior, behavior can alter the brain. Behavioral treatments focus on key environmental factors that influence how a person acts. As behavior changes in response to treatment, the brain is affected as well.

Take, for example, the treatment for *generalized anxiety disorders* attributed to chronic stress. People who endure a persistently high anxiety level often engage in

Clinical Focus 12-5 recounts a case of generalized anxiety disorder.

maladaptive behaviors to reduce it. While they require immediate treatment with anti-anxiety medication, long-term treatment entails changing their behavior. Generalized anxiety disorder is not simply a problem of abnormal brain activity but also of experiential and social factors that fundamentally alter the person's perception of the world.

Perhaps you are thinking that behavioral treatments may help somewhat in treating brain dysfunction, but the real solution must lie in altering brain activity. Since every aspect of behavior is the product of brain activity, behavioral treatments *do* act by changing brain function. If people can change how they think and feel about themselves or some aspect of their lives, this change has taken place because talking about their problems or resolving a problem alters how their brain functions. In a sense, then, a behavioral treatment is a biological intervention. Behavioral treatments may sometimes be helped along by drug treatments that make the brain more receptive to change through behavioral therapy. In this way, drug treatments and behavioral treatments have synergistic effects, each helping the other to be more effective.

Your behavior is a product of all your learning and social experiences. An obvious approach to developing a treatment is to re-create a learning environment that replaces a maladaptive behavior with an adaptive behavior. Thus, the various approaches to behavioral treatment use principles derived from experiment-based learning theory. Following is a sampling of these approaches.

BEHAVIOR MODIFICATION **Behavioral therapies** apply well-established learning principles to eliminate unwanted behaviors. Therapists apply principles developed in studying learning by reinforcement in laboratory settings, including operant and classical conditioning. For example, if a person is debilitated by a fear of insects, rather than looking for inner causes, the behavioral therapist tries to replace the maladaptive behaviors with more constructive ways of behaving. These might include training the patient to relax while systematically exposing him to unthreatening insects (butterflies), followed by gradual exposure to more threatening insects (bees). This form of habituation (adaption to a repeatedly presented stimulus) is called *systematic desensitization*.

COGNITIVE THERAPY **Cognitive therapy** operates from the perspective that thoughts intervene between events and emotions. Consider responses to losing a job. One reaction could be, "I'm a loser; life is hopeless," but an alternative thought is, "The job was a dead end. The boss did me a favor. I can do better." The former cognition might lead to depression, whereas the latter would not. Cognitive therapies challenge a person's self-defeating attitudes and assumptions and are important for people with brain injury, too, because it is easy for people to think they are crazy or stupid after suffering a brain injury. Equally powerful, if not more so, is cognitive-behavioral therapy, discussed in Section 16-2.

NEUROPSYCHOLOGICAL THERAPY If a relative or friend had a stroke and became aphasic, you would expect him or her to attend speech therapy—a behavioral treatment for an injured brain. The logic in speech therapy is that by practicing (relearning) the basic components of speech and language, the patient should be able to regain at least some lost function. The same logic can apply to other types of behavioral disorders, whether motor or cognitive.

Therapies for cognitive disorders resulting from brain trauma or dysfunction aim to retrain people in the fundamental cognitive processes they have lost. Although cognitive therapy seems as logical as speech therapy after a stroke, cognitive therapy assumes that we know what fundamental elements of cognitive activity are meaningful to the brain. Cognitive scientists are far from understanding these elements well enough to generate optimal therapies. Still, neuropsychologists are developing neurocognitive programs that can improve functional outcomes following TBI and stroke. Treatment effectiveness can be improved with computer-based tools and follow-up therapy.

EMOTIONAL THERAPY In the 1920s, Sigmund Freud developed the idea that talking about emotional problems enables people to gain insight into the causes of the problems and can serve as treatment also. Talk cures and other forms of psychological intervention may be broadly categorized as psychotherapies.

behavioral therapy Treatment that applies learning principles, such as conditioning, to eliminate unwanted behaviors.

cognitive therapy Psychotherapy based on the perspective that thoughts intervene between events and emotions, and thus the treatment of emotional disorders requires changing maladaptive patterns of thinking.

Since Freud's time, many ideas have been put forth about the best type of therapy for emotional disorders. Key here is that for many disorders, whether neurological or psychiatric, medical treatments are not effective unless patients also receive **psychotherapy**. Indeed, the only effective treatment in many cases lies in addressing the unwanted behaviors directly—in acquiring the skill rather than taking the pill.

Consider a 25-year-old woman pursuing a promising career as a musician who suffered a traumatic brain injury in an automobile accident. After the accident, she found that she was unable to read music. Not surprisingly, she soon became depressed. Part of her therapy required her to confront her disabling cognitive loss by talking about it rather than by simply stewing over it. Only when she pursued psychotherapy did she begin to recover from her intense depression.

For many people with emotional impairments resulting from brain disease or trauma, the most effective treatment for depression or anxiety is to help them adjust by encouraging them to talk about their difficulties. Group therapy provides such encouragement and is standard treatment in brain injury rehabilitation units.

PHYSICAL ACTIVITY AND MUSIC AS THERAPY Exercise and music have positive effects on peoples' attitudes, emotional well-being, and brain function. Physical exercise demands visual control of movement. Music affects arousal and activates the motor cortex and the premotor cortex. Listening to music can improve gait in Parkinson and stroke patients and reduce pain after surgery. Learning to play a musical instrument likewise is beneficial therapy. Singing, a useful adjunct to rehabilitative speech therapy, enhances the ability to enunciate. Physical activity, including dancing and playing sports, combined with other therapies, improves well-being and counteracts the effects of depression.

REAL-TIME fMRI Using real-time fMRI, individuals learn to change their behavior by controlling their own brain activation patterns. This behavior-modification technique was first used to treat intractable pain, which produces a characteristic brain activity pattern (deCharms, 2008). The researchers proposed that if subjects could see their brain activity via fMRI in real time as they felt pain, they could be trained to reduce the neural activity and lessen their pain. **Real-time fMRI (rt-fMRI)** uses a form of operant conditioning in which the gradual modification of a participant's behavior increases the probability of reward.

Think of rt-fMRI as a form of neural plasticity in which the individual learns new strategies, guided by brain activation information. When subjects decrease brain activation in regions associated with pain, they report decreased pain perception. Conversely, through learning to increase brain activation in these regions, they would be able to increase their pain—although it seems unlikely that this ability would be much cultivated! An actual potential application of rt-fMRI is in monitoring brain activation when treatment for disorders occurs in the context of behavioral therapy. Patients need not be consciously aware of the therapy's objectives: induced brain changes, whether conscious or unconscious, can prove beneficial.

VIRTUAL REALITY THERAPY The principle behind virtual reality (VR) therapy is that patients enter or interact with a virtual world displayed on a computer screen or through goggles. One example is the Virtual Iraq and Afghanistan Simulation described in Research Focus 16-1. The participant can experience sights, sounds, and even smells that mimic situations related to acquiring the behavioral disorder, in this case PTSD. In modified VR therapy, a patient interacts as a character in a computer game. Winning the game necessitates making adaptive choices; maladaptive choices result in losing the game.

psychotherapy Talk therapy derived from Freudian psychoanalysis and other psychological interventions.

real-time fMRI (rt-fMRI) Behavior-modification technique in which individuals learn to change their behavior by controlling their own patterns of brain activation.

Section 10-4 observes that practitioners have only begun to tap the power of music as a therapeutic tool.

GreatStock/Masterfile

Exercise boosts your mood because it boosts your dopamine levels.

Research Focus 11-5 describes an effective low-tech strategy for controlling phantom limb pain.

16-1 Review

Before you continue, check your understanding. Answers to Self-Test appear at the back of the book.

1. Neural correlates of Freud's id, ego, and superego could be, respectively, the _____, _____, and _____.

2. Causes of disordered behavior include _____, _____, _____, _____, and _____.

3. For most psychiatric disorders, the causes are unknown, but _____ is an exception.

4. How does the approach to classification taken by the RDoC contrast with the approach taken by the DSM?

For additional study tools, visit 📖 **LaunchPad** at launchpadworks.com

16-2

Psychiatric Disorders

Psychiatric disorders, which are assumed to be due to brain malfunction, include a wide range of disorders summarized by the DSM-5. We focus here on the three general behavioral categories—psychoses, mood disorders, and anxiety disorders—that are the best studied and understood. **Figure 16-2** summarizes their prevalence. Schizophrenia, bipolar disorder, and major depression affect a smaller number of people, but their costs—in loss of social relationships, productivity, and medical care—are disproportionate.

Schizophrenia Spectrum and Other Psychotic Disorders

Psychoses are disorders in which a person loses contact with reality and is subject to irrational ideas and distorted perceptions. Among the varieties of psychosis, schizophrenia is the most common and best understood. Schizophrenia takes many forms, and whether it is a single disorder or several disorders that share some symptoms is uncertain. The complexity of behavioral and neurobiological factors that characterize schizophrenia makes it especially difficult to diagnose and classify. Understanding schizophrenia is an evolving process and far from complete.

Diagnosing Schizophrenia

The DSM lists six diagnostic symptoms of schizophrenia:

1. Delusions—beliefs that distort reality
2. Hallucinations—distorted perceptions, such as hearing voices
3. Disorganized speech, such as incoherent statements or senselessly rhyming talk
4. Disorganized behavior or excessive agitation
5. Catatonic behavior—the opposite extreme of agitation
6. Negative symptoms, such as blunted emotions or loss of interest and drive, all characterized by the absence of some healthy response

Schizophrenia may produce a wide range of symptoms, and individual differences in behavioral effects exist as well. Voluminous research related to the origins and causes of schizophrenia has emerged, but the three lines of research summarized in this section have transformed ideas about its genetics, its development, and its associated brain correlates.

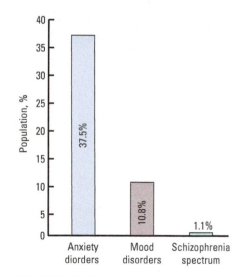

FIGURE 16-2 **Prevalence of Some Psychiatric Illnesses** Data from National Institute of Mental Health, http://www.nimh.nih.gov/health/statistics/index.shtml

GENETICS It is recognized that genetics contributes to schizophrenia, as does environment. The more closely related an individual is to someone diagnosed with schizophrenia, the more likely he or she is to develop the condition. The concordance of schizophrenia in identical twins is high: 50 percent is often cited. That the concordance for schizophrenia is not 100 percent means that environmental factors also play a role (Shorter & Miller, 2015).

Mutations on a number of chromosomes (candidates are 1, 6, 8, 13, and 22) predispose an individual to schizophrenia, and many mutations in candidate genes on those chromosomes are involved. Genetic studies suggest that schizophrenia is probably a family of disorders that may include other conditions, such as major depression and bipolar disorder (XiangWei et al., 2018). What may be common to the genes involved is that they contribute to brain development, and therefore mutations in these genes may contribute to various abnormalities in brain development.

DEVELOPMENT Typically, schizophrenia is diagnosed in young adulthood, but a body of evidence suggests that it originates much earlier, even prenatally. Its expression in adulthood must therefore await the conclusion of a host of developmental processes that ultimately shape the adult human brain. That schizophrenia has developmental origins has many implications.

First, environmental factors acting through epigenetic mechanisms are likely to influence brain development such that a subset of at-risk individuals develops adult schizophrenia. Second, identifying developmental factors that contribute to schizophrenia provides the best opportunity for intervention to reduce the risks of developing it. Any potential cure for schizophrenia will depend on early detection and remediation through epigenetic mechanisms.

BRAIN CORRELATES The following lines of evidence show that anatomical changes in the brain are associated with schizophrenia:

1. The schizophrenic brain generally has large ventricles and thinner cortex in the medial temporal regions and frontal cortex, suggesting cell loss in these areas. The PET images in **Figure 16-3** illustrate metabolic changes in adult-onset schizophrenia. The scan on the left reveals an obvious abnormality in prefrontal cortex activity compared with the scan on the right, from an adult who does not have schizophrenia.

2. Imaging technology suggests that there are similarities in the brain changes associated with schizophrenia across a wide range of ages. Some aspects of neuronal and fiber composition of the temporal lobes and the frontal lobes are changed, as indicated by changes in their density, imaged by MRI (Watsky et al., 2018). Cortical maps derived by Judith Rapoport and coworkers (2012) reveal

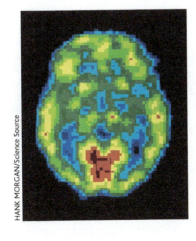
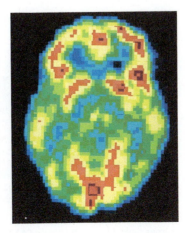

HANK MORGAN/Science Source

FIGURE 16-3 **Adult-Onset Schizophrenia** Note the abnormally low blood flow in the prefrontal cortex at the top of the PET scan in the brain of an adult schizophrenia patient (*left*) compared with that of an adult who does not have schizophrenia (*right*).

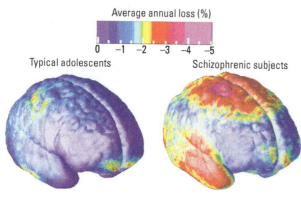

Average annual loss (%)

0   −1   −2   −3   −4   −5

Typical adolescents   Schizophrenic subjects

FIGURE 16-4 **Childhood-Onset Schizophrenia** Comparison of three-dimensional maps derived from MRI scans reveals that, compared with healthy teenagers aged 13 to 18 (*left*), patients with childhood-onset schizophrenia (*right*) have widespread loss of gray matter across the cerebral hemispheres. Courtesy of Paul Thompson and Arthur W. Toga, Laboratory of Neuro Imaging, Keck School of Medicine of USC and Judith L. Rapoport, National Institute of Mental Health.

The dopamine hypothesis of schizophrenia is discussed in Section 6-2.

GABA is the brain's main inhibitory neurotransmitter. Section 6-2 discusses GABAergic agonists and their effects at the GABA receptor.

that children who developed schizophrenia showed a remarkable loss of gray matter in the cerebral cortex between the ages of 13 and 18 (**Figure 16-4**). Imaging of subjects with childhood-onset schizophrenia suggests that the condition begins *in utero* and is characterized by excessive pruning of short-distance cortical connections (Rao et al., 2015). Research by Watsky and colleagues (2018) finds many similarities in brain changes in childhood-onset schizophrenia and adult-onset schizophrenia, which shows that there is continuity between the conditions.

3. Alterations in neuronal structure show abnormal dendritic fields in cells in the dorsal prefrontal regions, as shown in **Figure 16-5**, in the hippocampus (Cho et al., 2004) and in the entorhinal cortex (Arnold et al., 1997).

In sum, this evidence almost definitively shows that schizophrenia is associated in the main with alteration in the temporal region and the frontal cortex. As you have learned, the temporal region and frontal cortex are associated with memory, language, and decision making.

Neurochemical Correlates of Schizophrenia

Neuroscientists also consider the neurochemical correlates of brain–behavior relationships in schizophrenia. Dopamine abnormalities were the first to be linked to schizophrenia, through two lines of evidence. First, most neuroleptic drugs (drugs used to treat schizophrenia) act on the dopamine synapse. Second, drugs that enhance dopamine synaptic activity, such as amphetamine, can produce psychotic symptoms reminiscent of schizophrenia.

This dopamine theory of schizophrenia appears too simple, however, because many other neurochemical abnormalities, summarized in **Table 16-4**, are also associated with schizophrenia—in particular, abnormalities in dopamine and dopamine receptors and in GABA and GABA-binding sites. Recent evidence also suggests changes in the NMDA receptor in schizophrenia, a finding that is leading to the development of new classes of glutamate drug therapy. Patients vary widely in the extent of each abnormality, however. How these neurochemical variations might relate to the presence or absence of specific symptoms is not yet known (Morrison & Murray, 2018).

To summarize, schizophrenia is a complex disorder associated with abnormalities in brain structure and with neurochemical abnormalities in dopamine, glutamate, and GABA. Given the complexity of all these factors, it is not surprising that schizophrenia is so difficult to characterize and to treat.

TABLE 16-4 **Biochemical Changes Associated with Schizophrenia**

Decreased dopamine metabolites in cerebrospinal fluid
Increased striatal D_2 receptors
Decreased expression of D_3 and D_4 mRNA in specific cortical regions
Decreased cortical glutamate
Increased cortical glutamate receptors
Decreased glutamate uptake sites in cingulate cortex
Decreased mRNA for synthesizing GABA in prefrontal cortex
Increased $GABA_A$-binding sites in cingulate cortex

Source: Information from Byne et al., 1999.

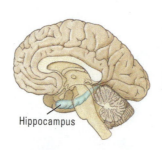

Hippocampus

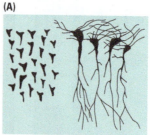

(A)

Organized (healthy) pyramidal neurons

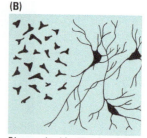

(B)

Disorganized (schizophrenic) pyramidal neurons

FIGURE 16-5 **Organic Dysfunction** Rather than the consistently parallel orientation of hippocampal neurons typical in healthy brains **(A)**, the orientation of hippocampal neurons in the brain of a person with schizophrenia is haphazard **(B)**. Information from Kovelman & Scheibel, 1984.

Mood Disorders

Mood disorders include major depressive disorders, bipolar disorder, and anxiety disorders. The main symptoms of **major depression** are prolonged feelings of worthlessness and guilt, disruption of normal eating habits, sleep disturbances, a general slowing of behavior, and frequent thoughts of suicide. **Bipolar disorder** is a condition in which periods of mood often change, sometimes abruptly, to depression and back again to mania. **Mania**, the opposite mood extreme from depression, is characterized by excessive euphoria. The affected person often formulates grandiose plans and is uncontrollably hyperactive. **Anxiety disorders** include a number of conditions in which unhelpful anxiety has a negative effect on daily life.

Major Depression

Brain and environment both contribute to major depression. Predisposing factors related to brain anatomy and chemistry thus may contribute more to mood changes in some people, whereas life experiences contribute mainly to mood changes in other people. As a result, a bewildering number of life, health, and brain factors have been related to depression. These factors include economic or social failure, disruption of circadian rhythm, deficiencies of vitamin D and other nutrients, pregnancy, brain injury, diabetes, cardiovascular events, and childhood abuse, among many others.

One approach in neurobiological studies of depression is to ask whether a common brain substrate exists for depression. Antidepressant drugs acutely increase the synaptic levels of norepinephrine and serotonin, a finding that led to the idea that depression results from decreased availability of one or both neurotransmitters. Lowering their levels in healthy participants does not produce depression, however. And while antidepressant medications may increase the level of norepinephrine and serotonin within days, it takes weeks for the drugs to start relieving depression. Furthermore, there are now numerous drugs available for the treatment of depression, and it is not certain that they influence only levels of norepinephrine and serotonin (Andrade, 2018).

Mood and Reactivity to Stress

A significant psychological factor in understanding depression is reactivity to stress. Monoamines—the noradrenergic and serotoninergic activating systems diagrammed in **Figure 16-6A**—modulate hormone secretion by the hypothalamic–pituitary–adrenal system, or the **HPA axis**, illustrated in Figure 16-6B. When we are stressed, the HPA axis is stimulated to secrete corticotropin-releasing hormone, which stimulates the pituitary to produce adrenocorticotropic hormone (ACTH). ACTH circulates through the blood and stimulates the adrenal medulla to produce cortisol. Normally, cortisol helps us deal with stress. If we cannot cope, or if stress is intense, excessive cortisol can wield a negative influence on the brain, damaging the feedback loops the brain uses to turn off the stress response.

Excessive stress early in life may be especially detrimental. During critical periods in early childhood, abuse or other severe environmental stress can permanently disrupt HPA axis reactivity: it becomes constantly overactive. Overactivity in the HPA axis results in oversecretion of cortisol. Patrick McGowan and Moshe Szyf (2010) wondered if early experiences could alter gene expression related to cortisol activity in the HPA axis. They compared, postmortem, hippocampi obtained from suicide victims with a history of childhood abuse and hippocampi from other suicide

major depression Mood disorder characterized by prolonged feelings of worthlessness and guilt, disruption of normal eating habits, sleep disturbances, a general slowing of behavior, and frequent thoughts of suicide.

bipolar disorder Mood disorder characterized by periods of depression alternating with normal periods and periods of intense excitation, or *mania*.

mania Disordered mental state of extreme excitement.

anxiety disorder A disorder that includes a number of conditions in which unhelpful anxiety has a negative effect on daily life.

HPA axis Hypothalamic–pituitary–adrenal circuit that controls the production and release of hormones related to stress.

Clinical Focus 6-3 explains the threat of suicide attendant to untreated major depression.

Section 6-2 discusses medications used to treat depression.

FIGURE 16-6 **Stress-Activating System** **(A)** Medial view showing that in the brainstem, cell bodies of noradrenergic (norepinephrine) neurons emanate from the locus coeruleus (*top*), and cell bodies of the serotonergic activating system emanate from the raphe nuclei (*bottom*). **(B)** When activated, the HPA axis affects mood, thinking, and, indirectly, cortisol secretion by the adrenal glands. HPA deactivation begins when cortisol binds to hypothalamic receptors.

(A)

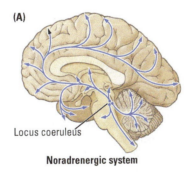

Locus coeruleus

Noradrenergic system

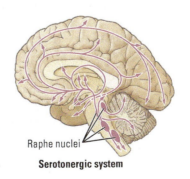

Raphe nuclei

Serotonergic system

(B)

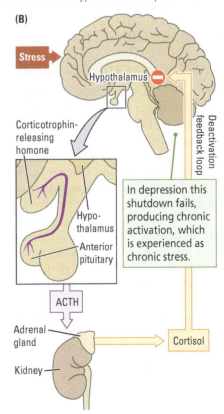

Stress

Hypothalamus

Corticotrophin-releasing homone

Hypo-thalamus

Anterior pituitary

ACTH

Adrenal gland

Kidney

Cortisol

Deactivation feedback loop

In depression this shutdown fails, producing chronic activation, which is experienced as chronic stress.

cognitive-behavioral therapy (CBT) Problem-focused, action-oriented, structured treatment for eliminating dysfunctional thoughts and maladaptive behaviors.

Section 6-5 explains the neurobiology of the stress response—how it begins and ends.

This research confirms studies on the effects of stress on hippocampal function reported in Sections 6-5, 7-5, and 8-4.

Principle 2: Neuroplasticity is the hallmark of nervous system functioning.

victims with no childhood abuse and from controls. Abused suicide victims showed decreased gene expression for cortisol receptors compared to the other suicide victims with no childhood abuse and the controls. These results suggest that early neglect or abuse alters the HPA axis for life (Marzi et al., 2018).

To summarize, the diffuse distribution of the norepinephrine- and serotonin-activating systems makes relating depression to a single brain structure impossible. Findings from neuroimaging studies show that depression is accompanied by increased blood flow and glucose metabolism in the orbitofrontal cortex, anterior cingulate cortex, and amygdala. Blood flow drops as the symptoms of depression remit when a patient takes antidepressant medication (Drevets et al., 2004). Antidepressants effectively increase the amount of serotonin in the cortex and may also stimulate brain repair. For example, fluoxetine (Prozac) stimulates both brain-derived neurotrophic factor (BDNF) production and neurogenesis in the hippocampus, resulting in a net increase in granule cells, described in Research Focus 16-2, Antidepressant Action and Brain Repair.

Although we have emphasized biological correlates of depression, the best treatment need not be a direct biological intervention. **Cognitive-behavioral therapy (CBT)** is an excellent—arguably the best—therapy for depression. It focuses on challenging the patient's beliefs and perceptions. The objective is to identify dysfunctional thoughts and beliefs that accompany negative emotions and to replace them with more realistic ones.

Simply pointing out that a person's beliefs are faulty is not likely to be effective, however, because it probably took months or years to develop those beliefs. The neural circuits underlying faulty beliefs must change, just as the strategies for developing new ones must change. In a real sense, then, CBT is effective if it induces neural plasticity and changes brain activity.

Anxiety Disorders

Anxiety often accompanies depression, but anxiety disorders can also occur as a separate condition. Anxiety disorders include phobias, panic disorders, agoraphobia, obsessive-compulsive disorder, PTSD, and generalized anxiety disorder.

We are all subject to anxiety, usually acutely in response to stress or less commonly as chronic reactivity—an increased anxiety response—even to seemingly minor stressors.

⊙ **RESEARCH FOCUS** 16-2

Antidepressant Action and Brain Repair

Excessive stress and poor coping skills contribute to excessive cortisol levels in the brain and to depression and anxiety. Granule cells in the hippocampus, which are especially sensitive to cortisol, can die when cortisol levels are either reduced, as shown in the figure, or increased excessively.

These hippocampal cells may themselves play a role in regulating cortisol levels: they may be the switch that turns off the brain's stress response. Their absence leaves the HPA axis unchecked. Then increased cortisol levels contribute to more neuron death and to depression and anxiety. It's a vicious circle.

A remarkable finding emerged from studying how antidepressants such as fluoxetine and other selective serotonin reuptake inhibitors (SSRIs) affect the hippocampus. The SSRIs increased neurogenesis in the subgranular zone, cell migration into the dentate gyrus, and the number of functioning cells there (Kraus et al., 2017).

That antidepressants take some weeks to produce their positive effects on behavior and that new neurons take some weeks to migrate and incorporate into the hippocampus suggest that the antidepressants' mechanism of action is to enhance hippocampal function—in essence, to replace the neural switch that turns off the stress response.

The literature on hippocampal neurogenesis is the most prolific in neuroscience, encompassing more than 3000 papers. This research indicates that phenomena we perceive as bad (deprivation in infancy, conflict, stress, poor diet, most drugs) depress neurogenesis, and phenomena we perceive as good (exercise, enriched environment, sufficient sleep, healthy diet) enhance neurogenesis. Finding the signaling pathways that enhance neurogenesis may reveal the relationships among altered cognition, memory, depression, and the effects of antidepressant drugs (Caron, 2018).

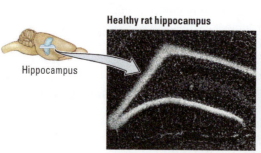

Hippocampus

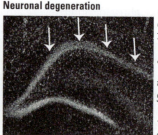

Healthy rat hippocampus   Neuronal degeneration

Courtesy of Dr. Simon Spanswick, Dept. of Psychology, University of Calgary

Anxiety reactions certainly are not pathological; they are likely an evolutionary adaptation for coping with adverse conditions. But anxiety can become pathological and make life miserable. Anxiety disorders are the most common psychiatric conditions. The DSM-5 lists 10 classes of anxiety disorders that together affect 15 percent to 35 percent of the population at some point in their lives (see Figure 16-2).

Imaging studies of people with anxiety disorders record increased baseline activity in a number of brain structures, including the amygdala and frontal cortex. Because drugs that enhance the inhibitory transmitter GABA are particularly effective in reducing anxiety, researchers hypothesize that excessive excitatory neurotransmission in these brain regions is the cause of anxiety.

Considerable interest has developed in investigating why some people show pathological anxiety to stimuli to which others have a milder response. One hypothesis, covered in the earlier section on depression, is that stressful experiences early in life increase susceptibility to a variety of behavioral disorders, especially anxiety disorders.

Although anxiety disorders used to be treated primarily with GABA-enhancing benzodiazepines, such as Valium, they can also be treated with SSRIs, such as Prozac, Paxil, Celexa, and Zoloft, that act on noradrenaline and serotonin. Antidepressant drugs do not act immediately, however, suggesting that the treatments must stimulate some gradual change in brain structure, much as these drugs act in treating depression.

Cognitive-behavioral therapy, which we described in the discussion of depression, is also effective in treating anxiety. The most effective behavioral therapies expose and re-expose patients to their fears. For example, treating a phobic fear of germs requires exposing the patient repeatedly to potentially germy environments, such as public washrooms, until the discomfort abates.

Clinical Focus 12-5 describes symptoms of anxiety disorders.

Figure 12-11 diagrams these limbic system structures and charts their major connections.

One more time: a pill is not a skill.

16-2 Review

Before you continue, check your understanding. Answers to Self-Test appear at the back of the book.

1. Schizophrenia is a complex disorder associated with neurochemical abnormalities in _____, _____, and _____ receptors.

2. Schizophrenia is associated with pronounced anatomical changes in the _____ and _____ cortices.

3. The monoamine-activating systems that have received the most investigation related to understanding depression are _____ and _____.

4. The most effective treatment for depression and anxiety disorders is _____.

5. Describe the main difficulty in linking genes to schizophrenia.

For additional study tools, visit **LaunchPad** at launchpadworks.com

---

16-3

Neurological Disorders

Neurological disorders are disorders in which the brain is damaged. They include traumatic brain injury, stroke, epilepsy, multiple sclerosis, and neurocognitive disorders.

Traumatic Brain Injury

Traumatic brain injury (TBI), a wound to the brain that usually results from a blow to the head, is the most common form of brain damage in people under age 40. TBI commonly results from the head making impact with other objects—as can occur in automobile and industrial accidents and in sports injuries. TBI can also follow blows to the chest that result in a rapid increase in blood pressure, which can damage the brain indirectly.

The two most important factors in the incidence of head trauma are age and sex. Children and elderly people are more likely to injure their head in a fall than are others,

TABLE 16-5 **Signs and Symptoms of Concussion**

Headache or a feeling of pressure in the head
Temporary loss of consciousness
Confusion or feeling as if in a fog
Amnesia surrounding the traumatic event
Dizziness or "seeing stars"
Ringing in the ears
Nausea
Vomiting
Slurred speech
Delayed response to questions
Appearing dazed
Fatigue

Section 14-5 details a dancer's recovery from TBI.

In longitudinal research, over time investigators repeatedly observe or examine subjects with respect to the study's variable(s).

FIGURE 16-8 **Mechanics of TBI** Pink and blue shading mark brain regions most frequently damaged in closed-head injury. A blow can produce a contusion both at the site of impact and on the opposite side of the brain, due to rebound compression.

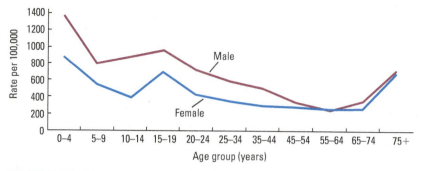

FIGURE 16-7 **Incidence Rates of Head Trauma** Based on combined reports of emergency room visits, hospitalizations, and deaths, this chart graphs the estimated frequency of TBI in males and females across the life span. Information from the Centers for Disease Control and Prevention, 2005.

and males between 15 and 30 incur brain injury especially in automobile and motorcycle accidents (**Figure 16-7**). A child's chance of having significant traumatic brain injury before he or she is old enough to drive is 1 in 30.

Concussion, the common term for mild traumatic brain injury (MTBI), is a critical concern for both professional and amateur athletes—especially those who play football, ice hockey, lacrosse, and soccer—and no less for those on active military duty. Sports incidents account for about 20 percent of TBIs, and the U.S. Army Institute of Surgical Research reports that traumatic brain injury affects more than 1 in 5 U.S. soldiers wounded in war. Concussion results from a blow to the head or body that may or may not result in loss of consciousness. It is possible to have a concussion and not know it. Some of the symptoms of concussion are listed in **Table 16-5**.

A large-scale longitudinal study is under way, involving football and ice hockey players who have a history of concussion and who have agreed to donate their brains for postmortem analysis (Broglio et al., 2018). Preliminary examination of the brains of deceased professional football players who had a history of concussion and severe postconcussion symptoms (described in Clinical Focus 16-3, Concussion) reveals extensive, diffuse loss of cerebral tissue. It is important to recognize that the study of the relationship between concussion and brain changes is in its infancy, and there is debate about the interpretation of emerging findings for sports and for the brain (Schwab & Hazrati, 2018).

Symptoms and Outcomes of Brain Trauma

TBI can cause direct damage to the brain. Trauma can disrupt the brain's blood supply, induce bleeding and cause swelling (leading to increased intracranial pressure), expose the brain to infection, and scar brain tissue (the scar being a focus for later epileptic seizures). The disruption in blood supply tends to be brief, but a parallel disruption of energy production by neuronal mitochondria, which can persist for weeks, is related to many postconcussion behavioral symptoms.

Traumatic brain injury is commonly accompanied by a loss of consciousness that may be brief (minutes) or prolonged (coma). Duration of unconsciousness can serve as a measure of the severity of damage because it correlates directly with mortality, intellectual impairment, and deficits in social skills. The longer a coma lasts, the greater the possibility of serious impairment or death.

Two kinds of behavioral effects result from TBI: (1) impairment of specific functions mediated by the cortex at the coup (the site of impact) or contrecoup (opposite side) lesion, as illustrated in **Figure 16-8**, and (2) more generalized impairments from widespread trauma throughout the brain. Discrete

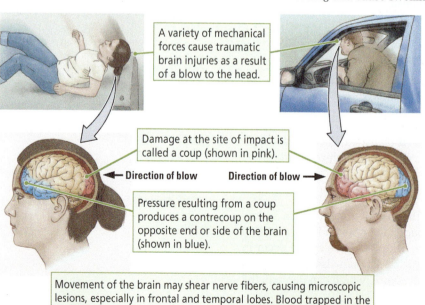

A variety of mechanical forces cause traumatic brain injuries as a result of a blow to the head.

Damage at the site of impact is called a coup (shown in pink).

← **Direction of blow**   **Direction of blow** →

Pressure resulting from a coup produces a contrecoup on the opposite end or side of the brain (shown in blue).

Movement of the brain may shear nerve fibers, causing microscopic lesions, especially in frontal and temporal lobes. Blood trapped in the skull (hematoma) and swelling (edema) cause pressure on the brain.

⊙ CLINICAL FOCUS 16-3

Concussion

Early in 2011, 50-year-old former Chicago Bears defensive back Dave Duerson shot himself in the chest and died. He left a note asking that his brain be studied. Duerson had played 11 years in the National Football League, won two Super Bowls, and received numerous awards.

As a pro player, he endured at least 10 concussions, but each did not seem serious enough to cause him to leave a game. After retiring from football, he went to Harvard and obtained a business degree. He pursued a successful business career until he began to have trouble making decisions and controlling his temper.

Eventually, Duerson's business and marriage failed. After his suicide, the Center for the Study of Traumatic Encephalopathy in Boston did study his brain. The center is conducting postmortem anatomical analyses of the brains of other former athletes as part of a long-term longitudinal study.

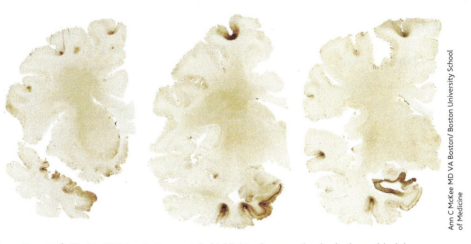

Ann C McKee MD VA Boston/ Boston University School of Medicine

Dave Duerson's Brain Staining for tau protein highlights degenerating brain tissue (dark brown areas) in the frontal cortex and medial temporal lobe of these coronal sections through Duerson's anterior right hemisphere. Damage to the subcortical basal ganglia in the sections' central portions (yellowish areas) is sparse by comparison.

Duerson's diagnosis, **chronic traumatic encephalopathy (CTE)**, is a progressive degenerative disease found in individuals with a history of multiple concussions and other closed-head injuries. (A variant long associated with boxing is *dementia pugilistica*, or *DP*.)

Concussion (mild traumatic brain injury) is common in sports, especially contact sports, including American and European football, ice hockey, and rugby (Solomon, 2018). Concussion also results from falls in many other sports and from vehicular accidents. It is likely that the incidence of concussion is higher than 6 per 1000 individuals.

Concussion often goes unrecognized. For those that are diagnosed, little apparent pathology appears after relatively short periods of rest, the usual treatment. Nevertheless, the relationship is well established between concussion and a range of degenerative diseases that occur later in life—neurocognitive disorders, including Alzheimer disease, as well as Parkinson disease, motor neuron disease, and CTE.

The relationship between concussion in early life and later degenerative brain disease suggests that concussion can initiate a cascade of pathological events that, over years, develop into CTE. CTE is characterized by neurofibrillary tangles, plaques, and neuronal death. Cerebral atrophy and expanded ventricles due to cell loss are typical in advanced cases. As shown in the illustration, researchers test for cell death by staining for accumulation of the tau protein, which is associated with neuronal death and so is a sensitive marker for brain trauma.

The unknowns about CTE are many. Can just one concussion initiate a cascade that results in CTE, or are many concussions required? Are individuals who get CTE especially susceptible? What constitutes a concussion? Should blows to the head that result in no pronounced symptoms be distinguished from blows that result in loss of consciousness?

What we do know is that many well-known athletes, especially football and ice hockey players, have developed CTE. This fact has generated public awareness of the consequences of concussion that is causing people to reconsider their participation in these sports and is leading to changes in sports to make them safe for the brain (Broglio et al., 2018).

impairment is most commonly associated with damage to the frontal and temporal lobes, the brain areas most susceptible to TBI. (See the tissue samples in Clinical Focus 16-3.)

More generalized impairment results from minute lesions and lacerations scattered throughout the brain. Movement of the hemispheres in relationship to one another causes connecting fibers to tear, especially those of the corpus callosum. This results in a decrease in complex cognitive function, including mental speed, concentration, and overall cognitive efficiency.

TBI patients generally complain of poor concentration or lack of ability. They fail to do things as well as they could before the injury. People with highly developed skills may be the most affected by TBI, in large part because they are acutely aware of the loss of a skill that prevents them from returning to their former competence level.

Traumatic brain injury that damages the frontal and temporal lobes also affects personality and social behavior. Few victims of TBI who have sustained severe head

chronic traumatic encephalopathy (CTE) Progressive degenerative disease caused by multiple concussions and other closed-head injuries, characterized by neurofibrillary tangles, plaques, cerebral atrophy, and expanded ventricles due to cell loss.

Section 1-1 presents a case study on recovering consciousness following TBI.

magnetic resonance spectroscopy (MRS) Modification of MRI used to identify changes in specific markers of neuronal function; promising for accurate diagnosis of traumatic brain injuries.

ischemic stroke A stroke resulting from a blocked blood vessel.

hemorrhagic stroke A stroke resulting from bleeding from a blood vessel.

Section 7-3 introduces the MRS technique.

injuries ever resume their studies or return to gainful employment. If they do re-enter the workforce, they do so at a lower level than before their accident.

One frustrating problem with traumatic brain injury is misdiagnosis: chronic effects of injuries are often unaccompanied by any obvious neurological signs or abnormalities in CT or MRI scans. Patients may therefore be referred for psychiatric or neuropsychological evaluation. Nevertheless, there are a number of ways to assess TBI.

Magnetic resonance spectroscopy (MRS), a modification of MRI, can identify changes in specific markers of neuronal function. One such marker is *N*-acetylaspartate (NAA), the second-most-abundant amino acid in the human brain. Assessing the level of NAA expression provides a measure of neuronal integrity, and deviations from normal levels (up or down) can be taken as markers of abnormal brain function. People with traumatic brain injury show a chronic decrease in NAA that correlates with the severity of the injury. Although not yet in wide clinical use, MRS is a promising tool, not only for identifying brain abnormalities but also for monitoring cellular response to therapeutic interventions, as is PET (Omalu et al., 2018). Other research suggests that resting patterns of EEG activity may provide a sensitive measure of traumatic brain injury (Dunkley et al., 2018).

Recovery from Traumatic Brain Injury

Recovery from head trauma may continue for 2 to 3 years following the initial event, but most cognitive recovery occurs in the first 6 to 9 months. Recovery of memory functions appears to be slower than recovery of general intelligence, and recovery of memory is poorer than for other cognitive functions. People with brainstem damage, as inferred from oculomotor disturbance, have a poorer cognitive outcome, and a poorer outcome is probably true of people with initial speech difficulties or motor impairments.

Although the prognosis for significant recovery of cognitive functions is good, optimism about the recovery of social skills or personality traits, areas that often show significant change, is less rosy. Numerous studies support the conclusions that quality of life—in social interactions, perceived stress levels, and enjoyment of leisure—is reduced after TBI and that this reduction is chronic.

Stroke

Stroke is an interruption of blood flow due to either blockage or bleeding of a vessel. **Ischemic stroke** is a result of blockage to a vessel; **hemorrhagic stroke** is a result of bleeding from a vessel. Bleeding could result from a cerebral aneurysm, a bulge with resulting weakening of a blood vessel (see Clinical Focus 16-4, Cerebral Aneurysms).

A stroke sets off a sequence of damage that progresses, even if the blood flow is restored, as might occur after ischemic stroke. Changes at the cellular level can seriously compromise not only the injured part of the brain but other brain regions as well.

Effects of Stroke

Consider what happens after a stroke interrupts the blood supply to the affected portion of the brain. In the first seconds to minutes, as illustrated in **Figure 16-9**, changes begin in the affected regions' ionic balance, including changes in pH and in the properties of the cell membrane. These ionic changes result in several pathological events:

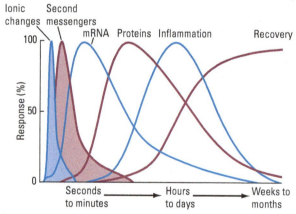

FIGURE 16-9 Results of Ischemic Stroke A cascade of events takes place after blood flow is blocked as a result of stroke. Within seconds, ionic changes at the cellular level spur changes in second-messenger molecules and RNA production. Changes in protein production and inflammation follow and resolve slowly, in hours to days. Recovery begins within hours to days and continues for weeks to months or years.

1. Release of massive amounts of glutamate results in prolonged opening of calcium channels in cell membranes.

2. Open calcium channels in turn allow toxic levels of calcium to enter the cell, not only producing direct toxic effects but also instigating various second-messenger pathways that can harm neurons. In the ensuing minutes to hours, mRNA is stimulated, altering protein production in the neurons and possibly proving toxic to the cells.

3. Brain tissues become inflamed and swollen, threatening the integrity of cells that may be far removed from the stroke site. As in TBI, an energy crisis ensues as mitochondria reduce their production of ATP, resulting in less cerebral energy.

Cerebral Aneurysms

C. N. was a 35-year-old nurse described by Isabelle Peretz and her colleagues (1994). In December 1986, C. N. suddenly developed severe neck pain and a headache. A neurological examination revealed an aneurysm in the middle cerebral artery on the right side of her brain.

An *aneurysm* is a bulge in a blood vessel wall caused by weakening of the tissue, much like the bulge that appears in a bicycle tire at a weakened spot. Aneurysms in a cerebral artery are dangerous: if they burst, severe bleeding and consequent brain damage result.

In February 1987, C. N.'s aneurysm was surgically repaired, and she appeared to have few adverse effects. Postoperative brain imaging revealed, however, that a new aneurysm had formed in the same location but in the middle cerebral artery on the opposite side of the brain. This second aneurysm was repaired 2 weeks later.

After her surgery, C. N. had temporary difficulty finding the right words when she spoke, but more importantly, her perception of music was deranged. She could no longer sing, nor could she recognize familiar tunes. In fact, singers sounded to her as if they were talking instead of singing. But C. N. could still dance to music.

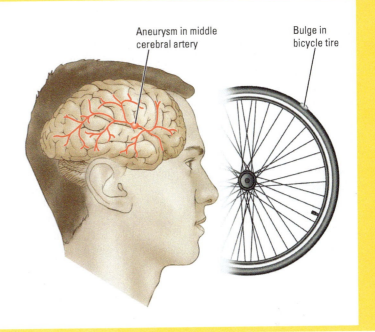

Aneurysm in middle cerebral artery

Bulge in bicycle tire

4. A form of neural shock occurs. During this **diaschisis**, areas distant from the damage are functionally depressed. Thus, not only are local neural tissue and its function lost, but areas related to the damaged region also undergo sudden withdrawal of excitation or inhibition.

5. Stroke may also be followed by changes in the injured hemisphere's metabolism, its glucose utilization, or both. These changes may persist for days. As with diaschisis, the metabolic changes can severely affect the functioning of otherwise healthy tissue. For example, after a cortical stroke, metabolic rate has been shown to decrease about 25 percent throughout the hemisphere.

Figure 5-4 shows how calcium affects neurotransmitter release; Figure 5-15, how metabotropic receptors can activate second messengers.

Clinical Focus 2-3 describes the symptoms and aftereffects of stroke.

Treatments for Stroke

The ideal treatment for stroke is to restore blood flow before the cascade of pathological events begins, which is really only effective for ischemic stroke. One clot-busting drug is tissue plasminogen activator (t-PA), but t-PA must be administered within 3 to 5 hours to be effective. Currently, only a small percentage of stroke patients arrive at the hospital soon enough—in large part because stroke is not quickly identified, transportation is slow, or the stroke is not considered an emergency. (The table to the right offers some suggestions for identifying a potential stroke event.)

Other drugs, called **neuroprotectants**, can be used to try to block the cascade of postinjury events, but to date there are no truly effective drugs. Clinical trials based on animal studies are targeted to a search for effective neuroprotectant drugs.

When the course of a stroke leads to dead brain tissue, the only treatments that can be beneficial are those that facilitate plastic changes in the remaining living brain tissue. Examples include speech therapy and physical therapy, virtual reality, computer games, and robotic machines (Laver et al., 2015).

Still, some simple treatments are surprisingly effective. One is *constraint-induced therapy*, pioneered by Edward Taub in the 1990s (Uswatte et al., 2018). Its logic confronts a problem in poststroke recovery related to *learned nonuse*. Stroke patients with motor deficits in a limb often compensate by overusing the intact limb, with an accompanying decrease in the use of the impaired limb such that the function of that impaired limb actually regresses.

Use the F.A.S.T. Test to Spot Stroke
Face Ask for a smile to check both understanding and muscle control.
Arms Check if one arm is weak by asking the person to raise both arms.
Speech Listen for slurred speech.
Time If you see any symptom, call 911 or the local emergency services number right away.

diaschisis Neural shock that follows brain damage in which areas connected to the site of damage show a temporary arrest of function.

neuroprotectant Drug used to try to block the cascade of poststroke neural events.

Experiment 11-3 describes research with monkeys that contributed to developing constraint-induced therapy for people.

focal seizure Seizure that arises at a synchronous, hyperactive, localized brain region (at a focus).

generalized seizure Seizure that starts at a focal location then spreads rapidly and bilaterally to distributed networks in both hemispheres.

TABLE 16-6 **Factors That May Precipitate Seizures in Susceptible Persons**

Emotional stress
Sleep deprivation
Tiredness
Alcohol
Fever
Flickering lights
Noncompliance
Menstruation
Physical exercise
Health

Source: Information from Ferlisi & Shorvon (2014).

In constraint-induced therapy, the intact limb is held in a sling for several hours per day, forcing the patient to use the impaired limb. Nothing about the procedure is magical: virtually any treatment that forces patients to practice behaviors extensively is successful. An important component of these treatments, however, is a posttreatment contract in which the patients continue to practice after the formal therapy is over. If they fail to do so, the chances for learned nonuse and a return of symptoms are high.

Another common effect of stroke is loss of speech. Specific speech therapy programs can aid in the recovery of speech. Music and singing, mediated in part by the right hemisphere, can augment speech therapy after left hemisphere stroke.

Therapies using pharmacological interventions (such as noradrenergic, dopaminergic, and cholinergic agonists) combined with behavioral therapies provide equivocal gains in stroke patients. The bulk of evidence suggests that patients with small gray-matter strokes are most likely to show benefits from these treatments, whereas those with large strokes that include white matter show little benefit.

Finally, there have been many attempts to use either direct cortical stimulation or transcranial magnetic stimulation (TMS) in combination with behavioral therapy as a stroke treatment. The idea is to induce plasticity in regions adjacent to the dead tissue, with the goal of enhancing the efficiency of the residual parts of the neuronal networks. These treatments have proved beneficial in patients with good residual motor control, but again, those with larger injuries show much less benefit, presumably because the residual neuronal network is insufficient.

Epilepsy

Epilepsy is characterized by recurrent seizures, which register on an electroencephalogram (EEG) as highly synchronized neuronal firing indicated by a variety of abnormal waves. About 1 person in 20 has at least one seizure in his or her lifetime, usually associated with an infection, fever, and hyperventilation during childhood (6 months to 5 years of age). Most children who experience a seizure do not develop epilepsy, which affects between 0.2 percent and 4.1 percent of the population. Developed nations record a lower prevalence and incidence of epilepsy compared with developing nations.

Classifying Seizures

Causes of epileptic seizures are categorized as genetic, structural/metabolic, or unknown. *Genetic epilepsy* results directly from a known genetic defect. Causes of *structural/metabolic epilepsy* include brain malformations and tumors (see **Figure 16-10** for one example), acquired disorders such as stroke and trauma, and infections. The *unknown* category encompasses causes yet to be identified.

Table 16-6 summarizes the great variety of circumstances that appear to precipitate seizures. The range of circumstances is striking, but seizures do have a consistent feature: they are most likely to occur when a person is sleeping.

Seizures are classified with respect to the amount of the brain engaged in the abnormal activity. **Focal seizures** arise from a synchronous, hyperactive local brain region. Thus, focal seizures may have motor, sensory, autonomic, and/or psychogenic features, depending on where they are located. If focal seizures involve memory regions of the brain, memory and awareness can be altered (impaired awareness seizure). **Generalized seizures** start at a focal location and then spread rapidly and bilaterally to distributed networks in both hemispheres. In *primary generalized epilepsy*, seizures begin in more widespread

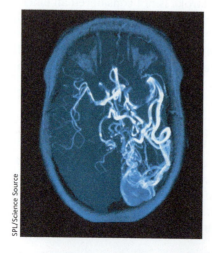

FIGURE 16-10 **MRI Showing Angioma** Structural or metabolic epilepsy may result from brain malformations such as angioma, or AV malformation, shown on this dorsal view MRI. Abnormal cerebral blood vessels (in white) form a convoluted pattern, including a balloon-like structure (blue area at lower right) that caused the death of brain tissue around it in the right occipital cortex.

SPL/Science Source

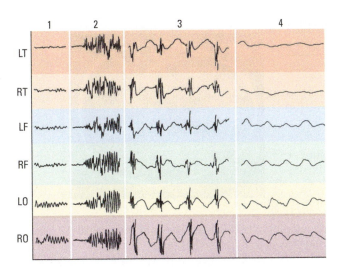

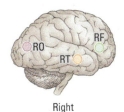
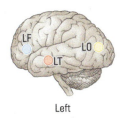

FIGURE 16-11 **Generalized Seizure Patterns** Examples of EEG patterns recorded during a generalized seizure. Dots on the hemispheres below indicate the approximate recording sites. Column numbers mark the seizure's stages: (1) normal record before the attack; (2) onset of seizure and tonic phase; (3) clonic phase; and (4) a period of depressed EEG activity after the seizure ends. *Abbreviations:* LT and RT, left temporal and right temporal; LF and RF, left frontal and right frontal; LO and RO, left occipital and right occipital.

Left   Right

neural networks. Seizure diagnosis is improved by the use of a wearable EEG recording device that records their time, duration, and location (Gubbi et al., 2015).

People having a generalized seizure may cycle through the four stages charted in **Figure 16-11**: (1) normal EEG record before onset; (2) onset and tonic phase, in which the body stiffens; (3) clonic phase, in which the person makes rhythmic movements in time with the large, highly synchronized discharges; and (4) a period of depressed EEG activity after the seizure ends.

For the most part, seizures self-terminate. In some cases, termed *status epilepticus*, the seizure's driving force does not abate, often due to a brain insult or to drug withdrawal. This can be a life-threatening condition, and drug intervention with a fast-acting GABA agonist or glutamate antagonist is required to end the seizure. Death due to status epilepticus is much more common in adults than in children (26 percent versus 3 percent, respectively), and survivors often live with significant brain damage. The recommended time limit before intervention is 5 minutes. Longer-lasting seizures are unlikely to self-terminate.

People with epilepsy die unexpectedly at a rate 24 times that of the general population (Shankar et al., 2018). *Sudden unexpected death in epilepsy* (*SUDEP*) has no identifiable cause (such as status epilepticus, or drowning or falling as a result of the loss of motor control). Most evidence suggests that SUDEP occurs during or more often after a seizure. Respiratory and cardiac failure may be common causes, but events leading up to SUDEP have yet to be characterized.

Clinical Focus 4-1 describes a diagnosis of epilepsy and shows an EEG being recorded.

Treating Epilepsy

The first-line treatment for epilepsy is drugs to inhibit seizure development and propagation. Among the diverse range of mechanisms that drugs employ to raise seizure thresholds are enhancing the action of the inhibitory neurotransmitter GABA and stabilizing the inactive state of sodium channels. Most people with epilepsy work with their physician to find a drug and dosage that cause few side effects. In 30 percent to 40 percent of people with epilepsy, however, antiseizure drugs fail to completely control the condition; this is known as *intractable epilepsy*. The most common treatment for intractable epilepsy in adults is surgical resection of epileptogenic tissue, which has a success rate of about 70 percent. Deep brain stimulation (DBS) may prove useful for intractable epilepsy: bilateral stimulation of the anterior thalamus has been successful in reducing seizure frequency. While DBS shows promise, however, more research is needed (Kwon et al., 2018).

Multiple Sclerosis

In multiple sclerosis (MS), the myelin that encases axons is damaged, and neuronal functions are disrupted. MS is characterized by myelin loss in both motor and sensory tracts and nerves. The oligodendroglia that form the myelin sheath, and in some cases

FIGURE 16-12 **Diagnosing MS** Imaged by MRI, discrete multiple sclerosis lesions appear as dark patches all around the lateral ventricles and in the brain's white matter.

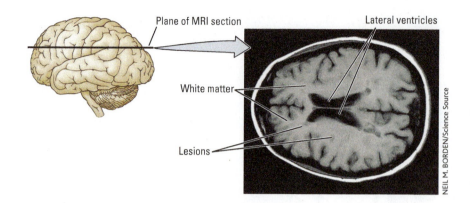

Plane of MRI section

Lateral ventricles

White matter

Lesions

NEIL M. BORDEN/Science Source

autoimmune disease Illness resulting from the loss of the immune system's ability to discriminate between foreign pathogens in the body and the body itself.

Section 4-2 discusses the function of the myelin sheath, and Clinical Focus 4-2 elaborates on multiple sclerosis as an autoimmune disease.

the axons, are destroyed. Brain imaging with MRI, as shown in **Figure 16-12**, identifies areas of sclerosis in the brain as well as in the spinal cord.

Remission followed by relapse is a striking feature of MS: in many cases, early symptoms initially are followed by improvement. The course varies, running from a few years to as long as 50 years. A person with MS may eventually be affected by paraplegia and confined to a wheelchair or to bed.

Worldwide, about 2 million people have MS; women outnumber men about 2 to 1. Multiple sclerosis is most prevalent in Northern Europe and northern North America, and it is rare in Japan and in more equatorial countries. Depending on region, incidence of MS ranges from 2 to 150 per 100,000 people, making it one of the most common structural nervous system diseases.

Proposed causes of MS include bacterial infection, virus, environmental factors including pesticides, an immune response of the central nervous system, misfolded proteins, and lack of vitamin D. Often, multiple cases occur in a single family. Many genes have been associated with MS, but no clear evidence indicates as yet that MS is inherited or transmitted from one person to another.

Research has focused on the relationship between MS and the immune system and has determined that MS is an **autoimmune disease.** The ability to discriminate between a foreign pathogen in the body and the body itself is central to immune system functioning. If this discrimination fails, the immune system makes antibodies to the person's own body; in the case of MS, the immune system makes antibodies to myelin.

As various organisms' genomes have been sequenced, it has become apparent that all have many genes in common. Thus, the proteins found in different organisms are surprisingly similar. And here is the problem for the human immune system: a foreign microbe may contain a protein that is nearly identical to the body's own protein. If microbe and human have a common gene sequence, the immune system, in attacking that microbe, can end up attacking itself. This process is known as *horror autotoxicus* (Latin for "horrible self-toxicity"). The idea is that some microbial protein sequences are homologous with structures found in myelin, which leads to an attack against the microbe and a person's own myelin, as illustrated in **Figure 16-13**. Research showing the important role of the immune system in MS has intensified work on developing treatments that selectively target immune pathways that attack myelin (Pegoretti et al., 2018).

The fact that MS is more common in extreme northern and southern latitudes has raised the possibility that inadequate direct sunlight, which is necessary for the body to synthesize vitamin D, factors into precipitating the condition (Evans et al., 2018). The question remains whether an acute or a longstanding vitamin D deficiency is relevant to this relationship. Perhaps a vitamin D deficiency interacts with other factors to increase susceptibility to MS. For example, a number of genes are involved in the transport and absorption of vitamin D, and variants of these genes are related to low levels of vitamin D, even in individuals who consume diets containing adequate amounts of vitamin D and/or are exposed to adequate amounts of sunlight.

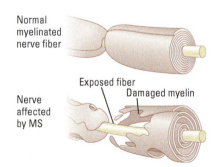

Normal myelinated nerve fiber

Exposed fiber

Damaged myelin

Nerve affected by MS

FIGURE 16-13 **Damage to the Myelin Sheath Caused by MS** *Sclerosis* comes from the Greek word for "hardness."

Neurocognitive Disorders

Neurocognitive disorders are those in which there is progressive loss of function in neurons and/or loss of neurons themselves. They are classified as either Major or Mild, depending on the extent to which they allow a person to live independently. Human societies have never before undergone the age-related demographic shifts now developing. Since 1900, the percentage of older people in the general population has increased steadily. In 1900, about 4 percent of the population had attained 65 years of age. By 2030, approximately 20 percent will be older than 65—about 50 million people in the United States alone. The increase in the percentage of older people has significant implications related to age-related neurocognitive disorders. Neurocogntive disorders affect 1 percent to 6 percent of the population older than age 65 and 10 percent to 20 percent of those older than age 80.

For every person diagnosed with a major neurocognitive disorder, it is estimated that several others have mild neurocognitive disorder that affects their quality of life. Currently, more than 6 million people in the United States have a major diagnosis—a number projected to rise to about 15 million by 2050. By then, 1 million new U.S. cases per year will be emerging. Extending these projections across the rest of the developed world portends staggering social and economic costs (Khachaturian & Khachaturian, 2015). The World Health Organization estimates that by 2050, the incidence of neurocognitive disorder will balloon to 135.5 million people worldwide.

Neurocognitive disorders are a relatively new classification of disorders previously known as *dementias*. Because many professional classifications continue to use this older subcategory designation, we will discuss this classification briefly before discussing two major neurocognitive diseases characterized by symptoms associated with dementia: Alzheimer and Parkinson.

Dementia

Dementia is an acquired and persistent syndrome of intellectual impairment. Its two essential features are (1) loss of memory and other cognitive deficits and (2) impairment in social and occupational functioning. Dementia is featured in a number of neurocognitive disorders. Causes of dementia can be divided into two broad categories: degenerative and nondegenerative (**Table 16-7**).

Nondegenerative dementias, a heterogeneous group of disorders with diverse causes—including diseases of the vascular and endocrine systems, inflammation, nutritional deficiency, and toxins—are summarized in the right column of Table 16-7. The most prevalent cause is vascular. The most significant risk factors for nondegenerative dementias—and for cardiovascular disease as well—are chronic hypertension, obesity, sedentary lifestyle, smoking, and diabetes. *Degenerative dementias*, listed in the left column of the table, also have various causes, including genetic and toxic causes, as well trauma to the nervous system.

dementia Acquired and persistent syndrome of intellectual impairment characterized by memory and other cognitive deficits and impairment in social and occupational functioning.

Alzheimer Disease

Alzheimer disease is a major neurocognitive disorder and one of the most common causes of degenerative dementia. Given the increasing population of elderly people and thus of Alzheimer disease, which accounts for about 65 percent of all neurocognitive disorders, research is directed toward potential causes (Kumar & Tsao, 2018). Personal lifestyle, environmental toxins, high levels of trace elements such as aluminum in the blood, an autoimmune response, a slow-acting virus, reduced blood flow to the cerebral hemispheres, and genetic predisposition are targets of ongoing research. Incidence of Alzheimer disease is high in some families, suggesting that genetic causes may be a factor in 40 percent to 70 percent of cases.

Until recently, the only way to identify and study Alzheimer disease was via postmortem pathology examination, and this method is still the only way to provide a definitive diagnosis. Early diagnosis in the course of the disease, or even before disease onset, is an obvious goal that aids in treatment and prevention. As the disease progresses, widespread changes occur

TABLE 16-7 Degenerative and Nondegenerative Dementias

Degenerative	Nondegenerative
Alzheimer disease	Vascular dementias (e.g., multi-infarct dementia)
Extrapyramidal syndromes (e.g., progressive supernuclear palsy)	Infectious dementia (e.g., AIDS dementia)
Wilson disease	Neurosyphilis
Huntington disease	Posttraumatic dementia
Parkinson disease	Demyelinating dementia (e.g., multiple sclerosis)
Frontal temporal dementia	Toxic or metabolic disorders (e.g., vitamin B_{12} and niacin deficiencies)
Corticobasal degeneration	
Leukodystrophies (e.g., adrenoleukodystrophy)	Chronic alcohol or drug abuse (e.g., Korsakoff syndrome)
Prion-related dementias (e.g., Creutzfeldt-Jakob disease)	
Chronic traumatic encephalopathy (CTE)	

Information from Charney et al., 2017.

FIGURE 16-14 **Cortical Degeneration in Alzheimer Disease** Brain of **(A)** a healthy elderly adult contrasted with **(B)** an elderly adult's brain that shows shriveling due to cell shrinkage characteristic of Alzheimer disease.

(A) Healthy brain

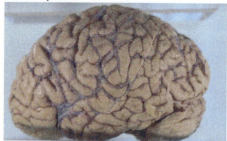

(B) Brain characteristic of Alzheimer disease

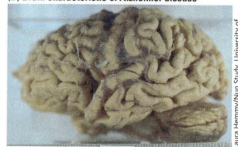

Laura Hemmy/Nun Study, University of Minnesota

Clinical Focus 14-3, on Alzheimer etiology, includes a micrograph of an amyloid plaque.

Neurofilaments are a type of *tubule* that reinforces cell structure, aids its movement, and transports proteins.

in cortical structures and in many neurotransmitter systems. Neuropsychological testing and brain imaging are thus helpful in diagnosis, as are blood tests (Nakamura et al., 2018).

The principal neuroanatomical change in Alzheimer disease is the emergence of amyloid plaques (clumps of protein from dead neurons and astrocytes), chiefly in cortical areas. Increased plaque concentration in the cortex has been correlated with the magnitude of cognitive deterioration. Plaques are generally considered nonspecific phenomena because they can be found in non-Alzheimer patients and in neurocognitive disorders caused by other known events.

Another anatomical correlate of Alzheimer disease is neurofibrillary tangles (accumulations of microtubules from dead cells) found in both neocortex and allocortex, where the posterior half of the hippocampus is affected more severely than the anterior half. Neurofibrillary tangles have been described mainly in human tissue and have also been observed in patients with Down syndrome and Parkinson disease.

Finally, neocortical changes that correlate with Alzheimer disease are not uniform. As **Figure 16-14** shows plainly, the cortex atrophies and can lose as much as one-third of its volume as the disease progresses. But cellular analyses at the microscopic level reveal that some areas, including the primary sensory and motor cortices (especially the visual and sensorimotor cortices), are relatively spared. The frontal lobes are less affected than is the posterior cortex.

Cortical areas show the most extensive change. The entorhinal cortex is affected earliest and most severely. The entorhinal cortex is the major information relay between the hippocampus and related structures and the neocortex. Entorhinal damage is associated with memory loss, an early and enduring symptom of Alzheimer disease.

Many studies describe cell loss in the cortices of Alzheimer patients, yet this finding is disputed. There seems to be a substantial reduction in large neurons, but these

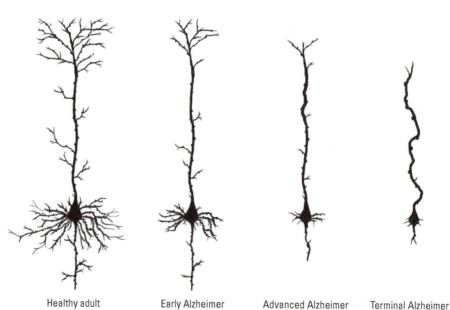

FIGURE 16-15 **Stripped Branches** Alzheimer patients' dendritic trees degenerate and their neurons atrophy, worsening their symptoms, including memory loss and personality changes.

Healthy adult pattern

Early Alzheimer disease

Advanced Alzheimer disease

Terminal Alzheimer disease

cells may shrink rather than disappear. The more widespread cause of cortical atrophy appears to be a loss of dendritic arborization (**Figure 16-15**).

In addition to cell loss and shrinkage, changes take place in the remaining cells' neurotransmitters. In the 1970s, researchers believed that a treatment paralleling L-dopa treatment of Parkinson disease could be found for Alzheimer disease. The prime candidate neurotransmitter was, and still is, acetylcholine, and one treatment developed for Alzheimer disease is medication that increases acetylcholine levels in the forebrain. Cholinergic agonists given orally or as a skin patch can be helpful early in the disease. Unfortunately, Alzheimer has proved far more complex because transmitters other than ACh clearly are changed as well. Noradrenaline, dopamine, and serotonin are reduced, as are the NMDA and AMPA receptors for glutamate. Clinical trials of treatments for Alzheimer disease number in the hundreds but show limited success in producing a cure or treatment (Knight et al., 2018).

Figure 14-18 shows how glutamate can affect NMDA and AMPA receptors to promote learning by association.

Parkinson Disease

Parkinson disease, another major neurocognitive disorder, is a condition in which movement is slowed, but this condition is also associated with many other alterations in movement, emotion, and cognition. Parkinson disease is estimated to afflict up to 1 percent of the population. Because the incidence rises sharply in old age, rates are certain to grow in coming decades as populations age. The disease is related to degeneration of the substantia nigra and attendant loss of the neurotransmitter dopamine produced there and released in the striatum. The disease therefore offers insight into the roles played by the substantia nigra and dopamine in movement control.

That Parkinson symptoms vary enormously illustrates the complexity inherent in understanding a neurological disorder. The degeneration of a well-defined set of cells is central to the disease, but many other brain areas are also affected, so the symptoms are not the same in every patient. Many symptoms strikingly resemble changes in motor activity that occur as a consequence of aging. Thus, Parkinson disease offers indirect insight into more general problems of age-related neural changes.

Symptoms begin insidiously, often with a tremor in one hand and slight stiffness in distal parts of the limbs. Movements may become slower, the face becoming masklike, eventually with loss of eye blinking and facial emotional expression. Thereafter, the body may stoop and the gait may become a shuffle, with arms hanging motionless at the sides. Speech may slow and become monotonous, and difficulty swallowing may cause drooling. At the onset of symptoms, a person may display symptoms neglect— they may not be aware of the changes.

Although the disease is progressive, the rate at which symptoms worsen varies; only rarely is progression so rapid that a person becomes disabled within 5 years. Usually 10 to 20 years elapse before symptoms cause incapacity. A distinctive aspect of Parkinson disease is its on-again–off-again quality: symptoms may appear suddenly and then just as suddenly disappear.

Momentary partial remission may also occur in response to interesting or stimulating situations. Neurologist Oliver Sacks (1998) recounted an incident in which a stationary Parkinson patient leaped from his wheelchair at the seaside and rushed into the breakers to save a drowning man, only to fall back into his chair immediately afterward and become inactive again. Remission of some symptoms in activating situations is common but usually not as dramatic as this case. Simply listening to familiar music can help an otherwise inactive patient get up and dance, for example. Or a patient who has difficulty walking may ride a bicycle or skate, seemingly effortlessly. A person who seems immobilized can quickly catch a ball that is thrown. The ability of a patient to respond to these activating stimuli is useful in physical therapy, and physical therapy is important because it may slow disease progression.

Figure 7-5 diagrams degeneration in the substantia nigra associated with Parkinson symptoms. Section 5-2 discusses neurotransmitters associated with dopamine, and Clinical Focus 5-2 discusses the discoveries that led researchers to understand the connection between Parkinson and dopamine.

Clinical Focus 5-3 describes Sacks's case history administering L-dopa to Parkinson patients. Sacks, whose writings enriched the neurological literature, died in 2015.

The four major symptoms of Parkinson disease are tremor, rigidity, loss of spontaneous movement (*hypokinesia*), and postural disturbances. Each symptom may manifest in different body parts in different combinations. Because some symptoms entail the appearance of abnormal behaviors (positive symptoms) and others the loss of normal behaviors (negative symptoms), we consider both major categories.

Positive symptoms are behaviors not typically seen in people. *Negative symptoms* are the absence of typical behaviors or inability to engage in an activity.

Principle 10: The nervous system works by juxtaposing excitation and inhibition.

POSITIVE SYMPTOMS Because positive symptoms are common in Parkinson disease, they are thought to be inhibited, or held in check, in unaffected people but released from inhibition in the process of the disease. Following are the three most common:

1. *Tremor at rest.* Alternating movements of the limbs occur when they are at rest and stop during voluntary movements or sleep. Hand tremors often have a pill-rolling quality, as if a pill were being rolled between the thumb and forefinger.

2. *Muscular rigidity.* Increased muscle tone simultaneously in both extensor and flexor muscles is particularly evident when the limbs are moved passively at a joint. Movement is resisted, but with sufficient force the muscles yield for a short distance and then resist movement again. Thus, complete passive flexion or extension of a joint occurs in a series of steps, giving rise to the term *cogwheel rigidity*. Rigidity may be severe enough to make all movements difficult—like moving in slow motion and being unable to speed up the process.

3. *Involuntary movements.* Small movements or changes in posture, sometimes referred to as **akathesia**, or *cruel restlessness*, may accompany general inactivity to relieve tremor and sometimes to relieve stiffness—but these often occur for no apparent reason. Other involuntary movements are distortions of posture, such as occur during *oculogyric crisis* (involuntary turns of the head and eyes to one side), which last minutes to hours.

NEGATIVE SYMPTOMS After detailed analysis of negative symptoms, Jean Prudin Martin (1967) divided patients severely affected with Parkinson disease into five groups:

1. *Disorders of posture.* A subcategory is *disorder of fixation*, which presents as an inability or difficulty to maintain a part of the body in its normal position in relationship to other parts. A person's head may droop forward, or a standing person may gradually bend forward, ending up on his or her knees. Disorders in a second subcategory, *disorders of equilibrium*, cause difficulties in standing or even sitting unsupported. In less severe cases, people may have difficulty standing on one leg, or, if pushed lightly on the shoulders, they may fall passively without taking corrective steps or attempting to catch themselves.

2. *Disorders of righting.* A person in a supine position has difficulty standing. Many advanced patients have difficulty even rolling over.

3. *Disorders of locomotion.* Normal locomotion requires support of the body against gravity, stepping, balancing while the weight of the body is transferred from one leg to the other, and pushing forward. Parkinson patients have difficulty initiating stepping. When they do walk, they shuffle with short footsteps on a fairly wide base of support because they have trouble maintaining equilibrium when shifting weight from one leg to the other. On beginning to walk, Parkinson patients often demonstrate **festination**: they take faster and faster steps and end up running forward.

4. *Speech disturbances.* One symptom most noticeable to relatives is the almost complete absence of prosody (rhythm and pitch) in the speaker's voice.

5. *Hypokinesia.* A lack of or slow movement may also manifest in a blankness of facial expression, a lack of blinking or of swinging the arms when walking, a lack of spontaneous speech, or an absence of normal fidgeting. Akinesia also manifests in difficulty making repetitive movements, such as tapping, even in the absence of rigidity. People who sit motionless for hours show hypokinesia in its most striking manifestation.

COGNITIVE SYMPTOMS Although Parkinson disease is usually viewed as a motor disorder, changes in cognition occur as well. Psychological symptoms in Parkinson patients are as variable as the motor symptoms. Nonetheless, a significant percentage of patients show cognitive symptoms in emotion, memory, and thought processes. People may sit for hours, apparently lacking the will to begin or continue any activity. Thinking seems generally to

---

akathesia Small, involuntary movements or changes in posture; motor restlessness.

festination Tendency to engage in a behavior, such as walking, faster and faster.

be slowed and Parkinson disease is often thought to be a neurocognitive disorder because patients do not appear to be processing the content of conversations. In fact, they may simply be processing very slowly.

Cognitive slowing in Parkinson patients has some parallels to Alzheimer disease.

CAUSES OF PARKINSONISM The ultimate cause of Parkinson disease—loss of cells in the substantia nigra—may result from disease (such as encephalitis or syphilis), from drugs (such as MPTP), or from unknown causes. *Idiopathic* causes—those related to the individual—may include environmental pollutants, insecticides and herbicides, concussion, or genetic factors. Demographic studies of patients who contract the disease at a relatively young age have prompted the suggestion that water and air might contain environmental toxins that work in a fashion similar to MPTP (1-methyl-4-phenylpyridinium), a contaminant that has been found in synthetic heroin and causes Parkinson disease.

Actor Michael J. Fox, a native of Canada pictured in Clinical Focus 5-2, was diagnosed with young-onset Parkinson disease at age 30.

TREATING PARKINSON DISEASE The cure for Parkinson disease is either to stop degeneration of cells in the substantia nigra or to replace them. Neither goal is achievable at present. Thus, current treatment is pharmacological and directed toward support and comfort.

Psychological factors influence Parkinsonism's major symptoms, and outcome depends on how well a person copes. Patients should seek behaviorally oriented treatment early—counseling on the meaning of symptoms, the nature of the disease, and the potential for most patients to lead long, productive lives. Physical therapy consists of simple measures, such as heat and massage, to alleviate painful muscle cramps, as well as training and exercise to cope with debilitating movement changes. Used therapeutically, music and exercise can improve other aspects of behavior, including balance and walking, and may actually slow the course of the disease.

The prime objective of pharmacological treatment is increasing the activity in whatever dopamine synapses remain. L-Dopa, a precursor of dopamine, is converted into dopamine in the brain and enhances effective dopamine transmission, thereby lessening the patient's symptoms. Drugs such as amantadine, amphetamine, monoamine oxidase inhibitors, and tricyclic antidepressants can stimulate remaining dopamine neurons, and thus they may also lessen symptoms. Anticholinergic drugs, such as atropine, scopolamine, benztropine (Cogentin), and trihexyphenidyl (Artane), block the brain cholinergic systems that seem to show heightened activity in the absence of adequate dopamine activity.

Rhythmic movement helps Parkinson patients restore the balance between positive and negative symptoms. Patients who participate in specially designed Dance for Parkinson groups led by the Mark Morris Dance Center, like the one pictured here, report that moving to music helps them regain muscle control. Exercise, including tai chi and boxing, also reinforces treatments directed toward replacing depleted dopamine.

As the disease progresses, however, drug therapies become less effective because there are fewer dopamine neurons to stimulate. One effect of the decrease in available dopamine is that the number of dopamine receptors increases. Consequently, the action of remaining dopamine on the increased number of receptors begins to produce side effects that include abnormal movements. Once the side effects become severe, treatments that stimulate dopamine release are no longer useful. Some drug treatments that directly stimulate dopamine receptors have been reported to result in increased sexuality and an increased incidence of compulsive gambling, again because there are so many receptors.

Two surgical treatments described later in this section are based on the idea that increased activity of globus pallidus (GPi) neurons inhibits motor function. A lesion of the internal part of the GPi can reduce rigidity and tremor. Hyperactivity of GPi neurons can also be reduced neurosurgically by electrically stimulating the neurons via deep brain stimulation (see Figure 16-18 later in this section). A stimulating electrode is permanently implanted in the GPi or an adjacent area, the subthalamic nucleus. Patients carry a small electric stimulator that they can turn on to induce DBS and so reduce rigidity and tremor. These two treatments may be used sequentially: when DBS becomes less effective as the disease progresses, a GPi lesion may be induced.

Figure 11-13 charts how the globus pallidus internal, a structure in the basal ganglia, regulates movement force.

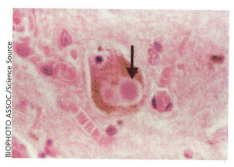

FIGURE 16-16 **Midbrain Lewy Body**   Lewy bodies (arrow) characteristic of Parkinson disease are found in the brains of patients with other disorders as well.

A promising prospective Parkinson treatment involves increasing the population of dopamine-producing cells. One way is to transplant embryonic dopamine cells into the basal ganglia. In the 1980s and 1990s, this treatment was reported to have varying degrees of success; the results were blurred, however, by many poorly conducted studies with inadequate preassessment and postassessment procedures. A newer treatment course proposes either transplanting stem cells that could then be induced to take a dopaminergic phenotype or stimulating endogenous stem cells to migrate to the basal ganglia. The advantage is that these stem cells need not be derived from embryonic tissue but can come from a variety of sources, including the person's own body.

All these treatments are experimental, and the fascinating story of this research is told by pioneers in this research, Björklund and Lindvall (2017). Before cell replacement can become a useful therapy, many questions must be resolved—including which cell source is best, where in the brain to put grafts, and how new cells can be integrated into existing brain circuits. Stem cells are not a quick fix for Parkinson disease, but the pioneering work on this disease will be instrumental in applying such technology to other diseases.

Are All Neurocognitive Disorders Aspects of a Single Disease?

Neither Parkinson disease nor Alzheimer disease is related to a single brain structure or region, although dopamine in the case of the former and acetylcholine in the case of the latter seem more affected. Other similarities in their pathology suggest some common neurodegenerative processes. Donald Calne (Calne & Mizuno, 2004) noted that when scientists traveled to Guam at the end of World War II to investigate a reportedly widespread dementia described as being similar to Alzheimer disease, they did indeed report a high incidence of Alzheimer. Many years later, Calne and his colleagues, also experts in Parkinson disease, examined the same general group of people and found that they had Parkinson disease. Calne noted that, if you look for Alzheimer symptoms in these people, you find them and miss the Parkinson symptoms—and vice versa.

The best-studied similarity between the two diseases is the **Lewy body** (**Figure 16-16**), a fibrous ring that forms within neuronal cytoplasm and is thought to correspond to abnormal neurofilament metabolism. Until recently, the Lewy body was most often found in the region of the midbrain substantia nigra and believed to be a hallmark of Parkinson disease, as amyloid plaques were viewed as a marker of Alzheimer disease. In fact, Lewy bodies appear in several neurocognitive disorders, including Alzheimer disease. There are even reports of people with Alzheimer-like neurocognitive disorders who have no plaques and tangles but who do have extensive Lewy bodies in the cortex.

The Prion Theory of Progressive Neurocognitive Disorder

Alzheimer and Parkinson symptoms may be similar because both diseases have similar origins. Indeed, the idea that several diseases marked by brain degeneration—including Huntington disease, MS, and ALS—may have a similar origin is central to *prion* theory (the term *prion* is short for "proteinaceous infectious particle"), advanced in 1982 by Stanley B. Prusiner, who received the 1997 Nobel Prize for his work. A **prion** is an abnormally folded protein that causes other similar proteins to adopt the abnormal fold (**Figure 16-17**). The abnormal fold renders the protein less functional.

Prions tend to clump together, forming protein aggregates that contribute to cell death. Prions can also infect neighboring brain and body cells, resulting in general brain degeneration and muscle wasting. As this gradual infection proceeds, it causes progressive neurodegeneration. A prion can have a genetic origin, have spontaneous origin, result from trauma and other causes, or be acquired by ingesting food that contains a prion.

Prions were identified during investigation of various degenerative brain diseases in humans and other animals. Creutzfeldt-Jakob disease, a rare human degenerative disease

Infection as referred to in the definition is not one caused by casual contact.

Lewy body   Circular fibrous structure found in several neurocognitive disorders; forms within the cytoplasm of neurons and is thought to result from abnormal neurofilament metabolism.

prion   From *proteinaceous* and *infectious*, an abnormally folded protein that causes progressive neurocognitive disorders.

that progresses rapidly, gained public prominence in the 1990s. People were contracting a similar condition after eating beef from cattle that had displayed symptoms of *bovine spongiform encephalopathy* (*BSE*), a degenerative brain condition accompanied by muscle wasting. BSE in turn is similar to a condition in sheep called *scrapies* (because the animals scrape or scratch themselves) that also features wasting of brain and body. *Chronic wasting disease* is a similar condition found in deer and elk.

The infectious nature of one such infection was observed in the Fore tribe of Papua New Guinea in the 1950s. A large number of Fore were dying of a muscle-wasting condition called *kuru* (meaning "to shake" in Fore). It turned out that the Fore were contracting kuru by practicing ritual cannibalism: they ate the brains of dead relatives (some of whom had died of kuru), which the Fore believed would preserve their spirits. In an experiment to investigate the condition, body parts from kuru victims were fed to a chimp that then contracted the disease. The infectious agent in the condition is a prion.

In Parkinson disease, the misfolded protein is proposed to be *alpha-synuclein*. It accumulates, largely in substantia nigra cells, to form a Lewy body. In Alzheimer disease, the accumulating protein forms amyloid plaques and mainly affects cortical cells. Misfolded proteins in oligodendroglia may be responsible for the cell demyelination characteristic of MS and ALS.

The prion theory opens new avenues for investigating degenerative disease treatments, including drugs that remove prions, block prion formation, or alter proteins that are prone to misfolding (Ullah & Khan, 2018). In addition, the many lifestyle attributes—including healthy diet, exercise, and education—that seem to confer some resistance to degenerative diseases may be effective because they help the body resist the formation and effects of prions. Selective cattle breeding for protein alleles that do not produce misfolding prevents BSE. Inserting a misfolding-resistant human protein allele into mice renders them resistant to prion disease. Any treatment developed for humans could potentially treat BSE in cattle, scrapie in sheep, and wasting disease in deer and elk.

Preventing protein misfolding could even arrest, in part, degenerative consequences of traumatic brain injury and concussion. An infectious prion can pass from one individual to another and even from one species to another—but only if the normal proteins in the two individuals are similar. Investigations show that among several alleles of the gene that produces normal proteins, some are more susceptible to misfolding than are others. Individuals with alleles that are not susceptible to misfolding, such as the Fore tribespeople who did not contract kuru, are resistant to prion disease.

Age-Related Cognitive Loss

Most people who grow old do not develop a neurocogntive disorder, but virtually everyone acquires age-related cognitive loss, even while living an active, healthy, productive life. Aging is associated with declines in perceptual functions (especially vision, hearing, and olfaction) and declining motor, cognitive, and executive (planning) functions as well. Older people tend to learn at a slower pace and typically do not attain the same mastery of new skills as do younger adults.

Noninvasive imaging studies reveal that aging is correlated with decreased white matter volume, probably related to myelin loss. This condition is reparable. There is little evidence of neuronal loss in typical aging, although a reduction in neurogenesis in the hippocampus does occur. Compared with younger people, older people tend to activate larger regions of their attentional and executive networks (parietal and prefrontal cortices) when they perform complex cognitive and executive tasks. This increased activation correlates with reduced performance on tests of working memory, as well as on attentional and executive tasks.

Two lines of evidence suggest that age-related declines in function can be slowed. The first is aerobic exercise to enhance general health and improve the brain's plasticity via increased neurogenesis, gliogenesis, and trophic factor support. The second treatment is brain exercise employing training strategies that enhance neural plasticity and reverse learned nonuse.

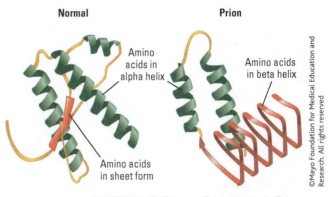

FIGURE 16-17 **Disease Process** *Left:* Prion proteins typically fold into helices and pleated sheets. *Right:* In misfolding, part of the normal protein changes into a beta helix. The result is an infectious disease-causing prion.

Brain Workout Engaging in cognitively stimulating activities can prevent neural networks and general cognitive function from declining with age.

View the progression of these microbleeds, or silent strokes, at https://www.youtube.com /watch?v=J3fb0CaDpEk.

deep brain stimulation (DBS) Neurosurgery in which electrodes permanently implanted in the brain stimulate a targeted area with a low-voltage electrical current to facilitate behavior.

Brain tumors are the topic of Clinical Focus 3-2. AV malformation, or angioma, is imaged in Figure 16-10.

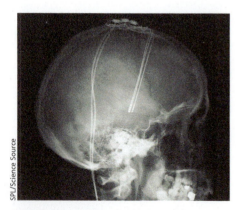

FIGURE 16-18 **Deep Brain Stimulation** X-ray of a human brain showing electrodes implanted in the thalamus for DBS.

Most of us know the frustration of losing a skill—whether it's trigonometry or tennis—after getting out of practice. Skill loss does not reflect neurocogntive disorder but simply a use-it-or-lose-it effect. Training programs designed to stimulate plasticity in the appropriate cerebral circuitry include motor, auditory, or visual system–based cognitive and/or attentional training. Brain training is designed to stimulate plasticity rather than to rehabilitate specific losses.

Brain-aging changes take place in the context of the entire body's aging. For example, neurocognitive disorder may reflect a chronic cerebrovascular disorder, marginal high blood pressure. Marginal elevations in blood pressure can lead to cerebral microbleeds, especially in white matter. The cumulative effect of years or even decades of tiny bleeds would lead eventually to increasingly disturbed cognition. The condition may first appear as a *mild cognitive impairment (MCI)* that slowly progresses, with cumulative microbleeds, toward neurocognitive disorder. For this reason, a healthy lifestyle that preserves the healthy function of the body also contributes to an enduring healthy brain.

Treatments for Neurocognitive Disorders

The ultimate goal for behavioral neurosciene is to apply knowledge to generate treatments that can restore a disordered brain to a range of healthy functioning. This goal is daunting because the first task—learning what causes a particular behavioral disturbance—is so difficult. Few behavioral disorders have a cause as simple as PKU does. Most, like schizophrenia, are complex. A more achievable goal is to make small advances by improving current treatments, developing new treatments, and to analyzing the causes of disease. Available treatments, while extensive, fall into four general categories:

1. *Neurosurgical.* The skull is opened, and some intervention is performed on the brain.
2. *Electrophysiological.* Brain function is modified by stimulation through the skull.
3. *Pharmacological.* A chemical that affects the brain is either ingested or injected.
4. *Behavioral.* Treatment manipulates the body or the experience, which in turn influences the brain.

Neurosurgical Treatments

Neurosurgical manipulation of the nervous system is largely reparative, as when tumors are removed or arteriovenous (AV) malformations corrected. Typically, such neurosurgical interventions are successful. Advances include improved imaging of a target for surgery—as the surgery takes place—and methods that allow diseased tissue to be destroyed without opening the skull. For example, *radiosurgery* uses energy, such as X-rays directed from different sources, to converge on a target and destroy abnormal cells. Individual X-rays lack the energy to damage healthy cells through which they pass: tissue is destroyed only where multiple beams converge.

Treatment for Parkinson disease entails inactivating brain regions that produce tremors and regions participating in the production of muscular rigidity that impairs movement. An electrode is placed in the motor thalamus, and an electric current is used to damage neurons responsible for producing the unwanted effects. Alternatively, in **deep brain stimulation (DBS)**, an electrode fixed in place in the globus pallidus or subthalamic nucleus is connected to an external electrical stimulator that the patient can activate (**Figure 16-18**). The stimulation can inactivate cells responsible for unwanted effects and so restore more normal movement (Knight et al., 2015).

DBS is also used experimentally to treat TBI and behavioral dysfunctions such as obsessive-compulsive disorder (OCD) and major depression (Cleary et al., 2015). Electrodes implanted in the brain are well tolerated and remain effective for several years. Electrical stimulation can have an activating effect and so relieve depression or compulsive behaviors. Stimulation may also make brain tissue more plastic and receptive to other treatments. During stimulation, patients can learn more effective thought and behavioral patterns. For many conditions, DBS remains an experimental option of last resort. It is not a permanent cure: when the stimulation stops, beneficial effects are reduced—hence the importance of coupling DBS with cognitive-behavioral therapy.

Another highly experimental neurosurgical strategy draws on the fixed sequence of prenatal brain development from cell division and cell differentiation to cell migration and synaptogenesis. If a brain region is functioning abnormally or if it is diseased or dead, as occurs in TBI or after a stroke, it should be possible to return this region to the embryonic state and regrow a healthy region. The use of so-called *induced neurogenesis* has a science fiction ring but may someday be feasible. In laboratory rats, for example, stem cells can be induced by *neurotrophic factors* to generate new cells that can migrate to the site of an injury.

In the 1980s, neurosurgeons experimented with implanting fetal stem cells in adult brains. Success was limited due to difficulties in cell placement, connections, and rejection by the patient's immune system. Another restorative idea comes from the discovery that multipotent stem cells in other body regions, such as bone marrow and skin, appear capable of manufacturing neural stem cells. Indeed, using appropriate manipulations, any cell can potentially be returned to a stem cell state. The advantage is that the patient's own cells are not rejected by the immune system.

If people's own multipotent stem cells prove able to generate neural stem cells, it should be possible to extract stem cells, place them in a special culture medium to generate thousands or millions of cells, and place these stem cells in the damaged brain. The cells would be instructed to differentiate appropriately and develop the correct connections. Stem cell transplantation is taken seriously today as a potential treatment for many neurological conditions, including Parkinson disease, TBI, and stroke, but it remains largely at an investigative stage (Savitz, 2015).

Figure 14-26 shows neurogenesis induced in a rat brain to repair a cortical stroke.

Figure 8-8 diagrams the origins of specialized brain cells from multipotent neural stem cells.

Electrophysiological Treatments

Treating the mind by treating the body is an ancient notion. In the 1930s, researchers used insulin to lower blood sugar and produce seizures as a treatment for depression. By the 1950s, insulin therapy had been replaced by electroconvulsive therapy (ECT), the first electrical brain stimulation treatment.

ECT was developed as a treatment for otherwise untreatable depression, and although its mode of action was not understood, it did prove useful. Less frequently used today, ECT sometimes remains the only treatment for people with severe depression. One reason may be that it stimulates the production of a variety of neurotrophic factors, especially brain-derived neurotrophic factor (BDNF), which in turn restore inactive cells to a more active mode.

Problems with ECT include the massive convulsions that electrical stimulation causes. Large doses of medication are required to prevent them. ECT also leads to memory loss, a symptom that can be troublesome with repeated treatments. A noninvasive technique called transcranial magnetic stimulation (TMS) uses magnetic rather than electrical stimulation. Magnetic stimulation can be applied to a localized brain region. Anesthesia is not necessary. TMS is an FDA-approved treatment for depression. Clinical applications, reviewed in Research Focus 16-5, Treating Behavioral Disorders with Transcranial Magnetic Stimulation, are growing.

Neurotrophic factors, nourishing chemical compounds, support neuronal growth, development, and viability.

Figure 7-7 diagrams how TMS works.

Pharmacological Treatments

Several accidental discoveries, beginning in the 1950s, led to a pharmacological revolution in the treatment of behavioral disorders. Here are some key examples:

1. The development of phenothiazines (neuroleptics) to treat schizophrenia stemmed from a drug used to premedicate surgical patients. In the decades that followed, new neuroleptic drugs became increasingly more selective, and they remain effective today.

2. A new class of antianxiety drugs was invented: the anxiolytics. Medications such as Valium quickly became—and remain—the most widely prescribed drugs in the United States.

⊙ RESEARCH FOCUS 16-5

Treating Behavioral Disorders with Transcranial Magnetic Stimulation

In transcranial magnetic stimulation (TMS), a magnetic coil placed over the scalp induces an electrical current in underlying brain regions. TMS can be applied to localized brain regions (focal areas) thought to be implicated in specific disorders. Manipulation of the magnetic field can stimulate an area of cortex as small as a quarter, the cortical surface only, or deeper layers of brain tissue.

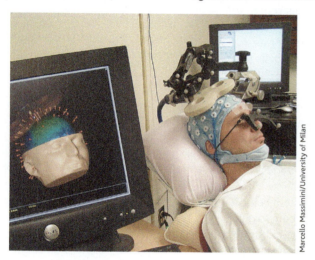

In clinical therapy for depression, TMS influences neural activity in a localized brain area.

Marcello Massimini/University of Milan

The primary clinical use of TMS, which the U.S. Food and Drug Administration formally approved in 2008, is for depression. Numerous studies report positive effects using TMS, but the required duration of treatment and the duration of beneficial effects remains under investigation.

The effects of brief pulses of TMS do not outlive the stimulation. *Repetitive TMS* (rTMS), which involves continuous stimulation for up to several minutes, produces longer-lasting effects than TMS. Small but promising studies have also extended the possible benefits of TMS to schizophrenic auditory hallucinations, anxiety disorders, neurocognitive disorders, hemiparesis, and pain syndrome (Boes et al., 2018).

Among the problems in all studies of TMS are questions related to the duration and intensity of stimulation, as well as to the area stimulated. Each person's brain is slightly different, and to ensure that appropriate structures are stimulated, an MRI must be performed on each subject.

Does TMS stimulation make the brain more plastic? If so, can learning be enhanced? The idea is that, when TMS is delivered, it produces a change in cortical excitability. This change in turn facilitates learning. Indeed, the therapeutic effects of motor or cognitive training can be improved when combined with TMS (Brem et al., 2018).

---

3. L-Dopa provided the first drug treatment for serious motor dysfunction in Parkinson disease. Once taken, L-dopa is converted into and replaces dopamine lost due to Parkinson disease.

The power of drugs to change disordered behavior revolutionized the pharmaceutical industry. The central goal is to develop drugs that can act as "magic bullets" to correct the chemical imbalances found in various disorders and that have fewer side effects than the drugs currently available. Both goals have proved difficult to achieve.

Pharmacological treatments have significant downsides. Acute and chronic side effects top the list, and long-term use may cause new problems. Consider a person who receives antidepressant medication. The drug may ease the depression, but it may also produce decreased sexual desire, fatigue, sleep disturbance, and reduced cognitive functioning.

Thus, although a medication may be useful for getting a person out of a depressed state, it may produce other symptoms that are themselves disturbing. Furthermore, in depression related to a person's life events, a drug does not provide the behavioral tools needed to cope with an adverse situation. One final time, "A pill is not a skill."

Negative side effects of drug treatments are evident in many people whose schizophrenia is being treated with neuroleptics. Antipsychotic drugs act on the mesolimbic dopamine system, which affects motivation, among other functions. The side effect emerges because the drugs also act on the nigrostriatal dopaminergic system, which controls movement. Patients who take neuroleptics also eventually develop motor disturbances. **Tardive dyskinesia**, an inability to stop the tongue, hands, or other body parts from moving, is a motor symptom of long-term neuroleptic administration. Side effects of movement disorders can persist after treatment with the psychoactive medication has stopped. Taking drugs for behavioral disorders, then, does carry risk. Rather than being magic bullets, these medications often act like shotguns.

Despite their drawbacks, drugs do prove beneficial for many people. Improved drug chemistry will reduce side effects, as will improved delivery modes that bring a drug to a target system with minimal effects on other systems. One improved delivery system,

Section 6-2 classifies psychoactive drugs and their therapeutic effects.

tardive dyskinesia Inability to stop the tongue or other body parts from moving; motor side effect of neuroleptic drugs.

illustrated in **Figure 16-19**, uses nanoparticles called *liposomes*, which are biosynthetic molecules 1 to 100 nm (nanometers, or billionths of a meter) in size. One natural biological nanoparticle, with a radius of about 40 nm, is the synaptic vesicle that houses a neurotransmitter for delivery into the cell's extracellular space. Liposomes consisting of a synthetic vesicle with a homing peptide on the surface can, in principle, be constructed to carry a drug across the blood–brain barrier and deliver it to specified types of neuron or glial cells within the nervous system.

16-3 Review

Before you continue, check your understanding. Answers to Self-Test appear at the back of the book.

1. _____, a wound to the brain resulting from a blow to the head, is the most common form of brain damage for people under age 40.

2. The four general categories of treatment of neurocognitive disorders are _____, _____, _____, and _____.

3. Interruption of blood to the brain is called _____, and if prolonged, it can result in _____.

4. Although superficially appearing to be very different diseases, Parkinson and Alzheimer have similarities such as _____ and _____ that suggest they may be part of a common disease spectrum.

5. Name two strategies that can reduce or reverse neurological and cognitive decline with aging.

For additional study tools, visit ⓜ **LaunchPad** at launchpadworks.com

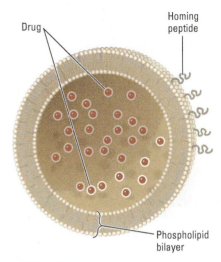

FIGURE 16-19 **Liposome for Drug Delivery** Biosynthetic vesicles can deliver microscopic drugs or DNA to the body's cells. Synthetic biology is discussed in Section 7-1.

16-4

Research Challenges

Even if the problems of diagnosis were solved, major obstacles to investigating behavioral disorders would still exist. Following is a partial list.

Organizational Complexity

The nervous system far outstrips other body systems in terms of complexity. The brain has a wider variety of cell types than does any other body organ, and nervous system cells and their connections are plastic: they change with experience. These features present a complex challenge to understanding healthy and disordered functioning.

Systemic Complexity

As our understanding of brain and behavior has progressed, it has become apparent that multiple receptor systems serve widely varied functions. For example, the brain's major activating systems—those that employ acetylcholine, dopamine, norepinephrine, serotonin, and GABA—are diffuse, with little specificity between biochemistry and behavior. The neurotransmitter GABA affects some 30 percent of the brain's synapses. When people ingest a GABA agonist (such as a benzodiazepine) to treat anxiety, multiple effects on behavior become apparent. So it is with most drug treatments.

Figure 5-18 summarizes major neural activating systems; Figure 6-7, how psychoactive drugs affect the GABA$_A$ receptor.

Neuronal Plasticity

The nervous system can adapt to extreme stress or injury. Even the nigrostriatal dopaminergic system's close relationship to Parkinson disease is enigmatic. It is impossible to tie dopamine depletion to a consistent behavioral syndrome. Two people with Parkinson disease can exhibit vastly different symptoms, even though the common basis of the disease is a loss of neurons from the substantia nigra (Fereshtehnejad et al., 2015). Furthermore, only when the loss of dopamine neurons exceeds about

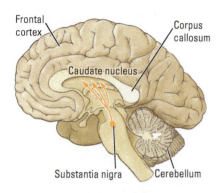

Frontal cortex

Corpus callosum

Caudate nucleus

Substantia nigra

Cerebellum

Nigrostriatal Dopamine Pathways Axons of neurons in the midbrain substantia nigra project to the basal ganglia, supplying dopamine to maintain healthy motor behavior. Dopamine loss contributes to muscle rigidity and dyskinesia in Parkinson disease.

Section 7-7 reviews the benefits of creating animal models of disorders.

60 percent to 80 percent do investigators see clinical signs of Parkinson disease. Are all those dopamine cells not needed? That is unlikely, but this finding shows that the brain's compensatory plasticity is considerable. When a disease progresses slowly, the brain has a remarkable capacity for adapting.

Compensatory Plasticity

Even the best technology produces uncertain relationships. Magnetic resonance imaging may show that a person with multiple sclerosis has many nervous system lesions, yet behaviorally that person may at the same time display few outward symptoms. Just as brain lesions do not always produce behavioral symptoms, behavioral symptoms are not always linked to obvious neuropathology. Clearly, people display compensatory plasticity: they can change their behavior to adapt to neural change just as they can display disordered behavior without obvious brain pathology.

Technological Resolution

Some people have notable behavioral problems after a brain trauma, yet no obvious signs of brain damage appear on an MRI. An infant's brain may seem healthy, only to display severe cerebral palsy later. The resolution of an imaging technology may lack sufficient power to detect subtle neuronal change, such as a drop in dendritic spine density or injury so diffuse that it is hard to identify. Given the current diagnostic methods for both behavioral disorders and neuropathology, identifying disorders and their causes is seldom easy.

Modeling Simplicity

A major avenue for investigating the causes of disorders is to develop and study animal models. Monkeys, rats, and mice with specific lesions of the nigrostriatal dopamine system are used to model Parkinson disease. Animal models lead to significant advances in understanding neural conditions and their treatment. But the insights they provide into the neurobiology behind behavioral disorders can be oversimplified.

The fact that a drug reduces symptoms does not necessarily mean that it is acting on a key biochemical aspect of the pathology. Aspirin can get rid of a headache, but that does not mean the headache is caused by the receptors on which aspirin acts. Similarly, antipsychotic drugs block dopamine D_2 receptors, but that does not mean schizophrenia is caused by abnormal D_2 receptors. Schizophrenia quite possibly results from a disturbance in glutamatergic systems, and for some reason dopamine antagonists can either rectify the abnormality or, alternatively, produce effects on behavior that counteract the behavioral effects of schizophrenia.

Modeling Limitations

Modeling human disorders is complex, and critical thinking is imperative when you encounter media reports about studies that describe possible cures for human behavioral diseases. Caution is especially in order when it comes to psychiatric disorders whose causes remain unknown. Furthermore, many symptoms of disorders such as schizophrenia and anxiety are largely cognitive. Objectively identifying any cognitive processes mimicked by a laboratory model is a difficult task.

16-5

Is Misbehavior Always Bad?

You know this movie plot: a person sustains a blow to the head and then becomes a better person. Do pathological changes in brain and behavior sometimes lead to behavioral improvement in real life? A report by Jim Giles (2004) on Tommy McHugh's case is thought provoking.

McHugh (1949–2012), a heroin addict, committed multiple serious crimes and spent a great deal of time in jail. Later, he suffered a cerebral hemorrhage (bleeding into the brain) from an aneurysm. The bleeding was repaired surgically with a metal clip on the leaking artery. After he recovered from the injury, McHugh's personality changed dramatically. He took up painting, which he had never done before, and became a successful artist.

McHugh's injury-induced brain changes appear to have been beneficial, but the exact nature of his brain injury has not been identified. The metal clip in his brain precluded the use of MRI. Aspects of his cognitive behavior suggest that he may have had frontal lobe damage.

The phenomenon in which an individual acquires a new skill after an injury is called *acquired savant syndrome*. There are many other reports of people who have developed new musical or artistic talents after their injuries; a registry has been created to document cases of congenital and acquired savant syndrome (Treffert & Rebedew, 2015). Corrigan and colleagues (2012) propose that allied savant skills can be acquired by depressing inhibitory systems in the brain so that new skill strategies can be activated. In experiments, for example, depressing participants' left hemispheres with TMS briefly improved mathematical skills, which are subserved by the right hemisphere.

The general idea of artificially manipulating the brain for the better is controversial (Heinz et al., 2012). Influencing brain function through a strategy loosely described as **cognitive enhancement** enlists current knowledge of pharmacology, brain plasticity, brain stimulation, neurogenetics, and other specialties to boost brain functioning. Of course, people already use drugs to alter brain function, and the basis of many therapies is to enhance brain function. Psychosurgical techniques such as frontal lobotomy were based on the general idea that brain function could be improved. As yet, however, evidence is lacking that cognitive enhancement for the average person is better than old-fashioned but readily available methods: learning, practice, and a healthy lifestyle.

To learn more and view McHugh's art, go to http://www.tommymchugh.co.uk.

cognitive enhancement Brain function enhancement by pharmacological, physiological, or surgical manipulation.

In Clinical Focus 6-1, a brief history of cognitive enhancers is context for a trend: procuring medication prescribed for ADHD as a study aid.

Summary

16-1 Multidisciplinary Contributions to Brain and Behavior

Contemporary understanding of brain and behavior provides new insights, explanations, and treatments for brain disorders. Health professionals who treat behavioral disorders are forging a unified understanding of mind and brain. Clinical neuroscience is a specialty that focuses on the diagnosis and treatment of diseases and disorders affecting the brain and central nervous system.

Disorders can be classified according to presumed etiology (cause), symptomatology, or pathology. The classification systems developed by psychologists, psychiatrists, and neurologists overlap, and each is revised from time to time. Clearly, better comprehension of the causes of disorders will lead to better classification systems. Advances in genetics and brain imaging will aid this effort. The table summarizes the range of available treatments, from highly invasive neurosurgery to noninvasive electrophysiology, from moderately invasive pharmacology to behavioral treatments.

General Treatment Categories

Neurosurgical	Behavioral
Direct intervention	*Manipulation of experience*
DBS	Behavior modification
Stem cell transplantation	Cognitive, cognitive-behavioral therapy
Tissue removal or repair	Neuropsychological
Electrophysiological	Emotional therapy, psychotherapy
Noninvasive manipulation	Physical activity, music
ECT	rt-fMRI
TMS, rTMS	VR exposure and other computer-based simulations
Pharmacological	
Chemical administration	
Antibiotics or antivirals	
Psychoactive drugs	
Neurotrophic factors	
Nutrition	

16-2 Psychiatric Disorders

Psychiatric disorders, including psychoses, mood disorders (such as major depression), and anxiety disorders, are assumed to be caused by brain malfunction. Psychoses, of which schizophrenia is the most common and best understood, are characterized by loss of contact with reality. Schizophrenia can produce a wide range of symptoms, influenced by individual differences, and its causes have genetic, developmental,

anatomical, and neurochemical correlates. Mood disorders include major depression and anxiety disorders. Psychological factors in understanding depression relate to the brain's reactivity to stress. Anxiety disorders often accompany depression but can occur separately.

16-3 Neurocognitive Disorders

Neurocognitive disorders are the result of damage to the brain. Traumatic brain injury (TBI) is a wound to the brain as a result of a blow to the head or body. Mild TBI, which includes concussion, is currently the subject of a large-scale longitudinal study. Stroke is an interruption of blood flow due to blockage (ischemic) or bleeding (hemorrhagic) of a vessel, which can cause a cascade of pathological events. Epilepsy is characterized by recurrent seizures, which can be recorded on an EEG. Seizures can be focal or generalized, and treatment can be pharmacological or, in cases of intractable epilepsy, surgical. Multiple sclerosis is an autoimmune disorder that results in damage to the myelin sheaths that encase the axons, and eventually leads to paraplegia.

Neurocognitive disorders involve progressive loss of function in neurons, or the loss of neurons themselves. Memory loss and an acquired and persistent syndrome of intellectual impairment characterizes many neurocogntive disorders, including Alzheimer and Parkinson diseases. The prion theory of progressive neurocognitive disorder suggests that these disorders may be causes by abnormally folded proteins. Treatments for neurocognitive disorders include neurosurgical treatments, electrophysiological treatments, and pharmacological treatments.

16-4 Research Challenges

Most behavioral disorders have multiple causes—genetic, epigenetic, biochemical, anatomical, social–environmental variables—all of them interacting. Research methods directed toward these causes include family studies designed to find a genetic abnormality that might be corrected, biochemical anomalies that might be reversed by drug or hormone therapy, anatomical pathologies that might account for behavioral changes, and social–environmental variables.

Investigators rely increasingly on neuroimaging (fMRI, PET, TMS, ERP) to examine brain–behavior relationships in vivo in healthy participants as well as in people with disorders. Interest in more refined behavioral measurements is growing, especially for cognitive behavior, the better to understand behavioral symptoms.

16-5 Is Misbehavior Always Bad?

In rare cases, people with a behavioral disorder also have some benefit. An individual who has a brain injury, for example, may suddenly display an artistic talent. The explanation for this acquired savant syndrome is that depressing the brain's inhibitory systems can activate new skill strategies. Artificially manipulating the brain with cognitive enhancers is a controversial approach to improving brain function.

❙ Key Terms

akathesia, p. 582

anxiety disorder, p. 569

autoimmune disease, p. 578

behavioral therapy, p. 564

bipolar disorder, p. 569

chronic traumatic encephalopathy (CTE), p. 573

clinical neuroscience, p. 560

cognitive enhancement, p. 591

cognitive therapy, p. 564

cognitive-behavioral therapy (CBT), p. 570

deep brain stimulation (DBS), p. 586

dementia, p. 579

diaschisis, p. 575

Diagnostic and Statistical Manual of Mental Disorders (DSM), p. 562

festination, p. 582

focal seizure, p. 576

generalized seizure, p. 576

hemorrhagic stroke, p. 574

HPA axis, p. 569

ischemic stroke, p. 574

Lewy body, p. 584

magnetic resonance spectroscopy (MRS), p. 574

major depression, p. 569

mania, p. 569

neuroprotectant, p. 575

phenylketonuria (PKU), p. 559

posttraumatic stress disorder (PTSD), p. 558

prion, p. 584

psychotherapy, p. 565

real-time fMRI (rt-fMRI), p. 565

tardive dyskinesia, p. 588

virtual reality (VR) exposure therapy, p. 558

Visit ❧ **LaunchPad** to access the e-Book, videos, ❧ **LearningCurve** adaptive quizzing, flashcards, and more at launchpadworks.com

ANSWERS TO SECTION REVIEW SELF-TESTS

CHAPTER 1

REVIEW 1-1
1. Traumatic brain injury (TBI); concussion
2. central nervous system (CNS); peripheral nervous system (PNS)
3. cerebrum; forebrain; hemispheres; brainstem
4. inherited; learning
5. Research on embodied behavior proposes that we understand each other not only by listening to words but also by observing gestures and other body language; it also proposes that we think not only with silent language but also with overt gestures and body language.

REVIEW 1-2
1. mentalism; dualism; Materialism
2. natural selection; Charles Darwin
3. minimally conscious state *or* MCS; persistent vegetative state *or* PVS
4. In formulating the theory of natural selection, Darwin relied on observation to conclude that living organisms are related and pass traits from parents to offspring. Mendel used experimentation to show that heritable factors underlie phenotypic variation among species.

REVIEW 1-3
1. nervous systems
2. nerve net; bilaterally symmetrical; ganglia; chordate
3. cladogram
4. Humans possess the largest brain of all animals relative to body size and the most complex brain structure.

REVIEW 1-4
1. common ancestor; chimpanzee
2. hominid; *Australopithecus*; *Homo habilis*; *Homo erectus*
3. encephalization quotient (EQ); counting brain cells (neurons)
4. *in any order:* climate changes; changes in lifestyle skills; physiological changes; delayed maturation *or* neoteny
5. Changes in climate may have driven many physical changes in hominids, including the nearly threefold increase in brain size from apes to modern humans. Evidence suggests that each new hominid species appeared after climate changes devastated old environments and produced new ones. Eventually, modern humans evolved adaptability sufficient to allow us to populate almost every climatic region on Earth.

REVIEW 1-5
1. species-typical behavior
2. culture; memes
3. *g*; multiple intelligences
4. In comparing different species, a larger brain correlates with more complex behavior. In comparing individuals within a species, brain size and intelligence are only remotely related. Rather, the complexity of different brain regions is related to behavioral abilities. Humans, for example, vary widely in body size and in brain size, as well as in having different kinds of intelligence. All these factors make any simple comparison of individuals' brain sizes and intelligence impossible.

CHAPTER 2

REVIEW 2-1
1. behavior; brain
2. *in any order:* frontal; temporal; parietal; occipital
3. neuroplasticity (*or* plasticity)
4. white matter; gray matter
5. tracts; nerves
6. Compare your diagram with Figure 2-2B.

REVIEW 2-2
1. *in any order:* forebrain; midbrain; hindbrain
2. behavior
3. The forebrain has grown dramatically over the course of vertebrate evolution. But archaic forms have not been discarded and replaced as more complex nervous systems have emerged. The forebrain's growth thus is an elaboration of functions already present in the other brain regions and leads to its functioning on multiple levels.

REVIEW 2-3
1. levels of function
2. spinal cord
3. hindbrain; midbrain; diencephalon
4. cerebellum
5. basal ganglia; allocortex *or* limbic system structures
6. allocortex; neocortex; *in any order:* sensory; motor; integrative
7. The forebrain regulates cognitive activity, including thought and memory, and it holds ultimate control over movement (behavior).

REVIEW 2-4
1. cranial nerves; spinal (peripheral) nerves
2. same
3. *in any order:* head; internal organs and glands
4. The law of Bell and Magendie states that sensory (afferent) spinal nerve fibers are dorsal (in humans, posterior) and that motor (efferent) spinal fibers are ventral (in humans, anterior). This law is important because it allows neurologists to predict the location of spinal cord damage accurately, based on changes in sensation or movement.

REVIEW 2-5
1. ganglia
2. sympathetic; parasympathetic; in opposition
3. The ANS operates largely outside our conscious awareness, whether we are awake or asleep, to regulate the vegetative functions essential to life.
4. numbers and types of neurons and glia and of chemical transmitters
5. microbiome; nutrients; chemicals
6. Psychobiotics are live organisms that, when ingested in adequate amounts, can benefit people who have psychiatric illness.

REVIEW 2-6
1. *in any order:* olfactory system; somatic nervous system; ANS; ENS
2. multiple levels of functioning
3. excitation; inhibition
4. Any individual's perceived reality is only an approximation of what is actually present. An animal's representation of the world depends on the nature of the information sent to the animal's brain.

CHAPTER 3

REVIEW 3-1
1. *in either order:* neurons; glial cells
2. *in either order:* exciting; inhibiting
3. *in any order:* sensory neurons [, which] detect and convey incoming stimuli into the CNS; interneurons [, which] form links between sensory and motor neurons; motor neurons [, which] make muscles move
4. *in any order:* ependymal cells; astrocytes; microglia; oligodendroglia; Schwann cells; *in any order:* nourishing; removing waste; insulating; supporting; repairing
5. Robots are capable of producing goal-oriented actions, as well as sensing the world around them and coordinating actions in response, much as animals do.

Researchers can thus construct robotic models to confirm hypotheses about human nervous system function, such as the excitation and inhibition of neurons.

REVIEW 3-2

1. *in any order:* cell membrane; nucleus; endoplasmic reticulum (*or* ER); Golgi bodies; microtubules (*or* tubules); vesicles

2. *in any order:* channels; gates; pumps

3. DNA; RNA; protein

4. endoplasmic reticulum (*or* ER); Golgi bodies; microtubules; exocytosis

5. By using most of the proteins that it makes, a cell enables itself to interact with other cells and to modify their behavior. The collective action of cells mediates behavior.

REVIEW 3-3

1. 23; protein

2. alleles; proteins

3. mutation; Down syndrome; trisomy

4. recessive; dominant

5. CRISPR (*or* Clustered Regularly Interspaced Short Palindromic Repeat); DNA; DNA base sequence

6. Gene methylation *or* DNA methylation

7. Mendelian genetics concentrates on inheritance patterns—on which genes parents pass to their offspring and offspring pass to succeeding generations. Epigenetics is the study of how the environment and experience can affect the inherited genome.

CHAPTER 4

REVIEW 4-1

1. René Descartes

2. stimulation; recording

3. *in any order:* how to record from the giant axons of the North Atlantic squid; how to use an oscilloscope to measure small changes in voltage; how to craft microelectrodes small enough to place on or in an axon

4. *in either order:* concentration gradient, from an area of relatively high concentration to an area of lower concentration; voltage gradient, from an area of relatively high charge to an area of lower charge

5. Ion channels in cell membranes may open to facilitate ion movement, close to impede ion movement, or pump ions across the membrane.

REVIEW 4-2

1. resting potential; ions

2. semipermeable; negative

3. hyperpolarization; depolarization

4. action potential; nerve impulse

5. Nerve impulses travel more rapidly on myelinated axons because of saltatory conduction: action potentials leap between the nodes separating the glial cells that form the axon's myelin sheath.

REVIEW 4-3

1. excitatory postsynaptic potentials (EPSPs); inhibitory postsynaptic potentials (IPSPs)

2. *in either order:* time, space; integrates

3. cell body; initial segment; axon

4. Some neurons have voltage-activated channels on their dendrites that allow the reverse movement of an action potential into the neurons' dendritic fields.

REVIEW 4-4

1. action potential

2. sensory receptor cell; voltage-activated

3. motor; muscles

4. autoimmune; acetylcholine

5. The varieties of membrane channels generate the transmembrane charge, mediate graded potentials, and trigger the action potential.

CHAPTER 5

REVIEW 5-1

1. chemical synapses; gap junction

2. experience; learning

3. axodendritic; axosomatic; axomuscular; axoaxonic; axosynaptic; axoextracellular; axosecretory; dendrodendritic

4. dendrite; cell body *or* soma

5. When an action potential reaches an axon terminal, (1) a chemical transmitter that is synthesized inside the neuron and (2) then packaged and stored in the axon terminal. Next, it is (3) transported to the presynaptic membrane and released into the synaptic cleft. The transmitter (4) binds to and activates receptors on the postsynaptic membrane. The transmitter is (5) degraded or removed.

REVIEW 5-2

1. *in any order:* synthesis; release; receptor action; inactivation

2. *in any order:* small-molecule transmitters; peptide transmitters; gaseous transmitters; lipid transmitters; ion transmitters

3. *in either order:* acetate, choline; acetylcholinesterase *or* AChE

4. lipid; postsynaptic

5. An ionotropic receptor's pore or channel can be opened or closed to regulate the flow-through of ions, directly effecting rapid and usually excitatory voltage changes on the cell membrane. Metabotropic receptors, which are

generally inhibitory and slow acting, activate second messengers to indirectly produce changes in cell function and structure.

REVIEW 5-3

1. neurotransmitter; neurotransmitter

2. acetylcholine *or* ACh; cholinergic; norepinephrine *or* NE

3. *in either order:* serotonin *or* 5-HT; dopamine *or* DA

4. *in any order:* cholinergic; dopaminergic; noradrenergic; serotonergic

5. This idea has been attractive for a long time because a clear relationship exists between DA loss in the substantia nigra and Parkinson disease and because acetylcholine and norepinephrine are clearly related to somatic and autonomic behaviors. But for other neurotransmitter systems in the brain, establishing clear one-to-one relationships has been difficult.

REVIEW 5-4

1. synapse; learning

2. *in either order:* habituation; sensitization

3. presynaptic axon terminal; sensory; calcium; less

4. interneurons; potassium *or* K; calcium ions *or* Ca^{2+}

5. posttraumatic stress disorder *or* PTSD; sensitization

6. Permanent responses to frequently occurring stimuli are biologically (*or* behaviorally *and/or* metabolically) efficient, but if stimuli change suddenly, a lack of flexibility becomes maladaptive.

CHAPTER 6

REVIEW 6-1

1. Psychoactive drugs; psychopharmacology

2. blood–brain barrier; brain

3. synapses; agonists; antagonists

4. tolerance; sensitization

5. *in any order:* feces; urine; sweat; breath; breast milk

6. (a) Drug use at home is unlikely to condition drug-taking behavior to familiar home cues, so tolerance is likely to occur.
(b) Novel cues in a work setting may enhance conditioning and so sensitize the occasional drug user.

REVIEW 6-2

1. Caffeine; adenosine

2. $GABA_A$; Cl^- *or* chloride ion

3. seroton

4. endorphins

5. release; reuptake; D_2

ANSWERS TO SECTION REVIEW SELF-TESTS

CHAPTER 1

REVIEW 1-1

1. Traumatic brain injury (TBI); concussion
2. central nervous system (CNS); peripheral nervous system (PNS)
3. cerebrum; forebrain; hemispheres; brainstem
4. inherited; learning
5. Research on embodied behavior proposes that we understand each other not only by listening to words but also by observing gestures and other body language; it also proposes that we think not only with silent language but also with overt gestures and body language.

REVIEW 1-2

1. mentalism; dualism; Materialism
2. natural selection; Charles Darwin
3. minimally conscious state or MCS; persistent vegetative state or PVS
4. In formulating the theory of natural selection, Darwin relied on observation to conclude that living organisms are related and pass traits from parents to offspring. Mendel used experimentation to show that heritable factors underlie phenotypic variation among species.

REVIEW 1-3

1. nervous systems
2. nerve net; bilaterally symmetrical; ganglia; chordate
3. cladogram
4. Humans possess the largest brain of all animals relative to body size and the most complex brain structure.

REVIEW 1-4

1. common ancestor; chimpanzee
2. hominid; *Australopithecus*; *Homo habilis*; *Homo erectus*
3. encephalization quotient (EQ); counting brain cells (neurons)
4. *in any order:* climate changes; changes in lifestyle skills; physiological changes; delayed maturation *or* neoteny
5. Changes in climate may have driven many physical changes in hominids, including the nearly threefold increase in brain size from apes to modern humans. Evidence suggests that each new hominid species appeared after climate changes devastated old environments and produced new ones. Eventually, modern humans evolved adaptability sufficient to allow us to populate almost every climatic region on Earth.

REVIEW 1-5

1. species-typical behavior
2. culture; memes
3. *g*; multiple intelligences
4. In comparing different species, a larger brain correlates with more complex behavior. In comparing individuals within a species, brain size and intelligence are only remotely related. Rather, the complexity of different brain regions is related to behavioral abilities. Humans, for example, vary widely in body size and in brain size, as well as in having different kinds of intelligence. All these factors make any simple comparison of individuals' brain sizes and intelligence impossible.

CHAPTER 2

REVIEW 2-1

1. behavior; brain
2. *in any order:* frontal; temporal; parietal; occipital
3. neuroplasticity (*or* plasticity)
4. white matter; gray matter
5. tracts; nerves
6. Compare your diagram with Figure 2-2B.

REVIEW 2-2

1. *in any order:* forebrain; midbrain; hindbrain
2. behavior
3. The forebrain has grown dramatically over the course of vertebrate evolution. But archaic forms have not been discarded and replaced as more complex nervous systems have emerged. The forebrain's growth thus is an elaboration of functions already present in the other brain regions and leads to its functioning on multiple levels.

REVIEW 2-3

1. levels of function
2. spinal cord
3. hindbrain; midbrain; diencephalon
4. cerebellum
5. basal ganglia; allocortex *or* limbic system structures
6. allocortex; neocortex; *in any order:* sensory; motor; integrative
7. The forebrain regulates cognitive activity, including thought and memory, and it holds ultimate control over movement (behavior).

REVIEW 2-4

1. cranial nerves; spinal (peripheral) nerves
2. same

3. *in any order:* head; internal organs and glands
4. The law of Bell and Magendie states that sensory (afferent) spinal nerve fibers are dorsal (in humans, posterior) and that motor (efferent) spinal fibers are ventral (in humans, anterior). This law is important because it allows neurologists to predict the location of spinal cord damage accurately, based on changes in sensation or movement.

REVIEW 2-5

1. ganglia
2. sympathetic; parasympathetic; in opposition
3. The ANS operates largely outside our conscious awareness, whether we are awake or asleep, to regulate the vegetative functions essential to life.
4. numbers and types of neurons and glia and of chemical transmitters
5. microbiome; nutrients; chemicals
6. Psychobiotics are live organisms that, when ingested in adequate amounts, can benefit people who have psychiatric illness.

REVIEW 2-6

1. *in any order:* olfactory system; somatic nervous system; ANS; ENS
2. multiple levels of functioning
3. excitation; inhibition
4. Any individual's perceived reality is only an approximation of what is actually present. An animal's representation of the world depends on the nature of the information sent to the animal's brain.

CHAPTER 3

REVIEW 3-1

1. *in either order:* neurons; glial cells
2. *in either order:* exciting; inhibiting
3. *in any order:* sensory neurons [, which] detect and convey incoming stimuli into the CNS; interneurons [, which] form links between sensory and motor neurons; motor neurons [, which] make muscles move
4. *in any order:* ependymal cells; astrocytes; microglia; oligodendroglia; Schwann cells; *in any order:* nourishing; removing waste; insulating; supporting; repairing
5. Robots are capable of producing goal-oriented actions, as well as sensing the world around them and coordinating actions in response, much as animals do.

Researchers can thus construct robotic models to confirm hypotheses about human nervous system function, such as the excitation and inhibition of neurons.

REVIEW 3-2
1. *in any order:* cell membrane; nucleus; endoplasmic reticulum (*or* ER); Golgi bodies; microtubules (*or* tubules); vesicles
2. *in any order:* channels; gates; pumps
3. DNA; RNA; protein
4. endoplasmic reticulum (*or* ER); Golgi bodies; microtubules; exocytosis
5. By using most of the proteins that it makes, a cell enables itself to interact with other cells and to modify their behavior. The collective action of cells mediates behavior.

REVIEW 3-3
1. 23; protein
2. alleles; proteins
3. mutation; Down syndrome; trisomy
4. recessive; dominant
5. CRISPR (*or* Clustered Regularly Interspaced Short Palindromic Repeat); DNA; DNA base sequence
6. Gene methylation *or* DNA methylation
7. Mendelian genetics concentrates on inheritance patterns—on which genes parents pass to their offspring and offspring pass to succeeding generations. Epigenetics is the study of how the environment and experience can affect the inherited genome.

CHAPTER 4

REVIEW 4-1
1. René Descartes
2. stimulation; recording
3. *in any order:* how to record from the giant axons of the North Atlantic squid; how to use an oscilloscope to measure small changes in voltage; how to craft microelectrodes small enough to place on or in an axon
4. *in either order:* concentration gradient, from an area of relatively high concentration to an area of lower concentration; voltage gradient, from an area of relatively high charge to an area of lower charge
5. Ion channels in cell membranes may open to facilitate ion movement, close to impede ion movement, or pump ions across the membrane.

REVIEW 4-2
1. resting potential; ions
2. semipermeable; negative
3. hyperpolarization; depolarization
4. action potential; nerve impulse

5. Nerve impulses travel more rapidly on myelinated axons because of saltatory conduction: action potentials leap between the nodes separating the glial cells that form the axon's myelin sheath.

REVIEW 4-3
1. excitatory postsynaptic potentials (EPSPs); inhibitory postsynaptic potentials (IPSPs)
2. *in either order:* time, space; integrates
3. cell body; initial segment; axon
4. Some neurons have voltage-activated channels on their dendrites that allow the reverse movement of an action potential into the neurons' dendritic fields.

REVIEW 4-4
1. action potential
2. sensory receptor cell; voltage-activated
3. motor; muscles
4. autoimmune; acetylcholine
5. The varieties of membrane channels generate the transmembrane charge, mediate graded potentials, and trigger the action potential.

CHAPTER 5

REVIEW 5-1
1. chemical synapses; gap junction
2. experience; learning
3. axodendritic; axosomatic; axomuscular; axoaxonic; axosynaptic; axoextracellular; axosecretory; dendrodendritic
4. dendrite; cell body *or* soma
5. When an action potential reaches an axon terminal, (1) a chemical transmitter that is synthesized inside the neuron and (2) then packaged and stored in the axon terminal. Next, it is (3) transported to the presynaptic membrane and released into the synaptic cleft. The transmitter (4) binds to and activates receptors on the postsynaptic membrane. The transmitter is (5) degraded or removed.

REVIEW 5-2
1. *in any order:* synthesis; release; receptor action; inactivation
2. *in any order:* small-molecule transmitters; peptide transmitters; gaseous transmitters; lipid transmitters; ion transmitters
3. *in either order:* acetate, choline; acetylcholinesterase *or* AChE
4. lipid; postsynaptic
5. An ionotropic receptor's pore or channel can be opened or closed to regulate the flow-through of ions, directly effecting rapid and usually excitatory voltage changes on the cell membrane. Metabotropic receptors, which are

generally inhibitory and slow acting, activate second messengers to indirectly produce changes in cell function and structure.

REVIEW 5-3
1. neurotransmitter; neurotransmitter
2. acetylcholine *or* ACh; cholinergic; norepinephrine *or* NE
3. *in either order:* serotonin *or* 5-HT; dopamine *or* DA
4. *in any order:* cholinergic; dopaminergic; noradrenergic; serotonergic
5. This idea has been attractive for a long time because a clear relationship exists between DA loss in the substantia nigra and Parkinson disease and because acetylcholine and norepinephrine are clearly related to somatic and autonomic behaviors. But for other neurotransmitter systems in the brain, establishing clear one-to-one relationships has been difficult.

REVIEW 5-4
1. synapse; learning
2. *in either order:* habituation; sensitization
3. presynaptic axon terminal; sensory; calcium; less
4. interneurons; potassium *or* K; calcium ions *or* Ca^{2+}
5. posttraumatic stress disorder *or* PTSD; sensitization
6. Permanent responses to frequently occurring stimuli are biologically (*or* behaviorally *and/or* metabolically) efficient, but if stimuli change suddenly, a lack of flexibility becomes maladaptive.

CHAPTER 6

REVIEW 6-1
1. Psychoactive drugs; psychopharmacology
2. blood–brain barrier; brain
3. synapses; agonists; antagonists
4. tolerance; sensitization
5. *in any order:* feces; urine; sweat; breath; breast milk
6. (a) Drug use at home is unlikely to condition drug-taking behavior to familiar home cues, so tolerance is likely to occur.
(b) Novel cues in a work setting may enhance conditioning and so sensitize the occasional drug user.

REVIEW 6-2
1. Caffeine; adenosine
2. $GABA_A$; Cl^- *or* chloride ion
3. seroton
4. endorphins
5. release; reuptake; D_2

6. Psychotropic drugs act on many neurotransmitters, including acetylcholine, anandamide, dopamine, epinephrine, glutamate, norepinephrine, and serotonin.

REVIEW 6-3

1. Behavioral myopia
2. Substance abuse; addiction *or* substance dependence
3. psychomotor activation; mesolimbic dopamine system
4. females; males
5. Behavioral myopia theory suggests that intoxicated individuals are unusually responsive to local and immediate cues, so the environment excessively influences their behavior, while consequences go ignored.

REVIEW 6-4

1. liking (pleasure); tolerance; wanting (craving); sensitization
2. frontal cortex; brainstem; mesolimbic dopamine system (pathways); basal ganglia
3. epigenetics
4. drugs; other life experiences
5. A reasonable approach to treatment views drug addiction in the same way as chronic behavioral addictions and medical problems are viewed: as a lifelong challenge for most people.

REVIEW 6-5

1. neurohormones; pituitary gland; releasing hormones; brain
2. *in either order:* steroids; peptides
3. homeostatic; gonadal; glucocorticoids
4. anabolic (*or* anabolic–androgenic) steroids; muscle mass; masculinizing
5. epinephrine; cortisol
6. The hippocampus is important in ending the stress response by regulating cortisol levels. If cortisol remains elevated by prolonged stress, eventually it damages the hippocampus.

CHAPTER 7

REVIEW 7-1

1. *in either order:* brain function; behavior
2. sectioning and staining; multiphoton imaging
3. touchscreen platforms
4. Brain-stimulation methods include using electrical pulses, as in DBS; magnetic fields, such as in TMS; ultrasonic beams, as in HIFU; chemicals, by administering drugs; or in the transgenic techniques of optogenetics (which employs light), chemogenetics (which employs synthetic drugs to interact exclusively with designer receptors), or genetic engineering, in the case of CRISPR-Cas9 techniques.

REVIEW 7-2

1. *in any order:* single-cell recording; EEG; ERP; MEG
2. action
3. graded
4. magnetic activity of many neurons; three-dimensional localization of the cell groups generating the measured field
5. EEG is much less expensive than MEG.

REVIEW 7-3

1. *in either order:* computed tomography *or* CT scan; magnetic resonance imaging *or* MRI
2. neural connections *or* fiber pathways; concentrations of brain metabolites
3. brain injury *or* brain damage
4. CT produces X-ray images of one object from many angles and then uses scanning software to combine them into a three-dimensional image of the brain.

REVIEW 7-4

1. *in any order:* functional magnetic resonance imaging *or* fMRI; optical tomography *or* fNIRS; functional positron emission tomography *or* PET
2. radioactively labeled molecules; neurochemical
3. cerebral blood flow
4. Resting-state images in PET and rs-fMRI can identify abnormalities in brain function. rs-fMRI can also identify functional connections in the resting brain.

REVIEW 7-5

1. biochemical; *in either order:* microdialysis; voltammetry
2. concordance rates
3. DNA; gene expression
4. Epigenetic studies show that life experience can alter gene expression and that these changes are associated with changes in neuronal structure and connectivity. Altered neuronal organization in turn is associated with changes in behavior.

REVIEW 7-6

1. *in any order:* temporal resolution; spatial resolution; degree of invasiveness
2. *any one or more:* EEG, ERP, *and/or* fNIRS; less expensive *or* inexpensive
3. Answers will vary but should touch on one or more of the methods described in Table 7-2. For example, cerebral voltammetry can be used to measure the change in dopamine concentration in the nucleus accumbens following the introduction of corticosterone, as was done by Wheeler and his colleagues.

REVIEW 7-7

1. behavioral
2. Animal Welfare Act
3. Animal experimentation can help researchers better understand the functions of human and nonhuman body, brain, and behavior, as well as develop medicines and treatments for humans and other animals.

CHAPTER 8

REVIEW 8-1

1. behavior
2. neural circuits
3. *any three in any order:* hormones; sensory experience; injuries; genes
4. Behaviors cannot emerge until the requisite neural structures are sufficiently mature.

REVIEW 8-2

1. neural tube
2. neurogenesis; gliogenesis
3. *in either order:* cell adhesion molecules *or* CAMs; tropic factors
4. *in either order:* myelination; synaptic pruning
5. Dynamic changes in frontal lobe structure (morphology) are related to the development of intelligence.

REVIEW 8-3

1. independent finger movements *or* the pincer grasp
2. vocabulary; sound processing
3. Piaget's stages of cognitive development
4. temporal lobe; basal ganglia
5. Correlation does not prove causation.

REVIEW 8-4

1. chemoaffinity hypothesis
2. amblyopia
3. testosterone
4. critical periods *or* sensitive periods
5. Adolescence is a time of rapid brain change related to pubertal hormones and psychosocial stressors, both of which make the brain vulnerable to disorders.

REVIEW 8-5

1. critical
2. SIDS *or* sudden infant death syndrome
3. visual *or* sensory
4. The brain retains its plasticity, or capacity to change, adapt, and learn, throughout our lifetimes.
5. Egg cells are formed early in female development and are not easily

changed by experience; because sperm is constantly being renewed, gene expression is more likely to be altered by experience and passed on through the germline.

CHAPTER 9

REVIEW 9-1
1. Sensory receptors
2. Receptive; density
3. brain
4. subjective
5. Each modality has many receptors and sends information to the cortex to form topographic maps.

REVIEW 9-2
1. retinal ganglion cells *or* RGCs
2. P *or* Parvocellular; M *or* magnocellular
3. *in either order:* geniculostriate; tectopulvinar
4. facial agnosia *or* prosopagnosia
5. The dorsal stream to the parietal lobe processes the visual guidance of movements (the *how*). The ventral stream to the temporal lobe processes the visual perception of objects (the *what*).

REVIEW 9-3
1. receptive fields
2. *in any order:* photoreceptors; retinal ganglion cells; lateral geniculate neurons; cortical neurons
3. topographic map
4. corpus callosum
5. The fovea is represented by a larger area in the cortex than the visual field's periphery, and thus there is more processing of foveal information in region V1 than of peripheral information.

REVIEW 9-4
1. bars of light
2. temporal
3. trichromatic theory
4. opponent
5. RGCs are excited by one wavelength of light and inhibited by another, producing two pairs of what seem to be color opposites—red versus green and blue versus yellow.

REVIEW 9-5
1. hemianopia
2. scotomas
3. monocular blindness
4. optic ataxia
5. Damage to the dorsal stream produces deficits in visually guided movements. Damage to the ventral stream produces deficits in object recognition.

CHAPTER 10

REVIEW 10-1
1. air pressure waves *or* compression waves *or* sound waves
2. *in any order:* frequency; amplitude; complexity
3. *in any order:* loudness; pitch; prosody; quality *or* timbre
4. temporal
5. Delivery speed, or the number of sound segments that can be analyzed per second, distinguishes speech and musical sounds from other auditory inputs. Nonlanguage sounds that are faster than 5 segments per second are heard as a buzz, yet we are capable of understanding speech delivered at nearly 30 segments per second. Random or aperiodic sounds are perceived as noise.

REVIEW 10-2
1. ossicles *or, in any order,* hammer, anvil, and stirrup
2. inner hair cells; cochlea *or* organ of Corti
3. *in either order:* basilar; tectorial
4. auditory *or* cochlear; auditory vestibular *or* eighth
5. inferior colliculus; medial geniculate nucleus
6. The planum temporale is larger in the left hemisphere, and Heschl's gyrus is larger in the right. In most people, this anatomical asymmetry correlates to a functional asymmetry: the left temporal cortex analyzes language-related sounds, whereas the right temporal cortex analyzes music-related ones.

REVIEW 10-3
1. tonotopic
2. cochlea
3. *in either order:* superior olive; trapezoid body
4. audition for action
5. The brain detects a sound's location via two mechanisms. Neurons in the brainstem (hindbrain) compute the ITD, the time difference in a sound wave's arrival at each ear. Other neurons in the brainstem compute IID, the difference in sound amplitude (loudness) in each ear.

REVIEW 10-4
1. language; music
2. *in any order:* Broca's area; supplementary speech area; face area of motor cortex
3. Wernicke's
4. Broca's
5. perfect (*or* absolute) pitch; amusic *or* tone deaf
6. Three lines of evidence support the idea that language is innate: the universality of language, the natural acquisition by

children, and the presence of syntax in all languages.

REVIEW 10-5
1. epigenetic mechanisms
2. left
3. spectrogram
4. Birdsong dialects demonstrate that the songs young birds hear influence how they sing.

CHAPTER 11

REVIEW 11-1
1. *in either order:* hierarchical; parallel
2. prefrontal; premotor; motor *or* M1
3. brainstem
4. spinal cord
5. Lower-level functions in the motor hierarchy can continue in the absence of higher-level ones, but the higher levels provide voluntary control over movements. When the brain is disconnected from the spinal cord, movement can no longer be controlled at will.

REVIEW 11-2
1. topographic; homunculus; larger
2. Position-point
3. lateral; anterior
4. trunk; *in either order:* arm, finger
5. muscles; *in either order:* flexes, extends
6. The motor cortex, M1, is organized into a set of functional categories that encode a movement lexicon, or dictionary. Used in different combinations, these few movements enable more complex movements.

REVIEW 11-3
1. basal ganglia; force
2. hyperkinetic; hypokinetic
3. accuracy; skills
4. The cerebellum compares an intended movement with the actual movement, calculates any necessary corrections, and informs the cortex to correct the movement.

REVIEW 11-4
1. hapsis; proprioception; nociception
2. posterior; anterior
3. pain gate
4. periaqueductal gray matter *or* PAG
5. vestibular; balance
6. Without proprioception, sensory information about body location and movement is lost and can be regained by only using vision.

REVIEW 11-5

1. primary; secondary; *in either order:* visual, auditory

2. apraxia

3. dorsal visual; ventral visual

4. Studies have demonstrated that unpredictability plays a role in the tickle perception, and because we can predict when we are about to tickle ourselves, we do not perceive the tickle sensation in these cases.

CHAPTER 12

REVIEW 12-1

1. rewarding

2. stimulation

3. androgen levels

4. innate releasing mechanisms *or* IRMs

5. In general, behavior is controlled by neural circuits that are modulated by a wide range of factors.

REVIEW 12-2

1. olfactory epithelium

2. orbitofrontal cortex *or* orbital frontal cortex *or* OFC

3. pheromones

4. allele of the taste receptor gene *TAS2R38;* taste buds

5. There is a vital link between human olfaction and social behavior. Growing evidence indicates that humans can identify their own odor, the odor of kin vs. non-kin, and the odor of friends vs. strangers, and that these different odors activate different regions of the brain.

REVIEW 12-3

1. regulatory; nonregulatory

2. hypothalamus

3. hormones

4. The behavioral column is composed of brainstem regions devoted to social behaviors, ingesting, and exploration and foraging behaviors. These functions are modulated by the cerebral hemispheres. The hypothalamus acts to organize these cerebral inputs and produce feedback loops that regulate cerebral information to orchestrate homeostasis and motivate behaviors.

REVIEW 12-4

1. *in any order:* lateral hypothalamus; ventromedial hypothalamus; paraventricular nucleus

2. enteric

3. Osmotic; hypovolemic

4. Cognitive factors that control eating include thinking about food and the association between environmental cues and the act of eating. The constant pairing of environmental cues with eating can result in the cues alone motivating eating behavior. Some eating disorders have a cognitive component.

REVIEW 12-5

1. *in either order:* hypothalamus; amygdala

2. *in either order:* organizing effects; activating effects

3. medial preoptic area; the amygdala

4. Variations in epigenetics effects could lead to different architecture and function of the hypothalamus among heterosexual, homosexual, and transgender individuals.

REVIEW 12-6

1. *in any order:* constructivist; appraisal; neuropsychological

2. *in any order:* hypothalamus; amygdala; prefrontal cortex

3. Transorbital leukotomy

4. (1) Tameness and loss of fear; (2) indiscriminate dietary behavior (eating many types of formerly rejected foods); (3) greatly increased autoerotic, homosexual, and heterosexual activity with inappropriate object choice (e.g., the sexual mounting of chairs); (4) tendency to attend and react to every visual stimulus; (5) tendency to examine all objects by mouth; (6) visual agnosia, an inability to recognize objects or drawings of objects.

REVIEW 12-7

1. rewarding

2. wanting; liking

3. dopamine; *in either order:* opioid, endocannabinoid

4. Intracranial self-stimulation is a phenomenon whereby animals learn to turn on a stimulating electric current to their brain, presumably because it activates the neural system that underlies reward.

CHAPTER 13

REVIEW 13-1

1. circannual; circadian

2. free-running; Zeitgebers

3. *any two in any order:* Light pollution; jet lag; working swing shifts; working night shifts

4. Circadian rhythm allows us to synchronize our behavior with our body's metabolic processes—so that we are hungry at optimal times for eating, for example, and tired at optimal sleep times.

REVIEW 13-2

1. superchiasmatic nucleus *or* SCN

2. retinohypothalamic; melanopsin ganglion *or* photosensitive retinal ganglion

3. shell; chemical; anatomical

4. Experimental evidence suggests that the circadian rhythm can put a time stamp on a behavioral event, rendering it easier to recall at the same time in the circadian cycle that it occurred in previously.

REVIEW 13-3

1. W (Waking); N-1 (NREM stage 1); N-2 (NREM stage 2); N-3 (NREM stage 3); R (REM)

2. EOG *or* electrooculogram; EMG *or* electromyogram; EEG *or* electroencephalogram

3. five; longer

4. Interpreting dreams is difficult because it is possible that the interpreter will impose his or her own explanation, or spin, on the dreams.

REVIEW 13-4

1. biological; restorative; memories

2. Explicit; implicit

3. place cells; NREM

4. microsleep

5. There are many types of memory and many types of sleep, which poses problems for any attempt to relate memory to sleep.

REVIEW 13-5

1. reticular activating system *or* RAS

2. coma

3. REM

4. subcoerulear

5. We have separate neural systems for keeping us awake while we are still (cholinergic) and awake when we move (serotonergic). Movement activates our serotonergic neurons, restoring arousal levels.

REVIEW 13-6

1. insomnia; narcolepsy

2. drug-dependent insomnia

3. sleep paralysis; cataplexy

4. REM sleep behavioral disorder *or* REM (R-sleep) without atonia; subcoerulear

5. Orexin is a peptide neurotransmitter that helps to maintain wakefulness, and orexin cells project to many brain regions to activate related systems. Orexin is probably one of many factors related to waking behavior, as animals with narcolepsy can be awake but then collapse into sleep.

CHAPTER 14

REVIEW 14-1

1. Pavlovian *or* classical

2. operant *or* instrumental

3. implicit; explicit

4. Episodic

5. Memory is not localized to any particular brain circuit or region. Rather, multiple memory circuits vary with the requirements of the memory task.

REVIEW 14-2

1. *in either order:* hippocampus; amygdala

2. basal ganglia

3. Lashley searched for explicit memory in the perceptual and motor systems of his animal subjects using invasive tests designed mostly for implicit memory. Milner studied a patient with medial temporal removal and used behavioral tests of both explicit and implicit memory.

REVIEW 14-3

1. *in either order:* hippocampus; neocortex or cortex

2. implicit

3. amygdala

4. consolidation

5. Emotional experiences stimulate hormonal and neurochemical activating systems that stimulate the amygdala. The amygdala in turn modulates the laying down of memory circuits in the rest of the brain.

REVIEW 14-4

1. long-term potentiation *or* LTP; long-term depression *or* LTD

2. GABAergic *or* inhibitory

3. *in either order:* synapse number; neuron number

4. hippocampus

5. behavioral sensitization

6. Plastic changes in neural networks can interfere with behavior essentially by learning behaviors that interfere with healthy function. Examples are addiction and PTSD.

REVIEW 14-5

1. *in any order:* learning new ways to solve problems; reorganizing the brain to do more with less; replacing the lost neurons

2. *in either order:* direct cortical stimulation; deep brain stimulation *or* DBS

3. neurotrophic

4. Functional improvement after brain injury reflects compensation rather than recovery.

CHAPTER 15

REVIEW 15-1

1. *in order:* attending to; identifying; making meaningful responses to

2. language; flexibility

3. neuron

4. Much of human thought is verbal. Language allows us to categorize information and provides a way to organize our behavior around time.

REVIEW 15-2

1. knowledge; cognition

2. temporal; parietal

3. *in either order:* plan movements; organize behavior over time

4. Mirror

5. Multimodal cortex allows the brain to combine characteristics of stimuli across different sensory modalities, whether we encounter the different stimuli together or separately.

REVIEW 15-3

1. cognitive neuroscience

2. brain connectome

3. cerebellum

4. social interactions

5. theory of mind

6. decision making

7. *in any order:* Understanding others; understanding oneself; self-regulation; social living

REVIEW 15-4

1. *in either order:* spatial behavior; music

2. *in either order:* controlling voluntary movement sequences; language

3. corpus callosum

4. Because the hemispheres process information differently, they think differently. The existence of language in the left hemisphere allows it to label computations and thus make inferences that the right hemisphere cannot. Our understanding of this asymmetry has implications for our study of certain behaviors and disorders.

REVIEW 15-5

1. *in either order:* sex; handedness

2. neural circuits

3. synesthesia

4. Gonadal hormones influence brain development and shape neural circuits in adulthood.

REVIEW 15-6

1. *g* factor *or* general intelligence; convergent; divergent; intelligence A; intelligence B; Parieto-Frontal Integration

2. structural; functional

3. epigenetic

4. Neuroimaging studies show that efficiency of prefrontal–parietal circuits is related to standard intelligence measures and that executive function is related to gray matter volume in the frontal lobe. The Parieto-Frontal Integration Theory proposes that specific cortical regions connected by white matter underlie intelligence and that individual differences in intelligence are related to structural and functional differences in these regions.

REVIEW 15-7

1. Consciousness

2. ventral visual stream

3. a semantic pointer

4. *Evolutionary theory* suggests that as organisms became more complex, more complex nervous systems were needed to coordinate activity, which led to the development of incentives and rewards, and thus to emotions, and eventually to a sense of self, or consciousness. *Information integration theory* suggests consciousness emerges from our ability to integrate information. *Semantic pointer competition theory* suggests that consciousness is a neural process emerging from complex neural networks.

CHAPTER 16

REVIEW 16-1

1. brainstem and limbic system; neocortex; dorsal frontal cortex

2. *in any order:* genetic errors; epigenetic mechanisms; progressive cell death; rapid cell death; loss of neural connections

3. PKU *or* phenylketonuria

4. The RDoC seeks to understand biological functions as a way to understand disorders and their treatment. The DSM begins by identifying a condition and then seeks to understand and treat that condition.

REVIEW 16-2

1. *in any order:* dopamine; glutamate; GABA

2. *in either order:* temporal; frontal

3. *in either order:* norepinephrine; serotonin

4. cognitive-behavioral therapy *or* CBT

5. Many genetic and epigenetic influences contribute to every behavior, including schizophrenia.

REVIEW 16-3

1. TBI *or* Traumatic brain injury

2. *in any order:* neurosurgical; electrophysiological; pharmacological; behavioral

3. ischemia; stroke

4. *in either order:* loss of cells from the substantia nigra; accumulation of Lewy bodies

5. Aerobic exercise and brain training are strategies for enhancing or stimulating neuroplasticity as we age.

GLOSSARY

A

absolutely refractory The state of an axon in the repolarizing period, during which a new action potential cannot be elicited (with some exceptions) because gate 2 of sodium channels, which are not voltage activated, are closed.

acetylcholine (ACh) First neurotransmitter discovered in the PNS and CNS; activates skeletal muscles in the SNS; either excites or inhibits internal organs in the ANS.

action potential Large, brief reversal in the polarity of an axon membrane.

activating effects Hormonal actions that influence activities in the adult brain.

activating system Neural pathways that coordinate brain activity through a single neurotransmitter; its cell bodies lie in a brainstem nucleus; axons are distributed through a wide CNS region.

adaptations Evolved anatomical/functional features that solved long-standing historical problems.

addiction A complex brain disorder characterized by escalation, compulsive drug taking, and relapse; called *substance use disorder* per the DSM-5.

afferent Conducting toward a CNS structure.

agonist Substance that enhances neurotransmitter function.

akathesia Small, involuntary movements or changes in posture; motor restlessness.

allele Alternative form of a gene; a gene pair contains two alleles.

allocortex Part of the cerebral cortex ("outer bark"), composed of three or four layers; plays a role in controlling motivational and emotional states as well as in certain forms of memory.

alpha rhythm Large, extremely regular brain waves with a frequency ranging from 7 to 11 Hz; found in most people when they are relaxed with eyes closed.

Alzheimer disease Degenerative brain disorder related to aging; first appears as progressive memory loss and later develops into generalized dementia.

amblyopia Condition in which vision in one eye is reduced as a result of disuse; usually caused by a failure of the two eyes to look in the same direction.

amnesia Partial or total loss of memory.

amphetamine Synthetic compound that increases the neurotransmitter dopamine in the synaptic cleft by reversing the dopamine transporter.

amplitude Stimulus intensity; in audition, roughly equivalent to loudness, graphed by the increasing height of a sound wave.

amusia Tone deafness—inability to distinguish between musical notes.

amygdala The part of the brain that participates in species-typical behaviors, emotion, and emotional memory. From the Greek word for *almond*, reflecting the general shape in the medial temporal lobe.

anabolic steroid Class of synthetic hormones related to testosterone that have both muscle-building (anabolic) and masculinizing (androgenic) effects; also called *anabolic–androgenic steroid*.

androgen Class of hormones that stimulates or controls masculine characteristics; related to level of sexual interest.

anencephaly Failure of the forebrain to develop.

anomalous speech representation Condition in which a person's speech zones are located in the right hemisphere or in both hemispheres.

anorexia nervosa Exaggerated concern with being overweight that leads to inadequate food intake and often excessive exercising; can lead to severe weight loss and even starvation.

antagonist Substance that blocks neurotransmitter function.

anterior spinothalamic tract Pathway from the spinal cord to the thalamus that carries information about pain and temperature toward the brain.

anterograde amnesia Inability to remember events subsequent to a disturbance of the brain such as head trauma, electroconvulsive shock, or neurodegenerative disease.

anterograde synaptic transmission Process that occurs when a neurotransmitter is released from a presynaptic neuron and binds to a receptor on the postsynaptic neuron.

anxiety disorder A disorder that includes a number of conditions in which unhelpful anxiety has a negative effect on daily life.

aphagia Failure to eat; may be due to an unwillingness to eat or to motor difficulties, especially with swallowing.

aphasia Inability to speak or comprehend language despite the presence of normal comprehension and intact vocal mechanisms. *Broca's aphasia* is the inability to speak fluently despite the presence of normal comprehension and intact vocal mechanisms. *Wernicke's aphasia* is the inability to understand or to produce meaningful language even though word production remains intact.

apoptosis Genetically programmed cell death.

apraxia Inability to make voluntary movements in the absence of paralysis or other motor or sensory impairment, especially an inability to make proper use of an object.

association cortex Neocortex outside primary sensory and motor cortices; functions to produce cognition.

associative learning Linkage of two or more unrelated stimuli to elicit a behavioral response.

astrocyte Star-shaped glial cell that provides structural support to CNS neurons and transports substances between neurons and blood vessels.

atonia Reduced muscle tone; condition of maximally low muscle inactivity produced by motor neuron inhibition.

attention Narrowing or focusing awareness to a part of the sensory environment or to a class of stimuli.

attention-deficit/hyperactivity disorder (ADHD) Developmental disorder characterized by core behavioral symptoms including impulsivity, hyperactivity, and/or inattention.

autism spectrum disorder (ASD) Range of cognitive symptoms from mild to severe that characterize autism; severe symptoms include greatly impaired social interaction, a bizarre and narrow range of interests, marked abnormalities in language and communication, and fixed, repetitive movements.

autoimmune disease Illness resulting from the loss of the immune system's ability to discriminate between foreign pathogens in the body and the body itself; abnormal immune response by the body against substances and tissues normally present in the body.

autonomic nervous system (ANS) Part of the PNS that regulates the functioning of internal organs and glands.

autoreceptor Self-receptor in a neuronal membrane; that is, it responds to the same transmitter released by the neuron; part of a negative feedback loop allowing the neuron to adjust its output.

axon Root, or single fiber, of a neuron that carries messages to other neurons.

axon collateral Branch of an axon.

axon hillock Juncture of soma and axon.

B

back propagation Reverse movement of an action potential into the soma and dendritic field of a neuron; postulated to play a role in plastic changes that underlie learning.

basal ganglia Subcortical forebrain nuclei that coordinate voluntary movements of the limbs and body; connected to the thalamus and to the midbrain.

basic rest–activity cycle (BRAC) Recurring cycle of temporal packets (about 90-minute periods in humans), during which an animal's level of arousal waxes and wanes.

basilar membrane Receptor surface in the cochlea that transduces sound waves into neural activity.

behavioral myopia "Nearsighted" behavior displayed under the influence of alcohol, wherein local and immediate cues become prominent; remote cues and consequences are ignored.

behavioral neuroscience Study of the biological bases of behavior in humans and other animals.

behavioral sensitization Escalating behavioral response to the repeated administration of a psychomotor stimulant such as amphetamine, cocaine, or nicotine; also called *drug-induced behavioral sensitization*.

behavioral therapy Treatment that applies learning principles, such as conditioning, to eliminate unwanted behaviors.

beta rhythm Fast brain-wave activity pattern associated with a waking EEG.

bilateral symmetry Body plan in which organs or parts present on both sides of the body are mirror images in appearance. For example, the hands are bilaterally symmetrical, whereas the heart is not.

binding problem Philosophical question focused on how the brain ties single and varied sensory and motor events together into a unified perception or behavior.

biological clock Neural system that times behavior by producing biorhythms.

biorhythm A natural rhythm in behavior or bodily process.

bipolar disorder Mood disorder characterized by periods of depression alternating with normal periods and periods of intense excitation, or *mania*.

bipolar neuron Sensory neuron with one axon and one dendrite.

blind spot Retinal region where axons forming the optic nerve leave the eye and where blood vessels enter and leave; has no photoreceptors and is thus said to be blind.

blob Region in V1 that contains color-sensitive neurons, as revealed by staining for cytochrome oxidase.

blood–brain barrier Protective partition between blood vessels and the brain formed by tight junctions between the cells that compose blood vessels in the brain; prohibits entry of an array of substances, including toxins, into the brain.

brain connectome Map of the complete structural and functional fiber pathways of the human brain in vivo.

brainstem Central structure of the brain (including the hindbrain, midbrain, thalamus, and hypothalamus) that is responsible for most life-sustaining, unconscious behavior.

Broca's area Anterior left-hemisphere speech area that functions with the motor cortex to produce movements needed for speaking.

C

carbon monoxide (CO) Gaseous neurotransmitter; activates cellular metabolism.

cataplexy State of atonia, as in R-sleep, occurring while a person is awake and active; linked to strong emotional stimulation.

cell adhesion molecule (CAM) Chemical molecule to which specific cells can adhere, thus aiding in migration.

cell assembly Hypothetical group of neurons that become functionally connected via common sensory inputs; proposed by Hebb as the basis of perception, memory, and thought.

cell body (soma) Core region of the cell containing the nucleus and other organelles for making proteins.

central nervous system (CNS) The brain and spinal cord, which together mediate behavior.

cerebellum Major brainstem structure specialized for learning and coordinating movements; assists the cerebrum in generating many behaviors.

cerebral cortex Heavily folded and layered tissue that is the outer structure of the forebrain; composed of neocortex and allocortex.

cerebral palsy (CP) Group of disorders that result from brain damage acquired perinatally (at or near birth).

cerebral voltammetry Technique used to identify the concentration of specific chemicals in the brain as animals behave freely.

cerebrospinal fluid (CSF) Clear solution of sodium, chloride, and other ions that is produced in the ventricles inside the brain and circulates around the brain and spinal cord until it is absorbed beneath the arachnoid layer in the subarachnoid space.

cerebrum (forebrain) Major structure of the forebrain that consists of two mirror-image hemispheres (left and right) and is responsible for most conscious behavior.

channel Opening in a protein embedded in the cell membrane that allows the passage of ions.

chemical synapse Junction at which messenger molecules are released when stimulated by an action potential.

chemoaffinity hypothesis Proposal that neurons or their axons and dendrites are drawn toward a signaling chemical that indicates the correct pathway.

chemogenetics Transgenic technique that combines genetics and synthetic drugs to activate targeted cells in living tissue.

cholinergic neuron Neuron that uses acetylcholine as its main neurotransmitter; *cholinergic* applies to any neuron that uses ACh as its main transmitter.

chordate Animal that has both a brain and a spinal cord.

chronic traumatic encephalopathy (CTE) Progressive degenerative disease caused by multiple concussions and other closed-head injuries, characterized by neurofibrillary tangles, plaques, cerebral atrophy, and expanded ventricles due to cell loss.

chronotype Time type; individual variations in circadian activity.

circadian rhythm Day–night rhythm.

cladogram Phylogenetic tree that branches repeatedly, suggesting a taxonomy of organisms based on the time sequence in which evolutionary branches arise.

clinical neuroscience Specialty in the field of neuroscience that focuses on the diagnosis and treatment of diseases and disorders affecting the brain and central nervous system.

clinical trial Consensual experiment directed toward developing a treatment.

cochlea Inner ear structure containing the auditory receptor cells.

cochlear implant Electronic device implanted surgically into the inner ear to transduce sound waves to neural activity and allow a deaf person to hear.

cognition Act or process of knowing or coming to know; in psychology, refers to thought processes; in behavioral neuroscience, refers to identification and planned response to stimuli.

cognitive enhancement Brain function enhancement by pharmacological, physiological, or surgical manipulation.

cognitive neuroscience Study of the neural bases of cognition.

cognitive therapy Psychotherapy based on the perspective that thoughts intervene between events and emotions, and thus the treatment of emotional disorders requires changing maladaptive patterns of thinking.

cognitive-behavioral therapy (CBT) Problem-focused, action-oriented, structured treatment for eliminating dysfunctional thoughts and maladaptive behaviors.

color constancy Phenomenon whereby an object's perceived color tends to remain constant relative to other colors, regardless of changes in illumination.

coma Prolonged state of deep unconsciousness resembling sleep.

common ancestor Forebear of two or more lineages or family groups; ancestral to both groups.

compensation Following brain damage, the neuroplastic ability to modify behavior from that used prior to the damage.

competitive inhibitor Drug used to treat overdoses and opioid addiction; an example is naloxone, which acts quickly to block opioid action by competing with the opioid for binding sites.

computed tomography (CT) X-ray technique that produces a static three-dimensional image (called a CT scan) of the brain in cross section.

concentration gradient Difference in the relative abundance of a substance among regions of a container; allows the substance to diffuse from an area of higher concentration to an area of lower concentration.

concussion Damage to the brain caused by a blow to the head.

conditioned response (CR) In Pavlovian conditioning, the learned response to a formerly neutral conditioned stimulus (CS).

conditioned stimulus (CS) In Pavlovian conditioning, an originally neutral stimulus that, after association with an unconditioned stimulus (UCS), triggers a conditioned response (CR).

cone Photoreceptor specialized for color and high visual acuity.

connectome All the pathways connecting regions of the CNS.

consciousness The mind's level of responsiveness to impressions made by the senses.

consolidation Process of stabilizing a memory trace after learning.

constraint-induced therapy Procedure in which restraint of a healthy limb forces a patient to use an impaired limb to enhance recovery of function.

contralateral neglect Ignoring a part of the body or world on the side opposite (contralateral to) that of a brain injury.

convergent thinking Form of thinking that searches for a single answer to a question (such as 2+2=?); contrasts with *divergent thinking*.

corpus callosum Band of white matter containing about 200 million nerve fibers that connects the two cerebral hemispheres to provide a route for direct communication between them.

cortical column Anatomic organization that represents a functional unit six cortical layers deep and approximately 0.5 mm square, perpendicular to the cortical surface.

corticospinal tract Bundle of nerve fibers directly connecting the cerebral cortex to the spinal cord, branching at the brainstem into an opposite-side lateral tract that informs movement of limbs and digits and a same-side anterior tract that informs movement of the trunk; also called *pyramidal tract*.

cranial nerves The 12 nerve pairs that control sensory and motor functions of the head, neck, and internal organs.

critical period Developmental window during which some event has a long-lasting influence on the brain; also, *sensitive period*.

culture Learned behaviors that are passed on from one generation to the next through teaching and imitation.

cytoarchitectonic map Map of the neocortex based on the organization, structure, and distribution of the cells.

D

deafferentation Loss of incoming sensory input, usually due to damage to sensory fibers; also, loss of any afferent input to a structure.

decibel (dB) Measure of the relative physical intensity of sounds.

declarative memory Ability to recount what one knows, to detail the time, place, and circumstances of events; often lost in amnesia.

deep brain stimulation (DBS) Neurosurgery in which electrodes implanted in the brain stimulate a targeted area with a low-voltage electrical current to produce or facilitate behavior.

default network Brain network of interacting regions of the frontal and parietal lobes that have highly correlated activity.

delta rhythm Slow brain-wave activity pattern associated with deep sleep.

dementia Acquired and persistent syndrome of intellectual impairment characterized by memory and other cognitive deficits and impairment in social and occupational functioning.

dendrite Branching extension of a neuron's cell membrane; greatly increases the cell's surface area; collects information from other cells.

dendritic spine Protrusion that greatly increases the dendrite's surface area; typical point of dendritic contact with the axons of other cells.

depolarization Decrease in electrical charge across a membrane, usually due to the inward flow of sodium ions.

dermatome Body segment corresponding to a segment of the spinal cord.

Diagnostic and Statistical Manual of Mental Disorders (DSM) The American Psychiatric Association's classification system for psychiatric disorders.

diaschisis Neural shock that follows brain damage in which areas connected to the site of damage show a temporary arrest of function.

dichotic listening Experimental procedure for simultaneously presenting a different auditory input to each ear through stereophonic earphones.

diencephalon The between brain, which integrates sensory and motor information on its way to the cerebral cortex.

diffusion tensor imaging (DTI) Magnetic resonance imaging method that can image fiber pathways in the brain by detecting the directional movements of water molecules.

diffusion Movement of ions from an area of higher concentration to an area of lower concentration through random motion.

dimer Two proteins combined into one.

disinhibition theory Explanation holding that alcohol has a selective depressant effect on the brain's frontal cortex, which controls judgment, while sparing subcortical structures responsible for more instinctual behaviors, such as desire.

diurnal animal Organism that is active chiefly during daylight.

divergent thinking Form of thinking that searches for multiple solutions to a problem (how many ways can a pen be used?); contrasts with *convergent thinking*.

dopamine (DA) Amine neurotransmitter involved in coordinating movement, attention, learning, and reinforcing behaviors.

dopamine hypothesis of schizophrenia Idea that excess dopamine activity causes symptoms of schizophrenia.

dorsal stream Visual processing pathway from V1 to the parietal lobe; guides movements relative to objects.

dorsolateral prefrontal cortex (DLPFC) Brodmann areas 9 and 46; makes reciprocal connections with posterior parietal cortex and superior temporal sulcus; responsible for selecting behavior and movement with respect to temporal memory.

Down syndrome Chromosomal abnormality resulting in intellectual impairment and other abnormalities, usually caused by an extra chromosome 21.

dualism Philosophical position that both a nonmaterial mind and a material body contribute to behavior.

dyslexia Impairment in learning to read and write; probably the most common learning disability.

E

echolocation The ability to use sound to locate objects in space.

efferent Conducting away from a CNS structure.

electrical stimulation Passage of an electrical current from the uninsulated tip of an electrode through tissue, resulting in changes in the electrical activity of the tissue.

electrocorticography (ECoG) Graded potentials recorded with electrodes placed directly on the surface of the brain.

electroencephalogram (EEG) Graph of electrical activity from the brain, which is mainly composed of graded potentials from many neurons.

electrographic seizures Abnormal rhythmic neuronal discharges; may be recorded by an electroencephalogram.

embodied behavior Theory that the movements we make and the movements we perceive in others are central to communication with others.

emotion Cognitive interpretation of subjective experiences that can influence thought and behavior.

emotional memory Memory for the affective properties of stimuli or events.

encephalization quotient (EQ) Jerison's quantitative measure of brain size obtained from the ratio of actual brain size to expected brain size, according to the principle of proper mass, for an animal of a particular body size.

end plate On a muscle, the receptor–ion complex that is activated by the release of the neurotransmitter acetylcholine from the terminal of a motor neuron.

endocannabinoid Class of lipid neurotransmitters, including anandamide and 2-AG, synthesized at the postsynaptic membrane to act on receptors at the presynaptic membrane; affects appetite, pain, sleep, mood, memory, anxiety, and the stress response.

enteric nervous system (ENS) Mesh of neurons embedded in the lining of the gut, running from the esophagus through the colon; controls the gut.

entorhinal cortex Cortex located on the medial temporal lobe surface; provides a major route for neocortical input to the hippocampal formation; often degenerates in Alzheimer disease.

entrain To determine or modify the period of a biorhythm.

ependymal cell Glial cell that makes and secretes CSF; found on the walls of the brain's ventricles.

epidermal growth factor (EGF) Neurotrophic factor; stimulates the subventricular zone to generate cells that migrate into the striatum and eventually differentiate into neurons and glia.

epigenetics Differences in gene expression related to environment and experience.

epinephrine (EP) Chemical messenger that acts as a neurotransmitter in the CNS and as a hormone to mobilize the body for fight or flight during times of stress; also known as *adrenaline*.

episodic memory Autobiographical memory for events pegged to specific place and time contexts.

estrogen Variety of sex hormones responsible for the distinguishing characteristics of the female.

event-related potential (ERP) Complex electroencephalographic waveform related in time to a specific sensory event.

evolutionary psychology Discipline that seeks to apply principles of natural selection to understand the causes of human behavior.

excitation Increase in the activity of a neuron or brain area.

excitatory postsynaptic potential (EPSP) Brief depolarization of a neuron membrane in response to stimulation, making the neuron more likely to produce an action potential.

explicit memory Conscious memory: subjects can retrieve an item and indicate that they know the retrieved item is the correct one.

extinction In neurology, neglect of information on one side of the body when presented simultaneously with similar information on the other side of the body.

extrastriate (secondary visual) cortex (V2–V5) Visual cortical areas in the occipital lobe outside the striate cortex.

eyeblink conditioning Experimental technique in which subjects learn to pair a formerly neutral stimulus with a defensive blinking response.

F

facial agnosia Face blindness—the inability to recognize faces; also called *prosopagnosia*.

fear conditioning Conditioned emotional response between a neutral stimulus and an unpleasant event, such as a shock, that results in a learned association.

festination Tendency to engage in a behavior, such as walking, faster and faster.

fetal alcohol spectrum disorder (FASD) Range of physical and intellectual impairments observed in some children born to alcoholic parents.

filopod (pl. filopodia) Process at the end of a developing axon that reaches out to search for a potential target or to sample the intercellular environment.

focal seizure Seizure that arises at a synchronous, hyperactive, localized brain region (at a focus).

forebrain Evolutionarily the most recent addition to the brain; coordinates advanced cognitive functions such as thinking, planning, and language; contains the allocortex, neocortex, and basal ganglia.

fovea Central region of the retina specialized for high visual acuity; its receptive fields are at the center of the eye's visual field.

free-running rhythm Rhythm of the body's own devising in the absence of all external cues.

frequency Number of cycles a wave completes in a given time.

frontal lobe Part of the cerebral cortex, which performs the brain's executive functions, such as decision making, and voluntary movement; lies anterior to the central sulcus and beneath the frontal bone of the skull.

functional magnetic resonance imaging (fMRI) Magnetic resonance imaging technique that measures brain activity indirectly by detecting changes associated with blood flow; often used to measure cerebral blood flow during cognitive testing or resting.

functional near-infrared spectroscopy (fNIRS) Noninvasive technique that gathers light transmitted through cortical tissue to image oxygen consumption; form of optical tomography.

G

G protein Guanyl nucleotide–binding protein coupled to a metabotropic receptor; when activated, binds to other proteins.

gamma-aminobutyric acid (GABA) Amino acid neurotransmitter; typically inhibits neurons.

ganglia Collection of nerve cells that functions somewhat like a brain.

gap junction Area of contact between adjacent cells in which connexin proteins in each cell form connecting hemichannels, which, when open, allow ions to pass between the two cells; also called an *electrical synapse*.

gate Protein embedded in a cell membrane that allows substances to pass through the membrane on some occasions but not on others.

gender identity The degree to which a person feels male or female.

gene (DNA) methylation Epigenetic process in which a methyl group attaches to the DNA sequence, suppressing or enabling gene expression.

gene DNA segment that encodes the synthesis of a particular protein.

generalized anxiety disorder Persistently high levels of anxiety often accompanied by maladaptive behaviors to reduce anxiety; thought to be caused by chronic stress.

generalized seizure Seizure that starts at a focal location then spreads rapidly and bilaterally to distributed networks in both hemispheres.

geniculostriate system Projections from the retina to the lateral geniculate nucleus to the visual cortex.

genotype Particular genetic makeup of an individual.

glabrous skin Skin that does not have hair follicles but contains larger numbers of sensory receptors than do hairy skin areas.

glial cell Nervous system cell that provides insulation, nutrients, and support and that aids in repairing neurons and eliminating waste products.

glioblast Product of a progenitor cell that gives rise to different types of glial cells.

glucocorticoid One of a group of steroid hormones, such as cortisol, secreted in times of stress; important in protein and carbohydrate metabolism.

glutamate (Glu) Amino acid neurotransmitter; typically excites neurons.

gonadal (sex) hormone One of a group of hormones, such as testosterone, that control reproductive functions and bestow sexual appearance and identity as male or female.

graded potential Small voltage fluctuation across the cell membrane.

gray matter Areas of the nervous system composed predominantly of neuronal cell bodies that collect and modify information and capillary blood vessels that support this activity.

growth cone Growing tip of an axon.

growth spurt Sporadic period of sudden growth that lasts for a finite time.

gyri (sing. gyrus) Small protrusions or bumps formed by the folding of the cerebral cortex.

H

habituation Learned behavior in which the response to a stimulus weakens with repeated presentations.

hair cell Specialized neurons in the cochlea tipped by cilia; when stimulated by waves in the cochlear fluid, the cilia bend and generate graded potentials in inner hair cells, the auditory receptor cells.

hapsis Perceptual ability to discriminate objects on the basis of touch.

hemisphere Literally, half a sphere, referring to one side of the cerebrum.

hemorrhagic stroke A stroke resulting from bleeding from a blood vessel.

hertz (Hz) Measure of sound wave frequency (repetition rate); 1 hertz equals 1 cycle per second.

heterozygous Having two different alleles for the same trait.

hindbrain Evolutionarily the oldest part of the brain; contains the pons, medulla, reticular formation, and cerebellum, the structures that coordinate and control most voluntary and involuntary movements.

hippocampus From the Greek word for *seahorse*; distinctive allocortical structure lying in the medial temporal lobe; participates in species-typical behaviors, memory, and spatial navigation and is vulnerable to the effects of stress.

histamine (H) Neurotransmitter that controls arousal and waking; can cause the constriction of smooth muscles; when activated in allergic reactions, constricts airway and contributes to asthma.

homeostatic hormone One of a group of hormones that maintain internal metabolic balance and regulate physiological systems in an organism.

homeostatic mechanism Process that maintains critical body functions within a narrow, fixed range.

hominid General term referring to primates that walk upright, including all forms of humans, living and extinct.

homonymous hemianopia Blindness of the entire left or right visual field.

homozygous Having two identical alleles for a trait.

homunculus Representation of the human body in the sensory or motor cortex; also any topographical representation of the body by a neural area.

HPA axis Hypothalamic–pituitary–adrenal circuit that controls the production and release of hormones related to stress.

Huntington disease Hereditary disease characterized by chorea (ceaseless involuntary jerky movements) and progressive dementia, ending in death.

hydrocephalus Buildup of fluid pressure in the brain and, in infants, swelling of the head, if the flow of CSF is blocked; can result in intellectual impairment.

hydrogen sulfide (H₂S) Gaseous neurotransmitter; slows cellular metabolism.

hyperconnectivity Increased local connections between two related brain regions.

hyperkinetic symptom Excessive involuntary movement, as seen in Tourette syndrome.

hyperphagia Overeating that leads to significant weight gain.

hyperpolarization Increase in electrical charge across a membrane, usually due to the inward flow of chloride ions or the outward flow of potassium ions.

hypersomnia Disorder of falling asleep at inappropriate times, or a difficulty staying awake.

hypnagogic hallucination Dreamlike event occurring as sleep begins or while a person is in a state of cataplexy.

hypokinetic symptom Paucity of movement, as seen in Parkinson disease.

hypothalamus Diencephalon structure that contains many nuclei associated with temperature regulation, eating, drinking, and sexual behavior.

hypovolemic thirst Thirst produced by a loss of overall fluid volume from the body.

I

implicit memory Unconscious memory: subjects can demonstrate knowledge, such as a skill, conditioned response, or recall of events on prompting but cannot explicitly retrieve the information.

imprinting Formation of an attachment by an animal to one or more objects or animals at a critical period in development.

inhibition Decrease in the activity of a neuron or brain area.

inhibitory postsynaptic potential (IPSP) Brief hyperpolarization of a neuron membrane in response to stimulation, making the neuron less likely to produce an action potential.

initial segment Area near where the axon meets the cell body that is rich in voltage-gated channels, which generate the action potential.

innate releasing mechanism (IRM) Hypothetical mechanism that detects specific sensory stimuli and directs an organism to take a particular action.

insomnia Symptom of a number of disorders characterized by an inability to fall asleep or stay asleep.

insula Multifunctional cortical tissue located within the lateral fissure; contains language and taste perception–related regions and neural structures underlying social cognition.

intelligence A Hebb's term for innate intellectual potential, which is highly heritable and cannot be measured directly.

intelligence B Hebb's term for observed intelligence, influenced by experience and other factors in the course of development; measured by intelligence tests.

interneuron Association cell interposed between a sensory neuron and a motor neuron; in mammals, interneurons constitute most of the brain's neurons.

ionotropic receptor Embedded membrane protein; acts as (1) a binding site for a neurotransmitter and (2) a pore that regulates ion flow to directly and rapidly change membrane voltage.

ischemic stroke A stroke resulting from a blocked blood vessel.

J

jet lag Fatigue and disorientation resulting from rapid travel through time zones and exposure to a changed light–dark cycle.

K

Klüver–Bucy syndrome Behavioral syndrome, characterized especially by hypersexuality, that results from bilateral injury to the temporal lobe.

Korsakoff syndrome Permanent loss of the ability to learn new information (anterograde amnesia) and to retrieve old information (retrograde amnesia) caused by diencephalic damage resulting from chronic alcoholism or malnutrition that produces a vitamin B 1 deficiency.

L

lateralization Localization of function primarily on one side of the brain.

law of Bell and Magendie Sensory fibers are dorsal and motor fibers are ventral.

learned taste aversion Acquired association between a specific taste or odor and illness; leads to an aversion to foods that have the taste or odor.

learning set Rules of the game; implicit understanding of how a problem can be solved with a rule that can be applied in many different situations.

learning Relatively persistent or even permanent change in behavior that results from experience.

Lewy body Circular fibrous structure found in several neurocognitive disorders; forms within the cytoplasm of neurons and is thought to result from abnormal neurofilament metabolism.

light pollution Exposure to artificial light that changes activity patterns and so disrupts circadian rhythms.

limbic system A conceptual system controlling affective and motivated behaviors and certain forms of memory with key anatomy lying between the neocortex and brainstem; includes the cingulate cortex, amygdala, and hippocampus, among other structures.

locked-in syndrome Condition in which a patient is aware and awake but cannot move or communicate verbally because of complete paralysis of nearly all voluntary muscles except the eyes.

long-term depression (LTD) Long-lasting decrease in synaptic effectiveness after low-frequency electrical stimulation.

long-term potentiation (LTP) Long-lasting increase in synaptic effectiveness after high-frequency stimulation.

luminance contrast Amount of light an object reflects relative to its surroundings.

M

magnetic resonance imaging (MRI) Technique that produces a static three-dimensional brain image by passing a strong magnetic field through the brain, followed by a radio wave, then measuring a radiofrequency signal emitted from hydrogen atoms.

magnetic resonance spectroscopy (MRS) Magnetic resonance imaging method that uses the hydrogen proton signal to determine the concentration of brain metabolites; used to identify changes in specific markers of neuronal function, which is promising for accurate diagnosis of traumatic brain injuries.

magnetoencephalogram (MEG) Magnetic potentials recorded from detectors placed outside the skull.

magnocellular (M) cell Large visual system neuron sensitive to moving stimuli.

major depression Mood disorder characterized by prolonged feelings of worthlessness and guilt, disruption of normal eating habits, insomnia, a general slowing of behavior, and frequent thoughts of suicide.

masculinization Process by which exposure to androgens (male sex hormones) alters the brain, rendering it identifiably male.

materialism Philosophical position that behavior can be explained as a function of the nervous system without recourse to the mind.

medial forebrain bundle (MFB) Tract that connects brainstem structures with various parts of the limbic system; forms the activating projections that run from the brainstem to the basal ganglia and frontal cortex.

medial geniculate nucleus Major thalamic region concerned with audition.

medial pontine reticular formation (MPRF) Nucleus in the pons that participates in R-sleep.

melatonin Hormone secreted by the pineal gland during the dark phase of the day–night cycle; influences daily and seasonal biorhythms.

meme An idea, a behavior, or a style that spreads from person to person within a culture.

memory Ability to recall or recognize previous experience.

Ménière disease Disorder of the middle ear resulting in vertigo and loss of balance.

meninges Three layers of protective tissue—dura mater, arachnoid, and pia mater—that encase the brain and spinal cord.

mentalism Explanation of behavior as a function of the nonmaterial mind.

metabolic syndrome Combinations of medical disorders, including obesity and insulin abnormalities, that collectively increase the risk of developing cardiovascular disease and diabetes.

metabotropic receptor Embedded membrane protein with a binding site for a neurotransmitter linked to a G protein; can affect other receptors or act with second messengers to affect other cellular processes, including opening a pore.

metaplasticity Interaction among different plastic changes in the brain.

microdialysis Technique used to determine the chemical constituents of extracellular fluid in freely moving animals.

microelectrode A microscopic insulated wire or a saltwater-filled glass tube whose uninsulated tip is used to stimulate or record from neurons.

microglia Glial cells that originate in the blood, aid in cell repair, and scavenge debris in the nervous system.

microsleep Brief sleep period lasting a second or so.

midbrain Central part of the brain; contains neural circuits for hearing and seeing as well as for orienting movements.

mind–body problem Difficulty of explaining how a nonmaterial mind and a material body interact.

minimally conscious state (MCS) Condition in which a person can display some rudimentary behaviors, such as smiling or uttering a few words, but is otherwise not conscious.

mirror neuron Cell in the primate premotor and parietal cortex that fires when an individual observes an action taken by another individual.

monoamine oxidase (MAO) inhibitor Drug that blocks the enzyme monoamine oxidase from degrading such neurotransmitters as 5-HT, NE, and DA.

monosynaptic reflex Reflex requiring one synapse between sensory input and movement.

motor neuron Cell that carries efferent information from the brain and spinal cord to make muscles contract.

motor sequence Movement modules preprogrammed by the brain and produced as a unit.

multiple sclerosis (MS) Nervous system disorder resulting from the loss of myelin around axons in the CNS.

mutation Alteration of an allele that yields a different version of its protein.

myelin Glial coating that surrounds axons in the central and peripheral nervous systems; prevents adjacent neurons from short-circuiting.

N

narcolepsy A rare condition with symptoms that can include sleep paralysis and cataplexy.

natural selection Darwin's theory explaining how new species evolve and how existing species change over time. Differential success in the reproduction of different characteristics (phenotypes) results from the interaction of organisms with their environment.

neocortex Most recently expanded outer layer ("new bark") of the forebrain, composed of about six layers of gray matter. Its name is a misnomer, as it actually isn't newer because it arose at the same time during evolution as other forms of cortex. It is also called *isocortex* because it is almost always six-layered, with few exceptions.

neoteny Process in which juvenile stages of predecessors become adult features of descendants; idea derived from the observation that more recently evolved species resemble the young of their common ancestors.

nerve Large collection of axons coursing together *outside* the CNS.

nerve growth factor (NGF) Neurotrophic factor that stimulates neurons to grow dendrites and synapses and in some cases promotes the survival of neurons.

nerve impulse Propagation of an action potential on the membrane of an axon.

nerve net Simple nervous system that has no center but consists of neurons that receive sensory information and connect directly to other neurons that move muscles.

netrin Member of chemoattractive tropic molecules that guide axon growth.

neural Darwinism Hypothesis that the processes of cell death and synaptic pruning are, like natural selection in species, the outcome of competition among neurons for connections and metabolic resources in a neural environment.

neural network Functional group of neurons that connects wide areas of the brain and spinal cord.

neural plate Primitive neural tissue that gives rise to the neural tube.

neural stem cell Self-renewing multipotential cell that gives rise to any of the different types of neurons and glia in the nervous system.

neural tube Structure in the early stage of brain development from which the brain and spinal cord develop.

neuritic plaque Area of incomplete necrosis (dead tissue) consisting of a central protein core (amyloid) surrounded by degenerative cellular fragments; often seen in the cortex of people with neurocognitive disorders such as Alzheimer disease.

neuroblast Product of a progenitor cell that gives rise to any of the different types of neurons.

neuroeconomics Interdisciplinary field that seeks to understand how the brain makes decisions.

neuron Specialized nerve cell engaged in information processing.

neuropeptide Short, multifunctional amino acid chain (fewer than 100 amino acids); acts as a neurotransmitter and can act as a hormone; may contribute to learning.

neuroplasticity The nervous system's potential to physically or chemically modify itself in response to environmental change and to compensate for age-related changes and injury.

neuroprosthetics Field that develops computer-assisted devices to replace lost biological function.

neuroprotectant Drug used to try to block the cascade of poststroke neural events.

neuropsychology Study of the relationships between brain function and behavior, especially in humans.

neurotransmitter Chemical with an excitatory or inhibitory effect when released by a neuron onto a target.

neurotrophic factor Chemical compound that supports growth and differentiation in developing neurons and may act to keep certain neurons alive in adulthood.

nitric oxide (NO) Gaseous neurotransmitter; acts, for example, to dilate blood vessels, aid digestion, and activate cellular metabolism.

nociception Perception of pain, temperature, and itch.

node of Ranvier The part of an axon that is not covered by myelin.

nonregulatory behavior Behavior unnecessary to an animal's basic survival needs.

non-REM sleep (N-sleep) Slow-wave sleep associated with rhythms having slower waves with larger amplitude.

noradrenergic neuron From *adrenaline*, Latin for *epinephrine*; a neuron containing norepinephrine.

norepinephrine (NE) Neurotransmitter that accelerates heart rate in mammals; found in the brain and in the sympathetic division of the ANS; also known as *noradrenaline*.

nuclei (sing. nucleus) A group of neurons forming a cluster that can be identified using special stains.

O

obesity Excessive accumulation of body fat.

obsessive-compulsive disorder (OCD) Behavior characterized by compulsively repeated acts (such as hand washing) and repetitive, often unpleasant, thoughts (obsessions).

occipital lobe Part of the cerebral cortex where visual scene processing begins; the most posterior part of the neocortex, it lies beneath the occipital bone.

ocular dominance column Functional column in the visual cortex maximally responsive to information coming from one eye.

oligodendroglia Glial cells in the CNS that myelinate axons.

operant conditioning Learning procedure in which the consequences (such as obtaining a reward) of a particular behavior (such as pressing a bar) increase or decrease the probability of the behavior occurring again; also called *instrumental conditioning*.

opponent process Explanation of color vision that emphasizes the importance of the apparently opposing color pairs: red versus green and blue versus yellow.

optic ataxia Deficit in the visual control of reaching and other movements.

optic chiasm Junction of the optic nerves, one from each eye, at which the axons from the nasal halves of the retinas cross to the brain's opposite side.

optogenetics Transgenic technique that combines genetics and light to excite or inhibit targeted cells in living tissue.

orbitofrontal cortex (OFC) Prefrontal cortex behind the eye sockets (the *orbits*); receives projections from the dorsomedial nucleus of the thalamus; central to a variety of emotional and social behaviors, including eating; also called *orbital frontal cortex*.

organizing effects Hormonal actions that influence the organizational development of the fetal brain.

orienting movement Movement related to sensory inputs, such as turning the head to see the source of a sound.

oscilloscope Specialized device that serves as a sensitive voltmeter, registering changes in voltage over time.

osmotic thirst Thirst that results from a high concentration of dissolved chemicals, or *solutes*, in body fluids.

ossicle Bone of the middle ear; includes hammer, anvil, and stirrup.

otoacoustic emissions Spontaneous or evoked sound waves produced within the ear by the cochlea that escape from the ear.

P

pain gate Hypothetical neural circuit in which activity in fine-touch and pressure pathways diminishes the activity in pain and temperature pathways.

panic disorder Recurrent attacks of intense terror that come on without warning and without any apparent relationship to external circumstances.

parahippocampal cortex Cortex located along the dorsal medial temporal lobe surface.

paralysis Loss of sensation and movement due to nervous system injury.

paraplegia Paralysis of the legs due to spinal cord injury.

parasympathetic division Part of the autonomic nervous system that acts in opposition to the sympathetic division—for example, preparing the body to rest and digest by reversing the alarm response or stimulating digestion.

parietal lobe Part of the cerebral cortex that directs movements toward a goal or to perform a task, such as grasping an object; lies posterior to the central sulcus and beneath the parietal bone at the top of the skull.

Parkinson disease Disorder of the motor system correlated with a loss of dopamine from the substantia nigra and characterized by tremors, muscular rigidity, and a reduction in voluntary movement.

parvocellular (P) cell Small visual system neuron sensitive to differences in form and color.

Pavlovian conditioning Learning achieved when a neutral stimulus (such as a tone) comes to elicit a response after its repeated pairing with some event (such as delivery of food); also called *classical conditioning* or *respondent conditioning*.

peptide hormone Chemical messenger synthesized by cellular DNA that acts to affect the target cell's physiology.

perception Subjective interpretation of sensations by the brain.

periaqueductal gray matter (PAG) Nuclei in the midbrain that surround the cerebral aqueduct joining the third and fourth ventricles; PAG neurons contain circuits for species-typical behaviors (e.g., female sexual behavior) and play an important role in the modulation of pain.

peribrachial area Cholinergic nucleus in the dorsal brainstem having a role in R-sleep behaviors; projects to medial pontine reticular formation.

period Time required to complete an activity cycle.

peripheral nervous system (PNS) All the neurons in the body outside the brain and spinal cord; provides sensory and motor connections to and from the central nervous system.

perirhinal cortex Cortex lying next to the rhinal fissure on the ventral surface of the brain.

perseveration Tendency to emit repeatedly the same verbal or motor response to varied stimuli.

persistent vegetative state (PVS) Condition in which a person is alive but unaware, unable to communicate or to function independently at even the most basic level.

phenotype Set of individual characteristics that can be seen or measured.

phenotypic plasticity An individual's capacity to develop into a range of phenotypes.

phenylketonuria (PKU) Behavioral disorder caused by elevated levels of the amino acid phenylalanine in the blood and resulting from a defect in the gene for the enzyme phenylalanine hydroxylase; the major symptom is severe developmental disability.

pheromone Odorant biochemical released by one animal that acts as a chemosignal and can affect the physiology or behavior of another animal.

phobia Fear of a clearly defined object or situation.

photoreceptor Specialized retinal neuron that transduces light into neural activity.

pituitary gland Endocrine gland attached to the bottom of the hypothalamus; its secretions control the activities of many other endocrine glands; associated with biological rhythms.

place cells Hippocampal neurons maximally responsive to specific locations in the world.

plasticity Body's potential for physical or chemical change; enhances its adaptability to environmental change and its ability to compensate for injury. (In the brain and nervous system, this potential is called *neuroplasticity*.)

position-point theory Idea that the motor cortex allows an appropriate body part to be moved to a point in space.

positron emission tomography (PET) Imaging technique that detects changes in blood flow by measuring changes in the uptake of compounds such as oxygen or glucose; used to analyze the metabolic activity of neurons.

posterior spinothalamic tract Pathway that carries fine-touch and pressure fibers toward the brain.

postsynaptic membrane Membrane on the transmitter, or input, side of a synapse.

posttraumatic stress disorder (PTSD) Syndrome characterized by physiological arousal associated with recurrent memories and dreams arising from a traumatic event that occurred months or years earlier.

preparedness Predisposition to respond to certain stimuli differently from other stimuli.

presynaptic membrane Axon terminal membrane on the transmitter, or output, side of a synapse.

primary auditory cortex (area A1) Asymmetrical structures within Heschl's gyrus in the temporal lobes; receives input from the ventral region of the medial geniculate nucleus.

primary visual cortex (V1) Striate cortex in the occipital lobe that receives input from the lateral geniculate nucleus.

priming Using a stimulus to sensitize the nervous system to a later presentation of the same or a similar stimulus.

prion From *proteinaceous* and *infectious*; an abnormally folded protein that causes progressive neurocognitive disorders.

procedural memory Ability to recall a movement sequence or how to perform some act or behavior.

progenitor cell (precursor cell) Cell derived from a stem cell that migrates and produces a neuron or a glial cell.

proprioception Perception of the position and movement of the body, limbs, and head.

prosody Melodic tone of the speaking voice.

protein Folded-up polypeptide chain that serves a particular function in the body.

psyche Synonym for *mind*; an entity once proposed to be the source of human behavior.

psychoactive drug Substance that acts to alter mood, thought, or behavior; is used to manage neuropsychological illness, and may be taken recreationally.

psychobiotics Treatment that uses live bacteria (probiotics) or compounds to enhance the growth of gut bacteria (prebiotics).

psychological construct Idea or set of impressions that some mental ability exists as an entity; memory, language, and emotion are examples.

psychomotor activation Increased behavioral and cognitive activity so that at certain levels of consumption, the drug user feels energetic and in control.

psychopharmacology Study of how drugs affect the nervous system and behavior.

psychosurgery Any neurosurgical technique intended to alter behavior.

psychotherapy Talk therapy derived from Freudian psychoanalysis and other psychological interventions.

pump Protein in the cell membrane that actively transports a substance across the membrane.

Purkinje cell Distinctively shaped interneuron found in the cerebellum.

pyramidal cell Distinctively shaped interneuron found in the cerebral cortex.

Q

quadrantanopia Blindness of one quadrant of the visual field.

quadriplegia Paralysis of the legs and arms due to spinal cord injury.

quantum (pl. quanta) Number of neurotransmitter molecules, equivalent to the content of a single synaptic vesicle, that produces a just-observable change in postsynaptic electric potential.

R

radial glial cell Path-making cell that a migrating neuron follows to its appropriate destination.

rapidly adapting receptor Body sensory receptor that responds briefly to the onset of a stimulus on the body.

rate-limiting factor Any chemical in limited supply that restricts the pace at which another chemical can be synthesized.

real-time fMRI (rt-fMRI) Behavior-modification technique in which individuals learn to change their behavior by controlling their own patterns of brain activation.

receptive field Region of sensory space (for example, skin surface) in which a stimulus modifies a receptor's activity.

reconsolidation Process of restabilizing a memory trace after the memory is revisited.

referred pain Pain that arises in one of the internal organs but is felt on the surface of the body.

regulatory behavior Behavior motivated to meet an animal's survival needs.

reinforcer In operant conditioning, any event that strengthens the behavior it follows.

relatively refractory The state of an axon in the later phase of an action potential, during which higher-intensity electrical current is required to produce another action potential; a phase during which potassium channels are still open.

releasing hormone Peptide released by the hypothalamus that increases or decreases hormone release from the anterior pituitary.

REM sleep (R-sleep) Faster brain-wave pattern displayed by the neocortical EEG record during sleep.

resting potential Electrical charge across the insulating cell membrane in the absence of stimulation; a store of potential energy produced by a greater negative charge on the intracellular side relative to the extracellular side.

resting-state fMRI (rs-fMRI) Magnetic resonance imaging method that measures changes in oxygen when the individual is resting (not engaged in a specific task).

reticular activating system (RAS) Large reticulum (mixture of cell nuclei and nerve fibers) that runs through the center of the brainstem; associated with sleep–wake behavior and behavioral arousal; also called the *reticular formation*.

reticular formation Midbrain area in which nuclei and fiber pathways are mixed, producing a netlike appearance; associated with sleep–wake behavior and behavioral arousal; also called the *reticular activating system (RAS)*

retina Light-sensitive surface at the back of the eye, consisting of neurons and photoreceptor cells.

retinal ganglion cell (RGC) One of a group of retinal neurons with axons that give rise to the optic nerve.

retinohypothalamic tract Neural route formed by axons of photosensitive retinal ganglion cells (pRGCs) from the retina to the suprachiasmatic nucleus; allows light to entrain the SCN's rhythmic activity.

retrograde amnesia Inability to remember events that took place before the onset of amnesia.

reuptake Inactivation of a neurotransmitter when membrane transporter proteins bring the transmitter back into the presynaptic axon terminal for reuse.

rod Photoreceptor specialized for functioning at low light levels.

S

saccades Small, fast, random eye movements designed to keep photoreceptors exposed to ever-changing visual stimuli to prevent habituation.

saltatory conduction Fast propagation of an action potential at successive nodes of Ranvier; *saltatory* means "leaping."

schizophrenia Behavioral disorder characterized by delusions, hallucinations, disorganized speech, blunted emotion, agitation or immobility, and a host of associated symptoms.

Schwann cell Glial cell in the PNS that myelinates sensory and motor axons.

scotoma Small blind spot in the visual field caused by migraine or by a small lesion of the visual cortex.

scratch reflex Automatic response in which an animal's hind limb reaches to remove a stimulus from the surface of its body.

second messenger Chemical that initiates a biochemical process when activated by a neurotransmitter (the first messenger).

segmentation Division into a number of parts that are similar; refers to the idea that many animals, including vertebrates, are composed of similarly organized body segments.

selective serotonin reuptake inhibitor (SSRI) Drug that blocks 5-HT reuptake into the presynaptic terminal and most commonly used to treat depression.

semaphorins Class of chemorepulsive molecules that deflect axons from inappropriate regions.

sensation Registration by the sensory organs of physical stimuli from the environment.

sensitization Learned behavior in which the response to a stimulus strengthens with repeated presentations.

sensory neuron Cell that detects or carries sensory information into the spinal cord and brain.

serotonin (5-HT) Amine neurotransmitter; helps to regulate mood and aggression, appetite and arousal, perception of pain, and respiration.

sexual dimorphism Differential development of brain areas in the two sexes.

sexual orientation A person's pattern of sexual attraction—to the opposite sex or to the same sex or to both sexes.

sleep apnea Inability to breathe during sleep, causing a sleeper to wake up to breathe.

sleep paralysis Atonia and dreaming that occur when a person is awake, usually just falling asleep or waking up.

sleeping beauty syndrome A rare condition in which the sufferer has recurring bouts of excessive sleeping.

slowly adapting receptor Body sensory receptor that responds as long as a sensory stimulus is on the body.

small-molecule transmitter Quick-acting neurotransmitter synthesized in the axon terminal from products derived from the diet.

social neuroscience Interdisciplinary field that seeks to understand how the brain mediates social interactions.

somatic nervous system (SNS) Part of the PNS that includes the cranial and spinal nerves to and from the muscles, joints, and skin, which produce movement, transmit incoming sensory input, and inform the CNS about the position and movement of body parts.

somatosensory neuron Brain cell that brings sensory information from the body into the spinal cord.

sound wave Mechanical displacement of molecules caused by changing pressure that possesses the physical properties of frequency, amplitude, and complexity. Also referred to as a *compression wave.*

spatial summation Addition of one graded potential to another that occur close in space.

species Group of organisms that can interbreed.

species-typical behavior Behavior that is characteristic of all members of a species, such as walking in salamanders.

stereotaxic apparatus Surgical instrument that permits a researcher or neurosurgeon to target a specific part of the brain.

steroid hormone Fat-soluble chemical messenger synthesized from cholesterol.

storage granule Membranous compartment that holds several vesicles containing a neurotransmitter.

stretch-activated channel Ion channel on a tactile sensory neuron that activates in response to stretching of the membrane, initiating a nerve impulse.

striate cortex Primary visual cortex (V1) in the occipital lobe; shows stripes (striations) on staining.

striatum Caudate nucleus and putamen of the basal ganglia.

stroke Sudden appearance of neurological symptoms as a result of severely reduced blood flow.

substance abuse A pattern of drug use in which people rely on a drug chronically and excessively, allowing it to occupy a central place in their life.

subunit Protein molecule that assembles with other protein molecules.

subventricular zone Lining of neural stem cells surrounding the ventricles in adults.

sudden infant death syndrome (SIDS) Unexplained death while asleep of a seemingly healthy infant less than 1 year old.

sulci (sing. *sulcus*) Grooves in brain matter; most are in the neocortex or cerebellum.

supplementary speech area Speech production region on the left frontal lobe dorsal surface.

sympathetic division Part of the autonomic nervous system that arouses the body for action, such as mediating the involuntary fight-or-flight response to alarm by increasing heart rate and blood pressure.

synapse Spatial junction between one neuron and another; forms the information transfer site between neurons.

synaptic cleft Gap separating the neuronal presynaptic membrane from the postsynaptic membrane.

synaptic vesicle Membranous compartment that encloses a fixed number (called a *quantum*) of neurotransmitter molecules.

synesthesia Ability to perceive a stimulus of one sense as the sensation of a different sense, as when sound produces a sensation of color; literally, *feeling together.*

syntax Sets of rules for putting together words; proposed to be unique to human language.

synthetic biology Design and construction of biological devices, systems, and machines not found in nature.

T

tardive dyskinesia Inability to stop the tongue or other body parts from moving; motor side effect of neuroleptic drugs.

Tay-Sachs disease Inherited birth defect caused by the loss of genes that encode the enzyme necessary for breaking down certain fatty substances; appears 4 to 6 months after birth and results in intellectual disability, physical changes, and death by about age 5.

tectopulvinar system Projections from the retina to the superior colliculus to the pulvinar (thalamus) to the parietal and temporal visual areas.

tectum Roof (area above the ventricle) of the midbrain; its functions are sensory processing, particularly visual and auditory, and the production of orienting movements.

tegmentum Floor (area below the ventricle) of the midbrain; a collection of nuclei with movement-related, species-specific, and pain perception functions.

temporal lobe Part of the cerebral cortex that includes hearing, language, musical abilities, facial recognition, and emotional processing; lies below the lateral fissure, beneath the temporal bone at the side of the skull.

temporal summation Addition of one graded potential to another that occur close in time.

terminal button (end foot) Knob at the tip of an axon that conveys information to other neurons.

testosterone Sex hormone secreted by the testes and responsible for the distinguishing characteristics of the male.

thalamus Diencephalon structure through which information from all sensory systems is organized, integrated, and projected into the appropriate region of the neocortex.

theory of mind Ability to attribute mental states to others.

threshold potential Voltage on a neural membrane at which an action potential is triggered by the opening of sodium and potassium voltage-activated channels; about –50 mV relative to extracellular surround. Also called *threshold limit*.

tonotopic representation In audition, structural organization for processing of sound waves from lower to higher frequencies.

topographic Representing the different functional areas of the CNS.

topographic map Spatially organized neural representation of the external world.

topographic organization Neural spatial representation of the body or areas of the sensory world perceived by a sensory organ.

Tourette syndrome Disorder of the motor system, characterized by involuntary vocalizations (sometimes including curse words and grunting sounds) and odd, involuntary movements of the body, especially of the face and head.

tract Large collection of axons coursing together *in* the CNS.

transcranial magnetic stimulation (TMS) Procedure in which a magnetic coil is placed over the skull to stimulate the underlying brain; used either to induce behavior or to disrupt ongoing behavior.

transgender Possessing personal characteristics that transcend traditional gender boundaries and corresponding sexual norms; a person's belief that he or she was born the wrong sex.

transgenic animal Product of technology in which one or more genes from one species is introduced into the genome of another species to be passed along and expressed in subsequent generations.

transmitter-activated channel Receptor complex that has both a receptor site for a chemical and a pore through which ions can flow.

transmitter-activated receptor Protein that has a binding site for a specific neurotransmitter and is embedded in the membrane of a cell.

transporter Protein molecule that pumps substances across a membrane.

traumatic brain injury (TBI) Damage to the brain that results from a blow to the head.

tricyclic Drug, characterized by its three-ring chemical structure, that blocks 5-HT reuptake transporter proteins.

tripartite synapse Functional integration and physical proximity of the presynaptic membrane, postsynaptic membrane, and their intimate association with surrounding astrocytes.

tropic molecule Signaling molecule that attracts or repels growth cones.

tumor Mass of new tissue that grows uncontrolled and independent of surrounding structures.

U

unconditioned response (UCR) Unlearned, naturally occurring response to an unconditioned stimulus (UCS), such as salivation when food is in the mouth.

unconditioned stimulus (UCS) A stimulus that naturally and automatically (unconditionally) triggers an unconditioned response (UCR).

V

ventral stream Visual processing pathway from V1 to the temporal lobe for object identification and perceiving related movements.

ventricles Cavities in the brain that make and contain CSF.

ventrolateral thalamus Part of the thalamus that carries information about body senses to the somatosensory cortex.

vertebrae (sing. vertebra) The bones that form the spinal column.

vestibular system Somatosensory system comprising a set of receptors in each inner ear that respond to body position and to movement of the head.

virtual reality (VR) exposure therapy Controlled virtual immersion environment that, by allowing individuals to relive traumatic events, gradually desensitizes them to stress.

visual field Region of the visual world seen by the eyes.

visual-form agnosia Inability to recognize objects or drawings of objects.

visuospatial memory Use of visual information to recall an object's location in space.

voltage gradient Difference in charge between two regions that allows a flow of current if the two regions are connected.

voltage-activated channel Gated protein channel that opens or closes only at specific membrane voltages.

voltmeter Device that measures the strength of electrical voltage by recording the difference in electrical potential between two points.

vomeronasal organ (VNO) Collection of neurons that detect pheromones; this organ plays a role in reproduction and social behavior in many mammals, though its specific function in humans is disputed.

W

wanting-and-liking theory Explanation holding that when a drug is associated with certain cues, the cues themselves elicit desire for the drug; also called *incentive sensitization theory*.

Wernicke's area Secondary auditory cortex (planum temporale) lying behind Heschl's gyrus at the rear of the left temporal lobe; regulates language comprehension. Also known as the *posterior speech zone*.

white matter Areas of the nervous system with fat-rich, myelin-sheathed neuronal axons that form the connections between neurons.

wild type Typical allele (most common in a population).

withdrawal symptom Physical and psychological behavior displayed by a user when drug use ends.

Z

Zeitgeber Environmental event that entrains biological rhythms; German for "time giver."

zinc An ion transmitter that is packaged and stored in vesicles and that is then released and interacts with several receptors.

zoopharmacognosy Behavior in which non-human animals self-medicate.

REFERENCES

CHAPTER 1

Berwick, R., & Chomsky, N. (2016). *Why only us: Language and evolution.* Cambridge, MA: MIT Press.

Bianchi, S, Reyes, L. D., Hopkins, W. D., Taglialatela, J. P., & Sherwood, C. C. (2016). Neocortical grey matter distribution underlying voluntary, flexible vocalizations in chimpanzees. *Scientific Reports, 6,* 34733.

Darwin, C. (1871). *The descent of man, and selection in relation to sex.* London: J. Murray.

Darwin, C. (1963). *On the origin of species by means of natural selection, or the preservation of favored races in the struggle for life.* New York: New American Library. (Original work published 1859.)

Darwin, C. (1965). *The expression of the emotions in man and animals.* Chicago: University of Chicago Press. (Original work published 1872.)

Deary, I. J. (2000). *Looking down on human intelligence: From psychometrics to the brain.* Oxford Psychology Series, No. 34. New York: Oxford University Press.

Dennett, D. (1978). *The intentional stance.* Cambridge, MA: MIT Press.

Descartes, R. (1972). *Treatise on man* (T. S. Hall, Trans.). Cambridge, MA: Harvard University Press. (Original work published 1664.)

Dunbar, R. (1998). *Grooming, gossip, and the evolution of language.* Cambridge, MA: Harvard University Press.

Eibl-Eibesfeldt, I. (1970). *Ethology: The biology of behavior.* New York: Holt, Rinehart and Winston.

Flynn, J. R. (2012). *Are we getting smarter? Rising IQ in the twenty-first century.* Cambridge: Cambridge University Press.

Fonseca-Azevedo K., & Herculano-Houzel, S. (2012). Metabolic constraint imposes tradeoff between body size and number of brain neurons in human evolution. *Proceedings of the National Academy of Sciences of the United States of America, 109,* 18571–18576.

Gardner, H. (2006). *Multiple intelligences: New horizons.* New York: Basic Books.

Gardner, R. A., & Gardner, B. T. (1969). Teaching sign language to a chimpanzee. *Science, 165,* 664–672.

Gordon, A. D., Nevell, L., & Wood, B. (2008). The *Homo floresiensis* cranium (LB1): Size, scaling, and early *Homo* affinities. *Proceedings of the National Academy of Sciences of the United States of America, 105,* 4650–4655.

Gould, S. J. (1981). *The mismeasure of man.* New York: Norton.

Gross, C. G. (1995). Aristotle on the brain. *The Neuroscientist, 1*(4), 245–250.

Grove, M. (2017). Environmental complexity, life history, and encephalisation in human evolution. *Biology and Philosophy, 32*(3), 395–420.

Hampshire, A., Highfield, R. R., Parkin, B. L., & Owen, A. M. (2012). Fractionating human intelligence. *Neuron, 76,* 1225–1237.

Hebb, D. O. (1949). *The organization of behavior: A neuropsychological theory.* New York: Wiley.

Herculano-Houzel, S., Avelino-de-Souza, K., Neves, K., Porfirio, J., Messeder, D., Mattos Feijo, L., et al. (2014). The elephant brain in numbers. *Frontiers in Neuroanatomy, 12,* 8–46.

Heron, W. (1957). The pathology of boredom. *Scientific American, 196*(1), 52–56.

Herringa, R. J., Birn, R. M., Ruttle, P. L., Burghy, C. A., Stodola, D. E., Davidson, R. J., & Essex, M. J. (2013). Childhood maltreatment is associated with altered fear circuitry and increased internalizing symptoms by late adolescence. *Proceedings of the National Academy of Sciences of the United States of America, 110,* 19119–19124.

Jacobson, E. (1932). Electrophysiology of mental activities. *American Journal of Psychology, 44,* 677–694.

Jerison, H. J. (1973). *The evolution of the brain and intelligence.* New York: Academic Press.

Johanson, D., & Edey, M. (1981). *Lucy: The beginnings of humankind.* New York: Warner Books.

Kisser, J., Waldstein, S. R, Evans, M. K., & Zonderman, A. B. (2017). Lifetime prevalence of traumatic brain injury in a demographically diverse community sample. *Brain Injury, 31*(5), 620–623.

Kunz, A. R., & Iliadis, C. (2007). Hominid evolution of the arteriovenous system through the cranial base and its relevance for craniosynostosis. *Child's Nervous System, 23,* 1367–1377.

Levchenko, A., Kanapin, A., Samsonova, A., & Gainetdinov, R. (2018). Human accelerated regions and other human-specific sequence variations in the context of evolution and their relevance for brain development. *Genome Biology and Evolution, 10*(1), 166–188.

Linge, F. R. (1990). Faith, hope, and love: Nontraditional therapy in recovery from serious head injury, a personal account. *Canadian Journal of Psychology, 44,* 116–129.

Mesoudi, A., Whiten, A., & Laland, K. N. (2006). Towards a unified science of cultural evolution. *Behavioural and Brain Sciences, 29,* 329–347.

Milton, K. (2003). The critical role played by animal source foods in human (*Homo*) evolution. *Journal of Nutrition, 133*(Suppl. 2), 3886S–3892S.

Owen, A. M. (2015). Using functional magnetic resonance imaging and electroencephalography to detect consciousness after severe brain injury. *Handbook of Clinical Neurology, 127,* 277–293.

Pickering, R., Dirks, P. H., Jinnah, Z., de Ruiter, D. J., Churchill, S. E., Herries, A. I., et al. (2011). *Australopithecus sediba* at 1.977 Ma and implications for the origins of the genus *Homo. Science, 333,* 1421–1423.

Prinz, J. (2008). Is consciousness embodied? In P. Robbins and. M. Aydede (Eds.), *Cambridge handbook of situated cognition* (pp. 419–436). Cambridge: Cambridge University Press.

Sankararaman, S., Mallick, S., Dannemann, M., Prüfer, K., Kelso, J., Pääbo, S., et al. (2014). The genomic landscape of Neanderthal ancestry in present-day humans. *Nature, 507,* 354–357.

Savage-Rumbaugh, S. (1999). Ape communication: Between a rock and a hard place in origins of language—What non-human primates can tell us. In B. J. King (Ed.), *Origins of language: What non-human primates can tell us* (pp. 115–188). Santa Fe, NM: School of American Research Press.

Schiff, N. D., & Fins, J. J. (2007). Deep brain stimulation and cognition: Moving from animal to patient. *Current Opinion in Neurology, 20,* 638–642.

Stedman, H. H., Kozyak, B. W., Nelson, A., Thesier, D. M., Su, L. T., Low, D. W., et al. (2004). Myosin gene mutation correlates with anatomical changes in the human lineage. *Nature, 428,* 415–418.

Stout, D., & Hecht, E. E. (2017). Evolutionary neuroscience of cumulative culture. *Proceedings of the National Academy of Sciences of the United States of America, 114*(30), 7861–7868.

Tattersall, I. (2017). Why was human evolution so rapid? In A. Marom & E. Hovers (Eds.), *Human paleontology and prehistory: Contributions in honor of Yoel Rak* (pp. 1–9). Amsterdam: Springer.

Terkel, J. (1995). Cultural transmission in the black rat: Pinecone feeding. *Advances in the Study of Behavior, 24,* 119–154.

Villmoare, B., Kimbel, W. H., Seyoum, C., Campisano, C. J., DiMaggio, E. J., Rowan, J., et al. (2015). Early *Homo* at 2.8 Ma from Ledi-Geraru, Afar, Ethiopia. *Science, 20,* 1352–1355.

Watson, S. K., Townsend, S. W., Schel, A. M., Wilke, C., Wallace, E. K., Cheng, L., et al. (2015). Vocal learning in the functionally referential food grunts of chimpanzees. *Current Biology, 5,* 495–499.

Weiner, J. (1995). *The beak of the finch.* New York: Vintage.

Workman, A. D., Charvet, C. J., Clancy, B., Darlington, R. B., & Finlay, B. L. (2013). Modeling transformations of neurodevelopmental sequences across mammalian species. *Journal of Neuroscience, 33,* 7368–7380.

Zollikofer, C. P. (2012). Evolution of hominid cranial ontogeny. *Progress in Brain Research, 195,* 273–292.

CHAPTER 2

Avetisyan, M., Schill, E. M., & Heuchkeroth, R. O. (2015). Building a second brain in the bowel. *Journal of Clinical Investigation, 125,* 899–907.

Barton, R. A. (2012). Embodied cognitive evolution and the cerebellum. *Philosophical Transactions of the Royal Society B, 367,* 2097–2107.

Baumann, O., Borra, R. J., Bower, J. M., Cullen, K. E., Habas, C., Ivry, R. B., et al. (2015). Consensus paper: The role of the cerebellum in perceptual processes. *Cerebellum, 14,* 197–220.

Brodmann, K. (1909). *Vergleichende Lokalisationlehr der Grosshirnrinde in ihren Prinzipien dargestellt auf Grund des Zellenbaues.* Leipzig: J. A. Barth.

Fiorito, G., & Scotto, P. (1992). Observational learning in *Octopus vulgaris. Science, 256,* 545–547.

GBD 2015 Mortality and Causes of Death Collaborators. (2016). Global, regional, and national life expectancy, all-cause mortality, and cause-specific mortality for 249 causes of death, 1980–2015: A systematic analysis for the Global Burden of Disease Study 2015. *Lancet 388*(10053), 1459–1544.

Gilbert, S. F., & Epel, D. (2009). *Ecological developmental biology: Integrating epigenetics, medicine, and evolution.* New York: Sinauer.

Goyal, M., Demchuk, A. M., Menon, B. K., Eesa, M., Rempel, J. L., Thornton, J., et al. (2015). Randomized assessment of rapid endovascular treatment of ischemic stroke. *New England Journal of Medicine, 372*(11), 1019–1030.

Hatcher, M. A., & Starr, J. A. (2011). Role of tissue plasminogen activator in ischemic stroke. *Annals of Pharmacotherapy, 45,* 364–371.

Langhorne, P., Bernhardt, J., & Kwakkel, G. (2011). Stroke rehabilitation. *Lancet, 277,* 1693–1702.

Sender, R., Fuchs, S., & Milo, R. (2016). Are we really vastly outnumbered? Revisiting the ratio of bacterial to host cells in humans. *Cell, 164*(3), 337–340.

Schmahmann, J. D. (2010). The role of the cerebellum in cognition and emotion: Personal reflections since 1982 on the dysmetria of thought hypothesis, and its historical evolution from theory to therapy. *Neuropsychology Reviews, 20,* 236–260.

CHAPTER 3

Adinolfi, A., Carbone, C., Leo, D., Gainetdinov, R. R., Laviola, G., & Adriani, W. (2018). Novelty-related behavior of young and adult DAT-KO rats: Implication for cognitive and emotional phenotypic patterns. *Genes, Brain and Behavior, 17*(4), e12463.

Belykh, E., Miller, E. J., Hu, D., Martirosyan, N. L., Woolf, E. C., Scheck, A. C., et al. (2018). Scanning fiber endoscope improves detection of 5-ALA induced protoporphyrin IX fluorescence at the boundary of infiltrative glioma. *World Neurosurgery, 113,* e51–e69.

Carulli, D. (2018). Perineuronal nets, a mechanism to control brain plasticity. *The Scientist, 32,* https://www.the-scientist.com.

Di Lorenzo, R., & Ahluwalia, M. S. (2017). Targeted therapy of brain metastases: Latest evidence and clinical implications. *Therapeutic Advances in Medical Oncology, 9,* 781–796.

Eddy, C. M., & Rickards, H. E. (2015). Theory of mind can be impaired prior to motor onset in Huntington's disease. *Neuropsychology, 29,* 792–798.

Guerrero-Bosagna, C. (2017). Evolution with no reason: A neutral view on epigenetic changes, genomic variability and evolutionary novelty. *Bioscience, 67,* 469–476.

Hayes, P. (2017). *Advancing health care through personalized medicine.* New York: Taylor & Francis.

Herculano-Houzel, S., Manger, P. R., & Kaas, J. H. (2014). Brain scaling in mammalian evolution as a consequence of concerted and mosaic changes in numbers of neurons and average neuronal cell size. *Frontiers in Neuroanatomy, 8,* 77.

Hirokawa, T., Zou, Y., Kurihara, Y., Jiang, Z., Sakakibara, Y., Ito, H., et al. (2017). Regulation of axonal regeneration by the level of function of the endogenous Nogo receptor antagonist LOTUS. *Scientific Reports, 7,* 12119.

Iwano, S., Sugiyama, M., Hama, H., Watakabe, A., Hasegawa, N., Kuchimaru, T., et al. (2018). Single-cell bioluminescence imaging of deep tissue in freely moving animals. *Science, 359*(6378), 935–939.

Jardim-Messeder, D., Lambert, K., Noctor, S., Pestana, F. M., de Castro Leal, M. E., Bertelsen, M. F., et al. (2017). Dogs have the most neurons, though not the largest brain: Trade-off between body mass and number of neurons in the cerebral cortex of large carnivoran species. *Frontiers in Neuroanatomy, 11,* 118.

Kaati, G., Bygren, L. O., Pembrey, M., & Sjöström, M. (2007). Transgenerational response to nutrition, early life circumstances and longevity. *European Journal of Human Genetics, 15,* 784–790.

Kenny, A., Plank, M. J., & David, T. (2018). The role of astrocytic calcium and TRPV4 channels in neurovascular coupling. *Journal of Computer Neuroscience, 44,* 97–114.

Lannes, N., Eppler, E., Etemad, S., Yotovski, P., & Filgueira, L. (2017). Microglia at center stage: A comprehensive review about the versatile and unique residential macrophages of the central nervous system. *Oncotarget, 8,* 114393–114413.

Lodato, M. A., Rodin, R. E., Bohrson, C. L., Coulter, M. E., Barton, A. R., Kwon, M., et al. (2018). Aging and neurodegeneration are associated with increased mutations in single human neurons. *Science, 359*(6375), 555–559.

Mathews, N., Christensen, A. L., O'Grady, R., Mondada, F., & Dorigo, M. (2017). Mergeable nervous systems for robots. *Nature Communications, 8,* 1754.

Mimori, T., Nariai, N., Kojima, K., Sato, Y., Kawai, Y., Yamaguchi-Kabata, Y., et al. (2015). Estimating copy numbers of alleles from population-scale high-throughput sequencing data. *BMC Bioinformatics, 16*(Suppl. 1), S4.

Ostrom, Q. T., Gittleman, H., Xu, J., Kromer, C., Wolinsky, Y., Kruchko, C., & Barnholtz-Sloan, J. S. (2016). CBTRUS statistical report: Primary brain and other central nervous system tumors diagnosed in the United States in 2009–2013. *Neuro-Oncology, 18*(Suppl. 5), v1–v75.

Ramón y Cajal, S. (1909–1911). *Histologie du systeme nerveux de l'homme et des vertebres.* Paris: Maloine.

Reeve, R., van Schaik, A., Jin, C., Hamilton, T., Torben-Neilsen, B., & Webb, B. (2007). Directional hearing in a silicon cricket. *Biosystems, 87,* 307–313.

Rogers, J. (2018). The behavioral genetics of nonhuman primates: Status and prospects. *American Journal of Physical Anthropology, 65,* 23–36.

Stricker-Shaver, J., Novati, A., Yu-Taeger, L., & Nguyen, H. P. (2018). Genetic rodent models of Huntington disease. *Advances in Experimental Medicine and Biology, 1049,* 29–57.

Vinauger, C., Lahondère, C., Wolff, G. H., Locke, L. T., Liaw, J. E., Parrish, J. Z., et al. (2018). Modulation of host learning in *Aedes aegypti* mosquitoes. *Current Biology, 28,* 333–344.

Wahlsten, D., & Ozaki, H. S. (1994). Defects of the fetal forebrain in acallosal mice. In M. Lassonde & M. A. Jeeves (Eds.), *Callosal agenesis* (pp. 125–132). New York: Plenum.

Yapijakis, C. (2017). Huntington disease: Genetics, prevention, and therapy approaches. *Advances in Experimental Medicine and Biology, 987,* 55–65.

CHAPTER 4

Bartholow, R. (1874). Experimental investigation into the functions of the human brain. *American Journal of Medical Sciences, 67,* 305–313.

Bender, K. J., & Trussell, L. O. (2012). The physiology of the axon initial segment. *Annual Review of Neuroscience, 35,* 249–265.

Bhalla, D., Godet, B., Druet-Cabanac, M., & Preux, P. M. (2011). Etiologies of epilepsy: A comprehensive review. *Expert Review of Neurotherapeutics, 11,* 861–876.

Cendes, F., Theodore, W. H., Brinkmann, B. H., Sulc, V., & Cascino, G. D. (2016). Neuroimaging of epilepsy. *Handbook of Clinical Neurology, 136,* 985–1014.

Crotty, P., Sangrey, T., & Levy, W. B. (2006). Metabolic energy cost of action potential velocity. *Journal of Neurophysiology, 96,* 1237–1246.

Descartes, R. (1972). *Treatise on man* (T. S. Hall, Trans.). Cambridge, MA: Harvard University Press. (Original work published 1664.)

Eccles, J. (1965). The synapse. *Scientific American, 21*(1), 56–66.

Hodgkin, A. L., & Huxley, A. F. (1939). Action potentials recorded from inside nerve fiber. *Nature, 144,* 710–711.

Höfflin, F., Jack, A., Riedel, C., Mack-Bucher, J., Roos, J., Corcelli C., et al. (2017). Heterogeneity of the axon initial segment in interneurons and pyramidal cells of rodent visual cortex. *Front Cell Neuroscience, 11,* 332.

Khalilov, I., Minlebaev, M., Mukhtarov, M., & Khazipov, R. (2015). Dynamic changes from depolarizing to hyperpolarizing GABAergic actions during giant depolarizing potentials in the neonatal rat hippocampus. *Journal of Neuroscience, 37,* 12635–12642.

Pan, Z.-H., Lu, Q., Bi, A., Dizhoor, A. M., & Abrams, G. W. (2015). Optogenetic approaches to restoring vision. *Annual Reviews of Vision Science, 1,* 185–210.

Reich, D. S., Lucchinetti, C. F., & Calabresi, P. A. (2018). Multiple sclerosis. *The New England Journal of Medicine, 378*(2), 169–180.

Rezania, K., Soliven, B., Baron, J., Lin, H., Penumalli, V., & van Besien, K. (2012). Myasthenia gravis, an autoimmune manifestation of lymphoma and lymphoproliferative disorders: Case reports and review of literature. *Leukemia & Lymphoma, 53,* 371–380.

Rho, J., Sankar, R., & Stafstrom, C. E. (Eds.). (2010). *Epilepsy: Mechanisms, models, and translational perspectives.* Boca Raton, FL: CRC Press.

Schiess, M., Urbanczik, R., & Senn, W. (2016). Somato-dendritic synaptic plasticity and error-backpropagation in active dendrites. *PLOS Computational Biology, 12*(2), e1004638.

Sterley, T.-L., Baimoukhametova, D., Füzesi, T., Zurek, A. A., Daviu, N., Rasiah, N. P., et al. (2018). Social transmission and buffering of synaptic changes after stress. *Nature Neuroscience, 21,* 393–403.

Stys, P. K. (2013). Pathoetiology of multiple sclerosis: Are we barking up the wrong tree? *F1000Prime Reports, 5,* 20.

CHAPTER 5

Anand, A., Patience, A. A., Sharma, N., & Khurana, N. (2017). The present and future of pharmacotherapy of Alzheimer's disease: A comprehensive review. *European Journal of Pharmacology, 815,* 364–375.

Bailey, C. H., Kandel, E. R., & Harris, K. M. (2015). Structural components of synaptic plasticity and memory consolidation. *Cold Spring Harbor Perspectives in Biology, 7*(7), a021758.

Ballard, A., Tetrud, J. W., & Langston, J. W. (1985). Permanent human parkinsonism due to 1-methyl-4-phenyl-1, 2, 3, 6-tetrahydropyridine (MPTP). *Neurology, 35,* 949–956.

Barbeau, A., Murphy, G. F., & Sourkes, T. L. (1961). Excretion of dopamine in diseases of basal ganglia. *Science, 133,* 1706–1707.

Birkmayer, W., & Hornykiewicz, O. (1961). Der L-3, 4-Dioxyphenylalanin (L-DOPA) Effekt bei der Parkinson A Kinase. *Wiener Klinische, 73,* 787–789.

Bosch, M., & Hayashi, Y. (2012). Structural plasticity of dendritic spines. *Current Opinion in Neurobiology, 22,* 383–388.

Dere, E., & Zlomuzica, A. (2012). The role of gap junctions in the brain in health and disease. *Neuroscience & Biobehavioral Reviews, 36,* 206–217.

Ehringer, H., & Hornykiewicz, O. (1960/1974). Distribution of noradrenaline and dopamine (3-hydroxytyramine) in the human brain and their behavior in the presence of disease affecting the extrapyramidal system. In J. Marks (Ed.), *The treatment of Parkinsonism with L-dopa* (pp. 45–56). Lancaster, U.K.: MTP Medical and Technical Publishing.

Hamilton, T. J., Wheatley, B. M., Sinclair, D. B., Bachmann, M., Larkum, M. E., & Colmers, W. F. (2010). Dopamine modulates synaptic plasticity in dendrites of rat and human dentate granule cells. *Proceedings of the National Academy of Sciences of the United States of America, 107*(42), 18185–18190.

Hebb, D. O. (1949). *The organization of behavior.* New York: Wiley.

Heuser, J. E., & Reese, T. S. (1977). Structure of the synapse. In E. R. Kandel (Ed.), *Handbook of physiology. The nervous system. Cellular biology of neurons* (Sect. 1, Vol. I, pp. 261–294). Bethesda, MD: American Physiological Society.

Lane, E. L., Björklund, A., Dunnett, S. B., & Winkler, C. (2010). Neural grafting in Parkinson's disease unraveling the mechanisms underlying graft-induced dyskinesia. *Progress in Brain Research, 184,* 295–309.

Langston, J. W. (2008). *The case of the frozen addicts.* New York: Pantheon Books. (Original work published 1995.)

Magee, J. C., & Cook, E. P. (2000). Somatic EPSP amplitude is independent of synapse location in hippocampal pyramidal neurons. *Nature Neuroscience, 3,* 895–903.

McAllister, B. B, & Dyck, R. H. (2017). Zinc transporter 3 (ZnT3) and vesicular zinc in central nervous system function. *Neurosciences & Biobehavioral Reviews, 80,* 329–350.

Mechoulam, R., & Gaoni, Y. (1967). The absolute configuration of delta-1-tetrahydrocannabinol, the major active constituent of hashish. *Tetrahedron Letters, 12,* 1109–1111.

Mechoulam, R., Hanus, L. O., Pertwee, R., & Howlett, A. C. (2014). Early phytocannabinoid chemistry to endocannabinoids and beyond. *Nature Neuroscience Reviews, 15,* 757–764.

Moore, T. J., Glenmullen, J., & Mattison, D. R. (2014). Reports of pathological gambling, hypersexuality and compulsive shopping associated with dopamine receptor agonist drugs. *JAMA Internal Medicine, 174,* 1930–1933.

Nagy, J. I., Pereda, A. E., & Rash, J. E. (2017). On the occurrence and enigmatic functions of mixed (chemical plus electrical) synapses in the mammalian CNS. *Neuroscience Letters, S0304-3940*(17), 30755-3.

Parkinson, J. (1989). An essay on the shaking palsy. In A. D. Morris & F. C. Rose (Eds.), *James Parkinson: His life and times* (pp. 151–175). Boston: Birkhauser. (Original work published 1817.)

Sacks, O. (1976). *Awakenings*. New York: Doubleday.

Scudellari, M. (2017). Your body is teeming with weed receptors. *The Scientist*. https://www.the-scientist.com/?articles.view/articleNo/49810/title/Your-Body-Is-Teeming-with-Weed-Receptors/.

Tréatikoff, C. (1974). Thesis for doctorate in medicine. In J. Marks (Ed.), *The treatment of Parkinsonism with L-dopa* (pp. 29–38). Lancaster, U.K.: MTP Medical and Technical Publishing. (Original work published 1919.)

Ungerstedt, U. (1971). Adipsia and aphagia after 6-hydroxydopamine induced degeneration of the nigrostriatal dopamine system in the rat brain. *Acta Physiologica (Scandinavia), 82*(Suppl. 367), 95–122.

Weilinger, N. L., Lohman, A. W., Rakai, B. D., Ma, E. M., Bialecki, J., Maslieieva, V., et al. (2016). Metabotropic NMDA receptor signaling couples Src family kinases to pannexin-1 during excitotoxicity. *Nature Neuroscience, 19*, 432–442.

Widner, H., Tetrud, J., Rehngrona, S., Snow, B., Brundin, P., Gustavii, B., et al. (1992). Bilateral fetal mesencephalic grafting in two patients with Parkinsonism induced by 1-methyl-4-phenyl-1, 2, 3, 6-tetrahydropyridine (MPTP). *New England Journal of Medicine, 327*, 1556–1563.

CHAPTER 6

Aagaard, L., & Hansen, E. H. (2011). The occurrence of adverse drug reactions reported for attention deficit hyperactivity disorder (ADHD) medications in the pediatric population: A qualitative review of empirical studies. *Neuropsychiatric Disease and Treatment, 7*, 729–744.

Asarnow, J. R., Porta, G., Spirito, A., Emslie, G., Clarke, G., Wagner, K. D., et al. (2011). Suicide attempts and nonsuicidal self-injury in the treatment of resistant depression in adolescents: Findings from the TORDIA study. *Journal of the American Academy of Child and Adolescent Psychiatry, 50*, 772–781.

Barth, C., Villringer, A., & Sacher, J. (2015). Sex hormones affect neurotransmitters and shape the adult female brain during hormonal transition periods. *Frontiers in Neuroscience, 20*, 9–37.

Becker, J. B., & Hu, M. (2008). Sex differences in drug abuse. *Frontiers in Neuroendocrinology, 29*(1), 36–47.

Berninger, J. P., LaLone, C. A., Villeneuve, D. L., & Ankley, G. T. (2016). Prioritization of pharmaceuticals for potential environmental hazard through leveraging a large scale mammalian pharmacological dataset. *Environmental Toxicology and Chemistry, 35*(4), 1007–1020

Birks, J. S., Chong, L. Y., & Grimley Evans, J. (2015). Rivastigmine for Alzheimer's disease. *The Cochrane Database of Systematic Reviews, 4*, CD001191.

Bourgin, J., Cachia, A., Boumezbeur, F., Djemaï, B., Bottlaender, M., Duchesnay, E., et al. (2015). Hyper-responsivity to stress in rats is associated with a large increase in amygdala volume: A 7T MRI study. *European Journal of Neuropsychopharmacology, 25*(6), 828–835.

Bradley, C. (1937). The behavior of children receiving Benzedrine. *American Journal of Psychiatry, 94*, 577–581.

Brown, A. R., Owen, S. F., Peters, J., Zhang, Y., Soffker, M., Paull, G. C., et al. (2015). Climate change and pollution speed declines in zebrafish populations. *Proceedings of the National Academy of Science of the United States of America, 112*, 1237–1246.

Büttner, A. (2011). Review: The neuropathology of drug abuse. *Neuropathology and Applied Neurobiology, 37*, 118–134.

Caddy, C., Giaroli, G., White, T. P., Shergill, S. S., & Tracy, D. K. (2014). Ketamine as the prototype glutamatergic antidepressant: Pharmacodynamics actions, and a systematic review and meta-analysis of efficacy. *Therapeutic Advances in Psychopharmacology, 4*(2), 75–99.

Campbell, N. A. (1996). An interview with Eloy Rodriguez. In *Biology* (4th ed., p. 23). New York: Benjamin Cummings.

Clauss, J. A., Avery, S. N., & Blackford, J. U. (2015). The nature of individual differences in inhibited temperament and risk for psychiatric disease: A review and meta-analysis. *Progress in Neurobiology, 127–128*, 23–45.

Comer, R. J. (2011). *Fundamentals of abnormal psychology* (7th ed.). New York: Worth.

Cowan, R. L., Roberts, D. M., & Joers, J. M. (2008). Neuroimaging in human MDMA (Ecstasy) users. *Annals of the New York Academy of Sciences, 1139*, 291–298.

Dube, S. R., Felitti, V. J., Dong, M., Chapman, D. P., Giles, W. H., & Anda, R. F. (2003). Childhood abuse, neglect, and household dysfunction and the risk of illicit drug use: The adverse childhood experiences study. *Pediatrics, 111*(3), 564–572.

Durell, T. M., Kroutil, L. A., Crits-Christoph, P., Barchha, N., & Van Brunt, D. E. (2008). Prevalence of nonmedical methamphetamine use in the United States. *Substance Abuse Treatment, Prevention, and Policy, 3*, 19.

Everitt, B. J. (2014). Neural and psychological mechanisms underlying compulsive drug seeking habits and drug memories: Indications for novel treatments of addiction. *European Journal of Neuroscience, 40*, 2163–2182.

Fraioli, S., Crombag, H. S., Badiani, A., & Robinson, T. E. (1999). Susceptibility to amphetamine-induced locomotor sensitization is modulated by environmental stimuli. *Neuropsychopharmacology, 20*, 533–541.

Freud, S. (1974). *Cocaine papers* (R. Byck, Ed.). New York: Penguin. (Original work published 1884.)

Griffin, J. A., Umstattd, M. R., & Usdan, S. L. (2010). Alcohol use and high-risk sexual behavior among collegiate women: A review of research on alcohol myopia theory. *Journal of American College Health, 58*, 523–532.

Han, B., Compton, W. M., Mojtabai, R., Colpe, L., & Hughes, A. (2016). Trends in receipt of mental health treatments among adults in the United States, 2008–2013. *Journal of Clinical Psychiatry, 77*(10), 1365–1371.

Hardee, J. E., Weiland, B. J., Nichols, T. E., Welsh, R. C., Soules, M. E., Steinberg, D. B., et al. (2014). Development of impulse control circuitry in children of alcoholics. *Biological Psychiatry, 76*, 708–716.

Hill, A. S., Sahay, A., & Hen, R. (2015). Increasing adult hippocampal neurogenesis is sufficient to reduce anxiety and depression-like behaviors. *Neuropsychopharmacology, 40*, 2368–2378.

Hillemacher, T., Weinland, C., Lenz, B., Kraus, T., Heberlein, A., Glahn, A., et al. (2015). DNA methylation of the LEP gene is associated with craving during alcohol withdrawal. *Psychoneuroendocrinology, 51*, 371–377.

Isacsson, G., & Rich, C. L. (2014). Antidepressant drugs and the risk of suicide in children and adolescents. *Paediatric Drugs, 16*, 115–122.

Isbell, H., Fraser, H. F., Wikler, R. E., Belleville, R. E., & Eisenman, A. J. (1955). An experimental study of the etiology of "rum fits" and delirium tremens. *Quarterly Journal of Studies on Alcohol, 16*, 1–35.

Kapadia, M., Zhao, H., Ma, D., Hatkar, R., Marchese, M., & Sakic, B. (2014). Zoopharmacognosy in diseased laboratory mice: Conflicting evidence. *PLOS ONE, 9*(6), e100684.

Kenny, P. J. (2007). Brain reward systems and compulsive drug use. *Trends in Pharmacological Sciences, 28*(3), 135–141.

Koob, G. F., Buck, C. L., Cohen, A., Edwards, S., Park, P. E., Schlosburg, J. E., et al. (2014). Addiction as a stress surfeit disorder. *Neuropharmacology, 76*, 370–382.

Krasnova, I. N., & Cadet, J. L. (2009). Methamphetamine toxicity and messengers of death. *Brain Research Reviews, 60*(2), 379–407.

Lajud, N., & Torner, L. (2015). Early life stress and hippocampal neurogenesis in the neonate: Sexual dimorphism, long-term consequences and possible mediators. *Frontiers in Molecular Neuroscience, 8*, 3.

Landré, L., Destrieux, C., Baudry, M., Barantin, L., Cottier, J. P., Martineau, J., et al. (2010). Preserved subcortical volumes and cortical thickness in women with sexual abuse-related PTSD. *Psychiatry Research, 183*, 181–186.

Lee, B. Y., Park, S. Y., Ryu, H. M., Shin, C. Y., Ko, K. N., Han, J. Y., et al. (2015). Changes in the methylation status of DAT, SERT, and MeCP2 gene promoters in the blood cell in families exposed to alcohol during the periconceptional period. *Alcohol: Clinical and Experimental Research, 39*, 239–250.

Liu, P., Lu, H., Filbey, F. M., Tamminga, C. A., Cao, Y., & Adinoff, B. (2014). MRI assessment of cerebral oxygen metabolism in cocaine-addicted individuals: Hypoactivity and dose dependence. *NMR Biomedicine, 27*, 726–732.

MacAndrew, C., & Edgerton, R. B. (1969). *Drunken comportment: A social explanation.* Chicago: Aldine.

MacDonald, T. K., MacDonald, G., Zanna, M. P., & Fong, G. T. (2000). Alcohol, sexual arousal, and intentions to use condoms in young men: Applying alcohol myopia theory to risky sexual behavior. *Health Psychology, 19*, 290–298.

McGowan, P. O., Sasaki, A., D'Alessio, A. C., Dymov, S., Labonté, B., Szyf, M., et al. (2009). Epigenetic regulation of the glucocorticoid receptor in human brain associates with childhood abuse. *Nature Neurosciences, 12*, 342–348.

National Institute on Drug Abuse, National Institutes of Health. (2016). *2015–2016 National Survey of Drug Use and Health*, https://www.drugabuse.gov/national-survey-drug-use-health.

Nehlig, A. (2010). Is caffeine a cognitive enhancer? *Journal of Alzheimer's Disease, 20*(Suppl. 1), S85–S94.

Nguyen, B. M., Kim, D., Bricker, S., Bongard, F., Neville, A., Putnam, B., et al. (2014). Effect of marijuana use on outcomes in traumatic brain injury. *American Surgery, 80*, 979–983.

Nugent, B. M., Tobet, S. A., Lara, H. E., Lucion, A. B., Wilson, M. E., Recabarren, S. E., et al. (2012). Hormonal programming across the lifespan. *Hormone and Metabolic Research, 44*, 577–586.

Oleson, E. B., & Roberts, D. C. (2009). Parsing the addiction phenomenon: Self-administration procedures modeling enhanced motivation for drug and escalation of drug intake. *Drug Discovery Today: Disease Models, 5*(4), 217–226.

Popova, S., Lange, S., Bekmuradov, D., Mihic, A., & Rehm, J. (2011). Fetal alcohol spectrum disorder prevalence estimates in correctional systems: A systematic literature review. *Canadian Journal of Public Health, 102*, 336–340.

Reinstatler, L., & Youssef, N. A. (2015). Ketamine as a potential treatment for suicidal ideation: A systematic review of the literature. *Drugs, 15*, 37–43.

Roberts, N. P., Roberts, P. A., Jones, N., & Bisson, J. I. (2015). Psychological interventions for post-traumatic stress disorder and comorbid substance use disorder: A systematic review and meta-analysis. *Clinical Psychological Reviews, 38*, 25–38.

Robinson, T. E., & Becker, J. B. (1986). Enduring changes in brain and behavior produced by chronic amphetamine administration: A review and evaluation of animal models of amphetamine psychosis. *Brain Research Reviews, 11*, 157–198.

Robinson, T. E., & Berridge, K. C. (2008). Incentive sensitization theory. *Philosophical Transactions of the Royal Society of London, 363*, 3137–3146.

Roitman, P., Mechoulam, R., Cooper-Kazaz, R., & Shalev, A. (2014). Preliminary, open-label, pilot study of add-on oral Δ9-tetrahydrocannabinol in chronic post-traumatic stress disorder. *Clinical Drug Investigations, 34*, 587–591.

Sacks, J. J., Gonzales, K. R., Bouchery, E. E., Tomedi, L. E., & Brewer, R. D. (2015). 2010 national and state costs of excessive alcohol consumption. *American Journal of Preventive Medicine, 49*(5), e73–e79.

Sapolsky, R. M. (2004). *Why zebras don't get ulcers* (3rd ed.). New York: Henry Holt.

Sapolsky, R. M. (2005). The influence of social hierarchy on primate health. *Science, 308*(5722), 648–652.

Sevincer, A. T., & Oettingen, G. (2014). Alcohol myopia and goal commitment. *Frontiers in Psychology, 4*, 169–175.

Steen, E., Terry, B. M., Rivera, E. J., Cannon, J. L., Neely, T. R., Tavares, R., et al. (2005). Impaired insulin and insulin-like growth factor expression and signaling mechanisms in Alzheimer's disease: Is this type 3 diabetes? *Journal of Alzheimer's Disease, 7*, 63–80.

Substance Abuse and Mental Health Services Administration (SAMHSA). (2015). National Survey on Drug Use and Health (NSDUH). Table 5.6B—Substance use disorder in past year among persons aged 18 or older, by demographic characteristics: Percentages, 2014 and 2015.

Teixeira-Gomes, A., Costa, V. M., Feio-Azevedo, R., Bastos, M. L., Carvalho, F., & Capela, J. P. (2015). The neurotoxicity of amphetamines during the adolescent period. *International Journal of Developmental Neuroscience, 41*, 44–62.

Vevelstad, M., Oiestad, E. L., Middelkoop, G., Hasvold, I., Lilleng, P., Delaveris, G. J., et al. (2012). The PMMA epidemic in Norway: Comparison of fatal and non-fatal intoxications. *Forensic Science International, 219*, 151–157.

Wadgave, U., & Nagesh, L. (2016). Nicotine replacement therapy: An overview. *International Journal of Health Sciences, 10*(3), 425–435.

Wenger, J. R., Tiffany, T. M., Bombardier, C., Nicholls, K., & Woods, S. C. (1981). Ethanol tolerance in the rat is learned. *Science, 213*, 575–577.

Whishaw, I. Q., Mittleman, G., & Evenden, J. L. (1989). Training-dependent decay in performance produced by the neuroleptic *cis*(Z)-flupentixol on spatial navigation by rats in a swimming pool. *Pharmacology Biochemistry and Behavior, 32*, 211–220.

Wright, G. A., Baker, D. D., Palmer, M. J., Stabler, D., Mustard, J. A., Power, E. F., et al. (2013). Caffeine in floral nectar enhances a pollinator's memory of reward. *Science, 339*(6124), 1202–1204.

Yager, L. M., Pitchers, K. K., Flagel, S. B., & Robinson, T. E. (2015). Individual variation in the motivational and neurobiological effects of an opioid cue. *Neuropsychopharmacology, 40*, 1269–1277.

CHAPTER 7

Brown, A. R., Antle, M. C., Hu, B., & Teskey, G. C. (2011). High frequency stimulation of the subthalamic nucleus acutely rescues neocortical movement representations and motor deficits following 6-hydroxydopamine administration in rats. *Experimental Neurology, 231*, 82–90.

Bueller, J. A., Aftab, M., Sen, S., Gomez-Hassan, D., Burmeister, M., & Zubieta, J.-K. (2006). BDNF Val66Met allele is associated with reduced hippocampal volume in healthy subjects. *Biological Psychiatry, 59*, 812–815.

Cacucci, F., Yi, M., Wills, T. J., Chapmans, P., & O'Keefe, J. (2008). Place cell firing correlates with memory deficits and amyloid plaque burden in Tg2576 Alzheimer mouse model. *Proceedings of the National Academy of Sciences of the United States of America, 105*, 7863–7868.

Damasio, H., & Damasio, A. R. (1989). *Lesion analysis in neuropsychology.* New York: Oxford University Press.

Fox, P. T., & Raichle, M. E. (1986). Focal physiological uncoupling of cerebral blood flow and oxidative metabolism during somatosensory stimulation in human subjects. *Proceedings of the National*

Academy of Sciences of the United States of America, 83, 1140–1144.

Fraga, M. F., Ballestar, E., Paz, M. F., Ropero, S., Setien, F., Ballestar, M. L., et al. (2005). Epigenetic differences arise during the lifetime of monozygotic twins. *Proceedings of the National Academy of Sciences of the United States of America, 102,* 10604–10609.

Ghosh, K. K., Burns, L. D., Cocker, E. D., Nimmerjahn, A., Ziv, Y., Gamal, A. E., & Schnitzer, M. J. (2011). Miniaturized integration of a fluorescence microscope. *Nature Methods, 8,* 871–878.

Gonzalez, C. L. R., Gharbawie, O. A., & Kolb, B. (2006). Chronic low-dose administration of nicotine facilitates recovery and synaptic change after focal ischemia in rats. *Neuropharmacology, 50,* 777–787.

Haubensak, W., Kunwar, P. S., Cai, H., Ciocchi, S., Wall, N. R., Ponnusamy, R., et al. (2010). Genetic dissection of an amygdala microcircuit that gates conditioned fear. *Nature, 468,* 270–276.

Kolb, B., & Walkey, J. (1987). Behavioural and anatomical studies of the posterior parietal cortex of the rat. *Behavioural Brain Research, 23,* 127–145.

Kut, C., Chaichana, K. L., Xi, J., Raza, S. M., Ye, X., McVeigh, E. R., et al. (2015). Detection of human brain cancer infiltration ex vivo and in vivo using quantitative optical coherence tomography. *Science Translational Medicine, 7*(292), 292ra100.

Lecendreux, M., Konofal, E., Cortese, S., & Faraone, S. V. (2015). A 4-year follow-up of attention-deficit/hyperactivity disorder in a population sample. *Journal of Clinical Psychiatry, 76,* 712–719.

Livet, J., Weissman, T. A., Kang, H., Draft, R. W., Lu, J., Bennis, R. A., et al. (2007). Transgenic strategies for combinatorial expression of fluorescent proteins in the nervous system. *Nature, 450,* 56–62.

Lomber, S. G., & Payne, B. R. (1996). Removal of two halves restores the whole: Reversal of visual hemineglect during bilateral cortical or collicular inactivation in the cat. *Visual Neuroscience, 13,* 1143–1156.

May, L., Byers-Heinlein, K., Gervain, J., & Werker, J. F. (2011). Language and the newborn brain: Does prenatal language experience shape the neonate neural response to speech? *Frontiers in Psychology, 2,* 1–9.

McGowan, P. O., Sasaki, A., D'Alessio, A. C., Dymov, S., Labonté, B., Szyf, M., et al. (2009). Epigenetic regulation of the glucocorticoid receptor in human brain associates with childhood abuse. *Nature Neuroscience, 12,* 342–348.

Morris, R. G. M. (1981). Spatial localization does not require the presence of local cues. *Learning and Motivation, 12,* 239–260.

Mychasiuk, R., Schmold, N., Ilnytskyy, S., Kovalchuk, O., Kolb, B., & Gibb, R. (2011). Prenatal bystander stress alters brain, behavior, and the epigenome of developing rat offspring. *Developmental Neuroscience, 33,* 159–169.

National Research Council of the National Academies. (2011). *Guide for the care and use of laboratory animals* (8th ed.). Washington, DC: The National Academies Press.

Ogawa, S., Lee, T. M., Kay, A. R., & Tank, D. W. (1990). Brain magnetic resonance imaging with contrast dependent on blood oxygenation. *Proceedings of the National Academy of Sciences of the United States of America, 87,* 9868–9872.

O'Keefe, J., & Dostrovsky, J. (1971). The hippocampus as a spatial map. *Brain Research, 34,* 171–175.

Oomen, C. A., Hvoslef-Eidem, M., Heath, C. J., Mar, A. C., Horner, A. E., Bussey, T. J., & Saksida, L. M. (2013). The touchscreen operant platform for testing working memory and pattern separation in rats and mice. *Nature Protocols, 8,* 2006–2021.

Penfield, W., & Jasper, H. H. (1954). *Epilepsy and the functional anatomy of the human brain.* Boston: Little, Brown.

Phillips, B. U., Lopez-Cruz, L., Hailwood, J., Heath, C. J., Saksida, L. M., & Bussey, T. J. (2018). Translational approaches to evaluating motivation in laboratory rodents: Conventional and touchscreen-based procedures. *Current Opinion in Behavioral Sciences, 22,* 21–27.

Posner, M. I., & Raichle, M. E. (1997). *Images of mind.* New York: W. H. Freeman.

Quadri, S. A., Waqas, M., Khan, I., Khan, M. A., Suriya, S. S., Farooqui, M., & Fiani, B. (2018). High-intensity focused ultrasound: Past, present, and future in neurosurgery. *Neurosurgery Focus, 44*(2), E16.

Reza, M. F., Ikoma, K., Ito, T., Ogawa, T., & Mano, Y. (2007). N200 latency and P300 amplitude in depressed mood post-traumatic brain injury patients. *Neuropsychological Rehabilitation, 17,* 723–734.

Rojczyk-Gołębiewska, E., Pałasz, A., Worthington, J. J., Markowski, G., & Wiaderkiewicz, R. (2015). Neurolight: Astonishing advances in brain imaging. *International Journal of Neuroscience, 125,* 91–99.

Schlaepfer, T. E., Bewernick, B. H., Kayser, S., Mädler, B., & Coenen, V. A. (2013). Rapid effects of deep brain stimulation for treatment-resistant major depression. *Biological Psychiatry, 73,* 1204–1212.

Scoville, W. B., & Milner, B. (1957). Loss of recent memory after bilateral hippocampal lesions. *Journal of Neurology, Neurosurgery, and Psychiatry, 20,* 11–21.

Spanswick, S., Lehmann, H., & Sutherland, R. J. (2011). A novel animal model of hippocampal cognitive deficits, slow neurodegeneration, and neuroregeneration. *Journal of Biomedicine and Biotechnology.* doi: 10.1155/2011/527201

Spanswick, S., & Sutherland, R. J. (2010). Object/context-specific memory deficits associated with loss of hippocampal granule cells after adrenalectomy in rats. *Learning and Memory, 17,* 241–245.

Spinney, L. (2005). Optical topography and the color of blood. *The Scientist, 19,* 25–27.

Szyf, M., McGowan, P., & Meaney, M. J. (2008). The social environment and the epigenome. *Environmental Molecular Mutagenetics, 49,* 46–60.

Takamura, T., & Hanakawa, T. (2017). Clinical utility of resting-state functional connectivity magnetic resonance imaging for mood and cognitive disorders. *Journal of Neural Transmission, 124,* 821–839.

Tisdall, M. M., & Smith, M. (2006). Cerebral microdialysis: Research technique or clinical tool. *British Journal of Anaesthesia, 97,* 18–25.

Wess, J., Nakajima, K., & Jain, S. (2013). Novel designer receptors to probe GPCR signaling and physiology. *Trends in Pharmacological Sciences, 34,* 385–392.

Wheeler, D. S., Ebben, A. L., Kurtoglu, B., Lovell, M. E., Bohn, A. T., Jasek, I. A., et al. (2017). Corticosterone regulates both naturally occurring and cocaine-induced dopamine signaling by selectively decreasing dopamine update. *European Journal of Neuroscience, 46,* 2638–2646.

Whishaw, I. Q. (1989). Dissociating performance and learning deficits in spatial navigation tasks in rats subjected to cholinergic muscarinic blockade. *Brain Research Bulletin, 23,* 347–358.

Whishaw, I. Q., & Kolb, B. (2005). *The behavior of the laboratory rat.* New York: Oxford University Press.

CHAPTER 8

Agate, R. J., Grisham, W., Wade, J., Mann, S., Wingfield, J., Schanen, C., et al. (2003). Neural, but not gonadal, origin of brain sex differences in a gynandromorphic finch. *Proceedings of the National Academy of Sciences of the United States of America, 100,* 4873–4878.

Ames, E. W. (1997). *The development of Romanian orphanage children adopted to Canada.* Final report to Human Resources Development, Canada.

Anda, R. F., Felitti, V. J., Bremner, J. D., Walker, J. D., Whitfield, C., et al. (2006). The enduring effects of abuse and related adverse experiences in childhood: A convergence of evidence from neurobiology and epidemiology. *European Archives of Psychiatry and Clinical Neuroscience, 256,* 174–186.

Arai, K., & Lo, E. H. (2017). Gliogenesis. In L. R. Caplan, J. Biller, M. C. Leary, E. H. Lo, A. Thomas, M. Yenari, & J. H. Zhang (Eds.), *Primer on cerebrovascular diseases* (2nd ed., pp 91–95). New York: Elsevier.

Berens, A. E., & Nelson, C. A. (2015). The science of early adversity: Is there a role for large institutions in the care of vulnerable children? *Lancet, 386*(9991), 388–398.

Bock, J., Rether, K., Grogerr, N., Xie, L., & Braun, K. (2014). Perinatal programming of emotional brain circuits: An integrative view from systems to molecules. *Frontiers of Neuroscience, 11*, 1–15.

Bond, A. M., Ming, G.-L., & Song, H. (2015). Adult mammalian neural stem cells and neurogenesis: Five decades later. *Cell Stem Cell, 17*, 385–395.

Bourgeois, J.-P. (2001). Synaptogenesis in the neocortex of the newborn: The ultimate frontier for individuation? In C. A. Nelson & M. Luciana (Eds.), *Handbook of developmental cognitive neuroscience* (pp. 23–34). Cambridge, MA: MIT Press.

Casey, B. J., Galvan, A., & Somerville, L. H. (2015). Beyond simple models of adolescence to an integrated circuit-based account: A commentary. *Developmental Cognitive Neuroscience, 17*, 128–130.

Changeux, J.-P., & Danchin, A. (1976). Selective stabilization of developing synapses as a mechanism for the specification of neuronal networks. *Nature, 264*, 705–712.

Charil, A., Laplante, D. P., Vaillancourt, C., & King, S. (2010). Prenatal stress and brain development. *Brain Research Reviews, 65*, 56–79.

Chen, R., Jiao, Y., & Herskovits, E. H. (2011). Structural MRI in autism spectrum disorder. *Pediatric Research, 69*, 63R–68R.

Clarke, R. S., Heron, W., Fetherstonhaugh, M. L., Forgays, D. G., & Hebb, D. O. (1951). Individual differences in dogs: Preliminary report on the effects of early experience. *Canadian Journal of Psychology, 5*(4), 150–156.

Cowan, C. S. M., Callaghan, B. L., & Richardson, R. (2016). The effects of probiotic formulation (*Lactobacillus rhamnosus* and *L. helveticus*) on developmental trajectories of emotional learning in stressed infant rats. *Translational Psychiatry, 6*(5), e823.

Cowan, W. M. (1979). The development of the brain. *Scientific American, 241*(3), 116.

Dean, D. C., Planalp, E. M, Wooten, W., Schmidt, C. K., Kecskemeti, S. R., Frye, C., et al. (2018). Investigation of brain structure in the 1-month infant. *Brain Structure and Function, 223*(4), 1953–1970.

Dettmer, A. M., & Suomi, S. J. (2014). Nonhuman primates models of neuropsychiatric disorders: Influences of early rearing, genetics, and epigenetics. *ILAR Journal, 55*, 361–370.

Dias, B. G., & Ressler, K. J. (2014). Parental olfactory experience influences behavior and neural structure in subsequent generations. *Nature Neuroscience, 17*, 89–96.

Dietsche, B., Kircher, T., & Falkenberg, I. (2017). Structural brain changes in schizophrenia at different stages of illness: A selective review of longitudinal magnetic resonance imaging studies. *Australia and New Zealand Journal of Psychiatry, 51*, 500–508.

Epstein, H. T. (1979). Correlated brain and intelligence development in humans. In M. E. Hahn, C. Jensen, & B. C. Dudek (Eds.), *Development and evolution of brain size: Behavioral implications* (pp. 111–131). New York: Academic Press.

Faiz, M., & Morshead, C. M. (2017). Stem cells to function. In R. Gibb & B. Kolb (Eds.), *The neurobiology of brain and behavioral development* (pp. 99–132). New York: Elsevier.

Foster, J. A., Rinaman, L., & Cryan, J. F. (2017). Stress & the gut–brain axis: Regulation by the microbiome. *Neurobiology of Stress, 7*, 124–136.

Franke, K., Ristow, M., & Gaser, C. (2014). Gender-specific impact of personal health parameters on individual brain aging in cognitively unimpaired elderly subjects. *Frontiers in Aging Neuroscience, 6*, 94.

Fuhrmann, D., Knoll, L. J., & Blakemore, S.-J. (2015). Adolescence as a sensitive period of brain development. *Trends in Cognitive Sciences, 19*, 558–566.

Gershon, E. S., & Rieder, R. O. (1992). Major disorders of mind and brain. *Scientific American, 267*(3), 126–133.

Geschwind, D. H., & Rakic, P. (2013). Cortical evolution: Judge the brain by its cover. *Neuron, 80*, 633–647.

Gibb, R., Gonzalez, C., & Kolb, B. (2014). Prenatal enrichment and recovery from perinatal cortical damage: Effects of maternal complex housing. *Frontiers in Behavioral Neuroscience, 8*, 223.

Goldstein, J. M., Seidman, L. J., Horton, N. J., Makris, N., Kennedy, D. N., Caviness, V. S., Jr., et al. (2001). Normal sexual dimorphism of the adult human brain assessed by in vivo magnetic resonance imaging. *Cerebral Cortex, 11*, 490–497.

Guerrini, R., Dobyns, W. B., & Barkovich, A. J. (2007). Abnormal development of the human cerebral cortex: Genetics, functional consequences and treatment options. *Trends in Neurosciences, 31*, 154–162.

Harlow, H. F. (1971). *Learning to love*. San Francisco: Albion.

Hebb, D. O. (1947). The effects of early experience on problem solving at maturity. *American Psychologist, 2*, 737–745.

Hensch, T. K. (2017). Critical periods in cortical development. In R. Gibb & B. Kolb (Eds.), *The neurobiology of brain and behavioral development* (pp. 133–152). New York: Academic Press.

Herholz, S. C., & Zatorre, R. J. (2012). Musical training as a framework for brain plasticity: Behavior, function, and structure. *Neuron, 76*, 486–502.

Hodel, A. S., Hunt, R. H., Cowell, R. A., van den Heuvel, S. E., Gunnar, M. R., & Thomas, K. M. (2015). Duration of early adversity and structural brain development in post-institutionalized adolescents. *Neuroimage, 105*, 112–119.

Horn, G., Bradley, P., & McCabe, B. J. (1985). Changes in the structure of synapses associated with learning. *Journal of Neuroscience, 5*, 3161–3168.

Huttenlocher, P. R. (1994). Synaptogenesis in human cerebral cortex. In G. Dawson & K. W. Fischer (Eds.), *Human behavior and the developing brain* (pp. 137–152). New York: Guilford Press.

Juraska, J. M. (1990). The structure of the cerebral cortex: Effects of gender and the environment. In B. Kolb & R. Tees (Eds.), *The cerebral cortex of the rat* (pp. 483–506). Cambridge, MA: MIT Press.

Kelly, J. R., Minuto, C., Cryan, J. F., Clarke, G., & Dinan, T. G. (2017). Cross talk: The microbiota and neurodevelopmental disorders. *Frontiers in Neuroscience, 11*, 490.

Kinney, H. C. (2009). Brainstem mechanisms underlying the sudden infant death syndrome: Evidence from human pathologic studies. *Developmental Psychobiology, 51*, 223–233.

Kolb, B., & Gibb, R. (1993). Possible anatomical basis of recovery of function after neonatal frontal lesions in rats. *Behavioral Neuroscience, 107*, 799–811.

Kolb, B., & Gibb, R. (2015). Childhood poverty and brain development. *Human Development, 58*, 215–217.

Kolb, B., Gibb, R., & Gorny, G. (2003). Experience-dependent changes in dendritic arbor and spine density in neocortex vary with age and sex. *Neurobiology of Learning and Memory, 791*, 1–10.

Kolb, B., Mychasiuk, R., Muhammad, A., Li, Y., Frost, D. O., & Gibb, R. (2012). Experience and the developing prefrontal cortex. *Proceedings of the National Academy of Sciences of the United States of America, 109*(Suppl. 2), 17186–17193.

Kovelman, J. A., & Scheibel, A. B. (1984). A neurohistologic correlate of schizophrenia. *Biological Psychiatry, 19*, 1601–1621.

Kuhl, P. K. (2011). Early language learning and literacy: Neuroscience implications for education. *Mind, Brain, and Education, 5*, 128–142.

Lenneberg, E. H. (1967). *Biological foundations of language*. New York: Wiley.

Lenroot, R. K., Gogtay, N., Greenstein, D. K., Wells, E. M., Wallace, G. L.,

Clasen, L. S., et al. (2007). Sexual dimorphism of brain development trajectories during childhood and adolescence. *NeuroImage, 36,* 1065–1073.

Levitin, D. J., & Rogers, S. E. (2005). Absolute pitch: Perception, coding, and controversies. *Trends in Cognitive Science, 9,* 26–33.

Lorenz, K. (1970). *Studies on animal and human behavior* (Vols. 1 and 2). Cambridge, MA: Harvard University Press.

Lu, L. H., Leonard, C. M., Thompson, P. M., Kan, E., Jolley, J., Welcome, S. E., et al. (2007). Normal developmental changes in inferior frontal gray matter are associated with improvement in phonological processing: A longitudinal MRI analysis. *Cerebral Cortex, 17,* 1092–1099.

Malanga, C. J., & Kosofsky, B. E. (2003). Does drug abuse beget drug abuse? Behavioral analysis of addiction liability in animal models of prenatal drug exposure. *Developmental Brain Research, 147,* 47–57.

Marin-Padilla, M. (1993). Pathogenesis of late-acquired leptomeningeal heterotopias and secondary cortical alterations: A Golgi study. In A. M. Galaburda (Ed.), *Dyslexia and development: Neurobiological aspects of extraordinary brains* (pp. 64–88). Cambridge, MA: Harvard University Press.

Minnes, S., Singer, L. T., Min, M. O., Wu, M., Lang, A., & Yoon, S. (2014). Effects of prenatal cocaine/polydrug exposure on substance abuse by age 15. *Drug and Alcohol Dependence, 134,* 201–210.

Moore, K. L. (1988). *The developing human: Clinically oriented embryology* (4th ed.). Philadelphia: Saunders.

Mychasiuk, R., Gibb, R., & Kolb, B. (2011). Prenatal stress produces sexually dimorphic and regionally specific changes in gene expression in hippocampus and frontal cortex of developing rat offspring. *Developmental Neuroscience, 33,* 531–538.

Mychasiuk, R., Muhammad, A., & Kolb, B. (2014). Environmental enrichment alters structural plasticity of the adolescent brain but does not remediate the effects of prenatal nicotine exposure. *Synapse, 68,* 293–305.

Myers, D. G. (2015). *Psychology* (11th ed.). New York: Worth Publishers.

National Institute on Drug Abuse. (2012). *What are the risks of smoking during pregnancy?* http://www.drugabuse.gov/ publications/research-reports/tobacco/ smoking-pregnancy-what-are-risks.

Nelson, C. A., Zeanah, C. H., Fox, N. A., Marshall, P. J., Smyke, A. T., & Guthrie, D. (2007). Cognitive recovery in socially deprived young children: The Bucharest Early Intervention Project. *Science, 318,* 1937–1940.

Noble, K. G., Houston, S. M., Brito, N. H., Bartsch, H., Kan, E., Kuperman, J. M., et al. (2015). Family income, parental education and brain structure in children and adolescents. *Nature Neuroscience, 18,* 773–778.

Nordahl, C. W., Scholz, R., Yang, X., Buonocore, M. H., Simon, T., Rogers S., et al. (2012). Increased rate of amygdala growth in children aged 2 to 4 years with autism spectrum disorders: A longitudinal study. *Archives of General Psychiatry, 69,* 53–61.

O'Hare, E. D., & Sowell, E. R. (2008). Imaging developmental changes in gray and white matter in the human brain. In C. A. Nelson and M. Luciana (Eds.), *Handbook of developmental cognitive neuroscience* (pp. 23–38), Cambridge, MA: MIT Press.

Overman, W., Bachevalier, J., Schuhmann, E., & Ryan, P. (1996). Cognitive gender differences in very young children parallel biologically based cognitive gender differences in monkeys. *Behavioral Neuroscience, 110,* 673–684.

Overman, W., Bachevalier, J., Turner, M., & Peuster, A. (1992). Object recognition versus object discrimination: Comparison between human infants and infant monkeys. *Behavioral Neuroscience, 106,* 15–29.

Paterson, D. S., Trachtenberg, F. L., Thompson, E. G., Belliveau, R. A., Beggs, A. H., Dranall, et al. (2006). Multiple serotonergic brainstem abnormalities in sudden infant death syndrome. *Journal of the American Medical Association, 296,* 2124–2132.

Payne, B. R., & Lomber, S. G. (2001). Reconstructing functional systems after lesions of cerebral cortex. *Nature Reviews Neuroscience, 2,* 911–919.

Petanjek, Z., Judaš, M., Šimić, G., Rašin, M. R., Uylings, H. B. M., Rakic, P., & Kostović, I. (2011). Extraordinary neoteny of synaptic spines in the human prefrontal cortex. *Proceedings of the National Academy of Sciences of the United States of America, 108,* 13281–13286.

Piaget, J. (1952). *The origins of intelligence in children.* New York: Norton.

Piccolo, L. R., Merz, E. C., He, X., Sowell, E. R., & Noble, K. G. (2016). Age-related differences in cortical thickness vary by socioeconomic status. *PLOS ONE, 11,* e0162511

Purpura, D. P. (1974). Dendritic spine "dysgenesis" and mental retardation. *Science, 186,* 1126–1127.

Raizada, R. D. S., Richards, T. L., Meltzoff, A., & Kuhl, P. K. (2008). Socioeconomic status predicts hemispheric specialization of the left inferior frontal gyrus in young children. *NeuroImage, 40,* 1392–1401.

Rakic, P. (1974). Neurons in rhesus monkey cerebral cortex: Systematic relation between time of origin and eventual disposition. *Science, 183,* 425.

Rapoport, J. L., Giedd, J. N., & Gogtay, N. (2012). Neurodevelopmental model of schizophrenia: Update 2012. *Molecular Psychiatry, 17,* 1228–1238.

Raza, S., Harker, A., Richards, S., Kolb, B., & Gibb, R. (2015). Tactile stimulation improves neuroanatomical pathology but not behaviour in rats prenatally exposed to valproic acid. *Behavioural Brain Research, 282,* 25–36.

Riesen, A. H. (1982). Effects of environments on development in sensory systems. In W. D. Neff (Ed.), *Contributions to sensory physiology* (Vol. 6, pp. 45–77). New York: Academic Press.

Rogenmoser, L., Kernbach, J., Schlaug, G., & Gaser, C. (2018). Keeping brains young with making music. *Brain Structure and Function, 223*(1), 297–305.

Ross, E. J., Graham, D. L., Money, K. M., & Stanwood, G. D. (2015). Developmental consequences of fetal exposure to drugs: What we know and what we still must learn. *Neuropsychopharmacology, 40,* 61–87.

Rutter, M. (1998). Developmental catch-up, and deficit, following adoption after severe global early privation. *Journal of Child Psychology and Psychiatry, 39,* 465–476.

Schnack, H. G., van Haren, N. E., Brouwer, R. M., Evans, A., Durston, S., Boomsma, D. I., et al. (2014). Changes in thickness and surface area of the human cortex and their relationship with intelligence. *Cerebral Cortex, 25,* 1608–1617.

Sherman, L. E., Rudie, J. D., Pfeifer, J. H., Masten, C. L., McNealy, K., & Dapretto, M. (2014). Development of the default mode and central executive networks across early adolescence: A longitudinal study. *Developmental Cognitive Neuroscience, 10,* 148–159.

Smyke, A. T., Zeanah, C. H., Gleason, M. M., Drury, S. S., Fox, N. A., Nelson, C. A., & Guthrie, D. (2012). A randomized controlled trial comparing foster care and institutional care for children with signs of reactive attachment disorder. *American Journal of Psychiatry, 169,* 508–514.

Sowell, E. R., Thompson, P. M., Leonard, C. M., Welcome, S. E., Kan, E., & Toga, A. W. (2004). Longitudinal mapping of cortical thickness and brain growth in normal children. *Journal of Neuroscience, 24,* 8223–8231.

Sowell, E. R., Thompson, P. M., & Toga, A. W. (2004). Mapping changes in the human cortex throughout the span of life. *The Neuroscientist, 10,* 372–392.

Sperry, R. W. (1963). Chemoaffinity in the orderly growth of nerve fiber patterns and connections. *Proceedings of the National Academy of Sciences of the United States of America, 50,* 703–710.

Tottenham, N. (2014). The importance of early experiences for neuro-affective development. *Current Topics in Behavioral Neuroscience, 16,* 109–129.

Tottenham, N., & Galvan, A. (2016). Stress and the adolescent brain: Amygdala-prefrontal cortex circuitry and ventral striatum as developmental targets. *Neuroscience and Biobehavioral Reviews, 70,* 217–227.

Twitchell, T. E. (1965). The automatic grasping response of infants. *Neuropsychologia, 3,* 247–259.

Ursache, A., & Noble, K. G. (2016). Socioeconomic status, white matter, and executive function in children. *Brain and Behavior, 6*(10), e00531.

Wallace, P. S., & Whishaw, I. Q. (2003). Independent digit movements and precision grip patterns in 1–5-month-old human infants: Hand-babbling, including vacuous then self-directed hand and digit movements, precedes targeted reaching. *Neuropsychologia, 41,* 1912–1918.

Weiss, S., Reynolds, B. A., Vescovi, A. L., Morshead, C., Craig, C. G., & van der Kooy, D. (1996). Is there a neural stem cell in the mammalian forebrain? *Trends in Neurosciences, 19*(9), 387–393.

Werker, J. F., & Tees, R. C. (1992). The organization and reorganization of human speech perception. *Annual Review of Neuroscience, 15,* 377–402.

Yakovlev, P. E., & Lecours, A.-R. (1967). The myelogenetic cycles of regional maturation of the brain. In A. Minkowski (Ed.), *Regional development of the brain in early life* (pp. 3–70). Oxford: Blackwell.

Zuccolo, L., DeRoo, L. A., Wills, A., Smith, G. D., Suren, P., Roth, C., et al. (2016). Preconception and prenatal alcohol exposure from mothers and fathers drinking and head circumference: Results from the Norwegian Mother–Child Study (MoBa). *Scientific Reports, 6,* 39535.

Zuchero, J. B., & Barres, B. A. (2015). Glia in mammalian development and disease. *Development, 142,* 3805–3809.

CHAPTER 9

Bálint, R. (1909). Seelenlähmung des "Schauens," optische Ataxie, räumliche Störung der Aufmerksamkeit. *Monatschrift für Psychiatrie und Neurologie, 25,* 51–81.

de Gelder, B., Tamietto, M., van Boxtel, G., Goebel, R., Sahraie, A., van den Stock, J., et al. (2008). Intact navigation skills after bilateral loss of striate cortex. *Current Biology, 18,* R1128–R1129.

Farah, M. J. (1990). *Visual agnosia.* Cambridge, MA: MIT Press.

Freud, E., Culham, J. C., Plaut, D. C., & Behrmann, M. (2017). The large-scale organization of shape processing in the ventral and dorsal pathways. *eLife, 6,* e27576.

Goodale, M. A., Milner, D. A., Jakobson, L. S., & Carey, J. D. P. (1991). A kinematic analysis of reaching and grasping movements in a patient recovering from optic ataxia. *Nature, 349,* 154–156.

Hamilton, R. H., Shenton, J. T., & Coslett, H. B. (2006). An acquired deficit of audiovisual speech processing. *Brain and Language, 98,* 66–73.

Hasson, U., Nir, Y., Levy, I., Fuhrmann, G., & Malach, R. (2004). Intersubject synchronization of cortical activity during natural vision. *Science, 303,* 1634–1640.

Held, R. (1968). Dissociation of visual function by deprivation and rearrangement. *Psychologische Forschung, 31,* 338–348.

Jerison, H. J. (1973). *The evolution of the brain and intelligence.* New York: Academic Press.

Kline, D. W. (1994). Optimizing the visibility of displays for older observers. *Experimental Aging Research, 20,* 11–23.

Kuffler, S. W. (1952). Neurons in the retina: Organization, inhibition and excitatory problems. *Cold Spring Harbor Symposia on Quantitative Biology, 17,* 281–292.

Laha, B., Stafford, B. K., & Huberman, A. D. (2017). Regenerating optic pathways from the eye to the brain. *Science, 356,* 1031–1034.

Lim, J.-H. A., Stafford, B. K., Nguyen, P. L., Lien, B. V., Wang, C., Zukor, K., et al. (2016). Neural activity promotes long distance, target-specific regeneration of adult retinal axons. *Nature Neuroscience, 19,* 1073–1084.

Milner, A. D., & Goodale, M. A. (2006). *The visual brain in action* (2nd ed.). Oxford: Oxford University Press.

Purves, D., Augustine, G. J., Fitzpatrick, D., Katz, L. C., LaMantia, A.-S., & McNamara, J. O. (Eds.). (1997). *Neuroscience.* Sunderland, MA: Sinauer.

Sacks, O., & Wasserman, R. (1987). The case of the colorblind painter. *The New York Review of Books, 34,* 25–33.

Szentagothai, J. (1975). The "module-concept" in cerebral cortex architecture. *Brain Research, 95,* 475–496.

Tanaka, K. (1993). Neuronal mechanisms of object recognition. *Science, 262,* 685–688.

Venugoplalan, P., Wang, Y., Nguyen, T., Huang, A., Muller, K. J., & Goldberg, J. L. (2016). Transplanted neurons integrate into adult retinas and respond to light. *Nature Communications, 7,* 10472.

Wallisch, P. (2017). Illumination assumptions account for individual differences in the perceptual interpretation of a profoundly ambiguous stimulus in the color domain: "The dress." *Journal of Vision, 17,* 5.

Weizkrantz, L. (1986). *Blindsight: A case study and implications.* Oxford: Oxford University Press.

Wong-Riley, M. T. T., Hevner, R. F., Cutlan, R., Earnest, M., Egan, R., Frost, J., & Nguyen, T. (1993). Cytochrome oxidase in the human visual cortex: Distribution in the developing and the adult brain. *Visual Neuroscience, 10,* 41–58.

Yu, W., Mookherjee, S., Chaitankar, V., Hiriyanna, S., Kim, J.-W., Brooks, M., et al. (2017). *Nrl* knockdown by AAV-delivered CRISPR/Cas9 prevents retinal degeneration in mice. *Nature Communications, 8,* 14716.

Zaidi, F. H., Hull, J. T., Peirson, S. N., Wulff, K., Aeschbach, D., Gooley, J. J., et al. (2007). Short-wavelength light sensitivity of circadian, pupillary, and visual awareness in humans lacking an outer retina. *Current Biology, 17,* 2122–2128.

Zhu, J., Ming, C., Fu, X., Duan, Y., Hiang, D. A., Rutgard, J., et al. (2017). Gene and mutation independent therapy via CRISPR-Cas9 mediated cellular reprogramming in rod photoreceptors. *Cell Research, 27,* 830–833.

Zihl, J., von Cramon, D., & Mai, N. (1983). Selective disturbance of movement vision after bilateral brain damage. *Brain, 106,* 313–340.

CHAPTER 10

Bermudez, P., Lerch, J. P., Evans, A. C., & Zatorre, R. J. (2009). Neuroanatomical correlates of musicianship as revealed by cortical thickness and voxel-based morphometry. *Cerebral Cortex, 19,* 1583–1596.

Bregman, A. S. (2005). Auditory scene analysis and the role of phenomenology in experimental psychology. *Canadian Psychology, 46*(1), 32–40.

Chomsky, N. (1965). *Aspects of the theory of syntax.* Cambridge, MA: MIT Press.

Clark, G. M. (2015). The multi-channel cochlear implant: Multi-disciplinary development of electrical stimulation of the cochlea and the resulting clinical benefit. *Hearing Research, 322,* 4–13.

Daniel, E. (2007). Noise and hearing loss: A review. *The Journal of School Health, 77,* 225–231.

Drake-Lee, A. B. (1992). Beyond music: Auditory temporary threshold shift in rock musicians after a heavy metal concert. *Journal of the Royal Society of Medicine, 85,* 617–619.

Geissmann, T. (2001). Gibbon songs and human music from an evolutionary perspective. In N. L. Wallin, B. Merker, & S. Brown (Eds.), *The origins of music* (pp. 103–124). Cambridge, MA: MIT Press.

Hyde, K. L., Lerch, J. P., Zatorre, R. J., Griffiths, T. D., Evans, A. C., & Peretz, I. (2007). Cortical thickness in congenital amusia: When less is better than more. *Journal of Neuroscience, 27,* 13028–13032.

Johansson, B. B. (2012). Multisensory stimulation in stroke rehabilitation. *Frontiers in Human Neuroscience, 6,* 60.

Kim, K. H. S., Relkin, N. R., Young-Min Lee, K., & Hirsch, J. (1997). Distinct cortical areas associated with native and second languages. *Nature, 388,* 171–174.

Knudsen, E. I. (1981). The hearing of the barn owl. *Scientific American, 245*(6), 113–125.

Loeb, G. E. (1990). Cochlear prosthetics. *Annual Review of Neuroscience, 13,* 357–371.

Marler, P. (1991). The instinct to learn. In S. Carey and R. German (Eds.), *The epigenesis of mind: Essays on biology and cognition* (p. 39). Hillsdale, NJ: Erlbaum.

Nottebohm, F., & Arnold, A. P. (1976). Sexual dimorphism in vocal control areas of the songbird brain. *Science, 194,* 211–213.

Penfield, W., & Roberts, L. (1956). *Speech and brain mechanisms.* Oxford: Oxford University Press.

Pinker, S. (1997). *How the mind works.* New York: Norton.

Rauschecker, J. P. (2012). Ventral and dorsal streams in the evolution of speech and language. *Frontiers in Evolutionary Neuroscience, 4,* 7.

Romanski, L. M., Tian, B., Fritz, J., Mishkin, M., Goldman-Rakic, P. S., & Rauschecker, J. P. (1999). Dual streams of auditory afferents target multiple domains in the primate prefrontal cortex. *Nature Neuroscience, 2,* 1131–1136.

Sunitha Suresh, B. S., De Oliveira, G. S. Jr., & Suresh, S. (2015). The effect of audio therapy to treat postoperative pain in children undergoing major surgery: A randomized controlled trial. *Pediatric Surgical International, 31,* 197–201.

Teie, P. U. (1998). Noise-induced hearing loss and symphony orchestra musicians: Risk factors, effects, and management. *Maryland Medical Journal, 47,* 13–18.

Teng, S., & Whitney, D. (2011). The acuity of echolocation: Spatial resolution in the sighted compared to expert performance. *Journal of Visual Impairment & Blindness, 105,* 20–32.

Thaler, L., Arnott, S. R., & Goodale, M. A. (2011). Neural correlates of natural human echolocation in early and late blind echolocation experts. *PLOS ONE, 6,* e20162.

Thompson, C. K., Meitzen, J., Replogle, K., Drnevich, J., Lent, K. L., et al. (2012). Seasonal changes in patterns of gene expression in avian song control brain regions. *PLOS ONE, 7,* e35119.

Trehub, S., Schellenberg, E. G., & Ramenetsky, G. B. (1999). Infants' and adults' perception of scale structures. *Journal of Experimental Psychology: Human Perception and Performance, 25,* 965–975.

Zatorre, R. J., Evans, A. C., & Meyer, E. (1994). Neural mechanisms underlying melodic perception and memory for pitch. *Journal of Neuroscience, 14,* 1908–1919.

Zatorre, R. J., Evans, A. C., Meyer, E., & Gjedde, A. (1992). Lateralization of phonetic and pitch discrimination in speech processing. *Science, 256,* 846–849.

Zatorre, R. J., Meyer, E., Gjedde, A., & Evans, A. C. (1996). PET studies of phonetic processing of speech: Review, replication, and reanalysis. *Cerebral Cortex, 6,* 21–30.

CHAPTER 11

Aflalo, T. N., & Graziano, M. S. (2007). Relationship between unconstrained arm movements and single-neuron firing in the macaque motor cortex. *Journal of Neuroscience, 127,* 2760–2780.

Alessandria, M., Vetrugno, R., Cortelli, P., & Montagna, P. (2011). Normal body scheme and absent phantom limb experience in amputees while dreaming. *Consciousness and Cognition, 20,* 831–834.

Alexander, R. E., & Crutcher, M. D. (1990). Functional architecture of basal ganglia circuits: Neural substrates of parallel processing. *Trends in Neuroscience, 13,* 269.

Asanuma, H. (1989). *The motor cortex.* New York: Raven Press.

Ballester-Plané, J., Schmidt, R., Laporta-Hoyos, O., Junqué, C., Vázquez, É., Delgado, I., et al. (2017). Whole-brain structural connectivity in dyskinetic cerebral palsy and its association with motor and cognitive function. *Human Brain Mapping, 38*(9), 4594–4612.

Blakemore, S. J., Wolpert, D. M., & Frith, C. D. (1998). Central cancellation of self-produced tickle sensation. *Nature Neuroscience, 1,* 635–640.

Brinkman, C. (1984). Supplementary motor area of the monkey's cerebral cortex: Short- and long-term deficits after unilateral ablation and the effects of subsequent callosal section. *Journal of Neuroscience, 4,* 918–992.

Brown, B. J., Kim, S., Saunders, H., Bachmann, C., Thompson, J., Ropar, D., et al. (2017). Neural basis for contagious yawning. *Current Biology, 27*(17), 2713–2717.

Casartelli, L., Federici, A., Biffi, E., Molteni, M., & Ronconi, L. (2017). Are we "motorically" wired to others? High-level motor computations and their role in autism. *Neuroscientist.* doi: 10.1177/1073858417750466

Cole, J. (1995). *Pride and a daily marathon.* Cambridge, MA: MIT Press.

Corkin, S., Milner, B., & Rasmussen, T. (1970). Somatosensory thresholds. *Archives of Neurology, 23,* 41–58.

Critchley, M. (1953). *The parietal lobes.* London: Arnold.

Dalamagkas, K., Tsintou, M., & Seifalian, A. M. (2018). Stem cells for spinal cord injuries bearing translational potential. *Neural Regeneration Research, 13*(1), 35–42.

Evarts, E. V. (1968). Relation of pyramidal tract activity to force exerted during voluntary movement. *Journal of Neurophysiology, 31,* 14–27.

Fisher, P., Pogosyan, A., Cheeran, B., Green, A. L., Aziz, T. Z., Hyam, J., et al. (2017). Subthalamic nucleus beta and gamma activity is modulated depending on the level of imagined grip force. *Journal of Experimental Neuroscience, 293,* 53–61.

Foster, E., Wildner, H., Tudeau, L., Haueter, S., Ralvenius, W. T., Jegen, M., et al. (2015). Targeted ablation, silencing, and activation establish glycinergic dorsal horn neurons as key components of a spinal gate for pain and itch. *Neuron, 85,* 1289–1304.

Gillick, B., Rich, T., Nemanich, S., Chen, C. Y., Menk, J., Mueller, B., et al. (2018). Transcranial direct current stimulation and constrain-induced therapy in cerebral palsy: A randomized, blinded, sham-controlled clinical trial. *European Journal of Paediatric Neurology, 22*(3), 358–368.

Graziano, M. S. A. (2009). *The intelligent movement machine: An ethological perspective on the primate motor system.* New York: Oxford University Press.

Guell, X., Gabrieli, J. D. E, & Schmahmann, J. D. (2018). Triple representation of language, working memory, social and emotion processing in the cerebellum: Convergent evidence from task and seed-based resting-state fMRI analyses in a single large cohort. *Neuroimage, 172,* 437–449.

Hellman, R. B., Chang, E., Tanner, J., Helms Tillery, S. I., & Santos, V. J. (2015). A robot hand testbed designed for enhancing embodiment and functional neurorehabilitation of body schema in subjects with upper limb impairment or loss. *Frontiers in Human Neuroscience, 9,* 1–26.

Hess, W. R. (1957). *The functional organization of the diencephalon.* London: Grune & Stratton.

Hikosaka, O., Kim, H. F., Amita, H., Yasuda, M., Isoda, M., Tachibana, Y., & Yoshida, A. (2018). Direct and indirect pathways for choosing objects and actions. *European Journal of Neuroscience.* doi: 10.1111/ejn.13876

Ishijima, K., & Negayama, K. (2017). Development of mother–infant interaction in tickling play: The relationship between infants' ticklishness and social behaviors. *Infant Behavior and Development, 49,* 161–167.

Kaas, J. H. (1987). The organization and evolution of neocortex. In S. P. Wise (Ed.), *Higher brain functions* (pp. 237–298). New York: Wiley.

Kalueff, A. V., Stewart, A. M., Song, C., Berridge, K. C., Graybiel, A. M., & Fentress, J. C. (2016). Neurobiology of rodent self-grooming and its value for translational neuroscience. *Nature Reviews Neuroscience, 17*(1), 45–59.

Karl, J. M., Kuntz, J. R., Lenhart, L. A., & Whishaw, I. Q. (2018). Frame-by-frame video analysis of idiosyncratic reach-to-grasp movements in humans. *Journal of Visualized Experiments, 131.* doi: 10.3791/56733

Kern, U., Busch, V., Rockland, M., Kohl, M., & Birklein, F. (2009). Prevalence and risk factors of phantom limb pain and phantom limb sensations in Germany: A nationwide field survey. *Schmerz, 23,* 479–488.

Kuntz, J. R., Karl, J. M., Doan, J. B., & Whishaw, I. Q. (2018). Gaze anchoring guides real but not pantomime reach-to-grasp: Support for the action-perception theory. *Experimental Brain Research, 236*(4), 1091–1103.

LaFollette, M. R., O'Haire, M. E., Cloutier, S., Blankenberger, W. B., & Gaskill, B. N. (2017). Rat tickling: A systematic review of applications, outcomes, and moderators. *PLOS ONE, 12*(4), e0175320.

Lashley, K. S. (1951). The problem of serial order in behavior. In L. A. Jeffress (Ed.), *Cerebral mechanisms and behavior* (pp. 112–136). New York: Wiley.

Lazarou, I., Nikolopoulos, S., Petrantonakis, P. C., Kompatsiaris, I., & Tsolaki, M. (2018). EEG-based brain–computer interfaces for communication and rehabilitation of people with motor impairment: A novel approach of the 21st century. *Frontiers in Human Neuroscience, 12,* 14.

Meier, J. D., Aflalo, T. N., Kastner, S., & Graziano, M. S. (2008). Complex organization of human primary motor cortex: A high-resolution fMRI study. *Journal of Neurophysiology, 100*(4), 1800–1812.

Melzack, R. (1973). *The puzzle of pain.* New York: Basic Books.

Melzack, R., & Wall, P. D. (1965). Pain mechanisms: A new theory. *Science, 150,* 971–979.

Moisello, C., Perfetti, B., Marinelli, L., Sanguineti, V., Bove, M., Feigin, A., Di Rocco, A., Eidelberg, D., Ghilardi, M. F. (2011). Basal ganglia and kinematics modulation: Insights from Parkinson's and Huntington's diseases. *Parkinsonism & Related Disorders, 17*(8), 642–644.

Mountcastle, V. B. (1978). An organizing principle for cerebral function: The unit module and the distributed system. In G. M. Edelman & V. B. Mountcastle (Eds.), *The mindful brain* (pp. 7–50). Cambridge, MA: MIT Press.

Nevoux, J., Barbara, M., Dornhoffer, J., Gibson, W., Kitahara, T., & Darrouzet, V. (2018). International consensus (ICON) on treatment of Ménière's disease. *European Annals of Otorhinolaryngology, Head and Neck Diseases, 135*(1S), S29–S32.

Nudo, R. J., Wise, B. M., SiFuentes, F., & Milliken, G. W. (1996). Neural substrates for the effects of rehabilitative training on motor recovery after ischemic infarct. *Science, 272,* 1791–1794.

Penfield, W., & Boldrey, E. (1958). Somatic motor and sensory representation in the cerebral cortex as studied by electrical stimulation. *Brain, 60,* 389–443.

Pons, T. P., Garraghty, P. E., Ommaya, A. K., Kaas, J. H., Taum, E., & Mishkin, M. (1991). Massive cortical reorganization after sensory deafferentation in adult macaques. *Science, 252,* 1857–1860.

Ramachandran, V. S., & Rogers-Ramachandran, D. (1996). Synaesthesia in phantom limbs induced with mirrors. *Proceedings of the Royal Society, Biological Science, 263*(1369), 377–386.

Riva, D., Taddei, M., & Bulgheroni, S. (2018). The neurophysiology of basal ganglia. *European Journal of Paediatric Neurology, 22*(2), 321–326.

Roland, P. E. (1993). *Brain activation.* New York: Wiley-Liss.

Ross, M. D., Owren, M. J., & Zimmermann, E. (2010). The evolution of laughter in great apes and humans. *Communicative & Integrative Biology, 3*(2), 191–194.

Rothwell, J. C., Taube, M. M., Day, B. L., Obeso, J. A., Thomas, P. K., & Marsden, C. D. (1982). Manual motor performance in a deafferented man. *Brain, 105,* 515–542.

Sacks, O. W. (1998). *The man who mistook his wife for a hat: And other clinical tales.* New York: Touchstone Books.

Schieber, M. H. (2011). Dissociating motor cortex from the motor. *Journal of Physiology, 589*(Pt. 23), 5613–5624.

Thach, W. T. (2007). On the mechanism of cerebellar contributions to cognition. *Cerebellum, 6,* 163–167.

Thach, W. T., Goodkin, H. P., & Keating, J. G. (1992). The cerebellum and the adaptive coordination of movement. *Annual Review of Neuroscience, 15,* 403–442.

Therrien, A. S., & Bastian, A. J. (2015). Cerebellar damage impairs internal predictions for sensory and motor function. *Current Opinion in Neurobiology, 33,* 127–133.

van Nispen, K., Mieke, W. M. E., van de Sandt-Koenderman, E., & Krahmer, E. (2018). The comprehensibility of pantomimes produced by people with aphasia. *International Journal of Language and Communication Disorders, 53*(1), 85–100.

van Wensen, E., & van de Warrenburg, B. P. (2018). The yips: A movement disorder among golfers. *Nederlands Tijdschrift Voor Geneeskunde, 162,* D2204.

von Holst, E. (1973). *The collected papers of Erich von Holst* (R. Martin, Trans.). Coral Gables, FL: University of Miami Press.

Windt, J. M., Harkness, D. L., & Lenggenhager, B. (2015). Tickle me, I think I might be dreaming! Sensory attenuation, self-other distinction, and predictive processing in lucid dreams. *Frontiers in Human Neuroscience, 8,* 717.

Wolbrecht, E. T., Rowe, J. B., Chan, V., Ingemanson, M. L., Cramer, S. C., & Reinkensmeyer, D. J. (2018). Finger strength, individuation, and their interaction: Relationship to hand function and corticospinal tract injury after stroke. *Clinical Neurophysiology, 129*(4), 797–808.

CHAPTER 12

Ackerly, S. S. (1964). A case of paranatal bilateral frontal lobe defect observed for thirty years. In J. M. Warren & K. Akert (Eds.), *The frontal granular cortex and behavior* (pp. 192–218). New York: McGraw-Hill.

Anderson, D. J., & Adolphs, R. (2014). A framework for studying emotions across species. *Cell, 157,* 187–200.

Arnold, A. P., Reue, K., Eghbali, M., Vilain, E., Chen, X., Ghahramani, N., et al. (2016). The importance of having two X chromosomes. *Philosophical Transactions of the Royal Society of London B: Biological Sciences, 371*(1688), 20150113.

Bao, A.-M., & Swaab, D. F. (2011). Sexual differentiation of the human brain: Relation to gender identity, sexual orientation and neuropsychiatric disorders. *Frontiers in Neuroendocrinology, 32,* 214–226.

Bartoshuk, L. M. (2000). Comparing sensory experiences across individuals: Recent psychophysical advances illuminate genetic variation in taste perception. *Chemical Senses, 25,* 447–460.

Beatty, J. (1995). *Principles of behavioral neuroscience.* Dubuque, IA: Brown & Benchmark.

Bechara, A. (2017). Revisiting Phineas Gage: Lessons we learned from damaged brains. In B. Kolb & I. Q. Whishaw (Eds.), *Brain & Behaviour: Revisiting the Classic Studies* (pp. 113–129). London: Sage.

Berridge, K. C. (1996). Food reward: Brain substrates of wanting and liking. *Neuroscience and Biobehavioral Reviews, 20,* 6.

Berridge, K. C., & Kringelbach, M. L. (2015). Pleasure systems in the brain. *Neuron, 86,* 646–664.

Berridge, K. C., & Robinson, T. E. (1998). What is the role of dopamine in reward: Hedonic impact, reward learning, or incentive salience? *Brain Research Reviews, 28*, 309–369.

Berridge, K. C., & Robinson, T. E. (2003). Parsing reward. *Trends in Neuroscience, 26*, 507–513.

Berridge, K. C., & Robinson, T. E. (2016). Liking, wanting and the incentive-sensitization theory of addiction. *American Psychologist, 71*, 670–679.

Brunetti, M., Babiloni, C., Ferretti, A., Del Gratta, C., Merla, A., Olivetti Belardinelli, M., & Romani, G. L. (2008). Hypothalamus, sexual arousal and psychosexual identity in human males: A functional magnetic resonance imaging study. *European Journal of Neuroscience, 27*, 2922–2927.

Buss, D. (2014). *Evolutionary psychology: The new science of the mind* (5th ed.). New York: Taylor & Francis.

Butler, R. A., & Harlow, H. F. (1954). Persistence of visual exploration in monkeys. *Journal of Comparative and Physiological Psychology, 47*, 257–263.

Buzaki, G. (2011). *Rhythms of the brain.* New York: Oxford University Press.

Carus-Cadavieco, M., Gorbati, M., Ye, L., Bender, F., van der Veldt, S., Kosse, C., et al. (2017). Gamma oscillations organize top-down signaling to hypothalamus and enable food seeking. *Nature, 542*, 232–236.

Clark-Polner, E., Johnson, T. D., & Barrett, L. F. (2017). Multivoxel pattern analysis does not provide evidence to support the existence of basic emotions. *Cerebral Cortex, 27*, 1944–1948.

Daly, M., & Wilson, M. (1988). *Homicide.* New York: Aldine.

Day, J. J., & Sweatt, J. D. (2011). Cognitive neuroepigenetics: A role for epigenetic mechanisms in learning and memory. *Neurobiology of Learning and Memory, 96*, 2–12.

Dubois, J., Oya, H., Tyszka, J. M., Howard, M., Eberhardt, F., & Adolphs, R. (2017). Causal mapping of emotion networks in the human brain: Framework and initial findings. *Neuropsychologia.* doi:10.1016/j.neuropsychologia.2017.11.015

Eisenberger, N. I., Jarcho, J. M., Lieberman, M. D., & Naliboff, B. D. (2006). An experimental study of shared sensitivity to physical pain and social rejection. *Pain, 126*, 132–138.

Eisenberger, N. I., Lieberman, M. D., & Williams, K. D. (2003). Does rejection hurt? An fMRI study of social exclusion. *Science, 302*, 290–292.

Everitt, B. J. (1990). Sexual motivation: A neural and behavioral analysis of the mechanisms underlying appetitive and copulatory responses of male rats. *Neuroscience and Biobehavioral Reviews, 14*, 217–232.

Field, T. M., Woodson, R., Greenberg, R., & Cohen, D. (1982). Discrimination and imitation of facial expression by neonates. *Science, 218*, 179–181.

Garcia, J., & Koelling, R. A. (1966). Relation of cue to consequences in avoidance learning. *Psychonomic Science, 4*, 123–124.

Garrison, K. A., Zeffiro, T. A., Scheinost, D., Constable, R. T., & Brewer, J. A. (2015). Meditation leads to reduced default mode network activity beyond an active task. *Cognitive Affective Behavioral Neuroscience, 15*, 712–720.

Gerkin, R. C., & Castro, J. B. (2015). The number of olfactory stimuli that humans can discriminate is still unknown. *eLife, 4*, e08127.

Glickman, S. E., & Schiff, B. B. (1967). A biological theory of reinforcement. *Psychological Review, 74*, 81–109.

Gorski, R. A. (1984). Critical role for the medial preoptic area in the sexual differentiation of the brain. *Progress in Brain Research, 61*, 129–146.

Hummer, T. A., Phan, K. L., Kern, D. W., & McClintock, M. K. (2017). A human chemosignal modulates frontolimbic activity and connectivity in response to social stimuli. *Psychoneuroendocrinology, 75*, 15–25.

Insel, T. R., & Fernald, R. D. (2004). How the brain processes social information: Searching for the social brain. *Annual Review of Neuroscience, 27*, 697–722.

Jacobsen, C. F. (1936). Studies of cerebral function in primates. *Comparative Psychology Monographs, 13*, 1–68.

Kagan, J. (2018). Brain and emotion. *Emotion Review, 10*, 79–86.

Klüver, H., & Bucy, P. C. (1939). Preliminary analysis of the temporal lobes in monkeys. *Archives of Neurology and Psychiatry, 42*, 979–1000.

Kolb, B., & Nonneman, A. J. (1975). The development of social responsiveness in kittens. *Animal Behavior, 23*, 368–374.

Kolb, B., & Whishaw, I. Q. (2015). *Fundamentals of human neuropsychology* (7th ed.). New York: Worth.

Kragel, P. A., Kano, M., van Oudenhove, L., Ly, H. G., Dupont, P., Rubio, A., et al. (2018). Generalizable representations of pain, cognitive control, and negative emotion in medial frontal cortex. *Nature Neuroscience, 21*, 283–289.

Kringelbach, M. L., & Berridge, K. C. (2017). The affective core of emotion: Linking pleasure, subjective well-being, and optimal metastability in the brain. *Emotion Review, 9*, 191–199.

Kringelbach, M. L., & Phillips, H. (2014). *Emotion: Pleasure and pain in the brain.* Oxford: Oxford University Press.

Kross, E., Berman, M. G., Mischel, W., Smith, E. E., & Water, T. D. (2011). Social rejection shares somatosensory representations with physical pain. *Proceedings of the National Academy of Sciences of the United States of America, 108*, 6270–6275.

Kung, K. T. F., Brown, W. V., Constantinescu, M., Noorderhaven, R. M., & Hines, M. (2016). Early postnatal testosterone predicts sex-related differences in early expressive vocabulary. *Psychoneuroendocrinology, 68*, 111–116.

LeDoux, J. E. (2014). Evolution of human emotion: A view through fear. *Progress in Brain Research, 195*, 431–442.

Levenson, R. W., Lwi, S. J., Brown, C. L., Ford, B. Q., Otero, M. C., & Vertaen, A. (2017). Emotion. In J. T. Cacippo, L. G. Tassinary, & G. G. Berntson (Eds.), *Handbook of psychophysiology* (4th ed., pp. 444–464). Cambridge: Cambridge University Press.

Lundstrom, J. N., Boyle, J. A., Zatorre, R. J., & Jones-Gotman, M. (2008). Functional neuronal processing of body odors differs from that of similar common odors. *Cerebral Cortex, 18*, 1466–1474.

MacLean, P. D. (1949). Psychosomatic disease and the "visceral brain": Recent developments bearing on the Papez theory of emotion. *Psychosomatic Medicine, 11*, 338–353.

McCarthy, M., de Vries, G. J., & Forger, N. G. (2017). Sexual differentiation of the brain: A fresh look at mode, mechanisms, and meaning. In D. W. Pfaff & M. Joels (Eds.), *Hormones, brain, and behavior* (3rd ed., pp. 3–32). Oxford, U.K.: Academic Press.

McCarthy, M. M., Auger, A. P., Bale, T. L., De Vries, G. J., Dunn, G. A., et al. (2009). The epigenetics of sex differences in the brain. *Journal of Neuroscience, 29*, 12815–12823.

Money, J., & Ehrhardt, A. A. (1972). *Man and woman, boy and girl.* Baltimore: Johns Hopkins University Press.

Moors, A., Ellsworth, P. C., Scherer, K. R., & Frijda, N. H. (2013). Appraisal theories of emotion: State of the art and future development. *Emotion Review, 5*, 119–124.

Narayanan, N. S., & DiLeone, R. J. (2017). Lip sync: Gamma rhythms orchestrate top-down control of feeding circuits. *Cell Metabolism, 25*(3), 497–498.

Olds, J., & Milner, P. (1954). Positive reinforcement produced by electrical stimulation of septal area and other regions of rat brain. *Journal of Comparative and Physiological Psychology, 47*, 419–427.

Olsson, S. B., Barnard, J., & Turri, L. (2006). Olfaction and identification of unrelated individuals: Examination of the mysteries of human odor recognition. *Journal of Chemical Ecology, 32*, 1635–1645.

Phoenix, C. H., Goy, R. W., Gerall, A. A., & Young, W. C. (1959). Organizing action of prenatally administered testosterone propionate on the tissues mediating mating behavior in the female guinea pig. *Endocrinology, 65,* 365–382.

Ritchie, S. J., Cox, S. R., Shen, X., Lombardo, M. V., Reus, L. M., Alloza, C., et al. (2018). Sex differences in the adult human brain: Evidence from 5216 UK biobank participants. *Cerebral Cortex, 28*(8), 2959–2975.

Schroeder, M., Krebs, M. O., Bleich, S., & Frieling, H. (2010). Epigenetics and depression. *Current Opinion in Psychiatry, 23,* 588–592.

Seeley, R. J., & Woods, S. C. (2003). Monitoring of stored and available fuel by the CNS: Implications for obesity. *Nature Reviews Neuroscience, 4,* 885–909.

Skinner, B. F. (1938). *The behavior of organisms.* New York: Appleton-Century-Crofts.

Smith, D. V., & Shepherd, G. M. (2003). Chemical senses: Taste and olfaction. In L. R. Squiare, F. E. Bloom, S. K. McConnell, J. L. Roberts, N. C. Spitzer, & M. J. Zigmond (Eds.), *Fundamental neuroscience* (2nd ed., pp. 631–667). New York: Academic Press.

Swanson, L. W. (2000). Cerebral hemisphere regulation of motivated behavior. *Brain Research Reviews, 886,* 113–164.

Wise, R. A. (1980). The dopamine synapse and the notion of "pleasure centers" in the brain. *Trends in Neuroscience, 3,* 91–95.

Woolley, C. S., Gould, E., Frankfurt, M., & McEwen, B. (1990). Naturally occurring fluctuation in dendritic spine density on adult hippocampal pyramidal neurons. *Journal of Neuroscience, 10,* 4035–4039.

World Health Organization. (2000). *Obesity: Preventing and managing the global epidemic.* WHO Technical Report Series, No. 894, 1–253.

CHAPTER 13

Amariei, C., Tomita, M., & Murray, D. B. (2014). Quantifying periodicity in omics data. *Frontiers in Cellular Developmental Biology, 19*(2), 40.

Aschoff, J. (1978). Circadian rhythms within and outside their ranges of entrainment. In I. Assenmacher & D. S. Farner (Eds.), *Environmental endocrinology* (pp. 171–181). Berlin: Springer.

Batterink, L. J., Oudiette, D., Reber, P. J., & Paller, K. A. (2014). Sleep facilitates learning a new linguistic rule. *Neuropsychologia, 65,* 169–179.

Binkley, S. (1990). *The clockwork sparrow.* Englewood Cliffs, NJ: Prentice Hall.

Blumberg, M. S. (2015). Developing sensorimotor systems in our sleep. *Current Directions in Psychological Science, 24,* 32–37.

Bosler, O., Girardet, C., Franc, J. L., Becquet, D., & François-Bellan, A. M. (2015). Structural plasticity of the circadian timing system: An overview from flies to mammals. *Frontiers in Neuroendocrinology, 38,* 50–64.

Cain, S. W., Verwey, M., Szybowska, M., Ralph, M. R., & Yeomans, J. S. (2007). Carbachol injections into the intergeniculate leaflet induce nonphotic phase shifts. *Brain Research, 1177,* 59–65.

Carter, K. A., Hathaway, N. E., & Lettieri, C. F. (2014). Common sleep disorders in children. *American Family Physician, 89,* 368–377.

Corrêa C. C., Blasca, W. Q., & Berretin-Felix, G. (2015). Health promotion in obstructive sleep apnea syndrome. *International Archives of Otorhinolaryngology, 19,* 166–170.

de Lavilléon, G., Lacroix, M. M., Rondi-Reig, L., & Benchenane, K. (2015). Explicit memory creation during sleep demonstrates a causal role of place cells in navigation. *Nature Neuroscience, 18,* 493–495.

Dement, W. C. (1972). *Some must watch while some must sleep.* Stanford, CA: Stanford Alumni Association.

Diekman, C. O., & Bose, A. (2018). Reentrainment of the circadian pacemaker during jet lag: East–west asymmetry and the effects of north–south travel. *Journal of Theoretical Biology, 437,* 261–285.

Dissel, S., Angadi, V., Kirszenblat, L., Suzuki, Y., Donlea, J., Klose, M., et al. (2015). Sleep restores behavioral plasticity to *Drosophila* mutants. *Current Biology, 25,* 1270–1280.

Edwards, C. L., Ruby, P. M., Malinowski, J. E., Bennett, P. D., & Blagrove, M. T. (2013). Dreaming and insight. *Frontiers in Psychology, 24,* 974–979.

Elliott, A. S., Huber, J. D., O'Callaghan, J. P., Rosen, C. L., & Miller, D. B. (2014). A review of sleep deprivation studies evaluating the brain transcriptome. *Springerplus, 3,* 728.

Fadda, A., El Anbari, M., & Ptitsyn, A. (2018). Circadian succession of molecular processes in living tissues. *BMC Medical Genomics, 11*(Suppl. 1), 14.

Filevich, E., Dresler, M., Brick, T. R., & Kühn, S. (2015). Metacognitive mechanisms underlying lucid dreaming. *Journal of Neuroscience, 35,* 1082–1088.

Foulkes, D., & Domhoff, G. W. (2014). Bottom-up or top-down in dream neuroscience? A top-down critique of two bottom-up studies. *Conscious Cognition, 27,* 168–171.

Freud, S. (1900). *The interpretation of dreams.* Leipzig and Vienna: Franz Deuticke.

Gale, C., & Martyn, C. (1998). Larks and owls and health, wealth, and wisdom. *BMJ, 317,* 1675–1677.

Gaucher, J., Montellier, E., & Sassone-Corsi, P. (2018). Molecular cogs: Interplay between circadian clock and cell cycle. *Trends in Cell Biology, 28*(5), 368–379.

Gerrard, J. L., Burke, S. N., McNaughton, B. L., & Barnes, C. A. (2008). Sequence reactivation in the hippocampus is impaired in aged rats. *Journal of Neuroscience, 30,* 7883–7890.

Hall, C. S., Domhoff, G. W., Blick, K. A., & Weesner, K. E. (1982). The dreams of college men and women in 1950 and 1980: A comparison of dream contents and sex differences. *Sleep, 5,* 188–194.

Hobson, J. A. (1989). *Sleep.* New York: Scientific American Library.

Hobson, J. A. (2002). Sleep and dream suppression following a lateral medullary infarct: A first-person account. *Consciousness and Cognition, 11,* 377–390.

Hobson, J. A. (2004). *13 dreams Freud never had: A new mind science.* New York: Pi Press.

Honma, S. (2018). The mammalian circadian system: A hierarchical multi-oscillator structure for generating circadian rhythm. *Journal of Physiological Sciences, 68*(3), 207–219.

Jagannath, A., Taylor, L., Wakaf, Z., Vasudevan, S. R., & Foster, R. G. (2017). The genetics of circadian rhythms, sleep and health. *Human Molecular Genetics, 26*(R2), R128–R138.

Jones, B. E. (1993). The organization of central cholinergic systems and their functional importance in sleep–waking states. *Progress in Brain Research, 98,* 61–71.

Jouvet, M. (1972). The role of monoamines and acetylcholine-containing neurons in the regulation of the sleep–waking cycle. *Ergebnisse der Physiologie, 64,* 166–307.

Kay, D. B., & Buysse, D. J. (2017). Hyperarousal and beyond: New insights to the pathophysiology of insomnia disorder through functional neuroimaging studies. *Brain Sciences, 7*(23), 1–19.

Kelley, D. D. (1991). Sleep and dreaming. In E. R. Kandel, J. H. Schwartz, & T. M. Jessell (Eds.), *Principles of neuroscience* (pp. 741–777). New York: Elsevier.

Kerr, D. C., Zava, D. T., Piper, W. T., Saturn, S. R., Frei, B., & Gombart, A. F. (2015). Associations between vitamin D levels and depressive symptoms in healthy young adult women. *Psychiatry Research, 227,* 46–51.

Klinger, E. (1990). *Daydreaming.* Los Angeles: Tarcher (Putnam).

Kreutzmann, J., Havekes, R., Abel, T., & Meerlo, P. (2015). Sleep deprivation and hippocampal vulnerability: Changes in neuronal plasticity, neurogenesis and cognitive function. *Neuroscience, 309,* 173–190.

Lajoie, P., Aronson, K. J., Day, A., & Tranmer, J. (2015). A cross-sectional study of shift work, sleep quality and cardiometabolic risk in female hospital employees. *BMJ Open Science, 5*(3), e007327.

Lamberg, L. (2003). Scientists never dreamed finding would shape half-century of sleep research. *Journal of the American Medical Association, 290,* 2652–2654.

Lan, K. C., Chang, D. W., Kuo, C. E., Wei, M. Z., Li, Y. H., Shaw, F. Z., et al. (2015). Using off-the-shelf lossy compression for wireless home sleep staging. *Journal of Neuroscience Methods, 246,* 142–152.

Li, Y., Ma, W., Kang, Q., Qiao, L., Tang, D., Qiu, J., et al. (2015). Night or darkness, which intensifies the feeling of fear? *International Journal of Psychophysiology, 97*(1), 46–57.

Lucas, S. J., Michel, C. B., Marra, V., Smalley, J. L., Hennig, M. H., Graham, B. P., & Forsythe, I. D. (2018). Glucose and lactate as metabolic constraints on pre-synaptic transmission at an excitatory synapse. *The Journal of Physiology, 596*(9), 1699–1721.

Lungato, L., Gazarini, M. L, Paredes-Gamero, E. J., Tufik, S., & D'Almeida, V. (2015). Paradoxical sleep deprivation impairs mouse survival after infection with malaria parasites. *Malaria Journal, 14,* 183.

Mahowald, M. W., & Schenck, C. H. (2015). REM sleep behaviour disorder: A window on the sleeping brain. *Brain, 138,* 1131–1133.

Malcolm-Smith, S., Koopowitz, S., Pantelis, E., & Solms, M. (2012). Approach/avoidance in dreams. *Consciousness and Cognition, 21,* 408–412.

Maquet, P., Laureys, S., Peigneux, P., Fuchs, S., Petiau, C., Phillips, C., et al. (2000). Experience-dependent changes in cerebral activation during human REM sleep. *Nature Neuroscience, 3,* 831–836.

Mårtensson, B., Pettersson, A., Berglund, L., & Ekselius, L. (2015). Bright white light therapy in depression: A critical review of the evidence. *Journal of Affective Disorders, 182,* 1–7.

Mieda, M. (2017). The roles of orexins in sleep/wake regulation. *Neuroscience Research, 118,* 56–65.

Monecke, S., Brewer, J. M., Krug, S., & Bittman, E. L. (2011). Duper: A mutation that shortens hamster circadian period. *Biological Rhythms, 26,* 283–292.

Moruzzi, G., & Magoun, H .W. (1949). Brain stem reticular formation and activation of the EEG. *Electroencephalography and Clinical Neurophysiology, 1,* 455–473.

Mulder, C. K., Reckman, G. A., Gerkema, M. P., & Van der Zee, E. A. (2015). Time–place learning over a lifetime: Absence of memory loss in trained old mice. *Learning and Memory, 22,* 278–288.

Nelini, C., Bobbo, D., & Mascetti, G. G. (2012). Monocular learning of a spatial task enhances sleep in the right hemisphere of domestic chicks (*Gallus gallus*). *Experimental Brain Research, 18,* 381–388.

Osorio, I., & Daroff, R. B. (1980). Absence of REM and altered NREM sleep in patients with spinocerebellar degeneration and slow saccades. *Annals of Neurology, 7,* 277–280.

Paganelli, R., Petrarca, C., & Di Gioacchino, M. (2018). Biological clocks: Their relevance to immune-allergic diseases. *Clinical and Molecular Allergy, 16,* 1.

Phillips, A. J., Czeisler, C. A., & Klerman, E. B. (2011). Revisiting spontaneous internal desynchrony using a quantitative model of sleep physiology. *Journal of Biological Rhythms, 26*(5), 441–453.

Postuma, R. B., Gagnon, J. F., Tuineaig, M., Bertrand, J. A., Latreille, V., Desjardins, C., et al. (2013). Antidepressants and REM sleep behavior disorder: Isolated side effect or neurodegenerative signal? *Sleep, 36,* 1579–1585.

Putilov, A. A., Dorokhov, V. B., & Poluektov, M. G. (2017). How have our clocks evolved? Adaptive and demographic history of the out-of-African dispersal told by polymorphic loci in circadian genes. *Chronobiology International, 35*(4), 511–532.

Quinlan, J., & Quinlan, J. (1977). *Karen Ann: The Quinlans tell their story.* Toronto: Doubleday.

Ralph, M. R., & Lehman, M. N. (1991). Transplantation: A new tool in the analysis of the mammalian hypothalamic circadian pacemaker. *Trends in Neurosciences, 14,* 363–366.

Rasch, B., & Born, J. (2013). About sleep's role in memory. *Physiological Reviews, 93,* 681–766.

Raven, P. H., Evert, R. F., & Eichorn, S. E. (1992). *Biology of plants.* New York: Worth Publishers.

Reiter, R. J. (1980). The pineal and its hormones in the control of reproduction in mammals. *Endocrinology Review, 1,* 120.

Richter, C. P. (1965). *Biological clocks in medicine and psychiatry.* Springfield, IL: Charles C. Thomas.

Roffward, H. P., Muzio, J., & Dement, W. C. (1966). Ontogenetic development of the human sleep–dream cycle. *Science, 152,* 604–619.

Sateia, M. J. (2014). International Classification of Sleep Disorders, Third Edition. *Chest Journal, 146,* 1387–1394.

Schenck, C. H., Bundlie, S. R., Ettinger, M. G., & Mahowald, M. W. (1986). Chronic behavioral disorders of human REM sleep: A new category of parasomnia. *Sleep, 25,* 293–308.

Schmidt, C., Peigneux, P., Cajochen, C., & Collette, F. (2012). Adapting test timing to the sleep–wake schedule: Effects on diurnal neurobehavioral performance changes in young evening and older morning chronotypes. *Chronobiology International, 29,* 482–490.

Siegel, J. (2004). Brain mechanisms that control sleep and waking. *Naturwissenschaften, 91,* 355–365.

Tononi, G., & Cirelli, C. (2016). Sleep and synaptic down-selection. In G. Buzsáki & Y. Christen (Eds.), *Micro-, meso-, and macro-dynamics of the brain* (pp. 99–106). Cham, Switzerland: Springer.

Valli, K., & Revonsuo, A. (2009). The threat simulation theory in light of recent empirical evidence: A review. *American Journal of Psychology, 122,* 17–38.

Vanderwolf, C. H. (2002). *An odyssey through the brain, behavior and the mind.* Amsterdam: Kluwer Academic.

Van Dongen, H. P., Baynard, M. D., Maislin, G., & Dinges, D. F. (2004). Systematic interindividual differences in neurobehavioral impairment from sleep loss: Evidence of trait-like differential vulnerability. *Sleep, 27*(3), 423–433.

Wijemanne, S., & Jankovic, J. (2015). Restless legs syndrome: Clinical presentation diagnosis and treatment. *Sleep Medicine, 16*(6), 678–690.

Wilson, M. A., & McNaughton, B. L. (1994). Reactivation of hippocampal ensemble memories during sleep. *Science, 265,* 676–679.

Wilson, S., & Argyropoulos, S. (2005). Antidepressants and sleep: A qualitative review of the literature. *Drugs, 65,* 927–947.

Zaidi, F. H., Hull, J. T., Peirson, S. N., Wulff, K., Aeschbach, D., Gooley, J. J., et al. (2007). Short-wavelength light sensitivity of circadian, pupillary, and visual awareness in humans lacking an outer retina. *Current Biology, 17*(24), 2122–2128

Zhang, L., Hirano, A., Hsu, P.-K., Jones, C. R., Sakai, N., Okuro, M., et al. (2016). A PERIOD3 variant causes a circadian phenotype and is associated with a seasonal mood trait. *Proceedings of the National Academy of Sciences of the United States of America, 113*(11), E1536–E1544.

Zwart, T. C., Smits, M. G., Egberts, T. C. G, Rademaker, C. M. A, & van Geijlswijk, I. M. (2018). Long-term melatonin therapy for adolescents and young adults with chronic sleep onset insomnia and late melatonin onset: Evaluation of sleep quality, chronotype, and lifestyle factors compared to age-related randomly selected population cohorts. *Healthcare (Basel), 6,* E23.

CHAPTER 14

Arvanitakis, Z., Capuano, A. W., Lamar, M., Shah, R. C., Barnes, L. L., Bennett, D. A., & Schneider, J. A. (2018). Late-life blood pressure association with cerebrovascular and Alzheimer disease pathology. *Neurology, 91*(6), e517–e525.

Binder, J. R., Desai, R. H., Graves, W. W., & Conant, L. L. (2009). Where is the semantic system? A critical review and meta-analysis of 120 functional neuroimaging systems. *Cerebral Cortex, 19,* 2767–2796.

Bliss, T. V., & Lømø, T. (1973). Long-lasting potentiation of synaptic transmission in the dentate are of the anaesthetized rabbit following stimulation of the perforant path. *Journal of Physiology, 232,* 331–356.

Bonnici, H. M., Chadwick, M. J., Lutti, A., Hassabis, D., Weiskopg, N., & Maguire, E. A. (2012). Detecting representations of recent and remote autobiographical memories in vmPFC and hippocampus. *Journal of Neuroscience, 32,* 16982–16991.

Bonnici, H. M., & Maguire, E. A. (2018). Two years later—Revisiting autobiographical memory representations in vmPFC and hippocampus. *Neuropsychologia, 110,* 159–169.

Cahill, L., Babinsky, R., Markowitsch, H. J., & McGaugh, J. L. (1995). The amygdala and emotional memory. *Nature, 377,* 295–296.

Candia, V., Wienbruch, C., Elbert, T., Rockstroh, B., & Ray, W. (2003). Effective behavioral treatment of focal hand dystonia in musicians alters somatosensory cortical organization. *Proceedings of the National Academy of Sciences of the United States of America, 100,* 7942–7946.

Chang, F.-L. F., & Greenough, W. T. (1982). Lateralized effects of monocular training on dendritic branching in adult split-brain rats. *Brain Research, 232,* 283–292.

Corkin, S. (2002). What's new with the amnesic patient H. M.? *Nature Reviews Neuroscience, 3,* 153–160.

Corkin, S., Amaral, D. G., Gonzalez, R. G., Johnson, K. A., & Hyman, B. T. (1997). H. M.'s medial temporal lobe lesion: Findings from magnetic resonance imaging. *Journal of Neuroscience, 17,* 3964–3979.

Damasio, A. R., Tranel, D., & Damasio, H. (1989). Amnesia caused by herpes simplex encephalitis, infarctions in basal forebrain, Alzheimer's disease and anoxia/ischemia. In F. Boller & J. Grafman (Eds.), *Handbook of neuropsychology* (Vol. 3, pp. 149–166). New York: Elsevier.

Davis, M. (1992). The role of the amygdala in fear and anxiety. *Annual Review of Neuroscience, 15,* 353–375.

Day, J. J., Kennedy, A. J., & Sweatt, J. D. (2015). DNA methylation and its implications and accessibility for neuropsychiatric therapeutics. *Annual Review of Pharmacology and Toxicology, 55,* 591–611.

Dias, B. G., Maddox, S., Klengel, T., & Kessler, K. J. (2015). Epigenetic mechanisms underlying learning and the inheritance of learned behaviors. *Trends in Neuroscience, 38,* 96–107.

Dittrich, L. (2016). *Patient H. M.: A story of memory, madness, and family secrets.* New York: Random House.

Eriksson, P. S., Perfilieva, E., Bjork-Eriksson, T., Alborn, A. M., Nordborg, C., Peterson, D. A., et al. (1998). Neurogenesis in the adult human hippocampus. *Nature Medicine, 4,* 1313–1317.

Fuster, J. M. (1995). *Memory in the cerebral cortex.* Cambridge, MA: MIT Press.

Fuster, J. M., Bodner, M., & Kroger, J. K. (2000). Cross-modal and cross-temporal association in neurons of frontal cortex. *Nature, 405,* 347–351.

Gapp, K., Jawaid, A., Sarkies, P., Bohacke, J., Pelczar, P., Prados, J., et al. (2014). Implication of sperm RNAs in transgenerational inheritance of the effects of early trauma in mice. *Nature Neuroscience, 17,* 667–669.

Gazzaniga, M. S. (Ed.). (2000). *The new cognitive neurosciences.* Cambridge, MA: MIT Press.

Gould, E., Tanapat, P., Hastings, N. B., & Shors, T. J. (1999). Neurogenesis in adulthood: A possible role in learning. *Trends in Cognitive Sciences, 3,* 186–191.

Gould, E., Tanapat, P., McEwen, B. S., Flugge, G., & Fuchs, E. (1998). Proliferation of granule cell precursors in the dentate gyrus of adult monkeys is diminished by stress. *Proceedings of the National Academy of Sciences of the United States of America, 95,* 3168–3171.

Hampson, E., & Kimura, D. (1988). Reciprocal effects of hormonal fluctuations on human motor and perceptual-spatial skills. *Behavioral Neuroscience, 102,* 456–459.

Hebb, D. O. (1947). The effects of early experience on problem solving at maturity. *American Psychologist, 2,* 737–745.

Hebb, D. O. (1949). *The organization of behavior: A neuropsychological theory.* New York: Wiley.

Hornickel, J., Zecker, S. G., Bradlow, A. R., & Kraus, N. (2012). Assistive listening devices drive neuroplasticity in children with dyslexia. *Proceedings of the National Academy of Sciences of the United States of America, 109,* 16731–16736.

Jacobs, B., Schall, M., & Scheibel, A. B. (1993). A quantitative dendritic analysis of Wernicke's area in humans: II. Gender, hemispheric, and environmental factors. *Journal of Comparative Neurology, 327,* 97–111.

Jacobs, B., & Scheibel, A. B. (1993). A quantitative dendritic analysis of Wernicke's area in humans: I. Lifespan changes. *Journal of Comparative Neurology, 327,* 83–96.

Josselyn, S. A., Kohler, S., & Frankland, P. W. (2017). Heroes of the engram. *Journal of Neuroscience, 37,* 4647–4657.

Kaas, J. (2000). The reorganization of sensory and motor maps after injury in adult mammals. In M. S. Gazzaniga (Ed.), *The cognitive neurosciences* (pp. 223–236). Cambridge, MA: MIT Press.

Kempermann, G., Kuhn, H. G., & Gage, F. H. (1998). Experience-induced neurogenesis in the senescent dentate gyrus. *Journal of Neuroscience, 18,* 3206–3212.

Kolb, B., Cote, S., Ribeiro-da-Silva, A., & Cuello, A. C. (1997). Nerve growth factor treatment prevents dendritic atrophy and promotes recovery of function after cortical injury. *Neuroscience, 76,* 1146.

Kolb, B., & Gibb, R. (2014). Searching for principles of brain plasticity and behavior. *Cortex, 58,* 251–260.

Kolb, B., Gibb, R., & Gorny, G. (2003). Experience-dependent changes in dendritic arbor and spine density in neocortex vary with age and sex. *Neurobiology of Learning and Memory, 79,* 1–10.

Kolb, B., Li, Y. Robinson, T. E., & Parker, L. A. (2018). THC alters morphology of neurons in medical prefrontal cortex, orbital prefrontal cortex, and nucleus accumbens and alters the ability of later experience to promote structural plasticity. *Synapse, 72*(3).

Kolb, B., Morshead, C., Gonzalez, C., Kim, N., Shingo, T., & Weiss, S. (2007). Growth factor–stimulated generation of new cortical tissue and functional recovery after stroke damage to the motor cortex of rats. *Journal of Cerebral Blood Flow and Metabolism, 27,* 983–397.

Kronbichler, L., & Kronbichler, M. (2018). The importance of the left occipitotemporal cortex in developmental dyslexia. *Current Developmental Disorders Reports, 5,* 1–8.

Lashley, K. S. (1960). In search of the engram. Symposium No. 4 of the Society of Experimental Biology. In F. A. Beach, D. O. Hebb, C. T. Morgan, & H. T. Nissen (Eds.), *The neuropsychology of Lashley* (pp. 478–505). New York: McGraw-Hill. (Reprinted from R. Sutton (Ed.), *Physiological mechanisms of animal behavior,* pp. 454–482, 1951. Cambridge: Cambridge University Press.)

LeDoux, J. E. (1995). In search of an emotional system in the brain: Leaping from fear to emotion and consciousness. In M. S. Gazzaniga (Ed.), *The cognitive neurosciences* (pp. 1047–1061). Cambridge, MA: MIT Press.

LePort, A. K., Mattfeld, A. T., Dickinson-Anson, H., Falon, J. H., Stark, C. E.,

Kruggle, F., et al. (2012). Behavioral and neuroanatomical investigation of highly superior autobiographical memory (HSAM). *Neurobiology of Learning and Memory, 98,* 78–92.

LePort, A. K. R., Stark, S. M., McGaugh, J. L., & Stark, C. E. L. (2017). A cognitive assessment of highly superior autobiographical memory. *Memory, 25,* 276–288.

Loftus, E. F. (1997). Creating false memories. *Scientific American, 277*(3), 70–75.

MacDougall, M., & Fine, A. (2014). The expression of long-term potentiation: Reconciling the priests and the positivists. *Philosophic Transactions of the Royal Society B Biological Science, 369*(1633), 20130135.

Maguire, E. A., Gadian, D. G., Johnsrude, I. S., Good, C. D., Ashburner, J., Frackowiak, R. S., et al. (2000). Navigation-related structural change in the hippocampi of taxi drivers. *Proceedings of the National Academy of Sciences of the United States of America, 97,* 4398–4403.

Mahncke, H. W., Bronstone, A., & Merzenich, M. M. (2006). Brain plasticity and functional losses in the aged: Scientific bases for a novel intervention. *Progress in Brain Research, 157,* 81–109.

Martin, A., Kronbichler, M., & Richlan, F. (2016). Dyslexic brain activation abnormalities in deep and shallow orthographies: A meta-analysis of 28 functional neuroimaging studies. *Human Brain Mapping, 37,* 2676–2699.

McCormick, C., Moscovitch, M., Valiante, T. A., Cohn, M., & McAndrews, M. P. (2018). Different neural routes to autobiographical memory recall in healthy people and individuals with left medical temporal lobe epilepsy. *Neuropsychologia, 110,* 26–36.

McGaugh, J. (2004). The amygdala modulates the consolidation of memories of emotionally arousing experiences. *Annual Review of Neuroscience, 27,* 1–28.

McKenzie, S., & Eichenbaum, H. (2011). Consolidation and reconsolidation: Two lives of memories? *Neuron, 71,* 224–233.

Meloni, E. G., Gillis, T. E., Manoukian, J., & Kaufman, M. J. (2014). Xenon impairs reconsolidation of fear memories in a rat model of post-traumatic stress disorder (PTSD). *PLOS ONE, 9*(8), e106189.

Miller, C. A., Gavin, C. F., White, J. A., Parrish, R. R., Honasoge, A., Yancey, C. R., et al. (2010). Cortical DNA methylation maintains remote memory. *Nature Neuroscience, 13,* 664–666.

Milner, B., Corkin, S., & Teuber, H. (1968). Further analysis of the hippocampal amnesic syndrome: 14-year follow-up study of H.M. *Neuropsychologia, 6,* 215–234.

Mishkin, M. (1982). A memory system in the brain. *Philosophical Transactions of the Royal Society of London, Biological Sciences, 298,* 83–95.

Mishkin, M., Suzuki, W. A., Gadian, D. G., & Vargha-Khadem, F. (1997). Hierarchical organization of cognitive memory. *Philosophical Transactions of the Royal Society of London, Biological Sciences, 352,* 1461–1467.

Murray, E. (2000). Memory for objects in nonhuman primates. In M. S. Gazzaniga (Ed.), *The new cognitive neurosciences* (pp. 753–763). Cambridge, MA: MIT Press.

Murray, E. A., Wise, S. P., & Graham, K. S. (2017). *The evolution of memory systems.* Oxford: Oxford University Press.

Mychasiuk, R., Muhammad, A., Ilnystskyy, S., & Kolb, B. (2013). Persistent gene expression changes in NAc, mPFC, and OFC associated with previous nicotine or amphetamine exposure. *Behavioural Brain Research, 256,* 655–661.

Mychasiuk, R., Muhammad, A., Ilnystskyy, S., Kovalchuk, O., & Kolb, B. (2016). Chronic stress induces persistent changes in global DNA methylation and gene expression in the medial prefrontal cortex, orbitofrontal cortex, and hippocampus. *Neuroscience, 322,* 489–499.

Nudo, R. J., Plautz, E. J., & Milliken, G. W. (1997). Adaptive plasticity in primate motor cortex as a consequence of behavioral experience and neuronal injury. *Seminars in Neuroscience, 9,* 13–23.

O'Keefe, J. (2006). Hippocampal neurophysiology in the behaving animal. In P. Andersen, R. Morris, D. Amaral, T. Bliss, & J. O'Keefe (Eds.), *The hippocampus book* (pp. 475–548). New York: Oxford University Press.

O'Keefe, J., & Nadel, L. (1978). *The hippocampus as a spatial map.* New York: Oxford University Press.

Patihis, L., Frenda, S. J., LePort, A. K. R., Petersen, N., Nichols, R. M., Stark, C. E. L., et al. (2013). False memories in highly superior autobiographical memory individuals. *Proceedings of the National Academy of Sciences of the United States of America, 110,* 20947–20952.

Purves, D., & Voyvodic, J. T. (1987). Imaging mammalian nerve cells and their connections over time in living animals. *Trends in Neurosciences, 10,* 398–404.

Ragert, P., Schmidt, A., Altenmuller, E., & Dinse, H. R. (2003). Superior tactile performance and learning in professional pianists: Evidence for meta-plasticity in musicians. *European Journal of Neuroscience, 19,* 473–478.

Ramachandran, V. S. (1993). Behavioral and magnetoencephalographic correlates of plasticity in the adult human brain. *Proceedings of the National Academy of Sciences of the United States of America, 90,* 10413–10420.

Ramón y Cajal, S. (1928). *Degeneration and regeneration of the nervous system.* London: Oxford University Press.

Reynolds, B., & Weiss, S. (1992). Generation of neurons and astrocytes from isolated cells of the adult mammalian central nervous system. *Science, 255,* 1707–1710.

Robinson, T. E., & Kolb, B. (1997). Persistent structural adaptations in nucleus accumbens and prefrontal cortex neurons produced by prior experience with amphetamine. *Journal of Neuroscience, 17,* 8491–8498.

Robinson, T. E., & Kolb, B. (2004). Structural plasticity associated with drugs of abuse. *Neuropharmacology, 47*(Suppl. 1), 33–46.

Sainsbury, R. S., & Coristine, M. (1986). Affective discrimination in moderately to severely demented patients. *Canadian Journal on Aging, 5,* 99–104.

Sapolsky, R. M. (1992). *Stress, the aging brain, and the mechanisms of neuron death.* Cambridge, MA: MIT Press.

Schacter, D. L. (1983). Amnesia observed: Remembering and forgetting in a natural environment. *Journal of Abnormal Psychology, 92,* 236–242.

Sherry, D. F., Jacobs, L. F., & Gaulin, S. J. C. (1992). Spatial memory and adaptive specialization of the hippocampus. *Trends in Neuroscience, 15,* 298–303.

Sirevaag, A. M., & Greenough, W. T. (1987). Differential rearing effects on rat visual cortex synapses: III. Neuronal and glial nuclei, boutons, dendrites, and capillaries. *Brain Research, 424,* 320–332.

Sirevaag, A. M., & Greenough, W. T. (1988). A multivariate statistical summary of synaptic plasticity measures in rats exposed to complex, social and individual environments. *Brain Research, 441,* 386–392.

Skinner, B. F. (1938). *The behavior of organisms.* New York: Appleton-Century-Crofts.

Squire, L. R., Genzel, L., Wixted, J. T., & Morris, R. G. (2015). Memory consolidation. *Cold Spring Harbor Perspectives in Biology, 7*(8), a021766.

Stewart, J., & Kolb, B. (1994). Dendritic branching in cortical pyramidal cells in response to ovariectomy in adult female rats: Suppression by neonatal exposure to testosterone. *Brain Research, 654,* 149–154.

Sutherland, R. J., Sparks, F. T., & Lehmann, H. (2010). Hippocampus and retrograde amnesia in the rat model: A modest proposal for the situation of systems consolidation. *Neuropsychologia, 48,* 2357–2369.

Tallal, P. (2012). Improving neural response to sound improves reading. *Proceedings of the National Academy of Sciences of the United States of America, 109,* 16404–16407.

Temple, E., Deutsch, G. K., Poldrack, R. A., Miller, S. L., Tallal, P., Merzenich, M. M., et al. (2003). Neural deficits in children with dyslexia ameliorated by behavioral remediation: Evidence from functional MRI. *Proceedings of the National Academy of Sciences of the United States of America, 100,* 2860–2865.

Thorndike, E. L. (1898). Animal intelligence: An experimental study of the associative processes in animals. *Psychological Review Monograph Supplements, 2,* 1–109.

Tulving, E. (2002). Episodic memory: From mind to brain. *Annual Review of Psychology, 53,* 1–25.

Turner, A., & Greenough, W. T. (1985). Differential rearing effects on rat visual cortex synapses: I. Synaptic and neuronal density and synapses per neuron. *Brain Research, 329,* 195–203.

Walker, L. C., & Jucker, M. (2015). Neurodegenerative diseases: Expanding the prion concept. *Annual Review of Neuroscience, 38,* 87–103.

Wisniewski, T., & Goni, F. (2015). Immunotherapeutic approaches for Alzheimer's disease. *Neuron, 85,* 1162–1176.

Woolley, C. S., Gould, E., Frankfurt, M., & McEwen, B. S. (1990). Naturally occurring fluctuation in dendritic spine density on adult hippocampal pyramidal neurons. *Journal of Neuroscience, 10,* 4035–4039.

Woollett, K., & Maguire, E. A. (2011). Acquiring "the knowledge" of London's layout drives structural brain changes. *Current Biology, 21,* 2109–2114.

CHAPTER 15

Adamaszek, M., D'Agata, F., Ferrucci, R., Habas, C. Keulen, S., Kirkby, K. C., et al. (2017). Consensus paper: Cerebellum and emotion. *Cerebellum, 16,* 552–576.

Adolphs, R., Gosselin, F., Buchanan, T. W., Tranel, D., Schyns, P., & Damasio, A. R. (2005). A mechanism for impaired fear recognition after amygdala damage. *Nature, 433,* 68–72.

Barton, R. A. (2012). Embodied cognitive evolution and the cerebellum. *Philosophical Transactions of the Royal Society B, 367,* 2097–2107.

Basten, U., Hilger, K., & Fiebach, C. J. (2015). Where smart brains are different: A quantitative meta-analysis of functional and structural brain imaging studies on intelligence. *Intelligence, 51,* 10–27.

Baumann, O., Borra, B. J., Bower, J. M., Cullen, K. E., Habas, C., Ivry, R. B., et al. (2015). Consensus paper: The role of the cerebellum in perceptual processes. *Cerebellum, 14,* 197–220.

Bugnar, T., Reber, S. A., & Buckner, C. (2016). Ravens attribute visual access to unseen competitors. *Nature Communications, 7,* 10506. doi: 10.1038/ncomms10506.

Calvin, W. H. (1996). *How brains think.* New York: Basic Books.

Castiello, U., Paulignan, Y., & Jeannerod, M. (1991). Temporal dissociation of motor responses and subjective awareness. *Brain, 114,* 2639–2655.

Chomsky, N. (2010). Some simple evo-devo theses: How true might they be for language. In Larson, R., Deprez, V., & Yamakido, H. (Eds.). *The evolution of human language* (p. 54–62). Cambridge: Cambridge University Press.

Crick, F., & Koch, C. (1998). Consciousness and neuroscience. *Cerebral Cortex, 8,* 97–107.

Csibra, G. (2007). Action mirroring and action understanding: An alternative account. In P. Haggard, Y. Rosetti, & M. Kawato (Eds.), *Sensorimotor foundations of higher cognition: Attention and Performance XII* (pp. 453–459). Oxford: Oxford University Press.

Damasio, A. (2012). *Self comes to mind: Constructing the conscious brain.* New York: Vintage.

Dediu, D., & Levinson, S. C. (2013). On the antiquity of language: the reinterpretation of Neandertal linguistic capacities and its consequences. *Frontiers in Psychology, 4.* doi: 10.3389/fpsyg.2013.00397

Diamond, M. C., Scheibel, A. B., Murphy, G. M., Jr., & Harvey, T. (1985). On the brain of a scientist: Albert Einstein. *Experimental Neurology, 88,* 198–204.

Dolins, F. L., Klimowicz, C., Kelley, J., & Menzel, C. R. (2014). Using virtual reality to investigate comparative spatial cognitive abilities in chimpanzees and humans. *American Journal of Primatology, 76,* 496–513.

Duncan, J., Seitz, R. J., Kolodny, J., Bor, D., Herzog, H., Ahmed, A., Newell, F. N., & Emslie, H. (2000). A neural basis for general intelligence. *Science, 289,* 457–459.

Frith, C., Perry, R., & Lumer, E. (1999). The neural correlations of conscious experience. *Trends in Cognitive Sciences, 3,* 105–114.

Gaulin, S. J. (1992). Evolution of sex differences in spatial ability. *Yearbook of Physical Anthropology, 35,* 125–131.

Gazzaniga, M. S. (1970). *The bisected brain.* New York: Appleton-Century-Crofts.

Gazzaniga, M. S. (1992). *Nature's mind.* New York: Basic Books.

Gazzaniga, M. S., Ivry, R. B., & Mangun, G. R. (1999). *Cognitive science: The biology of the mind.* New York: Norton.

Genc, E., Fraenz, C., Schluter, C., Friedrich, P., Hossiep, R., Voekle, M. C., et al. (2018). Diffusion markers of dendritic density and arborization in gray matter predict differences in intelligence. *Nature Communications, 9*(1), 1905.

Ghanzanfar, A. A., & Schroeder, C. E. (2006). Is neocortex essentially multisensory? *Trends in Cognitive Science, 10,* 278–285.

Glasser, M. F., Coalson, T. S., Robinson, E. C., Hacker, C. D., Harwell, J., Yacoub, E., et al. (2016). A multi-modal parcellation of human cerebral cortex. *Nature, 536,* 171–178.

Goldstein, J. M., Seidman, J. L., Horton, N. J., Makris, N., Kennedy, D. N., et al. (2001). Normal sexual dimorphism of the adult human brain assessed by in vivo magnetic resonance imaging. *Cerebral Cortex, 11,* 490–497.

Gray, J. R., & Thompson, P. M. (2004). Neurobiology of intelligence: Science and ethics. *Nature Reviews Neuroscience, 5,* 471–482.

Guilford, J. P. (1967). *The nature of human intelligence.* New York: McGraw-Hill.

Haier, R. J. (2017). *The neuroscience of intelligence.* New York: Cambridge University Press.

Hebb, D. O. (1949). *The organization of behavior.* New York: McGraw-Hill.

Hebb, D. O. (1980). *Essay on mind.* Hillsdale, NJ: Lawrence Erlbaum.

Heyes, C. (2015). Animal mindreading: What's the problem? *Psychonomic Bulletin and Review, 22,* 313–327.

Hickok, G. (2013). Do mirror neurons subserve action understanding? *Neuroscience Letters, 540,* 56–58.

Hickok, G. (2014). *The myth of motor neurons.* New York: Norton.

Hubbard, E. W. (2007). Neurophysiology of synesthesia. *Current Psychiatry Reports, 9,* 193–199.

Ingalhalikar, M., Smith, A., Parker, D., Satterthwaite, P. D., Elliott, M. A., Ruparel, K., et al. (2014). Sex differences in the structural connectome of the human brain. *Proceedings of the National Academy of Sciences of the United States of America, 111,* 823–828.

Jung, R. E., & Haier, R. J. (2007). The parieto-frontal integration theory (P-FIT) of intelligence: Converging neuroimaging evidence. *The Behavioral and Brain Sciences, 30,* 135–154.

Kelly, C., Biswal, B. B., Craddock, R. C., Castellanos, F. X., & Milham, M. P. (2012). Characterizing variation in the functional connectome: Promise and pitfalls. *Trends in Cognitive Science, 16,* 181–188.

Kimura, D. (1967). Functional asymmetry of the brain in dichotic listening. *Cortex, 3,* 163–178.

Kimura, D. (1973). The asymmetry of the human brain. *Scientific American, 228*(3), 70–78.

Kimura, D. (1999). *Sex and cognition.* Cambridge, MA: MIT Press.

Kolb, B., & Stewart, J. (1991). Sex-related differences in dendritic branching of cells in the prefrontal cortex of rats. *Journal of Neuroendocrinology, 3,* 95–99.

Kolb, B., & Whishaw, I. Q. (2015). *Fundamentals of human neuropsychology* (7th ed.). New York: Worth.

Kranz, G. S., Hahn, A., Kaufmann, U., Kublbock, M., Hummer, A., Ganger S., et al. (2014). White matter microstructure in transsexuals and controls investigated by diffusion tensor imaging. *Journal of Neuroscience, 34,* 15466–15474.

Lieberman, M. D. (2007). Social cognitive neuroscience: A review of core processes. *Annual Review of Psychology, 58,* 259–289.

Lieberman, M. D., & Eisenberger, N. I. (2015). The dorsal anterior cingulate cortex is selective for pain: Results from large-scale reverse inference. *Proceedings of the National Academy of Sciences of the United States of America, 112,* 15250–15255.

Loui, P., Li, H. C., Hohmann, A., & Schlaug, G. (2011). Enhanced cortical connectivity in absolute pitch musicians: A model for local hyperconnectivity. *Journal of Cognitive Neuroscience, 23,* 1015–1026.

Luria, A. R. (1972). *The man with a shattered world.* New York: Basic Books.

Maginnity, M. E., & Grace, R. C. (2014). Visual perspective taking by dogs (*Canis familiaris*) in a Guesser–Knower task: Evidence for a canine theory of mind? *Animal Cognition, 17,* 1375–1392.

Mlodinow, L. (2009). *The drunkard's walk: How randomness rules our lives.* New York: Vintage Books.

Moran, J., & Desimone, R. (1985). Selective attention gates visual processing in the extrastriate cortex. *Science, 229,* 782–784.

Mukerjee, M. (1996). Interview with a parrot [field note]. *Scientific American, 274*(4), 24.

Newsome, W. T., Shadlen, M. N., Zohary, E., Britten, K. H., & Movshon, J. A. (1995). Visual motion: Linking neuronal activity to psychophysical performance. In M. Gazzaniga (Ed.), *The cognitive neurosciences* (pp. 401–414). Cambridge, MA: MIT Press.

Pepperberg, I. M. (1990). Some cognitive capacities of an African grey parrot (*Psittacus erithacus*). In P. J. B. Slater, J. S. Rosenblatt, & C. Beer (Eds.), *Advances in the study of behavior* (Vol. 19, pp. 357–409). New York: Academic Press.

Pepperberg, I. M. (1999). *The Alex studies.* Cambridge, MA: Harvard University Press.

Pepperberg, I. M. (2006). Ordinality and inferential ability of a grey parrot (*Psittacus erithacus*). *Journal of Comparative Psychology, 120,* 205–216.

Poldrack, R. A., Baker, C. I., Durnez, J., Gorgolewski, K. J., Matthews, P. M., Munafo, M. R., et al. (2017). Scanning the horizon towards transparent and reproducible neuroimaging research. *Nature Reviews Neuroscience, 18,* 115–126.

Proulx, M. J., Todorov, O. S., Aiken, A. T. M., & deSousa, A. A. (2016). Where am I? Who am I? The relation between spatial cognition, social cognition, and individual differences in the built environment. *Frontiers of Psychology, 7,* 64.

Ramachandran, V. S., & Oberman, L. M. (2006). Broken mirrors: A theory of autism. *Scientific American, 295,* 62–69.

Rameson, L. T., Morellis, S. A., & Lieberman, M. D. (2012). The neural correlates of empathy: Experience, automaticity, and prosocial behavior. *Journal of Cognitive Neuroscience, 24,* 235–245.

Rasmussen, T., & Milner, B. (1977). The role of early left brain injury in determining lateralization of cerebral speech functions. *Annals of the New York Academy of Sciences, 299,* 355–369.

Ritchie, S. J., Cox, S. R., Shen, X., Lombardo, M. V., Reus, L. M., Alloza, C., et al. (2018). Sex differences in the adult human brain: Evidence from 5216 UK biobank participants. *Cerebral Cortex, 28*(8), 2959–2975.

Rizzolatti, G. (2007). *Mirrors on the mind.* New York: Oxford University Press.

Rizzolatti, G., & Craighero, L. (2004). The mirror-neuron system. *Annual Review of Neuroscience, 27,* 169–192.

Sacks, O. (1989). *Seeing voices.* Los Angeles: University of California Press.

Sala-Llonch, R., Bartres-Faz, D., & Junque, C. (2015). Reorganization of brain networks in aging: A review of functional connectivity studies. *Frontiers in Psychology, 6,* 553.

Sawamoto, N., Honda, M., Okada, T., Hanakawa, T., Kanda, M., et al. (2000). Expectation of pain enhances responses to nonpainful somatosensory stimulation in the anterior cingulate cortex and parietal operculum/posterior insula: An event-related functional magnetic resonance imaging study. *Journal of Neuroscience, 20,* 7438–7445.

Sperry, R. (1968). Mental unity following surgical disconnection of the cerebral hemispheres. *Harvey Lectures, 62,* 293–323.

Stein, B. E., & Rowland, B. A. (2011). Organization and plasticity in multisensory integration: Early and late experience affects its governing principles. *Progress in Brain Research, 191,* 145–163.

Stewart, J., & Kolb, B. (1994). Dendritic branching in cortical pyramidal cells in response to ovariectomy in adult female rats: Suppression by neonatal exposure to testosterone. *Brain Research, 654,* 149–154.

Storm, J. F., Boly, M., Casali, A. G., Massimini, M., Olcese, U., Pennartz, C. M. A., & Wilke, M. (2017). Consciousness regained: Disentangling mechanisms, brain systems, and behavioral responses. *Journal of Neuroscience, 37,* 10882–10893.

Thagard, P., & Stewart, T. C. (2014). Two theories of consciousness: Semantic pointer competition vs. information integration. *Consciousness and Cognition, 30,* 73–90.

Wada, J., & Rasmussen, T. (1960). Intracarotid injection of sodium amytal for the lateralization of cerebral speech dominance: Experimental and clinical observations. *Journal of Neurosurgery, 17,* 266–282.

Waller, D., & Nadel, L. (Eds.). (2013). *Handbook of spatial cognition.* Washington, DC: American Psychological Association.

Witelson, S. F., & Goldsmith, C. H. (1991). The relationship of hand preference to anatomy of the corpus callosum in men. *Brain Research, 545,* 175–182.

Witelson, S. F., Kigar, D. L., & Harvey, T. (1999). The exceptional brain of Albert Einstein. *Lancet, 353,* 2149–2153.

Woollett, K., Spiers, H. J., & Maguire, E. A. (2009). Talent in the taxi: A model system for exploring expertise. *Philosophical Transactions of the Royal Society B, 364,* 1407–1416.

Yeo, B. T. T., Fienen, F. M., Sepulcre, J., Sabuncu, M. R., Lashkari, D., Hollinshead, M., et al. (2011). The organization of the human cerebral cortex estimated by intrinsic functional connectivity. *Journal of Neurophysiology, 106,* 1125–1165.

CHAPTER 16

American Psychiatric Association. (2013). *Diagnostic and statistical manual of mental disorders* (5th ed.). Washington, DC: American Psychiatric Association.

Andrade, C. (2018). Relative efficacy and acceptability of antidepressant drugs in adults with major depressive disorder: Commentary on a network meta-analysis. *Journal of Clinical Psychiatry, 79*(2), 18f12254.

Arnold, S. E., Rushinsky, D. D., & Han, L. Y. (1997). Further evidence of abnormal cytoarchitecture in the entorhinal cortex in schizophrenia using spatial point analyses. *Biological Psychiatry, 142,* 639–647.

Björklund, A., & Lindvall, O. (2017). Replacing dopamine neurons in Parkinson's disease: How did it happen? *Journal of Parkinson's Disease, 7*(S1), S23–S33.

Boes, A. D., Kelly, M. S., Trapp, N. T., Stern, A. P., Press, D. Z., & Pascual-Leone, A. (2018). Noninvasive brain stimulation: Challenges and opportunities for a new clinical specialty. *The Journal of Neuropsychiatry and Clinical Neurosciences, 30*(3), 173–179.

Brem, A. K., Almquist, J. N., Mansfield, K., Plessow, F., Sella, F., Santarnecchi, E., et al. (2018). Modulating fluid intelligence performance through combined cognitive training and brain stimulation. *Neuropsychologia*. doi: 10.1016/j.neuropsychologia.2018.04.008.

Broglio, S. P., Kontos, A. P., Levin, H., Schneider, K., Wilde, E. A., Cantu, R. C., et al. (2018). The National Institute of Neurological Disorders and Stroke and Department of Defense Sport-Related Concussion Common Data Elements Version 1.0 recommendations. *Journal of Neurotrauma*. doi: 10.1089/neu.2018.5643.

Byne, W., Kemegther, E., Jones, L., Harouthunian, V., & Davis, K. L. (1999). The neurochemistry of schizophrenia. In D. S. Charney, E. J. Nesthler, & B. S. Bunney (Eds.), *The neurobiology of mental illness* (p. 242). New York: Oxford University Press.

Calne, D. B., & Mizuno, Y. (2004). The neuromythology of Parkinson's disease. *Parkinsonism and Related Disorders, 10,* 319–322.

Caron, N., Genin, E. C., Marlier, Q., Verteneuil, S., Beukelaers, P., Morel, L., et al. (2018). Proliferation of hippocampal progenitors relies on p27-dependent regulation of Cdk6 kinase activity. *Cellular and Molecular Life Sciences*. doi: 10.1007/s00018-018-2832-x

Centers for Disease Control and Prevention. (2005). *TBI in the United States: Emergency department visits, hospitalizations, and deaths, 2004.*

Charney, D. S., Nestler, E. J., Sklar, P., & Buxbaum, D. (Eds.). (2017). *The neurobiology of mental illness*. New York: Oxford University Press.

Cho, R. Y., Gilbert, H., & Lewis, D. A. (2004). The neurobiology of schizophrenia. In D. S. Charney & F. J. Nestler (Eds.), *The Neurobiology of Mental Illness* (2nd ed., pp. 299–310). New York: Oxford University Press.

Cleary, D. R., Ozpinar, A., Raslan, A. M., & Ko, A. L. (2015). Deep brain stimulation for psychiatric disorders: Where we are now. *Neurosurgical Focus, 38,* E2.

Corrigan, N. M., Richards, T. L., Treffert, D. A., & Dager, S. R. (2012). Toward a better understanding of the savant brain. *Comprehensive Psychiatry, 53,* 706–717.

Daskalakis, N. P., Rijal, C. M., King, C., Huckins, L. M., & Ressler, K. J. (2018). Recent genetics and epigenetics approaches to PTSD. *Current Psychiatry Reports, 20*(5), 30.

deCharms, R. C. (2008). Applications of real-time fMRI. *Nature Reviews Neuroscience, 9,* 720–729.

Drevets, W. C., Kishore, M. G., & Krishman, K. R. R. (2004). Neuroimaging studies of mood disorders. In D. S. Charney & E. J. Nestler (Eds.), *The neurobiology of mental illness* (2nd ed., pp. 461–490). New York: Oxford University Press.

Dunkley, B. T., Urban, K., Da Costa, L., Wong, S. M., Pang, E. W., & Taylor, M. J. (2018). Default mode network oscillatory coupling is increased following concussion. *Frontiers in Neurology, 9,* 280.

Evans, E., Piccio, L., & Cross, A. H. (2018). Use of vitamins and dietary supplements by patients with multiple sclerosis: A review. *JAMA Neurology, 75*(8), 1013–1021.

Fereshtehnejad, S. M., Romenets, S. R., Anang, J. B., Latreille, V., Gagnon, J. F., & Postuma, R. B. (2015). New clinical subtypes of Parkinson disease and their longitudinal progression: A prospective cohort comparison with other phenotypes. *JAMA Neurology, 72*(8), 863–873.

Ferlisi, M., & Shorvon, S. (2014). Seizure precipitants (triggering factors) in patients with epilepsy. *Epilepsy & Behavior, 33,* 101–105.

Giles J. (2004). Neuroscience: Change of mind. *Nature, 430,* 14.

Gubbi, J., Kusmakar, S., Rao, A., Yan, B., O'Brien, T., & Palaniswami, M. (2015). Automatic detection and classification of convulsive psychogenic non-epileptic seizures using a wearable device. *IEEE Journal of Biomedical and Health Information, 20*(4), 1061–1072.

Heinz, A., Kipke, R., Heimann, H., & Wiesing, U. (2012). Cognitive neuroenhancement: False assumptions in the ethical debate. *Journal of Medical Ethics, 38,* 372–375.

Horn, S. R., & Feder, A. (2018). Understanding resilience and preventing and treating PTSD. *Harvard Review of Psychiatry, 26*(3), 158–174.

Khachaturian, Z. S., & Khachaturian, A. S. (2015). Politics of science: Progress toward prevention of the dementia-Alzheimer's syndrome (review). *Molecular Aspects of Medicine, 43–44,* 3–15.

Knight, E. J., Testini, P., Min, H. K., Gibson, W. S., Gorny, K. R., Favazza, C. P., et al. (2015). Motor and nonmotor circuitry activation induced by subthalamic nucleus deep brain stimulation in patients with Parkinson disease: Intraoperative functional magnetic resonance imaging for deep brain stimulation. *Mayo Clinic Proceedings, 90,* 773–785.

Knight, R., Khondoker, M., Magill, N., Stewart, R., & Landau, S. (2018). A systematic review and meta-analysis of the effectiveness of acetylcholinesterase inhibitors and memantine in treating the cognitive symptoms of dementia. *Dementia and Geriatric Cognitive Disorders, 45*(3–4), 131–151.

Kovelman, J. A., & Scheibel, A. B. (1984). A neurohistologic correlate of schizophrenia. *Biological Psychiatry, 19,* 1601–1621.

Kraus, C., Castrén, E., Kasper, S., & Lanzenberger, R. (2017). Serotonin and neuroplasticity—Links between molecular, functional and structural pathophysiology in depression. *Neuroscience & Biobehavioral Reviews, 77,* 317–326.

Kumar, A., & Tsao, J. W. (2018). *Alzheimer disease*. Treasure Island, FL: StatPearls Publishing.

Kwon, C. S., Ripa, V., Al-Awar, O., Panov, F., Ghatan, S., & Jetté, N. (2018). Epilepsy and neuromodulation-randomized controlled trials. *Brain Sciences, 8*(4), E69.

Laver, K. E., George, S., Thomas, S., Deutsch, J. E., & Crotty, M. (2015). Virtual reality for stroke rehabilitation. *Cochrane Database Systems Review, 9,* CD008349.

Martin, J. P. (1967). *The basal ganglia and posture*. London: Ritman Medical.

Marzi, S. J., Sugden, K., Arseneault, L., Belsky, D. W., Burrage, J., Corcoran, D. L., et al. (2018). Analysis of DNA methylation in young people: Limited evidence for an association between victimization stress and epigenetic variation in blood. *American Journal of Psychiatry, 175*(6), 517–529.

McGowan, P. O., & Szyf, M. (2010). Environmental epigenomics: Understanding the effects of parental care on the epigenome. *Essays in Biochemistry, 48,* 275–287.

Morrison, P. D., & Murray, R. M. (2018). The antipsychotic landscape: Dopamine and beyond. *Therapeutic Advances in Psychopharmacology, 8*(4), 127–135.

Nakamura, A., Kaneko, N., Villemagne, V. L., Kato, T., Doecke, J., Doré, V., et al. (2018). High performance plasma amyloid-β biomarkers for Alzheimer's disease. *Nature, 554*(7691), 249–254.

National Institute of Mental Health website: http://www.nimh.nih.gov/health/statistics/index.shtml

Norr, A. M., Smolenski, D. J., Katz, A. C., Rizzo, A. A., Rothbaum, B. O., Difede, J., et al. (2018). Virtual reality exposure versus prolonged exposure for PTSD: Which treatment for whom? *Depression and Anxiety, 35*(6), 523–529.

Omalu, B., Small, G. W., Bailes, J., Ercoli, L. M., Merrill, D. A., Wong, K., et al. (2018). Postmortem autopsy-confirmation of antemortem [F-18]FDDNP-PET scans in a football player with chronic traumatic encephalopathy. *Neurosurgery, 82*(2), 237–246.

Pegoretti, V., Baron, W., Laman, J. D., & Eisel, U. L. M. (2018). Selective modulation of TNF-TNFRs signaling: Insights for multiple sclerosis treatment. *Frontiers in Immunology, 9,* 925.

Peretz, I., Kolinsky, R., Tramo, M., Labrecque, R., Hublet, C., Demeurisse, G., et al. (1994). Functional dissociations following bilateral lesions of auditory cortex. *Brain, 117,* 1283–1301.

Rao, J., Chiappelli, J., Kochunov, P., Regenold, W. T., Rapoport, S. I., & Hong, L. E. (2015). Is schizophrenia a neurodegenerative disease? Evidence from age-related decline of brain-derived neurotrophic factor in the brains of schizophrenia patients and matched non-psychiatric controls. *Neurodegenerative Diseases, 15,* 38–44.

Rapoport, J. L., Giedd, J. N., & Gogtay, N. (2012). Neurodevelopmental model of schizophrenia: Update 2012. *Molecular Psychiatry, 17,* 1228–1238.

Sacks, O. (1998). *The man who mistook his wife for a hat: And other clinical tales.* New York: Touchstone.

Sacrey, L. A., Zwaigenbaum, L., Bryson, S., Brian, J., Smith, I. M., Roberts, W., et al. (2015). Can parents' concerns predict autism spectrum disorder? A prospective study of high-risk siblings from 6 to 36 months of age. *Journal of the American Academy of Child and Adolescent Psychiatry, 54*(6), 470–478.

Savitz, S. I. (2015). Developing cellular therapies for stroke. *Stroke, 46,* 2026–2031.

Schwab, N., & Hazrati, L. N. (2018). Assessing the limitations and biases in the current understanding of chronic traumatic encephalopathy. *Journal of Alzheimer's Disease, 64*(4), 1067–1076.

Shankar, R., Newman, C., Gales, A., McLean, B. N., Hanna, J., Ashby, S., et al. (2018). Has the time come to stratify and score SUDEP risk to inform people with epilepsy of their changes in safety? *Frontiers of Neurology, 9,* 281.

Shorter, K. R., & Miller, B. H. (2015). Epigenetic mechanisms in schizophrenia. *Progress in Biophysics and Molecular Biology, 118,* 1–7.

Solms, M. & Turnbull, O. (2002). *The brain and the inner world: An introduction to the neuroscience of subjective experience.* Karnac Books, London, UK.

Solomon, G. L. (2018). Chronic traumatic encephalopathy in sports: A historical and narrative review. *Developmental Neuropsychology, 43*(4), 279–311.

Treffert, D. A., & Rebedew, D. L. (2015). The savant syndrome registry: A preliminary report. *WMJ, 114*(4), 158–162.

Ullah, H., & Khan, H. (2018). Anti-Parkinson potential of silymarin: Mechanistic insight and therapeutic standing. *Frontiers in Pharmacology, 9,* 422.

Uswatte, G., Taub, E., Bowman, M. H., Delgado, A., Bryson, C., Morris, D. M., et al. (2018). Rehabilitation of stroke patients with plegic hands: Randomized controlled trial of expanded constraint-induced movement therapy. *Restorative Neurology and Neuroscience, 36*(2), 225–244.

Watsky, R. E., Gotts, S. J., Berman, R. A., McAdams, H. M., Zhou, X., Greenstein, D., et al. (2018). Attenuated resting-state functional connectivity in patients with childhood- and adult-onset schizophrenia. *Schizophrenia Research, 197,* 219–225.

XiangWei, W., Jiang, Y., & Yuan, H. (2018). De novo mutations and rare variants occurring in NMDA receptors. *Current Opinion in Physiology, 2,* 27–35.

Youssef, N. A., Lockwood, L., Su, S., Hao, G., & Rutten, B. P. F. (2018). The effects of trauma, with or without PTSD, on the transgenerational DNA methylation alterations in human offsprings. *Brain Science, 8*(5), E83.

Zong, Y., Liu, N., Ma, S., Bai, Y., Guan, F., & Kong, X. (2018). Three novel variants (p.Glu178Lys, p.Val245Met, p.Ser250Phe) of the phenylalanine hydroxylase (PAH) gene impair protein expression and function in vitro. *Gene, 668,* 135–139.

NAME INDEX